Frommer's®

Caribbean

23rd Edition

by Christina Paulette Colón,
Alexis Lipsitz Flippin, John Marino,
Darwin Porter & Danforth Prince

John Wiley & Sons, Inc.

Published by:

JOHN WILEY & SONS, INC.
111 River St.
Hoboken, NJ 07030-5774

ISBN 978-1-118-00427-2 (paper); ISBN 978-1-118-10736-2 (ebk); ISBN 978-1-118-10735-5 (ebk); ISBN 978-1-118-10734-8 (ebk)

Editor: William Travis, with Naomi Kraus
Production Editor: Lindsay Conner
Cartographer: Anton Crane
Photo Editor: Richard Fox
Production by Wiley Indianapolis Composition Services

Front Cover Photo: Man diving off U.S. Virgin Islands © John Kelly / Getty Images.
Back Cover Photo: View from the top of Gros Piton peak Petit Piton in St. Lucia © Blaine Harrington Photography.

For information on our other products and services or to obtain technical support, please contact our Customer Care Department within the U.S. at 877/762-2974, outside the U.S. at 317/572-3993 or fax 317/572-4002.

Wiley also publishes its books in a variety of electronic formats. Some content that appears in print may not be available in electronic formats.

Manufactured in the United States of America

5 4 3 2 1

CONTENTS

5 BARBADOS 93

6 BONAIRE 126

7 THE BRITISH VIRGIN ISLANDS 145

8 THE CAYMAN ISLANDS 173

9 CURAÇAO 205

10 DOMINICA 227

11 THE DOMINICAN REPUBLIC 244

12 GRENADA 282

13 GUADELOUPE 301

14 JAMAICA 333

15 MARTINIQUE 390

16 PUERTO RICO 418

17 SABA 476

18 ST. BARTHÉLEMY 486

19 ST. EUSTATIUS 506

20 ST. KITTS & NEVIS 515

21 ST. LUCIA 545

22 ST. MAARTEN/ST. MARTIN 572

23 ST. VINCENT & THE GRENADINES 605

24 TRINIDAD & TOBAGO 627

25 TURKS & CAICOS 655

26 THE U.S. VIRGIN ISLANDS 684

27 PLANNING YOUR TRIP TO THE CARIBBEAN 747

LIST OF MAPS

ABOUT THE AUTHORS

Christina Paulette Colón has three great passions in life: nature, teaching, and travel. She has been everywhere from Borneo (where she lived for 2 years) to Bonaire. With a Ph.D. in Ecology and a Master's in Environmental Education, she is a talented educator, accomplished writer, and experienced editor (of everything from scientific articles to children's books).

Alexis Lipsitz Flippin is a freelance writer and former Frommer's senior editor. She is the author of *Frommer's Portable St. Maarten/St. Martin, Anguilla & St. Barts* and *Frommer's Portable Turks & Caicos* and has written and edited for consumer magazines including *Self, American Health,* and *Rolling Stone.*

John Marino, the author of *Frommer's Puerto Rico,* lives in San Juan, where he covers local and political news for the *San Juan Star* as city editor. He has written about Puerto Rico for the *New York Times, Conde Nast Traveler,* and other publications.

As a team of veteran travel writers, **Darwin Porter** and **Danforth Prince** have produced various titles for Frommer's, including guides to Italy, France, England, and Germany. A film critic, columnist, and broadcaster, Porter is also a Hollywood biographer. His recent releases include *Brando Unzipped,* documenting the private life of Marlon Brando, and *Jacko: His Rise and Fall,* the first complete biography ever written on the tumultuous life of Michael Jackson. Prince was formerly employed by the Paris bureau of the *New York Times* and is today the president of Blood Moon Productions. Porter and Prince's latest non-travel-related venture, jointly co-authored and published in 2008 by Blood Moon, is *Hollywood Babylon—It's Back!,* which one critic described as "the hottest compilation of intergenerational scandal in the history of Hollywood."

HOW TO CONTACT US

In researching this book, we discovered many wonderful places—hotels, restaurants, shops, and more. We're sure you'll find others. Please tell us about them, so we can share the information with your fellow travelers in upcoming editions. If you were disappointed with a recommendation, we'd love to know that, too. Please write to:

Frommer's Caribbean, 23rd Edition
John Wiley & Sons, Inc. • 111 River St. • Hoboken, NJ 07030-5774
frommersfeedback@wiley.com

ADVISORY & DISCLAIMER

Travel information can change quickly and unexpectedly, and we strongly advise you to confirm important details locally before traveling, including information on visas, health and safety, traffic and transport, accommodation, shopping, and eating out. We also encourage you to stay alert while traveling and to remain aware of your surroundings. Avoid civil disturbances, and keep a close eye on cameras, purses, wallets, and other valuables.

While we have endeavored to ensure that the information contained within this guide is accurate and up-to-date at the time of publication, we make no representations or warranties with respect to the accuracy or completeness of the contents of this work and specifically disclaim all warranties, including without limitation warranties of fitness for a particular purpose. We accept no responsibility or liability for any inaccuracy or errors or omissions, or for any inconvenience, loss, damage, costs, or expenses of any nature whatsoever incurred or suffered by anyone as a result of any advice or information contained in this guide.

The inclusion of a company, organization or Website in this guide as a service provider and/or potential source of further information does not mean that we endorse them or the information they provide. Be aware that information provided through some Websites may be unreliable and can change without notice. Neither the publisher or author shall be liable for any damages arising herefrom.

FROMMER'S STAR RATINGS, ICONS & ABBREVIATIONS

Every hotel, restaurant, and attraction listing in this guide has been ranked for quality, value, service, amenities, and special features using a star-rating system. In country, state, and regional guides, we also rate towns and regions to help you narrow down your choices and budget your time accordingly. Hotels and restaurants are rated on a scale of zero (recommended) to three stars (exceptional). Attractions, shopping, nightlife, towns, and regions are rated according to the following scale: zero stars (recommended), one star (highly recommended), two stars (very highly recommended), and three stars (must-see).

In addition to the star-rating system, we also use seven feature icons that point you to the great deals, in-the-know advice, and unique experiences that separate travelers from tourists. Throughout the book, look for:

special finds—those places only insiders know about

fun facts—details that make travelers more informed and their trips more fun

kids—best bets for kids and advice for the whole family

special moments—those experiences that memories are made of

overrated—places or experiences not worth your time or money

insider tips—great ways to save time and money

great values—where to get the best deals

The following abbreviations are used for credit cards:

AE	American Express	DISC	Discover	V	Visa
DC	Diners Club	MC	MasterCard		

TRAVEL RESOURCES AT FROMMERS.COM

Frommer's travel resources don't end with this guide. Frommer's website, **www.frommers.com,** has travel information on more than 4,000 destinations. We update features regularly, giving you access to the most current trip-planning information and the best airfare, lodging, and car-rental bargains. You can also listen to podcasts, connect with other Frommers.com members through our active-reader forums, share your travel photos, read blogs from guidebook editors and fellow travelers, and much more.

1

THE BEST OF THE CARIBBEAN

The Caribbean dream of days spent lolling on palm-tree-shaded sandy beaches or snorkeling in crystalline waters and of nights spent dining and dancing to steel-band rhythms is real enough. It exists only a few hours by plane from North America on this string of islands.

THE best BEACHES

Good beaches with soul-warming sun, crystal-clear waters, and fragrant sea air can be found on virtually every island of the Caribbean, with the possible exceptions of Saba (which has rocky shores) and Dominica (where the few beaches have dramatically black sands that absorb the hot sun).

- **Shoal Bay (Anguilla):** This luscious stretch of silvery sand helped put Anguilla on the world-tourism map. Snorkelers are drawn to the schools of iridescent fish that dart among the coral gardens offshore. You can take the trail walk from Old Ta to little-known Katouche Beach, which provides perfect snorkeling and is also a prime site for a beach picnic under shade trees. See chapter 2.
- **Antigua:** Legend has it that there is a beach here for every day of the year. Antiguans claim, with justifiable pride, that their two best are Dickenson Bay, in the northwest corner of the island, and Half Moon Bay, which stretches for a white-sandy mile along the eastern coast. Most major hotels open directly onto a good beach, so chances are good yours will be built on or near a strip of sand. See chapter 3.
- **Palm Beach (Aruba):** This superb white-sand beach put Aruba on the tourist map. Several publications, including *Condé Nast Traveler,* have hailed it as one of the 12 best beaches in the world. It's likely to be crowded in winter, but for swimming, sailing, or fishing, it's idyllic. See chapter 4.
- **The Gold Coast (Barbados):** Some of the finest beaches in the Caribbean lie along the so-called Gold Coast of Barbados (now often called the Platinum Coast), site of some of the swankiest deluxe hotels in the Northern Hemisphere. Our favorites include Paynes Bay, Brandon's Beach, Paradise Beach, and Brighton Beach—all open to the public. See chapter 5.

The Caribbean Islands

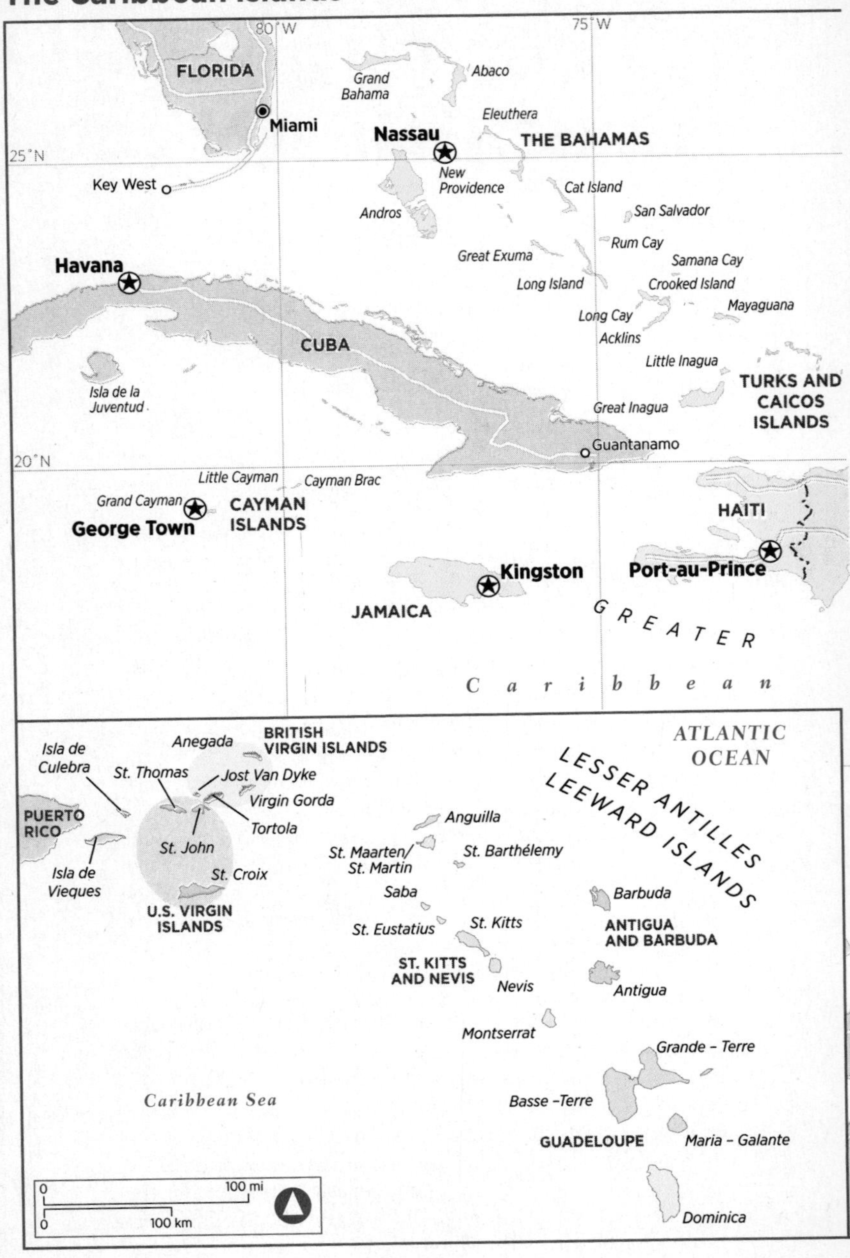

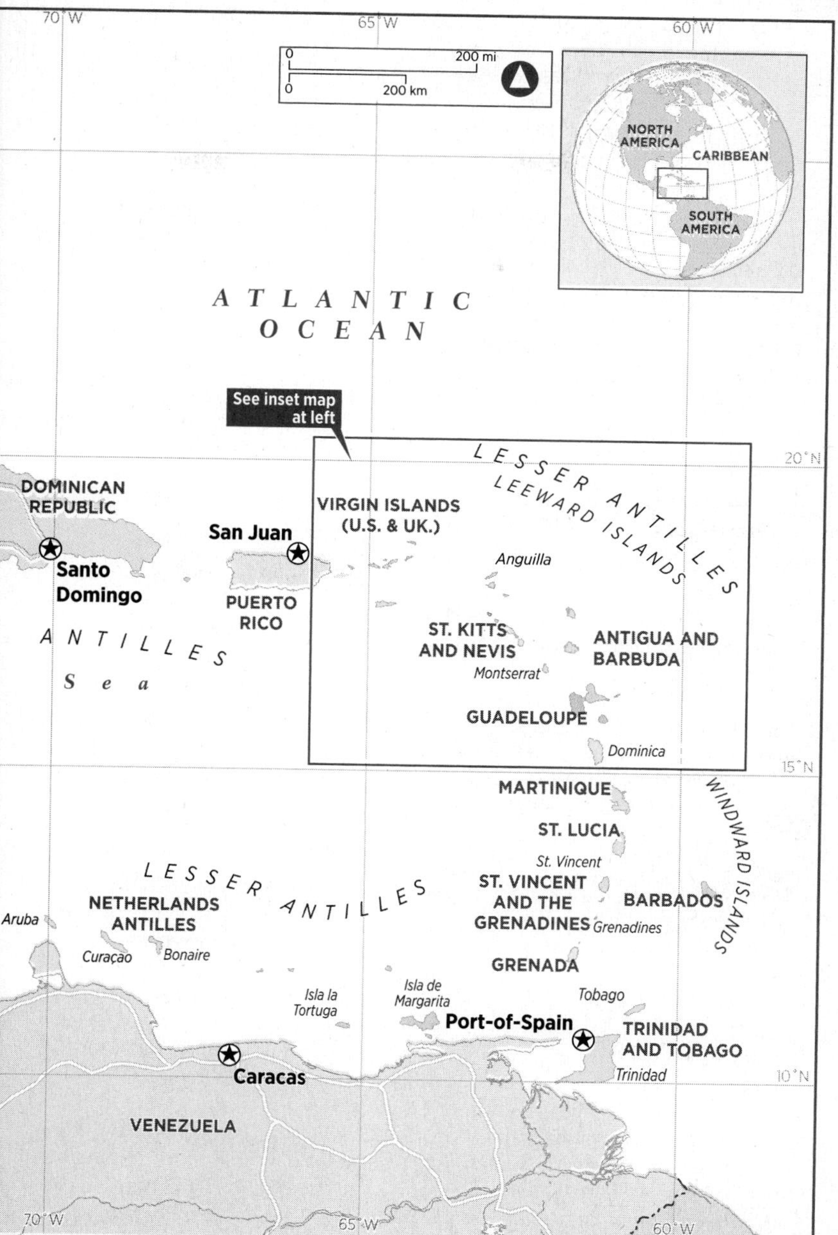
70° W
65° W
60° W
0
200 mi
0
200 km
NORTH AMERICA
CARIBBEAN
SOUTH AMERICA
ATLANTIC OCEAN
See inset map at left
LESSER ANTILLES
LEEWARD ISLANDS
20° N
DOMINICAN REPUBLIC
VIRGIN ISLANDS (U.S. & UK.)
San Juan
Santo Domingo
PUERTO RICO
Anguilla
ANTILLES
Sea
ST. KITTS AND NEVIS
ANTIGUA AND BARBUDA
Montserrat
GUADELOUPE
Dominica
15° N
MARTINIQUE
WINDWARD ISLANDS
ST. LUCIA
St. Vincent
LESSER ANTILLES
ST. VINCENT AND THE GRENADINES
BARBADOS
Grenadines
Aruba
NETHERLANDS ANTILLES
Curaçao
Bonaire
GRENADA
Isla la Tortuga
Isla de Margarita
Tobago
Port-of-Spain
TRINIDAD AND TOBAGO
Caracas
Trinidad
10° N
VENEZUELA

- **Cane Garden Bay (Tortola, British Virgin Islands):** One of the Caribbean's most spectacular stretches, Cane Garden Bay has 2km (1¼ miles) of white sand and is a jogger's favorite. It's a much better choice than the more crowded Magens Bay beach on neighboring St. Thomas. See chapter 7.
- **Seven Mile Beach (Grand Cayman, Cayman Islands):** It's really about 9km (5½ miles) long, but who's counting? Lined with condos and plush resorts, this beach is known for its array of watersports and its translucent aquamarine waters. Australian pines dot the background, and the average winter temperature of the water is a perfect 80°F (27°C). See chapter 8.
- **The Dominican Republic:** There are two great options here: the beaches of resort-riddled Punta Cana at the easternmost tip of the island, or those at Playa Dorada along the northern coast, which fronts the Atlantic. Punta Cana is a 30km (19-mile) strip of oyster-white sand set against a backdrop of palm trees, and Playa Dorada is filled with beaches of white or beige sands. See chapter 11.
- **Grand Anse Beach (Grenada):** This 3km (2-mile) beach is reason enough to go to Grenada. Although the island has some 45 beaches, most with white sand, this is the fabled one, and rightly so. There's enough space and so few visitors that you'll probably find a spot just for yourself. The sugary sands of Grand Anse extend into deep waters far offshore. Most of the island's best hotels are within walking distance. See chapter 12.
- **Seven Mile Beach (Negril, Jamaica):** In the northwestern section of the island, this beach stretches for 11km (6¾ miles) along the sea and is backed by some of the most hedonistic resorts in the Caribbean. Not for the conservative, the beach also contains some nudist sections, along with bare-all Booby Cay offshore. See chapter 14.
- **Diamond Beach (Martinique):** This bright-white beach stretches for about 10km (6¼ miles), much of it developed. It faces a rocky offshore island, Diamond Rock, which has uninhabited shores. See chapter 15.
- **Luquillo Beach (Puerto Rico):** Luquillo, 48km (30 miles) east of San Juan, is a vast sandy beach opening onto a crescent-shaped bay edged by a coconut grove. Coral reefs protect the crystal-clear lagoon from the often rough Atlantic waters that can buffet the northern coast. Much photographed because of its white sands, Luquillo has a snack bar, picnic areas with changing rooms, lockers, and showers. See chapter 16.
- **St-Jean Beach (St. Barthélemy):** A somewhat narrow golden-sand beach, St-Jean is the gem of the island, reminiscent of the French Riviera (though you're supposed to keep your top on). Reefs protect the beach, making it ideal for swimming. See chapter 18.
- **St. Maarten/St. Martin:** Take your pick: This island, divided about equally between France and the Netherlands, has 39 white-sand beaches. Our favorites include Orient Beach (clothing optional), Pinel Island, Long Bay, and Friar's Bay on the French Side; and Dawn Beach, Mullet Bay Beach, Maho Beach, and Great Bay Beach on the Dutch side. See chapter 22.
- **Canouan (The Grenadines):** Most of the other beaches recommended in this section may be crowded in winter. But if you're looking for an idyllic, secluded stretch of perfect white sand, head for the remote and tiny island of Canouan, one of the pearls of the Grenadines, a string of islands lying south of its parent, St. Vincent. You'll have the beaches and the crystal-clear waters to yourself, even in winter. See chapter 23.

- **Tobago:** For your Robinson Crusoe holiday in the southern Caribbean, head to the little island of Tobago. Even Trinidadians fly here on weekends to enjoy the beach life. It doesn't get any better than Pigeon Point, a long coral beach on the northwestern coast. Other good beaches on Tobago include Back Bay (site of an old coconut plantation) and Man-O-War Bay, with a beautiful natural harbor and long stretch of sand. See chapter 24.
- **Grace Bay Beach (Providenciales, Turks and Caicos):** These 20km (12 miles) of pale sands are the pride of Provo; the beach has been named the "World's Leading Beach" at the World Travel Awards for 4 years running. It's such a spectacular setting that increasing numbers of resorts have sprung up along the shore. A couple of miles out from the northern shore, the beach is fringed by a reef with fabulous snorkeling. See chapter 25.
- **Trunk Bay (St. John, U.S. Virgin Islands):** Protected by the U.S. National Park Service, this beach is one of the Caribbean's most popular. A favorite with cruise-ship passengers, it's known for its underwater snorkeling trail, where markers guide you along the reef just off the white sands; you're sure to see a gorgeous rainbow of tropical fish. See chapter 26.

THE best SNORKELING

The Virgin Islands offer some particularly outstanding sites, but there are many other great places for snorkeling in the Caribbean.

- **Antigua:** This is a snorkeler's dream. Most of its lovely beaches open onto clear, calm waters populated by rainbow-hued tropical fish. The marine life offshore is particularly dense, including colorful sea anemones. The rich types of different elk and brain coral make snorkeling particularly rewarding. See chapter 3.
- **Bonaire Marine Park (Bonaire):** All the attributes that make Bonaire a world-class diving destination apply to its snorkeling, too. Snorkelers can wade from the shores off their hotels to the reefs and view an array of coral and colorful fish. In particular, the reefs just off Klein Bonaire receive rave reviews. See chapter 6.
- **Stingray City (Grand Cayman, Cayman Islands):** Stingray City is an easy 4m (13-ft.) diving site that can also be seen while snorkeling. It's an extraordinary experience to meet the dozens of tame, gentle stingrays that glide around you in the warm, crystal-clear waters. See chapter 8.
- **Curaçao Underwater Marine Park (Curaçao):** In contrast to Curaçao's arid terrain, the marine life that rings the island is rich and spectacular. The best-known snorkeling sites, in the Curaçao Underwater Marine Park, stretch for 20km (12 miles) along Curaçao's southern coastline, and there are many other highly desirable sites as well. Sunken ships, gardens of hard and soft coral, and millions of fish are a snorkeler's treat. See chapter 9.
- **St. Martin:** The best snorkeling on the island lies on the French side, where the government religiously protects the calm waters, which are populated with schools of brilliantly colored fish. Find a tiny cove and explore the shallow reefs along its shores, especially in the northeastern underwater nature reserve. See chapter 22.
- **The Grenadines:** Every island here offers great snorkeling possibilities right off magnificent white-sand beaches. In most places you'll have the waters to yourself. One of the best is the reef stretching for 1.5km (1 mile) along the island of Canouan, where waters are filled with beautiful brain coral and vibrant fish. The snorkeling is also good at Palm Island and Petit St. Vincent. See chapter 23.

- **Tobago:** Enormous colonies of marine life inhabit the shallow, sun-dappled waters off the coastline facing Venezuela. Buccoo Reef on Tobago is especially noteworthy, and many local entrepreneurs offer snorkeling cruises. See chapter 24.
- **Provo (Turks and Caicos):** Although this island is known primarily as one of the world's best dive sites, it also provides a number of fine snorkeling possibilities, many in and around the islets of the Caicos Cays but a handful right off of Provo's spectacular Grace Bay Beach (at Smith's Reef and Bight Reef). The TCI reefs provide easy access to the fragile but stunningly beautiful world of coral gardens, the most dramatic in the vast area immediately south of the Bahamas. See chapter 25.
- **Buck Island (St. Croix, U.S.V.I.):** More than 250 species of fish, as well as a variety of sponges, corals, and crustaceans, have been found at this 340-hectare (840-acre) island and reef system, 3km (2 miles) off St. Croix's north shore. The reef is strictly protected by the U.S. National Park Service. See chapter 26.
- **Cane Bay (St. Croix, U.S.V.I.):** One of the best diving and snorkeling sites on St. Croix is off this breezy north-shore beach. On a clear day, you can swim out 140m (459 ft.) and see the Cane Bay Wall that drops off dramatically to deep waters below. Multicolored fish, elkhorn, and brain coral abound. See chapter 26.
- **Trunk Bay (St. John, U.S.V.I.):** Trunk Bay's self-guided 205m-long (673-ft.) trail has large underwater signs that identify species of coral and other items of interest. The beach has showers, changing rooms, equipment rentals, and a lifeguard. See chapter 26.
- **Haulover Bay (St. John):** A favorite with locals, this small bay is rougher than Leinster and often deserted. The snorkeling is dramatic, with ledges, walls, nooks, and sandy areas set close together. At this spot, only about 180m (591 ft.) of land separates the Atlantic Ocean from the Caribbean Sea. See chapter 26.
- **Coki Point Beach (St. Thomas, U.S.V.I.):** On the north shore of St. Thomas, this beach offers excellent snorkeling, especially around the coral ledges near Coral World's underwater tower, a favorite with cruise-ship passengers. See chapter 26.

THE best DIVING

All the major islands offer diving trips, lessons, and equipment, but here are the top picks.

- **Bonaire:** The highly accessible reefs that surround Bonaire are pristine, and the island's environmentally conscious diving industry ensures they will remain that way. Created from volcanic eruptions, the island is an underwater mountain, with fringe reefs right off the beach of every hotel on any part of the island. See chapter 6.
- **Virgin Gorda (B.V.I.):** Many divers plan their entire vacations around exploring the famed wreck of the HMS *Rhone,* off Salt Island. This royal mail steamer, which went down in 1867, is the most celebrated diving site in the Caribbean. See chapter 7.
- **Grand Cayman:** This is a world-class diving destination. There are 34 dive operators on Grand Cayman (with five more on Little Cayman, plus three on Cayman Brac). A full range of professional diving services is available, including equipment sales, rentals, and repairs; instruction at all levels; underwater photography; and video schools. See chapter 8.

- **Puerto Rico:** With the continental shelf surrounding it on three sides, Puerto Rico has an abundance of coral reefs, caves, sea walls, and trenches for divers of all experience levels to explore. In southern Puerto Rico, the continental shelf drops off precipitously several miles off the southern coast, producing a dramatic wall 32km (20 miles) long and teeming with marine life. See chapter 16.
- **Saba:** Islanders can't brag about its beaches, but Saba is blessed with some of the Caribbean's richest marine life. It's one of the premier diving locations in the Caribbean, with 38 official diving sites. The unusual setting includes underwater lava flows, black sand, large strands of black coral, millions of fish, and underwater mountaintops submerged under 27m (89 ft.) of water. See chapter 17.
- **Turks and Caicos:** These islands provide a rich assortment of relatively unexplored underwater sites, including sea lanes where boaters and divers often spot whales from January to March. A collection of unusual underwater wrecks and miles of reefs house colorful marine life. Right off Grand Turk, experienced divers explore the many miles of "drop-off" diving, where the sea walls plunge into the uncharted depths of blue holes more than 2,100m (6,890 ft.) below sea level. As you descend, you'll see colonies of black coral, rare forms of anemone, purple sponges, stunning gorgonian, endless forms of coral, and thousands of fish. See chapter 25.
- **St. Croix:** Increasingly known as a top diving destination, St. Croix hasn't yet overtaken Grand Cayman but has a lot going for it. Beach dives, reef dives, wreck dives, nighttime dives, wall dives—they're all here. The highlight is the underwater trails of the national park at Buck Island, off St. Croix's mainland. Other desirable sites include the drop-offs and coral canyons at Cane Bay and Salt River. Davis Bay is the location of the 3,600m-deep (11,811-ft.) Puerto Rico Trench, the fifth-deepest body of water on earth. See chapter 26.

THE best SAILING

Virtually every large-scale hotel in the Caribbean provides small sailboats (most often Sunfish, Sailfish, and small, one-masted catamarans) for its guests. For larger craft, the almost-ideal sailing conditions in the Virgin Islands and the Grenadines come instantly to mind. These two regions offer many options for dropping anchor at secluded coves surrounded by relatively calm waters. Both areas are spectacular, but whereas the Virgin Islands have more dramatic, mountainous terrain, the Grenadines offer insights into island cultures little touched by the modern world.

Other places to sail in the Caribbean include Antigua, Barbados, St. Martin, and the French-speaking islands. But if you plan on a lot of sailing, know that the strongest currents and biggest waves are usually on the northern and eastern sides of most islands—the Atlantic (as opposed to the Caribbean) side.

- **The Grenadines:** Boating is a way of life in the Grenadines, partly because access to many of the tiny remote islands is difficult or impossible by airplane. One of the most prominent local charter agents is **Nicholson Yacht Charters** (© **305/433-5533,** or 268/460-1530 from Antigua; www.nicholson-charters.com), headquartered in nearby St. Vincent. On Bequia, Mustique, Petit St. Vincent, and Union Island, all the hotels can put you in touch with local entrepreneurs who rent sailing craft. See chapter 23 for more details.

- **The British Virgin Islands:** Perhaps because of their well-developed marina facilities (and those of the nearby U.S. Virgins), the Virgin Islands receive the lion's share of devoted yachties. The reigning capital for sailing is Tortola, the largest island of the British Virgins. On-site are about 300 well-maintained sailing craft available for bareboat rentals and perhaps 100 charter yachts. The largest of the Caribbean's yacht-chartering services is the **Moorings** (✆ **888/952-8420** or 284/494-2331; www.moorings.com). On the island of Virgin Gorda, in the British Virgin Islands, the best bet for both boat rentals and accommodations, as well as for a range of instruction, is the **Bitter End Yacht Club** (✆ **800/872-2392** in the U.S., or 312/506-6205; www.beyc.com). The outfits in this paragraph are described more fully in chapter 7.
- **The U.S. Virgin Islands:** Some of the biggest charter business in the Caribbean is conducted on St. Thomas, especially at **American Yacht Harbor,** Red Hook (✆ **340/775-6454;** www.igy-americanyachtharbor.com), which offers bareboat and fully crewed charters. Other reliable rental agents include **Charter Yacht League,** at Flagship (✆ **800/524-2061** in the U.S., or 340/774-3944; www.vicl.org). On St. Croix, boating is less essential to the local economy than it is on St. Thomas or in the British Virgins, so if you're taking a Virgin Islands sailing trip, plan accordingly. The U.S. Virgin Islands are covered in chapter 26.

THE best GOLF COURSES

Some of the world's most famous golf architects, including Robert Trent Jones (both Jr. and Sr.), Pete Dye, and Gary Player, have designed challenging courses in the Caribbean.

- **Tierra del Sol Golf Course** (Aruba; ✆ **866/978-5158** in the U.S., or 297/586-0978; www.tierradelsol.com): Robert Trent Jones, Jr., has designed an 18-hole, par-71, 6,811-yard course that is one of the grandest in the southern Caribbean. On the northwest coast of this arid, cactus-studded island, the course takes in Aruba's indigenous flora, including the divi-divi tree. See p. 86.
- **Teeth of the Dog and the Links** (Casa de Campo, Dominican Republic; ✆ **809/523-3333;** www.casadecampo.com.do): Teeth of the Dog is one of designer Pete Dye's masterpieces. Seven holes are set adjacent to the sea, whereas the other 11 are confoundedly labyrinthine. The resort also has a second golf course, the Links, which some claim is even more difficult. See p. 251.
- **Golf de St-François** (Guadeloupe; ✆ **590/88-41-87;** www.lesilesdeguadeloupe.com): Six of its 18 holes are ringed with water traps, the winds are devilishly unpredictable, and the par is a sweat-inducing 71. This fearsome course displays the wit and skill of its designer, Robert Trent Jones, Sr. Most of the staff is multilingual, and because the course is owned by the local municipality, it's a lot less snobby than you might expect. See p. 325.
- **Tryall Club Jamaica** (Montego Bay, Jamaica; ✆ **876/956-5660;** www.tryallclub.com): This is the finest golf course on an island known for its tricky breezes. The site occupied by the Tryall Club was once the home of one of Jamaica's best-known sugar plantations, the only remnant of which is a ruined waterwheel. The promoters of Johnnie Walker Scotch, who know a lot about golfing, use this place for their most prestigious competition. In winter the course is usually open only to guests of the Tryall Club. See p. 350.

- **Cinnamon Hill** (Rose Hall, Jamaica; ✆ **876/953-2984;** http://cinnamonhilljamaica.com): This is one of the top five courses in the world, even though it faces tough competition in Montego Bay. The signature hole is no. 8, which doglegs onto a promontory and a green that thrusts about 180m (591 ft.) into the sea. The back 9, however, are the most scenic and most challenging, rising into steep slopes and deep ravines on Mount Zion. See p. 350.
- **Four Seasons Resort Nevis** (Nevis; ✆ **800/332-3442;** www.fourseasons.com/nevis): We consider this our personal favorite in all of the Caribbean. It was carved out of a coconut plantation and tropical rainforest in the 1980s, and its undulating beauty is virtually unequaled. Designed by Robert Trent Jones, Jr., the course begins at sea level, rises to a point midway up the slopes of Mount Nevis, and then slants gracefully back down near the beachfront clubhouse. Electric carts carry golfers through a maze of well-groomed paths, some of which skirt steep ravines. See p. 541.

THE best TENNIS FACILITIES

- **Curtain Bluff** (Antigua; ✆ **888/289-9898** in the U.S., or 268/462-8400; www.curtainbluff.com): Small, select, and carefully run by people who love tennis, this is also the annual site of a well-known spring tournament. The courts are set in a low-lying valley. See p. 46.
- **Casa de Campo** (Dominican Republic; ✆ **800/877-3643** or 809/523-3333; www.casadecampo.com.do): The facilities here include 13 clay courts (10 are lit, and two are ringed with stadium seating), four all-weather Laykold courts, a resident pro, ball machines, and tennis pros who are usually available to play with guests. Midwinter, residents and clients of Casa de Campo have first crack at court times. See p. 249.
- **Half Moon** (Montego Bay, Jamaica; ✆ **888/830-5974** in the U.S., or 876/953-2211; http://halfmoon.rockresorts.com): This resort sprawls over hundreds of acres, with about a dozen tennis courts and at least four squash and/or racquetball courts. Jamaica has a strong, British-based affinity for tennis, and Half Moon keeps the tradition alive. See p. 342.
- **The Buccaneer** (St. Croix; ✆ **800/255-3881** in the U.S., or 340/712-2100; www.thebuccaneer.com): Hailed as having the best tennis facilities in the Virgin Islands, this resort hosts several tournaments every year. There are eight all-weather Laykold courts, two of which are illuminated at night; there's also a pro shop. Nonguests can play here for a fee. See p. 728.
- **Wyndham Sugar Bay Resort & Spa** (St. Thomas; ✆ **877/999-3223** or 340/777-7100; www.wyndham.com/hotels/STTSB/main.wnt): This resort offers the first stadium tennis court in the U.S. Virgin Islands, with a capacity of 220 spectators. In addition, it has four Laykold courts, each of which is lit for night play. There's an on-site pro shop, and lessons are available. See p. 691.

THE best HONEYMOON SPOTS

More and more couples are exchanging their vows in the Caribbean. Many resorts will arrange everything from the preacher to the flowers, so we've included in the following list some outfits that provide wedding services.

- **Cap Juluca** (Anguilla; www.capjuluca.com; ✆ **888/858-5822** in the U.S., or 264/497-6666): This 72-hectare (178-acre) resort looks like a Saharan Casbah, with milky domed villas that seem to float against the scrubland and azure sky. It's an extremely stylish setting for romance. More than any other resort on Anguilla, Cap Juluca affords privacy: In their secluded villas, honeymooners can enjoy private pools and oversize tubs for two. Much of the resort and all of the rooms were given a thorough "reinvisioning" in 2009—even the beach is impeccably groomed on a regular basis.
- **St. James's Club** (Antigua; www.stjamesclubantigua.com; ✆ **866/237-2071** in the U.S., or 268/460-5000): There are enough diversions at this very posh British-style resort to keep a honeymooning couple up and about for weeks. Breakfast, lunch, and dinner are included, along with unlimited drinks. Among the perks is a private, candlelit dinner for two in a romantic setting. Honeymooners are greeted with a bottle of champagne and freshly cut bougainvillea in their rooms, which can be private villas, suites, or, for complete isolation, a hillside home. Unlike Cap Juluca, which promotes seclusion, this is for honeymooners who prefer an active lifestyle, gambling at the casino, taking in the beach, or enjoying the widest array of dining and drinking options of any hotel on the island. See p. 48.
- **Biras Creek Resort** (Virgin Gorda; www.biras.com; ✆ **877/883-0756** in the U.S., or 284/494-3555): If you're eager to escape your in-laws and bridesmaids after a wedding ceremony, this is the place. It's a quintessential mariner's hideaway that can be reached only via a several-mile boat ride across the open sea. Perched on a narrow promontory jutting into the Caribbean, it's an intensely private retreat set on 60 hectares (148 acres), with a crisscrossing network of signposted nature trails. Spacious, open-air, walled showers are provided in each bathroom. Honeymooners come here not to be pampered, but to be left alone to do their thing—don't expect a lot of activities. Entertainment and dancing enliven some evenings, but for the most part, you'll enjoy utter tranquillity. Its king-size beds are the best on the island. See p. 160.
- **Peter Island Resort** (Peter Island, B.V.I.; www.peterisland.com; ✆ **800/346-4451** or 284/495-2000): Romantics appreciate the isolation of this resort, on a 720-hectare (1,779-acre) private island south of Tortola and east of St. John. Reaching it requires a 30-minute waterborne transfer, which many urban refugees consider part of the fun. It's very laid-back—bring your new spouse and a good book, and enjoy the comings and goings of yachts at the island's private marina while you recover from the stress of your wedding. See p. 171.
- **Casa Colonial** (Dominican Republic; www.casacolonialhotel.com; ✆ **866/376-7831** or 809/320-3232): On the north coast of the Dominican Republic, this boutique hotel is the most elegant in the country, a member of Small Luxury Hotels of the World. Your marriage will last longer if you check into one of the lavish oceanfront master suites with a private entrance. See p. 259.
- **Sandals Royal Caribbean** (Jamaica; www.sandals.com; ✆ **888/SANDALS** [726-3257] in the U.S., or 876/953-2231): There are a handful of members of this resort chain in Jamaica alone (plus three others on St. Lucia, one in Turks and Caicos, and yet another one on the island of Antigua that is far less grand). Each prides itself on providing an all-inclusive (cash-free) environment where meals are provided in abundance. Enthusiastic members of the staff bring heroic amounts of

community spirit to ceremonies celebrated on-site. Sandals provides everything from a preacher to petunias (as well as champagne, a cake, and all the legalities) for you to get hitched here. See p. 343.

- **Horned Dorset Primavera** (Puerto Rico; www.horneddorset.com; © **800/633-1857** or 787/823-4030): The most romantic place for a honeymoon on the island, this small, tranquil estate lies on the Mona Passage in western Puerto Rico, a pocket of posh where privacy is almost guaranteed. Spanish neocolonial accommodations are luxurious, and the property opens onto a long, secluded beach of white sand. There are no phones, TVs, or radios in the rooms to interfere with the soft sounds of pillow talk. This is a retreat for adults only, with no facilities for children. See p. 471.
- **Four Seasons Resort Nevis** (Nevis; www.fourseasons.com/nevis; © **800/332-3442**): Though not as historic as some of the island's plantation-style inns, the Four Seasons rules without peer as the most deluxe hotel on the island, with the most extensive facilities. Set in a palm grove adjacent to the island's finest beach, it has the atmosphere of a supremely indulgent country club. The Four Seasons offers a 4-day wedding package with a choice of ceremony styles (in a church or on a beach, with a judge or with a civil magistrate). The resort's pastry chef designs each wedding cake individually, and the staff can arrange music, photographs, flowers, legalities, and virtually anything else you want. See p. 532.
- **Anse Chastanet Resort** (St. Lucia; www.ansechastanet.com; © **800/223-1108** in the U.S., or 758/459-7000): Offering panoramic views of mountains and jungle, this intimate hotel is a winner with romantics. With its small size, it provides a lot of privacy and rustic charm. Its wedding package includes all legal processing, a wedding cake, and champagne, and add-ons cover everything from photography to a postwedding sunset sail. See p. 550.
- **Petit St. Vincent Resort** (the Grenadines; www.psvresort.com; © **800/654-9326** or 954/963-7401): If your idea of a honeymoon is to run away from everybody except your new spouse, this is the place. It takes about three planes and a boat to reach it, but the effort to get here is worth it if you want total isolation and privacy. Even the staff doesn't bother you unless you raise a flag for room service. If the honeymoon is going well, you may never have to leave your stone cottage by the beach. The artfully built clubhouses and bungalows were crafted from tropical woods and local stone; the results are simultaneously rustic and lavish. See p. 626.
- **Le Grand Courlan Spa Resort** (Tobago; www.legrandtobago.com; © **868/639-9667**): This is the favorite honeymoon retreat on Tobago. If you want to be fussed over, you and your new spouse can attend the spa for relaxing massages, or you can be left entirely alone to enjoy the bay outside your window or the sandy beach at your doorstep. From Guyanan hardwood to Italian porcelain, the decor is refined and elegant. See p. 646.
- **Parrot Cay** (Parrot Cay, Turks and Caicos; www.parrotcay.com; © **866/388-0036**): Never mind about the celebrity cachet—*you* are the ultrapampered one on this private-island getaway ringed by sparkling green seas. Beachside villas are spacious and ultraprivate, with polished wood floors, four-posters draped in billowing white voile, and private heated plunge pools. The spa is world class. See p. 664.

- **The Buccaneer** (St. Croix; www.thebuccaneer.com; ✆ **800/255-3881** in the U.S., or 340/712-2100): Posh and discreet, this resort has some of the most extensive vacation facilities on St. Croix—three beaches, eight tennis courts, a spa and fitness center, an 18-hole golf course, and 3km (2 miles) of carefully maintained jogging trails. The accommodations include beachside rooms with fieldstone terraces leading toward the sea. The resort's stone sugar mill (originally built in 1658) is one of the most popular sites for weddings and visiting honeymooners on the island. See p. 728.

THE best PLACES TO ESCAPE

In addition to the choices below, see the listings under "The Best Places to Honeymoon," above, for information on Peter Island Resort in the British Virgin Islands and Petit St. Vincent Resort in the Grenadines.

- **Biras Creek Resort** (Virgin Gorda; www.biras.com; ✆ **877/883-0756** in the U.S., or 284/494-3555): The only access to this resort is by private launch. The sea air and the views over islets, cays, and deep blue waters will relax you in your charming guest room. The nautical atmosphere will quickly remove all thoughts of the 9-to-5 job you left behind. See p. 160.
- **Guana Island Club** (Guana Island, B.V.I.; www.guana.com; ✆ **800/544-8262** in the U.S., or 284/494-2354): One of the most secluded hideaways in the entire Caribbean, this resort occupies a privately owned 340-hectare (840-acre) bird sanctuary with nature trails. Head here for views of rare plant and animal life and for several excellent uncrowded beaches. See p. 171.
- **Little Cayman Beach Resort** (Little Cayman; www.littlecayman.com; ✆ **800/327-3835** in the U.S. and Canada, or 345/948-1033): The only practical way to reach the 26-sq.-km (10-sq.-mile) island where this resort is located is by airplane. Snorkelers will marvel at some of the most spectacular and colorful marine life in the Caribbean. The resort has the most complete watersports facilities on the island, and bikes are available for exploring. See p. 202.
- **Rawlins Plantation Inn** (St. Kitts; www.rawlinsplantation.com; ✆ **869/465-6221**): Surrounded by 5 hectares (12 acres) of carefully manicured lawns and tropical shrubbery, and set on a panoramic hillock about 100m (328 ft.) above sea level, this hotel, with its rugs of locally woven rushes and carved four-poster beds, evokes a 19th-century plantation. You'll be separated from the rest of the island by hundreds of acres of sugar cane, and there are few phones and no televisions. See p. 521.

THE best FAMILY VACATIONS

- **Hyatt Regency Aruba Resort & Casino** (Aruba; www.hyatt.com; ✆ **888/591-1234** in the U.S. and Canada, or 297/586-1234): Designed like a luxurious hacienda, with award-winning gardens, this resort is the most upscale on Aruba. Supervised activities for children 3 to 12 include games and contests such as crab races and hula-hoop competitions. See p. 75.
- **Amaryllis Beach Resort** (Barbados; www.amaryllisbeachresort.com; ✆ **246/438-8000**): From its kiddie pool to its activity-filled children's club, this hotel along

Palm Beach is the most family friendly on the island. The complex has an abundance of two-bedroom suites, ideal for the family trade. The chefs also prepare meals for families with young children. See p. 104.

- **The Ritz-Carlton** (Grand Cayman; www.ritzcarlton.com; ✆ **800/542-8680** in the U.S. and Canada, or 345/943-9000): No one coddles families with children as much as this plush hotel. With 58 hectares (143 acres) of grounds to romp on, it's almost like staying in a landscaped park. Plus, the hotel opens onto the activity-filled Seven Mile Beach. It also offers the best children's program on island and, of course, can easily arrange babysitting. See p. 179.
- **Sunset at the Palms Resort & Spa** (Negril, Jamaica; www.sunsetatthepalms.com; ✆ **877/734-3486** in the U.S., or 876/957-5350): Rising on stilts, these wooden cottages with private decks add a sense of adventure to a beach vacation. Surrounded by tropical vegetation, it still puts families only steps from the beach. Features for kids include a playground, computer games, arts and crafts lessons, and even storytelling sessions. Children 2 and under stay free if they share a room with their parent; children 3 to 12 are $100 extra. See p. 357.
- **FDR** (Runaway Bay, Jamaica; www.fdrholidays.com; ✆ **888/337-5437**): FDR gives you a suite with its own kitchen and a "vacation nanny" whose duties include babysitting. Neither its beach nor its pool is the most appealing on Jamaica, but the price is right, and the babysitting is part of the all-inclusive deal. Programs for children include dress-up parties, donkey rides, basketball, tennis, and snorkeling. See p. 375.
- **El Conquistador Resort & Golden Door Spa** (Puerto Rico; www.elconresort.com; ✆ **888/543-1282** or 787/863-1000): Located 50km (31 miles) east of San Juan, this resort offers Camp Coquí on Palomino Island for children 3 to 12 years of age. The hotel's free water taxi takes kids to the island for a half- or full day of watersports and nature hikes. A new water park also adds to the family appeal, boasting a 790-sq.-m (8,504-sq.-ft.) pool, several slides, a rope bridge, and a winding river attraction. This resort has some of the best facilities and restaurants in eastern Puerto Rico and, in fact, all of the Caribbean. See p. 460.
- **Four Seasons Resort Nevis** (Nevis; www.fourseasons.com/nevis; ✆ **800/332-3442**): The staff of the Kids for All Seasons day camp are kindly, matronly souls who work well with children. During the adult cocktail hour, when parents might opt for a romantic sundowner, kids attend a supervised children's hour that resembles a really good birthday bash. Other kid-friendly activities include tennis lessons, watersports, and storytelling. See p. 532.
- **Beaches Turks & Caicos Resort & Spa** (Lower Bight Road, Provo; www.beaches.com; ✆ **888/232-2437** or 649/946-8000): Beaches just walked away with another World Travel Award for best family resort. And why not? It's got *Sesame Street* characters showing up all over the place, camps and activities for kids of all ages, kid-centric restaurants, and a full-service nursery. See p. 666.
- **The Buccaneer** (St. Croix; www.thebuccaneer.com; ✆ **800/255-3881** in the U.S., or 340/712-2100): Posh, upscale, and with extremely good service, this hotel is a longtime favorite that occupies a 96-hectare (237-acre) former sugar estate. Its kids' programs (ages 2–12) include a half-day sailing excursion to Buck Island Reef and guided nature walks that let kids touch, smell, and taste tropical fruit. See p. 728.

THE best INNS

- **The Admiral's Inn** (Antigua; http://admiralsantigua.com; ✆ **268/460-1027**): The most historically evocative corner of Antigua is Nelson's Dockyard, which was originally built in the 1700s to repair His Majesty's ships. The brick-and-stone inn that flourishes here today was once a warehouse for turpentine and pitch. In the late 1960s, it was transformed into a well-designed and very charming hotel. ***Note:*** If you're sensitive to noise, you might be bothered by the sometimes raucous bar and restaurant. See p. 50.
- **Avila Hotel** (Curaçao; www.avilahotel.com; ✆ **800/747-8162** or 599/9-461-4377): This hotel's historic core, built in 1780 as the "country house" of the island's governor, retains its dignity and elegance. Although it's been a hotel since the end of World War II, 150 bedrooms in outbuildings and upgraded sports and dining facilities were artfully added in recent years. Today the Avila provides a sandy beach and easy access to the shops and distractions of nearby Willemstad. See p. 209.
- **Spice Island Beach Resort** (Grenada; www.spicebeachresort.com; ✆ **473/444-4258**): Each of this hotel's 64 units is a suite (with Jacuzzi) either beside the beach (one of Grenada's best) or near a swimming pool. Friday night features live music from the island's most popular bands. See p. 288.
- **Gallery Inn at Galería San Juan** (Puerto Rico; www.thegalleryinn.com; ✆ **866/572-ARTE** [2783] or 787/722-1808): The most whimsically bohemian hotel in the Caribbean sits on a coastal bluff. Once the home of an aristocratic Spanish family, it is today filled with sculptures, silk screens, and original paintings by artist Jan D'esopo, who, along with husband Manuco Gandía, owns the inn. Many of the rooms have dramatic views of the coast, with two historic Spanish forts framing the view. Staying in one of the comfortable rooms here is like living in an art gallery. See p. 430.
- **Ottley's Plantation Inn** (St. Kitts; www.ottleys.com; ✆ **800/772-3039** in the U.S., or 869/465-7234): As you approach, the inn's dignified verandas appear majestically at the crest of 14 hectares (35 acres) of impeccably maintained lawns and gardens. It's one of the most charming plantation-house inns anywhere in the world, maintained with style and humor by its expatriate U.S. owners. The food is the best on the island, and the setting will soothe your tired nerves within a few hours of your arrival. See p. 520.
- **Montpelier Plantation Inn** (Nevis; www.montpeliernevis.com; ✆ **888/334-7609** or 869/469-3462): Style and grace are the hallmarks of this former 18th-century plantation, now converted to an inn and set on a 12-hectare (30-acre) estate. Guests have included the late Princess of Wales. Cottage rooms are spread across 4 hectares (10 acres) of ornamental gardens. Swimming, horseback riding, windsurfing, a private beach, and "eco-rambles" fill the agenda. See p. 533.
- **The Hermitage Plantation Inn** (Nevis; www.hermitagenevis.com; ✆ **800/682-4025** in the U.S., or 869/469-3477): Guests stay in clapboard-sided cottages separated by carefully maintained bougainvillea and grasslands. The beach is a short drive away, but this slice of 19th-century plantation life (complete with candlelit dinners amid the antiques and polished silver of the main house) is decidedly romantic. See p. 533.

- **The Frangipani** (Bequia, the Grenadines; www.frangipanibequia.com; ✆ **784/458-3255**): This is the century-old homestead of the Mitchell family, whose most famous scion later became prime minister of St. Vincent. Today it's a small, very relaxed inn. It's fun to watch the yachts setting out to sea from the nearby marina. See p. 618.

THE best ECO-RESORTS

- **Brac Reef Beach Resort** (Cayman Brac; www.bracreef.com; ✆ **800/594-0843** or 345/948-1323): Cayman Brac is a little, unspoiled island off the coast of the much larger Grand Cayman. Here at this small resort, you can take a series of nature trails that cut through lush vegetation, including sea grapes, to explore the wilderness and enjoy some of the best bird-watching in the islands. This family-friendly resort also offers some of the best snorkeling in the islands. See p. 200.
- **Papillote Wilderness Retreat** (Dominica; www.papillote.dm; ✆ **767/448-2287**): In the middle of one of the Caribbean's most lush rainforests, at the foot of a mountain, this intimate inn returns you to nature in its remote setting of exotic fruits, flowers, and herb gardens. You'll feel like Adam and Eve in the Garden of Eden. Natural hot mineral baths are offered, and you can follow a trail to a secluded waterfall for a river swim. Rooms are rustic but comfortable. See p. 233.
- **Natura Cabañas & the Attabeyra Spa** (Cabarete, Dominican Republic; www.naturacabana.com; ✆ **809/571-1507**): The most eco-sensitive hotel in the Dominican Republic lies between Cabarete and Sosúa, attracting New Age patrons drawn to its setting. Some guests are housed in mushroom-shaped organic-looking structures. During the day, guests can swim, enjoy the spa, or go horseback riding. Mountain bikes or jeeps also can be used to explore this remote part of the country. Or you can just spend the day in a hammock. See p. 269.
- **Asa Wright Nature Centre & Lodge** (Trinidad; www.asawright.org; ✆ **800/426-7781** or 868/667-4655): Known to bird-watchers around the world, this is the most legendary eco-retreat in the Caribbean, standing on 74 hectares (183 acres) of protected land at an elevation of 360m (1,181 ft.) in a rainforest in a mountain range in Trinidad. Nature lovers from all over the world flock here to see the vast array of bird life, including hummingbirds, toucans, manikins, tanagers, and even the rare oilbird. Guided tours are available along trails to a natural waterfall. Accommodations are in a 1908 Edwardian house and various cottages. See p. 632.
- **Cinnamon Bay Campground** (St. John; www.cinnamonbay.com; ✆ **800/539-9998** or 340/776-6330): This National Park Service campground is the best in the Caribbean, and it's set directly on a sandy beach surrounded by thousands of acres of tropical vegetation. You can stay here in a cottage or a tent, or else rent a bare site. Guests take cool water showers and cook their own meals when not swimming, sailing, snorkeling, windsurfing, or hiking through trails in the national park. See p. 718.

THE best DINING

- **Veya** (Anguilla; ✆ **264/498-8392;** www.veya-axa.com): On an island blessed with top-caliber chefs and the Caribbean's best dining scene, this Sandy Ground "treehouse" is one of the best—and it's only been around since 2007. The Pennsylvania chef/owners call their food the "cuisine of the sun," and it's a minxy fusion of exotic flavors from hot spots around the globe, from Moroccan-spiced shrimp "cigars" to vanilla-cured duck in guavaberry sauce. See p. 32.
- **The Reef Grill at Royal Palms** (Grand Cayman; ✆ **345/945-6358;** www.reefgrill.com): Elegant and hip, this hotshot restaurant in the Royal Palms Beach Club opens onto the fabled Seven Mile Beach. Adjacent to a beachfront bar and grill, it is a citadel of fine cuisine, specializing in seafood recently plucked from the nearby sea. The chefs treat seasonal products with care, turning out technically precise dishes that also have imagination—anyone for mashed potatoes garnished with chunks of lobster tail? See p. 188.
- **Sugar Mill Restaurant** (Jamaica; ✆ **888/830-5974;** http://halfmoon.rockresorts.com): At Half Moon, this first-rate restaurant has been created from the ruins of what used to be a water wheel for a sugar plantation. The cuisine is exquisite as you dine by candlelight on an open terrace under the moon. The chef is inspired, roaming the globe for his culinary creations. See p. 347.
- **Wall House** (St. Barts; ✆ **590/27-71-83;** www.wallhouserestaurant.com): It's neither coolly elegant nor dripping with chic. It doesn't cost an arm and a leg to eat here, either. It is, however, a perfect representation of the kind of invitingly atmospheric French *boîte* that people want to come back to again and again. New ownership has not diminished the Wall House traditions of warm service, lively ambience, and bistro fare with flair at reasonable prices. The dazzling harbor views certainly don't hurt, either. See p. 500.
- **The Edge** (St. Lucia; ✆ **758/450-3343;** www.edge-restaurant.com): Swedish-born Bobo Bergström is hailed as St. Lucia's finest chef—and the competition is keen. His European fusion cuisine produces thrilling gastronomic delights, and he also offers the first and only sushi bar ever set up on St. Lucia. In 2003 he was designated as Caribbean Chef of the Year. We'll let you in on a secret: He's gotten even better since then. See p. 562.

THE best SHOPPING

Because the U.S. government allows its citizens to take (or send) home more duty-free goods from the U.S. Virgins than from other ports of call, the islands remain the shopping bazaar of the Caribbean. U.S. citizens may carry home $1,400 worth of goods untaxed, as opposed to only $400 to $600 worth of goods from most other islands in the Caribbean. (The only exception to this rule is Puerto Rico, where any purchase, regardless of the amount, can be carried tax-free back to the U.S. mainland.) St. Maarten/St. Martin, which is ruled jointly by France and the Netherlands, gives the Virgins some serious competition. It is virtually a shopper's mall, especially on the Dutch side. Although the U.S. doesn't grant the generous Customs allowances to St. Maarten/St. Martin that it does to its own islands, the island doesn't have duty, so you can find some attractive bargains.

- **Aruba:** The wisest shoppers on Aruba are cost-conscious souls who have carefully checked the prices of comparable goods before leaving home. Duty is relatively low (only 3.3%). Much of the European china, jewelry, perfumes, and watches have a disconcerting habit of reappearing in every shopping mall and hotel boutique on the island, so after you determine exactly what brand of watch or china you want, you can comparison-shop. See chapter 4.
- **Barbados:** Local shops seem to specialize in all things English. Merchandise includes bone china from British and Irish manufacturers, watches, jewelry, and perfumes. Bridgetown's Broad Street is the shopping headquarters of the island, although some of the stores here maintain boutiques (with similar prices but a less extensive range of merchandise) at many of the island's hotels and in malls along the congested southwestern coast. Except for cigarettes and tobacco, duty-free items can be hauled off by any buyer as soon as they're paid for. Duty-free status is extended to anyone showing a passport or ID and an airline ticket with a date of departure from Barbados. See chapter 5.
- **The Cayman Islands:** Goods are sold tax-free from a daunting collection of malls and minimalls throughout Grand Cayman. Most of these are along the highway that parallels Seven Mile Beach; you'll need a car to shop around. There are also lots of stores in George Town, which you can explore on foot, poking in and out of some large emporiums in your search for bargains. See chapter 8.
- **Curaçao:** In the island's capital, tidy and prosperous Willemstad, hundreds of merchants are only too happy to cater to your needs. A handful of malls lies on Willemstad's outskirts, but most shops are clustered within a few blocks of the center of town. During seasonal sales, goods might be up to 50% less than comparable prices in the United States; most of the year, you'll find luxury items (porcelain, crystal, watches, and gemstones) priced at about 25% less than in the U.S. Technically, you'll pay import duties on virtually everything you buy, but rates are so low you may not even notice. See chapter 9.
- **The Dominican Republic:** The island's best buys include handicrafts, amber from Dominican mines, and the distinctive pale-blue semiprecious gemstone known as larimar. The amber sold by street vendors may be nothing more than orange-colored, transparent plastic; buy only from well-established shops if your investment is a large one. Other charming souvenirs might include a Dominican rocking chair (JFK used to sit in one), which is sold boxed, in ready-to-assemble pieces. Malls and souvenir stands abound in Santo Domingo, in Puerto Plata, and along the country's northern coast. See chapter 11.
- **Jamaica:** The shopping was better in the good old days, before taxes added a 10% surcharge. Despite that, Jamaica offers a wealth of desirable goods, including flavored rums, Jamaican coffees, handicrafts (such as woodcarvings, woven baskets, and sandals), original paintings and sculpture, cameras, watches, and DVD players. Unless you're a glutton for handmade souvenirs (which are available on virtually every beach and street corner), you'd be wise to limit most of your purchases to bona fide merchants and stores. See chapter 14.
- **St. Maarten/St. Martin:** Because of the massive influx of cruise ships, shopping in Dutch St. Maarten is now about the finest in the Caribbean for deals in electronics, cameras, designer fashions, watches, and crystal, along with linens and jewelry.

Because there's no duty, prices can be 30% to 40% lower than in the U.S. Philipsburg, capital of the island's Dutch side, is the best place to shop. Although it can't compete with Dutch St. Maarten, French St. Martin is becoming a more popular shopping destination, especially for goods such as fashion or perfumes imported from France. See chapter 22.

- **St. Croix:** This island doesn't have the massive shopping development of St. Thomas, but its merchandise has never been more wide-ranging than it is today. Even though most cruise ships call at Frederiksted, with its urban mall, our favorite shops are in Christiansted, which has many one-of-a-kind boutiques and a lot of special finds. Prices are about the same here as on St. Thomas. See chapter 26.
- **St. Thomas:** Many of its busiest shops are in restored warehouses that were originally built in the 1700s. Charlotte Amalie, the capital, is a shopper's town, with a staggering number of stores stocked with more merchandise than anywhere else in the entire Caribbean. However, despite all the fanfare, real bargains are hard to come by. Regardless, the island attracts hordes of cruise-ship passengers on a sometimes-frantic hunt for bargains, real or imagined. Look for two local publications, *This Week* and *Best Buys;* either might steer you to the type of merchandise you're seeking. If at all possible, try to avoid shopping when more than one cruise ship is in port—the shopping district is a madhouse on those days. See chapter 26.

THE best NIGHTLIFE

Nighttime is sleep time on the British Virgins, Montserrat, Nevis, Anguilla, St. Eustatius, Saba, St. Barts, Dominica, Bonaire, St. Vincent, and all of the Grenadines. The serious partier will probably want to choose one of the following destinations.

- **Aruba:** This island has 12 casinos, each with its own unique decor and each with a following of devoted gamblers. They offer cabarets and comedy shows, dance floors with live or recorded music, restaurants of all degrees of formality, and bars. The casinos are big, splashy, and colorful, and, yes, people even occasionally win. Drinks are usually free while you play. The legal tender in most of Aruba's casinos is the U.S. dollar. See chapter 4.
- **Barbados:** Bridgetown is home to rum-and-reggae cruises, as well as oversize music bars like Harbour Lights. Otherwise, a host of bars, British-style pubs, dozens of restaurants, and dance clubs (both within and outside large hotels) beckon from St. Lawrence Gap or the crowded southwest coast. See chapter 5.
- **Curaçao:** Although outdistanced by Aruba, the action spinning around the island's casinos makes this one of the southern Caribbean's hot spots for gamblers. Salinja, a sector of Willemstad, has lively bars where locals and visitors drink and party until the wee hours, and live jazz often fills the air. See chapter 9.
- **The Dominican Republic:** Large resort hotels in the Dominican Republic evoke a Latino version of Las Vegas. If cabaret shows aren't your thing, there are enough dance clubs in the major towns and resorts to keep nightclubbers busy for weeks. The tourist areas of Puerto Plata and Santo Domingo are sprinkled with casinos, and the island's ever-developing north shore contains its share of jingle-jangle, too. See chapter 11.

- **Jamaica:** Many visitors are drawn here by a love for the island's distinct musical forms. Foremost among these are reggae and soca, both of which are performed at hotels, resorts, and raffish dives all over the island. Hotels often stage folkloric shows that include entertainers who sing, dance, swallow torches, and walk on broken glass. There are also plenty of indoor/outdoor bars where you might actually be able to talk to people. See chapter 14.
- **Puerto Rico:** Puerto Rico contains all the raw ingredients for great nightlife, including casinos, endless rows of bars and taverns, cabaret shows with girls and glitter, and dance clubs that feature everything from New York imports to some of the best salsa and merengue anywhere. The country's gaming headquarters lie along the Condado in San Juan, although there are also casinos in megaresorts scattered throughout the island. The casinos here are the most fun in the Caribbean. Each contains lots of sideshows (restaurants, merengue bars, art galleries, piano bars, and shops) that can distract you from the roulette and slots. Puerto Ricans take pride in dressing well at their local casinos, which enhances an evening's glamour. (***Note:*** You can't drink at the tables.) If you're a really serious partier, you'll have lots of company in Puerto Rico. Be prepared to stay out very late; you can recover from your Bacardi hangover on a palm-fringed beach the next day. See chapter 16.
- **St. Maarten/St. Martin:** This cosmopolitan island has an active nightlife, with 14 casinos (on the Dutch side) and countless beach bar/restaurants featuring live soca or reggae. Nightclubs are often indoor/outdoor affairs, with pools, international DJs, and statuesque servers hoisting bottles of champagne ablaze with sparklers. See chapter 22.
- **St. Thomas:** The Virgin Islands' most active nightlife is found here. Don't expect glitzy shows like those in San Juan's Condado area, and don't expect any kind of casino. But you can find plenty of fun at the beach bars, restaurants, concerts, clubs, and folklore and reggae shows. See chapter 26.

ANGUILLA

2

For years one of the Caribbean's best-kept secrets, this small, serene island is a top-end destination with only a handful of resorts. Anguilla (rhymes with "vanilla") has deliberately turned its back on the package tours, glitzy casinos, and cruise ships of neighboring Dutch St. Maarten. It's a chic but unaffected island destination, with dozens of powdery-soft sand beaches and sparkling green seas.

Beaches **Shoal Bay East** offers both activity and seclusion: Beach bars and barbecue shacks line one section, while you can snorkel about undisturbed on its less-crowded eastern side. Sunbathers have three miles of curving white sand at **Rendezvous Bay.** Watch fisherman haul silver bonito onto the sugary crescent at **Meads Bay.** Don a mask and fins and snorkel in the calm, sparkling waters of **Maundys Bay.** Take a day trip to idyllic offshore islands such as **Sandy Isle** or **Prickly Pear.**

Things to Do Take a **taxi tour** of this small island with your driver as your local guide. Arawak Indian tools and slave shackles are part of the **Heritage Museum Collection** at Pond Ground. Snorkel about in the gin-clear shallows at **Junk's Hole** until your lobster comes off the grill at **Nat Richardson's Palm Grove.** Watch fishermen bring up their nets as the sun sets at **Sandy Ground.** Enjoy music at a **beach bar** like **Smokey's.**

Eating & Drinking Dine on fresh, **locally caught fish**—red snapper, yellowfin tuna, grouper, mahimahi—**Anguillian lobster,** and sweet local **crayfish.** Anguilla has some of the region's best beach bars and grills, serving up ribs at **Uncle Ernie's** in Shoal Bay, grilled spiny lobster at **Smitty's** in Island Harbour, or barbecued chicken at **Gwen's Reggae Bar & Grill** in Upper Shoal Bay.

Shopping Anguilla has a thriving arts and crafts scene, with a number of art galleries, including that of American painter Lynne Bernbaum in George Hill; Louise Brooks' Alak Gallery on Shoal Bay East; Devonish Art Gallery in Long Bay, with work by Anguillian potter and sculptor Courtney Devonish; and the Stone Cellar Art Gallery in The Valley, a former 1868 cotton gin and home to Sir Roland Richardson's Caribbean Impressionistic paintings.

ESSENTIALS

Visitor Information

The **Anguilla Tourist Board,** Coronation Avenue, The Valley, Anguilla, B.W.I. (✆ **800/553-4939** or 264/497-2759; fax 264/497-2710; www.anguilla-vacation.com), is open Monday to Friday from 8am to 5pm.

Anguilla

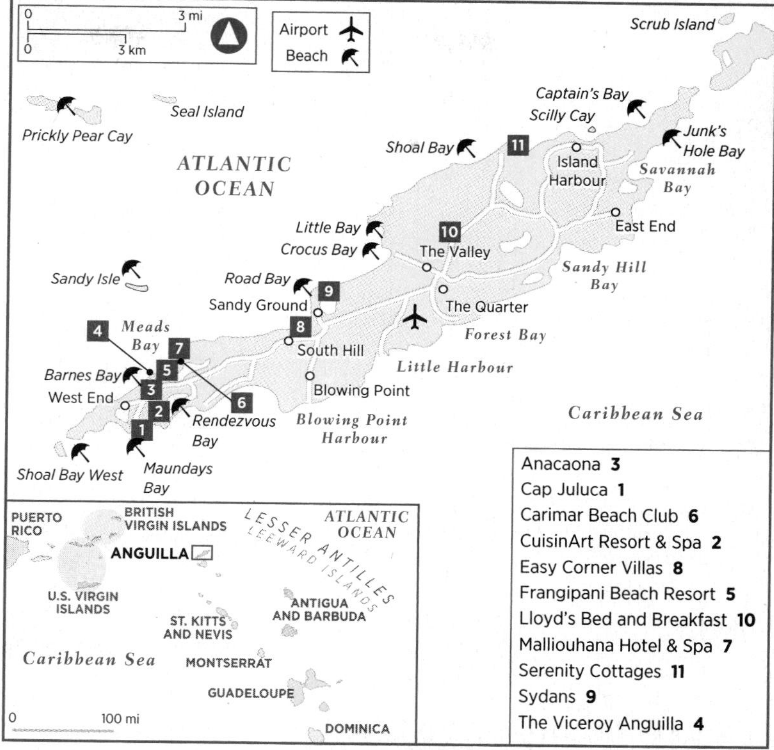

In the United States, contact Marie Walker at the Anguilla Tourist Board, 246 Central Ave., White Plains, NY 10606 (✆ **877/426-4845** or 914/287-2400; mturnstyle@aol.com). For U.S. travelers who need quick answers to questions about Anguilla, contact the toll-free **Anguilla Hotline** (✆ **800/418-4620**).

In the United Kingdom, contact the **Anguilla Tourist Board,** 7A Crealock St., London SW18 2BS (✆ **020/8871-0012**).

USEFUL WEBSITES In addition to the website above, other helpful sites include **www.gov.ai** (Anguilla government), **www.anguillahta.com** (Anguilla Hotel and Tourism Association) and the ***Anguillian* newspaper** (www.anguillian.com). The **Anguilla Guide** (www.anguillaguide.com) and the **Anguilla Forum** (www.anguillaforum.com) are very helpful—the message boards often contain invaluable travel tips.

USEFUL READING In The Valley, the **Anguilla Arts and Crafts Center** (✆ **264/497-2200**) and the **National Trust Office** (✆ **264/497-5297;** www.axanationaltrust.org) stock books on Anguilla, including guides to the local flora and fauna. Of note is Brenda Carty and Colville Petty's *Anguilla, an Introduction and Guide,* which is also available at Petty's **Heritage Museum Collection** ★ in the island's East End (p. 37).

Getting There

BY PLANE During high season, Anguilla's **Wallblake Airport** (www.gov.ai/airport.htm), located just outside The Valley, is abuzz with private Gulfstreams and Fortune 500 executive jets purring on the runway. There are no nonstop flights from mainland North America into Anguilla, so visitors either transfer through San Juan, Puerto Rico, or the Princess Juliana International Airport in St. Maarten, or fly in by private charter.

Currently, three commercial airlines are flying connecting flights into Wallblake. **LIAT** (✆ **888/844-5428** or 264/497-5001; www.liatairline.com) flies to Anguilla daily from Antigua, St. Kitts, and St. Thomas. **Winair (Windward Islands Airways International;** ✆ **866/466-0410** in the U.S. and Canada, or 599/545-4237; www.fly-winair.com) has daily flights to Anguilla from Dutch St. Maarten. In late 2010, New England–based **Cape Air** (✆ **866/227-3247;** www.capeair.net) entered the Anguilla market with twice-day flights between Wallblake and San Juan. ***Note:*** At press time, **American Eagle** (✆ **800/433-7300** in the U.S. and Canada; www.aa.com), the commuter partner of American Airlines, had suspended its nonstop daily flight into Anguilla from American's San Juan hub.

A fast and convenient option is to hop on one of the handful of private regional airlines that offer chartered plane service from St. Maarten/St. Martin or other nearby islands directly to Anguilla. At press time, **Anguilla Air Services** (✆ **264/498-5922;** www.anguillaairservices.com) was offering one-way flights at rates of $80. Offering comparable fares is the other Anguillian airlines, **Trans Anguilla Airways** (✆ **264/497-8690;** www.transanguilla.com). **Rainbow International Airlines** (✆ **866/966-1881;** www.rainbowinternationalairlines.com) flies out of San Juan.

BY FERRY Most people coming in to Anguilla arrive via the Blowing Point ferry port. Public ferries run between Marigot Bay, St. Martin, and Anguilla (✆ **264/497-6070**), every 30 minutes. The trip takes 20 to 25 minutes, making day trips a snap. Usually, the first ferry leaves St. Martin at 8am and the last at 7pm; from Blowing Point, the first ferry leaves at 7:30am and the last at 6:15pm. The one-way fare is $15 ($10 children 2–18) plus a $3 departure tax. A departure tax of $20 (children $10) is charged on your return trip to St. Martin; day-trippers and visiting yachts pay a $5 departure tax. No reservations are necessary. Ferries vary in size, and none take passenger vehicles. ***Tip:*** Keep in mind that if you have a late-arriving flight, you may quite literally miss the (ferry) boat. You can either spend the night in St. Maarten/St. Martin or arrange a charter plane connection (see above) into Anguilla.

A convenient option is to take one of the **privately run charter boats and ferries** that shuttle passengers between Anguilla and the airport in St. Maarten. Anguilla-based charter boats will pick you up at the Princess Juliana airport in St. Maarten and transport you and your luggage to Blowing Point or a hotel on the south side of Anguilla. These boats are more expensive than the public ferries, but they let you avoid having to travel from the airport to the ferry port in Marigot by taxi (a 10- to 15-min. trip)—a smart option for travelers with lots of luggage or lots of kids. Plus, the privately run boats are smaller and have fewer passengers and can even arrange full-boat charters for groups or families. Keep in mind that these boats do not run as frequently as the government-run ferry, but most do include ground transportation. ***Good news:*** In 2010 an agreement was reached between the St. Maarten and Anguilla governments designed to greatly facilitate the ease of private-boat transfers (and passing through immigration) from the airport. This means that, ideally, you will be able to get off the plane and jump on a boat straight to Anguila in under 30 minutes.

Check out the ***GB Express*** (✆ **264/235-6205** in Anguilla, or 599/581-3568 in St. Maarten; www.anguillaferryandcharter.com; $55 one-way, $90 round-trip); the ***M.V. Shauna VI*** (✆ **264/476-0975** or 264/772-2031 in Anguilla; myshauna6@hotmail.com; round-trip fare $60 adults, $40 children 2–12); or **Funtime Charters** (✆ **866/334-0047** or 264/497-6511; www.funtime-charters.com; $55 per person one-way; half-price for children 11 and under). Reservations required.

Most Anguilla hotels will also arrange (for a fee) private-boat charters between the airport in St. Maarten and the ferry dock at Blowing Point, Anguilla, with door-to-door ground transportation.

Tip: If you'd like to do some shopping and have lunch in Marigot before you take your ferry to Anguilla, simply store your bags at the ferry landing. The Port de Marigot has a small baggage storage area ($5, plus tip).

Getting Around

BY RENTAL CAR To explore the island in any depth, I highly recommend you rent a car, though be prepared for some badly paved roads. Four-wheel-drive vehicles are a real bonus for exploring the island's unpaved and pitted back roads, but not necessary elsewhere. Rental agencies on the island can issue the mandatory Anguillian driver's license, which is valid for 3 months. You can also get a license at police headquarters in the island's administrative center, The Valley, and at ports of entry. You'll need to present a valid driver's license from your home country and pay a one-time fee of $20.

Remember: Drive on the left side of the road.

Most visitors take a taxi from the airport to their hotel and arrange, at no extra charge, for a rental agency to deliver a car there the following day. All rental companies offer discounts for rentals of 7 days or more. Renting a car is not cheap on Anguilla, beginning at about $40 a day plus insurance and taxes, which can be steep.

Avis (✆ **800/331-1212** in the U.S. and Canada, or 264/497-2642; www.avisanguilla.com), which is represented by **Apex** in The Valley, offers regular cars and some four-wheel-drive vehicles, as does **Hertz**'s representative, **Triple K Car Rental,** Airport Road (✆ **800/654-3001** in the U.S. and Canada, or 264/497-2934; www.hertz.com). Local firms include **Connor's Car Rental,** South Hill (✆ **264/497-6433**), and **Island Car Rentals,** Airport Road (✆ **264/497-2723**).

Note: It's worth pricing a car rental with one of the larger agencies and then checking with your hotel to see what price they can get for you. Many hotels and inns on Anguilla rent all their customers' cars from one or more small local agencies. Your car may not be as new and shiny as some of the other rentals available, but your savings may be considerable.

BY TAXI Taxi fares are posted at Walblake Airport, at the Blowing Point ferry, and in most taxis. Taxis can be pricey, so don't take it out on your driver if you think your fare is, well, unfair. Not only does each driver have to pay costly insurance to insure you, the passenger, but gas is astronomically expensive, at press time nearly $5 a gallon, and most drivers have vans—which can cost $75 to fill up. Plus, Anguilla taxis don't have meters, so if a customer is dragging his feet, drivers are not compensated to wait. But the main reason a taxi ride costs what it does is that the government has parceled the island into 10 strictly delineated taxi zones, with a set fee schedule based

Festivals: Carnival, Boat Races & Moonsplash

Anguilla's most colorful annual festival is Carnival. The festival begins on the Thursday before the first Monday in August and lasts 10 days, with spectacular parades of floats and elaborately costumed dancers. Carnival harks back to Emancipation Day, or "August Monday," in 1834, when enslaved Africans all throughout the British colonies were freed. Boat races are Anguilla's national sport, and the distinctive swift, high-masted, brightly painted open boats—many of them made here on the island—stage a number of exciting races during Carnival. In early May, the Anguilla Regatta (www.anguillaregatta.com) features competitive races over a 3-day weekend, with free entertainment and barbecues every night. Anguilla's other major festivals are late March's 4-day Moonsplash Music Festival (www.bankiebanx.net), founded by Anguilla's best-known musician, Bankie Banx, and Tranquility Jazz Festival (www.anguillajazz.org), held the second week of November. On an early April weekend, Island Harbor celebrates fishing and the sea in the Festival del Mar.

on travel within and out of each zone. So, for example, Zone 1 covers the West End, where many of the top resorts and restaurants are located. Within that zone, a taxi ride will cost $10 (plus an additional $4 after 6pm). But from Zone 1 to Zone 2—another busy resort area 5 minutes away—the fare jumps to $14 (plus $4 after 6pm).

Tipping is at the discretion of the customer. You can check out the latest rate schedules by going to the **Anguilla Hotel & Tourism Association** website (www.ahta.ai/Taxi_Service.html). You can also get a cab through the **Airport Taxi Stand** at ✆ **264/497-5054** or **Blowing Point Ferry Taxi Stand** at ✆ **264/497-6089.** A $4 surcharge goes into effect between 6pm and 6am.

If you find a taxi driver you like, ask for his card and cellphone number for future rides. I highly recommend the taxi services of **Accelyn Connor** (✆ **264/497-0515** or 264/235-8931; premiertaxiandtour@hotmail.com), a gentleman and a stickler for service. Taxi drivers also make great tour guides; check out "Exploring the Island," later in this chapter.

[FastFACTS] ANGUILLA

Banks Banks with ATMs are open Monday to Thursday 8am to 3pm, Friday 8am to 5pm. Several banks, including **Scotiabank,** The Valley, Fairplay Commercial Complex (✆ **264/497-3333**), and **First Caribbean,** The Valley (✆ **264/497-2301**), have ATMs usually accessible after hours.

Currency The **Eastern Caribbean dollar (EC$)** is the official currency of Anguilla, although U.S. dollars are the actual "coin of the realm." Some restaurants and small establishments may present prices in EC$. When you inquire about a price, make sure you know the type of dollars quoted. The exchange rate is permanently fixed at EC$2.70 to each US$1 (EC$1 = US37¢). *Prices in this chapter are quoted in U.S. dollars ($).*

Customs Even for tourists, duties are levied on imported goods at varying rates, from 5% on foodstuffs to 30% on luxury goods, wines, and liquors.

Documents All visitors must have an onward or return ticket. U.S., British, and Canadian citizens must have a valid passport.

Electricity The electricity is 110-volt AC (60 cycles), so no transformers or adapters are necessary to use U.S. appliances.

Hospitals For medical services, consult the **Princess Alexandra Hospital,** Stoney Ground (✆ **264/497-2551** or -2552).

Language The language spoken on Anguilla is English.

Liquor Laws Beer, wine, and liquor are sold 7 days a week during regular business hours. It's legal to have an open container on the beach.

Pharmacies The Princess Alexandra Hospital Pharmacy, Stoney Ground (✆ **264/497-2551**), is open weekdays 8am to 5pm and Saturday 10am to noon. The **Paramount Pharmacy** has branches at Water Swamp (✆ **264/497-2366**) and South Hill (✆ **264/498-2366**).

Police You can reach the police at their headquarters in The Valley (✆ **264/497-2333**) or the substation at Sandy Ground (✆ **264/497-2354**). For emergencies, dial ✆ **911.**

Post Office The main post office is on Wallblake Road, The Valley (✆ **264/497-2528;** www.aps.ai). Collectors consider Anguilla's stamps valuable, and the post office also operates a philatelic bureau, open Monday to Friday 8am to 4:45pm. Airmail postcards and letters cost EC$1.50 to the U.S., Canada, and the United Kingdom. ***Note:*** In January 2009, Anguilla got its first postal code: AI-2640. So if you're *sending* a letter to Anguilla from another country, you'll place the new postal code after "Anguilla" and before "British West Indies" (or "BWI").

Safety Although crime is rare here, secure your valuables; never leave them in a parked car.

Taxes The government collects a 10% tax on rooms, and hotels tack on a 10% service charge. All visitors traveling through the seaports are required to pay an embarkation tax of $20 per adult and $10 for children 13–18 (children 12 and under are free).

Telephone Telephone, cable, and Telex services are offered by **LIME** (formerly Cable & Wireless Ltd.), Wallblake Road, The Valley (✆ **264/497-3100**), open Monday to Friday 8am to 5pm. To call the United States from Anguilla, dial **1,** the area code, and the seven-digit number. **Digicel** (✆ **264/498-3444**), with its main office by the public library in The Valley, often has more competitive rates for renting or buying a cellphone than LIME.

Time Anguilla is on Atlantic Standard Time year-round, which means it's usually 1 hour ahead of the U.S. East Coast—except when the U.S. is on daylight saving time, when the clocks are the same.

Weather The hottest months in Anguilla are July to October; the coolest, December to February. The mean monthly temperature is about 80°F (27°C).

WHERE TO STAY

Very Expensive

Cap Juluca ★★★ New ownership and new management have things percolating at Cap Juluca, and a savvy refashioning of the resort's main public spaces has given this much-loved resort fresh vigor. This is one of the premier properties on the island and a favorite honeymoon destination. Of course, having one of the best beaches on the island doesn't hurt; here, beachside pampering is a daylong affair. Encircling Maundays Bay's lovely white-sand beach and nestled in luxuriantly landscaped 72-hectare (179-acre) grounds, Cap Juluca defines excellence: It employs 375 people for only 98 rooms. A $29-million renovation in 2009 completely repositioned the Main House, capped by a soaring domed ceiling and a Moroccan chandelier. Just outside is the new Maundays Bay bar. The architectural style throughout is quasi-Moorish, with sun-blasted exteriors, white domes, arched doorways, and walled courtyards. All of the spacious rooms and villas have luxurious Frette-sheathed beds, ceramic tile floors, and colonial-style louvered doors opening onto patios, many with pathways leading directly to the sea. All are outfitted with the essential mod cons of 21st-century life—flatscreen TVs, Wi-Fi, iPod docks, Bose Wave music systems—and a number of villas have private plunge pools. Bathrooms are enormous and sheathed in marble. And plans are underway for the building of five new villas. Pimm's features "Eurobbean" cuisine—a marriage of European and Caribbean styles and flavors. Blue replaces George's as the casual alfresco beach-front spot, and the pan-Asian Spice has replaced Kemia.

Maundays Bay (P.O. Box 240), Anguilla, B.W.I. www.capjuluca.com. ✆ **888/858-5822** in the U.S., or 264/497-6666. Fax 264/497-6617. 71 units. Winter/spring $995–$1,195 double, from $1,595 suite; off season $425–$695 double, from $695 suite. Children 11 and under stay free in parent's room. Airport boat/taxi transfers: $75 one-way per person semi-private boat; $425 (1–4 persons) private boat. AE, MC, V. **Amenities:** 3 restaurants; 2 bars; babysitting; children's programs (in summer only); fitness center; driving range; golf course; outdoor pool; room service; spa; 3 tennis courts; watersports equipment (extensive). *In room:* A/C, TV/DVD, CD player, hair dryer, minibar, MP3 docking station, Wi-Fi (free).

CuisinArt Resort & Spa ★★★ ☺ Pillowed in the sand dunes that line a lovely stretch of Rendezvous Bay beach, CuisinArt's whitewashed villas seem transplanted from some sunny Greek isle. This handsomely landscaped resort has an infinity pool that flows all the way to the beach—its long stretches of shallow water are perfect for toddling kids. CuisinArt has a happy, comfortable vibe, with roosters crowing in the morning and lizards skittering in the underbrush, and a palm-fringed patio that faces the gleaming pool. And, yes, it is owned by CuisinArt (of blender fame), and yes, it takes its food seriously, with Anguilla's first and only hydroponic farm, an herb garden, and twice-weekly **barbecue buffets ★★**, piled high with grilled lobster, spit-roasted chicken, and ribs. The rooms are sun-splashed and cheerful, with comfy wicker and dark-wood furniture and colorful Haitian paintings on the walls. Bathrooms are spacious, with lots of marble and fluffy towels. Patios have spectacular ocean views. Six new luxury villas have been built on the resort's eastern flank. The resort's main dining room, Santorini, serves dinner only. The poolside Mediterraneo has more casual fare, with breakfasts that include delicious corn pancakes and fresh fruit smoothies. The newly renovated and expanded Venus Spa features 16 treatment rooms, a Thalasso pool of heated seawater, and an oceanfront relaxation room.

Rendezvous Bay (P.O. Box 2000), Anguilla, B.W.I. www.cuisinartresort.com. ✆ **800/943-3210** or 264/498-2000. Fax 264/498-2010. 93 units. Winter/spring $740 double, $920–$2,270 suite, $3,150–$3,670 penthouse; off season $400–$495 double, $495–$1,500 suite, $1,700–$2,550 penthouse. Children 11 and under stay free in parent's room. Airport boat/taxi transfers: $65 one-way per person semi-private boat; $350 (1–4 persons) private boat; additional person $25. AE, MC, V. Closed Sept–Oct. **Amenities:** 3 restaurants; 3 bars; babysitting; mountain bikes; children's playground; fitness center; bocce court; croquet; billiards room; Jacuzzi; outdoor pool; room service; salon; spa; 3 tennis courts; watersports equipment (extensive); Wi-Fi (free, in lobby). *In room:* A/C, TV/VCR (DVD in some), CD player, hair dryer, high-speed Internet ($15/day), minibar.

Malliouhana Hotel & Spa ★★★ ☺ The island's oldest and most celebrated resort resides over a magical setting, its sun-blasted limestone villas terraced on a bluff overlooking the broad sweep of Meads Bay. Cradled amid cliffside gardens between two crescent beaches, Malliouhana's 10 hectares (25 acres) hold pools, tiled walkways, and fountains in a carefully tended landscape of palms, sea grape, agave, and banks of flowers. All 55 rooms have sea or garden views—sometimes both—and spacious marbled bathrooms. Rooms are decadently large, with closet space designed for steamer trunks and entourages. The Meads Bay beaches at the foot of the resort are some of the island's best, with terrific off-the-beach snorkeling around the rocks. Equally fine is the Michel Rostang at Mallíouhana restaurant, which garnered a top spot on *Condé Nast Traveler*'s Gold List in 2010 as one of the best hotels for food in the Americas and the Caribbean. The stellar wine cellar is the largest in the Caribbean, capable of holding 25,000 to 35,000 bottles. If you're traveling with a child, a terrific supervised playground surrounds a faux pirate ship (nonguests $25 per person per day). The spa is world-class, with 15,000 square feet of oceanfront pampering. Is the resort a little tired? Perhaps. But Malliouhana has solid bones. The setting alone is magic. It's hard to argue with a sunset cocktail on your terrace, enveloped in that vast ocean of turquoise, as the pelicans swoop in for the night.

Meads Bay (P.O. Box 173), Anguilla, B.W.I. www.malliouhana.com. ✆ **800/835-0796** in the U.S., or 264/497-6111. Fax 264/497-6011. 55 units. Winter $860–$1,220 double, $1,175–$3,660 suite; off season $430–$670 double, $660–$2,360 suite. Airport boat/taxi transfers: $70 one-way per person. AE, MC, V. Closed Sept–Oct. **Amenities:** 2 restaurants; 2 bars; babysitting; children's playground; concierge; fitness center/gym; basketball court; Jacuzzi; 3 freshwater outdoor pools; room service; salon; spa; 4 lighted tennis courts; watersports equipment (extensive). *In room:* A/C, ceiling fan, hair dryer, minibar, Wi-Fi ($10/day).

The Viceroy Anguilla ★★ The sleek white lines and hyperdesigned interiors may not be your cup of tea, but Viceroy has brought a new level of modern luxe to Anguilla—you can't deny the property's wow factor. The Viceroy delivers what it promises: a lifestyle immersion in high chic, 21st-century style. From afar the 14-hectare (35-acre) resort looks like a small city has landed on the promontory between Meads Bay and Barnes Bay. It all comes into focus up close, the crisp white structures smartly juxtaposed against the blue Anguillian sea and sky. Rooms and suites are outfitted with every high-tech toy and furnished in a palette of cream, sand, and brown, punctuated with Kelly Wearstler sunbursts (the Viceroy logo). Every suite (except the Viceroy King) has its own plunge pool. Six "rooftop" suites have second-story terraces with plunge pools and dizzying sea views. The villas are luxe dialed to 11. Each four- and five-bedroom villa comes with a designer kitchen, master baths with deep soaking tubs and outdoor showers, a pool and outdoor cabana, a grill, and a hot tub. Coba, the main restaurant, is encased in glass for a seamless panorama view. An entire second, self-contained family-friendly section has at its center a sprawling pool and restaurant, Aleta. One issue: Erosion has eaten away much of the beach around the Viceroy (it's expected to build up again); the resort's best beach is a short walk (or hotel shuttle) away on Meads Bay. The Viceroy is open year-round.

Barnes Bay (P.O. Box 8028), Anguilla, B.W.I. www.viceroyhotelsandresorts.com/anguilla. ✆ **800/578-0283** in the U.S., or 264/497-7000. Fax 264/497-7001. 166 units. Winter $695–$995 double, $1,095–$1,195 1-bedroom suite, $2,295–$2,695 2-bedroom suite, $4,750–$6,500 3-bedroom suite, $7,500–$9,500 villa; off season $495–$795 double, $895–$995 1-bedroom suite, $1,095–$1,295 2-bedroom suite, $1,795–$2,095 3-bedroom suite, $2,500–$4,500 villa. Airport boat/taxi transfers: $85 one-way per person. AE, DC, MC, V. **Amenities:** 3 restaurants; 2 bars; babysitting; children's programs; concierge; fitness center/gym/spinning room; 3 outdoor pools; room service; spa; watersports equipment (extensive). *In room:* A/C, ceiling fan, TV, hair dryer, kitchen or kitchenette (in 2-bedroom deluxe suites, 3-bedroom suites, and villas), minibar, plunge pools (except in Viceroy King rooms), Wi-Fi (free).

Expensive

Frangipani Beach Resort ★ Set on a spectacular stretch of Meads Bay beach, this appealing pink-hued resort has upgraded its rooms and public spaces to stay competitive in an increasingly competitive market. The Spanish Mediterranean–style buildings feature one-, two-, and three-bedroom configurations. The one-bedroom suites are the best, with gleaming stainless steel kitchens, ocean views, and spacious living quarters. (All junior, one-bedroom, and two-bedroom suites have full kitchens and washer/dryers.) It has a nice big infinity pool, and the Straw Hat restaurant (which moved here in 2009) is an island favorite.

Meads Bay (P.O. Box 1378), Anguilla, B.W.I. www.frangipaniresort.com. ✆ **877/593-8988** in the U.S., or 264/497-6442. Fax 264/497-6440. 18 units. Winter $385–$525 double, from $685 suite; off season $325–$425 double, from $525 suite. Rates include continental breakfast. AE, MC, V. Closed Sept–Nov. **Amenities:** Restaurant; bar; babysitting; 2 pools; tennis court; watersports equipment. *In room:* A/C, ceiling fan, TV/DVD, CD player, hair dryer, full kitchen (in suites only), washer/dryer (in suites only), Wi-Fi (free).

Moderate

Anacaona ★ In 2010, Robin and Sue Ricketts, co-developers of Anguilla's best-known posh resorts, Cap Juluca and Malliouhana, bought the Sirena Hotel, renaming it Anacaona (pronounced an-nah-kay-*oh*-nah). The Ricketts' goal: to provide an oasis of "affordable chic" on glorious Meads Bay beach. This they have done, with excellent package deals and seriously discounted off-season rates. Their other goal—to make Anacaona the "cultural entertainment center of Anguilla"—is as yet a goal, not a reality, although longtime favorite Mayoumba dinner-theater dance troupe still performs on Thursday evenings. The Anacaona's rooms have crisp new bedding and large flatscreen TVs, but only the suites have kitchen facilities. Standard and superior rooms have just a small fridge and coffeemaker. The new Fire Fly restaurant offers an ambitious menu of nouvelle Caribbean dishes as well as old favorites, such as Scrub Island goat. Service is swift and helpful. That said, like its predecessor, the Sirena, Anacaona has some serious drawbacks: The lobby, bar, and restaurant share one space, and the beach is a 5-minute stroll away, circumnavigating clusters of villas and the immense Viceroy complex.

Meads Bay (P.O. Box 200), Anguilla, B.W.I. www.anacaonahotel.com. ✆ **877/647-4736** in the U.S., or 264/497-6827. Fax 264/497-6829. 27 units. Winter $250–$350 double, $400–$480 suite, $500–$600 villa; off season $150–$180 double, $220–$250 suite, $230–$360 villa. MAP (breakfast and dinner) $70 per person. AE, MC, V. **Amenities:** Restaurant; bar; babysitting; dive center; 2 outdoor pools; room service; watersports equipment. *In room:* A/C, ceiling fan, TV/DVD, hair dryer, kitchen (in villas), minibar (in rooms), Wi-Fi (free).

Carimar Beach Club This 24-apartment resort is sitting pretty on one of the loveliest stretches of beach on the island. It's a small, folksy place, broken into six villas surrounding a flower-filled courtyard. It has no pool or restaurant, but Blanchards and Jacala are just next door; within easy walking distance are the restaurants at Malliouhana and Frangipani. Villas 1 and 6 are oceanfront, with the priciest rates. The suites are simply but comfortably furnished one- or two-bedroom apartments with fully equipped kitchens; the two-bedroom apartments have two baths, which makes them ideal for families. Guests gather on their patios or balconies for drinks, or else stay glued to their beach lounges for the fabulous sunsets.

Meads Bay, Anguilla, B.W.I. www.carimar.com. ✆ **866/270-3764** for reservations only, or 264/497-6881. Fax 264/497-6071. 24 units. Winter $390–$470 1-bedroom suite, $515–$600 2-bedroom suite; off season $200–$295 1-bedroom suite, $295–$395 2-bedroom suite. Extra person $75. AE, DISC, MC, V. **Amenities:** Babysitting; bike rental; concierge; 2 tennis courts; watersports equipment. *In room:* A/C (in bedrooms only), ceiling fan, TV/VCR, hair dryer, full kitchen, Wi-Fi (free).

Serenity Cottages ★ With a great location at the quiet end of Shoal Bay Beach, Serenity is one place that lives up to its name. The crowds at Uncle Ernie's and Kú are a brisk 15-minute beach stroll away. Anguillian owner Kenneth Rogers keeps a sharp eye on every detail here. The two cottages are surrounded by lovingly tended flowers and trees (at least one unit's shower has a glass wall brushed by palm fronds). The furnishings have a solid, understated elegance, with lots of dark wood offset by cheerful floral upholstery, and the views from the rooms and balconies through the gardens to the sea are marvelous. The open-air restaurant/bar functions as a meeting place. Serenity also has a toes-in-the-sand beach hut serving drinks and snacks, and Gwen's Reggae Grill is just steps away down the beach. One thing to keep in mind: There are coral reefs here, and seas can be rough; a short walk will take you past the reefs to Shoal Bay's calmer waters.

Shoal Bay East (P.O. Box 309, The Valley), Anguilla, B.W.I. www.serenity.ai. ✆ **264/497-3328.** Fax 264/497-3867. 18 units. Winter $325–$350 studio, $425–$450 1-bedroom suite, $525–$550 2-bedroom suite; off season $195–$225 studio, $295–$325 1-bedroom suite, $395–$425 2-bedroom suite. Extra person $100. MC, V. **Amenities:** 2 restaurants; beach bar; babysitting; limited room service; Wi-Fi (lfree). *In room:* Ceiling fan, TV, fridge, hair dryer (in some units), kitchen (in suites only).

Inexpensive

Easy Corner Villas On a bluff overlooking Sandy Ground (aka Road Bay), this place is a good 15-minute drive from the best beaches, so you'll definitely want a car. No problem: The owner is Anguillian Maurice Connor, the same entrepreneur who owns Connor's Car Rentals (ask about car/villa packages). Easy Corner's one-, two-, and three-bedroom apartments (known as villas) are set on modestly landscaped grounds with beach views from some of the private porches. Each comes with kitchen facilities, an airy combination living/dining room, good storage space, and simple furnishings. Maid service is available for an extra charge, except on Sunday. Note that new buildings below partially obstruct the views of Sandy Ground and the sea from a number of units—but even with less of a view, this is still a good value spot.

South Hill (P.O. Box 65, The Valley), Anguilla, B.W.I. www.easycornervilla.com. ✆ **264/497-6433.** Fax 264/497-6410. 12 units. Winter $210 suite, $190 1-bedroom villa, $230 2-bedroom villa, $295 3-bedroom villa; off season $175 suite, $155 1-bedroom villa, $195 2-bedroom villa, $255 3-bedroom villa. AE, MC, V. *In room:* A/C, ceiling fan, TV/VCR, kitchen.

Lloyd's Bed and Breakfast The island's oldest inn opened in 1959 on the crest of Crocus Hill in The Valley. This family-owned B&B is the sort of place that makes you feel at home the moment you walk through the door. The bright yellow exterior, with lime-green shutters and a wide, inviting veranda, is exuberantly Caribbean. Inside the smallish rooms have filmy curtains at the windows and hand-crocheted bedspreads. Lloyd's main room, with its traditional wood and cane furniture, old prints, and small library, is the perfect place for island travelers (many are repeat guests) to trade tall tales. There's only one drawback here: Lloyd's is not on a beach. Still, an excellent beach lies just down the hill at Crocus Bay (site of restaurant/bar Da'Vida; see below). A full, family-style breakfast is included in the price, which makes Lloyd's one of the most charming bargains in the Caribbean.

Crocus Hill (P.O. Box 52, The Valley), Anguilla, B.W.I. www.lloyds.ai. ✆ **264/497-2351.** Fax 264/497-3028. 9 units. Year-round $135 double. MC, V. **Amenities:** Restaurant (breakfast only); bar; Internet (free). *In room:* A/C, ceiling fan, TV.

Sydans Anguillian Anne Edwards is the tirelessly helpful proprietor of Sydans, a hospitable family-run inn that overlooks Sandy Ground's large salt pond and is only steps from the sea. Some guests from the States and Europe have been coming here every year for 20 years; others use this as a long-term home away from home. All rooms have kitchens (some stoves have burners, but not ovens), bathrooms with tub/shower combinations, and homey bed- and sitting rooms. The second-floor units overlooking the salt pond are a birder's delight, with spottings of pelicans, cranes, herons, and seasonal birds; ground-floor rooms open into a central courtyard, lack the pond view, and are less quiet. Sydans is very much part of the Sandy Ground neighborhood: You'll hear roosters at sunrise, see the school bus drop off neighborhood children in the afternoon, and know when Johnno's or the Pumphouse has live music until the wee hours. Things are casual here (water outages are not unknown), but if you ask Ms. Edwards for an extra reading lamp or towels, they'll be in your room by the time you're back from the beach.

Sandy Ground, Anguilla, B.W.I. www.inns.ai/sydans. ✆ **264/497-3180** or 264/235-7740. Year-round from $100 double. MC, V. **Amenities:** Shop. *In room:* A/C, ceiling fan, TV, kitchen.

WHERE TO DINE

Very Expensive

Blanchards ★★★ INTERNATIONAL In 1994, when Anguilla was just beginning to attract high-spending foodies, Bob and Melinda Blanchard opened a restaurant at the end of a dirt track to the sea. It was elegantly casual and offered a fresh and inventive haute cuisine. Since then, this place with indoor-outdoor dining on the beach has become the island's must-do place to eat. It's not uncommon to see dinner guests arrive here clutching copies of the Blanchards' book *A Trip to the Beach,* a charming account of how they created their restaurant. Now Blanchards' only problem is how to live up to its reputation. No problem: The crackerjack staff keeps the engine humming night after night. Behind tall teal shutters (open to the sea breezes), diners enjoy sophisticated but unfussy food with a spirited Caribbean flair. Among the perpetual favorites are sublime lobster-and-shrimp cakes—worth the trip alone. The Caribbean sampler features oven-crisped mahimahi with coconut, lime, and ginger; roasted Anguilla lobster; and jerk chicken with cinnamon-rum bananas. You can buy one of the Blanchards' newest tomes on the way out, and son Jesse's colorful paintings hang on the walls. At press time, Blanchards was offering a recession-friendly three-course prix fixe in the off season.

Meads Bay. ✆ **264/497-6100.** www.blanchardsrestaurant.com. Reservations required. Main courses $38–$58. AE, MC, V. Mon–Sat 6:30–10pm. Closed Sept 1–Nov 1 and Sun–Mon in off season.

Expensive

Hibernia ★★ FRENCH/INDOCHINESE Anguillian residents since 1987, chef Raoul Rodriguez and his wife, hostess Mary Pat O'Hanlon, have converted a traditional West Indian cottage at the east end of Anguilla into an inventive restaurant decorated with French- and Indonesian-inspired objets d'art collected from their annual world travels. The food here is equally international, with touches of the West Indies, Thailand, and France. It's tempting to make a meal of starters, perhaps the Caribbean fish soup and a terrine of foie gras with aged rum, cashews, and dates. Main courses include tender duck breast, classic beef tenderloin, and Caribbean seafood prepared Thai style. Save room for the homemade ice cream in a selection of dreamy flavors that includes mint, lavender, and chestnut. Reserve early: Hibernia has only 11 tables.

Island Harbour. ✆ **264/497-4290.** www.hiberniarestaurant.com. Reservations recommended. Main courses $32–$45. AE, MC, V. Tues–Sat noon–2pm and 7–9pm; Sun 7–9pm. Closed Aug–Sept and Mon–Tues during low season.

Jacala ★★ 🎁 FRENCH/INTUITIVE CUISINE The new kid on the Meads Bay block was opened by two veterans of the local restaurant scene, Jacques Borderon and Alain Laurent, who worked at Malliouhana, practically next door, for 24 years. It's right on the beach; you can almost reach out and grasp the last rays of sun melting into the sea. The menu is simple and straightforward, from fettucine with sautéed fresh tomato, garlic, and basil to a steak tartar to grilled lobster or whole snapper; the brilliance is in the execution.

Meads Bay. ✆ **264/498-5888.** Reservations recommended. Main courses $16–$44. MC, V. Tues–Sat noon–2pm and 7–9pm.

Michel Rostang at Malliouhana ★★★ FRENCH MEDITERRANEAN You dine ever so dramatically in a sweeping open-sided pavilion set on a promontory over the sea; down below big bass float, mesmerized by the lights illuminating the rocks. It makes for a memorable night, and the food lives up to the magical setting. The menu—classic Mediterranean infused with Caribbean accents—is supervised by Parisian two-star Michelin chef Michel Rostang and prepared by head chef Fred Cougnon and a staff of 26. The house specialty is a whole snapper baked in a case of salt with vegetables in papilotte (for two). Equally good are pan-seared scallops on a bed of buttery leeks. Start with lobster and sweet-pea soup under a golden crust of pastry, or marinated snapper and scallop tartar. Kids dine on a special children's menu from 6 to 7pm, after which they are whisked away so the grown-ups can have some fun. The extraordinary wine cellar—overseen by sommelier Albert Lake for the past 20 years—holds 25,000 to 35,000 bottles, many of them rare vintages.

Meads Bay. ✆ **264/497-6111.** www.malliouhana.com. Reservations required. Main courses $36–$44. AE, MC, V. Daily 7–11:30am, 12:30–3pm, and 7:30–10:30pm.

Straw Hat ★ CARIBBEAN/INTERNATIONAL In its location at the Frangipani Beach Resort, the Straw Hat continues to be one of the island's most satisfying spots to dine. Perched on a deck overlooking Meads Bay, the Straw Hat does a brisk business indeed, with consistently solid food and that sizzling setting. The indoor dining area is light, bright, open to the beach and sea, and hung with paintings by local artist Lynne Bernbaum. Food preparation is straightforward; sauces may be drizzled, but, as yet, there is no foam. Try the seafood stew: shrimp, crayfish, fresh local fish simmered with ginger, coconut milk, cilantro, and tomatoes, served over coconut rice. Smart buys include snapper, tuna, chicken, or shrimp "plain grilled" with two sides (fried plantains, Caesar salad, garlic mashed potatoes, or Anguillian rice and peas).

Frangipani Beach Resort, Meads Bay. ✆ **264/497-8300.** www.strawhat.com. Reservations recommended. Main courses $23–$48. AE, DC, MC, V. Daily 7:30–10am, noon–3pm, and 6:30–9pm.

Veya ★★★ CARIBBEAN/ASIAN With a transporting ambience that one writer likened to an "Indonesian treehouse," Veya is perched on the hillside above Sandy Ground and enveloped in bamboo, date and coconut palms, and flowering fangipani trees. The restaurant has lots of interesting nooks. Veya's fans—and there are lots of them—love looking out into tropical greenery and prize the fact the food and service here are consistently excellent. Detractors find the setting more memorable than the food. Veya serves what owners Carrie and Jerry Bogar call the "cuisine of the sun," with ingredients and styles of preparation taken from a wide range of sunny countries straddling the Equator. You might start with the grilled watermelon and poached shrimp appetizer, sprinkled with spiced pecans and mint. Favorite entrees include local crayfish with a ginger beurre blanc, vanilla-cured duck breast, and five-spice pork tenderloin. Veya's tasting menu ($85), a five-course medley of the chef's current favorites, is a good way to sample the offerings. **Veya's Café** (✆ **264/498-2233;** Mon–Sat 9am–5pm), a cluster of shaded outdoor tables downstairs, serves great panini and salads ($8–$14) and freshly baked johnnycakes and does a brisk take-out business (whole jerk, tandoori, or garlic-herb rotisserie chicken).

Sandy Ground. ✆ **264/498-8392.** www.veya-axa.com. Reservations required. Main courses $28–$46. AE, MC, V. Mon–Sat 6–10pm.

Moderate

Da'Vida ★★ ASIAN/CARIBBEAN Does it really matter that this place is slicker than other island beach bars? Nah, not with this sunny vibe and beautiful setting—and admirable efforts at cooking sustainably with local ingredients. After Roy's casual beachside restaurant moved to Sandy Ground a few years ago, Crocus Bay had no restaurant and fell into decline—until the Da'Vida complex opened in 2009 directly on the beach. Anguillian chef Guy Gumbs' restaurant quickly became one of the island's favorite places for celebratory dinners. Da'Vida—whose motto is "Celebrate life"—comprises an upscale restaurant and the more casual Bayside Grill. Both are just steps from shimmering Crocus Bay. The main restaurant is open to the sea on three sides, but the dark wood tables, crisp linen, and crystal make the mood more elegant than casual. The menu leans heavily on local seafood (crayfish, snapper, grouper) and offers creative twists on traditional island cuisine. Start with lobster bisque with corn fritters and cinnamon cream, or sweet potato gnocchi with sweet basil and tomato coulis. Mains include coconut-crusted scallops and grilled local fish (snapper, grouper, lobster, crayfish). Whatever you do, ask for an order of johnnycakes. The more casual Bayside Grill has that same seaside setting, albeit with picnic tables under the palms, clusters of tables under umbrellas, and a menu of grilled favorites (barbecued chicken or ribs, with rice and peas and salad). Beach chairs and umbrellas mean that guests here can alternate dining with dipping in the sea.

Crocus Bay. (✆ **264/498-5433.** www.davidaanguilla.com. Main courses Bayside Grill $18–$20, restaurant $32–$39. Restaurant Tues–Sun 11am–3pm and 6:30–9pm. Bayside Grill 11am–5pm.

Roy's Bayside Grill CARIBBEAN/ENGLISH PUB GRUB This is one of the best places at Sandy Ground for sunset watching, especially on Happy Hour Fridays (5:30–7pm), when the early-bird specials often include fish and chips, shepherd's pie, steak-and-kidney pie, and—perhaps the only spot where you can find this dish on Anguilla—haggis. The regular menu is packed with Caribbean favorites like grilled local lobster or crayfish, or conch chowder. Roy's also has free Wi-Fi and tables both on the beach and under a long wooden roof.

Sandy Ground. ✆ **264/498-0154.** www.roysbaysidegrill.com. Main courses $12–$32 (filet $42); Happy Hour Fridays specials $14. MC, V. Mon 5pm–midnight; Tues–Sun noon–3pm and 5pm–midnight.

Tasty's ★★ CARIBBEAN/AMERICAN Set inside a Creole cottage in teal, blue, and lavender hues is Dale Carty's uplifting hymn to the local cuisine. It's located on the right as you head through South Hill along the main road toward the East End. Colorful island murals by artist Susan Croft line the walls. Trained in international cuisine in the kitchen in Malliouhana, the award-winning chef prepares food that is indeed tasty. In Carty's hands, local specialties sing with flavor. Conch creole is paired with coconut dumplings; grilled snapper is elevated with a savory onion-pepper-tomato herb sauce. Tasty's shrimp are sautéed in coconut curry sauce and served with a sweet potato puree. Among the delicious breakfast entrees is a Caribbean sampler breakfast: fried and salt fish, johnnycakes, fried plantains, and bush tea. Okay, you're not dining by the sea—you're on a main road, and the soundtrack is passing traffic—but the interior's bright pastels are welcoming and the food is superb.

South Hill. ✆ **264/497-2737.** www.tastysrestaurant.com. Dinner reservations recommended. Main courses $18–$30 (lobster $36–$40). AE, MC, V. Daily 7:30am–3pm and 7–10pm.

Trattoria Tramonto ★ ☺ NORTHERN ITALIAN This favorite of many, serving solid Italian food, is on the tip of the west end of the island. There's even a Bellini, to make Italophiles remember the ones they drank at Harry's Bar in Venice. The chef takes special care with his appetizers, including sautéed shrimp with saffron and a porcini-mushroom sauce, and spicy-hot penne with a garlic, tomato, and red-pepper sauce. The house specialty is a sublime lobster-filled ravioli in a heart-stopping cream sauce. Kids are treated like celebrities here.

Shoal Bay West. ✆ **264/497-8819.** www.trattoriatramonto.com. Reservations required. Main courses lunch $16–$36, dinner $24–$38. MC, V. Tues–Sun noon–3pm and 6:30–9pm. Closed Sept–Oct.

Inexpensive

Delicious, affordable food is served at Anguilla's fabulous beachside bars and barbecue shacks. See "Anguilla After Dark," p. 39, for details.

E's Oven ★ CARIBBEAN/INTERNATIONAL Darting from beach to beach, it's easy to neglect some of Anguilla's inland restaurants. This place at South Hill (by the big curve in the main road) is very popular with locals, and when you eat here, you'll know why. The coconut-flavored pumpkin soup and garlic-crusted crayfish tails are yummy, and the seafood pasta is one of the main reasons some friends of mine say they keep coming back to Anguilla! The dining room is simple, with tables and chairs—nothing fancy, but perfectly pleasant.

South Hill. ✆ **264/498-8258.** Main courses $10–$20. MC, V. Wed–Mon 11am–midnight.

Ripples ★ CARIBBEAN/INTERNATIONAL Set in a restored clapboard house, Ripples has a raised deck, comfy wicker chairs, a casual West Indian decor, and a nightly crowd of regulars and drop-ins (including Brad Pitt and Jennifer Aniston the night before they announced their separation). No wonder: Caribbean Chef of the Year Glendon Carty is behind the stove. You can get anything from a burger to fresh local fish—mahimahi, snapper, tuna, and grouper—prepared any way you like. The weekly early-bird special, offering a choice of three entrees (usually one veggie, one seafood, and one traditional English roast) for $15, is one of the island's best bargains. The bar scene gets increasingly lively as the night wears on.

Sandy Ground. ✆ **264/497-3380.** Dinner reservations recommended. Main courses $15–$25. MC, V. Daily noon–midnight.

ANGUILLA'S BEACHES

Superb beaches are what put Anguilla on the tourist map. And there are dozens of them, plus another handful on offshore islets, like Sandy Isle and Prickly Pear. We love Anguilla's limestone-and-scrub interior, its roaming goats, salt ponds teeming with birds, and the wildflowers that spring up after the rains. Still, it's the beaches that bring us here. Miles and miles of pristine, powdery-soft sands open onto crystal-clear waters. As new roads are built, fewer beaches are reached via the bone-jarring dirt paths. All beaches—even those of the fanciest resorts—are open to the public.

Note: At press time, the effects of Hurricane Earl were evident in the erosion of beaches on the western end of Rendezvous Bay in front of Dune Preserve and CuisinArt, and along Shoal Bay. The natural accretion of sand is expected to eventually return the beaches to pre-Earl conditions, but contact your hotel for status updates before you leave home.

Most of the best beaches (Barnes, Maundays, Meads, Rendezvous Bay, Shoal Bay West) are on the west end of the island, site of the most expensive hotels. **Rendezvous Bay ★★** is a long, curving ribbon of satiny, pale-gold sand that stretches along the bay for 4km (2½ miles). For now you will probably have to enter the beach from the public access near the Anguilla Great House or Bankie Banx's Dune Preserve—and pray that future construction does not ruin this beach forever. **Meads Bay ★★★** is lined with a number of resorts and beachside restaurants—Malliouhana, Frangipani, Carimar, the Viceroy, Blanchards, Jacala—but it never feels crowded. We've been here on May mornings when fishermen in wooden skiffs with boat bottoms filled with silvery bonito are the only souls on the beach. This is one sweet stretch of beach, with surprisingly good snorkeling around the rocks of Malliouhana.

In the northeast, 3km (2-mile) **Shoal Bay ★★★** is Anguilla's most popular beach, a Caribbean classic, with silver-white, powder-soft sands and a backdrop of sea grapes. This beach is often called Shoal Bay East to distinguish it from Shoal Bay West (see below). The luminous waters are brilliantly blue and populated by enough fish to make most casual snorkelers happy. At noon the sands are blindingly white, but at sunrise and sunset they turn a pink to rival any beach in Bermuda. Rental umbrellas, beach chairs, and other equipment are available just behind Uncle Ernie's at the long-established **Skyline Beach Rentals** (**© 264/497-8644**). And no trip to Anguilla is really complete without at least one order of ribs (washed down with a Ting or a Red Stripe) at Uncle Ernie's.

Shoal Bay West ★ has pristine white sands tinged with pink on the southwest coast. You'll find deluxe accommodations and superior snorkeling at its western tip. Adjoining it is 1.5km-long (1-mile), white-sand **Maundays Bay ★★**, site of Cap Juluca and justifiably one of the island's most popular shorelines, with gentle surf for good snorkeling and swimming. Though the waters are usually calm, sometimes the wind blows enough to attract windsurfers and sailboats. Most days you see St. Martin across the way; some days you can see the peak of Saba in the distance.

Sandy Isle, on the northwest coast, is a tiny islet with a few palms surrounded by a coral reef, a beach bar and restaurant, and a place to rent snorkeling gear and buy underwater cameras. During the high season, a speedboat from **Sandy Ground** (which has its own long sand beach) brings visitors back and forth to Sandy Isle almost hourly from around 9am to 4pm.

The northwest coast has a number of other beaches worth seeking out, notably the glittering white stretch of **Barnes Bay** beneath a bullying bluff. You can admire the offshore islands silhouetted against the horizon or join the windsurfers and snorkelers.

Little Bay Beach ★ is at the foot of Anguilla's steepest cliffs. The sands are not the characteristic Anguillian white but, well, *sandy.* That said, none of us who have been there, including serious bird-watchers, snorkelers, and scuba divers, seems to mind. You can get a boat here most days from about 9am to 4pm from Crocus Bay for around $10 round-trip.

Sandy Ground (aka Road Bay), also on the northwest coast, paints an idyllic old-time Caribbean scene, right down to meandering goats, spectacular sunsets, and clear blue waters, often dotted with yachts coming from St. Martin and beyond. You can watch fishermen and lobstermen set out in fishing boats as brightly colored as children's finger paints. **Johnno's** is arguably the archetypal beach bar, serving burgers

Grilled Lobster on a Remote Cay

As beautiful as Anguilla's beaches are, there's something about boating off to a desert island that is both exhilarating and liberating. (Cruising along in that clear turquoise sea is certainly a big part of it.) Visiting one of Anguilla's tiny offshore gems is a must-do during your visit—and none is more than 20 minutes from shore. Here you can snorkel in gin-clear waters, beachcomb, and generally putter about a spit of sand in the castaway spirit. A handful even have ramshackle beach restaurants, where fresh lobster and fish are sizzling on the grill.

Some resorts, like Malliouhana, have their own powerboats to get you out to the cays. Otherwise book an offshore excursion with **Shoal Bay Scuba** ✆ **264/235-1482; www.shoalbayscuba.com)** or **Gotcha! Garfield's Sea Tours (**✆ **264/235-7902; www.gotcha-garfields-sea-tours-anguilla.com)**. The most westerly cay is the privately owned **Dog Island,** truly a deserted isle—500 acres of sugary-sand beaches, salt ponds, and limestone cliffs. **Prickly Pear** has great snorkeling and two beach restaurants: an offshoot of **Johnno's** (on Sandy Ground), and the **Prickly Pear Restaurant & Bar** (www.pricklypearanguilla.com), where drinks are whipped up in a solar-powered blender. Both Shoal Bay Scuba and Gotcha! Garfield's Sea Tours offer twice-weekly trips to Prickly Pear for $55 to $65 per person (including lunch).

Sandy Island, on the northwest coast, is a tiny islet with a few palms surrounded by a coral reef, and a dilapidated beach bar and restaurant. During the high season, a $5 speedboat from **Sandy Ground** takes visitors back and forth to Sandy Island almost hourly from around 9am to 4pm. The closest cay lies just 150m (492 ft.) off the pier at Island Harbour. To get to tiny **Scilly Cay** (pronounced "silly key"), just go out on the pier and wave your arms (or dial ✆ **264/497-5123**) and a boatman will pick you up. Five minutes later, you're at Eudoxie and Sandra Wallace's glorified tiki hut, **Gorgeous Scilly Cay** (www.scillycayanguilla.com), picking out a fresh spiny lobster or crayfish (or chicken or veggies). You can snorkel around the reef or just relax over one of Eudoxie's Rhum Punches and watch the pelicans dive for fish. Lunch is daily Tuesday to Sunday from noon to 3pm, with live music Wednesdays and Sundays. This is a place to laze away the day; by the time you leave, you may have spent $100 per person—but what a day.

and grilled fish and rocking at night. Indeed, many of the weathered wooden Antillean houses around here shaded by turpentine trees and oleander hold casual bars, making Sandy Ground party central on Friday nights. **Island Harbor** is still a working fishing port, with island-made boats bobbing by the pier. For centuries Anguillians have set out from these shores to haul in spiny lobster, which are still cooked up here at **Smitty's** (✆ **264/497-4300;** www.smittys.com). It was Smitty who set up generators and started the tradition of live music and grilled lobster at his toes-in-the-water restaurant back in the 1970s, before Anguilla had electricity. Islanders of a certain age remember walking for hours to get to Smitty's on the weekend to hear the music—and then walking back home after dark by the light of the moon.

Savannah Bay (aka Junk's Hole) ★ offers a long stretch of uncrowded white sand and offshore reefs full of eels, squid, and manta rays. The one attraction here is Nat Richardson's **Palm Grove Bar & Grill,** with its perfectly boiled or grilled lobster, crayfish, or shrimp. Chances are you'll have **Captain's Bay** ★ all to yourself. Here's why: There's no shade, and the undertow is very dangerous. The rock formations are starkly beautiful, but this is a spot for a stroll, *not* a swim.

SPORTS & OUTDOOR PURSUITS

BICYCLE TOURS Accelyn Conner's **Premier Taxi & Tours** (✆ **264/497-0515** or 264/235-8931) offers 1½-hour bike tours that travel the scenic route overlooking the harbor and down to Shoal Bay, with a professional cyclist as your guide. Helmets and bikes provided. Tours start at your hotel ($60/couple).

CRUISES & BOATING At Sandy Ground, **Sandy Island Enterprises** (✆ **264/476-6534**), **Shoal Bay Scuba** (✆ **264/235-1482;** www.shoalbayscuba.com), and **Gotcha! Garfield's Sea Tours** (✆ **264/235-7902;** www.gotcha-garfields-sea-tours-anguilla.com) all arrange excursions and offer boat charters.

FISHING Your hotel can arrange for you to cast your line with a local guide, but you should bring your own tackle. Agree on the cost before setting out, however, to avoid the "misunderstandings" that are commonly reported.

GOLF The 18-hole, par-72 Greg Norman–designed **Temenos Golf Course,** between Long and Rendezvous bays (✆ **264/498-5602;** www.capjuluca.com), sits on a sprawling 111-hectare (274-acre) site that sputtered as a megaresort but is now under the management of Cap Juluca. Bill Clinton has played here, and so can you—for greens fees of around $225 per person during peak hours. Check with your hotel concierge or the tourist office for the latest details on this development.

HORSEBACK RIDING First-time and advanced riders can go horseback riding on the beach or "through the bush" with **Seaside Stables,** located on Paradise Drive (next to Paradise Cove in western Anguilla), Cove Bay (✆ **264/235-3667;** www.seaside-stables-anguilla.com). Per-person rates for scheduled beach rides are $70 to $80; kids' half-hour pony rides to the beach $35; moonlight rides $90; rides including a swim on horseback $90.

SAILING Sailing is the island's national sport, and local kids learn the ropes from a young age. **The Anguilla Sailing Association** (✆ **264/584-7245;** www.sailanguilla.com) is the force behind the Anguilla Regatta in early May and offers sailing lessons for kids and adults at its Optimist Sailing School on Sandy Ground.

SCUBA DIVING & SNORKELING Most of the coastline is fringed with coral reefs, and the crystalline waters are rich in marine life: brilliantly colored fish, greenback turtles, and stingrays. Thus, conditions for scuba diving and snorkeling are ideal. Over the years, the government of Anguilla has artificially enlarged the existing reef system, a first for the Caribbean. Battered and outmoded ships, deliberately sunk in carefully designated places, act as nurseries for fish and lobster populations and provide new dive sites. At **Stoney Ground Marine Park,** off the northeast coast, you can explore the ruins of a Spanish galleon that sank in 1772. Offshore cays **(Anguillita, Prickley Pear, Sandy Island, Dog Island)** offer pristine conditions.

Shoal Bay Scuba (✆ **264/235-1482;** www.shoalbayscuba.com) has a custom-built, state-of-the-art boat. A two-tank dive costs $90, plus $10 for equipment. They also provide snorkel trips, fishing charters, sunset cruises, and windsurfer rentals and lessons. At Sandy Ground, ask around for PADI-trained **Doug Carty** (✆ **264/235-8438** or 264/497-4567; www.dougcarty.com), who with his company **Special D** takes visitors on scuba excursions; a single-tank dive costs from $50. At Meads Bay, **Anguillian Divers** (✆ **264/497-4750** or 264/235-7742; www.anguilliandiver.com), is a one-stop dive shop that answers most diving needs. PADI instructors are on hand, with a two-tank dive costing $85, plus another $10 for equipment.

Most hotels provide snorkeling gear. Several places, such as long-established **Skyline Beach Rentals** (✆ **264/497-8644**) at Shoal Bay, rent snorkeling gear, if your hotel doesn't provide it. The snorkeling is great off the beach at Shoal Bay, Maundays Bay, Barnes Bay, Little Bay, Road Bay, and Mead Bay beneath the rocks at the Malliouhana resort.

TENNIS Most of the resorts have their own tennis courts (see "Where to Stay," earlier in this chapter). **Malliouhana,** Meads Bay (✆ **264/497-6111**), has a pro shop and four championship Laykold tennis courts. All courts are lit for night games.

EXPLORING THE ISLAND

The best way to get an overview of the island (if you don't have local friends) is on a **taxi tour.** In about 2 hours, a local driver (all of them are guides) will show you everything for around $60 (tip expected). The driver will also arrange to let you off at your favorite beach after a look around, and then pick you up and return you to your hotel or the airport. I highly recommend **Accelyn Connor** (✆ **264/497-0515** or 264/235-8931; premiertaxiandtour@hotmail.com), whose personable and informative tours make him a sought-after guide. His Premier Property Tour includes drinks (including beer), snacks, and admission to the museum ($70 single or double; $10 each additional person).

It's easy to combine a great lunch at the Palm Grove Bar & Grill at Junk's Hole with a visit to the **Heritage Museum Collection ★**, East End at Pond Ground (✆ **264/497-4092**), open Monday to Saturday 10am to 5pm, charging $5 admission ($3 children 11 and under). The modest look of the museum belies the range of fascinating artifacts inside, from Arawak Indian tools to slave shackles. If Mr. Colville Petty, who founded the museum, is here when you visit, you will have an especially memorable visit—he collected many of these artifacts himself and was awarded an OBE from Queen Elizabeth II. Ask at the museum for information on the **Heritage Trail,** which takes in 10 historic Anguillian landmarks, including Wallblake House, Anguilla's one surviving Great House, and the Pumphouse, now a popular Sandy Ground restaurant (see "Anguilla after Dark," below), where salt was once produced. Each stop on the trail is marked by a small white sign with an H surrounded by three dolphins.

The **Anguilla National Trust** offers daily **wildlife and eco tours ★** to places like Big Spring, with 1,000-year-old rock carvings and an underwater spring; and East End Pond, a richly inhabited wildlife conservation site. Call **✆ 264/497-5297** to book a spot ($25 adults, $10 children 2–12). Also ask whether former chief minister Sir Emile Gumbs, an Anguilla National Trust volunteer, is giving his delightful **eco-tours** (**✆ 264/497-2711**), spiked with wry, wonderful historical and political anecdotes.

SHOPPING

For serious shopping (Gucci, Louis Vuitton, and the like), take the ferry (see "Getting There," under "Essentials," earlier in this chapter) and visit the shops in Marigot on French St. Martin. St. Martin is also a good place to stock up on French wines and cheeses if you're planning a long stay on Anguilla and have self-catering capabilities.

Piled to the rafters with everything you need to be a stylin' Anguillian—silky kurtas, bejeweled caftans, scads of fine and costume jewelry, slinky bathing suits—is **ZaZAA ★**, in three locations: next to Ku Resort in Shoal Bay (**✆ 264/497-0460**); Lower South Hill (**✆ 264/497-6049**); and at the Anacaona resort (**✆ 264/497-6827**). If you need a bathing suit, T-shirt, stylish sandals, or any beach gear, you'll find it in the colorful cottage at **Irie Life** (**✆ 264/498-6526**), on the cliffside road at South Hill. ("Irie" is Rastafarian for "cool.")

Anguilla has a thriving local arts and crafts scene. On Shoal Bay East Road, **Alak Gallery** (**✆ 264/497-7270**) showcases the work of local artist Louise Brooks, who paints genre island scenes and Caribbean flora and fauna in vivid, saturated hues. For a good selection of paintings by Anguillian and Caribbean artists, try the **Savannah Gallery,** Coronation Street, Lower Valley (**✆ 264/497-2263;** www.savannahgallery.com), on the road to Crocus Bay. **Devonish Art Gallery,** in its new, larger location in Long Bay opposite CuisinArt Road (**✆ 264/497-2949**), features the work of Courtney Devonish, the well-known Anguillian potter and sculptor, as well as a good collection of paintings from local artists. **Cheddie's Carving Studio,** West End Road, the Cove (**✆ 264/497-6027;** www.cheddieonline.com), is the domain of self-taught Cheddie Richardson, who sculpts intricate, whimsical figures from driftwood, stone, and coral. In Island Harbour, check out the intriguing rotating art exhibits and delicious food at the **Art Café** (Coconut Paradise Building; **264/497-8595**). Inside a former 1868 cotton gin, the **Stone Cellar Art Gallery,** at Government Corner in The Valley (**✆ 264/498-0123;** www.oldfactory-anguilla.ai), houses rotating art exhibits (on the second floor) and Sir Roland Richardson's Caribbean Impressionistic paintings on the first.

As you explore the island, you'll see a surprising number of small art galleries. That's because Anguilla has a number of talented resident artists from around the world. One of the best is American **Lynne Bernbaum** (**✆ 264/497-5211;** www.lynnebernbaum.com), whose George Hill studio features her bold images of Anguilla, the Caribbean, and France. In addition to paintings, Bernbaum sells prints of her works, including some very Anguillian cacti and goats.

ANGUILLA AFTER DARK

Anguilla has no casinos or other gambling spots—it's said that the local Church Council holds sway in matters such as this. If you feel the need for some casino action, St. Maarten and its 14 casinos are just a 20-minute ferry ride (and then a short cab ride) away.

In high season, various hotels host barbecues or feature live music, both local and imported, for entertainment. But you should really get out and sample the island's casual **beach bars and grills ★★**, which serve great food and drink and feature live music at least one day a week. (You can have a light meal and a drink for around $20.) Look for such popular soca/reggae/calypso entertainers as the Musical Brothers, Darvin & His DC Band, and the British Dependency. Dancing the night away—well, until around 2am, when things wind down—is absolutely de rigueur. These places are about as casual as casual can be, but remember, this is modest Anguilla; if you've been swimming, cover up before you sit down to eat.

At Upper Shoal Bay, check out **Gwen's Reggae Bar & Grill** (✆ **264/497-2120**), which features Gwen Webster's barbecue daily into the early evening; on Sunday it showcases live reggae. Ask for a side order of Gwen's special slaw. The palm grove here is one of the few naturally shady seaside spots on the island, and it comes with hammocks. (***Note:*** At press time, Gwen's was rebuilding after a fire; call to make sure she's back in business.) At the more populated end of Shoal, island institution **Uncle Ernie's** (✆ **264/497-3907;** www.uncleerniesbeachbar.com) is open from morning 'til at least sunset, serving up generous plates of chicken and ribs, fresh fish, fries, slaw, and cold beer.

At the west end of the island, a sign points off the main road down a bumpy road to Nat Richardson's **Palm Grove Bar & Grill** (✆ **264/497-4224**) at Junk's Hole. Islanders and visitors flock here for what many think are Anguilla's most succulent grilled lobsters and lightest johnnycakes. If you're here for lunch, bring swimming gear and snorkel until your lobster comes off the grill. Reservations are required after dark; dinner is by appointment only.

Over at Sandy Ground, the **SandBar** (✆ **264/498-0171;** sandbar.anguilla@gmail.com) was opened in late 2009 by Anguillian husband and wife Joash Proctor and Denise Carr. This indoor/outdoor beach bar is the island hot spot for a sundowner and a wide range of tapas (including grilled shrimp, conch fritters with payaya chutney, and chicken or beef satay with peanut curry), priced from $6 to $12. SandBar is open from around 4pm to at least 10pm, and until at least midnight on nights when there is live music. Another island favorite, **Johnno's** (✆ **264/497-2728;** closed Mon) has live music most Wednesday evenings (reggae and soca) and Sunday afternoons (jazz). Burgers and grills are available all day, or you can just order a rum punch, plop down at one of the picnic tables on the beach, and watch the spectacular Sandy Ground sunset. A few minutes' stroll down the beach, **Elvis'** (✆ **264/476-0101;** www.elvisbeachbar.net) gives Johnno's some serious sunset competition. Elvis' bar occupies an Anguillian boat beached on the sand, with tables and chairs scattered nearby. Listen to live music several times a week, or join the crowds to watch cricket matches and American football on the island's largest outdoor TV. Warning: The rum punches, made by Elvis himself, are drop-dead dynamite.

Halfway between Johnno's and Elvis', overlooking the Salt Pond, the **Pumphouse** (✆ **264/497-5154;** www.pumphouse-anguilla.com; closed Sun) has rafter-shaking live music almost every night, enormous cheeseburgers, and crisp Caesar salads. This former rock-salt factory, with some of its original machinery still in place, is the funkiest bar on the island—unless that award should go to Bankie Banx's **Dune Preserve** (✆ **264/729-4215;** www.bankiebanx.net/Dunepreserve.html) at Rendezvous Bay, with its own salvaged boats and the island's most seriously relaxed musician. Reggae star Bankie Banx is usually in attendance and joins in the live music performances here several times a week. Heading from Dune Preserve toward the east end of the island, keep an eye out for the small sign that points from the main road to **Smokey's** (✆ **264/497-6582;** wwwsmokeysatthecove.com) at Cove Bay. Delicious crayfish, lobster, ribs, and spicy wings are served up most days; this is one of the island's top spots to chill. Smokey's has live music Saturday afternoons and Sunday evenings.

ANTIGUA & BARBUDA

There's a beach for every day of the year on the Caribbean island of Antigua (An-tee-gah), many of them stunning sugar-white strands protected by coral reefs. Although this former British colony is now an independent nation, it still retains many English traditions. The capital, St. John's, is dotted with weathered wooden houses with corrugated iron roofs and louvered verandas. Beaches, resorts, and dramatic scenery attract visitors just north of the capital, while the historic harbors of the southern coast bear vestiges of the country's glory days as a strategic naval port.

Beaches **Dickenson Bay,** in the northwest, is a favorite for its wide strip of powder-soft sand and tranquil turquoise waters, perfect for families with small children. Solitude, schools of rainbow-colored fish and stark white sand greet you at **Johnson's Point,** near Jolly Harbour. Take a ferry to "the last frontier of the Caribbean," **Barbuda,** the sister island of Antigua, for undisturbed lounging on pink-and-white sandy beaches.

Things to Do The white baroque towers of **St. John's Cathedral** occupy the capital's skyline. The **Saturday Morning Market** in St. John's brings islanders together to sell luscious fruits, fragrant flowers, and handicrafts. One of the eastern Caribbean's biggest attractions, **Nelson Dockyard's National Park,** near English Harbour, is perfect for history and cinema buffs alike: Think 18th-century *Pirates of the Caribbean.* Follow Lookout Trail from English Harbour to **Shirley Heights;** its summit reveals panoramic views of nearby Montserrat.

Eating & Drinking For a bit of old-fashioned British charm, complete with an atmospheric dark-wood bar, try the lobster or pumpkin soup at the 17th-century hotel **Admiral's Inn,** in English Harbour. Splurge at **East,** in St John's, the most gastronomically sophisticated restaurant on Antigua, with a menu inspired by the best of Asian cuisine. The popular **Sticky Wicket** in Coolidge serves up good, stick-to-your-ribs West Indian fare (including ribs) while you watch a match next door at the Stanford Cricket Grounds.

Nature **Indian Town,** one of Antigua's national parks, is home to **Devil's Bridge,** a natural bridge carved over time by the lashing of breakers; look for the numerous blowholes created by the pounding surf. Birders love the park for its 36 different species. On Barbuda, the **Frigate Bird Sanctuary** is worth the diversion for bird lovers—it has one of the Caribbean's largest nesting colonies of frigates, seabirds also known as man-o'-war birds.

ANTIGUA

Essentials

VISITOR INFORMATION

You can contact the **Antigua and Barbuda Department of Tourism** at 305 E. 47th St., 6A, New York, NY 10017 (✆ **212/541-4117;** fax 212/541-4789; www.antigua-barbuda.org); or 25 SE Second Ave., Ste. 300, Miami, FL 33131 (✆ **305/381-6762;** fax 305/381-7908). A toll-free number also gives information: ✆ **888/268-4227.** Operators are available Monday to Friday 9am to 5pm Eastern Standard Time.

In Canada, contact the **Antigua and Barbuda Department of Tourism and Trade,** 60 St. Claire Ave. E., Ste. 304, Toronto, ON M4T 1N5 (✆ **416/961-3085;** fax 416/961-7218). In England, the tourist office is at Victoria House, Fourth Floor, Victoria Road, Chelmsford, Essex CM1 1JR (✆ **1245/707-471**). On the island, the **Antigua and Barbuda Ministry of Tourism,** Queen Elizabeth Highway (✆ **268/462-0480;** fax 268/462-2483), is open Monday to Thursday 8am to 4:30pm and Friday 8am to 3pm.

GETTING THERE

The major airline that flies to Antigua's V. C. Bird Airport is **American Airlines** (✆ **800/433-7300** in the U.S. and Canada; www.aa.com), which makes four daily nonstop flights to Antigua from its hub in San Juan, Puerto Rico. A flight takes about 1½ hours, and each departs late enough in the day to allow easy transfers.

Continental (✆ **800/231-0856** in the U.S. and Canada; www.continental.com) flies 3 days a week out of Newark, New Jersey. **Delta** (✆ **800/221-1212;** www.delta.com) flies twice weekly from Atlanta in winter.

British Airways (✆ **800/247-9297** in the U.S. and Canada; www.britishairways.com) flies daily from London's Gatwick Airport. **Virgin Atlantic Airways** (✆ **800/821-5438** in the U.S. or Canada, 0844/209-7777 in the U.K.; www.virgin-atlantic.com) also offers nonstop flights from London.

Air Canada (✆ **888/247-2262;** www.aircanada.com) has regularly scheduled flights from Toronto to Antigua on Saturdays.

US Airways (✆ **800/622-1015;** www.usairways.com) flies nonstop flights from Philadelphia and Baltimore.

The not-always-reliable **LIAT** (✆ **888/844-LIAT** [5428] in the Caribbean, 268/480-5601 outside the Caribbean; www.liatairline.com) flies from several Caribbean islands into Antigua, notably from San Juan and St. Thomas.

GETTING AROUND

BY TAXI Taxis meet every airplane, and drivers wait outside the major hotels. If you're going to spend a few days here, a particular driver may try to "adopt" you. The typical one-way fare from the airport to St. John's is $7, but to English Harbour it's $31 and up. The government of Antigua fixes rates, and taxis are meterless.

Taxis aren't cheap, but they're the best way to see Antigua, as the drivers also act as guides. Most taxi tours go from the St. John's area to English Harbour. Drivers generally charge a flat rate of $24 for three or four passengers and often wait 30 minutes or more while you sightsee around English Harbour. If you split the cost with another couple, these tours become more affordable.

To call a taxi in St. John's, dial ✆ **268/460-8300.**

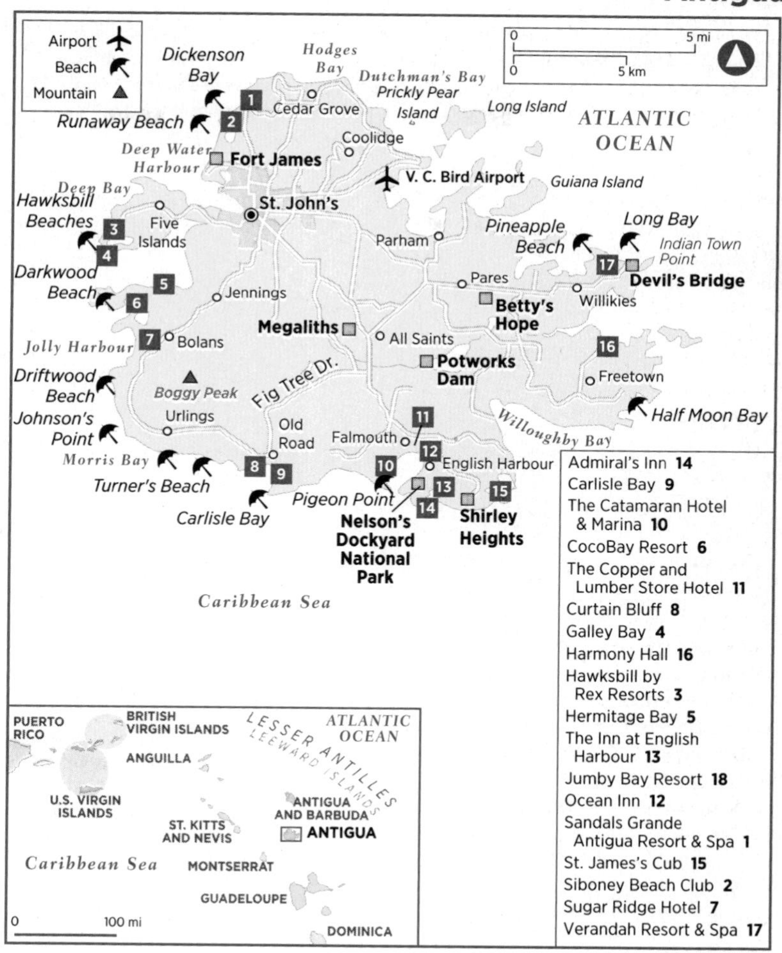

BY RENTAL CAR To drive on island, you must obtain an Antiguan license, which costs $12 and requires a valid driver's license from home. Most car rental firms can issue you an Antiguan license, which they usually do without a surcharge. ***Remember:*** Drive on the left.

It's best to stick with the major U.S. rental companies rather than using a local agency. Try **Avis** (✆ **800/331-1084** in the U.S. and Canada, or 268/462-2840; www.avisantigua.com) or **Hertz** (✆ **800/654-3001** in the U.S. and Canada, or 268/462-4114; www.hertz.com) for service at the airport. Another agency to try is **Dollar,** 40 Factory Rd., St. John's (✆ **800/800-3665** in the U.S. and Canada, or 268/462-0362; www.dollarantigua.com).

Special Events

The week before the first Tuesday in August, summer Carnival brings exotic costumes that recall Antiguans' African heritage. Festivities include a beauty competition and calypso- and steel-band competitions. The big event in spring is Sailing Week (www.sailingweek.com), in late April or early May.

BY BUS Although buses are a cheap option, we don't recommend them for the average visitor. Service is erratic and undependable, and roads are impossibly bumpy. In theory, buses operate between St. John's and the villages daily from 5:30am to 6pm, and on a relatively limited number of runs between St. John's and far-flung regions of the island till as late as 10pm, but don't count on it. In St. John's, buses leave from two different "stations"—on Market Street near the Central Market, and on Independence Avenue adjacent to the Botanical Gardens. Most fares are $1. There is no central information bureau to call for schedules.

[FastFACTS] ANTIGUA & BARBUDA

Banks Banks are usually open Monday to Thursday 8am to 2pm and on Friday 8am to 4pm. Try RBC **Royal Bank of Canada** (✆ **268/480-1150;** www.rbcroyalbank.com) and **Scotiabank** (✆ **268/480-1514;** www.scotiabank.com), across the street from one another at the corner of High and Market streets in St. John's. You'll find several ATMs here, each of them dispensing EC dollars but not U.S. dollars.

Currency These islands use the **Eastern Caribbean dollar (EC$).** Nearly all hotels bill in U.S. dollars, however, and only certain tiny restaurants present their prices in EC dollars. When you inquire about a price, make sure you know the type of dollars quoted. The EC dollar is worth about 37¢ in U.S. currency (EC$2.70 = US$1). *Prices in this chapter are quoted in U.S. dollars ($).*

Customs Arriving visitors are allowed to bring in 200 cigarettes or 50 cigars, 1 liter of wine or spirits, and 6 ounces of perfume.

Documents A valid passport is required from U.S., British, and Canadian nationals. All arriving visitors must have a departing ticket.

Electricity Most of the island's electricity is 220-volt AC (60 cycles), which means that U.S. appliances require transformers. The Hodges Bay area and some hotels, however, are supplied with 110-volt AC (60 cycles).

Emergencies In an emergency, contact the police (✆ **268/462-0125**), the fire department (✆ **268/462-0044**), or an ambulance (✆ **268/462-0251**). You can also call ✆ **911** or ✆ **999** for any type of emergency.

Hospital The principal medical facility on Antigua is **Holberton Hospital,** on Queen Elizabeth Highway, St. John's (✆ **268/462-0251**). A respected private hospital is **Adelin Medical Centre,** Fort Road, St. John's (✆ **268/462-0866**).

Language The official language is English.

Liquor Laws Beer and liquor are sold in many stores 7 days a week. It's legal to have an open container on the beach.

Safety Antigua is generally safe, but that doesn't mean you should wander alone at night on St. John's near-deserted streets. Don't leave valuables unguarded on the beach, either.

Taxes & Service Charges Visitors must pay a departure tax of $20 and an 8.5% government tax on hotel bills. Most hotels also add a service charge of between 10% and 15%. Most goods sold on island come with a "built-in" sales tax of around 15%, but since prices quoted on island invariably include the sales tax, it's likely you'll never even know you're paying it.

Telephone Telephone calls can be made from hotels or the office of **LIME,** at the corner of Long and Thames streets in St. John's (✆ **268/480-4206;** www.time4lime.com). Whereas LIME is responsible for international calls to and from Antigua, local on-island telephone service is provided by a local, quasi-governmental entity known as APUA, which competes with several on-island cell-phone carriers. To call Antigua from the United States, dial **1268** and then the number. To call the United States from Antigua, dial **1,** the area code, and then the number. You might want to purchase a phone card, which you can use to connect with an American long-distance company. You can reach **MCI** at ✆ **800/888-8000** and **Sprint** at ✆ **800/829-0965.**

Time Antigua is on Atlantic Standard Time year-round, so it's 1 hour ahead of U.S. Eastern Standard Time (EST). When daylight saving time takes over in the U.S., then Antigua's time is the same as the eastern United States.

Water Tap water is generally safe to drink here, but many visitors prefer to drink only bottled water.

Weather The average year-round temperature ranges from 75°F to 85°F (24°C–29°C).

Where to Stay

Antigua's hotels are generally small, and many are closed during the summer. Owners may decide to shut down early if business isn't good. There is a high percentage of upscale boutique hotels on Antigua, and competition among them is fierce.

An 8.5% government tax and a service charge of between 10% and 15%, depending on your hotel, are added to your hotel bill, which makes quite a difference in your final tab.

Antigua has lots of shockingly expensive hotels and resorts, but there are ways you can bring down the prices. Consider booking a package if you're interested in one of those pricey places.

Because getting around the island is difficult, your choice of where to stay is crucial. (The hotels are all plotted on the island map on p. 43.) Those who prefer high winds, breaking waves, and dramatic scenery should stay on the northwest side, north of the capital of St. John's. This is an area of middle-bracket resorts such as Sandals. If you want to spend most of your vacation at one resort, venturing out only occasionally, and can afford it, try one of the superexclusive places such as Curtain Bluff, Carlisle Bay, or St. James's Club on the remote southern coast. History buffs interested in atmospheric B&Bs should try either Admiral's Inn or the Inn at English Harbour, unless a good beach is crucial. If it is, then head for any of the big, mass-market resorts, all of which are on sandy beaches.

VERY EXPENSIVE

Carlisle Bay ★★★ ☺ Giving every first-class resort in the Caribbean a serious run for its money is this stunner. It's the most opulent, most luxurious, and best-accessorized hotel in Antigua, with a European flair that fits into what's left of the island's English colonial overlay. Set on a picture-perfect bay, the resort offers every luxe amenity, from a world-class spa and a movie theater, to tennis pros, to serious cuisine. The Beach Suites are steps away from the water. Best of all, there's a sense of whimsical fun associated with a stay at this resort. The Carlisle Suites are the biggest units, with three bedrooms, a sitting room, and a kitchen. The resort's entire collection of furniture, all dark Indonesian teak and creamy Italian upholstery, is custom made, all of it supremely comfortable, stylish, and with lots of pizzazz.

Old Rd., St. Mary's, Antigua, W.I. www.carlisle-bay.com. ✆ **866/502-2855** or 268/484-0000. Fax 268/484-0001. 82 suites. Winter $805–$3,700 double; off season $555–$2,300 double. Special packages available. AE, DC, MC, V. Closed Sept. **Amenities:** 2 restaurants; 3 bars; boat excursions; children's programs; movie theater; dive shop; state-of-the-art fitness center; outdoor pool; room service; 9 tennis courts (4 lit for night play). *In room:* A/C, DVD, CD player, hair dryer, minibar, Wi-Fi (free).

Curtain Bluff ★★★ ☺ This serene oasis, which is rivaled in glamour by only Carlisle Bay and Jumby Bay, is one of the island's premier resorts, with a price tag to match and enough ambience and class to make St. James's Club (see below) look like a glorified Holiday Inn. Residing 24km (15 miles) from the airport on the southwest shore, the hotel occupies the most lushly tropical section of the island, in the village of Old Road, and sits on two beautiful beaches (one turbulent, the other calm). This place is for a mature America-based, old-money crowd that likes the clubby feel. The beautifully furnished accommodations include deluxe units with king-size beds; a terrace room with a king-size, four-poster bed; and spacious suites with two balconies. Accommodations in the newer units are more spacious, with upgraded furnishings and two double beds. The two-story suites are among the most luxurious in the Caribbean.

Morris Bay (P.O. Box 288), Antigua, W.I. www.curtainbluff.com. ✆ **888/289-9898** in the U.S., or 268/462-8400. Fax 268/462-8409. 72 units. Winter $1,050–$1,500 double, $1,395–$3,900 suite; off season $685–$850 double, $795–$1,650 suite. Rates are all-inclusive. AE, MC, V. **Amenities:** 2 restaurants; 2 bars; babysitting; children's programs; outdoor pool; room service; 4 tennis courts (lit); TV room; watersports equipment/rental. *In room:* A/C, sauna (in suites), Wi-Fi (free).

Galley Bay ★ This all-inclusive has none of that toga-party hysteria associated with such lesser all-inclusives. Though celebrities are no longer photographed topless on the hotel beach, the resort still has an aura of exclusivity. The Gauguin-inspired Tahitian-style rentals are a bit faded. These intimate rooms open onto 16 secluded hectares (40 acres) of beachfront gardens, a bird sanctuary, and a lagoon, with the biggest draw, of course, being 1.2km (¾ mile) of white-sand beach. Choose among beachfront bungalows, the Gauguin rondavels (tikilike huts) with thatched roofs, or accommodations and suites in the two-story wings.

Five Islands (P.O. Box 305), St. John's, Antigua, W.I. www.galleybayresort.com. ✆ **866/237-1644** or 268/462-0302. Fax 268/462-4551. 98 units. Winter $965–$1,145 double, $1,145–$1,225 suite; off season $840–$965 double, $1,045 suite. Rates are all-inclusive. 5-night minimum in winter, 7-night minimum in Feb, 8-night minimum during holiday season. AE, DISC, MC, V. Children 15 and under not allowed except during holiday season. **Amenities:** 3 restaurants; 3 bars; bikes; exercise room; outdoor pool; room service; tennis court (lit); watersports equipment/rentals. *In room:* A/C, TV/DVD, fridge, hair dryer, MP3 docking station, Wi-Fi (free).

Hawksbill by Rex Resorts ★ ☺ Named after an offshore rock that resembles a hawksbill turtle, this 15-hectare (37-acre) all-inclusive resort is about 15km (9¼ miles) west of the airport and 6km (3¾ miles) southwest of St. John's. Set on four beaches (one reserved for those who want to go home sans tan lines), it caters to active types and is popular for weddings and honeymoons. This resort draws families and happy couples who like its informality and might feel uncomfortable in the atmosphere of pretension and social climbing that you get at Curtain Bluff. The hotel revolves around an open-air, breezy central core. Bedrooms are small and comfortably furnished, and the least expensive accommodations open onto a garden. The beach club rooms are the only units with air-conditioning and phone.

Five Islands Village (P.O. Box 108), St. John's, Antigua, W.I. www.rexresorts.com. ✆ **268/462-0301.** Fax 268/462-1515. 111 units. Winter $445–$585 double, $590–$720 triple; off season $330–$465 double, $450–$590 triple. Rates are all-inclusive. AE, MC, V. **Amenities:** 2 restaurants; 2 bars; exercise room; tennis court (lit); watersports equipment/rentals. *In room:* A/C (in some), ceiling fan, fridge, hair dryer, Wi-Fi (free).

Hermitage Bay ★ This small-scale cottage colony is set on a grassy, sloping hillside above a sandy beach in a remote and isolated part of southwestern Antigua down a potholed access road. It sits on 8 hectares (20 acres) of windswept coastline. Lodgings are stylish and upscale, each a freestanding wood-sheathed cottage with views of panoramic beauty. Your biggest choice involves your selection of a hillside villa high up on the slope (with a private plunge pool of its own and a sweeping view of the sea), or a beachfront unit within earshot of the waves (with a beach but no pool of its own).

Hermitage Bay (P.O. Box 60), St. John's, Antigua, W.I. www.hermitagebay.com. ✆ **268/562-5500,** or 268/562-8080 for reservations. Fax 268/562-5505. 25 units. Winter $1,200–$1,900 suites; off season $830–$1,265 suites. AE, DC, MC, V. Children 11 and under not allowed Sept–June. **Amenities:** Restaurant; room service; spa; free use of Sunfish and Hobie Cats. *In room:* A/C, TV/DVD, hair dryer, minibar, MP3 docking station, Wi-Fi (free).

The Inn at English Harbour ★ This small inn occupies one of the finest and most historic sites on Antigua, 4 hectares (10 acres) that directly flank a beach, with views over Nelson's Dockyard and English Harbour. This inn is tranquil, informal, and unpretentious. Bedrooms have been updated with modern conveniences, yet they retain a traditional style, with marble and mahogany floors, canopied beds, screened plantation style shutters, and wide verandas inviting you to linger. If you prefer, you can rent a quartet of beach cabanas opening onto the water. The most luxurious way to live here, however, is in one of the four regally appointed suites. A complimentary water shuttle takes you to Nelson's Dockyard for sightseeing and shopping.

English Harbour (P.O. Box 187), St. John's, Antigua, W.I. www.theinn.ag. ✆ **268/460-1014**. Fax 268/460-1603. 28 units. Winter $600 double, $940–$1,100 suite; off season $450 double, $705–$825 suite. A 3-night minimum stay is required. AE, MC, V. Children 11 and under not allowed. From St. John's, head south, through All Saints and Liberta, until you reach the south coast. **Amenities:** Restaurant; 2 bars; babysitting; bikes; exercise room; outdoor pool; room service; spa; 2 tennis courts (lit); watersports equipment/rentals. *In room:* A/C, ceiling fan, TV, hair dryer, minibar, MP3 docking station, Wi-Fi (free).

Jumby Bay Resort ★★★ This sybaritic retreat, set on a 132-hectare (326-acre) offshore island, attracts a celebrity-and-CEO crowd that can afford its pricey rates. Boats filled with the rich and famous depart from the Antiguan "mainland" every hour from 7am to midnight daily (trip time only 10 min.). With three secluded white sandy beaches along a coastline protected by coral reefs, the grounds have been luxuriantly planted with loblolly and white cedar. A haven for naturalists, the resort features Pasture Bay Beach on the island's windward side, home to endangered species of turtles, rare birds, and sheep. In late 2010, the resort reopened following a $28 million renovation, retaining its high standard of Caribbean luxury. No amenity is spared, and guests are coddled and pampered. Most suites and villas have ocean views and outdoor bathtubs in lush private courtyards. An exciting new addition is its first-ever spa, Sense, an open-air facility with a garden just 50 feet from a beach.

Jumby Bay (P.O. Box 243), St. John's, Antigua, W.I. www.jumbybayresort.com. ✆ **888/767-3966** or 268/462-6000. Fax 268/462-6020. 56 units. Winter $1,420-$2,200 double, $2,200-$3,200 suite, from $4,000 villa; off season $975-$1,125 double, $1,150-$1,900 suite, from $3,000 villa. **Amenities:** 2 restaurants; bar; concierge; exercise room; outdoor pool; room service; spa. *In room:* A/C, TV, hair dryer, minibar, MP3 docking station, Wi-Fi (free).

St. James's Club ☺ This remote, 40-hectare (99-acre) resort on Mamora Bay on two sand beaches tries for glamour, but it falls far behind Carlisle Bay, Curtain Bluff, and Jumby Bay, and it doesn't have the state-of-the-art maintenance of those properties, either. Midrange package tours from Britain and America continue to fill many of the rooms on occasions. But the sports facilities are among the Caribbean's best. Some of the rooms are standard and medium size, but others are spacious. The resort has never been able to escape the architectural curse of its former existence as a somewhat banal-looking Holiday Inn. Despite that, all units have sliding-glass doors that open onto private balconies or patios. Pricey two-bedroom villas and hillside homes are also available. If you're looking into a package all-inclusive deal, be aware that the cuisine here is merely average. Many enjoy gambling in the glamorous but small European-style casino.

Mamora Bay (P.O. Box 63), St. John's, Antigua, W.I. www.stjamesclubantigua.com. ✆ **866/237-2071** in the U.S., or 268/460-5000. Fax 268/460-3142. 257 units, including 73 villas. Winter $395–$755 double, $855–$915 suite, $890–$1,335 2-bedroom villa; off season $315 double, $525–$750 suite, $810–$1,070 2-bedroom villa. Children 2 and under stay free in parent's room. AE, MC, V. **Amenities:** 4 restaurants; 5 bars; dance club; babysitting; kids' playground; exercise room; Jacuzzi; 4 outdoor pools; casino; room service; sauna; spa; 6 tennis courts (lit); watersports equipment/rentals. *In room:* A/C, ceiling fan, TV, hair dryer, Wi-Fi (free).

Sandals Grande Antigua Resort & Spa ★ If you like sprawling megaresorts where everything's paid in advance and you live in a virtual walled compound with lots of organized activities, this might be for you. The older wings are low-rise, comfortable, and serviceable affairs, costing a bit less than accommodations in the newer wings, which are grandly Mediterranean in their aura. Public areas have trompe-l'oeil ceilings, tile work, and wrought-iron and masonry details. In the center of the newer section is one of the largest pools in the eastern Caribbean, whose free-form, serpentine edges encase an "island" with an oversize gazebo. If you opt for a holiday here, you'll find lots to do and a wide variety of comfortable accommodations in different price ranges.

Dickenson Bay (P.O. Box 147), St. John's, Antigua, W.I. www.sandals.com. ✆ **888/726-3257** or 268/484-0100. Fax 268/462-4135. 374 units. Winter $875–$1,210 double, $1,385–$3,045 suite; off season $875–$1,220 double, $1,360–$3,045 suite. 7-night minimum. Rates are all-inclusive. AE, DC, MC, V. **Amenities:** 9 restaurants; 10 bars; exercise room; 7 outdoor pools; 6 whirlpools; spa; 2 tennis courts (lit); watersports equipment/rentals. *In room:* A/C, TV, hair dryer, Wi-Fi ($14 per day).

EXPENSIVE

CocoBay Resort ★ Set on a soaring headland that rises above a trio of sandy beaches, this hillside compound of colorful wood-sided, tin-roofed cottages lies on 4 steeply inclined hectares (10 acres) of land that's crisscrossed and traversed with boardwalks, staircases, and tropical landscaping. When this all-inclusive opened, it gave Sandals some real competition. Understated elegance and a touch or two of funky West Indian charm combine in this cliffside setting on the "sunset side" of the island. Accommodations are comfortable but unpretentious, often within clapboard-sided buildings modeled on traditional vernacular houses, many of which are raised on stilts, with hand-carved furnishings and island art. Guests stay in cottages or in one of four "plantation houses," suitable for up to four occupants, on the hill. Each cottage has a four-poster king-size bed and a private porch.

Valley Church (P.O. Box 431), St. John's, Antigua, W.I. www.cocobayresort.com. ✆ **877/385-6516** in the U.S. or Canada, or 268/562-2400. Fax 268/562-2424. 53 units. Winter $360–$430 double, $840 plantation house; off season $270–$350 double, $680 plantation house. Rates include all meals and watersports. AE, MC, V. **Amenities:** 2 restaurants; 2 bars; exercise room; outdoor pool; spa; watersports equipment/rentals; Wi-Fi (free). *In room:* Ceiling fan, fridge, hair dryer, no phone.

The Copper and Lumber Store Hotel ★ Forget a pool. Forget a beach. This is the 18th-century "museum hotel" of English Harbour. It was originally a warehouse that stored wood and copper for the repair of British sailing ships. The hotel and its adjacent harborfront structures were built of brick that once was used as ships' ballast. Each unit evokes the British colonial era of Antigua's 19th-century history, with exposed bricks and heavy timbers, and with fine Chippendale and Queen Anne reproductions, antiques, brass chandeliers, hardwood paneling, and hand-stenciled floors. Each suite has a kitchen with aging equipment. The downside to a sojourn here involves a stream of visitors who view the place as a museum rather than an inn.

Nelson's Dockyard, English Harbour (P.O. Box 1283), St. John's, Antigua, W.I. www.copperandlumberhotel.com. ✆ **268/460-1058** or 460-1160. Fax 268/460-1529. 14 units. Winter $195–$275 double, $215–$325 suite; off season $135–$195 double, $145–$275 suite. AE, MC, V. From St. John's, follow the signs southeast to English Harbour. **Amenities:** Restaurant (June–Oct); pub; babysitting; ferry service to Galleon Beach. *In room:* A/C, hair dryer, kitchen (in suites), Wi-Fi (free).

Siboney Beach Club ★ The inn is named for the Amerindian tribe who predated the Arawaks. Set north of St. John's on .4 hectares (10 acres) of thickly foliated land fronting the 1.5km-long (1-mile) white-sand beach of Dickenson Bay, the resort is shielded on the inland side by a tall, verdant hedge. The club's social center is the Coconut Grove restaurant (p. 53). The comfortable suites are in a three-story balconied building draped with bougainvillea. The suites have louvered windows for natural ventilation. All units have separate bedrooms, living rooms, and balconies or patios, plus tiny kitchens. There's also a treehouse: a single room with a king-size bed and jungle decor perched high in a *Ficus benjamina* tree.

Dickenson Bay (P.O. Box 222), St. John's, Antigua, W.I. www.caribbean-resort-antigua-hotel-siboney-beach.com. ✆ **800/533-0234** in the U.S., or 268/462-0806. Fax 268/462-3356. 12 suites. Winter $190–$325 double; off season $150–$205 double. AE, MC, V. **Amenities:** Restaurant; bar; babysitting; outdoor pool. *In room:* A/C, TV (on request), hair dryer, kitchenette, Wi-Fi (free).

Sugar Ridge Hotel ★ Antigua's newest boutique hotel stands on a hillside bordered with sugar cane on the west coast, close to palm-lined beaches. All the rooms are grouped into sets of four, each with its own entrance. Units on the upper floors open onto a large veranda and dining deck; accommodations on the lower floor have the same facilities plus a private plunge pool. Rooms are stylishly furnished with muslin-draped, king-size, four-poster beds, and dressed in natural tones and rich, dark woods. All the latest amenities and technologies have been installed, including electronic safes. The island's first Aveda spa is on the ground floor, with modern equipment and four treatment rooms, two of which are reserved for couples. The on-site Carmichael's Restaurant serves imaginative fusion cuisine, including the fresh catch of the day.

Jolly Harbour (P.O. Box 153), Antigua, W.I. www.sugarridgeantigua.com. ✆ **866/591-4881** in the U.S., or 268/562-7700. Fax 268/562-5946. 60 units. Year-round $260-$350 double. Rates include breakfast. AE, MC, V. **Amenities:** Restaurant; bar; concierge; exercise room; 3 outdoor pools; room service; spa. *In room:* A/C, TV, MP3 docking station, Wi-Fi (free).

Verandah Resort & Spa ★ ☺ For those tired of the dreary Sandals format, this government-rated five-star all-inclusive has opened at Dian Bay on the east coast. Walking trails are cut across a 12-hectare (30-acre) site, and the chic resort borders Devil's Bridge, a natural park where the sea has carved an arch into the limestone coast. The Verandah combines luxurious amenities with an eco-friendly plant. The accommodations are in charming cottages—each with a private veranda—constructed on pillars rising above lush foliage. Fronting two beaches, the resort has its own desalination plant and an array of facilities that make it a somewhat self-sufficient unit.

Dian Bay, Antigua, W.I. www.verandahresortandspa.com. ✆ **866/237-1785** in the U.S. or Canada, or 268/562-6848. Fax 268/562-6609. 200 suites. Winter $350–$750 double; off season $280–$640 double. Rates are all-inclusive. AE, DC, MC, V. **Amenities:** 3 restaurants; 4 bars; kids' club; outdoor pool; room service; spa; Wi-Fi (free). *In room:* A/C, TV, hair dryer, minibar.

MODERATE

The Admiral's Inn ★★ This place is full of character and atmosphere, and it reopened in 2011 following a massive renovation. Designed in 1785, the year Horatio Nelson sailed into the harbor as captain of the HMS *Boreas,* and completed in 1788, the building here once housed British officers stationed at the dockyards, with a ground floor devoted to the storage of tar and boat-repair supplies. Loaded with West Indian charm, this place in the heart of Nelson's Dockyard is constructed of weathered brick that was brought from England to be used as ships' ballast. There are three types of accommodations. The most expensive are the ground-floor rooms in a tiny brick building across the courtyard from the main structure. The front rooms on the first floor of the main building, with views of the lawn and harbor, are also more expensive. The back rooms on this floor are less pricey. With dormer-window views over the yacht-filled harbor, the least expensive rooms on the top floor are smaller and quiet, but they can get warm on summer afternoons.

English Harbour (P.O. Box 713), St. John's, Antigua, W.I. http://admiralsantigua.com. ✆ **268/460-1027.** Fax 268/460-1534. 16 units. Winter $150-$190 double; off season $105–$130 double. AE, MC, V. Closed Sept to mid-Oct. Take the road southeast from St. John's, following the signs to English Harbour. **Amenities:** Restaurant; bar; room service; snorkeling. *In room:* A/C (in some), ceiling fan, no phone (in some), Wi-Fi (free).

The Catamaran Hotel A favorite since the 1970s, the Catamaran opens onto a palm-lined beach at Falmouth Harbour, a 3km (2-mile) drive from English Harbour. Peace, tranquillity, and lots of bougainvillea plants prevail. On the second floor, each of eight self-contained, motel-style rooms has a comfortable bed (in many cases, a four-poster) and a balcony overlooking the water. The Captain's Cabin is the most luxurious. The ground-floor rooms are small but comfortable, and additional units are within a waterside annex.

Falmouth Harbour (P.O. Box 958), St. John's, Antigua, W.I. www.catamaran-antigua.com. ✆ **268/460-1036.** Fax 268/460-1339. 14 units. Winter $170–$250 double, $240 Captain's Cabin; off season $145–$210 double, $210 Captain's Cabin. Children 9 and under stay free in parent's room. DISC, MC, V. **Amenities:** Restaurant; bar; babysitting; outdoor pool; sportfishing. *In room:* A/C (in 2 units), ceiling fan, TV, hair dryer, kitchenette (in most), no phone (prepaid cellphones can be rented), Wi-Fi (free).

Harmony Hall ★ 🎁 This art gallery and restaurant-cum-hotel was constructed around a former sugar mill. Standing on 2.5 hectares (6¼ acres) of land, secluded and tranquil Harmony Hall opens onto Brown's Bay, part of the greater body of water Nonsuch Bay. Its Neapolitan owners have restored two separate villas, carving each into six large bedrooms with high ceilings. It's not on the beach, but some good sands are just down the hill. Complimentary boat trips are arranged to the uninhabited Green Island, with its lovely beaches and idyllic snorkeling conditions.

Brown's Bay (P.O. Box 1558), St. John's, Antigua, W.I. www.harmonyhallantigua.com. ✆ **268/460-4120.** Fax 268/460-4406. 6 units. Year-round $200 double. Rates include breakfast. MC, V. Closed mid-May to Nov. **Amenities:** Restaurant (Fri–Sat only for dinner); bar; babysitting; outdoor pool; room service; tennis court (lit). *In room:* A/C, ceiling fan, minibar.

Ocean Inn ★ This is Antigua's premier B&B, just a 10-minute walk from some golden sandy beaches. It's a special place, with the coziest and most homelike decor on the island. Accommodations are either in the main building or in one of the cottages on the grounds; each comes with a little deck opening onto the marina. The garden of the hotel overlooks the historic dockyard. Guests share the communal swimming pool or meet for drinks in the Tree Trunk Bar. The most popular night here is Thursday, when there's an open-air barbecue.

English Harbour (P.O. Box 838), Antigua, W.I. www.theoceaninn.com. ✆ **268/463-7950.** Fax 268/460-1263. 12 units. Winter $110–$170 double, $170 double room in cottage; off season $100–$125 double, $125 double room in cottage. Rates include continental breakfast. AE, MC, V. **Amenities:** Restaurant (breakfast only); bar; babysitting; exercise room; outdoor pool. *In room:* A/C, TV (in most), hair dryer, no phone.

Where to Dine

Although the Eastern Caribbean dollar is used on these islands, only certain tiny restaurants present their prices in the local currency. When you inquire about a price, make sure you know which type of dollar is being quoted.

IN ST. JOHN'S

Cecilia's High Point Café CONTINENTAL This is a great place to hang out, lying just 2 minutes from the airport. It perches right on the edge of the water opening onto views of the ocean, with easy access to the soft sandy beach. If you'd like to combine some beaching with lunch, the cafe has a shower where you can rinse off before drinks and food. It also has free Wi-Fi and the best espresso on island. As jazz, R&B, or soul music plays in the background, you can peruse the short menu, perhaps starting with the chef's soup or else the antipasti platter for two. The chef's specials are written on a blackboard and might include a homemade mushroom ravioli or filet of salmon with dill sauce and white asparagus. The owner, a former model from Sweden, offers a dish from her homeland—Swedish hash (beef tenderloin) sautéed with potatoes and onions and served with pickled red beets. For dessert, try perhaps the "drunk raisins" ice cream. Dinner is served only on Monday nights.

Dutchman's Bay. ✆ **268/562-7070.** www.highpointantigua.com. Reservations required. Main courses $19–$32. MC, V. Mon noon–3pm and 7–10pm; Thurs-Sun noon–3pm.

Commissioner Grill ANTIGUAN/INTERNATIONAL Convenient to the cruise-ship docks, this restaurant was established by Conroy White, a busy entrepreneur known by virtually everyone on Antigua. His premises occupy a 200-year-old white-painted clapboard-covered house that functioned 40 years ago as a bottle factory. Today its cool, thick-walled interior is an inviting and restful place for drinks and for menu items that include lobster club sandwiches, fish soup, Caesar salads, grilled mahimahi, mixed seafood grills, baked snapper, marinated conch, and burgers. The food never rises to greatness but is always reliable and satisfying.

Redcliffe St. ✆ **268/462-1883.** Reservations not necessary. Salads, sandwiches, and burgers $10–$30; main courses $18–$35. MC, V. Daily 10am–11pm.

East ★★★ PAN ASIAN This is the most gastronomically sophisticated restaurant on Antigua, the kind of upscale Asian-restaurant-cum-celebrity-hangout you might expect from London's West End. You'll push through a pair of antique, intricately carved Thai doors and encounter a decor that's dark with tones of crimson. Choose from four different Asian soups; starters inspired by Japan, Thailand, Malaysia, and Vietnam; salads garnished with Thai-style beef, cucumber, and mint; or four different preparations of curry, including an unusual version from Java made with lamb, cinnamon, and cardamom. Main courses include Chinese-lacquered pork with hoisin-and-chili sauce, or grilled filet of mahimahi with tamarind and lemon grass sauce. The best dessert is a chocolate-and-ginger version of "molten lava," wherein deliberately undercooked chocolate cake is lightened with orange sauce and lemon-grass ice cream.

In the Carlisle Bay Resort, Old Rd., St. Mary's. ✆ **268/484-0000.** www.carlisle-bay.com. Reservations recommended. Main courses $10–$30. AE, DC, MC, V. Daily 7–10pm.

Papa Zouk ★ 🎁 SEAFOOD If you like seafood, *zouk* (French Creole music with strong African influences), and rum, you've come to the right place. To the strains of zouk music, you can have a New Orleans–type Creole party in the Caribbean. This dive is known for its extensive collection of rums. Its signature tropical fruit drink is called ti-punch and is well worth a try. After cocktails, try the stuffed clams baked with cheese or a selection of tapas for a starter. For dinner, you might order the savory bouillabaisse or a delectable pan-fried red snapper. The house special is the Carnival Platter, a medley of seafood such as mussels, scallops, and shrimp. The service is among the friendliest in town.

Hilda Davis Dr., St. John's. ✆ **268/464-6044.** Reservations recommended. Main courses $20–$28. No credit cards. Tues–Sat 7–10pm; off season Thurs-Sat 7–10pm.

ELSEWHERE AROUND THE ISLAND

Admiral's Inn ★ AMERICAN/CREOLE Enjoy lobster, seafood, and steaks in this 17th-century hotel (p. 50), and make sure to try our favorite appetizer, the pumpkin soup. The chefs use quality ingredients to create four or five main courses daily. Though the atmosphere is sometimes more exciting than the cuisine, the service is agreeable. Before dinner, order a drink in the bar and read the names of sailors carved into the wood 100 years ago.

Nelson's Dockyard, English Harbour. ✆ **268/460-1027.** Reservations recommended, especially for dinner in high season. Main courses $13–$24 lunch, $21–$36 dinner. AE, MC, V. Daily 8am–10pm. Closed Sept to mid-Oct.

Bay House INTERNATIONAL This is an intimate dining room linked with a family-owned hotel set in a garden on a hillside, a 10-minute walk uphill from the beach at Dickenson Bay. Surrounded by lattices and potted plants, it is an open-sided room with sweeping views of the jagged coastline. Lunch consists of freshly made salads, stuffed baguette sandwiches, and grills. The kitchen's culinary flair is more obvious at nighttime, when meals might begin with a salad of baby shrimp with grapefruit segments and truffle oil, or fresh chicken livers flambéed with brandy. Main dinner courses feature grilled fish, as well as fresh local lobster that's either grilled and served with lime-and-garlic sauce or prepared thermidor style. Steaks are served in a light soy sauce with braised Chinese cabbage. For vegetarians, there's a platter piled high with grilled Provençal-style vegetables.

In the Tradewinds Hotel, Dickenson Bay. ✆ **268/462-1223.** Reservations recommended. Main courses $17–$36 lunch, $24–$36 dinner. AE, MC, V. Daily 7am–11pm.

Coconut Grove ★★ INTERNATIONAL/SEAFOOD Found north of St. John's in a coconut grove right on the beach, its simple tables on a flagstone floor beneath a thatched roof are cooled by sea breezes. This is most visitors' dream of what a Caribbean restaurant should be—and it's one of the island's best. Soup is prepared fresh daily from local ingredients like ginger, carrot, and pumpkin. Lobster and shrimp dishes figure prominently, along with a catch of the day and a daily vegetarian special. Lunch fare is lighter. During happy hour at the bar (4–7pm), all drinks are half price.

In the Siboney Beach Club, Dickenson Bay. ✆ **268/462-1538.** www.coconutgroveantigua.net. Reservations required. Main courses $13–$32 lunch, $19–$39 dinner. MC, V. Daily 7:30am–11pm.

Cocos CARIBBEAN/INTERNATIONAL This restaurant is built on pilings sunk into the beachfront, granting diners an unimpeded view over the Caribbean and Antigua's westward-facing headlands, including Indian Mountain. Because it's within an all-inclusive resort, management urges diners who aren't hotel guests to phone in advance of arrival. Diners eat at tables sheathed in azure-colored tiles. Lunches focus on salads, burgers, sandwiches, and pastas. The best dinner items are usually the grilled catch of the day, marinated and covered with butter. Also recommended is grilled mahimahi prepared in puff pastry, like a beef Wellington, and served with a slow-simmered Creole sauce of fresh tomatoes, sweet garden peppers, and onions.

Valley Church. ✆ **268/462-9700.** Reservations required. Main courses $19–$35; 3-course dinner $33. MC, V. Daily 7:30–10am, noon–2:30pm, and 7–9:30pm.

The Cove ★ 🎁 INTERNATIONAL This gastronomic hideaway is one of the most romantic evening spots on Antigua. It occupies a gracefully proportioned pavilion adjacent to the sea. It's the kind of place where concierges at upscale resorts send their clients when they ask for an independent restaurant that's a change from a hotel dining room. Some of the best-tasting menu items include a carpaccio of marlin, sautéed calamari, pan-fried loin of yellowfin tuna with lemon grass, and loin of black-faced lamb with red-grape-and-apple chutney. Unusual desserts include a trio of summer sorbets or a golden apple tart flambéed with Calvados.

At the Blue Waters Resort, Soldiers' Bay. ✆ **268/562-2683.** www.thecove-antigua.com. Reservations recommended. Main courses $27–$36. AE, MC, V. Mon–Tues and Fri–Sat 7–10pm.

JohnnyCocoNat ★ CARIBBEAN In the heart of English Harbour, this waterside restaurant is an idyllic spot for a meal overlooking Nelson's Dockyard. It's a vibrant and animated place, filled with locals and visitors throughout the day; yachties drop in for hearty breakfasts beginning at 9am. For subtle, sophisticated flavors, you can stick around for lunch, and it's also a very romantic setting in the evening. Appetizers are the best in the area, including a real tasty treat, mango gazpacho. You can also order such starters as fish carpaccio or fresh sautéed local clams. Main courses have a certain zest, especially the soul chicken with couscous and arugula, or the grilled catch of the day served with lemon syrup. You can also order 20 imaginatively conceived pizzas hot from the oven. Lunch can be lighter fare, as the chef prepares the best salads on island, made with everything from fresh fish to chicken. The finest rib-eye burgers in town are served here on a focaccia bun.

Slipway, English Harbour. ✆ **268/562-5012.** www.johnnycoconat.com. Main courses $18–$28. MC, V. Thurs–Tues 9am–10pm.

Le Bistro ★ FRENCH Less than a kilometer (½ mile) inland from the coast of Hodges Bay, this restaurant occupies a stone-sided structure built as a clubhouse for a now-defunct golf course. Sporting informal charm, it's Antigua's oldest continuously operated restaurant (since 1981). The owners are English-born Philippa Esposito and her husband, Raffaele, from Capri. As the first authentic French restaurant on island, Le Bistro changes its menus twice a year, but each one is highly creative and innovative, a kind of fusion of West Indian and French recipes. Start with such appetizers as a homemade onion soup or a duet of fresh salmon and tuna sashimi. Prepared with flair are such mains as fresh grilled filet of snapper or a whole grilled fresh local lobster. Crispy Long Island duck is flamed in Grand Marnier and served with a caramelized orange sauce.

Hodges Bay. ✆ **268/462-3881.** www.antigualebistro.com. Reservations recommended. Main courses $24–$52. AE, MC, V. Tues–Sun 7pm–1am.

The Pavilion ★★★ CONTINENTAL Although it's located in the dreary area of the airport, this restaurant of a talented chef, Andrew Knoll, serves the most imaginative cuisine not only on Antigua, but also in this part of the Caribbean. The building that houses the restaurant evokes a plantation great house. The setting is one of elegance, with a skilled staff offering silver service. The chef knows how to balance textures, colors, and flavors, and he creates happy marriages of market-fresh ingredients from caviar to delectable desserts. The wine cellar contains more than 8,000 of the world's finest vintages. For a memorable main course, sample rack of lamb with a goat-cheese-and-potato custard or pan-roasted red snapper with black mussels, Maine lobster, Gulf shrimp, and Spanish chorizo. You can even order a fork-tender, 12-ounce Japanese Kobe rib-eye. Nothing quite tops the chef's specialty, a pan-fried blue crab cake with ham-hock black-bean ragout accompanied by roasted chili-lime-butter sauce and crispy plantain chips. Another of his classics is a foie gras pan roast with Antiguan black pineapple marmalade and macadamia-buttered crêpes.

7 Pavilion Dr., Coolidge. ✆ **268/480-6800.** Reservations essential. Main courses $30–$36. AE, DC, MC, V. Jacket required for men. Mon–Sat 7–11pm.

Shirley Heights Lookout Restaurant & Bar AMERICAN/CARIBBEAN To reach this place requires an uphill (vehicular) trek through the arid landscapes and ruined 18th-century military fortifications of what used to be one of England's mightiest naval bases. At the top, you'll find a stone house that once housed sailors; today the site houses a bar and a restaurant. We consider this place a charming venue for lunch, dinner, or a series of cocktails timed to coincide with sundown. It's far from gastronomic, though—food mostly consists of simple island fare, and there's the distinct sense that this is a working, sometimes raucous bar for locals. Sundays from around 4 to 9:30pm, the hilltop becomes the biggest outdoor party and "be-in" in Antigua. Menu items include pumpkin soup, Creole-style fresh fish, grilled lobster with garlic butter, goat stew or curried goat, and, occasionally, tapas.

At the Shirley Heights Lookout, above English Harbour. ✆ **268/728-0636.** www.shirleyheightslookout.com. Reservations not necessary except Sun afternoon and evening. Main courses $4.50–$13 lunch, $6–$20 dinner. No credit cards. Mon 9am–6:30pm (last order); Tues–Sun 9am–9:30pm (last order).

Sticky Wicket ★ INTERNATIONAL/CARIBBEAN Lying next to the Stanford Cricket Grounds, close to the island's international airport, this restaurant allows you to watch a match while you eat. Known for serving large portions of earthy, rib-sticking food, it's one of the island's most popular sports-oriented gathering spots, but its lounge, decorated with cricket memorabilia, and the courtyard overlooking the sports arena are posh. The food is far better than at most sports bars, as exemplified by the West Indian pork rib plate or the grilled lamb souvlakia. You might launch your meal with a chili-flavored tomato dipping sauce, or tasty shrimp and seafood fritters with a rémoulade. The soups and salads are always fresh and homemade, including Antiguan lobster bisque or an East Indian curried chicken salad mixed with toasted coconut and fresh fruit. Nothing quite tops the Key lime cheesecake for dessert.

20 Pavilion Dr., Coolidge. © **268/481-7000.** Reservations recommended. Main courses $18–$30. AE, MC, V. Tues 11am–11pm; Thurs–Sat 11am–12:30am; Sun 11am–11pm. Closed Mon and Wed.

Antigua's Beaches

There's a lovely white-sand beach on **Pigeon Point** at Falmouth Harbour, about a 4-minute drive from Admiral's Inn. With calm waters and pristine sands, this is the best beach near English Harbour, but it's often crowded, especially when a cruise ship is in port. It's ideal for snorkelers and swimmers of most ages and abilities.

Dickenson Bay ★★, in the northwest, directly north of St. John's, is one of the island's finest beaches, with its wide strip of powder-soft sand and blissfully calm turquoise waters. This safe beach attracts families with small children. You can rent watersports equipment at the **Rex Halcyon Cove Beach Resort** (© **268/462-0256**). Refreshments are available at the hotel, or mosey over to the casual bars and restaurants nearby.

On the north side of Dickenson Bay, you'll find more secluded beaches and some ideal snorkeling areas along the fan-shaped northern crown of Antigua. For a fee, locals will sometimes take beachcombers to one of the uninhabited offshore islets, such as **Prickly Pear Island,** surrounded by beautiful coral gardens. One of the island's best snorkeling spots is **Paradise Reef,** a 1.5km-long (1-mile) coral garden of stunning beauty north of Dickenson Bay (see "Scuba Diving, Snorkeling & Other Watersports," under "Sports & Outdoor Pursuits," below).

If you're seeking solitude, flee to **Johnson's Point.** Between the hamlets of Johnson's Point and Urlings at Antigua's southwestern tip below Jolly Harbour, this beach opens onto the tranquil Caribbean Sea. There are no facilities, but the sand is dazzling white, and the waters, usually clear and calm, are populated with schools of rainbow-hued tropical fish.

Near Johnson's Point on the southwest coast, **Turner's Beach** is idyllic. This is one of the best places to lie out in the tropical sun, cooled by trade winds. The beach has fine white sand and gin-clear waters. If the day is clear (as it usually is), you can see the volcanic island of Montserrat.

If you head east of Urlings and go past the hamlet of Old Road, you'll reach **Carlisle Bay,** site of one of the island's most celebrated shores. Against a backdrop of coconut groves, two long beaches extend from the spot where Curtain Bluff, the island's most deluxe hotel, sits atop a bluff. Here, where the calm Caribbean meets the more turbulent Atlantic, the water is impossibly blue.

South of Jolly Harbour, **Driftwood Beach** is directly north of Johnson's Point, in the southwest. The white sands and calm, clear waters are delightful. It is close to all the villas at Jolly Harbour Beach Resort Marina, however, and can be overcrowded.

In the same vicinity is **Darkwood Beach,** a 5-minute drive south of Jolly Harbour Marina and the Jolly Harbour Golf Club. Here the shimmering waters are almost crystal blue. The snorkeling is great, and you can bet that gentle trade winds will keep you cool. Located in a tourist zone, it is likely to be crowded—almost unbearably so when cruise ships are in port.

If you continue north toward St. John's and cut west at the turnoff for Five Islands, you'll reach the four secluded **Hawksbill Beaches** on the Five Islands peninsula. The beaches here have white sands, dazzling blue-and-green waters, and coral reefs ideal for snorkeling. On one of them, you can sunbathe and swim in the buff. The Five Islands peninsula is the site of major hotel developments. Though it's secluded, the beaches are sometimes crowded.

Perhaps Antigua's most beautiful beach, **Half Moon Bay ★★** stretches for nearly 1.5km (1 mile) on the southeastern coast, a 5-minute drive from Freetown village. The Atlantic surf is liable to be rough, but that doesn't stop a never-ending stream of windsurfers, who head out beyond the reef, which shelters protected waters for snorkeling. The beach is now a public park and ideal for a family outing. Half Moon Bay lies east of English Harbour near Mill Reef.

Directly north of Half Moon Bay, east of the village of Willikies, **Long Bay** fronts the Atlantic on the far eastern coast of Antigua. Guests of the Long Bay Hotel and the Pineapple Beach Club usually populate this sandy strip. The shallow waters are home to stunning coral reefs and offer great snorkeling.

In the same vicinity, **Pineapple Beach** is a 5-minute drive heading northeast from Willikies. It opens onto **Long Bay** and the west coast (Atlantic side) of Antigua. Crystal-blue waters make it ideal for snorkeling. Most beach buffs come here just to sun on nearly perfect white sands.

Sports & Outdoor Pursuits

ADVENTURE TOURS Eco-tourism is all the rage. The best and most thrilling eco-adventure in Antigua is the **Rainforest Canopy Tour ★★**, headquartered at Fig Tree Drive in Wallings (✆ **268/562-6363;** www.antiguarainforest.com). Think Tarzan in a harness in a high-altitude, vertigo-challenged transit on an interconnected series of twin cables high above the island's treetops. The tour is recommended only for the physically fit and those with no undue fear of heights. The shortest of the nine cables stretches for 91m (299 ft.), the longest for 107m (351 ft.) above a gorge. Four options range in price from $30 to $110, timed at 30 minutes to 2½ hours. The most popular costs $80, lasting 90 minutes. At the end, you have to climb 170 steps to your original point of departure. Monday to Saturday departures are at 9am, 10am, 11am, 1pm, and 3pm; call for a reservation.

In a less daunting adventure, you can take an **Antigua Adventures** tour (✆ **268/726-6355;** www.antiguaadventures.com). The cost is $90 per person. The tour takes you around the lush island in air-conditioned comfort, visiting a sugar mill, national parks, Nelson's Dockyard, Falmouth Harbour, and Shirley Heights, among other attractions.

BOATING & YACHT CHARTERS If you're contemplating serious yachting around Antigua, as many well-heeled visitors do, make arrangements through **Nicholson Yacht Charters** (✆ **305/433-5533** in the U.S. and Canada, or 268/460-1530; www.nicholson-charters.com) well in advance of your trip. It offers boats of all sizes. Once on Antigua, if you plan only minor sailing such as in a Sunfish or small catamaran like Hobie Waves, or windsurfing, contact **Sea Sports,** on the beach in front of the Rex Halcyon Cove Beach Resort at Dickenson Bay (✆ **268/462-3355**).

CRUISES All the major hotel desks can book boat cruises, the most popular and most frequently patronized of which is **Pirates of Antigua** (**© 268/562-7946;** www.piratesofantigua.com). Departing daily at 9am and 1pm aboard a romanticized replica of a pirate ship (the fact that it's motorized isn't immediately obvious), it simultaneously sails the water and plies its participants with rum-based drinks so strong that after two or three of them, you'll be hallucinating. The cost is $60 for adults, $30 for ages 5 to 12, and free for those 4 and under. There are Saturday night sails from 8pm to midnight at a cost of $90 per passenger. You can also call **Tropical Adventures** (**© 268/480-1225;** www.tropicalad.com), which offers day trips to neighboring Barbuda aboard a motorized catamaran, the *Excellence*, that's suitable for up to 70 passengers at a time. Departures are every Saturday at 9:30am, returning the same day around 4:30pm. The price is $150 ($120 for teenagers 13–16; $90 for children 4–12, free for children 3 and under), which includes lunch, use of snorkeling equipment, and a visit to Barbuda's bird sanctuary. **Barbuda-bound cruises** depart from **Tony's Water Sports** at Dickenson Bay (**© 268/462-6326;** fax 268/462-2065).

FISHING Many anglers visit Antigua just for the big game fishing offshore, where wahoo, tuna, and marlin abound. The best deep-sea fishing charter is ***Overdraft*** (**© 268/464-4954;** www.antiguafishing.com), a large 12m (39-ft.) fiberglass boat that goes in hunt of dolphin (the fish), shark, barracuda, wahoo, and other creatures of the deep. Captain Frank Hart knows his fishing grounds. Up to six fishermen are accommodated at one time; a 4-hour charter costs $495, and an 8-hour charter goes for $790.

GOLF Antigua's golf facilities are not on par with some of the other islands', but its foremost and most popular course, the 18-hole, par-70 **Cedar Valley Golf Club,** Friar's Hill Road (**© 268/462-0161;** www.cedarvalleygolf.ag), is good. This course was designed by the late Richard Aldridge and is 5km (3 miles) east of St. John's, near the airport. It has panoramic views of Antigua's northern coast. Daily greens fees are $49 for 18 holes, with cart rentals going for $42.

Another course worth playing is the **Jolly Harbour Golf Course** at Jolly Harbour (**© 268/462-3085**), though we prefer this less than Cedar Valley. Jolly Harbour is a par-71, 6,000-yard, 18-hole course plotted by golf designer Karl Litten on a hilly, tropically landscaped setting. The maintenance of the course is not always the best, however. Greens fees are $23 for 9 holes, or $46 for 18 holes.

PARASAILING Parasailing is gaining popularity on Antigua. Facilities are available during the day, Monday to Saturday, on the beach at Dickenson Bay.

SCUBA DIVING, SNORKELING & OTHER WATERSPORTS The reefs that fringe Antigua are home to beautiful, brilliantly colored fish. Many of the island's beaches (see "Beaches," above) have clear, pure, calm waters that make for great snorkeling. The most popular, such as Dickenson Bay, have concessions where you can rent snorkel gear and other equipment if it isn't available from your hotel.

Scuba diving is best arranged through **Jolly Dive Center,** Jolly Harbour (**© 268/462-8305**). A single-tank dive costs $85, including all equipment except wet suit, with a two-tank dive going for $120. Dive packages are also available, with two-tank deals going for $325.

Splish Splash (**© 268/462-3483**) regularly conducts 2-hour snorkeling jaunts over to Paradise Reef for $40 per person. Departures are daily at 11am and again at 1pm.

TENNIS Well-off tennis buffs check into **Curtain Bluff** (p. 46). Its courts, rivaled by the nine courts at **Carlisle Bay** (p. 45), are the finest on the island. Most of the major hotels have courts as well, and some are lit for night games. (We don't recommend playing tennis at midday—it's just too hot!) Hotel guests usually play for free; if you're not a guest, you'll have to book a court and pay charges that vary from place to place.

Exploring the Island

IN ST. JOHN'S

The most colorful sight of St. John's is the **Saturday morning market,** when many islanders come into the capital to hawk everything from birds and luscious fruits to beautiful flowers and handicrafts. The sights, sounds, and smells of Antigua are at their photographic best here from 8am to noon. However, don't snap a picture of any market person without asking permission first. Most will want a tip for the privilege of taking their photograph. The public market lies on Market Street at the southern end of St. John's, at the point where it intersects with All Saints and Valley roads.

St. John's Cathedral, the Anglican church between Long and Newgate streets at Church Lane (✆ **268/462-4686**), has resurrected itself time and again—it's been destroyed by earthquakes and rebuilt on the same site at least three times since it was first constructed in 1683. The present structure dates from 1845. In 2005 the clock on its facade was restored and made workable again. Exhibits at the **Museum of Antigua & Barbuda,** at Market and Long streets (✆ **268/462-1469**), are within one of Antigua's oldest buildings, built by English colonials in 1750 as a courthouse. The museum covers the island's history, from prehistoric days up to its independence from Britain in 1981. Exhibitions include examples of each of the semiprecious stones (especially jade) you can find on Antigua, as well as models of sugar plantations, steam engines, paintings, and historical prints. It's open Monday through Friday from 8:30am to 1pm and on Saturday from 10am to 2pm. The entrance fee is $3 for adults; students and children 11 and under enter free.

AROUND THE ISLAND

Eighteen kilometers (11 miles) southeast of St. John's is **Nelson's Dockyard National Park ★★★** (✆ **268/481-5028;** www.nationalparksantigua.com), one of the eastern Caribbean's biggest attractions and the world's most visible symbol of the once-formidable power of England's navy within the West Indies. Because of its almost constant state of archeological restoration, it's defined by its curators as "a continuing cultural landscape," with many aspects of "a living park" that's permanently associated in a major way with the expansion and protection of Britain's once-formidable empire. English ships took refuge from the hurricanes in this harbor as early as 1671. The park's centerpiece is the restored Georgian naval dockyard, which was used by admirals Nelson, Rodney, and Hood, and was the home of the British fleet during the Napoleonic Wars. From 1784 to 1787, Nelson commanded the British navy in the Leeward Islands and made his headquarters at English Harbour. The dockyard museum, the gem within a landscape that's almost constantly in a state of restoration, recaptures the 18th-century era of privateers, pirates, and battles at sea. Its colonial naval buildings remain as they were when Nelson was here. Although Nelson never lived at **Admiral House** (✆ **268/481-5028**)—it was built in 1855—his telescope and tea caddy are on display, along with other nautical memorabilia.

The park itself has sandy beaches and tropical vegetation, with various species of cactus as well as mangroves. A migrating colony of African cattle egrets shelters in the

Forts & Photo Ops

In the 1700s, Antigua's coastline was ringed with British forts. Although they're in ruins today, the views from these former military strongholds are among the most panoramic in the Caribbean—and you can visit them for free. You can begin at St. John's harbor (the capital), which was once guarded by **Fort Barrington** on the south and **Fort James** on the north. Later you can head down to **Fort James Bay,** where you'll find a couple of bars right on the sand. The most evocative of these is **Russell's Beach Bar:** Positioned directly within the ruins of the 18th-century Fort of St. Johns, it's at its most active on Sunday afternoon. Its funky West Indian setting, smack in the center of a ruined English colonial fort, makes it an appealing place to unwind with a beer and perhaps a platter of grilled fish. In the south, near English Harbour, check out the view from **Shirley Heights.**

mangroves. Archaeological sites here predate Christ. Nature trails, with coastal views, lead you through the flora. Tours of the dockyard last 15 to 20 minutes; nature walks along the trails can last anywhere from 30 minutes to 5 hours. The dockyard and all the buildings noted in this section are open daily from 9am to 5pm. Children 12 and under are admitted free. The admission price of $5 includes the Admiral House and the Shirley Heights Lookout.

The best **nature trail** on Antigua, a well-tended footpath, goes up the hill from English Harbour to **Shirley Heights ★**, beginning at the Galleon Beach Hotel. Follow the sign that points to the lookout. The trail is marked with yellow and/or green tape tied to the branches of trees and shrubs surviving in the blinding sunlight of these arid altitudes. Eventually you reach a summit of nearly 150m (492 ft.), where you're rewarded with a panoramic view. If you'd like to get more information about the walk, you can pick up a free brochure at the dockyard at the office of the National Parks Authority. This walk is easy; it takes less than an hour to reach the peak.

On the way back, take **Fig Tree Drive ★**, a 32km (20-mile) circular drive across the main mountain range. It passes through lush tropical hills and fishing villages along the southern coast. You can pick up the road just outside Liberta, north of Falmouth. Winding through a rainforest, it passes thatched villages, every one with a church and lots of goats and children running about. But don't expect fig trees: *Fig* is an Antiguan name for bananas.

Betty's Hope (**© 268/462-1469**), a picturesque ruin just outside the village of Pares on the eastbound route to Long Bay, was Antigua's first sugar plantation (from 1650). You can tour it Tuesday to Saturday from 10am to 4pm ($2 for adults, free for children). Exhibits in the visitor center trace the sugar era, and you can also see the full restoration of one of the original plantation's two windmills. If you visit, you may see the local masons, who are sporadically involved in the restoration of the curing and boiling plant, where sugar cane used to be processed into sugar, rum, and molasses.

Indian Town is one of Antigua's national parks, on the island's northeastern point. Over the centuries, Atlantic breakers have lashed the rocks and carved a natural bridge known as **Devil's Bridge.** It's surrounded by numerous blowholes spouting surf, a dramatic sight. An environmentally protected area, Indian Town Point lies at the tip of a deep cove, Indian Town Creek. The park fronts the Atlantic at Long Bay, just west of Indian Town Creek at the eastern side of Antigua. Birders flock here to see some 36 different species. The park is blanketed mainly by the acacia tree, a dry shrub locally known as "cassie." A large, meadowed headland around Devil's Bridge makes a great spot for a **picnic.** Arm yourself with directions and a good map before you start out. The main highway ends at Long Bay, but several **hiking trails** lead to the coastline. Our favorite hike is to Indian Town Point at a distance of 2km (1¼ miles). This is the most scenic walk in the park, passing through a protected area of exceptional natural beauty. Long Bay is great for snorkeling, but you'll need to bring your gear.

Shopping

Most of Antigua's shops are clustered on **St. Mary's Street** or **High Street** in St. John's. Some stores are open Monday to Saturday from 8:30am to noon and 1 to 4pm, but this varies greatly from place to place—Antiguan shopkeepers are an independent lot. Many of them close at noon on Thursday.

Duty-free items include English woolens and linens. You can also purchase Antiguan goods: local pottery, straw work, rum, floppy foldable hats, shell curios, and hand-printed fabrics.

If you're in St. John's on a Saturday morning, visit the **fruit and vegetable market** at the south end of Market Street. The juicy Antiguan black pineapple alone is worth the trip.

One prime hunting ground in St. John's is the **Redcliffe Quay** ★ waterfront on the southern edge of town, where nearly three dozen boutiques are housed in former warehouses set around tree-shaded, landscaped courtyards. Our favorite is **A Thousand Flowers** (**✆ 268/462-4264**), which sells linens, all-natural fiber, rayon, and other fabrics.

At the **Gazebo** (**✆ 268/460-2776**), expect a little bit of everything, from a mass of south-of-the-border pottery to Indonesian wood items, and (our favorite) stunning blue-glaze plates. Additional Redcliffe Quay shops include **Isis** (**✆ 268/462-4602**) for unique Egyptian jewelry, cotton gowns, handicrafts, inlaid marquetry work, and Afghan jewelry. It's often worth checking out **the Goldsmitty** (**✆ 268/462-4601;** www.goldsmitty.com), where precious stones are set in unique, exquisite creations of 14- and 18-karat gold.

Noreen Phillips, Redcliffe Quay (**✆ 268/462-3127;** www.noreenphillips.com), an entity entirely based in Antigua, is one of the island's major fashion outlets. Cruise-ship passengers beeline here for both casual wear and beaded glitzy dress clothes. **Exotic Antigua,** Radcliffe Quay, St. Mary's Street (**✆ 268/562-1288**), specializes in Caribbean-made gifts and clothing, including T-shirts and casual wear, and handicrafts.

At **Lipstick,** Heritage Quay (**✆ 268/562-1133**), you can browse a daunting array of cosmetics and perfumes, some of them locally made, many of the others imported from the U.S., Britain, and France. **Shoul's Chief Store,** St. Mary's Street at Market Street (**✆ 268/462-1140**), is an all-purpose department store selling fabric, appliances, souvenirs (more than 300 kinds), and general merchandise.

Heritage Quay ★★, Antigua's premier shopping-and-entertainment complex, is a well-maintained neighborhood close to the cruise-ship piers that features some 40 duty-free shops and an arcade for local artists and artisans. Its restaurants and food court offer a range of cuisines and views of St. John's Harbour. Many shops are open all day, at least from 9am to 5:30pm Monday to Saturday, and later, including on Sunday, if there's a cruise ship in port.

Tucked away within Heritage Quay are a number of shops. The **Camera Shop** (✆ **268/462-3619**), a Kodak distributor and photofinisher, sells sunglasses, film, and brand-name cameras. **Fashiondock** (✆ **268/462-9672**) is known for its duty-free Prada, Moschino, and Gucci accessories, plus other Italian styles. **Sunseekers** (✆ **268/462-4523**) carries the largest collection of duty-free swimwear in the Caribbean. **Colombian Emeralds** (✆ **268/462-3462**) is the world's biggest retailer of these gemstones. **Abbott's Jewelry** (✆ **268/462-3107**) sells the best selection of watches on Antigua, plus china and crystal. Nick Maley, a makeup artist who worked on *Star Wars* and *The Empire Strikes Back,* founded **Island Arts,** upstairs at Heritage Quay (✆ **268/462-2787**). You can purchase his own fine-art reproductions or browse through everything from low-cost prints to works by artists exhibited at the Museum of Modern Art in New York.

Rain Boutique, Lower St. Mary's (✆ **268/462-0118**), sells casual clothes, formal wear, hats, scarves, shoes, jewelry, and handbags.

At Falmouth Harbour, **Seahorse Studios & Gift Shop** (✆ **268/460-1457**) specializes in batiks, T-shirts, signs, and table linens. Its affiliated branch at English Harbour, **Seahorse Art Gallery** (✆ **268/460-1457**), sells paintings, engravings, and watercolors, with lots of emphasis on seascapes.

The best for last: Head for **Harmony Hall ★**, in Brown's Bay Mill, near Freetown (✆ **268/460-4120**), following the signs along the road to Freetown and Half Moon Bay. This restored 1843 plantation house and sugar mill overlooking Nonsuch Bay is ideal for a lunch stopover, a shopping expedition, even an overnight (p. 50). It displays an excellent selection of Caribbean arts and crafts. Lunch is served daily from noon to 3:30pm, featuring Green Island lobster, flying fish, and other specialties. Sunday is barbecue day.

Antigua After Dark

Steel bands, limbo dancers, calypso singers, folkloric groups—there's always something happening by night on Antigua. Your hotel can probably tell you where to go on any given night. If you want to roam Antigua at night looking for that hot local club, arrange to have a taxi pick you up so you're not stranded in the wilds somewhere. The following clubs are reliable hot spots.

The best and most elaborate gambling joint on island is **Grand Princess Casino,** Jolly Harbour (✆ **268/562-9900**), spread across three floors, offering a lot more than gambling. You can dine in the first-class Bellagio Restaurant, patronize an Internet cafe, get down in a dance club, enjoy flashy Las Vegas entertainment in a lounge, or even work out at the rooftop fitness center. A small but flamboyant alternative is the **St. James's Club** at Mamora Bay (✆ **268/460-5000**). Other action is found at **King's Casino** on Heritage Quay (✆ **268/462-1727**), the only casino in St. John's proper. Entrance is free and no ID is required. You must be 18 to play.

The best place to be on island on Sunday afternoon is the bar and restaurant at the **Shirley Heights Lookout** at Shirley Heights (p. 54; ✆ **268/728-0636**). Beginning at 4pm, a barbecue is offered here, followed by a reggae and steel-pan band for dancing later in the evening. Celebrities such as Chuck Norris, R&B singer Bobbie Brown, Sting, and even Whitney Houston have joined in a weekly be-in that sometimes evolves into the island's largest and most free-form social event. Many locals arrive on any late afternoon, grab a sundowner, and head for the patio in the rear for a sweeping view over the arid landscapes surrounding English Harbour and Antigua's most spectacular sunset. Sunday's $6 cover charge includes the first drink.

Antigua's hippest nighttime venue is the **Coast ★**, Heritage Quay, St. John's (✆ **268/562-6278;** www.coast.ag), drawing both islanders and visitors to its precincts, where they are entertained by Antiguan live bands, especially techno music, in a raucous setting of good times with plenty of drink and local specialties. No admission is charged.

Another venue is **Rush Nightclub & Connors Sports Bar,** Runaway Bay (✆ **268/562-7874**), open Thursday to Saturday. Doors open nightly and the cover is free on Thursday and Saturday, rising to $10 on Friday. Resident DJs entertain the mostly young crowd with hip-hop, soca, reggae, and R&B music.

At English Harbour, the joint is always rocking at **Abracadabra Restaurant & Disco-Bar ★**, Nelson's Dockyard (✆ **268/460-2701;** www.theabracadabra.com). Trattoria such as homemade pastas and fresh seafood, even lobster from an aquarium, launch the night, which becomes a dance party as the evening progresses. There's always something happening here: live jazz, reggae performances, even costume parties. Check it out.

Admiral's Inn (✆ **268/460-1027**) is a barefoot-friendly kind of place. You can always play a game of darts, and there's live music Thursday and Saturday nights, usually a local 14-piece steel band. Try one of Norman's daiquiris (the island's best), and ask the bartender about the famous guests he's served. Another much-frequented English Harbour watering hole is the **Life Bar,** Nelson's Dockyard, VHF no. 68 (✆ **268/562-2353**), the most popular spot for visitors arriving aboard yachts. We like its nautical atmosphere and the wooden pier that the action centers on. On occasion it's West Indian party time, with live groups performing. The most authentic British pub at Nelson's Dockyard is **Mainbrace** (✆ **268/460-1058**), with darts, of course; fish and chips; and, on some nights, live jazz. The pub is part of the Copper and Lumber Store Hotel (p. 49).

18 Carat, Lower Church Street, St. John's (✆ **268/562-1858**), is the most popular and sought-after dance club and night bar on the island. Expect a cover charge, ranging from $4 to $8 per person, an indoor-outdoor format that's open to a view of the night air of downtown St. John's, and a barrage of music that includes lots of reggae and soca. It's open Friday to Sunday 8pm to 1am.

Sand Haven, Runaway Bay (✆ **268/771-6803;** www.sandhavenantigua.com), is the hangout of local cricketers and always attracts a fun-loving bevy of patrons who dance the night away after ordering Tex-Mex fare. The beach bar associated with this place is especially busy on weekends.

Live nightly entertainment takes place right on the beach at **Millers by the Sea,** at Runaway Beach (✆ **268/462-9414**). Its happy hour is the best in town.

BARBUDA

Barbuda is part of the independent nation of Antigua and Barbuda. It's the Caribbean's last frontier, even though it is home to two of the region's most expensive and exclusive resorts: the K-Club, which is reviewed below, and the Coco Point Beach Resort, which we don't recommend because we think it has an exclusive, snobby atmosphere. Charted by Columbus in 1493, the island is 42km (26 miles) north of Antigua. Twenty-four kilometers (15 miles) long by 8km (5 miles) wide, it has a population of only 1,200 hardy souls, most of whom live around the unattractive village of Codrington. There's no lush tropical scenery, no paved roads, few hotels, and only a handful of restaurants.

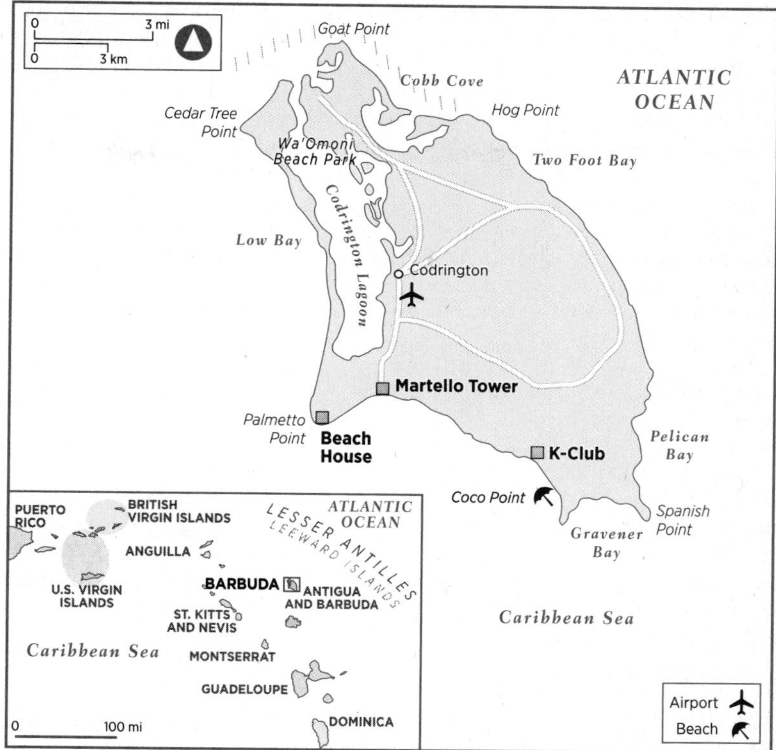

So what's the attraction? The island's 27km (17 miles) of pink- and white-sand beaches—almost like those of Bermuda. (We prefer the sands north of Palmetto Point.) Barrier reefs protect the island and keep most of the waters tranquil. Beaches on the southwestern shore stretch uninterrupted for 15km (9¼ miles); these are the best for swimming. The beaches on the island's eastern shore fronting the Atlantic are somewhat rougher, but they're good for beachcombing and shell collecting. The water temperature seldom falls below the average of 75°F (24°C).

Visitors gravitate to Barbuda to see fallow deer, guinea fowl, pigeons, and wild pigs. Anglers can also negotiate with small-boat owners to fish for bonefish and tarpon.

Day visitors usually head for **Wa'Omoni Beach Park ★** to visit the frigate bird sanctuary, snorkel for lobster, and eat barbecue. The frigate bird sanctuary is one of the world's largest and a very impressive sight. You can see the birds, *Fregata magnificens,* sitting on their eggs in the mangrove bushes, which stretch for miles in a long lagoon accessible only by small motorboat. Various hotels and resorts on Antigua arrange tours to the sanctuary. The island attracts about 150 other species of birds, including pelicans, herons, and tropical mockingbirds.

While you're here, look into the **Dividing Wall,** which once separated the imperial Codrington family from the African islanders. Also visit the **Martello Tower,** which predates the known history of the island. Purportedly the Spanish erected it before the British occupied the island. Several tours explore interesting **underground caves** on Barbuda. Stamp collectors might want to stop in at the **philatelic bureau** in Codrington (no phone).

Essentials

GETTING THERE The island is a 15-minute flight from Antigua's Bird Airport. Barbuda has two airfields: one at Codrington and the other a private facility, the Coco Point Airstrip, which is some 13km (8 miles) from Codrington at the Coco Point Lodge.

To reach Barbuda from Antigua, you can contact **Winair** (**© 866/466-0410;** www.fly-winair.com), a carrier that flies twice a day from Antigua's Bird Airport to Barbuda's Codrington Airport. The ride takes between 15 and 20 minutes one way. Round-trip passage costs around $104 per person, depending on restrictions.

GETTING AROUND Many locals rent small four-wheel-drive Suzukis, which are the best way to get around the island. They meet incoming flights at Codrington Airport, and prices are negotiable. You'll need an Antiguan driver's license (see "Essentials," under "Antigua," earlier in the chapter) if you plan to drive.

Where to Stay & Dine

K-Club ★★ The beachfront K-Club brings a chic Italian panache to one of the most far-flung backwaters of the Antilles. The resort is the "temple in the desert" of Italy's Krizia Mariuccia Mandelli, empress of a sports- and evening-wear empire. The resort is set on more than 80 hectares (198 acres). Conceived by Italian architect Gianni Gamondi, the cottages and main clubhouse have roofs supported by a forest of white columns. Accommodations come in a huge range of styles and shapes, with Caribbean rattan furnishings.

Barbuda, Antigua, W.I. www.kclubbarbuda.com. © **268/460-0300.** Fax 268/460-0305. 29 units. Winter $1,400 golf lodge for 2, $2,000 suite for 2; off season $950 golf lodge for 2, $1,400 suite for 2. Rates include all meals. AE, DC, MC, V. Closed Sept to mid-Nov. Children 11 and under not accepted. **Amenities:** Restaurant; bar; airport transfers; exercise room; Jacuzzi; outdoor pool; room service; 2 tennis courts (lit); watersports equipment/rentals. *In room:* A/C, ceiling fan, TV, fridge, hair dryer, minibar, Wi-Fi (free).

MONTSERRAT

Adventurous, eccentric, and eco-minded visitors are returning to the partially destroyed island of Montserrat. Formerly known as the "Emerald Isle of the Caribbean," partly because of its verdant vegetation and partly because of its historic links to Ireland, Montserrat is 19km (12 miles) long and 11km (6¾ miles) wide, about the size of Manhattan. In the aftermath of one of the worst natural disasters to hit the Caribbean during recorded history, two-thirds of the population of 12,000 had to be evacuated in 1995 and 1996 after the island's volcano, Soufrière Hills, blew its top, smothering the southern portion of the island with pyroclastic flows of hot gases and boiling hot ash, sometimes traveling downhill at hurricane velocity. In the aftermath, much of the island's southern tier—including the island's only airport—was burned, buried, or rendered uninhabitable. Another destructive blast occurred in 1997.

Since the explosions, only about a third of the original population has stayed on island, the others having been evacuated, or emigrating of their own volition, to the

U.K. or, less frequently, to such neighboring islands as Antigua. Today, thanks to enormous investment of time and energy from local and international geologists, the path of future pyroclastic flows can more or less be predicted. That has allowed tourism to return to the island, albeit in very small volumes. In fact, the volcanic eruptions have defined Montserrat as one of the most haunting and upsetting natural and geological spectacles in the Caribbean.

The volcano's last major eruption occurred on July 12, 2003, when almost two-thirds of the Soufrière Hills volcanic dome collapsed, sending ash and rocky debris as much as 15,000m (49,213 ft.) into the sky over Montserrat. In the aftermath, some islanders found themselves shoveling 1.5m (5-ft.) "drifts" of volcanic debris off their verandas and out from the bottom of their swimming pools. Today a visit to Montserrat can solicit hundreds of stories about heroism, endurance, disappointment, sacrifice, and backbreaking labor. About half the island is earmarked as an "exclusion zone," which you're supposed to avoid. In contrast, the other half is luxuriant and tropical.

Since the destruction of Plymouth, the island's historic and once-charming capital, Montserrat's commercial center and gerrymandered capital is Brades, on the island's north coast. Overall, you'll get the sense of a small community galvanized into new forms of self-reliance and cooperation, with lots of emphasis on somewhat gritty business-related visits from construction crews and British and international relief agencies.

Pear-shaped and mountainous, and most definitely volcanic in origin, Montserrat lies 43km (27 miles) southwest of Antigua, about midway between Nevis and Guadeloupe. Before the volcanic eruptions, Montserrat was known as the place where such musicians as Elton John, the Rolling Stones, and Stevie Wonder recorded. They, along with much of the rest of Montserrat's glitterati, moved long ago to safer, and more convenient, sites.

English is the island's official language, although it's spoken with a faint Irish brogue, a holdover from the island's early Irish settlers. The Eastern Caribbean dollar is the official unit of currency, although U.S. dollars are widely accepted. The island's biggest and most comprehensive travel agency is **Runaway Travel,** P.O. Box 54, Brades, Montserrat, B.W.I. (✆ **664/491-2776**). They'll arrange access to Federal Express shipments, sell a limited roster of airline tickets, and perform a limited array of financial services, including foreign exchange. A valid passport is required for everyone.

Essentials

INFORMATION Contact the **Montserrat Tourist Board,** 7 Farara Plaza (P.O. Box 7), Brades, Montserrat, B.W.I. (✆ **664/491-2230;** www.visitmontserrat.com). For up-to-the-minute information specifically related to the island's volcanic activity, check out www.mvo.ms.

GETTING THERE Montserrat is most easily reached from Antigua. **Gerald's Airport,** a latter-day, postmillennium replacement for the one that was rendered unusable during the searing pyroclastic flows, opened in 2005 near a hamlet on the north side of the island. **Winair** (✆ **866/466-0410;** www.fly-winair.com) wings in several times daily on the 20-minute flight from Antigua, using 19-seat Twin Otters. There is also ferry service from Antigua's Heritage Quay; the hour-long trip runs twice daily, three times a week, for $90 roundtrip. For more information, contact **Twin Islands Ferry Service** (✆ **268/464-8474**).

There is a departure tax of $21 per person leaving Montserrat.

GETTING AROUND Although the island has about 25km (16 miles) of surfaced roads, most of the island's vehicular traffic is limited to the route between Jack Boy Hill, on the island's northeasterly tip, and the village of Fleming, incorporating the island's airport and most points within the designated "northern safety zone" en route. The typical **taxi** fare from the airport to any of the hotels in the northern tier is $8 to $29.

The only regular **buses** are those running from Salem, near the island's southernmost tip, to Lookout, on the island's northern end—passing through hamlets that include Brades, Sweeney's, and St. John's en route. (Sweeney's is the site of a government-funded residential community on the island's northern tip.) The fare is 75¢ between any two points along this route. Don't expect the conventional buses you find in large North American cities. These are usually 15-seater minivans, each individually painted. If you want the bus to make a reasonable detour from the designated route, the driver will usually do it for an additional, negotiable fee, pending the approval of the other passengers.

BY RENTAL CAR None of the major U.S.-based car rental companies operates on Montserrat, although you can find a handful of privately owned agencies. You are required to buy a local Montserrat driver's license for $19, which should accompany your own valid license. Rarely are these available directly from the rental agency. More often, you'll need to purchase a license from the immigration office at either the heliport or the ferryboat terminal, or from the island's **Police Traffic Department** in Salem (✆ **664/491-2555**), which is open 24 hours a day.

Most island car rental agencies stock a battered roster of Toyota Corollas, Toyota RAV4s, Suzuki jeeps, or Mazdas, which rent for $48 and up a day, or from $213 per week, depending on the make and model, and the duration of your rental. A collision-damage waiver costs from $9 to $19 per day. Even if you buy it, you'll still be liable for the cost of some of the repairs to your vehicle if you damage it, for any reason, during your tenure.

Be-Beeps Car Rentals (✆ **664/491-3787**) is in the hamlet of Olveston, near Salem, close to the Vue Pointe Hotel, recommended below. **M.S. Osborne,** Brades (✆ **664/491-2494**), has a virtual monopoly on supplying most of the Nissans and Suzukis, including some SUVs, on the island.

Warning: Before you begin driving here, be aware that you must drive on the left and you should be careful of the steep, winding roads, which can be treacherous. In addition, volcanic ash on the roads, sometimes identified as "gray snow," can make for slippery driving conditions.

Where to Stay

Accommodations are extremely limited—so limited, in fact, that it leaves us wondering what lodgers would do in the event of a sudden and unexpected influx of new business. The island's finest accommodations are within the **Tropical Mansions Suites** (www.tropicalmansion.com; ✆ **664/491-8767;** fax 664/491-8275), in the hamlet of Sweeney's and with its own outdoor pool and an airy, somewhat sterile and decent-looking restaurant (the Tropical Mansion Restaurant; daily 7:30am–9:30pm). Built in 1999 as a kind of 18-unit neo-Palladian motel, it's identified by a soaring front portico, a modern no-nonsense kind of efficiency, and a series of breezeways and arcades that surround an ornamental pool. A double room with breakfast costs $140 to $190 per night and includes free Wi-Fi. American Express, MasterCard, and Visa are accepted. In the restaurant, lunch main courses cost $10 to $20 each, and dinner main courses cost $20 to $35 each. Creole-style fried fish, especially snapper, is a specialty.

Grand View Bed & Breakfast, Baker Hill (http://mnigrandview.com; ✆ **664/491-2284;** fax 664/491-7858), is for those who'd rather have a homelike place to stay. One of the island's best hosts, Theresa Silcott, will also prepare you a great dinner if you make a reservation. Overlooking Little Bay, the B&B has six units (including three suites), which are simple but well maintained and comfortable. In lieu of air-conditioning, you get fresh mountain air. Each of these spacious rooms comes with TV and phone. Double rooms with private bath cost $65, with suites going for $95 and including free Wi-Fi.

Gingerbread Hill, P.O. Box 246, St. Peter's (www.volcano-island.com; ✆ **664/491-5812**), is a four-room, tranquil mountainside retreat that evokes a hippie compound of the late 1960s. Each member of the Lea family pitches in, doing his or her own thing, from conducting tours to making fresh bread. On the grounds are hydroponic gardens, and you can enjoy the luxuriant growth of bananas, oranges, papaya, and mangoes. Even fresh eggs come from the family's chickens. This is the most eco-friendly lodging on island. You can stay here most comfortably in one of the villas, each imaginatively decorated, or else in two comfortable units. Some of the accommodations have a fridge and kitchenette. Double rates are $65 in a one-room apartment, $65 in the cottage, or $125 in a suite or villa, each with free Wi-Fi. No credit cards are accepted, and bikes and laundry facilities are available.

RENTING A HOUSE ON MONTSERRAT

Montserrat real estate, thanks to the recent volcanic explosions, has disappointed more real estate investors than virtually any other island in the Caribbean. But what that means for you is now you can select from a pool of affordable buildings (at least 100) of all sizes, shapes, and degrees of comfort and maintenance that can be rented for anywhere from a few days to a season or more. We firmly believe that if you're tempted to rent a house for a Caribbean holiday, you should stay for the first time on island within a conventional hotel, and then—for a second- or third-time holiday—consider renting from a reputable agent. Two of the best agencies are **Trade Winds Real Estate,** P.O. Box 365, Olveston (✆ **664/491-2004;** fax 664/491-6229; www.tradewindsmontserrat.com); and **Montserrat Enterprises, Ltd.,** P.O. Box 58, Old Towne (✆ **664/491-2004;** fax 664/491-6229; www.montserratenterprises.com).

Where to Dine

ANFA Restaurant & Bar CHINESE On virtually any other island, this restaurant would be viewed as a minor, not particularly noticeable hideaway, favored by locals and forgotten in the mainstream tourist crush. On Montserrat, however, where restaurants aren't very common, it's a major player on the local dining scene. About 80% of the food sold within its basic, cement-and-Formica interior is takeaway. But for clients who want to eat in, there's a bar, a blaring TV set, and a menu listing all the staples of Canton and China's south.

St. John's Main Rd. ✆ **664/491-2200.** Reservations not necessary. Main courses $7–$24. No credit cards. Daily 11am–10pm.

JJ's Cuisine CARIBBEAN Dominica-born Zephrina Jnofinn owns and operates this popular restaurant, in a low-slung roadside building that's within a 5-minute drive of the airport. Inside the Formica-clad dining room, you can order lobster, a worthy version of mountain chicken (frogs' legs) sautéed in garlic and butter, sandwiches, and excellent burgers that Jnofinn concocts herself with a few secret ingredients. Her signature cocktail is an "energy punch," ingredients for which include grated sweet potato, tannia root and arrowroot, Frangelica liqueur, and rum.

St. John's Main Rd., Sweeney's Center. © **664/491-9024.** Reservations recommended. Burgers and sandwiches $4–$8, platters $9–$24. No credit cards. Mon–Sat 8am–midnight.

Tina's Restaurant CARIBBEAN Set within a green-and-white Antillean house, this place is less than a 5-minute drive uphill from the ferryboat terminal. Tina Farrell established it in 1998 after she was evacuated from her home on Montserrat's southern tier. Expect a clean, decent, cozy, down-home Caribbean feel, with savory portions of chicken or beef, as well as burgers, grilled-chicken salads or lobster salads, and whatever fresh fish was hauled in by local fishermen that day.

Brades Main Rd. © **664/491-3538.** Reservations recommended only on national holidays. Lunch main courses $7.40–$10, set menu $17, pizzas $9–$24; dinner set menu and main courses $17–$24. MC, V. Mon–Sat 8am–midnight.

Ziggy's ★ MONTSERRATIAN Ziggy's is the island's most elegant, upscale, and elaborate restaurant, though hard to find. Accessible after a drive along some of the most winding and shadowy roads on Montserrat, it lies within a traditionally designed house in the high and isolated altitudes above Mount Pleasant Woodlands. Menu items emerge in an idiosyncratic rhythm all their own, including green banana soup, butterfly shrimp, Scottish smoked salmon, sirloin steak, rack of lamb, and grilled sea bass.

Mahogany Lane, Mount Pleasant Woodlands. © **664/491-8282.** www.ziggysrestaurant.com. Reservations recommended. Main courses $26–$35. AE, MC, V. Daily 7–10pm.

Exploring the Island

SCUBA DIVING Montserrat offers 30 excellent dive sites, each with a rich assortment of marine life, including spotted drums and copper sweepers, and perhaps a large sea turtle. At the rim of the island's marine shelf, where relatively shallow waters suddenly drop off to great depths, divers can plunge into 21m-deep (69-ft.) waters to see mammoth sponges along with large star- and brain-coral reefs.

A particularly well-managed dive and watersports operation is the **Green Monkey,** which operates from a wood-sided shack adjacent to Festival Village at Little Bay (© **664/491-2628;** www.divemontserrat.com). From its premises, Midwest-born Troy Deppermann and his wife, Melanie, conduct PADI-approved snorkeling and dive trips with a conscious eye toward safety and the transfer of information about life below sea level. On their premises is a cubbyhole-size bar, which maintains a thriving business completely independent from anything to do with underwater explorations. On island their most visible competitors are Emmy and Andrew, who operate the well-respected **Seawolf Diving School** (© **268/783-3466;** www.seawolfdivingschool.com). Prices at both outfits are roughly comparable: One-tank dives cost $55, two-tank dives cost $88, and one-tank night dives go for $70. Snorkeling equipment can be rented for $35, but it's a lot more fun and informative to participate in a supervised snorkeling trip, by boat, to nearby Rendezvous Bay, site of a teeming offshore reef, for $45 per person.

SIGHTS An active volcano can itself be a point of interest. The **Soufrière Hills Volcano** in the still-restricted southern part of the island is eerily fascinating, but by no means should any novice visitor to Montserrat venture into this region. The only

Beaches

Montserrat isn't known for its white-sand beaches. Most of its beaches have black volcanic sand, and they lie on the northern rim of the island, the part not threatened by volcanic activity. Many observers have noted that the beaches have actually improved, becoming bigger, sandier, and wider since the volcano deposited millions of tons of sand, ash, and debris upon them. The best beach on the island—and the only one with white sand—is Rendezvous Bay, which is accessible only via water taxis that depart from both Little Bay and the nearly adjacent Carr's Bay, or after a half-hour hike. If you want to walk, the routes to Rendezvous Bay are especially convenient from either Little Bay or the hamlet of Drummond's, adjacent to the airport. More readily accessible but less popular and hotter on bare feet are the dark-sand (a slate-gray color) beaches at Carr's Bay, Woodlands Beach, Lime Kiln Bay, Little Bay (near the arrival of the ferryboats from Antigua), and Bunkum Bay. The staff at Tropical Mansions Suites (✆ 664/491-8767) or the Vue Pointe Hotel (✆ 664/491-5210) can arrange day sails to these beaches.

deaths suffered during the island's volcanic explosions occurred on June 25, 1997, when 19 people were farming in an area that had been declared an exclusion zone.

Nevertheless, much to the regret of amateur volcano watchers, the government is very strict about discouraging anyone from visiting, under virtually any circumstances, the southern two-thirds of the island, which includes, regrettably, the once-bustling capital of Plymouth. Not only does the southern zone lack electricity and running water, but the government also wishes to prevent squatters from settling on land abandoned by the many homeowners who evacuated the island. The exclusion zone has also been deemed unsafe for transit on foot and, in multiple instances, in conventional vehicles or even all-terrain vehicles equipped with four-wheel-drive.

A good place to learn about the volcanic catastrophe is the **Montserrat Volcano Observatory** ★ (✆ **664/491-5647;** www.mvo.ms), which is in Flemings, above the village of Salem, on the island's north coast. The observatory is accessible via a winding, rutted road, about a 25-minute drive from the ferry terminal and about a 30-minute jaunt from the airport. Some of the staff here are busy recording and analyzing the seismic information emanating from the volcano, and aren't usually available for conversations and dialogue. But on-site are a series of exhibitions, including videos that document life on Montserrat before and after the seismic explosions, and close-up video views of the almost unimaginable geologic forces that spewed mud and debris many thousands of feet into the air. Unfortunately, because of the instability of the terrain affected by the explosions, no tours, either by jeep or on foot, are allowed onto the regions of Montserrat that were ruined by the explosions.

ARUBA

The most popular island in the Dutch Caribbean, Aruba draws droves of honeymooners and sun worshippers to its sandy shores. This small, 32km-long (20-mile) island dances to salsa, dines on red snapper, gambles in glitzy casinos, and surfs and sunbathes year-round. Aruba's past unfolds in the Dutch architecture of its bustling capital, Oranjestad, and on a hike past the abandoned gold mines in Arikok National Park. Platinum-blonde sandy beaches line its west coast, but the east coast is rugged, with craggy limestone cliffs, sand dunes, and crashing breakers.

Things to Do Some of Aruba's best white sugary stretches are found on the western and southern shores, including **Palm Beach** and **Eagle Beach.** For something secluded, head for the shallow, half-moon cove of **Baby Beach,** where the locals go. Slip through the heart-shaped entrance of the **Tunnel of Love** cave system in **Arikok National Park,** picnic on a boat, then dive with parrot fish around rusting wrecks. East of Oranjestad, trek around the mysterious **Ayo and Casibari rock formations** and see the wind-swept divi-divi trees.

Shopping Spend your florins on hand-painted boxes of dominos (the national game), Delft china, and plastic iguanas in Oranjestad's relaxed **harborside market,** or splash out on diamonds along **Main Street**—the gingerbread, pastel-colored buildings are impossible to miss. To soothe your sunburn, you'll want cooling aloe vera from the **Aruba Aloe Museum & Factory.** Buy something dazzling for a night at the casinos from the couture boutiques at the **Renaissance Mall.**

Nightlife & Entertainment At night the air is filled with the infectious sounds of salsa, reggaeton (South American raga), merengue, and the island's own tumba in Oranjestad. Down an Aruban Sunset cocktail at Mambo Jambo, one of the island's liveliest clubs, or don heels for a waltz at Bon Bini Festival every Tuesday at Fort Zoutman. Play a game of Caribbean stud poker at one of the casinos. Remember: Locals love to dress up and don't appreciate beachwear in the clubs.

Eating & Drinking Dining in Aruba is a ritual of indulgence and romance. Its proximity to South America brings *escabeche* (marinated poached or fried fish) and Spanish spices. Stewed **green papaya** is a specialty, as is crispy-yet-soft **corn bread.** Fresh seafood is abundant, especially in the comfortable confines of **Old Fisherman,** an island institution. Whether you dine at a beachside bar in **Palm Beach** or an opulent antique house in **Oranjestad,** you are guaranteed to stagger back to your hotel room sated and happy.

ESSENTIALS

Visitor Information

Before you leave home, contact the **Aruba Tourism Authority** at the following locations: 100 Plaza Dr., First Floor, Secaucus, NJ 07094 (✆ **201/558-1110;** fax 201/558-4768; ata.newjersey@aruba.com); and in the U.K., the Copperfields, 25 Copperfield St., London SE1 0EN (✆ **020/7928-1600;** fax 020/7928-1700; aruba@saltmarshpr.co.uk).

Information is available at **www.aruba.com** or by calling ✆ **800/TO-ARUBA** (862-7822).

Once on the island, you can go to the **Aruba Tourism Authority** at L. G. Smith Blvd. 172, Oranjestad (✆ **297/582-3777;** ata.aruba@aruba.com), for information. It's open Monday to Friday 8am to 5pm.

Getting There

American Airlines (✆ **800/433-7300** in the U.S. and Canada; www.aa.com) has a nonstop flight from New York's JFK Airport on Tuesdays, Thursdays, and Saturdays. American also flies nonstop from Miami.

US Airways (✆ **800/622-1015** in the U.S. and Canada; www.usairways.com) flies nonstop from Charlotte, North Carolina, and Philadelphia several days a week. **Continental Airlines** (✆ **800/231-0856** in the U.S. and Canada; www.continental.com) flies to Aruba via nonstop flights daily from Newark, New Jersey, and also from Houston on Saturdays. **United Airlines** (✆ **800/538-2929** in the U.S. and Canada; www.united.com) has weekend service from Chicago O'Hare and Washington Dulles. **Delta** (✆ **800/221-1212** in the U.S. and Canada; www.delta.com) flies daily to Aruba from its hub in Atlanta. The airline also offers Saturday flights from New York's JFK Airport. **JetBlue** (✆ **800-JETBLUE** [538-2583]; www.jetblue.com) has direct flights from Boston and from New York's JFK Airport every day. **Airtran** (✆ **800/AIR-TRAN** [247-8726]; www.airtran.com) flies nonstop from Orlando and Atlanta.

Air Canada (✆ **888/247-2262** in the U.S. and Canada; www.aircanada.com) has connections from Toronto to Aruba on Saturdays.

From Europe, the carrier **Martinair** (www.martinair.com) has taken over the routes previously serviced by KLM, flying nonstop from Amsterdam to Aruba.

Getting Around

BY RENTAL CAR It's easy to rent a car in Aruba. Excellent roads connect major tourist attractions, and all the major rental companies accept valid U.S. or Canadian driver's licenses. Major U.S. car rental companies maintain offices on Aruba at the airport and at major hotels. No taxes are imposed on car rentals on Aruba, but insurance can be tricky. Even when you purchase a $15 per day collision-damage waiver, you are still responsible for the first $500 to $600 worth of damage. Some companies offer deductible protection (D.P.) for an additional $5 per day. Rental rates range between $45 and $95 per day.

Try **Budget Rent-a-Car,** at Queen Beatrix Airport (✆ **800/472-3325** in the U.S. and Canada, or 297/582-8600; www.budgetaruba.com); **Hertz,** Sabana Blanca 35 (✆ **800/654-3001** in the U.S. and Canada, or 297/582-1845; www.arubarentcar.com); **Thrifty Car Rental,** L. G. Smith Blvd. 9 (✆ **800/THRIFTY** [847-4389] in the U.S. and Canada, or 297/585-5300; www.thriftyaruba.com); **Avis,** Queen Beatrix

Carnival

Many visitors come here for the annual pre-Lenten Carnival, a 2-month-long festival held in January and February, with events day and night. The music, dancing, parades, costumes, and "jump-ups" (Caribbean hoedowns) make Carnival the highlight of Aruba's winter season. For more information, contact the tourist office (see above).

Airport (✆ **800/331-1212** in the U.S. and Canada, or 297/582-5496; www.avis.aw); **Dollar Rent-a-Car,** Queen Beatrix Airport (✆ **800/800-3665** in the U.S. and Canada, or 297/583-0101; www.dollar.com); and **National** (✆ **877/222-9058** in the U.S. and Canada; www.nationalcar.com), with branches at the Oranjestad Holiday Inn (✆ 297/586-3768) and at the Queen Beatrix Airport (✆ 297/582-5451).

BY BUS Aruba has excellent bus service, with regular daily service from 6am to midnight. Round-trip fare between the beach hotels and Oranjestad is around 4AFl. Bus schedules are available at the **Arubus Terminal** at the central bus station on Zoutmanstraat. Your hotel reception desk will know when the buses pass by. They run about every 15 minutes during the day or every 30 minutes in the evenings, with limited service on Sundays. Try to have exact change. For schedules and information, call Arubus Co. (✆ **297/588-2300;** www.arubus.com).

BY TAXI Taxis are unmetered but rates are fixed, so tell the driver your destination and ask the fare before you get in. The main office is near Palm Beach; a dispatch office is located at the Pos Abao (✆ **297/582-2116**). A ride from the airport to most of the hotels, including those at Palm Beach, costs about $30 per car, with a five-passenger maximum. Some locals don't tip, but we suggest you do, especially if the driver has helped you with luggage. On some parts of the island, it's next to impossible to locate a taxi and you'll have to call. If you're going to a remote location, it's a good idea to ask the driver to return for you at a certain time.

The English-speaking drivers are usually willing tour guides. Most seem well informed and eager to share their knowledge with you. A 1-hour tour (you don't need much more than that) costs from $50 for a maximum of five passengers.

BY MOTORCYCLE & MOPED Because Aruba's roads are good and the terrain is flat, many visitors like to rent mopeds and motorcycles. At **George's Cycle Rental,** L. G. Smith Blvd. 124 (✆ **297/593-2202;** www.georgecycles.com), rental scooters begin at $40 per day for a single, $50 for a double. If you're a fan of the Fatboy or like to be king of the road, **Big Twin Harley Davidson Motor Cycle,** L. G. Smith Blvd. 106 (✆ **297/582-8660;** www.harleydavidson-aruba.com) offers half-day tours for $150 and full-day tours for $183.

[FastFACTS] ARUBA

Banks Banks are open Monday to Friday from 8am to 4pm. The most centrally located bank is **Aruba Bank** at Caya Betico Croes 41 (✆ **297/527-7926**). It's not hard to find an ATM (since there are over 50 on the island and they dispense money in either florins or U.S. dollars, depending on your preference).

Currency The currency is the **Aruba florin (AFl),** which is divided into 100 cents. Silver coins are in denominations of 5¢, 10¢, 25¢, and 50¢, and 1 and 2½

Aruba

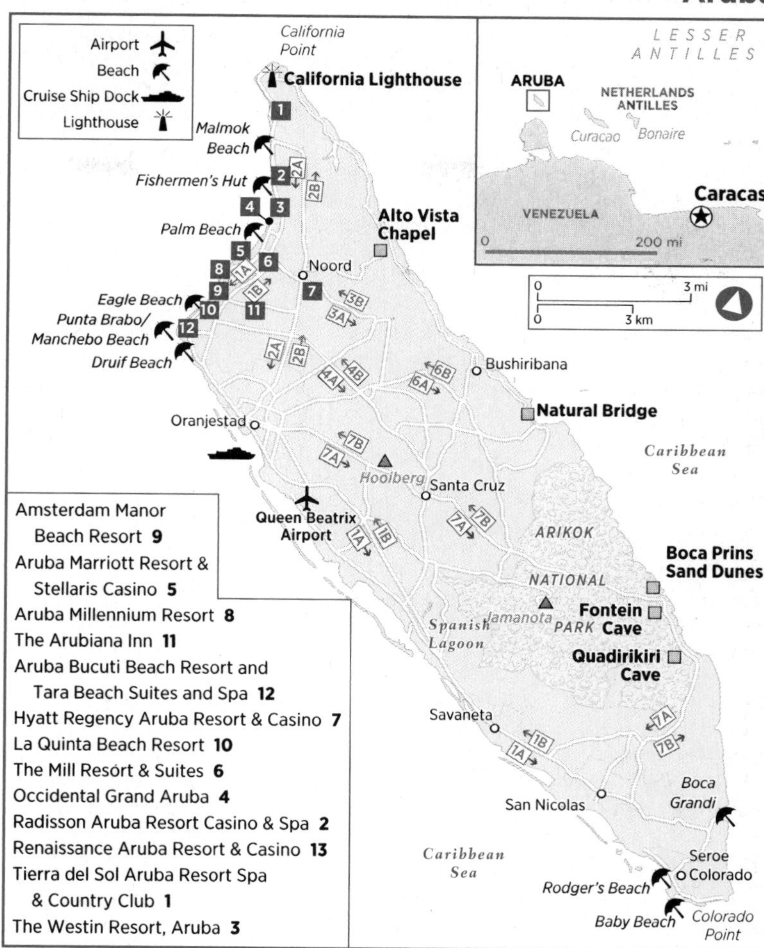

florins. The 50-cent piece, the square *yotin,* is Aruba's best-known coin. At press time, the exchange rate, fairly consistent over the years, was 1.78AFl to US$1 (1AFl is worth about 56¢). U.S. dollars, euros, traveler's checks, and major credit cards are widely accepted on the island. Change is usually given in local currency, so pay for your purchases in small bills if you want to avoid winding up with a pocketful of florins. *Unless otherwise specified, prices in this chapter are quoted in U.S. dollars.*

Documents To enter Aruba, U.S. and Canadian citizens and British subjects must submit a valid passport. Citizens of a member country of the European Union need a passport and an E.U. Travel Card.

Electricity The electricity is 110–120 volts AC (60 cycles), the same as in the United States.

Emergencies For the police or fire department, or a medical emergency, dial ✆ **911.**

Hospital For medical care, go to the **Horacio Oduber Hospital** on L. G. Smith Boulevard (✆ **587-4300;** this is also the number to call in case of a medical emergency). This modern building near Eagle Beach has excellent medical facilities. Hotels also have medical doctors on call, and there are good dental facilities as well (appointments can be made through your hotel).

Language The official languages are Dutch and the local dialect Papiamento, but nearly everybody speaks English. Spanish is also widely spoken.

Liquor Laws The minimum legal drinking and gambling age is 18. Liquor is sold on any day of the week throughout the island in most stores, including grocery stores and delis. By law (which doesn't seem to be strictly enforced), you can have an open container on the beach only if the liquor is purchased at one of the bars of the resort hotels lining the beachfront.

Safety Aruba is one of the Caribbean's safest destinations, in spite of its numerous hotels and casinos. Pickpockets and purse snatchers are around, of course, but they're rare. Still, it's wise to guard your valuables. Never leave them unattended on the beach or even in a locked car. Also, never hitchhike, and ladies out on the town should use the buddy system.

Taxes & Service Charges Hotels tack on a variety of additional charges that include a 6% government tax on rooms, and another 10% to 15% for "service," which may also include an energy surcharge of $4 to $8 per unit per night. Sales tax is 1.5%.

Telephone To call Aruba from the United States, dial ✆ **011** (the international access code), then **297** (the country code for Aruba), then **58** (the area code), and the five-digit local number. If you're in Aruba, you have to dial **58** followed by the five-digit local number. If you want to really keep in touch while on island, rent a local cellphone or get a local SIM card if you have a GSM phone. Visit the **SETAR** (✆ **297/525-1000;** www.setar.aw) or **Digicel** (✆ **297/522-2200;** www.digicelaruba.com) kiosks at the airport or in town. Another option is to dial **188** at any SETAR pay phone to make a credit card call home.

Time Aruba is on Atlantic Standard Time year-round; when all time zones are on standard time, Aruba is 1 hour ahead of Eastern Standard Time (when it's 10am in Aruba, it's 9am in New York). When daylight saving time is in effect in the United States, clocks in New York and Aruba show the same time.

Water The water, which comes from the world's second-largest desalination plant, is not only pure, but among the best in the world.

Weather The island lies outside the hurricane belt, so there is no threat of tropical storms. The average annual temperature is 82°F (28°C).

WHERE TO STAY

Most of Aruba's hotels are bustling, self-contained resorts. There's a dearth of family or budget hotels. Guesthouses are also rare and tend to fill up early in winter with faithful return visitors.

In season it's imperative to make reservations well in advance. Don't ever arrive expecting to find a room on the spot. You must give Immigration the address where you'll be staying when you arrive.

Don't forget to ask if the room tax and service charge (see "Fast Facts," above) are included in the rates quoted when you make your reservation. Also, lots of the big resorts in Aruba are frequently featured in packages, which can bring their rates down dramatically.

In lieu of renting an actual house or villa, which you can do on some islands, your best bet here is to rent an apartment or condo. Amsterdam Manor Beach Resort (p. 78) is a good place for such rentals.

Very Expensive

Aruba Marriott Resort & Stellaris Casino ★★ ☺ The Marriott's airy, tastefully subdued rooms are the largest in any of Aruba's luxury high-rise hotels. Its 9-sq.-m (97-sq.-ft.) balconies are also the most commodious in the area. As the last resort along Palm Beach, the Marriott offers a beach that's ideal for sunbathers craving space. Built in 1995 and constantly upgraded, the hotel has a quiet and discerning tone; guests run the gamut from honeymooners to retirees to corporate-incentive rewardees. There are plenty of families, too, but children here are well behaved. The eight-story complex forms a U that overlooks a large free-form pool, a waterfall, and lush palm, banana, and jacaranda trees. The Mandara Spa offers Aruba's most spiritually transformative indoor experience.

L. G. Smith Blvd. 101, Palm Beach, Aruba. www.marriott.com. ✆ **800/223-6388** in the U.S. and Canada, or 297/586-9000. Fax 297/520-6227. 413 units. Christmas/New Year's $800–$1,190 double, from $1,990 suite; Jan–Apr $490–$740 double, from $1,695 suite; May to mid-Dec $300–$750 double, from $1,000 suite. Packages available. Children 11 and under stay free in parent's room. AE, DISC, MC, V. **Amenities:** 5 restaurants (including a Ruth's Chris Steak House); 3 bars; babysitting; children's center; children's pool; concierge; 18-hole championship golf course nearby; well-equipped health club and spa; large outdoor pool w/waterfall; casino; room service; 2 tennis courts (lit); extensive watersports equipment/rentals. *In room:* A/C, TV, fridge, hair dryer, Wi-Fi ($15 per day).

Hyatt Regency Aruba Resort & Casino ★★★ ☺ This elegant nine-story beachfront resort has stunning spaces and a stellar reputation. It offers first-rate amenities and some of the most elaborate guest programs on the island. The elaborate water feature allows guests to gently meander through interconnected pools and water slides. Although attractively furnished with Deco-inspired furniture and modern carnival colors, the rooms are significantly smaller than the Marriott's. And the "Parisian" balconies offer just enough room for one person to stand. Standard rooms overlook the pool area but have no balconies. Other rooms provide vistas of the pool and ocean, while garden units have views of the lush tropical foliage. The 18 suites vary in size, but all are spacious, with good balconies; some feature such extras as stereo systems and in-room fitness equipment.

J. E. Irausquin Blvd. 85, Palm Beach, Aruba. www.aruba.hyatt.com. ✆ **888/591-1234** in the U.S. and Canada, or 297/586-1234. Fax 297/586-1682. 360 units. Winter $630–$880 double, $890–$3,650 suite;

Freebies for Kids

The One Cool Family Vacation (OCFV) program entices families to visit Aruba during the summer (June–Sept). Here's the deal: If you bring kids 12 and under, you'll get an assortment of freebies—breakfast, daily activities, sightseeing tours, cruises, snorkeling, and scuba lessons. In addition, discounts may be offered for submarine rides, horseback riding, car rentals, and even film developing. The program covers two children for every paying adult. Contact Aruba Tourism (✆ 800/TO-ARUBA [862-7822]; www.aruba.com) for a list of participating resorts.

off season $315–$540 double, $615–$2,450 suite. AE, DISC, MC, V. **Amenities:** 4 restaurants; 4 bars; babysitting; horseback riding; canoes; children's center and programs; dive shop; health club; Jacuzzi; outdoor pool/lagoon complex; casino; room service; scuba diving; smoke-free rooms; snorkeling; spa; 2 tennis courts (lit). *In room:* A/C, ceiling fan, TV, hair dryer, minibar, Wi-Fi ($10 per day).

Occidental Grand Aruba ★ ☺ The lobby is this resort combines Moroccan- and European-style furnishing and fixtures. Guest rooms have tile and marble floors, and private balconies or terraces. The pool has retained its bustling feel, so if you're looking for a casual house-party atmosphere with lots of action and organized activities, this good-times place is for you. The resort is popular with almost everybody: families with kids, young couples, middle-aged folks, and some elderly guests; most people choose an all-inclusive package. The hotel also has a wide range of restaurants—Mexican, Pan-Asian, Caribbean fusion, and, our favorite, **L'Olio,** with a finely tuned Italian cuisine and an impressive wine list.

J. E. Irausquin Blvd. 83, Palm Beach, Aruba. www.occidentalhotels.com/grand/Aruba.asp. ✆ **800/858-2258** in the U.S., or 297/586-4500. Fax 297/586-3191. 391 units. Winter $570–$950 double, $1,150–$1,550 suite; off season $522–$729 double, $826–$1,229 suite. Rates are all-inclusive. AE, MC, V. **Amenities:** 6 restaurants; deli; 6 bars (1 swim-up); babysitting; boating; children's club; dive shop; fitness center; Jacuzzi; outdoor pool; casino; room service; smoke-free rooms; snorkeling; 2 tennis courts (lit); windsurfing. *In room:* A/C, hair dryer, minibar.

Radisson Aruba Resort Casino & Spa ★★★ ☺ One of the 10 most luxurious resorts in the southern Caribbean, this eight-story hotel has the most stylish and beautiful rooms in Aruba. Integrating Caribbean plantation and South Beach Art Deco elements, the complex is both sophisticated and personal. Because the lush gardens, lagoons, and waterfalls ramble over more than 6 hectares, the tone is tranquil and the feel is spacious. The guest rooms aren't large, but they're remarkable: West Indian colonial louvered doors, rather than drapes, cover the terrace doors, and intricately carved finials crown the mahogany four-poster beds. The reading chairs' retractable ottomans and floor lamps mix Bauhaus and plantation influences. Elegance stretches out to the balconies, too, where mahogany slatted chairs and flagstone floors enhance the view over the gardens or sea. The Radisson adds such touches as frosted drinking glasses, silver ice buckets, and earth-toned pottery.

J. E. Irausquin Blvd. 81, Palm Beach, Aruba. www.radisson.com/aruba. ✆ **800/395-7046** in the U.S. and Canada, or 297/586-6555. Fax 297/586-3260. 353 units. Winter $582–$630 double, $955–$1085 suite; off season $290–$425 double, $680–$840 suite. AE, DC, DISC, MC, V. **Amenities:** 3 restaurants; 2 bars; babysitting; children's center; dive shop; golf privileges; fitness center; 2 outdoor pools; casino: room service; spa; 2 tennis courts. *In room:* A/C, TV, hair dryer, minibar, Wi-Fi (free).

Tierra del Sol Aruba Resort Spa & Country Club ★★ If you think more about sand traps than sand castles, Tierra del Sol tops the board. This resort, with its championship 18-hole golf course designed by Robert Trent Jones, Jr., combines the sun and golf of Scottsdale with the waves and dunes of Aruba's north coast. The Mediterranean-style condominiums, villas, and homes clustered in intimate neighborhoods, spread over acres of desert landscaping, have golf-course or ocean views, living rooms, dining rooms, kitchens, master suites with full bathrooms, guest rooms with another bathroom, covered terraces, and washers and dryers. Some also feature walk-in closets, saunas, balconies, outdoor Jacuzzis, private pools, and garages. You can arrive to a fully stocked kitchen by ordering items online beforehand.

Caya di Solo 10, Malmokweg, Noord, Aruba. www.tierradelsol.com. ✆ **866/978-5158** or 297/586-7800. Fax 297/586-4970. 112 units. Winter $590–$675 2-bedroom condo, $550–$790 2-bedroom villa, $750 3-bedroom condo, $750–$975 3-bedroom villa, $1,600–$1,850 4-bedroom estate home; off season

Spa Retreats

Diamonds may be a girl's best friend, but corporeal indulgence is a close second. The Mandara Spa at Marriott's Aruba Ocean Club, L. G. Smith Blvd. 99, Palm Beach (✆ 297/586-9000), recreates the tranquillity of a Japanese rainforest with Thai silk wall hangings, soft Balinese gamelan music, and the scents of clove and cinnamon. Personal attention is the hallmark of this meditative retreat, which offers state-of-the-art massages, body wraps, and facials. Programs cater to couples and men, who make up a hefty portion of the clientele. Other upscale spas can be found at Tierra del Sol (✆ 297/586-4861), the Hyatt (✆ 297/586-1234), and the Larimar Spa at the Renaissance (✆ 297/583-6000). For a more rustic pampering experience, try Spa del Sol at the Manchebo Beach Resort and Spa, J. E. Irausquin Blvd. 55 (✆ 297/582-6145), a garden sanctuary by the sea featuring massages, yoga, reflexology, and other treatments in beachside cabanas. The training of masseurs and masseuses on the island varies greatly. Be sure to ask for the most experienced person available.

$430–$530 2-bedroom condo, $550–$675 2-bedroom villa, $575 3-bedroom condo, $750 3-bedroom villa, $1,000–$1,250 4-bedroom estate home. AE, MC, V. **Amenities:** 2 restaurants; 3 bars; golf; fitness center; outdoor pool; spa; 2 tennis courts. *In room:* A/C, TV, kitchen.

The Westin Resort, Aruba ★★★ Built in 1975, this hotel was renovated in 2006. Today olive, beige, and mustard fabrics accent the cherry-wood furniture, while subtle carpeting, flatscreen TVs, and modern rectangular lamps add more Miami style. Plus, the trademark Westin "heavenly" beds provide a fluffy retreat from the world. The terraces on the top floors mean superb ocean views—with 18 floors, this is Aruba's tallest building. Guests include the usual suspects—couples, honeymooners, a fair number of business groups, and families. The kids' program includes scuba lessons in the pool, and the iguanas that patrol the pool area are adorable. But you'll have to wait in line in the morning to reserve a beach hut, and one never gets used to the sad sight of parrots, toucans, and cockatoos squawking in their cages.

J. E. Irausquin Blvd. 77, Palm Beach, Aruba. www.westinaruba.com. ✆ **800/937-8461** in the U.S., or 297/586-4466. Fax 297/586-0928. 481 units. Winter $490–$800 double; off season $260–$490 double; year-round $840–$1,110 suite. AE, MC, V. **Amenities:** 6 restaurants; 4 bars; babysitting; children's program; health club; outdoor pool; casino; room service; smoke-free rooms; spa; 2 tennis courts; watersports. *In room:* A/C, TV, hair dryer, minibar, Wi-Fi (free).

Expensive

Aruba Bucuti Beach Resort and Tara Beach Suites & Spa ★★ This elegant oasis provides Aruba's most adult ambience. Set on one of the Caribbean's best beaches, a serene 5.6-hectare (14-acre) expanse of sand, it's a favored retreat for sophisticated couples of all ages, especially honeymooners. And though most guests are straight, the Bucuti is both appealing and welcoming to gay couples. Contemporary minimalist design with walnut and linen tones warm the spacious rooms, and the large balconies overlook gardens or the beach. Penthouses and the junior suites have kitchenettes. Because the owner is the driving force behind many environmental initiatives, the hotel is one of Aruba's greenest: Recycling bins, water-conservation measures, and beachwide cleanups are part of the effort. Beach lovers appreciate the

Bucuti's *palapa*-to-guest ratio—it's the highest on the island. At the breezy, open-air fitness area, nature and exercise go hand in hand.

L. G. Smith Blvd. 55B, Eagle Beach, Aruba. www.bucuti.com. ✆ **888/4BUCUTI** [428-2884] or 297/583-1100. Fax 297/582-5272. 104 units. Winter $450–$490 double, $565 bungalow or junior suite, $660 penthouse; off season $310–$345 double, $415 bungalow or junior suite, $515 penthouse. All rooms include a full American breakfast buffet daily. AE, DISC, MC, V. **Amenities:** Restaurant; 2 bars; babysitting; open-air health club; outdoor pool; spa. *In room:* A/C, TV, fridge, hair dryer, minibar, Wi-Fi ($10 per day).

Renaissance Aruba Resort & Casino ★★★ The anchor of a second mall, the six-story Marina Tower hotel at the Renaissance Resort in the thick of the capital is popular with business travelers and vacationing couples. The compact rooms feature thick carpeting, modern colors, stylish furniture, and step-out balconies. The bathrooms are small but have separate sink and bath areas. On the waterfront and favored by groups, the Ocean Suites feel more like a resort and are family-friendly. This part of the complex features a small man-made beach, a pool with slides, and 258 one-bedroom suites with living rooms, large bathrooms, balconies or patios, and stocked wet bars. Carpeted floors, solid pastels, and glass bricks brighten the rooms. Hop the free water taxi to Renaissance Island (a 10-min. ride) for a relaxing day on the beach. Also on the premises are two casinos (including the island's only 24-hr. facility).

L. G. Smith Blvd. 82, Oranjestad, Aruba. www.marriott.com. ✆ **800/421-8188** in the U.S. and Canada, or 297/583-6000. Fax 297/582-5317. 558 units in 2 resorts. Winter $350–$550 double, from $895 suite; off season $230–$380 double, from $420 suite. Extra person $50. Children 16 and under stay free in parent's suite. Meal plans and packages available. AE, DC, DISC, MC, V. **Amenities:** 4 restaurants; 4 bars; children's programs; exercise room; fishing; 2 outdoor pools; casino; room service; scuba diving; smoke-free rooms; spa; 2 tennis courts; water-skiing; windsurfing. *In room:* A/C, TV, hair dryer, Internet ($15 per day), minibar.

Moderate

Amsterdam Manor Beach Resort ★★ ☺ This cheerful gem is a refreshing alternative to cookie-cutter uniformity. With a strong European accent and couples-friendly slant, the Amsterdam Manor features a quiet atmosphere and boutique size that's perfect for independent travelers. The last low-rise resort across the street from Eagle Beach, it's near the bus stop for easy access to town. Bird lovers enjoy the proximity to the Bubali Pond bird sanctuary. The architecture of the three-floor complex is Dutch gingerbread with quaint gabled roofs and whimsical turrets. Scattered around a series of intimate courtyards, the studios and one- and two-bedroom suites feature oak furniture and stylish wicker sofa sets. All units feature a balcony or terrace and kitchen or kitchenette. Standard studios have shower-only bathrooms, while superior units have a Jacuzzi and an ocean view. Suites on the top floor boast high barn ceilings. An environmental leader, the resort is Green Globe certified.

J. E. Irausquin Blvd. 252 (P.O. Box 1302), Oranjestad, Aruba. www.amsterdammanor.com. ✆ **800/969-2310** in the U.S., or 297/527-1100. Fax 297/527-1112. 72 units. Winter $295–$325 studio, $375–$475 suite; off season $190–$220 studio, $270–$360 suite. Children 11 and under stay free in parent's room. MC, V. **Amenities:** 2 restaurants; 2 bars; concierge; 2 pools (outdoor and kiddie); smoke-free rooms. *In room:* A/C, TV, fridge, hair dryer, kitchenette, Wi-Fi (free).

La Quinta Beach Resort Built in 1991, this small timeshare is across the road from Eagle Beach. Most owners are older couples, but there are a fair number of families as well. The atmosphere at the two five-floor buildings is sedate. All units have large balconies, but the closets are small. The furnishings are tropical and modular—lots of bamboo, pink tile, and nondescript floral prints. The wooden louvered windows and paned windows and doors are a nice touch, though. All units have a kitchenette, and two-bedroom deluxe units have a loft bedroom. The pool in the executive complex is much larger than the one in front. For those looking for a touch of luxury, some of the one-bedroom executive suites have balcony Jacuzzis.

J. E. Irausquin Blvd. 228, Oranjestad, Aruba. www.laquintaaruba.net. ✆ **297/587-5010.** Fax 297/587-6263. 54 units. Winter $125–$155 double, $185–$215 1-bedroom suite, $255–$430 2-bedroom suite, $480 3-bedroom suite; summer $85–$95 double, $110–$130 1-bedroom suite, $155–$185 2-bedroom suite, $265 3-bedroom suite. AE, DISC, MC, V. **Amenities:** Restaurant; bar; babysitting; Jacuzzis; 2 pools; Wi-Fi (free). *In room:* A/C, TV/VCR, video rentals, hair dryer, kitchen or kitchenette.

The Mill Resort & Suites ★ The only low-rise in a high-rise area, this resort combines Dutch efficiency and Aruban warmth. Opened in 1990, the two-story complex lies opposite Palm Beach and the Westin. Its strengths include personal service, easy access to amenities, and reasonable prices. Guests vary from honeymooning couples to singles looking to have a good time. The sunny units feature bamboo furniture and tile floors. Junior rooms have king-size beds, full bathrooms, sitting areas with sofa beds, good-size porches or balconies, and kitchenettes. Studios have one king-size bed, a pullout sofa, a shower-only bathroom, a dining/sitting area, and a kitchen. A Jacuzzi is steps away from a king-size bed in the Royal rooms. Garden- and pool-view rooms cost the same; the pool's party atmosphere wanes later in the day, but garden rooms are quieter around the clock. Beach access is directly across the street.

J. E. Irausquin Blvd. 330, Palm Beach, Aruba. www.millresort.com. ✆ **800/992-2015** in the U.S. and Canada, or 297/526-7700. Fax 297/586-7271. 200 units. Dec–Mar $275 royal room, $295 studio, $315 junior suite, $480 1-bedroom suite, $655 2-bedroom suite; Apr–Nov $140 royal room, $150 studio, $190 junior suite, $295 1-bedroom suite, $435 2-bedroom suite. Children 11 and under stay free in parent's room. Packages available. AE, MC, V. Children not accepted in royal room. **Amenities:** Restaurant; bar; babysitting; concierge; exercise room; 2 pools (1 for children); smoke-free rooms; spa; 2 tennis courts (lit); Wi-Fi ($7 per day, around pool and lobby areas). *In room:* A/C, TV, hair dryer.

Inexpensive

Aruba Millennium Resort This two-story bright-yellow motel is a 10-minute walk inland from Palm Beach. The studios and one-bedroom units, each with a kitchenette, face either a small pool or one of two cozy courtyards. Each of the courtyards features two minuscule Jacuzzis with rickety wooden decks. All rooms have either a balcony or a raised rustic-wood terrace with patio furniture and a blue-and-white-striped awning. Inside, well-worn blue-and-yellow floral prints accent the white wicker and bamboo furniture. Ask for a smoke-free room to avoid the smell, which has permeated the drapes, and ask to face the pool. The motel's quiet ambience makes it popular with budget-conscious families, locals, and couples looking to zone out by the pool. Restaurants and other shops are also within easy walking distance.

Palm Beach 33, Palm Beach, Aruba. ✆ **297/586-3700.** Fax 297/586-2506. 20 units. Dec–Apr $130 studio, $175 1-bedroom; May–Nov $60 studio, $95 1-bedroom. $20 per night extra per child. AE, MC, V. **Amenities:** Small outdoor pool. *In room:* A/C, TV, kitchenette.

The Arubiana Inn A 15-minute walk inland from Eagle Beach, this quiet, tidy motel lies in wild, cactus-covered terrain a few hundred feet from a main road. The single-story structure of coral stucco and terra-cotta tile encloses a central pool area with plenty of chairs and tables. Each of the squeaky-clean studio units opens to this palm-lined courtyard. The cozy rooms feature white-tile floors, white-wicker furniture, and pastel floral prints. The small bathrooms are blindingly white with salmon accents. A minimart supplies food and other items. Restaurants, a supermarket, and miniature golf are a few minutes away by foot.

Bubali 74, Oranjestad, Aruba. www.arubianainn.com. ✆ **297/587-7700.** Fax 297/587-1770. 18 units. Winter $102 double; off season $85 double. AE, MC, V. Children 5 and under not accepted. **Amenities:** Babysitting; outdoor pool. *In room:* A/C, TV, fridge.

WHERE TO DINE

Sometimes—at least on off-season package deals—visitors on the Modified American Plan (breakfast and dinner) are allowed to dine around on an exchange plan with other hotels. Ask your hotel for details.

In Oranjestad

EXPENSIVE

Cuba's Cookin' ★ CUBAN This fun, informal spot is plenty hip. Original art captures whimsical scenes of Cuban street life, while up-tempo live Cuban music keeps the warm staff smiling. Sip a mojito and start with the plantain chips; they're great with the *muy picante* salsa. Your conga cocktail appetizer should arrive just in time to extinguish the fire in your mouth. Served in a half-shell, it features cold lobster, crab, red onions, and carrots in a light vinaigrette. The seafood boat is a winning main course: Lightly grilled shrimp, calamari, conch, and mussels rise from a flavorful ragout of green and red peppers, onions, garlic, tomatoes, and cucumbers. Other Cuban specialties include *ropa vieja* (shredded skirt steak sautéed in tomatoes, onions, and green peppers) and *picadillo de res* (ground beef with raisins and olives). For dessert, try the *tres leches* pound cake, then light up a Cuban cigar with your *café con leche.*

Wilhelminastraat 27 (across from the police station). ✆ **297/588-0627.** www.cubascookin.com. Reservations recommended. Main courses $20–$40. AE, DISC, MC, V. Mon–Sat noon–3pm and 5:30–11pm.

Driftwood ★ SEAFOOD/ARUBAN The married partners who run this restaurant have an unusual setup: Herbert Merryweather spends the day on the high seas catching the fish served that night in the restaurant, while Francine Merryweather stays on-site, directing the sometimes busy traffic in the dining room. The setting is an Aruban-style antique house in the center of Oranjestad, with interior walls covered with (guess what) pieces of driftwood. The menu items always available include Argentine filet mignon served with a bacon-flavored mushroom sauce; boneless breast of chicken with Parmesan and linguine; stewed conch; and shrimp in Creole sauce. But the composition of the fish menu varies according to the day's catch. It might include mahimahi, wahoo, kingfish, grouper, or lobster. These will be prepared after a consultation with a staff member, usually Francine, who will propose any of several methods of preparation—either blackened, meunière, fried, or baked, along with appropriate garnishes and sauces.

Klipstraat 12. ✆ **297/583-2515.** www.driftwoodaruba.com. Reservations recommended. Main courses $23–$47. AE, DISC, MC, V. Wed–Mon 5–10:30pm (last order at 10pm).

Gasparito Restaurant and Art Gallery ★ ARUBAN/SEAFOOD Here's a favorite with people in love. Located in a restored *cunucu* (farmhouse), Gasparito features intimate dining rooms inside and a breezy outdoor patio and bar. The tinkling of a fountain, comfortable patio chairs, and candlelight enhance the courtyard's warmth. Inside, vaulted ceilings embrace cozy rooms. Local art, much of it for sale, graces the interior walls. The *keri keri* ravioli, a favorite appetizer, features shredded fish (dry like *bacalão*) in a creamy tomato-and-basil sauce. Main courses focus on seafood and Aruban dishes, but the menu makes a special nod to vegetarians, and the filet mignon has vocal fans. For dessert you can't go wrong with *banana na forno,* a whole banana baked with cinnamon.

Gasparito 3. ✆ **297/586-7044.** www.gasparito.com. Reservations recommended. Main courses $18–$38. AE, DISC, MC, V. Daily 5:30–11pm.

L. G. Smith's Steak & Chop House ★★ STEAK/SEAFOOD The dining choices at the Renaissance Aruba Resort & Casino (p. 78) are vast, but nothing quite tops this hip and sophisticated venue, with its wood paneling, waterfall wall, quartzite-stone columns, black furniture with white-leatherette cushions, and panoramic view of the Oranjestad marina. Located next to the upper level of the casino entrance, the restaurant doesn't survive on its trendy decor alone, but serves one of the best selections of meat in Aruba, ranging from porterhouse to New York strip. Naturally, you expect surf and turf on the menu, but the chef goes far beyond the routine, offering such dishes as locally caught mahimahi with a mango salsa or free-range chicken with a red-pepper-laced cranberry juice. If you passed on the thick chocolate cake, you might opt for the signature mascarpone tart. The early bird special at $79 is a bargain but is available only from 5:30 to 7pm.

In the Renaissance Aruba Resort & Casino, L. G. Smith Blvd. 82. ✆ **297/523-6115.** www.lgsmiths.com. Reservations recommended. Main courses $19–$36. AE, DISC, MC, V. Daily 5:30–11pm.

Pinchos Grill & Bar ★ GRILL Hovering over the water at the end of a short pier at the Surfside Marina, this open-air restaurant is little more than a circular bar surrounded by a ring of dining tables and low-profile sofas nestled dangerously close to the calm water below. Yet two things make this family-run venue remarkable. One is the spectacular setting, with a SoBe feel and unrestricted views of nearby Oranjestad, passing cruise ships, and incoming flights. The other is the fact that they dish up a full menu from the small grill behind the bar—they prep much of the food off-site but always grill the crab cakes or marinated, tender steak and shrimp *pinchos* (skewers) to order. While the salads are uninspiring and the portions are a bit small, the desserts more than make up for it, and the atmosphere is as romantic as it gets.

L. G. Smith Blvd. 7 (at Aruba Surfside Marina Hotel). ✆ **297/583-2666.** Reservations recommended. Main courses $19–$44. AE, DISC, MC, V. Daily 5–11pm. Bar open till midnight (Fri–Sat until 1am).

MODERATE

Eetcafe the Paddock INTERNATIONAL In the heart of Oranjestad, this cafe and bistro overlooks the harbor, a short walk from virtually every shop in town. Much of the staff is hip and European. No one will mind whether you opt for a drink, a cup of tea or coffee, a snack, or a full-fledged meal. The menu is dizzying in its international offerings, ranging from pasta to stir-fry, salads to *shawarma* (pita-bread sandwiches stuffed with chicken and a garlic sauce with plenty of tang). For dinner, try the fresh poached or sautéed fish, or glazed tenderloin of pork.

L. G. Smith Blvd. 13. ✆ **297/583-2334.** www.paddock-aruba.com. Main courses $12–$23. MC, V. Daily 9am–11pm.

Near Palm Beach

EXPENSIVE

Chalet Suisse ★ SWISS/INTERNATIONAL This alpine-chalet restaurant feels like an old-fashioned Swiss dining room. In deliberate contrast to the arid scrublands that surround it, the restaurant is an air-conditioned refuge of pinewood panels and *gemutlichkeit* (comfort). Tempting menu items include Dutch pea soup, beef stroganoff, a pasta of the day, Wiener schnitzel, roast duckling with orange sauce, red snapper with Creole sauce, and an array of high-calorie desserts. The chefs claim they serve the best rack of lamb in the Southern Hemisphere; we can't vouch for that, but it's really good. The Swiss fare is hearty, if a bit heavy for the Tropics. Finish off with a smooth chocolate fondue or the eternal favorite, Swiss apple strudel. Most dishes are at the lower end of the price scale.

J. E. Irausquin Blvd. 246, Eagle Beach. ✆ **297/587-5054.** www.chaletsuisse-aruba.com. Reservations recommended. Main courses $19–$45. AE, DISC, MC, V. Mon–Sat 5:30–10pm.

Madame Janette ★★ 🎁 ARUBAN/CARIBBEAN/INTERNATIONAL In a low-slung Aruban-style house a short ride from Palm Beach, this elegant restaurant exudes island atmosphere, attracting a laid-back crowd to its tables set in a desert courtyard. The European chef has created a buzz among local foodies with his imaginative menu and clever blending of ingredients; we recommend Madame's Hot Shrimps, succulent prawns baked in a well-flavored marinara sauce topped with Gouda and Gorgonzola. Even though the delicate texture of the seafood is overpowered by the Gouda, the taste is still delightful. The rack of lamb is the chef's masterpiece, with a family-secret marinade. Finish off with such desserts as the Austrian *kaiserschmarrn,* which is a thick pancake covered with plum sauce, or the Mama Jamaica: fresh pineapple marinated in old Appleton rum and served with vanilla ice cream topped with roasted coconut flakes.

Cunuco Abao 37 (next to the Blue Village Villas). ✆ **297/587-0184.** www.madamejanette.info. Reservations recommended. Main courses $26–$68. AE, MC, V. Wed–Mon 5:30–10pm.

Screaming Eagle ★ FRENCH FUSION If the idea of fine dining while luxuriating on white beds and at intimate tables shrouded in gauzy drapes sounds romantic, make a pilgrimage to this sleek new restaurant. Start with a drink at the bar, where the award-winning bartender will whip you up something from his list of 110 cocktails, or just order from the selection of 150 wines. Appetizers that stand out are the carpaccio of artichoke with goat cheese and the ahi tuna tartare with soft-shell crab and spicy papaya mayonnaise. As a main course, the chef recommends the fresh local wahoo with shrimp ginger risotto, asparagus, and creamy Cajun sauce, or the black Angus tenderloin with shiitake pine-nut sauce. For a dessert almost too beautiful to eat, try *la tazza famosa:* a cup and saucer made of chocolate filled with Tia Maria, orange sherbet, and chocolate mousse.

J. E. Irausquin Blvd. 228, Eagle Beach. ✆ **297/587-8021.** www.screaming-eagle.net. Reservations recommended. Main courses $26–$59. AE, DISC, MC, V. Daily 6–11pm.

In or Near Noord

Buccaneer ★ SEAFOOD/INTERNATIONAL In a rustic building near the hamlet of Noord, close to many of the island's biggest high-rise hotels, the Buccaneer is one of Aruba's most popular seafood restaurants. Inside you'll find a nautical decor and a dozen bubbling aquariums. There are a number of tempting appetizers, such as crabmeat cocktail or a savory plate of escargot with an infusion of Pernod. Seafood thermidor appears on the menu, or you can try the land-and-sea platter with fresh fish, shrimp, and tender beef tenderloin. The food is hearty and delicious. A spacious bar shaped like a sailing ship is a good place to linger over drinks.

Gasparito 11-C, Noord. ✆ **297/586-6172.** Reservations recommended. Main courses $18–$40. AE, DISC, MC, V. Mon–Sat 5:30–11pm.

La Trattoria "El Faro Blanco" ★ ITALIAN Charming and authentically Italian, this restaurant, built in 1914, was originally the local lighthouse keeper's home. The staff is mostly European, and the head chef studied in Italy. Views sweep out over the sea, the island's northern coastline, and the island's largest golf course. The menu covers a full range of Italian cuisine, with a heavy dose of aromatic Neapolitan specialties. The best examples include heaping platters of fish and vegetable antipasti; linguine with shrimp, octopus, scallops, clams, and tomatoes (our vote for the island's best pasta); red snapper cooked in a potato crust with olive oil and rosemary; and *osso buco* (veal shank) served with Parmesan-laced risotto Milanese. The desserts are excellent; we recommend tiramisu or pears poached in red wine served with ice cream.

At the California Lighthouse, Noord. ✆ **297/586-0786.** www.aruba-latrattoria.com. Reservations recommended. Main courses $22–$48. AE, DISC, MC, V. Daily 8:30am–midnight; pizza served until 5:30pm.

The Old Cunucu House ★ ARUBAN/INTERNATIONAL When originally constructed as a private house in the 1920s, this was the only building in the neighborhood. Today it retains a warm, traditional feeling, with original decor of very thick plaster-coated walls, ultrasimple furniture, and tile floors. Many visitors start with a cocktail under a shed-style roof in front, where chairs and tables overlook a well-kept garden studded with desert plants. The skilled chef knows how to embellish a traditional repertoire with first-class ingredients; the kitchen focuses on local and international recipes, including fish soup, fried squid, and coconut fried shrimp. Several dishes are also served with *funchi* (Caribbean polenta) and *pan bati* (a local pancake).

Palm Beach 150, Noord. ✆ **297/586-1666.** www.theoldcunucuhouse.com. Reservations recommended. Main courses $19–$40. AE, DISC, MC, V. Daily 11:30am–3pm and 5–11pm.

Papiamento ★★ INTERNATIONAL/CARIBBEAN/SEAFOOD Originally from Holland, the Ellis family has served award-winning Caribbean food in their 200-year-old *cunucu* home for almost 2 decades. Over the years, tables have spilled out from the thick-walled, antiques-filled interiors to the large, fairy lit palm garden. At twilight birds serenade outdoor diners around the luminescent pool. When Beatrix, queen of the Netherlands, is in Aruba, she sups inside on the former veranda, now dubbed the Queen's Room. You might start with the smoked-salmon appetizer, garnished with capers, caviar, basil, passion fruit, and radicchio. The crudités platter features prosciutto, aged Gouda, and marinated peppers and onions. Mango, onion, and chili-pepper chutney accompanies *pisca arubiana* (fish Aruban style). Best bets for dessert are *cocobana,* an ephemeral coconut mousse, and flaky-crusted Dutch apple pie. Coffee snobs, take note: Papiamento's espresso may be the island's best.

Washington 61, Noord. ✆ **297/586-4544.** www.papiamentorestaurant.com. Reservations recommended. Main courses $26–$52. AE, DISC, MC, V. Mon–Sat 6–10:30pm.

East of Oranjestad

Charlie's Bar and Restaurant SEAFOOD/ARUBAN Charlie's is the best reason to visit San Nicolas—but come for the good times and the brew, not the food. The bar dates from 1941 and is the most overly decorated joint in the West Indies, sporting an array of memorabilia and local souvenirs. Where roustabouts and roughnecks once brawled, you'll now find tables filled with visitors admiring thousands of pennants, banners, and trophies dangling from the high ceiling. Two-fisted drinks are still served, but the menu has improved since the good old days, when San Nicolas was one of the toughest towns in the Caribbean. You can enjoy freshly made soup, grilled scampi, Creole-style squid, and churrasco. Sirloin steak and red snapper are usually featured.

Main St., San Nicolas (25-min. drive east of Oranjestad). ✆ **297/584-5086.** Main courses $23–$30. MC, V. Mon–Sat 11:30am–9:30pm. Bar till 10pm or later.

ARUBA'S BEACHES

The western and southern shores of Aruba are called the Turquoise Coast. Along this stretch, Palm Beach and Eagle Beach (the latter closer to Oranjestad) are the best. No hotel along the strip owns these beaches, all of which are open to the public. (If you use any of the hotel's facilities, however, you'll be charged.) The major resort hotels are built on the southwestern and more tranquil strip of Aruba. These beaches open onto calm waters that are ideal for swimming. The beaches on the northern side of Aruba, although quite beautiful, face choppy waters with stronger waves.

Palm Beach ★★★ is a superb stretch of wide white sand. It's great for swimming, sunbathing, sailing, fishing, and snorkeling. It's crowded in the winter, but there's plenty of room for all. The waters off this beach are incredibly blue. Along Palm Beach, all the resorts are set away from the beach by flowering gardens, which take on a special beauty because the island is so dry. As you walk along the beach, you can wander past a rainbow of red, yellow, and pink bushes, which attract some colorful native bird life. If you stop to have a drink at one of the open-air bars, chances are, you'll be joined by a yellow banaquit hoping to steal some sugar from you.

Also worth seeking out is **Fisherman's Huts,** where billowing rainbow-colored kite and windsurf sails abound. Conditions for windsurfing and kitesurfing are excellent here. For this reason, the strip is dominated by both, making swimming unadvisable. This beach is known for some of the finest windsurfing on island and is a great place to watch the local talent leap, flip, and sail through the air at breakneck speed. It's the site of the annual **Hi-Winds Pro-Am Windsurfing Competition** and is a great place for beginners to take a lesson or get in some practice.

Quite similar to Palm Beach, **Eagle Beach ★** is next door on the west coast, fronting a number of timeshare units. With gentle surf along miles of white-powder sand, swimming conditions here are excellent. Hotels along the strip organize non-motorized watersports and beach activities, but it's more low-key than Palm Beach.

The white-powder sands of **Punta Brabo,** also called **Manchebo Beach,** are a favorite among topless sunbathers. Actually, Manchebo is part of the greater Eagle Beach, and the Manchebo Beach Resort is a good place to stop, as it offers a dive shop and rents snorkeling gear. It's also set amid 40 hectares (99 acres) of gardens, filled with everything from cacti to bougainvillea.

Practically every visitor winds up on Eagle Beach for an uncrowded quiet escape or Palm Beach for a livelier bar and boating scene. If you'd like something more private, head for **Baby Beach ★** on the eastern end of Aruba. The beach has white-powder sand and tranquil, shallow waters, making it ideal for swimming, and it's the best place on the island for beach-based snorkeling. There are no facilities other than restrooms, a refreshment stand, and shaded areas. You'll spot the Arubans themselves here on weekends. Baby Beach opens onto a vast lagoon shielded by coral rocks that rise from the water. Bring your own towels and snorkeling gear, or rent the latter from the small stand where they also sell you bread to lure in the sizeable fish.

Next to Baby Beach on the eastern tip of the island, **Rodger's Beach** also has white-powder sand and excellent swimming conditions. The backdrop, however, is an oil refinery at the far side of the bay. But the waters remain unpolluted (so they say),

Sunset at Bubali Pond

The Bubali Pond bird sanctuary lies on the north side of Eagle Beach at Post Chikito, south of De Olde Molen (a 19th-c. windmill, now Aruba's most famous landmark). Flocks of birds cluster at this freshwater pond, particularly at sunset, which makes for a memorable sight. You can see pelicans galore; black olivaceous cormorants; black-crowned night herons; great egrets with long, black legs and yellow bills; and spotted sandpipers. The large wood stork and the glossy scarlet ibis sometimes fly in from Venezuela. While tempting to climb, the rickety viewing tower is in dire need of repair and should not be scaled.

and you can admire both large and small multicolored fish and strange coral formations. The trade winds will keep you cool.

SPORTS & OUTDOOR PURSUITS

CRUISES For a boat ride and a few hours of snorkeling, contact **De Palm Tours,** which has offices in eight of the island's hotels. Its main office is at L. G. Smith Blvd. 142, in Oranjestad (✆ **800/609-7374** in the U.S. and Canada, or 297/582-4400; www.depalmtours.com). De Palm Tours offers a 4-hour cruise that visits two coral reefs and the German shipwreck *Antilla* daily. The cost is $77 per person, half price for children 12 and under. **Red Sail Sports** (✆ **297/586-1603;** www.redsailaruba.com) has three catamarans and several sailing options. The 4-hour luncheon snorkel sail visits three snorkeling sites and includes a deli lunch and an open bar (daily at 9:15am; $69 adults, $39 children 3–11). The 2½-hour snorkel sail includes snacks and beverages (daily at 2:30pm; $49 adults, $29 children 3–11). **Pelican Adventures** (✆ **297/587-2302;** www.pelican-aruba.com) gives morning, afternoon, and sunset cruises on four different catamarans. The 2½-hour snorkel cruise departs daily at 2:30pm and includes snacks and open bar ($48 adults, $28 children 4–12). The 3½-hour brunch cruise features continental breakfast, champagne lunch, snorkeling, and open bar (Wed, Fri, and Sun 9:30am; $75 adults, $50 children). The sunset booze cruise lasts 2 hours and includes snacks and drinks (daily 5pm; $45 adults, $25 children).

Jolly Pirates ★ (✆ **297/586-8107;** www.jolly-pirates.com) features unique 4½-hour sail, snorkel, lunch, and rope-swing excursions. Friendly and athletic deckhands will astound you with their mast-climbing antics, followed by an acrobatic swing into the sea—think Tarzan meets Aquaman. Morning cruises embark daily ($56, including tasty, full-service barbecue lunch), as do 2-hour sunset trips (Mon and Fri; $27) and 3-hour afternoon sail and snorkel tours (daily; $38).

Mi Dushi Sailing Adventures (✆ **297/586-2010;** www.arubaadventures.com) offers three cruises on a 23m (75-ft) sailing vessel built in 1925. The 5-hour morning cruise combines sailing, snorkeling, swimming, and a rope swing with continental breakfast, barbecue lunch, and open bar. The boat departs from the De Palm Pier daily at 9:30am. The price is $59 for adults, $20 for children 6 to 12, and free for children 5 and under (though they get no lunch, and parents are strongly discouraged from bringing children 3 and under). The afternoon snorkel sail is only $39 ($20 for children 6–12).

DEEP-SEA FISHING In the deep waters off the coast of Aruba, you can test your skill and wits against the big ones—wahoo, marlin, tuna, bonito, and sailfish. **De Palm Tours** (see above) takes 4 to 10 people on one of its eight boats, which range in length from 10 to 16m (33–53 ft). Half-day tours, with all equipment included, begin at $350 for up to four people. The price for a full-day trip starts at $700. Boats leave from the docks in Oranjestad. De Palm maintains 13 branches, most of which are located in Aruba's major hotels. At **Renaisssance Marina** (✆ **297/588-0260;** www.renaissancemarina.com) you can find charter boats in a wide range of sizes and prices.

GOLF Aruba's **Tierra del Sol Golf Course** (✆ **866/978-5158** or 297/586-0978; www.tierradelsol.com), designed by Robert Trent Jones, Jr., is on the northwest coast near the California Lighthouse. The 18-hole, par-71, 6,811-yard course combines lush greens with the island's indigenous flora, such as the swaying divi-divi tree. Facilities include a restaurant and lounge in the clubhouse and a swimming pool. In winter, greens fees are a whopping $159, including golf cart, or $124 after noon. Off-season greens fees are $132, or $105 after noon. The course is open daily from 7am to 7pm.

Opened in 2005, **Links at Divi Aruba,** near Druif Beach, across the street from the Divi Aruba Resort (✆ **297/581-4653;** www.divigolf.com), offers a less pricey yet elegant alternative. Although it has only 9 holes, the course allows a second pass to simulate an 18-hole round. The course has two par-5 holes, two par-3 holes, and five par-4 holes. Six holes play either over or alongside the numerous man-made lagoons, and each hole has three tees for different-level players. Fees are $124 for 18 holes, $85 for 9 holes. The course is open daily from 6:30am to 5:30pm. Start before 1pm to complete 18 holes. Golf carts can be rented at the on-site pro shop, and clubs are included with the green fees; however, caddies are not available.

HORSEBACK RIDING You can ride at **Rancho Notorious** (✆ **297/586-0508;** www.ranchonotorious.com). The price is $45 for a 1-hour tour (daily 11am, 3pm, and 5pm) and $100 for a 2-hour tour (daily 9am, 3pm, and sunset). The minimum age is 6 for children to ride their own horses. **The Gold Mine Ranch** (✆ **297/585-9870;** www.thegoldmineranch.com) offers 2-hour tours starting at $65 and offers free transportation.

OFF-ROADING If a jeep tour is too slow and an ATV is too fast, then a TomCar is *juuuust* right. These dune-buggies drive like a car, have four-point seatbelts, and are so stable, you can't flip them if you try (yes, we tried). Feel free to play Mad Max as your convoy snakes along gravel slopes, dirt roads, and sand dunes on one of two routes. **Green Zebra Adventures** (✆ **297/585-0027**) is based at the Aruba Ostrich Farm and offers two daily tours. The morning drive, $119 per person for the first two passengers and $59 each for the back-seat passengers, takes you to Seroe Colorado, Baby Beach, and Guadrikiri Caves, and includes a tasty lunch at Boca Prins. The afternoon expedition is $99 and winds its way through Ayo Rock Formation, Bushiribana Gold Mine, Baby Natural Bridge, Alto Vista Chappel, California Lighthouse, and Boca Catalina Beach.

TENNIS Most of the island's beachfront hotels have tennis courts, often cooled by trade winds, and some have top pros on hand to give instruction. Many of the courts can also be lit for night games. (We don't advise playing in Aruba's hot noonday sun.) Some hotels allow only guests on their courts.

Volunteer Vacations

If you want to have fun while doing good, you can log on to www.aruba.com/specializedvacations/volunteervacations.aspx and find out about volunteer opportunities that you can participate in while on vacation to help protect the wildlife and habitat of Aruba. There's everything from beach cleanups to help in caring for those adorable donkeys at the donkey sanctuary.

The best tennis is at the **Aruba Racquet Club** (✆ **297/586-0215;** www.arc.aw), the island's first world-class tennis facility, with eight courts, an exhibition center court, a swimming pool, a bar, a small restaurant, an aerobics center, and a fitness center. The club is open Monday through Friday 6am to 9pm, and Saturday 1 to 5pm. Rates are $10 per hour per court, or you may purchase a $20 day pass. Lessons are available by appointment only. The location is Rooi Santo 21 on Aruba's northwest coast, near the California Lighthouse.

WATERSPORTS You can snorkel in the shallow waters here, and scuba divers find stunning marine life with endless varieties of coral and tropical fish in myriad hues; at some points, visibility extends up to 30m (98 ft.). Most divers set out for the German freighter ***Antilla*** ★★, which was scuttled in the early years of World War II off the northwestern tip of Aruba, not too far from Palm Beach. It's a spectacular sight to see and should not be missed. In December it shifted due to strong tides and is now showing signs of collapsing further, an inevitable process of aging and exposure.

Red Sail Sports, Palm Beach (✆ **297/586-1603;** www.redsailaruba.com), is the island's biggest watersports center. The activities offered here include sailing and scuba diving. Red Sail dive packages include shipwreck dives and marine-reef explorations. Their dive prices are competitive: Two-tank morning boat dives are $79, one-tank morning or afternoon boat dives are $49, and one-tank night dives are $55. More dive packages include 5-, 8-, and 10-tank dives, starting at $188. Nondiving boat passengers pay $20, space permitting. Snorkelers are charged $30, including equipment, but Red Sail Sports offers an array of snorkeling-only excursions that visit multiple sites. They also offer a half-day "Discover Scuba Resort" course and refresher courses that include instructions and a pool session for $99. Pool-only introductory courses are available for children for $49. The PADI open-water certification course is $425 and now is offered with an online component, so you can spend less time in the classroom once on island—and less money, since it's only $325.

EXPLORING THE ISLAND

In Oranjestad ★

Aruba's capital, Oranjestad, attracts more shoppers than sightseers. The bustling city has a very Caribbean flavor, with part-Spanish, part-Dutch architecture. The main thoroughfare, **L. G. Smith Boulevard,** runs along the waterfront and on to Palm Beach, changing its name along the way to **J. E. Irausquin Boulevard.** Most visitors stroll along it, then head for **Caya G. F. Betico Croes** and the best duty-free shopping.

After a shopping trip, you might return to the **harbor,** where fishing boats, many from Venezuela, and some high-end yachts are moored. Most newcomers to Aruba photograph the colorful gingerbread architecture that looks out over the scenic harbor. Colorful boats dock along the quay, and local merchants display their wares in open stalls. A little farther along, fresh fish is hauled in from small boats. **Wilhelmina Park,** named after Queen Wilhelmina of the Netherlands, is on the sea side of Oranjestad, next to the helipad used to take tourists on a whirlwind tour of the island. The park features a tropical garden along the water and a sculpture of the queen mother. The area also attracts an unnatural number of iguanas, who rest nonchalantly on the rocks.

An Underwater Journey

One of the island's most fun activities is an underwater journey on one of the world's few passenger submarines, operated by **Atlantis Adventures** ★, located at the Seaport Marina (opposite the Renaissance Hotel), Oranjestad (✆ **297/588-6881;** www.atlantisadventures.com). Even nondivers can witness a coral reef firsthand without risking the obstacles and dangers of a scuba expedition. Carrying 46 passengers to a depth of up to 45m (148 ft.), the ride provides all the thrills of an underwater dive—but keeps you dry. In 1995 an old Danish fishing vessel was sunk to create a fascinating view for divers and submariners.

There are two departures daily from the Oranjestad harborfront. Each tour includes a 30-minute catamaran ride to Barcadera Reef, 3km (2 miles) southeast of Aruba—a site chosen for the huge variety of its underwater flora and fauna. At the reef, participants are transferred to the submarine for a 50-minute underwater lecture and tour. Allow 2 hours for the complete experience. The cost is $99 for adults, $49 for children 12 and under (children under 1m tall are not admitted). Advance reservations are essential. A staff member will ask for a credit card number (and give you a confirmation number) to hold the booking for you.

In the Countryside

If you can lift yourself from the sands for an afternoon, you might enjoy driving into the country. Here Arubans live in modest, colorful, pastel-washed houses, decorated with tropical plants that require expensive desalinated water. Visitors who venture into the center of Aruba will want to see the strange **divi-divi trees,** with their tradewind-blown coiffure.

You probably will want to visit Aruba's best-known peak, **Hooiberg,** affectionately known as the "Haystack." From Oranjestad, take Caya G. F. Croes (7A) toward Santa Cruz. Anybody with the stamina can climb steps to the top of this 160m-high (525-ft.) hill. On a clear day, you can see Venezuela from here.

The island's best-known natural landmark was the **Natural Bridge,** but it collapsed, so its smaller cousin, **Baby Bridge** ★★, now holds that title. While it lacks the dramatic arch of its predecessor, it's pretty cool and is sturdy enough (so far) to stand on and view the rugged sea below. The nearby "thirst-aid" station supplies refreshments and souvenirs.

Aruba is studded with massive boulders. You can see the most impressive ones at **Ayo** and **Casibari,** northeast of Hooiberg. Diorite boulders stack up as high as urban buildings. The rocks weigh several thousand tons, and their peculiar shapes puzzle geologists. Ancient Amerindian drawings appear on the rocks at Ayo. At Casibari you can climb to the top for a panoramic view of the island or a close look at rocks that nature has carved into seats. Pay special attention to the island's unusual species of lizards and cacti. Casibari is open daily from 9am to 5pm, with no admission charge. There's a lodge at Casibari where you can buy souvenirs, snacks, soft drinks, and beer.

Guides can also point out drawings on the walls and ceiling of the **Caves of Canashito,** south of Hooiberg. You may see some giant green parakeets here, too.

Arikok National Park ★★★ (✆ **297/585-1234;** www.arubanationalpark.org), Aruba's showcase ecological preserve, sprawls across roughly 20% of the island. Rock outcrops, boulders, and crevices create microclimates that support animal species found only in Aruba, including the Aruban rattlesnake, Aruban cat-eyed snake, Aruban whiptail lizard, Aruban burrowing owl, and Aruban parakeet. Iguanas and many species of migratory birds live in the park as well, and goats and donkeys graze on the hills. Examples of early Amerindian art, abandoned mines from Aruba's gold-rush past, and remains of early farms dot the park. Sand dunes and limestone cliffs ornament the coast. It's easy to explore the preserve, but bring water, sunscreen, and food, and wear a hat and comfortable walking shoes. Birds and animals are most active in the morning, so go as early in the day as you can. You can see cave drawings at the **Guadarikiri Cave** and **Fontein Cave.** These caves are open to the public, and many companies offer tours and guides. There are a number of other caves, including **Huliba Cave** and the famous **Tunnel of Love;** however, both of these caves are closed indefinitely to protect and replenish the bat population.

Near San Nicolas

As you drive along the highway toward the island's southernmost section, you may want to stop at the **Spanish Lagoon,** where pirates hid and waited to plunder rich cargo ships in the Caribbean. Today it's an ideal place for snorkeling, and you can picnic at tables under the mangrove trees.

Boca Grandi, on the windward side of the island, is a favorite windsurfing location; if you prefer quieter waters, try Baby Beach and Rodgers Beach, on Aruba's leeward side. **Seroe Colorado** (Colorado Point) overlooks the two beaches. From here you can see the Venezuelan coastline and the pounding surf on the windward side. If you climb down the cliffs, you're likely to spot an iguana; protected by law, the once-endangered saurians now proliferate in peace.

SHOPPING

Aruba manages to offer goods from six continents along L. G. Smith Boulevard, starting at Renaissance Marina and ending at the Arubus Depot. The .8km-long (½-mile) **Caya G. F. Betico Croes** is Oranjestad's main shopping street for locals, but the shops here are less Gucci and more Payless. Technically, this is not a free port, but the duty is so low (3.3%) that prices are attractive. The main shopping zones in town are the very high-end **Renaissance Mall** and the less pricey **Royal Plaza Mall** and **Renaissance Marketplace** (next to the Marina). The former features such shops as **Gucci, Carolina Hererra, Ralph Lauren, Salvatore Ferregamo,** and **Lacoste.** The **Port of Call Marketplace,** at the cruise-ship pier, is rather rundown, while the new mall next door was, at press time, entirely bereft of shops due to legal and financial delays that have dragged on for years. At the dozens of jewelry and gift shops that line the main strip, you can find the usual array of Swiss watches; German and Japanese cameras; jewelry; liquor; English bone china and porcelain; Dutch, Swedish, and Danish silver and pewter; French perfume; British woolens; Indonesian specialties; and Madeira embroidery. Delft blue pottery is an especially good buy. Other good buys include Dutch cheese (Edam and Gouda), Dutch chocolate, and English cigarettes in the airport departure area.

Paseo Herencia (Aruba's Pride), on the High-Rise District's main street, contains a plethora of shops on two levels, a multiplex cinema, and a jazz restaurant and club on the upper level. The center contains a small swimming pool and a fountain, which offers a mini–dancing water show once a night and several times on weekends.

Another new shopping mall called **The Village Center** (J. E. Irausquin Blvd. 348A) has recently opened in Palm Beach. The atmosphere lends itself toward entertainment and ambience. In the early evening, the plaza fills up with art vendors and street performers. Here you can find retail shops, souvenir shops, a large **Red Sail Sports** (see "Sports & Outdoor Pursuits," earlier in this chapter) and a number of restaurants, including an open-air, French fusion bistro called **Papillon** (✆ **297/586-5400;** www.papillonaruba.com).

ARUBA AFTER DARK

Casinos: Let the Good Times Roll ★★

The casinos in the big hotels along Palm Beach are the liveliest nighttime destinations. Most stay open into the wee hours. In plush gaming parlors, guests try their luck at roulette, craps, blackjack, and, of course, slots. Limits and odds are about the same as in the United States. The newest casino at press time is **Cool Casino** (✆ **297/528-0993;** www.coolcasinogaming.com) at the Riu Palace. Slot machines open at 10am, and table games start at noon.

Palm Beach Casino, at the Westin Aruba Resort, J. E. Irausquin Blvd. 77, Palm Beach (✆ **297/586-2283;** www.westinaruba.com), formerly the Casablanca Casino, boasts 300 high-tech slots, hyperlink machines, roulette, craps, and blackjack. Casablanca may be gone, but the Moroccan-style Rick's Café remains; specialty drinks are still a feature at the bar, along with sports broadcasts on multiple TV screens and live entertainment.

Excelsior Casino, J. E. Irausquin Blvd. 230 (✆ **866/358-6518** or 297/586-7777; www.excelsiorcasino.com), wins the prize for all-around action. Its casino doors are open daily from 8am to 4am. The poker room may stay open later if there's action.

Another of the island's best is the **Crystal Casino** at the Renaissance Aruba Resort & Casino (✆ **297/583-6000**), open daily 24 hours. The 1,260-sq.-m (13,563-sq.-ft.) casino has luxurious furnishings, ornate moldings, marble, and crystal chandeliers.

One of the largest and splashiest casinos is the **Copacabana,** found at the **Hyatt Regency Aruba,** J. E. Irausquin Blvd. 85 (✆ **297/586-1234;** www.hyattcasinoaruba.com). The casino is open from 10am to 4am.

The **Occidental Grand Aruba Casino,** J. E. Irausquin Blvd. 83 (✆ **297/586-4500**), at press time, had just undergone a full face-lift. It is still known for its Caribbean stud poker, blackjack, roulette, baccarat, and craps, and its computerized slot machines are still open for action at noon; tables and other games open at 5pm.

Another choice, the **Stellaris Casino,** at the Aruba Marriott Resort, L. G. Smith Blvd. 101, Palm Beach (✆ **297/586-9000;** www.stellariscasino.com), is a large casino that starts to get busy daily at 2pm, when gamblers arrive to play roulette, craps, and Caribbean stud poker. This Casino offers gaming kiosks and the island's only Wheel of Fortune slot machines.

The Club & Bar Scene

We like to begin our Aruban nights at **Salt and Pepper,** J. E. Irausquin Blvd. 368A (✆ **297/586-3280;** www.saltandpepperaruba.com), where we can order the island's best tapas. Three or four of these appetizers are large enough to make a meal. If you bring in a set of original salt and pepper shakers for the owners to keep, you get your first glass of sangria free with your dinner. ***Note:*** Sets can't be "borrowed" from local restaurants and hotels. Sangria, consumed in an alfresco courtyard, is the usual drink of choice, and the bar stays open until 1am. From here you can wander around the corner to **Soprano's Piano Bar** (✆ **297/586-8622;** www.sopranospianobar.com/aruba) to see if there is any piano music left.

Mambo Jambo, in the Royal Plaza Mall, L. G. Smith Boulevard (✆ **297/583-3632;** www.mambojamboaruba.com), is sultry and relaxing. Expect a blend of Dutch and Latino visitors, and lots of Latin rhythms. The volume is kept at a tolerable level for anyone who wants to have a conversation. There's an array of specialty drinks, though none are particularly noteworthy; imagine coconut shells, very colorful straws, and large fruit. It's open daily 11am to 4am.

Iguana Joe's, Royal Plaza Mall, L. G. Smith Boulevard (✆ **297/583-9373;** www.iguanajoesaruba.com), enjoys an equal vogue among visitors and islanders. It's known for its huge array of specialty drinks, including the Pink Iguana, Grandma Joe's Pink Lemonade, and the aptly named Lethal Lizard, packing four shots of liquor in a half-liter carafe. Line your stomach with fresh salads, pastas, fresh mahimahi, sizzling fajitas, and rich homemade desserts. Hours are Monday to Saturday 11am to midnight, and Sunday 5pm to midnight.

Aruba's most-talked-about attraction is **Kukoo Kunuku** (✆ **297/586-2010;** www.kukookunuku.com), a psychedelically painted 1957 Chevy party bus that hits half a dozen of the island's hottest bars. The carousing begins at "sundowner" time at 6pm and goes on until around midnight, Monday to Saturday. Every reveler gets maracas for this pub crawl on wheels. The cost of $59 per person includes dinner, a champagne toast on the beach, a free drink at the three bars, and a pickup at your hotel.

Señor Frogs, The Village, J. E. Irausquin Blvd 348A (✆ **297/586-8900;** www.senorfrogs.com), is a great place to party if you are eager to relive your college years. It offers such corn-pone antics as dancing in the conga line with the crazy waiters. Part of a chain, the bar/restaurant appeals mostly to singles, young couples, and vacation revelers. Hours are Sunday to Thursday from 11pm to 1am, and Friday and Saturday from 11pm to 3am. For some late-night revelry favored by Dutch locals and frequented by a broad range of ages, the hip place in town is **Café Rembrandt,** South Beach Centre, Palm Beach 55 (✆ **297/586-4747;** www.rembrandt-aruba.com).

For a rock-'n'-roll scene and to check out the game, head over to **Buster's Garage Sports Bar and Grill,** Palm Beach 55 (✆ **297/586-0104**).

If a beach party is your scene, then there is nothing to do but go to **Moomba Beach Bar,** J. E. Irausquin Blvd. 230, at De Palm Pier in front of the Marriott (✆ **297/586-5365;** www.moombabeach.com). It has live music around 5 or 6pm most nights, but Mondays are the big night to party.

Zissles Aruba, L. G. Smith Blvd. 382-A, 2nd Floor, Paseo Herencia (✆ **888/723-3410** or 297/586-3800; www.zissles.com), starts the night off as a dinner-show venue, which turns into a nightclub afterward. Show tickets cost $50 per person without dinner, or $85 to $95 per person with dinner. The shows start at 8pm, but if you just want to come for drinks, dancing, and tapas, then plan to arrive after 9:30pm.

BARBADOS

Though independent, Barbados embraces its British Empire roots. Afternoon tea remains a tradition, cricket is the national sport, and many Bajans speak with a British accent. The past is alive everywhere, including 18th- and 19th-century homes scattered around the island. A-listers and budget travelers alike flock to the island's natural pink and white sands and turquoise waters. Here a dynamic culture is built on a reef of coral, colonialism, Christianity, and the former slave trade—with a calypso beat.

5

Things to Do The low-lying **west coast,** gently washed by a Caribbean breeze, shimmers with star-studded beaches and provides divers with a colorful haven of marine life. The windblown Atlantic **east coast** is great for cliffhanging hikes, secret beach picnics, and surfing. Relive colonial days at the **Sunbury Plantation House,** or visit a rare Jacobean mansion at **St. Nicholas Abbey.** On land, **Flower Forest** is a fragrant oasis of exotic flowers and spice trees, and the **Andromeda Botanical Garden** and **Farley Hill National Park** offer even more quiet respite. Taste the island's famous libation with a tour of the **Mount Gay Rum Factory.**

Shopping For the best in duty-free shopping, **Bridgetown** is a smorgasbord of cameras, watches, crystal, gold jewelry, and local Mount Gay rum. Buy straw bags and rum cakes from the **Pelican Crafts Centre** and whimsical, vibrantly colored ceramics from **Earthworks,** a longtime artistic highlight. Find quintessential Barbados handicrafts like black-coral jewelry and clay pottery on the **east coast,** near Chalky Mountain. Shops across the island brim with a fine selection of locally made vases, pots, mugs, glazed plates, and ornaments.

Nightlife & Entertainment Nightlife on the **west coast** revolves around the big resorts, many of which have waterfront pubs and wine bars. For an authentic Bajan evening, try **Baxters Road** in Bridgetown for a "caf crawl." The **south coast** buzzes with sports bars and clubs, where margaritas and the local Banks beer flow freely. When the sun sets, join the party for **lime,** a Bajan street party.

Eating & Drinking Seafood, like snapper, shellfish, and the popular national emblem, **the flying fish,** is on every menu, from five-star restaurants to beachside cafes. It's usually served with spicy ***cou-cou*** (cornmeal and okra), but **pudding 'n souse** (pickled pork, breadfruit, and sweet potato pudding) and **macaroni pie** are local specialties worth trying, too. For fresh grilled fish, rum, and reggae, **Oistins Friday Night Fish Fry** is a must.

ESSENTIALS

Visitor Information

In the United States, you can contact the following offices of the **Barbados Tourism Authority:** 820 Second Ave., 5th Floor, New York, NY 10017 (✆ **800/221-9831** or 212/551-4350); or 2121 Ponce de Leon Blvd., Ste. 1300, Coral Gables, FL 33134 (✆ **786/515-1226**). The Canadian office is at 105 Adelaide St. W., Ste. 1010, Toronto, Ontario M5H 1P9 (✆ **800/268-9122** or 416/214-9880). In the United Kingdom, contact the Barbados Tourism Authority at 263 Tottenham Court Rd., London W1T 7LA (✆ **020/7636-9448**).

On the Internet, go to **www.barbados.org** or **www.visitbarbados.org**. The tourism office may be able to help you track down condo and villa rentals.

On the island, the local **Barbados Tourism Authority** office is on Harbour Road (P.O. Box 242), Bridgetown (✆ **800/744-6244** or 246/427-2623).

Getting There

More than 20 flights arrive on Barbados from all over the world every day. **Grantley Adams International Airport** (✆ **246/418-4242**) is on Hwy. 7, on the southern tip of the island at Long Bay, between Oistins and a village called the Crane. From North America, the four major gateways to Barbados are New York; Miami; Toronto; and San Juan, Puerto Rico. Flying time to Barbados is 4½ hours from New York, 3½ hours from Miami, 5 hours from Toronto, and 1½ hours from San Juan.

Virgin Atlantic Airways (✆ **800/821-5438** in the U.S. and Canada; www.virgin-atlantic.com) flies daily from London's Gatwick Airport to Barbados.

American Airlines (✆ **800/433-7300** in the U.S. and Canada; www.aa.com) has dozens of connections passing through San Juan, plus daily nonstop flights to Barbados from Miami. **US Airways** (✆ **800/622-1015** in the U.S. and Canada; www.usairways.com) flies daily from New York's LaGuardia to Philadelphia, Washington, or Baltimore, then on to Barbados. There are no nonstop flights on US Airways from New York to Barbados.

All flights are nonstop from Toronto to Barbados. **Air Canada** (✆ **888/247-2262** in the U.S. and Canada; www.aircanada.com) flies daily from Toronto in winter. From Montréal, connections are made through Toronto.

Barbados is a major hub of the Caribbean-based airline **LIAT** (✆ **888/844-LIAT** [5428] from most destinations within the Caribbean, 268/480-5601 for reservations, or 246/428-8888 at the Barbados airport; www.liatairline.com), which flies to most points within the Caribbean but provides generally poor service to Barbados from a handful of neighboring islands, including St. Vincent and the Grenadines, St. Lucia, Antigua, and Dominica.

Air Jamaica (✆ **800/523-5585** in North America and the Caribbean; www.airjamaica.com) offers daily flights that link Barbados to Atlanta, Baltimore, Boston, Chicago, and Miami through the airline's Montego Bay hub. Air Jamaica also flies between Los Angeles and Barbados on Monday and Wednesday (but it requires an overnight stay in Montego Bay). Nonstop flights from New York to Barbados are available at least 4 days a week (Mon, Wed, Fri, and Sun).

Cayman Airways and **Air Jamaica** have joined forces to provide an air link from Grand Cayman to Barbados and Trinidad, via Kingston in Jamaica. Flights wing out of Grand Cayman Sunday, Monday, Thursday, and Friday, linking up in Kingston with continuing flights to Barbados and Port-of-Spain, with daily return flights. For reservations and information, call Air Jamaica at © **800/523-5585.**

British Airways (© **800/247-9297** in the U.S. and Canada; www.britishairways.com) flies nonstop daily to Barbados from London's Gatwick Airport.

Getting Around

BY RENTAL CAR If you don't mind **driving on the left,** you may find a rental car ideal on Barbados. You'll need a temporary permit if you don't have an international driver's license. The rental agencies listed below all can issue this visitor's permit, or you can go to the police desk upon your arrival at the airport. You must have a license from home and pay a registration fee of $5. Within a city or town, the speed limit is 20kmph (12 mph), going up to 60kmph (37 mph) on secondary roads, and rising to 80kmph (50 mph) on major highways. Because of frequent delays at airport counters, we suggest taking a taxi from the airport to your hotel and then calling to have your rental car delivered. A 15% tax is levied upon all car rentals in Barbados.

None of the major U.S.-based car rental agencies operate on Barbados, but a host of local companies rent vehicles. Except in the peak midwinter season, cars are usually readily available without prior reservations. Be forewarned that many local companies continue to draw serious complaints from readers, both for overcharging and for the poor conditions of their vehicles. Proceed very carefully with rentals on this island. Check the insurance and liability issues carefully when you rent.

The island's most frequently recommended agency is **Drive-A-Matic,** Lower Carlton, St. James (© **800/581-8773** or 246/422-3000; www.carhire.tv), which has a wide selection of Japanese cars. The agency is located 15km (9¼ miles) north of Bridgetown, near the main highway (Hwy. 1); it delivers cars to almost any location on the island, and the driver who delivers it will carry the necessary forms for the Bajan driver's license, priced at $5 per registered driver and valid for 2 months.

Another comparable company is **Sunny Isle Motors,** Dayton, Worthing Main Road, Christ Church (© **246/435-7979**).

BY TAXI Taxis aren't metered, but rates are fixed by the government; one cab can carry up to four passengers for the same fare. Taxis are plentiful and easily identifiable by the letter z on their license plates. Drivers will produce a list of standard rates ($25–$35 per hr.). To call a taxi, contact one of the following services: **Paramount Taxi Service** (© **246/429-3718**), **Independence Taxi Service** (© **246/426-0090**), **Royal Pavilion Taxi Service** (© **246/422-1260**), or **Lyndhurst Taxi Service** (© **246/436-2639**). A typical taxi ride from the airport to Bridgetown costs $18; to Holetown, along the western Gold Coast, $23; and to St. Lawrence Gap, site of many of the less expensive hotels, $13.

BY BUS Take a bus only as a last resort, as the service is unreliable, in spite of the fact that many Bajans depend on this service to get to and from work. The nationally owned buses of Barbados are blue with yellow stripes. They're not numbered, but their destinations are marked on the front. On most major routes, buses run every 30 minutes or so. Wherever you go, the fare is BD$1.50, exact Barbados change required. Departures are from Bridgetown, leaving from Fairchild Street for the south and east, and from Lower Green and the Princess Alice Highway for the north going along the west coast. Call the **Barbados Transport Board** (© **246/436-6820**) for schedules and information.

Barbados

North Point
Archer's Bay
River Bay
Stroud Bay
Harrison Point
ST. LUCY
Cuckold Point
Gay's Cove
Pico Teneriffe
1B
Maycock's Bay
Fairfield
Coleton
1C
Charles Duncan O'Neale Hwy.
St. Nicholas Abbey
Half Moon Fort
Morgan Lewis Beach
Morgan Lewis Sugar Mill
Six Men's Bay
Heywoods Beach
ST. PETER
2
Greenland
St. Andrew's Church
Speightstown
SCOTLAND DISTRICT
ST. ANDREW
East Coast Rd.
1
Chalky Mount
Mullins Beach
Weston
Gibbs Beach
2
2A
1
Turner's Hall Woods
Cattlewash
8
Tent Bay
Lower Carlton
3A
9
Bathsheba
3
ST. JAMES
Flower Forest
Andromeda Botanic Gardens
Church Point
Welchman Hall Gully
ST. JOSEPH
FOLKESTONE UNDERWATER PARK
Hackleton's Cliff
4
5
1A
Welchman Hall
3
Holetown
6
ST. THOMAS
Blackmans
Sunset Crest
7
Harrison's Cave
ST.
Paynes Bay
3B
2
Groves
Lazaretto
Francia Plantation
2A
4
Locust Hall
Prospect
Warrens
Gun Hill Signal Stati
Paradise Beach
3
Brighton Beach
ST. GEORGE
Black Rock
Brandon's Beach
2
4B
Spring Garden Hwy.
Errol Barrow Hwy.
4
5
Deep Water Harbour
ST. MICHAEL
Queen's Park
CHRIST CHURCH
Caribbean Sea
Bridgetown
10
6
11
Tyrol Cot Heritage Village
Carlisle Bay
6
Tom Adams Hwy.
Hastings
12
Worthing
St. Lawrence
Needham's Point
13
14
17
Maxwell
7
Rockley Beach
Sandy Beach
Pink Pearl Beach
Casuarina Beach
Oistins
15
18
16
South Point
19
Silver Sands Beach

Airport
Beach
Church
Lighthouse

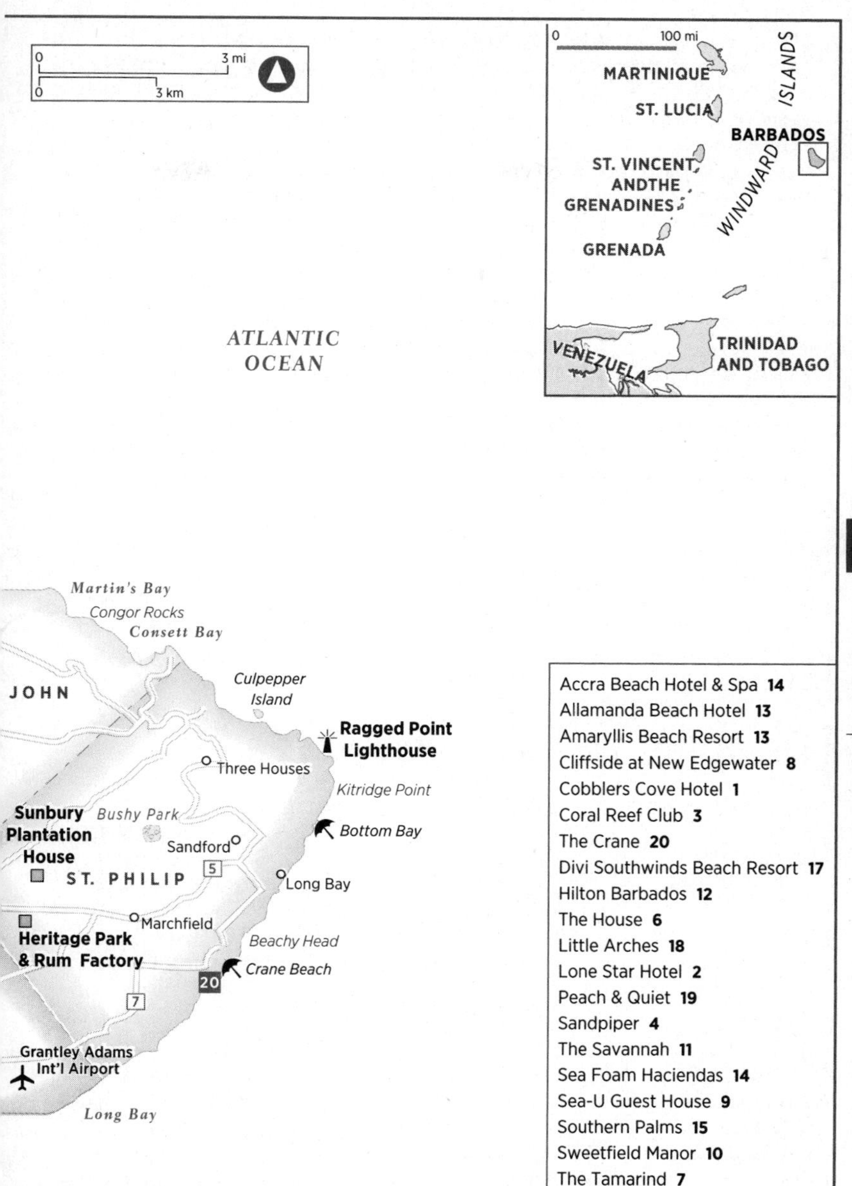
0
3 mi
0
3 km
0
100 mi
MARTINIQUE
ST. LUCIA
WINDWARD ISLANDS
BARBADOS
ST. VINCENT AND THE GRENADINES
GRENADA
VENEZUELA
TRINIDAD AND TOBAGO
ATLANTIC OCEAN
Martin's Bay
Congor Rocks
Consett Bay
Culpepper Island
JOHN
Ragged Point Lighthouse
Three Houses
Kitridge Point
Sunbury Plantation House
Bushy Park
Bottom Bay
Sandford
5
ST. PHILIP
Long Bay
Marchfield
Heritage Park & Rum Factory
Beachy Head
Crane Beach
20
7
Grantley Adams Int'l Airport
Long Bay
Accra Beach Hotel & Spa 14
Allamanda Beach Hotel 13
Amaryllis Beach Resort 13
Cliffside at New Edgewater 8
Cobblers Cove Hotel 1
Coral Reef Club 3
The Crane 20
Divi Southwinds Beach Resort 17
Hilton Barbados 12
The House 6
Little Arches 18
Lone Star Hotel 2
Peach & Quiet 19
Sandpiper 4
The Savannah 11
Sea Foam Haciendas 14
Sea-U Guest House 9
Southern Palms 15
Sweetfield Manor 10
The Tamarind 7
Traveller's Palm 5
Turtle Beach Resort 16

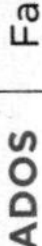

SPECIAL EVENTS

In mid-February, the **Holetown Festival** (**www.holetownfestivalbarbados.com**) at St. James is a weeklong event commemorating the landing of the first European settlers at Holetown in 1627. Highlights include street fairs, police band concerts, a music festival in the parish church, and a road race.

During the first week of April, the **Oistins Fish Festival** commemorates the signing of the charter of Barbados with fishing, boat racing, fish-boning competitions, a Coast Guard exhibition, food stalls, arts and crafts, dancing, singing, and road races.

Beginning in mid-July and lasting until the first week of August, the **Crop Over Festival** is the island's major national festival, celebrating the completion of the sugar-cane harvest and recognizing the hardworking men and women in the sugar industry. Communities all over the island participate in fairs, concerts, calypso competitions, car parades, and other cultural events. The climax of the festival occurs at **Kadooment Day,** a national holiday on the first Monday in August, which becomes the biggest party of the year in Barbados.

Visit www.visitbarbados.org for additional festivals.

Privately operated **minibuses,** usually painted yellow, run shorter distances and travel more frequently. They are bright yellow with blue stripes, with their destinations displayed on the bottom-left corner of the windshield. Minibuses in Bridgetown are boarded at River Road, Temple Yard, and Probyn Street. The fare is BD$1.50, and unlike the larger, blue-sided government-operated buses, exact change is appreciated but not required.

[Fast FACTS] BARBADOS

American Express There is no officially designated exclusive Amex representative on Barbados, but a reputable travel agency that can fulfill most travel-related services is **St. James Travel,** West Plaza, Sunset Crest, St. James (✆ **246/432-6725;** www.stjamestravel.com).

Banks Most banks are open Monday to Thursday 8am to 3pm, and Friday 8am to 5pm. The major banks of Barbados, **all with ATMs,** are found along Broad Street in Bridgetown, including branches of First Caribbean Bank, the Barbados National Bank, Scotiabank, and the Butterfield Bank. These banks also have branch offices in Holetown, Speightstown, and along the St. Lawrence Gap south of Bridgetown. There are ATMs at the airport as well, plus at bank branches throughout the island.

Consulates & High Commissions The **Embassy of the United States** is in the Wildey Business Park, Wildey, St. Michael (✆ **246/227-4000;** http://barbados.usembassy.gov); the **Canadian High Commission** at Bishop's Court Hill, St. Michael (✆ **246/429-3550;** www.barbados.gc.ca); and the **British High Commission** at Lower Collymore Rock, St. Michael (✆ **246/430-7800;** http://ukinbarbados.fco.gov.uk).

Currency The **Barbados dollar (BD$)** is the official currency, available in $5, $10, $20, and $100 notes, as well as 10¢, 25¢, and $1 silver coins, plus 1¢ and 5¢ copper coins. The Barbados dollar is permanently fixed because of an international agreement, at the rate of approximately 50¢ in U.S. currency. In contrast, the value of the British pound is not permanently fixed, and as such, it floats freely, going up or down in relation to a wide range of political and economic factors that change from day to day. At press time for this edition, £1 equaled a little more than BD$3. Most stores take traveler's checks or U.S. dollars. However, it may be best to convert your money at banks and pay in Barbados dollars, since you could save over U.S. dollars. *Prices in this chapter are quoted in U.S. dollars.*

Customs Most items for personal use (within reason, of course) are allowed into Barbados, except agricultural products and firearms. You can bring in perfume for your use if it's not for sale. You're also allowed a carton of cigarettes and a liter of liquor.

Documents Citizens of all countries need a passport to enter Barbados, including those from the United States and Canada. Cruise-ship passengers need only the ship's magnetic identification card. However, if a cruise begins and ends in Barbados, a passport is required.

Electricity Most electrical outlets are wired with 110-volt AC (50 cycles) current, same as within the U.S., so you can use your U.S.-made appliances. The very few electrical outlets that follow the British and European systems (220-volt AC) are rare, and when they do appear, they're clearly marked and designated with a plug configuration that makes it virtually impossible to plug a U.S.-made appliance into it without a special adapter and/or converter.

Emergencies In an emergency, dial the police at ✆ **211,** the fire department at ✆ **311,** and an ambulance at ✆ **511.**

Hospitals The **Queen Elizabeth Hospital** is located on Martinsdale Road in St. Michael (✆ **246/436-6450;** www.qehconnect.com). Of the several private clinics, one of the most expensive and best recommended is the **Bayview Hospital,** St. Paul's Avenue, Bayville, St. Michael (✆ **246/436-5446;** www.bayviewhospital.com.bb).

Language The Bajans speak English, but with their own island lilt.

Liquor Laws Liquor, beer, and wine are sold throughout the island at every outlet, from grocery stores to convenience stores, on any day the stores are open. Open containers are illegal on the beach.

Safety Crimes against visitors used to be rare, but today there are reports of pickpocketing, armed robbery, and even sexual assault. Avoid leaving cash or valuables in your hotel room, beware of purse snatchers when walking, exercise caution on the beach or at attractions, and be wary of driving in isolated areas.

Taxes A 7.5% government sales tax is tacked onto hotel bills. A 15% VAT (value-added tax) is levied on all meals. (For example, if your hotel costs $200 per night and you are charged $50 per person for a MAP, you'll have to pay a 7.5% government tax plus the 10% additional service charge for the $200 room rate, and then an additional 15% VAT on the MAP rate.) Some visitors view these additional charges as "larcenous." They certainly won't make you happy when you go to pay your final bill. There's a departure tax of BD$27.50 or US$14, payable in either currency.

Telephone To call Barbados from the United States, dial **1,** then **246** (the area code for Barbados) and the local number. Once on Barbados, to call another number on the island, only the seven-digit local number is necessary.

Time Barbados is on Atlantic Standard Time year-round, so it's 1 hour ahead of New York except during daylight saving time, when Barbados's time is the same as the eastern United States.

Tipping Most hotels and restaurants add at least a 10% service charge to your bill. If service is extremely good, you may want to supplement that. If it has not been included, you may want to tip your waiter 10% to 15%. Taxi drivers expect a 10% tip.

Water Barbados has a pure water supply. It's pumped from underground sources in the coral rock that covers most of the island, and it's safe to drink.

Weather Daytime temperatures are in the 75°F to 85°F (24°C–29°C) range throughout the year.

WHERE TO STAY

Barbados has some of the best hotels in the Caribbean, many of which are small and personally run.

Most of our recommendations are on fashionable St. James Beach, which is the entire strip of beachfront bordering the parish of St. James. Although hotels are scattered around Barbados, most of them lie on the tranquil west coast as opposed to opening onto the turbulent Atlantic in the east. If you're in Barbados on business, you may want a hotel in Bridgetown, the capital. If you're into the grand life, head for one of the fashionable resorts north of Bridgetown, all of which open onto sandy beaches. Otherwise, if you want something more informal and less expensive, go to the lower south coast, especially around the busy strip of St. Lawrence Gap, where you can find the most reasonably priced nightlife, restaurants, and local bars. This area also has beaches, although they're not as fabulous as those claimed by the pricey resorts north of Bridgetown. The prices of many of Barbados's hotels are among the most celestial in the Caribbean, rivaled by only Anguilla and St. Barts. Just when you think a hotelier won't dare raise prices any more than they already are, he adds another $200 or so to your daily room cost.

If you want a holiday in the southern Caribbean but haven't come into your inheritance, consider such neighboring islands as St. Vincent or Grenada.

To rent your own villa, cottage, or house on Barbados, contact **Jennifer Alleyne Ltd.,** Weston, St. James, Barbados, W.I. (✆ **246/432-1159;** www.jalbarbados.com), which represents about two dozen rental properties scattered throughout the island in a wide range of prices.

On the West Coast

VERY EXPENSIVE

Cobblers Cove Hotel ★★★ This former mansion on a white-sand beach is built in a mock-medieval style on the site of a former British fort. A member of Relais & Châteaux, and originally built by members of the Jock Haines family, the hotel is a favorite honeymoon retreat. Elegant suites are housed in 10 Iberian-style villas, situated throughout lush gardens. Each unit is fully renovated, and each has a spacious living room and bathroom, a private balcony or patio, and a wet bar. To keep the property in top-notch condition, nine bedrooms are completely redecorated each year. Two of the most exclusive accommodations on the entire island are the Camelot and Colleton suites, on the rooftop of the original mansion; they're beautifully decorated and offer panoramic views of both the beach and the garden. Both have their own pool.

Road View, Speightstown, St. Peter, Barbados, W.I. www.cobblerscove.com. ✆ **800/890-6060** in the U.S. and Canada, or 246/422-2291. Fax 246/422-1460. 40 suites. Winter $770–$1,105 double, $2,205–$2,575 Camelot or Colleton suite; off season $490–$645 double, $1,080–$1,200 Camelot or Colleton suite. Rates include American breakfast. MAP $82 extra per person per day. AE, MC, V. Closed Sept to mid-Oct. Children 11 and under not allowed Jan–Mar. **Amenities:** Restaurant; bar; babysitting; exercise room; outdoor pool; room service; tennis court (lit); watersports equipment/rentals. *In room:* A/C, hair dryer, minibar, Wi-Fi (free).

Coral Reef Club ★★★ This family-owned and -managed luxury hotel is one of the best and most luxurious on the island, set on elegantly landscaped grounds beside a white-sand beach for swimming. A collection of veranda-fronted private units, most of them renovated in 2007 and 2008, is scattered about the main building and clubhouse on 5 hectares (12 acres), fronting the ocean. Rental units, housed in cottages, in the main building, or in small coral-stone wings in the gardens, can vary greatly, but each has a luxurious bed (a king-size, twins, or a four-poster) and a tiled bathroom. All units have private patios, and some have separate dressing rooms.

Hwy. 1, Porter's, St. James, Barbados, W.I. www.coralreefbarbados.com. ✆ **800/223-1108** in the U.S., 800/567-5327 in Canada, or 246/422-2372. Fax 246/422-1776. 88 units. Winter $760–$870 double, $915–$2,595 suite; off season $420-$550 double, $475–$1,410 suite. AE, MC, V. Closed June to mid-July. Drive 5 min. north of Holetown on Hwy. 1. Children 11 and under not allowed between late Jan and Mar. **Amenities:** Restaurant; bar; babysitting; dive shop; exercise room; 2 outdoor pools; room service; 2 tennis courts (lit). *In room:* A/C, TV (in most), CD player, hair dryer, minibar, Wi-Fi (free).

The House ★★★ This exclusive retreat, a sophisticated sanctuary of tranquillity and privacy strictly reserved for adults, calls itself not a hotel, but "a concept." That manages to combine the best of posh upscale Britain with überhip Miami Beach. At the moment you arrive, a cheerful and attractive "ambassador," clad in white linen, materializes to serve you during your stay. It boasts the most exotic-looking facade in Barbados, a plan that was activated by previous owners who transformed a then-somewhat-banal waterfront hotel into a mock-medieval fortress, replete with stone archways, dozens of flickering torches, and a trussed wooden drawbridge spanning a "defensive" moat studded with water lilies. Living units manage to be both plush and high-tech at the same time, each configured as a luxuriously furnished suite with granite surfaces and lots of teak.

Hwy. 1, Paynes Bay, St. James, Barbados, W.I. www.thehousebarbados.com. ✆ **888/996-9948** in the U.S., or 246/432-5525. Fax 246/432-5255. 34 units. Winter $595–$1,895 suite; off season $665–$1,180 suite. Rates include full breakfast. AE, DC, MC, V. Children 17 and under not allowed. **Amenities:** Restaurant; bar; Jacuzzi; outdoor pool; room service; watersports equipment/rentals; Wi-Fi (free). *In room:* A/C, TV/DVD, hair dryer.

Lone Star Hotel ★ It's the most retro-chic spot on Barbados. It originated in the 1940s as a concrete-sided gas station and auto repair shop, and despite thousands of dollars' worth of improvements since then, the original look of the place was carefully (even defiantly) preserved. Within a much-battered concrete annex, which one British critic defined as "rock-industry chic, as opposed to the *Tatler*-toting crowd at the Coral Reef Club," the Lone Star offers suites, two opening directly onto a narrow beachfront, the others set upstairs. Each is whimsically outfitted in a combination of four-poster beds, white muslin, and a mixture of antique and modern. Upper suites open onto large furnished balconies.

Hwy. 1, Mount Standfast, St. James, Barbados, W.I. www.thelonestar.com. ✆ **246/419-0599.** Fax 246/419-0597. 4 suites. Winter $600–$900 double; off season $350–$500 double. Extra person $80. Rates include full breakfast. Children 13 and under stay free in parent's room. AE, MC, V. Closed June and Sept. **Amenities:** Restaurant; bar; babysitting; Internet (free); room service. *In room:* A/C, TV, hair dryer, minibar.

Sandpiper ★ The Coral Reef Club (see above) does it better, but if it's full, this South Seas resort on a white-sand beach evokes an earlier Barbados. For this self-contained, intimate resort sits in a small grove of coconut palms and flowering trees. A cluster of rustic-chic units surrounds the pool; some have fine sea views. The rooms open onto little terraces that stretch along the second story. Accommodations are large, consisting of superior rooms and one- or two-bedroom suites beautifully furnished with tropical pieces, each with a private terrace.

Holetown (a 3-min. walk north of town), St. James, Barbados, W.I. www.sandpiperbarbados.com. ✆ **800/223-1108** in the U.S., 800/567-5327 in Canada, or 246/422-2251. Fax 246/422-0900. 47 units.

Winter $760–$870 double, $1,070–$2,595 suite; off season $420–$550 double, $550–$1,465 suite. AE, MC, V. Closed Aug–Oct. Children 11 and under not allowed Jan–Mar. **Amenities:** Restaurant; 2 bars; babysitting; children's programs; exercise room; outdoor pool; room service; 2 tennis courts (lit). *In room:* A/C, fridge, hair dryer, Wi-Fi (free).

The Tamarind ★ On 240m (787 ft.) of prime beachfront, this hotel reopened in late 2010 after an extensive renovation, including the addition of an intimate spa. Attracting an upmarket clientele, the hotel occupies a choice location on St. James Beach, 2km (1¼ miles) south of Holetown. Rooms are spread out in a number of three-story Mediterranean-style buildings designed for privacy and linked by a labyrinth of covered walkways, each interspersed with vegetation and fountains. All of the guest rooms have been renovated and modernized, and each opens out onto a private balcony overlooking the gardens or ocean.

Hwy. 1, Paynes Bay, St. James, Barbados, W.I. www.tamarindbarbados.com. ✆ **888/996-9948** in the U.S., or 246/432-1332. Fax 246/432-6317. 110 units. Winter $580–$660 double, $760–$830 junior suite, $990–$1,090 suite; off season $365–$410 double, $485–$535 junior suite, $660–$740 suite. Rates include breakfast. AE, MC, V. **Amenities:** 3 restaurants; bar; babysitting; children's programs; golf privileges; exercise room; 3 outdoor pools; room service; 2 nearby tennis courts (lit); watersports equipment/rentals, Wi-Fi (free). *In room:* A/C, TV, fridge, hair dryer, Internet ($20 per day), MP3 docking station.

MODERATE

Traveller's Palm Within a 10-minute walk of a good beach, this is for self-sufficient types who are not too demanding and want to save money. There's a choice of simply furnished one-bedroom apartments with fully equipped kitchens and well-maintained bathrooms. Apartments are almost aggressively unpretentious, but each has been renovated, and each represents good value within this high-rent district. The apartments have living and dining areas, as well as patios where you can have breakfast or a candlelit dinner you've prepared yourself. No meals are served here, but there are many restaurants within this densely populated district.

265 Palm Ave., Sunset Crest, St. James, Barbados, W.I. www.thepalmsresort.net. ✆ **246/432-6750.** Fax 246/432-7229. 16 units. Winter $165 apt for 2; off season $125 apt for 2. MC, V. **Amenities:** Babysitting; outdoor pool. *In room:* Token-operated A/C, kitchenette, Wi-Fi ($8 per hr.).

South of Bridgetown/the South Coast

VERY EXPENSIVE

Divi Southwinds Beach Resort ★ ☺ Midway between Bridgetown and Oistins on a .8km-long (½-mile) sandy beach, this resort was created when two distinctly different complexes were combined. The present resort consists of buildings scattered over 20 hectares (49 acres) of sandy flatlands. The showpiece is the newer (inland) complex, housing one- and two-bedroom suites with full kitchens—perfect for small families. These units look like a connected series of town houses, with wooden balconies and views of a large L-shaped pool. The beach is through two groves of palm trees and across a narrow lane. The more modestly furnished older units lie directly on the beachfront, ringed with palm trees, near an oval pool.

St. Lawrence Main Rd., Christ Church, Barbados, W.I. www.diviresorts.com. ✆ **800/367-3484** in the U.S., or 246/428-7181. Fax 246/428-4674. 160 units. Winter $340–$420 double, $495–$825 suite; off season $220–$235 double, $325 suite. Children 11 and under stay free in parent's room. AE, DC, MC, V. **Amenities:** 2 restaurants; 2 bars; beach snack bar; exercise room; 3 outdoor pools (poolside activities for kids); 2 tennis courts (lit); watersports equipment/rentals. *In room:* A/C, TV, kitchen, Wi-Fi (free).

Hilton Barbados ★★ ☺ The Hilton Barbados lies on a rocky peninsula near the island's only airport, at the site of one of the most important 17th-century British military installations in the Caribbean, Fort Charles. Flanked with more than 5.7 hectares (14 acres) of land at the southern edge of Bridgetown, the hotel has direct access to a very good white-sand beach, as well as the much-reconstructed site of the 1650 fort. The Hilton's architecture incorporates jutting balconies and wide expanses of glass; bedrooms are arranged around a central atrium filled with tropical gardens. Each of the well-furnished units has a view of Carlisle Bay on the north side or the Atlantic on the south. Guests staying on the Executive Floor enjoy access to a luxurious lounge overlooking the bay. An oceanview spa opens on to the sixth floor, with panoramic views.

Needham's Point, St. Michael, Barbados, W.I. www.hiltoncaribbean.com. ✆ **800/HILTONS** (445-8667) in the U.S., or 246/426-0200. Fax 246/434-5792. 350 units. Winter $310–$380 double, from $460 suite; off season $250–$320 double, from $400 suite. Rates include breakfast. **Amenities:** 3 restaurants; 2 bars; children's programs; health club; spa; 3 tennis courts (lit). *In room:* A/C, TV, minibar, Wi-Fi ($15 per day).

The Savannah ★ Blending traditional with the contemporary, this hotel, whose accommodations rise on land that seems to ripple uphill from its beachfront, is a 10-minute drive from Bridgetown. Sections of this complex, like the much-rebuilt plantation house (location of nine of the accommodations) that functions as its core, for example, have been standing here for 2 centuries. Today two modern extensions reach toward the sea on the well-landscaped grounds of tropical foliage. The waterfalls cascading into the lagoon-style pool are particularly lovely. Some historians cite this as the most historic hotel in Barbados, with roots extending back to the days when it functioned as a barracks for the 18th-century military garrison next door. Opening onto views of the pool, garden, or ocean, bedrooms are elegantly furnished with mahogany four-poster beds and modern amenities. Rooms also have spacious patios or balconies.

Garrison Main Rd., Hastings, Christ Church, Barbados, W.I. www.gemsbarbados.com. ✆ **800/868-9429** in the U.S., or 246/435-9473. Fax 246/435-8822. 98 units. Year-round $280–$560 double. Children 11 and under stay free in parent's room. Rates include continental breakfast. AE, MC, V. **Amenities:** 2 restaurant; 2 bars (1 swim-up); babysitting; children's programs; exercise room; outdoor pool; room service; spa services. *In room:* A/C, ceiling fan, TV/VCR, hair dryer, Wi-Fi (free).

Turtle Beach Resort ★★ ☺ Opening onto 450m (1,476 ft.) of white-sand beach, this posh south-coast resort opened in 1998 and was named after the turtles that sometimes nest on the nearby sands. It's an all-inclusive property, drawing families, couples, and honeymooners. An open-air lobby opens onto the beach. All midsize rooms have ocean views, wicker furniture, ceiling fans, and voice mail. For diversity Turtle Beach offers a dine-around program with its other tony properties, including Crystal Cove and Coconut Creek. There's also nightly entertainment—calypso, jazz, cabaret, and more.

Dover (near St. Lawrence Gap), Barbados, W.I. www.turtlebeachresortbarbados.com. ✆ **888/996-9948** in the U.S., or 246/428-7131. Fax 246/428-6089. 164 units. Winter $505–$795 suite; off season $410–$690 suite. Rates are all-inclusive. AE, DC, MC, V. **Amenities:** 3 restaurants; 3 bars; babysitting; children's club and playground; golf privileges; gym; Jacuzzi; 3 outdoor pools; room service; 2 tennis courts (lit); watersports equipment/rentals. *In room:* A/C, ceiling fan, TV, fridge, hair dryer, Wi-Fi (free).

EXPENSIVE

Accra Beach Hotel & Spa ★ This hotel, totally rebuilt in 1996, lies on the prettiest beach on the south coast, only 10 minutes from the airport, with Bridgetown about 3km (2 miles) to the west. The three-story property is tastefully laid out in a West Indian style and offers spacious rooms opening onto a view of the pool or ocean. The units have large balconies and wooden shutters. The look is a bit sterile, more corporate hotel than island escape. Steer clear of units marked "island view," as the panorama is of the parking lot. A barbecue and floor show every Thursday is a highlight. ***Note:*** Much of the hotel is open-air (including a dance floor), and the mosquitoes appreciate that fact.

Hwy. 7, Rockley, Christ Church, Barbados, W.I. www.accrabeachhotel.com. ✆ **888/712-2272** in the U.S. and Canada, or 246/435-8920. Fax 246/435-6794. 146 units. Winter $215–$270 double, $280 junior suite, $430–$1,090 suite; off season $175–$260 double, $235 junior suite, $315–$865 suite. AE, MC, V. **Amenities:** 3 restaurants; 2 bars (1 swim-up); babysitting; exercise room; nearby golf; outdoor pool; room service; snorkeling. *In room:* A/C, ceiling fan, TV, hair dryer, Wi-Fi (free).

Amaryllis Beach Resort ☺ Recycled from an older resort, this complex on the south coast is a more affordable option than some of the gold-plated properties farther north. Right on the beach in the historic Garrison area, the Amaryllis Beach Resort has very appealing tropical gardens and a deluxe pool. Bedrooms are midsize to spacious and furnished in a tasteful Caribbean motif. You have various accommodation options, ranging from regular hotel rooms to studios, or even one- or two-bedroom suites for families or groups. Bedrooms open onto balconies or patios, with views of the landscaped grounds or the ocean.

Hastings, Barbados, W.I. www.amaryllisbeachresort.com. ✆ **246/438-8000.** Fax 246/426-9566. 150 units. Winter $230–$345 double, $465–$615 suite; off season $190–$230 double, $295–$455 suite. AE, MC, V. **Amenities:** 4 restaurants; beach bar; children's club; exercise room; 3 pools (2 outdoor, 1 children's); tennis court (lit). *In room:* A/C, TV, hair dryer, Internet ($25 per day), kitchenette (in some).

Little Arches ★★ 🎁 A real discovery, this adults-only boutique hotel overlooks white-sand Enterprise Beach on the south coast. It's a charmer for those who seek out personalized hotels. The oceanview bedrooms are individually styled with four-poster king-size beds, along with such extras as private Jacuzzi sun decks. Italian fabrics and well-chosen furnishings grace the bedrooms. The extras make this place really thrive: a roof-deck swimming pool, a holistic massage therapist, an alfresco restaurant run by an international chef, and free use of mountain bikes. The location is a short walk from the village of Oistins at a point 6.5km (4 miles) from St. Lawrence Gap and 13km (8 miles) from the airport.

Enterprise Beach Rd., Christ Church, Barbados, W.I. www.littlearches.com. ✆ **246/420-4689.** Fax 246/418-0207. 10 units. Winter $295–$375 double, $370–$590 suite; off season $195–$215 double, $245–$340 suite. AE, MC, V. **Amenities:** Restaurant; bar; mountain bikes; outdoor pool; room service; Wi-Fi (free). *In room:* A/C, TV, hair dryer, kitchenette (in 3 units).

Southern Palms A seafront club on 300m (984 ft.) of sand, with a distinct personality, Southern Palms is a pink-and-white manor house built in the Dutch style, with a garden-level colonnade of arches. Spread along the sands are arched two- and three-story buildings, with Italian fountains and statues creating a Mediterranean feel. In its more modern block, an eclectic mixture of rooms includes some with kitchenettes, some facing the ocean, others opening onto the garden, and some with penthouse luxury. A cluster of straw-roofed buildings, housing the drinking and dining facilities, links the accommodations. A local band often entertains with merengue, calypso, and steel-band music.

St. Lawrence Gap, Christ Church, Barbados, W.I. www.southernpalms.net. ✆ **246/428-7171.** Fax 246/428-7175. 92 units. Winter $310–$360 double, $450–$520 suite; off season $195–$240 double, $320–$360 suite. AE, DC, MC, V. **Amenities:** Restaurant; bar; babysitting; exercise room; 2 outdoor pools; room service; 2 tennis courts (lit); watersports equipment/rentals; Wi-Fi (free). *In room:* A/C, TV, fridge, hair dryer, kitchenette (in suites).

Sweetfield Manor ★★ George Clarke, whose British relatives were among the early settlers of Barbados, and his wife, Ann—a gourmet cook, author of children's books, and an interior designer—operate the island's most delightful B&B. They took a manse constructed at the beginning of the 20th century and converted it to receive guests. The location overlooks Carlisle Bay, about a mile from white-sand beaches and Bridgetown itself. The centerpiece of the B&B is a gorgeous tropical-lagoon-styled pool, surrounded by banana trees and West Indian flora. Bedrooms are one of a kind, each furnished with flair, including, for example, the Island Room with its original plantation wood floors and with a Tommy Bahama Queen Sleigh Bed. Ann prepares one of the island's best breakfasts, with such treats as prosciutto-wrapped eggs or lemon ricotta pancakes.

Brittons New Rd., St. Michael, Barbados, W.I. www.sweetfieldmanor.com. ✆ **246/429-8356** or 246/825-0050. 7 units, 4 with bathroom. Year-round $245–$325 double; $495–$595 carriage house. 2-night minimum. AE, DISC, MC, V. **Amenities:** Bar; outdoor pool. *In room:* A/C (in some); no phone, Wi-Fi (free).

MODERATE

Allamanda Beach Hotel ☺ This complex, while not particularly imaginative or exciting in its design, offers some of the best hotel-room bargains on Barbados, and as such, it's ideal for families. Directly on a rocky shoreline 4km (2½ miles) southeast of Bridgetown, the hotel is in the heart of the village of Hastings. The U-shaped complex is built around a pool terrace overlooking the sea. Functional and minimalist in decor, the accommodations are comfortable, each with a compact but fully equipped kitchenette. You face a choice of either a regular hotel room or a one-bedroom suite. All have balconies or decks. Although some athletic guests attempt to swim off the nearby rocks, most walk 5 minutes to the white sands of nearby Rockley (Accra) Beach. For even softer and wider sands, the hotel offers free shuttle-van service to and from the beach that fronts the Amaryllis Beach Resort (p. 104).

Hastings, Christ Church, Barbados, W.I. www.allamandabeach.com. ✆ **246/438-1000.** Fax 246/435-9211. 50 units. Winter $220 double, $280 suite; off season $150 double, $190 suite. Extra person $39. AE, MC, V. **Amenities:** Restaurant; bar; babysitting; outdoor pool; room service. *In room:* A/C, ceiling fan, TV, fridge, hair dryer, Internet ($20 per day), kitchenette.

Sea Foam Haciendas At this compound on the south coast, wide balconies open onto ocean views and white sands, from suites that come with well-equipped kitchens and maid service. Many guests purchase food at the nearby markets and cook in their accommodations. A maximum of six persons per suite is permitted. Most apartments are furnished in a tropical rattan decor, with floors in Italian ceramic tile. If you don't want to cook, the hotel can arrange for you to have a cook for the half-day or even a full day. A bus stops in front, carrying passengers along the beach-lined western coast into Bridgetown.

Worthing, Christ Church, Barbados, W.I. www.seafoamhaciendas.com. ✆ **246/435-7380.** Fax 246/435-7384. 12 units. Winter $260 for 1–4 persons; off season $185 for 1–4 persons. MC, V. **Amenities:** Babysitting. *In room:* A/C, TV, kitchen, Wi-Fi (free).

INEXPENSIVE

Peach & Quiet ★ The name alone attracted us to this little hideaway, an oceanfront property lying in 1.5 hectares (3¾ acres) of gardens at the southern tip of Barbados. Peach and Quiet is about a 15-minute drive from the restaurants and bars at St. Lawrence Gap. Guests can walk to the beaches in about 5 minutes, and they are also drawn to a rock pool that attracts some 100 species of rainbow-hued fish. All the spacious units are suites, each furnished in a style evocative of a Greek island. Your fan-cooled bedroom comes with a king-size bed, a double, or else two doubles, along with a minimum of furnishings (although it's very comfortable). Each room opens onto a terrace or private balcony.

Inch Marlow Main Rd., Christ Church, Barbados, W.I. www.peachandquiet.com. ✆ **246/428-5682.** Fax 246/428-2467. 22 units. Year-round up to $110 double. MC, V. **Amenities:** Restaurant; bar; outdoor pool. *In room:* Ceiling fan, fridge.

On the East Coast

VERY EXPENSIVE

The Crane ★ It's so old it's new again. Opened in 1887, this is arguably the Caribbean's first resort hotel. Near the easternmost end of the island, 23km (14 miles) east of Bridgetown, the hotel has bounced back for a new lease on life. What hasn't changed is Crane Beach—called by many the most beautiful spot on earth, its spectacular powder-soft white sand can look pink in certain lights. In the main house are 18 rooms with hardwood floors, resting under 3.5m (11-ft.) ceilings. These are graced with antiques and four-poster beds. Some of these accommodations offer wraparound balconies; we prefer these units, but you can also book into one of the three modern buildings with a series of one-, two-, and three-bedroom rooms. These, too, have such lovely features as Jacuzzis, Asian carpets, plunge pools, and handcrafted furnishings.

Crane Bay, St. Philip, Barbados, W.I. www.thecrane.com. ✆ **866 978-5942** in the U.S. and Canada, or 246/423-6220. Fax 246/423-5343. 98 units. Winter $230–$380 double, $350–$1,100 suite; off season $160–$250 double, $240–$520 suite. 3-night minimum in summer and 7-night minimum in winter. AE, MC, V. **Amenities:** 2 restaurants; 2 bars; babysitting; exercise room; outdoor pool; room service. *In room:* A/C, TV/DVD, hair dryer, kitchenette (in 1 suite), minibar, Wi-Fi (free).

MODERATE

Sea-U Guest House Far from the south coast, this guesthouse is a retreat from the world. It's the lazy life here. Your biggest challenge will be to lie in a hammock strung between palms, taking in the view of the nearby waves or checking out the monkeys scampering about. This east coast hideaway is built in the traditional two-story Bajan plantation style. In lieu of air-conditioning, the comfortably furnished and rather traditional bedrooms are cooled by sea breezes. The spacious accommodations are either studio apartments or guest cottages.

Tent Bay, Bathsheba, St. Joseph, Barbados, W.I. www.seaubarbados.com. ✆ **246/433-9450.** Fax 246/433-9210. 7 units. Winter $159–$189 double, $189–$438 suite; off season $119–$149 double, $149–$338 suite. MC, V. **Amenities:** Restaurant; bar; natural dipping pools. *In room:* A/C (in cottages), ceiling fan, kitchenette, Wi-Fi (free).

INEXPENSIVE

Cliffside at New Edgewater This scenic outpost is one of the best bets for those who'd like to avoid the hordes and hide out here in a sort of beachhouse atmosphere. Even if you don't stay here, consider it for the best luncheon stopover during your tour of the east coast. From noon to 3pm daily, the kitchen prepares one of the best Bajan buffets on island on Saturday and Sunday, or by reservations with a large group during the week. It's also a good venue for afternoon tea with freshly baked scones and pastries served daily from 3:30 to 6pm. Adjoining Cliffside is the 34.4 hectare (85-acre) Joe's Tropical Rain Forest, which rises to a height of 1,000 feet. Rooms, furnished in a Caribbean motif with a blend of antique and modern appointments, are on the main floor and the story above; the latter rooms have views of either the ocean or the rainforest.

Bathsheba, St. Joseph, Barbados, W.I. www.newedgewater.com. ✆ **866/978-5067** in the U.S., or 246/433-9900. Fax 246/433-9902. 24 units. Winter $125–$230 double; off season $90–$175 double. AE, MC, V. **Amenities:** Restaurant; bar. *In room:* A/C, TV, fridge, hair dryer.

WHERE TO DINE

On the West Coast

VERY EXPENSIVE

The Cliff ★★ INTERNATIONAL/THAI Built atop a 3m (10-ft.) coral cliff, this open-air restaurant features a three-level dining room crafted with terra-cotta tiles and coral stone. It is the snobbiest restaurant on Barbados, but it also enjoys the most dramatic setting. The culinary technique is impeccably sharp, and the chefs select only the finest cuts of beef, the freshest seafood, and the choicest vegetables. The best items are grilled snapper drizzled with three types of coriander sauce (cream-based, oil-based, and vinaigrette style), accompanied with garlic mashed potatoes and Thai-style curried shrimp. For sheer innovation, dishes such as this put the Cliff near the top. Also try the fresh sushi, when available. As you dine, watch for stingrays, which glide through the illuminated waters below; a sighting is considered good luck.

Hwy. 1, Derricks, St. James. ✆ **246/432-1922.** www.thecliffbarbados.com. Reservations required in winter. Prix-fixe menu $122 for 2 courses, $147 for 3 courses. AE, MC, V. Daily 6:30pm–midnight.

EXPENSIVE

Daphne's ★★ MODERN ITALIAN The owners of the House hotel (p. 101) operate this sexy, intimate outpost of the fabled London eatery. The service is flawless, and the setting on the beach idyllic. The coconut-shell lampshades and Indonesian batiks evoke Bali. For greater privacy, muslin curtains surround the tables. The chef is a whiz, turning out memorable dishes based on fresh ingredients, either local or imported. The pasta dishes get raves, especially the linguine with seafood and the *pappardelle* (wide-ribbon noodles) with rabbit ragout and black olives. The chef's most successful main dishes are grilled mahimahi with Marsala, *peperonata* (stewed peppers), and zucchini; or the sesame-seed-encrusted tuna with arugula and tomatoes. We've also enjoyed the grilled tiger shrimp with Mediterranean salsa and couscous.

Paynes Bay, St. James. ✆ **246/432-2731.** www.daphnesbarbados.com. Reservations required. Main courses $15–$26 lunch, $17–$35 dinner. AE, MC, V. Daily 12:30–3pm and 6:30–10pm. Closed Mon off season and June–Nov.

The Fish Pot ★ 🎁 SEAFOOD/INTERNATIONAL Just minutes north of the port of St. Charles, this restaurant lies in a little fishing community called Shermans. The restaurant is in a family-run oceanfront hotel but is so special that even non-guests should visit. The complex was constructed on the site of a 17th-century fort that later was used to store sugar. The food is intensely flavored and produced with finesse. The appetizers are among the most imaginative on the coast, everything from Canadian scallops seared with chutney spices and cilantro oil to baked king prawns with a garnish of tomato. Other delights include cracker-crusted tuna, grilled swordfish, a seafood platter for two, and braised lamb shanks.

You may fall in love with the place and want to stay in its one-, two-, or three-bedroom chattel-style cottages, each furnished to a high standard with a living room and a spacious covered dining terrace off a fully equipped kitchen. Winter rates begin at $419 for a double but are lowered to $249 in the off season.

In Little Good Harbour, Shermans, St. Peter. ✆ **246/439-3000.** www.littlegoodharbourbarbados.com. Main courses $23–$45. MC, V. Daily 8:30–10am, noon–3pm, and 6:30–9pm.

Lone Star Restaurant ★ INTERNATIONAL This theatrical roofed-over deck fronting the beach has a casual atmosphere during the day, which becomes more elegant in the evening. This space, within the Lone Star Hotel (p. 101), is one of the most sought-after hipster dining spots on Barbados, more hip than the Cliff and a lot more fun. Top chefs cooking for a discerning international clientele turn out tuna tartare with vegetarian spring rolls; Caesar salad with tempura shrimp; blackened mahimahi, dorado, or dolphinfish; chicken tikka masala; Caribbean fish pie (especially delectable with its cheesy mashed potatoes); and such fusion dishes as a Thai green king-prawn curry. For the überchic and über-rich, there's a dizzyingly expensive platter that features five kinds of caviar, as well as one with several species of fresh oysters—though the prices aren't particularly daunting for the rock-'n'-roll, media, and entertainment-industry types and the upscale Europeans that mingle here.

Hwy. 1, Mount Standfast, St. James. ✆ **246/419-0599.** Reservations required. Main courses $20–$45. MC. V. Daily 11:30am–3:30pm and 6:30–10:30pm. Closed lunch June and Sept.

The Mews INTERNATIONAL Known as a hideaway among the eateries of First and Second streets, this intimate restaurant occupies a small and somewhat cramped wood-and-masonry house. Behind a violet-colored doorway, it offers good-tasting menu items such as Thai-style green-curry shrimp; chicken breast stuffed with cream cheese, smoked salmon, and herb-flavored pâté; and seafood chowder in puff pastry. In a separate dining area, with somewhat easier access to a bar, is the bistro, where "pub grub" dishes include chicken and mushroom pie, or pork tenderloin stuffed with plantain and spinach.

Second St., Holetown, St. James. ✆ **246/432-1122.** www.diningwithus.net/mews. Reservations recommended. Main courses $29–$47 in restaurant, $17–$26 in bistro area. AE, MC, V. Daily 6:30–10:30pm.

Olives Bar & Bistro ★ MEDITERRANEAN/CARIBBEAN Olive oil is used to prepare almost all the dishes here, and olives are the only snack served in the bar, where there's a welcome rowdiness. The street-level, air-conditioned dining room (where no smoking is permitted) spills out from its original coral-stone walls and scrubbed-pine floorboards into a pleasant garden. The cuisine celebrates the warm climates of southern Europe and the Antilles, and does so exceedingly well. Even some local chefs like to dine here on their nights off. The best items include yellowfin tuna, marinated and seared rare and served on a bed of roasted-garlic mashed potatoes with grilled ratatouille. You can also order roast lamb, flavored with honey, garlic, and fresh herbs; or, for something more Caribbean, jerk tenderloin of pork. The pizza oven is kept busy at night.

Second St. at the corner of Hwy. 1, Holetown, St. James. ✆ **246/432-2112.** Reservations required in winter. Main courses $20–$35; pizza $11–$16. AE, MC, V. Daily 6:30–10pm.

Ragamuffins ★ CARIBBEAN This is a real discovery: an affordable, lively place that serves authentic island cuisine. With an exterior that's painted a bright shade of blue, and jammed between two more substantial neighbors, it's one of the few restaurants in Barbados occupying a traditional chattel house (a rectangular clapboard-sided cabin that's small enough and light enough that in the old days could be easily moved atop rolling logs from one location to another). The broiled T-bones are juicy and perfectly flavored, there's always an offering of fresh fish, and vegetarians can enjoy stir-fried vegetables with noodles. Other highlights include blackened fish, the local version of a spicy West Indian curry, and a zesty jerk chicken salad.

First St., Holetown, St. James. ✆ **246/432-1295.** www.ragamuffinsbarbados.com. Reservations recommended. Main courses $20–$33. AE, MC, V. Daily 6:30–10pm (sometimes until midnight).

The Tides ★ INTERNATIONAL/CARIBBEAN This former beachfront villa is now occupied by a graceful restaurant that serves fine food. The chef and owner, Guy Beasley, fine-tuned his culinary skills with the Roux brothers in England—arguably a couple of the top chefs there. Nearly 100 people can dine here at any given time, each enjoying a sea view from the restaurant's lush, candlelit gardens. The chef specializes in seafood but also offers finely honed meat, poultry, and vegetarian dishes. When not appreciating the art collection displayed, you can enjoy crab cakes with a Thai sauce or the homemade Caribbean seafood chowder for starters. Follow with the fresh catch of the day—grilled, blackened, pan-fried, or poached. Other dishes to which we'd award a star include honey-and-mustard-coated roast of lamb with bacon-scented scalloped potatoes, and the chargrilled filet of pork with Mexican rice, citrus juice, and a tangy orange salsa.

Holetown, St. James. ✆ **246/432-8356.** www.tidesbarbados.com. Reservations required. 3-course dinner $65–$80. MC, V. Mon–Sat 6:30–9:30pm. Closed Sept.

MODERATE

Angry Annie's Restaurant & Bar ★ INTERNATIONAL Annie may be angry, but the atmosphere here is friendly, cozy, uninhibited, and whimsical. Originally built about a century ago as a simple wooden cabin, Annie's now rests amid one of the densest concentrations of restaurants in Barbados. It's outfitted in almost violently tropical colors, with a bar that features a playlist of rock-'n'-roll classics. The dishes are uncomplicated, tasty, and permeated with local flavor. The place is especially known for its "famous" ribs, the most savory on the island, and roasted Bajan chicken. We like the garlic-cream potatoes and the fresh local vegetables. Annie also turns out fresh fish and excellent pasta dishes.

First St., Holetown, St. James. ✆ **246/432-2119.** Main courses $10–$30. MC, V. Daily 6–9:30pm.

Brown Sugar ★ BAJAN Brown Sugar serves the tastiest Bajan specialties on the island. The alfresco restaurant is hidden behind lush foliage in a turn-of-the-century coral limestone bungalow. The ceiling is latticed, with slow-turning fans, and there's an open veranda for dining by candlelight beneath hanging plants. We suggest starting with gungo-peak soup (pigeon peas cooked in chicken broth and zested with fresh coconut milk, herbs, and a touch of white wine). Among the main dishes we like, Creole orange chicken is the best, or you might like the stuffed crab backs. A selection of locally grown vegetables is also offered. Only the lobster is expensive; most of the other dishes are reasonably priced. For dessert we recommend walnut-rum pie with rum sauce. The restaurant is known for its buffet-style lunches, popular with local businesspeople for their value.

Aquatic Gap, St. Michael. ✆ **246/426-7684.** www.brownsugarbarbados.com. Reservations recommended. Main courses $18–$45; fixed-price buffet lunch $26–$33. AE, DC, DISC, MC, V. Mon–Fri noon–2:30pm and 6–9:30pm; Sat 6–9:30pm; Sun noon–2:30pm.

Calabaza ★ CARIBBEAN In vibrant colors in a Moroccan-style building, this restaurant lies on a cliff overlooking the water. East meets West defines the menu, which the chef labels a "Caribblend" style of cuisine. The appetizers are indeed appetizing, especially the pumpkin soup with crystallized ginger. Among the more tempting main courses are the red snapper, baked and flavored with a lime-and-jalapeño syrup;

The Island's Most Convivial Outdoor Fish Fry

Savvy locals can guide you to the historic Oistins Fish Market, southeast of Bridgetown and past the settlements of Hastings and Worthing. This is where Bajan fishermen unload their daily catches and sell directly to the customer—ideal if you have accommodations with a kitchen. If not, you can find nearly a dozen cottages selling fresh-cooked fish: Flying fish is in the fryer, and fish steaks such as wahoo are on the grill. On Friday night, when it seems that about a third of the island shows up to meet and greet one another, the local vendors sponsor live bands and a medley of food stalls from 6 to 10:30pm.

and crispy Bajan pork belly with tiger prawns and apple purée. A tantalizing choice is a vegetarian risotto with wild mushrooms and truffles.

Prospect, St. James. ✆ **246/424-4557.** www.calabazarestaurant.com. Reservations recommended. Main courses $17–$32. AE, MC, V. Daily 6:30–9:30pm. Closed in summer.

Mango's by the Sea ★★ INTERNATIONAL/SEAFOOD This restaurant and bar is set on the second story of a clapboard-sided building overlooking the water in the downtown center of Speightstown. Its exterior is painted a shade of mango pink. The owners, Montréal natives Gail and Pierre Spenard, buy the catch of the day directly from the fishermen's boats. The venue is whimsical and airy, and the food is exceedingly good. The seasonings aren't as overpowering as they are at many other Bajan restaurants. Appetizers might include French-style chicken liver pâté, ocean crepes with dill sauce, smoked salmon, and pumpkin soup. As a main course, you might opt for the 8-ounce U.S. tenderloin steak cooked to perfection, or the fall-off-the-bone barbecued baby back ribs, or any of several kinds of local fish prepared the way you want it. Top off your meal with passion fruit cheesecake or star-fruit torte. There's live entertainment on some nights.

2 West End, Queen St., Speightstown, St. Peter. ✆ **246/422-0704.** www.mangosbythesea.com. Reservations required. Main courses $13–$45. AE, MC, V. Daily 6–10pm. Closed Sun June–Oct.

Bridgetown

Waterfront Café INTERNATIONAL/BAJAN This is a good bet if you're in Bridgetown shopping or sightseeing. In a historic warehouse originally built to store bananas and freeze fish, this cafe serves international fare with a strong emphasis on Bajan specialties, as well as Creole. Try the fresh catch of the day prepared Creole style, or pan-seared steak. For vegetarians, the menu features three-mushroom pasta, vegetable soup, and usually a special of the day. Tuesday nights bring live steel-band music and a Bajan buffet. There's jazz on Wednesday, Friday, and Saturday.

Cavans Lane, the Carenage, Bridgetown. ✆ **246/427-0093.** www.waterfrontcafe.com.bb. Reservations required. Main courses $16–$40 lunch, $20–$46 dinner. AE, DC, MC, V. Mon–Sat 10am–10pm.

On the South Coast

EXPENSIVE

Aqua ★ BAJAN FUSION The designers of this ultratrendy restaurant combined the best of London's hip West End with a tropical climate. Once inside the (you guessed it) aqua-colored and artfully lit interior, two tiers of tables descend to a view off the deck of crashing waves. The cuisine is trendy, market fresh whenever possible, and imaginative in concept, and there is always a selection of fresh fish. Some of the best dishes include Thai-style yellow-curry coconut soup with seafood and enoki, pan-seared "dived" sea scallops with fava bean purée, New Zealand lamb with whipped polenta and toasted pine nuts, and a wide selection (at lunch Mon–Fri) of sushi.

Hastings Main Rd., Christ Church. ✆ **246/420-2995.** www.aquabarbados.com. Reservations recommended. Main courses $31–$60. AE, DC, MC, V. Restaurant Mon–Fri noon–2:30pm and 6–10:30pm; Sat 6–10:30pm; Sun 11:30am–2:30pm and 6–10:30pm. Cocktail lounge nightly till 1am.

Bellini's Trattoria ★ NORTHERN ITALIAN You're greeted with a *buon appetito*, as you walk through the doors of this restaurant on the main floor of Little Bay Hotel. Try for a table on the open-air veranda, a particularly romantic setting in the evening. Launch your night out with a Bellini cocktail, which has been compared favorably to those served at the famous Harry's Bar in Venice, Italy. The chefs prepare their specialties with precision and sensitivity, turning out an array of savory dishes beginning with the antipasti. You might try their fresh tender calamari with lemon wedges or their *bruschetta*, with freshly baked Italian bread spread with marinated vine-ripened tomatoes, fresh garlic and leafy green basil. Their pizzas are among the best on the island, and the pastas are succulent, including linguine with fresh seasonal fish, clams, calamari, jumbo shrimp, and scallops. Meat eaters will relish the filet mignon char-grilled and served with green peppercorn sauce.

Little Bay Hotel, St. Lawrence Gap, Dover, Christ Church. ✆ **246/420-7587.** www.bellinisbarbados.com. Reservations required. Main courses $21–$39. AE, DISC, MC, V. Daily 6–10pm.

Champers Wine Bar and Restaurant ★ INTERNATIONAL This is one of our favorite restaurants on Barbados's south shore, with good food, relatively moderate prices, and an unpretentious venue. You enter through a cocktail bar that invites you to linger, past a collection of paintings by local artists that are for sale. A sprawling deck stretches toward the sea with both indoor (a la air-conditioning) and outdoor (a la trade winds) dining areas. Menu items change often but may include spiced deep-fried calamari with ginger-teriyaki sauce, Parmesan-crusted barracuda with mashed potatoes and seasonal vegetables, oven-roasted rack of lamb, veal chops with Stilton blue-cheese garnish, and penne pasta with cream sauce and grilled shrimp.

Skeetes Hill, Christ Church. ✆ **246/434-3463.** www.champersbarbados.com. Reservations recommended. Sandwiches $14–$19; main courses $20–$37 at lunch, $26–$49 at dinner. AE, DC, MC, V. Mon–Sat 11:30am–3pm and 6–10pm.

On the East Coast

MODERATE

The Cove ★ 🎁 CARIBBEAN/BAJAN LaurelAnn Morley, author of *Caribbean Recipes: Old and New,* is one of the great characters of the island—a Bajan-style grande dame. Expect home-spun dialogue and lots of passion for time-tested Bajan cuisine at her restaurant. Only a tiny sign points uphill to the modest premises—actually her home, above a hillside over the coastal highway. For clients who phone in advance, LaurelAnn will prepare a lunch of stuffed crab backs, calaloo soup, fried filets of flying fish, three different preparations of shrimp, and fresh fish of the day hauled in from the Oistins Fish Market, often served with her signature orange-and-ginger glaze.

27 Atlantic Park, Cattlewash-on-Sea, St. Joseph. ✆ **246/433-9495.** Reservations required. Main courses $18–$26; fixed-price Sun buffet $38. MC, V. Wed–Thurs and Sat–Sun noon–3pm.

Plantation Dining the Way It Used to Be

For a unique dining adventure, phone Fisher Pond Great House ★★★, St. Thomas (✆ 246/433-1754), an early-17th-century plantation house, where John Chandler and his charming wife, Rain, invite, for a fee, anyone who's interested for lunch every Sunday. Some of the art and antiques are derived from silver-screen legend Claudette Colbert, who retired from Hollywood to Barbados and died in an ocean-fronting villa in 1996. The Sheraton-style dining table here, built of mahogany in 1705, has since hosted formal dinners for Queen Elizabeth II and Prince Philip. Expect a lavish array of between 25 and 30 mostly West Indian dishes laid out like a five-course buffet, and floral "eye candy" gathered from more than 300 species of hibiscus and bougainvillea. The cost, per person, is $60. MasterCard and Visa are accepted, and since the event can host a maximum of only about 80 participants, advance reservations are essential. Everything begins at 12:30pm Sundays, winding up at around 4pm.

Round House Inn Restaurant & Bar INTERNATIONAL/BAJAN Built in 1832, this restaurant lies on sloping, grass-covered lawns punctuated with solid, coral-stone retaining walls. The owners, Robert and Gail Manley, usher you to a table perched atop a rocky ledge opening onto the Bathsheba "Soup Bowl," the best surfing beach, only a half-hour drive from Bridgetown. The freshest of ingredients go into the wholesome food, which is made all the more delightful by a reggae band on Saturday nights or a guitarist on Sundays. Tuck into such appetizers as flying fish pâté or brie baked in a light-rum-and-walnut sauce. For your main course, try either the oven-baked dolphin steak or the blackened catch of the day.

Bathsheba, St. Joseph. ✆ **246/433-9678.** www.roundhousebarbados.com. Reservations required on Sun, recommended at all other times. Main courses $21–$26. MC, V. Mon–Sat 8–10am, 11:30am–3:30pm, and 6:30–9:30pm; Sun 8–10am and 11:30am–5pm.

BARBADOS'S BEACHES

The island's beaches are all open to the public—even those in front of the big resort hotels and private homes—and the government requires that there be access to all beaches via roads along the property line or through hotel entrances. The beaches on the west coast—also known as the **Gold Coast,** or in recent years, **Platinum Coast ★★**—are the most popular.

ON THE WEST (PLATINUM) COAST The waters are calm here. Major beaches include **Paynes Bay,** which is accessed from the Coach House, south of Holetown, and has a parking area. This is a good choice for watersports, especially snorkeling. The beach can get rather crowded, but the beautiful bay is worth the effort. Directly south of Payne's Bay, at Fresh Water Bay, are three of the best west-coast beaches: **Brighton Beach, Brandon's Beach,** and **Paradise Beach.**

We also recommend **Mullins Beach,** where the glassy-blue waters attract snorkelers. There's parking on the main road and some shady areas. At the Mullins Beach Bar, you can order that rum drink you've been craving.

ON THE SOUTH COAST **Almond Beach** (also known as **Casuarina Beach**) is accessed from Maxwell Coast Road, behind the Casuarina Beach Hotel. This is one of Barbados's wider beaches, and it's cooled by trade winds even on the hottest August days. Windsurfers are especially fond of this one. Food and drink can be ordered at the hotel.

Silver Sands Beach, to the east of Oistins, is near the southernmost point of Barbados, directly east of South Point Lighthouse and near the Silver Rock Hotel. This white-sand beach is a favorite with many Bajans (who would probably like to keep it a secret from tourists). The Silver Rock Bar sells drinks.

Sandy Beach, accessible via the parking lot on the Worthing main road, has tranquil waters opening onto a lagoon. It's a family favorite, and especially boisterous on weekends. Food and drinks are available.

ON THE SOUTHEAST COAST The southeast coast is the site of big waves, especially at **Crane Beach,** the white-sand strip set against a backdrop of palms that you may have seen in travel magazines. The beach is spectacular, and Prince Andrew, who has a house overlooking it, might agree. It offers excellent bodysurfing, but at times the waters may be too rough for all but the strongest swimmers; take appropriate precautions. The beach is set against cliffs, and Crane Beach Hotel towers above.

Bottom Bay ★★, north of Sam Lord's Castle Resort, is one of our Bajan favorites. Park on top of a cliff, then walk down the steps to this much-photographed tropical beach with its grove of coconut palms; there's even a cave. The sand is brilliantly white against the aquamarine sea, a picture-postcard-perfect beach paradise.

ON THE EAST (ATLANTIC) COAST The miles and miles of uncrowded beaches on the rougher Atlantic side are ideal for strolling, but swimming can be dangerous. Waves are extremely high, and the bottom tends to be rocky. The currents are also unpredictable. Many travelers enjoy the rugged grandeur of these beaches, especially those in the **Bathsheba/Cattlewash** areas.

SPORTS & OUTDOOR PURSUITS

GOLF Open to all is the Tom Fazio 18-hole championship golf course of **Sandy Lane Hotel ★★**, St. James (✆ **246/444-2000**), on the west coast. Greens fees for 18 holes are $235 for nonguests and $200 for guests in winter, and $190 for nonguests and $170 for guests in summer. For its famed "Old Nine" holes, which wind through the estate grounds, cost is $100 for nonguests and $85 for guests year-round.

The **Royal Westmoreland Golf and Country Club ★★★**, Westmoreland, St. James (✆ **246/422-4653;** www.royalwestmoreland.com), is the island's premier golf course. Designed by Robert Trent Jones, Jr., this 18-hole course is spread across 200 hectares (494 acres) overlooking the Gold Coast. It is part of a private residential community, but it's open for use by any nonmember who agrees to pay the requisite fees and who agrees to tee off any day between 10:20 and 11am. With rental of a golf cart included, the fee for 18 holes is $250.

Barbados Golf Club, Durants, Christ Church (✆ **246/428-8463;** fax 256/420-8205; www.barbadosgolfclub.com), on the south coast, opened as Barbados's first public championship golf course in 2000. The 6,800-yard, par-72 course, designed by Ron Kirby, hosted the PGA Seniors Tournament in 2003. Greens fees for 18 holes are $120 (includes cart). A 3-day unlimited golf pass is $300 (includes cart).

HIKING The **Barbados National Trust** (✆ **246/426-2421;** http://trust.funbarbados.com) gives Sunday morning hikes throughout the year. Led by young Bajans and members of the National Trust, the popular hikes cover a different area of the island each week. The guides give brief talks on subjects such as geography, history, geology, and agriculture. The hikes, free and open to all ages, are divided into fast, medium, and slow categories, with groups of no more than 10. Hikes leave promptly at 6am and take about 3 hours to complete. There are also hikes at 3:30 and 5:30pm, the latter conducted only on moonlit nights. For more information, contact the Barbados National Trust.

The **Arbib Nature & Heritage Trail** explores the natural history and heritage of Speightstown, once a major sugar port and even today a fishing town with old houses and a bustling waterfront. The trail takes you through town, the mysterious gully known as "the Whim," and the surrounding districts. The first marked trail is an 8km (5-mile) trek, which begins outside St. Peter's Church in Speightstown, traverses the Whim, crosses one of the last working plantations in Barbados (Warleight), and leads to historic 18th-century Dover Fort, following along white-sand beaches at Heywoods before ending up back in town. For information and reservations, call the Barbados National Trust, and ask for a trail map at the tourist office.

The rugged, dramatic **east coast** stretches about 25km (16 miles) from the lighthouse at Ragged Point, the easternmost point of Barbados, north along the Atlantic coast to Bathsheba and Pico Teneriffe. This is the island's most panoramic hiking area. Some hardy souls do the entire coast; if your time is limited, try the 6km (3.75-mile) stretch from Ragged Point to Consett Bay, along a rough, stony trail that requires only moderate endurance. Allow at least 2½ hours. A small picnic facility just north of Bathsheba is a popular spot for Bajan families, especially on Sundays. As for information, you're on your own, but if you stick to the coastline, you won't get lost.

HORSEBACK RIDING A different view of Barbados is provided by **Caribbean International Riding Centre,** St. Andrew, Sarely Hill (✆ **246/422-7433**). With nearly 40 horses, it offers a variety of trail rides for all levels of experience, ranging from a 1½-hour jaunt for $80 to a 2½-hour trek for $100. You'll ride through the hilly terrain of the Scotland district; along the way, you can see wild ducks and water lilies, with the rhythm of the Atlantic as background music.

SCUBA DIVING & SNORKELING The clear waters off Barbados have a visibility of more than 30m (98 ft.) most of the year. More than 50 varieties of fish are found on the shallow inside reefs, and there's an unusually high concentration of hawksbill turtles. On night dives, you can spot sleeping fish, night anemones, lobsters, moray eels, and octopuses. Diving is concentrated on the leeward west and south coasts, where hard corals grow thick along the crest of the reef, and orange elephant ear, barrel sponge, and rope sponge cascade down the drop-off of the outer reef.

On a 2km-long (1¼-mile) coral reef 2 minutes by boat from **Sandy Beach,** sea fans, corals, gorgonians, and reef fish are plentiful. *J.R.*, a dredge barge sunk as an artificial reef in 1983, is popular with beginners for its coral, fish life, and 6m (20-ft.) depth. The *Berwyn,* a coral-encrusted tugboat that sank in Carlisle Bay in 1916, attracts photographers for its variety of reef fish, shallow depth, good light, and visibility.

Asta Reef, made from another wreck that was sunk in 1986, has a drop of 24m (79 ft.), as well as coral, sea fans, and reef fish in abundance. **Dottins,** the most beautiful reef on the west coast, stretches 8km (5 miles) from Holetown to Bridgetown and has numerous dive sites at an average depth of 12m (39 ft.), with drop-offs of 30m (98 ft.). The SS *Stavronikita,* a Greek freighter, is a popular site for advanced divers. Crippled by fire in 1976, the 106m (348-ft.) freighter was sunk

.4km (¼ mile) off the west coast to become an artificial reef in **Folkestone Underwater Park,** north of Holetown. The mast is 12m high (39 ft.), the deck 24m (79 ft.), and the keel 36m (118 ft.). You might spot barracuda, moray eels, and a vibrant coat of bright yellow tube sponge, delicate pink rope sponge, and crimson encrusting sponge there. The park offers an underwater snorkel trail, plus glass-bottom boat rides, making it a family favorite.

The **Dive Shop,** Pebbles Beach, Aquatic Gap, St. Michael (✆ **888/898-3483** in the U.S., or 246/426-9947; www.divebds.com), offers some of the best scuba diving on Barbados, charging $60 for a one-tank dive and $100 for a two-tank dive, including equipment. Every day three dive trips go out to the nearby reefs and wrecks; snorkeling trips and equipment rentals are also available. Visitors with reasonable swimming skills who have never dived before can sign up for a resort course. Priced at $85, these include pool training, safety instructions, and a one-tank open-water dive. The establishment is NAUI- and PADI-certified and is open Sunday to Friday from 8:30am to 4:30pm. Other dive shops in Barbados that rent or sell snorkeling equipment include **Hazell's Water World,** Bridgetown, St. Michael (✆ **246/426-4043**).

Several companies also operate snorkeling cruises that take you to particularly picturesque areas; see "Tours & Cruises" under "Exploring the Island," below.

TENNIS The big hotels have tennis courts that can be reserved even if you're not a guest. In Barbados most tennis players still wear traditional whites. **Folkestone Park,** Holetown (✆ **246/422-2314**), has a free public tennis court. Courts at the **Barbados Squash Club,** Marine Gardens, Hastings, St. Michael (✆ **246/427-7913;** www.squashbarbados.org), can be reserved for $20 for 45 minutes.

WINDSURFING Experts say the windsurfing off Barbados is as good as any this side of Hawaii, and has turned into a very big business between November and April, attracting windsurfers from as far away as Finland, Argentina, and Japan. The shifting of the trade winds between November and May and the shallow offshore reef of **Silver Sands** create unique conditions of wind and wave swells. This allows windsurfers to reach speeds of up to 50 knots and do complete loops off the waves. Silver Sands is rated the best spot in the Caribbean for advanced windsurfing (skill rating of 5–6).

EXPLORING THE ISLAND

Tours & Cruises

Barbados is worth exploring, either in a rental car or with a taxi-driver guide. Unlike many Caribbean islands, Barbados has fair roads. They are, however, poorly signposted, and newcomers invariably get lost—not once, but several times. If you lose your way, you can generally find people in the countryside helpful.

CRUISES Luxury catamaran cruises are offered on five spacious and custom-built vessels owned by the Tiami Catamaran Fleet and operated by **Tall Ships** (✆ **246/430-0900;** www.tallshipscruises.com), located at Shallow Draught near Bridgetown Harbour. A wide range of options is available, including both lunch and dinner cruises, sunset cocktail cruises, and even turtle snorkel cruises. The lunch cruises are the most popular, operated daily from 10am to 3pm, costing $85 per person. A starlight dinner cruise from 7 to 11pm is even cheaper, at $80 per person.

Part cruise ship, part nightclub, the **MV *Harbour Master Blockbuster*** (✆ **246/430-0900**) is a 30m (98-ft.), three-story vessel with theme decks, a modern galley, and two bars. It has a dance floor and also offers formal buffets on its Calypso Deck. On the Harbour Master Deck, there's a bank of TVs for sports buffs. The showpiece of the vessel is an onboard semisubmersible, which is lowered hydraulically to 2m (6½ ft.) beneath the ship. This is, in effect, a "boat in a boat," with 30 seats. Lunch and dinner cruises cost $68 and $80 per person; the semisubmersible experience costs another $20. This cruise is offered on Wednesday 11am to 4pm.

SUBMERGED SIGHTSEEING You no longer have to be an experienced diver to see what lives 45m (148 ft.) below the surface of the sea; you can simply sail aboard one of the vessels operated by **Atlantis Submarines,** Shallow Draught, Bridgetown (✆ **246/436-8929;** www.atlantisadventures.com). The air-conditioned sightseeing submarines seat 28 to 48 passengers and make several dives daily from 9am to 1pm Monday, Tuesday, Thursday, and Friday; and 9am to 4pm on Wednesday. Passengers are transported aboard a ferryboat from the Carenage in downtown Bridgetown to the submarine site, about 2km (1¼ miles) from the west coast of Barbados. The ride offers a view of the west coast of the island. The submarine, *Atlantic III,* features viewing ports that allow you to see a rainbow of colors, tropical fish, plants, and even a shipwreck that lies upright and intact below the surface. The cost is $102 for adults, $47 for children 17 and under.

Exploring Bridgetown

Often hot and clogged with traffic, the capital, Bridgetown, merits a morning's shopping jaunt (see "Shopping," later in this chapter), plus a visit to some of its major sights.

Since about half a million visitors arrive on Barbados by cruise ship every year, the bustling **cruise-ship terminal** houses about 30 duty-free shops, 13 local retail stores, and scads of vendors. Cruise passengers can choose from a range of products, including the arts and crafts of Barbados, jewelry, liquor, china, crystal, electronics, perfume, and leather goods. The interior was designed to re-create an island street scene; some storefronts appear as traditional chattel houses in brilliant island colors, complete with streetlights, tropical landscaping, benches, and pushcarts.

Begin your tour at the waterfront, called the **Carenage** (French for "turning vessels on their side for cleaning"). This was a haven for clipper ships, and even though today it doesn't have the color of yesteryear, it's still worth exploring.

At **Heroes Square** (formerly known as **Trafalgar Square**), the long tradition of British colonization is immortalized. The monument here honoring Lord Nelson was created by Sir Richard Westmacott and erected in 1813. The great gray Victorian/Gothic **Public Buildings** on the square look like ones you might find in London. The east wing contains the meeting halls of the Senate and the House of Assembly, with some stained-glass windows representing the sovereigns of England. Look for the "Great Protector" himself, Oliver Cromwell.

Behind the Financial Building, **St. Michael's Cathedral,** east of Heroes Square, is the symbol of the Church of England. This Anglican church was built in 1655 but was completely destroyed in a 1780 hurricane. Reconstructed in 1789, it was again damaged by a hurricane in 1831. George Washington supposedly worshipped here during his visit to Barbados.

The **Synagogue,** Synagogue Lane (✆ **246/426-5792;** http://haruth.com/jw/JewsBarbados.html), is one of the oldest synagogues in the Western Hemisphere and is surrounded by a burial ground of early Jewish settlers. The present building dates from 1833. It was constructed on the site of an even older synagogue, erected by Jews

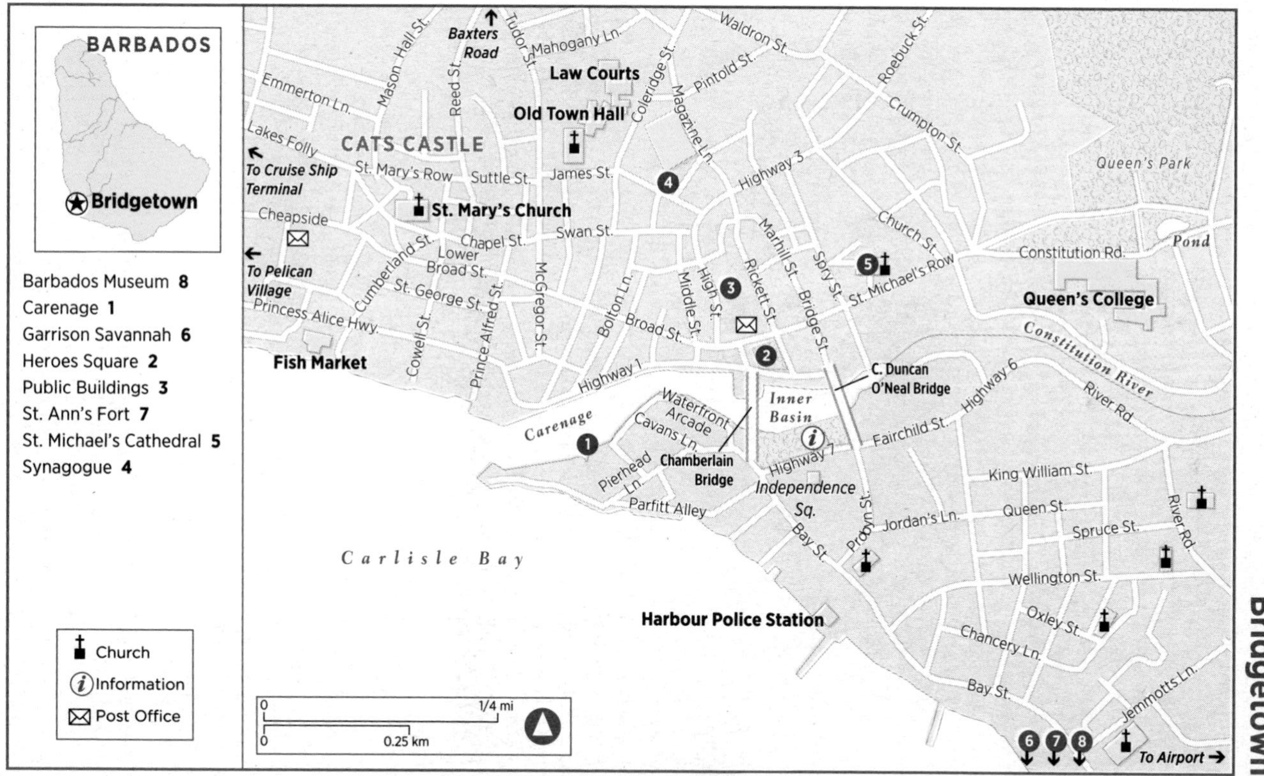
BARBADOS
Bridgetown
Barbados Museum 8
Carenage 1
Garrison Savannah 6
Heroes Square 2
Public Buildings 3
St. Ann's Fort 7
St. Michael's Cathedral 5
Synagogue 4
Church
Information
Post Office
0
1/4 mi
0
0.25 km
Baxters Road
Tudor St.
Mahogany Ln.
Waldron St.
Roebuck St.
Mason Hall St.
Reed St.
Law Courts
Coleridge St.
Pintold St.
Emmerton Ln.
Old Town Hall
Magazine Ln.
Crumpton St.
Lakes Folly
CATS CASTLE
To Cruise Ship Terminal
St. Mary's Row
Suttle St.
James St.
Highway 3
Queen's Park
St. Mary's Church
Cheapside
Swan St.
Church St.
Chapel St.
Lower Broad St.
Marhill St.
Pond
Constitution Rd.
To Pelican Village
Cumberland St.
St. George St.
Spry St.
St. Michael's Row
Princess Alice Hwy.
McGregor St.
Bolton Ln.
Middle St.
High St.
Rickett St.
Bridge St.
Queen's College
Broad St.
Constitution River
Fish Market
Cowell St.
Prince Alfred St.
Highway 1
C. Duncan O'Neal Bridge
Highway 6
Waterfront Arcade
Inner Basin
River Rd.
Carenage
Cavans Ln.
Fairchild St.
Highway 7
Pierhead Ln.
Chamberlain Bridge
King William St.
Independence Sq.
Parfitt Alley
Probyn St.
Jordan's Ln.
Queen St.
Spruce St.
Carlisle Bay
Bay St.
Wellington St.
Harbour Police Station
Oxley St.
Chancery Ln.
Jemmotts Ln.
To Airport

from Brazil in 1654. It's now part of the National Trust of Barbados—and a synagogue once again. It's open Monday to Friday from 9am to 3pm; a donation is appreciated.

First made popular in 1870, **cricket** is the national pastime on Barbados. Matches can last from 1 to 5 days. If you'd like to see one, watch for announcements in the newspapers or ask at the **Barbados Cricket Association,** at the nation's state-of-the-art and futuristic-looking stadium, Kensington Oval, St. Michael (✆ **246/436-1325;** www.bcacricket.org).

From Bridgetown you can take a taxi to **Garrison Savannah,** just south of the capital, a venue for horse races.

Barbados Museum, St. Ann's Garrison, St. Michael (✆ **246/427-0201;** www.barbmuse.org.bb), is in a former military prison. Extensive collections show the island's development from prehistoric to modern times and give fascinating glimpses into the natural environment and fine examples of West Indian maps. The museum sells a variety of quality publications, reproductions, and handicrafts. Hours are Monday to Saturday 9am to 5pm, Sunday 2 to 6pm. Admission is $7.50 for adults, $3.75 for children.

Nearby, the russet-red **St. Ann's Fort,** on the fringe of the savanna, garrisoned British soldiers in 1694. The fort wasn't completed until 1703. The **Clock House** survived the hurricane of 1831.

Seeing the Inland Sights

IN THE CENTER OF THE ISLAND ★★

Many visitors stay on those fabulous west-coast beaches, but the island's true beauty is its lush interior. If you have time, we highly recommend a hike, drive, or tour through such rarely visited parishes as St. Thomas and St. George (both are landlocked) and the wild Atlantic coast parishes of St. Andrews, St. Joseph, and St. John.

Flower Forest ★ This former sugar plantation stands 255m (837 ft.) above sea level near the western edge of the Scotland district, 2km (1¼ miles) from Harrison's Cave. Set in one of the most scenic parts of Barbados, it's more than just a botanical garden; it's where people and nature unite to create something beautiful. After viewing the grounds, visitors can purchase handicrafts at Best of Barbados.

Richmond Plantation, St. Joseph. ✆ **246/433-8152.** Admission $10 adults, $5 children 6–14, free for children 5 and under. Daily 9am–5pm.

Harrison's Cave ★★ ☺ The underground world here, the number-one tourist attraction of Barbados, is viewed from aboard an electric tram and trailer. You'll see bubbling streams, tumbling cascades, and subtly lit deep pools, while all around stalactites hang overhead like icicles, and stalagmites rise from the floor. Visitors may disembark and get a closer look at this natural phenomenon at the Rotunda Room and the Cascade Pool. Although it's interesting, it may not impress those who have been to the far more spectacular Carlsbad or Luray caverns back in the United States.

Welchman Hall, St. Thomas. ✆ **246/417-3700.** www.harrisonscave.com. Admission $30 adults, $15 children 16 and under. Daily 9am–4pm.

Orchid World ★ Set on 2.6 landscaped hectares (6½ acres) of highland, this is a botanical garden with the largest collection of orchids in the West Indies, with a diversity that's rivaled by only one or two equivalent organizations in Trinidad. The site was selected for its relatively cool temperatures and abundant rainfall. Although it originated as a place for strolls through tropical wetlands, past an astonishing variety of orchids, it has evolved into one of the most popular places in Barbados for weddings and anniversary parties. We recommend that you devote at least an hour to

The Great Tour

From mid-January through the first week of April, you can tour a different great house every Wednesday afternoon from 2:30 to 5:30pm, many rarely seen by the public. You'll see a great array of plantation antiques and get a feeling for the elegant colonial lifestyle once commonplace on Barbados. For more information, call ✆ 246/426-2421.

wandering through this site's labyrinth of paths and glens. Both it and the above-recommended Flower Forest, with which it is associated, are wheelchair accessible.

Groves, St. George. ✆ **246/433-0306.** Admission $10 adults, $5 children 5–13, free for children 4 and under. Daily 9am–5pm.

Welchman Hall Gully ★ The Barbados National Trust owns this lush tropical garden, which contains specimens of plants—many of them labeled—that were here before the English settlers landed in 1627 and later imports that include cocoa bushes, and trees from which both cloves and nutmeg are produced. Occasionally, you'll spot a wild monkey amid the flora. You can also see breadfruit trees that are supposedly descendants of the seedlings brought ashore by Captain Bligh, of *Bounty* fame.

Welchman Hall, St. Thomas. ✆ **246/438-6671.** www.welchmanhallgullybarbados.com. Admission $9 adults, $4 children 5–12, free for children 4 and under. Daily 9am–5pm. Take Hwy. 2 from Bridgetown.

SIGHTS ALONG THE WEST COAST

The Cockspur Beach Club Lying to the north of Bridgetown, this manufacturer of white rum has been going strong since 1897. The distillery is known for producing the popular island drink, coconut rum. To make this tour even more enticing, the center is constructed on an idyllic stretch of white-sand beach set against a backdrop of sea-grape and almond trees. Also on-site is a beachside grill where lunch and rum punches are served. The price of the tour includes a rum drink and the use of a beach chair. In contrast to the sunny beach, the distillery is dark with a lot of old equipment, including a century-old copper-pot still.

Black Rock, Brighton, St. Michael. ✆ **246/425-9393.** Admission $10, or $40 with lunch and transportation from your hotel. Mon–Fri 9am–5pm (off season till 4pm).

Folkestone Marine Park & Visitor Centre ☺ Set beside a shimmering stretch of coral sand beach, this is a "water park" lying just north of Holetown. It combines a museum and aquarium to illustrate the rich marine life of Barbados. An underwater snorkeling trail goes around a reef, and you can see the same sights in a glass-bottom boat. A number of beachfront restaurants and bars are nearby, and there is an on-site gift shop open Monday to Friday 9am to 5pm.

Church Point, Holetown, St. James. ✆ **246/422-2871.** Museum admission 65¢ adults, 25¢ children. Snorkeling with equipment $10. Mon–Fri 9am–5pm.

The Mount Gay Rum Tour & Gift Shop On the northern edge of Bridgetown, you can learn the story of island rum, produced here more or less since the British first settled on the island in 1627. By 1655, Barbados was producing some 900,000 gallons of rum annually. The actual distillery is in St. Lucy Parish to the north, but at this center you can see both old and contemporary equipment used in rum making, along with rows and rows of barrels. First you view a video about Mount Gay's history,

A Beautiful Picnic Spot

Farley Hill National Park surrounds what used to be one of the great houses of Barbados, Farley Hill, a mansion now in ruins. The park is north of the parish of St. Peter, directly across the road leading into the Barbados Wildlife Reserve. You can bring in a picnic and wander in the park, overlooking the turbulent waters of the Atlantic. You can enter the park for free if you're walking, but it costs $2 to enter by car. Hours are daily 8:30am to 5pm.

followed by a 15-minute crash course in rum making. The tour concludes with a rum tasting. Rum, along with gift items, is for sale in the on-site shop. You can make a reservation for an admission-free tour of the actual Mount Gay refinery, which is located in the northern part of St. Lucy Parish, by calling ✆ **246/425-9066.**

Spring Garden Hwy., Brandons, St. Michael. ✆ **246/425-9066.** Admission $7, or $50 including lunch and transportation from your hotel; free for children 11 and under. Mon–Fri 9:30am–3:30pm.

IN THE SOUTHEAST (ST. PHILIP)

Heritage Park & Rum Factory After driving through cane fields, you'll arrive at the first rum distillery to be launched on the island since the 19th century. Inaugurated in 1996, this factory is located on a former molasses and sugar plantation dating back some 350 years. Produced on-site is ESA Field, a white rum praised by connoisseurs. Adjacent is an admission-free park where Bajan handicrafts are displayed. You'll also find an array of shops and carts selling food, handicrafts, and products.

Foursquare Plantation, St. Philip. ✆ **246/420-1977.** Free admission. Mon–Fri 9am–4:30pm.

Sunbury Plantation House ★ This mid-17th-century plantation house is steeped in history, featuring mahogany antiques, old prints, and a unique collection of horse-drawn carriages. Take the informative tour, then stop in the Courtyard Restaurant and Bar for a meal or drinks; there's also a gift shop. A candlelight dinner is offered at least once a week, usually on either Tuesday or Thursday nights. Served atop an impressive antique mahogany table, this five-course meal costs $100 per person, inclusive of wine.

Sunbury, off 6 Cross Rd., St. Philip. ✆ **246/423-6270.** www.barbadosgreathouse.com. Admission $9 adults, $4.50 children 5–12. Daily 9:30am–4pm (last tour).

IN THE NORTHEAST

Andromeda Botanic Gardens ★ On a cliff overlooking the town of Bathsheba on the rugged east coast, limestone boulders make for a natural 3-hectare (7½-acre) rock-garden setting. Thousands of orchids, hundreds of hibiscus and heliconia, and many varieties of ferns, begonias, palms, and other species grow here in splendid profusion. You'll occasionally see toads, frogs, herons, lizards, hummingbirds, and sometimes a mongoose or a monkey.

Bathsheba, St. Joseph. ✆ **246/433-9384.** http://andromeda.cavehill.uwi.edu. Admission $10 adults, $5 children 6–12, free for children 5 and under. Daily 9am–4:30pm.

St. Nicholas Abbey ★★ Surrounded by sugar-cane fields, this Jacobean plantation great house has been around since about 1650. It was never actually an abbey—around 1820, a socially ambitious owner simply christened it as such. More than 80 hectares (198 acres) are still cultivated each year. The house, characterized by its curved gables, is believed to be one of three authentically Jacobean houses in the

Western Hemisphere. Recent restorations have transformed this spectacularly historic site into one of the Caribbean's genuine architectural treasures. On some days, you're likely to see smoke billowing from the chimneys of the reconstructed on-site sugar refinery. It's wise to phone in advance, as the place sometimes closes unexpectedly because of inclement weather or the absence of the hard-working owners.

On Cherry Tree Hill, Hwy. 1, St. Peter. ✆ **246/422-8725.** www.stnicholasabbey.com. Admission $15 adults, $10 children 11 and under. Sun–Fri 10am–3:30pm.

SHOPPING

You may find duty-free merchandise here at prices 20% to 40% lower than in the United States and Canada—but you've got to be a smart shopper to spot bargains, and you should be familiar with prices back in your hometown. Duty-free shops have two prices listed on items of merchandise: the local retail price, and the local retail price less the government-imposed tax.

Some of the best duty-free buys include cameras, watches, crystal, gold jewelry, bone china, cosmetics and perfumes, and liquor (including locally produced Barbados rum and liqueurs), along with tobacco products and cashmere sweaters, tweeds, and sportswear from Britain. Items made on Barbados are duty-free.

The quintessential Barbados handicrafts are black-coral jewelry and clay pottery. The latter originates at **Highland Pottery, Inc.** ★ (✆ **246/422-9818**), which is worth a visit. Potters turn out different products, some based on designs that are centuries old. The potteries (which are signposted) are north of Bathsheba on the east coast, most of them within or immediately adjacent to the hamlet of Chalky Mountain, in St. Andrew's Parish. In shops across the island, you'll also find a selection of locally made vases, pots, pottery mugs, glazed plates, and ornaments.

Island artisans weave wall hangings from local grasses and dried flowers, and also turn out straw mats, baskets, and bags with raffia embroidery. Leatherwork—particularly handbags, belts, and sandals—is also found on Barbados.

IN BRIDGETOWN Cruise passengers generally head for the **cruise-ship terminal** at Bridgetown Harbour, which has some 20 duty-free shops, 13 local shops, and many vendors (see "Exploring Bridgetown" under "Exploring the Island," p. 116).

At **Articrafts** ★, Norman Center Mall, Broad Street (✆ **246/427-5767**), John and Roslyn Watson have assembled an impressive display of Bajan arts and crafts. Roslyn's distinctive wall hangings are decorated with objects from the island, including sea fans and coral.

Cave Shepherd ★, Broad Street (✆ **246/227-1330;** www.caveshepherd.com), is the largest department store on the island and the best place for duty-free merchandise. There are branches at Sunset Crest in Holetown, Da Costas Mall, Grantley Adams Airport, and the Bridgetown cruise-ship terminal, but if your time is limited, try this outlet, as it has the widest selection. The store sells perfumes, cosmetics, fine crystal and bone china, cameras, jewelry, swimwear, leather goods, men's designer clothing, handicrafts, liquor, and souvenirs. Take a break in the cool comfort of the **Balcony,** overlooking Broad Street, which serves vegetarian dishes and has a salad bar and beer garden.

Harrison's, 10–14 Broad St. (✆ **246/431-5500**), has six branch stores, all selling a wide variety of duty-free merchandise, including china, crystal, jewelry, watches, liquor, and perfumes—all at fair prices. Also for sale are some fine leather products handcrafted in Colombia.

Little Switzerland, in the Da Costas Mall, Broad Street (✆ **246/431-0030;** www.littleswitzerland.com), offers a wide selection of watches, fine jewelry, and an array of goodies from Waterford, Lalique, Swarovski, Baccarat, and others.

Pelican Craft Centre, Harbour Road (✆ **246/427-5350**), consists of about 20 somewhat disorganized crafts boutiques, each of them clustered tightly into a folkloric/ethnic blend of thatched roofs, dust, and commercial hubbub. It's been accused of being somewhat overpriced and something of a tourist trap, but there are occasional moments of charm among the handcrafted items on display. Most of the shops here are gimmicky, but a few intriguing items can be found if you search hard enough. Sometimes you can see craftspeople at work. In Bridgetown, go down Princess Alice Highway to the city's Deep Water Harbour, where you'll find this tiny colony of thatched-roof shops.

ELSEWHERE ON THE ISLAND **The Watering Hole,** Hwy. 7, St. Lawrence Main Road, close to the entrance to St. Lawrence's Gap (✆ **246/435-6375**), is not only the best place to purchase bottles of Bajan rum at duty-free prices, but is also a great dive for hanging out. A small bottle of rum (about 6 oz.) sells for around $8. Some locals as well as savvy visitors come here and make an evening of it, sampling the various rum drinks. Of course, you may need someone to carry you back to your hotel, as these punches are lethal. Opening times vary—call to be sure—but we've seen this place going strong at 3am. One of the more interesting shopping jaunts in Barbados involves a visit to the very laid-back vendors at **Tyrol Cot Heritage Village,** Codrington Hill, St. Michael (✆ **246/424-2074**), the former home of Bajan national hero Sir Grantley Adams. On the grounds of the former prime minister's estate is a colony of artisans, who turn out an array of articles for sale ranging from paintings to pottery, from baskets to handmade figurines.

Earthworks Pottery/On the Wall Gallery ★, Edgehill Heights 2, St. Thomas (✆ **246/425-0223;** www.earthworks-pottery.com), is one of the artistic highlights of Barbados. Deep in the island's central highlands, Canadian-born Goldie Spieler and her son, David, in business at this site since 1978, create whimsical ceramics in the colors of the sea and sky, with touches of watermelon pink. Many are decorated with Antillean-inspired swirls and zigzags. On the premises are a studio and a showroom that sells the output of at least half a dozen other island potters. Purchases can be shipped. Immediately next door is the **Ins and Outs Gift Emporium** (✆ **246/438-3438**), where jars of locally made condiments—jams, jellies, sauces, and spices—are sold along with a small selection of island-inspired reading materials.

The **Shell Gallery "Contentment,"** Gibbes Hill, St. Peter (✆ **246/422-2593**), has the best collection of shells in the West Indies. Also offered are shell jewelry, and local pottery and ceramics.

Greenwich House Antiques, Greenwich Village, Trents Hill, St. James (✆ **246/432-1169**), a 25-minute drive from Bridgetown, feels like a genteel private home where the objects for sale seem to have come from the attic of your slightly dotty great aunt. The building that contains the shop is at least a century old, the historic centerpiece of what used to be a sugar plantation. Dozens of objects, both utilitarian and decorative, including some good examples of Barbados-made mahogany furniture, fill every available inch of display space.

BARBADOS AFTER DARK

ON THE WEST COAST A lot of the evening entertainment around here revolves around the big resorts, many of which have lovely bars, some of which host bands and beach parties in the evening. See "Where to Stay," p. 100.

Some say the green-and-yellow **Coach House,** on the main Bridgetown-Holetown road, just south of Sandy Lane, about 10km (6¼ miles) north of Bridgetown, Paynes Bay, St. James (✆ **246/432-1163**), is 200 years old. Attracting mostly visitors, this is a Bajan version of an English pub, with an outdoor garden bar. Every day from noon to 6pm you can order bar meals, including flying-fish burgers, priced at $14 to $20 and up. On-site, there's also a well-attended Saturday night buffet costing $35.

Scarlet (✆ **246/432-3663;** www.scarletbarbados.com) is a wine bar and bistro-style restaurant that's positioned in a scarlet-colored old-fashioned house across the coastal road from the House and Tamarind Bay resorts. Frankly, we prefer it as a drinking hangout and wine emporium instead of as a full-fledged restaurant, ordering a glass or two from the comprehensive wine list or perhaps any of the staggeringly potent cocktails. Try, for example, an "elderflower Collins" or a passion fruit Caipirhumba (they call it "a caipirinha revisited"). At the bar, you'll find Warhol portraits of the women who got intimate with JFK, including Jackie O. and Marilyn Monroe. Know in advance that you don't "sit" here, you "perch" somewhat uncomfortably, on a high bar stool overlooking the crowds of urbanized 30-somethings that make the place their hangout. Cocktails cost from $8 to $18. Small *amuse-bouche* platters of decidedly stylish food (flying-fish lollipops, smoked-salmon sushi with wasabi) cost from $8 to $14. It's open Tuesday to Sunday 5 to 10:30pm as a restaurant, till around midnight as a bar.

John Moore Bar ★, on the waterfront, Weston, St. James (✆ **246/422-2258**), is the most atmospheric and least pretentious bar on Barbados. Open to the sea breezes and very weather-beaten, it's the nerve center of this waterfront town, filled day and night with a congenial group of neighborhood residents and a scattering of tourists. You might even find Barbados's prime minister hanging out here—the bar is a stronghold of his island constituency, and since he won his office, things around this bar became a lot more interesting. Most visitors opt for a rum punch or beer, but you can order up a plate of local fish if you don't mind waiting.

Another worthy drinking spot is the previously recommended **Olives Bar & Bistro ★**, Second Street at the corner of Hwy. 1, in Holetown (✆ **246/432-2112**). Not only is it a fine restaurant, but it's also a good place to spend an hour before or after dinner—maybe both. Within a *Casablanca*-like setting of potted palms, coral stone walls, and whirling ceiling fans, it draws a convivial international crowd, mostly expats, Americans, and English visitors in their 30s and 40s. Unfortunately, it's open as a restaurant only during relatively limited hours of 6:30 to 9:30pm daily, and as a bar daily from 6:30 till around 11:30pm. The kitchen is known for its roasted mutton derived from the local blackbelly sheep, a variety for which Barbados is well known.

What's our ultimate fave in the "raffish bars on the waterfront" category? It's **Fisherman's Pub & Beach Bar,** Queen Street, Speightstown, St. Peter (✆ **246/422-2703**). Set within a dilapidated wood-and-corrugated-steel building directly on the waterfront, it's a local hangout for Bajan residents and the politicians who serve them, as well as an occasional rock, soccer, or cricket bigwig. There has been a bar here since the 1940s, with chairs and battered tables set on a covered wooden deck built over the water. Beer costs $2.50, rum punch costs $3.50, and full meals, served by an employee, cafeteria style, from a steam tray in a corner, cost from $5 to $15 each. Expect boiled chicken, shepherd's pie, flying-fish filets, and various preparations of beef. It's open Monday to Saturday 11am to 9pm as a restaurant and till around midnight as a bar. A steel band plays here on Wednesday nights.

IN BRIDGETOWN For the most authentic Bajan evening possible, head for **Baxters Road ★** in Bridgetown, where there's always something cooking Friday and Saturday nights after 11pm. In fact, if you stick around until dawn, you'll find the party's still going strong. Some old-time visitors have compared Baxters Road to the back streets of New Orleans in the 1930s. If you fall in love with the place, you can "caf crawl" up and down the street, where nearly every bar is run by a Bajan mama.

The most popular "caf" on Baxters Road is **Patsy** (she has a phone, "but it doesn't work"), a little ramshackle establishment where Bajans come for fried chicken throughout the evening between around 5pm till as late as 2am, depending on business. Even if you're not particularly hungry, consider stopping in for a Banks beer.

Boatyard Bar & South Deck Grill, Bay Street in Bridgetown (✆ **246/436-2622;** www.theboatyard.com), is one of the busiest and most hard-drinking of the youth-oriented bars in Bridgetown. Occupying the beachfront, the interior is lavishly decorated in bright Creole colors of yellow, blue, and pink. If you want food, the menu features simple platters of fish, chicken, or burgers. If you want to go swimming, the beach lies almost directly adjacent to the foundations of this place. Expect a 5-minute trek from central Bridgetown; hordes of dancers jiving to the DJ every Tuesday, Wednesday, Friday, and Saturday; and lots of local gossip. It's open daily 9am to sometimes as late as 3am, depending on business.

Harbour Lights, Marine Villa, Lower Bay Street, 2km (1¼ miles) southeast of Bridgetown (✆ **246/436-7225;** www.harbourlightsbarbados.com), is the island's most popular weekend spot for dancing, drinking, and flirting. In a modern seafront building with an oceanfront patio (which gives dancers a chance to cool off), the place plays recorded versions of reggae, soca, and whatever else is popular until the wee hours nightly. Monday is Beach Party Night; the $73 charge includes transportation to and from your hotel, a barbecue buffet, drinks, a live band, and lots of theme-derived entertainment that includes limbo contests and fire-eaters. On Wednesday and Friday, the cover is $25.

ON THE SOUTH COAST The bustling activity at **Cafe Sol,** St. Lawrence Gap, Christ Church (✆ **246/420-7655;** www.cafesolbarbados.com), attracts a very convivial crowd. As a specialty of the house, the bartender rubs the margarita glasses with Bajan sugar instead of the usual salt. There's an on-site local restaurant as well.

Plantation Theatre Restaurant, Main Road (Hwy. 7), St. Lawrence Main Road, Christ Church (✆ **246/428-5048;** www.plantationtheatre.com), is the island's main showcase for evening dinner theater and Caribbean cabaret. It's completely touristy, but enjoyable nonetheless. Every Wednesday and Friday, dinner is served at 7:15pm, followed at 8:15pm by a show, *Bajan Roots and Rhythm*. Expect elaborate costumes and reggae, calypso, and limbo. For $98 you get dinner, the show, and transportation to and from your hotel; the show alone costs $58. Reserve in advance.

The Ship Inn, St. Lawrence Gap, Christ Church, near Oistins (✆ **246/420-7447;** www.shipinnbarbados.com), is among the leading drinking, dining, and entertainment centers on the south coast. The pub is the hot spot: Top local bands perform 3 nights a week, offering reggae, calypso, and pop music. Otherwise, there's a live DJ. The entrance fee ranges from free (if you're eating dinner) to between $5 and $10. The place draws an equal number of visitors and locals.

The biggest and best sports bar in Barbados, without equal, is **Bubba's Sports Bar,** Rockley Main Road, Christ Church (✆ **246/435-6217;** www.bubbassportsbar.net), which offers a couple of satellite dishes, a 3m (10-ft.) video screen, and a dozen TVs. Wash a Bubba burger down with a Banks beer.

6

BONAIRE

In the Caribbean Sea north of Venezuela, Bonaire is the "B" of the ABC islands. Bonaire lacks Aruba's glitzy diversions, but avid scuba divers have preferred this unspoiled treasure for years. With its clear waters, stunning coral reef just feet from shore and vibrant marine life, tiny Bonaire is one of the best places in the Caribbean for diving and snorkeling. Its capital city, Kralendijk, is a sleepy little seafront town with the best shopping and nightlife options. Those who come to Bonaire for quiet beach time find a laid-back island.

Beaches Swimmers prefer the tranquil leeward coast; the east coast is rough and dangerous. **No Name Beach** on Klein Bonaire has a pretty white-sand strip and is popular with divers and snorkelers. In Lac Bay, both **Lac Bay Beach** and **Sorbon Beach** aren't too deep, which make them ideal destinations for families. For a traditional beach experience, **Eden Beach** has a bar and restaurant, but snorkelers will want to view the wealth of marine life in the shallow water.

Things to Do Bonaire is prized for what the island's license plate boasts: a DIVER'S PARADISE. Most of the 80 **dive sites** are accessible by shore and house a rich marine ecosystem, including anemones, parrotfish, sea horses, and corals. Snorkelers aren't slighted, with opportunities to swim among sea turtles. Kralendijk's **Fort Oranje** may be small, but the quaint building is the oldest on Bonaire. Walk among fanciful stalactites and stalagmites in the island's many caves, such as **Barcadera.**

Eating & Drinking Despite Bonaire's size, dining options are more diverse than you might think—the restaurant scene includes cuisines from Continental to French to Asian. Try local specialties such as ***keshi yena,*** cheese stuffed with meat, or ***kabritu stoba,*** goat stew. Go for casual meals at **Kon Tiki** and **Rum Runners,** but don't skip the fresh seafood at **La Balandra,** designed after a Spanish schooner. Dutch beer and extravagant umbrella drinks top the beverage menus at island bars.

Nature Bonaire has some of the region's best bird watching. Look for Caribbean pink flamingos at the **Salina Matijs,** or parakeets at **Bronswinkel Well,** situated at the foot of **Mount Brandaris,** the island's highest peak. The **Washington-Slagbaai National Park** fills much of Bonaire's northern end. The land, formerly a plantation, is home to cacti, iguanas, blue lizards, parakeets, and parrots. Talk to the animals at Bonaire's **Donkey Sanctuary,** home to the wild donkeys that used to roam the island.

ESSENTIALS

Visitor Information

Before you go, contact the **Bonaire Government Tourist Office** (✆ **800/ BONAIRE** [266-2473] in the U.S.), or go online to **www.tourismbonaire.com** for information.

On the island, the **Bonaire Government Tourist Bureau,** Kaya Grandi 2 (✆ **599/717-8322**), is open Monday to Friday from 8am to noon and 1:30 to 5pm.

Pick up a copy of ***Bonaire Affair, Bonaire Nights,*** the ***Bonaire Dining Guide,*** and ***Bonaire Update*** for information on where to shop, play, eat, and stay. The ***Bonaire Dive Guide*** provides up-to-date information on the best dive and snorkel sites.

Getting There

Continental Airlines (✆ **800/231-0856** in the U.S. and Canada; www.continental.com) flies nonstop to and from Newark, New Jersey, and Houston to Bonaire on weekends during the high season. Through its American Eagle subsidiary, **American Airlines** (✆ **800/433-7300** in the U.S. and Canada; www.aa.com) offers three weekly round-trip flights between San Juan, Puerto Rico, and Bonaire. It also provides one-stop service to Bonaire from many U.S. gateway cities.

An airline based in Bonaire, **Dutch Antilles Express** (✆ **599/717-0808;** www.flydae.com) has numerous flights per day between Bonaire and Curaçao and between Bonaire and Aruba. Two other local carriers serving the ABC islands are **Tiara Air** (✆ **599/717-3008;** www.tiara-air.com) and **Insel Air** (✆ **800/386-4800** in the U.S., or 599/737-0444; www.fly-inselair.com), so check rates and itineraries with them.

Getting Around

Even though most of the island is flat and renting a moped or motor scooter is fun, be prepared for some unpaved, pitted, and rocky roads.

BY RENTAL CAR Consider renting a four-wheel-drive vehicle, especially from October to January, when it can be muddy.

Budget (✆ **800/472-3325** in the U.S. and Canada, or 599/717-4700; www.bonaire-budgetcar.com) and **Hertz** (✆ **800/654-3001** in the U.S. and Canada, or 599/717-7221; www.interislandcarrental.com) have desks at Flamingo Airport. Weekly arrangements are cheaper, but daily rates range from $50 to $60, with unlimited mileage. Also at the airport, **Total Car Rental** (✆ **599/717-7424;** www.totalcarrentalbonaire.com) rents cars and pickup trucks. Some automatic, air-conditioned four-door sedans are available. **Island Car Rentals,** J.A. Blvd. 80 (✆ **599/717-2100;** www.islandcarrentalbonaire.com), rents SUVs and jeeps from $24 a day. It pays to shop around: Sometimes—but not always—you can make a better deal with a local agency.

Your valid U.S., British (you must have had it for 2 years), or Canadian driver's license is acceptable for driving on Bonaire. Drive on the right and keep an eye out for goats, chickens, lizards, and donkeys that frequently dart out in front of cars.

BY TAXI Taxis are unmetered, but the government has established rates. All taxis carry a license plate with the letters TX. Every driver must produce a price list upon request. As many as four passengers can go along for the ride, unless there's too much luggage. A trip from the airport to your hotel should cost about $10 to $25. From midnight to 6am, fares go up by 50%.

Most taxi drivers can take you on a tour of the island, but you'll have to negotiate a price according to how long a trip you want and what you want to see. For more information, call **Taxi Central Dispatch** (✆ **599/717-8100**).

BY BICYCLE If you're in good shape, you might consider renting a bike, although you'll have to contend with the hot sun and powerful trade winds. Nevertheless, much of the island is flat, and if you follow the main road, you'll go along the water's edge.

[Fast FACTS] BONAIRE

Banks Banks are usually open Monday to Friday from 8am to 3:30 or 4pm. **RBTT Bank,** Kaya Korona 15 (✆ **599/717-4500**), is the most convenient facility for visitors, and it has an ATM. There's also an ATM at the airport and several along Kaya Grandi.

Currency In February 2011, Bonaire switched their official currency from the Netherlands Antillean florin (NAf) to the **U.S. dollar.** *As such, prices in this chapter are quoted in U.S. dollars.*

Customs Besides articles for personal use, visitors over 15 are allowed 400 cigarettes, 50 cigars, 250 grams of tobacco, 2 liters of distilled beverages, and 2 liters of wine.

Documents U.S. and Canadian citizens need a passport. A return or continuing ticket is also required along with sufficient means to support yourself during your stay. (Maximum stay is 14 days, with the possibility of extending the visit to 90 days.)

Electricity The electricity on Bonaire is slightly different from that used in North America—110–130 volts/50 cycles, as opposed to U.S. and Canadian voltages of 110 volts/60 cycles. Adapters and transformers are not necessary for North American appliances, but because of the erratic current, you should still proceed with caution and be aware plug-in clocks may run slow. ***Warning:*** Electrical current used to feed or recharge finely calibrated diving equipment should be stabilized with a specially engineered electrical stabilizer. Every diving operation on the island has one of these as part of its standard equipment for visiting divers.

Emergencies Call ✆ **911** in case of fire or for the police, and **912** for an ambulance.

Hospital The **Hospitaal San Francisco** is located at Kaya Soeur Bartola 2 in Kralendijk (✆ **599/717-8900**). A recompression chamber is on-site. A plane on standby at the airport takes seriously ill patients to Curaçao for treatment.

Language English is widely spoken, but you'll hear Dutch, Spanish, and Papiamento, the local dialect, as well.

Liquor Laws The minimum drinking age is 18. Beer, wine, and liquor are sold in all kinds of stores 7 days a week. It's legal to have an open container on the beach. The minimum age for gambling is 21.

Safety Bonaire is quite a safe haven in this crime-infested world. But remember, any place that attracts tourists also attracts people who prey on them. Safeguard your valuables.

Taxes The government requires a $5.50-per-person daily room tax on all hotel rooms, but some hotels charge $6.50 as members of a local hotel organization. Upon leaving Bonaire, you'll be charged an airport departure tax of $35, so don't spend every penny. There's also an interisland departure tax of $5.75 if you are flying to Curaçao.

Telephone To call Bonaire from the United States, dial **011** (the international access code), then **599** (the area code for Bonaire), and then **717** (the exchange) and the four-digit local number. Once on

Bonaire, to call another number on the island, only the four-digit local number is necessary. There are three cellphone providers on island: TELBO is the central phone company servicing land lines, while Chippie and Digicell are cellphone competitors. While you can purchase a SIM card for your existing phone, it's easier to rent a cellphone from a local agency such as **Chat 'n' Browse** (✆ **599/717-2281;** www.chatnbrowse.com) to make local calls.

Time Bonaire is on Atlantic Standard Time year-round, 1 hour ahead of Eastern Standard Time. (When it's noon on Bonaire, it's 11am in Miami.) When daylight saving time is in effect in the United States, clocks in Miami and Bonaire show the same time.

Tipping Most hotels and guesthouses add a 10% service charge in lieu of tipping. Restaurants generally add a service charge of 15% to the bill. Taxi drivers expect a 10% tip.

Water Drinking water comes from desalinated seawater and is perfectly safe.

Weather Bonaire is known for its warm climate, with temperatures hovering around 82°F (28°C). The water temperature averages 80°F (27°C). It's warmest in August and September, coolest in January and February. The average rainfall is 22 inches, and December to March are the rainiest months. Like all the Dutch ABC (Aruba, Bonaire, and Curaçao) islands, Bonaire lies outside the hurricane belt, which comes as a relief to many visitors planning to visit the Caribbean during the hurricane season.

WHERE TO STAY

Hotels, all facing the sea and in many cases opening onto the waterfront, are low-key, personally run operations where everybody gets to know everybody else in no time. They are concentrated on the west coast of the island immediately north or immediately south of the capital of Kralendijk.

Remember that taxes and service charges are seldom included in the prices you're quoted, so ask about them when making your reservations.

Your best deal at one of the dive resorts, such as Captain Don's Habitat, is to book a package deal, often for a week. Depending on the house count, more limited bookings can be accommodated if rooms are available.

Very Expensive

Harbour Village Bonaire ★★★ Conceived by one of the largest land developers in Venezuela, this exclusive complex, the most stylish on the island, is designed like an Iberian village, opening onto a sandy beach. It's upscale and well managed, offering services and resort amenities to well-heeled divers who don't want the more laid-back atmosphere of Captain Don's Habitat (see below). Accommodations are in Spanish-style villas painted in pastels, with red-tile roofs and terraced balconies. Guest rooms have tropical decor, four-poster beds, white-tile floors, natural-wood furniture, and marble bathrooms with deluxe toiletries, shower stalls, and robes.

A wide array of very good food awaits you. Our favorite restaurant is La Balandra Beach Bar and Restaurant, a gazebo-like structure set beside a massive pier; an octagonal bar area flanked by an open grill and salad bar is open to the sea view and breezes.

Kaya Gobernador N. Debrot 71, Playa Lechi (P.O. Box 312), Bonaire, N.A. www.harbourvillage.com. ✆ **800/424-0004** in the U.S. and Canada, or 599/717-7500. Fax 599/717-7507. 42 units. Winter $385–$415 double, $675 1-bedroom suite, $865 2-bedroom suite; off season $330–$365 double, $590 1-bedroom suite, $645 2-bedroom suite. Children 16 and under stay free in parent's room. AE, DC, DISC, MC, V. **Amenities:** 2 restaurants; bar; airport transfers; babysitting; bikes; dive shop; fitness center; marina; outdoor pool; room service; spa; 4 tennis courts. *In room:* A/C, ceiling fan, flatscreen TV, hair dryer, kitchenette (in suites), MP3 docking station, Wi-Fi (free).

Expensive

Plaza Resort Bonaire ★ This luxury resort lies a short drive from the airport, on a strip of land midway between a saltwater lagoon and a sandy stretch of Caribbean beachfront. Designed in 1995 by a team of Italian architects, it resembles a white-sided village along the coast of southern Portugal, thanks to terra-cotta roofs and a pair of bridges that traverse the lagoon for easy access to the 5 hectares (12 acres) of grounds. It's an extremely large property for Bonaire, where most hotels are more intimate. Rooms are quite large, though be aware that suites are actually very large bedrooms, without interior dividers. The one- and two-bedroom villas contain fully equipped kitchens, ceiling fans, and simple, spartan summery furnishings. Most units are large and airy, with private balconies and queen-size beds. Bathrooms are roomy and luxurious, with showers and deep tubs and a separate "water closet" that contains the toilet.

J. A. Abraham Blvd. 80, Bonaire, N.A. www.plazaresortbonaire.com. ✆ **800/766-6016** in the U.S. and Canada, or 599/717-2500. Fax 599/717-7133. 174 units. Winter $240–$270 suite, $290 1-bedroom villa, $370 2-bedroom villa; off season $190–$220 suite, $230 1-bedroom villa, $300 2-bedroom villa. Extra person $30. AE, MC, V. **Amenities:** 2 restaurants; 2 bars; babysitting; bikes; boats; children's programs; dive shop; health club; marina; outdoor pool; room service; sailing; spa; 4 tennis courts; windsurfing. *In room:* A/C, TV, fridge, hair dryer, Wi-Fi (free).

Moderate

Bellafonte Chateau de la Mer ★ As you enter the courtyard, you are greeted by a *bella fonte* (beautiful fountain) surrounded by three-story buildings that replicate a small Mediterranean villa. Though it is on the waterfront, the hotel has no beach—only a pool and a long pier over the water good for sunbathing and swimming in the sea below. Except for its pool, it lacks the amenities of the larger resorts, but it is a bastion of comfort, style, and grace in all other respects. The rooms are decorated not only with taste, but also with a sense of glamour; the trendy decor includes teak wood and stainless steel. The limited space and lack of guardrails indicate that the destination is more suited to couples than families. The richly appointed units with balconies or terraces seem intended to lure honeymooners whose desire is to relax and escape from the crowds.

E. E. G. Blvd. 10, Belnem, Bonaire, N.A. www.bellafontebonaire.com. ✆ **599/717-3333.** Fax 599/717-8581. 20 units. Winter $145–$275 double, $325–$495 2-bedroom suite; off season $125–$235 double, $275–$425 2-bedroom suite. AE, DISC, MC, V. **Amenities:** Bikes; dive shop; grocery service; Jacuzzi; private pier; outdoor pool. *In room:* A/C, TV, kitchen (in some), Wi-Fi (free).

Captain Don's Habitat ★ Built on a coral bluff overlooking the sea and a tiny beach about 5 minutes north of Kralendijk, this divers' resort, with an air of congenial informality, is for those whose souls belong to the sea. Habitat and its accompanying dive shop are the creation of Capt. Don Stewart, who sailed his schooner from San Francisco through the Panama Canal, arriving in Bonaire in 1962—and he's been here ever since. Known on the island as the "godfather of diving," Captain Don was instrumental in the formation of the Bonaire Marine Park, whereby the entire island became a protected reef.

More than 90% of the guests here opt for a package, which incorporates a variable number of dives, with accommodations ranging from standard doubles to villas with full kitchens and oceanview verandas. Often the hotel hosts live entertainment as well as occasional reef ecology slide shows by local experts and enthusiasts.

Kaya Gobernador N. Debrot 103, Pier 7, Bonaire, N.A. www.habitatbonaire.com. ✆ **800/327-6709** in the U.S. or Canada, or 599/717-8290. Fax 599/717-8240. 63 units. Winter $190 double, $220 suite; off season $149 double, $175 suite. AE, DISC, MC, V. **Amenities:** Restaurant; bar; babysitting; dive program; outdoor pool. *In room:* A/C, TV, fridge, kitchenette (in some), no phone (in some), Wi-Fi (free).

Divi Flamingo Beach Resort & Casino ★ ☺ Modern furnishings, paint, tiles, and rejuvenated air-conditioning have made this once-tired waterfront hostelry quite comfortable. Originally a cluster of flimsy wooden bungalows used to intern German prisoners in World War II, today the resort consists of individual cottages and seafront rooms with private balconies. These accommodations rest on piers above the surf so you can stand on your balcony and watch rainbow-hued tropical fish in the waters below. The resort's original rooms are supplemented timeshare units, forming Club Flamingo. These are the best accommodations, and all can be rented by the day or week. The timeshare units are clustered in a neo-Victorian pavilion facing a curving pool, and each comes with a kitchenette. Chibi-Chibi and Calabas provide satisfying, straightforward meals featuring fresh local seafood and Continental specialties.

J. A. Abraham Blvd. 40, Bonaire, N.A. www.diviflamingo.com. ✆ **800/367-3484** in the U.S., or 599/717-8285. Fax 599/717-8238. 129 units. Winter $200–$230 double, from $240 studio; off season $140–$170 double, from $190 studio. Children 11 and under stay free in parent's room. AE, DISC, MC, V. **Amenities:** 2 restaurants; 2 bars; babysitting; children's programs; dive shop; fitness center; Internet access in lobby; 2 outdoor pools; casino; room service; snorkeling; spa services. *In room:* A/C, TV.

Inexpensive

Coco Palm Garden & Casa Oleander ★ In the tranquil residential area of Belnem, south of the airport and Kralendijk, these vacation homes are a real discovery. Two friendly neighbors, Brigitte and Marin, combined their two properties into a cohesive whole and opened their affordable guesthouses to the world, drawing divers and windsurfers or anyone wanting to get away from the bigger resort hotels. Their accommodations consist of a series of little houses, studios, and apartments. A typical studio comes with one queen-size bed, a kitchen, a porch with tables and chairs, and a small garden with hammock and sun bed. Rooms are well furnished and have small bathrooms with showers. Even though each of the accommodations is self-sufficient, there are public areas, including a terrace for sunning, a pool, and a bar for guests only. The only TV is at the bar.

Kaya Statius van Eps 9, Belnem, Bonaire, N.A. www.cocopalmgarden.com. ✆ **599/717-2108.** Fax 599/717-8193. 23 units. Year-round $66–$76 studio; $76–$86 1 bedroom; $106 2-bedroom house; $211 4-bedroom house. Extra person $16. Children 11 and under $10 extra in parent's room. AE, DISC, MC, V. **Amenities:** Buffet restaurant (Mon and Thurs only); bar; babysitting; outdoor pool; Wi-Fi (free). *In room:* A/C ($12 per day), kitchen, no phone.

Eden Beach Resort ★ ☺ Located directly on one of Bonaire's nicer beaches, this tiny resort provides all the essentials and more at a price that's right. The clean and spacious rooms, studios, and apartments feature simple decor; tile floors; a functional, well-equipped kitchen; and plenty of comfort. Most units have their own private porch or terrace and are only steps away from the beach, pool, patio, restaurant, and bar. A dive shop is located on the premises, and an activity center offers bike, kayak, and windsurf rentals.

Kaya Gobernador N. Debrot 73, Bonaire, N.A. www.edenbeach.com. ✆ **599/717-6720.** Fax 599/717-6710. 46 units. Mid-Apr to mid-Dec $120 studio, $145 1 bedroom, $225 2 bedroom; mid-Dec to mid-Apr $120 studio, $165 1 bedroom, $250 2 bedroom. AE, MC, V. **Amenities:** Restaurant; bar; babysitting; fitness center; outdoor pool. *In room:* A/C, TV, kitchen.

Hotel Rochaline Located in the heart of town and attached to the popular City Café, the Rochaline is Bonaire's take on an urban backpacker/youth hostel. (The name is a merging of the names of the owners' four children.) The rooms upstairs are sparse but clean. Noise from festivities below can be an issue, so bring earplugs if you are a light sleeper.

Kaya Grandi 7, Bonaire, N.A. www.hotelrochaline.com. ✆ **599/717-6886.** Fax 599/717-8265. 17 units. Year-round $69 double. **Amenities:** Restaurant; bar. *In room:* A/C, TV.

WHERE TO DINE

Expensive

La Guernica Fish and Tapas ★ TAPAS In a 150-year-old building, this chic corner restaurant and lounge bar serves the island's finest tapas. The interior is decorated like a hacienda in Mexico, with tiles and artifacts, and outdoor seating overlooks the harbor. La Guernica specializes in seafood, so the best bets are the fried calamari—which makes for a good appetizer or main course—the coconut shrimp with ginger sauce, or the fresh tuna sashimi. There's also a selection of appetizers with an Italian flair.

Kaya Bonaire 4C. ✆ **599/717-5022.** www.laguernica.com. Reservations recommended. Main courses $20–$24. AE, MC, V. Daily 6–10pm.

Mona Lisa ★ FRENCH/INTERNATIONAL A local favorite on the main street of town, this is one of the best places for food that tastes homemade. The prices are more than reasonable, considering the quality of the food and the generous portions. Although many regulars come just to patronize the Dutch bar and catch up on the latest gossip, the old-fashioned dining room deserves serious attention. Guests enjoy the fresh fish of the day (often wahoo) or such meat dishes as a rack of lamb and sirloin steak. The most popular appetizers are onion soup and the shrimp cocktail. Mona Lisa is known for serving fresh vegetables on an island where nearly everything is imported.

Kaya Grandi 15. ✆ **599/717-8718.** Reservations recommended. Main courses $20–$40. AE, MC, V. Restaurant Mon–Fri 6–10pm. Bar Mon–Fri 4pm–2am.

Sunset Bar & Grill SEAFOOD Located next to the Sand Dollar Condominium Resort, this relatively new spot serves some of the freshest seafood in Bonaire. The tables are set on a breezy terrace, where you can watch the waves hit the small beach or watch the ethereal underwater glow as night divers emerge from the sea with their powerful lamps. In addition to seafood and meat, there are vegetarian options. The local goat-cheese fritters and the beef carpaccio is top notch. Follow with a trio of seafood brochette in smoked-tomato-and-crab-butter sauce, or fresh tuna steak prepared to order (try it blackened for a spicy option). Select from the extensive wine list that includes bottles from almost every continent. Cheesecake topped with passion fruit coulis ends the meal on a tangy note.

Kaya Gobernador N. Debrot 77. ✆ **599/788-2698.** www.sunsetrestaurantbonaire.com. Main courses $17–$32. DISC, MC, V. Thurs–Tues 11:30am–3pm and 5–10pm.

Eating Responsibly in Bonaire

Due to the decline of local species, many restaurants have made a choice to stop serving Caribbean lobster and conch. It's also recommended that reef fish (such as grouper, snapper, and grunt) be avoided, even if the server tells you it's okay. Tasty, fresh, and eco-friendly alternatives are pelagic species that live out in open water, such as dorado, wahoo, and barracuda. If seafood isn't your game, don't be afraid to try some local goat cheese or goat stew; while cute, goats are abundant!

Moderate

Bistro De Paris FRENCH This tiny roadside restaurant with indoor and outdoor seating has a casual European feel. The main courses add a healthy twist to traditional French recipes, with plenty of vegetarian options. Try the fish with artichoke and roasted tomatoes, or the rib-eye steak with sun-dried tomatoes. The apple tarte tatin, with caramelized sugar and served a la mode, is exquisite.

Kaya Gobernador N. Debrot 46. ✆ **599/717-7070.** www.bistrodeparis.com. Main courses $15–$25. AE, DISC, MC, V. Mon–Fri 11:30am–2:30pm and 6–10pm; Sat 6–10pm.

Rum Runners ★ INTERNATIONAL/SEAFOOD This casual waterfront restaurant has a breezy yet intimate feel and sits above the water, which happens to be inhabited by a pack of skulking tarpon. The pizza is said to be the best on the island. As a starter, try the calamari or beef yakitori. Seafood lovers should sample the shrimp-and-scallop skewers served with beurre blanc. The filet mignon with a red-wine sauce with strong nutmeg overtones gets rave reviews from carnivores. Save room for the heavenly *fiesta de fruitas:* Bavaros crème topped with strawberry coulis, bathed in a melon soup and garnished with a fresh-fruit kebab.

At Captain Don's Habitat, Kaya Gobernador N. Debrot 103. ✆ **599/717-8290** or 717-7303. www.habitatbonaire.com. Reservations recommended. Main courses $12–$30. AE, MC, V. Daily 7am–10pm.

Zeezicht Restaurant INTERNATIONAL This is the best place in the capital to see the sunset. Join the old salts to watch the sun go down, and look out for the "green flash" that Hemingway wrote about, just after the sun sets. Zeezicht (pronounced *Zay*-zikt, meaning "sea view") has long been popular for its local cooking. It has an extensive menu that includes fresh fish from the nearby market, plus burgers and steak. The restaurant runs an adjacent bistro that serves Asian and Mexican food.

Kaya J. N. E. Craane 12. ✆ **599/717-8434.** Main courses $10–$48. AE, MC, V. Daily 8am–11pm.

BONAIRE'S BEACHES

For the most part, the beaches in Bonaire are full of coral and feel gritty to bare feet. Those on the leeward side (the more tranquil side of the island) are often narrow strips. To compensate, some hotels have shipped in extra sand for their guests.

Bonaire's offshore island—tiny, uninhabited **Klein Bonaire ★★**, just 1.5km (1 mile) off the west coast—has some pristine beaches. Popular for snorkeling, scuba diving, and picnicking, **No Name Beach,** on the north side of Klein Bonaire, features a 273m (896-ft.) white-sand beach. Snorkelers can see a rainbow of colorful fish darting through stunning formations of elkhorn coral. Accessible only by boat, Klein Bonaire is home to sea turtles and other spectacular marine life. Ask at your hotel if arrangements can be made for a trip to the island.

Playa Funchi, within Washington Slagbaai National Park, is good for snorkeling. Regrettably, it has almost no sand and no facilities, and the area surrounding the beach is a bit smelly. On one side of the beach, there's a lagoon where flamingos nest; the other side is good for snorkeling. Also within the park, the more appealing **Boca Slagbaai ★** is picturesque and draws swimmers, snorkelers, and picnickers. You can spot flamingos nearby. A 19th-century building has decent toilets and a small bar and restaurant. Don't venture into the waters barefoot, as the coral beach can be quite rough. A final beach at the national park is **Boca Cocolishi,** a black-sand strip on the northern coast. This is the windiest beach on Bonaire; you'll certainly stay cool as

The *Hooker*

The waters off the coast of Bonaire received an additional attraction in 1984: A rust-bottomed 24m-long (79-ft.) general cargo ship was confiscated by the police, along with its contraband cargo, about 25,000 pounds of marijuana. Known as the *Hilma Hooker* (familiarly dubbed *The Hooker* by everyone on the island), it sank unclaimed (obviously) and without fanfare one calm day, in 30m (98 ft.) of water. Lying just off the southern shore near the capital, its wreck is now a popular dive site.

the trade winds whip up the surf. The waters are too rough for swimming, but it's a good picnic spot.

Many of Bonaire's beaches are along the east coast. The best spot for windsurfers and a favorite for locals and for families with children is **Lac Bay Beach,** on the southern shore of Lac Bay and adjacent **Sourbon.** There are mangroves at the north end of the bay. A couple of windsurfing concessions usually operate here, and food and drink are readily available. One unusual spot is **Nukove Beach,** a minicave in a limestone cliff with a small white-sand channel, which cuts through the dense wall of elkhorn coral near the shore, giving divers and snorkelers easy access to the water. Farther north is **1,000 Steps Beach,** where 67 steps (although it can feel like 1,000 on the way back up) carved out of the limestone cliff lead to a white-sand beach. This beach offers good snorkeling and diving, a unique location and view, and nearly perfect solitude.

DIVING & SNORKELING ★★★

Much of Bonaire's allure is based on its teeming offshore reefs and dive sites. Its true beauty is under the sea, where visibility is 30m (98 ft.) 365 days of the year, and the water temperatures range from 78°F to 82°F (26°C–28°C). One of the richest reef communities in the entire West Indies, Bonaire has plunging walls that descend to a sand bottom at 40m (131 ft.) or so. The reefs are home to various coral formations that grow at different depths, ranging from the knobby brain coral at .9m (3 ft.), to staghorn and elkhorn up to about 3m (10 ft.) deeper, and gorgonians, giant brain, and others. Swarms of rainbow-hued tropical fish inhabit the reefs, and the deep reef slope is home to a range of basket sponges, groupers, and moray eels. Most of the diving is done on the leeward side, where the ocean is calm and usually flat. There are more than 40 dive sites on sharply sloping reefs. Divers from around the world leave with a sense of awe about how good the diving really is.

Bonaire Marine Park ★★ was created to protect the coral-reef ecosystem off Bonaire. The park incorporates the entire coastline of Bonaire and neighboring **Klein Bonaire.** The park is policed, and services and facilities include a visitor information center at the **Karpata Ecological Center,** lectures, slide presentations, films, and permanent dive-site moorings.

Visitors are asked to respect the marine environment and to refrain from activities that may damage it, including sitting or walking on the coral. Even a thin layer of silt can prove fatal to these delicate colonial marine animals that make up the fragile living surface of the coral formations. Because these ecosystems are so fragile, all marine life in and around Bonaire is completely protected. This means no fishing or collecting fish, shells, or corals—dead or alive. Feeding the fish is also illegal, not to mention unhealthy for the fish. Spearfishing is forbidden, as is anchoring; all craft must use permanent moorings, except for emergency stops. (Boats shorter than 13 ft. may use a stone anchor.) Most recreational activity in the marine park takes place on the island's leeward side and among the reefs surrounding Klein Bonaire. Due to safety regulations in a post–September 11 era, diving or snorkeling near any commercial piers requires an additional permit from the harbor master. (In other words, you really should go elsewhere, or hire a guide.)

Because protecting nature is taken seriously here, all divers, snorkelers, windsurfers, and swimmers are required to pay a **nature fee** of $10 for nondivers and $25 for divers. Tags are good for 1 calendar year and also permit admission into Washington Slagbaai National Park. Nondivers 12 and under and residents of the Netherlands are exempt. Tags can be purchased at all dive shops, as well as the STINAPA office in Barcadera. An orientation dive is required for all divers. For more information, contact **STINAPA Bonaire** (**© 599/717-8444;** www.stinapa.org).

The major hotels offer personalized, close-up encounters with the island's fish and other marine life under the expertise of Bonaire's dive guides. **Divi Dive Bonaire,** on the beachfront of the Divi Flamingo Beach Resort & Casino, J. A. Abraham Blvd. 40, north of Kralendijk (**© 800/367-3484** in the U.S., or 599/717-8285; www.diviflamingo.com), is among the island's most complete scuba facilities. It's open daily from 8am to 5pm. It operates out of a well-stocked beachfront building, renting diving equipment and offering expeditions. A resort course for first-time divers costs $93; for experienced divers, a one-tank dive goes for $47, a two-tank dive for $67.

Captain Don's Habitat Dive Shop, Kaya Gobernador N. Debrot 103 (**© 599/717-8290;** www.habitatbonaire.com), is a PADI five-star training facility. The open-air, full-service dive shop includes a classroom, photo/video lab, camera rental facility, equipment repair, and compressor rooms. Habitat's slogan is "Diving Freedom": Divers can take their tanks and dive anywhere, day or night. Most head for the Pike, .8km (½ mile) of protected reef right in front of the property. The highly qualified staff is here to assist and advise, but not to police or dictate dive plans. Diving packages include boat dives, unlimited offshore diving (24 hr. a day), unlimited air tanks, weights, and belts. Some dive packages also include accommodations and meals. If you're not staying at the hotel as part of a dive package, you can visit for a beach dive, costing $52. A boat dive, not including equipment, goes for $62.

Bonaire Dive and Adventure, adjacent to the Sand Dollar Condominium Retreat, Kaya Gobernador N. Debrot 77A (**© 599/717-2229;** www.bonairediveandadventure.com), is open daily from 8:30am to 4:30pm. It offers dive packages, PADI and SSI instruction, and equipment rental and repairs; boat and shore trips with an instructor are available by appointment. A beginning course, including two dives, costs $120 per person. The photo shop offers underwater photo and video shoots, PADI specialty courses by appointment, E-6 slide processing, print developing, and equipment rental and repair.

If you are an experienced diver and have training doing reef cleanups, you can participate in a cleanup dive through **Bonaire Marine Park** (**© 599/717-8444;** www.bmp.org). You must send an e-mail to **marinepark@stinapa.org** to make special arrangements. Additionally, every few months, **Dive Friends Bonaire** (**© 599/717-2929;** www.dive-friends-bonaire.com), together with NetTech NV, organizes cleanup dives. If the timing is wrong and you still want to "do your part" for

Sea Turtle Etiquette

Sea turtles are some of the most highly endangered species in the oceans, and catching even a passing glimpse is a magical experience, so some basics apply if or when you encounter a sea turtle. When you first spot one, resist the urge to move in and get a closer look; you will only scare it off and ruin the opportunity for others to see it. Instead, stay still and watch at a respectful distance as it goes about its business or glides along gracefully. Keep an eye out for identification tags on their flippers or shells, a sure sign these creatures are being closely studied and well protected. It goes without saying, but never approach a turtle or its nest, and never touch or try to touch one—for your safety and theirs. While it seems harmless, it is, in fact, quite stressful for the turtles. (How'd you like to be chased around by strangers all day while holding your breath?)

To learn more about the sea turtles or to learn about current conservation action and how you can participate, contact Sea Turtle Conservation Bonaire (✆ 599/717-2225; www.bonaireturtles.org).

the reef, check out **REEF,** the **Reef Environmental Education Foundation** (www.reef.org), a volunteer monitoring program where divers can log in and add their fish sightings to a global database used by scientists to monitor populations.

Bonaire's coral reefs are also an underwater paradise for snorkelers. They start in just inches of water and, therefore, have dense coral formations in very shallow surf. Most snorkeling on the island is conducted in 5m (16 ft.) of water or less, and there's plenty to see even at this depth. As you travel around the island, particularly in the northern area, you'll see evidence of prehistoric reefs now 12 to 30m (39–98 ft.) above sea level, having lived submerged for hundreds of thousands of years and then uplifted as the island slowly rose.

Snorkeling equipment can be rented at **Bonaire Dive and Adventure,** Kaya Gobernador N. Debrot 77A (**✆ 599/717-2229;** www.bonairediveandadventure.com), and **Captain Don's Habitat Dive Shop** (p. 136). A full day's rental of mask, fins, and snorkel costs $10. Most snorkelers swim out to reefs from points directly offshore, but most of the dive operators will also allow snorkelers to ride out to dive sites with scuba divers for $12, plus the equipment rental cost. For those who want to try something different, **Outdoor Bonaire ★** (**✆ 599/791-6272;** www.outdoorbonaire.com) offers cave snorkeling, which combines rock climbing and spelunking with exploration of small subterranean pools.

For a relaxing morning or afternoon sail and snorkel trip, board the ***Woodwind*** (**✆ 599/786-7055;** www.woodwindbonaire.com). For $45 (4 hr.) or $50 (5 hr.) per person, the trip includes snorkel gear, lunch, and nonalcoholic beverages. Or try **Pirate Cruises** (**✆ 599/780-9933**) with Captain Mike, aboard a 17m (56-ft.) privateer ship that offers half-day sail and snorkel trips, as well as sunset or dinner cruises daily. If you are eager to finally see a wild turtle, he offers a turtle lover's snorkel trip aboard an 11m (36-ft.) dive boat to some of the best sites for turtle encounters. All trips leave from Karel's Beach Bar Pier downtown on the waterfront, and reservations can be made at Zeezicht Restaurant across the street.

SPORTS & OUTDOOR PURSUITS

Bonaire is most striking underwater, but the sailing and birding are great, too.

BIRD-WATCHING Bonaire is home to about 200 species of birds, 80 of which are indigenous to the island. Most famous are its flamingos, which can number 15,000 during the mating season. For great places to bring your binoculars, see "Exploring the Island," below. **Bonaire Dive & Adventure,** Kaya Gobernador N. Debrot 77A (✆ **599/717-2229**; www.bonairediveandadventure.com), offers expertly guided trips to the island's best bird havens for $50.

FISHING Bonaire's offshore fishing grounds have some of the best fishing in the Caribbean, and the Bonaire Marine Park allows line fishing. A good day's catch might include mackerel, tuna, wahoo, dolphin (mahimahi), blue marlin, amberjack, grouper, sailfish, or snapper. Bonaire is also one of the best-kept secrets of bonefishing enthusiasts, a challenging style of fishing that is strictly catch and release—given global decline of fishing stocks, a far preferable option for fish and humans alike.

Your best bet is Chris Morkos of **Piscatur Fishing Supplies,** Kaya Herman 4, Playa Pabao (✆ **599/717-8774;** www.piscatur.com). A native Bonairean, he has fished all his life. A half-day deep-sea or reef charter (up to 5 hr.) with up to six people runs $400, a three-quarter day (6½ hr.) is $475, and a full day (8 hr.) is $550. A half-day wading trip is $400 for one or two people up to 4 hours, and $475 for a half-day shore trip up to 5 hours with three people. If your group has more than six people, they can be added for $25 each. Strict regulations on fishing and size limits, as well as high levels of concern about the reef fish, mean that catch and release may be the best way to go, even if your guide says otherwise.

HIKING **Washington Slagbaai National Park** (see "Exploring the Island," below) has a varied terrain; those ambitious enough to climb some of its steep hills are rewarded with panoramic views. The hiking possibilities are seemingly endless. Small hidden beaches with crashing waters by the cliffs provide ideal spots for picnics. After going on patrol with a ranger, we could see that this is a big park, and it's surprisingly easy to get lost, injured, or dehydrated, so it may be best for beginners to go with a guide. **Outdoor Bonaire** (✆ **599/791-6272;** www.outdoorbonaire.com) can arrange hiking, free climbing, and overnight camping adventures in the national park.

KAYAKING Paddle the protected waters of Lac Bay, or head for the miles of flats and mangroves in the south (the island's nursery), where you can see baby fish and wildlife. Kayak rentals are available at **Jibe City,** Lac Bay (✆ **599/717-5233;** www.jibecity.com), for $30 per half-day or $40 for a full day. One-man kayaks rent by the hour for $10, double kayaks are $15 per hour, and stand-up paddle boards are $15 per hour. A half-day guided tour through the mangroves can be arranged through **Mangrove Info and Kayak Center** (✆ **599/780-5353;** www.mangrovecenter.com). A 1-hour tour is $27, and a 2-hour tour costs $46. For those who are not able to kayak but still want to see the ecosystem, it gives tours on a solar-powered boat for $26 per hour. It's closed on Sundays. **Outdoor Bonaire** (✆ **599/791-6272;** www.outdoorbonaire.com) runs guided kayak tours through the mangroves or out to Klein Bonaire for $50 per person. It can even do a night kayak or custom build a tour for your specific interests.

KITEBOARDING This relatively extreme sport combines windsurfing with kite flying and allows boarders to sail, leap, and flip along the water's surface. On Atlantis Beach, at the southern end of the island, **Kiteboarding Bonaire** (✆ **599/786-6138**

or 701-5483; www.kiteboardingbonaire.com) helps beginners get started with 3-hour intro lessons or multiday packages. Those who've already taken an intro course and received a certification are allowed to rent equipment and go it alone.

LANDSAILING ★ With less than 5 minutes of instruction and even less experience, you can be cruising at top speed around the largest landsailing track in the world. This fun sport requires little knowledge of sailing and just a rudimentary understanding of physics. Let the natural trade winds speed you along an .8km (½-mile) oval track. **Landsailing Bonaire** (✆ **599/786-8122** or 717-8122; www.landsailingbonaire.com) can be found on the road to Rincón. An hour rental plus a 15-minute lesson will cost $50, or $30 for a half-hour.

MOUNTAIN BIKING Biking is an ideal way to see Bonaire's hidden beauty; you can explore more than 300km (186 miles) of trails and dirt roads, venturing off the beaten path to enjoy the scenery. Ask at the tourist office for a trail map that outlines the most scenic routes. You can check with your hotel about arranging a trip, or call **Bonaire Wellness Connexions** (✆ **599/717-4241** or 599/785-0767; www.bonairewellness.com), which offers guided bike excursions for every skill and endurance level, from the leisurely pedal-pusher to the grit-in-your-teeth, mud-splattered enthusiast. Mountain bikes can also be rented from a number of other locations, including the **Bike Shop** (✆ **599/560-7000**) and **Buddy Dive Resort** (✆ **599/717-5080;** www.buddydive.com), which has mountain-bike rentals for $16. Bikes can also be rented for Washington Slagbaai National Park through **Caribbean Sports Bonaire** (✆ **599/787-0270;** www.caribbeansportsbonaire.com) for $18 per day.

WINDSURFING Lac Bay's consistent conditions and shallow, calm waters are suitable for windsurfers with a wide range of skill levels. **Jibe City** (✆ **599/717-5233;** www.jibecity.com) and **Bonaire Windsurf Place** (✆ **599/717-2288;** www.bonairewindsurfplace.com) rent equipment; boards and sails are $75 for a full day. Beginner lessons at 10am, 1pm, and 4pm are $50 each, including equipment. Packages are available.

EXPLORING THE ISLAND

Bonaire Tours and Vacations (✆ **599/717-8778;** www.bonairetours.com) will show you the island, both north and south, taking in the flamingos, slave huts, conch shells, Goto Lake, the Amerindian inscriptions, and other sights. You can take a half-day Island Journey Tour, lasting 3 hours and costing from $28 per person, which allows you to see the entire northern section and the southern part as far as the slave huts.

Kralendijk

Because Bonaire has always been off the beaten track, highlights are modest and few. You can walk the length of sleepy Kralendijk—the name translates literally into "dyke made of coral"—in less than half an hour. Stroll along the seafront, with its views and restaurants, and along Kaya Grandi, the major shopping district. Just south of the town square, tiny Fort Oranje boasts a cannon dating from the time of Napoleon. The town has some charming Dutch Caribbean architecture—gabled roofs painted ochre and terra cotta. If you've got a yen for fruit, visit the waterfront food market.

Bonaire's minuscule **Fort Oranje** takes more time to find than to explore, but provides a pleasant diversion. The tiny fort—Bonaire's oldest building—is quaint and makes for a pleasant walking destination.

A 10-minute walk away, the **Museo Boneriano (Bonaire Museum),** Kaya J. C. van der Ree 7 (© **599/717-8868**), displays a haphazard collection of shells from local species, excavated human remains from a Caicetto burial site, and various antiques and artifacts of European settlement that offer clues into the island's colonial history. With few signs to make sense of the collection, a guided tour is recommended. The museum is open weekdays 8am to noon and 2 to 4:30pm. Admission is $2.

The Tour North

The road north is one of the most beautiful stretches in the Antilles, with turquoise waters on your left and coral cliffs on your right. You can stop at several points along this road, where there are paved paths for strolling or bicycling.

There are plans to erect giant white windmills to harness the abundant wind power and reduce dependency on oil, which is currently imported via massive oil tankers from Venezuela. The long-term goal is to reduce dependence on fossil fuels by as much as 80%, which may impact some of the island's scenic vistas but will be a net gain for this eco-friendly island.

After leaving Kralendijk and passing the Sunset Beach Hotel and the desalination plant, you'll come to **Radio Nederland Wereld Omroep (Dutch World Radio).** It's a 13-tower 300,000-watter. Opposite the transmitting station is a lovers' promenade. Built by nature, it's an ideal spot for a picnic.

Continuing, you'll pass the storage tanks of the Bonaire Petroleum Corporation and the road heading to **Goto Meer,** the island's inland sector with a saltwater lake. Several flamingos prefer this spot to the salt flats in the south.

Just north of Kralendijk, **Barcadera** is an old cave once used to trap goats. Take the stone steps down to the cave and examine the stalactites. Farther north, just past the Radio Nederland towers, **1,000 Steps Beach** offers picturesque coves, a craggy coastline, and tropical waters of changing hues.

Bonaire's oldest village is **Rincón.** Slaves who used to work in the salt flats in the south once lived here. Today the quiet village is home to the **Rincón Ice Cream Parlour,** which makes homemade ice cream in a variety of interesting flavors, and a couple of very local bars. Above the bright roofs of the village is the crest of a hill called **Para Mira,** which means "stop and look." If you're hungry, stop for a traditional lunch of *stoba* (stew) and *funchi* (polenta), or slimy but tasty cactus soup at the famous **Rose Inn,** Kaya Buyaba 4 (© **599/717-6420**). It's open for lunch Thursday to Monday 11am till 4pm.

A side path outside Rincón takes you to some **Arawak inscriptions** supposedly 500 years old. The petroglyph designs are in pink-red dye. At nearby **Boca Onima,** you'll find craggy grottoes of coral. You can also take a short bypass to **Seroe Largu,** which has a good view of Kralendijk and the sea. Lovers frequent this spot at night. Stop at the home of **Sherman Gibbs,** Kaminda Tras di Montaña. Sherman com-

Name That Street Theme

As you meander along, read the street signs and try to figure out their theme. Each town will designate a certain theme (musical instruments, women's names, gemstones, fish, and so on). This makes it easy to figure out someone's location if you know only their street address!

bines plastic bottles, boat motors, buoys, car seats, and just about everything to create an "outsider's" art exhibit worth a brief gander. How exactly did he get that motorcycle onto the top of that enormous cactus anyway?

On the outskirts of Rincón, a large white building marks the spot of a new and not-to-be-missed highlight of any island tour. **Magazina di Rei** (**© 599/786-2101;** www.magazinadirei.com) translates as the "King's Warehouse" and is the second-oldest building on the island (the first is Fort Oranje back in town). Once used to store provisions for slaves, it has been restored and transformed into a small museum and cultural center that preserves and depicts the culture, history, architecture, and traditions of early Bonaire. Drop by for a tour guided by the friendly staff, then have a wander through the gardens, where re-creations of houses from different eras are on display. Local children learn traditional crafts, dances, and recipes from elders, so don't be surprised if you're offered some homemade tamarind juice or ice-cold limeade and invited to try a few local dance steps. The center is open Monday to Saturday from 9am to 5pm.

Washington Slagbaai National Park ★★

Washington Slagbaai National Park (**© 599/788-9015;** www.washingtonpark-bonaire.org) has varied terrain that includes desertlike areas, secluded beaches, caverns, a visitor center, and a bird sanctuary. It's easy to find—just look for the yellow-and-green lizards painted on telephone polls along the road. They lead you to the park entrance. Occupying about 6,000 hectares (14,826 acres) of Bonaire's northwesternmost territory, the park was once plantation land, producing divi-divi, aloe, and charcoal; today it functions as a wildlife preserve. The reserve showcases Bonaire's geology, animals, and vegetation. Residents include 203 bird species, thousands of organ-pipe and prickly-pear cacti, endemic parrots, parakeets, flamingos, iguanas, and blue lizards. Feral goats and donkeys, left over from the colonial period, continue to roam the hills browsing voraciously on native and declining plant species, though the park is attempting to remove these invasive species over time.

You can see the park in a few hours, although it takes days to appreciate it fully. If you want to drive through the park, you must use a four-wheel-drive vehicle. Even so, you may want to reconsider going if it has rained recently, as the roads quickly become deeply mired in mud and difficult to navigate—even in a four-wheel-drive. There are two routes: a 24km (15-mile) "short" route, marked by green arrows, and a 35km (22-mile) "long" route, marked by yellow arrows. The roads are well marked and safe, but somewhat rugged, although improvements are ongoing. For those wanting a closer look, the hiking possibilities are nearly endless. Park entrance is gained through purchase of a **nature/squire tag** (the mandatory pass costs $15; free for children 12 and under) for general park entry or $25 if you wish to snorkel, swim, or dive. The park is open daily except holidays from 8am to 5pm. You must enter before 2:45pm. Guide booklets, maps, and a small museum are at the gate. For those looking to leave the island just a tad tidier than it was when they arrived, volunteer opportunities to paint, prune, and mend fences can be arranged by sending an e-mail to **washingtonpark@stinapa.org**.

Whatever route you take, there are a few important stops you shouldn't miss. Just past the gate is **Salina Matijs,** a salt flat that's home to flamingos during the rainy season. Beyond the salt flat on the road to the right is **Boka Chikitu,** a white-sand beach and bay. A few miles up the beach lies **Boka Cocolishi,** a two-part black-sand beach. Many a couple has raved about their romantic memories of this beach, perfect for a secluded picnic. A ridge of calcareous algae separates its deep, rough seaward side and calm, shallow basin. The basin and the beach were formed by small pieces of coral and mollusk shells (*cocolishi* means "shells"), thus the black sand. The basin itself has no current, so it's perfect for snorkeling close to shore. **Boka Slagbaai** has a picturesque beach and positively charming restaurant where you can cool off with a bite, a beer, and a view of the ocean on one side and a serene lake teeming with shore birds such as flamingos, egrets, and herons on the other.

The main road leads to **Boka Bartol,** a bay full of living and dead elkhorn coral, sea fans, and reef fish. A popular watering hole good for bird-watching is **Poos Mangel. Wajaca** is a remote reef, perfect for divers and home to the island's most exciting sea creatures, including turtles, octopus, and triggerfish. Immediately inland is **Mount Brandaris;** at 235m (771 ft.), it's Bonaire's highest peak. At its foot is **Bronswinkel Well,** a watering spot for pigeons and parakeets. About 200 species of birds live in the park, many with such exotic names as banaquit and black-faced grassquit. Bonaire has few mammals, but you'll likely see a few goats and donkeys. If you encounter donkeys outside of the sanctuary or inside the park, remember that it's illegal to feed them and advisable to not approach or touch them, as they can be quite dangerous if frightened. Not touching is particularly important when encountering a colt whose mother is probably nearby watching, and who may abandon her young if your smell masks its natural odor, used to help Mom recognize her baby.

The Tour South

Just south of Kralendijk, next to the airport down a dirt road, the **Donkey Sanctuary ★** (**© 599/956-7607;** www.donkeysanctuary.org) is a sure bet for donkey spotting, and provides a safe haven for many of the island's 300 to 400 feral donkeys that previously roamed the entire island and fell victim to car accidents with increasing frequency. The park is open daily from 10am to 5pm; drive-through closes at 4pm. Entrance fee is $6 for adults and $3 for children, but additional donations are welcomed, as are a volunteered hour or two helping to clean out a few stalls, or feed or brush these adorable orphans.

Heading south, you then come to the **salt flats ★**, where the brilliantly colored Caribbean pink flamingos live. Bonaire shelters the largest accessible nesting and breeding grounds in the world. The flamingos build high mud mounds to hold their eggs. The best time to see the birds is in spring, when they're nesting and tending their young. Slaves once worked the salt flats, and you can still see the pinkish pools where the salt is slowly extracted from the water, then piled in huge glistening white **salt pyramids** ready for export. The government has rebuilt some primitive **slave huts,** bare shelters little more than waist high. The slaves slept in these huts, and returned to their homes in Rincón in the north on weekends. The centuries-old salt pans have been reactivated by the International Salt Company. Near the salt pans, you'll see some 9m (30-ft.) obelisks in white, blue, and orange, built in 1838 to help mariners locate their proper anchorages.

Farther down the coast is the island's oldest lighthouse, **Willemstoren,** built in 1837. Still farther along, **Sorobon Beach, Lac Bay Beach,** and **Boka Cai** come into view. They're at landlocked Lac Bay, which is ideal for swimming and snorkeling. Conch shells are stacked up on the beach. The water here is so vivid and clear, you can see coral 20 to 36m (66–118 ft.) down in the reef-protected waters.

Hungry after your drive? Follow the signs heading back to town to **Maiky Snack** (**© 599/786-0086** or 599/700-6785) for a local lunch under the shade of a divi-divi tree. The papaya and cucumber *stobas* (stews) with goat meat are served with rice or

Boogie with Moogie

Local musician Moogie plays bongos while serenading the crowd with familiar favorites and original tunes. His sound is distinctive and he lends a fun, relaxed vibe to every venue. He plays during dinner on Wednesdays at Cactus Blue restaurant (✆ 599/717-4564; www.cactusbluebonaire.com) and Thursdays at Rum Runners (✆ 599/717-8290).

funchi (polenta), and the fresh fish of the day is topped with a sweet Creole sauce. It's open Friday to Wednesday for lunch from 11:30am to 4pm.

SHOPPING

Aruba has more stores and better prices than Bonaire, but dive-related items such as dive watches, underwater cameras, and marine-themed jewelry are abundant. Most shops are in the Harborside Mall and on Kaya Grandi in Kralendijk. Most shops are open 9am to noon and 2 to 6pm. ***Tip:*** When a cruise ship is in harbor, shops stay open longer, and small stands selling local wares and affordable jewelry appear in the town square.

Benetton, Kaya Grandi 29 (✆ **599/717-5107**), claims to offer its brightly colored merchandise at prices about a quarter less than at most U.S. outlets.

Littman Jewelers, Kaya Grandi 33 (✆ **599/717-7750;** www.bonairelittmanstores.com), sells Tag Heuer dive watches and also carries exquisite jewelry. **Atlantis,** down the street at Kaya Grandi 32B (✆ **599/717-7730;** www.atlantisbonaire.com), has a similar selection of jewelry and watches.

Next door is Littman's **Anything Artistique** (✆ **599/717-7750;** www.bonairelittmanstores.com), selling standard and hand-painted T-shirts, plus sandals, hats, Gottex swimsuits, gift items, costume jewelry, and toys, as well as original glass and metal sculptures and plenty of casual jewelry.

Other stores you might want to visit include **Jewel of Bonaire,** Kaya Grandi 36 (✆ **599/717-8890**), which sells handmade marine-themed jewelry; and **Best Pearls Bonaire,** Kaya Grandi 32 (✆ **599/796-7451;** www.bestpearlsbonaire.com), which carries pearls, casual wear, and gifts. **Bamali,** Kaya Grandi 26A (✆ **599/717-4833**), sells men's and women's clothing, silver jewelry, and accessories imported from Indonesia, as well as buttery leather handbags and belts from South America.

BONAIRE AFTER DARK

Bonaire's nightlife is, for the most part, subdued and relaxed. Head out along the waterfront in Kralendjik and follow the small crowd to find the fun; then order the island's signature beer, Heineken Bright, or try a Polar, brewed in Venezuela.

To learn more about Bonaire's spectacular marine life, or just to meet fellow nature lovers and dive enthusiasts, ask about the slide and video shows given by local experts. They usually take place around 6:30pm about once a week, are commonly held at either **Captain Don's Habitat** (p. 136) or **Buddy Dive** (p. 139), and are free and open to the public. Look in the back of *Bonaire Nights* for dates, times, and locations.

Divi Flamingo Beach Resort & Casino, J. A. Abraham Blvd. 40 (✆ **599/717-8285;** www.diviflamingo.com), has blackjack tables, roulette, poker, Wheel of Fortune, video games, and slot machines. Hours are Monday to Saturday from 8pm to 4am and Sunday 7pm to 3am. If the slots don't inspire you or you're overwhelmed by the smell of smoke, walk over to their beach bar and indulge in a glass of house wine.

Karel's Beach Bar and Cappuccino Bar, on the waterfront (✆ **599/717-8434**), perches above the sea on stilts. Zeezicht's full menu (p. 134) is also available to patrons of Karel's, as Johan Visser owns both restaurants. You can sit at the long rectangular bar with many of the island's dive and boating professionals, or select a table near the balustrades overlooking the illuminated surf. Local bands entertain on Fridays, and a flat-screen TV is tuned to ESPN.

Down the road, **City Café,** Kaya Isla Riba 3 (no phone; www.citybonaire.com), remains the island's most popular casual hangout and is the place to see and be seen, whether you're a tourist, a local, or a resident American med student taking a well-earned study break.

Little Havana, Kaya Bonaire 4 (✆ **599/700-5927;** www.littlehavanabonaire.com), with its dark-wood furniture and Cuban feel, is another hot spot on the island's tiny nightlife scene. Live jazz on weekends and mellow jazz vinyl spun by a DJ during the week attract people to the indoor and outdoor tables just steps away from the waterfront.

To really get away from it all, try some romance on the high seas aboard the ***Samur*** (✆ **599/717-5592;** www.samursailing.com), an authentic Siamese junk that offers starlight evening sails with champagne, appetizers, or a full seven-course homemade Thai dinner. Charters leave from the pier in between the Sand Dollar Condominiums and Den Laman Restaurant at Kaya Gobernador N. Debrot 77.

THE BRITISH VIRGIN ISLANDS

7

With its small bays and hidden coves, once havens for pirates, the British Virgin Islands are among the world's loveliest cruising areas. The B.V.I. include some 50 islands (although that figure includes small, uninhabited cays or spits of land). Only three are of any significant size: Tortola (which means "Dove of Peace"), Virgin Gorda ("Fat Virgin"), and Jost Van Dyke. The smaller islands have colorful names, such as Fallen Jerusalem and Ginger.

ESSENTIALS

Visitor Information

Before you go, contact the **British Virgin Islands Tourist Board,** 1 W. 34th St., Ste. 303, New York, NY 10001 (✆ **800/835-8530** or 212/563-3117). Other branches of the **British Virgin Islands Information Office** are in the United Kingdom; contact the **B.V.I. Information Office,** 15 Upper Grosvenor St., London W1K 7PJ (✆ 0**20/7355-9585**).

The tourist board's official website is **www.bvitourism.com**. On Tortola, the **B.V.I. Tourist Board** is in the Akara Building, De Castro Street, Road Town (✆ **284/494-3134**).

Getting There

BY PLANE **Beef Island,** the site of the major airport serving the British Virgins, the Terrence B. Lettsome Terminal, is connected to Tortola by the one-lane **Queen Elizabeth Bridge.**

There are no nonstop flights from the U.S. to the British Virgin Islands, but you can make connections from San Juan, Puerto Rico, and St. Thomas to Beef Island/Tortola. (See chapters 16 and 26 for information on flying to these islands.)

Your best bet to reach Beef Island/Tortola is **American Eagle** (✆ **800/433-7300** in the U.S. and Canada, or 284/495-2559; www.aa.com), which has dozens of flights to its hub in San Juan, and at least four daily trips from San Juan to Beef Island/Tortola.

Another choice, if you're on one of Tortola's neighboring islands, is the much less reliable **LIAT** (✆ **888/844-LIAT** [5428]; www.liatairline.com). This Caribbean carrier makes the short hop to Tortola from Antigua and St. Maarten in small planes not known for their frequency or careful scheduling. Reservations are made through travel agents or through the larger U.S.-based airlines that connect with LIAT hubs.

Air Sunshine (✆ **800/327-8900** in the U.S. and Canada, or 284/495-8900; www.airsunshine.com) flies between San Juan or St. Thomas to Beef Island/Tortola and Virgin Gorda.

BY FERRY You can travel from Charlotte Amalie, St. Thomas, by public ferry to West End and Road Town on Tortola, a 45-minute voyage along Drake's Channel through the islands. One-way crossings range from $25 to $28, with round-trips costing from $49. Boats making this run include **Native Son** (✆ **284/494-5674;** www.nativesonferry.com) and **Smith's Ferry Service** (✆ **284/495-4495**). **Inter-Island Boat Services** (✆ **284/495-4166**) has routes from St. John to the West End on Tortola.

[FastFACTS] THE BRITISH VIRGIN ISLANDS

Banks Banks are generally open Monday to Thursday 8am to 3pm, Friday from 9am to 5pm. Most banks have ATMs.

Currency The U.S. dollar is the legal currency in the B.V.I., much to the surprise of British travelers. *Prices in this chapter are quoted in U.S. dollars.*

Customs You can bring items intended for your personal use into the British Virgin Islands, but only in discreet amounts. In other words, yes to a bottle of perfume or even two, but no to two suitcases filled with unopened fragrances. For returning U.S. residents, the duty-free allowance is only $800, providing you have been out of the country for 48 hours. You can send unsolicited gifts home if they total less than $100 per day to any single address. You don't have to pay duty on items classified as handicrafts, art, or antiques.

Electricity The electrical current is 110-volt AC (60 cycles), as in the United States.

Emergencies Dial ✆ **999** in the event of an emergency.

Entry Requirements U.S. citizens and Canadians, plus others, need a valid passport.

Language The official language is English.

Liquor Laws Alcoholic beverages can be sold any day of the week, including Sunday. You can have an open container on the beach, but be careful not to litter, or you will be fined.

Mail Postal rates in the British Virgin Islands are 50¢ for either an airmail postcard or a first-class airmail letter (½ oz.) to the United States or Canada

Maps The best map of the British Virgin Islands is published by Vigilate and is sold at most bookstores in Road Town.

Medical Assistance The B.V.I.'s major hospital is **Peebles Hospital** in Road Town (✆ **284/494-3497**) on Tortola; the island has more than a dozen doctors. If you need medical help, your hotel will put you in touch with the islands' medical staff.

Newspapers & Magazines The B.V.I. has no daily newspaper, but the *Island Sun,* published Wednesday and Friday, is a good source of information on local entertainment, as is the *BVI Beacon,* published on Thursday. *Standpoint* is another helpful publication that comes out on Monday and Saturday.

Safety Crime is rare here; in fact, the British Virgin Islands are among the safest places in the Caribbean. Still, you should take all the usual precautions you would anywhere, and don't leave items unattended on the beach.

The British Virgin Islands

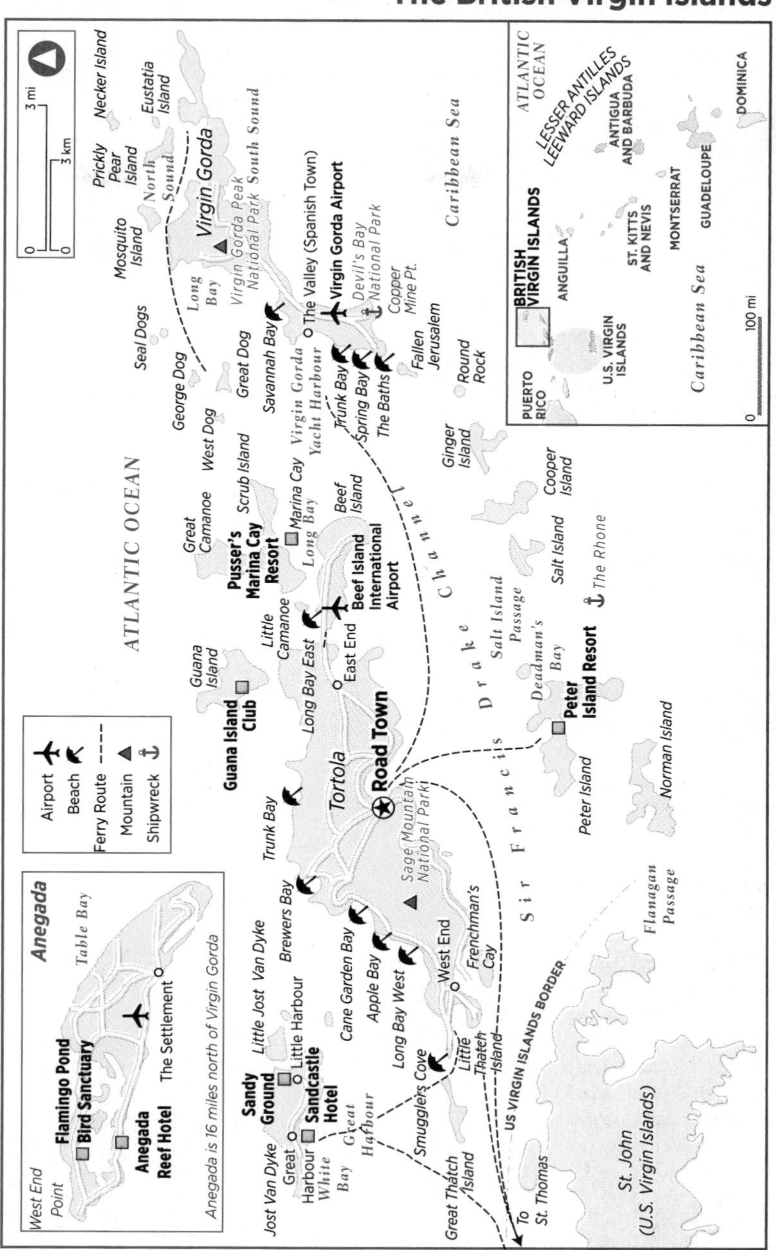

Taxes There is no sales tax. A government tax of 7% is imposed on all hotel rooms. A $20 departure tax is collected from everyone leaving by air, $5 for those departing by ferry, or $7 if departing by cruise ship.

Telephone You can call the British Virgins from the United States by just dialing **1,** the area code **284,** and the number. From all public phones and from some hotels, you can access **MCI** by dialing ✆ **800/888-8000.** You can reach **Sprint** at ✆ **800/877-4646** and **AT&T** at ✆ **800/225-5288.**

Time The islands operate on Atlantic Standard Time year-round. In the peak winter season, when it's 10am in the British Virgins, it's 9am on the U.S. East Coast (EST). However, when the U.S. goes on daylight saving time, EST is the same as B.V.I. time.

Tipping & Service Charges Most hotels add on a 5% to 15% service charge; ask if it's already included when you're initially quoted a price. A 10% service charge is often (but not always) added on to restaurant bills; you can leave another 5% if you thought the service was unusually good. You usually don't need to tip taxi drivers, since most own their own cabs, but you can tip 10% if they've been unusually helpful.

Water The tap water in the British Virgin Islands is safe to drink.

Weather During the winter, temperatures in the British Virgin Islands range between 72°F and 82°F (22°C–28°C). September is the warmest month, with temperatures averaging 90°F (32°C). Temperatures rarely drop below 77°F (25°C) in winter or rise above 90°F (32°C) in summer.

TORTOLA ★★

There's no better place to launch your own sailing adventure than in the bareboat capital of the world: Tortola, the largest (13 miles by 3 miles) and most populous of the British Virgin Islands. But you don't have to be a sailor to appreciate the quiet, understated beauty of Tortola, no matter how many flocks of sails bob in the Road Town harbor. Unwind to the soft caress of trade winds, the gentle green hills that slope down to sparkling waters, the secluded white-sand beaches and hidden coves.

Beaches Beaches are rarely crowded on Tortola. You'll have to navigate roller-coaster hills to get to the island's finest, **Cane Garden Bay**, but its fine white sand and sheltering palms are well worth the trip. **Smugglers Cove**, at the extreme western end of Tortola, is a crescent of white sand with calm turquoise waters. A favorite with locals, Smugglers Cove is also popular with snorkelers, who explore a world of sea fans, sponges, parrotfish, and elkhorn and brain corals.

Things to Do **Charter a sailboat** if you haven't already arrived in your own boat -- these are some of the world's best cruising waters, and exploring the island's cays and coves by boat is serendipity unbound. Across **Drake Channel** lies **Norman Isle**, the inspiration for Robert Louis Stevenson's *Treasure Island*, for great snorkeling. No visit to Tortola is complete without a trip to **Sage Mountain National Park**, a primeval rainforest where you can picnic while overlooking neighboring cays.

Eating & Drinking While many guests rarely dine outside their hotels, a venture out to one of the local restaurants is highly recommended. **Road Town** offers the largest concentration of cheap and authentic Caribbean eateries in the B.V.I. Be sure to sample the **roti**—Caribbean/Indian-style burritos or turnovers stuffed with curried chicken or goat, potatoes and peas or carrots. **Rum punch** is the island

Tortola

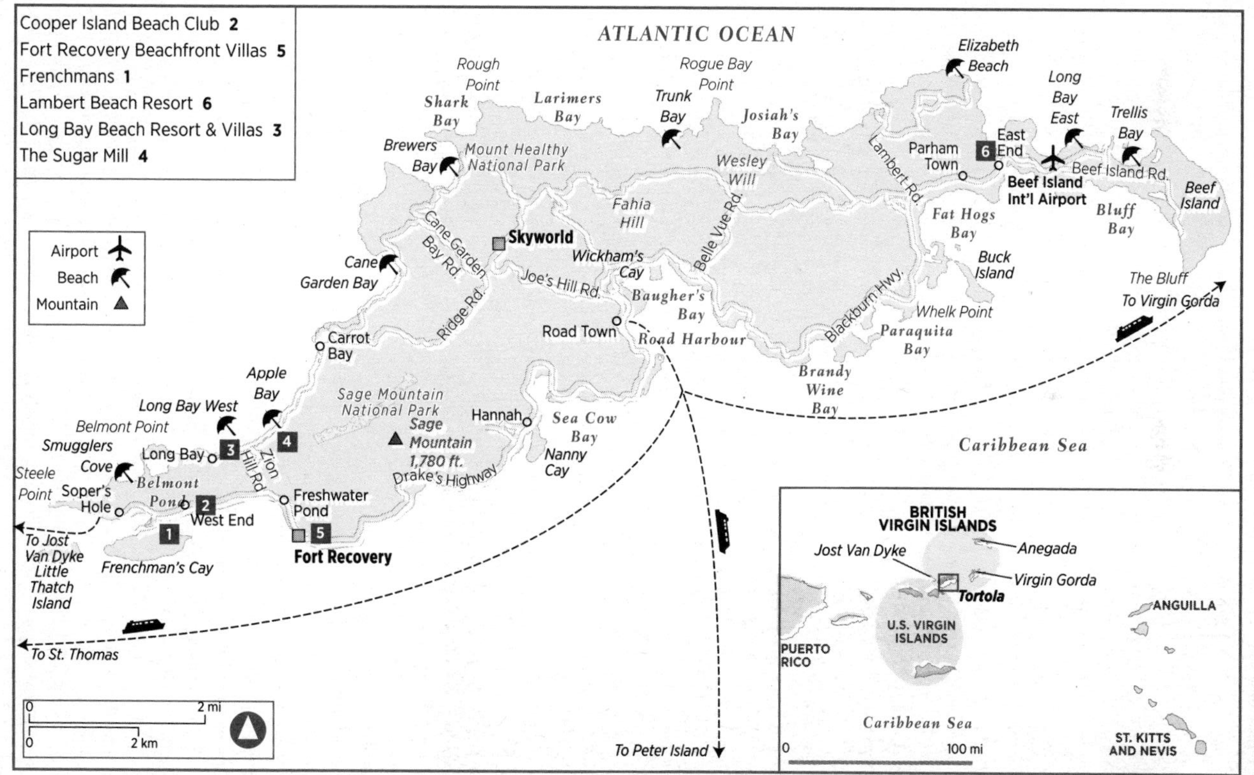

Cooper Island Beach Club 2
Fort Recovery Beachfront Villas 5
Frenchmans 1
Lambert Beach Resort 6
Long Bay Beach Resort & Villas 3
The Sugar Mill 4
Airport
Beach
Mountain
ATLANTIC OCEAN
Rough Point
Shark Bay
Larimers Bay
Trunk Bay
Rogue Bay Point
Josiah's Bay
Elizabeth Beach
Long Bay East
Trellis Bay
Brewers Bay
Mount Healthy National Park
Wesley Will
Lambert Rd.
Parham Town
East End
Beef Island Rd.
Beef Island Int'l Airport
Beef Island
Bluff Bay
Fahia Hill
Belle Vue Rd.
Fat Hogs Bay
Skyworld
Cane Garden Bay Rd.
Wickham's Cay
Cane Garden Bay
Joe's Hill Rd.
Baugher's Bay
Buck Island
Blackburn Hwy.
The Bluff
To Virgin Gorda
Whelk Point
Paraquita Bay
Ridge Rd.
Road Town
Road Harbour
Carrot Bay
Brandy Wine Bay
Apple Bay
Long Bay West
Sage Mountain National Park
Belmont Point
Hannah
Sea Cow Bay
Sage Mountain 1,780 ft.
Smugglers Cove
Long Bay
Zion Hill Rd
Nanny Cay
Drake's Highway
Caribbean Sea
Steele Point
Soper's Hole
Belmont Pond
West End
Freshwater Pond
Fort Recovery
To Jost Van Dyke
Little Thatch Island
Frenchman's Cay
To St. Thomas
To Peter Island
0 2 mi
0 2 km
BRITISH VIRGIN ISLANDS
Jost Van Dyke
Anegada
Virgin Gorda
Tortola
ANGUILLA
U.S. VIRGIN ISLANDS
PUERTO RICO
Caribbean Sea
0 100 mi
ST. KITTS AND NEVIS

cocktail of choice, but beware; it can be deceptively strong. **Conch** and **lobster** are top seafood selections.

Nightlife & Entertainment Nightlife on Tortola is of the laidback, **beach bar** variety; you'll have to go elsewhere for clanging casinos and big entertainment complexes. Head to a popular hangout like the **Bomba Shack** in Apple Bay—a surfside shack constructed of driftwood and broken surfboards—for rollicking full-moon parties. Steel bands and scratch bands appear regularly around **Road Town**, hammered oil drums or steel "pans" in tow. Pick up a copy of *Limin' Times*, an events listing, at your hotel.

Essentials

VISITOR INFORMATION A **B.V.I. Tourist Board Office,** at the center of Road Town near the ferry dock (✆ **284/494-3134**), has information about hotels, restaurants, tours, and more. Pick up a copy of *The Welcome Tourist Guide,* which has a useful map of the island.

GETTING THERE Because Tortola is the gateway to the British Virgin Islands, the information on how to get here is covered in "Getting There," under "Essentials," earlier in this chapter.

GETTING AROUND **Taxis** meet every arriving flight. Government regulations prohibit renting a car at the airport, so you'll have to take a taxi to your hotel. Fares are set by the government, and taxis are unmetered. The fare from the Beef Island airport to Road Town is $30 each for one to three passengers. A **taxi tour** lasting 2½ hours costs $65 to $85 for one to three people. To call a taxi in Road Town, dial ✆ **284/494-2322;** on Beef Island, call ✆ **284/495-1982.**

A handful of local companies and U.S.-based chains rent cars. **Itgo** (✆ **284/494-5150;** www.itgobvi.com) is located at 1 Wickham's Cay, Road Town; **Avis** (✆ **800/331-1084** in the U.S. and Canada, or 284/494-3322; www.avis.com) maintains offices opposite police headquarters in Road Town; and **Hertz** (✆ **800/654-3001** in the U.S. and Canada, or 284/495-4405; www.hertz.com) has offices outside Road Town, on the island's west end, near the ferryboat landing dock. Rental companies will usually deliver your car to your hotel. All three companies require a valid driver's license and a temporary B.V.I. driver's license, which the car rental agency can sell you for $10; it's valid for 3 months. Because of the volume of tourism to Tortola, you should reserve a car in advance, especially in winter.

Remember: Drive on the left. Roads are pretty well paved, but they're often narrow, windy, and poorly lit, and they have few, if any, lines, so driving at night can be tricky. It's a good idea to take a taxi to that difficult-to-find beach, restaurant, or bar.

FAST FACTS The local **American Express** representative is Travel Plan, Waterfront Drive (✆ **284/494-2872**).

Local bank branches include the **Bank of Nova Scotia (Scotiabank),** Wickham's Cay (✆ **284/494-2526**), or **First Caribbean National Bank,** Wickham's Cay (✆ **284/494-2171**), both near Road Town. There's also a branch of **First Bank** at Road Town on Wickham's Cay 1 (✆ **284/494-2662**). Each has its own ATM.

The best place for camera supplies on Tortola is **Bolos Department Store,** Wickham's Cay (✆ **284/494-2867**).

For dental emergencies, contact **Dental Surgery,** Stevens Corner in Road Town (✆ **284/494-3474**), behind the Skeleton Building and next to the *BVI Beacon,* the local newspaper.

Peebles Hospital, Porter Road, Road Town (✆ **284/494-3497**), has X-ray, emergency, and laboratory facilities. The best pharmacy is **Medicure Pharmacy,** Road Town (✆ **284/494-6189**).

The main **police headquarters** is on Waterfront Drive near the ferry docks on Sir Olva Georges Plaza, with a branch office in Road Town in the town center (✆ **284/494-3822**).

Where to Stay

None of the island's hotels is as big or splashy as the hotels in the U.S. Virgin Islands, and that's just fine with most of Tortola's repeat visitors. All rates are subject to between a 10% and 16% service charge, depending on the hotel, and a 7% government tax on the room.

VERY EXPENSIVE

Fort Recovery Beachfront Villas & Suites ★ Nestled in a small palm grove about 12km (7½ miles) from Road Town, this property faces the Sir Francis Drake Channel and fronts one of the best small beaches on this side of the island, ideal for swimming and snorkeling. The estate contains the remnants of an old Dutch fort, including the stone lookout tower. Accommodations include villas and two houses, which are suitable for families. The large house has an art gallery hallway and a large wraparound porch. The resort offers its own yoga instructor and classes are complimentary to guests, in case the sea breezes and the beach aren't relaxing enough. If you book for 7 or more nights, dinner and a snorkeling trip are on the house.

The Towers, West End (P.O. Box 239), Road Town, Tortola, B.V.I. www.fortrecovery.com. ✆ **800/367-8455** or 284/541-0955. Fax 284/495-4036. 30 units. Winter $310–$360 suite, $520 villa for 4, $750 villa for 6–8; off season $210–$250 villa for 2, $360 villa for 4, from $560 villa for 6–8. Extra person $50 per night. Children 11 and under $35 per night. MAP (breakfast and dinner) $45 per day. AE, MC, V. **Amenities:** Restaurant; babysitting; bikes; exercise room; pool (outdoor); watersports equipment/rentals. *In room:* A/C, TV, hair dryer, kitchenette, Wi-Fi (free).

Frenchmans ★ This little boutique hotel has a certain chic. It is the latest reincarnation of the old Frenchman's Cay Hotel, which had become almost a landmark before it was shut down. After a dramatic renovation and under different owners, the emerging resort is far better than the older property. Standing on a 4.8-hectare (12-acre) peninsula, it is a cluster of luxurious cottages. You get some of the benefits of a larger resort, but with a lot more privacy. The hotel lies within walking distance of Soper's Hole, with its various marina services, markets, shops, and dining choices. Cottages open onto a private beach and a view of Sir Francis Drake Channel. All cottages contain full kitchens with modern appliances and accessories. The clubhouse restaurant on-site is open Monday, Wednesday, and Friday, featuring set menus costing from $40 to $65.

West End, Road Town, Tortola, B.V.I. www.frenchmansbvi.com. ✆ **284/494-8811.** 9 units. Winter $380–$545 1-bedroom villa, $550–$985 2-bedroom villa; off season $305 1-bedroom villa, $470 2-bedroom villa. Rates include continental breakfast. MC, V. **Amenities:** Restaurant; bar; concierge; pool (outdoor); tennis court (lit). *In room:* A/C, ceiling fan, TV/DVD, MP3 docking station, Wi-Fi (free).

Long Bay Beach Resort & Villas ★ This resort lies on a 2km-long (1¼-mile) sandy beach. In a setting on the north shore, about 10 minutes from West End, it's the only full-service resort on the island, a low-rise complex set in a 21-hectare (52-acre) estate. The accommodations include hillside rooms and studios; the smallest and most basic have simple furnishings, while the deluxe beachfront rooms and cabanas are tastefully elegant. All rooms have either balconies or patios overlooking the ocean. The resort also offers two- and three-bedroom villas complete with a kitchen, living area, and large deck with a gas grill.

Long Bay, Road Town, Tortola, B.V.I. www.longbay.com. ✆ **866/237-3491.** 156 units. Winter $250–$395 double, $430 junior suite, $610–$900 2-bedroom villa; off season $195–$345 double, $375 junior suite, $570 2-bedroom villa. AE, DISC, MC, V. **Amenities:** 3 restaurants; 3 bars; babysitting; health club; outdoor pool; sauna; snorkeling; spa; 2 tennis courts (lit). *In room:* A/C, TV, hair dryer, kitchen (in villas), Wi-Fi (free).

The Sugar Mill ★ Set in a lush tropical garden on the site of a 300-year-old sugar mill on the north side of Tortola, this secluded cottage colony sweeps down the hillside to its own little beach, with vibrant flowers and fruits brightening the grounds. The accommodations are contemporary and well designed, ranging from suites and cottages to studios, all self-contained with kitchenettes and private terraces with views. Rooms have twin or king-size beds. Four units are suitable for families of four. The latest addition, the Plantation House suites, evokes traditional Caribbean architecture, with fine stonework, breezy porches, and lacy gingerbread. Just steps from the beach, a pair of two-bedroom air-conditioned suites has tropical decor and sea views.

Apple Bay (P.O. Box 425), Road Town, Tortola, B.V.I. www.sugarmillhotel.com. ✆ **800/462-8834** in the U.S., or 284/495-4355. Fax 284/495-4696. 23 units. Winter $340 double, $380 triple, $395 quad, $695 2-bedroom villa; off season $255–$280 double, $305 triple, $330–$350 quad, $535–$585 2-bedroom villa. MAP (breakfast and dinner) $85 per person extra. AE, MC, V. Closed Aug–Sept. From Road Town, drive west 11km (6¾ miles), turn right (north) over Zion Hill, and turn right at the T-junction opposite Sebastian's; Sugar Mill is .8km (½ mile) down the road. Children 11 and under not accepted in winter. **Amenities:** 2 restaurants; 2 bars; babysitting; concierge; outdoor pool; scuba diving; snorkeling; windsurfing. *In room:* A/C, ceiling fan, TV (in villa and master suite), fridge, hair dryer, kitchenette (in some), Wi-Fi (free).

EXPENSIVE

Cooper Island Beach Club ★ This ultimate escapist's retreat is far from luxurious, but is the perfect place for those who want to experience simplicity. This one-of-a-kind hotel lies on a hilly island on the southern tier of the Sir Francis Drake Channel, about 8km (5 miles) south of Tortola. There are no roads, shopping centers, nightclubs, or other diversions on the island. The midsize units come with a bedroom and a kitchen, plus a balcony. The property is powered by a generator. Thus, lighting and ceiling fans are powered by 12-volt DC, and there is one 110-volt outlet in every room. The freshwater supply comes from rain and is stored in a cistern under every room. Every building uses a solar heater, and all toilets are flushed with sea water.

Manchioneel Bay, Road Town, Tortola, B.V.I. www.cooper-island.com. ✆ **800/542-4624** in the U.S. and Canada, or 284/495-9084. Fax 284/495-9180. 8 units. Winter $250 double; off season $200 double. Extra person $25. No credit cards. **Amenities:** 2 restaurants; bar; watersports equipment/rental. *In room:* Kitchenette, no phone, Wi-Fi (free).

Lambert Beach Resort ★ On the remote northeastern section of the island, this is the place for escapists who want isolation. Perched in an amphitheater sloping to the water, the resort opens onto a .8km (½-mile) beach of white sand set against a backdrop of palm trees. To reach the resort, you'll need to rent a car or take a taxi; it's about a 15-minute car ride from Road Town. Once here you'll find some of the B.V.I.'s best white-sand cove beaches, along with a large swimming pool. Playground facilities for children make this a family favorite. The Mediterranean-style cottage cluster spreads across eight one-floor structures, each containing a combination of suites with a living room, veranda, and bedrooms. Bedrooms are spacious and feature sand-hued walls, stained wood, ceramic-tiled floors, and tropical motifs.

Lambert Bay, East End, Tortola, B.V.I. www.lambertresort.com. ✆ **284/495-2877.** Fax 284/495-2876. 38 units. Winter $169–$270 double, $400 suite; off season $120–$215 double, $300 suite. AE, DC, MC, V. **Amenities:** Restaurant; bar; outdoor pool; room service; tennis court (lit); watersports equipment/rentals. *In room:* A/C, ceiling fan, fridge, Wi-Fi (free).

MODERATE

Sebastian's on the Beach This hotel is at Little Apple Bay, about a 15-minute drive from Road Town, on a long beach that has some of the best surfing in the British Virgin Islands. The rooms are housed in three buildings, with only one on the beach. All come with Indonesian furniture and balconies or porches. Most sought after are the beachfront rooms, only steps from the surf; they have an airy tropical vibe, with tile floors, balconies, patios, and screened jalousies. The rear accommodations on the beach side are less desirable—not only do they lack views, but they're also subject to traffic noise. The dozen spartan rooms in the back of the main building lack views.

Little Apple Bay (P.O. Box 441), West End, Tortola, B.V.I. www.sebastiansbvi.com. ✆ **800/336-4870** in the U.S., or 284/495-4212. Fax 284/495-4466. 26 units. Winter $110–$235 double; off season $85–$135 double. Breakfast and dinner $50 per person extra. AE, DISC, MC, V. **Amenities:** Restaurant; bar; Wi-Fi (free). *In room:* A/C, ceiling fan, TV, fridge (in some), minibar, phone (in some).

Where to Dine

Lobster is becoming scarce in the B.V.I., and restaurants will serve it only during lobster "season"—November to July.

EXPENSIVE

Brandywine Bay Restaurant ★★ ITALIAN/INTERNATIONAL Set on a cobblestone garden terrace along the south shore overlooking Sir Francis Drake Channel, this is one of Tortola's most elegant, romantic restaurants. Davide Pugliese, the chef, and his wife, Cele, have earned a reputation for their outstanding Florentine fare. Davide changes his menu daily, based on the availability of fresh produce. The best dishes include beef carpaccio, roast duck, homemade pasta, his own special calf-liver dish (the recipe is a secret), and homemade mozzarella with fresh basil and tomatoes. The skillful cooking ranges from classic to inspired.

Brandywine Estate, Sir Francis Drake Hwy. ✆ **284/495-2301.** www.brandywinebay.com. Reservations required. Appropriate dress required. Main courses $20–$28. AE, MC, V. Tues–Sat 6–10pm. Closed Aug–Oct. Drive 5km (3 miles) east of Road Town (toward the airport) on South Shore Rd.

Le Grand Cafe FRENCH Islanders and visitors gather at this restaurant and bar to enjoy good French food on the outdoor patio. Delicious appetizers include Mediterranean fish soup with rouille, herring-and-potato salad, and Camembert flambé with Calvados. Much of the menu is classically inclined, including dishes such as snapper meunière. Especially tasty options include the almond-curried Madras chicken, the Chilean sea bass with wasabi sauce, and the yellowfin tuna in a soy-and-basil sauce. For dessert, finish off with a crème brûlée or the chocolate mousse, accurately billed as "heavenly" on the menu.

Waterfront Dr. ✆ **284/494-8660.** Reservations recommended. Main courses $23–$38. MC, V. Mon–Fri 9am–3pm; Mon–Sat 7pm–midnight. Closed Sept.

1748 Restaurant CONTINENTAL At the Long Bay Beach Resort, this alfresco dining room is the beachfront restaurant here. Invitingly casual, the much frequented deck spot was the site of an 18th-century sugar mill. Beginning with one of the island's most lavish breakfast buffets, the restaurant serves both lunch and dinner from a daily changing menu. Popular starters include the creamy seafood soup and the chef's seafood salad. For mains, try the baby back ribs, prepared with the chef's secret sauce, the catch of the day, often lobster, or the pan-seared red snapper. For dessert, the pastry chef bakes about a half dozen luscious desserts—try his fluffy coconut lemon cake, most delicious. Two nights a week, special lavish buffets are offered, featuring live entertainment from a local band.

In the Long Bay Beach Resort, Long Bay, Road Town. ✆ **284/495-4252.** www.longbay.com. Reservations recommended. Main courses lunch $15–$30; dinner $15–$45. AE, DISC, MC, V. Daily 7:30–10am,noon–3pm, and 6:30–9pm.

Sugar Mill Restaurant ★ CALIFORNIAN/CARIBBEAN Transformed from a 3-century-old sugar mill (p. 152), this hotel is a romantic spot for dining. Colorful works by Haitian painters hang on the old stone walls, and big copper basins have been planted with tropical flowers. Before going to the dining room, once part of the old boiling house, visit the open-air bar on a deck that overlooks the sea. Your hosts, the Morgans, know a lot about food and wine. One of their most popular creations, published in *Bon Appétit,* is curried banana soup. You might also begin with the roasted-pepper salad or the especially tasty wild-mushroom soup. For a main course, we recommend such dishes as pan-roasted duck breast served with Asian coleslaw and soba noodles, or grilled fresh fish with a pineapple-pepper salsa.

Apple Bay. ✆ **284/495-4355.** Reservations required. Main courses $25–$45. AE, MC, V. Daily 8–10am, noon–2pm, and 7–9pm. Closed Aug–Sept. From Road Town, drive west 11km (6¾ miles), turn right (north) over Zion Hill, and turn right at the T-junction opposite Sebastian's; Sugar Mill is .8km (½ mile) down the road.

MODERATE

Gourmet picnic, anyone? **Bobby's Market Place,** Nanny Cay (✆ **284/494-2894**), offers fabulous fixings, including cheeses, snacks, groceries, wines, beer, breads, and fine chocolates. It's open daily 7am to 6pm.

Capriccio di Mare ★ ITALIAN Created in a moment of whimsy by the more upscale Brandywine Bay Restaurant (see above), this place is small, casual, laid-back, and a local favorite. It's the most authentic-looking Italian cafe in the Virgin Islands. At breakfast time, many locals stop in for a refreshing Italian pastry and a cup of cappuccino, or else a full breakfast. If it's evening, you might try the mango Bellini, a variation of the famous cocktail served at Harry's Bar in Venice. Begin with such appetizers as *piedini* (flour tortillas with various toppings), then move on to fresh pastas with succulent sauces, the best pizza on the island (our favorite is the one topped with grilled eggplant), or even well-stuffed sandwiches. If you arrive on the right night, you might even be treated to stuffed Cornish hen with scalloped potatoes.

Waterfront Dr., Road Town. ✆ **284/494-5369.** Main courses $8–$15. MC, V. Mon–Sat 8am–9pm.

The Pub INTERNATIONAL This establishment is housed in a low-slung timbered building on a narrow strip of land between the coastal road and the southern edge of Road Town's harbor. It has a barnlike interior and a rambling veranda built on piers over the water. The pub attracts many of the island's yachties, as well as the local sports teams, who celebrate here after their games. More than 25 different kinds of beer are available. If you're here for a meal, some of the best options include Bahamian fritters, Caesar or Greek salads, pastas, four kinds of steaks, and burgers. Locals who frequent this place are especially fond of the chef's jerk chicken and his combo platter of spareribs, chicken, and fried shrimp. The chef also prepares a catch of the day. Happy hour brings discounted drinks daily from 5 to 7pm, and on Friday hot wings and raw vegetable platters are offered.

Fort Burt Marina, Harbour Rd. ✆ **284/494-2608.** Reservations recommended. Main courses $8–$35. AE, DISC, MC, V. Mon–Sat 6am–midnight, Sun 5pm–midnight.

Pusser's Landing CARIBBEAN This location in West End, which opens onto the water, is nicer than the original location on the waterfront across from the ferry dock. In this nautical setting, you can enjoy fresh grilled fish of the day cooked to your requirements. Begin with a hearty soup, perhaps pumpkin or freshly made seafood chowder. Many of the main courses, most of which are moderate in price, have real island flavor, the most justifiably popular being jerk chicken Jamaican style, or the grilled chicken breast with fresh pineapple salsa. A classic is the curried shrimp over rice. Mud pie remains the choice dessert here, but the Key lime pie and mango soufflé are also appealing. Happy hour is daily from 5 to 7pm.

Frenchman's Cay, West End. ✆ **284/495-4554.** Reservations required. Main courses $17–$34. AE, MC, V. Daily 11am–9:30pm.

Hitting the Beach

Beaches are rarely crowded on Tortola unless a cruise ship is in port. You can rent a car or a jeep to reach them, or take a taxi (but arrange for a time to be picked up).

Tortola's finest beach is **Cane Garden Bay ★★★**, on Cane Garden Bay Road directly west of Road Town. You'll have to navigate some roller-coaster hills to get there, but these fine white sands with sheltering palm trees are among the most popular in the B.V.I., and the lovely bay is beloved by yachties. Outfitters here rent Hobie Cats, kayaks, and sailboards. Windsurfing is possible as well. This is one beach that may get crowded, especially during high season. There are several places to eat, along with a handful of bars. **Rhymer's** (✆ **284/495-4639**) is our favorite, dispensing cold beer and refreshing rum drinks. If you're hungry, try the conch or lobster, black-bean gazpacho, or barbecued spareribs. The beach bar and restaurant is open daily from 8am to 9pm. Ice and freshwater showers are available, and you can rent towels. Ask about renting Sunfish sailboats and windsurfers next door.

Surfers like **Apple Bay,** west of Cane Garden Bay, along North Shore Road. The beach isn't very big, but that doesn't diminish activity when the surf's up. Conditions are best in January and February. After enjoying the white sands here, stop for a drink at **Bomba's Surfside Shack,** a classic dive of a beach bar at the water's edge (see "Tortola After Dark," below).

Smugglers Cove, known for its tranquillity and beautiful sands, lies at the extreme western end of Tortola, opposite the offshore island of Great Thatch and just north of St. John. It's a lovely crescent of white sand, with calm turquoise waters. A favorite local beach, it's at the end of bumpy Belmont Road. Once you get here, a little worse for wear, we think you'll agree that the crystal-clear water and the beautiful palm trees are worth the effort. Snorkelers like this beach, which is sometimes called Lower Belmont Bay. It's especially good for beginners, since the reef is close to shore and easily reached. You'll see parrotfish, sea fans, sponges, and elkhorn and brain corals.

East of Cane Garden Bay and site of a campground, **Brewers Bay,** accessed from long, steep Brewers Bay Road, is ideal for snorkelers and surfers. This clean white-sand beach is a great place to enjoy walks in the early morning or at sunset. Sip a rum punch from the beach bar, and watch the world go by.

The 2km-long (1¼-mile) white-sand beach at **Long Bay West,** reached along Long Bay Road, is one of the most beautiful in the B.V.I. Joggers run along the water's edge, and spectacular sunsets make it perfect for romantic strolls. The Long Bay Beach Resort (p. 151) stands on the northeast side of the beach; many visitors like to book a table at the resort's restaurant overlooking the water.

At the very east end of the island, **Long Bay East,** reached along Beef Island Road, is a great spot for swimming. Cross Queen Elizabeth Bridge to reach this 2km-long (1¼-mile) beach with great views and white sands.

Exploring the Island

Travel Plan Tours, Romasco Place, Harbour House (P.O. Box 437), Road Town (✆ **284/494-2872;** www.aroundthebvi.com), offers two islandwide tours, the first taking 3 hours, the second 3½ hours, costing $32 to $50 per person. The company also runs 3-hour **snorkeling tours** for $70 per person (with snacks included). A full-day **sailing tour** aboard a catamaran that goes from Tortola to either Peter Island or Norman Island costs $165 per person; a full-day tour, which goes as far afield as the Baths at Virgin Gorda and includes lunch, costs $125 per person. And if **deep-sea fishing** appeals to you, you can go for a half-day excursion, with equipment, for four fishermen and up to two "nonfishing observers" for $900, or the full day for $1,300.

A **taxi tour** costs $60 to $85 for two passengers. To call a taxi in Road Town, dial ✆ **284/494-2322;** on Beef Island, call ✆ **284/495-1982.**

J. R. O'Neal Botanic Gardens ★, Botanic Station, Road Town (no phone), fills up a 1.6-hectare (4-acre) site of lush tropical growth. Wander at leisure, taking in the pergola walk, a waterfall, a lily pond, tropical birdhouses, and miniature rainforests. Of course, you can also enjoy the rich plant life that ranges here, from exotic orchids to gardens of medicinal herbs. Admission is free; the gardens are open Monday to Saturday 9am to 4:30pm.

No visit to Tortola is complete without a trip to **Sage Mountain National Park ★**, rising to an elevation of 534m (1,752 ft.). Here you'll find traces of a primeval rainforest, and you can enjoy a picnic while overlooking neighboring islets and cays. Go west from Road Town to reach the mountain. Before you head out, stop by the tourist office and pick up the brochure *Sage Mountain National Park;* it has a location map, directions to the forest and parking, and an outline of the main trails through the park. Covering 37 hectares (91 acres), the park protects the remnants of Tortola's original forests not burned or cleared during the island's plantation era. From the parking lot, a trail leads to the main park entrance. The two main trails are the Rainforest Trail and the Mahogany Forest Trail.

The Wreck of the Rhone & Other Top Dive Sites

The one site in the British Virgin Islands that lures divers from St. Thomas is the wreck of the **HMS *Rhone* ★★**, which sank in 1867 near the western point of Salt Island. *Skin Diver* magazine called it "the world's most fantastic shipwreck dive." It teems with marine life and coral formations, and was featured in the 1977 movie *The Deep.*

Although it's no *Rhone,* **Chikuzen** is another intriguing dive site off Tortola. This 81m (266-foot) steel-hulled refrigerator ship sank off the island's east end in 1981. The hull, still intact under about 24m (79 ft.) of water, is now home to a vast array of tropical fish, including yellowtail, barracuda, black-tip sharks, octopus, and drum fish.

South of Ginger Island, **Alice's Wonderland** is a deep-dive site with a wall that begins at around 3.6m (12 ft.) and slopes gently to 30m (98 ft.). It abounds with marine life such as lobsters, crabs, rainbow-hued fan coral, and mammoth mushroom-shaped coral. **Spyglass Wall** is another offshore dive site dropping to a sandy bottom and filled with sea fans and large coral heads. The drop is from 3 to 18m (9¾–59 ft.). Divers here seek out tarpon, eagle rays, and stingrays.

Blue Waters Divers, Nanny Cay Marina, Road Town (✆ **284/494-2847;** www.bluewaterdiversbvi.com), is a PADI outfitter, offering various dive packages, including to the wreck of the *Rhone*. A resort course costs $115, a PADI open-water certification $410.

Yacht Charters

Tortola boasts the largest fleet of bareboat sailing charters in the world. The best place to get outfitted is the **Moorings,** Wickham's Cay (✆ **888/952-8420** in the U.S. and Canada, or 284/494-2331; www.moorings.com). This outfit, along with a handful of others, makes the British Virgins the cruising capital of the world. You can choose from a fleet of sailing yachts, which can accommodate up to six couples in comfort and style. Depending on your nautical knowledge and skills, you can arrange a bareboat rental (with no crew) or a fully crewed rental with a skipper, a staff, and a cook. Boats come equipped with a portable barbecue, snorkeling gear, dinghy, linens, and galley equipment. The Moorings has an experienced staff of mechanics, electricians, riggers, and cleaners. If you're going out on your own, you'll get a thorough briefing session on Virgin Island waters and anchorages.

If you'd like sailing lessons, consider **Steve Colgate's Offshore Sailing School** (✆ **888/454-7015** in the U.S. and Canada; www.offshoresailing.com), which offers courses in seamanship year-round.

Shopping

Most of Tortola's shops are on Road Town's Main Street. Unfortunately, the British Virgins have no duty-free shopping. British goods are imported, and you can find some good buys among these imported items, especially in English china. In general, store hours are Monday to Saturday from 9am to 5:30pm.

You might start your shopping expedition at **Crafts Alive,** an open-air market lying in the center of Road Town and impossible to miss. It consists of a series of old-fashioned West Indian–style buildings that are stocked with crafts, ranging from Caribbean dolls to straw hats, from crocheted doilies to pottery—plus, of course, the inevitable B.V.I. T-shirts. Very few of these items, however, are made on island; we noted that some, in fact, come from Panama.

Sunny Caribbee Herb and Spice Company, 119 Main St., Road Town (✆ **284/494-2178;** www.sunnycaribbee.com), in an old West Indian building, was the first hotel on Tortola. It's now a shop specializing in Caribbean spices, seasonings, teas, condiments, and handicrafts. With an aroma of spices permeating the air, this factory is an attraction in itself. You can buy two famous specialties here: the West Indian hangover cure and the Arawak love potion. A Caribbean cosmetics collection, Sunsations, includes herbal bath gels, island perfume, and sunscreens. There's a daily sampling of island products—perhaps tea, coffee, sauces, or dips.

Samarkand Jewelers, 94 Main St., Road Town (✆ **284/494-6415**), evokes an exotic land but is actually an unusually good bet for jewelry and other items. Look for an intriguing selection of bracelets, pins, pendants in both silver and gold, and pierced earrings. Caribbean motifs such as palms and sea birds often appear in the designs of the jewelry.

Pusser's Company Store, Main Street and Waterfront Road, Road Town (✆ **284/494-2467**), sells gourmet food items, including meats, spices, fish, and a nice selection of wines. Pusser's Rum is one of the best-selling items here.

Arawak Boutique & Gift Shop, Nanny Cay Marina (✆ **284/494-5240**), is known for its household furnishings such as placemats and candleholders, but it also sells sporty clothing for adults and kids, along with a selection of gifts and souvenirs.

Flamboyance, Waterfront Drive (✆ **284/494-4099**), is the best place to shop for perfume and upscale cosmetics.

If you've rented a villa or condo, or even if your accommodations have a kitchenette, consider a visit to **Ample Hamper,** Inner Harbour Marina, Wickham's Cay 1, Road Town (✆ **284/494-2494;** www.amplehamper.com). This outlet stocks some of the best-packaged food and bottled wines on the island. It also has fresh fruit and a tasty selection of cheeses.

Philatelists from all over the world flock to the **British Virgin Islands Post Office,** Main Street, Road Town (✆ **284/468-5165,** ext. 4996), for its exquisite, unusual stamps in beautiful designs. Even though the stamps carry U.S. monetary designations, they can be used only in the B.V.I. Most stamp collectors, however, collect the stamps rather than actually using them.

Tortola After Dark

Ask around to find out which hotel might have entertainment on any given evening. Steel bands and fungi or scratch bands (African Caribbean musicians who improvise on locally available instruments) appear regularly, and nonresidents are usually welcome. Pick up a copy of *Limin' Times,* an entertainment magazine listing what's happening locally; it's usually available at hotels.

Bomba's Surfside Shack, Cappoon's Bay (✆ **284/495-4148**), is the oldest, most memorable, and most uninhibited hangout on the island. Sitting on the beach near the West End, it's covered with Day-Glo graffiti and odds and ends of plywood, driftwood, and abandoned rubber tires. Despite its makeshift appearance, the shack has the sound system to create a really great party. Every month (dates vary), Bomba's stages a full-moon party, with free house tea spiked with hallucinogenic mushrooms. (The tea is free because it's illegal to sell it.) The place is also wild on Wednesday and Sunday nights, when there's live music and a $10 all-you-can-eat barbecue. It's open daily from 10am to midnight (or later, depending on business).

The bar at the **Mariner Inn,** Wickham's Cay (✆ **284/494-2333;** www.bvimarinerinnhotel.com), is the preferred watering hole for upscale yacht owners, but drink prices are low. Open to a view of its own marina, and bathed in a dim and flattering light, the place is relaxed.

Other places worth a stop on a bar-hopping jaunt include the **Jolly Roger Inn,** West End (✆ **284/495-4559;** www.jollyrogerbvi.com), where you can hear local or sometimes American bands playing everything from reggae to blues. In the same area, visit **Stanley's Welcome Bar,** Cane Garden Bay (✆ **284/495-9424**), where a rowdy frat-boy crowd gathers to drink, talk, and drink some more. Finally, check out **Sebastian's,** Apple Bay (✆ **284/495-4212;** www.sebastiansbvi.com), especially on Sunday, when you can dance to live music under the stars, at least in winter.

Rhymer's, on the popular stretch of beach at Cane Garden Bay (✆ **284/495-4639**), serves cold beer or tropical rum concoctions, along with a casual menu of ribs, conch chowder, and more. It's open daily from 8am to 9pm.

VIRGIN GORDA ★★★

Virgin Gorda is where you come to relax and escape, at some of the poshest and most self-contained inns in the Caribbean, if you can afford them. Life here is much slower-paced than on Tortola, without much shopping or nightlife. The island gets far less rain, making some sections of it quite arid. Goats wander among a landscape of cactus and scrub brush.

In 1493, on his second voyage to the New World, Columbus named this island Virgin Gorda, or "Fat Virgin" (from a distance, the island looks like a reclining woman with a protruding stomach). The third-largest island in the cluster of British Virgin Islands, Virgin Gorda is about 15km (9¼ miles) long and 3km (2 miles) wide, with a population of some 1,400. It's 19km (12 miles) east of Tortola and 42km (26 miles) from St. Thomas.

The island was a fairly desolate agricultural community until Laurance S. Rockefeller established the Little Dix Bay Hotel here in the early 1960s, following his success with the Caneel Bay resort on St. John in the 1950s. He envisioned a "wilderness beach," where privacy and solitude would reign. In 1971 the Virgin Gorda Yacht Harbour opened, turning the island into a world-class destination for yachties. Operated by the Little Dix Bay Hotel, it accommodates 120 yachts today.

Try to visit Virgin Gorda, if only for the day, to see the **Baths,** gigantic rocks and boulders shaped by volcanic pressures millions of years ago. The beach at the Baths is simply spectacular. Virgin Gorda is also quite mountainous; if you're tired of flat Caribbean islands, you'll love the gorgeous, dramatic scenery here.

Essentials

GETTING THERE **Speedy's Fantasy** (✆ **284/495-5240;** www.speedysbvi.com) runs a ferry service between Road Town and Virgin Gorda. Monday to Saturday, at least five ferries a day leave from Road Town (three per day on Sun). The cost is $20 one-way or $30 round-trip. From St. Thomas to Virgin Gorda, it offers service Tuesday, Thursday, and Saturday, costing $40 one-way or $70 round-trip.

Most of the luxurious resorts have their own boats to take you from the airport on Beef Island to Virgin Gorda.

GETTING AROUND Independently operated open-sided **safari buses** run along the main road. Holding up to 22 passengers, these buses charge upward of $3 to $5 per person to transport a passenger from, say, the Valley to the Baths. Additional taxi service is provided by **African Pride Taxi Service** (✆ **284/499-3127**) and **Mahogany Rentals & Taxi Service** (✆ **284/495-5469;** http://mahoganyrentals.puzzlepiece.net), both in the Valley.

If you'd like to rent a car, try one of the local firms, including **Mahogany Rentals,** the Valley, Spanish Town (✆ **284/495-5469;** http://mahoganyrentals.puzzlepiece.net), across from the yacht harbor. This company is the least expensive on the island, beginning at $55 daily for a Suzuki Sidekick. Road conditions on Virgin Gorda range from good to extremely poor; you're probably better off renting a four-wheel-drive vehicle. ***Remember:*** Drive on the left.

FAST FACTS You can reach the **police station** by calling ✆ **284/495-7584. First Caribbean International Bank** (✆ **284/495-5217**) is located in Spanish Town at the Virgin Gorda Shopping Centre. It has an ATM.

Where to Stay

VERY EXPENSIVE

Biras Creek Resort ★★★ This private, romantic resort is the classiest place on the island (Bitter End is more family oriented, and Little Dix Bay more conventional). It stands at the northern end of Virgin Gorda like a hilltop fortress. On a 60-hectare (148-acre) estate with its own marina, it occupies a narrow neck of land flanked by the sea on three sides. All the tropically decorated units are well-furnished bedrooms with private patios. There are no TVs in the rooms, but you get such luxuries as oceanview verandas. You get your own bikes while you're there, plus you have lots of hiking trails near the property to explore.

North Sound (P.O. Box 54), Virgin Gorda, B.V.I. www.biras.com. ✆ **877/883-0756** or 284/494-3555. Fax 284/494-3557. 31 units. Winter $850–$2,500 suite; off season $700–$1,950 suite. Rates include all meals (no drinks). Ask about packages. AE, MC, V. Children 7 and under not accepted. **Amenities:** Restaurant; bar; airport transfers ($95); bikes; exercise room; outdoor pool; 2 tennis courts (lit); watersports equipment/rentals. *In room:* A/C, ceiling fan, TV/DVD, fridge, hair dryer, MP3 docking station (in some), Wi-Fi (free).

Bitter End Yacht Club ★★★ This is the liveliest of the B.V.I. resorts and even better equipped than the more exclusive Biras Creek. It's the best sailing and diving complex in the British chain. It opens onto one of the most unspoiled and secluded deep-water harbors in the Caribbean. Guests have unlimited use of the resort's million-dollar fleet and a complimentary introductory course at the Nick Trotter Sailing and Windsurfing School. The Bitter End offers an informal yet elegant experience in either a hillside chalet or a well-appointed beachfront overlooking the sound. Most units have varnished hardwood floors, sliding-glass doors, and wicker furnishings.

John O Point, North Sound (P.O. Box 46), Virgin Gorda, B.V.I. www.beyc.com. ✆ **800/872-2392** in the U.S., or 312/506-6205;. Fax 284/494-4756. 85 units. Winter $700–$1,840 double; off season $530–$1,360 double. Rates include all meals. AE, MC, V. Take the private ferry from the Beef Island airport ($30 per person one-way). **Amenities:** 3 restaurants; pub; babysitting; exercise room; outdoor pool; watersports equipment/rentals. *In room:* A/C (in some), ceiling fan (in some), TV (on request), fridge, Wi-Fi (free).

Rosewood Little Dix Bay Hotel ★★ Full of low-key luxury, along a curving white-sand beach, Little Dix Bay Hotel is a resort scattered along a .8km (½-mile) crescent-shaped private bay on a 200-hectare (494-acre) preserve. Many guests find this resort too pricey and stuffy; we prefer the more casual elegance of Biras Creek and the Bitter End Yacht Club, though Little Dix Bay does have an undeniably lovely setting, fine service, and a quiet elegance. All rooms, built in the woods, have private terraces with views of the sea or gardens. Units come with ceiling fans and air-conditioning, and louvers and screens let in sea breezes. Some units are two-story *rondavels* (like tiki huts) raised on stilts to form their own breezeways. Accommodations are roomy, airy, and decorated with tropical flair. Furnishings and fabrics evoke a Southeast Asian style with wicker or reed furniture, bamboo beds, and ceramic objets d'art.

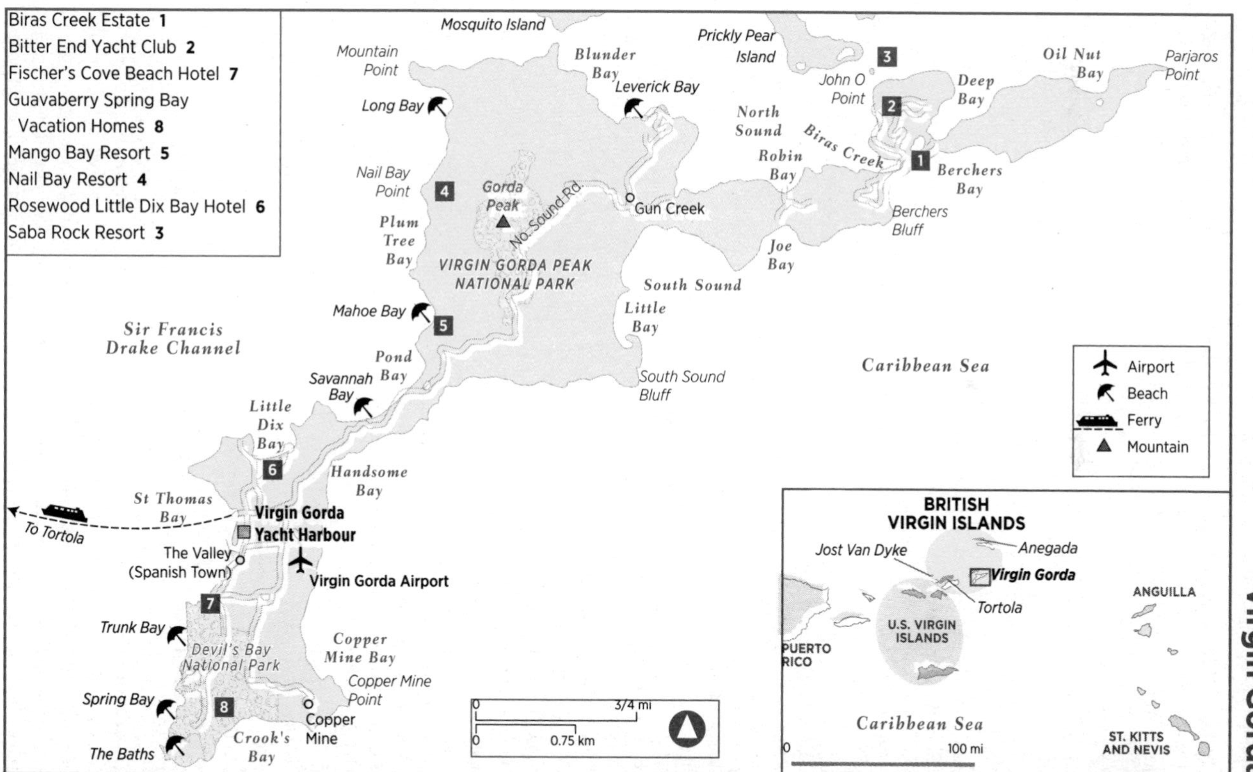

Biras Creek Estate 1
Bitter End Yacht Club 2
Fischer's Cove Beach Hotel 7
Guavaberry Spring Bay Vacation Homes 8
Mango Bay Resort 5
Nail Bay Resort 4
Rosewood Little Dix Bay Hotel 6
Saba Rock Resort 3
Mosquito Island
Mountain Point
Blunder Bay
Prickly Pear Island
Oil Nut Bay
Parjaros Point
John O Point
Deep Bay
Leverick Bay
Long Bay
North Sound
Biras Creek
Robin Bay
Berchers Bay
Berchers Bluff
Nail Bay Point
Gorda Peak
No. Sound Rd.
Gun Creek
Plum Tree Bay
VIRGIN GORDA PEAK NATIONAL PARK
Joe Bay
South Sound
Little Bay
Mahoe Bay
Sir Francis Drake Channel
Pond Bay
Savannah Bay
South Sound Bluff
Caribbean Sea
Airport
Beach
Ferry
Mountain
Little Dix Bay
Handsome Bay
St Thomas Bay
To Tortola
Virgin Gorda Yacht Harbour
The Valley (Spanish Town)
Virgin Gorda Airport
Trunk Bay
Devil's Bay National Park
Copper Mine Bay
Copper Mine Point
Spring Bay
Copper Mine
Crook's Bay
The Baths
0 3/4 mi
0 0.75 km
BRITISH VIRGIN ISLANDS
Jost Van Dyke
Anegada
Virgin Gorda
Tortola
ANGUILLA
U.S. VIRGIN ISLANDS
PUERTO RICO
Caribbean Sea
ST. KITTS AND NEVIS
0 100 mi

1km (½ mile) north of Spanish Town (P.O. Box 70), Virgin Gorda, B.V.I. www.littledixbay.com. ✆ **888/767-3966** in the U.S., or 284/495-5555. Fax 284/495-5661. 100 units. Winter $725–$1,150 double, from $2,300 suite; off season $540–$810 double, from $1,170 suite. Extra person $75. MAP (breakfast and dinner) $110 per person extra; AP (full board) $140 per person extra. AE, DISC, MC, V. Take the private ferry from the Beef Island airport ($95 per person round-trip). **Amenities:** 3 restaurants; 2 bars; babysitting; children's programs; exercise room; room service; 7 tennis courts (lit); watersports equipment/rentals. *In room:* A/C, ceiling fan, DVD (on request), fridge, Wi-Fi (free).

EXPENSIVE

Guavaberry Spring Bay Vacation Homes ★ Staying in one of these hexagonal, white-roofed redwood houses built on stilts is like living in a treehouse. Screened and louvered walls let in sea breezes, and the Baths, with its excellent sandy beach, is nearby. Each unique home, available for daily or weekly rental, has one or two bedrooms; all have private bathrooms with showers, full kitchens, and dining areas. And each has an elevated sun deck overlooking Sir Francis Drake Passage. The cottage colony is close to both the beach at Spring Bay and the Yacht Harbour Shopping Centre.

Spring Bay (P.O. Box 20), Virgin Gorda, B.V.I. www.guavaberryspringbay.com. ✆ **284/495-5227.** Fax 284/495-5283. 19 units. Winter $235 1-bedroom house, $300 2-bedroom house, $420 3-bedroom house; off season $150 1-bedroom house, $200 2-bedroom house, $320 3-bedroom house. Extra person $25. No credit cards. **Amenities:** Babysitting; boats; watersports equipment/rentals; Wi-Fi ($2 per 30 min.). *In room:* A/C (in some), ceiling fan, fridge, kitchen, no phone.

Mango Bay Resort ★ This well-designed compound of eight white-sided villas is set on lushly landscaped grounds overlooking the scattered islets of Drake Channel on the island's western shore. It's a good value for your money. The accommodations are the most adaptable on the island—doors can be locked or unlocked to divide each villa into as many as four independent units. Costs vary with the proximity of your unit to the nearby beach. Interiors are stylish yet simple, often dominated by the same turquoise as that of the seascape in front of you.

Mahoe Bay (P.O. Box 1062), Virgin Gorda, B.V.I. www.mangobayresort.com. ✆ **284/495-5672.** Fax 284/495-5674. 26 units. Winter $195–$1,150 villa or suite; off season $150–$695 villa or suite. MC, V. **Amenities:** Restaurant; bar; boats; watersports equipment/rentals. *In room:* A/C, kitchen.

Nail Bay Resort ★ Near Gorda Peak National Park, and a short walk from a trio of usually deserted beaches, this resort enjoys an idyllic position. From its 60-hectare (148-acre) site, you can take in some of the best sunset views of Sir Francis Drake Channel and the Dog Islands. The well-furnished units are comfortable and tasteful. Accommodations include deluxe bedrooms, suites, apartments, and villas. This villa community has a core of a dozen units in two structures on a hillside, with sitting areas amid old sugar-mill ruins. The most modest units are hotel-style bedrooms in the main building. The best accommodations are the five estate villas.

Nail Bay (P.O. Box 69), Virgin Gorda, B.V.I. www.nailbay.com. ✆ **800/871-3551** in the U.S., 800/487-1839 in Canada, or 284/494-8000. Fax 284/495-5875. 45 units. Winter $240–$495 double; summer $185–$395 double. AE, DISC, MC, V. **Amenities:** Restaurant; swim-up bar; babysitting; Jacuzzi; outdoor pool; snorkeling; tennis court (lit). *In room:* A/C, TV/DVD/VCR, hair dryer, kitchen, MP3 docking station, Wi-Fi ($5 per hour).

Saba Rock Resort ★ This idyllic retreat, perched on its own small cay and reached by a free ferry, offers tranquillity and privacy in an area ideal for swimming, sailing, or exploring. The island itself owned for 3 decades by Bert Kilbride, the Caribbean's most legendary diver. Queen Elizabeth herself named him "Receiver of

Wrecks," because he discovered some 90 shipwrecks in and around the BVI. His scuba-diving "resort course," created in the 1960s, is now taught around the world. Bert died in 2008 at the age of 93, and the island's new owners decided to turn his former private island into this rather luxurious compound of 1- and 2-bedroom suites. Furnishings are minimal and tasteful, with a breakfast of island fruits and fresh baked pastries served in an "over-the-water" dining room. Honeymooners prefer the Mustique House set in the back of the island (its king-size bed sees much activity). The restaurant prepares steaks grilled to order, succulent pastas, and local seafood. Just under a half a hectare (1 acre) in size at low tide, Saba Rock has its own nautical museum with shipwreck artifacts accumulated by Bert.

Saba Rock, North Sound (P.O. Box 67), Virgin Gorda, B.V.I. www.sabarock.com. ✆ **284/495-9966** for reservations, or 284/495-7711. Fax 284/495-7373. 9 units. Year-round $175–$225 double, $195–$375 quad. DC, MC, V. **Amenities:** Restaurant; bar; watersports equipment/rental. *In room:* A/C, TV, fridge, kitchenette (in some), MP3 docking station, no phone (in some), Wi-Fi (free).

MODERATE

Fischer's Cove Beach Hotel Swim from your doorstep in this group of units nestled near the sandy beach of St. Thomas Bay. Erected of native stone, each of the eight cottages is self-contained, with one or two bedrooms and a combination living/dining room with a kitchenette. You can stock up on provisions at a food store near the grounds. There are also 12 pleasant but simple rooms with views of Drake Channel. Each has its own private shower-only bathroom and private porch.

The Valley (P.O. Box 60), Virgin Gorda, B.V.I. www.fischerscove.com. ✆ **284/495-5252.** Fax 284/495-5820. 20 units. Winter $90–$125 double, $190–$315 studio cottage; off season $90 double, $125–$205 studio cottage. MAP (breakfast and dinner) $40 per person extra. AE, MC, V. **Amenities:** Restaurant; bar; babysitting; children's playground; scooter rental; watersports equipment/rentals. *In room:* A/C (in some), ceiling fan (in some), TV, fridge, kitchenette (in cottages), no phone (in cottages), Wi-Fi (free).

Where to Dine

VERY EXPENSIVE

Biras Creek Restaurant ★★ INTERNATIONAL With even better cuisine than that of Little Dix Bay Pavilion (see below), this hilltop restaurant is our longtime island favorite, and for good reason. The resort (p. 160) hires the island's finest chefs, who turn out superb cuisine based on quality ingredients. The menu changes every night, but the panoramic view of North Sound doesn't. A recent sampling of the appetizers turned up such delights as five-spice duck salad for starters, followed by such well-prepared main courses as pan-seared salmon wrapped in Parma ham in a lentil-cream sauce, or grilled grouper with an herby couscous. The chef's special grilled lobster is featured Sunday and Wednesday nights. Desserts are likely to range from a chilled green-apple parfait to a choice of sorbets served with a chilled cantaloupe soup.

In Biras Creek Resort, North Sound. ✆ **284/494-3555.** www.biras.com. Reservations required. Fixed-price dinner $85–$125. AE, MC, V. Seatings daily 6:30–9pm.

EXPENSIVE

Chez Bamboo ★ INTERNATIONAL Set within an antique Creole house—which its owner, Rose Giacinto, painted in vibrant tones of lime, peach, and turquoise—this likable eatery defines itself as an upscale Caribbean bistro with a view not of the sea, but of a verdant garden and a coconut grove. Positioned within a 5-minute walk south of the marina, it offers a bar where career mixologist Leonard makes award-winning martinis and sangria, the best on island. Savory menu items include conch gumbo, lobster bisque, wahoo cakes with tartar sauce, shrimp-stuffed ravioli, and steaks. There's live music every Friday.

Main Rd., Spanish Town. ✆ **284/495-5752.** Reservations not necessary. Main courses $23–$46. AE, MC, V. Daily 4–11pm. Closed Aug–Oct.

Little Dix Bay Pavilion ★ INTERNATIONAL The most romantic of the dining spots on Virgin Gorda, this pavilion is our preferred choice at this deluxe resort (p. 160). At the pavilion, the guests (most middle-aged and well heeled) sit under a large thatched roof with the doors open to the trade winds. The chefs change the menu daily. Although many of the ingredients are shipped in frozen, especially meats and some seafood, there is much that is fresh and good. The most expensive items on the menu are the rack of lamb and grilled salmon. Many vegetables evoke the Pacific Rim, and the seafood keeps us returning again and again.

In the Rosewood Little Dix Bay Hotel, 1km (½ mile) north of Spanish Town. ✆ **284/495-5555.** www.littledixbay.com. Reservations required. Main courses $20–$36. AE, MC, V. Daily 8–10:30am, 11:30am–3pm, and 6:30–9pm.

Mine Shaft Café AMERICAN Near Copper Mine Point, this little bistro draws diners who like a panoramic view, affordable prices, and well-prepared food. Count yourself lucky if you arrive for one of those all-you-can-eat Caribbean style barbecues staged at least once a month: Locals flock to the cafe on those nights for a riotous party time. The catch of the day is usually your best bet, and it can be grilled to your specifications. The chef also turns out succulent steaks and some zestily flavored baby back ribs. Fresh lobster is also a feature, as is grilled shrimp. Throughout the day you can drop in for sandwiches and juicy burgers.

Copper Mine Point, The Valley. ✆ **284/495-5260.** www.mineshaftbvi.com. Reservations not needed. Main courses $19–$34; sandwiches and burgers $7–$16. AE, DC, MC, V. Mon–Thurs 5–10pm; Fri–Sun noon–10pm.

MODERATE

The Flying Iguana MEDITERRANEAN/FRENCH/WEST INDIAN The owner of this place, Puck (also known as Orlington Baptiste), studied his craft in Kansas City with the Hilton Group before setting up this amiable restaurant overlooking the airport's landing strip and the sea. Potted hibiscus and many stuffed and carved iguanas ornament a room that's a celebration of West Indian mystique. The house drink is the Iguana Sunset, a concoction whose secret ingredients change according to the whim of the bartender. Whatever the recipe, it usually produces a lightheaded effect that goes well with the carefully conceived cuisine. The finest examples include fresh fish and all kinds of shellfish, including shrimp, scallops, and conch, often served in combination. Steak, chicken, and lamb are seasoned in a way that evokes both the Caribbean and the Mediterranean. Happy hour is from 4 to 6pm daily.

The Valley (at the airport). ✆ **284/495-5277.** www.flyingiguanabvi.com. Reservations recommended. Main courses $7–$15 breakfast, $12–$36 lunch and dinner. MC, V. Daily 6:30am–9pm (last order).

Rock Café CARIBBEAN/ITALIAN Although the name suggests otherwise, this is not some island clone of the ubiquitous Hard Rock Cafe. You can stop for a drink in the special tequila bar upstairs before heading for a table later. The setting is amid boulders like the ones at the Baths, the number-one sightseeing attraction on Virgin Gorda. The recessed lighting and boardwalks add to the theatrical allure at night. Fortunately, the chefs don't depend just on the setting. The menu is wisely balanced, the dishes well prepared and consumed with affordable wine from a respectable list whose vintages range from Italy to California. Freshly caught red snapper comes in a tangy marinade, and we're especially fond of the chicken piccata. Live entertainment, usually a local band, is featured on Friday night.

The Valley. ✆ **284/495-5482.** Reservations recommended. Main courses $19–$38. AE, MC, V. Daily 4–10:30pm.

INEXPENSIVE

The Bath & Turtle INTERNATIONAL At the end of the waterfront shopping plaza in Spanish Town sits the most popular pub on Virgin Gorda; it's packed with locals during the 4:30-to-6:30pm happy hour. Even if you don't care about food, you can join the regulars over midmorning mango coladas or peach daiquiris. There's live music every Wednesday night. From its handful of indoor and courtyard tables, you can order fried fish fingers, tamarind-ginger wings, very spicy chili, pizzas, fresh pasta, barbecue chicken, steak, lobster, and daily seafood specials such as conch fritters from the simple menu here.

Virgin Gorda Yacht Harbour, Spanish Town. ✆ **284/495-5239.** Reservations required. Main courses $7–$16 breakfast, $10–$19 lunch, $10–$24 dinner. AE, MC, V. Daily 7am–9pm.

The Restaurant at Leverick Bay ☺ CONTINENTAL A combined restaurant and beach bar, this is today's version of the old Pusser's, which now operates only a store here. During the day, you can enjoy all sorts of light meals, including croissant sandwiches, burgers, fried snapper, and pizza. There's also a children's menu. At night, the menu is more ambitious, featuring such intriguing appetizers as roasted pumpkin soup made with island-grown pumpkins and a splash of truffle oil. The chicken satay served with a spicy peanut dipping sauce is also enticing. The chef's main-dish specialty is a tender and slow-roasted prime rib of beef with mashed potatoes and fresh vegetables. The fresh ahi tuna with a tangy wasabi and sweet soy sauce is full of aromatic flavor. If it's featured, you might also opt for the grilled wahoo, caught in local waters, marinated in lime, and served with West Indian rice and fresh vegetables.

Leverick Bay, North Sound. ✆ **284/495-7154.** www.therestaurantatleverickbay.com. Reservations recommended. Main courses $9–$19 lunch, $25–$50 dinner; pizzas from $16. MC, V. Daily 9am–midnight.

Top of the Baths CARIBBEAN This aptly named green-and-white restaurant has a patio with a swimming pool. Locals gather here to enjoy the food they grew up on. At lunch you can order an array of appetizers, sandwiches, and salad plates. You're invited to swim in the pool either before or after dining. At night the kitchen turns out good home-style cookery, including fresh fish, lobster, chicken, and steaks. Look for one of the daily specials. And save room for a piece of that rum cake! Live steel bands perform on Sunday.

The Valley. ✆ **284/495-5497.** www.topofthebaths.com. Main courses $23–$40; sandwiches and salads $12–$18. AE, MC, V. Daily 9am–10:30pm.

Exploring the Island

The northern side of Virgin Gorda is mountainous, with Gorda Peak, at 411m (1,348 ft.), the highest spot on the island. However, the southern half of the island is flat, with large boulders at every turn.

The best way to see the island if you're over for a day trip is to call **Andy Flax** at the Fischers Cove Beach Hotel. He runs the **Virgin Gorda Tours Association** (✆ **284/495-5252;** www.virgingordatours.com), which will give you a tour for $50 per person. You can get picked up at the ferry dock if you give 24-hour notice.

HITTING THE BEACH The best beaches are at **the Baths ★★**, where giant boulders form a series of tranquil pools and grottoes flooded with seawater. (Nearby snorkeling is excellent, and you can rent gear on the beach.) Scientists think volcanic activity brought these boulders to the surface eons ago.

Devil's Bay National Park can be reached by a trail from the Baths. The walk to the secluded coral-sand beach takes about 15 minutes through boulders and dry coastal vegetation. The Baths and surrounding areas are part of a proposed system of parks and protected areas in the B.V.I. The protected area encompasses 273 hectares (675 acres) of land and includes sites at Little Fort, Spring Bay, the Baths, and Devil's Bay on the east coast.

Neighboring the Baths is **Spring Bay,** one of the best of the island's beaches, with white sand, clear water, and good snorkeling. **Trunk Bay** is a wide sandy beach reachable by boat or along a rough path from Spring Bay.

Savannah Bay is a sandy beach north of the yacht harbor, and **Mahoe Bay,** at the Mango Bay Resort, has a gently curving beach with neon-blue water.

DIVING **Kilbrides Sunchaser Scuba** is located at the Bitter End Yacht Club, North Sound (✆ **800/932-4286** in the U.S., or 284/495-9638; www.sunchaserscuba.com). Kilbrides offers the best diving in the British Virgin Islands, at 40 dive sites, including the wreck of the ill-fated HMS *Rhone*. Prices range from $100 to $110 for a two-tank dive on one of the coral reefs. A one-tank dive in the afternoon costs $75. Equipment, except wet suits, is supplied free. It's open daily 7:45am to 5:30pm.

HIKING Consider a trek up the stairs and hiking paths that crisscross Virgin Gorda's largest stretch of undeveloped land, **Virgin Gorda Peak National Park** (www.bvinationalparkstrust.org/vgparks.html). To reach the best departure point for your uphill trek, drive north of the Valley on the only road leading to North Sound for about 15 very hilly minutes. (Using a 4WD vehicle is a good idea.) Stop at the base of the stairway leading steeply uphill. There's a sign pointing to Virgin Gorda Peak National Park.

It takes between 25 and 40 minutes to reach the summit of Gorda Peak, the highest point on the island. You'll be rewarded with sweeping views of the many scattered islets of the Virgin archipelago. There's a tower at the summit, which you can climb for enhanced views. Admire the flora and the fauna (birds, lizards, nonpoisonous snakes) that you're likely to run across en route. Be sure to bring sunscreen, and consider taking a picnic, as tables are scattered along the hiking trails.

Virgin Gorda After Dark

There isn't a lot of action at night, unless you want to make some of your own. The **Bath & Turtle** pub, at Yacht Harbour (✆ **284/495-5239**), brings in local bands for dancing in the summer on Wednesday and Friday at 8:30pm. The **Bitter End Yacht Club** (✆ **284/494-2746;** www.beyc.com) has live music on Fridays. Reached only by boat, this is the best bar on the island. With its dark wood, it evokes an English pub and even serves British brews. Call to see what's happening at the time of your visit.

Andy's Chateau de Pirate, at the Fischer's Cove Beach Hotel, the Valley (✆ **284/495-5252**), is a sprawling, sparsely furnished local hangout. It has a simple stage, a very long bar, and huge oceanfront windows that almost never close.

JOST VAN DYKE

About 150 people live on the 10 sq. km (4 sq. miles) of this mountainous island, off the west side of Tortola. On the south shore, **White Bay** and **Great Harbour** are good beaches. Although there are only a handful of places to stay, several dining choices are available, as the island is a popular stop for the yachting set and many cruise ships, including Cunard (and often some all-gay cruises). The peace and tranquillity often disappear unless you're here when the cruise ships aren't.

In the 1700s, a Quaker colony settled here to develop sugar-cane plantations; one colonist, William Thornton, won the worldwide competition to design the U.S. Capitol in Washington, D.C. Smaller islands surround the place, including Little Jost Van Dyke, the birthplace of Dr. John Lettsome, founder of the London Medical Society.

Essentials

GETTING THERE Take the ferry to White Bay on Jost Van Dyke from either St. Thomas or Tortola. (***Be warned:*** Departure times can vary widely throughout the year and often don't adhere very closely to the printed timetables.) Ferries from St. Thomas depart from Red Hook 3 days a week (Fri, Sat, and Sun), usually twice daily. More convenient (and more frequent) are the daily ferryboat shuttles from Tortola's isolated West End. The latter departs five times a day for the 25-minute trip and costs $25 for adults round-trip, $15 for children 11 and under round-trip. Call the **Paradise New Horizons Ferry Service** (✆ **284/495-9278**) for information about departures from any of the above-mentioned points. If all else fails, carefully negotiate a transportation fee with one of the handful of privately operated water taxis.

EMERGENCIES In the unlikely event that you need the police, call ✆ **284/495-9345.**

Where to Stay

Sandcastle Hotel A retreat for escapists who want few neighbors and absolutely nothing to do, these six cottages are surrounded by flowering shrubbery and bougainvillea, have panoramic views, and open onto a white-sand beach. Bedrooms are spacious, light, and airy, furnished in a tropical motif, with tile floors, local art, rattan furnishings, day beds, and king-size beds. Some units have enclosed showers, outside off the bathroom. At the beachside bar, the Soggy Dollar, you mix your own drinks and keep your own tab. Visiting boaters often drop in to enjoy the beachside informality and order a drink called the Painkiller. A line in the guest book sums it up: "I thought places like this only existed in the movies."

White Bay, Jost Van Dyke, B.V.I. www.soggydollar.com. ✆ **284/495-9888.** Fax 284/495-9999. 6 units. Winter $295 double; off season $230 double. Extra person $50. 3-night minimum. MC, V. Children 15 and under not permitted. **Amenities:** Restaurant; bar; diving; fishing trips; sailing. *In room:* A/C (in 2 rooms), ceiling fan, no phone, Wi-Fi (free).

Sandy Ground These self-sufficient apartments are along the edge of a beach on a 7-hectare (17-acre) hill site on the eastern part of Jost Van Dyke. The complex rents two- and three-bedroom villas. One of our favorites was built on a cliff that seems to hang about 25m (82 ft.) over the beach. The airy villas, each privately owned, are fully equipped with refrigerators and stoves. The interiors vary widely, from rather fashionable to bare bones. The living space is generous, and extras include private balconies or terraces. Most rooms have showers only. The managers help guests with boat rentals and watersports. Diving, day sails, and other activities can also be arranged, and there are dinghies available. Snorkeling and hiking are among the more popular activities.

P.O. Box 594, West End, Tortola, B.V.I. www.sandyground.com. ✆ **284/494-3391.** Fax 284/495-9379. 7 units. Weekly rates: winter $1,950 villa for 2; off season $1,400 villa for 2. Extra person $500 per week in winter, $350 off season. MC, V. Take a private water taxi from Tortola or St. Thomas. **Amenities:** Boats; watersports equipment/rentals. *In room:* Ceiling fan, fridge, no phone.

Where to Dine

Abe's by the Sea WEST INDIAN In this local bar and restaurant, sailors are satisfied with a menu of fish, lobster, conch, ribs, and chicken. Prices are low, too, and it's money well spent. With each main course, you also get peas, rice, and coleslaw.

Little Harbour. ✆ **284/495-9329.** Reservations required for groups of 5 or more. Dinner $22–$45. DC, MC, V. Daily 8am–8pm.

Foxy's Tamarind Bar ★★ WEST INDIAN Arguably the most famous bar in the B.V.I., this mecca of yachties and other boat people is built entirely around sixth-generation Jost Van Dyke native Philicianno "Foxy" Callwood. He opened the place in the late 1960s, and guests have been coming back ever since. A songwriter and entertainer, Foxy is part of the draw. He creates impromptu calypso—almost in the Jamaican tradition—around his guests. If you're singled out, he'll embarrass you, but it's all in good fun. He also plays the guitar and takes a profound interest in preserving the environment of his native island. Thursday through Saturday nights, a live band entertains. On other evenings, it's rock 'n' roll, reggae, or soca. The food and drink aren't neglected, either—try Foxy's Painkiller Punch. During the day, flying-fish sandwiches, *rotis* (Caribbean burritos), and the usual burgers are served, but evenings might bring freshly caught lobster, spicy steamed shrimp, or even grilled fish, depending on the catch of the day.

Great Harbour. ✆ **284/495-9258.** www.foxysbar.com. Reservations recommended. Main courses $10–$15 lunch, $22–$28 dinner. AE, MC, V. Daily 11:30am–midnight. Closed Sept.

Sandcastle INTERNATIONAL/CARIBBEAN This hotel restaurant often serves food that has been frozen, but, even so, the flavors remain consistently good. Lunch is served in the open-air dining room, while lighter fare and snacks are available at the Soggy Dollar Bar. Dinner is by candlelight, featuring four courses, including such dishes as mahimahi Martinique (marinated in orange-lemon-lime juice and cooked with fennel, onions, and dill). Sandcastle hen is another specialty likely to appear on the menu: It's a grilled Cornish hen that's been marinated in rum, honey, lime, and garlic. But we'd skip all that for the sesame snapper, if available. Meals are served with seasonal vegetables and fresh pasta, along with a variety of salads and homemade desserts. Those desserts are luscious and include Key lime pie, Irish whiskey cheesecake, and mango mousse.

At the Sandcastle Hotel, White Bay. ✆ **284/495-9888.** Reservations required for dinner by 4pm. Main courses $7–$15 lunch; fixed-price dinner $22–$35. MC, V. Daily 11am–3pm, and 1 seating at 7pm.

Dive Sites

Increasingly, Jost Van Dyke has been attracting divers. They are drawn, in particular, to the north coast of Little Jost Van Dyke, with its Twin Towers, a pair of rock formations jutting up some 27m (89 ft.). The best dive operator is **JVD Scuba and BVI Eco-Tours,** Great Harbour (✆ **284/495-0271;** www.bvi-ecotours.com). A one-tank dive goes for $85, a two-tank dive for $115. You can also arrange rentals here for snorkel gear, scuba equipment, kayaks, surfboards, windsurfers, small boats, or fishing equipment. You can also arrange boat excursions to nearby islands, costing $750 for 1 day for four persons, including the services of a captain; half-day tours can also be taken, for $395.

ANEGADA

The most northerly and isolated of the British Virgins, 48km (30 miles) east of Tortola, Anegada has a population of about 250, none of whom has found the legendary treasure from the more than 500 wrecks lying off its notorious Horseshoe Reef. It's different from the other British Virgins in that it's a coral-and-limestone atoll, flat, with a 750m (2,461-ft.) airstrip. Its highest point reaches 8m (26 ft.), and it hardly appears on the horizon if you're sailing to it.

At the northern and western ends of the island are some good white-sand beaches, which might be your only reason for coming here. This is a remote little corner of the Caribbean: Don't expect a single frill, and be prepared to put up with some hardships, such as mosquitoes. Most of the island has been declared off-limits to settlement and reserved for birds and other wildlife. The B.V.I. National Parks Trust has established a flamingo colony in a bird sanctuary, which is also the protected home of several different varieties of heron, as well as ospreys and terns. It has also designated much of the interior of the island as a preserved habitat for Anegada's animal population of some 2,000 wild goats, donkeys, and cattle. Among the endangered species being given a new lease on life here is the rock iguana, a fierce-looking but quite harmless reptile that can grow to a length of 2m (6½ ft.). Although rarely seen, these creatures have called Anegada home for thousands of years.

Essentials

GETTING THERE **Fly BVI** (✆ **284/495-1747;** www.bviaircharters.com) operates a charter/sightseeing service between Anegada and Beef Island off Tortola. The one-way passage costs $175 per person.

GETTING AROUND Limited taxi service is available on the island—not that you'll have many places to go. **Tony's Taxis,** which you'll easily spot when you arrive, will take you around the island. It's also possible to rent **bicycles;** ask around.

Where to Stay

The Anegada Reef Hotel offers the only major accommodations on the island. Neptune's Treasure (see below) rents tents and basic rooms.

Anegada Reef Hotel ★ The only major hotel on the island is 5km (3 miles) west of the airport, right on the beachfront. It's one of the most remote places covered in this guide—guests who stay here are, in effect, hiding out. It's a favorite of the yachting set, who enjoy the hospitality. The hotel offers motel-like, basic rooms with private porches, with either a garden or ocean view. You can arrange to go inshore fishing, deep-sea fishing, or bonefishing (there's also a tackle shop); you can also set up snorkeling excursions and secure taxi service and jeep rentals.

There's a beach barbecue nightly; the house specialty is lobster, and many attendees arrive by boat. Reservations for the 7:30pm dinner must be made by 4pm.

Setting Point, Anegada, B.V.I. www.anegadareef.com. ✆ **284/495-8002.** Fax 284/495-9362. 14 units. Winter $265–$400 double; off season $240–$365 double. Rates include all meals. MC, V. **Amenities:** Restaurant; bar. *In room:* A/C, no phone.

Where to Dine

Cow Wreck Beach Bar & Grill ★ WEST INDIAN This laid-back, family-run, and definitely funky joint is a coveted address among yachties anchoring at Anegada. Ice-cold beer and the best lobster in the B.V.I. keep the patrons coming back. The crustaceans are kept in a cage under the water, waiting their "death summons" to the grill. Under a straw roof, diners sit at rough-hewn wooden tables placed outside on a terrace with a view of the water. If you go for lunch, you can tie in a visit with a snorkel trip. At night this is the most popular place on the island for a sundowner. Other standard dishes appear on the menu, but we've never known a guest to order anything but lobster for a main course.

Lower Cow Wreck Beach, Loblolly Bay East. ✆ **284/495-8047.** www.cowwreckbeach.com. Reservations required for dinner by 4pm. Main courses $18–$48. MC, V. Daily 7am–midnight; dinner seatings 6pm. Closing time for bar "when the last customer departs."

Neptune's Treasure INTERNATIONAL Set near its own 24-slip marina, near the southern tip of the island in the same cluster of buildings that includes the more high-priced Anegada Reef Hotel, this funky bar and restaurant usually hosts a mix of yacht owners and local residents. Dining is in a spacious indoor area whose focal point is a bar and lots of nautical memorabilia. The drink of choice is a Dark and Stormy, composed of ginger beer and rum. The Soares family and their staff serve platters of swordfish, lobster, fish fingers, chicken, steaks, and ribs; dispense information about local snorkeling sites; and generally maintain order and something approaching a (low-key) party atmosphere.

They also offer nine simple bedrooms with air-conditioning. Depending on the season, rooms with a private bathroom rent for $110 to $275 double. Discounts are offered for stays of a week or more.

Between Pomato and Saltheap points. ✆ **284/495-9439.** www.neptunestreasure.com. Reservations for dinner must be made by 4pm. Main courses $8–$12 breakfast, $6–$12 lunch, $18–$45 dinner. MC, V. Daily 8am–10pm.

PETER ISLAND ★

Half of this island, which has a good marina and docking facilities, is devoted to the yacht club. The other part is deserted. Beach facilities are found at palm-fringed Deadman's Bay, which faces the Atlantic but is protected by a reef. All goods and services are at the one resort (see below). The island is so private that, except for an occasional mason at work, about the only company you'll encounter will be an iguana or a feral cat whose ancestors were abandoned generations ago by shippers. (The cats are said to have virtually eliminated the island's rodent population.)

A complimentary, hotel-operated ferry, **Peter Island Ferry** (© **284/495-2000**), departs Tortola from the pier at Trellis Bay, near the airport. Other boats depart six or seven times a day from Baugher's Bay in Road Town. Passengers must notify the hotel 2 weeks before their arrival so transportation can be arranged.

Where to Stay & Dine

Peter Island Resort & Spa ★★★ This 720-hectare (1,779-acre) tropical island is solely dedicated to Peter Island Resort guests and yacht owners who moor their crafts here. The island's tropical gardens and hillside are bordered by five gorgeous private beaches, including Deadman's Beach. (In spite of its name, it's often voted one of the world's most romantic beaches in travel-magazine reader polls.)

The resort contains 32 rooms facing Sprat Bay and Sir Francis Drake Channel (oceanview rooms), and 20 larger rooms on Deadman's Bay Beach (beachfront). Designed with a casual elegance, each has a balcony or terrace. The least-desirable rooms are also the smallest and housed in two-story, A-frame structures next to the harbor. The Crow's Nest, a luxurious four-bedroom villa, overlooks the harbor and Deadman's Bay, and features a private swimming pool. The Hawk's Nest villas are three-bedroom villas set on a tropical hillside.

P.O. Box 211, Road Town, Tortola, B.V.I. www.peterisland.com. © **800/346-4451** in the U.S., or 284/495-2000. Fax 284/495-2500. 52 units. Winter $950–$1,375 double, $4,600 3-bedroom villa, $9,800 4-bedroom villa; off season $590–$900 double, $3,100 3-bedroom villa, $6,200 4-bedroom villa. Rates include all meals and transportation from the Tortola airport. AE, MC, V. **Amenities:** 2 restaurants; 2 bars; babysitting; bikes; boats; exercise room; outdoor pool; room service; spa; 4 tennis courts (lit); watersports equipment/rentals. *In room:* A/C, CD player (in suites), hair dryer, minibar, Wi-Fi (free).

GUANA ISLAND ★

This 340-hectare (840-acre) island, a nature preserve and wildlife sanctuary, is one of the most private hideaways in the Caribbean. Don't come here looking for action; rather, vacationing here is to retreat from the world. This small island right off the coast of Tortola offers seven virgin beaches and nature trails ideal for hiking; it abounds in unusual species of plant and animal life. Arawak relics have been found here. You can climb 242m (794-ft.) Sugarloaf Mountain for a panoramic view. It's said that the name of the island came from a jutting rock that resembled the head of an iguana.

The Guana Island Club will send a boat to meet arriving guests at the Beef Island airport (trip time is 10 min.).

Where to Stay & Dine

Guana Island Club ★★ The sixth- or seventh-largest of the British Virgin Islands, Guana Island was bought in 1974 by Henry and Gloria Jarecki, dedicated conservationists who run this resort as a nature preserve and wildlife sanctuary. The cluster of white cottages was built as a private club in the 1930s on the foundations of a Quaker homestead. The stone cottages have only two phones. Because the dwellings are staggered along a flower-dotted ridge overlooking the Caribbean and the Atlantic, the sense of privacy is almost absolute. Groups of up to 36 can rent the entire island. Although water is scarce, each of the airy accommodations has a shower. The decor is rattan and wicker. Renting North Beach cottage, the most luxurious of the accommodations, is like renting a private home. There are seven beaches, some of which require a boat to reach.

P.O. Box 32, Road Town, Tortola, B.V.I. www.guana.com. © **800/544-8262** in the U.S., or 284/494-2354. Fax 284/495-2900. (For reservations, write or call the Guana Island Club Reservations Office, 67 Irving Pl., 12th Floor, New York, NY 10003; © **212/482-6247;** fax 917/591-6631.) 15 units. Winter $1,250–$1,550 double, $2,325–$2,825 cottage, $4,325–$8,100 villa; off season $695–$950 double, $1,535–$2,165 cottage, $4,325–$6,500 villa. Rent the island for $19,585–$33,975 per day. Rates include all meals and drinks served with meals. MC, V. Closed Sept–Oct. Call ahead to see if children are being accepted. **Amenities:** Restaurant; self-service bar; babysitting; boats; fishing; nature trails; 2 tennis courts (lit); watersports equipment/rentals. *In room:* Ceiling fan, no phone, Wi-Fi (free).

THE CAYMAN ISLANDS

8

Ringed by coral reefs and pristine azure waters, the three islands that comprise the Cayman Islands are a marine paradise in the western Caribbean. You can swim with stingrays in sparkling shallows, dive amid rainbow-hued fish along coral reefs, or simply plunk yourself down on one of the islands' white-sand beaches with a rum punch in hand. The Caymans have a well-developed tourism infrastructure offering a range of lodgings, from funky West Indian cottages to luxury resorts, and diverse dining options.

Beaches A curling stretch of powdery white sand, **Seven Mile Beach** on Grand Cayman is picture-postcard beautiful; it's fringed by shady casuarina trees and blissfully free of litter and beach hawkers. Grab snorkel and fin and head to **Rum Point,** a secluded spot whose clear waters teem with rainbow-hued fish. **Point of Sand,** at the southeastern tip of Little Cayman, has luminescent pink sand—on many weekdays, you're likely to have the beach all to yourself.

Things to Do Take a walking tour of the historic capital city, **George Town,** with the National Trust. Visit the **Cayman Islands National Museum,** to learn about the cultural and natural history of the island. You don't need any special skills to take part in the national sport of the Caymans: **fishing.** Blue marlin, wahoo, dolphin, and tuna await those who cast their lines. This is one of the Caribbean's top diving destinations, with more than 200 **scuba diving sites** scattered throughout the islands.

Eating & Drinking Chow down on locally caught fish at a waterside shack, or indulge in a five-course meal in an upscale restaurant. For a taste of island cuisine, sample a bowl of **conch chowder,** a hearty tomato-based soup made with sweet peppers, onions, and a smidgeon of salt pork or bacon. The charming waterfront **Calypso Grill** is a local favorite for its marinated conch and Cuban-style shrimp. **Hemingway's,** serving paella, crab cakes, and the catch of the day, has garnered international accolades.

Nature Stroll the 200-year-old, 3km (2-mile) **Mastic Trail** on Grand Cayman, which slices through a dry subtropical forest. Here you'll find a native mangrove swamp, tall mahogany trees and royal palms, and birdlife that includes the Caribbean dove, the Cuban bullfinch, and the Grand Cayman parrot. The **Cayman Turtle Farm** is the protected habitat of thousands of green sea turtles, an endangered species. Enter a mesh-enclosed area where butterflies from all over the world fly freely at the **Butterfly Farm.**

ESSENTIALS

Visitor Information

The **Cayman Islands Department of Tourism** (© **800/263-5805**) has the following office in the United States: 3 Park Ave., 39th Floor, New York, NY 10116 (© **212/889-9009**). In Canada, 1200 Bay St., Ste. 1101, Toronto, ON M5R 2A5 (© **800/263-5805** or 416/485-1550; fax 416/485-0835). In the United Kingdom, the contact is **Cayman Islands Department of Tourism,** 6 Arlington St., London SW1 1RE (© **020/7491-7771;** fax 020/7409-7773).

Three websites that describe the Cayman Islands include **www.caymanislands.ky**, **www.divecayman.ky**, and **www.caymantripper.com**.

Getting There

The Cayman Islands are easily accessible. Flying time from Miami is 1 hour, 10 minutes; from Houston, 2 hours, 45 minutes; from Tampa, 1 hour, 40 minutes; and from Atlanta, 3 hours, 35 minutes. Only a handful of nonstop flights are available from the U.S. Midwest, so most visitors use Miami as their gateway.

Cayman Airways (© **800/422-9626** in the U.S. and Canada, or 345/949-8200; www.caymanairways.com) has the most frequent service to Grand Cayman, with three daily flights from Miami, four flights a week from Tampa, and occasional nonstop flights from Houston. Depending on bookings and the season, they also fly to Boston, Kingston (Jamaica), and Havana (Cuba). Since 2008, Cayman Airways has also been flying nonstop from Chicago to Grand Cayman, with twice-weekly flights departing and arriving on Wednesday and Sunday. It's also the only airline with regularly scheduled service between Grand Cayman and the sister islands of Cayman Brac and Little Cayman.

Many visitors also fly to Grand Cayman on **American Airlines** (© **800/433-7300** in the U.S. and Canada; www.aa.com), which flies once a day from Miami. **US Airways** (© **800/622-1015** in the U.S. and Canada; www.usairways.com) flies nonstop daily from Charlotte. **Delta** (© **800/221-1212** in the U.S. and Canada; www.delta.com) flies daily into Grand Cayman from its hub in Atlanta. **Continental Airlines** (© **800/231-0856** in the U.S. and Canada; www.continental.com) offers service between Houston and Grand Cayman on Wednesday, Friday, Saturday, and Sunday. **Air Canada** (© **888/247-2262** in the U.S. and Canada;

Ahoy, Matey!

Cayman Islands Pirates' Week is held during a 10-day period every year during early November. It's a national festival in which cutlass-bearing pirates and sassy wenches storm George Town, capture the governor, throng the streets, and stage a costume parade. The celebration, which is held throughout the Caymans, pays tribute to the nation's past and its cultural heritage. For exact dates and other information, contact the **Pirates Week Festival Office** (© **345/949-5078; www.piratesweekfestival.com**).

www.aircanada.com) flies nonstop from Toronto on Sunday (in winter only) and Wednesday (year-round). **British Airways** (✆ **800/247-9297** in the U.S. and Canada, or 0844/493-0787 in the U.K.; www.britishairways.com) offers between three and four weekly flights, depending on the season, from London's Gatwick Airport, with a stopover in Nassau.

[Fast FACTS] THE CAYMAN ISLANDS

Business Hours Normally, banks are open Monday to Thursday from 9am to 4pm and Friday 9am to 4:30pm. Shops are usually open Monday to Saturday 9am to 5pm.

Currency The legal tender is the Cayman Islands dollar **(CI$)**. Whereas the U.S. dollar and the Cayman Island dollar are more or less permanently fixed at a ratio of 1 to 1.25, the British pound and the Cayman dollar float freely, according to a complicated set of international economic factors. Canadian, U.S., and British currencies are accepted throughout the Cayman Islands, but you'll save money if you exchange your U.S. dollars for Cayman Islands dollars. The Cayman dollar breaks down into 100 cents. Coins come in 1¢, 5¢, 10¢, and 25¢ denominations. Bills come in denominations of CI$1, CI$5, CI$10, CI$25, CI$50, and CI$100 (there is no CI$20 bill). Most hotels quote rates in U.S. dollars. However, many restaurants quote prices in Cayman Islands dollars, which might lead you to think that food is much cheaper than it is. *Prices in this chapter are quoted in U.S. dollars.*

Documents Citizens of the United States should carry a valid passport, both for the purposes of entering the Cayman Islands and also for ease in returning to the U.S. at the end of their trip. Citizens of the United Kingdom and Canada should have at least a certified birth certificate with a raised seal and a photo ID, although a passport is preferred. All visitors need a return or ongoing ticket.

Electricity It's 110-volt AC (60 cycles), so U.S. and Canadian appliances will not need adapters or transformers.

Emergencies For medical, police, or fire-related emergencies, dial ✆ **911.**

Hospital There's a hospital on Grand Cayman and another small one on Cayman Brac. Seriously ill cases, or cases associated with a genuinely serious accident on Little Cayman, are usually transported by plane or helicopter to Grand Cayman. On Grand Cayman, the **Cayman Islands Hospital** is at 1 Hospital Rd. (✆ **345/949-8600;** www.hsa.ky); on Cayman Brac, the **Faith Hospital** is at Stake Bay (✆ **345/948-2243**); and on Little Cay, the **Little Cayman Clinic** (✆ **345/948-0072**) lies adjacent to the airport. You can summon emergency help on all three of the islands by dialing 911.

Language English is the official language of the islands.

Liquor Laws Beer, wine, and liquor are sold at most grocery and convenience stores Monday to Saturday. It is legal to have an open container on the beach.

Taxes A government tourist tax of 10% is added to your hotel bill. A departure tax of $25 is collected when you leave the Caymans, usually in the form of a fee that's automatically included in the price of your airplane ticket. There are no taxes on goods and services.

Telephone To call the Cayman Islands from the United States, dial **1,** then the **345** area code and the local number. Once you're on the island, to charge a long-distance call to a calling card, here are some access numbers: **AT&T** at ✆ **800/872-2881, Sprint** at ✆ **888/366-4663,** and **MCI** at ✆ **800/888-8000.** In lieu of any of these three carriers (some smaller hotels might not accept them), the access code for a local telephone carrier (Blue Skies) is **800/534-9718.**

Time U.S. Eastern Standard Time is in effect year-round; daylight saving time is not observed.

Tipping Virtually every restaurant in the Cayman Islands adds a 10% to 15% service charge in lieu of tipping, so check your bill carefully. Hotels also often add a 10% service charge to your bill. Taxi drivers expect a 10% to 15% tip.

Water According to most official statements, the water in the Cayman Islands is safe to drink directly from the tap, but we've found that many local residents opt, instead, for bottled water whenever possible, using tap water for only cooking and cleaning.

Weather The temperature in the Cayman Islands seldom goes lower than 70°F (21°C) or higher than 90°F (32°C). The daily average is between 77°F (25°C) and 84°F (29°C).

GRAND CAYMAN ★★

The largest of the three islands and a real diving mecca, Grand Cayman survives and flourishes thanks to a unique blend of tourism, financial services, low crime, conservatism, and political stability. Home to the branch offices of more than 500 banks and dozens of insurance companies, its capital, George Town, is the offshore banking center of the Caribbean. (No problems finding an ATM here!) Retirees are drawn to the peace and tranquillity of this British Crown Colony, site of many large-scale real estate and condominium developments. The overwhelming majority of the Cayman Islands' population lives on Grand Cayman. The manners and presuppositions of the locals reflect their British heritage.

Essentials

GETTING THERE See "Getting There," above.

GETTING AROUND All arriving flights are met by taxis. The fares are fixed by the director of civil aviation (✆ **345/949-7811**); typical one-way taxi fares from the airport to Seven Mile Beach for between one and three passengers and their luggage range from $20 to $30. Cabs are legally required to carry a printed version of the official rates established by the Caymanian government, usually inside the cab drivers' notebooks.

Taxis (which can hold a maximum of five people) can also take visitors on around-the-island tours. **Cayman Cab Team** (✆ **345/947-1173**) offers 24-hour service. You can also call **A.A. Transportation** at ✆ **345/949-7222.**

The island has limited **bus service,** with approximately 38 minibuses operated by 24 licensed operators, serving eight routes daily from 6am to midnight. The bus terminal lies adjacent to the public library on Edward Street in George Town. The one-way per-person fare from George Town to points within George Town and along most of Seven Mile Beach is $2.50. Fares from George Town to far-distance points of Grand Cayman—say, to the most distant tip of the East End—can go as high as $4.40 each way.

If you can safely and responsibly drive on the left, consider renting a car. Several car rental companies operate on the island, including **Avis,** through Avis Cisco

Grand Cayman Island

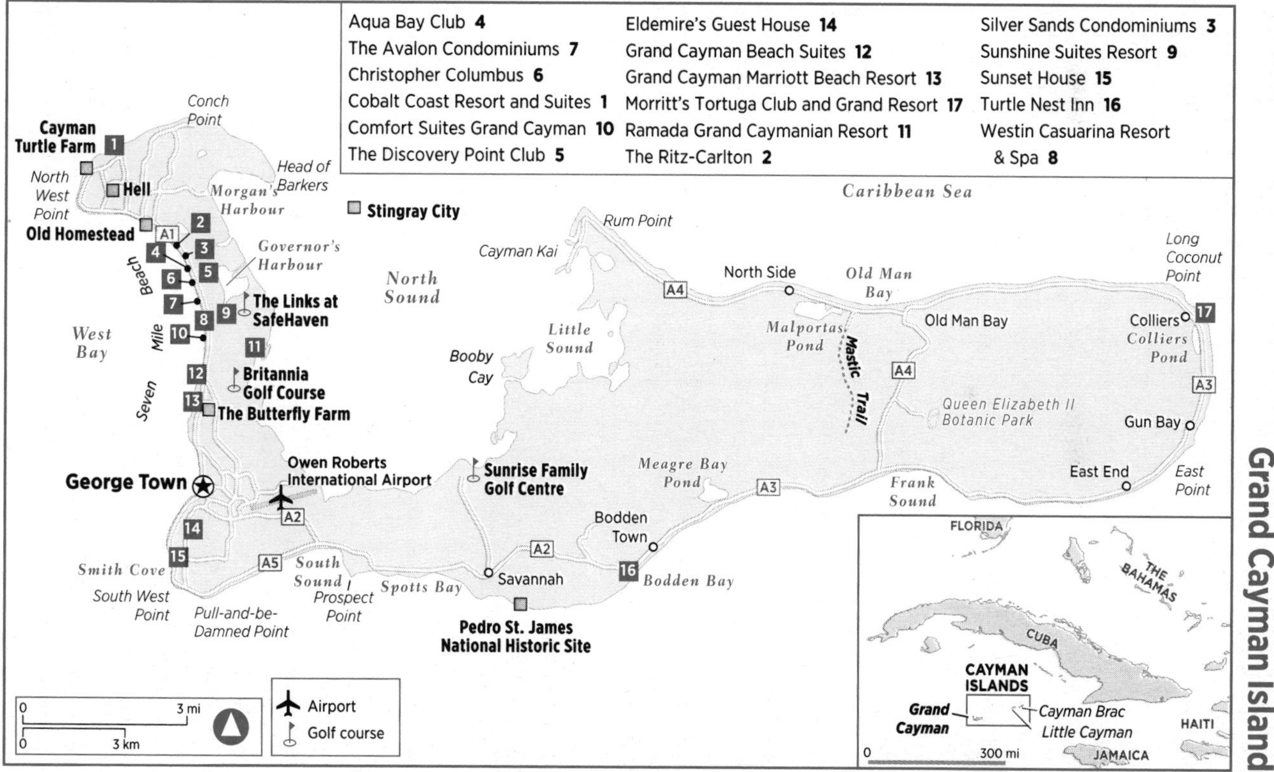

(✆ **800/331-1084** in the U.S. and Canada, or 345/949-2468; www.aviscayman.com); **Budget** (✆ **800/472-3325** in the U.S. and Canada, or 345/949-5605; www.budgetcayman.com); **Hertz,** through a local franchise, Ace Rent-a-Car (✆ **800/654-3001** or 345/949-2280; www.acerentacarltd.com); or **Andy's Rent-a-Car,** a well-respected local car rental company (✆ **345/949-8111;** www.andys.ky). Each will issue the mandatory Cayman Islands driving permit for an additional $7.50. All four require that you make reservations between 6 and 36 hours before pickup. Government regulations demand that drivers be at least 21 years old to rent a car, and some require that drivers be at least 25. Each of the outfits maintains rental kiosks and inventories of available cars within walking distance of the airport, although most visitors find it easier to take a taxi to their hotels and then arrange for the cars to be brought to them.

Remember to drive on the left and to reserve your car as far in advance as possible, especially in midwinter.

VISITOR INFORMATION The **Department of Tourism** is temporarily housed in the Regatta Office Park, Windward 3, West Bay Road, P.O. Box 67, Grand Cayman KY1-1102 (✆ **345/949-0623;** fax 345/949-4053). Hours are Monday to Friday 8:30am to 5pm.

FAST FACTS The only full-service hospital is the **Cayman Islands Hospital** (also known as the George Town Hospital), 1 Hospital Rd. (✆ **345/949-8600;** www.hsa.ky). The most central pharmacy is **Cayman Drug,** at Kirk Freeport Centre, George Town (✆ **345/949-2597**).

In George Town, the main branch of the **post office** and philatelic bureau is located at 14 Edward St. (✆ **345/949-2474**). It's open Monday to Friday from 8:15am to 5pm, Saturday 9am to 12:30pm. There are branch offices on Cayman Brac and Little Cayman, and a total of at least nine additional branch post offices on Grand Cayman as well, including branches at the airport, along Seven Mile Beach, and in the barren-looking, rock-studded neighborhood known as Hell, each maintaining the same hours as the main branch.

Where to Stay

Nearly all the hotels are lined up along Seven Mile Beach. Hotels, unlike many Caymanian restaurants, generally quote prices in U.S. dollars. When choosing a hotel, keep in mind that the quoted rates do not include the 10% government tax or the hotel service tax, which varies between 6% and 10%, depending on the hotel.

VERY EXPENSIVE

The Avalon Condominiums ★★ One of Grand Cayman's best condo complexes is the Avalon, which occupies prime real estate on a stretch of Seven Mile Beach. Painted a distinctive shade of blue-violet (the staff refers to it as "orchid"), it consists of 27 oceanfront three-bedroom/three-bathroom units, 19 of which can be rented. About a 10-minute drive from George Town, it's well maintained, pleasant, and stylish. Children 11 and under are allowed on-site, but overall, they're rather carefully "policed" for misbehavior and loud noises. The well-appointed, spacious units have an English colonial motif, durable flowered or pastel-colored upholsteries, plus king-size or twin beds. Each condo has a fully equipped open-sided kitchen and a large screened lanai that overlooks a stretch of the beach.

1371 West Bay Rd. (P.O. Box 31236), Grand Cayman, B.W.I. www.avaloncayman.com. ✆ **305/395-4503** in the U.S., or 345/945-4171. Fax 345/945-4189. 27 units. Winter $975 apt for 4, $1,175 apt for 6; off season $595 for all apt. AE, MC, V. **Amenities:** Exercise room; Jacuzzi; outdoor pool; sauna; tennis court (lit). *In room:* A/C, TV, hair dryer, kitchen, Wi-Fi (free).

Grand Cayman Beach Suites ★ ☺ It's stylish and an all-suite resort set directly on the sands of Seven Mile Beach. This property originated in the 1980s as a part of the 36-hectare (89-acre) resort development. The beach suites—originally conceived as an afterthought to a larger resort—are some of the most sought-after accommodations on Grand Cayman. And although the land on which the truncated resort sits is relatively compact, the owners have placed lots of distractions and diversions on-site, including two restaurants, and direct access to the beach. Rooms, each configured as a compact but artfully designed suite, are well upholstered and have private verandas with views of the sea. Restaurants lie nearby; there are also some convenient markets if you want to cook inside your suite.

George Town, Seven Mile Beach (P.O. Box 1588), Grand Cayman, B.W.I. www.grand-cayman-beach-suites.com. ✆ **345/949-1234.** Fax 345/949-8528. 53 suites. Winter $390–$450 1-bedroom suite, $870–$1,170 2-bedroom suite; off season $270–$330 1-bedroom suite, $540–$660 2-bedroom suite. AE, DC, DISC, MC, V. **Amenities:** 2 restaurants; 4 bars; babysitting; children's programs (3–12); 9-hole golf course; health club; Jacuzzi; 2 outdoor pools (1 with swim-up bar); room service; spa; watersports equipment/rentals. *In room:* A/C, TV, fridge, hair dryer, MP3 docking station, Wi-Fi ($13 per day).

The Ritz-Carlton ★★★ ☺ With amenities and a service level that's rivaled only by the Westin, the Ritz-Carlton is the largest, plushest, most prestigious, most spectacular, and most awe-inspiring resort in the Cayman Islands. Straddling both sides of the boulevard that parallels Seven Mile Beach, the hotel is divided into two regal and distinctly separate buildings. Binding the components together is a soundproofed, climate-controlled catwalk that stretches above the sometimes congested rush-hour traffic of West Bay Street. Everything is climate-controlled, meticulously manicured, and covered with marble, stone, expensive hardwoods, or ultraplush wall-to-wall carpeting. The Ritz covers 58 hectares (143 acres), the entire width of the island, from Seven Mile Beach to North Sands, including a Greg Norman–designed golf course and the world's first spa inspired by La Prairie's Silver Rain. All the rooms are blissful, but the especially luxurious ones are available at the Reserve, a collection of two dozen oceanfront condos with large living and dining areas and wide terraces. A $35 resort fee, in addition to the room rate, covers a host of extras, including the use of the spa and watersports equipment.

West Bay Rd., Grand Cayman, B.W.I. www.ritzcarlton.com. ✆ **800/542-8680** in the U.S. and Canada, or 345/943-9000. Fax 345/943-9001. 365 units. Winter $460–$960 double, $1,100-$3,400 suite; off season $450–$780 double, $900-$1,950 suite. AE, DC, MC, V. **Amenities:** 5 restaurants; 2 bars; babysitting; boats; children's programs (ages 4–18); golf course; 2 outdoor pools; room service; spa; watersports equipment/rentals. *In room:* A/C, TV, hair dryer, kitchen (in some), minibar, Wi-Fi (included in resort fee).

Silver Sands Condominiums ★ ☺ A good choice for families, this modern eight-building complex is arranged horseshoe fashion on a low-density stretch of sandy beachfront, 11km (6¾ miles) north of George Town. The well-maintained apartments are grouped around a rectangular freshwater pool. The eight three-story apartment blocks were solidly built to high standards in the late 1970s. Each is configured as either a two-bedroom/two-bathroom or three-bedroom/three-bathroom unit. The two-bedroom units can hold up to six people, and the three-bedroom units can house up to eight. Each apartment has a balcony and a fully equipped kitchen.

2131 West Bay Rd., Seven Mile Beach (P.O. Box 752WB), Grand Cayman, B.W.I. http://silversandscondos.com. ✆ **345/949-3343.** Fax 345/949-1223. 42 units. Winter $520–$570 2-bedroom apt, $610–$710 3-bedroom apt; off season $340–$570 2-bedroom apt, $410–$480 3-bedroom apt. Additional person $25 extra. Maximum two children 12 and under stay free in parent's room. 7-night minimum in winter, 3-night minimum in off season. AE, MC, V. **Amenities:** 2 tennis courts (lit). *In room:* A/C, ceiling fan, cable TV, kitchen, Wi-Fi (free).

Westin Casuarina Resort & Spa ★★ After the Ritz-Carlton, this is the best accessorized, most elegant, and plushest resort in the Cayman Islands. Set directly astride the sands of Seven Mile Beach, it has artfully landscaped gardens and grounds, plenty of facilities, and an oval-shaped, large pool. Most of the bedrooms have French doors that open onto private balconies and conservative, comfortable furnishings. Units are a bit small for such a luxury hotel but are well equipped and comfortable. Thanks to the building's layout in the form of a giant U, about two-thirds of the accommodations have sea views, a higher percentage than at the Ritz-Carlton; the others look out on the parking lot and West Bay Road, so ask when you reserve.

West Bay Rd., Seven Mile Beach (P.O. Box 30620), Grand Cayman, B.W.I. www.westincasuarina.com. ✆ **800/937-8461** in the U.S., or 345/945-3800. Fax 345/949-5825. 343 units. Winter $410–$580 double, $1,050 1-bedroom suite, from $1,450 2-bedroom suite; off season $324–$555 double, $650 1-bedroom suite, from $1,000 2-bedroom suite. AE, MC, V. **Amenities:** 3 restaurants; 3 bars; boats; children's programs (ages 4–12); dive shop; exercise room; golf; outdoor pool; room service; sauna; spa; watersports equipment/rentals. *In room:* A/C, cable TV, fridge, hair dryer, Internet ($15 per day), minibar.

EXPENSIVE

Aqua Bay Club ★ These privately owned oceanfront condos are located on the western end of Seven Mile Beach, about a 20-minute run from the airport. On well-kept grounds with coconut palms, the compound dates from 1989. Short-term rentals are arranged here while the owners are away. Each accommodation offers the same layout, and most of the units come with two bedrooms and two full bathrooms. In most cases, the master bedroom opens onto a terrace with a view of the water. Each accommodation comes with a well-equipped kitchen, including a dishwasher. Special features are machines for laundry, as well as grills for barbecuing near the beach. As an added bonus, a cellphone is provided for each rental. The location is a bit remote, so you'll probably have to rely on taxi service unless you rent a car.

Seven Mile Beach (P.O. Box 30091), Grand Cayman, B.W.I. www.aquabayclub.com. ✆ **800/825-8703** or 345/945-4728. Fax 345/945-5681. 21 units. Winter $325–$495 1-bedroom suite, $395–$625 2-bedroom suite; off season $275–$300 1-bedroom suite, $325–$375 2-bedroom suite. AE, MC, V. **Amenities:** Jacuzzi; outdoor pool. *In room:* A/C, ceiling fan, TV/DVD/VCR, CD player, Internet (free), kitchen.

Christopher Columbus ★ ☺ This intimate condo complex and hideaway, tucked at the northern end of Seven Mile Beach, has some of the best snorkeling right off its beach. The choice is idyllic for families because the lodgings consist of either two- or three-bedroom units. The condos come with spacious, well-equipped kitchens and large living rooms, decorated with pastel colors, handsomely furnished, and well-maintained. Thatched cabanas line the beach, and there is a private swimming pool. The complex has no restaurant; nearby dining options exist, but you'll need a car.

2013 West Bay Rd., Seven Mile Beach, Grand Cayman, B.W.I. www.christophercolumbuscondos.com. ✆ **866/311-5231** or 345/945-4354. Fax 345/945-5062. 30 units. Winter $340 2-bedroom, $490 3-bedroom, $540 penthouse; off season $250 2-bedroom, $325 3-bedroom, $350 penthouse. AE, DISC, MC, V. **Amenities:** Outdoor pool; 2 tennis courts (lit). *In room:* A/C, kitchen, Wi-Fi (free).

The Discovery Point Club ★ ☺ Located at the far end of the northern stretch of Seven Mile Beach, in West Bay (10km/6¼ miles from George Town), this tranquil and relatively isolated group of condos is entirely composed of ocean-bordering suites. The venue here is local, West Indian, and rural—if you're looking for big-city ways, forget it. Some of the best snorkeling along the beach is found just off the shores here. You can also retreat to the club's freshwater pool or heated Jacuzzi. The accommodations here are comfortable and well-maintained, and, in some cases, better than those offered by some nearby competitors. Condos feature tasteful furnishings and a screened-in patio. Each renovated unit is decorated by the individual owner, and all come with fully equipped kitchens. Children 5 and under stay free, and cribs and rollaways are available. Each condo receives daily maid service.

West Bay Rd., West Bay (P.O. Box 439), Grand Cayman, B.W.I. www.discoverypointclub.com. ✆ **866/384-9980** or 345/945-4724. Fax 345/945-5051. 45 units. Winter $495 double, $675 quad; off season $300 double, $345 quad. AE, DISC, MC, V. **Amenities:** Jacuzzi; outdoor pool; 2 tennis courts (lit). *In room:* A/C, cable TV, hair dryer, kitchen, Internet (free).

Grand Cayman Marriott Beach Resort ★ ☺ Way down in the pecking order from the Ritz-Carlton and the Westin Casuarina, this five-story choice on Seven Mile Beach is still among the top-ranked hotels on the island. A favorite with large package-tour groups and conventions, it's a 5-minute drive north of George Town. The resort has watersports facilities, and there's good snorkeling 15m (49 ft.) offshore. Its Hispanic design contains roofed-over loggias that open onto views of the sea and a landscaped interior courtyard. Regrettably, it sits astride a relatively narrow portion of Seven Mile Beach. The accommodations were all remodeled and are among the most spacious on the island. Each contains modern art, dark-grained wood furniture that includes an armoire, pastel walls, tropical-patterned fabrics, large closets, and private balconies.

389 West Bay Rd., Seven Mile Beach (P.O. Box 30371), Grand Cayman, B.W.I. www.marriott.com. ✆ **800/223-6388** in the U.S. or Canada, or 345/949-0088. Fax 345/949-0288. 295 units. Winter $340–$475 double, $740 junior suite, $1,150 suite; off season $199–$299 double, $570 junior suite, $950 suite. AE, DISC, MC, V. **Amenities:** 3 restaurants; 2 bars; boats; children's programs (Camp Coconuts); health club; Jacuzzi; outdoor pool; room service; sauna; watersports equipment/rentals. *In room:* A/C TV, fridge (in some), hair dryer, Wi-Fi ($9.95 per day).

Morritt's Tortuga Club and Grand Resort ★ On 3 beachfront hec acres) on the east end of the island, this resort offers some of the island surfing and some of its best diving. Tortuga Divers (p. 194), which r the premises, focuses on the dive trade and, to a lesser extent, th that has developed offshore. About a 40km (25-mile) drive fro is composed of clusters of three-story beachfront condos Each accommodation was built in the Antillean plantati a former hotel. And each is part of either the Tort There's a bit more space within units at the Gran 10% and 15% more from the rates noted belov those within the Tortuga Club. Many are comfortably furnished apartments has guests opt for meals in the complex's

East End (P.O. Box 496GT), Grand Cayman, B.W. 345/947-7449. Fax 345/947-3544. 160 units. Win 2-bedroom suite; off season $250 studio, $300 1-bedr MC, V. **Amenities:** Restaurant; 4 bars; babysitting; exe watersports equipment/rentals. *In room:* A/C, cable TV, kitc

MODERATE

Cobalt Coast Resort and Suites ★★ Fans of this resort liken it to a contemporary European bed-and-breakfast where most of the clients are deeply involved with diving. It's one of the best resorts for divers on Grand Cayman, thanks to the on-site presence of a full-service dive operation (Divetech) and the presence, a short distance offshore, of a deep drop-off (the North Wall) that's loaded with many different types of marine life. Don't expect a sand beach: The coastline is entirely composed of jagged rocks, with ladders and metal steps by which you'll lower yourself into the surf. Units include both oceanfront suites and standard rooms, which are roomy, modern, cozy, and soothing, with Marimekko fabrics from Finland and European plumbing fixtures.

18 Seafan Dr., West Bay (P.O. Box 159), Grand Cayman, B.W.I. www.cobaltcoast.com or www.divetech.com. ✆ **888/946-5656** in the U.S., 345/946-5656 for hotel, or 946-5658 for Divetech dive center. Fax 345/946-5657 for hotel, or 946-5659 for dive center. 18 units. Winter $290 double, $330 1-bedroom suite for 2, $525 2-bedroom suite or villa for 4; off-season $170 double, $195 1-bedroom suite for 2, $355 2-bedroom suite or villa for 4. Dive packages available. AE, DC, MC, V. **Amenities:** Restaurant; bar; Jacuzzi; outdoor pool; watersports equipment/rentals. *In room:* A/C, cable TV, fridge, hair dryer, Wi-Fi (free).

Comfort Suites Grand Cayman Streamlined, efficient, and relatively cost effective, this hotel is often cited as one of the less expensive accommodations along Seven Mile Beach. Rising five sand-colored stories above the southern end of the beach, it follows a familiar layout that has proven successful in hundreds of other locations. The comfortable bedrooms each have a large writing table and are comfortably but predictably outfitted. Unfortunately, none of the rooms has a balcony or veranda, and only some have worthwhile views. One- and two-bedroom suites also contain stoves and dishwashers. There's a small pool and sandy footpath.

West Bay Rd., Grand Cayman, B.W.I. www.caymancomfort.com. ✆ **800/517-4000** in the U.S., or 345/945-7300. Fax 345/945-7400. 108 units. Winter $210–$300 double; off season $145–$240 double. Rates include breakfast. AE, DC, MC, V. **Amenities:** Restaurant; bar; babysitting; bikes; exercise room; Jacuzzi; pool; watersports equipment/rentals. *In room:* A/C, TV, hair dryer, kitchenette (in studios), kitchen (in suites), Wi-Fi (free).

Ramada Grand Caymanian Resort ★ ☺ Opening in 2010, this became the first resort to occupy the shores of the North Sound Lagoon. The resort, which stands adjacent to the North Sound Golf Club, is loaded with amenities and attractions. From the hotel's own dock, you can easily commute by boat or jet skis to Stingray [illegible]y. Since its opening, the hotel has been a big hit with the family trade. Guests can [illegible]ct from a studio for two or else one- or two-bedroom suites, the latter with a full [illegible]en and washer and dryer. All suites contain balconies and whirlpool tubs. Inci[illegible]y, the one-bedroom sleeps four, while the two-bedroom suite can accommo[illegible] guests.

[illegible]n Dr., Crystal Harbour (P.O. Box 31495), Grand Cayman, B.V.I. www.grandcaymanian.ky. [illegible]-3100. Fax 345/949-3161. 170 units. Winter $160 studio, $190 1-bedroom suite, $230–$460 [illegible]ite; off season $140 studio, $170 1-bedroom suite, $210–$360 2-bedroom suite. AE, DISC, [illegible]s: Restaurant; bar; children's programs; concierge; outdoor pool; room service; water[illegible]t/rentals; Wi-Fi (free). *In room:* A/C, TV/DVD/VCR, hair dryer, kitchen (in some).

[illegible] Set on a coastal road about 1.2km (¾ mile) south of George Town, [illegible]mmended middle-bracket hotel whose rooms are divided among a [illegible]y pink-sided outbuildings. Accommodations are no nonsense and relatively comfortable. This place is favored by divers and snorkelers, who appreciate the jagged, mostly rocky shoreline (site of excellent snorkeling possibilities) and the diving programs. You're given a number of options for accommodations here, ranging from the cheapest (a unit opening onto the courtyard) to the most expensive (a roomy suite that contains extras such as private balconies, two double beds, a full kitchen, and a living room). The midrange standard bedrooms open onto views of the sea and contain more space than the courtyard units. Don't expect to swim here off sand: You must lower yourself via ladders directly into the sea.

390 S. Church St., George Town (P.O. Box 479), Grand Cayman, B.W.I. www.sunsethouse.com. ✆ **800/854-4767** or 345/949-7111. Fax 345/949-7101. 59 units. Winter $220–$310 double, $320 suite, $365 apt; off season $200–$250 double, $260 suite, $280 apt. AE, DISC, MC, V. **Amenities:** Restaurant; bar; Jacuzzi; outdoor pool; watersports equipment/rentals. *In room:* A/C, TV, fridge (in suites), kitchen (in apts), Wi-Fi (free).

Sunshine Suites Resort A 5-minute trek across the traffic of West Bay Street is required before reaching the sands of Seven Mile Beach, but this is a well-designed resort compound. Resembling a decent but somewhat anonymous and uncluttered apartment complex, it includes a relatively small pool. Both inside and out, the design reflects British colonial architecture. Each of the units has its own kitchen, so many guests prepare their meals on-site. Nestled in the compound's center are a handful of gazebos and the resort's simple restaurant.

1465 Esterley Tibbetts Hwy. (P.O. Box 30095), Grand Cayman, B.W.I. http://sunshinesuites.com. ✆ **877/786-1110** in the U.S. and Canada, or 345/949-3000. Fax 345/949-1200. 132 units. Winter $200–$220 studio, $230 suite; off season $125–$135 studio, $145 suite. Rates include continental breakfast. AE, DISC, MC, V. **Amenities:** Restaurant; bar; free use of nearby fitness center; outdoor pool; watersports equipment/rentals. *In room:* A/C, TV, hair dryer, kitchen, Wi-Fi (free).

Turtle Nest Inn This cluster of fully furnished studios and apartments opening onto a beach is an attractive and affordable alternative to the pricey condos and chain hotels such as the Marriott. The beach out front is a bit narrow but always has good snorkeling, and guests usually find it uncrowded. Otherwise, guests relax on the terrace. The architecture is vaguely Spanish, with arches and a red-tiled roof, along wit whitewashed walls and cooling terra-cotta tiles in the private, well-furnished u Lying a 10-minute drive from George Town and the airport, the location obscure in the village of Bodden Town, the first capital of the island.

166 Bodden Town Rd., Bodden Town (P.O. Box 187), Grand Cayman, B.W.I. www.t ✆ **345/947-8665.** Fax 345/947-6379. 8 units. Winter $149 double, $159–$299 apt double, $159–$219 apt. AE, DC, MC, V. **Amenities:** Bikes and mopeds; outdoor A/C, TV/DVD, CD player (in some), fridge, kitchen (in some), Wi-Fi (free).

INEXPENSIVE

Eldemire's Guest House Set within an unpre landward side of South Church Road, this B&B li town George Town. Basic and completely fre Eldemire Huddleston, a no-nonsense Jama arch") who lives just across the street. A house or a handful of outbuildings. I well-worn furniture and few frills. Smit Residents of the double rooms have acces each of the suites and apartments contains a s

18 Pebbles Way, George Town, Grand Cayman, B.W.I. www.eldemire.com. ✆ **704/469-2635** in the U.S. and Canada, or 345/916-8369. Fax 345/949-4595. 13 units. Winter $120–$145 double, $160 1-bedroom apt, $240 2-bedroom apt; off season $85–$105 double, $115 1-bedroom apt, $175 2-bedroom apt. MC, V. **Amenities:** Bikes; outdoor pool, Wi-Fi (free). *In room:* A/C, TV, ceiling fan, kitchenette (in suites and apts).

Where to Dine

Make sure you understand which currency the menu is printed in. If it's not written on the menu, ask the waiter if the prices are in U.S. dollars or Cayman Island dollars. It will make a big difference when you get your final bill.

Because virtually everything is shipped in, Cayman Islands restaurants are among the most expensive in the Caribbean. For the best value, opt for West Indian fare such as conch and grouper, which are invariably less expensive. Fewer and fewer restaurants offer turtle these days, although traditionally, it's been a culinary star in the Caymans. Today it appears most often as turtle steak, but sometimes in soups or stews.

VERY EXPENSIVE

Blue by Eric Ripert ★★★ SEAFOOD This is Grand Cayman's premier restaurant, a showcase for the deluxe culinary wares of master chef Eric Ripert. The mother restaurant is Le Bernardin, one of the most celebrated in Manhattan. At Blue you're presented with a choice of three-course fixed-price menus or else a fabulous tasting menu that food critics have labeled "hedonistic." The chef has perfected a wonderfully rich, inventive cuisine that is full of flavors and textures, all presented harmoniously and artistically on your plate. The seafood menus, inspired by the bounty of island fishermen, are presented with epicurean skill. The appetizers dazzle, including a trio of conch ceviche or a combo of yellowfin tuna and foie gras. The main courses are sensual delights, especially the sautéed cobia with an avocado and coconut cream, or bread-crusted striped bass with a grilled mango and roasted chili emulsion. The restaurant has one of the most awarded wine cellars in the Caribbean, with more than 650 selections.

In the Ritz-Carlton, West Bay Rd. ✆ **345/943-9000.** www.ritz-carlton.com. Reservations required. 3-course fixed-price dinner menus $82–$110; tasting menus $120–$165. AE, DC, MC, V. Tues–Sat 6–10pm.

Casa Havana ★★ CUBAN/ASIAN As you walk in, you may expect to see Ernest Hemingway reincarnated and sitting at the bar with his cronies telling tall fish tales.
n the Westin Casuarina, this sophisticated eatery recaptures some of the flavor of
-Castro Old Havana, with mahogany furnishings and crystal chandeliers. At Casa
ana, chef Jason Koppinger's creates Nuevo Latino Caribbean cuisine, served in
egant oceanfront setting. The highly personalized cuisine is fresh and inspired,
d inventive and sensual, with rich yet subtle flavors. As an appetizer, you might
ed to a seared foie gras with a caramelized apple salad that is earthy yet
followed by the chef's black cod specialty: crusted with ground macadamia
erved with a white truffle essence. The Key lime cheesecake is the dessert
hanced by a melba sauce.

asuarina, West Bay Rd. ✆ **345/945-3800.** www.westincasuarina.net. Reservations
urses $33–$51. AE, DC, MC, V. Daily 6–10pm.

E

★★ CARIBBEAN/CONTINENTAL Elegant and stylish, and
rs of Grand Cayman's investment community, this restaurant

seems very far removed from the tourist hubbub of Seven Mile Beach and other tourist-geared areas. Expect a Caribbean colonial decor with high ceilings, artfully carved teakwood and mahogany furniture, spinning ceiling fans, and a cool, breezy layout that might evoke an upscale private club in a long-gone British colonial empire. Lunches focus on upscale and upbeat salads such as a fresh yellowfin tuna tataki with pine nuts, feta cheese, and sweet-basil vinaigrette, and pastas or the fresh catch of the day. Dinners are more elaborate, featuring such appetizers as a slab of Hudson Valley foie gras with chocolate foam, or else warm white asparagus with prosciutto and a lemon veloute. Main courses are a Luccullan treat, especially the pan-seared scallops with a celeriac mouselline, or else braised lamb shank with roasted garlic mashed potatoes and red-wine cabbage.

171 Elgin Ave, Cricket Sq. ✆ **345/945-1815.** www.brasseriecayman.com. Reservations recommended, especially at lunch. Lunch salads and platters $8–$15; main courses $18–$31. AE, DC, MC, V. Mon–Fri 11:30am–2:30pm, tapas menu 4:30–7pm, and dinner 6–10pm; Sat–Sun tapas menu 4:30–7pm and dinner 6–10pm.

Calypso Grill ★★ 🎁 SEAFOOD/INTERNATIONAL At first glance, you might think this is little more than a waterfront shack. But when you enter, you'll find a charming, funky, and slightly psychedelic bar and restaurant that absolutely drips with Creole colors, a sense of whimsy, and even a bold and creative sense of elegance. If the wind isn't too brisk, you can sit on a wooden deck directly above the water, watching workaday fishing craft depositing their loads at West Bay's busiest fishing port. The venue is very authentic, with a clientele that derives from many walks of Caymanian life, from the monied to the bohemian—all of it a far cry from the congestion and glitter of Seven Mile Beach. Perch at the rectangular bar here for a cocktail or any of about a dozen kinds of wine by the glass, or, if a table isn't likely to become available, opt for a full meal. The best menu items include marinated conch; a creamy version of lobster bisque; Cuban-style shrimp with sherry-flavored cream sauce; fresh fish (ask the waiter what's available) that can be blackened, grilled, or sautéed; and a garlic-laced version of shrimp linguine. Favorite desserts include mango crepes and sticky toffee pudding.

Morgan's Harbour, West Bay. ✆ **345/949-3948.** www.calypsogrillcayman.com. Reservations rec for dinner. Main courses $25–$39. AE, DC, MC, V. Tues–Sat 11:30am–2:30pm and 6–10pm; Su 2:30pm and 6–10pm.

Casanova Restaurant ★ ITALIAN/SEAFOOD In the heart of Ge local favorite is owned and run by the Crescente family. Here the co the catch of the day, and they have also mastered the heart of lunch menu is enticing, with its salads and the homemade also order conch fritters with jerk mayonnaise and marin grows more enticing, with a choice of both hot and col sashimi style to sautéed mussels. Pastas include a center-cut yellowfin tuna in a light oregano sau

65 N. Church St., George Town. ✆ **345/949-7633** Main courses $14–$35. MC, V. Mon–Sat 11:30am–2

The Cracked Conch/MacaBuca O INTERNATIONAL This place reopene became the focus of recommendations acros ged rocks of West Bay, on the seacoast near th Beach, across the road from the Turtle Farm, it se seafood. It's also a dining and drinking destination in its own right, a magnet for young, attractive residents of Grand Cayman. The best way to appreciate this place involves drinks and perhaps a focus on the big-screen TVs at the MacaBuca Tiki Bar, and then a migration to a table on the open-sided veranda at the Cracked Conch. As a whole, the experience involves views of flickering torches and the sound of surf crashing against the jagged rocks nearby, hallucinatory rum punches and martinis, and very good food.

Informal menu items available throughout the day and evening at MacaBuca and at lunch at the Cracked Conch include salads, fried calamari, breaded and fried conch steaks, and beef, chicken, or conch burgers. More formal and elaborate dishes, available for dinner at the Cracked Conch, feature steamed conch and snapper coconut casserole, and a skillfully prepared roulade of conch and turtle steak. Sunday brunches here are festive, with buffet stations set up within the establishment's gleaming stainless steel kitchen. There's also an elegant indoor bar here.

N. West Point Rd., near Turtle Bay Farm, West Bay. ✆ **345/945-5217.** www.crackedconch.com.ky. Reservations required. MacaBuca platters, sandwiches, and salads $8–$23; Cracked Conch main courses $18–$48, all-you-can-eat buffet-style Sun brunch $35. AE, MC, V. Cracked Conch daily 11am–3pm and 5:30–10pm. MacaBuca Tiki Bar daily 10am–midnight (or later).

Grand Old House ★★ AMERICAN/CARIBBEAN/PACIFIC RIM The Grand Old House is the island's premier caterer and hosts everything from lavish weddings and political functions to informal family celebrations. This former plantation house lies amid venerable trees 2km (1¼ miles) south of George Town, past Jackson Point. Built on bedrock near the edge of the sea, it stands on 129 ironwood posts that support the main house and a bevy of gazebos.

For appetizers, we recommend the roasted lobster Napoleon or the marinated conch Cayman Island–style with tomato, cilantro, and Key lime flavorings. Also worthwhile is the tequila-infused snow crab and lobster laid on a mango gazpacho with spicy cucumber noodles. A signature main course is a platter of baked shrimp and scallops gratin in white wine, or the Cayman-style turtle steak in a tomato-and-white-wine sauce. Among fish dishes, we like the fire-roasted Chilean sea bass in balsamic syrup on a sweet-potato mash with a candied lemon-and-mango beurre blanc.

Petra Plantation, 648 S. Church St. ✆ **345/949-9333.** www.grandoldhouse.com. Reservations required. Main courses $26–$49. AE, DISC, MC, V. Mon–Sat 11:30am–2pm and 6–10pm.

Hemingway's ★★ SEAFOOD/INTERNATIONAL Some of the best seafood on [illegible]e island is at the premier restaurant of the Grand Cayman Beach Suites, 3km (2 [illegible]es) north of George Town. It occupies a rambling, single-story annex of the hotel, [illegible] spot shoehorned between the beach and two swimming pools. There's a rather [illegible] bar inside, a favorite after-work hangout that's favored by managers of compet[illegible]naffiliated restaurants nearby; a big-windowed, air-conditioned dining room; [illegible]es set outside, on a shaded colonnade near trails of bougainvillea and spinning [illegible] fans. The menu is among the most imaginative on the island and has won [illegible]m *Gourmet* magazine. Appetizers include a tasty coconut shrimp with a [illegible]alade accent; Cuban-style barbecued turtle steak; well-spiced crab cakes; [illegible]tely fantastic deep-fried version of a whole red snapper that's deboned [illegible]sented like a piece of sculpture, with pickled onions, bell peppers, and [illegible]hed potatoes. There's also catch of the day, prepared any way you want [illegible]kened, and citrus-and-cumin-marinated pork tenderloin.

In the Grand Cayman Beach Suites, West Bay Rd. ✆ **345/949-1234.** www.grand-cayman-beach-suites.com. Reservations required. Main courses $15–$23 lunch, $26–$53 dinner. AE, DC, DISC, MC, V. Daily 11:30am–2:30pm and 6–10pm.

Lighthouse at Breakers ★ CARIBBEAN/ITALIAN/SEAFOOD On the south shore of the island, this cozy, elegant, and nautically decorated landmark lies about a 30-minute drive east from George Town. Its creative menu mainly features fresh local seafood. A well-trained chef, backed up by a skilled staff, offers well-prepared meals, attracting both locals and visitors. Put yourself in the hands of the mostly European staff, and sit back to enjoy such tempting appetizers as penne pasta with shrimp, asparagus, tomatoes, and pesto; or tuna sushi rolled in sesame seeds. For your main course, opt for the mixed grill of Caribbean seafood, lobster with gnocchi and shrimp, filet mignon with brandy-flavored cream sauce, or a veal chop topped with Gorgonzola and pancetta ham. The restaurant has one of the best wine cellars on the island. Immediately adjacent to the restaurant is a towering life-size replica of a lighthouse, its trademark and signature, that's visible for many miles out to sea.

Breakers. ✆ **345/947-2047.** www.lighthouse.ky. Reservations recommended. Main courses $9–$16 lunch, $19–$50 dinner. AE, DISC, MC, V. Daily 11:30am–3:30pm and 5:30–10pm.

Lobster Pot ★ SEAFOOD/INTERNATIONAL Folksy and charming, but not quite as good or as polished as Hemingway's, Lobster Pot is still an island favorite. It overlooks the water from its second-floor perch at the northern perimeter of George Town, directly beside the road that funnels traffic into the capital from Seven Mile Beach. As its name suggests, it serves lobster prepared in many different ways: Cayman style, broiled in its shell, as lobster bisque, and as a mouth-watering salad. Braised jerk chicken, turtle steak, and stuffed Chilean salmon are also on the menu. Most dishes are right on the mark. A house specialty is the "Cayman Trio," with portions of broiled lobster tail, garlic-sautéed shrimp, and grilled fresh local fish piled onto the same platter. For lunch, you might opt for English-style fish and chips, or perhaps lobster quesadillas or lobster-studded pasta.

245 N. Church St. ✆ **345/949-2736.** www.lobsterpot.ky. Reservations recommended in winter. Main courses $14–$35 lunch, $22–$49 dinner. AE, DISC, MC, V. Mon–Fri 11:30am–2:30pm and 5–10pm; Sat–Sun 5–10pm.

Portofino Wreckview Restaurant ★ ITALIAN/INTERNATIONAL/CARIBBEAN In 1962 an American cargo ship, the *Liberty,* sank during a storm on a reef close to Grand Cayman's eastern shore. Today, split into three thoroughly rusted separate sections that rest in shallow water, it provides a focal point for the panoramas that open before you from the terrace of this restaurant. The most popular independent restaurant on Grand Cayman's East End, it draws clients from the hotel and resort complexes nearby. You might begin a meal here with a satay of beef or chicken, served with a cucumber-and-peanut sauce, then follow with a savory version of *zuppa di pesce* (fish soup); breaded conch steak served in traditional East End style; turtle steak; any of several kinds of pasta; and the house specialty, baked seafood Portofino, which delectably combines lobster, tiger shrimp, scallops, and mousseline potatoes au gratin. Lunches are simpler than dinners, focusing on salads, sandwiches, pastas, and grilled fish.

898 Austin Connolly Dr. (in Colliers), East End. ✆ **345/947-2700.** Reservations recommended. Main courses $14–$28; lunch platters $6–$16. AE, DISC, MC, V. Daily 11:30am–10pm.

The Reef Grill at Royal Palms ★★★ SEAFOOD This is one of the island's finest, and one of our favorite, restaurants on Grand Cayman, a site that manages to be chic, savvy, elegant, hip, and fun all at the same time. It's positioned on a strategic plot of land in the heart of the Seven Mile Beach "golden strip." The savvy entrepreneurs who rent the space maintain a compound of one- and two-story buildings that include a beachfront bar and grill, a nightclub, and a classy citadel of gourmet cuisine. To fully appreciate the place, we recommend a brisk walk-through as a means of determining which corner of the place you'd most like to occupy. The inland, "landlocked" bar and dining area is elegant, red, and evocative of an upscale corner of Europe, but the seafront bar offers dance-floor views of Grand Cayman's most nubile and flirtatious chatterboxes.

Favorites here include Maytag blue cheese salad with chopped Granny Smith apples and spiced pecans; conch fritters with jerk-flavored mayonnaise; a melt-in-your-mouth honey-and-soy-glazed sea bass with Thai-style curried vinaigrette; and lobster risotto with coconut reduction. At lunch you can order well-stuffed sandwiches, freshly made salads, and from-the-oven pizzas. If you opt to dine under the stars, and if it's a Friday or Saturday, you'll hear some of the most talented local musicians playing soca and calypso in the bar pavilion about a hundred paces away.

537 W. Bay Rd. (in the Royal Palms Beach Club), Seven Mile Beach. ✆ **345/945-6358.** www.reefgrill.com. Reservations recommended. Main courses $9–$16 lunch, $22–$32 dinner. AE, MC, V. Daily 11am–3pm and 5:30–10pm. Closed Sun night May–Dec.

Ristorante Pappagallo ★ NORTHERN ITALIAN/SEAFOOD One of the island's most memorable restaurants lies on a 6-hectare (15-acre) bird sanctuary overlooking a natural lagoon, 15 minutes north of George Town. Its designers incorporated Caymanian and Aztec weaving techniques in its thatched roof. Glass doors, black marble, and polished brass mix a kind of Edwardian opulence with a Tahitian decor. Inside you'll see some of the most beautiful (caged) parrots on the island, separated from the dining and drinking area (for sanitary reasons) by plate-glass windows. The lobster-and-scallop bisque in coconut cream and the carpaccio of raw beef with arugula are appealing appetizers. Pastas are full of flavor, especially the fettuccine with lemon-grilled chicken and sun-dried tomatoes, and the penne with homemade sausage. Fish and shellfish are well prepared, or you can opt for either the peppered West Indian pork tenderloin in an apple-bourbon sauce, or a combination of lobster and shrimp, prepared in the style of the chef, with pepper, garlic, diced tomatoes, mushrooms, and a flaming brandy-and-tarragon-flavored cream sauce.

Conch Point Rd., Barkers, West Bay (near the northern terminus of West Bay Rd., 13km/8 miles north of George Town). ✆ **345/949-1119.** www.pappagallo.ky. Reservations recommended. Main courses $10–$40. AE, MC, V. Daily 6–10:30pm.

The Wharf ★ CARIBBEAN/CONTINENTAL On the northern fringe of George Town, at the southernmost edge of Seven Mile Beach, this dining, drinking, and nightlife emporium is fun, tropical, artfully illuminated, and occasionally hip. More than half of the place is built on wharves and piers that jut seaward, allowing fish to swim under your dining table as you eat, and even to make appearances in an open area that's the target of a plethora of spotlights that catch their every silvery movement. (The feeding of the tarpon, something approaching an underwater frenzy, occurs every night at 9pm.) The restaurant is decorated in tones of turquoise and blue, and offers dining within an air-conditioned interior, or outside on either an elevated veranda or a waterside terrace. The sound of the surf mingles with chatter from the Ports of Call Bar and music from the strolling Paraguayan harpist, Eugenio Leon.

Many diners begin with the blue-crab-and-shrimp salad with cucumber and mango, or the golden-fried Caribbean lobster cake with a roasted-corn relish. Main dishes are a delight, especially the basil-and-pistachio-crusted sea bass in a creamy champagne sauce, or the grilled-turtle-and-lobster pie with rice and vegetables. A local favorite is the pork tenderloin Tortuga, baked between sugar cane and served with a dark-rum sauce. Fresh fish can be prepared any way you want: blackened, almondine, grilled, or "island style." The kitchen makes a laudable effort to break away from typical, dull menu items, and for the most part, it succeeds.

43 West Bay Rd., Seven Mile Beach. ✆ **345/949-2231.** www.wharf.ky. Reservations recommended. Main courses $23–$44. AE, MC, V. Daily 6–10pm.

MODERATE

Kaibo INTERNATIONAL Isolated on Grand Cayman's northern coast, in a location that's adjacent to a busy marina, this place offers good food and an irreverent and gregarious atmosphere. Some aspects of the place evoke a beach compound in Polynesia, thanks to flaming torches, multilevel terraces, and cabanas roofed in palm thatch. Menu items focus on juicy burgers, fresh salads, seafood prepared any way you want, steaks, and pastas, any of which can be accompanied by sunset-colored drinks that tend to get the party roaring.

585 Water Cay Rd. (in the Kaibo Yacht Club), Cayman Kai, North Side. ✆ **345/947-9975.** www.kaibo.ky. Reservations not necessary. Main courses $23–$48; lunchtime platters, salads, and sandwiches $10–$15. AE, MC, V. Grill daily 11am–11pm. Bar 11am–1am.

Mezza INTERNATIONAL Hip, breezy, Europeanized, and urban, this restaurant sits one floor above a landmark liquor store (Big Daddy's), immediately adjacent to the Treasure Island Hotel. This is a venue that you might expect to find in South Beach, Miami. Lunches are simple, featuring steak sandwiches, burgers, Caesar salads, and seafood pasta. The dinner menu is more artful, with dishes that include bacon-wrapped mahimahi, basil-encrusted salmon steaks, sautéed shrimp with wine sauce and asparagus, steak au poivre with pommes frites, and fettuccine with jerk chicken. Caramel pecan fudge cake or crème brûlée make for enticing desserts.

233 West Bay Rd. ✆ **345/946-3992.** www.mezza.com.ky. Reservations recommended. Main courses $18–$26. AE, DC, MC, V. Mon noon–4pm; Tues-Sat noon–4pm and 6–10pm; Sun noon–3pm.

Rackam's Waterfront AMERICAN/CARIBBEAN If you're interested in an extensive menu and open-air dining with a beautiful view, then you should try this place. In the morning you can watch boats coming to port, and in the evening you can see their lights as they head back out to sea. Your best bets here are the Caribbean shrimp, fish and chips, grilled mahimahi marinated in jerk sauce, Caesar salad, pan-fried grouper with rice and beans, and a wide array of curries and pastas.

93 N. Church St., George Town. ✆ **345/945-3860.** http://rackamswaterfront.ky. Reservations recommended for parties of 6 or more. Main courses $11–$38. AE, MC, V. Kitchen daily 10:30am–11pm. Bar Mon–Fri 9am–1am; Sat 10am–midnight; Sun 10:30am–midnight.

INEXPENSIVE

Chicken! Chicken! ☺ AMERICAN This venue completely lacks glamour, but within its cheerful and unpretentious premises (it looks like the interior of a brightly painted Creole cottage), you can feed a family for less money than at virtually any other restaurant on the island. The specialty, and the only available main course, is tender, richly seasoned, perfectly cooked chicken. As many as 32 chickens at a time rotate enticingly in the glare of the island's biggest and most theatrical rotisserie, prominently positioned near the restaurant's entrance. Each chicken is flavored with herbs and a touch of garlic. After placing your order at the stand-up counter, you can opt to dine in the restaurant, or you can haul your chicken away for consumption somewhere else. The chicken (breast, thigh, or whole roasted birds, depending on your order) is accompanied by corn bread and your choice of coleslaw, rice, or beans. In the West Shore Shopping Plaza, West Bay Rd. ✆ **345/945-2290.** www.chicken2.com. Main courses $9–$10 lunch, $11–$15 dinner. AE, MC, V. Daily 11am–10pm.

Hitting the Beach

One of the finest beaches in the Caribbean, Grand Cayman's **Seven Mile Beach ★★★**, which begins north of George Town, has sparkling white sands rimmed with Australian pines and palms. (Technically, it's called West Bay Beach, but everybody just says Seven Mile Beach.) Although it's not actually as long as its name claims, it is still a honey: 9km (5½ miles) of white, white sands stretching all the way to George Town. It tends to be crowded near the big resorts, but the beach is so big you can always find some room to spread out your towel. There are no peddlers to hassle you, and the beach is, for the most part, kelp-free and beautifully maintained.

Because the beach is on a relatively tranquil side of Grand Cayman, there is no great tide and the water is generally placid and inviting, ideal for families, even those with small children. A sandy bottom slopes gently to deep water. The water's so clear that you can usually see what's swimming in it. It's great for snorkelers and swimmers of most ages and abilities.

From one end of the beach to the other, most immediately adjacent to their neighbors, there are hotels and condos, many with beachside bars that you can visit. Originally, only buildings with three stories or less were allowed on the beach, but that changed in the 1990s with the construction of several six- and even seven-story towers. The increased "population density" has added greater numbers of people to the sands during periods of high occupancy, which you may or may not like, depending on your values, aesthetics, and lifestyle. All sorts of watersports concessions can be found along this beach, including kiosks that rent snorkel gear, boats, windsurfers, WaveRunners, paddlecats, and aqua trikes. Parasailing and water-skiing are also available. Even if you're staying in a relatively obscure guesthouse or condominium, most watersports outfits, including members of the well-respected Red Sail group, will shuttle you from any point along Seven Mile Beach to the departure point for your particular excursion.

Grand Cayman also has a number of minor beaches, although their allures pale in comparison to Seven Mile Beach. Visit these if you want to escape the crowds. Many beaches on the east and north coasts of Grand Cayman are relatively desirable, layered in many cases with pale sand and protected in some cases by offshore barrier reefs, so waters are generally tranquil. The best windsurfing on Grand Cayman is off the eastern shore, with particularly good conditions on the beaches adjacent to the separately recommended Morritt's resorts.

One of our favorites is on the north coast, bordering **Cayman Kai.** This beach is a Caribbean cliché of charm, with palm trees and beautiful sands, along with changing facilities. You can snorkel along the reef to Rum Point. The beach is also ideal as a Sunday afternoon picnic spot. **Red Sail Sports,** at Rum Point, offers windsurfers, WaveRunners, sailboats, water-skiing, and even glass-bottom boat tours to see the stingrays offshore. It also offers scuba diving.

Sports & Outdoor Pursuits

What they lack in nightlife, the Caymans make up for in watersports—the fishing, swimming, water-skiing, snorkeling, and especially diving are among the finest in the Caribbean. Coral reefs and coral formations encircle the islands and are filled with lots of marine life (which scuba divers and snorkelers are forbidden to disturb, by the way).

It's easy to dive close to shore, so boats aren't necessary, but there are plenty of boats and scuba facilities available. On certain excursions, we recommend a trip with a qualified dive master. There are many dive rental shops, but they won't rent you scuba gear or supply air unless you have a card from one of the national diving schools, such as NAUI or PADI. Hotels also rent diving equipment to their guests, as well as arrange snorkeling and scuba-diving trips.

Universally regarded as the most up-to-date and best-equipped watersports facility in the Cayman Islands, **Red Sail Sports** maintains its administrative headquarters at Coconut Place, P.O. Box 31473, Grand Cayman KY1-1206 (© **877/506-6368** in the U.S., or 345/623-5965; www.redsailcayman.com), and its largest, best-accessorized branch at the Grand Cayman Beach Suites, West Bay Road (© **345/945-0178**). Other locations are at the Westin Casuarina (© **345/949-8767**), at Rum Point (© **345/947-2082**), at the Marriott Beach Resort (© **345/949-8938**), at the Courtyard by Marriott (© **345/946-5481**), and at Morritt's Tortuga Club (© **345/947-9827**). Red Sail has a wide range of offerings, from deep-sea fishing to sailing, windsurfing, diving, and more. Red Sail can also arrange water-skiing for $120 per half-hour (the cost can be divided among several people), and parasailing is offered at $80 to $180 per person.

The following are the best options for a gamut of outdoor activities.

CRUISES **Red Sail Sports** (see above) has a number of inexpensive ways you can go sailing in Cayman waters, including a glass-bottom-boat ride costing $35 without snorkeling equipment or $45 with snorkeling equipment. It also offers sunset cruises costing $40, as well as a 9am-to-1:15pm sail to Stingray City, with snorkeling equipment and lunch included in the price of $88 per person. Children 3 to 11 pay half price.

FISHING Grouper and snapper are most plentiful for those who bottom-fish along the reef. Deeper waters turn up barracuda and bonito. Sport-fishers from all over the world come to the Caymans for the big ones: tuna, wahoo, and marlin. Most hotels can make arrangements for charter boats; experienced guides are also available. **Bayside Water Sports,** from a base at the Morgan's Harbour Marina (© **345/949-3200;** www.baysidewatersports.com), offers deep-sea-fishing excursions in search of tuna, marlin, and wahoo on a variety of air-conditioned vessels with an experienced crew. Tours depart at 7am and noon, last half a day, and cost around $500 to $1,000; a full day costs $900 to $1,900. The fee can be split among four to six people.

GOLF Your best bet is **Britannia Golf Club** (© **345/745-4653;** www.britannia-golf.com), located across the avenue from Grand Cayman Beach Suites on West Bay Road. This is actually a three-in-one course, including a 9-hole, par-35 course; an 18-hole, par-57 course; and a special course played with a Cayman ball that goes half

INTO THE DEEP: SUBMARINE DIVES

So scuba diving is not enough for you? You want to see the real undiscovered depths of the ocean? On Grand Cayman, you can take the *Atlantis* reef dive. It's expensive and, in some participants, can induce severe feelings of claustrophobia, but it's a unique way to go underwater—and one of the island's most popular attractions.

The ***Atlantis XI,*** Harbour Avenue (© **800/887-8571** or 345/949-7700; www.atlantissubmarinescayman.com), is a submersible that's 66 feet long, weighs 80 tons, and was built to carry 48 passengers. You can view the reefs and colorful tropical fish through the 26 large viewpoints .6m (2 ft.) in diameter, as it cruises at a depth of 30m (98 ft.) through the maze of coral gardens at a speed of 1½ knots; a guide keeps you informed.

On the *Atlantis* Expedition dive, operated both day and night, you'll experience the reef and see the famous Cayman Wall; the dive lasts 45 minutes and costs $99. Children 4 to 12 are charged $59. *Atlantis XI* dives between five and nine times a day, depending on the number of cruise ships moored offshore on any particular day. Reservations are recommended at least 2 days in advance.

the distance of a regular golf ball. Greens fees are $65 to $150 for 18 holes. The course was designed by the famous Jack Nicklaus.

Yet another course, **North Sound Golf Club,** off West Bay Road (© **345/947-4653;** www.northsoundclub.com), designed by Roy Case, is an 18-hole, par-71 course charging greens fees of $175. Expect lots of sand traps here.

A final course, the 9-hole **Blue Tip,** West Bay Road (© **345/815-6500**), is reserved for guests of the Ritz-Carlton, charging greens fees of $125 to $215 per player. Designed by Greg Norman, Blue Tip also has the best pro shop on island.

HIKING The **Mastic Trail** is a restored 200-year-old footpath through a woodland area in the heart of the island. The trail lies west of Frank Sound Road, about a 45-minute drive from the heart of George Town, and showcases the reserve's natural attractions, including a native mangrove swamp, traditional agriculture, and an ancient woodland area—home to the largest variety of native plant and animal life found in the Cayman Islands.

Although the trail is supervised and maintained, during periods of heavy rain, the southern end is likely to be flooded. The government therefore recommends hikers approach the trail from the northern end, off Further Road, as opposed to via the southern end, off Frank Sound Road.

Guided tours of the trail, organized by the **Cayman Islands National Trust,** are scheduled every Wednesday and every fourth Saturday at 9am. Tours last 2 to 3 hours each and are limited to a maximum of 15 participants. Reservations are strongly recommended, and the cost is $25 per person. The hike is not recommended for children 5 and under, seniors, or persons with physical disabilities. Wear comfortable, sturdy shoes and carry water and insect repellent. For reservations, call the National Trust (© **345/749-1121;** www.nationaltrust.org.ky). If the scheduled departure time for these organized tours isn't practical or convenient, you can stop into the headquarters of the National Trust, on South Church Street, Monday to Friday from 9am to 5pm for a self-guided walking tour/map of the trail. The guidebook, which describes the botanical and geological features you're likely to see en route, costs $6.30.

SCUBA DIVING & SNORKELING Divers rate Grand Cayman as one of the world's top dive sites, and the island has some of the best scuba-diving outfitters in the Caribbean. Its coral reefs and nearly vertical coral walls teeming with marine life are justifiably famous.

These natural attractions surround not only Grand Cayman, but Little Cayman and Cayman Brac as well. In some cases, experienced divers who are familiar with local waters shun boats altogether and begin their dives from the shore, but we recommend guided expeditions as an enhancement to your pleasure, convenience, and safety. You can call the dive shops recommended in this chapter, or you can ask your hotel to make the arrangements for you.

The waters off Grand Cayman also abound in shipwrecks, many of them so close to the surface that they can even be viewed from the water's surface by snorkelers.

To avoid subpar outfitters, stick to our list of recommendations and avoid concessions that spring up every year along Seven Mile Beach. Since scuba diving, of course, is a potentially dangerous sport, it is best to patronize well-established dive outfitters with an established record of diver satisfaction and a good safety record.

The nation's reefs and marine life are justifiably considered one of the Cayman Island's most valuable resources and, as such, are rigidly—even fanatically—protected by the government; violators are often prosecuted. If you're unclear about any of the rules, you can contact the **Department of Environment** (© **345/949-8469**), an agency that also regulates fishing offshore. If you see violators vandalizing or destroying the reefs or taking coral (which is prohibited), you are asked to report them to **Marine Enforcement** by calling © **345/948-1042.**

The basic rule is that the reefs and coral are here for your enjoyment—you're to look but not touch. Obviously, the "theft" of a reserve that took thousands of years to produce is prohibited.

The offshore waters of Grand Cayman are home to one of the most unusual underwater attractions in the world, **Stingray City ★★**. Set in the sun-flooded, 4m-deep (13-ft.) waters of North Sound, about 3km (2 miles) east of the island's northwestern tip, the site originated in the mid-1980s when local fishers cleaned their catch and dumped the offal overboard. They quickly noticed scores of stingrays (which usually eat marine crabs) feeding on the debris, a phenomenon that quickly attracted local divers and marine zoologists. Today between 30 and 50 relatively tame stingrays hover in the waters around the site for daily handouts of squid and ballyhoo from increasing hordes of snorkelers and divers. To capitalize on the phenomenon, about half a dozen entrepreneurs lead expeditions from points along Seven Mile Beach, traveling around the landmass of Conch Point to the feeding grounds. The previously recommended **Red Sail Sports** offers one-tank scuba dives to Stingray City, priced at $75, including tank and weights equipment, and snorkeling excursions to the site as well. Snorkel excursions cost between $55 and $80, depending on the time you intend to spend there, the distance the shuttle bus will have to travel to retrieve you at your hotel, and whether lunch is included as part of the experience. ***Warning:*** Stingrays possess deeply penetrating and viciously barbed stingers capable of inflicting painful damage to anyone who mistreats them. If you encounter one, be alert, and don't make any fast moves. (The rays can panic, we're told.) And above all, as the divers say, never try to grab one by the tail and never, ever, when you're wading in shallow waters at Stingray City, step on one.)

Despite the potential dangers, divers and snorkelers seem amazingly adept at feeding, petting, and stroking the velvet surfaces of these batlike creatures while avoiding unpleasant incidents.

You'll find plenty of concessions offering snorkel gear for rent along Seven Mile Beach. The snorkeling is great in the clear, warm waters here. Other popular sites are Parrot's Reef and Smith's Cove, south of George Town. Lush reefs abound with parrotfish, coral, sea fans, and sponges. Also great for snorkelers is Turtle Farm Reef, a short swim from shore, with a miniwall rising from a sandy bottom.

Red Sail Sports (see earlier in this chapter) offers beginners' scuba diving as well as excursions for the experienced. A two-tank morning dive includes exploration of two different dive sites at depths ranging from 15 to 30m (49–98 ft.), and costs $120. Beginners can take a daily course that costs $150 per person. See "Cruises," above, for information on Red Sail Sports snorkel cruises.

Another good dive outfit, **Tortuga Divers** (© **877/506-6368** or 345/947-2097; www.tortugadivers.com), operates out of Morritt's Tortuga Club and Grand Resort at East End, site of what's described as the best windsurfing conditions in the Cayman Islands, with easy access to the rich marine life. This outfitter caters to both experienced and novice divers, offering dives, whenever business justifies it, at 9am and 2pm. Half-day or full-day snorkeling adventures can also be arranged at the same time, and all types of gear are available for rent. The morning two-tank scuba dive costs $120; the afternoon one-tank dive goes for $75. A 1½-hour snorkeling excursion costs $35 to $45, going up to $40 to $55 for 2 to 2½ hours, including lunch.

Ambassador Divers, at the Comfort Suites, West Bay Road, East End (p. 182; © **345/743-5513;** www.ambassadordivers.com), is a small dive operation that usually takes out no more than eight passengers at a time. Trips feature the North and South Wall diving areas. PADI certification courses are offered, and dive packages are available; a 2-day deal goes for $90 per person. A two-tank dive is $105 plus equipment.

Cayman Aggressor IV (© **800/348-2628** or 985/385-2628; www.aggressor.com) was designed by divers for divers. Participants are taken out for week-long cruises aboard a 110-foot boat. The living is simple, and the chow is basic. The boat has private cabins and an on-board cook. An inclusive package ranges from $2,495 to $2,895.

Divetech, at the Cobalt Coast Resort and Suites, 18A Sea Fan Dr., West Bay (© **888/946-5656** or 345/946-5658; www.divetech.com), offers daily two-tank boat trips priced at $110 per person. The highlight of most adventures here involves diving down along the side of Grand Cayman's vertiginous North Wall. We especially like this outfitter because of its association with Cobalt Coast (p. 182), a resort that caters almost exclusively to divers, and its personalized, hands-on approach. One-tank trips to Stingray City cost $60, and snorkeling trips are also featured. There's also a series of programs designed for kids.

Don Foster's Dive, 218 S. Church St., George Town (© **345/949-5679;** www.donfosters.com), operates from the waterfront at Casuarina Point in George Town. At its headquarters, there is also a pool with a shower. Boat dives are featured, as well as offshore snorkeling. A two-tank dive costs $95, with night dives going for $55.

Eden Rock Diving Center, 124 S. Church St., George Town (© **345/949-7243;** www.edenrockdive.com), specializes in dives to Eden Rock and Devil's Grotto, both of them hailed as two of the best dive sites in the Caribbean. A full line of scuba and snorkeling equipment is available for rent, with a two-tank dive going for $90 to $125. Snorkeling trips cost $35.

Ocean Frontiers Reef Resort, 346 Austin Connelly Dr., East End (✆ **800/348-6096** or 345/947-0000; www.oceanfrontiers.com), is a well-run outfitter highlighting underwater attractions in the East End, offshore from which are pristine reefs and easy access to wall diving. This tends to be a less crowded dive center than around the West End. Its specialty is PADI-certified open water dive instruction priced at $399. A half-day program, which includes classroom instruction and pool practice, followed by a shallow reef dive, goes for $149.

TENNIS A total of nine tennis courts are available to the public at the **Cayman Islands Tennis Club,** Ann Bonney Crescent, South Sound (✆ **345/949-9464;** www.tennis.ky). The fee for up to 2 hours' use of either asphalt or "classic clay" courts is $15 per person. Hours can vary, according to the season and the weather, so call ahead before coming here.

WINDSURFING The best place for windsurfing on the island is the beachfront resort of **Morritt's Tortuga Club and Grand Resort** at the East End (p. 181; ✆ **345/947-7449**). There, Tortuga Divers, an outfit that's associated with Red Sail Sports, charges $40 for 1 hour, $90 for 3 hours, and $145 for 5 hours. A 1-hour lesson can be arranged for $65, which is followed by a 1-hour practice session that's included in the price. The favorable windsurfing conditions here result from nearly constant winds blowing in from offshore, and an offshore reef that protects the waters of the lagoon in most cases from unpredictable waves.

Exploring the Island

The capital, **George Town,** can easily be explored in an afternoon; stop by for its restaurants and shops (and banks!)—not sights. The town does have a clock monument to King George V, and the post office on Edward Street is the oldest government building in use in the Caymans. Stamps sold here are collected avidly.

The island's premier museum, the **Cayman Islands National Museum,** Harbor Drive (✆ **345/949-8368;** www.museum.ky), occupies an antique building directly on the water. The veranda-fronted building once served as the island's courthouse. Today the formal exhibits include a collection of Caymanian artifacts collected by Ira Thompson beginning in the 1930s, and the museum incorporates a gift shop, theater, cafe, and more than 2,000 items portraying the natural, social, and cultural history of the Caymans. Hours are Monday to Friday 9am to 5pm and Saturday 10am to 2pm, with an admission of $5.

You might also go to **Hell!** At the north end of West Bay Beach is a jagged piece of rock named Hell by a former commissioner. There the postmistress will stamp "Hell, Grand Cayman" on your postcard to send back to the U.S.

Cayman Turtle Farm ★, at Boatswain's Beach, 786 Northwest Point Rd., West Bay (✆ **345/949-3894;** www.turtle.ky), in the heart of the West Bay district, about a 25-minute drive north of George Town, is the only green-sea-turtle farm of its kind in the world. Once the islands had a multitude of turtles in the surrounding waters (which is why Columbus called the islands Las Tortugas), but, sadly, today these creatures are few in number, and the green sea turtle has been designated an endangered species. (You cannot bring turtle products into the United States.) Its main function involves providing the local market with edible turtle meat (preventing the need to hunt turtles in the wild) and replenishing the waters with hatchling and yearling turtles. Visitors today can observe about a hundred circular concrete tanks in which these sea creatures exist in every stage of development; the hope is that one day their population in the sea will regain its former status. Turtles here range in size from 170g (6 oz.) to 272 kg (600 lb.).

At Touch Tanks, you can hold yearling turtles in your hands; they are about the size of a mature cat. The compound also has a walk-through aviary with birds native to the Caymans. Adjoining it is the Iguana Exhibit, with indigenous blue and gray rock iguanas. Yet another exhibit is the Butterfly Farm, where you can mingle with these fluttery creatures.

More attractions include the Breaker's Lagoon, the largest swimming pool in the Caymans, with two waterfalls. Swimmers can jump in and cool off. Snorkeling is possible at Boatswain's Lagoon, where a synthetic reef system supports rainbow-hued marine life. Close encounters via underwater viewing panels are possible at Predator Reef. At a snack bar and restaurant, you can sample turtle dishes. There's a well-stocked gift shop on-site. The turtle farm is open daily from 8am to 5:30pm (last admission is at 4:30pm). A tour of the turtle farm costs $30 for adults and $20 for kids 4 to 12; use of the entire park, including lagoons, pools, and other animal exhibits, is $45 for adults or $25 for ages 4 to 12.

If you're driving, you might want to go along **South Sound Road,** which is lined with pines and, in places, old wooden Caymanian houses. After leaving the houses behind, you'll find good spots for a picnic.

Pedro St. James National Historic Site, Savannah (**© 345/947-3329;** www.pedrostjames.ky), is a restored great house dating from 1780, when only 400 people lived on the island. It lasted until 1970, when it was destroyed by fire. Now rebuilt, it is the centerpiece of a new heritage park, with a visitor center and an audiovisual theater with a laser light show. Because of its size, the great house was called "the Castle" by generations of Caymanians. Its primary historic importance dates from December 5, 1831, when residents met here to elect Cayman's first legislative assembly. The great house sits atop a limestone bluff with a panoramic view of the sea. Guests enter via a visitor center with a landscaped courtyard, gift shop, and cafe. Self-guided tours are possible. You can explore the house's wide verandas, rough-hewn timber beams, gabled framework, mahogany floors and staircases, and wide-beam wooden ceilings. Guides in 18th-century costumes are on hand to answer questions. Admission is $10 for adults and free for those 12 and under. Hours are daily from 9am to 5pm. A video, which describes the site's role within the history of the nation and the labor expended to restore it, is screened every hour on the hour, daily from 10am to 4pm.

On the road again, you reach **Bodden Town,** once the largest settlement on the island. At Gun Square, two cannons commanded the channel through the reef. They are now stuck muzzle first into the ground.

On the way to **East End,** just before Old Isaac Village, you'll see the onshore sprays of water shooting up like geysers. These are called blowholes, and they sound like the roar of a lion.

Later you'll spot the fluke of an anchor sticking up from the ocean floor. As the story goes, this is a relic of the famous "Wreck of the Ten Sails" in 1788. A more recent wreck can also be seen—the *Ridgefield,* a 7,500-ton Liberty ship from New England, which struck the reef in 1943.

Old Man Bay is reached by a road that opened in 1983. From here you can travel along the north shore of the island to **Rum Point,** which has a good beach and is a fine place to end your island tour. Rum Point got its name from barrels of rum that once washed ashore here after a shipwreck. Today it is dreamy and quaint, surrounded by towering casuarina trees blowing in the trade winds. Most of these trees have hammocks hanging from their trunks, inviting you to partake of the leisurely life. With its cays, reefs, mangroves, and shallows, Rum Point is a refuge that extends west and south for 11km (6¾ miles). It divides the two "arms" of Grand Cayman. The sound's many spits of land and its plentiful lagoons are ideal for snorkeling, swimming, wading, and birding. It you get hungry, drop in to the Wreck Bar for a juicy burger. After visiting Rum Point, you can head back toward **Old Man Village,** where you can go south along a cross-island road through savanna country that will eventually lead you west to George Town.

On 24 hectares (59 acres) of rugged wooded land off Frank Sound Road, North Side, a 45-minute drive east from Georgetown, the **Queen Elizabeth II Botanic Park ★** (**✆ 345/947-9462;** www.botanic-park.ky) offers visitors a short walk through a tract that includes wetland, swamp, dry thicket, mahogany trees, orchids, and bromeliads. The walking trail is 1km (½ mile) long. You'll probably see chickatees, which are freshwater turtles found only on the Caymans and in Cuba. Occasionally, you'll spot the rare Grand Cayman parrot, or perhaps the anole lizard, with its cobalt-blue throat pouch. Even rarer is the endangered blue iguana. The park is open daily April to September 9am to 6:30pm, October to March 9am to 5:30pm. The last ticket is sold an hour before closing. Admission is $10 for adults and free for children 12 and under. There's a visitor center with changing exhibitions, plus a canteen for food and refreshments. It's set adjacent to the woodland trail and includes a heritage garden with a re-creation of a traditional Cayman home, garden, and farm; a floral garden with .6 hectares (15 acres) of flowering plants; and a .8-hectare (2-acre) lake with three islands, home to many native birds.

Grand Cayman After Dark

Lone Star Bar & Grill, West Bay Road (**✆ 345/945-5175;** www.lonestarbargrill.com), across the road from the Grand Cayman Beach Suites, is a transplanted corner of the Texas Panhandle. You can enjoy burgers in the dining room or head immediately for the bar in back. Here, beneath murals of Lone Star beauties, lime and strawberry margaritas and the 14 different TV screens are the top sellers. Monday and Thursday are all-you-can-eat fajita nights, costing $19; Tuesday is all-you-can-eat spicy tacos, for $15; and Wednesday is all-you-can-eat surf and turf, priced at $52. Classier and, in its own way, more intriguing is the **Reef Grill** (p. 188) at the **Royal Palms Beach Club,** West Bay Road (**✆ 345/945-6358**), with a beachfront bar that's open to the trade winds where you can dance the night away in the moonlight. Local bands play here every Friday night beginning at 9pm, and every Thursday and Saturday night beginning at 8pm.

The most authentic local bar, a regular hangout for locals after the cruise ships have departed, is **Calico Jack's,** West Bay Road, Seven Mile Beach (**✆ 345/945-7850**), outside the hotel zone. It's a barefoot-in-the-sand type of place, with a tin roof fending off the occasional rain, and rock music playing on the radio. Stiff drinks are served to the diverse clientele. There's an open-mic jam on Tuesday nights, with occasional live music on Fridays or DJs on Saturday nights. Full-moon parties are riotous fun here when you're invited to let your hair down.

My Bar, on the grounds of the Sunset House Hotel, 390 S. Church St., on the southern periphery of George Town (© **345/949-7111;** www.sunsethouse.com), is a place that's very far removed from Seven Mile Beach. It attracts the local dive-shop staff and lots of lawyers, especially on Fridays. It has the highest Polynesian-style thatched roof on Grand Cayman and some of the stiffest drinks. It's open Monday to Thursday and Saturday from 9am to midnight, Friday 9am to 1am.

Fidel Murphy's, in the Queen's Court Shopping Center, West Bay Road (© **345/949-5189**), is the unofficial Irish capital on Grand Cayman, with a wood-paneled premises that would have made James Joyce feel at home and foaming mugs full of every imaginable kind of beer. Hours are Monday to Friday from 10:30am to 1am, Saturday and Sunday from 10:30am to midnight.

The Bamboo Lounge, on the ground floor of the Grand Cayman Beach Suites, West Bay Road (p. 179; © **345/949-1234**), is about as urban and trendy a venue as you'll find on island, with a red-and-black, high-octane decor that's as pan-Asian and fusion as its cuisine.

An earthier and more down-to-earth alternative is the bar at **Morgan's Harbour Marina,** Morgan's Harbour (© **345/946-7049**). Thanks to the raffish charm of its Austrian-born owner, Richard Schweiger, it's developed a fast reputation for throwing into the same workaday setting millionaires from New York with local roustabouts and marina crew members in ways that can lead to unexpectedly surreal dialogues. Shoehorned between gas pumps at the nearby marina and stocks of provisions for outfitting boats, there's a battered bar area serving stiff drinks, fresh lobster, and unassuming platters of burgers, salads, and steaks, priced at $11 to $40. It's open daily from 7am to 1am.

CAYMAN BRAC ★

The "middle" island of the Caymans was given the name Brac (Gaelic for "bluff") by 17th-century Scottish fishermen who settled here. The bluff for which the 19km-long (12-mile) island was named is a towering limestone plateau rising 42m (138 ft.) above the sea, covering the eastern half of Cayman Brac. Caymanians refer to the island simply as Brac, and its 1,400 inhabitants, a hospitable bunch, are known as Brackers. In the early 18th century the Caymans were occupied by pirates, and Edward Teach, the infamous Blackbeard, is supposed to have spent quite a bit of time around Cayman Brac. The island is about 145km (90 miles) east of Grand Cayman.

There are more than 170 caves honeycombing the limestone heights of the island. Some of the caves are at the bluff's foot; others can be reached only by climbing over jagged limestone rock. One of the biggest is Great Cave, which has a number of chambers. Harmless fruit bats cling to the roofs of the caverns.

On the south side of the bluff, you won't see many people, and the only sounds are the sea crashing against the lavalike shore. The island's herons, wild green parrots, and a wide diversity of other bird species can be seen here. Most of the Brackers live on the north side, many in traditional wooden seaside cottages, some built by the island's pioneers. Given the variety of flowers, shrubs, and fruit trees in many of the

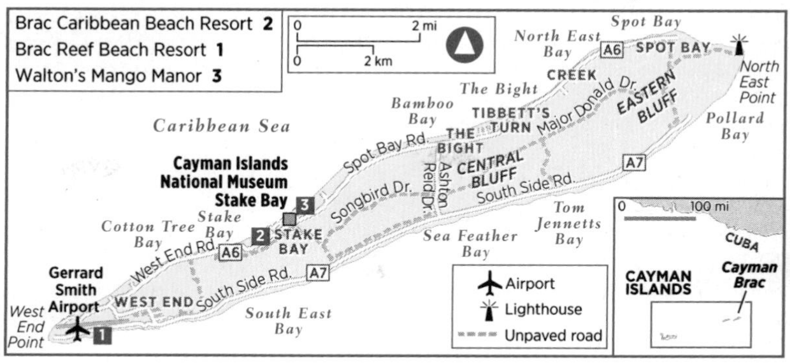

yards, the islanders must all have green thumbs. You'll see poinciana trees, bougainvillea, Cayman orchids, croton, hibiscus, aloe, sea grapes, cactus, and coconut and cabbage palms. Gardeners grow cassava, pumpkins, breadfruit, yams, and sweet potatoes.

There are no actual towns, only settlements, such as Stake Bay (the "capital"), Spot Bay, the Creek, Tibbitts Turn, the Bight, and West End, where the airport is.

Essentials

GETTING THERE Flights from Grand Cayman to Cayman Brac are operated by **Cayman Airways** and its affiliate, **Cayman Express** (✆ **800/422-9626** in the U.S. and Canada, or 345/949-8200; www.caymanairways.com). Between the two companies, there are between four and seven flights a day, depending on the day of the week, between Grand Cayman and Cayman Brac. The cost of a one-way ticket ranges from $67 to $106 per person. Note in advance that the larger planes (such as the 737s, with 122 seats) flying this route allow twice the luggage allotment per passenger, so if you have a lot of luggage, it's wise to opt for a flight on one of the 737s.

VISITOR INFORMATION A little office, the **Cayman Brac Tourist Office,** has opened at West End Community Park (✆ **345/948-1649**). If you're stopping in, call first to see if anybody's going to be there.

EMERGENCIES There's a small hospital, the 18-bed **Faith Hospital** at Stake Bay (✆ **345/948-2243;** www.hsa.ky). For emergencies of any kind on Cayman Brac, dial ✆ **911.**

Where to Stay

Brac Caribbean Beach Resort ★ The largest condo structure on the island offers 16 bright, spacious two-bedroom/two-bathroom or two-bedroom/three-bathroom condos on a white-sand beach, along with a pool and scuba-diving program. Each unit has a full-size refrigerator with an icemaker and a microwave, and 12 units open onto private balconies. A variety of items, including breakfast food, are stocked before your arrival. The master bedroom is furnished with a queen-size bed, the guest bedrooms with twin beds. The units are rather simply furnished in a Caribbean tropical motif. The hotel offers some of the best dining on the island, at the Captain's Table (see below).

Stake Bay (P.O. Box 4), Cayman Brac, Cayman Islands, B.W.I. www.866thebrac.com. ✆ **866/843-2722** or 345/948-2265. Fax 345/948-1111. 16 units. Winter $185 apt for 2, $245 apt for 4 (weekly $1,100 apt for 2, $1,600 apt for 4); off season $140 apt for 2, $185 apt for 4 (weekly $825 apt for 2, $1,200 apt for 4). Dive packages from $890 per person double occupancy, including 7 nights' stay and 5 days of 2-tank dives. AE, MC, V. **Amenities:** Restaurant; bar; outdoor pool; watersports equipment/rentals. *In room:* A/C, ceiling fan, TV, kitchen, Wi-Fi (free).

Brac Reef Beach Resort ★ On a sandy plot of land on the south shore 3km (2 miles) east of the airport, near some of the best snorkeling in the region, this family-friendly, family-run resort contains motel-style units comfortably furnished with carpeting and ceiling fans. Durable and resilient, it's the most visible hotel on Cayman Brac. Once the location was little more than a maze of sea grapes, a few of whose venerable trunks still rise amid the picnic tables, hammocks, and boardwalks. There are still lots of nature trails surrounding the resort, good for bird-watching. Don't expect grandeur or anything approaching urban style or posh: It simply isn't part of the equation here.

P.O. Box 56, Cayman Brac, Cayman Islands, B.W.I. www.bracreef.com. ✆ **800/594-0843** in the U.S. and Canada, or 345/948-1323. 40 units. Year-round $145–$180 double; $175–$205 triple. AE, MC, V. **Amenities:** Restaurant; bar; babysitting; Jacuzzi; pool; day spa; tennis court (lit); watersports equipment/rentals. *In room:* A/C, cable TV, hair dryer, Wi-Fi (free).

Walton's Mango Manor ★★ Unique on Cayman Brac, this is a personalized, intimate B&B that's more richly decorated, more elegant, and more appealing than you might have thought possible in such a remote place. Originally the home of a sea captain, it was moved to a less exposed location and rebuilt from salvaged materials shortly after the disastrous hurricane of 1932. Set on 1.6 hectares (4 acres) on the island's north shore, within a lush garden, it contains intriguing touches such as a banister salvaged from the mast of a 19th-century schooner. The best accommodations are on the upper floor and have narrow balconies with sea views. There is also a two-bedroom, two-bathroom luxury villa, the perfect getaway for two to four guests. The villa contains a kitchen, washer/dryer, phone, TV, and both air-conditioning and ceiling fans. Your hosts are Brooklyn-born Lynne Walton and her husband, George, a former USAF major who retired to his native Cayman Brac.

Stake Bay (P.O. Box 56), Cayman Brac, Cayman Islands, B.W.I. www.waltonsmangomanor.com. ✆ **888/866-5809** or 345/948-0518. Fax 345/948-0518. 6 units. Winter $120–$130 double; off season $105–$115 double; year-round villa $185 daily or $1,200 weekly for 1–2 people, $210 per night or $1,400 per week for 3–4 people. Rates for doubles include full breakfast. MC, V. *In room:* A/C, no phone, Wi-Fi (free).

Where to Dine

Biggie's AMERICAN/CONTINENTAL A newcomer on the island, Biggie's is the kind of place that generated a lot of buzz when it first opened, and a place whose staff and owner (Kent Rankin) work hard to keep clients happy. It faces a traffic roundabout on the island's West End, occupying a peachy-white dining room with clean white napery and glass-topped tables. Lunches focus on an all-you-can-eat American-style buffet of salads and hot foods; dinners are more elaborate, more formal, and permeated with Continental flair, with lots of emphasis on seafood, chicken, beef, and pastas, some of them all vegetarian.

West End. ✆ **345/948-2449.** Reservations recommended. Main courses $16–$30; lunch buffet $10–$16. MC, V. Daily 11am–2:30pm and 5:30–9pm.

Captain's Table AMERICAN The decor here is vaguely nautical, with oars over and around the bar and pieces of boats forming the restaurant's entryway. The restaurant offers both indoor, air-conditioned seating and outdoor, poolside dining. Every Saturday night, its karaoke party draws in more business than any other bar on the island. Begin a meal here with shrimp and lobster cocktail or a conch fritter, and then try one of the soups, such as black bean or a tomato-based conch chowder. Main dishes include everything from the catch of the day, often served pan-fried, to barbecue ribs. Lunch features burgers, salads, and sandwiches.

In Brac Caribbean Beach Village, Stake Bay. ✆ **345/948-1418.** Reservations recommended. Main courses $10–$15 lunch, $20–$42 dinner. AE, MC, V. Daily 11am–3pm and 6–9:30pm. Bar daily 11:30am–midnight.

Fun On & Off the Beach

The biggest lure on Cayman Brac is the variety of **watersports**—swimming, fishing, snorkeling, and some of the world's best diving. There are undersea walls on both the north and south sides of the island, with stunning specimens lining their sides. The big attraction for divers is the **MV *Tibbetts*,** a 98m-long (322-ft.) Russian frigate resting in 30m (98 ft.) of water, a relic of the Cold War sunk in September 1996. Hatches into the ship have been barred off to promote diver safety. Over the years, marine life has become more and more pronounced on this relic. For information on diving in Cayman Brac, visit **www.divecayman.ky**.

History buffs might want to check out the **Cayman Brac Museum,** in the former Government Administration Building, Stake Bay (✆ **345/948-2622;** www.naturecayman.com), which has an interesting collection of Caymanian antiques, including pieces rescued from shipwrecks and items from the 18th century. Hours are Monday to Friday from 9am to noon and 1 to 4pm, Saturday from 9am to noon. Admission is free, but donations are accepted.

LITTLE CAYMAN ★

The smallest of the Cayman Islands, cigar-shaped Little Cayman has only about 170 permanent inhabitants. About 15km (9¼ miles) long and 2km (1¼ miles) across at its widest point, it lies about 120km (75 miles) northeast of Grand Cayman and some 8km (5 miles) from Cayman Brac. The entire island is coral and sand.

The islands of the Caymans are mountaintops of the long-submerged Sierra Maestra Range, which runs north and into Cuba. Coral formed layers over the underwater peaks, eventually creating the islands. Beneath Little Cayman's Bloody Bay is one of the mountain's walls—a stunning sight for snorkelers and divers.

This is a near-perfect place for diving and fishing. The late Jacques Cousteau hailed the waters around the little island as one of the three finest diving spots in the world. The flats on Little Cayman are said to offer the best bonefishing in the world, and a brackish inland pool can be fished for tarpon. Even if you don't dive or fish, you can row 182m (597 ft.) off Little Cayman to isolated and uninhabited Owen Island, where you can swim at the sandy beach and picnic by a blue lagoon.

There may still be pirate treasure buried on the island, but it's thought to be in the dense interior of what is now the largest bird sanctuary in the Caribbean. In addition to having the largest population of rock iguanas in the entire Caribbean, which are easy to spot, Little Cayman is home to one of the oldest species of reptiles in the New World—the tree-climbing *Anolis maynardi* (which is known by no other name). This rare lizard is difficult to spot because the females are green, the males brown, and both blend into local vegetation.

Blossom Village, the island's "capital," is on the southwest coast.

Most visitors fly from Grand Cayman to Little Cayman aboard any of the several daily flights operated by Cayman Express, a subdivision of **Cayman Airways** (✆ **800/422-9626** in the U.S. and Canada, or 345/949-8200; www.caymanairways.com), the national carrier. The cost of a one-way passage aboard any of its 18-seater planes is $66 to $91. Since luggage is limited (without payment of an additional surcharge) to two suitcases per person, totaling no more than 55 pounds for both bags, it's wise to pack lightly. Airplanes land and take off on Little Cayman only during daylight hours.

Where to Stay

Little Cayman Beach Resort ★★ Lying on the south coast, this resort was built in 1991 and enlarged and renovated in 2008. It's close to many of the island's diving and sporting attractions, including the South Hole Sound Lagoon's bonefishing. It's popular with anglers, divers, bird-watchers, and adventurous types. The hotel, owned by Michael Tibbetts, lies only 1.5km (1 mile) from the Edward Bodden Airport, and it has a white-sand beach fringing a shallow, reef-protected bay. It is divided into three pastel, coral-colored two-story buildings with gingerbread trim. The most desirable units are the 12 oceanfront rooms. Each unit has a ceiling fan, a harmonious color scheme, and an inviting, airy atmosphere. Each unit has one king-size or two double beds.

Blossom Village, Little Cayman, Cayman Islands, B.W.I. www.littlecayman.com. ✆ **800/327-3835** in the U.S. and Canada, or 345/948-1033. Fax 345/948-0124. 40 units. Winter $585–$700 for nondiver, $810–$980 for diver; off season $475–$610 for nondiver, $690–$880 for diver. Rates are per person and include a stay of 3 nights with breakfast and dinner; diver rates include 3 1-tank dives per day. AE, MC, V. **Amenities:** Restaurant; bar; babysitting; bikes; health club; Jacuzzi; outdoor pool; sauna; spa; tennis court (lit); watersports equipment/rentals; Wi-Fi (free). *In room:* A/C, ceiling fan, TV, hair dryer, kitchenette, MP3 docking station (in some), no phone.

Pirates Point Resort & Dive Center ★ For watersports or just relaxing, this resort near West End Point offers a family environment with gourmet cuisine, although it's a notch down from Little Cayman Beach Resort. The place has remodeled rooms and a non-air-conditioned family cottage with two large rooms. In addition, it has four seaside cottages, with balconies overlooking Preston Bay. The resort's packages include a room, three excellent meals per day with appropriate wines and all alcoholic beverages, and two-tank boat dives daily, featuring tours of the Bloody Bay Wall and Jackson Reef. Other activities include snorkeling, bird-watching, and exploring.

The food is excellent; the owner and manager, Texas-born Gladys Howard, is an award-winning cookbook author and a graduate of Cordon Bleu in Paris. She has

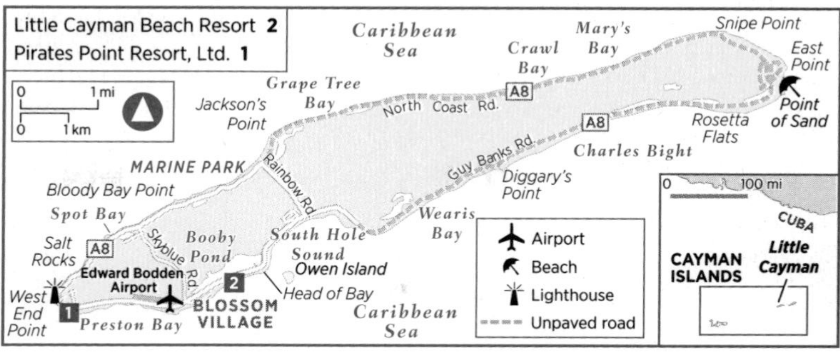

studied with such stars as Julia Child, Jacques Pepin, and James Beard. She uses fresh fruits and vegetables grown locally, as well as local seafood.

Preston Bay, Little Cayman, Cayman Islands, B.W.I. www.piratespointresort.com. ✆ **345/948-1010.** Fax 345/948-1011. 11 units. Winter $1,995 per person 7-day dive package, $1,595 per person 7-day nondiver package; off season $1,895 per person 7-day dive package, $1,595 7-day nondiver package. Children 5–12 free in parent's room. MC, V. Children 4 and under not accepted. **Amenities:** Restaurant; bar; Internet (free); Jacuzzi; outdoor pool; sauna; watersports equipment/rentals. *In room:* A/C (in some), hair dryer, no phone.

Where to Dine

Birds of Paradise AMERICAN/CONTINENTAL This spot caters primarily to Little Cayman Beach Resort guests but welcomes anyone. The specialty is buffet-style dinners—the kind your parents might have enjoyed back in the 1950s or 1960s. Saturday night features the island's most generous barbecue spread—all the ribs, fish, and Jamaican-style jerk chicken you'd want. On other nights, try the prime rib, fresh fish Caribbean style (your best bet), or chicken (either Kiev or *cordon bleu*). There's a freshly made salad bar, and homemade desserts are yummy, especially the Key lime pie. At night, opt for an outdoor table under the stars.

At Little Cayman Beach Resort. ✆ **345/948-1033.** Reservations recommended for dinner for non-guests. Main courses $15 breakfast, $21 lunch, $44 dinner. AE, MC, V. Daily 7–8:30am, 12:30–1:30pm, and 6:30–8pm.

The Hungry Iguana AMERICAN/CARIBBEAN At the beach, you'll spot the mammoth iguana mural that marks this place immediately. The island's tastiest dishes are served here, a winning combination of standard American fare and some zesty flavors from islands to the south. It's the rowdiest place on Little Cayman, especially the sports bar, with its satellite TV in the corner, a sort of T.G.I. Friday's atmosphere. Lunch is the usual burgers and fries, along with some well-stuffed sandwiches. We prefer the grilled chicken salad. Dinner gets a little more elaborate—there's usually a special meat dish of the day, depending on the market (supplies are shipped in once a week by barge). The chef always seems willing to prepare a steak as you like it. Marinated conch with homemade chips is another tasty choice.

Paradise Resort. ✆ **345/948-0007.** Reservations recommended. Main courses $8–$15 lunch, $18–$36 dinner. AE, MC, V. Daily noon–2:30pm and 5:30–9pm. Bar Mon–Fri noon–1am; Sat–Sun noon–midnight.

Sports & Outdoor Pursuits

The **Governor Gore Bird Sanctuary ★** is home to some 5,000 pairs of red-footed boobies. As far as it is known, this is the largest colony of such birds in the Western Hemisphere. The sanctuary, which is near the small airport, is also home to dramatic colonies of snowy egrets and black frigates. Many bird-watchers from the U.S. fly into Little Cayman just to see these bird colonies.

The best **fishing** is at Bloody Bay, lying off the island's north coast. It is especially noted for its bonefishing and tarpon catches. Most hotels will help you arrange for a fishing adventure.

The **Bloody Bay Wall ★★**, the best dive site on island and one of the great dive spots in the Caymans, lies just 20 minutes offshore by boat. The drop here begins at only 6m (20 ft.) but plunges to more than 360m (1,181 ft.). For more information about how to enjoy it, click on www.divecayman.ky or call **Conch Club Divers** (**✆ 345/948-1026;** www.conchclubdivers.com).

CURAÇAO

The "C" in the Dutch ABC islands, Curaçao is the largest, most populous, and most cosmopolitan of the former Lesser Antilles. It has in the colorful capital of Willemstad a picturesque trove of colonial Dutch architecture and a World Heritage Site. Like Aruba, Curaçao boasts a warm, friendly polyglot populace, but it also offers a rich history, a vibrant art scene, and world-class diving. Just 10km (six miles) wide and 60km (37 miles) long, this semi-arid landscape is dotted with spiny-leaf aloe, mesquite, and divi-divi trees.

9

Beaches Curaçao has nearly 40 beaches, ranging from tranquil bays to secluded coves. **Seaquarium Beach** (Mambo Beach), just east of Willemstad, offers placid waters perfect for swimming and bars and restaurants on-site. The largest and most popular destination for sunbathing, **Blauwbaai** has showers and changing facilities and plenty of shade. Hang with the locals on pristine sand at **Daaibooi,** south of Willemstad, where you can snorkel in clear reef waters. Shallow, tranquil seas tucked inside a narrow cove make **Playa Lagun** a prime spot for families.

Things to Do Sip a cool drink at a Willemstad cafe as you gaze upon the colored lights illuminating the **Queen Emma Bridge,** a floating pontoon across Saint Anna Bay. A short walk away, scores of schooners parked along the canal compose a **Floating Market** selling crafts and tropical fruits and vegetables. Admire the colorful Dutch architecture in the colonial capital, **Willemstad.** The unusual collection of artifacts and oddities in the **Museum Kurá Hulanda** includes fertility dolls, fossils, musical instruments, and even slave quarters.

Eating & Drinking The island's Dutch heritage surfaces in specialties such as ***keshi yena,*** a traditional baked dish with spicy chicken, dates, raisins, olives, and Gouda cheese. Feel the warm breeze at the open-air **Belle Terrace,** a 200-year-old mansion where you can dine on international fare fused with such island flourishes as *tu tu* (local polenta with beans). Soul-satisfying Creole cooking reigns at rustic, leisurely **Jaanchie's Restaurant** in Westpunt, with iguana soup, goat stew, and fresh fish served with rice and beans.

Nightlife & Entertainment Locals kick back here more than the tourists—or so it seems. The biggest party is **Carnival,** which runs for several weeks and ends on Mardi Gras. Otherwise, the capital's **Salinja** district forms the scene's thumping heart. In Penstraat, **Blues,** a restaurant and bar perched over the water, features live jazz. Sundays are devoted to salsa at **Mambo Beach's** bar, which sometimes shows classic movies under the stars. Casinos offer live music nightly and great people-watching.

ESSENTIALS

Visitor Information

In the United States, contact the **Curaçao Tourist Board** at One Gateway Center, Ste. 2600, Newark, NJ 07102 (✆ **800/3-CURACAO** [328-7222]). You can also point your Web browser to **www.curacao.com**.

Once you're on the island, go to the **Curaçao Tourist Board,** Pietermaai 19 (✆ **599/9-434-8200**). The readily available and free glossy magazines ***Curaçao Events*** and ***Curaçao Nights*** are published by the tourism board and provide a good overview of where to go and what to see. Also pick up a copy of the weekly dining and entertainment guide ***K-Pasa*** (www.k-pasa.com) at any tourism office, hotel lobby, or many shops and restaurants.

Getting There

The air routes to the modern **Hato International Airport,** Plaza Margareth Abraham (✆ **599/9-839-1000**), are firmly linked to those leading to nearby Aruba. In recent years, however, some airlines have initiated nonstop routings into Curaçao from such international hubs as Miami.

American Airlines (✆ **800/433-7300** in the U.S. and Canada; www.aa.com) flies daily to Curaçao from Miami; it departs late enough in the day to permit easy connections from cities all over the northeastern U.S. American also flies to neighboring Aruba from New York, Miami, and San Juan, Puerto Rico. American Airlines also offers discounted hotel/airfare packages. **Air Jamaica** (✆ **800/523-5585;** www.airjamaica.com) flies nonstop from Montego Bay on Tuesdays, Saturdays, and Sundays. **Continental** (✆ **800/231-0856** in the U.S. and Canada; www.continental.com) flies to Curaçao on Saturdays via nonstop flights from Newark, New Jersey. **Delta** (✆ **800/221-1212** in the U.S. and Canada; www.delta.com) flies to Curaçao from its hub in Atlanta on Saturdays.

Getting Around

BY RENTAL CAR Because all points of interest on Curaçao are easily accessible via paved roads, you may want to rent a car. U.S., British, and Canadian visitors can use their own licenses, if valid. The minimum age to rent for many companies is 25. ***Note:*** Traffic moves on the right. International road signs are observed.

Special Events

The big event of the year is the **Curaçao Carnival,** which starts on New Year's Day, with various festivities and dozens of parades extending until Mardi Gras and the **Grand Farewell Parade.** The schedule is available at the tourism office. The most fun events, similar to hoedowns, are called "jump-ups." The highlight of Carnival is the **Festival di Tumba,** the second week in February, in which the island's musicians vie for prizes. Other Carnival events include the crowning of a queen and king, street parades, concerts, and even a children's parade.

Curaçao

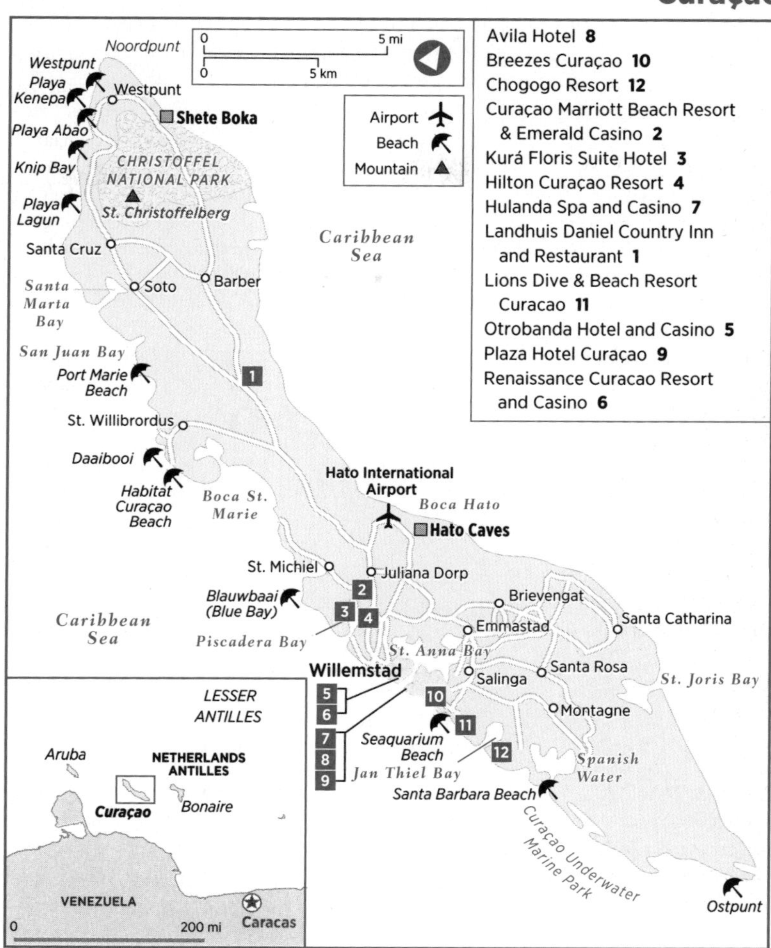

Avis (✆ **800/331-1084** in the U.S. and Canada, or 599/9-839-1500; www.aviscuracao.com) and **Budget** (✆ **800/472-3325** in the U.S. and Canada, or 599/9-868-3466; www.curacao-budgetcar.com) offer some of the lowest rates. Budget usually offers the best deal if it has compact cars with manual transmissions in stock. **Hertz** (✆ **800/654-3001** in the U.S. and Canada, or 599/9-888-0188; www.curacaocarrental.com) is also on island. **National** (✆ **599/9-869-4433;** www.nationalcuracao.com) has an office at the airport. Rentals are cheaper if you reserve from North America at least a week before your departure, and rates vary depending on the times of the year and seasonal promotions.

BY TAXI Most taxis are metered, and all drivers carry an official rate sheet. Charges go up by 20% after 8pm. Tipping isn't customary among islanders, but from tourists, drivers will appreciate a discretionary 10% tip, especially if they've helped with your luggage. The fare from the airport to Willemstad is about $20, and the cost can be split among four passengers. Each piece of luggage bears a surcharge of $1.

In town the best place to get a taxi is on the Otrabanda side of the floating bridge. To summon a cab, call the dispatch office (✆ **599/9-869-0752**). Cabbies will usually give you a tour of the island for around $50 per hour for up to four passengers. **Taber Tours** (✆ **599/9-868-7012;** www.tabertours.nl) specializes in hotel transfers and island tours for big groups.

BY BUS Most of the large hotels operate a free shuttle that takes you from the suburbs to the shopping district of Willemstad. A fleet of DAF yellow buses (also called "convoys") operates from Wilhelmina Plein, near the shopping center, to most parts of Curaçao. Some minivans function as buses. If you see one listing your destination, you can hail it at any of the designated bus stops.

[FastFACTS] CURAÇAO

Banks Normal bank hours are Monday to Friday from 9am to 3:30 or 4:30pm. Banks and ATMs can be found in Willemstad.

Currency While U.S. dollars are accepted for purchases on the island, the official currency is the **Netherlands Antillean florin (NAf),** also called a **guilder,** which is divided into 100 NA (Netherlands Antillean) cents. You will most likely be handed change in guilders. The exchange rate as of this writing is US$1 to 1.78 NAf (1 NAf = 55¢). Shops, hotels, and restaurants usually accept most major U.S. and Canadian credit cards. While American Express, Visa, and Master Card are preferred, Discover is gaining ground, while Diner's Club is rarely accepted. *Prices in this chapter are quoted in U.S. dollars.*

Documents To enter Curaçao, U.S., British, and Canadian citizens need a passport, along with a return or continuing airline ticket out of the country and photo ID.

Electricity The electricity is both 220 and 110–130 volts AC (50 cycles), the same as in both Europe and North America, and most hotels have plugs that fit North American and European appliances.

Emergencies For **police,** call ✆ **911.** For an **ambulance,** call ✆ **912.** For **fire,** call ✆ **115.**

Hospital The **St. Elisabeth Hospital,** Breedestraat 193 (✆ **599/9-462-4900**), near Otrabanda in Willemstad, is one of the most up-to-date facilities in the Caribbean. It has a recompression chamber.

Language Dutch, Spanish, and English are spoken on Curaçao, along with Papiamento, a patois that combines the three major tongues with Amerindian and African dialects. Most people in the tourism industry speak English, but you can always thank them by saying *masha danki* (*mas*-ha *dan*-key).

Safety Although Curaçao is not plagued with crime, it's wise to safeguard your valuables.

Taxes Curaçao levies a room tax of 5%, plus a 12% service fee on accommodations and a $3 daily (per room) energy tax on all hotels. There's a departure tax of $22, but it's usually built into the price of your ticket.

Telephone To call Curaçao from the United States, dial **011** (the international access code), then **599** (the country code for Curaçao), and then **9** (the area code) and the local number. Once on Curaçao, to call another number on the island, only the local seven-digit number is necessary; to make calls to an off-island destination, dial **021** and then the area code and number.

Time Curaçao is on Atlantic Standard Time year-round, 1 hour ahead of Eastern Standard Time and the same as eastern daylight saving time.

Water The water comes from a modern desalination plant and is safe to drink.

Weather Curaçao has an average temperature of 81°F (27°C); trade winds keep the island quite comfortable. It's flat and arid, with an average rainfall of only 22 inches per year.

WHERE TO STAY

A few hotels are in the capital of Willemstad, but most are in the suburbs, which lie only 10 to 15 minutes from the shopping center. The bigger hotels often have free shuttle buses running into town, and most have their own beaches and pools. Some hotels cater primarily to American and Canadian tourists, while others are occupied almost exclusively by the many Dutch visitors. The latter tend toward a quiet self-service atmosphere, with kitchenettes in the rooms and shuttles to local shopping markets. Many of these are clustered near the Jan Thiel Beach area. South Americans are an increasingly significant percentage of the tourist population, so many hotel desks can greet you in Spanish and Portuguese. Hotels listed here are a mixture, but the larger chain hotels are really U.S.-centric.

Curaçao is a bustling commercial center, and the downtown hotels often fill up fast with business travelers as well as visitors from neighboring countries such as Venezuela. It's important to reserve well in advance. When making reservations, ask if the room tax and service charge are included in the price you're quoted.

Very Expensive

Renaissance Curacao Resort & Casino This modern, upscale resort adjacent to the Riffort is responsible for the influx of new shops, restaurants, and bars to the area. The rainbow-hued lobby has a colorful frenetic feel that matches the sounds and lights emanating from the hotel's appropriately named Carnival casino. A restaurant and bar are also integrated into the spacious lobby and look out over the outdoor plaza. The rooms are spacious, colorful, and loaded with comfortable linens, pillows, and plush chairs with ottomans. Bathrooms are cheerfully painted and well appointed, though the doors are irritatingly determined to shut on their own. The infinity beach is a new concept and works well in this urban setting, creating a serene respite to swim, sunbathe, and relax before hitting the casino.

Baden Powellweg 1, Willemstad, Curaçao, N.A. www.renaissancecuracao.com. ✆ **888/236-2427** in the U.S., or 599/9-435-5000. Fax 599/9-435-5001. 223 units. Late Dec to Mar $410–$575 double, $790–$1,780 suite; Apr to mid-Dec $220–$425 double, $380–$1,140 suite. AE, MC, V. **Amenities:** Restaurant; 2 bars; babysitting; dive shop; casino; room service; Wi-Fi (free, in lobby); rooms for those w/limited mobility. *In room:* A/C, TV, hair dryer, high-speed Internet.

Expensive

Avila Hotel ★★ The Avila Hotel consists of four separate structures: a beautifully restored 200-year-old colonial mansion; a large extension of deluxe rooms called La Belle Alliance wing; the Blues Wing, an all-wood complex of deluxe rooms built on a pier off of the beach, each with a private terrace or balcony overlooking the sea; and the new contemporary-style Octagon Wing. Converted into a hotel in 1949, the Avila regularly hosts members of the Dutch royal family, including the queen of the

Netherlands. The Blues Wing rooms have a full bathroom, kitchenette, Jacuzzi tub, and balcony or terrace with an ocean view. Similarly, the recently refurnished La Belle Alliance units have full bathrooms and balconies; some have kitchenettes. Rooms in the Octagon Wing have a chic South Beach feel, with beige suede headboards, flatscreen TVs, and frosted-glass bathroom walls and doors.

Penstraat 130 (P.O. Box 791), Willemstad, Curaçao, N.A. www.avilahotel.com. ✆ **800/747-8162** or 599/9-461-4377. Fax 599/9-461-1493. 150 units. Dec 16–Apr 15 $430 1 bedroom, $575 2 bedroom; Apr 16–Sept 15 $360 1 bedroom, $475 2 bedroom; Sept 16–Dec 15 $370 1 bedroom, $485 2 bedroom. Meal plans available. AE, MC, V. **Amenities:** 2 restaurants; 2 bars; babysitting; pool; spa/wellness center; tennis court; rooms for those w/limited mobility. *In room:* A/C, TV, hair dryer, high-speed Internet.

Breezes Curaçao ★ ☺ Adjacent to both the Undersea National Park and Sea Aquarium, this big all-inclusive resort—a member of SuperClubs—opens onto one of Curaçao's longest beaches, with good snorkeling offshore. Although it caters to couples and singles, the resort also welcomes families, and its Camp Breezes has the best children's program on island. For those who like to gamble, Breezes also has Curacao's largest casino. Dive enthusiasts get one free shore dive per day. In the rooms, bathrooms come with either showers or complete tub/showers, and all open onto private patios or balconies. If the food isn't gourmet, there is at least plenty of it. It's a real all-you-can-eat type of place, from breakfast buffets in the morning to lavish dinner feasts at night.

Dr. Martin Luther King Blvd. 8, Willemstad, Curaçao, N.A. www.breezes.com. ✆ **877/273-3937** or 599/9-736-7888. Fax 599/9-461-4003. 339 units. Winter $325–$365 double, $460–$540 suite; off season $310–$350 double, $440–$560 suite. Rates are all-inclusive (no tipping). AE, DC, DISC, MC, V. **Amenities:** 4 restaurants; 4 bars; babysitting; children's program (kids' snack bar, playground); dive shop; fitness center; Jacuzzi; 3 outdoor pools; casino; smoke-free rooms; snorkeling; spa; 2 tennis courts; windsurfing. *In room:* A/C, TV, hair dryer, Wi-Fi ($15 per day).

Curaçao Marriott Beach Resort & Emerald Casino ★★ ☺ This is the most glamorous and most prominent hotel on the island, set beside the largest beach on Curaçao. It's 10 minutes from both the airport and Willemstad. The hotel is a cluster of three-story buildings whose distinctive shape and ocher color were adapted from traditional Dutch colonial architecture. The open-sided lobby was designed for optimum views of the beach and the hotel's many fountains. Scattered throughout the property are unusual, often monumental, artworks by local and international artists, and a collection of unfussy, overstuffed furniture. Most of the colorful rooms have a view of the ocean and one king-size or two double beds, plus a spacious bathroom with a tub/shower. Although never rising to any great imagination or flair, the food here is consistently good, with quality ingredients. There's an expansive beach with postcard-perfect beach bar complete with bar swings. There's also a big casino.

Piscadera Bay (P.O. Box 6003), Willemstad, Curaçao, N.A. www.curacaomarriott.com. ✆ **800/223-6388** in the U.S., or 599/9-736-8800. Fax 599/9-462-7502. 247 units. Late Dec to Mar $275–$340 double, from $490 suite; Apr to mid-Dec $170–$200 double, from $390 suite. AE, MC, V. **Amenities:** 3 restaurants; 2 bars; children's program; concierge; health club; 2 open-air Jacuzzis; outdoor pool; casino; room service; sauna; spa; watersports; rooms for those w/limited mobility. *In room:* A/C, TV, hair dryer, minibar, Wi-Fi ($14.95 per day).

Kurá Hulanda Spa & Casino ★★ 🎁 Curaçao's most imaginative and unusual hotel, in the heart of the city's Dutch colonial historic district, is part of the Kurá Hulanda museum complex (p. 221). The hotel's Dutch colonial architecture dates from the 18th and 19th centuries. Both the museum and the hotel are the brainchild of the Dutch millionaire Dr. Jacob Gelt Dekker, whose passion for preserving the architecture of Curaçao and the history and culture of its people is palpable. It's not on a beach, but this hotel offers the Dutch Caribbean's best West Indian character. The gorgeous rooms feature hand-woven linens from India and hand-carved mahogany and teak furniture. A free daily shuttle runs to nearby Blaubai Beach and Blue Bay Golf Course, and to a sister property, the Lodge Kurá Hulanda, where visitors can escape the city and enjoy an idyllic day at the beach or a relaxed meal at their waterside eatery, Watamula Restaurant.

Langestraat 8, Willemstad, Curaçao, N.A. www.kurahulanda.com. ✆ **877/264-3106** in the U.S., or 599/9-434-7700. Fax 599/9-434-7701. 80 units. Winter $200 double, $460–$1,100 suite; off season from $145 double, $425–$1,000 suite. AE, MC, V. **Amenities:** 3 restaurants; cafe; bar; babysitting; fitness center; 2 outdoor pools; casino; room service; smoke-free rooms. *In room:* A/C, ceiling fan, TV, CD player, hair dryer, kitchenette (in some), minifridge, Wi-Fi (free).

Moderate

Floris Suite Hotel ★★ The Dutch philanthropist and architect Jan des Bouvrie created this gem of a boutique hotel in the vicinity of the Curaçao World Trade Center. Unlike any hotel on island, the all-suite hotel blends aspects of European colonial with West Indian architecture. Natural stone tiles are wedded with solid mahogany doors and windows. The compound is enveloped by a tropical garden whose focal point is a swimming pool. A good private sandy beach is just across the street. The standard of luxury differs from suite to suite. For example, the Royal Suites offer a separate bedroom with one king-size bed. In the living area, there is yet another queen-size sleeper sofa, and a fully equipped kitchen with a large covered porch or balcony. Everything is designed for comfort and convenience. A spa center is within walking distance, and a dive headquarters is just across from the hotel. Because the hotel has adopted an eco-friendly mentality, air-conditioning units turn off when guests leave the rooms.

John F. Kennedy Blvd., Piscadera Bay, Curaçao, N.A. www.florissuitehotel.com. ✆ **800/411-0170** in the U.S. and Canada, or 599/9-462-6111. Fax 599/9-462-6211. 71 units. Dec–Apr $130–$270 suite; off season $145–$240 suite. AE, MC, V. **Amenities:** Restaurant; 2 bars; babysitting; fitness room; outdoor pool; smoke-free rooms; tennis court. *In room:* A/C, TV, hair dryer, high-speed Internet, kitchenette.

Hilton Curaçao Resort ★★ ☺ Built in 1965 and once a Sheraton, this hotel resort got an updated look when Hilton took it over. Today it rises five floors above the northern perimeter of Willemstad, amid rocky bluffs. Glass-enclosed elevators cling to the outside walls of the hotel, offering a panoramic view as you're whisked to your room. Each of the midsize accommodations has a view of either the ocean or the garden. Outfitted in pastel colors, the rooms contain traditional colorful furnishings, carpeting, plush bedding, private balconies, and generously proportioned bathrooms with tubs and showers. Rooms on the executive floor are somewhat better furnished and offer amenities such as fax machines. The hotel opens onto two private sandy beaches.

The food isn't great, but it's varied—everything from Italian trattoria favorites to fresh seafood. A social director organizes theme nights based on Mexican or Antillean food and dance music. There's a lively casino on-site.

Piscadera Bay, John F. Kennedy Blvd. (P.O. Box 2133), Willemstad, Curaçao, N.A. www.hiltoncaribbean.com/curacao. ✆ **800/HILTONS** [445-8667] in the U.S. and Canada, or 599/9-462-5000. Fax 599/9-462-5846. 196 units. Late Dec to Mar $190–$265 double, $250–$380 suite; Apr to mid-Dec $150–$170 double, $210–$250 suite. AE, MC, V. **Amenities:** 3 restaurants; 2 bars; children's program and playground; 18-hole minigolf course; health club; outdoor pool; casino; room service; smoke-free rooms; 2

tennis courts (lit); watersports; rooms for those w/limited mobility. *In room:* A/C, TV, hair dryer, high-speed Internet ($7.35 for 5 hr., $15.75 for 24 hrs.).

Lions Dive & Beach Resort Curacao On the island's largest white-sand beach, this hotel lies a 30-minute taxi ride southeast of the airport. The complete dive resort features programs supervised by the Underwater Curaçao staff. Each of its comfortable though standard accommodations has a sea and/or garden view, a balcony or terrace, two double beds, and a shower-only bathroom.

Bapor Kibrá, Willemstad, Curaçao, N.A. www.lionsdive.com. ✆ **599/9-434-8888.** Fax 599/9-434-8889. 137 units. Jan to mid-Dec $195 double, $440 apt, $405–$490 suite; mid-Dec to late Dec $280 double, $520 apt, $640 suite. Extra bed in room $25. Dive packages and meal plans available. AE, MC, V. **Amenities:** 3 restaurants; beach bar; babysitting; dive shop; health club; outdoor pool; sailing. *In room:* A/C, TV, fridge, kitchenette (in some); Wi-Fi ($12 per day).

Plaza Hotel Curaçao Standing guard over the Punda side of St. Anna Bay, right in the heart of Willemstad, the 14-story Plaza is nestled in the ramparts of an 18th-century waterside fort on the eastern tip of the harbor entrance. As one of the harbor's two "lighthouses," the hotel has to carry marine collision insurance (the only accommodations in the Caribbean with that distinction). The original part of the hotel was built in 1954, and the quirky lobby complete with fish pond, enormous rotating ceiling fans, and open-air balcony retains the 1950s look. However, now there's a modern tower of rooms stacked 15 stories high. Each of the smallish bedrooms is comfortably furnished and contains a small tub/shower.

The pool, with a bar and sun-tanning area, is inches away from the parapet of the fort. The Waterfort Terrace serves standard American and Continental dishes.

Plaza Piar (P.O. Box 813), Willemstad, Curaçao, N.A. www.plazahotelcuracao.com ✆ **599/9-461-2500.** Fax 599/9-461-6543. 252 units. Winter $180–$235 double, $255–$450 suite; off season $150–$180 double, $210–$315 suite. Breakfast included. Children 13 and under stay free. AE, DC, DISC, MC, V. **Amenities:** 2 restaurants; 3 bars; outdoor pool; casino; room service; Sunset sailboats; smoke-free rooms. *In room:* A/C, TV, hair dryer, kitchenette (in some), Wi-Fi ($3 per day).

Inexpensive

Chogogo Resort In Curaçao's east end, a 2-minute walk from the busy and Dutch-dominated Jan Thiel Beach, this resort is for visitors seeking an apartment or a bungalow. It is named after a species of local flamingo and set within an arid landscape between the oceanfront beaches and a shallow saltwater bay southeast of Willemstad. One- and two-story buildings dot the grounds; these contain the guest bungalows, studios, and apartments, each with a kitchenette, airy and unpretentious furniture, and a compact shower-only bathroom.

Jan Thiel Beach, Curaçao, N.A. www.chogogo.com. ✆ **599/9-747-2844.** Fax 599/9-747-2424. 120 units. Year-round $135–$160 studio for 2, $135–$160 apt for 2, $210–$280 bungalow for 4. 3-night minimum. AE, MC, V. **Amenities:** Restaurant; bar; outdoor pool; children's wading pool. *In room:* A/C, TV, kitchenette, Wi-Fi ($10 per day).

Landhuis Daniel Country Inn and Restaurant Situated on the narrow middle part of the island, this mustard-colored plantation house is a 15-minute drive from the beach, but it offers the best value in Curaçao. Simple but comfortable guest rooms are tidily maintained and have small private bathrooms with showers. Only six rooms are air-conditioned, but all units have ceiling fans. The basic rooms and communal TV room give this simple country inn the aura of a youth hostel; guests also play billiards.

Weg naar, Westpunt z/n, Curaçao, N.A. www.landhuisdaniel.com. ✆ **599/9-864-8400.** Fax 599/9-864-7284. 8 units. Year-round $60–$70 double. MC, V. **Amenities:** Restaurant (see below); bar; dive shop; pool. *In room:* A/C, no phone, Wi-Fi (free).

Otrobanda Hotel & Casino Situated in the heart of town, this small hotel is more geared toward local business travelers than American tourists, but it provides an inexpensive way to stay in town for a few nights on the cheap, great for those who just need a crash pad close to the city bustle. The small guest rooms overlook the harbor, and even the pocket-size pool has great views of town. Prices include breakfast at the restaurant, which also affords stupendous photo ops of the waterfront and the mouth of the harbor. The sad casino is not worth more than a glance, but at the other end of town, there are glitzy shops, restaurants, a piano bar, and a new casino at the Renaissance in the Riffort.

Breedestraat O (P.O. Box 2092) Willemstad, Curaçao, N.A. www.otrobandahotel.com. ✆ **599/9-462-7400.** Fax 599/9-462-7299. 45 units. Year-round $135 single, $160 double, $225 triple. AE, DISC, MC, V. **Amenities:** Restaurant; bar; pool; small casino. *In room:* A/C, TV, Wi-Fi ($10 for 2-day minimum).

WHERE TO DINE

Expensive

Bistro Le Clochard ★ FRENCH/SWISS This restaurant fits snugly into the grim ramparts of Riffort, at the gateway to the harbor. Its entrance is marked with a canopy leading to a series of rooms, each built under the vaulting of the old Dutch fort. This appealingly formal restaurant has several seating options, including a glassed-in dining room near the entrance and an outdoor terrace. Appetizers such as snails marinated in cognac, frogs' legs, or crepes stuffed with a seafood ragout with a hollandaise sauce seem more appropriate to a Paris bistro than a tropical island. The kitchen staff is at its best when preparing beef dishes; the tenderloin with mushrooms in a cream sauce is recommended. The signature dish is La Potence, a swinging, red-hot metal ball covered with bits of sizzling tenderloin, served with various dipping sauces. The catch of the day always comes with a lemon-butter sauce.

Rif Fort, on the Otrobanda side of the pontoon bridge. ✆ **599/9-462-5666.** www.bistroleclochard.com. Reservations recommended. Main courses $35–$46. AE, MC, V. Daily noon–3pm and 6:30–10:45pm. Harborside Terrace daily noon–10:45pm.

Blues SEAFOOD/INTERNATIONAL As you dine on a pier jutting far out from the beachfront of the Avila Hotel, water ripples beneath your seat, and heaping platters of fresh seafood challenge even the heartiest of appetites. You may enjoy homemade wild-mushroom ravioli or chargrilled swordfish filet with a garlic-butter crust. An especially impressive dish is the seafood special, compiled from three different types of fish, depending on the catch of the day. If after all this hearty fare you still have room, the chef makes great desserts, including one of our favorites, a lemon panna cotta.

In the Avila Hotel, Penstraat 130, Willemstad. ✆ **599/9-461-4377.** www.avilahotel.com. Reservations recommended. Main courses $16–$26. AE, MC, V. Tues–Sun 7–10:30pm. Live jazz Thurs and Sat. From the center of town, drive east along the Pieter Maai Weg (which becomes Pennstraat) for about 1.5km (1 mile).

Landhuis Daniel ★ 🎁 FRENCH/MEDITERRANEAN/CREOLE This restaurant serves a unique combination of loosely French, Mediterranean, and Creole flavors using fresh produce organically grown on the premises. Surrounded by arid scrubland about 3km (2 miles) south of Westpunt, near the island's most northwesterly tip, this place was originally built in 1711 as an inn and tavern. Today its mustard-colored facade, white columns, terra-cotta roof, and old-fashioned green-and-yellow dining room are carefully preserved and historically authentic. Their three-course menu changes weekly, and items are cooked slowly, to order, in a setting of sea breezes and sunlight streaming in the big windows. Launch your repast with a spicy Caribbean seafood bisque, then order the dover sole in butter or locally raised rabbit in stewed pears; another favorite is the Argentine beef tenderloin with spicy pumpkin sauce.

In the Landhuis Daniel Inn, Weg naar, Westpunt. ✆ **599/9-864-8400.** www.landhuisdaniel.com. Reservations recommended. Main courses $19–$30 lunch, $24–$43 dinner. AE, MC, V. Daily 8:30am–2pm and 5–10pm.

Watamula Restaurant SEAFOOD/INTERNATIONAL Perched over lapping water with views of the beach below, this breezy open-air restaurant features fresh local food prepared with a continental flair. The seared tuna or shrimp tempura appetizers work well to open your palate before the ostrich filet with teriyaki sambal or blackened swordfish with blue-cheese mashed potatoes. Seafood is not the only option; the jerk chicken, spiced New Zealand rack of lamb, and wild-forest-mushroom linguini are just as satisfying. For dessert, tease your palate with the banana crepe flavored with local rum and served with rum-raisin ice cream.

At the Lodge Kurá Hulanda, Playa Kalki 1, Westpunt. ✆ **599/9-839-3600.** www.kurahulanda.com. Reservations recommended. Main courses $22–$40. AE, MC, V. Daily noon–3pm and 6–10pm.

Moderate

Belle Terrace ★ INTERNATIONAL This open-air restaurant, in a 200-year-old mansion on the beachfront of Willemstad, offers superb dining in a relaxed and informal atmosphere. The beachfront Schooner Bar, where you can enjoy rum punch, is shaped like a weather-beaten ship's prow looking out to sea. The restaurant, sheltered by an arbor of flamboyant branches, serves such specialties as pickled herring, smoked salmon, and a Danish lunch platter. Local dishes, such as *keshi yena* (baked Gouda cheese with a spicy chicken filling), are also on the lunch menu. The fish is always fresh, and the chef prepares it to perfection, whether grilled, poached, or meunière. On Saturday night, there's a mixed grill and a serve-yourself salad bar, all accompanied by live music.

In the Avila Hotel, Penstraat 130, Willemstad. ✆ **599/9-461-4377.** www.avilahotel.com. Reservations required. Main courses $21–$34. AE, MC, V. Daily noon–2:30pm and 7–10pm. From the center of town, drive east along the Pieter Maai Weg (which becomes Pennstraat) for about 1.5km (1 mile).

Gouverneur DeRouville INTERNATIONAL Overlooking the waterfront, this spectacular three-story structure was the residence of the original governor of Willemstad. Whether you sit on the balcony overlooking the water, in the courtyard next to the fountain, or inside the main dining room beneath the ornate chandelier, you will likely appreciate the charming Dutch architecture almost as much as you'll enjoy the well-prepared local and international food and professional service. The *keshi yena* (stuffed cheese) is worth the wait, and the mixed grill is cooked to perfection.

De Rouvilleweg 9. ✆ **599/9-462-5999.** www.de-gouverneur.com. Reservations recommended. Main courses $17–$28. AE, MC, V. Daily 10am–midnight.

Jaanchie's Restaurant SEAFOOD/CREOLE The proprietor of this establishment is likely to greet you himself, and to inform you that his iguana soup is the best on island. Since the iguana is not deboned and does not taste like chicken, you might want to take his word for it. On the other hand, iguana is reputed to have the same aphrodisiac properties as the legendary oyster. In a rustic country-style setting with antiques and oak walls, diners are treated to a savory local cuisine. The fish is among the freshest around; our recent sampling of the grilled wahoo was perfection itself. You can also order delectable garlic shrimp or stewed goat. Most visitors drop in for lunch, and locals swear by this place.

Westpunt 15, Westpunt. ✆ **599/9-864-0126.** Reservations required for dinner. Main courses $14–$20. Daily noon–7pm (last seating).

Jaipur INDIAN Within the breezy, European Kurá Hulanda "village" sits this fine Indian restaurant. With its terra-cotta walls, teak chairs, marble tabletops, and location beside the babbling eco-pool, Jaipur offers Indian fare with a pan-Asian flair and an unusually thorough wine list. The food—particularly the fresh naan, curries, and chicken and seafood, which emerge steaming from the tandoori oven—is finely honed, with details (bright chutneys, peppery purées) that show unexpected kitchen finesse.

Langestraat 8, within the Hotel Kurá Hulanda complex. ✆ **599/9-434-7700.** www.kurahulanda.com. Reservations recommended. Main courses $13–$35. AE, MC, V. Wed–Mon 7–11pm.

Rijsttafel Indonesia ★ INDONESIAN This is the best place on the island to sample Indonesian *rijstafel,* the traditional rice table served here with 16, 20, or 25 zesty side dishes. The spicy food is a good change of pace when you tire of seafood and steak. Warming trays are placed on your table; the service is buffet style. You can season your plate with peppers rated hot, very hot, and palate melting. It's best to go with a party so that all of you can share in the feast, although at lunchtime, the selection of dishes is more modest.

Mercuriusstraat 13, Salinja. ✆ **599/9-461-6361.** Reservations recommended. Main courses $18–$32; *rijsttafel* $22 for 16 dishes, $27 for 20 dishes, $43 for 25 dishes; vegetarian *rijsttafel* $23 for 16 dishes. AE, MC, V. Tues–Sun noon–2pm and 6–10pm. Take a taxi to this villa in the suburbs near Salinja, near Breezes Curaçao, southeast of Willemstad.

The Wine Cellar ★ FRENCH Near the center of town is the domain of Nico and Angela Cornelisse and their son, Daniel, who offer one of the most extensive wine lists on the island. The atmosphere is reminiscent of an old-fashioned Dutch home. The kitchen turns out an excellent lobster salad and a sole meunière in a butter-and-herb sauce. You might also try fresh red snapper in garlic sauce, filet mignon from Argentina, or the rack of lamb with rosemary-port sauce. Game dishes, imported throughout the year from Holland, usually include venison roasted with mushrooms, hare, and roast goose. After years of dining here, we have found the food commendable in every way—dishes are hearty and full of flavor, and there are selections for lighter appetites as well. Of course, as good as the food is, it never matches the impressive wine list.

Intersection of Ooststraat and Concordiastraat, Willemstad. ✆ **599/9-461-2178.** www.winecellar.an. Reservations required. Main courses $20–$40. AE, DC, MC, V. Mon–Fri noon–2pm and 6pm–midnight; Sat 6pm–midnight.

Zanzibar Restaurant INTERNATIONAL This stylish beach bar and restaurant caters to patrons at Jan Thiel Beach on the east side of the island. It has a global vibe and features Moroccan decor, under a large open African hut, and serves an international menu, with a Mediterranean flair, to mostly Dutch patrons. Shish kebab and seafood are good, but pizza is its specialty.

Jan Theil Beach. ✆ **599/9-747-0633.** www.zanzibar-curacao.com. Reservations recommended. Main courses $12–$37. MC, V. Daily 8am–10pm.

CURAÇAO'S BEACHES

Curaçao beaches (called *playas* or *bocas*) aren't the best in the Dutch Leewards, but there are nearly 40 of them on island, ranging from hotel sands to secluded coves. *Playas* are the larger, classic sandy beaches, and *bocas* are small inlets between two large rock formations. The northwest coast is generally rugged and difficult for swimming, but the more tranquil waters of the west coast are filled with sheltered bays, offering excellent swimming and snorkeling.

Seaquarium Beach (also known as Mambo Beach), just to the east of the center of Willemstad, charges a fee of $3 for access to its complete facilities, including two bars, two restaurants, a watersports shop, beach-chair rentals, changing facilities, and showers. The calm waters make this beach ideal for swimming.

Just northwest of Willemstad, **Blauwbaai (Blue Bay)** is the largest and most popular beach on Curaçao, with enough white sand for everybody. Along with showers and changing facilities, there are plenty of shady places to retreat from the noonday sun. To get here, follow the road that goes past the Holiday Beach Hotel, heading in the direction of Juliandorp. Follow the sign that tells you to bear left for Blauwbaai and the fishing village of San Michiel.

Farther up the west coast, about 30 minutes from Willemstad in the Willibrordus area on the west side of Curaçao, **Daaibooi** is a good beach, though there are no showers or changing rooms. Wooden umbrellas provide shade. Snorkelers are attracted to the sides of the bay, as the cliffs rise out of the surf. Small multicolored fish are commonplace, and many varying corals cover the rocks. This beach gets very crowded with locals on Sunday.

A beach popular with families and a base for fishing boats, **Playa Lagun** lies well concealed in the corner of the village of Lagun as you approach from Santa Cruz. The narrow cove is excellent for swimming because of the tranquil, shallow water. Rainbow-hued fish appear everywhere, so the beach is also a favorite with snorkelers. Some concrete huts provide shelter from the scorching sun; a snack bar is open on weekends.

Knip Bay, just north of Playa Lagun, has white sands, rocky sides, and beautiful turquoise waters, making it suitable for snorkeling, swimming, and sunbathing. The

A Word of Caution to Swimmers

Beware of stepping on the spines of the sea urchins that sometimes abound in these waters. To give temporary first aid for an embedded urchin's spine, try the local remedies of vinegar or lime juice. Locals advise a burning match if you're tough. Although the urchin spines are not dangerous, they can give you several days of real discomfort.

beach tends to be crowded on weekends, often with locals. Changing facilities and refreshments are available. ***Warning:*** Manchineel trees provide some shade, but their fruit is poisonous; never seek shelter under the trees when it rains, as drops falling off the leaves will cause major skin irritation.

Playa Abao, with crystal turquoise waters, is at the northern tip of the island. One of Curaçao's most popular strands, this is often called Playa Grandi (Big Beach). It can get very, very hot at midday, but thatched shade umbrellas provide some protection. A stairway and ramp lead down to the excellent white sands. There's a snack bar in the parking lot. Near the large cove at Playa Abao is **Playa Kenepa ★**, which is much smaller but gets our nod as one of the island's most beautiful strips. Partially shaded by trees, it's a good place for sunbathing, swimming, and shore diving. A 10-minute swim from the beach leads to a reef where visibility is frequently 30m (98 ft.). Baby sea turtles are often spotted here. A snack bar is open on weekends.

Westpunt, a public beach on the northwestern tip of the island, is known for the Sunday divers who jump from its gigantic cliffs into the ocean below. You can spot little rainbow-hued boats and fishermen's nets hanging out to dry here. There are no facilities at this beach, which tends to be exceptionally hot and has no shade trees (bring lots of sunscreen). The calm waters offer excellent swimming, though they're not good for snorkeling.

South of Willemstad is **Santa Barbara Beach.** It's between the open sea and the island's primary watersports and recreational area known as Spanish Water. A mining company owns this land, which also contains Table Mountain, a remarkable landmark, and an old phosphate mine. The natural beach has pure-white sand and calm water. A buoy line protects swimmers from boats. Facilities include restrooms, changing rooms, a snack bar, and a terrace; water bicycles and small motorboats are available for rent. The beach, open daily from 8am to 6pm, has access to the Curaçao Underwater Marine Park.

SPORTS & OUTDOOR PURSUITS

CRUISES Travelers looking for an experience similar to the sailing days of yore should book a trip on the ***Insulinde,*** Handelskade (© **599/9-560-1340** [note that this is a cellular phone and the connection may be poor]; fax 599/9-461-1538; www.insulinde.com). This 120-foot traditionally rigged clipper offers afternoon snorkel, scenic tour, beach swim, and sail safaris for $50 (children $30), and day trips to the island of Klein Curaçao for $75 (children $45). These depart at 6:30am and return at 6:30pm, and include breakfast and lunch. Boats leave from right next to the Queen Emma pontoon bridge in town.

Like a ghost ship from ancient times, a dual-masted, five-sailed wooden schooner cruises silently through the waters of Curaçao. It carries a name steeped in legend—the ***Bounty*** (© **599/9-767-9998;** www.bountyadventures.com)—though it's not a replica of its famous namesake. Operated by Bounty Adventures, it gives 4-hour snorkel, swim, and swing outings that include lunch, an open bar, a rope swing, snorkel gear, and a guided snorkel safari at both a tugboat wreck and shallow reef. *Bounty* sails Tuesday through Friday from 10am to 2:30pm. The fare is $69 for adults and $35 for children 4 to 12. Bounty Adventures also has two catamarans that sail to Klein Curaçao on Tuesday, Wednesday, Thursday, Saturday, and Sunday; the cost is $89 for adults and $45 for children 4 to 12. The trip includes BBQ lunch, open bar, and snorkel gear. All boats leave from the Boathouse, Brakkeput Ariba z/n. Hotel pickup and drop-off can be arranged for an additional charge.

Diving with a Soft Touch

Warning: **Touching any coral, including soft corals such as sea fans, in any marine protected area is forbidden. Even the softest contact can be deadly to the coral, and it can result in scrapes, cuts, rashes, and stings much like that of a jellyfish (coral's closest kin). It's also prohibited to touch, pet, or otherwise harass any fish, including eels and rays. The delicate skin of marine organisms is coated with antibacterial slime, which protects them from potentially deadly skin infections. Even the use of sunscreen or insect repellent before entering the water adds harmful chemicals to the water that can irritate and harm these sensitive creatures.**

DIVING & SNORKELING Curaçao is a close second to Bonaire when it comes to marine environments, where scuba divers and snorkelers can enjoy healthy reefs and good visibility. Stretching along 20km (12 miles) of Curaçao's southern coastline, the **Curaçao Underwater Marine Park ★** features steep walls, shallow wrecks, gardens of soft coral, and more than 30 species of hard coral. A snorkel trail with underwater interpretive markers is laid out just east of the Breezes Resort and is accessible from shore.

The two most spectacular dive sites are the **Mushroom Forest** and **Sponge Forest,** where oversized coral heads and sponges abound. Two good wreck dives are the ***Superior Producer,*** a sunken vessel near Willemstad Harbor, and **Tugboat** near Caracas Bay. Dramatic vertical drops abound and can be explored at **Knipbai** and **Blauwbaai.** Due to the abundance of marine life, night dives are particularly rewarding in Curaçao.

Ocean Encounters Diving (**© 599/9-461-8131;** www.oceanencounters.com) offers the most complete dive facilities and services at many hotels, including Breezes, Lions Dive & Beach Resort, Sea Aquarium Resort, Kontiki Dive and Beach Resort, Hilton Curaçao Resort, and both Kurá Hulanda properties. They offer daily two-tank dives for $92 and afternoon snorkel trips for $50; wreck dives (Fridays) and night dives run $80. Ocean Encounters can even arrange interactive open-water dolphin dives together with the Dolphin Academy for $266 (Mondays and Fridays). Weekly trips to Mushroom Forest (Thursdays), East Punt (Tuesdays), and Klein Curaçao (reservation only) are also offered for $150 with its fleet of seven custom dive boats. The Kid's Sea Camp offers underwater educational activities for children.

FISHING Proximity to the continental shelf of South America and wanton overfishing significantly limit the likelihood of catching large pelagic fish, and their rarity significantly limits the pleasure of hauling these spectacular top predators from the sea as either a prize or a meal—plus it ain't cheap. Deep-sea fishing is $400 to $700 for a half-day tour (six-person maximum) and $600 to $1,200 for a full-day tour, drinks and equipment included. **Let's Fish** (**© 599/9-561-1812;** www.letsfish.net) offers fishing charters on either the 32-foot *Let's Fish* or the 50-foot *Princess Alexia.*

GOLF An 18-hole course lies at **Blue Bay Golf Course,** a par-72 course at Landhuis Blauw, on the road to Bullenbaai (**© 599/9-868-1755;** www.bluebaygolf.com). This challenging course, designed by Rocky Roquemore, takes advantage of Curaçao's seaside terrain and views of the Caribbean. Some shots are over water. Depending on the time of year, greens fees range from $65 for 9 holes to $105 for 18 holes, including a cart. Hours are daily from 7am to 7pm.

HORSEBACK RIDING **Criadero El Hijo de David,** at Seru Lora naast 175 (✆ **599/9-465-1166**), can arrange 2-hour tours along scenic trails near Salt Lakes at Jan Theil Bay for $60. They also offer beginner lessons in an outdoor ring. Call ahead for appointments.

MOUNTAIN BIKING Curaçao hosted the Union Cycliste Internationale's 2006 Mountain Bike World Cup, so it should come as no surprise that the trails here can be pretty challenging. **Wanna Bike ★** (✆ **599/9-527-3720;** www.wannabike.com) gives guided tours for riders of all levels. In addition to well-equipped bikes and helmets, the knowledgeable guides provide an insightful historic narrative of key historic sites and ruins. Bike tours lasting from 8 to 11am cost $38.

OFF-ROADING ATV excursions into rugged off-road areas can be arranged through **Eric's ATV Adventures,** Martin Luther King Boulevard across from Lion's Dive (✆ **599/9-524-7418;** www.curacao-atv.com). The cost for a half-day tour is $90 for a single and $140 for a two-person machine suitable for two adults or one adult and one child. These hefty four-wheel behemoths, reminiscent of a large tractor mower, can take on the steepest and rockiest terrain. The vehicle is relatively easy to operate, if rather loud and extremely hot underneath you. Goggles and helmets are provided. Sunscreen, eye protection, long pants, and closed shoes are highly recommended. A valid U.S. or international driver's license is required, and all drivers must be at least 16 years of age. **The Bike Shop Curaçao,** Sta. Rosawegn 27a (✆ **599/9-560-7000;** www.thebikeshop.nl), also rents motorcycles and scooters.

EXPLORING THE ISLAND

Most cruise-ship passengers see only Willemstad—or, more accurately, its shops—but you may want to get out into the *cunucu,* or countryside, and explore the towering cacti and rolling hills topped by *landhuizen* (plantation houses) built more than 3 centuries ago.

Willemstad ★★

Willemstad was originally founded as Santa Ana by the Spanish in the 1500s. Dutch traders found a vast natural harbor, a perfect hideaway along the Spanish Main, and they renamed it Willemstad in the 17th century. Not only is Willemstad the capital of Curaçao, but it's also the seat of government for the Netherlands Antilles. Today rows of pastel-colored, red-roofed town houses adorn the downtown area. After 10

Coral Above and Below

After emerging from an awe-inspiring dive to a healthy patchwork of pink, purple, and green coral reefs; waving fans; and a Carnival frenzy of topaz, yellow, and pink fish, I glanced skyward. As if not to be outdone, a flock of coral-hued flamingos silently glided overhead in a synchronized single-file display that would surely take first prize in any marching parade. Thank goodness saltwater conveniently masked the tears of awe that welled up.

The Floating Market

A few minutes' walk from the pontoon bridge, at the north end of Handelskade, is the Floating Market ★, where scores of fishing boats tie up alongside the canal, a few yards from the main shopping area. Boats arrive from Venezuela and Colombia, as well as other West Indian islands, to dock here and sell tropical fruits and vegetables. Across the street is a little market square where handicrafts from Haiti and South America are sold.

years of restoration, the historic center of Willemstad and the island's natural harbor, Schottegat, were inscribed on UNESCO's World Heritage list.

The easiest way to go exploring is to take a 1¼-hour **trolley tour,** visiting the highlights of the city. The open-sided cars, pulled by a silent "locomotive," make several trips every week. Tours leave at 10 or 11am. The tour begins at Fort Amsterdam near the Queen Emma Pontoon Bridge. The cost is $25 for adults, $20 for children 2 to 12. Call ✆ **599/9-461-0011** for more information.

The city developed on both sides of the canal. It's divided into **Punda** (old-world Dutch ambience and the best shopping) and **Otrabanda** (the "Other Side," the more contemporary side). A pedestrian walkway, the **Queen Emma Pontoon Bridge,** connects both sections. It is so unique, it was declared a World Heritage Site and was recently restored. Powered by a diesel engine at one end and operated by a driver, it swings open many times a day to let ships pass in and out of the harbor.

From the bridge, there's a view of the old **gabled houses** in harmonized pastel shades. The bright colors, according to legend, are a holdover from the time when one of the island's early governors had eye trouble, and flat white gave him headaches. The colonial-style architecture, reflecting the Dutch influence, gives the town a storybook look. The houses, built three or four stories high, are crowned by steep gables and roofed with orange Spanish tiles. Hemmed in by the sea, a tiny canal, and an inlet, the streets are narrow, and they're crosshatched by still narrower alleyways.

Except for the pastel colors, Willemstad may remind you of old Amsterdam. It has one of the most intriguing townscapes in the Caribbean. But don't let the colors deceive you: Up close, the city can be rather dirty.

A **statue of Pedro Luis Brion** dominates the square known as Brionplein right at the Otrabanda end of the pontoon bridge. Born in Curaçao in 1782, Brion became the island's favorite son and best-known war hero. Under Simon Bolivar, he was an admiral of the fleet and fought for the independence of Venezuela and Colombia.

In addition to the pontoon bridge, the **Queen Juliana Bridge** opened to vehicular traffic in 1973. Spanning the harbor, it rises 59m (194 ft.), which makes it the highest bridge in the Caribbean and one of the tallest in the world.

The Waterfront originally guarded the mouth of the canal on the eastern or Punda side, but now it has been incorporated into the Plaza Hotel. The task of standing guard has been taken over by **Fort Amsterdam,** site of the Governor's Palace and the 1769 Dutch Reformed church. The church still has a British cannonball embedded in it. The arches leading to the fort were tunneled under the official residence of the governor.

A corner of Fort Amsterdam stands at the intersection of Breedestraat and Handelskade, the starting point for a plunge into the island's major **shopping district.**

At some point, visit the **Waterfort Arches,** which stretch for .4km (¼ mile). They rise 9m (30 ft.) high and are built of barrel-vaulted 17th-century stone set against the sea. At Waterfort you can explore a handful of small boutiques. The breezy terrace on the sea here is perfect for a local Amstel beer or dinner at a choice of restaurants. The grand buildings and cobbled walkways are illuminated at night.

Between the I. H. (Sha) Capriles Kade and Fort Amsterdam, at Hanechi di Snoa 29, stands the **Mikvé Israel-Emanuel Synagogue** (✆ **599/9-461-1067;** www.snoa.com), the oldest extant synagogue in the Western Hemisphere. Consecrated on the eve of Passover in 1732, it houses the oldest Jewish congregation in the New World. Joaño d'Illan led the first Jewish settlers (13 families) to the island in 1651, almost half a century after their expulsion from Portugal by the Inquisition. The settlers came via Amsterdam to Curaçao. This synagogue, a fine example of Dutch colonial architecture, covers about a square block in the heart of Willemstad; it was built in a Spanish-style walled courtyard, with four large portals. Following a Portuguese Sephardic custom, sand covers the sanctuary floor, representing the desert where Israelites camped when the Jews passed from slavery to freedom. The highlight of the east wall is the Holy Ark, rising 5m (16 ft.).

Adjacent to the synagogue courtyard is the **Jewish Cultural Historical Museum,** Hanechi di Snoa 29 (✆ **599/9-461-1633;** www.snoa.com), housed in two buildings dating from 1728. They were originally the rabbi's residence and the bathhouse. The 250-year-old *mikvah* (a bath for religious purification purposes) was in constant use until around 1850, when the buildings were sold. They have since been reacquired through the Foundation for the Preservation of Historic Monuments and turned into the present museum. On display are ritual, ceremonial, and cultural objects, many of which date from the 17th and 18th centuries and are still used by the congregation for holidays and events.

The synagogue and museum are open to visitors Monday through Friday from 9am to 4pm and, if there's a cruise ship in port, Sunday from 9am to 4:30pm. Services are Friday at 6:30pm and Saturday at 10am. Visitors are welcome, with appropriate dress required. There's a $10 museum entrance fee for adults (includes synagogue); it's free for children 13 and under.

Museum Kurá Hulanda, Klipstraat 9 (✆ **599/9-434-7765;** www.kurahulanda.com/museum), is one of the most unusual—and one of the largest—museums in the Caribbean, housed in once-dilapidated 1800s buildings rescued from oblivion. The exhibits reflect the passion of Dr. Jacob Gelt Dekker, a Dutchman who has spent a great deal of his life devoted to the history and culture of Africa, and he has roamed that continent in search of cultural artifacts. At the site of one of the Caribbean's largest slave trading hubs, he has assembled his prize collection, including its most interesting exhibit: a life-size reconstruction of a slave ship that once sailed from the Ivory Coast carrying captured slaves into bondage and often death. Hours are daily 10am to 5pm; admission is $9 for adults, $7 for students, and $6 for children and seniors.

You can walk the distance or take a short cab ride to the sleepy **Curaçao Museum,** Van Leeuwenhoekstraat (✆ **599/9-462-3873**), from the Queen Emma Pontoon Bridge. Built in 1853 by the Royal Dutch Army Corps of Engineers as a military quarantine hospital, the building was carefully restored in the 1940s and is a fine example of 19th-century Dutch architecture, now housing paintings, objets d'art, and furniture crafted in the 19th century by local cabinetmakers. There's also a large collection from the Caiquetio tribes, the early inhabitants described by Amerigo Vespucci as 2m-tall (6½-ft.) giants, and a reconstruction of a traditional music pavilion in the garden, where Curaçao musicians give regular performances. It's open Tuesday to Friday 8:30am to 7pm, Saturday and Sunday 10am to 7pm. Admission is $5 for adults, free for children 11 and under.

Maritime Museum, Van De Brandhofstraat 7 (© **599/9-465-2327;** www.curacaomaritime.com), is in the historic Scharloo neighborhood of Willemstad, just off the old harbor of St. Anna Bay. More than 40 permanent displays trace the story of Curaçao, beginning with the arrival of the island's original inhabitants in 600 B.C. Video presentations cover the development of Curaçao's harbor and the role of the island as one of the largest slave depots in the Caribbean. There are also five oral histories (one from a 97-yr.-old Curaçaoan who served on the cargo vessel *Normandie*), antique miniatures, 17th-century ship models, and a collection of maps. Admission is $6 for adults and free for children 6 and under. Hours are Tuesday to Saturday from 9am to 4pm.

West of Willemstad

On Schottegatweg West, northwest of Willemstad, past the oil refineries, lies the **Beth Haim Cemetery,** the oldest Caucasian burial site still in use in the Western Hemisphere. Meaning "House of Life," the cemetery was consecrated before 1659. There are some 2,500 graves on about 1 hectare (2½ acres) here. The carving on some of the 17th- and 18th-century tombstones is exceptional.

En route to Westpunt, you'll come across a seaside cavern known as **Boca Tabla,** one of many such grottoes on this rugged, uninhabited northwest coast. In the Westpunt area, a 45-minute ride from Punda in Willemstad, **Playa Forti** is a stark region characterized by soaring hills and towering cacti, along with 200-year-old Dutch land houses, the former mansions that housed slave owners.

Out toward the western tip of Curaçao, a high-wire fence surrounds the entrance to the 1,800-hectare (4,448-acre) **Christoffel National Park ★★** in Savonet (© **599/9-864-0363**), about a 45-minute drive from the capital. A macadam road gives way to dirt, surrounded on all sides by abundant cacti and bromeliads. In the higher regions, you can spot rare orchids. Rising from flat, arid countryside, 369m-high (1,211-ft.) **St. Christoffelberg** is the highest point in the Dutch Leewards. Donkeys, wild goats, iguanas, the Curaçao deer, and many species of birds thrive in this preserve, and there are some Arawak paintings on a coral cliff near the two caves. The park has 32km (20 miles) of one-way trail-like roads, with lots of flora and fauna along the way. The shortest trail is about 8km (5 miles) long and, because of the rough terrain, takes about 40 minutes to drive through. There are also various walking trails; one takes you to the top of St. Christoffelberg in about 1½ hours. (Come early in the morning, when it isn't too hot.) The park is open Monday to Saturday from 7:30am to 4pm, Sunday from 6:30am to 3pm. The entrance fee is $8 per person.

Next door, the park has opened the **National Park Shete Boka.** This turtle sanctuary, whose name translates to "Seven Mouths" or inlets, contains a cave with pounding waves off the choppy north coast. Admission to the park is $2 per person. To learn more about nature, conservation, and history in Curaçao, and to participate in exciting nature exploration for the whole family, such as deer spotting, a pickup truck safari, or day hike up the mountain, contact the **Caribbean Research and Management of Biodiversity Foundation** (© **599/9-462-4242;** www.carmabi.org).

North & East of Willemstad

Just northeast of the capital, **Fort Nassau** was completed in 1797 and christened Fort Republic by the Dutch. Built high on a hill overlooking the harbor entrance to the south and St. Anna Bay to the north, it was fortified as a second line of defense in case the waterfront gave way. When the British invaded in 1807, they renamed it Fort George in honor of their own king. Later, when the Dutch regained control, they renamed it Orange Nassau in honor of the Dutch royal family. Today diners have replaced soldiers.

Curaçao Liqueur Distillery, Landhuis Chobolobo, Saliña a Arriba (✆ **599/9-461-3526**), offers a chance to visit Chobolobo, the 17th-century *landhuis* where the famous Curaçao liqueur is made. The cordial is a distillate of dried peel of a particular strain of orange found only on Curaçao. Several herbs are added to give it an aromatic bouquet. One of the rewards of a visit here is a free sample of the liqueur, offered Monday to Friday from 8am to noon and 1 to 5pm. Some recently introduced flavors include chocolate, coffee, and rum raisin, but the original orange flavor (regardless of the blue color) is still our favorite. Another interesting product made from the orange oil is a cooling spray called **Alcolodo Glacial,** great to soothe hot skin and ward off insects, and reputed to have many curative properties.

Curaçao Seaquarium, off Dr. Martin Luther King Boulevard at a site called Bapor Kibrá (✆ **599/9-461-6666;** www.curacao-sea-aquarium.com), has more than 400 species of fish, crabs, anemones, sponges, and coral on display in a natural environment. Located a few minutes' walk along the rocky coast from the Breezes Curaçao Resort (p. 210), the Seaquarium is open daily from 8:30am to 5:30pm. Admission is $19 for adults, $9.50 for children 5 to 12.

Special features of the aquarium are sea lion and dolphin encounters, costing $99 to $300 for divers or $49 to $159 for snorkelers. Divers, snorkelers, and experienced swimmers can feed, film, and photograph sharks, which are separated from them by a large window with feeding holes. In the animal-encounters section, you can swim among stingrays, grouper, sea turtles, and other marine life, feeding and photographing these creatures in a controlled environment where safety is always a consideration. The less adventurous can watch a dolphin show and pet marine invertebrates in a kid-friendly touch tank. The Seaquarium is also the site of Curaçao's only full-facility, palm-shaded, white-sand beach.

For those who swear by the curative properties of aloe, a visit to the **Aloe Vera Plantation** (✆ **599/9-767-5577;** www.aloecuracao.com) may be just what the doctor ordered. Not surprisingly, all guided tours, which describe the production process from plantation to shelf, conveniently end in the factory shop. It's open Monday through Saturday 9am to 4pm. Admission is free, though you may be inclined to purchase an aloe product—even without any sales pressure from the friendly staff.

The **Hato Caves,** F. D. Rooseveltweg (✆ **599/9-868-0379**), have been called mystical. Every hour guides take visitors through this world of stalagmites and stalactites, found in the highest limestone terrace of the island. Actually, they were once old coral reefs and were formed when the ocean water fell and the landmass was lifted up over the years. Over thousands of years, limestone formations were created, some mirrored in an underground lake. After crossing the lake, you enter the Cathedral, an underground cavern. The largest hall of the cave is called La Ventana (The Window). Also on display are samples of ancient Indian petroglyph drawings. The caves are open daily from 9am to 4pm; admission is $8 for adults and $6 for children 4 to 11.

SHOPPING ★★

Curaçao is a shopper's paradise. Some 200 shops line the major shopping streets such as Heerenstraat and Breedestraat. Right in the heart of Willemstad is the 5-block **Punda** shopping district. Most stores are open Monday through Saturday from 8am to noon and 2 to 6pm (some 8am–6pm). When cruise ships are in port, stores are also open for a few hours on Sundays and holidays. To avoid the cruise-ship crowds, do your shopping in the morning.

Look for good buys on French perfumes, Dutch Delft blue souvenirs, finely woven Italian silks, Japanese and German cameras, jewelry, silver, Swiss watches, linens, leather goods, liquor, and island-made rum and liqueurs, especially Curaçao liqueur, some of which has a distinctive blue color. The island is famous for its 2.3kg (5-lb.) wheels of Gouda and Edam cheeses. Some of the stores also stock some deals on intricate lacework imported from Portugal, China, and everywhere in between. If you're a street shopper and want something colorful, consider one of the woodcarvings or flamboyant paintings from Haiti or the Dominican Republic. Both are hawked by street vendors at any of the main plazas.

Incidentally, Curaçao is not technically a free port, but its prices are often inexpensive because of its low import duty.

The Art of Nena Sanchez, Schottegatweg-Oost 17 (✆ **599/9-738-2377;** www.nenasanchez.com), displays the artist's vibrant Caribbean still-lifes and striking portraits, as well as affordable prints. Every garment sold in **Bamali,** Breedestraat Punda 2 (✆ **599/9-461-2258;** www.bamali-fashion.com), is designed and, in many cases, crafted by the store owners. Influenced largely by Indonesian patterns, the airy attire includes V-neck cotton pullovers perfect for a casual, hot-weather climate, as well as linen shifts, often in batik prints, appropriate for a glamorous cocktail party. Most pieces here are for women; all are made from all-natural materials, such as cotton, silk, and linen, and there's also a limited array of sandals, hats, scarves, and leather bags. **Benetton,** Schottegatweg-Oost 148, Salinas (✆ **599/9-461-4619**), has invaded Curaçao with all its many colors. Some items are marked down by about 20% below U.S. prices (this is done to get rid of surplus stock from the previous season); in-season clothing is available as well.

Electronics are a good buy on Curaçao, as they can be sold duty-free; we recommend the very reliable **Boolchand's,** Breederstraat 50, Punda (✆ **599/9-461-6233**), in business since 1930. **Gandelman Jewelers,** Breedestraat 35, Punda (✆ **599/9-461-1854**), is the island's best and most reliable source for jewelry, often exquisitely designed and set with diamonds, rubies, emeralds, sapphires, and other gemstones. You can also find watches and the unique line of Prima Classe leather goods embossed with the world map.

Little Holland, Breedestraat 37, Punda (✆ **599/9-461-1413**), reputedly changed hands but still specializes in silk neckties, Panama hats, Nautica shorts and shirts, Swiss Army knives, and, most important, a sophisticated array of cigars. Crafted in Cuba, the Dominican Republic, and Brazil, they include some of the most prestigious names in smoke, including Montecristos, Cohiba, and Churchills. ***Remember:*** It's still illegal to bring Cuban cigars into the United States, so be sure to smoke them before you fly home.

As the name implies, **Mr. Tablecloth,** Handelskade 3, on the waterfront (✆ **599/9-462-9588**), is where the finest linens on the island can be found.

Penha & Sons, Heerenstraat 1 (✆ **599/9-461-2266;** www.jlpenha.com), is in the oldest building in town (1708). It has long been known for its fine selection of perfumes, cosmetics, and designer clothing (for both men and women). It distributes such names as Calvin Klein, Yves Saint Laurent, Elizabeth Arden, Clarins, and Estée Lauder, among others.

For some truly unique nature-inspired jewelry and artistic prints, head over to **Maravia** (✆ **599/9-461-9866**), at Handelskade no. 1 in Punda, near the swing bridge.

Wulfsen and Wulfsen, Gomezplein 7 at Gomez Square (✆ **599/9-461-2302**), sells fashionable ladies' clothing from Germany and Holland, and crisp men's shirts in every color of the rainbow.

La Casa Amarilla (the Yellow House), Breedestraat 46 (✆ **599/9-461-3222**), which has been operating since 1887 in a yellow-and-white building, sells an intriguing collection of perfume and cosmetics from all over the world and is an agent of Christian Dior, Guerlain, Gucci, and Versace.

In Otrobanda there are a slew of high-end shops in **Riffort Village** next to the new Renaissance, including Brietling, Tiffany, and a Little Switzerland.

CURAÇAO AFTER DARK ★★

Most of the action on Curaçao spins around the island's **casinos.** These hotel gaming houses usually start their action at 4pm, and some of them remain open until 3am.

Emerald Casino at the **Marriott Beach Resort,** Piscadera Bay (✆ **599/9-736-8800**), is especially popular, designed to resemble a Monte Carlo casino. It features 149 slot machines; 4 blackjack tables; 2 roulette wheels; 2 Caribbean stud, 1 Texas Bonus, and 2 Texas Hold'em tables; and a craps table. The **Princess Casino** at the **Breezes Curaçao Resort,** Dr. Martin Luther King Blvd. 8 (✆ **599/9-736-7888**), is the liveliest on the island. But the newest and flashiest casino on the island is the **Carnival Casino** at the **Renaissance Curacao Resort** (✆ **599/9-435-5000**). The flashing lights and noise from the slot machines (which feature hilarious themes such as Betti the Yetti and Revenge of the Moolah, featuring cows in space ships) spill into the hotel lobby. Nightly live music is a nice touch.

The landlocked, flat, and somewhat dusty neighborhood of **Saliña** is now the nightlife capital of Curaçao, but the island nightlife works on a timeshare system: Each club has its unofficial "night" when the crowds gather under its roof and the fun lasts long into the early morning hours. Pick up a copy of the weekly dining and entertainment guide ***K-Pasa*** at any tourism office or hotel lobby, or log on to **www.k-pasa.com** to find out what's happening where.

Blues, in the Avila Hotel, Penstraat 130 (✆ **599/9-461-4377**), is a restaurant with a hopping bar that's packed every night except Monday. Live jazz is offered Thursday from 7 to 11pm and Saturday from 8 to 11pm, with no cover.

Mambo Beach, at the **Seaquarium Beach** (✆ **599/9-461-8999**), features food, music, and a great beach bar that, on Tuesday nights, shows classic movies under the stars a mere stone's throw from the water. Sunday night is salsa night, and the place is usually packed. **Asia de Cuba,** Zuikertuintjeweg z/n (✆ **599/9-747-9009**), has live Cuban music and a pan-Asian decor and cuisine. Grab a mojito and belly up to a high-top table near the dance floor to watch the locals as they show off Latin moves so good you'll think you're in old Havana. **The Sopranos Piano Bar,**

at the Renaissance Rif Fort Mall (✆ **599/9-465-4007;** www.sopranospianobar.com), has nightly dancing, cocktails, and live music. The bar is open from 10am till 3am (or later). Live piano music plays from 9pm to 2am.

A pontoon boat, ***Mi Dushi,*** on Baya Beach at the end of Caracas Bai Street (✆ **599/9-747-4489;** www.midushi.com), is a floating club with a dance floor, three bars, and a full barbecue. *Mi Dushi* sails every Friday, costing $34 for adults and $20 for children 6 to 14.

DOMINICA

The pristine island of Dominica—the wildest in the Caribbean—was green long before anyone heard of ecotourism. The government of Dominica has been preserving its shoreline and protecting its mountain rainforests since the 1960s, even while other Caribbean islands, including Barbados and Aruba, were in the process of extensive development. Should you visit, you'll find clear rivers, waterfalls, hot springs, and boiling lakes.

Beaches Beaches are rocky with gray-black volcanic sand in Dominica but still provide ample snorkeling and diving in the turquoise waters. Swimmers should head for **Champagne** or **Picard Beach.** Snorkelers and scuba divers should make their way to **Soufrière Bay Beach** and **Scotts Head Beach** for the clear waters and the stunning underwater walls.

Things to Do Get acquainted with Caribe history, culture, and native customs in the **Carib Indian Territory,** the last remaining turf of the original Caribbean tribe. Spot dolphins and sperm whales on a whale-watching cruise off the island's coast. If you're a hiker, you'll find much to explore amid the lush rainforests. Hike to **Boiling Lake** and spot rare Sisserou and Jacquot parrots, monkeys, and vines along the way.

Eating & Drinking Chow down on locally caught fish at a West Indian house, or indulge in **Creole delicacies** with a gorgeous rainforest vista of mountains and rivers. The charming **Crystal Terrace Restaurant & Bar** is a local favorite for its stuffed crab backs and other authentic island favorites.

Nature Nature lovers can experience a wild, rugged Caribbean setting in Dominica. Plan an escape to **Morne Trois Pitons National Park,** where mists rise gently over lush, dark-green growth, rivers rush and tumble, and sunlight filters down through trees. Immerse yourself in natural springs at **Papillote Wilderness Retreat,** the botanical garden of which is worth the trip as are the views of mountains and lush valleys.

ESSENTIALS

Visitor Information

Before you go, Americans and Canadians can contact the **Dominica Tourist Office** (✆ **866/522-4057;** fax 767/448-5840; www.dominica.dm).

In England, information is available from **Tom Panagos** at the Dominica Tourist Office (✆ **020/7928-1600;** fax 020/7928-1700).

On the island, the **Dominica Tourist Information Office** is on the Old Market Plaza, Roseau, with administrative offices at the National

National Day

National Day celebrations on November 3 commemorate both Columbus's 1493 discovery of the island and its independence, in 1978. Cultural celebrations of Dominica's traditional dance, music, song, and storytelling begin in mid-October and continue to Community Day, November 4, when people undertake community-based projects.

Development Corporation offices, Valley Road (✆ **767/448-2045;** fax 767/448-5840); it's open Tuesday to Friday 8am to 4pm, Monday from 8am to 5pm.

There are also information bureaus at **Melville Hall Airport** (✆ **767/445-7051**) and **Canefield Airport** (✆ **767/449-1199**).

Getting There

BY PLANE Neither of the two airports on Dominica is large enough to handle a jet, so there are no nonstop flights from the U.S. or Canada. The **Melville Hall Airport** (✆ **767/445-7101**) is on the northeastern coast, a 1½-hour taxi ride from Roseau on the southwestern coast. The drive takes you across the island through the forest and coastal villages; the fare is around $26 per person when there are four passengers. On your own, the fare could be $60.

The more modern **Canefield Airport** (✆ **767/449-1199**) is about a 15-minute taxi ride north of Roseau. The 600m (1,969-ft.) airstrip accommodates smaller planes than those that can land at Melville Hall. From here, the typical taxi fare into town is $10.

For many from the U.S., the easiest way to reach Dominica is via the daily **American Airline** (✆ **800/433-7300** in the U.S. and Canada; www.aa.com) flight from American's hub in San Juan, Puerto Rico.

If you're already in the Caribbean, you can fly to Dominica from several other islands aboard **LIAT** (✆ **888/844-LIAT** [5428]; www.liat.com). The little airline flies nonstop from St. Lucia, daily from Antigua, and daily from Barbados. There is one flight daily, but with a stopover, from the islands of St. Kitts, St. Maarten, St. Vincent, Tortola (B.V.I.), and Trinidad.

BY BOAT The ***L'Express*** (✆ **767/448-2181;** www.express-des-iles.com), sailing from the French West Indies, runs between Guadeloupe in the north to Martinique in the south; Dominica is a port of call along the way. Departures are 6 days a week; call for exact schedules. For schedule information, contact **Whitchurch Travel,** 5 Great Marlborough St., Roseau (✆ **767/448-2181**). A one-way fare costs $25.

Getting Around

BY RENTAL CAR If you rent a car, there's a fee of $12 to obtain a driver's license, which is available at the airports. The island has 500km (311 miles) of paved roads, and only in a few areas is a four-wheel-drive vehicle necessary. ***Note:*** Driving is on the left.

There are a handful of small, usually family-owned car rental companies, the condition and price of whose vehicles vary widely. They include **Valley Rent-a-Car,** Goodwill Road, Roseau (✆ **767/448-3233;** www.valleyrentacar.com); and **Best Deal Rent-A-Car,** 15 Hanover St., Roseau (✆ **767/449-9204**).

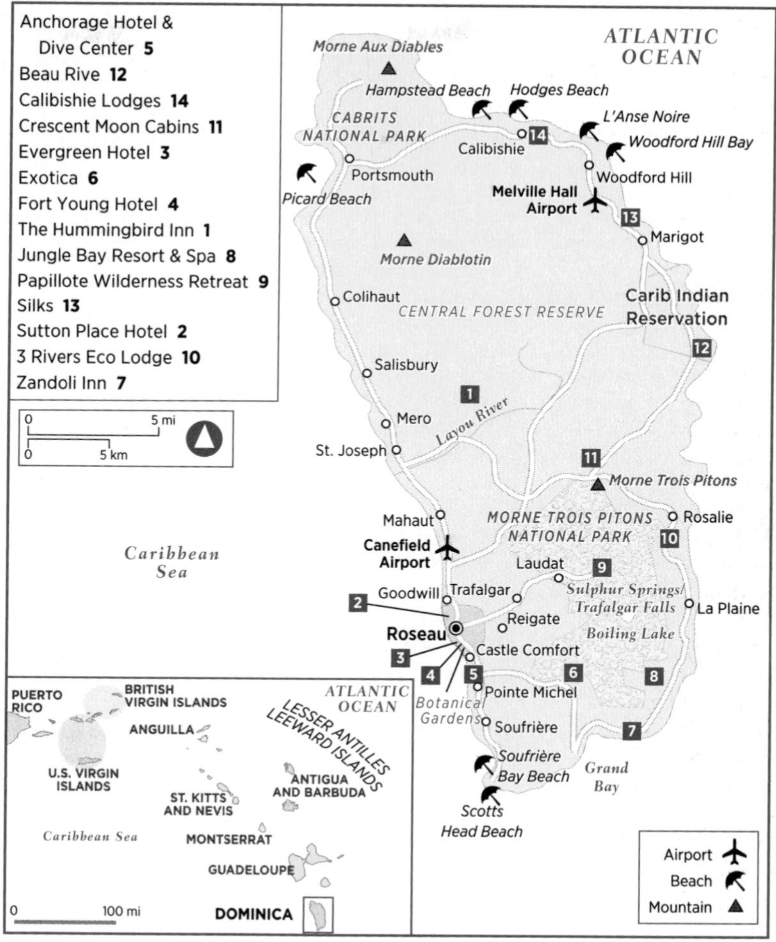

BY TAXI You can hire a taxi at either the Melville Hall or Canefield airports. Prices are regulated by the government (see "Getting There," above, for airport fares). If you want to see the island by taxi, the driver will charge from $70 to $120 for a tour that lasts between 4 and 5 hours. Rates are usually valid for up to four passengers. After 6pm, taxis may be hard to find, so call ahead.

BY MINIBUS The public transportation system consists of private minibus service between Roseau and the rest of Dominica. These flamboyantly painted minibuses are filled mainly with schoolchildren, workers, and country people who need to come into Roseau. On most Caribbean islands, we don't recommend buses, but on Dominica they afford terrific insights into local life. Taxis may be a more reliable means of transport for visitors, but there are hotels at which buses call during the course of the day. You can also just hail a bus when you see it and tell the driver where you want to go. Fares range from 55¢ to $3.80. Buses are identified by the letter H that precedes their license numbers.

[FastFACTS] DOMINICA

Banks Banks are open Monday to Thursday from 8am to 2pm, Friday from 8am to 5pm. There are several major bank branches in Roseau, complete with ATMs that dispense EC dollars.

Currency Dominica uses the **Eastern Caribbean dollar (EC$),** worth about EC$2.70 to US$1 (EC$1 = US37¢). At press time, the Eastern Caribbean dollar was trading to the British pound at the rate of EC$1 = 23p. (Stated differently, £1 = EC$4.27.) U.S. dollars are readily accepted throughout the island, though you'll usually get change in EC dollars. *Unless otherwise specified, prices in this chapter are quoted in U.S. dollars.*

Customs Dominica is lenient, allowing you to bring personal and household effects, plus 200 cigarettes, 50 cigars, and 40 ounces of liquor or wine per person.

Documents To enter, U.S. and Canadian citizens must have a passport. In addition, an ongoing or return ticket must be shown. British visitors should have a valid passport.

Electricity The electricity is 220–240-volt AC (50 cycles), so both adapters and transformers are necessary for U.S.-made appliances. It's smart to bring a flashlight with you, in case of power outages.

Emergencies To call the police, report a fire, or summon an ambulance, dial ✆ **999.**

Hospital There's **Princess Margaret Hospital,** Federation Drive, Goodwill (✆ **767/448-2231**), but those with serious medical conditions may want to forego a visit to the hospital in Dominica, as island medical facilities are often inadequate.

Language English is the official language. Locals often speak a Creole-French patois.

Pharmacies The island's best-stocked drugstore is **Jolly's Pharmacy,** in Roseau at 36 Great George St. and 12 King George V St. Both branches share the same phone number and hours (✆ **767/448-3388**). They're open Monday to Friday from 8:30am to 5:30pm, and Saturday from 8:30am to 2:30pm.

Safety Although crime is rare here, you should still safeguard your valuables. Never leave them unattended on the beach or in a locked car.

Taxes A 10% government room tax is added on accommodations, and a 15% tax applies to alcoholic drinks and food items. Anyone who remains on Dominica for more than 24 hours must pay a $22 departure tax.

Telephone To call Dominica from the United States, dial **1,** then **767** (the country code for Dominica) and the local number. To call Dominica from another island within the Caribbean, just dial **767** plus the seven-digit local number. International direct dialing is available on Dominica, as well as U.S. direct service through AT&T. You can contact **AT&T** in Dominica by dialing ✆ **800/225-5288.** Most hotel telephone operators throw up their hands at even placing a long-distance call for a resident. Instead, they connect their clients to the island's long-distance phone operator, who dials the call for a client, and then calls are billed directly to a client's room.

Time Dominica is on Atlantic Standard Time, 1 hour ahead of Eastern Standard Time in the United States. Dominica does not observe daylight saving time, so when the United States changes to daylight saving time, clocks in Dominica and the U.S. East Coast tell the same time.

Tipping Most hotels and restaurants add a 10%

service charge to bills; check carefully to see if it's been added. If this charge has not been included, tipping is up to you, though an additional 15% for particularly good service is always welcome.

Water Tap water is generally considered safe to drink, but because it's different from what you're used to, it still might cause a stomach disorder. Better stick to bottled water, to be on the safe side.

Weather Daytime temperatures average between 70° and 85°F (21°C–29°C). Nights are much cooler, especially in the mountains. The rainy season is June to October, when there can be hurricane activity. Dominica lies in the hurricane belt, and fierce storms have taken their toll on the island over the years.

WHERE TO STAY

The government imposes a 10% tax on hotel rooms and a 5% tax on beverages and food, which will be added to your hotel bill. On top of that, most hotels add a 10% service charge.

If you don't want to rent a car, it's best to stay in Roseau, where you can get around better. But if you'd like to experience nature, head for one of the remote inns in exotic tropical settings.

In Roseau & Castle Comfort

Anchorage Hotel & Dive Center The Anchorage, established in 1971, is at Castle Comfort, .8km (½ mile) south of Roseau. For the active traveler, there is no better choice, as scuba diving, whale-watching, hiking, fishing, and bird-watching are emphasized. The Armour family provides small, rather basic rooms with balconies overlooking a pool. The best open onto a view of the Caribbean and contain two double beds. The others are more standard, each with comfortable twin beds or one double. Although it's at the shore, there's little or no sandy beach available, so guests spend their days around the pool. However, the hotel has its own jetty, you can swim off the pebble beach, and there's a squash court. The hotel's French and Caribbean cuisine is simple, with an emphasis on fresh fish and vegetables.

Castle Comfort (P.O. Box 34), Roseau, Dominica, W.I. www.anchoragehotel.dm. ✆ **888/790-5264** in the U.S., or 767/448-2638. Fax 767/440-2639. 32 units. Winter $110–$145 double; off season $90 double. Children 11 and under 50% deduction on meals. Dive packages available. AE, MC, V. **Amenities:** Restaurant; bar; babysitting; outdoor pool; room service; watersports equipment/rentals. *In room:* A/C, TV, fridge (in some), Internet (free).

Evergreen Hotel This seafront, family-run hotel looks a bit like a Swiss chalet from the outside, but inside there's an open-air restaurant with bright jungle prints, crystal teardrop chandeliers, and an Art Deco bar. It lies 1.5km (1 mile) south of Roseau. A more modern-looking annex, though sterile, has better rooms than the main building. A few units have wraparound tile-floored verandas; all have stone accents. Accommodations are bright and airy, with most rooms having two double beds and ample storage space. The nicest is the Honeymoon Hut, an exotic and charming retreat for either honeymooners or off-the-record weekenders. A stony beach is visible a few steps beyond the garden. Inside and out, the airy, comfortably modern place is trimmed with local gommier wood.

Mosquito Alert

At night you are likely to be plagued with mosquitoes. If that's a real problem for you, check into the Fort Young Hotel (see below), which is above the "mosquito line." Most hotels offer mosquito netting. Remember, you came to Dominica for unspoiled nature, right?

Castle Comfort (P.O. Box 309), Roseau, Dominica, W.I. www.evergreenhoteldominica.com. ✆ **767/448-3288.** Fax 767/448-6800. 16 units. Winter $140–$190 double; off season $125–$170 double. Children 11 and under stay free in parent's room. Rates include full breakfast. AE, MC, V. **Amenities:** Restaurant; bar; babysitting; outdoor pool; room service; watersports equipment/rentals. *In room:* A/C, TV, hair dryer, Wi-Fi (free).

Fort Young Hotel ★ Occupying a cliffside setting, this modern hotel grew from the ruins of the 1770 Fort Young, once the island's major military installation. Traces of its former historic role remain, including cannons at the entrance. It's always attracted business travelers, but now more and more tourists are drawn to the comfortable bedrooms with ceiling fans and balconies. Here you are elevated far above the "mosquito line," so you can actually sit out and enjoy the balmy Caribbean air without being attacked. The hotel has 18 oceanfront guest rooms and three one-bedroom suites at the base of a cliff below the existing fort; it's worth the extra money to ask for one of these suites, which have direct ocean views and a sitting area.

Victoria St. (P.O. Box 519), Roseau, Dominica, W.I. www.fortyounghotel.com. ✆ **800/581-2034** or 767/448-5000. Fax 767/448-5006. 70 units. Winter $115–$250 double; off season $85–$175 double. AE, MC, V. **Amenities:** 2 restaurants; bar; dive shop; exercise room; Jacuzzi; outdoor pool; room service; sauna; spa. *In room:* A/C, ceiling fan, TV, hair dryer, kitchenette (in some), minibar (in some), Wi-Fi (free).

Sutton Place Hotel ★★ This small historic property stands in the center of town and was once a 1930s guesthouse run by "Mother" Harris, a matriarch who became a local legend. Destroyed by Hurricane David in 1979, Sutton Place was rebuilt in a traditional Caribbean style by the same Harris family, which continues the old traditions but with far greater style. Rooms are tastefully furnished with antiques, including four-poster beds, brass desk lamps, and teak furnishings in the shower-only bathrooms. Suites contain fully equipped kitchenettes. The staircase and floors of the suites are laid with a fine hardwood, tauroniro, from South America. Stylized floral arrangements, exotic prints, and luxurious fabrics contribute to the upscale style. The nearest beach is about 2km (1¼ mile) away.

25 Old St. (P.O. Box 2333), Roseau, Dominica, W.I. www.suttonplacehoteldominica.com. ✆ **767/449-8700** or 767/448-4313. Fax 767/448-3045. 8 units. Year-round $95 double; $135 suite. Extra person $30. Rates include breakfast. AE, DISC, MC, V. **Amenities:** Restaurant; bar; room service. *In room:* A/C, ceiling fan, TV, hair dryer, Internet (free), kitchenette (in suites).

Near Marigot

Silks ★ Dominica's pocket of posh was converted from a 17th-century estate and a former rum distillery. Surrounded by .6 hectares (1½ acres) of gardens, Silks lies between two freshwater estuaries. Sensitively restored and completely modernized, it lies about an hour's drive from Roseau. Both African and Creole styles are reflected in the public rooms. Bedrooms are roomy and beautifully decorated, often in a plantation-era style. Painting and sculpture fill the hotel, setting off the wooden floors and French tiles.

Hatton Garden, Marigot, Dominica, W.I. www.silkshotel.com. ✆ **767/445-8846.** 9 units. Year-round $220 double. Rates include continental breakfast. MC, V. **Amenities:** Restaurant; bar; airport transfers ($20–$60); Internet (free); kayak and bamboo rentals; outdoor pool. *In room:* A/C, Wi-Fi (free).

In the Rainforest

Papillote Wilderness Retreat ★ This eco-inn is run by the Jean-Baptiste family: Cuthbert, who handles the restaurant, and his wife, Anne Grey, a marine scientist. Their unique resort, 6km (3¾ miles) east of Roseau, stands right in the middle of Papillote Forest, at the foothills of Morne Macaque. In this remote setting, you're surrounded by exotic fruits, flowers, and herb gardens. The rooms are most inviting, with their hardwood floors, jungle-painted walls, floral quilts, and fresh flowers. Don't expect constantly sunny weather, since this part of the jungle is known for its downpours; however, that's what keeps the orchids, begonias, and brilliantly colored bromeliads lush. The 5 hectares (12 acres) of sloping and forested land have a labyrinth of stone walls and trails, beside which flow freshwater streams, a few of which originate in hot mineral springs. Natural hot mineral baths are available, and you'll be directed to a secluded waterfall where you can swim in the river.

Trafalgar Falls Rd. (P.O. Box 2287), Roseau, Dominica, W.I. www.papillote.dm. ✆ **767/448-2287.** Fax 767/448-2285. 7 units. Year-round $115 double; $120–$130 suite. MAP (breakfast and dinner) $15 per person extra. AE, DISC, MC, V. Closed Sept–Oct 15. **Amenities:** Restaurant; bar; 3 hot mineral pools; room service. *In room:* Ceiling fan, no phone, Wi-Fi (free).

3 Rivers Eco Lodge Significantly more rustic than Jungle Bay Resort & Spa (below), this eco-friendly lodge lies in a rainforest valley where three rivers meet. Secluded cottages are set in an organic garden with fruit trees, and the hot showers are solar-powered. Three Rivers even generates its own power with river currents. One covered building contains bunks and hammocks strung up dormitory style. You can even pitch your own tent on the grounds. A communal kitchen is also at the disposal of guests. Hiking, horseback riding, bird-watching, even whale- and turtle-watching will fill your social calendar. You can take dips in a trio of river ponds.

Newfoundland Estate (P.O. Box 1292), Rosalie, Dominica, W.I. www.3riversdominica.com. ✆ **767/446-1886.** Fax 510/578-6578. 6 units. Year-round $70–$90 double; $25 per person dormitory; $35 per person tent. DC, MC. V. **Amenities:** Restaurant; bar. *In room:* No phone.

In Stowe

Zandoli Inn ★ Picture this: A small hideaway inn anchored on a scenic cliff on the southeast coast overlooking the Atlantic, set on 2.4 hectares (6 acres) of tropical gardens with lush mountains as a backdrop. This oasis is crisscrossed with forest trails, and stairs take you to a 610m (2,001-ft.) boulder shoreline. Near the fishing village of Fond St. Jean, the inn lies 21km (13 miles) southeast of Roseau. A red-roofed building in the Caribbean/Mediterranean style, the well-furnished bedrooms are spacious opening onto scenic views and have mosquito netting and ceiling fans.

Roche Cassée Stowe, Dominica, W.I. www.zandoli.com. ✆ **767/446-3161.** Fax 767/446-3344. 5 units. Year-round $145 double. AE, MC, V. Children 11 and under not allowed. **Amenities:** Dining room; bar; outdoor plunge pool. *In room:* Internet (free), no phone.

In Morne Anglais

Exotica ★ 🎁 This tropical setting is home to what's called an "agro-eco" resort, with some 38 different flowers and fruit trees growing on the 2-hectare (5-acre) organic farm. You can enjoy the cool mountain breezes 480m (1,575 ft.) above sea level, at a point some 8km (5 miles) from Roseau. In 1995, Fae and Altherton Martin built this cluster of cottages on the western slope of Mount Anglais in the southern half of the island. The resort's cottages are constructed from hardwoods, cured pine, and stone. Accommodations are comfortable and tastefully furnished, each with a private porch, spacious living room, kitchen, large bedroom with two double beds, and private bathrooms with tub/shower.

Morne Anglais (P.O. Box 109), Roseau, Dominica, W.I. www.exotica-cottages.com. ✆ **767/448-8839** or 767/448-8849. Fax 767/448-8829. 6 units. Winter $168 double; off season $130 double. Extra person $24. Children 11 and under stay free in parent's room. MAP (breakfast and dinner) $43 per person extra. AE, DISC, MC, V. **Amenities:** Restaurant; bar. *In room:* Ceiling fan, hair dryer, kitchen, Wi-Fi (free).

In Point Mulatre

Jungle Bay Resort & Spa ★ This is a so-called "wellness" and adventure retreat, one of the finest on this eco-friendly island. Opened in 2005, the resort is a holistic health spa with a mammoth "yoga terrace." Rustically outfitted cottages with wood furnishings are perched like birds' nests on the hillside. The structures were made from volcanic stone and tropical hardwoods. The resort also features the Spa du Soleil, yoga studios, two restaurants serving health food, and hiking trails shooting out in all directions. Hikes cover a 23-hectare (57-acre) sanctuary filled with tropical birds and an array of exotic plant life. A spring-fed stream cascades along the valley below the hotel. Cottages are accessed through a series of stone stairways and footpaths. At your semioutdoor shower, your body communes with nature, or so they say. Organized activities include a full range of spa treatments, yoga classes, and even cultural activities such as live entertainment and dancing.

Point Mulatre, Dominica, W.I. www.junglebaydominica.com. ✆ **767/446-1789**. Fax 767/446-1090. 35 units. Winter $195–$220 single or double cottage, $260–$285 per person double; off season $190–$205 single or double cottage, $230–$260 per person double. 7-night honeymoon and eco-adventure packages available. MC, V. **Amenities:** 2 restaurants; beach bar; fitness classes; outdoor pool; spa. *In room:* Ceiling fan, no phone, Wi-Fi (free).

In Morne Daniel

The Hummingbird Inn A 3km (2-mile) drive from Roseau and the Canefield Airport and a 2-minute walk to the beach, this hilltop retreat is a great little bargain. Opening onto panoramic views, the rooms are in two bungalows and have louvered windows and doors to capture the breezes in lieu of air-conditioning. Ceiling fans hum day and night, and you can also retreat to terraces with hammocks. Each of the accommodations has bedside tables and reading lamps (not always a guarantee on Dominica). The handmade quilts on the beds add a homey touch. One four-poster bed, a mammoth wooden affair, is 250 years old. This is a friendly, family-style place, and there are lovely gardens with exotic plants that attract both hummingbirds and iguanas.

Rock-a-way, Canefield, Roseau, Dominica, W.I. www.thehummingbirdinn.com. ✆/fax **767/449-1042.** 10 units. Year-round $98 double; $140 suite. Extra person $20. Children 11 and under stay free in parent's room. AE, DC, DISC, MC, V. **Amenities:** Restaurant; bar; babysitting; Internet (free); room service. *In room:* Ceiling fan.

In Morne Trois Pitons

Crescent Moon Cabins ★ 🎁 A stay here puts you in the midst of "Me Tarzan, You Jane" country. In a setting of a roaring river and cascades of waterfalls, this eco-friendly resort lies in the foothills of Morne Trois Pitons National Park, midway between Melville Hall Airport and Roseau. Hiking trails branch out in every direction. If your vehicle can survive the road getting here, you will have arrived at a tropical paradise with dozens of fruit plants such as the mango or papaya. Accommodations are in wood-built cabins or else a stone-built cottage, each opening onto a panoramic view. Your hosts are nature-loving Ron and Jean Viveralli (he's a master chef and makes the world's best mango ice cream).

Sylvania (P.O. Box 2400), Roseau, Dominica, W.I. www.crescentmooncabins.com. ✆ **767/449-3449.** 4 units. Year-round $145 double cabin. 2-night minimum. Rates include continental breakfast; dinner $35 extra. **Amenities:** Dining room; Internet (free); outdoor pool. *In room:* No phone, Wi-Fi (free).

In Calibishie

Calibishie Lodges ★ About an hour's drive northeast of Roseau, you can stay at this isolated Caribbean retreat, its rooms opening onto panoramic views of land and sea. It is near a typical village with banana and coconut plantations, with fine white-sand beaches nearby. Accommodations are in small lodges on a hillside, each opening onto a balcony. The apartments here are self-contained and well furnished. Honeymooners are often attracted to this retreat, as are divers, hikers, bird-watchers, whale- and dolphin-watchers, and nature lovers in general. Lodges can house four guests comfortably. Features include mosquito screens, deck chairs on the veranda, and cooling by ceiling fans. Food and drink are served at the Bamboo Bar & Restaurant.

Calibishie Main Rd., Calibishie, Dominica, W.I. www.calibishie-lodges.com. ✆ **767/445-8537.** Fax 767/445-8074. 6 units. Winter $125–$215 double; off season $110–$180 double. Extra person $15. Rates include breakfast. DC, MC, V. **Amenities:** Restaurant; bar; outdoor pool. *In room:* Ceiling fan, kitchenette, Wi-Fi (free).

In Castle Bruce

Beau Rive ★ 🎁 Just south of the Carib Indian Territory, this is a wonderful little guesthouse on the east coast where owner Mark Steele welcomes you into his Zen world. Moving from England, he achieved his dream, which was to "create the hotel I've always hoped to discover on a tropical island." He's succeeded brilliantly with what is truly a "green hotel." The hot water is solar-heated, and even the soap in your bathroom is locally made. As much as possible, produce and fish are purchased from locals, and Steele planted 170 fruit and flowering trees, attracting a wide variety of birds. Every guest room is comfortably and attractively furnished with an ocean view and a private shower room.

Near Castle Bruce (P.O. Box 2424), Roseau, Dominica, W.I. www.beaurive.com. ✆ **767/445-8992.** 8 units. Year-round $180 double; $209 triple. Dinner $30 extra. MC, V. Closed Aug–Sept. Children 15 and under not allowed. **Amenities:** Dining room; bar; outdoor pool; Wi-Fi (free). *In room:* No phone.

WHERE TO DINE

If you're going out in the evening, always call to make sure the restaurant you want to visit is open. You'll also have to arrange transportation there and back; you probably don't want to drive yourself because of the bad lighting, hairpin turns, and blind corners.

Dominica is a lush island like Grenada and grows a lot of its own foodstuff, but fish and meats are generally shipped in frozen.

In Roseau

Cocorico FRENCH This breakfast and lunch cafe is often referred to as the living room of Roseau. Most items are given "the French touch here," beginning at breakfast with a series of omelettes, crepes, French sausage, Breton ham, and chaucuterie, along with café au lait. Diners sit at umbrella-covered tables like a Parisian cafe along the bayfront. Some visitors drop in to surf the Internet at one of the on-site computers. Lunch offers everything from a chicken Caesar salad to stewed shrimp with sauce on a succulent pasta. A Creole beef stew is regularly featured. Other Gallic delights include cigars, French bread, pâtés, cheeses, and chocolates. Downstairs in the cellar is a wine store with vintages from eight countries, most of which are French.

Bay Front at Kennedy Ave., Roseau. ✆ **767/449-8686.** www.natureisle.com/cocorico. Main courses EC$13–EC$30 breakfast, EC$33–EC $48 lunch; sandwiches EC$11–EC$21. MC, V. Mon–Fri 8:30am–4pm; Sat 8:30am–2pm.

Crystal Terrace Restaurant & Bar ★ DOMINICAN At this previously recommended family-run hotel, you can order authentic island cuisine, using home-grown products when available. Most guests begin their evening with a drink in the open-air lounge. At elegant table settings, open to the breezes, you can sample the cuisine, which features local specialties such as stuffed crab backs. Preparations of the main courses—chicken, beef, or fish—change on the daily menus, ending with a homemade cake and ice cream. Fresh soups are always made daily. The menu is limited yet generous, most often with a good choice. For example, there are four different meat options featured at dinner.

In the Evergreen Hotel, Castle Comfort. ✆ **767/448-3288.** www.evergreenhoteldominica.com. Reservations recommended. Breakfast EC$43; 3-course lunch EC$57; 3-course dinner EC$58. AE, MC, V. Daily 7:15–9am, 1–2pm, and 7–9pm.

Guiyave CREOLE This airy lunch restaurant occupies a wood-frame West Indian house. Rows of tables almost completely fill the narrow balcony overlooking the street outside. You can enjoy a drink at the stand-up bar on the second floor. Specialties include various Creole grills and different preparations of conch, octopus, lobster, spareribs, chicken, and pork chops. On Saturday, *rotis* (Caribbean burritos) and "goat water" (a local goat stew) are available. The place is known for refreshing juices like soursop, tamarind, sorrel, cherry, and strawberry. There's also a patisserie specializing in local pastries.

15 Cork St. ✆ **767/448-2930.** Reservations recommended. Lunch buffet EC$40. AE, MC, V. Sun-Fri 8am–3pm.

Pearl's Cuisine ★ 🎁 CARIBBEAN Come to this restored Creole house with a veranda for a true taste of Dominica: Chef Pearl's island delicacies are renowned locally. Begin with one of her tropical fruit juices, followed by perhaps freshly caught crayfish as an appetizer. Whenever lobster is available, it's served at dinner any way you want it. She also makes some mean pork chops, and her curried goat will put hair on your chest. Try the potato salad and spareribs, or the codfish and plantains, if you want to really go local.

55 King George V St. ✆ **767/448-8707.** Lunch EC$20. DC, MC, V. Mon–Sat 12:15–5pm.

Waterfront Restaurant DOMINICAN/INTERNATIONAL Jermaine Mitchell, a talented chef imported from neighboring St. Lucia, has awakened the taste buds of Roseau, for both guests of the Fort Young Hotel and nonguests as well. The restaurant, with its elegant place settings, opens onto romantic views of Roseau at night. Although Mitchell prepares wonderful regional fare, such as callaloo soup and guava tarts, the chef can roam the world borrowing from Thailand, Italy, East India, or wherever. A medley of seafood is presented along with good barbecue, even duck and lamb specialties. A live steel band often presents entertainment.

Victoria St., Roseau. ✆ **767/448-5000.** www.fortyounghotel.com. Main courses EC$13–$62. AE, MC, V. Daily 7–10pm.

In the Rainforest

Papillote Wilderness Retreat CREOLE/CARIBBEAN Even if you're not staying here (p. 233), come by taxi for lunch; it's only 6km (3¾ miles) east of Roseau. For dinner, you'll need to make reservations. Amid exotic flowers, century-old trees, and filtered sunlight, you'll dine overlooking a gorgeous vista of rivers and mountains. The array of healthful food includes flying fish and truly delectable freshwater prawns known as *bookh.* Freshly caught kingfish is also a tasty treat. Breadfruit or dasheen puffs merit a try if you've never had them, and the tropical salads—we recommend the green papaya chicken salad—are filled with flavor.

Trafalgar Falls Rd. ✆ **767/448-2287.** www.papillote.dm. Reservations recommended for lunch, required for dinner. Main courses EC$20–EC$30. AE, DC, DISC, MC, V. Daily 7:30am–10:30pm (dinner served at 7:30pm).

SPORTS & OUTDOOR PURSUITS

BEACHES If you really want a great beach, you should choose another island. Dominica has some of the worst beaches in the Caribbean; most are rocky and have gray-black volcanic sand. But some beaches, even though they don't have great sand or shade, are still good for diving or snorkeling in the turquoise waters.

Although the beach itself is filled with stones, the best place for swimming is at **Champagne,** south of Roseau and south of Ponte Michel but north of the southernmost town of Soufrière. Snorkeling and scuba diving are also actively pursued at this west-coast beach. Why the name? Volcanic vents puff steam into the ocean, and swimmers have likened the effect to swimming in the bubbly. From the Soufrière Scotts Head Marine Reserve, you can take a boardwalk to the beach, where the stones discourage lying on the beach in the sun.

Another good place for swimming lies on the northwest coast. **Picard Beach** stretches for about 3km (2 miles), a strip of grayish sand with palm trees as a backdrop. It's ideal for snorkeling or windsurfing. You can drop in for food or a drink at one of the hotels along the beach.

On the northeast coast, four beaches—**Hampstead Beach, Hodges Beach, L'Anse Noire,** and **Woodford Hill Bay**—are among the island's most beautiful, although none is great for swimming. Divers and snorkelers often come here, even though the water can be rough. Watch out for the strong currents.

The southwest coast also has some beaches, but the sand here is black and rock-studded. Nonetheless, snorkelers and scuba divers flock to **Soufrière Bay Beach** and **Scotts Head Beach** for the clear waters and the stunning underwater walls.

HIKING Wild and untamed Dominica offers hikers some of the most bizarre geological oddities in the Caribbean. Sights include scalding lava covered with a hot, thin, and not-very-stable crust; a boiling lake where mountain streams turn to vapor as they come into contact with superheated volcanic fissures; and a barren wasteland known as the Valley of Desolation.

All these attractions are in the heavily forested 6,800 hectares (16,803 acres) of the **Morne Trois Pitons National Park ★**, in the island's south-central region. You should go with a guide—there are plenty of them waiting for your business in the village of Laudat. Few markers appear en route, but the trek, which includes a real assortment of geological oddities, stretches 10km (6¼ miles) in both directions from Laudat to the Boiling Lake. Ferns, orchids, trees, and epiphytes create a tangle of underbrush; insect, bird, and reptilian life is profuse.

The hill treks of Dominica have been described as "sometimes easy, sometimes hellish," and if it should happen to rain during your climb (and it rains very frequently on Dominica), the paths are likely to become very slippery. But botanists, geologists, and experienced hikers all agree that climbs through the jungles of Dominica are the most rewarding in the Caribbean. Hikers should walk cautiously, particularly in areas peppered with bubbling hot springs. Regardless of where you turn, you'll run into streams and waterfalls, the inevitable result of an island that receives up to 400 inches of rainfall a year. Winds on the summits are strong enough to have pushed one recreational climber to her death several years ago, so be careful.

An adventure only for the most serious and experienced hiker is to **Boiling Lake** and the **Titou Gorge,** a deep and very narrow ravine whose depths were created as lava flows cooled and contracted. En route you might spot rare Sisserou and Jacquot parrots, monkeys, and vines whose growth seems to increase visibly on an hourly basis. The lake itself lies 10km (6¼ miles) east of Roseau, but reaching it requires about 4 hours of hiking, some of it strenuous. Go only with a guide, which can be arranged through the tourist office. (See "Getting a Guide," below.)

Taking the Wotton Waven Road, you branch off in the direction of **Sulphur Springs,** volcanic hot springs that are evidence of Dominica's turbulent past. Jeeps and Land Rovers can get quite close. This bubbling pool of gray mud sometimes belches smelly sulfurous fumes. The trail begins at the **Titou Gorge,** where you can go for a cooling swim in a pool or enjoy the hot spring waters alongside the pool. A 5-minute swim will take you up the gorge to a small cave with a beautiful waterfall. After the gorge, the marked trail goes through the appropriately named **Valley of Desolation** and comes out at Boiling Lake on the far side, a trek of 2 to 3 hours one-way. Sulfuric fumes in the area have destroyed much of the once-flourishing vegetation in the region.

Boiling Lake is the world's second-largest solfatara lake, measuring 63m (207 ft.) across. It is a bubbling cauldron with vapor clouds rising above blue-gray water. The depth of the lake is not known. The water temperature in the lake averages around 190°F (88°C). The lake is not the crater of a former volcano, but a flooded fumarole.

Getting a Guide

Locals warn that to proceed along the island's badly marked trails into dangerous areas is not a good idea; climbing alone or even in pairs is not advised. Guides should be used for all unmarked trails. You can arrange for a guide at the office of the Dominica National Park, in the Botanical Gardens in Roseau (✆ 767/448-2401), or the Dominica Tourist Board. Forestry officials recommend Ken's Hinterland Adventure Tours & Taxi Service, Fort Young Hotel on Victoria Street, Roseau (✆ 767/448-1660; www.khattstours.com). You can also call Discover Dominica (✆ 767/448-2045) to arrange a tour. Depending on the destination and the attractions, treks cost $40 to $75 per person for up to four participants and require 4 to 8 hours round-trip. Minivan transportation from Roseau to the starting point of your hill climb is usually included in the price.

Getting here is extremely difficult and even hazardous. Some visitors have even stumbled and fallen to their deaths into the boiling waters. The trail is most often very slippery because of rainfall. You'll encounter few visitors along this trail and, if you do, will likely be glad for the company, especially if a hiker is returning from the area where you're heading. He or she can give you advance reports of the conditions ahead of you.

See "Exploring the Island," below, for details on gorgeous Cabrits National Park.

KAYAKING ★★ Dominica is probably the best place in all the Caribbean for kayaking. Depending on the size, you can rent a kayak for $26 to $50 for a half-day, then go on a unique adventure around the rivers and coastline of the lushest island in the West Indies. **Nature Island Dive,** in Roseau (✆ **767/449-8181;** www.natureislanddive.com), offers rentals and gives the best advice. You can combine bird-watching, swimming, and snorkeling as you glide along. Consider Soufrière Bay, a marine reserve in southwest Dominica. Off the west coast, you will discover tranquil Caribbean waters with rainbow-hued fish along the beaches in Mero, Salisbury, and in the region of the Layou and Macoucherie rivers.

SCUBA DIVING Diving has taken off on Dominica. The underwater terrain is spectacular. Most of the diving is on the southwestern end of the island, with its dramatic drop-offs, walls, and pinnacles. These volcanic formations are interwoven with cuts, arches, ledges, and overhangs, home to sponges, gorgonians, and corals. An abundance of invertebrates, reef fish, and unusual sea creatures such as sea horses, frogfish, batfish, and flying gunards attract underwater photographers.

Dive Dominica, in the **Castle Comfort Diving Lodge,** P.O. Box 2253, Castle Comfort, Roseau, Dominica, W.I. (✆ **767/448-2188;** www.divedominica.com), gives open-water certification (both NAUI and PADI) and instruction. Two diving catamarans and a handful of smaller boats get you to the dive sites in relative comfort. The dive outfit is part of a hotel, a 15-room lodge where at least 90% of the clientele checks in as part of a dive package. A 6-night dive package, double occupancy, begins at $960 per person, including breakfasts and dinners, five two-tank dives, and one night dive. A single-tank dive for nonguests goes for $62, a two-tank dive for $140, and a night dive for $68. All rooms in the lodge are air-conditioned and have TVs, phones, and Wi-Fi. On the premises are a bar (for residents and their guests only) and a Jacuzzi.

Divers from all over the world come to the **Dive Centre,** at the Anchorage Hotel in Castle Comfort (p. 231; ✆ **767/448-2638;** www.anchoragehotel.dm). With a pool, classrooms, a private dock, a miniflotilla of dive boats, and a fully qualified PADI staff, this is the most complete dive resort on Dominica. A single-tank dive costs $62; a double-tank dive, $86; and a one-tank night dive, $68. A whale- and dolphin-watch from 2pm to sunset is popular and costs $67 per person. There is an additional $4 charge for use of the marine park for two people. Rum punch is served.

SNORKELING Snorkeling sites are never far away, regardless of where you are on Dominica. In all there are some 30 first-rate snorkeling areas immediately off the coast. The western side of the island, where nearly all of the snorkeling takes place, is the lee side, meaning the waters are tranquil. You can explore the underwater hot springs at Champagne and Toucari, the Coral Gardens off Salisbury, and the southern shoreline of Scotts Head Beach, with more than 190 species of flamboyantly colored fish. The closeness of the reefs to shore makes snorkeling here some of the best in the Caribbean. Your hotel or one of the dive shops can set you up with gear.

SWIMMING The beaches may be lousy, but Dominica has some of the best river swimming in the Caribbean. Some say the little island has 365 rivers, one for every day of the year. The best places for swimming are the refreshing ponds at the base of a waterfall, of which there are dozens on the island. Your best bets are on the west coast at the **Picard** or the **Machoucherie rivers.** On the east coast, the finest spot is **White River,** near the hamlet of La Plaine. Consider also the **Layou River** and its gorges. Layou is the island's largest river, ranging from tranquil beach-lined pools ideal for swimming to deep gorges and turbulent rapids. All the rivers are pristine and make nice spots for a little sunbathing or perhaps a picnic lunch along their banks.

The staff at the tourist office (see "Visitor Information," p. 227) knows the island intimately and will help you map out a place for a picnic and a swim during your tour of the island, depending on where you're going. They'll also arm you with a good map and directions if you're heading out on your own.

Our favorite place for a dip is the **Emerald Pool Trail,** which lies in the Morne Trois Pitons National Park. You reach it northeast of Pont Casse, going for 6km (3¾ miles) along an unmarked road taking you north to Castle Bruce. Eventually, you reach a sign pointing to the Emerald Pool Trail, the most accessible trail in this lush national park. A 30-minute hike takes you to a stunning cascade of water dropping 6m (20 ft.). This is Emerald Falls, where you can go for a cooling swim. Chances are, you'll have it all to yourself.

EXPLORING THE ISLAND

Those making day trips to Dominica from other Caribbean islands will want to see the **Carib Indian Territory ★**, in the northeast. In 1903, Britain got the surviving Caribs to agree to live on 1,480 hectares (3,657 acres) of land. Today this reservation is the last remaining turf of the once-hostile tribe for whom the Caribbean was named. Today they survive by fishing, growing food, and weaving baskets and

Searching for Moby Dick

You'll see more sperm whales, pilot whales, killer whales, and dolphins during whale- and dolphin-watching trips ★ off Dominica than off any other island in the Caribbean. A pod of sperm whales can often be spotted just yards from your boat, since there are no laws here regarding the distance you must keep from the whales. The Anchorage Hotel, at Castle Comfort (p. 231; ✆ 767/448-2638), offers the best tours. A 3½-hour trip costs $57, but children 11 and under pay half price. The vessels leave the dock every Wednesday, Saturday, and Sunday at 2pm (call ahead for availability).

vetiver-grass mats, which they sell to the outside world. The baskets sold at roadside stands make especially good buys. An on-site cultural center, **Kalinago Barana Auté** (✆ **767/445-7979;** www.kalinagobaranaaute.com), acquaints you with the Carib history, culture, and native customs. A guided 45-minute tour is conducted, not only exploring the Indian village, but allowing you to watch the natives practice their local crafts. They even bake cassava bread for you. The tour costs $10, and the site is open year-round daily 9am to 5pm.

It's like going back in time when you explore **Morne Trois Pitons National Park ★★**, a primordial rainforest. Mists rise gently over lush, dark-green growth, drifting up to blue-green peaks that have earned Dominica the nickname "Switzerland of the Caribbean." Framed by banks of giant ferns, rivers rush and tumble, trees sprout orchids, green sunlight filters down through trees, and roaring waterfalls create a blue mist. One of the best starting points for a visit to the park is the village of **Laudat,** 11km (6¾ miles) from Roseau. (See also "Hiking," above.)

The best tour is the **Rain Forest Aerial Tram,** at the corner of Old Street and Great George Street in Laudat (✆ **767/448-8775**), but it's open only when cruise ships are in port. For $64 per person, you're taken on a 90-minute tour that starts at the village of Laudat, "sailing" over the rainforest through the Morne Trois Pitons National Park. Along the way, you're treated to exotic bird life, beautiful waterfalls, and much tropical flora.

Eight kilometers (5 miles) up from the **Roseau River Valley,** in the south-central sector of Dominica, **Trafalgar Falls** is reached after driving through the village of Trafalgar. Shortly beyond the hamlet of Trafalgar and up a short hill, there's a little kiosk where you can hire a guide to take you on the short walk to the actual falls. In all, allow about 1½ hours for the trip from Trafalgar to the falls. This is the only road or pathway into the falls, and you'll have to approach on foot, as the slopes are too steep for vehicles. After a 20-minute walk past ginger plants and vanilla orchids, you arrive at the base, where a trio of falls converges in a rock-strewn pool.

For another great way to spend half a day, head for the **Papillote Wilderness Retreat** (p. 233). The botanical garden alone is worth the trip, as are the views of mountains and lush valleys. Near the main dining terrace is a Jacuzzi-size pool, which is filled with the mineral-rich waters of a nearby hot spring. Nonguests can use the pool for $4.50. Bring sturdy walking shoes in addition to a bathing suit.

On the northwestern coast, **Portsmouth** is Dominica's second-largest settlement. Here you can row up the Indian River in native canoes, visit the ruins of old Fort Shirley in Cabrits National Park, and bathe at Sandy Beach on Douglas Bay and Prince Rupert Bay.

Cabrits National Park ★★ (no phone), on Dominica's northwestern coast, immediately adjacent to Douglas Bay, is a 525-hectare (1,297-acre) protected site, only about 25% of which is devoted to dry land. Here are low-rising hills, tropical forests, swampland, volcanic-sand beaches, coral reefs, and the sprawling ruins of a fortified, 18th-century garrison of British, then French, construction. This is one of the area's great natural attractions, and if your time is limited, you may want to head here even if you skip everything else in Dominica. The park's land extends over a panoramic promontory formed by the low-rising twin peaks of extinct volcanoes (known as East Cabrit and West Cabrit) overlooking beaches, with Douglas Bay on one side and Prince Rupert Bay across the headland. The marine section of the park extends over the teeming marine life of the shallow waters of Douglas Bay.

If you want to explore the park underwater, we strongly encourage you to take one of the scuba or snorkeling trips organized by the officially designated dive operator for the park, **Cabrit's Dive Center,** Picard Estate, Portsmouth (✆ **767/445-3010;** www.cabritsdive.com). If you're interested in hiking, you'll find about 3km (2 miles) of trails, each clearly marked with brown-and-yellow signs, pointing out the geological and architectural highlights of the park. Foremost among these is **Fort Shirley,** a forbidding-looking hulk that was last used as a military post in 1854. The park's **Welcome Center** (no phone) contains a small on-site **museum** (daily 9am–5pm; free admission) that highlights the natural and historic aspects of the park. The staff will make suggestions about the trails you might want to follow, but since the surface of the park is relatively limited in scope, it's hard to get lost. Signs point from the welcome center to the ruins of Fort Shirley and to the low summits of the East and West Cabrit hills, neither of which rises more than about 150m (492 ft.) above sea level.

SHOPPING

Store hours are usually Monday to Friday from 8am to 5pm and Saturday from 9am to 1pm.

In Roseau, the **Old Market Plaza,** of historical significance as a former slave-trading market and, more recently, the site of a Wednesday-, Friday-, and Saturday-morning vegetable market, now houses three craft shops, each specializing in coconut, straw, and Carib craft products.

The handmade Dominican vetiver-grass mats sold at **Tropicrafts Island Mats,** 41 Queen Mary St. and Turkey Lane (✆ **767/448-2747**), are known throughout the world, and you can watch the weaving process during store hours. They also sell dolls, shopping bags, and place mats, all appliquéd by hand.

Outlets for crafts include **Dominica Pottery,** Bayfront Street at Kennedy Avenue, Roseau (no phone), run by a local priest. An array of pottery made from local clays is on sale, as well as other handicrafts. **Ego Boutique,** 9 Hillsborough St., Roseau (✆ **767/448-2336**), has the best selection of clothing, much of it in the classic West Indian style, along with some locally made crafts and home accessories.

DOMINICA AFTER DARK

It's not very lively, but there is some evening activity. A couple of the major hotels have entertainment on weekends, usually a combo or "jing ping" (traditional local music). The clubs and bars in these hotels attract mainly foreign visitors, so if you'd like to go where the locals go, head for one of the following.

The **Balas Bar,** at the Fort Young Hotel (p. 232), Victoria Street, in Roseau (✆ **767/448-5000**), is the place to be every Friday between 6 and 8pm. Drink specials, usually rum punches, are the feature, along with a live local band. It's open every day from 10am to 11pm.

Another very happening bar is the **Cellars Bar** at the Sutton Place Hotel (p. 232), Old Street, in Roseau (✆ **767/449-8700**). Various events are staged here throughout the week, including karaoke on Friday night. Amateur bartenders tempt you with their specialties on Wednesday night.

Symes Zee's, 34 King George V St., Roseau (✆ **767/448-2494**), is the domain of Symes Zee, the island's best blues man. A local band entertains with blues, jazz, and reggae. Here's your chance to smoke a reasonably priced Cuban cigar.

11 THE DOMINICAN REPUBLIC

The Dominican Republic shares the island of Hispaniola with its lesser developed cousin, Haiti, and enjoys a year-round summer, with sugar-white beaches shaded by palm trees, crystalline waters teeming with rainbow-hued fish, and Spanish colonial history stretching back 500 years. Small fishing villages attract locals and backpackers, while larger all-inclusive resorts appeal to couples and families. Spicy food, spicier merengue, and a leisurely lifestyle draw more travelers to the Dominican Republic every year.

Things to Do The white-sand beaches and swaying coconut palm trees make exclusive **Punta Cana** a respite for sun worshippers. Scuba divers can plunge deep for shipwrecks in the translucent waters of **Bayahibe.** Inland, the vibrant **Santo Domingo,** one of the oldest cities in the Caribbean, has a 12-block Colonial Zone whose cobblestone streets take you past old stone buildings and museums. Away from the city, discover the thundering waterfall **Salto de Aguas Blancas** or observe marine life at **Manati Park.**

Shopping Stock up on the world's finest smokes in the cigar-making region in and around **Santiago,** or bring home a bottle or three of aged Dominican rum. In Santo Domingo, browse **El Mercado Modela,** a market stuffed with local crafts and spices. Check out **Harrison's** in Puerto Plata for amber jewelry, worn by Keith Richards and Madonna. Duck in the art galleries of **Altos de Chavon,** a re-created 16th-century village, then linger along the cliff for awesome Punta Cana views.

Nightlife & Entertainment Locals and visitors alike flock to the dance clubs after dinner in the city and the hotels along the beach. Move to DJ-driven beats in **Santo Domingo** or **Puerto Plata,** or taste umbrella-topped cocktails at a beach bar in **Cabrera** and **Barahona.** Casinos in the larger cities and resorts offer late-night gaming; players enjoy free drinks. **Baseball** is a way of life here, and fans can watch future Major Leaguers compete in the country's professional league.

Eating & Drinking Dig into fresh rock lobster or zesty braised red snapper in **Santo Domingo,** or head to **Puerto Plata** for crayfish or grilled shrimp kabobs. Locals love their national dish, *la bandera* (rice, beans, meat, vegetables, and fried plantains), as well as the subtle flavors of stewed fish and conch at **Samana,** the national coconut capital. Wash it down with a bottle of Dominican Republic Presidente beer or a rum cocktail.

ESSENTIALS

Visitor Information

In the United States, you can contact the **Dominican Republic Tourist Information Center** at 136 E. 57th St., Ste. 805, New York, NY 10022 (© **888/374-6361** or 212/588-1012); or 848 Brickell Ave., Suite 747, Miami, FL 33131 (© **888/358-9594** or 305/358-2899). In Canada, try the office at 2080 Rue Crescent, Montréal PQ, Quebec H3G 288 (© **800/563-1611** or 514/499-1918); don't expect too much specific information. In England, the office is at 18–21 Hand Court, London, WC1V 6JF (© **020/7242-7778**). For information online, check **www.godominican republic.com** or **www.dr1.com**.

Getting There

American Airlines (© **800/433-7300** in the U.S. and Canada; www.aa.com) has the most frequent service, offering at least a dozen flights daily from cities throughout North America to either Santo Domingo or Puerto Plata. Flights from hubs such as New York, Miami, or San Juan, Puerto Rico, are usually nonstop.

If you're heading to one of the Dominican Republic's smaller airports, your best bet is with **American Eagle,** American's local commuter carrier. Its small planes depart every day from San Juan, Puerto Rico, for airports throughout the Dominican Republic, including Santo Domingo, Puerto Plata, La Romana, and Punta Cana.

Continental Airlines (© **800/231-0856** in the U.S. and Canada; www.continental.com) flies daily between Newark, New Jersey, and Santo Domingo. **JetBlue Airlines** (© **800/538-2583** in the U.S. and Canada; www.jetblue.com) flies from New York to the Dominican Republic. **US Airways** (© **800/622-1015** in the U.S. and Canada; www.usairways.com) flies from Boston, Philadelphia, or Charlotte to the island. **Delta** (© **800/221-1212** in the U.S. and Canada; www.delta.com) flies from both New York and Miami to the Dominican Republic.

Other airlines servicing the area include **Air Transat** (© **866/847-1112** in the U.S. and Canada; www.airtransat.ca), which flies to Santo Domingo from Toronto, Vancouver, and Montréal.

Iberia (© **800/772-4642** in the U.S. and Canada; www.iberia.com) flies daily from Madrid to Santo Domingo, making a brief stop in San Juan.

For information on flights into Casa de Campo/La Romana, see the section "La Romana & Altos de Chavón," below.

Be warned: Arriving at Santo Domingo's **Las Américas International Airport** is confusing and chaotic. Customs officials, who tend to be rude and overworked, may give you a very thorough check. Stolen luggage is not uncommon here; beware of "porters" who offer to help with your bags. Arrival at **La Unión International Airport,** 37km (23 miles) east of Puerto Plata on the north coast, is generally much smoother and safer, but you should still be cautious.

Getting Around

Getting around the Dominican Republic is not always easy if your hotel is in a remote location. The most convenient modes of transport are shuttle flights, taxis, rental cars, *públicos* (multipassenger taxis), and *guaguas* (public buses).

BY RENTAL CAR The best way to see the Dominican Republic is to drive. Motorists drive on the right here. Although major highways are relatively smooth, the country's secondary roads, especially those in the east, are riddled with potholes and ruts. Roads also tend to be badly lit and poorly marked in both the city and the countryside. Drive carefully and give yourself plenty of time when traveling between island destinations. Watch out for policemen who may flag you down and accuse you (often wrongly) of some infraction. Many locals give these low-paid policemen a $5 *regalo,* or gift "for your children," and are then free to go.

The high accident and theft rate in recent years have helped to raise car rental rates here. Prices vary, so call around for last-minute quotes. Make sure you understand your insurance coverage (or lack thereof) before you leave home. Your credit card issuer may already provide you with insurance; call to find out.

For reservations and more information, call the rental companies at least a week before your departure: **Avis** (✆ **800/331-1084** in the U.S. and Canada, or 809/535-7191; www.avis.com), **Budget** (✆ **800/472-3325** in the U.S. and Canada, or 809/549-0351; www.budget.com), and **Hertz** (✆ **800/654-3001** in the U.S. and Canada, or 809/221-5333; www.hertz.com) all operate in the Dominican Republic. All three have offices at the Santo Domingo and Puerto Plata airports, as well as in downtown Santo Domingo. Avis and Hertz also have offices in La Romana and Punta Cana.

Although the cars may not be as well maintained as the big three above, you can often get a cheaper deal at one of the local firms, notably **McAuto Rental Cars** (✆ **809/688-6518**). If you want a car with seat belts, you must ask. Your Canadian or American driver's license is suitable documentation, along with a valid credit card or a substantial cash deposit.

BY TAXI Taxis aren't metered, and determining the fare in advance (which you should do) may be difficult if you and your driver have a language problem. You can easily hail a taxi at the airport and at most major hotels. ***Warning:*** Don't get into an unmarked street taxi. Many visitors, particularly in Santo Domingo, have been assaulted and robbed by doing just that. The minimum fare within Santo Domingo is $2.30. In Santo Domingo, the most reliable taxi company is **Tecni-Taxi** (✆ **809/567-2010**). In Puerto Plata, call **Tecni-Taxi** at ✆ **809/320-7621.**

BY PUBLIC TRANSPORTATION ***Públicos*** are unmetered multipassenger taxis that travel along main thoroughfares, stopping often to pick up people waving from the side of the street. A *público* is marked by a white seal on the front door. You must tell the driver your destination when you're picked up to make sure the *público* is going there. A ride is usually 20¢. The minimum fare is 10¢.

Public buses, often in the form of minivans or panel trucks, are called ***guaguas*** (pronounced *gwa-gwas*). For about the same price, they provide the same service as *públicos,* but they're generally more crowded. Larger buses provide service outside the towns. Beware of pickpockets on board.

[FastFACTS] THE DOMINICAN REPUBLIC

Banks Most banks are open Monday to Friday 8:30am to 4:30pm. **ATMs** are found at all branches of **Banco Popular.** Banks at the malls stay open until 6pm.

Currency The Dominican monetary unit is the **peso (RD$),** made up of 100 centavos. Coin denominations are 1, 5, 10, 25, and 50 centavos; 1 peso; and 5 pesos. Bill denominations are RD$5, RD$10, RD$20,

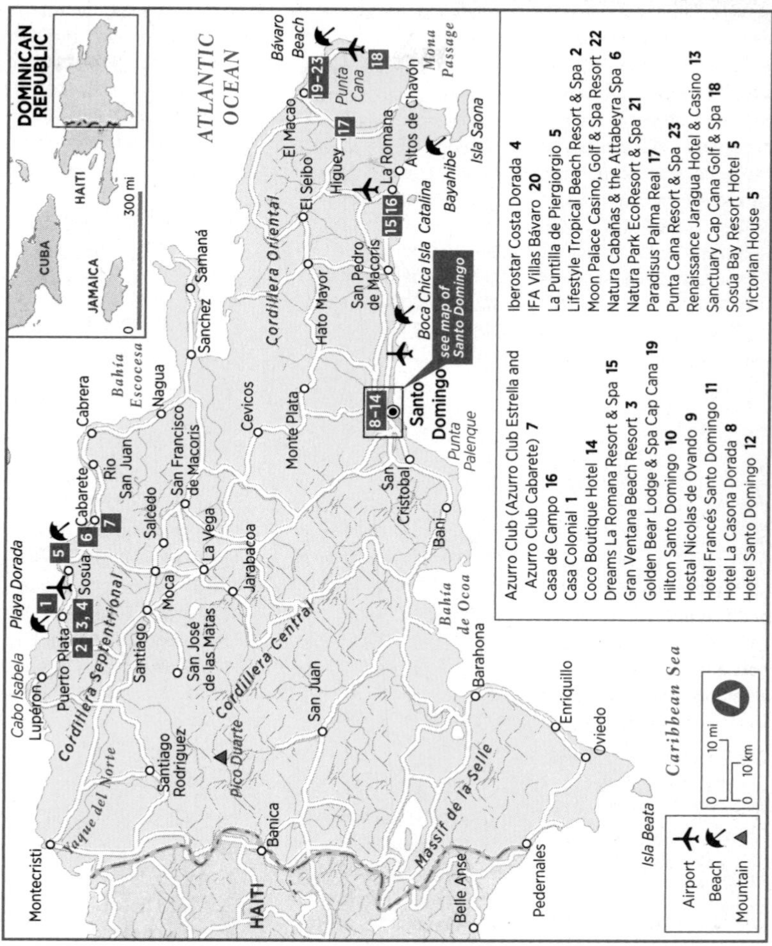

RD$50, RD$100, RD$500, RD$1,000, and RD$2,000. The use of any currency other than Dominican pesos is technically illegal, but few seem to heed this mandate. *As such, prices in this chapter are quoted in U.S. dollars.* At the time of this writing, the exchange rate was about RD$37 to US$1. Stated differently, RD$1 equals 2.6¢. The exchange of the RD$ and the British pound was approximately RD$1 to 1.6p, or, stated differently, £1 to RD$60. Technically, every peso is divided into 100 centavos, and you'll occasionally see centavos as part of the barter agreements among local residents, but many foreign visitors to the D.R. pass a holiday without ever seeing one. For most purposes, they're practically worthless. Bank booths at the international airports and major hotels will change your currency at the prevailing free-market rate.

Customs Visitors are allowed to bring in 200 cigarettes, 1 liter of alcohol, and gifts not exceeding a value of $100. Anything over that will be subjected to import taxes.

Documents To enter the Dominican Republic, citizens of the United States, Canada, the United Kingdom, Australia, New Zealand, and other countries need a valid passport. Upon your arrival at the airport in the Dominican Republic, you must purchase a tourist card for $10. You can avoid waiting in line by purchasing this card when checking in for your flight to the island.

Electricity The country generally uses 110-volt AC (60 cycles), so adapters and transformers are usually not necessary for U.S. appliances. To be safe, ask when booking your hotel.

Embassies All embassies are in Santo Domingo, the capital. The **U.S. Embassy** is on Calle Cesar Nicholas Penson at the corner of Máximo Gomez (✆ **809/221-2171;** http://santodomingo.usembassy.gov). The embassy of the **United Kingdom** is located at Av. 27 de Febrero 233, Edificio Corominas Pepin (✆ **809/472-7111;** http://ukindominicanrepublic.fco.gov.uk). The embassy of **Canada** is found at Av. Winston Churchill 1099 (✆ **809/262-3100;** canadainternational.gc.ca).

Emergencies Call ✆ **911.**

Language The official language is Spanish; many people also speak some English.

Safety The Dominican Republic has more than its fair share of crime. (See "Getting There," above, for a warning about crime at airports.) Avoid unmarked street taxis, especially in Santo Domingo; you could be targeted for assault and robbery. While strolling around the city, beware of hustlers selling various wares; pickpockets and muggers are common here, and visitors are easy targets. Don't walk in Santo Domingo at night. Locals like to offer their services as guides, and it is often difficult to decline. Hiring an official guide from the tourist office is your best bet. Lock valuables in your hotel safe, carry only a reasonable amount of cash or (better yet) one or two credit cards, and avoid dark, deserted places just like you would at home. (***One note:*** The single male will find more solicitations from prostitutes here than anywhere else in the Caribbean. Prostitutes are at their most visible and aggressive in such relatively unmonitored tourist zones as Cabarete, and within the bars and lounges of most of the deluxe hotels of Santo Domingo, especially the Jaragua.)

Taxes A departure tax of $20 is assessed and must be paid in U.S. currency. The government imposes a 16% tax on hotel rooms, which is usually topped by an automatic 10% service charge, bringing the total tax to staggering heights. That same tax is also levied on restaurant tabs, sports activities, rental cars, and many items purchased at stores. Visitors to the Dominican Republic are among the most heavily taxed in the Caribbean.

Telephone The area code for the Dominican Republic is **809.** You place calls to or from the Dominican Republic just as you would from any other area code in North America. You can access **AT&T Direct** by dialing ✆ **800/225-5288.** You can reach **MCI** at ✆ **800/888-8000** and **Sprint** at ✆ **800/751-7877.**

Time Atlantic Standard Time is observed year-round. Between November and March, when it's noon in New York and Miami, it's 1pm in Santo Domingo. However, during U.S. daylight saving time, it's the same time in the Dominican Republic and the U.S. East Coast.

Tipping Most restaurants and hotels add a 10% service charge to your check. Most people usually add 5% to 10% more, especially if the service has been good.

Water Stick to bottled water.

Weather The average temperature is 77°F (25°C). August is the warmest month and January the coolest month, although even then it's warm enough to swim.

LA ROMANA ★ & ALTOS DE CHAVON ★★★

On the southeast coast of the Dominican Republic, La Romana was once a sleepy sugar-cane town that specialized in cattle-raising. Visitors didn't come near the place until Gulf + Western Industries opened a luxurious tropical paradise resort, the Casa de Campo, about 2km (1¼ mile) east of town. It's the finest resort in the Dominican Republic, and especially popular among golfers.

Just east of Casa de Campo is Altos de Chavón, a charming and whimsical copy of what might have been a fortified medieval village in Spain, southern France, or Italy. It's the country's leading attraction.

Essentials

VISITOR INFORMATION The government maintains **La Romana Tourist Office** at Av. Libertad 7 (✆ **866/588-6856** or 809/550-6922), open Monday to Friday 8am to 3pm. The staff is earnest and hardworking, but don't expect to come away with a wealth of information.

GETTING THERE **By Plane** **American Airlines** (✆ **800/433-7300** in the U.S. and Canada; www.aa.com) flies once a day to the Casa de Campo/La Romana airport (its international code is LRM) from Miami, with a travel time of about 2½ hours each way. (Yes, it's a slow plane.) **American Eagle** (same phone number) operates at least two (and, in busy seasons, at least three) daily nonstop flights to Casa de Campo/La Romana airport (LRM) from San Juan, Puerto Rico. The flight takes about 45 minutes, and it departs late enough in the day to permit transfers from other flights.

By Car You can drive here in about an hour and 20 minutes from Santo Domingo's Las Américas International Airport (SDQ), along Las Américas Highway. (Allow another hour if you're in the center of the city.) Of course, everything depends on traffic conditions. (Watch for speed traps—low-paid police officers openly solicit bribes, whether you're speeding or not.)

GETTING AROUND Most visitors don't rent a car but rely on local transportation, which is very haphazard and operated by independent drivers. You'll find both taxis and *motoconchos* (motorized scooters) at the northeast corner of Parque Central in the heart of La Romana. A typical ride almost anywhere within town costs less than $2.20, with the average taxi ride costing less than $4.50. Prices are always to be negotiated, of course.

La Romana

WHERE TO STAY

Casa de Campo ★★★ Translated as "country house," Casa de Campo, on its own beach, functioned for many years as the most visible, most alluring, and most glamorous resort in the Dominican Republic. And although its preeminence has been challenged by newer, more cutting-edge resorts, it still exerts a powerful hold on the imagination of the country's image of itself as a tourist destination. There's a staggering variety of accommodations you can rent here, from a conventional but very comfortable hotel room to an entire house. Decor tends to be reasonably consistent throughout: Tiles, craft objects, mahogany furniture mostly built in the D.R., mahogany louvered doors, and neutral-toned fabrics, usually white, adorn the interior of both the public areas and the accommodations.

La Romana (P.O. Box 140), Dominican Republic. www.casadecampo.com.do. © **800/877-3643** in the U.S., or 809/523-3333. Fax 809/523-8394. 279 units. Winter $295–$645 double, $600–$1,886 suite; off season $195–$295 double, $350 suite. All-inclusive plans are extra. AE, DC, MC, V. **Amenities:** 8 restaurants; 5 bars; babysitting; bikes; children's center (ages 3-12); 4 18-hole golf courses; health club; horseback riding; 2 outdoor pools; 20 semiprivate pools; room service; 13 tennis courts (10 lit); watersports equipment/rentals. *In room:* A/C, TV, hair dryer, minibar, Wi-Fi (free).

Dreams La Romana Resort & Spa ★ ☺ This contender on a spectacular beach is giving the grande dame of Casa de Campo a run for the money. The golf and tennis facilities here aren't as elaborate as those at Casa de Campo, and there are no polo grounds, but the resort is beautifully landscaped and the beach is palm-fringed. Accommodations are in a well-designed series of three-story buildings with blue-tiled roofs. Decor inside features lots of tile, varnished hardwood, wicker, and rattan. Everything served in all of the resort's restaurants is covered by the all-inclusive price. This is one of the very rare all-inclusive resorts that offer the availability of a day pass, allowing up-close and personal access to the facilities.

Playa Bayahibe, La Romana (P.O. Box 80), Dominican Republic. www.dreamsresorts.com. © **866/2DREAMS** [237-3267] in the U.S., or 809/221-8880. Fax 809/221-2776. 751 units. Winter $462–$646 double, from $806 suite; off season $224–$345 double, $358–$500 suite. Day pass for nonresidents $50 per person. Rates are all-inclusive. AE, MC, V. **Amenities:** 8 restaurants; 7 bars; babysitting; bikes; children's programs; health club; horseback riding; Jacuzzi; 2 outdoor pools; disco; room service; sauna; 4 tennis courts (lit); watersports equipment/rentals. *In room:* A/C, TV/DVD, CD player, hair dryer, minibar, MP3 docking station, Wi-Fi ($16 per day).

WHERE TO DINE

The Beach Club by Le Cirque ★★★ SEAFOOD/INTERNATIONAL The Maccioni family of the world famous Le Cirque Restaurant in New York has combined forces with Casa de Campo to create this citadel of fine cuisine. Open to the breezes, the restaurant enjoys a scenic setting on the private Minitas Beach. The catch of the day is brought in that morning to be shaped into delectable seafood dishes, often from the grill. The chefs also grill succulent meats and create luscious pastas as well. Some of the freshest salads along the coast are also served here, and the pastry chef is known for his luscious desserts, which are prepared daily. Dishes reflect a light, contemporary touch, and the chefs update hearty classics with sunny, home-grown herbs and flavors into an array of appetizing selection. At lunch bathing suits are acceptable, but at dinner men should wear a collared shirt and long pants.

Minitas Beach, Casa de Campo. © **809/523-8698.** Reservations required. Main courses $25–$32. AE, DC, MC, V. Daily noon–4pm and 7–11pm.

La Casita ★ ITALIAN/INTERNATIONAL This is the most elegant and substantial restaurant in downtown La Romana, a stylish and well-managed enclave of chic that's the regular dining choice of some of the homeowners from nearby Casa de Campo. Established in the late 1980s and outfitted like a country tavern in the countryside of Italy, it has lined its walls with hand-painted porcelain collected during the owners' travels in Italy and Spain. We urge you to seek out the tiny corner bar of this place before or after your meal, where walls are lined with the sophisticated caricatures and cartoons of Dominican artist/architect Roberto Copa, the designer of Altos de Chavón. If you opt for a meal here, you'll be in rather upscale company: Menu items include lobster thermidor, filet of sea bass meunière, grilled salmon with white wine and herbs, and all manner of pastas.

Calle Francisco Richiez 57. ✆ **809/556-5932.** Reservations recommended. Main courses $7–$34. AE, DC, MC, V. Daily 11am–11pm.

HITTING THE BEACH

La Minitas, Casa de Campo's main beach and site of a series of bars and restaurants, is a small but immaculate beach and lagoon that requires a 10-minute shuttle-bus ride from the resort's central core. Bus transportation is provided, or you can rent an electric golf cart. A bit farther afield (a 30-min. bus ride, but only a 20-min. boat ride), **Bayahibe** is a large, palm-fringed sandy crescent on a point jutting out from the shoreline. Finally, **Catalina** is a fine beach on a deserted island, surrounded by turquoise waters; it's just 45 minutes away by motorboat. Unfortunately, many other visitors from Casa de Campo have learned of the glories of this latter retreat, so you're not likely to have the sands to yourself.

SPORTS & OUTDOOR PURSUITS

Casa de Campo is headquarters for just about any sporting activity or outdoor pursuit in the area. Call the resort's guest services staff at ✆ **809/523-8698** for more information. **Dreams La Romana Resort & Spa** weighs in with a heavy array of outdoor activities ranging from horseback riding to banana boating. Call **809/221-8880** for more details.

FISHING You can arrange **freshwater river–fishing trips** through Casa de Campo. Some of the biggest snook ever recorded have been caught around here. A 3-hour tour costs $36 per person and includes tackle, bait, and soft drinks. A 4-hour deep-sea fishing trip costs $708 to $2,621 per boat, with 8 hours going for $836 to $4,158.

GOLF *Golf* magazine declared Casa de Campo (✆ **809/523-3333** or 523-8698) "the finest golf resort in the world." The **Teeth of the Dog ★★★** course has been called "a thing of almighty beauty," and it is. The ruggedly natural terrain has 7 holes skirting the ocean. Opened in 1977, **the Links ★★★** is an inland course modeled after some of the seaside courses of Scotland. In the late 1990s, the resort added a third golf course to its repertoire, **La Romana Country Club,** which tends to be used almost exclusively by residents of the surrounding countryside rather than by guests of Casa de Campo.

The cost for 18 holes of golf is $150 at the Links and $170 at Teeth of the Dog and the La Romana Country Club. (Some golf privileges may be included in packages to Casa de Campo.) You can also buy a 3-day membership, which lets you play all courses for $420 per person (for Casa de Campo guests only). A 6-day membership costs $840. You can hire caddies for $25. Each course is open daily 7:30am to 5:30pm. Call far in advance to reserve a tee time if you're not staying at the resort.

HORSEBACK RIDING Trail rides at Casa de Campo or Casa del Mar cost $51 per person for 1 hour, $80 for 2 hours. The stables shelter 250 horses, although only about 40 of them are available for trail rides. For more information, call **Casa del Campo** at ✆ **809/523-3333** or 523-8698, or **Dreams La Romana** at ✆ **809/221-8880.**

SNORKELING **Casa de Campo** (✆ **809/523-3333** or 523-8698) has one of the most complete watersports facilities in the Dominican Republic. You can charter a boat for snorkeling, with a minimum of eight people. (The resort maintains eight charter vessels.) Full-day snorkeling trips to Isla Catalina cost $40 per snorkeler. Rental of fins and masks cost $11 per day; guests on all-inclusive plans use gear for free. Snorkeling is also included in the all-inclusive rates at **Dreams La Romana** (✆ **809/221-8880**).

TENNIS **Casa de Campo**'s (✆ **809/523-3333** or 523-8698) 13 clay courts are available from 7am to 9pm (they're lit at night). Charges are $28 per court per hour during the day or $35 at night. Lessons are $75 per hour with a tennis pro, and $60 with an assistant pro. Call far in advance to reserve a court if you're not staying at the resort. The four courts at **Dreams La Romana** (✆ **809/221-8880**) are reserved for the resort's all-inclusive guests.

Altos de Chavón: An Artists' Colony

In 1976 a plateau about 150km (93 miles) east of Santo Domingo was selected by Charles G. Bluhdorn, then chairman of Gulf + Western Industries, as the site for a remarkable project. Dominican stonecutters, woodworkers, and ironsmiths began the task that would produce **Altos de Chavón** (✆ **809/563-2802;** www.altosdechavon.com), a flourishing Caribbean art center set above the canyon of the Río Chavón and the Caribbean Sea.

A walk down one of the cobblestone paths of Altos de Chavón reveals architecture reminiscent of another era at every turn. Coral block and terra-cotta brick buildings house artists' studios, craft workshops, galleries, stores, and restaurants. Mosaics of black river pebbles, sun-bleached coral, and red sandstone spread out to the plazas. The **Church of St. Stanislaus** is the central attraction on the main plaza, with its fountain of the four lions, colonnade of obelisks, and panoramic views. Mass is held every Saturday and Sunday at 5pm.

The **galleries** (✆ **809/523-8011**) at Altos de Chavón offer an engaging mix of exhibits. In three distinct spaces—the Principal Gallery, the Rincón Gallery, and the Loggia—the work of well-known and emerging Dominican and international artists is showcased. The gallery has a consignment space where finely crafted silk-screen and other works are sold. Exhibits change about every month.

Altos de Chavón's *talleres* are craft ateliers, where local artisans produce ceramic, silk-screen, and woven-fiber products. From the clay apothecary jars with carnival devil lids to the colored tapestries of Dominican houses, the rich island folklore is much in evidence. The posters, notecards, and printed T-shirts that come from the silk-screen workshops are among the most sophisticated in the Caribbean. All the products of Altos de Chavón's *talleres* are sold at **La Tienda** (✆ **809/523-3333,** ext. 5398), the foundation village store.

The Altos de Chavón **Regional Museum of Archaeology** (✆ **809/523-8011**) houses the objects of Samuel Pion, an amateur archaeologist and collector of treasures from the vanished Taíno tribes, the island's first settlers. The timeless quality of some of the museum's objects makes them seem strangely contemporary in design—one discovers sculptural forms that recall the work of Brancusi or Arp. The museum is open Tuesday to Sunday from 9am to 8pm; entrance is free.

At the heart of the village's performing-arts complex is the 5,000-seat open-air **amphitheater.** Since its inauguration by Frank Sinatra and Carlos Santana, the amphitheater has hosted concerts (by Julio Iglesias and Gloria Estefan, among others), symphonies, theater, and festivals. The annual Heineken Jazz Festival has brought together such diverse talents as Dizzy Gillespie, Toots Thielmans, Randy Brecker, Shakira, Carlos Ponce, Carlo Vives, and Jon Secada.

The creations at **Everett Designs** (✆ **809/523-8331;** www.everettdesigns.com) are so original that many visitors mistake this place for a museum. Every piece of jewelry is handcrafted by Bill Everett in a minifactory at the rear of the shop.

WHERE TO DINE

Giacosa ★ ITALIAN/INTERNATIONAL This is one of the few restaurants within Altos de Chavón that's not owned and operated by Casa de Campo. Within a two-story stone Tuscan-style building whose windows open onto a spectacular view over the Chavón river's chasm, you can try Mediterranean dishes such as seafood soup studded with lobster and shrimp; eggplant filled with goat cheese, pine nuts, and prosciutto; and black Angus filet with wine sauce and truffles.

Altos de Chavón. ✆ **809/523-8466.** Reservations recommended. Main courses $13–$40. 6-course tasting menu $50. AE, MC, V. Daily noon–midnight.

La Piazzetta ITALIAN Much of the allure of this place derives from the way its outdoor tables are positioned on a stone terrace that showcases a spectacular view over the river valley of the Chavón. But if you prefer indoor dining, this restaurant offers an air-conditioned replica of an antique stone-sided farmhouse, the kind you'd have expected in Tuscany or perhaps Andalusía. Our favorites are the gnocchi stuffed with three kinds of cheeses; risotto flavored with pumpkin and shrimp; grilled chicken; filet of hake with local greens and sautéed potatoes; and lasagna Bolognese.

In Altos de Chavón, near the church. ✆ **809/523-8698.** Reservations recommended. Main courses $12–$30. AE, DC, MC, V. Daily 6–11pm.

PUNTA CANA ★

On the easternmost tip of the island is Punta Cana, site of several major vacation developments, with more scheduled to arrive in the near future. Known for its spectacular beaches and clear waters, Punta Cana is an escapist's dream. Its 32km (20 miles) of white sands, set against a backdrop of swaying palm trees, are unrivaled in the Caribbean.

Many Europeans (especially Spaniards) rushed to take advantage of Punta Cana's desirable climate—within one of the most arid landscapes in the Caribbean, it rarely rains during the day. Capitalizing on cheap land and the virtually insatiable desire of Europeans for sunny holidays during the depths of winter, European hotel chains participated in something akin to a land rush, acquiring large tracts of sugar-cane plantations and pastureland. Today at least a dozen megahotels, most with no fewer than 500 rooms, some with even more, attract a clientele that's about 70% European or Latin American. Some of them have among the most lavish beach and pool facilities in the Caribbean, spectacular gardens, and relatively new concepts in architecture (focusing on postmodern interplays between indoor and outdoor spaces).

Don't expect a real town here. Although the mailing address for most hotels is the dusty and distinctly unmemorable Higüey, very few guests ever spend time there. Most remain on the premises of their all-inclusive hotels.

If you choose to vacation in Punta Cana, you won't be alone, as increasing numbers of celebrities are making inroads, usually renting private villas within private compounds. Julio Iglesias has been a fixture here for a while. And one of the most widely publicized feuds in the Dominican Republic swirled a few years ago around celebrity designer Oscar de la Renta, who abandoned his familiar haunts at Casa de Campo for palm-studded new digs at Punta Cana.

Above all, don't expect a particularly North American vacation. The Europeans were here first, and many of them still have a sense of possessiveness about their secret hideaway. For the most part, the ambience is Europe in the Tropics, as seen through a Dominican filter. You'll find, for example, more formal dress codes, greater interest in soccer matches than in the big football game, and red wine rather than scotch and soda at dinner. Hotels are aware of the cultural differences between their North American and European guests, and sometimes strain to soften the differences that arise.

Essentials

GETTING THERE **American Eagle** (© **800/433-7300** in the U.S. and Canada; www.aa.com) offers two to six daily nonstop flights to Punta Cana from San Juan, Puerto Rico; flying time is about an hour. You can also opt for one of American Eagle's two or three (depending on the season) daily flights from San Juan to La Romana and then make the 90-minute drive to Punta Cana. **US Airways** (© **800/622-1015** in the U.S. and Canada; www.usairways.com) flies to Punta Cana from Boston, Philadelphia, and Charlotte, offering nonstop weekly service.

GETTING AROUND Most **taxi fares,** including those connecting the airport with most of the major hotels, range from $22 and up for up to four passengers. Your hotel can summon a cab for you. If you want to tour along the coast, you can **rent a car** on-site at the car rental desks of all the major resorts.

Where to Stay

Golden Bear Lodge & Spa Cap Cana ★★ Golfers flock here to Cap Cana, outside Puerto Cana, to enjoy two state-of-the-art, Jack Nicklaus-designed golf courses, Las Iguanas and Punta Espada. Punta Espada, opened in 2009, is an oceanfront course, and Las Iguanas, opened in 2010, incorporates many ecological areas into its design. If golf isn't your thing, there is an infinity pool, plus tennis courts, a full-service spa, and many more attractions. The bedrooms are spacious, with marble bathrooms and whirlpools for two, plus terraces or patios. Some of the suites have private plunge pools. A first-rate cuisine using quality ingredients is presented at tables where diners can enjoy panoramic views.

Proyecto Cap Cana, Juanillo, Punta Cana, Dominican Republic. www.capcana.com. © **809/469-7425.** Fax 809/469-7383. 124 units. Winter $350 double, from $1,600 suite; off season $220 double, from $890 suite. Rates are all-inclusive. AE, DC, MC, V. **Amenities:** 2 restaurants; 2 bars; free airport transfers; babysitting; concierge; 2 18-hole golf courses; outdoor pool; room service; sauna; spa; steam room; 4 tennis courts (lit); watersports equipment/rentals. *In room:* A/C, TV/DVD, CD player, hair dryer, kitchenette, MP3 docking station, Wi-Fi (free).

Hard Rock Hotel & Casino Punta Cana ★★ One of the largest hotels ever to open in the Caribbean made its debut in the spring of 2010. Opening onto Macao Beach, it's a virtual city unto itself, boasting a 5,574-sq.-m (60,000-sq.-ft.) spa, a 4,181-sq.-m (45,000-sq.-ft.) casino, a par-72 Jack Nicklaus golf course, eight pools, a lazy river, and 11 bars and restaurants serving a wide variety of food and drink. The spacious bedrooms open onto views of the Caribbean and a secluded lagoon. Most rooms feature private balconies, and each comes with satellite TV and a double Jacuzzi. There is also the Internet Cyber Café and Lounge. Luxury is the keynote here.

Blvd. Turístico del Este, Km 28, Macao Beach, Punta Cana, Dominican Republic. www.palaceresorts.com. © **800/635-1836** or 809/687-0000. Fax 809/731-0001. 1,791 units. Winter $460–$570 double; off season $385–$465 double. Rates are all-inclusive. AE, DC, MC, V. **Amenities:** 8 restaurants; 3 bars; free airport transfers; babysitting; beach club; concierge; 18-hole golf course; 8 outdoor pools; casino; room service; sauna; spa; 8 tennis courts (lit); watersports equipment/rentals. *In room:* A/C, TV/DVD, CD player, hair dryer, Wi-Fi (free).

IFA Villas Bávaro ★ ☺ This midsize resort is one of the most fun-loving along the coast. It's not the most tasteful—certainly not the most elegant—but those who like a party day and night check in here and often don't want to go home. The balconied rooms are midsize and spread over 23 villa-style houses, each with 10 rental units. Walls are white or cream, with the fabrics and draperies providing the tropical color accents. Parties, dancing, live shows with carnival themes, and a "Jungle Disco" are just some of the amusements provided.

Playa Bávaro, Punta Cana (P.O. Box 3177), Dominican Republic. www.ifahotels.com. ✆ **877/200-6102** or 809/221-8555. Fax 809/221-7040. 262 units. Year-round $160–$280 double. Children 2–12 $34 extra. AE, DC, MC, V. Free parking. **Amenities:** 4 restaurants; 5 bars; babysitting; beach club; bikes; health club; 3 outdoor pools (1 for kids); room service; 4 tennis courts (lit); watersports equipment/rentals. *In room:* A/C, ceiling fan, TV, fridge, hair dryer, Internet ($13 per day).

Natura Park EcoResort & Spa ★★ ☺ At last—a resort with originality, an escape from the imitative peas-in-a-pod of the Coconut Coast's hotel sprawl. Set near a protected island estuary, the resort opens onto one of the coast's premier white-sand beaches. Nature lovers flock to its 32 hectares (79 acres) of park grounds; the setting evokes *The Jungle Book*. Its rooms are distributed across 13 two-story buildings painted in blinding white and surrounded by an oasis of coconut palms. In general, accommodations are spacious and given homelike touches by the use of area rugs, comfy sitting areas, and king-size or paired double beds, the setting enhanced by tropical fabrics and the art of island artists.

Cabeza de Toro, Punta Cana, Dominican Republic. www.blauhotels.com. ✆ **809/221-2626.** Fax 809/221-6060. 490 units. Year-round $80–$270 double. Children 2–12 pay 50% of adult rate. AE, DC, MC, V. Free parking. **Amenities:** 4 restaurants; 6 bars; bikes; children's center; health club; 2 outdoor pools; disco; room service; sauna; spa; 3 tennis courts (lit); watersports equipment/rentals. *In room:* A/C, TV, hair dryer, minibar, Wi-Fi ($16 per day).

Paradisus Palma Real Resort ★★ ☺ This is our favorite all-inclusive hotel in Punta Cana. It's the beneficiary of one of the most sophisticated creative contemporary designs in the area. The hotel's Iberian architecture seems to ripple and undulate from its entrance, past multiple and highly theatrical staircases and five different restaurants, one of which remains open through the long Caribbean night. The pools are spectacular, as is the beach. A complicated structure of add-on luxuries (spa packages, additional attention from the concierge staff, upgraded children's diversions) are available and usually come with occupancy of somewhat upgraded accommodations.

Playas de Bávaro, Higüey, Dominican Republic. www.paradisuspalmareal.com. ✆ **888/741-5600** or 809/688-5000. Fax 809/688-5800. 554 units. Year-round $585–$2,020 double. Children 2–12 pay 50% of adult rate. Rates are all-inclusive. AE, DC, MC, V. Free parking. **Amenities:** 7 restaurants; 9 bars; children's center; nearby 18-hole golf club; horseback riding; 3 outdoor pools; casino; karaoke disco; room service; sauna; spa; 3 tennis courts (lit); watersports equipment/rentals. *In room:* A/C, TV, hair dryer, Internet ($13 per day), minibar.

Punta Cana Resort & Club ★★★ ☺ This sprawling complex is an oasis of luxury, opening onto 4.8km (3 miles) of white-sand beaches, all part of a massive 6,070-hectare (15,000-acre) residential community. The hotel itself stands on 42 hectares (104 acres) of lush gardens. The sprawling hotel complex comprises both three- and four-story buildings, each decorated with tropical flair, with gabled balconies attached. The choice is for a studio, suite, or villa, each with tropical "Dorothy Lamour fabrics," cool tile floors, and carved and painted headboards. The villas are also equipped with kitchenettes. Oscar de la Renta designed a pocket of posh within this complex. The Tortuga Bay complex offers 15 luxurious beachfront villas in two-, three-, or four-bedroom villas, with wicker and wood furnishings.

Carretera Punta Cana/Bávaro, Punta Cana, Dominican Republic. www.puntacana.com. ✆ **888/442-2262** or 809/959-2262. Fax 809/959-3951. 355 units. Year-round $96–$200 double; $280–$400 2-bedroom beach casitas for 4 adults; $360–$500 3-bedroom beach casitas for 6 adults. Rates include breakfast and dinner. AE, DC, MC, V. Free parking. **Amenities:** 7 restaurants; 5 bars; babysitting; children's center; 18-hole golf course; health club; 2 outdoor pools; room service; spa; 6 tennis courts (lit); watersports equipment/rentals. *In room:* A/C, TV, hair dryer, kitchenette (in some), minibar, Wi-Fi (free).

Secrets Sanctuary Cap Cana Golf & Spa ★★★ The biggest news coming out of the Caribbean Basin is the development of Cap Cana, of which Secrets, a government-rated five-star resort, was the first to open. Ultimate plans call for this luxurious compound, lying a 5-minute drive from the Punta Cana airport, to include condos and villas, as well as a casino and three Jack Nicklaus–designed golf courses, with several more hotels on the way. Bill and Hillary Clinton have already purchased property here.

The entire community, amazingly, will comprise an area the size of Manhattan, opening onto 4.8km (3 miles) of beachfront. Secrets is constructed in a Spanish colonial style, with luxurious and beautifully furnished suites. The spa is among the best in the D.R., and the adjoining marina is the largest in the Caribbean. From here you can go out on a fishing vessel to some of the best fishing spots in the world. Private residences feature one, two, or three bedrooms, with large outdoor sitting areas. The resort is set on a bluff overlooking the ocean and miles of pristine white-sand beaches.

Cap Cana, Dominican Republic. www.secretsresorts.com. ✆ **866/467-3273** or 809/544-4343. 176 suites and villas. Year-round $1,035–$1,295 junior suite; $1,190–$7,255 suite; $1,865–$5,180 villa. AE, MC, V. **Amenities:** 8 restaurants; 11 bars; beach club; Punta Espada golf course; horseback riding; 3 outdoor pools; room service; spa; watersports equipment/rentals. *In room:* A/C, TV/DVD, CD player, hair dryer, Internet ($12 per day), kitchen (in villas), minibar.

Where to Dine

Given the wealth of restaurants in the hotels listed above, many guests never leave the premises for meals. But the following are worth a special trip.

Blue Marlin ★★★ SEAFOOD At Punta Cana's most exclusive resort, Secrets Sanctuary (see above), you can dine on some of the freshest seafood on island. This thatched-roof restaurant evokes the South Pacific and sits at the end of a pier overlooking the waters. Blue Marlin even has its own fleet of fishing boats to harvest the fish and seafood delicacies from local waters. What is not caught in local waters is shipped in from all over the world, including the Pacific Rim, Chile, Spain, and Peru. Noted chefs and skilled mixologists make for an evening of scrumptious eats and tasty libations. For the meat eater, there's always a big steak with a dash of Creole sauce, or else you may dig into a Caribbean lobster. The catch of the day often is baked in spicy banana leaves or else a ginger-laced soy sauce. Finish off with a slice of rum cake and a side of tropical fruit.

In Secrets Sanctuary Cap Cana Golf & Spa, Cap Cana, Playa Juanillo. ✆ **809/562-9191.** Reservations required. Main courses $25–$45. AE, DC, DISC, MC, V. Daily 6:30–10:30pm.

Chez Palace ★ INTERNATIONAL This is the showcase restaurant of one of the biggest resort complexes in the Dominican Republic. If you're not staying here, you'll have to make reservations. The decor is cool and stylish, as if it were imported from a chic resort in the south of Spain. A formally dressed staff serves superb dishes that include salmon mousse in a prawn sauce, tartar of tenderloin, grilled red snapper, grouper with mustard sauce, and filet mignon with truffles and foie gras. The prix-fixe menu offers many different choices.

In the Barceló Bávaro Palace Deluxe, within the Barceló Bávaro Beach Resort. ✆ **809/686-5797.** Reservations required. Prix-fixe dinner $35. AE, DC, MC, V. Daily 7–11pm.

Hard Rock Cafe Punta Cana AMERICAN It was bound to happen, a Hard Rock Cafe in Punta Cana. This one follows the decor and cuisine of other Hard Rocks, lying in a high-end mall in Bavaró in the Palma Real Shopping Village. It features American fare and rock memorabilia, such as the shirt worn by Gwen Stefani on *Saturday Night Live,* as well as items that once belonged to Billy Joel. For your starters, the familiar nachos, quesadillas, potato skins, and chicken tenders appear, followed by such mains as New York strip steak, fajitas, burgers, and grilled wild salmon with garlic butter. From the smokehouse come the cafe's famous barbecue ribs.

Plaza Palma Real, Carretera el Cortecito 57, Higüey. ✆ **809/552-0594.** Reservations recommended. Main courses $16–$29. AE, DC, MC, V. Daily 11:30am–2am.

La Yola ★ MEDITERANEAN/CARIBBEAN Modeled after a local fisherman's boat, locally known as a *yola*, this breezy dining choice offers good food inspired by Mediterranean recipes, although every dish carries a Dominican touch. Right on the sea, the restaurant offers an elegant ambience and is ideal for a romantic dinner with views out over the water. The tavern boasts a glass-floor viewing portal to check up on the denizens of the deep. You can try some island beef and chicken selections, but mostly the chefs concentrate on the catch of the day. Start perhaps with a delectable and spicy tuna tartare with guacamole, or else fresh salads. Lobster is featured here, and it is prepared grilled or turned into a risotto. Baked Chilean sea bass is a much-ordered dish, served with a risotto made with cherry tomatoes and clams.

Punta Cana Resort & Club, Puntacana Marina. ✆ **809/959-2262.** Reservations required. Main courses $25–$45. AE, MC, V. Wed–Mon 11am–3pm and 7–11pm.

Hitting the Beaches

One of the Caribbean's great beaches stretches along the **Costa del Coco,** or Coconut Coast, covering more than 32km (20 miles). This beachfront is the stuff of travel magazines, with brilliant white sand and lots of coconut palms. Under an almost constant blue sky during the day, European, American, and Canadian guests frolic at the gin-clear waters. The major beaches include Playa Macao, Playa Cortecito, Playa Bávaro, Playa Punta Cana, and Playa Punta Juanillo. The all-inclusives have staked out the best beachfront properties, so everything is done for you here, including unlimited access to food and drinks, and watersports concessions at each hotel. For facilities, bars, and restaurants, you can use the hotel at which you are a guest.

The beaches at **Punta Cana** are wide, gorgeous, and safe to swim offshore throughout the year. An improvised series of barricades run parallel to some stretches of the coastal road, prohibiting access to the various beaches fronting the hotels. Entrances guarded by security forces prevent nonguests from entering, since once inside, you're entitled to unlimited food and drink.

Activities abound, not only scuba diving, but snorkeling, windsurfing, kayaking, water biking, sailing, beach volleyball or soccer, and even water polo, along with aqua aerobics and tons of children's activities.

Golf

The **Bávaro Golf Course,** at Barceló Bávaro Beach Resort, Bávaro Beach (✆ **809/686-5797;** www.barcelo.com), is the best golf course on this end of the island and bears the honor of being the golf course whose allure helped open eastern D.R. to the tourist boom. Greens fees are $70 for 18 holes; cart rentals are $50. Guests of the hotel pay only 50% of greens fees. The course is open daily 7am to 5pm.

Punta Cana Golf Club, near the Punta Cana Resort and Club (✆ **809/959-4653;** www.puntacana.com), is the best and most sought-after of the four golf courses now flourishing in Punta Cana. Fourteen of its holes open onto panoramic views of the Caribbean Sea, and 4 play along the ocean itself. For 18 holes, hotel guests pay $125, and nonguests are charged $165. In summer greens fees are reduced to $90 for hotel guests, $125 for nonguests.

Punta Cana After Dark

Bávaro Disco, on the grounds of the Barceló Bávaro Beach Resort (✆ **809/686-5797**), has emerged as the hottest, most popular, and sexiest dance club in Punta Cana, thanks to a superb sound system. The venue is more European than North American, with a heavy concentration of clients from Italy, Spain, and Holland. If you've been tempted to dress provocatively but never had the courage, the permissive and sexually charged ambience at this enormous club will give you the confidence to try. Painted black, with simulated stars overhead and lots of mirrors, the place is open nightly from 11pm to 5am. Entrance is free for residents of the Barceló Hotel complex; nonguests pay $40.

PUERTO PLATA ★★

Columbus wanted to establish a city at Puerto Plata and name it La Isabela. Unfortunately, a tempest detained him, so it wasn't until 1502 that Nicolás de Ovando founded Puerto Plata ("Port of Silver"), 209km (130 miles) northwest of Santo Domingo. The port became the last stop for ships going back to Europe, their holds laden with treasures taken from the New World.

Puerto Plata appeals to a mass-market crowd that prefers less expensive all-inclusives. More accommodations of this kind continue to pop up on this coast, and yet many are still booked solid almost year-round.

Most of the hotels are not actually in Puerto Plata itself, but in a tourist zone called Playa Dorada, which consists of major hotels, a scattering of secluded condominiums and villas, a Robert Trent Jones, Jr.–designed golf course, and a riding stable.

The government has spent millions of dollars to rejuvenate the beaches of the D.R., including several long stretches along the north coast. These improvements have made room for more sunbathers on the sands. But don't expect Robinson Crusoe–style isolation, either; you'll never be alone on a stretch of beach in Puerto Plata, since the beach is shared with the residents of at least nine hotels. However, if you enjoy beige sand that's rarely too hot to walk on, and a never-ending array of watersports kiosks, chaise longues, and loudspeakers projecting merengue music, you'll be happy here. ***One important note:*** It rains a lot in Puerto Plata during the winter. If you want guaranteed sun, go to Punta Cana or the beaches on the southern coast.

Essentials

GETTING THERE La Unión International Airport is east of Playa Dorada on the road to Sosúa. **American Eagle** (✆ **800/433-7300** in the U.S. and Canada; www.aa.com) has daily flights (1 hr., 40 min.) from San Juan, Puerto Rico, to Puerto Plata. American Airlines also flies daily from Miami (2 hr., 10 min.) and from New York (3½ hr.). Most Puerto Plata resorts are about a 40-minute drive from the airport.

From Santo Domingo, the 3½-hour drive directly north on Autopista Duarte passes through the lush Cibao Valley, home of the tobacco industry and Bermudez rum, and through Santiago de los Caballeros, the second-largest city in the country, 145km (90 miles) north of Santo Domingo.

GETTING AROUND **Avis** (✆ **800/331-1084** in the U.S. and Canada, or 809/586-0214; www.avis.com), **Budget** (✆ **800/472-3325** in the U.S. and Canada, or 809/586-0413; www.budget.com), and **Hertz** (✆ **800/654-3001** in the U.S. and Canada, or 809/586-0200; www.hertz.com) all have offices at the airport.

You probably won't need to rent a car, however, if you're staying at one of the all-inclusive resorts. You might just like to get around Puerto Plata by **motor scooter,** although the roads are potholed. You can rent a scooter at the guest services kiosk at just about any large hotel in Puerto Plata.

Minivans are another means of transport, especially if you're traveling outside town. They leave from Puerto Plata's Central Park and will take you all the way to Sosúa. Determine the fare before getting in. Usually a shared ride between Puerto Plata and Sosúa costs $1.45 to $2 per person. Service is daily from 6am to 9pm.

If you take a **taxi,** agree with the driver on the fare before your trip starts, as cabs are not metered. You'll find taxis on Central Park in Puerto Plata. At night, it's wise to rent your cab for a round-trip. If you go in the daytime by taxi to any of the other beach resorts or villages, check on reserving a vehicle for your return trip. A taxi from Puerto Plata to Sosúa will cost around $25 each way (for up to four occupants).

VISITOR INFORMATION There's an **Office of Tourism** on Calle José del Carmen Ariza 45 (✆ **809/586-3676;** www.puertoplata.com). Hours are Monday to Friday 8am to 3pm.

FAST FACTS 'Round-the-clock **drugstore** service is found at **Farmacia Deleyte,** Calle John F. Kennedy 89 (✆ **809/586-2583**). Emergency medical service is provided by **Clínica Dr. Brugal,** Calle José del Carmen Ariza 15 (✆ **809/586-2519**). To summon the **police,** Calle Luis Ginêbra in Puerto Plata, call ✆ **809/586-2331.**

Where to Stay

Casa Colonial ★★★ This is the most sophisticated, most intimate, and most socially prestigious hotel in the Dominican Republic. It was the first hotel in the country to join the Small Luxury Hotels of the World marketing group, and as an a la carte boutique hotel, it is distinctly and definitely never included within the roster of Puerto Plata's mass-market all-inclusives. Baronial and aristocratic looking, it evokes a combination of a Greek Orthodox church and a Palladian-style Renaissance villa, with hints of Andalusia and a definite sense of Spanish colonial chic. Its annex artfully combines lush gardens and a view of a primal-looking mangrove lagoon adjacent to a stretch of beachfront. Bedrooms are all-white retreats that are high-ceilinged and large—in some cases, very large. The best accommodations are the lavish oceanfront master suites with private entrances. This is a very adult kind of place, where children 12 and under are not encouraged.

Playa Dorada (P.O. Box 22), Puerto Plata, Dominican Republic. www.casacolonialhotel.com. ✆ **866/376-7831** or 809/320-3232. Fax 809/320-4017. 50 units. Year-round $260–$450 junior suites for 2; $460–$690 specialty suites for 2. AE, DC, MC, V. **Amenities:** 2 restaurants; 3 bars; babysitting; golf privileges; health club; room service; spa. *In room:* A/C, TV, CD player, hair dryer, Internet (free), minibar.

Gran Ventana Beach Resort ★ ☺ This is the largest of three nearly adjacent hotels that are each administered by the VH chain. Of the three, this has the most whimsical and least formal decor. It occupies 100 landscaped hectares (247 acres) of oceanfront that's divided into three clusters. The quietest and calmest of the three is the Beata Wing, which is just a bit removed but easily accessible, on foot, to the more animated Catalina and Saona clusters. You'll find a higher percentage of children here than at many other of Playa Dorada's resorts, thanks to the Kid's Klub and a day-care center. The resort is composed of a series of three-story buildings, softened with landscaping, that are each trimmed with latticework and vaguely Victorian-inspired fretwork; each unit has mahogany furniture, ceiling fans, a balcony or patio, and, in many cases, views of the sea.

Playa Dorada (P.O. Box 22), Puerto Plata, Dominican Republic. www.granventanahotel.com. ✆ **809/320-2111.** Fax 809/320-2112. 506 units. Year-round $255–$365 double; $310–$490 junior suites; $400–$570 suites. Rates are double occupancy and all-inclusive. AE, DC, MC, V. **Amenities:** 4 restaurants; 7 bars; babysitting; children's center; health club; horseback riding; 3 outdoor pools; room service; sauna; tennis court (lit); watersports equipment/rentals. *In room:* A/C, TV, ceiling fan, hair dryer, Internet ($3 per 30 min.), minibar.

Iberostar Costa Dorada ★ ☺ With easy access to the beach, this hotel is owned and operated by a Madrid-based chain, Iberostar. Elegant and striking, it has one of the most exciting designs of any hotel in Puerto Plata, with some of the most intricate stone, tile, and mosaic work, and a rambling combination of Taíno, Andalusian, and Moorish architecture. Several roofs of this hotel are covered with woven palm fronds, noteworthy for a hotel of this scale, sheltering a design that opens onto views of arcades, hidden courtyards, and fountains. A day or night pass, which entitles you to a meal, a round of drinks, and a view of the unusual design, costs $50 per adult (either 6pm–2am or 10am–6pm), or half-price per child age 11 and under. Rooms are cool and airy, with tilework floors, earth tones, brightly colored upholsteries, wall weavings inspired by Taíno designs, and big windows.

Costa Dorada, Carretera Luperón, Km 4, Marapicá, Puerto Plata, Dominican Republic. www.iberostar.com. ✆ **888/554-3215** or 809/320-1000. Fax 809/320-2023. 506 units. Winter $230–$250 double; off season $200–$280 double. Rates are all-inclusive. AE, MC, V. **Amenities:** 4 restaurants; 5 bars; children's activities; outdoor pool; watersports equipment/rentals. *In room:* A/C, TV, hair dryer, Internet ($5 per 30 min.), minibar.

Lifestyle Tropical Beach Resort & Spa ★ ☺ Opening onto the beautiful Cofresi Beach, this is a government-rated four-star, all-inclusive hotel that oozes with style and comfort. We are especially impressed with the activities desk, which can arrange excursions, horseback riding, yoga classes, and even aerobics. Guests also have access to a 9-hole executive golf course. Bedrooms are tastefully decorated, using local woods and handcrafts; most of them open onto a private balcony or terrace overlooking the beach. Each room has a lot of extras such as beverage makers and roll-away beds if you're traveling with kids. Suites come with four-poster beds, a sitting area, and a sofa that can be converted to a bed.

Playa Cofresi, Puerto Plata, Dominican Republic. www.lhvcresorts.com/tropical.html. ✆ **809/970-7777.** Fax 809/970-7100. 282 units. Winter $240–$320 double, $300–$360 suite; off season $242–$290 double, $282–$330 suite. Rates are all-inclusive. AE, DC, MC, V. **Amenities:** 6 restaurants; 7 bars; free airport transfers; babysitting; beach club; bikes; children's club; concierge; exercise room; 9-hole golf course; disco; spa; 4 tennis courts (lit); watersports equipment/rentals. *In room:* A/C, ceiling fan, TV, fridge, hair dryer, Internet ($15 per day).

Where to Dine

Chris & Mady's ★ SEAFOOD/INTERNATIONAL This eatery is reason enough to drive over to Playa Cofresi if you aren't staying here, with some of the best and freshest seafood along this part of the north shore. The price of freshly caught lobster changes daily based on market quotations, but it is among the most affordable in the area. We also like to come here to feast on Dominican crayfish (called *langostinos*). Guests sit at wood tables under a thatched roof, feasting on fettuccine with shrimp, Cajun-style chicken breast deep-fried and served with a zesty tomato sauce, or fat shrimp cooked and flavored only with fresh garlic and olive oil.

Playa Cofresi. ✆ **809/970-7502.** www.chrisandmadys.com/cofresi.html. Reservations recommended Dec–Apr. Main courses $8–$44. AE, MC, V. Daily 8am–11pm.

Hemingway Café INTERNATIONAL/MEXICAN The rough-hewn character of this place stands in stark contrast to the manicured exterior of the shopping center that contains it. Inside you'll find a dark and shadowy plank-sheathed bar and grill, dotted with accessories you might have found on a pier in Key West. The menu lists pastas, fajitas, quesadillas, meal-size salads, burgers, and generously portioned steaks. After around 9pm, a karaoke machine cranks out romantic or rock-'n'-roll favorites.

Playa Dorada Plaza. ✆ **809/320-2230.** Reservations not needed. Main courses $12–$32. AE, MC, V. Daily noon–2am.

Le Papillon CARIBBEAN/CONTINENTAL This is an unusual but charming restaurant set on a hillside in a residential neighborhood about 5km (3 miles) southwest of Puerto Plata. The expatriate German owner, Thomas Ackermann, manages to combine aspects of the Black Forest with merengue music. The best way to start a meal here is with a *caipirinha* (a Brazilian cocktail) at the bar beneath the cane-frond ceiling. Later, within an open-sided pavilion overlooking a forest, you'll be presented with a menu that's divided into categories that feature different preparations of pork, chicken, beef, seafood, rabbit, and even vegetarian offerings. Enduring favorites include fettuccine with lobster; "pirate" kabobs with shrimp, tenderloin of beef, and vegetables; an especially worthy chicken stuffed with shrimp and served with saffron sauce; and a four-fisted version of chateaubriand that's only prepared for two. Some savvy locals have complained that this restaurant can get just a bit pricier than it should, but in light of its cultural oddities, it's probably worth it.

Villas Cofresi. ✆ **809/970-7640.** Reservations recommended. Main courses $14–$36. MC, V. Tues–Sun 6–10:30pm. From the center of Puerto Plata, drive 5km (3 miles) south, following the signs to Santiago. Turn left at the signs to Villas Cofresi.

Sam's Bar & Grill STEAKHOUSE The *gringo* and *gringa* expats have made Sam's their favorite dive since way back in 1970, when it was first established. In the center of town, only a block and a half from Central Park and the Malecón, it lies in a Victorian building from 1896. Marilyn Monroe photographs and caricatures by local artists form the decor. Here is where you can order a plate of meatloaf like your mama made or, the eternal favorite, steak and eggs. The cook does a tasty filet of beefsteak and more ambitious dishes, such as chicken *cordon bleu*. Come here for the memories, the good times, and, of course, the good-tasting food. You can start your day with fluffy pancakes, and later enjoy freshly made soups, salads, and sandwiches for lunch, along with hot dishes.

Calle José del Carmen Ariza 34 (in the Castilla Hotel). ✆ **809/586-7267.** Main courses $6–$20. No credit cards. Daily 8am–10pm.

Veranda/Lucia ★★★ CARIBBEAN/CONTINENTAL/ASIAN FUSION Set within different areas of Puerto Plata's most upscale hotel, these are the two most elegant and sophisticated restaurants along the north shore of the Dominican Republic. Much of their allure derives from Chef Rafael Vasquez, whose earthy but elegant culinary style has earned him the justifiable title of the country's most celebrated chef. Both restaurants emanate high-design, cutting-edge charm, although their respective colors and decors are carefully calibrated for view in streaming sunlight (Veranda) or within the shadows of the evening (Lucia).

Veranda, beside the beach, is a study in angular lines and cool tones of aqua and turquoise; Lucia, with its acres of white linen, evokes the high-ceilinged, candle-lit, intensely Europeanized dining room of a land baron on a colonial plantation. The menu might include grilled red snapper with grilled pineapple, and slices of lobster tail prepared tempura style and served with avocados. Delectable desserts include mango tacos with pistachio ice cream. An even more decadent dessert choice is known as a "volcano"; combining in sculptural elegance a deep-fried pyramid of semi-melted chocolate with ice cream, it tastes even better than it looks.

In the Casa Colonial. ✆ **809/571-9727.** Reservations required. Veranda main courses $10–$29; Lucia main courses $12–$38. AE, DC, MC, V. Veranda daily 11:30am–5pm. Lucia daily 6pm–midnight.

Hitting the Beach

Although they face the sometimes-turbulent waters of the Atlantic, and it rains a lot in winter, it's the beaches that put the north coast on the tourist map. The beaches at **Playa Dorada** are known collectively as the "Amber Coast" for the deposits of amber that have been discovered here. Playa Dorada has one of the highest concentrations of hotels on the north coast, so the beaches here, though good, are almost always crowded with both tourists and locals. The beaches have lovely white or powdery beige sand, and the waters are very popular with water-skiers and windsurfers. Many concession stands along the beach rent equipment.

Another good choice in the area, **Luperón Beach** lies about an 80-minute drive to the west of Puerto Plata. This is a wide stretch of powdery white sand, set amid palm trees that provide wonderful shade when the noonday sun grows too fierce. It's better for windsurfing, scuba diving, and snorkeling than swimming. Various watersports concessions are found here, along with several snack bars.

Sports & Outdoor Pursuits

The north coast is a watersports scene, although the sea tends to be rough. Snorkeling is popular, and the windsurfing is among the best in the Caribbean.

GOLF Robert Trent Jones, Jr., designed the 18-hole **Playa Dorada** championship golf course (© **809/320-3472;** www.playadoradagolf.com), which surrounds the resorts and runs along the coast. Even nongolfers can stop at the clubhouse for a drink or a snack to enjoy the views. Greens fees are $54 to $77 for 18 holes, $31 to $51 for 9 holes; a caddy costs $8 to $15. It's best to make arrangements at the activities desk of your hotel.

TENNIS Nearly all the major resort hotels in this area have tennis courts.

WATERSPORTS Your watersports options in Puerto Plata are numerous. Most of the kiosks on the beaches are run by the same company, and prices don't vary among them. If there isn't one close to your hotel, try **Playa NACO Centro de Deportes Acuaticos** (© **809/320-2567**), a rustic clapboard-sided hut on the beachfront of the Playa Dorada hotel complex. Prices are as follows: banana-boat rides, $10 for a 10- to 12-minute ride; water skiing, $30 for a 10- to 15-minute ride; sea kayak and Sunfish sailboat rental, $20 per hour; sailboards, $20 a day; and paragliding, $85 for a 10-minute ride.

There are watersports kiosks about every 100m (328 ft.) along the beach, any of which will rent you snorkeling gear and tell you the best spots for seeing fish. Puerto Plata isn't great for snorkeling, but you can take a boat trip to some decent sites.

Exploring the Town

Ocean World ★★, Calle Principal 3 at Cofresi (© **809/291-1000;** www.oceanworld.net), is the largest entertainment complex in the country, lying 5km (3 miles) west of Puerto Plata. It combines a plush casino and a world-class marina with such mass-market venues as a kiddie park and an aquarium for marine life. There is a series of watery "pens" and habitats for the care, feeding, and display of dolphins, sea lions, sharks, stingrays, piranhas, and other denizens of the Amazon rainforest. A number of close encounters with these nautical creatures, especially dolphins, is offered, but these encounters are not cheap, ranging from $45 to $250 per person, depending on your age and the length of exposure you opt for. Supervision of these encounters is carefully monitored by trainers, and reservations are recommended. For those 13 and up, admission is $55, lowered to $40 for ages 4 to 12 and free for those 3 and under.

Fort San Felipe, the oldest fort in the New World, is a popular attraction (© **809/261-6043**). Philip II of Spain ordered its construction in 1564, a task that took 33 years to complete. Built with 2m-thick (6½-ft.) walls, the fort was virtually impenetrable, and the moat surrounding it was treacherous—the Spaniards sharpened swords and embedded them in coral below the surface of the water. The doors of the fort are only 1m (3¼ ft.) high, another deterrent to swift passage. During Trujillo's rule, Fort San Felipe was used as a prison. Standing at the end of the Malecón, the fort was restored in the early 1970s. Admission is 75¢, free for children 11 and under. It's open daily 8am to 5pm.

Isabel de Torres (© **809/970-0501**), an observation tower that was heavily fortified during the reign of Trujillo, affords a panoramic view of the Amber Coast from a point near the top, 780m (2,559 ft.) above sea level. You reach the observation point by *teleférico* (cable car), a 10-minute ascent. Once here, you're also treated to 3 hectares (7½ acres) of botanical gardens. The round-trip costs $7 for adults, $2.80 for children ages 12 and under. The aerial ride runs Thursday to Tuesday 8am to 5pm.

There's often a long wait in line for the cable car, and at certain times it's closed for repairs, so check at your hotel before you head out.

You can see a collection of rare amber specimens at the **Museo de Ambar Dominicano (Museum of Dominican Amber),** Calle Duarte 61 (✆ **809/586-2848;** www.ambermuseum.com), near Puerto Plata's Central Park. It's open Monday to Saturday 9am to 6pm. Guided tours in English are offered. Admission is $1.10, or 20¢ for children.

Shopping

The neoclassical house sheltering the Museo de Ambar Dominicano (see above) has the densest collection of **boutiques** in Puerto Plata. Many of the paintings here are from neighboring Haiti, but the amber, larimar, and mahogany woodcarvings are local.

Plaza Turisol Complex, the largest shopping center on the north coast, has about 80 different outlets and the most upscale and tasteful merchandise. Make this your first stop if you want to get an idea of what's available in Puerto Plata—make it your only stop if you don't have time to visit all the shopping centers. It's about 5 minutes from Puerto Plata and Playa Dorada, on the main road heading east. Nearby is a smaller shopping center, **Centro Commercial Playa Dorada** (✆ **809/320-8243**), with about 80 shops selling handicrafts, clothing, souvenirs, and gifts. Both it and the Plaza Turisol are open daily 9am to 9pm.

Plaza Isabela, in Playa Dorada about 450m (1,476 ft.) from the entrance to the Playa Dorada hotel complex, is a collection of small specialty shops constructed in Victorian gingerbread style, although much of its inventory has a Spanish inspiration or flair. Here you'll find the main branch of the Dominican Republic's premier jeweler, **Harrison's** (✆ **809/586-3933**), a specialist in platinum work. Madonna and Keith Richards have been spotted wearing Harrison's jewelry. The store has a special clearance area; tours are available. There's another branch in the Centro Comercial Playa Dorada (✆ **809/320-2219**).

Puerto Plata, Playa Dorada & Costa Dorada After Dark

Casino action dominates the night. The most imaginative decor is the **Casino at Ocean World ★★**, Calle Principal 3 at Cofresi (✆ **809/291-1000**). Its cabaret show, with gorgeous dancers, is the best in the D.R., rivaling some of the spectaculars in Las Vegas. A well-recommended way to experience the charms of this place involves booking a place on the "Ocean World Magical Nights." For $89 per person, you'll get round-trip transfers by minivan from most of Puerto Plata's hotels, unlimited access to a well-stocked dinner buffet, access to a dolphin night show and a sea lion night show, access to the casino and the location's many bars, and access to a Las Vegas–style review, replete with views of performers artfully outfitted in a minimalist style. Your hotel desk can usually book such tours for you.

The Playa Dorada Hotel complex itself contains about 14 hotels, some of which have **discos** that welcome anyone, guest or not. These after-dark diversions tend to be filled mainly with foreign visitors, although they occasionally attract locals looking to hook up with tourists. None charges a cover, and the almost-universal drink of choice, Presidente beer, costs $4.25 a bottle.

At least three discos pulse out dance music every night of the week within the Playa Dorada complex beginning at 10pm. The wildest, most animated, and most raucous is **Mangú** (✆ **809/320-3800**). You'll find an attractive blend of both local residents, many eager to score with an off-island visitor, and holidaymakers, who merge and mix in an animated blend of hot bodies and hot merengue. Entrance is free for residents of the Holiday Village, but around $3 for nonresidents. Expect flashing lights, hundreds of writhing bodies, and a skin, glitter, and feathers show that begins nightly at 11:30pm.

Mangu's most visible competitor is the **Roadway Western Bar and Mix Grill,** in the Playa Dorada Plaza (✆ **809/320-4502**). Set within a simulated re-creation of a log cabin, on the back side of the resort's busiest shopping center, its walls are outfitted with slogans like "Gringas are forever." There's no cover charge, but a Presidente beer goes for $4.20.

A final contender for the nightlife circuit in Puerto Plata is **Crazy Moon,** adjacent to the lobby of the Paradise Hotel (✆ **809/320-3663**). Though not as sweepingly popular as either Mangu or the Roadway Bar, it can be a lot of fun, and the music is always danceable.

SOSÚA ★

About 24km (15 miles) east of Puerto Plata is one of the finest beaches in the Dominican Republic, **Sosúa Beach.** A strip of soft, white sand more than .8km (½ mile) wide, it's tucked in a cove sheltered by coral cliffs and has crystal-clear water. The beach connects two strikingly disparate communities, which together make up the town known as Sosúa. As increasing numbers of visitors flock to Sosúa, mainly for its beach life, it is beginning to rival Puerto Plata. You won't find the superdeluxe resorts that are commonplace in Puerto Plata, but prices in Sosúa are half of what they are at the big resorts, and the beaches are just as lovely.

At one end of the beach is **El Batey,** an area with residential streets, gardens, restaurants, shops, and hotels. Real estate transactions have been booming in this area, and many villas have been constructed, fronted by newly paved streets.

At the other end of Sosúa Beach lies the typical village community of **Los Charamicos,** a sharp contrast to El Batey. Here you'll find tin-roofed shacks, vegetable stands, chickens scrabbling in the rubbish, and warm, friendly people.

Sosúa was founded in 1940 by European Jews seeking refuge from Hitler. Trujillo invited 100,000 of them to settle in his country on a banana plantation, but only 600 or so Jews were actually allowed to immigrate, and of those, only about a dozen or so remained on the plantation. There are some 20 Jewish families living in Sosúa today, and for the most part, they are engaged in the dairy and smoked-meat industries, which the refugees began during the war. Biweekly services are held in the local one-room synagogue. Many of the Jews intermarried with Dominicans, and the town has taken on an increasingly Spanish flavor; women of the town are often seen wearing both the Star of David and the Virgin de Altagracia, the patron saint of the Dominicans. Nowadays many German expatriates are also found in the town.

GETTING THERE To get here from Puerto Plata, take the *autopista* (Rte. 5) east for about 30 minutes. If you venture off the main highway, anticipate enormous potholes. Taxis, charter buses, and *públicos* from Puerto Plata and Playa Dorada let passengers off at the stairs leading down from the highway to Sosúa beach. Most rides cost $1.70 to $2.80.

Where to Stay

La Puntilla de Piergiorgio ★ This hotel lies in a residential neighborhood, within a 10-minute walk from the bustling commercial center of Sosúa. Built on a rocky promontory high above the beach, it has a neo-Victorian design that includes lots of enticing gingerbread, lattices, and whimsical grace. Accommodations are bright, large, well maintained, and outfitted with white-tile floors, flowered chintz upholsteries, and a semicircular veranda with views of either the garden or the ocean. Each room has a small but neatly arranged tiled private bathroom with shower stall.

Calle La Puntilla 1, El Batey, Sosúa, Dominican Republic. www.piergiorgiopalace.com. ✆ **809/571-2626.** Fax 809/571-2786. 51 units. Year-round $95–$125 double; $210–$310 suite. Rates include breakfast. AE, MC, V. **Amenities:** Restaurant; bar; babysitting; outdoor pool; room service. *In room:* A/C, TV, hair dryer, Wi-Fi (free).

Sosúa Bay Resort ★★ This handsome colonial-style hotel is all-inclusive, with some of the consistently best food at the resort and a view that opens directly onto the tranquil waters of Sosúa Bay. This is one of Sosúa's attempts to attract more upscale clients who might normally patronize Playa Dorada. The pillared lobby is the most impressive at the resort. You can start your breakfast with a mimosa and be wined and dined throughout the day, staying up late dancing to the sound of merengue. The midsize bedrooms, scattered across a three-floor building, are decorated with colonial-style wood furnishings and colorful bedspreads and draperies. If available, choose one of the superior doubles with an ocean view; others open onto lushly planted gardens. Most accommodations come with private balconies. The hotel also has some of the best entertainment at Sosúa and offers one of the most diversified activities programs.

Dr. Alejo Martínez 1, El Batey, Sosúa, Dominican Republic. www.sosuabayresort.com. ✆ **809/571-4000.** Fax 809/571-4545. 243 units. Winter $140–$220 double; off season $160–$180 double. Children 4–11 30% discount. Rates are all-inclusive. AE, MC, V. Free parking. **Amenities:** 6 restaurants; 5 bars; bikes; health club; 2 outdoor pools (1 for kids); watersports equipment/rentals; Wi-Fi (free). *In room:* A/C, TV, fridge.

Victorian House ★★ This is Sosúa's most delightful boutique hotel, enjoying a dramatic position on a cliff overlooking Soaúa Bay. A replica of a Victorian gingerbread house, it offers a variety of rooms that are open and breezy in a chic, modern style. Doubles come with balcony, ocean view, and two-queen-size beds. Even better are the junior suites with a terrace and a living area; some are equipped with a living room, kitchenette, and Jacuzzi.

Calle Dr, Alejo Martinez 1, El Batey, Sosúa, Dominican Republic. www.sosuabayresort.com. ✆ **809/571-4000.** Fax 809/571-4545. 47 units. Year-round $180 double; $250 junior suite. MC, V. **Amenities:** Restaurant; bar; bike rentals; exercise room; 2 outdoor pools; room service; watersports equipment/rentals. *In room:* A/C, TV, fridge, kitchen (in some).

Where to Dine

Morua Mai INTERNATIONAL This is the most visible, and most deeply entrenched, restaurant in downtown Sosúa. Established by German entrepreneurs in the 1970s and set at the town's busiest intersection, it manages to remain somewhat aloof from Sosúa's burgeoning sex industry, thanks to a location in a neighborhood that's a few blocks removed from the densest concentration of prostitutes and their pimps. It was designed of timbers and palm thatch like an enormous Taíno teepee, under which ceiling fans slowly spin, and wicker and wooden furniture help create an ambience conducive to the leisurely consumption of tropical drinks and well-prepared food. Steaks and seafood are staples here. Depending on the arrival of fresh supplies that day, the menu might also include four different preparations of lobster; several kinds of shrimp, including a version with spicy tomato sauce and fresh vegetables; four different preparations of sea bass, including a version flavored with Chablis; orange-flavored chicken spiced with ginger; steak Diana, flavored with bacon; and pork in mustard-flavored cream sauce. An excellent version of paella contains chunks of lobster and fresh shrimp.

Pedro Clisante 5, El Batey. ✆ **809/571-2966.** Main courses $10–$36; breakfast $3–$10; pizzas and pastas $6–$11. AE, MC, V. Daily 8am–midnight.

On the Waterfront ★★ INTERNATIONAL/SEAFOOD The memory of Marlon Brando's Oscar-winning 1954 movie, *On the Waterfront,* is perpetuated here. This informal yet elegant restaurant sits on a cliff side, serving the finest cuisine among the independent restaurants of Sosúa. To everyone's delight, especially the owners, ocean currents and tides unexpectedly deposited vast amounts of sand at the base of this restaurant, creating an "instant beach" that has added considerably to its allure. Take in the sweeping views before deciding on the best of the catch of the day, which might feature fresh lobster, sea bass, conch, calamari, or red snapper, the latter tasting delectable when perfectly grilled as it is here. If you don't want fish, try a tender steak in pepper sauce or some lamb chops grilled with aromatic herbs. Other menu highlights include filet of sole in a tangy orange sauce or fettuccine primavera.

Calle Dr. Rosen 1. ✆ **809/571-3024.** www.waterfrontrestaurantdr.com. Reservations recommended. Main courses $10–$38. AE, MC, V. Daily 7am–10pm.

Sports & Outdoor Pursuits

There are watersports kiosks about every 90m (295 ft.) along the beach, any of which will rent you snorkeling gear and tell you the best spots for seeing fish. You can also rent sailboats, windsurfers, and other watersports gear at any of the kiosks.

Gipsy Ranch, Carretera Sosúa-Cabarete, opposite the Coconut Palm Resort (✆ **809/571-1373**), is the region's largest and best-recommended **riding stable,** home to about 20 horses, which can be hired for equestrian treks of between 1 and 4 hours. You'll begin your experience at the stone corral about 7km (4¼ miles) from Sosúa and 5km (3 miles) from Cabarete. A 1-hour jaunt goes for $25; a 4-hour excursion through forests and along beaches costs $48. Reservations are strongly recommended.

Many divers are attracted to the waters off Sosúa. In town the best outfitter is **Northern Coast Diving,** Calle Pedro Clisante 8 (✆ **809/571-1028;** www.northerncoastdiving.com). There are more than a dozen diving sites off the coast, including a wreck, a canyon dive, and a wall dive. Northern Coast offers PADI-certified dive masters or instructors, featuring a two-tank boat dive for $80 with equipment, $50 without. For $300 you get 3 days of diving and certification training. The outfitter also offers 3-hour snorkeling excursions for $45 per person.

Shopping

Patrick's Silversmithy, Calle Pedro Clisante 9 (✆ **809/571-2121**), was established by British expatriate Patrick Fagg in 1973 as a showcase for his unusual jewelry

Serious Windsurfing

Cabarete hosts an annual weeklong windsurfing tournament every June. Only amateurs are allowed to participate. For more information, contact the **Happy Surf School,** Hotel Villa Taina, Calle Principal (✆ **809/571-0722;** www.villataina.com), or any staff member at the **Azurro Club** (✆ **809/571-0808;** www.starzresorts.com).

designs. At least half of the inventory here is made within his studios, and each incorporates such local stones as larimar, amber, and black coral. About 80% of the inventory is made from silver, making these one-of-a-kind creations affordable.

CABARETE

The winds that blow constantly southward off the Atlantic swept in a hip young crowd in the 1990s, when Cabarete emerged as the premier windsurfing site in the Caribbean. But only a small portion of the visitors who come here today are actually interested in the waves and jumping on a board. Many bask in the glory of the surfers by day and strut their stuff in the hyperhip town bars by night.

To service the needs of the growing number of visitors, the town has attracted some of the most aggressive prostitutes in the Dominican Republic: all ages, all skin tones, all degrees of blatancy. If you're a heterosexual male in Cabarete, you'll absolutely never, ever, lack for female companionship, paid or unpaid.

News of Cabarete's allure has spread among the 20-something populations of Europe. Especially prevalent are visitors from northern Europe; there are fewer North Americans here than you'd expect.

The big attraction is **Cabarete Beach,** with its white sands and ideal wind and surf conditions. Cabarete isn't particularly distinguished architecturally, consisting of a series of relatively small-scale hotels, restaurants, and gift shops lining either side of the highway that parallels the north coast. Virtually everything in town lies along this street (Calle Principal), with the exception of small-scale shops that are on narrow alleyways that bisect the main street. But as word of the resort has spread, there have been increasing numbers of large all-inclusive hotels built on the outskirts of town.

GETTING THERE To reach Cabarete from Sosúa, continue east along the *autopista* (Rte. 5) for about 13km (8 miles). Taxis and *públicos* from Sosúa will also take you here.

Where to Stay

Azurro Club (Azurro Club Estrella and Azurro Club Cabarete) ★ One of Cabarete's more deeply entrenched resorts was built in the late 1990s in a stylish, avant-garde design. Today you'll find slightly more upscale accommodations in the Azurro Cabarete, and lodgings that are just a notch less comfortable across the road, in the Azurro Estrella. With direct access to a wide beach on the outskirts of Cabarete's main commercial core, it's noted for a soaring network of steel girders and an attempt on the part of the staff to keep its guests amused with a variety of organized, although somewhat haphazard, daily activities. Despite a slightly disorganized staff, this is one of our favorite large-scale hotels in Cabarete, thanks to its convenient location and sense of style. The respective buildings of this resort rise in four-story designs, usually around well-landscaped central courtyards. Bedrooms are well maintained, attractive, and airy.

Calle Principal, Cabarete, Dominican Republic. www.starzresorts.com. © **809/571-0808.** Fax 809/571-0904. 272 units. Year-round $300 double. Rates are all-inclusive. AE, MC, V. **Amenities:** 3 restaurants; 3 bars; babysitting; exercise room; 3 outdoor pools; room service. *In room:* A/C, TV, hair dryer.

Natura Cabaña Boutique Hotel & Spa ★ This is the ultimate eco-sensitive boutique hotel. Located between Cabarete and Sosúa, the hotel occupies the site that was conceived as the owner's private home. In 1990 she opted to improve her acreage with a series of artfully rustic wood and concrete structures for the shelter and amusement of like-minded New Age friends. Some are mushroom-shaped organic-looking structures; others are more functional ones of wood clapboards and thick beams. Regardless of the shelter you select, you'll get a sense of living at a sunny, not particularly stressful summer camp for adults and their children. Yoga classes are conducted without charge for residents twice a week. The on-site spa is New Age–centered, small-scale, and personalized.

In the La Perla Marina Complex, Cabarete, Dominican Republic. www.naturacabana.com. © **809/571-1507.** Fax 809/571-1056. 11 units. Year-round $180 double; $240 triple; $280 quad. MC, V. **Amenities:** 2 restaurants; bar; mountain bikes; horseback riding; outdoor pool; spa. *In room:* Kitchen (in some), no phone.

Where to Dine

Casa del Pescador ★ SEAFOOD Since 1988, Casa del Pescador has served sophisticated seafood in an engagingly hip environment that's the domain of a Swiss expatriate. It's right on the beach, in the heart of town. To begin, sample the chef's flavor-filled fish consommé. He does very well with shrimp, too, either with pastis sauce or with curry and fresh garlic. On a hot day, the seafood salads are a welcome relief and tasty, too, as are the grilled octopus in spicy Creole sauce and fresh lobster in garlic sauce. (Unless you love garlic, you might find the latter overpowering; ask for butter instead.) Although there's a full wine list, Presidente beer seems the best accompaniment to the fish, especially on hot, sultry nights.

Calle Principal. © **809/571-0760.** Reservations recommended for dinner. Main courses $10–$25. AE, DC, MC, V. Daily 10am–11pm.

Sports & Outdoor Pursuits

Not surprisingly, Cabarete is home to one of the Caribbean's best **sailing schools, Carib Wind Center,** Playa Cabarete (© **809/571-0640;** www.caribwind.com). It's devoted to teaching proper techniques and to renting state-of-the-art equipment. Equipment rental costs $40 for 1 hour, and instruction is $50 to $200 per person. Clients who book a week or more in advance receive discounts of around 20%. A worthy competitor, located just a few doors away, is the **Fanatic Windsurfing Center,** Calle Principal (© **809/571-0861;** www.fanatic-cabarete.com). Fanatic offers windsurfing instruction and rentals.

Although windsurfing attracts more media attention than any other sport in Cabarete, conventional surfing is also big and getting bigger. Because of the prevailing tides and wind patterns, it's best undertaken at **Playa Encuentro,** a 2km (1¼-mile) stretch of beachfront that's 4km (2½ miles) west of Cabarete and 5km (3 miles) east of Sosúa. Here surfboards are rented from a crowd of active aficionados at the **Club M-Endy,** Playa El Encuentro, Carretera Sosúa-Cabarete (✆ **809/571-1625**). Renting a surfboard costs $25 per day, and lessons can be arranged for around $35 an hour.

Iguana Mama at Cabarete (✆ **809/571-0908;** www.iguanamama.com) offers the best **mountain biking** and **hiking.** Going strong since 1993, it features a trek to Mount Isabel de Torres with experienced guides that lasts a full day and costs $75 per person. If enough people book, this tour is offered daily. Another trek involves a 900m (2,952-ft.) downhill cruise, costing $90 per person and held only Monday, Wednesday, and Friday.

Finally, **Gipsy Ranch** (✆ **809/571-1373**) is the most complete riding stable in the Dominican Republic; they'll take you **horseback riding** at a cost of $25 per person for an hour or $48 for a 4-hour ride.

Cabarete After Dark

Las Brisas, Calle Principal (✆ **809/571-0614**), is the most popular nightlife venue in Cabarete. Arrive after 10:30pm, when the dance club action begins; from 8am to 10:30pm daily, food is served. The dance floor is illuminated with strobe lights and lasers, and the bar is always busy. Many patrons arrive with dates of their own, but if you're a man flying solo, never fear, as a bevy of attractive working women are invariably on hand to provide companionship.

Hip nightlife is also found at the little bars—shanties, really—along the beach. There's live music every night after sunset. Tuesday nights it's salsa and merengue at **Onno's Bar** (✆ **809/571-0461**). **The Bamboo Bar** is the place to be on Friday night, and on Saturday the new **Wave Bar** and **Tribal Café** (no phones) draw the most patrons. On virtually any night of the week, you can find dialogue and a sense of cosmopolitan hip at the **Café Pitu,** Calle Principal (✆ **809/571-0861;** www.cafepitu.com). Set a few steps from the also-recommended Onno's Bar, it's the bar that's almost always cited as a centerpiece of Cabarete nightlife. It also offers Wi-Fi access throughout its premises, thereby creating a sometimes studious venue of scantily clad athletes swigging rum punches and surfing the Net. ***Note:*** Only some of these bars have phone numbers, and none bears an individual street number on the Calle Principal, but each of them is easy to spot as you walk up and down either the beach or the town's main street.

SANTO DOMINGO ★★★

Santo Domingo is one of the Caribbean's most vibrant cities, with a 12-block Colonial Zone to rival that of Old San Juan in Puerto Rico. Come here to walk in the footsteps of Cortés, Ponce de León, and, of course, Columbus himself. Allow at least a day to capture some of the highlights of the old city, such as its Alcazar and its Catedral Santa Maria la Menor.

Santo Domingo is also one of the grand shopping bazaars of the Caribbean, with such "hot" items as hand-wrapped cigars for sale virtually everywhere, along with local handicrafts. Jewelry made of larimar or amber is also much sought after. From gambling to merengue, Santo Domingo is also one of the liveliest cities in the Caribbean after dark. Be careful, however: Most of the Dominican Republic's crime is concentrated in

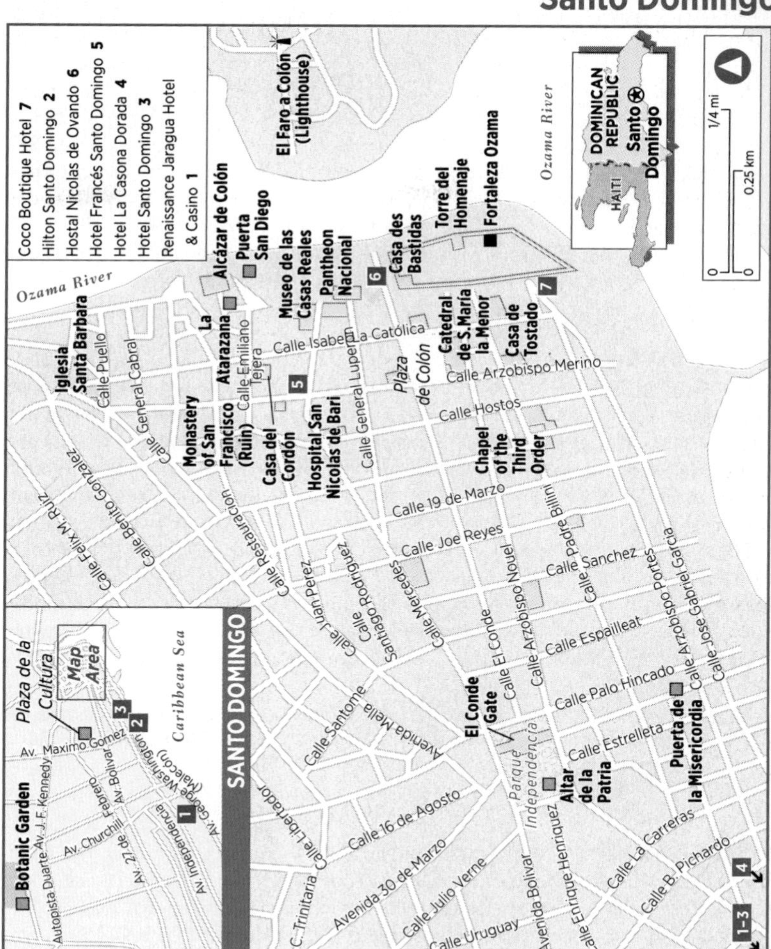

Santo Domingo. Keep valuables in your hotel safe, carry a minimum of cash with you, don't wear flashy jewelry, and if in doubt, take a cab.

Bartholomeo Columbus, brother of Christopher, founded the city of New Isabella (later renamed Santo Domingo) on the southeastern Caribbean coast in 1496. It's the oldest city in the New World and the capital of the Dominican Republic. Santo Domingo has had a long, sometimes glorious, more often sad history. At the peak of its power, Diego de Velázquez sailed from here to settle Cuba, Ponce de León went forth to conquer and settle Puerto Rico and Florida, and Cortés set out for Mexico. The city today still reflects its long history—French, Haitian, and especially Spanish.

Essentials

GETTING THERE See the beginning of this chapter for details on the airlines serving Santo Domingo.

VISITOR INFORMATION The **Tourist Office** is located at Avenida Mexico, Esquina Calle 30 de Marzo (✆ **809/221-4660**), open Monday to Friday from 8am to 3pm.

FAST FACTS There's a **24-hour drugstore** called **San Judas Tadeo,** Av. Independencia 57 (✆ **809/685-8165**). The best hospital in Santo Domingo, and the one recommended by the U.S. Embassy, is **Clinica Abreu,** Calle Beller 42 (✆ **809/688-4411;** www.clinicaabreu.com). Most of its English-speaking doctors trained in the United States, and it never closes. For the **police,** call ✆ **911.**

Where to Stay

EXPENSIVE

Hilton Santo Domingo ★★★ A soaring, artfully designed tower set directly on the seafront, this is the finest, tallest, and most desirable hotel in Santo Domingo. Its inauguration added the first new major hotel to the nation's capital in 15 years, and its location at the corner of the pivotal Maximo Gomez filled what had until then been a gaping dark hole on a key building site in one of the town's showplace neighborhoods. It was configured as part of the Malecón Center, a waterside development that includes three separate towers for condominiums, a 21-story hotel, the newest casino in town, and a small but choice shopping mall. We prefer its ultracomfortable rooms to any others in town. This hotel is not, and doesn't even try to be, a full-service resort, but if you want to play tennis or golf, the concierge can set it up for you. Rooms, which begin on the eighth floor and go upward from there, are richly furnished and plush.

Av. George Washington 500 (at the northwest corner of the Av. Maximo Gomez), Malecón Center, Santo Domingo, Dominican Republic. www.hiltoncaribbean.com. ✆ **877/GO-HILTON** (464-4586) in the U.S., or 809/685-0000. Fax 809/685-0202. 228 units. Winter $190–$240 double, from $260 suite; off season $130–$190 double, from $260 suite. AE, DC, MC, V. **Amenities:** Restaurant; 3 bars; exercise room; outdoor pool; casino; room service. *In room:* A/C, TV, hair dryer, Internet ($15 per day), minibar.

Hotel Santo Domingo ★★★ Run by Premier Resorts & Hotels, the Hotel Santo Domingo is tastefully extravagant without having the glitzy overtones of the Jaragua (see below). Those seeking local character in a home-grown hotel should check in here. This waterfront hotel sits on 6 tropical hectares (15 acres), 15 minutes from the downtown area, in the La Feria district. Oscar de la Renta helped design the interior. Most of the rooms have views of the sea, though some face the garden. Accommodations have bright floral carpets, tasteful Caribbean fabrics, and mirrored closets along with firm double beds. The superior Excel Club rooms offer seaview balconies and other amenities. Excel guests also have access to a private lounge.

Av. Independencia (at the corner of Av. Abraham Lincoln), Santo Domingo, Dominican Republic. www.hotelsantodomingo.com.do. ✆ **800/877-3643** in the U.S., or 809/221-1511. Fax 809/534-5584. 215 units. Year-round $95–$105 double; $125–$175 Excel Club double; $325 suite. Rates include American breakfast. AE, MC, V. **Amenities:** 3 restaurants; 2 bars; babysitting; exercise room; Olympic-size outdoor pool; room service; sauna; 3 tennis courts (lit). *In room:* A/C, TV, hair dryer, minibar, Wi-Fi (free in deluxe to suites, otherwise $12 per day).

Renaissance Jaragua Hotel & Casino ★★ A Las Vegas–style palace, this 10-story hotel lies on the 6-hectare (15-acre) site of the old Jaragua (Ha-*ra*-gwa) Hotel, which was popular in Trujillo's day. Open since 1988, it's a splashy pink waterfront palace that doesn't have the dignity and class of the Hotel Santo Domingo; for example, the casino and bars are often rife with prostitutes plying their trade. Located off the Malecón and convenient to the city's major attractions and shops, the hotel consists of two separate buildings: the 10-story Jaragua Tower and the two-level Jaragua Gardens Estate. Jaragua has the largest casino in the Caribbean, a 1,000-seat Vegas-style showroom, a cabaret theater, and a dance club. The luxurious rooms, the largest in Santo Domingo, feature multiple phones, refrigerators, and marble bathrooms with large makeup mirrors.

Av. George Washington 367, Santo Domingo, Dominican Republic. www.marriott.com. ✆ **800/331-3542** in the U.S. and Canada, or 809/221-2222. Fax 809/686-0528. 300 units. Year-round $80–$168 double; $240 junior suite; $280–$680 suite. AE, DC, MC, V. Valet parking $6. **Amenities:** 3 restaurants; 4 bars; dance club; babysitting; health club & spa; outdoor pool; casino; room service; tennis center w/4 clay courts (lit) and pro shop. *In room:* A/C, TV, fridge, hair dryer, kitchenette (in some), minibar, Wi-Fi ($15 per day).

MODERATE

Coco Boutique Hotel ★★ 🎁 This is a real discovery, a little B&B of charm and grace, decorated in earth tones with a brilliant use of white throughout. In the Zona Colonial, the hotel stands opposite the Plaza Pellerano Castro. Its rooftop terrace with Balinese sun beds is a magnet for guests. For such a small place, the hotel has a cosmopolitan atmosphere, and the service is most attentive. Each room, a few quite small, is individually decorated in a contemporary style. From the down pillows to the Egyptian cotton towels, extreme care went into the selection of each item in the hotel. The concierge can arrange excursions.

Calle Arzobispo Porte 7 (in the Zona Colonial), Santo Domingo, Dominican Republic. www.cocoboutiquehotel.com. ✆ **809/685-8467.** 5 units. Year-round $85–$100 double. AE, MC, V. **Amenities:** Bar; airport transfers ($40 for 2); concierge. *In room:* A/C, hair dryer, no phone, Wi-Fi (free).

Hostal Nicolas de Ovando ★★ In the heart of the colonial city, this 16th-century mansion was restored and opened as a hotel with all the modern amenities. For those seeking comfort among antiquity, this is an even better bet than the smaller Hotel Francés Santo Domingo (see below), another restoration. On the premises is a restaurant with a terrace facing a courtyard and two bars with a view of the pool. All the bedrooms are well furnished and handsomely maintained. The choice of accommodations ranges from standard doubles to spacious suites, which can also be used as family units. The classic architecture of the original mansion has been respected, although the property has been vastly enlarged.

Calle Las Damas, Santo Domingo, Dominican Republic. www.accorhotels.com. ✆ **800/515-5679** or 809/685-9955. Fax 809/686-6590. 104 units. Year-round $120–$290 double; from $250 suite. AE, DC, MC, V. **Amenities:** Restaurant; 2 bars; dance club; exercise room; outdoor pool; room service. *In room:* A/C, TV, hair dryer, Internet (free), minibar.

INEXPENSIVE

Hotel Francés Santo Domingo ★ A favorite small hotel in the old city, this intimate inn lies within a stone-fronted town house dating from the 16th century. Arches surround an Iberian-style fountain, and columns reach up to the second-floor patios, with palms and tropical plants surrounding the rooms. You'll think you've arrived in Seville. A gracefully winding stone staircase leads to the high-ceilinged and thick-walled bedrooms outfitted in a somber, rather dark colonial style. Accommodations are simple but tasteful, with rugs resting on tile floors.

Calle las Mercedes (corner of Calle Arzobispo Meriño), Santo Domingo, Dominican Republic. www.accorhotels.com. ✆ **800/515-5679** or 809/685-9331. Fax 809/685-1289. 19 units. Year-round $100–$150 double. Rates include breakfast. AE, MC, V. **Amenities:** Restaurant; bar; room service. *In room:* A/C, TV, hair dryer, Internet (free), minibar.

Hotel La Casona Dorada ★ This 18th-century building once belonged to former president Buenaventura Báez. A mansion converted to receive paying guests, the hotel lies on grounds set back from the street at the corner of Osvaldo Báez; it's a 5-minute ride to the Colonial Zone or a 30-minute ride to the beaches. Opened in 1993, the hotel caters to visitors and business clients. The small bedrooms are traditionally and comfortably decorated and are well maintained.

Av. Independencia 255 (at the corner of Osvaldo Báez), Santo Domingo, Dominican Republic. ✆ **809/221-3535.** Fax 809/221-3622. 51 units. Year-round $75 double. AE, MC, V. **Amenities:** Restaurant; bar; outdoor pool; room service. *In room:* A/C, TV, Wi-Fi (free).

Where to Dine

Most of Santo Domingo's restaurants stretch along the seaside, bordering Avenida George Washington, popularly known as the Malecón. Some of the best restaurants are in hotels. It's safest to take a taxi when dining out at night.

In most restaurants, casual dress is fine, although shorts are frowned upon at the fancier, more expensive spots. Many Dominicans prefer to dress up when dining out, especially in the capital.

EXPENSIVE

El Mesón de la Cava ★ DOMINICAN/INTERNATIONAL At first we thought this was a gimmicky club—you descend a perilous iron stairway into an actual cave with stalactites and stalagmites—but the cuisine is among the finest in the capital. The quality ingredients are well prepared and beautifully flavored. Recorded merengue, Latin jazz, blues, and salsa give the place a bit of festivity. Start with small shrimp sautéed in a delicate sauce of garlic or white wine, perhaps a mixed seafood or "sexy" conch gratinée. The gazpacho is also excellent, as is the bubbling *sopa de pescado* (red snapper chowder). Follow it up with the grilled Caribbean rock lobster or the double French lamb chops, which are done to tender perfection.

Mirador del Sur 1. ✆ **809/533-2818.** www.elmesondelacava.com. Reservations required. Main courses $20–$30. AE, DC, MC, V. Daily noon–midnight.

Paté Palo ★ INTERNATIONAL Part of Paté Palo's charm derives from its location, overlooking Plaza Colón, the graceful arcades of the Alcazar de Colón, where amiable clusters of Dominican families promenade every night at dusk. During the 1500s, the building was a bistro under the supervision of a mysterious Dutch buccaneer known as Peg-Leg (Paté Palo), who's credited with establishing the first tavern in the New World.

In the late 1990s, another Dutchman and his four partners transformed the place into a gregarious and engaging bistro that on weekends is one of the most crowded and popular singles bars in the country. Tables are thick-topped wooden affairs, set either on the plaza outside or within the antique walls of the dark and shadowy interior. The food is some of the best in the capital and is usually accompanied by live guitar music every Thursday to Sunday from 6 to 10pm. Having dined here many times, we can highly recommend the sautéed shrimp in coconut-curry sauce. On festive occasions, ask for the brochette of mixed meats; the meat has been marinated in fresh spices and herbs and is artfully flambéed at your table. The sea bass with white-wine sauce is perfectly prepared, although the fancy Continental dishes such as charbroiled steak with onion sauce and a grilled rack of lamb might be more suited for the cold Alps.

La Atarazana 21, Zona Colonial. ✆ **809/687-8089.** www.patepalo.com. Main courses $18–$36; burgers and salads $14–$16. AE, MC, V. Mon–Fri 4:30pm–1:30am; Sat–Sun noon–1:30am.

MODERATE

La Briciola ★★ ITALIAN/INTERNATIONAL This place has a touch of class, offering an elegant setting in two restored colonial palaces from the 16th century. Tables are romantically candlelit at night. In the Colonial Zone, it stands in front of Plazoleta Park. The menu reflects a commitment to prime ingredients and a determination not to let style overrule substance. The dishes here hardly test the creative culinary limits of the chefs but are tried-and-true favorites, beginning with many different pastas and sauces—all made fresh daily. Our favorite is the delectable linguini with "fruits of the sea." Sometimes you're in the mood just for a good steak, and the chefs oblige with a perfectly grilled T-bone cooked to your specifications. This is also a good place at which to order fresh fish. Dominican rice accompanies all the meat and fish courses. A piano bar overlooks a courtyard.

Calle Arzobispo Meriño 152-A. ✆ **809/688-5055.** www.labriciola.com.do. Reservations required. Main courses $12–$34. AE, DC, DISC, MC, V. Daily noon–3pm and 7pm–midnight. Closed Dec 24, 25, 31, and Jan 1.

La Résidence ★ 🎁 CONTINENTAL/CARIBBEAN It isn't particularly animated, but the food is surprisingly lavish at this showcase of local food. The setting is historic (a 1502 mansion transformed into a hotel), and if you happen to be within the historic zone, it's an excellent and easy-to-find dining choice. This is one of the few upscale restaurants in town offering spit-roasted lamb (rubbed with spices and served with bacon, garlic, and vinegar sauce) and rabbit (a boned saddle stuffed with bacon and mushrooms). Dominican-inspired dishes include roast lobster with wok-fried vegetables, a fricassee of pork chops with local spices, and braised "Dominican-style" red snapper. There's even a frequently changing array of vegetarian dishes.

In the Hostal Nicolas de Ovando, Calle Las Damas. ✆ **809/685-9955.** Reservations not necessary. Main courses $10–$30. AE, DC, MC, V. Daily noon–3pm and 7–11:30pm.

Lina Restaurant ★★ INTERNATIONAL/SPANISH This is one of the most prestigious restaurants in the Caribbean. Spanish-born Lina Aguado originally came to Santo Domingo as the personal chef of the dictator Trujillo, whom she served until opening her own restaurant. Today four master chefs, whom Dona Lina entrusted with her secret recipes, rule the kitchen of this modern hotel restaurant. The cuisine is international, with an emphasis on Spanish dishes, and the service is first-rate. Try the paella Valenciana, the finest in the Dominican Republic. We're equally enticed by the sea bass flambé with brandy, and few can resist the mixed seafood medley doused with Pernod. (It's cooked casserole style.) Lina's cuisine even wins the approval of hard-to-please Madrileños, who are a bit contemptuous of Spanish food served outside Spain.

In the Barceló Gran Hotel Lina, Máximo Gómez and 27 de Febrero aves. ✆ **809/563-5000,** ext. 7250. Reservations recommended. Main courses $12–$36. AE, DC, DISC, MC, V. Daily noon–4pm and 6:30pm–midnight.

Vesuvio I ★ ITALIAN Along the Malecón, the most famous Italian restaurant in the Dominican Republic draws crowds of visitors and local businesspeople in spite of its fading decor. What to order? That's always a problem, as the Neapolitan owners, the Bonarelli family, have worked since 1954 to perfect and enlarge the menu. They claim they catch it themselves, cook it from scratch, or even grow it if that's possible. Their homemade soups are excellent. Fresh red snapper, sea bass, and oysters are prepared in enticing ways. Specialties include Dominican crayfish *a la Vesuvio* (topped with garlic and bacon). Recent menu additions feature *pappardelle al Bosque* (noodles with porcini mushrooms, rosemary, and garlic), and black tallarini with shrimp *a la crema.*

The owner claims to be the pioneer of pizza in the Dominican Republic. At **Trattoria Vesuvio** next door (✆ **809/221-3000**), he makes a unique .9m-long (3-ft.) pizza! There's also **Vesuvio II** at Av. Tiradentes 17 (✆ **809/562-6060**).

Av. George Washington 521. ✆ **809/221-1954.** www.vesuvio.com.do. Reservations recommended. Main courses $12–$38. AE, MC, V. Daily 11am–midnight.

Sports & Outdoor Pursuits

BEACHES The Dominican Republic has some great beaches, but they aren't in Santo Domingo. The principal beach resort near the capital is at **Boca Chica,** less than 3km (2 miles) east of the airport and about 31km (19 miles) from the center of Santo Domingo. Here you'll find clear, shallow blue water, a white-sand beach, and a natural coral reef. The east side of the beach, known as "St-Tropez," is popular with Europeans. In recent years, the backdrop of the beach has become rather tacky, with an array of pizza and fast-food stands, beach cottages, chaise longues, watersports concessions, and plastic beach tables.

Slightly better maintained is the narrow white-sand beach of **Playa Juan Dolio** or **Playa Esmeralda,** a 20-minute drive east of Boca Chica. With all the hotels lining this beach, it's likely to be as crowded as Boca Chica any day of the week.

HORSE RACING Santo Domingo's racetrack, **Galapagos Hipódromo V Centenario,** on Avenida Las Américas, Km 14.5 (✆ **809/687-6060**), schedules races Tuesday, Thursday, and Saturday at 2pm. You can spend the day here and have lunch at the track's restaurant. Admission is free.

TENNIS You can often play on the courts at the major resorts if you ask your hotel desk to call in advance for you and make arrangements.

Exploring the Town

Prieto Tours, Av. Francia 125 (✆ **809/685-0102;** www.prieto-tours.com), one of the capital's leading tour operators, offers a 3-hour tour of the **Colonial Zone,** leaving most mornings at 9am and again at 3pm if there's sufficient demand; it costs $38. A 6-hour tour visits the Colonial Zone, the **Columbus Lighthouse,** the **Aquarium,**

and the city's modern neighborhoods; the $57 fee includes lunch and entrance to several well-known museums and monuments. About an hour of the tour is for shopping.

THE RELICS OF COLUMBUS & THE COLONIAL ERA

Santo Domingo—a treasure trove of historic, sometimes crumbling, buildings—is undergoing a major government-sponsored restoration. The old town is still partially enclosed by remnants of its original city wall. The narrow streets, old stone buildings, and forts are like nothing else in the Caribbean, except perhaps Old San Juan. The only thing missing is the clank of the conquistadors' armor.

Ancient and modern Santo Domingo meet at the **Parque Independencia,** a big city square whose most prominent feature is its **Altar de la Patria**—a national pantheon dedicated to the nation's heroes—Duarte, Sanchez, and Mella, who are buried here. These men led the country's fight for freedom from Haiti in 1844. As in provincial Spanish cities, the square is a popular family gathering place on Sunday afternoon. At the entrance to the plaza is **El Conde Gate,** named for El Conde (the count) de Penalva, the governor who resisted the forces of Admiral Penn, the leader of a British invasion. It was also the site of the March for Independence in 1844 and holds a special place in the hearts of Dominicans.

In the shadow of the Alcázar, **La Atarazana** is a fully restored section of one of the New World's finest arsenals. It extends for a city block, holding within it a catacomb of shops, art galleries, boutiques, and some good regional and international restaurants.

Just behind river moorings is the oldest street in the New World, **Calle Las Damas (Street of the Ladies),** named not because it was the red-light district, but for the elegant ladies of the viceregal court who used to promenade here in the evening. It's lined with colonial buildings.

Just north is the chapel of **Our Lady of Remedies,** where the first inhabitants of the city attended Mass before the cathedral was erected.

Try to see the **Puerta de la Misericordia** (Calle Palo Hincado, just north of Calle Arzobispo Portes). Part of the original city wall, this "Gate of Mercy" was once a refuge for colonists fleeing hurricanes and earthquakes.

The **Monastery of San Francisco** is a mere ruin, lit at night. That any part of it is still standing is a miracle; it was hit by earthquakes, pillaged by Drake, and bombarded by French artillery. To get here, go along Calle Hostos and across Calle Emiliano Tejera; continue up the hill, and about midway along you'll see the ruins.

You'll see a microcosm of Dominican life as you head east along **Calle El Conde** from Parque Independencia to **Plaza de Colón (Columbus Square),** which has a large bronze statue honoring the discoverer, made in 1882 by a French sculptor, and the **Catedral de Santa Maria la Menor** (see below).

Alcázar de Colón ★ The most outstanding structure in the old city is the Alcázar, a palace built for Columbus's son, Diego, and his wife, who was also niece to Ferdinand, king of Spain. Diego became the colony's governor in 1509, and Santo Domingo rose as the hub of Spanish commerce and culture in America. For more than 60 years, this coral limestone structure on the bluffs of the Ozama River was the center of the Spanish court, entertaining such distinguished visitors as Cortés, Ponce de León, and Balboa. The nearly two dozen rooms and open-air loggias are decorated with paintings, period tapestries, and 16th-century antiques.

Calle La Atarazana (at the foot of Calle Las Damas). ✆ **809/686-8657.** Admission $2. Tues–Sat 9am–5pm; Sun 9am–4pm.

Catedral de Santa Maria la Menor ★ The oldest cathedral in the Americas was begun in 1514 and completed in 1540. Fronted with a golden-tinted coral limestone facade, the church combines elements of both Gothic and baroque; the high altar is chiseled out of silver. The treasury has an excellent art collection of ancient wood-carvings, furnishings, funerary monuments, silver, and jewelry.

Calle Arzobispo Meriño (on the south side of Plaza de Colón). ✆ **809/689-1920.** Free admission. Cathedral Mon–Sat 9am–4:30pm; Sun Masses begin at noon. Treasury Mon–Sat 9am–4pm.

El Faro a Colón (Columbus Lighthouse) Built in the shape of a cross, the towering 206m-tall (676-ft.) Faro a Colón monument is both a sightseeing attraction and a cultural center. In the heart of the structure is a chapel containing the Columbus tomb and, some say, his mortal remains. The "bones" of Columbus were moved here from the Cathedral de Santa Maria la Menor. (Other locations, including the Cathedral of Seville, also claim to possess the explorer's remains.) The most outstanding and unique feature is the lighting system composed of 149 searchlights and a 70-kilowatt beam that circles out for nearly 70km (44 miles). When illuminated, the lights project a gigantic cross in the sky that can be seen as far away as Puerto Rico.

Although the concept of the memorial is 140 years old, the first stones were not laid until 1986, following the design submitted in 1929 by J. L. Gleave, the winner of the worldwide contest held to choose the architect. The monumental lighthouse was inaugurated on October 6, 1992, the day Columbus's "remains" were transferred from the cathedral.

Av. España (on the water side of Los Tres Ojos, near the airport in the Sans Souci district). ✆ **809/591-1492.** Admission $2 adults, 15¢ children 11 and under. Tues–Sun 9am–5:30pm.

Museo de las Casas Reales (Museum of the Royal Houses) Through artifacts, tapestries, maps, and re-created halls, including a courtroom, this museum traces Santo Domingo's history from 1492 to 1821. Gilded furniture, arms and armor, and other colonial artifacts make it the most interesting museum of Old Santo Domingo. It contains replicas of the *Niña,* the *Pinta,* and the *Santa Maria,* and one exhibit is said to hold some of Columbus's ashes. In addition to pre-Columbian art, you can see the main artifacts of two galleons sunk in 1724 on their way from Spain to Mexico, along with remnants of another 18th-century Spanish ship, the *Concepción.*

Calle Las Damas (at corner Las Mercedes). ✆ **809/682-4202.** Admission 85¢, children 11 and under free. Tues–Sun 9am–5pm.

You Call That a Bargain?

Always haggle over the price of handicrafts, particularly in the open-air markets. No stall keeper expects you to pay the first price asked. Remember the Spanish words for "too expensive": ***muy caro.***

Shopping

The best buys in Santo Domingo are handcrafted native items, especially amber jewelry.

Ever since the Dominicans presented John F. Kennedy with what became his favorite rocker, visitors have wanted to take home a **rocking chair.** These rockers are often sold unassembled, for easy shipping. Other good buys include Dominican rum, hand-knit articles, macramé, ceramics, and crafts in native mahogany.

The best shopping streets are **El Conde,** the oldest and most traditional shop-flanked avenue, and **Avenida Mella.** In the colonial section, **La Atarazana** is filled with galleries and gift and jewelry stores, charging inflated prices. Duty-free shops are found at the airport, in the capital at the **Centro de los Héroes,** and at both the Hotel Santo Domingo and the Hotel Embajador. Shopping hours are generally Monday to Saturday from 9am to 12:30pm and 2 to 5pm.

Head first for the National Market, **El Mercado Modelo,** Avenida Mella, filled with stall after stall of crafts, spices, and produce; you can easily get lost in the crush. The merchants are eager to sell, so remember to bargain. You'll see a lot of tortoiseshell work, but exercise caution, since many species, especially the hawksbill turtle, are on the endangered-species list and could be impounded by U.S. Customs if discovered in your luggage. Also for sale are rockers, mahogany, sandals, baskets, hats, and clay braziers for grilling fish.

Amber World Museum, Calle Arzobispo Meriño 452 (✆ **809/686-5700;** www.amberworldmuseum.com), lives up to its name. Many visitors flock here to see plants, insects, and even scorpions fossilized in resin millions of years ago. Although some of the displays are not for sale, in an adjoining salon you can watch craftspeople at work, polishing and shaping raw bits of ancient amber for sale. Entrance to the museum is free. It's open Monday to Saturday 8:30am to 6pm and Sunday 9am to 1pm.

Another reliable source for stunning amber, as well as coral, is **Ambar Nacional,** Calle Arzobispo Meriño (✆ **809/686-5700**). This is also the best source for purchasing larimar jewelry. In general, prices here are a bit less expensive than those at the more prestigious Amber World Museum nearby.

In the center of the most history-laden section of town is the well-known **Galería de Arte Nader,** Rafael Augusto Sanchez 22 (✆ **809/544-0878**), which displays so many Latin paintings that they're sometimes stacked in rows against the walls. The works of the country's best-known painters and most promising newcomers are displayed here (though, to be honest, the Dominican Republic is short on painters with international reputations). There is also a lot of tourist junk, shipped in by the truckload from Haiti. In the ancient courtyard in back, you can get a glimpse of how things looked in the Spanish colonies hundreds of years ago.

Nuebo, Fantino Falco 36, Naco (✆ **809/562-3333**), is patronized by some of the capital's most upscale buyers. This shop sells a carefully chosen assortment of art objects, lamps, and furnishings. With some persuasion, anything you buy here can be shipped.

Columbus Plaza (Decla, S.A.), Calle Arzobispo Meriño 204 (✆ **809/689-0565**), is one of the largest supermarket-style gift and artifacts stores in the country. Well organized and imaginative, with a helpful English-speaking staff, it sprawls over three floors of a modern building divided into boutiques specializing in amber, larimar, gold and silver jewelry, cigars, paintings and sculpture, plus craft items.

Cigars are big sellers in Santo Domingo. The best selection is at **Cigar King,** Calle Conde 208, Baguero Building (✆ **809/686-4987**), in the colonial city. Its selection of Dominican and Cuban cigars in a temperature-controlled room is wide ranging.

Santo Domingo After Dark

DANCE CLUBS

Local young people flock to the dance clubs in droves after dinner. Even the hotel dance clubs cater to locals as well as tourists. Great dancers abound, so go and watch even if you don't feel like dancing.

La Guácara Taína, Avenida Mirador del Sur, in Parque Mirador del Sur (✆ **809/533-1051**), is the best *discoteca* in the country, drawing equal numbers of locals and visitors. Set in an underground cave within a verdant park, the specialty is merengue, salsa, and other forms of Latin music. There are three bars, two dance floors, and banquettes and chairs nestled into the rocky walls. The cover is $8.40 and includes one drink. It's open Wednesday to Sunday from 9pm; closing time varies.

Fantasy Disco, Av. Heroes de Luperón 29, La Feria (✆ **809/535-5581**), is one of the capital's most popular dance clubs, about a block inland from the Malecón. Once you get past the vigilant security staff, you'll find lots of intimate nooks and crannies, a small dance floor, and one of the country's best-chosen medleys of non-stop merengue music. Entrance is free, and beer costs $2.10 to $2.80 a bottle. The place is open daily from 6pm to 4am.

Jet Set, Centro Comercial El Portal, Avenida Independencia (✆ **809/533-9707**), is one of the capital's most formal and elaborate nightclubs, admitting couples only, and nobody who is too rowdy. Most of the tables and chairs slope down toward an amphitheater-style dance floor, giving the place the feel of a bullfighting arena. The collection of live orchestras that play here is better than anywhere else in town. Entrance costs between $8.40 and $40, depending on the artist. The Jet Set takes off at 9pm and flies until the early morning.

ROLLING THE DICE

Santo Domingo has several major casinos, all of which are open nightly until 4 or 5am. Gambling here is a very minor attraction, and the odds are pretty much against you. If gambling is your raison d'être, you'd do better to plan a holiday in Puerto Rico.

The **Majestic Casino** in the Malecón Center, Av. George Washington 500 (✆ **809/687-4853**), manages to be somehow glittery but tasteful at the same time; it isn't the most animated casino in the capital, and on quiet nights it can be a bit staid, but you'll quickly get the feeling that it's deep into the process of finding a clientele of its own. It's open daily 4pm to 4am.

The **Renaissance Jaragua Hotel & Casino,** Av. George Washington 367 (✆ **809/535-9292**), has the most razzmatazz, and it's where Las Vegas–style gamblers converge to lose big bucks. You can't miss the brightly flashing sign; it's the most dazzling light along the Malecón. You can wager on blackjack, baccarat, roulette, and slot machines in either Dominican pesos or U.S. dollars. Daily hours are 4pm to 4am.

Another casino is at the **Hispaniola Hotel,** Avenida Independencia (✆ **809/221-7111**), open daily noon to 5am. One of the most stylish choices is the **Casino**

Diamante, in the Meliá Santo Domingo Hotel & Casino, Av. George Washington 365 (© **809/682-2102**). Its bilingual staff will help you play blackjack, craps, baccarat, and keno, among other games. There's also a piano bar. The casino is open daily noon to 6am.

GRENADA

12

The scent of nutmeg, vanilla, and cinnamon perfumes the air in sleepy Grenada, nicknamed the "Spice Island" for its fertile spice plantations. The largest of the three-island independent nation of Grenada (including Carriacou and Petit Martinique) tempts visitors with waterfalls, rainforests, and white-sand beaches. Devastated by Hurricane Ivan in 2004, the nutmeg crop is back in full flower, as is the island interior—a riot of blooms, from hibiscus to bougainvillea to frangipangi. The 18th-century harbor capital, St. George's, is one of the prettiest in the West Indies.

Beaches Some visitors never leave the sugary sands of **Grand Anse,** the two-mile stretch of beach near St. George's, which has watersports, craft vendors, and ice cream. **La Sagesse** has a tranquil olive-green horseshoe cove, and at **Magazine Beach** flickering schools of silver fish reward beachside snorkelers—both beaches have good restaurants. In the northeast, where the Atlantic meets the Caribbean, wild **Levera** is often deserted and fronts a miniature offshore cay, the moss-backed, cone-shaped **Sugar Island.**

Things to Do **Renting a car** is an excellent way to explore the island's **plantation houses** and **distilleries.** Watch sugar cane being crushed the old-fashioned way, by water-powered machinery, at the pungent **River Antoine Rum Distillery** in St. Andrew's. The idyllic **Belmont Estate** in the green hills of St. Patrick's is suffused with the scent of fermenting cocoa beans; see how chocolate is made, and try cocoa tea. Stock up on spices to take home at St. George's **Market Square.**

Eating & Drinking Grenada's national dish is the **"oil down"**: meat and vegetables lovingly simmered in spices and coconut milk over a fire in one enormous pot. Savory **stuffed crabs** and hot ***roti*** (filled pancakes) are mouth-watering island specialties. Don't miss the nutmeg ice cream at the **Aquarium,** a laid-back treat under the palms on beautiful Magazine Beach. Make friends over an icy **Carib beer**—but if you really want to get the party started, order a colorful **rum punch.**

Nature Watch as daredevil divers entertain tourists at **Annandale Waterfalls** near St. George's; the blissful walk through the steamy flower-filled rainforest to the higher falls at **Concord** or the **Seven Sisters** feels as rewarding as a dip in the sparkling water. Hike the trails of the **Grand Etang National Park** to see unexpected vistas of the coastline, kaleidoscopic bird life, and the extinct volcano's crater lake. Experienced divers explore the **"Titanic of the Caribbean,"** the coral-encrusted sunken remains of the passenger ship *Bianca C.*

ESSENTIALS

Visitor Information

In the United States, contact the **Grenada Tourist Office** at P.O. Box 1668, Lakeworth, FL 33460 (✆ **800/927-9554** or 561/588-8176; fax 561/588-7267).

In London, contact the **Grenada Board of Tourism,** 26–28 Hammersmith Grove, 4th Floor, London W6 7BA (✆ **020/8328-0650**).

On the island, pick up maps, guides, and general information at the **Grenada Board of Tourism,** Bums Point, in St. George's (✆ **473/440-2279**), open Monday to Friday from 8am to 4pm.

You can find information on the Internet at **www.grenadagrenadines.com**.

Getting There

Point Salines International Airport lies at the southwestern toe of Grenada. The airport is a 5- to 15-minute taxi ride from most of the major hotels.

American Airlines (✆ **800/433-7300** in the U.S. and Canada, or 473/444-2222; www.aa.com) flies from New York or Miami to San Juan, Puerto Rico, where you can take an **American Eagle** shuttle flight into Grenada. **US Airways** (✆ **800/622-1015** in the U.S. and Canada, or 473/439-0681; www.usairways.com) has weekly flights from Philadelphia.

British Airways (✆ **800/247-9297** in the U.S. and Canada; www.britishairways.com) flies to Grenada every Tuesday and Friday from London's Gatwick Airport, making a single stop at Antigua en route.

Air Jamaica (✆ **800/523-5585** in the U.S. and Canada; www.airjamaica.com) offers nonstop flights from New York to Grenada two to three times a week.

LIAT (✆ **888/844-LIAT** [5428] in most of the Caribbean, or 473/440-3967; www.liatairline.com), which early in the millennium incorporated the corporate structures of the regional airlines formerly known as Caribbean Star and SVG into its orbit, flies between Grenada, Carriacou, Petit Martinique, and several neighboring islands in the southern Caribbean. LIAT's twin hubs, into which most of the routes on its network are funneled, are Antigua and Barbados.

Finally, **Virgin Atlantic Airways** (✆ **800/862-8621** in the U.S. and Canada, or 800/744-7477 in Grenada; www.virgin-atlantic.com) flies nonstop once a week from London's Heathrow Airport.

Getting Around

BY TAXI Taxi rates are set by the government. Most arriving visitors take a cab at the airport to one of the hotels near St. George's, at a cost of $25 to $35. Add $4 to the fare from 6pm to 6am. You can also use most taxi drivers as a guide for a day of sightseeing; negotiate a price beforehand.

BY RENTAL CAR ***Remember:*** Drive on the left. A U.S., British, or Canadian driver's license is valid on Grenada; however, you must obtain a local permit, costing EC$30. These permits can be bought either from the car rental company or from the traffic department at the Carenage in St. George's. The Carenage is both the walkway and the road that loops around the horseshoe-shaped St. George's Harbour. It is the capital's principal thoroughfare.

Try **Dollar Rent-a-Car,** at the airport (✆ **800/800-3665** in the U.S. and Canada, or 473/444-4786; www.rocrentalsgrenada.com). You can also find a branch of **Avis**

Carnival on Grenada

The second weekend of August brings colorful Carnival parades, music, and dancing. The festivities begin on Friday, continuing practically nonstop through Tuesday. Steel bands and calypso groups perform at Queen's Park. Jouvert, one of the highlights of the festival, begins at 5am on Monday with a parade of Djab Djab/Djab Molassi, devil-costumed figures daubed with molasses. (*Be warned:* Don't wear nice clothes to attend this event—you may get sticky from close body contact.) The Carnival finale, a gigantic "jump-up" (like a hoedown), ends with a parade of bands from Tanteen through the Carenage into town.

(✆ **800/331-1084** in the U.S.; www.avis.com) at the airport, as well as an office for **Thrifty** (✆ **800/847-4389** in the U.S., or 473/444-4984; www.thrifty.com).

Warning: There's such a thing as Grenadian driving machismo; the local drivers take blind corners with abandon. An extraordinary number of accidents are reported in the lively local paper. Gird yourself with nerves of steel, and be on the lookout for children and pedestrians when driving at night. Many foreign visitors, in fact, find any night driving hazardous.

BY BUS Minivans, charging 60¢ to $5, are the cheapest way to get around. The most popular run is between St. George's and Grand Anse Beach. Most minivans depart from Market Square or from the Esplanade area of St. George's.

[FastFACTS] GRENADA

Banks Banks in St. George's, the capital, include **First Caribbean International Bank,** at Church and Halifax streets (✆ **473/440-3232**); **Scotiabank,** on Halifax Street (✆ **473/440-3274**); the **Public Bank of Grenada,** at Halifax and Hillsborough streets (✆ **473/440-3566**); and the **Grenada Cooperative Bank,** on Church Street (✆ **473/440-2111**). Most have ATMs that, in virtually every case, distribute only Eastern Caribbean dollars. Banking hours are usually Monday through Thursday from 8am to 3pm and Friday from 8am to 5pm.

Currency The official currency is the **Eastern Caribbean dollar (EC$),** which trades at a rate of EC$2.67 to US$1 (stated differently, EC$1 = 37¢), and at a rate of approximately EC$4.27 = £1 (stated differently, EC$1 = 23p). However, U.S. dollars are widely accepted on island. Always determine which dollars, EC or U.S., you're talking about when someone on Grenada quotes you a price. *Prices in this chapter are quoted in U.S. dollars.*

Documents A valid passport is required of U.S., British, and Canadian citizens entering Grenada, plus a return or ongoing ticket. Additionally, a valid U.S. passport is now required for readmission into the U.S.

Electricity Electricity is 220–240-volt AC (50 cycles), so transformers and adapters will be needed for U.S.-made appliances.

Embassies & High Commissions The **U.S. Embassy** is located at L'Anse aux Epines Salines, St. George's (✆ **473/444-1173**). The **British High Commission** is on Church Street, St. George's.

Emergencies Dial ✆ **911** for police, fire, or an ambulance.

Grenada

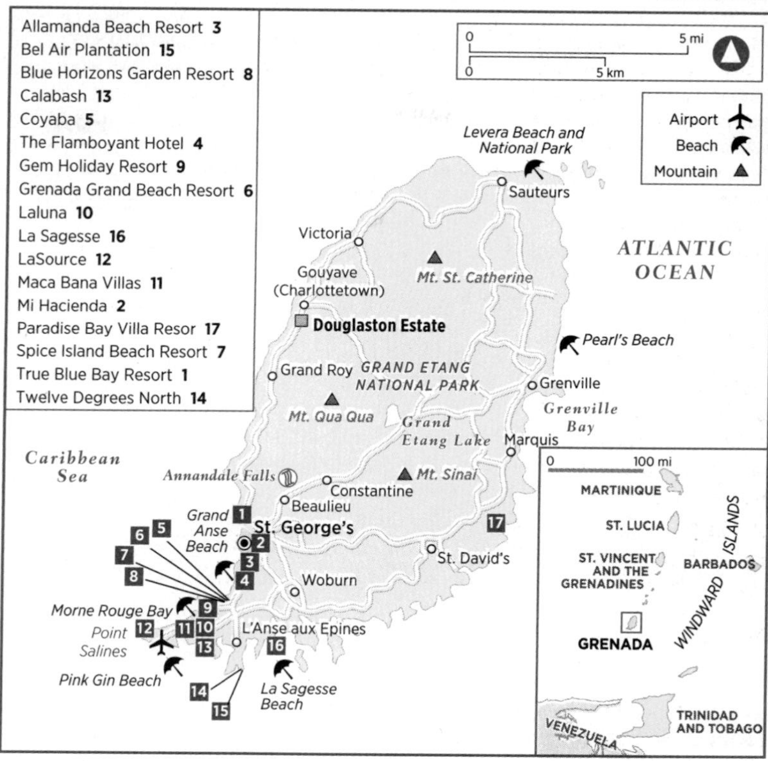

Hospital **St. George's General Hospital,** located on Grandetang Road, St. George's (✆ **473/440-2051**), has an X-ray department and operating room. Private doctors and nurses are available on call.

Language English is commonly spoken. Creole English, a mixture of several African dialects, English, and French, is spoken informally by most.

Pharmacies Try **Gittens Pharmacy,** which maintains its central headquarters on Halifax Street in St. George's and a branch on Wall Street in Grand-Anse (✆ **473/440-2165** for both branches), is open at both branches Monday to Thursday 7:30am to 7pm, Friday to 8pm, Saturday to 5pm, and Sunday 9am to noon.

Post Office The general post office, at the pier in St. George's, is open Monday to Friday from 8am to 4pm.

Safety Street crime occurs here, tourists have been victims of armed robbery in isolated areas, and thieves frequently steal U.S. passports and alien registration cards in addition to money. Muggings, purse snatchings, and other robberies occur in areas near hotels, beaches, and restaurants, particularly after dark. Don't leave valuables unattended at the beach. Be cautious when walking after dark, or take a taxi. Report a stolen or lost passport immediately to the local police and the embassy.

Taxes A 10% VAT (value-added tax) is imposed on food and beverages. Additionally, there's an 10% room tax. You'll pay a departure tax of $20 when you leave the island.

Telephone The area code for all of Grenada is **473.** You can call to or from Grenada as you would to or from any other area code in North America. Public phone and fax services are available at the Carenage offices of **Grenada Cable & Wireless** in St. George's (✆ **473/440-1000** for all offices). The office is open Monday to Thursday from 8am to 5pm, and Friday from 8am to 4pm.

Time Grenada is on Atlantic Standard Time year-round, which means it's usually 1 hour ahead of the U.S. East Coast—except during daylight saving time, when the clocks are the same.

Tipping A 10% service charge is added to most restaurant and hotel bills. No additional tip is expected.

Water Stick to bottled water.

Weather Grenada has two distinct seasons: dry and rainy. The dry season is from January to May; the rest of the year is the rainy season, although the rainfall doesn't last long. The average temperature is 80°F (27°C). Because of constant trade winds, there's little humidity.

WHERE TO STAY

Whether you're looking for a kitchenette apartment; a small, intimate inn; or a major resort, you'll find it waiting for you in Grenada, which has some of the best and most varied accommodations in the southern Caribbean. Unless you want to stay in an atmospheric inn tucked away somewhere, opt for a hotel lined up along Grand Anse Beach. All you'll have to do is walk out the door and head for the ocean.

Your hotel or inn will probably add a service charge of 10% to your bill—ask about this in advance.

Very Expensive

Bel Air Plantation ★★ This secluded hideaway stands on a 7-hectare (17-acre) tract of lush, sloping land on the southwestern side of the island. Beautifully integrated into an almost junglelike terraced waterfront landscape, this is a coterie of vibrantly colored gingerbread cottages built up and down the hillside overlooking St. David's Harbour. Surrounded by tropical gardens, each of the airy, spacious accommodations offers privacy and old-world charm, but also modern amenities. Each unit is furnished with its own character and personality, everything centering on a "waterfront village," complete with a restaurant, bar, gift shop, and a combination delicatessen and cafe. Even the simplest accommodations here, the cottages, are among the best-furnished accommodations on the island. You can live well by renting one of the two-bedroom villas with spacious master bedrooms and living rooms furnished in wicker and Indonesian teak.

St. David's Harbour, St. David's, Grenada, W.I. www.belairplantation.com. ✆ **866/504-3359** or 473/444-6305. Fax 473/444-6316. 11 units. Winter $375 cottage for 2, $475 villa for 2, $675 2-bedroom villa for 4; off season $295 cottage for 2, $380 villa for 2, $520 2-bedroom villa for 4. AE, MC, V. **Amenities:** Restaurant; bar; Internet (free); kayaks; outdoor pool; snorkeling. *In room:* A/C, ceiling fan, TV/DVD, CD player, hair dryer, kitchen.

Calabash ★★★ Set within a sinuously curved building that straddles a landscaped 3-hectare (7½-acre) beach, the posh and elegant Calabash is one of the leading boutique hotels on Grenada, even though the Spice Island Inn surpasses it in style and cutting-edge amenities. Everything is refined and low-key—nothing splashy. It occupies an isolated section of L'Anse aux Epines (Prickly Bay), 8km (5 miles) south of St. George's and only minutes from the airport. Foremost among the multitude of shrubs here are the scores of beautiful *calabashes* (gourds) for which the resort was named. The eight private plunge-pool suites and 22 whirlpool-bath suites all have verandas and either one king-size bed or two double beds.

L'Anse aux Epines (P.O. Box 382), St. George's, Grenada, W.I. www.calabashhotel.com. ✆ **473/444-4334.** Fax 473/444-5050. 30 units. Winter $570–$1,000 suite; off season $295–$660 suite. Children 16 and under stay free in parent's room. Dinner $65 to $75 per person extra. Rate includes breakfast. AE, MC, V. Children 12 and under not permitted Jan to mid-Mar. **Amenities:** 2 restaurants; 2 bars; babysitting; exercise room; golf privileges; outdoor pool; room service; sailboat rentals; snorkeling, tennis court (lit); Wi-Fi (free). *In room:* A/C, ceiling fan, TV, hair dryer, minibar.

Laluna ★★ One of Grenada's best hotels lies on an isolated, beautiful beach at Quarantine Point, near the extreme southern tip of the island. Designed along architectural lines you might expect in Indonesia, the resort consists of 16 thatch-covered, wood-and-stone-sided cottages, each with a small pool, artwork, and fabric-swathed four-poster beds imported from Bali. Scattered up and down a hillside, about 1.5km (1 mile) north of the Port Salines airport, they lie within a 2-minute walk of the beach. Bathrooms are light, airy, tropical affairs, often open to the breezes. The resort's social and architectural centerpiece is a clubhouse, the site of big verandas.

The resort is a glittery, hedonistic niche. The restaurant (p. 292), which is open to nonresidents who phone in advance, is less than 12m (39 ft.) from the beach.

Morne Rouge (P.O. Box 1500), St. George's, Grenada, W.I. www.laluna.com. ✆ **866/452-5862** in the U.S., or 473/439-0001. Fax 473/439-0600. 16 cottages. Winter $645–$1,290 double; off season $415–$1,105 double. MAP (breakfast and dinner) $95 per person extra. AE, MC, V. **Amenities:** Restaurant; bar; bikes; exercise room; room service; watersports equipment/rentals. *In room:* A/C, ceiling fan, TV/VCR, CD player, hair dryer, minibar, plunge pools (in some), Wi-Fi (free).

LaSource ★★★ There is no better place for a spa holiday that combines life on a secluded beach than this restored property, on the southern tip of Grenada. An adult retreat, it is for those seeking rejuvenation. The 17 spa treatment rooms offer a full range of facials, wraps, and massages. A host of services, including daily spa treatments, nightly entertainment, and food, is included. The resort, a 5-minute drive from the airport, stands in tropical gardens, surrounded on three sides by the ocean. Bedrooms are the epitome of luxury, with mahogany furniture, often four-poster beds, and private balconies or terraces with a view. All of the hotel's restaurants serve cuisine based on quality ingredients, light textures, and natural flavors.

Pink Gin Beach, Grenada, W.I. www.theamazingholiday.com. ✆ **888/527-0044** in the U.S. and Canada, or 473/444-2556. Fax 473/444-2561. 100 units. Winter $335–$525 double, $480–$670 suite; off season $235–$395 double, $360–$480 suite. Rates are per person. AE, MC, V. **Amenities:** 4 restaurants; 3 bars; airport transfers included; exercise room; 9-hole golf course; 3 pools (outdoor); room service; spa; 2 tennis courts (lit); watersports (included); Wi-Fi (free). *In room:* A/C, ceiling fan, fridge, hair dryer.

Maca Bana Villas ★ This is the most charming cottage colony on Grenada. It consists of seven artfully designed, artfully decorated, self-contained, self-catering cottages, clustered together on a hillside high above the sea, each with sprawling decks set amid verdant landscapings, and each themed in ways to correspond to the fruit trees that flourish nearby. The place is especially appropriate for people who seek privacy and independence. The smartest way to handle a rental here involves a phone dialogue with Rebecca Thompson, the British co-owner and artist who decorated each of the cottages. Expect one-of-a-kind decor, panoramic views, a supremely upscale kitchen, a private hot tub, and an environment that's conducive to relaxation and romance.

Point Salines (P.O. Box 496), St. George's G.P.O. Grenada, W.I. www.macabana.com. ✆ **473/439-5355.** Fax 473/439-6429. 7 units. Winter $515–$610 double, $580–$710 villa for 4; off season $295–$390 double, $490–$610 villa for 4. *In room:* Ceiling fan, TV, CD player, kitchen, Wi-Fi (free).

Spice Island Beach Resort ★★★ This is the most desirable resort in Grenada, the yardstick by which every other hotel on island is compared. Its location along a 360m (1,181-ft.) expanse of Grand Anse Beach is unequaled. The main house, a rambling series of open-air verandas and gracefully rambling arcades, is reserved for dining, socializing, sunbathing, and dancing. Of the accommodations, we prefer the location of the Sea Grape beach suites, but even more, we like the layout of the intimate pool suites, which are a few steps back from the beach. Least expensive are the second-floor suites, each of which has a terrace overlooking the ocean and the garden; 17 units have private plunge pools, and four offer private saunas.

Grand Anse Beach (P.O. Box 6), St. George's, Grenada, W.I. www.spiceislandbeachresort.com. ✆ **473/444-4258.** Fax 473/444-4807. 64 units. Winter $1,075 double, $1,045–$2,435 suite; off season $860–$950 double, $1,045–$1,700 suite. Rates are all-inclusive. Children 4 and under stay free in parent's room; children 5–11 $175 extra. AE, MC, V. **Amenities:** Restaurant; bar; fitness center; complimentary greens fees at Grenada Golf Course; swim-up Jacuzzi; outdoor pool; room service; sauna; spa; tennis court (lit). *In room:* A/C, ceiling fan, TV/DVD, CD player, hair dryer, Internet (free), minibar.

Expensive

Coyaba Beach Resort ★ On a flat, meticulously landscaped 2-hectare (5-acre) site on Grand Anse Beach, this is an upper-middle-bracket resort whose name means "heaven" in Arawak. Permeated with a Carib/Arawak theme, it evokes a white-walled Iberian-inspired apartment compound with lots of bustle. Set amid the densest concentration of resort hotels on the island, it lies 10km (6¼ miles) from St. George's and 5km (3 miles) north of the airport. The hotel has across-the-water views of town and of St. George's Harbour. All units have double beds plus verandas or patios.

Grand Anse Beach (P.O. Box 336), St. George's, Grenada, W.I. www.coyaba.com. ✆ **866/783-5413** or 473/444-2011. Fax 473/444-4808. 80 units. Winter $360–$425 double; off season $240–$265 double. Extra person winter $50, off season $25. MAP (breakfast and dinner) $82. AE, DC, MC, V. **Amenities:** 2 open-air restaurants; 3 bars (1 swim-up); golf; outdoor pool; room service; tennis court (lit); watersports equipment/rentals. *In room:* A/C, TV, ceiling fan, hair dryer, Wi-Fi (free).

Grenada Grand Beach Resort ★ Set on an 8-hectare (20-acre) tract of lush terrain, this resort stands within mature gardens upon a desirable stretch of white-sand beachfront. Guests, often groups, are ushered along garden paths to the various two- and three-story annexes containing the bedrooms, the floors of which are covered with either ceramic or marble tiles and furnished with English (usually Queen Anne–style) mahogany bed frames, dressers, and armoires. Each has a balcony or patio. The beachview rooms are the most desirable, naturally. The swimming pool here, incidentally, is the largest and most dramatic in Grenada, replete with waterfalls, two Jacuzzis, and a swim-up bar.

Grand Anse Beach (P.O. Box 441), Grenada, W.I. www.grenadagrand.com. ✆ **473/444-4371.** Fax 473/444-4800. 234 units. Winter $185–$350 double, $700–$1,000 suite; off season $130–$250 double, $245–$790 suite. Children 16 and under stay free in parent's room. AE, DISC, MC, V. **Amenities:** 2 restaurants; 3 bars (1 swim-up); babysitting; fitness center; 2 Jacuzzis; 2 pools; room service; 2 tennis courts (lit); watersports equipment/rentals. *In room:* A/C, cable TV, hair dryer, Wi-Fi (free).

True Blue Bay Resort This resort takes its name from an old indigo plantation that once stood here, but panoramic views of Prickly Bay's blue waters make the name appropriate today as well. English-born Russ Fielding and his South American–born wife, Magdelena, have infused the place with an Anglo-Hispanic charm that's vaguely reflected in the rooms' decor. Housing options include one-bedroom apartments with verandas overlooking the bay, or two-bedroom cottages nestled in tropical gardens. The accommodations are tastefully furnished in pastels and tropical rattan pieces.

Old Mill Rd., True Blue (P.O. Box 1414), St. George's, Grenada, W.I. www.truebluebay.com. ✆ **888/883-2482** in the U.S., or 473/443-8783. Fax 473/444-5929. 46 units. Winter $370–$595 double; off season $80–$200 double. Extra person $65. AE, MC, V. **Amenities:** Restaurant; 2 bars; dive shop; exercise room; 2 outdoor pools; room service; yacht charter. *In room:* A/C (in some), ceiling fan, TV, hair dryer, kitchenette, Wi-Fi (free).

Twelve Degrees North ★★ On a very private beach, this cluster of spotlessly clean efficiency apartments is owned and operated by Joseph and Patricia Gaylord, who personally greet visitors. Members of the staff cook breakfast, prepare lunch (perhaps pumpkin soup and flying fish), do the cleaning and laundry, and fix regional specialties for dinner (which you can heat up for yourself later). A housekeeper/cook, assigned to each unit, arrives as early as 8am (you determine the exact time) to perform the thousand small kindnesses that make Twelve Degrees North a favorite lair for repeat guests. All units are equipped with kitchens and large beds.

L'Anse aux Epines (P.O. Box 241), St. George's, Grenada, W.I. www.twelvedegreesnorth.com. ✆/fax **473/444-4580** (call collect to make reservations). 8 units. Winter $225 1-bedroom apt for 2, $350 2-bedroom apt for 4; off season $165 1-bedroom apt for 2, $285 2-bedroom apt for 4. Extra person $60–$70. MC, V. Children 14 and under not accepted. **Amenities:** Beach bar; outdoor pool; tennis court (lit); watersports equipment/rentals. *In room:* Ceiling fan, hair dryer, no phone, Wi-Fi (free).

Moderate

Allamanda Beach Resort ★ Opening onto a wide stretch of Grand Anse Beach, this is one of the best of the cost-conscious full-service operations on the island, with everything from a watersports center to a spa. Accommodations open onto views of the water. Units come with either a little terrace or a balcony. The decor is light and airy, in a Caribbean tropical motif, with tile floors and, in some cases, whirlpool baths. Although its amenities, plush and posh, fall far short of, say, Spice Island or the Coyaba (p. 288), the relatively low prices and good value ensure its ongoing popularity.

Grand Anse Beach (P.O. Box 27), St. George's, Grenada, W.I. www.allamandaresort.com. ✆ **473/444-0095.** Fax 473/444-0126. 50 units. Winter $140–$325 double, $250 suite; off season $100–$225 double, $180 suite. MC, V. **Amenities:** Restaurant; bar; gym; outdoor pool; room service; snorkeling; spa; tennis court (lit). *In room:* A/C, TV, fridge, hair dryer, kitchenette (in some), Wi-Fi (free).

Blue Horizons Garden Resort ★ Lying 8km (5 miles) south of Point Salines Airport, this is an eco-tourist resort, with energy-saving toilets, solar heaters, and a reputation for housing young U.K.- and U.S.-based families. A short walk from Grand Anse Beach, the resort also attracts both scuba divers and nature enthusiasts. Each efficiently furnished unit comes with a private terrace and a small kitchenette. Rentals are in two configurations—one with a king-size bed and pullout bed settee, the other with two queen beds plus a pullout. Trees and tropical plantings are spread across the handsomely landscaped 2.5-hectare (6¼-acre) grounds. It is estimated that nearly two dozen species of birds consider the property as home.

Grand Anse (P.O. Box 41), Grenada, W.I. www.grenadabluehorizons.com. ✆ **473/444-4316.** Fax 473/444-2815. 32 units. Winter $210–$230 double; off season $155–$165 double. Extra person winter

$60, off season $45. AE, DC, MC, V. **Amenities:** Restaurant; 2 bars; babysitting; outdoor pool. *In room:* A/C, TV, CD player, hair dryer, kitchenette, Wi-Fi (in some; free).

The Flamboyant Hotel Well established and completely unpretentious, this hotel occupies a relatively barren hillside that slopes down to Grand Anse Beach. It's a complex of 13 separate buildings, each low-slung, red-roofed, and modern, and each focusing on the resort's centerpiece, an outdoor swimming pool that's adjacent to the beach. Each medium-size unit has a loggia-style balcony overlooking the beach, tile floors, good beds, and floral-patterned curtains and upholsteries. Each unit was conceived as a self-sufficient private apartment with kitchenette.

Grand Anse Beach (P.O. Box 214), St. George's, Grenada, W.I. www.flamboyant.com. © **866/978-8013** in the U.S., or 473/444-4247. Fax 473/444-1234. 68 units. Winter $200–$290 double, from $210–$595 suite; off season $155–$194 double, from $205–$435 suite. Extra person $44. AE, DC, DISC, MC, V. **Amenities:** Restaurant; 2 bars; babysitting; outdoor pool; room service; watersports equipment/rentals. *In room:* A/C, TV, hair dryer, kitchenette (in about 40 units), minibar, Wi-Fi (free).

Mi Hacienda ★ Merle McEwen created this boutique hotel of charm and grace, filling her hacienda with her family's antiques and various furnishings and decorations. Lying in a residential neighborhood, the hotel offers a distant view of Grand Anse Beach, which is best seen from a veranda where food and drink are served. Each of the midsize bedrooms is individually decorated, often with antiques, and many have views of Grand Anse. On-site is an excellent restaurant serving such delights as chicken in coconut sauce or breaded snapper in orange sauce.

Grand Anse, St. George's, Grenada, W.I. www.mihacienda.gd. © **473/439-2799.** 20 units. Winter $90–$300 double; off season $75–$250. AE, MC, V. **Amenities:** Restaurant; bar; outdoor pool; spa. *In room:* Internet (free), kitchen (in some), no phone.

Inexpensive

Gem Holiday Beach Resort ☺ Opening onto Morne Rouge Beach, this complex of no-nonsense, ultrasimple, self-catering apartments is family-friendly, completely unpretentious, and, by island standards, reasonably priced. Its one- and two-bedroom apartments are a bit small, but they are fully equipped, with a kitchenette, comfortable beds, mahogany furnishings, and a private terrace opening onto the beach.

Morne Rouge Bay (P.O. Box 58), St. George's, Grenada, W.I. www.gembeachresort.com. © **473/444-4224.** Fax 473/444-1189. 20 units. Winter $126–$198 double or triple; off season $85–$150 double or triple. AE, DC, DISC, MC, V. **Amenities:** Restaurant; bar; dance club; babysitting. *In room:* A/C, TV, fridge, hair dryer, kitchen, Wi-Fi (free).

La Sagesse ★ On a tree-lined beach of black volcanic sand, 15km (9¼ miles) from the airport, La Sagesse is a small-scale, eco-friendly beach resort that includes a sea-fronting guesthouse; a simple, open-air restaurant serving Caribbean meals; a bar; and an art gallery. Nearby are trails for hiking and exploring, a haven for wading and shore birds, hummingbirds, hawks, and ducks. Rivers, mangroves, and a salt-pond sanctuary enhance its natural beauty. Scuba and snorkeling, and sailboat rentals, can be arranged on-site. The most impressive building is an imposing great house, built as a vacation home for a prominent Englishman (Peregrine Brownlow, the second cousin of Queen Elizabeth II). The Manor House now contains five accommodations, each with high ceilings and comfortable beds.

St. David's (P.O. Box 44), St. George's, Grenada, W.I. www.lasagesse.com. ©/fax **473/444-6458.** 12 units. Winter $185–$230 double; off season $125–$155 double. Extra person $20–$25. MC, V. **Amenities:**

Restaurant; bar; babysitting; watersports equipment/rentals; Wi-Fi (free). *In room:* A/C (1 room), ceiling fan, hair dryer, no phone.

Paradise Bay Beach Resort & Spa Surrounded by two good beaches on each side, this eco-friendly resort is a hidden-away retreat for the discerning traveler seeking comfort, good food, and an escape. This compound of villas is set on 3.2 lush hectares (8 acres), with forest trail hikes and easy walks along the beach readily available. It's an all-inclusive with fine island cooking with a French accent. House drinks, including occasional champagne, are served, and a roster of activities are featured, including massages, horseback riding, and such watersports as scuba diving. The midsize bedrooms are comfortably but rather simply furnished, the beds draped in mosquito netting plantation style.

La Tante, St. David, Grenada, W.I. www.paradisebayresort.com. © **473/405-8888.** 9 units. Year-round $143–$182 per person. Rates all-inclusive. MC, V. **Amenities:** Restaurant; beach bar; outdoor pool; tennis court. *In room:* Ceiling fan, no phone, Wi-Fi (free).

WHERE TO DINE

Expensive

Aquarium Restaurant ★★ SEAFOOD/INTERNATIONAL This is one of our favorite restaurants in Grenada, a whimsical, offbeat place that represents aspects of the West Indies and the funkiest charms of the homelands (England and Germany) of its owners. If Peter Pan were to design a Grenadian lair for himself, it would probably look like this combination of grotto and forest canopy with decking. It's the only custom-excavated restaurant on the island, carved as it was into a location midway between a cliff face, a jungle, and the beach. The menu is flavorful but unpretentious. Examples include calalloo cannelloni with Parmesan in a cream sauce, *spanakopita* (Greek-style puff pastry with callaloo and pesto), scallops wrapped in bacon with a bitter orange sauce, and Creole curried chicken. Although this restaurant occupies a shadowy spot under a canopy of trees, a sun-flooded beach bar is steps away.

In the Maca Bana Villa Complex, Magazine Beach, Point Salines. © **473/444-1410.** Reservations required. Main courses $20–$50. AE, MC, V. Tues–Sat 10am–10pm; Sun noon–10pm.

Coconut Beach Restaurant ★ FRENCH/CREOLE This informal restaurant occupies a green clapboard house set directly on the beach. From the dining room, you can watch the staff working in the exposed kitchen. They'll definitely be working on callaloo soup, made with local herbs and blended to a creamy smoothness. The kitchen specializes in various kinds of lobster, including the classic served with garlic butter, and an imaginative stir-fry with ginger chili. Fish dominates, including a catch of the day served with mango chutney. Almost anything prepared with fresh conch is terrific, but we also like the chicken breast cooked in local herbs and lime juice.

Warning: Because the restaurant is close to several major hotels, many people have opted to walk along the beach to reach it. Don't! Tourists have been robbed and had their lives threatened by machete-carrying thugs. Even if it's a short ride, take a taxi.

Grand Anse Beach (about .8km/½ mile north of St. George's). © **473/444-4644.** www.coconutbeach-grenada.com. Reservations recommended. Main courses $14–$33; lunch platters $7–$13. AE, MC, V. Wed–Mon 12:30–10pm.

La Belle Creole ★★ CARIBBEAN The inspired Creole cuisine and its romantic setting make this restored restaurant one of the island leaders. It's run by the Hopkins family, who still use recipes from the founding matriarch, who for years was hailed as the island's finest chef, especially in her use of homegrown products. Set in the lush tropical gardens of the Blue Horizons resort (p. 289), the restaurant offers both elegant surroundings and good service. Begin with the green banana soup (the finest version of this we've had). Lobster is prepared as you like it, and there are such other delights as a pork tenderloin with a spicy peanut sauce or fish mousse. Lunch is taken poolside.

At the Blue Horizons Garden Resort, Grand Anse. ✆ **473/444-4316.** Reservations recommended. Main courses $6–$32; breakfast or lunch $8–$17. Daily 7:30–10am, 12:30–2:30pm, and 7–9pm.

Laluna ITALIAN/INTERNATIONAL This is the restaurant that feeds, nourishes, and entertains the hedonistic international clientele of this stylish cottage compound (p. 287). And it does so exceedingly well. You'll dine in a thatch-covered setting, adjacent to the sea and a swimming pool, enjoying the cooking of a Sicily-born chef with wide-ranging experience in Asia. The best dishes include seafood gnocchi; sushi; pasta *a l'amatriciana* (with salami, ham, tomatoes, capers, and olives); and seafood Benedetto, a medley of wine-and-tomato-soaked seafood served over rice. A perfectly grilled steak or lobster almost invariably appears on the menu.

In the Laluna resort, Morne Rouge. ✆ **473/439-0001.** Reservations required. Main courses $24–$36. AE, MC, V. Daily 7am–11pm.

Oliver's Restaurant ★ CREOLE/SEAFOOD Want to dine within one of Grenada's most stylish resorts, facing an uncrowded beachfront, protected from sudden tropical showers? The parapet here, built of imported pine and cedar, looks like a Le Corbusier rooftop. Some of the best hotel food on the island is served in this winning open-air setting. Dinners are elegant, candlelit affairs; lunches are more casual, although service is very attentive regardless of when you happen to show up. Local seafood is featured on the constantly changing menu. The most generous buffet on the island, a real Grenadian spread, is served on Friday, along with live entertainment.

In the Spice Island Beach Resort, Grand Anse Beach. ✆ **473/444-4258.** Reservations required for nonguests. Full breakfast $25, continental breakfast $20; lunch main courses $15–$30; 6-course fixed-price dinner $85. AE, MC, V. Daily 7:30–10am, 12:30–3:00pm, and 7–9:30pm.

Red Crab ★ WEST INDIAN/INTERNATIONAL The food at the Red Crab isn't as good as that at other restaurants recommended here, but it's a fun, lively place to be at night, and many locals consider it a kind of landmark. Only a short taxi ride from the major hotels, it attracts visitors and locals alike and is especially popular with students from the medical college. Patrons can dine inside or out. The beefsteaks, especially the pepper steak, are among Grenada's finest. Other offerings include local lobster tail; *lambi* (conch); and locally caught fish such as snapper, dolphin (mahimahi), and grouper. If you weren't old enough to have dined in the '50s, you can at least experience that decade's popular cuisine and order beef stroganoff, veal *cordon bleu,* or lobster Newburg.

L'Anse aux Epines. ✆ **473/444-4424.** Reservations required. Main courses $15–$45. AE, MC, V. Mon–Sat 11am–2pm and 6–10pm.

Rhodes ★★★ INTERNATIONAL/SEAFOOD One of London's most exciting celebrity chefs, Gary Rhodes, has invaded Grenada. This chic and stylish restaurant is the most prestigious and manicured on the island. Rhodes came to Grenada to acquaint himself with its local produce and many spices. He then designed the menu around these flavors and trained local chefs in his cooking style. The actual recipes change daily but feature seafood. In London, Rhodes is known for his daring twists and creative flavors, so expect some delightful surprises if you show up here.

In the Calabash Hotel, L'anse aux Epines. © **473/444-4334.** Reservations required. Main courses $15–$36. AE, MC, V. Daily 7–11pm.

Water's Edge ★★ FUSION/SEAFOOD The aptly named Water's Edge is part of a deluxe property, the previously recommended Bel Air Plantation (p. 286). Veranda tables open onto St. David's harbor, although you can also dine more intimately in the courtyard garden. The chefs are skilled at getting the best of locally caught fish and seafood, even lobster. On their forever-changing menu, they season it with the locally grown herbs and spices for which Grenada is famous. Meats and poultry such as chicken, roast pork, and sirloin steak are imported. The kitchen also turns out a wonderfully flavored seafood curry, a specialty.

In the Bel Air Plantation, St. David's Harbour, St. David's. © **473/443-2822.** Reservations required. Main courses $11–$25 lunch, $21–$33 dinner. MC, V. Daily 11am–3pm and 6:30–9:30pm.

Moderate

La Boulangerie FRENCH/ITALIAN Don't be deterred by the shopping-center location, or the way this place resembles a coffee shop. It's an appropriate spot for a good breakfast or light lunch (served throughout the afternoon), and prices at dinner are very reasonable. In the early morning, visitors throng here for the freshly brewed coffee, pastries, and croissants. The lunch and dinner crowd devours well-stuffed baguettes, sandwiches, and pizzas.

In the Le Marquis Shopping Complex, Grand Anse Beach. © **473/444-1131.** Main courses $16–$43; sandwiches and pizzas $11–$15. No credit cards. Daily 8:30am–9:30pm.

La Sagesse ★ CARIBBEAN/CONTINENTAL Opening onto a sandy beach, this romantic open-air spot is one of the quirkiest places to dine on island. It is casually run and serves good food based on fresh ingredients. The seafood is some of the island's finest. You can order freshly made salads and well-stuffed sandwiches throughout the day. The *lambi* is an excellent choice, but on most nights, you can choose from a full range of fish, including mahimahi and grouper. In the evening, several Continental dishes appear. The restaurant also caters to vegetarians.

In the La Sagesse nature center, south of St. David's. © **473/444-6458.** Reservations not required. Main courses $16–$21; fixed-price menu $50. MC, V. Daily 8am–10pm.

Inexpensive

Belmont Estate ★ GRENADIAN Here is a rare opportunity to dine on a 4-centuries-old working plantation, producing nutmeg and cocoa. The location of this 160-hectare (395-acre) property lies in the green mountains between the parishes of St. Patrick and St. Andrew, in the northeast corner of the island. If you're touring the island, consider a luncheon stopover here to enjoy a plantation buffet of creatively prepared, home-cooked dishes. Many of the ingredients are grown on the estate, including the fresh fruit for the juices and fresh greens for the salads. The meal begins with a delectable homemade soup, followed by a choice of traditional chicken, beef, or mutton dishes or the catch of the day—everything enhanced by the locally grown vegetables. A scrumptious dessert brings an end to this skillfully blended and aromatic buffet seasoned with local spices. You can also tour the property from 9am to 4pm Sunday to Friday.

Belmont, St. Patrick. ✆ **473/442-9524.** www.belmontestate.net. Reservations recommended. Fixed-price lunch menu $20. MC, V. Sun–Fri noon–3pm.

Deyna's Tasty Food ★ 🎁 GRENADIAN This little eatery is a closely guarded secret among locals. It's reached by heading up Melville Street to a modest three-story building overlooking the sea. The chef, Deyna Hercules, resembles her namesake. Her savory stuffed crabs are the island's best, and you'll see her other specialties scribbled on a countertop chalkboard. She's known for her "fix up"—a sampling of the best food of the day, perhaps stewed fish, green plantains, and curried goat. She also serves Grenada's national dish, an "oil down," made with salted meat and breadfruit cooked in coconut milk. And where else could you get a tasty batch of *titiri,* minnow-size fish just plucked from the Caribbean? Wash them down with "bush tea" steeped from black sage leaves. Adventurous diners opt for one of the gamey specialties such as *manicou* (a cross between an opossum and a large rat).

Melville St., St. George's. ✆ **473/440-6795.** Reservations recommended. Main courses $12–$23. MC, V. Mon–Sat 6:30am–7pm; Sun 7am–4pm.

Morne Fendue Plantation House ★ 🎁 CREOLE This plantation house is the ancestral home of the late owner, Betty Mascoll. It was built in 1912 of carefully chiseled river rocks held together with a mixture of lime and molasses. Mascoll died in 1998, but her loyal staff carries on her tradition. They need time to prepare food for your arrival, so it's imperative to give them a call to let them know you're coming by. Lunch is likely to include yam-and-sweet-potato casserole, curried chicken with lots of hot spices, and a hot pot of pork and oxtail. Because this is very much a private home, tipping should be done tactfully. Nonetheless, the hardworking cook and maid seem genuinely appreciative of a gratuity.

St. Patrick's (40km/25 miles north of St. George's). ✆ **473/442-9330.** Reservations required. Fixed-price lunch $16. No credit cards. Daily 8am–4pm; dinner served upon request. Follow the coastal road north out of St. George's; after you pass through Nonpareil, turn inland (east) and continue through Sauteurs and follow the signs to Morne Fendue.

Patrick's Local Homestyle Restaurant GRENADIAN Set one floor above street level in a crumbling 1970s-era concrete house, this restaurant does a brisk trade with locals and yacht owners alike. It's not glamorous and it's anything but pretentious, but portions, as prepared by Patrick Levine, are large and flavorful, and many locals define it as their regular island bistro. It's been thriving in this unlikely spot since 2001, presenting a buffet-style cornucopia of as many as 15 to 20 different dishes every day, each served atop battered tables covered with linoleum, plastic tablecloths, and rusted metal chairs. Expect, as its name implies, strictly local cooking, including curried mutton, stewed beef, *lambi,* crayfish, rabbit, pork, chicken salad, and breadfruit salad.

Lagoon Rd., St. George's. ✆ **473/440-0364.** Reservations not necessary. Main courses $11–$30; fixed-price meals $23. MC, V. Daily 3–11pm.

GRENADA'S BEACHES

The best of Grenada's 45 beaches are in the southwestern part of the island. The granddaddy of them all is **Grand Anse Beach** ★★★, 3km (2 miles) of sugar-white sand fronting a sheltered bay. This beach is really the stuff of dreams—it's no surprise that many of the major resort hotels are here. A lot of visitors never leave this part of the island. Protected from strong winds and currents, the waters here are relatively safe, making Grand Anse a family favorite. The clear, gentle waters are populated with schools of rainbow-hued fish. Palms and sea-grape trees offer shade. Watersports concessions include water-skiing, parasailing, windsurfing, and scuba diving; vendors peddle coral jewelry, local crafts, and the inevitable T-shirts.

The beach at **Morne Rouge Bay ★** is less popular but just as nice, with white sands bordering clear waters. Morne Rouge, noted for its calm waters and some of the best snorkeling in Grenada, is about 2km (1¼ miles) south of Grand Anse Bay.

Pink Gin Beach lies near the airport at Point Salinas. This is also a white-sand beach with clear waters, ideal for swimming and snorkeling. (No one seems to know why it's called Pink Gin Beach.) You can find a restaurant and kayak rentals here.

Also on Grenada's southern coast, **La Sagesse Beach** is part of La Sagesse nature center. This strip of gray-and-black volcanic sand is a lovely, tranquil area; between sojourns on the beach, you can go for walks through the nearby countryside. A small restaurant, set beneath a veranda-style roof, opens onto the beach.

If you like your waters more turbulent, visit the dramatic **Pearl's Beach,** north of Grenville on the Atlantic coast. The light-gray sand stretches for miles and is lined with palm trees. You'll practically have the beach to yourself.

Part of Levera National Park, **Levera Beach,** at the northeastern tip of the island, is one of the most beautiful on Grenada. Its sands front the Atlantic, which usually means rough waters. Many locals come here for Sunday picnics.

SPORTS & OUTDOOR PURSUITS

DEEP-SEA FISHING Fishers visit from November to March in pursuit of both blue and white marlin, yellowfin tuna, wahoo, sailfish, and more. Most of the bigger hotels have a sports desk that arranges fishing trips. The **Spice Island BillFish Tournament,** held in January, attracts a number of regional and international participants. For more information, call Chairman Richard McIntyre (✆ **473/440-3753** or 415-0157; www.sibtgrenada.com).

GOLF At the **Grenada Golf Country Club,** Woodlands (✆ **473/444-4128**), you can tee off on a 9-hole course with views of both the Caribbean Sea and the Atlantic. Greens fees are only $23 for 9 holes, or $33 if you want to play it twice (to get 18 holes). Hours are Monday to Saturday 7:30am to 9pm.

HIKING Grenada's lushness and beauty make it one of the best Caribbean islands for hiking. If you have time for only one hike here, schedule it for points within the **Grand Etang National Park and Forest Preserve ★** (✆ **473/440-6160**). Its sheer scenic beauty makes the **Lake Circle Trail** our top choice on the island. The trail follows a 60-minute circuit along Grand Etang Lake, the crater of an extinct volcano, amid a forest preserve and bird sanctuary. You're likely to see the yellow-billed cuckoo and the emerald-throated hummingbird. The park is also a playground for Mona monkeys. Another easy hike, the **Morne LeBaye Trail,** originates at the park's center. The 15-minute trek affords a view of the 710m (2,329-ft.) Mount Sinai and the east coast. Of course, you can take longer hikes, perhaps to the peak of **Mount Qua Qua** at 712m (2,336 ft.), a trek which, round-trip, takes 3 to 3½ hours. Carry insect repellent and plenty of water, and remember that trails can be slippery after a rainfall (especially June–Nov), so wear good hiking shoes and bring a sense of humor.

You can hike the shorter trails independently, but you might wish to hire a guide for the ascent to Mount Qua Qua or the even more demanding hike to Mount Catherine, at 827m (2,713 ft.). The former costs $25 per person for a 4-hour hike, while the latter is $35. For information, call **Telfor Bedeau Hiking Tours** (✆ **473/442-6200**). Good hiking trails can also be found at **Levera National Park** (see "A Spectacular Rainforest & More," below).

SAILING Two large party boats, designed for 120 and 250 passengers, operate out of St. George's Harbour. The ***Rhum Runner*** and ***Rhum Runner II,*** c/o Best of Grenada, P.O. Box 188, St. George's, Grenada, W.I. (✆ **473/440-4386**), make one to three trips daily, depending on the season, with lots of emphasis on liquor, steel-band music, and good times. Conducted every morning and afternoon, the 3-hour tours coincide with the arrival of cruise ships and, as such, tend to be packed with passengers, but independent travelers are welcome if space is available. Depending on advance bookings, evening tours on Friday and Saturday from 7:30pm to midnight are much more frequently attended by island locals and are more bare-boned, louder, and usually less restrained. The cost is $15 per person.

SCUBA DIVING & SNORKELING Grenada provides divers with submarine gardens, exotic fish, and coral formations, sometimes with visibility stretching to 36m (118 ft.). Off the coast is the wreck of the ocean liner *Bianca C*, which is nearly 180m (591 ft.) long. Novice divers can stick to the west coast of Grenada, while more experienced divers might search out sights along the rougher Atlantic side.

Aquanauts, in the True Blue Bay, Grand Anse Beach (✆ **473/444-1126;** www.aquanautsgrenada.com), has night dives or two-tank dives for $55 to $95, respectively; PADI instructors offer an open-water certification program for $460 per person. They also offer **snorkeling trips** (1½–2 hr.) for $26. You can rent snorkel gear as well, even if you don't take the boat ride. Giving Aquanuts serious competition is affable **Eco-Dive,** at the Coyaba Beach Resort on Grand Anse Beach (✆ **473/444-7777;** www.ecodiveandtrek.com). There's a PADI instructor on-site, and the dive boat is well equipped. Both scuba diving and snorkeling jaunts to panoramic reefs and shipwrecks teeming with marine life are offered. A single dive costs $50, and a five-dive package $225. A **snorkeling trip** can be arranged for $36. Diving instruction, including a resort course, is available. **Dive Grenada,** Flamboyant Hotel, Grande Anse Beach (✆ **473/444-1092;** www.divegrenada.com), offers dives daily at 10am and 2pm, costing $50 for a one-tank dive and $95 for a two-tank dive. Snorkeling trips are also available for $35. The organization sank two rusted, terminally aged ships offshore as a catalyst for the creation of some underwater reefs.

If you'd rather strike out on your own, drive to Woburn and negotiate with a fisher for a ride to **Glovers Island,** an old whaling station, and snorkel away. Glovers Island is an uninhabited rock spit a few hundred yards offshore from the hamlet of Woburn.

TENNIS Most big resorts have tennis courts. There are public courts, as well, both at Grand Anse and in Tanteen in St. George's.

YACHT CHARTERS Grenada is increasingly known for the number and size of its yacht regatta. As such, the island is home to yacht-racing events throughout the year, including the Port Louis Grenada Sailing Festival in late January (www.grenada-sailingfestival.com), the Easter Round-the-Island Regatta (www.aroundgrenada.com), and the Carriacou Regatta Festival in late July (www.carriacouregatta.com).

If you'd like to sail the waters yourself, **Horizon Yacht Charters** at True Blue Resort, Old Mill Road, True Blue (✆ **473/439-1000;** www.horizonyachtcharters.com), specializes in bareboat or crewed charters, including 3-day trips to the Grenadines, arguably the best sailing waters in the Caribbean. Daily rates begin at $371, weekly rates at $2,395.

EXPLORING THE ISLAND

St. George's & Vicinity

The capital city of Grenada, **St. George's ★★** is the prettiest harbor town in the West Indies. Its landlocked inner harbor is actually the deep crater of a long-dead volcano. In the town, you can see some of the most charming Georgian colonial buildings in the Caribbean, still standing despite a devastating hurricane in 1955. The steep, narrow hillside streets are filled with houses of ballast bricks, wrought-iron balconies, and sloping, red-tile roofs. Many of the pastel warehouses date from the 18th century. Frangipani and flamboyant trees add to the palette of color. The port, which some compare to Portofino, Italy, is flanked by old forts and bold headlands. Among the town's attractions are an 18th-century pink **Anglican church,** on Church Street, and the **Market Square,** where colorfully attired farm women offer even more colorful produce for sale. **Fort George,** on Church Street, built by the French, stands at the entrance to the bay, with subterranean passageways and old guardrooms and cells.

Everyone strolls along the waterfront of the **Carenage ★**, on the inner harbor, or relaxes on its pedestrian plaza, with seats and hanging planters providing shade from the sun. From its large open windows, you'll have great views of the harbor activity. The hamburgers and rum drinks are great, too. On this side of town, the **Grenada National Museum,** at the corner of Young and Monckton streets (✆ **473/440-3725**), is set in the foundations of an old French army barracks and prison built in 1704. Small but interesting, it houses finds from archaeological digs, petroglyphs, native fauna, the first telegraph installed on the island, a rum still, and memorabilia depicting Grenada's history. The most comprehensive exhibit traces the native culture of Grenada. Hours are Monday through Friday from 9am to 4:30pm, Saturday from 10am to 1pm. Admission is $2.50 for adults, $1 ages 6 to 16, and free 5 and under.

You can drive up to Richmond Hill and **Fort Frederick** (✆ **473/440-6158**), begun by the French in 1779, completed by the English in 1791, and radically restored by the Canadian government in the late 1990s. From its battlements is a superb view of the harbor and yacht marina. Admission is $2 and includes the services of a guide, who will expect a small tip. Access to the fort is Monday to Friday 8am to 4pm.

An afternoon tour of St. George's and its environs might take you into the mountains north of the capital. A 15-minute drive delivers you to **Annandale Falls ★**, a tropical wonderland, with a cascade about 15m (49 ft.) high. You can enjoy a picnic surrounded by liana vines, elephant ears, and other tropical flora and spices. The

Annandale Falls Centre (✆ **473/440-2452**) offers gift items, handicrafts, and samples of the indigenous spices of Grenada. Nearby, an improved trail leads to the falls, where you can enjoy a refreshing swim. Swimmers can use the changing cubicles at the falls for free. The center is open daily 8am to 4pm.

A Spectacular Rainforest & More

If you head north out of St. George's along the western coast, you can take in beaches, spice plantations, and the fishing villages that are so typical of Grenada. You'll pass through **Gouyave,** a spice town that's the center of the nutmeg and mace industry. At the **Gouyave Nutmeg Processing Cooperative,** Gouvave, St. John (✆ **473/444-8337**), near the entrance to Gouyave, huge quantities of the spice are aged, graded, and processed. This is the best place to see spices being readied for market. Workers sit on stools in the natural light from the open windows of the aging factory and laboriously sort the raw nutmeg and its byproduct, mace, into different baskets for grinding, peeling, and aging. Jams, jellies, syrups, and more are sold. Hours are Monday to Friday 8am to 4pm; admission is $1.

In the northeast corner of the island (just east of Sauteurs) is palm-lined **Levera Beach,** an idyll of sand where the Atlantic meets the Caribbean. This is a great spot for a picnic lunch, but swimming can sometimes be dangerous. On the distant horizon, you'll see some of the Grenadines. The 180-hectare (445-acre) **Levera National Park** ★ actually has several white-sand beaches for swimming and snorkeling, although the surf is rough here where the Atlantic meets the Caribbean. It's a **hiker's paradise,** although you should go hiking here only after you've hiked Grand Etang National Park and Forest Preserve (see "Hiking," above), which is more lush and of far greater interest. Levera Park contains a mangrove swamp, a lake, and a bird sanctuary, where you might see a rare tropical parrot. Offshore are coral reefs and sea-grass beds.

Heading down the east coast of Grenada, you reach **Grenville,** the island's second city. If you pass through on a Saturday morning, you can enjoy the hubbub of the native produce market. There's also a fish market along the waterfront. A nutmeg factory here welcomes visitors. From Grenville you can cut inland into the heart of Grenada; here you're in a world of luxuriant foliage, and you pass nutmeg, banana, and cocoa plantations.

In the center of the island, reached along the major interior road between Grenville and St. George's, is **Grand Etang National Park** ★★ (✆ **473/440-6160**), containing the island's spectacular rainforest. The entrance fee of $2 per person is, according to local officials, merely a means of registering the identities of whomever opts to wander around these isolated landscapes, just in case someone should be injured or lost. For information about hikes in the park, see "Hiking," above.

Our favorite attraction north of St. Georges is the **River Antoine Rum Distillery** ★, St. Andrew Parish (✆ **473/442-7109**), which offers a set of almost bizarre visuals, each ripped directly from the pages of the colonial Caribbean's mid-19th-century Industrial Revolution. It's the oldest rum distillery in the world, replete with much of its original cane-crushing machinery and complicated network of siphons and distillation vats. Components of the facility include a late-18th-century water-powered mill whose groaning, creaking gears continue to mesh, connect, and crush the sugar cane. About 90 people are employed here, operating in low-tech, not particularly sanitary conditions. Tours depart whenever an interested observer happens to show up. Although tours are free, your guide will expect a tip of around $3. The finished product (River Antoine Rum) comes in strengths of 138 proof and 150 proof—and, in the locally famous Rivers brand, an alcohol content so high that it's too flammable to pass through the security screening devices at airports. Clearly signposted from the coastal road, the distillery is open Monday to Saturday 9am to 4pm.

On your descent from the mountains, you'll pass hanging carpets of mountain ferns. Going through the tiny hamlets of **Snug Corner** and **Beaulieu,** you eventually come back to the capital.

SHOPPING

Everybody who visits Grenada goes home with a basket of **spices,** better than any you're likely to find in your local supermarket. Vendors will besiege you wherever you go. Their hand-woven panniers of palm leaf or straw are full of items grown on the island, including the inevitable nutmeg, as well as mace, cloves, cinnamon, bay leaf, vanilla, and ginger.

If you like to attend Caribbean markets as much as we do, head for **Market Square ★**, at the foot of Young Street in St. George's. The market is at its liveliest on Saturday morning but is also open Monday to Friday. It's best to go between 8am and noon. An array of handicrafts is for sale, but fresh spices are more plentiful.

For something really special, visit **Arawak Islands Ltd. ★**, Upper Belmont Road, in St. George's (✆ **473/444-3577;** www.arawak-islands.com), founded in 1986 by Angelia Clements, a German woman. From the raw materials of Grenada, especially nutmeg and cinnamon, she manufactures delectable tropical perfumes and toiletries. The company is committed to natural products and minimal processing, and sells some items purchased from island companies and packaged here at the workshop.

If it's upscale, breezy, and insouciant resort wear you're looking to acquire, consider the twin retail outlets **Gatsby Male** and **Gatsby Female** (✆ **473/444-4258**), both of which lie a few steps from one another within the forecourt arcade of the previously recommended Spice Island Inn, on Grand Anse Beach. Inventories here include resort wear and bathing suits by Gottex, La Perla, and Paul & Shark.

Two crafts markets, which can be either bountiful sources of island crafts or sweaty, dusty repositories of things you'll eventually discard, include **the Spiceland Mall,** a 19-shop emporium on Grand Anse Beach, and the **Grand Anse Vendor Market** (✆ **473/439-6450**), also on Grand Anse Beach, wherein 80 vendors of spices, woodcarvings, batiks, and T-shirts are assembled into one intensely mercantile place.

Tikal, Young Street, St. George's (✆ **473/440-2310**), is the best place to shop for regional art. Its matriarch and founder is grande dame Jeanne Fisher, an American expat who founded this shop in 1959. About 85% of the paintings on display are by Grenadians, some of them untutored, others the product of formal training. There's also a variety of arts and crafts from Mexico and Latin America.

The merchandise at **Art Fabrik,** Young Street, St. George's (✆ **473/440-0568**), is quirky and eccentric and, in most cases, very appealing—quite simply, the finest and most comprehensive collection of island-made batiks in Grenada. Garments made from this ancient Indonesian dyeing technique tend to be airy, breathable, and appropriate for resort wear. There's an array of dresses and shirts for men and women, as well as table linens whose random patterns evoke the airy spontaneity of the islands.

GRENADA AFTER DARK

Regular evening entertainment is provided by the resort hotels and includes steel bands, calypso, reggae, folk dancing, and limbo—even crab racing. Ask at your hotel desk to find out what's happening at the time of your visit.

The island's most popular nightspot is **Fantazia 2001,** Morne Rouge Beach (✆ **473/444-2288;** http://fantazia2001niteclub.com). Although it gets progressively rougher as the evening progresses, it's air-conditioned, with state-of-the-art equipment, good acoustics, and fantastic lights, and plays the best in regional and international sounds. There are live shows Saturday. The cover ranges from $5 to $8.

Just as fun and a bit less gratuitously rowdy is **Club Banana,** True Blue, St. George's (✆ **473/444-4662**), down by the marina. Every Friday and Saturday night, it operates a disco from 10:30pm to 4am, charging a cover of $8. Some visitors have proclaimed Club Banana as the best nightlife hangout on the island.

The **Beachside Terrace** and the **Owl Sports Pub,** both at the Flamboyant Hotel, Grand Anse (✆ **473/444-4247**), have an amicable and sometimes boisterous clientele, a pair of pool tables, two wide-screen TVs, and a penchant for broadcasting cricket or soccer matches. They're the site of the island's longest happy hour (daily 4–7pm and again 11pm–midnight), during which prices are reduced by about 40%. Karaoke is featured Thursday and Friday nights beginning around 8:30pm. Full meals, including American burgers and Caribbean-style curries, are served in the Beachside Terrace daily from noon to 10:30pm.

Another favorite is **Aquarium Beach Club & Restaurant** ★ at Point Salines (✆ **473/444-1410**), which also serves delectable steaks (p. 291), with a special reputation for its Sunday barbecue specials. From the sprawl of decks open to the trade winds, you can enjoy the lights of St. George's Harbour here at night.

For those seeking culture, the 250-seat **Marryshow Folk Theatre** ★, Herbert Blaize Street near Bain Alley, St. George's (✆ **473/440-2385**), offers performances of Grenadian, American, and European folk music; drama; and West Indian interpretative folk dance. Tickets usually cost $12.

GUADELOUPE

If you have time for only one French island, should it be Martinique or Guadeloupe? The question's a tough one. Martinique is more sophisticated, with more culture, but Guadeloupe has more diversity and calmer leeward bathing beaches. You can also visit Guadeloupe's dependencies, the nearby islands of Marie Galante, Iles des Saintes, and La Désirade.

Beaches Guadeloupe is riddled with sandy beaches. Unwind at **Salako Beach**, with its lush backdrop of palms. Sunbathers and snorkelers gravitate to **Plage Caravelle,** filled with heaps of white sand and reef-protected waters. In Basse-Terre, **La Grande-Anse** offers powdery sands, tranquil waters, and palm trees.

Things to Do Climb to the 18th-century ruins of **Fort Fleur-d'Epée** to see its dungeons and battlements. Walk the ramparts of **Basse-Terre,** where panoramic vistas unfold in all directions. Don scuba gear and explore the colorful underwater world in the calm waters **La Réserve Cousteau**.

Eating & Drinking **Creole cuisine** on Guadeloupe is like nowhere else in the world, including land crab with hot peppers and fresh coconut, freshwater crayfish, and mashed bananas and breadfruit. The island's French heritage can be best sampled in the restaurants of **Pointe-à-Pitre, St-François,** and to **Basse-Terre.**

Nature Guadeloupe's mountains are covered with tropical forests, impenetrable in many places. Hike **Parc Naturel de Guadeloupe**, passing waterfalls and cool mountain pools, hot springs, and rugged gorges along the way. The big attraction of Basse-Terre is the famous sulfur-puffing **La Soufrière** volcano, which towers to a height of some 1,444m (4,737 ft.).

ESSENTIALS

Visitor Information

For information before you go, contact the **French Government Tourist Office** (© **202/659-7779;** www.francetourism.com). There are offices at 444 Madison Ave., 16th Floor, New York, NY 10022 (© **212/838-7800**); 9454 Wilshire Blvd., Ste. 715, Beverly Hills, CA 90212 (© **310/271-6665**); and 676 N. Michigan Ave., Ste. 3360, Chicago, IL 60611 (© **312/751-7800**).

Getting There

To get to Guadeloupe, most U.S. travelers will have to fly elsewhere in the Caribbean and transfer. You can take an **American Airlines**

(✆ **800/433-7300** in the U.S. and Canada; www.aa.com) flight to its hub in San Juan, Puerto Rico, and then get the one **American Eagle** flight daily on to Guadeloupe. There are also connections available through Martinique (see chapter 15). **Delta** (✆ **800/241-4141** in the U.S. and Canada; www.delta.com) also offers flights from Atlanta on Wednesday and Saturday.

Air Canada (✆ **888/247-2262** in the U.S. and Canada, or 590/21-12-77; www.aircanada.ca) flies between Montréal and Guadeloupe every Saturday year-round. Between December and April only, it also maintains an additional flight from Montréal to Guadeloupe every Wednesday. Passengers can also fly from Toronto on one of the daily nonstop flights to Barbados and transfer onto other carriers (usually LIAT), making the ongoing journey to points within the French West Indies.

Air France (✆ **800/237-2747** in the U.S. and Canada; www.airfrance.com) flies into Guadeloupe every day from Paris, with efficient connections from Britain and the rest of Europe. Air France also maintains direct service to Guadeloupe from Miami, via Port-au-Prince, Haiti, 3 days per week.

If you're already on the islands, you can wing into Guadeloupe on **LIAT** (✆ **888/844-LIAT** [5428] in most of the Caribbean, or 268/480-5601; www.liatairline.com), which flies from Antigua, St. Maarten, St. Croix, St. Lucia, Martinique, Barbados, Grenada, Trinidad, and Dominica. **Air Caraïbes** (✆ 590/82-47-47; www.aircaraibes.com) operates a half-dozen flights a day into Guadeloupe from Martinique, as well as at least one flight a day from St. Barts, French St. Martin, and Cayenne in French Guyana.

Consider arriving in Guadeloupe as many of the locals do, on one of the daily **ferryboats** operated by **Express des Iles** (✆ **0825/35-90-00;** www.express-des-iles.com), whose vessels originate every day in Fort-de-France, Martinique, at 2pm; make a 30-minute stopover in Dominica en route (departing from Dominica around 4pm); and then dock at the quays of Pointe-à-Pitre sometime around 5:45pm, depending on weather, tides, and the vagaries of island life.

One-way passage to Pointe-à-Pitre from Dominica costs 64€ per person each way; one-way passage to Guadeloupe from Martinique is 66€ and round-trip 100€, partly the result of government subsidies. For timetables and more information in Guadeloupe, call **Agence Penchard** (the local representative of Express des Iles). For timetables and information in Martinique, contact Express des Iles (✆ **0825/35-90-00;** www.express-des-iles.com).

Getting Around

BY RENTAL CAR You may want to rent a car on Guadeloupe so that you can explore Basse-Terre; the loop around the island is one of the most scenic drives in the Caribbean. Car-rental kiosks at the airport are open to meet international flights. Rental rates at local companies may appear lower, but several readers have complained of mechanical problems, billing irregularities, and difficulties in resolving insurance disputes in the event of accidents. We recommend reserving a car in advance through **Hertz** (✆ **800/654-3001** in the U.S. and Canada, or 590/21-13-46; www.hertz.com) or **Avis** (✆ **800/331-1084** in the U.S. and Canada, or 590/21-13-54; www.avis.com), both of which are headquartered at the airport. Many of the major hotels also have car rental desks. You'll have to pay a one-time airport surcharge of 20€ and VAT (value-added tax) of 8.5%. Prices are usually 20% to 25% lower between March and early December, excepting July and August.

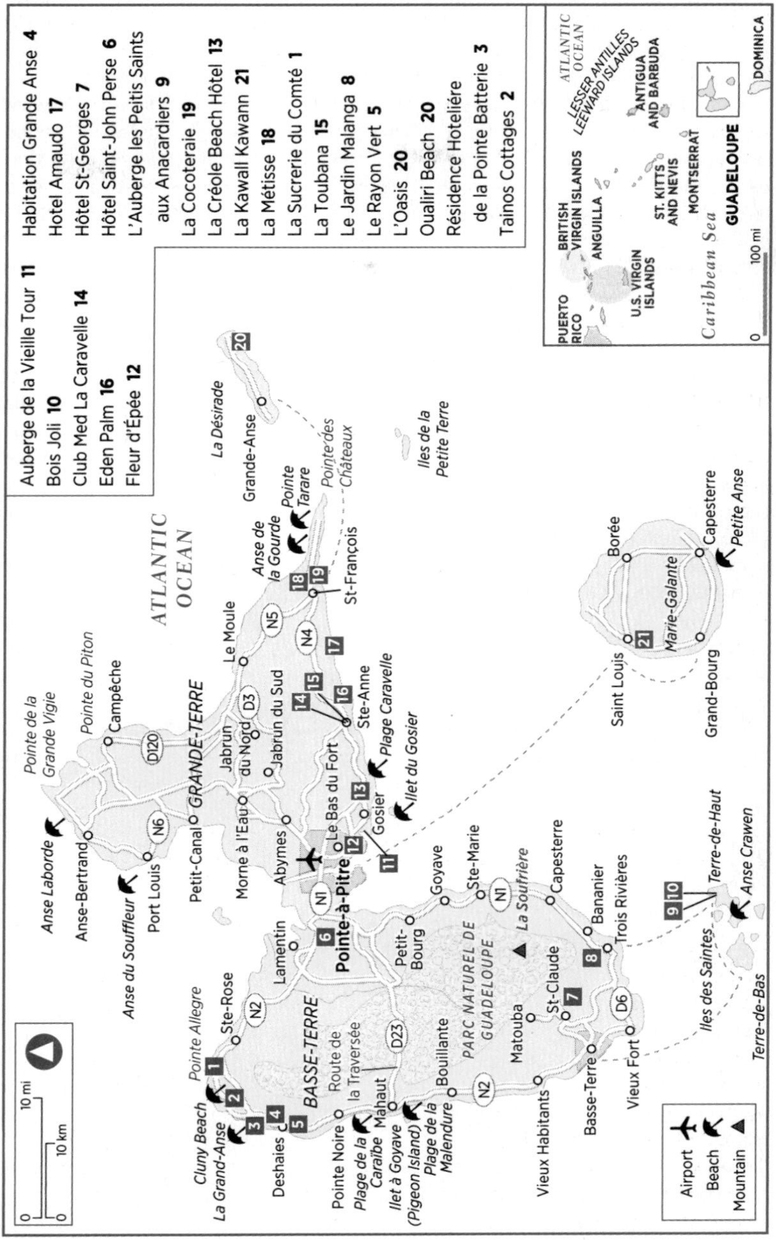

Guadeloupe

Auberge de la Vieille Tour **11**
Bois Joli **10**
Club Med La Caravelle **14**
Eden Palm **16**
Fleur d'Épée **12**
Habitation Grande Anse **4**
Hotel Amaudo **17**
Hôtel St-Georges **7**
Hôtel Saint-John Perse **6**
L'Auberge les Peitis Saints aux Anacardiers **9**
La Cocoteraie **19**
La Créole Beach Hôtel **13**
La Kawall Kawann **21**
La Métisse **18**
La Sucrerie du Comté **1**
La Toubana **15**
Le Jardin Malanga **8**
Le Rayon Vert **5**
L'Oasis **20**
Oualiri Beach **20**
Résidence Hoteliére de la Pointe Batterie **3**
Tainos Cottages **2**

0 10 mi
0 10 km
Anse Laborde
Pointe de la Grande Vigie
Anse-Bertrand
Pointe du Piton
Campêche
Anse du Souffleur
Port Louis
N6
D120
ATLANTIC OCEAN
Petit-Canal
GRANDE-TERRE
Cluny Beach
Pointe Allegre
La Grand-Anse
Ste-Rose
N2
Morne à l'Eau
Jabrun du Nord
D3
Le Moule
La Désirade
Grande-Anse
Deshaies
Lamentin
Abymes
Jabrun du Sud
N5
Anse de la Gourde
Pointe Tarare
BASSE-TERRE
N1
N4
Pointe des Châteaux
Pointe Noire
Route de la Traversée
Pointe-à-Pitre
Le Bas du Fort
St-François
Plage de la Caraïbe
Mahaut
Gosier
Ste-Anne
Plage Caravelle
Ilet à Goyave (Pigeon Island)
D23
Petit-Bourg
Ilet du Gosier
Plage de la Malendure
Bouillante
Goyave
Iles de la Petite Terre
PARC NATUREL DE GUADELOUPE
Ste-Marie
Matouba
La Soufrière
Vieux Habitants
St-Claude
Capesterre
Basse-Terre
Bananier
Saint Louis
Borée
Vieux Fort
D6
Trois Rivières
Marie-Galante
Iles des Saintes
Terre-de-Haut
Grand-Bourg
Capesterre
Petite Anse
Terre-de-Bas
Anse Crawen

Airport
Beach
Mountain

PUERTO RICO
BRITISH VIRGIN ISLANDS
ATLANTIC OCEAN
LESSER ANTILLES LEEWARD ISLANDS
ANGUILLA
U.S. VIRGIN ISLANDS
ST. KITTS AND NEVIS
ANTIGUA AND BARBUDA
MONTSERRAT
Caribbean Sea
GUADELOUPE
0 100 mi
DOMINICA

Driving is on the right-hand side of the road, and there are several gas stations along the island's main routes. Because of the distance between gas stations in outlying regions, try not to let your gas gauge fall below the halfway mark when driving outside of the capital.

BY TAXI You'll find taxis when you arrive at the airport, but no limousines or buses. From 7pm until 6am, cabbies are legally entitled to charge you 40% more than the regular fare. Some taxis in Guadeloupe have meters, although the driver will either activate them or not, depending on a complicated set of parameters involving the time of day, your destination, and his whim, even though fares are technically regulated by the French government. If the taxi you're about to enter doesn't have a working meter, always agree on a price before getting in. Approximate fares are 30€ from the airport to the hotels of Gosier, or about 20€ from the airport to anywhere within Pointe-à-Pitre. Taxis can be contacted throughout Guadeloupe by calling **Radio Cabs** at © **590/82-00-00.** It's possible, but very expensive, to sightsee by taxi. Usually, the concierge at your hotel will help you make arrangements. Fares are usually around 200€ for a 7-hour day for up to four passengers.

BY BUS Small buses link almost every hamlet to Pointe-à-Pitre. However, you may need to know some French to use the system. In Pointe-à-Pitre, you can catch a bus from the following departure points: If you're going anywhere in Basse-Terre, you'll depart from the Gare Routière de Bergevin. If the northern half of Grande-Terre is your destination, catch a bus at the Gare Routière de Mortenol. For the southern end of Grande-Terre, the buses depart from the *prolongement* (extension) of the Marché de la Darse. Infrequent and somewhat erratic service is available daily from 5:30am to 7:30pm. There is no direct bus service from the airport to Pointe-à-Pitre. To travel the entire island would cost around 5€. Many visitors find it easier, especially when they first arrive on Guadeloupe, to take a taxi.

[FastFACTS] GUADELOUPE

Banks Banks on Guadeloupe are usually open Monday to Friday 8am to 6pm, but in recent years, some, but not all, as a means of coordinating their hours with those of their clients, have begun operating Monday to Friday 8am to noon and 2 to 3:30pm. There are about a dozen banks in Pointe-à-Pitre, most with ATMs (they're called *distributeurs des billets*).

Currency Because the territory of Guadeloupe falls under the same monetary system as mainland France, the island uses the **euro (€)** as its mode of exchange. The current rate of exchange is 1€ to US$1.42. *Prices in this chapter are quoted in euros.*

Customs Items for personal use, such as tobacco, cameras, and film, are admitted without formalities or tax.

Documents U.S., British, or Canadian residents need a passport, plus a return or ongoing plane ticket.

Electricity The local electricity is 220-volt AC (50 cycles), which means that U.S.-made appliances will need a transformer and an adapter. Some of the big resorts may lend these to guests, but don't count on it.

Emergencies Call the **police** at © **17.** To report a **fire** or summon an **ambulance,** dial © **18.** For **medical emergencies,** dial © **15.**

Hospitals There are five modern hospitals on Guadeloupe, plus about two dozen clinics. Hotels and the Guadeloupe tourist office can assist in locating English-speaking doctors. A 24-hour emergency room is at the **Centre Hôpitalier**

Universitaire de Pointe-à-Pitre, Abymes (✆ **590/89-10-10**), on the northern fringe of Pointe-à-Pitre; for emergency services here, dial ✆ **15.**

Language The official language is French; Creole is the unofficial second language. English is spoken only in the major tourist centers, rarely in the countryside.

Liquor Laws Liquor is sold in grocery and liquor stores on any day of the week. It's legal to have an open container, though the authorities are very strict about littering, disorderly behavior, and drunk driving.

Pharmacies The pharmacies carry French medicines, and most over-the-counter U.S. drugs have French equivalents. Prescribed medicines can be purchased if you have the prescription with you. At least one drugstore is always open; the tourist office can tell you what pharmacies are open at what time.

Police In an emergency, call ✆ **17.** Otherwise, call ✆ **590/89-77-17.**

Safety Guadeloupe is relatively free of serious crime. But don't go wandering alone at night on the streets of Pointe-à-Pitre; by nightfall they are relatively deserted and might be dangerous. Purse-snatching by fast-riding motorcyclists has been reported, so exercise caution.

Taxes A departure tax, required on scheduled flights, is included in the airfares. Hotel taxes are included in all room rates.

Telephone To call Guadeloupe from the United States, dial **011** (the international access code), then **590** (the country code for Guadeloupe), then **590** again and the rest of the local number, which will be six digits. If you want to call another island of the French Antilles, be aware that St. Barts, French St. Martin, and offshore dependencies of Guadeloupe such as Ile des Saints or La Désirade are all directly linked to the phone network of Guadeloupe. Consequently, no telephone prefix is required, and you can dial any of those islands simply by dialing the six-digit local phone number. But if you're on Guadeloupe and want to dial someone in Martinique, you'll have to punch in the prefix for Martinique **(0596),** followed by the six-digit local number.

Time Guadeloupe is on Atlantic Standard Time year-round, 1 hour ahead of Eastern Standard Time (when it's 6am in New York, it's 7am on Guadeloupe). When daylight saving time is in effect in the U.S., clocks in New York and Guadeloupe show the same time.

Tipping Hotels usually add a 10% to 15% service charge. Restaurants always add a 15% service charge, and no additional tip is needed. Most taxi drivers who own their own cars do not expect a tip; if they've been especially helpful with your luggage, you might give them an additional 10%.

Water While on Guadeloupe, stick to bottled water only.

Weather The average temperature in Guadeloupe is 82°F (28°C) in summer, dropping to an average of 76°F (24°C) in winter. The rainiest months are between June and October.

POINTE-A-PITRE

The port and chief city of Guadeloupe, Pointe-à-Pitre, lies on Grande-Terre. Unfortunately, it doesn't have the old-world charm of Fort-de-France on Martinique, and what beauty it does possess is often hidden behind closed doors.

Having been burned and rebuilt so many times, the port now lacks character. Modern apartments and condominiums form a high-rise backdrop over jerry-built shacks and industrial suburbs. The rather narrow streets are crammed during the day with a colorful crowd that creates a permanent traffic jam. However, at sunset the town becomes quiet again and almost deserted. The only charm left is around the waterfront, where you half expect to see Bogie sipping rum at a cafe table.

Most visitors just drop in to Pointe-à-Pitre for **shopping.** It's best to visit the town in the morning (you can easily cover it in half a day), taking in the waterfront and outdoor market (the latter is livelier in the early hours).

The town center is **Place de la Victoire,** a park shaded by palm trees and poincianas. Here you'll see some old sandbox trees said to have been planted by Victor Hugues, the mulatto who organized a revolutionary army of both whites and blacks to establish a dictatorship. In this square he kept a guillotine busy, and the death-dealing instrument stood here until modern times.

With the completion of the **Centre Saint-John-Perse,** the waterfront of Pointe-à-Pitre has been transformed from a bastion of old warehouses and cruise-terminal buildings into an architectural complex comprising a hotel, 3 restaurants, 80 shops and boutiques, a bank, and the expanded headquarters of Guadeloupe's Port Authority. Named for Saint-John Perse, the 20th-century poet and Nobel Laureate who was born just a few blocks away, the center is designed in contemporary French Caribbean style, which blends with the traditional architecture of Pointe-à-Pitre. On the island, go to the local tourist office, the **Comité du Tourisme des Iles de la Guadeloupe,** Square de la Banque 5 (✆ **590/82-09-30;** www.go2guadeloupe.com), for maps, information, and advice.

Where to Stay

Hôtel Saint-John Perse Stay here only if you have business in town or need to be here for an early morning flight (it's 15 min. from the airport). This hotel rises four stories above the harborfront, near the quays. The small rooms are clean, simple, and furnished with locally crafted mahogany pieces. Very few have views of the sea. Bathrooms are small with no frills; about half have tub/showers. Once you check in, the laissez-faire staff will probably leave you alone until the end of your stay. There's a simple coffee shop/cafe on street level. To reach a beach, you'll have to travel 3km (2 miles) to the east to Le Bas du Fort and the Gosier area (see below).

Centre Saint-John-Perse, quai de Croisières (at the harborfront), 97110 Pointe-à-Pitre, Guadeloupe, F.W.I. www.saint-john-perse.com. ✆ **590/82-51-57.** Fax 590/82-52-61. 44 units. Winter 105€ double; off season 75€ double. Rates include continental breakfast. AE, MC, V. **Amenities:** Coffee shop. *In room:* A/C, TV, Wi-Fi (free).

Where to Dine

Côté Jardin ★ FRENCH This is one of the finest, most upscale independent restaurants in Guadeloupe, with an allegiance to the tenets of French cooking that you might expect on the French mainland. Because of its fine food and its sense of Gallic style, no one really cares that there isn't a water view. Surrounded by potted flowers and shrubs, with a view over palm trees and reproductions of paintings by Miró and Matisse, you'll dine in a white-and-green room with a hint of Provence. Menu items focus on fresh shellfish, much of which comes from fish tanks near the restaurant's entrance. Scallops with a Noilly Prat vermouth sauce, sweetbreads and morels in puff pastry, and several different preparations of foie gras (including a succulent version that's fried and served with a reduction of sweet Banyuls wine) make a flavorful beginning. This restaurant is particularly proud of specific European menu items, which include *boeuf charolais* imported from France, usually served with pepper sauce.

Your Own Villa

If you'd like to rent a villa on island, contact **Aquarelle's Villas,** 1 Domaine de Nogent, Ste-Rose (✆/fax **590/68-65-23;** www.aquarelles-villas.com), which offers 15 luxurious villas on the north coast of Basse-Terre. Each bungalow has a private pool and direct beach access. Villas contain two to five bedrooms and are an excellent choice for families. They range in price from 140€ to 690€. Each unit contains a fully equipped kitchen and two or three bathrooms. Room service is available from an on-site restaurant serving French and Creole specialities.

French Caribbean International (✆ **800/322-2223** in the U.S. and Canada; www.frenchcaribbean.com) is the largest resource for villa rentals in the French West Indies, with a wide variety of accomodations. Cottages are for rent in both Basse-Terre and Grand-Terre, starting at 115€ a night.

La Marina, Pointe-à-Pitre. ✆ **590/90-91-28.** Reservations recommended. Main courses 27€–36€; prix-fixe menus 40€–45€. AE, MC, V. Mon–Fri noon–2:30pm and 7:30–10pm; Sat 7:30–10pm.

Sucré-Salé TRADITIONAL FRENCH In the heart of Pointe-à-Pitre, adjacent to an Air France office and near several banks, this restaurant is always filled at lunchtime with deal makers and office workers. The theme revolves around jazz, with portraits of Louis Armstrong, Billie Holliday, and Miles Davis. A terrace overlooks the busy boulevard. The charming Marius Pheron, the Guadeloupéan-born owner who did an 18-year stint in Paris, offers filets of snapper served with pommes soufflés and black pepper, or meal-size salads, entrecôte steaks, and an impressive medley of grilled fish.

Bd. Légitimus, Pointe-à-Pitre. ✆ **590/21-22-55.** Reservations recommended. Main courses 8€–27€; fixed-price menu 17€. MC, V. Mon–Sat 7am–2:15pm.

Shopping

We suggest that you skip a shopping tour of Pointe-à-Pitre if you're going to Fort-de-France on Martinique, as you'll find far more merchandise there, and perhaps friendlier service. If you're not, however, we recommend the following shops, some of which line rue Frébault.

Your best buys will be anything French—perfumes from Chanel, silk scarves from Hermès, cosmetics from Dior, crystal from Lalique and Baccarat. Though they're still expensive, we've found some of these items discounted (but not often) as much as 30% below U.S. or Canadian prices. Most shops will accept U.S. dollars, but they'll give these discounts only for purchases made by traveler's check. Purchases are duty-free if brought directly from store to plane. In addition to the places below, there are also two duty-free shops at **Aéroport Guadeloupe Pôle Caraibes** (✆ **590/21-14-66**) selling liquor, rums, perfumes, crystal, and cigarettes.

Most shops open at 8:30am, close at 1pm, and then reopen between 3 and 5:30pm. They're closed on Saturday afternoons, Sundays, and holidays. When the cruise ships are in port, many shopkeepers stay open longer and on weekends, and sometimes remain open throughout the midday closing.

One of the best places to buy French perfumes, at prices often lower than those charged in Paris, is **Phoenicia,** 121 rue Frébault (✆ **590/82-25-75**), which has a

> **The Essence of Guadeloupe**
>
> **At some point as you stroll through the market, order a glass of *rhum agricole* from one of the local vendors. The drink is a pure form of rum that's fermented from sugar-cane juice. Savvy locals claim that the rum (whose brand name is Rhum Damoiseau) is the only kind you can drink without a hangover the next morning.**

good selection of imported cosmetics as well. Another leading perfume shop is **Au Bonheur des Dames,** 49 rue Frébault (✆ **590/82-00-30**), also known for its skin-care products.

If you're adventurous, you may want to seek out some native goods in little shops along the back streets of Pointe-à-Pitre. Look for the straw hats, or *salacos,* made in Les Saintes islands, usually created from split bamboo. Native **doudou dolls** are also popular gift items.

Open-air stalls surround the **Marché Couvert (covered market)** at the corner of rue Frébault and rue Peynier. Here you can discover the many fruits, spices, and vegetables that are fun to look at as well as to taste. In madras turbans, local Creole women make deals over their strings of fire-red pimientos. The bright fabrics they wear compete with the rich colors of oranges, papayas, bananas, mangos, and pineapples. Best times to visit are Monday to Saturday 7am to 1pm.

LE BAS DU FORT

Just 3km (2 miles) east of Pointe-à-Pitre is the tourist area of Le Bas du Fort, near Gosier. This is the best place to stay if you'd like to be near (but not in) the capital and if you'd like a location near the international airport. Although it has some good sandy beaches, there are far better ones farther out from the center. One drawback is that the area is rather built up and you may not find the tranquillity here you'll enjoy in other parts of Guadeloupe.

Aquarium de la Guadeloupe, place Créole, Marina Gosier (✆ **590/90-92-38;** www.guadeloupeaquarium.com), is one of the most modern aquariums in the Caribbean, and it can be visited in about an hour. Just off the highway near Le Bas du Fort Marina, the aquarium is home to tropical fish, coral, underwater plants, huge sharks, and other sea creatures. Hours are daily from 9am to 7pm. Admission is 9€ for adults, 6€ for children 5 to 12, and free for children 4 and under.

Where to Stay

Fleur d'Epée ☺ Few other hotels on Guadeloupe have been reconfigured and regrouped as often and as radically as this one. Originally built as a member of the chain hotel Novotel in the mid-1970s, it was combined with neighboring structures into a larger resort. That megaresort was carved up early in the millennium into condo units (now independent and positioned across the boulevard). Fleur d'Epée isn't the most stylish hotel on Guadeloupe, but its owners have spruced up the design (basically a chain-motel boxy look) with bright colors, especially tones of blue. Most units have tiled floors, an efficiently designed floor plan, and, in most cases, either a private terrace or a veranda. It sits directly beside a coastline dotted with a pair of crescent-shaped bays and a short, white-sand beach.

Le Bas du Fort, 97190 Gosier, Guadeloupe, F.W.I. www.hotel-fleur-depee.com. © **590/90-40-00.** Fax 590/90-99-07. 191 units. Winter 215€–260€ double; off season 145€–200€ double. Rates include breakfast. AE, DC, MC, V. **Amenities:** Restaurant; bar; children's programs; outdoor pool; free snorkeling. *In room:* A/C, TV, hair dryer, Wi-Fi (free).

Where to Dine

Rosini ★ ☺ NORTHERN ITALIAN/VENETIAN This is the best Italian restaurant in the French West Indies, thanks to the sophisticated father-in-law/son-in-law team of Venice-born Luciano Rosini and Christophe Giraud, from Provence. It's contained within two air-conditioned dining rooms, on the ground floor of an upscale condo complex across from the Fleur d'Eté in Le Bas du Fort. Recorded opera music sets the mood for succulent versions of tournedos layered with foie gras, *osso buco* (veal shanks), and freshwater prawns served *diavolo* style in a spicy tomato, garlic, and parsley sauce with freshly made fettuccine. Ravioli comes stuffed either with veal and herbs or with lobster. At least 10 types of pizza are available for kids. English is readily understood here.

La Porte des Caraïbes, Le Bas du Fort, Gosier. © **590/90-87-81.** Reservations recommended. Main courses 16€–49€. AE, MC, V. Daily noon–2:30pm and 7–10:30pm.

GOSIER

Gosier is where some of the best beachfront in Guadeloupe begins, and it has become one of the island's major resort centers, since it has nearly 8km (5 miles) of sandy but narrow beach, stretching east from Pointe-à-Pitre. All the hotels below are close to the sands. We like the funky charm of the town, which evokes a little resort along the French Riviera. Unlike many parts of the Caribbean, this area attracts mainly French visitors, so you'll feel as though you're on a Mediterranean holiday. Gosier also has some of the island's best dining and nightlife, plus a casino.

You can take a 15-minute climb to the 18th-century ruins of **Fort Fleur-d'Epée.** Its dungeons and battlements are testaments to the ferocious fighting between the French and British armies in 1794. The ruins command the crown of a hill, which affords good views over the bay of Pointe-à-Pitre in a gardenlike setting. If the visibility is good, you can see the neighboring offshore islands of Marie-Galante and Iles des Saintes.

Where to Stay

Auberge de la Vieille Tour ★ This place was once a family inn built around the shadow of an old sugar mill. Set on a 3-hectare (7½-acre) bluff, the property encompasses a small private beach. The older guest rooms are short on charm. The better-maintained units are usually within La Résidence, a series of town-house-style accommodations set near the pool. Their desirability is rivaled only by units referred to as "luxury class," set close to the water near the beach. Rooms have comfortable furnishings and compact bathrooms. The restaurants La Vieille Tour and Le Zagaya serve excellent French and Creole food, respectively, in relatively elegant, semiformal settings. L'Ajoupa is a grill-style indoor/outdoor affair.

Montauban, 97190 Gosier, Guadeloupe, F.W.I. www.mgallery.com. © **800/263-4835** in the U.S., or 590/84-23-23. Fax 590/84-33-43. 103 units. Winter 270€–490€ double; off season 180€–290€ double; year-round 455€–750€ suite. Rates include continental breakfast. AE, MC, V. **Amenities:** 3 restaurants; 2 bars; outdoor pool; room service; 2 tennis courts (lit); watersports equipment/rentals. *In room:* A/C, TV, hair dryer, minibar, Wi-Fi (free).

La Créole Beach Hôtel ☺ This is one of the largest resorts on Guadeloupe, but because it's divided into four distinct sections, you'll get a sense of isolation and privacy. It's alongside two sandy beaches within a lush setting of lawns, trees, hibiscus, and bougainvillea, and it has a strong French Creole flavor. The most upscale section is Les Palmes, which has the best furnishings and the most spacious rooms. Second is Le Creole, a three-story building with verandas influenced by French colonial architecture. Slightly less desirable is Le Mahogany, a comfortable compound with oceanfront rooms (most without kitchens). The most basic, Le Yucca, houses the family units with kitchens. Most rooms are spacious and contain two queen-size beds.

Pointe de la Verdure (B.P. 61), 97190 Gosier, Guadeloupe, F.W.I. www.creolebeach.com. ✆ **590/90-46-46.** Fax 590/90-46-66. 218 units. Winter 145€–325€ double, 475€ junior suite; off season 110€–215€ double, 235€ junior suite. Children 11 and under stay free in parent's room. Rates include continental breakfast. AE, DC, MC, V. **Amenities:** 2 restaurants; bar; babysitting; outdoor pool; room service; spa; watersports equipment/rentals. *In room:* A/C, TV, fridge, hair dryer, kitchenette (in some), minibar, Wi-Fi (in some; free).

Where to Dine

La Vielle Tour Restaurant ★ FRENCH The best dining in Gosier is at this first-class restaurant in the previously recommended hotel of the same name (see above). Installed in a former sugar mill, the restaurant presents a refined menu of sunny tastes, often using local produce. The menu is forever changing, but a few specialties appear regularly, including the highly touted fresh sea scallops; at the last minute, the chef douses them with vintage rum for extra flavor and tops the concoction with butter made with blood oranges. When available, fresh lobster is a feature, as is rack of lamb (imported from mainland France) and duck confit. Luscious desserts are made fresh daily.

Montauban, Gosier. ✆ **590/84-23-23.** Reservations required. Main courses 28€; 3-course *menu du jour* 50€. AE, MC, V. Daily noon–2pm and 7–10pm. Closed Wed and Sun off season.

STE-ANNE

About 14km (8¾ miles) east of Gosier, little Ste-Anne is a sugar town and a resort with many fine beaches and lodgings. In many ways, it's the most charming village of Guadeloupe, with its pastel-colored town hall, its church, and its principal square, **Place de la Victoire,** which features a statue of French abolitionist Victor Schoelcher.

Where to Stay & Dine

Club Med La Caravelle ★ ☺ This all-inclusive chain resort, covering 19 hectares (47 acres) along a peninsula dotted with palm trees, opens onto one of the finest beaches in the French West Indies. The renovated guest rooms tend to be small but have good beds. (All but 10 units have twin beds; the others have queen-size beds.) The building known as Marie-Galante contains the resort's largest and most comfortable rooms (each with a terrace or veranda). Children are welcome here, and there's been an upgrade in the facilities, including the Mini-Club with child minding and day-camp facilities. The resort also has an annex containing only single rooms. The meals here are nothing if not generous. The breakfast and lunch buffet tables overflow with French, Continental, and Creole food. Dinner is served in the main dining room or in the candlelit, more romantic annex restaurant beside the sea.

Begin the Beguine

The folkloric dance troupe **Les Ballets Guadeloupéens** makes frequent appearances at the big hotels, whirling and moving to the rhythms of island music in colorful costumes and well-choreographed routines. Some resorts, including the Club Med La Caravelle (p. 310), use their visit to set the theme for the evening, serving up a banquet of traditional island dishes to accompany the dance, music, and costumes.

Ask at your hotel where the Ballets Guadeloupéans will be appearing during your stay. Schedules vary widely according to the season and the touring agenda of the Ballets (part of their year is spent touring, usually in Europe or aboard some of the larger cruise ships), but you can usually catch them as they rotate through the Kalenda Resort, the Club Med La Caravelle, and—depending on a wide set of circumstances—the Creole Beach and/or the Novotel Coralia. On the night of any of these performances, you can order a drink at the bar and catch the show, or join in the hotel buffet for a flat price. Buffets usually start around 7:30pm, with the show beginning at 9:30pm.

97180 Ste-Anne, Guadeloupe, F.W.I. www.clubmed.com. ✆ **800/CLUB-MED** (258-2633) in the U.S., or 590/85-49-50. Fax 590/85-49-70. 300 units. Dec to early Jan and Aug 2,825€ per person; mid-Jan to July and Sept–Nov 1,635€ per person. Rates all-inclusive for 7-night stays, based on double occupancy. Children age 4–12 are charged 80% of the adult rate. Single supplement 10%–50% above the per-person double rate. AE, MC, V. **Amenities:** 2 restaurants; 2 bars; nightclub; children's program; exercise center; outdoor pool; 4 tennis courts (lit); watersports equipment/rentals. *In room:* A/C, TV, hair dryer, Wi-Fi (free).

Eden Palm ★ This hidden-away charmer grew up around an antique windmill of a former sugar plantation. Branching out from its core is a series of stylishly furnished cottages—actually duplex bungalows with two well-furnished guest rooms opening onto terraces fronting landscaped grounds. Accommodations are attractively furnished with tiles, Italian marble, and teak and mahogany wood furnishings. One of the reasons to stay here is to enjoy the tropical gardens of flowers and herbs, complete with a fish pond and enough water lilies to enchant Claude Monet. The hotel provides a golf cart to haul you to a white-sand beach about a 2-minute ride away. The most festive time to be here is at Sunday brunch, when island musicians entertain while diners enjoy a lavish buffet.

Lieu dit Le Helleux, Ste-Anne, 97180 Guadeloupe, F.W.I. www.edenpalm.com. ✆ **590/88-48-48.** Fax 590/88-48-49. 66 units. Winter 300€–365€ double, 350€–575€ suite; off season 102€–155€ double, 175€–380€ suite. Rates include breakfast. AE, MC, V. **Amenities:** Restaurant; bar; exercise room; outdoor pool; room service; tennis court (lit). *In room:* A/C, TV, minibar.

La Toubana ★ Built on 2 hectares (5 acres) of sloping land close to the beach (a 5-min. walk on a path carved into the cliff side), La Toubana is centered around a low-lying stone building on a rocky cliff overlooking the bay and Ste-Anne Beach. Many guests come for the panoramic view, which on a clear day encompasses Marie-Galante, Dominica, La Désirade, and the Iles des Saintes, but you'll quickly learn that there's more to this place than just a panorama. The red-roofed bungalows lie scattered among the tropical shrubs along the adjacent hillsides (*toubana* means "small house" in Arawak); there are 10 garden units and 12 more upscale oceanview units. Each has a kitchenette, comfortable French furnishings, a terrace, a rather compact bathroom, and either two twin beds or one king-size bed. Cots for kids are available on request.

Durivage (B.P. 63), 97180 Ste-Anne, Guadeloupe, F.W.I. www.toubana.com. ✆ **590/88-25-78.** Fax 590/88-38-90. 32 units. Winter 235€–420€ double; off season 140€–180€ double. Rates include continental breakfast. AE, MC, V. **Amenities:** Restaurant; bar; babysitting; deep-sea fishing; outdoor pool; scooters; snorkeling; tennis court (lit). *In room:* A/C, TV, hair dryer, kitchenette, Wi-Fi (free).

ST-FRANÇOIS ★

Continuing east from Ste-Anne, you'll notice many old round towers named for Father Labat, the Dominican founder of the sugar-cane industry. These towers were once used as mills to grind the cane. St-François, 40km (25 miles) east of Pointe-à-Pitre, used to be a sleepy fishing village; then Air France discovered it and opened a Meridien hotel with a casino. That was followed by the promotional activities of J. F. Rozan, a native who invested heavily to make St-François a jet-set resort. Now the once sleepy village has first-class accommodations, as well as an airport available to private jets, a golf course (it's the golfing center of the island), and a marina, where there's a casino (see "Guadeloupe After Dark," later in this chapter). It also has some good beaches and is known for its Creole restaurants.

Where to Stay

Hotel Amaudo ★ Outside the center of St. François, this discovery is built in the colonial style overlooking the bay Anse à la Barque. Facing the sea and surrounded by well-manicured gardens, it is a haven of peace and tranquillity, definitely not for those seeking action. The midsize bedrooms are rather homelike, each furnished with taste and decorated differently. From the hotel's terrace, you can enjoy a panoramic view of such offshore islands as Marie Galante and Les Saintes.

Anse à la Barque, 97118 St-François, Guadeloupe, F.W.I. www.amaudo.fr. ✆ **590/88-87-00.** 10 units. Winter 130€–175€ double; off season 100€–130€ double. MC, V. **Amenities:** Breakfast room. *In room:* A/C, TV, fridge, Wi-Fi (free).

La Cocoteraie ★★ This is a plush, suites-only resort, the island's finest choice for a luxury holiday. It opens onto a lagoon with two private but small white-sand beaches. The hotel hides behind a colonial plantation-style facade, flanked by a series of buildings, also in the colonial style. Twenty of the units are more desirable because they open right onto the beach. Across from the hotel lies the Robert Trent Jones, Sr., golf course. Each unit comes with a spacious patio or a balcony overlooking the water or else one of the largest hotel pools on Guadeloupe. Some of the accommodations are equipped with a duo of tub-only baths; others have tub/showers. Meals are served in a well-designed open-sided pavilion, La Varangue (see below).

Ave. de l'Europe, 97118 St-François, Guadeloupe, F.W.I. www.lacocoteraie.com. ✆ **590/88-79-81.** Fax 590/88-78-33. 50 suites. Year-round 120€–745€ suite. AE, DC, MC, V. Closed mid-Aug to mid-Oct. **Amenities:** Restaurant; bar; babysitting; exercise room; golf; outdoor pool; room service; 2 tennis courts (lit); Wi-Fi (in lobby; free). *In room:* A/C, TV, hair dryer, minibar.

La Métisse ★ ☺ The French would call this pink-stucco hotel with personalized service and tasteful accommodations a *hotel de charme*. It's not on the beach, but there is an artificially illuminated swimming pool with a raised hot tub, and the property's grounds are cooled by trade winds. The owners will transport you to the beach, into town, or to the nearby golf course. Doors can be opened to connect some of the units, which is a plus for families. The gardens are attractively planted with jasmine, gardenia, palms, hibiscus, and frangipani. The bar is noted for its fresh-fruit cocktails, including the cocktail Métisse (a blend of coconut, banana, maracudja, and cinnamon). Immaculate bedrooms are furnished with white-cane pieces.

66 Les Hauts de St-François, 97118 St-François, Guadeloupe, F.W.I. www.im-caraibes.com/metisse. ✆ **590/88-70-00.** Fax 590/88-59-08. 7 units. Winter 155€–340€ double; off season 136€–295€ double. Rates include continental breakfast. AE, MC, V. **Amenities:** Bar; babysitting; outdoor pool. *In room:* A/C, TV, hair dryer, minibar, Wi-Fi (free).

Where to Dine

La Porte des Indes ★ INDIAN/PAKISTANI In this beautifully restored Creole villa, you can treat your taste buds to a radical departure from the standard French/Creole cuisine served on island. You'll dine in an open-air pergola, sampling an array of tandoori, curry, and freshly baked Indian breads. The food is full of spice and flavor, and local produce is used when possible, though spices come from the East. Your waitress is likely to be wearing a sari as she guides you through the menu, which can be topped with Indian ice cream crowned with a ginger confit. Service can be slow when there's a full house, but it's worth the wait. The place can get very crowded on Friday or Saturday night, so reserve well in advance.

Lieu dit Devarieux, St-François. ✆ **590/21-30-87.** Reservations required. Main courses 20€–60€. V. Tues–Sat 7–10pm and Sun noon–2pm. Closed mid-Sept to mid-Oct.

La Varangue ★ FRENCH Named after the figureheads that used to grace the prows of pirate ships, this is the culinary showcase of La Cocoteraie hotel (p. 312). In many ways, it functions as the social and decorative showcase of the hotel as well, positioned adjacent to a low bridge that traverses the resort's swimming pool, near the reception desk, within full view of the beach and the gardens. Menu items at lunch revolve around fresh salads, pastas, and relatively simple versions of grilled fish and meats. Dinners are more elaborate, more leisurely, and more romantic, with flickering candles and such dishes as a crabmeat tart with exotic mushrooms; cream of shellfish soup; a confit of dorado (mahimahi) with tandoori spices and coconut milk; and an elegant version of lobster salad. And for any die-hard lover of Gallic food, there's even foie gras flash-seared in butter, similar to something you'd find on the French mainland.

In La Cocoteraie, ave. de l'Europe, St-François. ✆ **590/88-79-81.** Reservations recommended for nonresidents of the hotel. Main courses 20€–40€; lunch platters 12€–29€. AE, DC, MC, V. Daily noon–2pm and 7:30–10pm.

POINTE DES CHATEAUX

Eleven kilometers (6¾ miles) east of St-François is the rocky headland of Pointe des Châteaux, the easternmost tip of Grand-Terre, where the Atlantic meets the Caribbean. You'll see cliffs sculpted by the sea into dramatic castlelike formations, the erosion typical of France's Brittany coast. The view is panoramic. At the top is a cross erected in the 19th century.

You might want to walk to **Pointe des Colibris,** the extreme end of Guadeloupe. From here you'll have a view of the northeastern sector of the island, and to the east a look at La Désirade, an island that has the appearance of a huge vessel anchored far away. (See "Side Trips from Guadeloupe," p. 327.)

Pointe des Châteaux has miles of coved white-sand beaches. Most of these are safe for swimming, except at the point where the waves of the turbulent Atlantic

Nude Trysting

This part of Guadeloupe is studded with wind-carved coves. At **Anse Tarare,** the Caribbean Sea meets the Atlantic Ocean. From the signposted parking lot along the Route de la Pointe des Châteaux, you'll see a narrow pathway leading through scrub to the sea and Anse Tarare. If you want, you (and your loved one) can strip down here. Of course, it's wise to bring the makings of a French beachside picnic—a bottle of chilled rosé, a wheel of brie, and a freshly baked baguette.

encounter the tranquil Caribbean Sea, churning up the waters. Since there are no hotels here, you can come just for the day to enjoy the beaches.

Where to Dine

Iguane Café ★ FRENCH/INTERNATIONAL This bistro/cafe is one of the best dining choices on the island. Owners Marie Laure and Sylvan Serourt serve their creative cuisine at a point on the road connecting St-François with Pointe des Châteaux. The restaurant has a colorful West Indian decor, an open-air kitchen, and English-language menus. Don't come here in a rush, as food is cooked to order and the service is, well, relaxed. Mellow out at the bar, with its selection of nearly two dozen rum punches, including one flavored with cinnamon. A novelty drink comes from a large jar of rum with several hibiscus flowers floating inside. On the creative and varied menu, begin with a delectable sheep's cheese appetizer, battered in a crust with zesty Creole spices. You might also opt for the goose-liver pâté or a napoleon of sweet breads and lobster. We always gravitate to the fresh fish of the day, perhaps snapper, aromatically cooked in a puff pastry, or John Dory with Indian spices.

Route de la Pointe des Châteaux, St-François. ✆ **590/88-61-37.** Reservations recommended. Main courses 26€–32€; fixed-price menus 59€ and 79€. AE, MC, V. Wed–Mon 7:30–10pm; Sun 12:30–2pm. Closed Sept and 1st week of Oct.

A Stop in Le Moule

To go back to Pointe-à-Pitre from Pointe des Châteaux, you can use an alternative route, the N5 from St-François. After a 14km (8¾-mile) drive, you'll reach the village of **Le Moule,** which was founded at the end of the 17th century and known long before Pointe-à-Pitre. It used to be a major shipping port for sugar but was devastated in the hurricane of 1928 and never regained its importance. Now it's a tiny coastal fishing village. Because it offers more than 15km (9¼ miles) of crescent-shaped beach, it's developing as a destination.

Specialties of this Guadeloupean village are *palourdes,* clams that thrive in the semisalty mouths of freshwater rivers. Known for being more tender and less rubbery than saltwater clams, they have a distinct sulfur taste not unlike that of overpoached eggs. Local gastronomes prepare them with saffron and aged rum or cognac.

To return to Pointe-à-Pitre, we suggest that you use Route D3 toward Abymes. The road winds around as you plunge deeply into Grand-Terre. About halfway along the way a road is signposted to **Jabrun du Nord** and **Jabrun du Sud.** These two villages are inhabited by Caucasians with blond hair, said to be survivors of aristocrats slaughtered during the Revolution. Those who escaped found safety by hiding out in Les

Grands Fonds. The most important family here is named Matignon, and they gave their name to the colony known as "les Blancs Matignon." These citizens are said to be related to the late Prince Rainier of Monaco. Pointe-à-Pitre lies only 16km (10 miles) from Les Grand Fonds.

THE NORTH COAST OF GRANDE-TERRE ★★

From Pointe-à-Pitre, head northeast toward Abymes, passing next through Morne à l'Eau; you'll reach the small but not insignificant settlement of **Petit Canal** after 21km (13 miles). This is Guadeloupe's sugar-cane country, and a sweet smell fills the air.

Port Louis

Continuing northwest along the coast from Petit Canal, you come to Port Louis, well known for its beautiful beach, **Anse du Souffleur,** which lacks facilities. We like it best in spring, when the brilliant white sand is effectively shown off against the flaming red poinciana. During the week, the beach is an especially quiet spot. The little port town, though, has some good restaurants.

WHERE TO DINE

Le Poisson d'Or ★ CREOLE You enter this white-sided Antillean house by walking down a narrow corridor and emerging into a rustic dining room lined with varnished pine. Despite the simple setting, the food is well prepared and satisfying. You might begin with rillettes of marlin or stuffed crabs, followed by a heaping platter of raw shellfish, grilled lobster, or local fish, either grilled or prepared as a savory *court bouillon*. If you're in the mood for something French-inspired, consider a wine-flavored boeuf bourguignon, or an *entrecôte maître d'hotel* (grilled steak with butter and fresh herbs). Dessert might be a flambéed banana or a scoop of coconut-flavored ice cream. Don't even think of coming here at night without an advance reservation—you might find the place locked up and empty.

2 blvd. Achille René Boisneuf, Port Louis. ✆ **590/22-88-63.** Reservations required for dinner. Main courses 8€–35€; fixed-price menu 16€–45€. AE, MC, V. Daily 10am–5pm and 6:30–11pm. Closed Sept. Drive northwest from Petit-Canal along the coastal road.

Anse-Bertrand

About 8km (5 miles) from Port Louis is Anse-Bertrand, the northernmost village of Guadeloupe. What is now a fishing village was the last refuge of the Carib tribes, and a reserve was once created here. Everything now, however, is sleepy.

WHERE TO DINE

Les Tables d'Hote au Jardin de l'Eden ★ FRENCH/CARIBBEAN This little discovery lies 2.4km (1½ miles) from the sea, featuring dining on a large terrace centered in a well-landscaped garden. The menu depends on the catch of the day. Fish is market fresh and is featured with the vegetables of the season. The changing menu also offers a homemade soup of the day. For those not into seafood, a select few of pork, beef, and chicken dishes are also prepared for you. Eel is an occasional delicacy, as is lobster.

The little inn also rents four utterly simple bedrooms, costing only 25€ per person nightly. Cooling is by ceiling fan.

Rue Toussain Louverture. ✆ **590/22-16-66.** www.jardin-eden-guadeloupe.blogspot.com. Reservations required. Main courses 12€. No credit cards. Mon–Thurs noon–3pm (also Sun in winter); Fri–Sat noon–3pm and 7–10pm; Sun 7–10pm.

AROUND BASSE-TERRE ★★★

Leaving Pointe-à-Pitre by Route N1, you can explore the western coast and the island of Basse-Terre. Here you'll find views as panoramic as those along the corniche along the French Riviera, but without the heavy traffic and crowds. After 2km (1¼ miles), you cross the Rivière Salée at Pont de la Gabarre. This narrow strait separates the two islands that form Guadeloupe. For the next 6km (3¾ miles), the road runs straight through sugar-cane fields.

Turn right on Route N2 toward **Baie Mahault.** (Don't confuse this with the town of Mahault on Basse-Terre's westernmost coast.) Head northwest to **Lamentin,** a village settled by *corsairs* at the beginning of the 18th century. Scattered about are some colonial mansions, but neither of these villages merits a stopover.

Ste-Rose

From Lamentin, you can drive for 10km (6¼ miles) to Ste-Rose, where you'll find several good **beaches.** On your left, a small road leads in a few minutes to **Sofaia,** from which you'll have a panoramic view over the coast and forest preserve. You can easily skip this, however, if you're rushed for time.

WHERE TO STAY

La Sucrerie du Comté ★ Although you'll see the ruins of a 19th-century sugar factory (including a rusting locomotive) on this hotel's 5 hectares (12 acres) of forested land overlooking the sea, most of the resort is modern. The medium-size accommodations are in 26 red- or green-toned bungalows. Each cozy bungalow has chunky and rustic handmade furniture and a bay window overlooking either the sea or a garden. (Each bungalow contains two units, both with ceiling fans; none has a TV or phone.) The nearest major beach is La Grand-Anse, a 10- to 15-minute drive from the hotel. There's a small and narrow beach (Plage des Amandiers) within a 5-minute walk from the hotel, although the swimming here isn't very good.

Comté de Loheac, 97115 Ste-Rose, Guadeloupe, F.W.I. www.primeahotels.com. ✆ **590/28-60-17.** Fax 590/28-65-63. 52 units. Winter 90€–120€ double; off season 50€–80€ double. Rates include breakfast. AE, DC, MC, V. Closed Sept to early Oct. **Amenities:** Restaurant; bar; babysitting; outdoor pool; watersports equipment/rentals. *In room:* A/C, ceiling fan, hair dryer, minibar, no phone.

WHERE TO DINE

Restaurant Clara ★ CREOLE On the waterfront near the center of town is the culinary statement of Clara Lesueur. Clara lived for 12 years in Paris as a member of an experimental jazz dance troupe, but years ago she returned to Guadeloupe, her home, to set up this breezy restaurant. Try for a table on the open patio, where palm trees complement the color scheme. Clara artfully melds the classic French style of fine dining with authentic Creole flavors. Specialties include skate fish with rice and curry sauce, poached crayfish with Creole sauce and vegetables, brochette of swordfish and/or tuna, different preparations of conch, *salade de coffre* (made from a local fish whose name translates as "trunkfish"), braised chicken thighs stuffed with pulverized conch, or stuffed crab with avocado. The "sauce chien" that's served with many of the dishes is a blend of hot peppers, garlic, lime juice, and "secret things."

Bd. St. Charles, Ste-Rose. ✆ **590/28-72-99.** Reservations recommended. Main courses 12€–35€; fixed-price menu 15€. MC, V. Mon–Tues and Thurs–Sat noon–2:30pm and 7–10pm; Sun noon–2:30pm.

Deshaies/La Grand-Anse

A few miles farther along, you reach Pointe Allegre, the northernmost point of Basse-Terre. **Cluny Beach** is where the first settler landed on Guadeloupe, and it's a great place to break up your drive with a swim, although the waters are sometimes rough and there are no beach facilities.

Three kilometers (2 miles) farther will bring you to **La Grand-Anse ★**, one of the best beaches on Guadeloupe. It is very large and still secluded, sheltered by many tropical trees, especially palms. The place is ideal for either a swim or a picnic, although, again, there are no facilities.

At **Deshaies,** immediately to the south, snorkeling and fishing are popular, but you must bring your own equipment. The narrow road alongside the beach winds up and down and has a corniche look to it, with the blue sea underneath and the view of green mountains studded with colorful villages.

Fourteen kilometers (8¾ miles) from Deshaies, **Pointe Noire** comes into view; its name comes from the black volcanic rocks. Look for the odd polychrome cenotaph in town, the only reason to stop over.

WHERE TO STAY

Habitation Grande Anse ★ Lying across the coastal road from one of the island's best beaches, Grande-Anse, this somewhat battered assemblage of bungalows and studio apartments, each with natural-grained wood trim, is evocative of a Mediterranean village. All units have kitchenettes and contain rattan furniture, white walls, and a simple, summery decor that's well suited to life close to the beach. Don't expect too many activities here—the focus is on sunbathing surrounded by the tropical landscaping beside the beach. The on-site restaurant is, in theory, open for breakfast and dinner, but because the hotel does not have a full-time chef and because business is often slow, it may not be running when you visit. But since most guests are devoted to preparing their own meals, no one really seems to care.

Localité Ziotte, 97126 Deshaies, Guadeloupe, F.W.I. www.grande-anse.com. ✆ **590/28-45-36.** Fax 590/28-51-17. 60 units. Winter 90€-130€ double studio, 225€-250€ 2-bedroom apt for up to 6; off season 65€-90€ double studio, 180€ 2-bedroom apt for up to 6. AE, DC, MC, V. **Amenities:** Bar; outdoor pool; watersports equipment/rentals. *In room:* A/C, TV, kitchen, minibar, Wi-Fi (free).

Le Rayon Vert ★ 🎁 This boutique hotel is a favorite choice for honeymooners seeking a haven of tranquillity opening onto the water of Ferry Bay. You have a choice of spacious double rooms in the main building or bungalows set out on a hillside studded with tropical vegetation. Room furnishings are not luxurious—in fact, they could use some freshening—but the views from some of the units are almost incomparable on the island. You don't need to leave the premises at night to enjoy market-fresh cuisine, including the day's catch.

La Coque Ferry, 97126 Deshaies, Guadeloupe, F.W.I. www.hotels-deshaies.com. ✆ **590/28-43-23**. 22 units. Winter 165€–195€ double; off season 145€–165€ double. Rates include breakfast. MC, V. Closed June to mid-July and Sept. **Amenities:** Restaurant; bar; outdoor pool. *In room:* Ceiling fan, TV, fridge, hair dryer.

Résidence Hoteliére de la Pointe Batterie Built on steeply sloping land near the edge of both the rainforest and the sea, these all-wood villas each contain a veranda, a kitchen, ceiling fans, good beds, and summery furniture made from rattan, local hardwoods, and wicker. The nearest beach, La Grand-Anse, is a 3-minute drive (or a long uphill walk) away. In addition to the communal pool, some of the villas have their own private pools. Le Canon de la Baie specializes in Creole food from atop a wooden deck whose pilings are sunk directly into the seabed.

Chemin de la Batterie, 97126 Deshaies, Guadeloupe, F.W.I. www.pointe-batterie.com. ✆ **590/28-57-03.** Fax 590/28-57-28. 22 villas. Winter 130€ studio for 2, 230€–344€ units for 4–6 people; off season 70€ studio for 2, 160€–210€ units for 4–6 people. MC, V. **Amenities:** Restaurant; bar; outdoor pool; spa; tennis court (nearby). *In room:* A/C, ceiling fan, TV, kitchen, Wi-Fi (free).

Tainos Cottages ★ 🎁 This property, opening onto Grande-Anse Beach, is unique in Guadeloupe. Its seven cottages were actually made in Indonesia and shipped to Guadeloupe for reassembly. Each cottage has an exotic name such as Jaïba or Guana, and each is furnished with Indonesian pieces, including Persian carpeting and four-poster beds draped in mosquito netting. The tropical-style swimming pool overlooks the ocean. The cuisine is one of the reasons to stay here. You enjoy such dishes as filet of duck in a fresh mango coilis or medallions of crayfish.

Plage de Grande-Anse, 97126 Deshaies, Guadeloupe, F.W.I. www.tainoscottages.com. ✆ **590/28-44-42.** Fax 590/21-30-20. 7 units. Winter 300€ double; off season 150€ double. Rates include breakfast. MC, V. **Amenities:** Restaurant; bar; Internet (free); outdoor pool. *In room:* Ceiling fan, fridge.

WHERE TO DINE

La Caféière Beauséjour ★ 🎁 CREOLE In the green Pointe-Noire Valley on the site of a coffee plantation, this restaurant is one of Guadeloupe's dining secrets. It is the domain of Bernadette Hayot-Beauzelin, who grows the produce and herbs used in many of her nouvelle Creole dishes. Hayot-Beauzelin's home was constructed in 1764, years after Louis XIV sent the first coffee plant to Guadeloupe in 1721.

Don't expect a menu—you'll be told what the kitchen prepared that day. Starting in the early morning, Hayot-Beauzelin gathers the fresh fruits and vegetables that make her meals so special—everything from tomatoes and bananas to passion fruit and avocados. Your main course might be a delectable smoked duck served with some Pan-Asian sauce that tastes of ginger, with side dishes of fries from the breadfruit tree (cut like french fries) and pumpkin puree.

The restaurant also rents out two very basic bedrooms with air-conditioning and a terrace, costing 100€ per day in a double.

Acomat Pointe Noire. ✆ **590/98-10-09** or 069/61-94-04. www.cafeierebeausejour.com. Reservations required. Main courses 18€–30€. MC, V. Tues–Sun 10am–5pm. Closed Sept–Oct 15.

Les Gommiers CREOLE Named after the large rubber trees that grow nearby, this popular restaurant serves up well-flavored dishes in a dining room lined with plants. You can order such Creole staples as *accras de morue* (codfish beignets), *boudin Créole* (blood pudding), fricassee of freshwater crayfish, seafood paella, and a custardlike dessert known as *flan coco.* Dishes inspired by France include goat-meat stew, grilled steaks, and veal scallops. We return year after year and have never detected any lessening of quality. One chef told us, "We are not technically perfect, but we cook from the heart."

200 rue Baudot, Pointe Noire. ✆ **590/98-01-79.** Main courses 12€–30€; fixed-price lunch 15€. MC, V. Mon–Sat 10am–1pm and 7–11pm.

Parc Naturel de Guadeloupe: A Tropical Forest ★★

Six kilometers (3¾ miles) from Pointe Noire, you reach **Mahault.** On your left is the **Route de la Traversée ★★**, the Transcoastal Highway. This is the best way to explore the scenic wonders of **Parc Naturel de Guadeloupe,** passing through a tropical forest as you travel between the capital, Basse-Terre, and Pointe-à-Pitre.

To preserve Parc Naturel, Guadeloupe has set aside 30,000 hectares (74,132 acres), about a fifth of its entire terrain. Easily accessible via modern roads, this is a huge tract of mountains, tropical forests, and gorgeous scenery, and one of the largest and most spectacular parks in the Caribbean.

The park is home to a variety of tame animals, including *titi* (a raccoon, adopted as the park's official mascot) and such birds as the wood pigeon, turtledove, and thrush. Small exhibition huts, devoted to the volcano, to the forest, or to coffee, sugar cane, and rum, are scattered throughout the park. Parc Naturel has no gates, no opening or closing hours, and no admission fee.

You can hike for a mere 15 minutes or stretch out your adventure for an entire day. The 290km (180 miles) of trails here take in rainforests, hot springs, rugged gorges, rushing streams, and the wooded slopes of the 1,444m-high (4,738-ft.) Soufrière volcano. (See "Hiking" under "Sports & Outdoor Pursuits," p. 325.)

From Mahault, you drive slowly in a setting of giant ferns and luxuriant vegetation. Six kilometers (3¾ miles) after the fork, you reach **Les Deux Mamelles (the Two Breasts),** where you can park your car and go for a hike. Some of the trails are for experts only; others, such as the **Pigeon Trail,** will bring you to an impressive summit of about 780m (2,559 ft.). Expect to spend at least 3 hours going each way. Halfway along the trail, you can stop at **Forest House;** from that point, many lanes, all signposted, branch off on trails that will take anywhere from 20 minutes to 2 hours.

The most enthralling walk in the park is to the **Chute de l'Ecrevisse ★**, the "Crayfish Waterfall," a little pond of very cold water at the end of a .4km (.25-mile) path. This spot in the tropical forest is one of the most beautiful places on the island. The pool found at the base of the falls is an ideal place for a cooling swim. In just 10 minutes, you can reach this signposted attraction from the Corossol River Picnic Area. To the left of the Route de la Traversée, a short trail parallels the Corossol River, ending at the crayfish falls.

After the hike, the main road descends toward **Versailles,** a village about 8km (5 miles) from Pointe-à-Pitre.

Bouillante

If you don't take the Route de la Traversée at this time but want to continue exploring the west coast, you can head south from Mahault until you reach the village of Bouillante, which is exciting for only one reason: You might encounter former French film star and part-time resident Brigitte Bardot.

WHERE TO DINE

Le Rocher de Malendure FRENCH/CREOLE On a rocky peninsula 9m (30 ft.) above the rich offshore reefs near Pigeon Island, this restaurant offers gorgeous views. Each table is sheltered from direct sunlight (and rain) by a shed-style roof, which also affords a greater sense of privacy. Much of the cuisine served here is seafood caught in offshore waters: grilled red snapper, fondues of fish, marinated marlin steaks, and different preparations of crayfish and conch. There's a special emphasis here on marlin, with several creative adaptations—rillettes of marlin, marlin sushi, brochettes of marlin, and fried scallops of marlin, for example.

The restaurant also operates a small hotel on-site, **Le Jardin Tropical** (✆ **590/98-77-23**), renting 10 bungalows, which cost 80€ per night, single or double occupancy. Each small unit has a sea view, air-conditioning, a ceiling fan, a tiny bathroom with a shower, and a simple kitchenette, where many visitors cook most of their meals. Amenities include a pool, laundry service, and free Wi-Fi.

Malendure Pigeon, Bouillante. ✆ **590/98-70-84.** Reservations recommended. Main courses 17€–30€; fixed-price menus 19€, 29€, or 45€. AE, V. Thurs–Tues noon–4pm and 7–10:30pm. Closed Sept.

Basse-Terre ★

The winding coastal road brings you to **Vieux Habitants (Old Settlers),** one of the oldest villages on the island, founded in 1636. The name comes from its founders: After serving in the employment of the West Indies Company, they retired here, but they preferred to call themselves "inhabitants," so as not to be confused with slaves.

Another 15km (9¼ miles) of winding roads bring you to **Basse-Terre,** the capital of Guadeloupe. This sleepy town of some 15,000 inhabitants lies between the water and La Soufrière, the volcano. Founded in the 1640s, it's the oldest town on the island and still has a lot of charm. Tamarind and palm trees shade its market squares. Although there are many modern buildings, some grand old colonial structures are still standing.

The town suffered heavy damages at the hands of British troops in 1691 and again in 1702. It was also the center of fierce fighting during the French Revolution, when the political changes that swept across Europe caused explosive tensions on Guadeloupe. As it did in France, the guillotine claimed many lives on the island during the infamous Reign of Terror.

In spite of the town's history, there isn't much to see in Basse-Terre except for a 17th-century **cathedral** and **Fort St-Charles,** which has guarded the city (not always well) since it was established. Much modernized and reconstructed over the years, the cathedral is only of passing interest. On the narrow streets, you can still see old clapboard buildings, upper floors of shingle-wood tiles, and wrought-iron balconies. For the most interesting views, seek out the **Place du Champ d'Arbaud** and the **Jardin Pichon.** At the harbor on the southern tier of town, you can see **Fort Delgrès,** which once protected the island from the English. There are acres of ramparts to be walked, with panoramic vistas in all directions.

Originally selected as Guadeloupe's capital because of its prevailing breezes and location above the steaming lowlands of Pointe-à-Pitre, Basse-Terre today is a city that's curiously removed from the other parts of the French Antilles that it governs, and when the business of the day is concluded, it's an oddly calm and quiet town. The neighboring municipality of **St-Claude,** in the cool heights above the capital, was always where the island's oldest families proudly maintained their ancestral homes and where they continue to live today. These families, direct descendants of the white, slave-owning former plantation owners who originally hailed from such major French Atlantic ports as Bordeaux and Nantes, tend to live quietly, discreetly, and separately from both the island's blacks and the French *métropolitains* whose tourist ventures have helped change the face of Guadeloupe.

WHERE TO STAY & DINE

Hôtel St-Georges This tastefully modern inn is set on a hill with sweeping views over the town, the gardens, and, from the upper floors, the sea. A series of three-story buildings centers on a large swimming pool. The medium-size bedrooms are outfitted, Creole style, with dark-grained and rattan furniture, tiled floors, and small bathrooms trimmed with touches of marble. Overall, this place has the feel of a business hotel. Le Lamasure specializes in French, Continental, and Creole cuisine, serving dinner only.

Rue Gratien, Parize, 97120 St-Claude, Guadeloupe, F.W.I. www.hotelstgeorges.com. ✆ **590/80-10-10.** Fax 590/80-30-50. 40 units. Winter 110€ double; off season 80€ double; year-round 155€ suite. AE, DC, MC, V. **Amenities:** Restaurant; snack bar; fitness center; outdoor pool; squash court. *In room:* A/C, TV, minibar, Wi-Fi (24€ per day).

Le Jardin de Malanga ★ Clandestine lovers, honeymooners, and those passionate about nature view this as their secret hideaway in Guadeloupe. In a secluded location in the midst of a former banana plantation, it overlooks the Les Saintes archipelago. The nearest beach, La Plage de Trois Rivières, lies a 15-minute drive away. Wander in a secret garden of banana trees, birds of paradise flowers, rare orchids, hibiscus (the favorite food of iguanas), and flowering tropical foliage. Those who appreciate a place that looks like an outpost of French Guinea will gravitate to the main house of the inn, which was constructed in 1927 and contains a smattering of family antiques. Each of the bedrooms is comfortably and tastefully furnished, with bathrooms tiled in white. Some bathtubs open onto scenic views. The French Creole meals are often made with produce from the hotel's own gardens.

Route de Hermitage, 97114 Trois Rivières, Guadeloupe, F.W.I. www.jardinmalanga.com. ✆ **590/92-67-57.** Fax 590/92-67-58. 9 units. Year-round 230€ double in cottage; 265€ family unit in colonial house; 530€ quadruple. Rates include continental breakfast. AE, MC, V. **Amenities:** Restaurant; bar; outdoor pool. *In room:* A/C, hair dryer, minibar, Wi-Fi (free).

La Soufriere ★★

The big attraction of Basse-Terre is the famous sulfur-puffing **La Soufrière** volcano, which is currently dormant. Rising to a height of some 1,444m (4,737 ft.), it's flanked by banana plantations and lush foliage.

After leaving the capital at Basse-Terre, you can drive to **St-Claude,** a suburb 6km (3¾ miles) up the mountainside at a height of 570m (1,870 ft.). It has a reputation for a perfect climate and various privately owned tropical gardens.

From St-Claude, you can begin the climb up the narrow, winding road the Guadeloupéans say leads to hell—that is, **La Soufrière.** The road ends at a parking area at La Savane à Mulets, at an altitude of 990m (3,248 ft.). At this point, you have to leave your car and climb to the mouth of the volcano. Currently, the belching beast is quiet and it's presumed safe to climb to the summit, the tallest elevation in the Lesser Antilles. (Allow about 2 hr. for this climb.) In 1975 the appearance of ashes, mud, billowing smoke, and earthquakelike tremors proved that the old beast was still alive. In the resettlement process that followed the eruption, 75,000 inhabitants were relocated to safer terrain in Grande-Terre. No deaths were reported, but the inhabitants of Basse-Terre still keep a wary eye on this smoking giant.

Even in the parking lot, you can feel the heat of the volcano merely by touching the ground. Steam emerges from fumaroles and sulfurous fumes from the volcano's "burps." Of course, fumes come from its pit and mud cauldrons as well. Esoteric and technical information is available only with advance reservations, Fridays between 2 and 5pm, at a government-funded laboratory, **Observatoire Volcanologique le Houëlmont,** 97113 Gourbeyre (✆ **590/99-11-33**). Conceived as an observation post for seismic and volcanic activities, and staffed with geologists and volcanologists from the French mainland, it can be toured without charge by anyone who's interested in the technical aspects of this science. A visit here is best for children ages 10 and up.

WHERE TO DINE

Chez Paul de Matouba CREOLE/INTERNATIONAL You'll find good food in this family-run restaurant, which sits beside the banks of the small Rivière Rouge (Red River). The dining room on the second floor is enclosed by windows, which allow you to take in the surrounding dark-green foliage of the mountains. The cooking is Creole, and the specialty is crayfish dishes, though well-prepared East Indian meals are also available. By all means, drink the mineral or spring water of Matouba. Hearty meals include perfectly executed stuffed crab, *colombo* (curry) of chicken, and an array of French, Creole, and Hindu specialties. You're likely to find the place overcrowded in winter with the tour-bus crowd.

Rivière Rouge, Matouba, St-Claude. ✆ **590/80-01-77.** Main courses 13€–23€; fixed-price menu 16€–20€. No credit cards. Sun–Fri noon–3pm. Follow the clearly marked signs; it's beside a gully close to the center of the village.

The Windward Coast ★★

From Basse-Terre to Pointe-à-Pitre, the N1 road follows the east coast, called the Windward Coast. The country here is richer and greener than elsewhere on the island. There's no major sight or stopover along the way, so if your time is limited, you can simply savor the views along the coastal road, with the sea to your right and scenic landscapes to your left.

To reach the little town of **Trois Rivières,** you have a choice of two routes: One goes along the coastline, coming eventually to Vieux Fort, from which you can see Les Saintes archipelago. The other heads across the Monts Caraïbes hills.

Near the pier in Trois Rivières, you'll see the pre-Columbian petroglyphs carved by the original inhabitants, the Arawaks. They're called merely **Roches Gravées,** or "carved rocks." In this **Parc Archéologique** at Bord de la Mer (✆ **590/92-91-88**), the rock engravings are of animal and human figures, probably dating from A.D. 300 or 400. You can also see specimens of plants, including cocoa, pimento, and banana, that the Arawaks cultivated long before the Europeans set foot on Guadeloupe. Hours are Tuesday to Saturday 9am to noon and 2 to 5pm; admission is free.

After leaving Trois Rivières, continue north on N1. Passing through the village of Bananier after a 15-minute drive, you turn to your left at Anse Saint-Sauveur to reach the famous **Les Chutes du Carbet ★**, a trio of waterfalls that are wonderful to behold year-round. If you have time for only one stopover along the route, make it this one. The road to two of them is a narrow, winding one, along many steep hills, passing through banana plantations as you move deeper into a tropical forest.

Les Chutes du Carbet are the tallest falls in the Caribbean. The waters pour down from La Soufrière at 240m (787 ft.) in a trio of stages on the eastern slopes. The upper cascade falls 123m (404 ft.) through a steep crevice. Drawing the most visitors and the easiest to reach is the middle falls at 108m (354 ft.), dropping into a bigger canyon than the upper cascade. The second cascade in the falls is likely to be overrun with tours. The lower cascades drop only 20m (66 ft.) and are less interesting.

You can hike to each cascade. To reach the dramatic second stage from the little town of Saint-Sauveur, head inland via the village of Habituée, going to the end of the road. From here follow the signs for a 30-minute walk along a marked trailway to the foot of the falls. There is a picnic area nearby.

If you have plenty of time and are in good shape, you can also reach the upper falls from here. Follow a signposted trail, but note that this level of hiking takes about 1½ hours and is very steep, difficult, and often slippery.

After your hike, continue northeast on N1 to Capesterre. From there a 7km (4¼-mile) drive brings you to **Ste-Marie.** In the town square, you can see the statue of the first visitor who landed on Guadeloupe: Christopher Columbus, who anchored .4km (¼ mile) from Ste-Marie on November 4, 1493. If you'd like to see the same view that greeted Columbus, you can stop off here. The statue and that view are the only reasons to take a look.

After Ste-Marie, you pass through Goyave, then Petit-Bourg, seeing on your left the Route de la Traversée before reaching Pointe-à-Pitre.

GUADELOUPE'S BEACHES

Chances are your hotel will be right on a beach, or no more than 20 minutes from a good one. Plenty of natural beaches dot the island, from the surf-brushed dark strands of western Basse-Terre to the long stretches of white sand encircling Grande-Terre. Public beaches are generally free, but some charge for parking. Unlike hotel beaches, they have few facilities. Hotels welcome nonguests but charge for changing facilities, beach chairs, and towels. Sunday is family day at the beach. Topless sunbathing is common at hotels, less so on village beaches.

Most of the best beaches lie between Gosier and St-François on Grande Terre. Visitors usually head for the hotel beaches at **Gosier.** Stone jetties were constructed here to protect the beaches from erosion. Since this area has the largest concentration of tourists, it's likely to be crowded.

These beaches are not peas in a pod. There's no shade at the **Creole Beach** fronting Creole Beach Hotel, although you can retreat to the bar there for a drink. A stone retaining wall blocks access to the water. Nearby, the **Salako Beach** has more sand and is set against a backdrop of palms that provide some shade. Part of this beach also leads up to a jetty. This is a fine sandy beach (although a little too crowded at times), and it also contains a snack bar.

Also nearby, **Arawak Beach** is a gorgeous spot, with plenty of swaying palm trees providing a bit of shade on the beige sands. It, too, is protected by jetties. Close at hand, **Callinago Beach** is smaller than Arawak but still has a pleasant crescent of beige sand and palms.

Le Bas du Fort, 3km (2 miles) east of Pointe-à-Pitre and close to Gosier, is another popular area. Guests at the Hotels Fleu d'Eté and Marissol share its beaches, which are also protected by jetties. This is a picture-postcard tropical beach with tranquil waters, plenty of sand, and palms for shade. There are hotel bars as well as snack bars and vendors (some of whom are rather aggressive).

Some of Grande-Terre's best beaches are in the **Ste-Anne** area, site of Club Med La Caravelle. **Plage Caravelle** is heaped with white sand, attracting crowds of sunbathers; snorkelers, too, are drawn to the beach's reef-protected waters.

The French visitors here often like to go nude, and there is no finer nude beach than **Pointe Tarare,** a 45-minute drive from Gosier. This beach lies east of St-François at Pointe des Chateaux. It's one of the island's most pristine, tranquil beaches, but there's no shade to protect you from the fierce noonday sun. You can snorkel here if the water's not kicking up. There's a good restaurant by the car park. ***Warning:*** The tourist office doesn't recommend that women come here unaccompanied.

If you're not a nudist, you can enjoy the lovely strip of white sand at **Anse de la Gourde,** lying between St-François and Pointe des Chateaux. It has good sand, but it tends to become crowded on weekends.

The eastern coast of Grande-Terre is less desirable for swimming, as it fronts the more turbulent Atlantic. Nonetheless, the sands at **Le Moule** make for an idyllic beach because a reef protects the shoreline. There are also beach bars here—and the inevitable crowds, especially on weekends. You'll find a more secluded strip of sand north of here at **La Porte d'Enfer.**

There are two other excellent beaches on the northwestern coast: one at **Anse Laborde** just outside the village of Anse-Bertrand, the other called **Anse du Souffleur** at Port Louis. We especially like the beach at Souffleur for its brilliant, flamboyant trees that bloom in the summer. There are no facilities here, but you can pick up provisions in the shops in the little village, then enjoy a picnic on the beach.

In Basse-Terre, a highly desirable beach is **La Grande-Anse,** just outside Deshaies, reached by heading west from Sainte Rose along the N2. You won't find any facilities here, but we think you'll like the powdery sands, tranquil waters, and palm trees. Another desirable beach is **Plage de la Malendure,** on the west coast (the more tranquil side) of Basse-Terre across from Pigeon Island. This is a major center for scuba diving, but the sand tends to be dark here.

If you want to escape the crowds, seek out the spurs and shoulders produced by the mountains of Basse-Terre. In the northwest is a string of fine sandy beaches. Although small, these are highly desirable enclaves for sunbathing. Favorites include **La Plage de Cluny** (near Pointe Allegre), **Plage de la Tillette,** and **Plage de la Perle.** ***Warning:*** The beaches on the north coast of Basse-Terre are exceedingly dangerous for swimming. **Plage de Cluny** is especially treacherous (with very large waves), and there have been several deaths by drowning.

South of Pointe Noire, also on the west coast, is **Plage des Caraïbes,** with its calm waters and sandy strip. This beach has picnic facilities, a shower, and toilets.

Other good beaches are found on the offshore islands, **Iles des Saintes** and **Marie-Galante** (see "Side Trips from Guadeloupe," below).

SPORTS & OUTDOOR PURSUITS

DEEP-SEA FISHING Blue marlin, wahoo (known locally as *thazar*), and yellowfin tuna can be fished throughout the year; the season for *dorado* (mahimahi) is limited to November to May. Hotels can usually recommend a deep-sea outfitter or two. A well-recommended outfitter is **Le Manolo** (✆ **590/90-75-49**), who's usually moored offshore the Plage de Malendure, but who moves his craft to various ports on Guadeloupe and its offshore dependencies, depending on the tides, the season, and business. For a "very full" half-day experience at big game fishing, with a departure at 7:30am and a return scheduled for around 3pm, he charges 120€ per person, with all equipment included, minimum three passengers.

GOLF Guadeloupe's only golf course is the well-known **Golf de St-François ★★**, avenue de l'Europe, 97110 St-François (✆ **590/88-41-87**), opposite the Le Kalenda Resort. The course runs alongside a 320-hectare (791-acre) lagoon where windsurfing, water-skiing, and sailing prevail. Designed by Robert Trent Jones, Sr., it's a challenging 6,755-yard, par-71 course, with water traps on 6 of the 18 holes, not to mention massive bunkers, prevailing trade winds, and a particularly fiendish 400-yard, par-4 9th hole. The par-5 6th is the toughest hole on the course; its 450 yards must be negotiated in the constant easterly winds. Greens fees are 40€ per day per person. You can rent clubs for 15€ a day; an electric cart costs 36€ for 18 holes. Hours are daily from 7:30am to 6:30pm.

HIKING The 30,000-hectare (74,132-acre) **Parc Naturel de Guadeloupe** (✆ **590/80-86-00**) contains some of the best hiking trails in the Caribbean. The 290km (180 miles) of trails cut through the deep foliage of rainforest, passing waterfalls and cool mountain pools, hot springs, and rugged gorges along the way. The big excursion country, of course, is around the volcano, La Soufrière. Another highlight is Les Chutes du Carbet, one of the tallest waterfalls in the Caribbean, with a drop of 240m (787 ft.). More details are available in the notes on the Windward Coast near the end of "Around Basse-Terre," earlier in this chapter.

Hiking brochures are available from the tourist office. Hotel tour desks can make arrangements. For information about this and other hikes in the national park, contact **Organisation des Guides de Montagne de la Caraïbe,** Maison Forestière, Matouba (✆ **590/92-06-10**).

Warning: Hikers may experience heavy downpours. The annual precipitation on the higher slopes is 6.3m (248 in.) per year, so be prepared with rain gear.

SCUBA DIVING Guadeloupe is more popular for scuba diving than any other French-speaking island. The allure is the relatively calm seas and **La Réserve Cousteau,** a national park where the underwater environment is rigidly protected. Jacques Cousteau once described the waters off Guadeloupe's Pigeon Island as "one of the world's 10 best diving spots." Sergeant majors become visible at a depth of 9m (30 ft.); spiny sea urchins and green parrotfish at 18m (59 ft.); and magnificent stands of finger, black, brain, and star coral at 24m (79 ft.).

The most popular dive sites include Aquarium, Piscine, Jardin de Corail, Pointe Carrangue, Pointe Barracuda, and Jardin Japonais. Although scattered around the periphery of the island, many are in the bay of Petit Cul-de-Sac Marin, south of Rivière Salée, the channel that separates the two halves of Guadeloupe. North of the Salée is another bay, Grand Cul-de-Sac Marin, where the small islets of Fajou and Caret also boast fine diving.

Reacting to the rich diversity of underwater flora and fauna, which thrive at relatively shallow—and relatively safe—depths, several entrepreneurs have set up shop. One of these is **Les Heures Saines,** Rocher de Malendure, Bouillante (✆ **590/98-86-63;** www.heures-saines.gp), whose trio of dive boats departs two times a day at 10am and 2:30pm, for explorations of the waters within the reserve. With all equipment included, dives—depending on the level of expertise of the participants and the intended destination—cost from 45€ each. Novices, at least for the very first time they engage in the sport, pay 50€ for what is referred to as a *baptême* (baptism).

Les Heures Saines maintains its own 13-unit hotel, **Le Paradis Creole** (✆ **590/98-71-62;** www.guadeloupe-hotel.net). Here simple motel-style accommodations rent for 80€ in winter and 60€ off season. All have either air-conditioning or ceiling fans, but no TV or phone, and very few frills. Many of them are occupied almost exclusively by avid divers and, to a lesser degree, hill climbers, on tour-group holiday from the French mainland.

This outfit's slightly larger competitor, located a short distance away, is **Centre International de la Plongée (C.I.P. Bouillante),** Lieu-Dit Poirier, Malendure Plage, Pigeon, 97125 Bouillante (✆ **590/98-81-72;** www.cip-guadeloupe.com). It's acknowledged as the most professional dive operation on the island. In a wood-sided house on Malendure Plage, close to a well-known restaurant, Chez Loulouse, it's well positioned at the edge of the Cousteau Underwater Reserve. Certified divers pay 31€ for a one-tank dive. A "resort course" for first-time divers costs 46€ and is conducted one-on-one with an instructor. Packages of four dives are offered for 136€; PADI open-water certification costs 515€. It's usually awarded as part of an 8-day instruction ritual, but in a pinch, if its participants are extremely motivated, it can be passed in 3 days if you communicate your wishes and ambitions in advance.

WINDSURFING For an intensive immersion in the sport, consider enrolling (along with lots of like-minded aficionados) in one of the windsurfing programs at **UCPA (Union des Centres de Plein-Air),** 97118 St-François (✆ **590/99-54-94;** www.ucpa.com). This organization devoted to outdoor warm-weather sports has its own hotel-style bungalows, each of them beach-fronting affairs built in 1986, set close to a swimming pool and dining hall. They all contain simple and durable furniture and ceiling fans, but none have TVs, phones, air-conditioning, or any other grace notes. If you're already an experienced windsurfer, you can always drop in for a practice run—windsurfers rent for 30€ for a half-day—but participants are encouraged to remain on-site for between 5 and 7 days, buying sports packages whose arithmetic makes each individual session cost a lot less. With half-board included, per-person rates, double occupancy, cost from 380€ to 450€ per week. Packages can be built around windsurfing, surfing, kite surfing, and golf.

GUADELOUPE AFTER DARK

Guadeloupeans claim that *la biguine* was invented here, not on Martinique, and they dance it as if it truly was their own. Of course, there's also calypso, technically imported from points farther south such as Trinidad; merengue sounds from the Dominican Republic; salsa from Puerto Rico; and fusion jazz from Cuba, too—the islanders are known for their dancing.

Ask at your hotel for details on the folkloric **Ballets Guadeloupéens** performances (p. 311). This troupe makes frequent appearances at the big resorts.

The major casino, one of only two on the island, both administered by the same company, is **Casino Gosier-les-Bains,** 43 Pointe de la Verdure, Gosier (✆ **590/84-79-69**). A casually elegant spot, it's open daily from 10am until 3am (4am on Fri and Sat), although the hottest games—those associated with roulette, chemin de fer, and blackjack—don't open till 9pm. ID is requested. All areas of the casino are free of admission.

A smaller casino, with fewer slot machines, is **Casino de St-François,** avenue de l'Europe (✆ **590/88-41-31**), near the Le Kalenda Resort in St-François. It is open daily 10am to 2am.

If you don't like casino action, you can find other nighttime diversions in Guadeloupe, although these tend to be seasonal, with more offerings in the winter. Sheathed in wood and open to the outdoor breezes, the **Zoo Rock Café** at La

Marina in Gosier (✆ **590/90-77-77;** www.zoorockcafe.com) offers a revolving series of theme parties ("Midnight in Rio" and "Carnival in New Orleans") that might remind you of something in St-Tropez.

Cuban salsa and Latin dancing draw patrons to **Lollapalooza,** 122 Montauban, Gosier (✆ **590/84-56-18**), where pictures of dictator Fidel and the long-dead Che Guevara decorate the walls. If you get tired of this joint, try **Fanzy Bar,** Mathurin Poucette (✆ **590/84-41-34**), where musical styles might include 1980s-style French disco, Bob Marley reggae, and, in an occasional orgy of nostalgia, Edith Piaf singing songs from the 1940s and '50s. All these bars are free, but the island's dance clubs charge a uniform fee of about 20€, which includes the cost of a first drink. After that, most cocktails are a pricey 10€ to 15€.

The clientele and psychedelic colors of **Bar Americano,** sur la Plage in Ste-Anne (✆ **590/88-38-99**), might make you believe that the 1960s era of flower power is still alive and thriving. Set directly adjacent to the beach and artfully grungy, it's the kind of hangout that might remind you of your college years. More animated, but open only Friday and Saturday nights, is **La Cascade,** in Gosier (✆ **590/84-33-69**), which rocks and rolls, often to salsa or other Latin beats, for an audience of locals and short-term holidaymakers.

SIDE TRIPS FROM GUADELOUPE

Iles des Saintes ★

A cluster of eight islands off the southern coast of Guadeloupe, the Iles des Saintes are certainly off the beaten track. The two main islands and six rocks are Terre-de-Haut, Terre-de-Bas, Ilet-à-Cabrit, La Coche, Les Augustins, Grand Ilet, Le Redonde, and Le Pâté. Only Terre-de-Haut (Land of High) and, to a lesser extent, Terre-de-Bas (Land Below) attract visitors; **Terre-de-Haut** is the most interesting, and the only island with overnight accommodations.

Some claim that Iles des Saintes has one of the nicest bays in the world, a Lilliputian Rio de Janeiro. The isles, just 10km (6¼ miles) from the main island, were visited by Columbus on November 4, 1493, who named them Los Santos.

The history of Iles des Saintes is very much the history of Guadeloupe itself. In years past, the islands have been heavily fortified, as they were Guadeloupe's Gibraltar. The climate is very dry, and until the desalination plant opened, water was often rationed.

The population of Terre-de-Haut is mainly Caucasian, all fisherfolk or sailors and their families who are descended from Breton *corsairs* (pirates). The very skilled sailors maneuver large boats called *saintois* and wear hats called *salacos,* which are shallow and white, with sun shades covered in cloth built on radiating ribs of thick bamboo. Frankly, the hats look like small parasols. If you want to take a photograph of these sailors, please make a polite request (in French—otherwise, they won't know what you're talking about). Visitors often like to buy these hats (if they can find them) for use as beachwear.

The main tourist attraction of the island is **Fort Napoleon,** Bourg, Grand Bourg (✆ **590/37-99-59**), which is open daily 9am to 12:30pm, charging 4€. Walk uphill to enjoy the panoramic views and a garden filled with cacti and iguanas. Explore the barracks and former prison cells, and take in the collection of some 260 contemporary paintings, focusing largely on surrealism or cubism. As a curiosity, note the large exhibit of the world's greatest sea battles.

Some visitors travel to the Iles des Saintes for the day just to go scuba diving. The island's two leading dive outfitters are **Dive-Bouteille** (✆ **590/99-54-25;** www.dive-bouteille.com) and **Pisquettes** (✆ **590/99-88-80**). Both charge competitive rates and have staffs well versed in the esoterica of the region's many dive sites. Rates are 53€ for the first dive, with a three-dive package costing from 130€.

ESSENTIALS

GETTING THERE Since air connections from Grande-Terre to Terre-de-Haut are scheduled only 3 days a week (see above) and are expensive, most islanders reach Terre-de-Haut by ferryboat, for which there are two distinctly different departure points. Every Monday and Thursday at 8am, boats leave Pointe-à-Pitre's Gare Maritime de Bergevin, Centreville, across the street from the city's biggest open-air market, arriving an hour later on Terre-de-Haut. Round-trip passage costs 37€ per person. Returns from Terre-de-Haut for Pointe-à-Pitre are scheduled those same days (Mon and Thurs) at 4pm. For transit information, contact **Express des Iles** (✆ **0825/35-90-00;** www.express-des-iles.com).

Other ferryboats, operated by a different carrier, depart twice a day from Guadeloupe's port at Trois-Rivieres (near the southern point of Basse-Terre) at 6:45am and 3:45pm, taking 25 or 30 minutes for the transit to the quays at Bourg, on Terre-de-Haut, for a price of 20€ round-trip. Boats return to Trois-Rivieres from Terre-de-Haut every day at 8:30am and 6:30pm. For transit information, contact the **Societe Maritime des Iles du Sud** (✆ **590/98-30-08**).

GETTING AROUND On an island that doesn't have a single car rental agency, you get about by walking or riding a bike or motor scooter, which can be rented at hotels and in town near the pier.

There are also minibuses called ***taxis de l'Ile*** (eight in all), which take six to eight passengers. A taxi from the airport to the port at Bourg costs 12€.

VISITOR INFORMATION In the center of town and easy to spot is the **Office du Tourisme,** rue Jean Calot, Bourg, 97137 Terre-de-Haut (✆ **590/99-58-60**). Its information, mainly, is in French, but a map of the island might come in handy.

WHERE TO STAY ON TERRE-DE-HAUT

Bois Joli Set on the western edge of the island, about 3km (2 miles) from the village of Bourg, this complex of pink-stucco buildings forms one of the most isolated resorts on the island. Known for housing families from the French mainland, it offers both conventional bedrooms within the main house and eight outlying bungalows set into palm groves near the beach. Two of the bungalows have kitchenettes but don't cost more than the other units. Decor includes bold-patterned fabrics, comfortable chairs, and modern but blandly international furnishings, plus small bathrooms with a shower. The food served in the dining room emphasizes local Creole cuisine.

97137 Terre-de-Haut, Les Saintes, Guadeloupe, F.W.I. www.hotelboisjoli.fr. ✆ **590/99-50-38.** Fax 590/99-55-05. 31 units. Winter 145€ double, 205€ bungalow for 2; off season 90€ double, 140€ bungalow for 2. Rates include breakfast. MC, V. **Amenities:** Restaurant; bar; outdoor pool. *In room:* A/C, fridge, kitchen (in some), Wi-Fi (free).

L'Auberge les Petits Saints aux Anacardiers ★ The choice place to stay—and also to dine—is this antiques-filled former mayor's house set on a hillside site

An Escape to Pristine Beaches

There is no finer beach than Plage de Pompierre, which curves around the bay like a half-moon and is set against a backdrop of palms. The beach lies only a 15- to 20-minute walk from where the ferry from Basse-Terre docks. Unless a cruise ship is in port, the beach is generally uncrowded, filled with mainland French enjoying the powdery white sand wearing next to nothing. If you want to bare all, head for Anse Crawen, on the western coastline. It is the legal nudist beach, although people often go nude on the other beaches, too. The best snorkeling is on the southern coast at Plage Figuier, which, chances are, you'll have almost to yourself.

with a view of the turquoise bay and the adjacent beach. Surrounded by a tropical garden, a 5-minute walk north of Bourg, this is a tranquil retreat with much colonial charm. The owners, Jean Foraste and Laurence Nonjoie, have filled the house with their collection of furnishings and objects from around the world. All bedrooms, except a one-bedroom bungalow and a separate guesthouse, have queen-size or twin beds. The guesthouse has four spacious rooms and is suitable for friends traveling together or families. Well-prepared food (French and Creole) on the island is served for dinner here—the restaurant is open to the public, but you should call for a reservation.

La Savane, 97137 Terre-de-Haut, Les Saintes, Guadeloupe, F.W.I. www.petitssaints.com. ✆ **590/99-50-99.** Fax 590/99-54-51. 15 units. Winter 110€–140€ double, 160€–260€ suite; off season 90€–110€ double, 110€–190€ suite. Rates include breakfast. AE, MC, V. Closed 3 weeks in Sept. **Amenities:** Restaurant; bar; outdoor pool. *In room:* A/C, TV (in some), hair dryer, minibar, no phones (in some).

WHERE TO DINE ON TERRE-DE-HAUT

La Saladerie FRENCH/SEAFOOD With a decor of art painted on shipwreck parts, this restaurant serves the best and freshest fish on island. Naturally, most guests order the fish of the day, which can be simply grilled or else served in a delectable fondue with six homemade sauces. Begin perhaps with the local version of gazpacho, going on to such Creole-inspired dishes as shrimp cooked in coconut milk. You compose your own salad from a choice of ingredients. French music is played in the background if you want to linger, sipping Calvados imported from Normandy.

Anse Mire, Terre-de-Haut. ✆ **590/99-53-43.** Reservations recommended. Main courses 10€–18€. DC, MC, V. Wed–Sun 11:45am–2pm and 6:45–9pm. Closed mid-Sept to mid-Oct.

Les Amandiers CREOLE Across from the town hall on the main square of Bourg is the most traditional Creole bistro on Terre-de-Haut. Monsieur and Madame Brudey are your hosts in this blue-and-white building, which has tables and chairs on upper balconies for open-air dining. *Lambi* is prepared either in a fricassee or a *colombo,* a savory curry stew. Also offered are a court bouillon of fish, a *gâteau* (terrine) of fish, and a seemingly endless supply of grilled crayfish, a staple of the island. The catch of the day is also grilled the way you like it. You'll find an intriguing collection of stews, concocted from fish, bananas, and *christophene* (Caribbean squash). Knowledge of French is helpful around here.

Place de la Mairie. ✆ **590/99-51-77.** Reservations recommended. Main courses 8€–16€; fixed-price menu 15€–20€. AE, MC, V. Daily 9am–2:30pm and 7–9pm. Off season closed Fri evening.

DIVING OFF TERRE-DE-HAUT

Scuba diving is not limited to mainland Guadeloupe. The underwater world off Les Saintes has attracted deep-sea divers as renowned as Jacques Cousteau, but even the less experienced may explore its challenging depths and multicolored reefs. Intriguing underwater grottoes can be found near Fort Napoléon on Terre-de-Haut. Two well-recommended outfitters include **La Dive Bouteille,** Plage de la Colline (✆ **590/99-54-25;** www.dive-bouteille.com), and **Pisquettes,** Le Mouillage, in Bourg (✆ **590/99-88-80**). A resort course designed for unlicensed scuba divers costs 53€, and a one-tank dive for already-certified divers goes for 48€, with all equipment included.

Marie-Galante

Come to Marie-Galante to see the Caribbean the way it used to be before the advent of high-rise hotels and casinos. In just 1 hour from Pointe-à-Pitre, you can be transported to a world that time seems to have forgotten. This offshore dependency of Guadeloupe is an almost-perfect circle of about 155 sq. km (60 sq. miles). Almost exclusively French-speaking, it lies about 30km (19 miles) south of Guadeloupe's Grand-Terre and is full of rustic charm, including some 19th-century windmills dotting the island and an occasional ox-drawn cart. We could skip those Sunday cockfights, however.

Today some 12,500 inhabitants live here, making their living from sugar and rum, the latter said to be the best in the Caribbean. The best distillery to visit is **Distillerie Bielle,** Section Bielle, 97112 Grand-Bourg (✆ **590/97-93-62**). The island's climate is rather dry, and there are many good beaches, some of the finest in Guadeloupe's archipelago. One of these stretches of brilliantly white sand covers at least 8km (5 miles). However, swimming can be dangerous in some places. **Grand-Bourg,** the main town, is dominated by an 1845 baroque church. The island's best beach lies almost immediately adjacent to Grand-Bourg, **Plage de la Feuillère,** a 2km (1¼-mile) stretch of white sand that's favored by swimmers and sunbathers. Equally appealing, and more isolated, are the **Plages du Nord,** stretching across the island's northern tier. They include the **Plage du Vieux-Fort,** a 1km (½-mile) stretch of open white sand, and the **Place de l'Anse Canot,** a semicircular bay whose white sands encompass waters that are ideal for small sailcraft, thanks to wave-sheltered waters that are relatively calm.

ESSENTIALS

GETTING THERE **Express des Iles,** Gare Maritime, Bergevin, Pointe-à-Pitre (✆ **0825/35-90-00;** www.express-des-iles.com), operates boat service to the island with three daily round-trips between Point-à-Pitre and Grand-Bourg. The round-trip costs 40€. Monday to Saturday, ferryboats depart from Pointe-à-Pitre for Grand-Bourg on Marie Galante, at 8:15am, 12:30pm, and 5:15pm, with Sunday departures occurring at 8:15am, 5pm, and 7pm. Monday to Saturday, ferryboats to Pointe-à-Pitre depart from Marie-Galante at 6am, 9am, and 4pm, and on Sunday, ferryboats leave from Marie-Galante at 6am, 4pm, and 6pm.

GETTING AROUND A limited number of **taxis** are available at the airport, but be sure to negotiate the price before you drive off. Should you wish to rent a car, go to **Hertz** in Grand-Bourg (✆ **800/654-3001** in the U.S., or 590/97-59-80; www.hertz.com), where rentals range from 30€ to 60€ per day.

VISITOR INFORMATION The **Office de Tourisme** is at rue du Fort, B.P. 15, 97112 Grand-Bourg, Marie-Galante (✆ **590/97-56-51;** fax 590/97-56-54; www.ot-mariegalante.com).

WHERE TO STAY & DINE

Le Kawann On Folle Anse, an uncrowded white-sand beach, this completely renovated hotel is a comfortable nest. The beach is edged with sea-grape and mahogany trees. The hotel itself takes its name from the cohoba plant, known to the Caribs as a plant whose red pods have hallucinogenic powers. The hotel, the largest on Marie-Galante, has small, suitelike rooms decorated with white tile and ghost-white walls, along with bright Caribbean colors and tiny but efficient shower-only bathrooms. The superior rooms have kitchenettes.

Folle Anse (B.P. 59), 97112 Grand-Bourg, Guadeloupe, F.W.I. www.kawann-beach-hotel.com. ✆**590/97-50-50**. Fax 590/97-97-96. 100 units. Winter 125€–150€ double; off season 95€–125€ double. Rates include continental breakfast. AE, MC, V. **Amenities:** Restaurant; bar; babysitting; outdoor pool; 2 tennis courts (lit). *In room:* A/C, TV, hair dryer, kitchenette (in some), Wi-Fi (free).

Le Touloulou CREOLE Adjacent to the beach, with a hardworking staff and a casual crowd, Le Touloulou specializes in shellfish and crayfish culled from local waters. If sea urchins or lobster are your passion, you'll find them here in abundance, prepared virtually any way you want. Other standbys include a savory, and highly ethnic, version of *bébelé* (cow tripe enhanced with breadfruit, dumplings, and plantains) and conch served either as fricassee or in puff pastry.

The restaurant has five very basic bungalow-style accommodations, each with air-conditioning and a small private bathroom. Double occupancy costs 60€, with or without a kitchenette. A two-bedroom bungalow, with kitchenette, suitable for up to four occupants, costs 130€. Staff here tends to be blasé, bordering on terminally lethargic, so come armed with a sense of humor. At night the bar is transformed into the island's only dance club.

Petite Anse, Marie-Galante. ✆**590/97-32-63.** Fax 590/97-33-59. www.letouloulou.com. Main courses 16€–35€; fixed-price menu 30€. MC, V. Tues–Sun noon–3:30pm; Tues–Sat 7–10:30pm. Closed mid-Sept to mid-Oct.

La Desirade

La Désirade is one of the few islands in the Caribbean that is not touched by tourism of any significance. Most visitors come just for the day to enjoy the uncrowded white sandy beach, or perhaps to tour the island's barren expanses.

Columbus spotted this *terre désirée,* or "sought-after land," after his Atlantic crossing in 1493. The island, just 8km (5 miles) off the eastern tip of Guadeloupe proper, is less than 11km (6¾ miles) long and about 2km (1¼ miles) wide, and it has a single potholed road running along its length.

The island has fewer than 1,700 inhabitants, including the descendants of Europeans exiled here by royal command. There are a handful of exceptionally simple guesthouses charging from 50€ for overnight accommodations for two. Don't expect anything grand.

The main village is **Grande-Anse,** which has a small church with a presbytery and flower garden. **Le Souffleur** is a boat-building community, and at **Baie Mahault,** you'll see the ruins of the old leper colony (including a barely recognizable chapel) from the early 18th century.

The best **beaches** on the island's south side are **Souffleur,** a tranquil oasis near the boat-building center, and **Baie Mahault,** a small, quintessentially Caribbean beach with white sand and palm trees.

ESSENTIALS

GETTING THERE From Grand-Terre, most passengers opt for transit to La Désirade by **ferry,** which leaves from the wharves at St-François every day at 8am. Returns from La Désirade for St-François include a daily departure at 4:45pm, allowing convenient access for day-trippers. Trip time is around 50 minutes each way, depending on conditions at sea. Round-trip passage on the ferryboat costs 18€. Call ✆ **590/20-05-03** for schedules, but only from 4 to 7pm daily.

GETTING AROUND Three or four **minibuses** run between the dock and the towns. To get around, you might negotiate with a local driver. **Bicycles** are also available at the hotels.

WHERE TO STAY & DINE

L'Oasis One of the more suitable accommodations of a lackluster lot, lying .8km (½ mile) from the airport, this simple and boxy building is but a short walk from a good beach. It's decorated (if that is the word) in a plain, simple, yet comfortable way, almost how remote Caribbean inns looked in the 1950s. All bedrooms have a bathroom with a toilet, but little else other than a decent bed. Meals are taken at the Restaurant Lagranlang, specializing in Creole dishes and French cuisine, a typical menu usually with fresh fish, costing from 13€.

Beauséjour, 97127 La Désirade, Guadeloupe, F.W.I. www.oasisladesirade.com. ✆ **590/20-01-00.** 7 units. Year-round 48€ for 2 persons in a single; 60€ for 4 persons in a studio with kitchenette. Rates include breakfast. No credit cards. Closed Sept. **Amenities:** Restaurant; bar. *In room:* A/C, TV.

Oualiri Beach Its recent elevation to fame derives from its ownership and administration by Guadeloupe-born hotelier Theodore Compper, who retired to La Désirade after years successfully managing such large-scale hotels as The Holiday Inn and other blockbuster resorts on Guadeloupe. You'll find the ultimate minimalist hotel here, with few amenities other than access to the beach and the jetty of the hamlet of Beauséjour, each with a 270m (886-ft.) walk. Don't expect a raft of organized activities, as frankly, there's not a lot to do or see other than celebrate the sea, the clean air, and the ultra-laid-back island lifestyle. There's an on-site restaurant, open daily from 6:30am to 10pm, where set menus cost 18€ each. Menu items focus on fresh fish, shellfish, and whatever Creole recipes the locals are inspired to cook that day. Bedrooms have clear pale colors and concrete walls that were among the first erected on this island, more than 60 much-renovated years ago. Public areas are warmly decorated with Creole paintings, often in bright primary colors.

Beauséjour, 97127 La Désirade, Guadeloupe, F.W.I. www.im-caraibes.com/oualiri. ✆ **590/20-20-08.** Fax 590/89-68-50. 6 units. Winter 95€ double, 82€ triple; off season 66€ double, 70€ triple. Rates include breakfast. MC, V. **Amenities:** Restaurant; bar. *In room:* A/C, TV.

JAMAICA

There is more to Jamaica than reggae, Rastafarians, and honeymooners. Fringed with white-sand beaches, the island has year-round sunshine, misty mountains, a lush rainforest, and superb coffee. In the west, lazy Negril showcases its long beach, coconut groves, and clear waters. Partygoers gravitate to Montego Bay, with its colonial architecture, bars, and nightclubs. Cruise ships dock at Ocho Rios for its golf courses and water park, while Port Antonio's proximity to the lush Blue Mountains appeals to ecolovers. The capital, Kingston, is an edgy contrast.

14

Things to Do Head to the north and west coasts for diving and snorkeling in clear waters with reefs, garden grottoes, and deep drop-offs. Laze in the sun at **Doctor's Cave Beach,** where placid water invites leisurely swimming. Inland, **Rose Hall Great House,** perched on a hilltop overlooking Montego Bay, gives a glimpse of the heyday of plantation living and even has a resident ghost. Reggae legend Bob Marley's spirit is kept alive at his birthplace, the mountain village of **Nine Miles.**

Shopping Take a taste of Jamaica home with Blue Mountain coffee or Jamaican rum. Buy colorful art from the **Contemporary Art Centre** in Kingston, or go to the **Craft Market** in Negril for carvings, beads, and straw items. Arts and crafts range from alabaster and woodcarvings to weavings, and any outlet of **Things Jamaican** sells a reliable assortment, including its locations in Montego Bay and **Harmony Hall** outside Ocho Rios on the North Coast.

Nightlife & Entertainment Beach bars abound in Jamaica, and one of the most popular is the raffish **Time 'n' Place** in Falmouth, built of driftwood. The setting is so authentic that many fashion magazines, including *Vogue*, have used it for photo shoots. Dance on the sand at parties in **Negril** and **Montego Bay**'s Hip Strip, and hear soca, calypso, and reggae in hotels, roadside bars, and clubs. Serious reggae fans flock to one of **Kingston**'s sound-system discos for the real deal.

Eating & Drinking Jamaican flavors are often unexpected, zesty, and refreshing, and Jamaicans are increasingly proud of their island's culinary offerings. Try specialties such as jerk chicken, chowder with crabmeat, or conch in one of the many casual restaurants in **Montego Bay** or **Negril.** Taste island favorites ackee and salt fish at roadside stalls. Beachfront restaurants around the island serve fresh seafood and *escoveitch* (pickled fish fried with peppers and onions). Finally, cool off with a cold bottle of Red Stripe beer or a rum punch.

CHOOSING WHERE TO STAY

Jamaica is such a large island that you have a wide range of choices.

Jamaica's grande dame is **Montego Bay,** which has three of the leading and poshest resorts in the Caribbean (Half Moon, Round Hill, and Tryall), plus a very good selection of moderately priced hotels. The beaches are fabulous here, though often crowded in winter because of the hotel density. There are fine golf courses, and the shopping is excellent, but the nightlife is surprisingly lackluster.

Younger and hipper than Montego Bay, **Negril** is a sleepy town (with surprisingly little in the way of dining or nightlife) that has a freewheeling, sensual personality and a spectacular stretch of beach. A row of resorts, many of them lavish all-inclusives, has sprouted up along its shores.

To the west, **Ocho Rios** has some of the grandest and most traditional resorts in Jamaica, as well as some of the leading Sandals properties. But it doesn't have the best beaches, shops, or scenic attractions, and it's frequently overrun with cruise-ship passengers. Nonetheless, if you like the sound of a particular resort there and just plan to stay put on your resort's beach, this might be for you.

Port Antonio is for the upscale traveler who wants to escape the mass package tours of Ocho Rios or even Montego Bay. Come here for some good beaches plus great river rafting, scuba diving, or snorkeling.

Most visitors go to **Kingston** for business reasons. It does have interesting museums and historic sights, fine galleries, and a diverse nightlife scene. But it's a city with some serious urban problems, and not what you're looking for in an island vacation. You certainly wouldn't go to Kingston for beaches.

ESSENTIALS

Visitor Information

Before you go, you can get information from the **Jamaica Tourist Board** at 5201 Blue Lagoon Dr., Ste. 670, Miami, FL 33126 (✆ **800/526-2422** in the U.S., or 305/665-0557; fax 305/666-7239). In Canada, contact the office in Toronto at 303 Eglinton Ave. E, Ste. 200, Toronto, ON M4P 1L3 (✆ **800/465-2624** or 416/482-7850; fax 416/482-1730). Brits can contact the London office at 1–2 Prince Consort Rd., SW7 2BZ (✆ **020/7225-9090;** fax 020/7225-1020). The official website of the Jamaica Tourist Board is **www.visitjamaica.com**.

On the island, you can find tourist offices at 64 Knutsford Blvd., **Kingston** (✆ **876/929-9200**); and 18 Queens Dr., **Montego Bay** (✆ **876/952-4425**). For more information, check http://jamaica-guide.info.

Getting There

There are two **international airports** on Jamaica: **Donald Sangster Airport** in Montego Bay (✆ **876/952-3124;** www.mbjairport.com) and **Norman Manley Airport** in Kingston (✆ **876/924-8452;** www.nmia.aero). The most popular flights to Jamaica are from New York and Miami.

Among the most convenient service to Jamaica is that provided by **American Airlines** (✆ **800/433-7300** in the U.S. and Canada; www.aa.com) through its hubs in New York and Miami. Throughout the year, one daily nonstop flight departs from New York's JFK airport for Montego Bay, continuing on to Kingston. Return flights to New York usually depart from Montego Bay. From Miami, at least two daily flights

A True Taste of Jamaica

Wherever you go in Jamaica, you'll see ramshackle stands selling jerk pork. There is no more authentic local experience than to stop at one of these stands and order a lunch of jerk pork, preferably washed down with a Red Stripe beer. Jerk is a way of barbecuing spicy meats on slats of pimento wood, over a wood fire set in the ground. You can never be quite sure what goes into the seasoning, but the taste is definitely of peppers, pimento (allspice), and ginger. You can also order jerk chicken, sausage, fish, and even lobster. The cook will haul out a machete and chop the meat into bite-size pieces for you, then throw them into a paper bag.

depart for Kingston and three daily flights for Montego Bay. **US Airways** (✆ **800/622-1015** in the U.S. and Canada; www.usairways.com) has two daily flights from New York, stopping in Charlotte or Philadelphia. One daily flight leaves out of Baltimore, stopping in either Charlotte or Philadelphia before continuing to Jamaica. **Delta Airlines** (✆ **800/221-1212** in the U.S. and Canada; www.delta.com) flies directly to Montego Bay from Detroit or Minneapolis. **Continental Airlines** (✆ **800/231-0856** in the U.S. and Canada; www.continental.com) flies from its Houston hub at the George Bush Intercontinental Airport to Montego Bay.

Air Jamaica (✆ **800/523-5585** in the U.S. and Canada, or 876/922-3460; www.airjamaica.com) operates one or more flights daily to Montego Bay and Kingston from such cities as Miami, Fort Lauderdale, Orlando, Atlanta, Baltimore, Philadelphia, Chicago, Newark, Boston, Houston, Los Angeles, and New York. The airline has connecting service within Jamaica through its reservation network to **International Air Link** (✆ **876/940-6660;** www. intlairlink.net).

Air Canada (✆ **888/247-2262** in the U.S. and Canada; www.aircanada.com) flies from Toronto to Jamaica daily.

British Airways (✆ **800/247-9297;** www.britishairways.com) has three nonstop flights weekly to Kingston from London's Gatwick Airport.

Getting Around

Especially if you've booked a package at one of the big resorts, you're likely to have airport transfers from Montego Bay included. Many resorts send buses to pick up and drop off their arriving and departing guests.

BY TAXI Not all of Jamaica's taxis are metered; if yours is not, negotiate the price before you get in. Special taxis and buses for visitors are operated by **JUTA** (**Jamaica Union of Travelers Association;** ✆ **876/957-4620**) and have the union's emblem on the side of the vehicle. All prices are controlled, and any local JUTA office will supply a list of rates. JUTA drivers handle nearly all the ground transportation, and some offer sightseeing tours. A typical fare is $18 per person for an airport transfer between Montego Bay and Negril, or $80 for an airport transfer between Montego Bay and Ocho Rios. Rates are 25% higher after midnight.

BY RENTAL CAR Jamaica is big enough, and public transportation is unreliable enough, that a car is a necessity if you plan to do much independent sightseeing. You can also take an organized tour or a taxi tour to the major sights and spend the rest of the time on the beaches near your hotel.

Jamaica

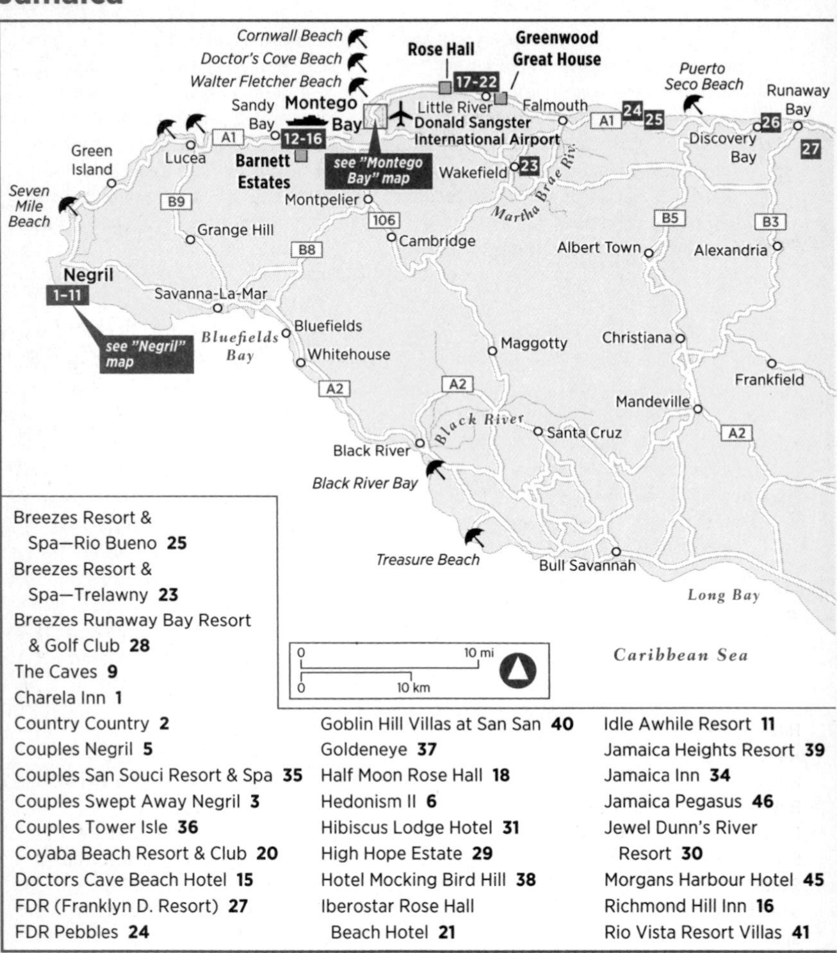

Depending on road conditions, driving time for the 80km (50 miles) from Montego Bay to Negril is 1½ hours; from Montego Bay to Ocho Rios, 1½ hours; from Ocho Rios to Port Antonio, 2½ hours; and from Ocho Rios to Kingston, 2 hours.

Unfortunately, car rental rates on Jamaica have skyrocketed recently, making it one of the most expensive rental scenes in the Caribbean. There's also a 15% government tax on rentals. Equally unfortunate are the unfavorable insurance policies that apply to virtually every car rental agency on Jamaica.

Try **Budget Rent-a-Car** (✆ **800/472-3325** in the U.S. and Canada, 876/952-3838 at the Montego Bay airport, or 876/924-8762 at the Kingston airport; www.budgetjamaica.com); with Budget, a daily collision-damage waiver is mandatory at $15 per day. **Hertz** (✆ **800/654-3001** in the U.S. and Canada; www.hertzja.com) operates branches at the airports at both Montego Bay (✆ **876/979-0438**) and

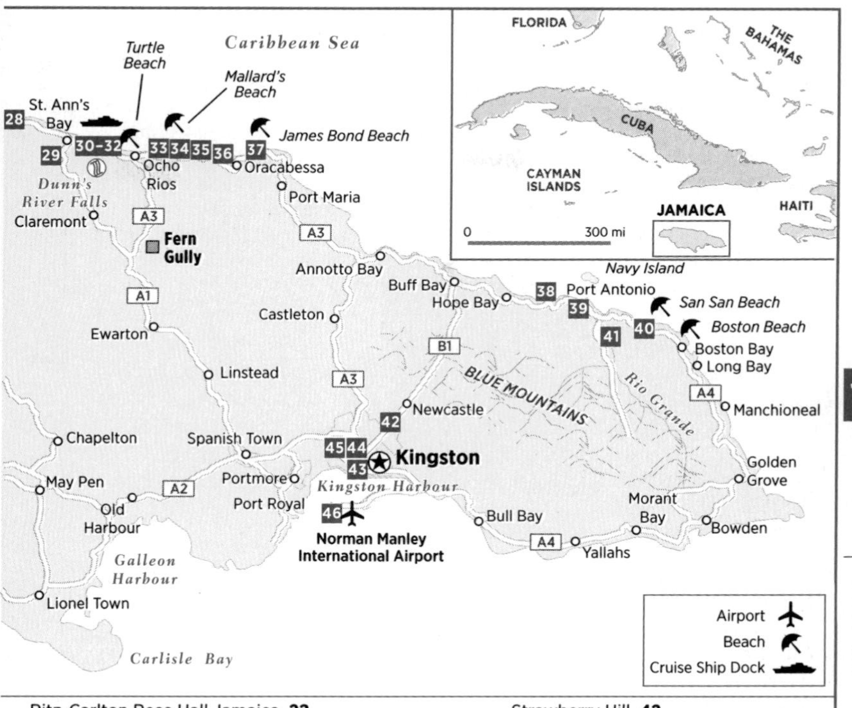

Ritz-Carlton Rose Hall Jamaica **22**
Rockhouse **7**
Round Hill Hotel and Villas **13**
Royal Plantation Spa & Golf Resort **32**
Runaway Bay H.E.A.R.T. Hotel **19**
Sandals Grande Ocho Rios Beach & Villa Resort **33**
Sandals Negril Beach Resort & Spa **4**
Sandals Royal Caribbean & Private Island **17**
Spanish Court Hotel **43**
Strawberry Hill **42**
Sunset at the Palms Resort & Spa **8**
Superfun Beach Resort & Spa **26**
Tensing Pen **10**
Terra Nova All Suite Hotel **44**
Tryall Golf, Tennis & Beach Club **12**
Wexford Court Hotel **14**
Whispering Bamboo Cove **42**

Kingston (✆ **876/924-8028**). A typical rental might be a Mitsubishi Mirage for $480 per week in winter, dropping to $330 weekly off season.

If you'd like to shop for a better deal with one of the local companies in Montego Bay, try **Jamaica Car Rental,** 23 Gloucester Ave. (✆ **866/735-1715;** www.jamaicacar.net), with a branch at the Sangster International Airport at Montego Bay (✆ **876/952-9496**). Daily rates range from $50 to $65. You can also try **United Car Rentals,** 49 Gloucester Ave. (✆ **876/952-3077**), which rents Toyotas and Hondas costing from $140 per 2 days for a four-door standard car with air-conditioning.

In Kingston, try **Island Car Rentals,** 17 Antigua Ave. (✆ **876/926-8012;** www.islandcarrentals.com), with a branch at Montego Bay's Sangster International Airport (✆ **876/952-7225**). It rents Hondas and Jimmys with rates beginning at $80 daily in winter, $60 in the off season.

A Word on Marijuana

You will almost certainly be approached by someone selling ganja (marijuana)—in fact, that's why many travelers come here. However, drugs, including marijuana, are illegal, and imprisonment is the penalty for possession. You don't want to experience the Jamaican penal system firsthand. Don't smoke pot openly in public. Of course, hundreds of visitors do and get away with it, but you may be the one who gets caught, and the person selling to you might even be a police informant. Above all, don't try to bring marijuana back into the United States. There are drug-sniffing dogs stationed at the Jamaican airports, and they will check your luggage. U.S. Customs agents, well aware of the drug situation on Jamaica, have arrested many tourists who have tried to bring some home.

Remember: Drive on the left, and exercise more than your usual caution here because of the unfamiliar terrain. Be especially cautious at night. Speed limits in town are 48kmph (30 mph), and 80kmph (50 mph) outside of town. Gas is measured in liters, and the charge is officially payable only in Jamaican dollars; some stations accept credit cards. Your own valid driver's license from back home is acceptable for short-term visits to Jamaica.

[Fast FACTS] JAMAICA

Banks Banks islandwide are open Monday to Friday from 9am to 5pm. You'll find **ATMs** in all the major resort areas and towns, including Port Antonio, Ocho Rios, and Kingston. There are several in Montego Bay, of course, and even one or two in sleepy Negril.

Currency The unit of currency on Jamaica is the **Jamaican dollar (J$),** and it uses the same symbol as the U.S. dollar ($). There is no fixed rate of exchange. Visitors to Jamaica can pay for most goods in U.S. dollars or with credit cards. Always check if prices are listed in U.S. dollars or Jamaican dollars.

Unless otherwise specified, prices in this chapter are quoted in U.S. dollars.

Jamaican currency is issued in banknotes of J$50, J$100, J$500, and J$1,000. Coins are available in denominations of J$1, J$5, J$10, and J$20. At press time, but subject to change, US$1 equaled approximately J$84, and 1£ equaled approximately J$135. As this will probably fluctuate a bit during the lifetime of this edition, use these rates for general guidance only.

There are Bank of Jamaica exchange bureaus at both international airports (Montego Bay and Kingston), at cruise-ship piers, and in most hotels.

Customs Do *not* bring in or take out illegal drugs to or from Jamaica. Your luggage will be searched; marijuana-sniffing police dogs are stationed at the airport. You cannot bring fresh foodstuffs into the U.S.; however, you can bring into Jamaica most items intended for personal use.

Documents U.S., British, and Canadian residents need a passport and a return or an ongoing ticket. Immigration cards, needed for bank transactions and currency exchange, are given to visitors at the airport arrival desks.

Electricity Most places have 110-volt AC (60 cycles), as in the United States. However, some establishments operate on 220-volt AC (50 cycles). If your hotel is on a different current from your U.S.-made appliance, ask for a transformer and an adapter.

Embassies, Consulates & High Commissions Calling embassies or consulates in Jamaica is a challenge. Phones will ring and ring before being picked up, if they are answered at all. Extreme patience is needed to reach a live voice on the other end. The embassy of the **United States** is located at 142 Old Hope Rd., Kingston 6 (✆ **876/702-6000**). The High Commission of **Canada** is situated at 3 W. Kings House Rd., Kingston 10 (✆ **876/926-1500**). The High Commission of the **United Kingdom** is found at 28 Trafalgar Rd., Kingston 10 (✆ **876/936-0700**).

Emergencies For the **police,** dial ✆ **119;** to report a **fire** or call an **ambulance,** dial ✆ **110.**

Language Jamaicans speak English with a lovely lilt. Among themselves, they also speak patois, a fast-spoken blend of French, English, and a number of other languages.

Safety Major resorts have security guards who protect the grounds, so most vacationers don't have any real problems. It's not wise to accept an invitation to see the "real Jamaica" from some stranger you meet on the beach. Exercise caution when traveling around Jamaica. Safeguard your valuables, and never leave them unattended on a beach. Likewise, never leave luggage or other valuables in a car, or even the trunk of a car. The U.S. State Department has issued a travel advisory about crime rates in Kingston, so don't walk around alone at night. Caution is also advisable in many north-coast tourist areas, especially remote houses and isolated villas that can't afford security.

Taxes The government imposes between 10% and 15% room tax, depending on your category of hotel. You'll be charged $20 departure tax at the airport, payable in either Jamaican or U.S. dollars. There's also a 20% government tax on rental cars and a 20% tax on all overseas phone calls.

Time Jamaica is on Eastern Standard Time year-round and doesn't follow daylight saving time. When the United States is on daylight saving time, at 6am in Miami it's 5am in Kingston.

Tipping A general 15% or 20% is expected in hotels and restaurants on occasions when you would normally tip. Some places add a service charge to the bill, so make sure you know whether it's already included. Tipping is not allowed in the all-inclusive hotels. Taxi drivers expect about 15%.

Water It's usually safe to drink piped-in water, islandwide, as it's filtered and chlorinated. However, it's prudent to drink bottled water if it's available.

Weather Expect temperatures around 77°F to 79°F (25°C–26°C) on the coast. Summer is a little warmer. In the mountains, it can get as low as 40°F (4°C). There is generally a breeze, which in winter is noticeably cool. The rainy periods generally are October and November (although it can extend into Dec), and May and June. Normally, rain comes in short, sharp showers; then the sun shines.

MONTEGO BAY ★★★

Situated on the northwestern coast of the island, Montego Bay (MoBay) first attracted tourists in the 1940s, when Doctor's Cave Beach became popular with wealthy vacationers who bathed in the warm water fed by mineral springs. It's now Jamaica's second-largest city. Despite the large influx of visitors, Montego Bay still retains its identity as a thriving business and commercial center, and it functions as the market town for most of western Jamaica. It has cruise-ship piers and a growing industrial center. Montego Bay has its own airport, so those who vacation here have little need to visit the capital, Kingston. MoBay is the most cosmopolitan of Jamaica's cities.

Montego Bay

JAMAICA
Montego Bay
Kingston

0 1 mi
0 1 km

Caribbean Sea

WHITEHOUSE VILLAGE
Donald Sangster International Airport
A1
The Queen's Drive
Claude Clarke Ave.
Hobbs Ave.
PARADISE PEN
Sunset Blvd.
Delliser Dr.
MANGO WALK
Hart Blvd.
Paradise Crescent
Leader
Park Ave.
The Queen's Dr.
Kent Ave.
Montego Beach
Cornwall Beach
Doctor's Cave Beach
NORWOOD
Norwood Ave.
MIRANDA HILL
NEWMARKET
Albion Playing Field
Albion Rd.
First St.
Second St.
DUNBAR PEN
ALBION
Corniche Rd.

For Tryall Club and Round Hill Hotel & Villas, see the "Jamaica" map.

ACCOMMODATIONS ■

Breezes Resort Spa-Trelawny **1**
Coyaba Beach Resort & Club **9**
Doctors Cave Beach Hotel **8**
FDR Pebbles **2**
Half Moon Rose Hall **6**
Iberostar Rose Hall Beach Hotel **4**
Richmond Hill Inn **15**
Ritz-Carlton Rose Hall Jamaica **5**
Round Hill Hotel & Villas **16**
Sandals Royal Caribbean & Private Island **3**
Tryall Golf, Tennis & Beach Club **17**
Wexford Court Hotel **10**

DINING ◆

Day-O Plantation Restaurant **18**
The Groovy Grouper Beach Bar & Grill **8**
Horizons **5**
Marguerite's Seafood by the Sea and Margueritaville Sports Bar & Grill **11**
The Native Restaurant **13**
The Pelican **12**
Pork Pit **14**
Sugar Mill Restaurant **7**

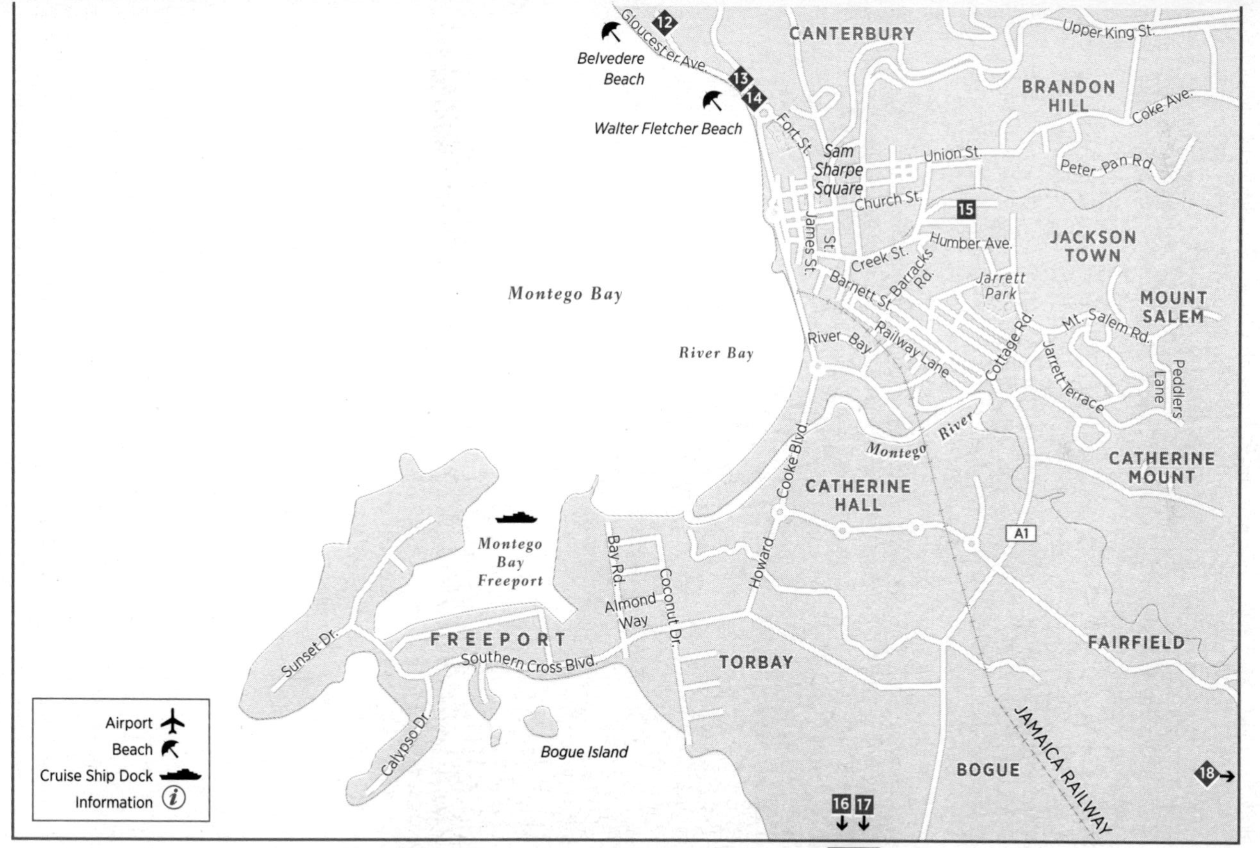
CANTERBURY
BRANDON HILL
JACKSON TOWN
MOUNT SALEM
CATHERINE MOUNT
FAIRFIELD
BOGUE
CATHERINE HALL
TORBAY
FREEPORT
JAMAICA RAILWAY
Upper King St.
Coke Ave.
Peter Pan Rd.
Peddlers Lane
Mt. Salem Rd.
Jarrett Terrace
Cottage Rd.
Jarrett Park
Humber Ave.
Union St.
Church St.
Barracks Rd.
Creek St.
Barnett St.
Railway Lane
Sam Sharpe Square
St. James St.
Fort St.
River Bay
Montego River
Cooke Blvd
Howard
A1
Gloucester Ave.
Belvedere Beach
Walter Fletcher Beach
Montego Bay
River Bay
Montego Bay Freeport
Coconut Dr.
Almond Way
Bay Rd.
Southern Cross Blvd.
Sunset Dr.
Calypso Dr.
Bogue Island
12
13
14
15
16
17
18
Airport
Beach
Cruise Ship Dock
Information

Essentials

MEDICAL FACILITIES The **Cornwall Regional Hospital** is at Mount Salem (✆ **876/952-5100**). For medicines and prescriptions, try the **Overton Pharmacy,** 49 Union St., Overton Plaza (✆ **876/952-2699**).

Where to Stay

VERY EXPENSIVE

Half Moon Rose Hall ★★★ ☺ Opening onto 160 hectares (395 acres) that take in a .8km (½-mile) stretch of white-sand beach, this is one of the Caribbean's grand hotels, without the snobbery of Round Hill or Tryall (see both below). One of the top 25 tropical resorts according to *Condé Nast Traveler,* it also has far more activities, excitement, amenities, restaurants, and a better beach. About 13km (8 miles) east of Montego Bay's city center and 10km (6¼ miles) from the international airport, it's a grand and appealing place, a true luxury hideaway with taste and style, and also highly acclaimed as an eco-sensitive resort. Accommodations include conventional hotel rooms, suites, and a collection of superbly accessorized private villas. (Most villas have private pools and a full-time staff.) Each unit is comfortably furnished with an English colonial/Caribbean motif and a private balcony or patio, plus a state-of-the-art bathroom. Queen Anne–inspired furniture is set off by vibrant Jamaican paintings, and many units contain mahogany four-poster beds.

Half Moon Post Office, Rose Hall, St. James, Montego Bay, Jamaica, W.I. http://halfmoon.rockresorts.com. ✆ **888/830-5974** in the U.S., or 876/953-2211. Fax 876/953-2731. 398 units. Winter $400–$470 double, $690–$1,680 suite; off season $250–$290 double, $420–$1,250 suite. Children 11 and under stay free in parent's room. MAP (breakfast and dinner) $85–$190 per person extra. Ask about golf and spa packages. AE, DC, DISC, MC, V. **Amenities:** 6 restaurants; 7 bars; babysitting; bikes; children's activities; deep-sea fishing; dive shop; exercise room; golf course; horseback riding; Jacuzzi; 4 outdoor pools; room service; 2 saunas; spa; 13 tennis courts (9 lit). *In room:* A/C, TV, hair dryer, kitchenette (in some), minibar, Wi-Fi ($14 per hour).

Ritz-Carlton Rose Hall Resort ★ ☺ This blockbuster complex is big, bustling, upscale, and impressive, sprawling across a wide stretch of white-sand beach. (Clients seeking a better beach are shuttled to the nearby Rose Hall Beach Club, site of many motorized and nonmotorized watersports.) One of its major draws is the White Witch golf course, a 15-minute shuttle ride away. Its public areas try to duplicate the ambience of a traditional Jamaican great house that's been updated and modernized. Come here if you're looking for a somewhat sanitized stopover in a big hotel with

Catch a Fire: Jamaica's Reggae Festival

For a week in mid-July, Montego Bay comes alive with the pulsating sounds of reggae: **Red Stripe Reggae Sumfest** (www.reggaesumfest.com) takes place at the Bob Marley Performing Arts Center, an open field set up with a temporary stage in the Freeport area. Performers have included some of the biggest names in reggae, both from Jamaica and abroad—Ziggy Marley, Cocoa Tea, the Melody Makers, Barefoot Hammond, the Mystic Revelers, and others. Many local hotels are fully booked for the festival, so advance reservations are necessary. The Jamaican Tourist Board's U.S. and Canadian offices can give you information about packages and group rates for the festivals and fill you in on other events held throughout the year on Jamaica.

international comforts, including a full-service spa. Frankly, this is not our favorite of the ultra-upscale resorts of Montego Bay—it lacks the sense of fantasy (gazebos, lavish gardens, bougainvillea burgeoning over lattices) of Half Moon and the intimacy of Round Hill. And for such a supposedly top-notch venue, the swimming pool isn't big enough. Accommodations, however, are appropriately luxurious, but with an upscale motif that could have been imported from virtually any luxury hotel in North America.

1 Ritz-Carlton Dr., Rose Hall, St. James, Jamaica, W.I. www.ritzcarlton.com. © **800/542-8680** in the U.S. or Canada, or 876/953-2800. Fax 876/684-0110. 427 units. Winter $330–$610 double, $400–$2,500 suite; off season $200–$300 double, $290–$2,500 suite. Children 11 and under stay free in parent's room. AE, DISC, MC, V. **Amenities:** 5 restaurants; 2 bars; babysitting; children's activities; golf course; health club; Jacuzzi; outdoor pool; room service; spa; 2 tennis courts (lit); watersports equipment/rentals. *In room:* A/C, TV, hair dryer, Internet (free), minibar.

Round Hill Hotel and Villas ★★★ Opened in 1953 on a small, private, white-sand beach, Round Hill is a legend, the most prestigious address in Jamaica, even though it lacks the extensive facilities (and, in some cases, the whimsical sense of romantic fantasy) of Half Moon. It originated as a small, clubby compound of private villas on the grounds of a 44-hectare (109-acre) plantation devoted to the production of pineapples and allspice, attracting the aristocracy of Europe and some of the biggest moguls of the New World. By far the most spectacular accommodations here are those cloistered away on the surrounding hillsides, within white-sided villas. Decors of these luxurious villas are elegant and theatrical, thanks to acres of mahogany and marble, the skill of some of the best architects in North America and Europe, and frequent renovations. Less grand accommodations in the Pineapple House, a rambling, two-story building set at the edge of the sea, overlook a swimming pool. Decor inside Pineapple House is all white, lighthearted, and airy, with four-poster bamboo beds.

John Pringle Drive (Rte. A1) (P.O. Box 64), Montego Bay, Jamaica, W.I. www.roundhill.com. © **800/972-2159** in the U.S., or 876/956-7050. Fax 876/956-7505. 124 units. Winter $560–$840 double, $760–$4,015 villa suite; off season $370–$490 double, from $480 villa suite. Breakfast and dinner $80 extra. AE, DC, DISC, MC, V. **Amenities:** Restaurant; 3 bars; babysitting; dive shop; health club; outdoor pool; room service; spa; 5 tennis courts (2 lit). *In room:* A/C, fridge, hair dryer, kitchen (in some), Wi-Fi (free).

Sandals Royal Caribbean & Private Island ★★ This all-inclusive, couples-only (any combination) tranquil resort lies on its own private beach. Some British colonialism remains here (formal tea in the afternoon), but there are modern touches as well, including a private, clothing-optional island reached by boat. The spacious rooms range from standard to superior to deluxe. Best are the grand luxe beachfront rooms, with private patios or balconies. The cuisine is more varied here than at other MoBay Sandals resorts, with, for example, Royal Thai, an Indonesian restaurant on the offshore island. The Regency and the Pavilion serve a rather good Jamaican-inspired cuisine, among other options.

Mahoe Bay (P.O. Box 167), Montego Bay, Jamaica, W.I. www.sandals.com. © **888/SANDALS** [726-3257] in the U.S. and Canada, or 876/953-2231. Fax 876/953-2788. 197 units. Winter $370–$1,020 double, from $735 suite; off season $335–$950 double, from $618 suite. Rates are for double and include all meals, drinks, and activities. 2-night minimum. AE, DISC, MC, V. Children 17 and under are not allowed. **Amenities:** 5 restaurants; 7 bars (2 swim-up); exercise room; 4 outdoor pools; 5 whirlpools; room service; sauna; 3 tennis courts (lit); watersports equipment/rentals. *In room:* A/C, TV, CD player, hair dryer, Wi-Fi ($14 per day).

Tryall Golf, Tennis & Beach Club ★★★ ☺ This is a top choice for vacationers who are serious about golf. With more spacious grounds than almost any other Jamaican hotel, this stylish and upscale resort sits 19km (12 miles) west of town on the site of an 880-hectare (2,175-acre) former sugar plantation. It has neither the fine beach of Half Moon nor the elegant house-party atmosphere of Round Hill, but it's one of Jamaica's grandest resorts. The property lies along a 2km (1¼-mile) beachfront and is presided over by a 165-year-old Georgian-style great house. The accommodations in luxurious villas are decorated in cool pastels with English colonial touches. Picture windows frame sea and mountain views. Bedrooms are spacious, with luxurious beds, private patios or terraces, and tile floors. The resort's villas are set amid lush foliage and are designed for privacy, each with a private pool. Nothing rents here for less than 5 days, and Tryall prefers weekly bookings. The most formal of the resort's dining areas is in the great house, but it's not the equal of the options available at Half Moon and the Ritz-Carlton. Tryall is gaining recognition as one of the most eco-sensitive resorts in the Caribbean, winning acclaim as a "Green Globe Hotel."

St. James (P.O. Box 1206), Montego Bay, Jamaica, W.I. www.tryallclub.com. ✆ **800/238-5290** in the U.S., or 876/956-5660. Fax 876/956-5673. 82 villas. Winter $550 1-bedroom villa, from $950 2-bedroom villa; off season $395 1-bedroom villa, from $475 2-bedroom villa. AE, DC, DISC, MC, V. **Amenities:** 2 restaurants; 4 bars (1 swim-up); babysitting; children's programs; exercise room; championship par-71 golf course; outdoor pool; 9 tennis courts (lit); watersports equipment/rentals. *In room:* A/C (in some), ceiling fan, TV, fridge, hair dryer, kitchen, Wi-Fi (free).

EXPENSIVE

Coyaba Beach Resort & Club ★★ On a lovely strip of private beachfront, this small all-inclusive resort evokes a British colonial atmosphere. East of the center of Montego Bay, it's centered on an adaptation of an 18th-century great house. Accommodations in the main building overlook the garden; those in the pair of three-story outbuildings lie closer to the beach and are more expensive. The decor is plantation style, with traditional prints, expensive chintz fabrics, French doors leading onto private patios or verandas, and mahogany furniture. Hand-carved bedsteads, often four-posters, are fitted with luxury coverings. Its bedrooms are modern and well maintained, and some units have been upgraded to junior suites with small refrigerators and sleeper sofas. The hotel's most formal restaurant, the Vineyard, serves first-rate Jamaican and Continental dinners. Less upscale is Docks Caribbean Bar & Grill.

Little River, Montego Bay, Jamaica, W.I. www.coyabaresortjamaica.com. ✆ **877/232-3224** or 876/953-9150. Fax 876/953-2244. 50 units. Winter $300–$340 double, $340–$380 suite; off season $200–$215 double, $215–$230 suite. Breakfast and dinner $108 per person. 2 children 11 and under stay free in parent's room. Children 11 and under get a 50% discount on meals. AE, MC, V. **Amenities:** 3 restaurants; 3 bars; babysitting; health club; Jacuzzi; outdoor pool; room service; spa; tennis court (lit) w/free tennis clinic; watersports equipment/rentals. *In room:* A/C, ceiling fan, CD player, TV, hair dryer, Wi-Fi (free).

FDR Pebbles ★ ☺ No, it's not named after the U.S. president. This resort invaded Montego Bay and quickly became the most family-friendly place in the area. It's even better than its parent outside Ocho Rios. FDR lies a 35-minute drive east of the airport, opening onto the waterfront and a beach. The resort is an all-inclusive property of cedarwood accommodations designed with real Jamaican flair, offering spacious living and bedroom areas, plus generous balconies opening onto a view. It's most suited for families with two children, although a larger family can be very comfortable in adjoining units. Everything is geared toward family fun, with an array of activities including fishing and swimming in a nearby river and hiking along nature trails. Each family is assigned a "vacation nanny," who helps with housekeeping and babysitting. In the restaurant, first-rate ingredients are fashioned into a rather standard repertoire of both Jamaican and American dishes. A 3-night minimum stay is required.

Main St., Runaway Bay (P.O. Box 201), St. Ann Jamaica, W.I. www.fdrholidays.com. ✆ **888/FDR-KIDS** [337-5437] in the U.S., or 876/617-2500. Fax 876/973-6987. 78 units. Winter $200–$235 per person double; off season $170–$210 per person double. Children 5 and under stay free in parent's room. Rates are all-inclusive. AE, DISC, MC, V. **Amenities:** 3 restaurants; 3 bars; dance club; babysitting; bikes; children's club; Jacuzzi; outdoor pool; teen center; tennis court (lit); watersports equipment/rentals. *In room:* A/C, TV, fridge, Wi-Fi (free).

Iberostar Rose Hall Beach Hotel ★★ Iberostar, the Spanish hotel chain, operates this resort as an all-inclusive, catering to well-heeled singles, couples, and families, and it's also aggressively pursuing honeymooners. A series of nearly three dozen suites are among Jamaica's finest, each elegantly decorated and spacious. Next in line is 100 oceanview rooms, each with balcony or terrace. The garden- and poolview rooms are also desirable and, of course, less expensive.

Rose Hall, Montego Bay, St. James, Jamaica, W.I. www.iberostar.com. ✆ **888/554-3215** in the U.S. and Canada, or 876/680-0000. Fax 876/680-0007. 366 units. Year-round $360–$420 double. AE, DC, MC, V. **Amenities:** 5 restaurants; 6 bars; golf; health club; 3 outdoor pools; watersports equipment/rentals. *In room:* A/C, TV, minibar, Wi-Fi ($5 for 30 min or $15 per hr.).

MODERATE

Breezes Resort & Spa—Trelawny ★ ☺ This all-inclusive resort is one of the best-value vacations on the island. Opening onto a stretch of powder-white, soft, sandy beach, it offers activities for both children and adults. The location is 37km (23 miles) east of MoBay airport. The most spacious rooms are the cottages at the rear of the hotel, which can house three adults and two children. For those who must have an ocean view, the resort rents some "superior" rooms, suitable for three adults and one child, with a balcony overlooking the beach. The least expensive units have a mountain or garden view, with a balcony, which can also accommodate three adults and a child. The wide range of sports and amenities makes this an alluring choice. The food is fairly standard, but there's a sushi bar with Teppanyaki tables and a pasta-and-pizza restaurant. Four-course gourmet dinners are served in the Casablanca Restaurant.

North Coast Hwy, Falmouth, Jamaica, W.I. www.breezes.com. ✆ **877/BREEZES** [273-3937] in the U.S. or 876/954-2450. Fax 876/518-6356. 349 units. Year round $1,315–$1,575 double. Rates are all-inclusive for 7 nights. AE, DC, MC, V. **Amenities:** 5 restaurants; 6 bars; dance club; babysitting; children's center; exercise room; Internet ($15 per day); 4 outdoor pools; sauna; spa; 4 tennis courts (lit); watersports equipment/rentals. *In room:* A/C, TV, hair dryer, minibar.

INEXPENSIVE

Doctors Cave Beach Hotel ★ This three-story hotel offers great value and lies in the bustle of the town's commercial zone. It's across from Doctor's Cave Beach, the busiest and most crowded beach, but with the best sands, in the Montego Bay area. It has 2 hectares (5 acres) of tropical gardens. The well-maintained rooms are simply but comfortably furnished, and suites have kitchenettes. Rooms are rated standard or superior; the latter are more spacious and have balconies with a view. All units have tile floors and queen-size or twin beds (suites have king-size beds). The food is more authentic than at the resorts recommended above.

Gloucester Ave. (P.O. Box 94), Montego Bay, Jamaica, W.I. www.doctorscave.com. ✆ **876/952-4355.** Fax 876/952-5204. 85 units. Winter $150–$160 double, $185 suite; off season $140–$155 double, $180 suite. Extra person $28. Breakfast and dinner $30 per person extra. AE, DC, MC, V. **Amenities:** Restaurant; bar; babysitting; exercise room; Internet ($5 per 15 min.); Jacuzzi; outdoor pool; room service. *In room:* A/C, TV, kitchenette (in some).

Going Native on the Street

MoBay has some of the finest and most expensive dining on the island. But if you're watching your wallet and have an adventurous streak, try the terrific street food. The densest concentration of street food in Montego Bay is available at the junction of Gloucester Avenue and Kent Road. (The .8km/½-mile strip of beach-fronting boulevard stretching along both sides of that junction is also known as Bottom Road or, less formally, the "Hip Strip.") It's lined with bars, food stands, and shops catering to the beach trade. At any of these stands, you might try authentic jerk pork or seasoned spareribs, grilled over charcoal fires and sold with extra-hot sauce. To complete the experience, order a Red Stripe beer to go with it. Cooked shrimp are also sold on the streets of downtown MoBay, especially along St. James Street. They don't look it, but they're very spicy, so be warned. And if you have an efficiency unit with a kitchenette, you can buy fresh lobster or the catch of the day and make your own dinner.

Richmond Hill Inn ★ If you're an avid beach lover, you should know in advance that the nearest beach is a 15-minute drive away from this hotel. It was built as the homestead of the Dewar family (the scions of scotch). Very little of the original villa remains, but what you'll find is a hilltop aerie ringed with urn-shaped concrete balustrades, a pool terrace suitable for sundowner cocktails, and comfortable, slightly fussy bedrooms done up in lace-trimmed curtains, homey bric-a-brac, and pastel colors. Both the bar and restaurant look out over Montego Bay.

Union St. (P.O. Box 362), Montego Bay, Jamaica, W.I. www.richmond-hill-inn.com. ✆ **876/952-3859.** Fax 876/952-6106. 20 units. Winter $115 double, $190–$450 suite; off season $90 double, $170–$400 suite. MC, V. **Amenities:** Restaurant; bar; babysitting; outdoor pool; room service; Wi-Fi (free). *In room:* A/C, TV, fridge (in some).

Wexford Court Hotel ☺ Especially good for families on a budget, this hotel lies within a 5-minute walk of Doctor's Cave Beach. All the rooms have patios shaded by gables and Swiss-chalet-style roofs, and each has a tiled, shower-only bathroom. The restaurant serves some zesty Jamaican dishes in a setting that evokes a 1950s Howard Johnson.

39 Gloucester Ave. (P.O. Box 108), Montego Bay, Jamaica, W.I. www.thewexfordhotel.com. ✆ **876/952-2854.** Fax 876/952-6714. 60 units. Winter $180–$350 double; off season $145–$350 double. 2 children 11 and under stay free in parent's room. MAP (breakfast and dinner) $34 per person extra. AE, DISC, MC, V. **Amenities:** Restaurant; bar; babysitting; outdoor pool; room service. *In room:* A/C, TV, Wi-Fi (free).

Where to Dine

EXPENSIVE

Horizons ★★ INTERNATIONAL This is the most upscale and fussed-over restaurant within the also-recommended Ritz-Carlton Rose Hall Resort (p. 342). What impresses here is the sense of stylish internationalism. Appetizers are enticing, including fresh fried calamari with a saffron mayonnaise or else a yellowtail snapper ceviche. The chefs prepare a soup of the day, although you can generally order clam minestrone. The array of fresh salads is among the best in any hotel. A limited selection of broiled meats and poultry is presented nightly, including New York steaks and braised lamb T-bones marinated in Barolo wine. The fresh catch of the day is the most ordered main dish—perhaps grilled cobia filet with roasted garlic.

In the Ritz-Carlton Rose Hall Hotel, Rose Hall, Montego Bay. © **876/953-2800.** Reservations recommended. Main courses $29–$38. AE, DC, MC, V. Daily 6:30–9:30pm.

Marguerite's Seafood by the Sea and Margueritaville Sports Bar & Grill INTERNATIONAL/SEAFOOD This two-in-one restaurant across from the Coral Cliff Hotel serves its seafood on a breeze-swept terrace overlooking the sea. There's also an air-conditioned lounge with an adjoining "Secret Garden." The chef specializes in exhibition cookery at a flambé grill. Although the menu is mainly devoted to seafood and fresh fish, there are also numerous innovative pastas and rather standard meat dishes. The Cheeseburger in Paradise is the most popular item on the menu, but you can also order Jamaican jerk chili, jerk burgers, and Jamaican pizza, even such Rastafarian dishes as Rasta Roots served with rice and peas. The homemade dessert options change, and a reasonable selection of wines is served. The DJ lives in a lair in the mouth of a faux great shark and, of course, plays more than just Jimmy Buffet tunes. The sports bar and grill features a 34m (112-ft.) water slide, live music, satellite TV, watersports, a sun deck, and a straightforward menu of seafood, sandwiches, pasta, pizza, salads, and snacks—nothing fussy. Naturally, the bartenders specialize in margaritas, which come in 52 different flavors.

Gloucester Ave. © **876/952-4777.** Reservations recommended for Marguerite's Seafood by the Sea. Main courses $25–$55; snacks and platters $12–$16. AE, MC, V. Restaurant daily 6–10:30pm. Sports bar daily 11am–10pm (club open until 3am).

Sugar Mill Restaurant ★★ INTERNATIONAL/CARIBBEAN After a drive through a rolling landscape, you'll come across this restaurant near the ruin of what used to be a water wheel for a sugar plantation. The lovely setting and exquisite cuisine make this place a perennial favorite. You can dine by candlelight either indoors or on an open terrace with a view of a pond, the water wheel, and plenty of greenery. Lunch can be a relatively simple affair—a daily a la carte offering is best preceded by Mama's pumpkin soup and followed with homemade rum-and-raisin ice cream. For dinner, try one of the chef's zesty versions of jerk pork, fish, or chicken. He also prepares the day's catch with considerable flair. Smoked north-coast marlin is a specialty. On any given day, you can ask the waiter what's cooking in the curry pot. Chances are, it will be a Jamaican specialty such as goat, full of flavor and served with island chutney.

At Half Moon Rose Hall. © **888/830-5974.** http://halfmoon.rockresorts.com. Reservations required. Main courses $30–$48. AE, MC, V. Daily 7–10pm. Private van transportation provided; ask when you reserve. Closed Sept–Oct.

MODERATE

Day-O Plantation Restaurant ★ 🎁 INTERNATIONAL/JAMAICAN Here's your chance to wander back to Jamaica's plantation heyday. This place was originally built in the 1920s as the home of the overseer of one of the region's largest sugar producers, the Barnett Plantation. It occupies a long indoor/outdoor dining room that's divided into two halves by a dance floor and a small stage. Owner Paul Hurlock performs as a one-man band, singing and entertaining the crowd, while his wife, Jennifer, and their three children manage the dining room and kitchen. Every dish is permeated with Jamaican spices. Try the plantation-style chicken, with red-wine sauce and herbs; the filet of red snapper Day-O style, with olives, white wine, tomatoes, and peppers; or, even better, some of the best jerked snapper in Jamaica. We also like the grilled rock lobster with garlic butter.

Day-O Plantation, Lot 1 Fairfield. © **876/952-1825.** www.dayorestaurant.com. Reservations suggested. Main courses $15–$40. AE, MC, V. Tues–Sun 11am–2pm and 6-11pm. 8-min. drive west of town off Rte. A1 toward Negril. Private van transportation provided; ask when you reserve.

The Native Restaurant ★ JAMAICAN/INTERNATIONAL Some of the finest Jamaican dishes in the area are served at this casual, open-air restaurant. While taking in the panoramic views, try some of the appetizers, including ackee and saltfish, jerk reggae chicken, and smoked marlin, which you can follow with steamed fish or jerk chicken. A more exotic specialty is Boonoonoonoos; billed as a "taste of Jamaica," it's a big platter with a little bit of everything—meat, fish, and vegetables.

29 Gloucester Ave. © **876/979-2769.** Reservations recommended. Main courses $10–$33. AE, DC, DISC, MC, V. Daily 7:30am–10:30pm.

The Pelican JAMAICAN A Montego Bay landmark, the family-friendly Pelican has been serving good food at reasonable prices for more than a 25 years. Most of the dishes are at the lower end of the price scale, unless you order shellfish. Many come here at lunch for the well-stuffed sandwiches, juicy burgers, or barbecued chicken. You can also choose from a wide array of Jamaican dishes, including stewed peas and rice, curried goat, Caribbean fish, and fried chicken. A "meatless menu" is also featured. The soda fountain serves old-fashioned sundaes with real whipped cream.

Gloucester Ave. © **876/952-3171.** Reservations recommended. Main courses $8–$37. AE, MC, V. Daily 7am–10:30pm.

INEXPENSIVE

The Groovy Grouper Beach Bar & Grill JAMAICAN/CARIBBEAN Lying at the beach club at Doctor's Cave Beach, this laid-back eatery is a favorite of visitors on the sands. Chef Hopeton James claims, "I have to create a carnival in the mouth when someone tastes something I prepared." Highlight of the week is the all-you-can-eat seafood feast on Friday. James invites you to "come feed your face." From burgers to spiny lobster, you get it all here, along with sea breezes. One specialty is escovietched fish—red snapper sautéed and topped off with a spicy veg. Fish is the obvious favorite, though there are also meat dishes, even pizza. Naturally, the chef's specialty is a 8-ounce grouper filet sprinkled with jerk spices, making for a zesty treat. You can even order a grouper burger, though you may prefer the conch fritters.

Gloucester Ave. © **876/952-8287.** Reservations not needed. Main courses $10–$14. MC, V. Daily 10am–10pm.

Pork Pit ★ JAMAICAN This joint—right in the heart of Montego Bay, near Walter Fletcher Beach—is the best place to go for jerk pork and jerk chicken. Many beachgoers desert their towels at noontime and head here for a big, reasonably priced lunch. Picnic tables encircle the building, and everything is open-air and informal. A half-pound of jerk meat, served with a baked yam or baked potato and a bottle of Red Stripe, is usually enough for a meal. The menu also includes steamed roast fish.

27 Gloucester Ave. © **876/940-3008.** 1 lb. of jerk pork $13. MC, V. Daily 11am–11pm.

Hitting the Beach

Doctor's Cave Beach, on Gloucester Avenue (© **876/952-2566;** www.doctorscavebathingclub.com for the beach club), is arguably the loveliest stretch of sand bordering Montego Bay. Its gentle surf, golden sands, and fresh turquoise water make it an inviting place to swim, and there's always a beach-party atmosphere. Placid and popular with families, it's the best all-around beach in Montego Bay. Sometimes schools of tropical fish weave in and out of the waters, but usually the crowds of frolicking people scare them away. Since it's almost always packed, especially in winter, you have to get there early to stake out a beach-blanket-size spot. Admission is $5 for adults, $2.50 for children 12 and under; it's open daily 8:30am to sunset. The beach club here has well-kept changing rooms, showers, restrooms, a food court, a bar, a cybercafe, and a sundries shop. Beach chairs and umbrellas can be rented daily.

Sports & Outdoor Pursuits

DEEP-SEA FISHING **Seaworld Resorts,** whose main office is at the Cariblue Hotel, Rose Hall Main Road (✆ **876/953-2180;** www.diveseaworld.com), operates flying-bridge cruisers, with deck lines and outriggers, for fishing expeditions. A half-day fishing trip costs $550 for up to four participants.

DIVING, SNORKELING & OTHER WATERSPORTS **Seaworld Resorts** (see above) operates scuba-diving, sailing, and windsurfing excursions. Its dives plunge to offshore coral reefs, among the most spectacular in the Caribbean. There are three certified dive guides, one dive boat, and all the necessary equipment for both inexperienced and already-certified divers. One-tank dives cost $70; night dives are $95.

Doctor's Cave Beach is part of the **Montego Bay Marine Park,** which was established to protect the wide variety of marine life among the coral reefs right offshore from the popular beaches. You can rent snorkel gear from the beach club at Doctor's Cave, or from the beach clubs at any of the local beaches.

You might also like to head across the channel to check out **Coyaba Reef, Seaworld Reef,** and **Royal Reef,** which are full of barjacks, blue and brown chromis, yellow-headed wrasses, and spotlight parrotfish. You must have a guide here, as the currents are strong and the wind picks up in the afternoon. If you're not staying at a resort offering snorkeling expeditions, then Seaworld is your best bet. For about $35 per hour, a guide swims with you and points out various fish.

A Waterworld for Families

For years, Walter Fletcher Beach was a sunny, well-maintained beach, without too many improvements, positioned a short walk from the heart of Montego Bay. In 2004 a team of entrepreneurs added a compound of entertainment options, fenced everything in, and renamed it **Aquasol Theme Park** (✆ **876/979-9447** or 876/940-1344). Its sands now bustle with scantily clad sunbathers and swimmers throughout the day. Beginning at around 8pm every Friday to Sunday, the site experiences a change of clientele, when mobs of both Jamaicans and foreign visitors hang out in the moonlight, jamming and gossiping till the wee hours. The entrance fee allows access to a watersports kiosk; a pier where glass-bottomed boats are moored; a strip of sand; a salon; a bar-and-grill-style restaurant; a gym/health club with a private local membership; and a dance club/bar with views of the sea, a collection of caged macaws, and surges of reggae and soca. Admission is $5 for adults, $3 for children 11 and under. Regardless of which of the facilities you opt to patronize, the entire compound is open Monday to Thursday 9am to 6pm, and 9am to at least 11pm (sometimes later, depending on business) on Friday to Sunday.

GOLF The **White Witch of Rose Hall Golf Course,** part of the Ritz-Carlton Rose Hall (✆ **876/684-0174;** www.whitewitchgolf.com), is one of the most spectacular courses in the Caribbean, set on 80 hectares (198 acres) of lush greenery in Jamaica's old plantation country. The course is named after Annie Palmer, the notorious "White Witch" and mistress of Rose Hall nearby. Ten minutes from the deluxe resort by wheels, the course was created by Robert von Hagge, who designed the course to wind up and down the mountains, with panoramic vistas of the sea visible from 16 of the 18 holes. Greens fees are $99 to $175 for hotel guests, $185 for nonguests.

Cinnamon Hill ★★, Rose Hall (✆ **876/953-2984**), has a noted course with an unusual and challenging seaside and mountain layout. Its 8th hole skirts the water, then doglegs onto a promontory and a green thrusting 180m (591 ft.) into the sea. The back 9 are the most scenic and interesting, rising up steep slopes and falling into deep ravines on Mount Zion. The 90m-high (295-ft.) 13th tee offers a rare panoramic view of the sea and the roof of the hotel, and the 15th green is next to a 12m (39-ft.) waterfall, once featured in a James Bond movie. Amenities include a fully stocked pro shop, a clubhouse, and a professional staff. Guests pay $99 to $119 for 18 holes, nonguests $129. Cart rental and the use of a caddy are included in the greens fees.

The excellent course at the **Tryall Club Jamaica ★★★** (✆ **876/956-5660**), 20km (12 miles) from Montego Bay, is so regal that it's often the site of major tournaments. For 18 holes, guests of Tryall are charged $100 in winter, $70 the rest of the year. Nonguests pay $110 to $145 year-round.

Half Moon, at Rose Hall (✆ **876/953-2211**), features a championship course designed by Robert Trent Jones, Sr., with manicured and diversely shaped greens. Half Moon hotel guests pay $85 for 18 holes, including caddy and cart. Nonguests pay $130 for 18 holes.

The **SuperClubs Ironshore Golf Club,** Ironshore, St. James, Montego Bay (✆ **876/953-3681**), is another well-known 18-hole, par-72 course. Privately owned, it's open to all golfers. Greens fees for 18 holes are $65.

HORSEBACK RIDING A good program is offered at the **Rocky Point Riding Stables,** at Half Moon, Rose Hall, Montego Bay (✆ **876/953-2286**). Housed in the most beautiful barn and stables in Jamaica are around 30 horses, with a helpful staff. A 90-minute beach or mountain ride costs $80.

RAFTING **Mountain Valley Rafting,** P.O. Box 23, Montego Bay (✆ **876/956-4920**), gives somewhat tame and touristy excursions on the Great River, which depart from the Lethe Plantation, about 15km (9¼ miles) south of Montego Bay. For a little more adventure, skip that and head over to Falmouth, 45km (28 miles) to the east, where you can raft on the **Martha Brae.** To reach the starting point from Falmouth, drive approximately 5km (3 miles) inland to **Martha Brae's Rafters Village** (✆ **876/952-0889;** www.jamaicarafting.com). The rafts are similar to those on the Rio Grande, near Port Antonio; you sit on a raised dais on bamboo logs. The cost is $60, with two riders allowed on a raft, plus a small child if accompanied by an adult (but use caution). The trips last 1¼ hours and operate daily from 9am to 4:30pm. It's not necessary to wear swimsuits. Along the way, you can stop and order cool drinks or beer along the banks of the river. There's a bar, a restaurant, and two souvenir shops in the village.

TENNIS **Half Moon ★★★**, outside Montego Bay (✆ **876/953-2211**), has the finest courts in the area. Its 13 state-of-the-art courts, 7 of which are lit for night games, attract tennis players from around the world. Lessons cost $30 per half-hour or $55 per hour. Residents play free, day or night. The pro shop, which accepts reservations for court times, is open daily from 7am to 9pm. If you want to play after those hours, you switch on the lights yourself. If you're not a hotel guest, you must purchase a day pass ($40 per person) at the front desk; it allows access to the resort's courts, gym, sauna, Jacuzzi, pools, and beach facilities.

Exploring the Town

TOURS & CRUISES

A **Hilton High Day Tour,** P.O. Box 161, Reading, St. James (© **876/952-3343**), showcases the rich sociology of plantation life in the Jamaican hinterlands. At 8am every Tuesday, Wednesday, Friday, and Sunday, an air-conditioned minivan picks up participants at hotels in both Montego Bay and Negril, and returns them to their hotels the same day—at around 3pm to Montego Bay, and at around 4pm to Negril. Breakfast and a buffet lunch of Jamaican food (such as spit-roasted pork and a dozen different Jamaican vegetables) are included. Lunch, during which a local calypso band performs, takes place on the grounds of an 18th-century citrus farm, Hilton Plantation, reminiscent of the Jamaica of long ago.

All-inclusive costs are $72 per person for participants picked up at hotels in Montego Bay, $75 for those picked up in Negril. Advance reservations are required.

THE GREAT HOUSES

Occupied by plantation owners, each great house of Jamaica was always built on high ground so that it overlooked the plantation itself and was in sight of the next house in the distance. It was the custom for the owners to offer hospitality to travelers crossing the island by road. While these homes are intriguing and beautiful, it's important to remember that they represent the sad legacy of slavery—they were built by slaves, and the lavish lifestyle of the original owners was supported by the profits of slave labor. The two great houses below can be toured in the same day.

Greenwood Great House ★ Some people find the 15-room Greenwood more interesting than Rose Hall (see below) because it has undergone less restoration and has more literary associations. Erected between 1780 and 1800, the Georgian-style building was the residence of Richard Barrett, cousin of poet Elizabeth Barrett Browning. Elizabeth herself never visited Jamaica, but her family was one of the largest landholders. An absentee planter who lived in England, her father owned close to 33,600 hectares (83,027 acres) and some 3,000 slaves. On display is the original library of the Barrett family, with rare books dating from 1697, along with oil paintings of the family, Wedgwood china, rare musical instruments, and antique furniture.

On Rte. A1, 23km (14 miles) east of Montego Bay. © **876/953-1077.** www.greenwoodgreathouse.com. Admission $14 adults, $7 children 11 and under. Daily 9am–6pm.

Rose Hall Great House ★ The legendary Rose Hall is the most famous great house on Jamaica. The subject of at least a dozen Gothic novels, it was immortalized in the H. G. de Lisser book *White Witch of Rose Hall.* The house was built from 1778 to 1790 by John Palmer, a wealthy British planter. At its peak, this was a 2,640-hectare (6,524-acre) plantation, with more than 2,000 slaves. However, it was Annie Palmer, wife of the builder's grandnephew, who became the focal point of fiction and fact. Called "Infamous Annie," she was said to have dabbled in witchcraft. She took slaves as lovers and then killed them off when they bored her. Servants called her the "Obeah woman" (*Obeah* is Jamaican for voodoo). Annie was said to have murdered several of her husbands while they slept and eventually suffered the same fate herself. Long in ruins, the house has now been restored. Annie's Pub is on the ground floor.

Rose Hall Hwy., 15km (9¼ miles) east of Montego Bay. ✆ **876/953-2323.** Admission $20 adults, $10 children 12 and under. Daily 9:15am–5:15pm (last tour at 5:15pm).

Shopping

Be prepared for aggressive vendors in Montego Bay, as in all of Jamaica. There's a feverish attempt to peddle goods to tourists, all of whom are viewed as rich. Therefore, prepare yourself for being pursued persistently.

Some so-called "duty-free" prices are lower than in the U.S., until you're hit with a 10% "general consumption tax" on all purchases. But you can still find good duty-free items here, including Swiss watches, Irish crystal, Italian handbags, Indian silks, and liquors and liqueurs. Appleton's rums are an excellent value. Tia Maria, laced with coffee, and rum-based Rumona are among the best of the traditional liqueurs. Increasingly popular additions to the liquor inventories of Jamaica include Smirnoff Black Ice, a light version of Red Stripe Beer, and delicious (and incredibly fattening) mudslides that are sold as individual servings in short brown bottles. Khus Khus is the most famous of the local perfumes. Jamaican arts and crafts are available throughout the resorts, from vendors on the beaches, and at the Crafts Market (see below).

The main shopping areas are at **Montego Freeport,** within easy walking distance of the pier; **City Centre,** where most of the duty-free shops are, aside from those at the large hotels; and the **Holiday Village Shopping Centre,** located across from the Holiday Inn, on Rose Hall Road, heading from Montego Bay toward Ocho Rios.

If you have time for only one shopping complex, make it **Old Fort Craft Park,** as its handicrafts are more varied. It's grazing country for souvenirs and more serious purchases. This shopping complex with 180 vendors (all licensed by the Jamaica Tourist Board) fronts Howard Cooke Boulevard (up from Gloucester Ave. in the heart of Montego Bay, on the site of Fort Montego). You can see wall hangings, hand-woven straw items, and wood sculptures. You can even get your hair braided. Be aware that vendors can be very aggressive. If you want something, be prepared to bargain.

At the **Crafts Market,** near Harbour Street in downtown Montego Bay, you can find a good selection of handmade souvenirs of Jamaica, including straw hats and bags, wooden platters, straw baskets, musical instruments, beads, carved objects, and toys. That *jipijapa* (Panama-style) straw hat is important if you're out in the island sun.

One of the most intriguing places for shopping is an upscale minimall, **Half Moon Shopping Village,** on the coastal road about 13km (8 miles) east of the commercial center of Montego Bay. It caters to the guests of Half Moon, and the carefully selected merchandise is expensive. A bank, about 25 relatively upscale boutiques, a private hospital, and a private and well-respected prep school named in honor of the long-time manager of Half Moon, Heinz Simonowitz, are on the premises.

The best selection of native art is found at the **Gallery of West Indian Art,** 11 Fairfield Rd. (✆ **876/952-4547;** www.galleryofwestindianart.com), with a wide selection of paintings from not only Haiti and Jamaica, but Cuba as well, along with Jamaican hand-carved wooden animals and even some painted, hand-turned pottery.

Montego Bay After Dark

Nightlife is not guaranteed at Montego Bay's top hotels. In winter the restaurants and bars of the Ritz-Carlton or Half Moon have the most diverse amusements. After dark, it's sleepy at Round Hill and Tryall.

Rum, Reggae & an Escape

When you want to escape, head for **Time 'n' Place,** just east of Falmouth (✆ **876/954-4371**). On an almost deserted 3km (2-mile) beach sits this funky beach bar, built of driftwood. From Montego Bay, you can spot the sign by the side of the road before you reach Falmouth: IF YOU GOT THE TIME, THEN WE GOT THE PLACE. Sit back in this relaxed, friendly spot and listen to the reggae from the local stations. You can order daiquiris made from fresh local fruit, or stick around for peppery jerk chicken or lobster. Of course, Time 'n' Place isn't completely undiscovered—the fashion editors of *Vogue* occasionally use it as a backdrop for beach fashion shots.

The top nightspot in MoBay is a two-in-one restaurant, **Marguerite's Seafood by the Sea** and **Margueritaville Sports Bar & Grill,** Gloucester Avenue (p. 347), which attracts mainly a crowd in their 20s to 40s.

Cricket Club, at Rose Hall (✆ **876/953-2650**), is more than just a sports bar; it's where people go to meet and mingle with a young, international crowd. Televised sports, karaoke sing-alongs, tournament darts, and backgammon are all part of the fun. It's open daily from 10pm to 2am; there's no cover.

The Brewery, Gloucester Avenue (✆ **876/940-2433**), is one of the city's most popular nightlife hangouts. It's a cross between an English pub and a Jamaican jerk-pork pit, but everyone is into Red Stripe and reggae. There's a woodsy-looking bar, lots of neo-Medieval memorabilia, and a covered veranda in back overlooking busy Gloucester Avenue.

Montego Bay's latest hot spot is the **Groovy Grouper,** at Doctor's Cave Bathing Club along Gloucester Avenue (✆ **876/952-8287**). It's a private club, but a $5 daytime admission can gain your entrance; after 5pm you can just walk right in. The lively bar and restaurant is located right on the sands of what is the best beach along the north coast of Jamaica. You can order some of the best rum punches in MoBay, especially the bartender's special, "Groovy Delight." Food includes conch chowder (or fritters), along with freshly made salads and wings. Jerk calamari is a specialty. The big night is Friday, when chefs present a $20 all-you-can-eat seafood beach buffet.

NEGRIL ★★★

This once-sleepy village is now a tourist mecca, with visitors drawn to its beaches along three well-protected bays: Long Bay, Bloody Bay (also known as Negril Harbour), and Orange Bay. There are really two Negrils: The **West End** is the site of many little local restaurants and funky cottages that still take in visitors. This is the area to head to if you want to recapture some of the charm and freewheeling spirit first publicized here in the '60s, but don't expect a lot of creature comforts here. The other Negril is on the **east end,** the first area you approach on the road from Montego Bay. Here are the upscale hotels and some of the most gorgeous beachfronts. Come here if you want to experience Negril from the confines of a luxury resort, particularly an all-inclusive.

Negril became famous in the late 1960s, when it attracted American and Canadian hippies, who liked the idea of a place with no phones and no electricity; they rented modest digs on the West End, where the local people extended their hospitality. But those days are long gone, and a strip of sophisticated hotels and all-inclusive resorts has sprouted along the sands of famous **Seven Mile Beach.**

Situated on the western tip of the island, Negril is 80km (50 miles) and about a 2-hour drive from Montego Bay's airport, along a winding road and past ruins of sugar estates and great houses.

Essentials

GETTING THERE If you're going to Negril, you will fly into **Donald Sangster Airport** in Montego Bay. Some hotels, particularly the all-inclusive resorts, will arrange for airport transfers from that point. Be sure to ask when you book.

The 1¼-hour **bus trip** costs $25. We recommend **Tour Wise** (✆ **876/974-2323** in Ocho Rios). The bus will drop you off at your final destination once you reach Negril.

MEDICAL SERVICES For a non-life-threatening emergency, try the **Negril Beach Medical Center,** Plaza Negril (✆ **876/957-4888**). **Negril Pharmacy,** Shop no. 14, in the Coral Seas Plaza (✆ **876/957-4076**), is open Monday to Saturday 9am to 7pm, and Sunday 10am to 4pm.

Where to Stay

VERY EXPENSIVE

The Caves ★ Although the nearest beach is a 12-minute ride away, Negril's most atmospheric and elegant small inn still attracts international celebrities. In spite of its fame, however, there are drawbacks. There's a sense of snobbishness at this member of Chris Blackwell's Island Outpost hotels, generally the finest in the Caribbean, and the prices are high compared to the competition's. The hotel is on 1 hectare (2½ acres) of land perched above a honeycombed network of cliffs, 10m (33 ft.) above the surf on a point near Negril's lighthouse, close to Jamaica's westernmost tip. The setting, though lavishly publicized, is difficult to negotiate with its stairwells and catwalks.

Accommodations, well suited for groups of friends traveling together, are in breezy units within five cement-and-wood-sided cottages, each with a thatched roof and sturdy furniture. Matisse could have designed them. None has air-conditioning, and the windows are without screens. A TV and VCR can be brought in if you request them. Many of the units contain alfresco showers.

Sumptuous meals are prepared only for guests and are included, along with domestic Jamaican drinks from the bar, as part of the all-inclusive price.

P.O. Box 3113, Lighthouse Rd., Negril, Jamaica, W.I. www.thecavesresort.com. ✆ **800/688-7678** in the U.S. and Canada, or 876/957-0270. Fax 876/957-4930. 10 units. Winter $475–$1,025 double; off season $420–$790 double. Rates include all meals and self-service bar. AE, MC, V. Children 15 and under not allowed. **Amenities:** 2 restaurants; bar; free airport transfers; bikes; Jacuzzi; outdoor saltwater pool; sauna; spa; snorkeling. *In room:* Ceiling fan, TV/DVD, CD player, hair dryer, minibar, Wi-Fi (free).

EXPENSIVE

Couples Negril ★ If you're a loving male-female couple, you're welcomed at this romantic resort, lying on around 300m (984 ft.) of white-sand beach, fronting Bloody Bay, 8km (5 miles) from the center of Negril. The formula worked at the Couples in Ocho Rios (p. 364), so it was repeated here. A rival of Sandals properties, this love nest is the site of many weddings and honeymoons. On 7 hectares (17 acres) facing crescent-shaped Negril Harbour, this resort caters to those who want back-to-back scheduled activities, ranging from tennis tournaments to fashion shows. Each

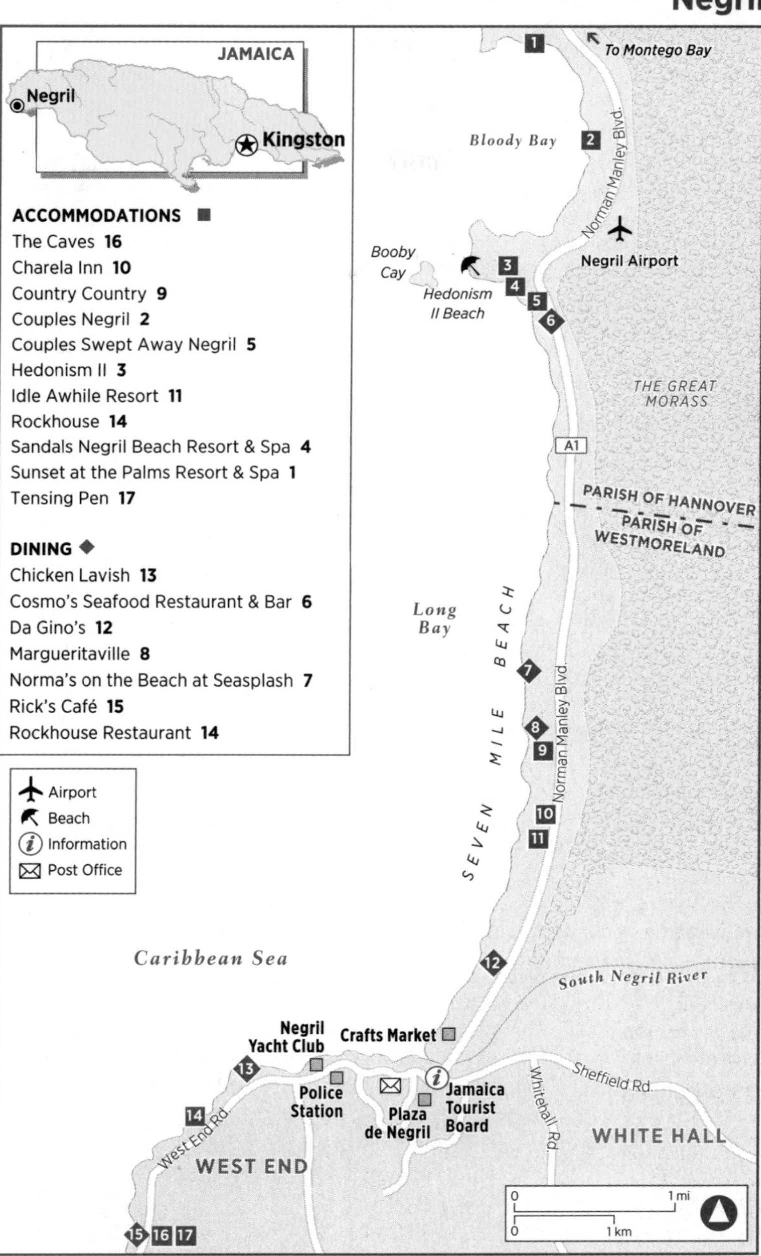
JAMAICA
Negril
Kingston
ACCOMMODATIONS
The Caves 16
Charela Inn 10
Country Country 9
Couples Negril 2
Couples Swept Away Negril 5
Hedonism II 3
Idle Awhile Resort 11
Rockhouse 14
Sandals Negril Beach Resort & Spa 4
Sunset at the Palms Resort & Spa 1
Tensing Pen 17
DINING
Chicken Lavish 13
Cosmo's Seafood Restaurant & Bar 6
Da Gino's 12
Margueritaville 8
Norma's on the Beach at Seasplash 7
Rick's Café 15
Rockhouse Restaurant 14
Airport
Beach
Information
Post Office
To Montego Bay
Bloody Bay
Norman Manley Blvd.
Negril Airport
Booby Cay
Hedonism II Beach
THE GREAT MORASS
A1
PARISH OF HANNOVER
PARISH OF WESTMORELAND
Long Bay
SEVEN MILE BEACH
Caribbean Sea
South Negril River
Negril Yacht Club
Crafts Market
Police Station
Plaza de Negril
Jamaica Tourist Board
Sheffield Rd.
Whitehall Rd.
West End Rd.
WEST END
WHITE HALL
0
1 mi
0
1 km

The Naked Truth

Nude bathing is allowed at a number of hotels, clubs, and beaches (especially in Negril), but only where there are signs stating SWIMSUITS OPTIONAL. Elsewhere the law prohibits even topless sunbathing.

good-size unit has a king-size bed and a CD player (bring your own tunes), plus a balcony or patio with a view of the bay or of the lush gardens. Furnishings, though standard, are comfortable, and everything is modern. The best doubles are the deluxe beachfront suites, which have Jacuzzis and hammocks. No building in the complex is higher than the tallest coconut tree. On the east side of the property, nude sunbathing is permitted.

Norman Manley Blvd. (P.O. Box 35), Hanover, Jamaica, W.I. www.couples.com. ✆ **800/268-7537** in the U.S. and Canada, or 876/957-5960. Fax 876/957-5858. 234 units. Winter $683–$791 double, $889–$1,072 suite; off season $635–$724 double, $795–$925 suite. Rates include all meals, drinks, and activities. 3-night minimum. AE, MC, V. Children 17 and under not allowed. **Amenities:** 5 restaurants; 4 bars (1 swim-up); exercise room; golf; 2 outdoor pools; room service; 14 tennis courts (lit); watersports equipment/rentals. *In room:* A/C, TV, hair dryer, minibar, MP3 docking station, Wi-Fi (free).

Couples Swept Away Negril ★★ This is one of the best beachside hotels in Negril—conscious of both sports and relaxation. All-inclusive, it caters to those eager for an ambience of all possible diversions available but absolutely no organized schedule and no pressure to participate if you just want to relax. Unlike the Couples above, this resort allows same-sex couples. The resort occupies 8 flat and sandy hectares (20 acres), which straddle both sides of the highway leading in from Montego Bay. The accommodations (called "veranda suites" because of their large balconies) are in 26 two-story villas clustered together and accented with flowering shrubs and vines, a few steps from Seven Mile Beach. Each lovely, airy, and spacious unit has a ceiling fan, a king-size bed, and (unless vegetation obscures it) sea views. Wooden shutters let sunlight and breezes in.

Norman Manley Blvd. (P.O. Box 3077), Westmoreland, Jamaica, W.I. www.couples.com. ✆ **800/268-7537** in the U.S. and Canada, or 876/957-4061. Fax 876/957-4060. 312 units. Winter $751–$943 double; off season $650–$800 double. Rates are all-inclusive. 3-night minimum. Ask about spa packages. AE, MC, V. Children 17 and under not allowed. **Amenities:** 6 restaurants; 8 bars; free airport transfers; bikes; health club; 2 Jacuzzis; 2 outdoor pools; room service; sauna; spa; 10 tennis courts (lit); watersports equipment/rentals. *In room:* A/C, hair dryer, MP3 docking station, Wi-Fi (free).

Hedonism II ★ Devoted to the pursuit of sophomoric pleasure, and with less class than Couples Negril, Hedonism II packs the works into a one-package deal, including all the drinks and partying anyone could want. The complex lies at the northern end of Negril Beach. Of all the members of the SuperClubs chain, this is the most raucous. It's a meat market, deliberately inviting its mainly single guests to go wild for a week. The rooms are stacked in dull two-story clusters dotted around a sloping 9-hectare (22-acre) site about 3km (2 miles) east of the town center. The hotel will find you a roommate if you'd like to book on the double-occupancy rate. Accommodations don't have balconies but are very spacious. On one section of this resort's beach, clothing is optional. It's called the "Nude" section; the other is known as the "Prude." The resort also has a secluded beach on nearby Booby Cay, where guests are taken twice a week for picnics.

Negril Beach Rd. (P.O. Box 25), Negril, Jamaica, W.I. www.hedonismresorts.com. © **877/467-8737** in the U.S., or 876/957-5070. Fax 876/957-5214. 280 units. Winter $2,220–$3,250 double; off season $1,904–$2,630 double. Rates include all meals, drinks, and activities for 7 days. AE, DC, DISC, MC, V. Children 17 and under not accepted. **Amenities:** 4 restaurants; 5 bars (1 swim-up); dance club; free airport transfers; exercise room; 2 indoor squash courts; Internet cafe; Jacuzzi; 2 outdoor pools; sauna; spa; 6 tennis courts (lit); watersports equipment/rentals. *In room:* A/C, TV, hair dryer, Wi-Fi ($15 per day).

Sandals Negril Beach Resort & Spa ★ On 5 hectares (12 acres) of prime beachfront land, a short drive east of the center of Negril, Sandals Negril is an all-inclusive, couples-only (straight and gay) resort that attracts a basically young, convivial, and unsophisticated audience. It's far more active and freewheeling than the more formal Sandals properties in Ocho Rios and Montego Bay. The casual, well-furnished rooms have a tropical motif and come in a wide range of styles, but are generally spacious. The best units open directly on the beach. Honeymooners usually end up in a Jamaican-built four-poster mahogany bed. For a balcony and sea view, you have to pay the top rates. In the typical Sandals style, the food is rather standard, but there is great variety and no one goes hungry.

Norman Manley Blvd. (P.O. Box 12), Negril, Jamaica, W.I. www.sandals.com. © **888/SANDALS** (726-3257) in the U.S. and Canada, or 876/957-5216. Fax 876/957-5338. 222 units. Winter $1,150–$3,700 double; off season $990–$3,200 double. Rates are per night and include all meals, drinks, and activities. AE, DISC, MC, V. Children 15 and under not allowed. **Amenities:** 5 restaurants; 5 bars (2 swim-up); free airport transfers; exercise room; 2 outdoor pools; 2 whirlpools; room service; sauna; spa; 4 tennis courts (lit); watersports equipment/rentals. *In room:* A/C, TV, hair dryer, minibar (in some), Wi-Fi ($31 per day).

Sunset at the Palms Resort & Spa This place appeals to eco-travelers who want to get away from it all without spending a fortune; it's an especially good choice for families with kids. The wooden cabins (which have been featured in *Architectural Digest*) are in a forest, across the road from a beach called Bloody Bay. The 4 hectares (10 acres) of gardens are planted with royal palms, bull thatch, and a rare variety of mango tree. The simple but stylish cabins are small timber cottages, none more than two stories high, rising on stilts. Each offers two spacious and comfortable bedrooms, plus a balcony. Units are brightened with vibrant Jamaican fabrics. The best are rented as "executive suites," with a sunken living and dining area, plus a pull-out queen-size sofa bed for small families. Simple but tasty Jamaican and international dishes are served.

Norman Manley Blvd. (P.O. Box 118), Negril, Jamaica, W.I. www.sunsetatthepalms.com. © **877/734-3486** in the U.S., or 876/957-5350. Fax 876/957-5381. 65 units. Winter $380 double, $580 suite; off season $350 double, $540 suite. Rates are all-inclusive. Children 2 and under stay free in parent's room; children 3–12 $75 extra. AE, MC, V. **Amenities:** 3 restaurants; 3 bars; bikes; exercise room; Jacuzzi; outdoor pool; room service; spa services; tennis court (lit); watersports equipment/rentals. *In room:* A/C, TV, hair dryer, Internet (free).

MODERATE

Charela Inn ★ Simplicity, a sense of calm, a well-managed restaurant, and good value are the hallmarks of this seafront inn reminiscent of a Spanish hacienda. The inn sits on the main beach strip on 1 hectare (2½ acres) of landscaped grounds. The building's inner courtyard, with a tropical garden and a round, freshwater pool, opens onto one of the widest (75m/246 ft.) sandy beaches in Negril. Try for one of the 20 or so rooms with a view of the sea. Accommodations are generally spacious, often with a bit of Jamaican character with wicker furnishings and ceiling fans. All have private patios or balconies. Le Vendôme, facing the sea and the garden, offers both an a la carte menu and a five-course fixed-price meal that changes daily. Several times a week in winter, the hotel offers some form of live entertainment.

Norman Manley Blvd. (P.O. Box 33), Negril, Jamaica, W.I. www.charela.com. ✆ **876/957-4277.** Fax 876/957-4414. 47 units. Winter $185–$271 double; off season $125–$190 double. MAP (breakfast and dinner) $45 per person extra. 5-night minimum in winter. AE, MC, V. **Amenities:** Restaurant; bar; outdoor pool; room service; watersports equipment/rentals. *In room:* A/C, ceiling fan, TV, hair dryer, Wi-Fi (free).

Idle Awhile Resort ★ Enjoying a choice but narrow spot in the middle of Seven Mile Beach, this is an intimate, personal inn. The inn offers deluxe bedrooms with king-size beds and large verandas, and eight junior suites, each with a kitchenette and enclosed patio. There are also larger suites available with more living area and a more spacious veranda. Catering to families, singles, or couples, the resort offers guest privileges at the large sports complex at the nearby Couples Swept Away (p. 356). Bedrooms are nestled in tropical gardens. On a luxury-living note, if you book a one-bedroom suite, you can hire a cook. For an extra $20 per day (plus groceries), the chef will go grocery shopping for you and prepare regional Jamaican dishes for you.

Norman Manley Blvd., Negril. www.idleawhile.com. ✆ **877/243-5352** or 876/957-3303. Fax 876/957-9567. 14 units. Winter $210 double, $250–$335 1-bedroom suite; off season $180 double, $190–$230 1-bedroom suite. AE, MC, V. **Amenities:** Restaurant; bar; babysitting; room service. *In room:* A/C, TV, kitchenette (in some rooms), minibar, Wi-Fi (free).

Tensing Pen ★★ Our favorite nest in Negril lies on the western tip and has grown and evolved since its hippie era in the early 1970s. On a cliff, a 10-minute stroll from the landmark lighthouse, it is 6km (3¾ miles) south of the center of Negril. Hidden away from the world, the place is a little gem. Those aggressive beach vendors will never find you here, tucked behind a high wall. On 1 hectare (2½ acres) of grounds, you're surrounded by tropical planting. Laze in the hammocks or sunbathe on the terraces hewn out of rock. Sleep in a rustic stone cottage covered in thatch in a four-poster draped in mosquito netting, plantation house style. Local tiles, tropical woods, bamboo rockers, ceiling fans, and louvered windows set the tone. There's a communal kitchen where guests sometimes cook for each other. The only minor downfalls here are that the nearest beach is a 10- to 15-minute drive or a 30-minute walk, and the staff tends to be disorganized.

Lighthouse Rd. (P.O. Box 3031), Negril, Jamaica, W.I. www.tensingpen.com. ✆ **800/957-0387** in the U.S., or 876/957-0387. Fax 876/957-0161. 21 units. Winter $195–$640 double; off season $115–$415 double. Rates include breakfast. AE, MC, V. **Amenities:** Restaurant; babysitting; communal kitchen. *In room:* A/C (in some), fridge, no phone, Wi-Fi (free).

INEXPENSIVE

Another low-budget option for lodging is found at **Da Gino's** (see "Dining," below).

Country Country ★ The owners of this intimate hotel were determined to outclass the competition, so they turned to celebrity architect Ann Hodges, the creative force behind the gorgeous decor in many of the much more expensive Island Outpost properties. A narrow meandering path stretches from the coastal boulevard to the white-sand beach, where watersports await. Along the way, a collection of neo-Creole, clapboard-sided buildings drip with elaborate gingerbread and cove moldings, each inspired by an idealized vision of vernacular Jamaican colonial architecture. The buildings are painted in a variety of peacock hues, highlighting their architectural features. Inside, concrete floors keep the spacious interiors cool. Each unit has a slight Victorian feel, with comfortable furnishings. There's a beachfront bar and grill.

Norman Manley Blvd. (P.O. Box 39), Negril, Jamaica, W.I. www.countryjamaica.com. ✆ **888/790-5264** in the U.S., or 876/957-4273. Fax 876/957-4342. 20 units. Winter $180–$200 double; off season $150–$170 double. Rates include breakfast. AE, MC, V. **Amenities:** Restaurant; bar; room service. *In room:* A/C, TV, fridge, hair dryer, Wi-Fi (free).

Rockhouse ★ This funky boutique inn stands in stark contrast to hedonistic all-inclusive resorts like Sandals, and it offers very affordable rates. It's a cross between a South Seas island retreat and an African village, with thatched roofs capping stone-and-pine huts. A team of enterprising young Aussies restored and expanded this place, which was one of Negril's first hotels (the Rolling Stones hung out here in the 1970s). The rooms have ceiling fans, four-poster beds draped in mosquito netting, and open-air showers. All units contain queen-size beds, and four cottages have sleeping lofts with extra queen-size beds. Less than half a kilometer (¼ mile) from the beach, Rockhouse has a ladder down to a cove where you can swim and snorkel. After a refreshing dip in the cliff-side pool, you can dine in the open-sided restaurant pavilion, serving excellent, spicy local fare three times a day.

West End Rd. (P.O. Box 3024), Negril, Jamaica, W.I. www.rockhousehotel.com. ✆ **876/957-4373.** Fax 876/957-0557. 34 units. Winter $160–$425 double; off season $125–$350 double. AE, MC, V. Children 11 and under not allowed. **Amenities:** Restaurant; 2 bars; outdoor pool; watersports equipment/rentals. *In room:* A/C, hair dryer, minibar, Wi-Fi (free).

Where to Dine

Along Seven Mile Beach, **Chill Awhile** (✆ **876/957-3303**) is luring beach devotees to its open-air precincts where they eat as the Rastas do—that is, a vegetarian cuisine with no salt, oil, or meat. The cooking is called *ital,* which is short for "vital food." An ital plate sells for $7, and you get an assortment of specialties from callaloo to rice, beans, squash, carrots, avocado, and tomato. It's eaten with a coconut-shell spoon and plenty of coconut milk; Scotch bonnet peppers add flavor.

EXPENSIVE

Da Gino's ITALIAN Four octagonal, open-sided dining pavilions, separated from Negril's beachfront by a strip of trees, evolved as the escapist dream of Gino Travaini, the Italy-born owner. Pastas and bread are made fresh daily. The best chef's specialties feature linguine with lobster, filet of beef with peppercorns, various forms of scaloppini, and huge platters of grilled seafood.

On the premises are a dozen very simple huts, each octagonal, rustic, and camplike, that rent for $60 to $150 double, depending on the season. Each has a TV, a very basic kitchenette, and a ceiling fan, but no air-conditioning.

In the Hotel Mariposa Hideaway, Norman Manley Blvd. ✆ **876/957-4918.** Reservations recommended. Main courses $18–$30. MC, V. Daily 7am–10pm.

Margaritaville Negril AMERICAN/INTERNATIONAL It's practically Disney gone Jamaican at this rowdy bar, restaurant, and entertainment complex. Thanks to the loaded buses that pull in for field trips from some of Negril's all-inclusive hotels, it's a destination in its own right. People party here all day and night. There's an on-site art gallery where most of the works are by the very talented U.S.-born artist Geraldine Robbins. Every evening beginning around 9pm, there's live music or perhaps karaoke. Permanently moored a few feet offshore is a pair of Jamaica's largest trampolines, whale-size floaters that feature high-jumping contests by any participant whose cocktails haven't affected them yet. Rock climbing is also available. Drinks are deceptively potent. With all this, you wouldn't expect the food to be that good, but you might be surprised (even though it consists of such fare as shrimp-and-tuna kabobs). You'll find Southern-fried chicken, along with the standard club steaks and burgers.

Norman Manley Blvd. ✆ **876/957-4467.** www.margaritavillecaribbean.com. Burgers and sandwiches $10–$13; main courses $19–$31. MC, V. Daily 8am–11pm.

Norma's on the Beach at Sea Splash ★★ INTERNATIONAL/JAMAICAN The durable matriarch, Norma Shirley, is hailed as the finest chef in Jamaica. Although it's unlikely that she'll appear on the premises at the time of your arrival, the chefs use her recipes for their inspiration—characterized by such regional products as callaloo (a spinachlike vegetable), papaya, and corn-fed free-range chicken. To reach the place, you proceed down a long, jungle-landscaped pathway from the parking lot (near the sea-hugging boulevard), through the gardens of the Sea Splash resort, to a pair of lattice-ringed wooden decks beside a stretch of Seven Mile Beach. Pick your preferred dining venue—there are at least two, one of which is at the top of a flight of wooden stairs. The menu is seasonally adjusted, with items that may include grilled red snapper served with a garlic-butter sauce, or jerk penne pasta with slivers of chicken, fresh basil leaves, and sun-dried tomatoes. A specialty is jerk pork marinated in jerk sauce and grilled and served with a pimento jerk glaze. That's a lot of jerk.

In the Sea Splash Resort, Norman Manley Blvd. ✆ **876/957-4041.** Reservations recommended. Main courses $4–$12 breakfast, $8–$16 lunch, $12–$28 dinner. AE, DC, MC, V. Daily 7am–10pm.

Rick's Café ★ SEAFOOD/STEAKS At sundown, everybody in Negril heads toward the lighthouse along the West End strip to Rick's Café, whether they want a meal or not. Of course, the name was inspired by the old watering hole of Bogie's *Casablanca*. There was a real Rick (Richard Hershman), who first opened this bar back in 1974, but he's long gone. This laid-back cafe was made famous in the '70s as a hippie hangout, and ever since it's attracted the bronzed and the beautiful (and some who want to be). Management claims the sunset here is the most glorious in Negril, and after a few fresh-fruit daiquiris, you'll agree with them. (Actually, the sunset is just as spectacular at any of the waterfront hangouts in Negril, if nothing is blocking the view.) Casual dress is the order of the day, and the background music comprises reggae and rock. If you want dinner, you can order imported steaks along with a complete menu of blackened dishes, Cajun style. The fish (red snapper, fresh lobster, or grouper) is always fresh. The food is rather standard, and expensive for what you get, but that doesn't keep the touristy crowds away from the sunset party. You can also buy plastic bar tokens at the door, which you can use instead of money, a la Club Med. A bit tacky, we'd say. Bogie would never have tolerated this.

West End Rd. ✆ **876/957-0380.** www.rickscafejamaica.com. Reservations accepted for parties of 6 or more. Main courses $14–$28. AE, MC, V. Daily noon–2am (food served until 10pm).

MODERATE

Cosmo's Seafood Restaurant & Bar ★ 🎁 SEAFOOD/JAMAICAN One of the best places to go for local seafood is this Polynesian thatched *bohîo* (beach hut) open to the sea and bordering the main beachfront. In this rustic setting, Cosmo Brown entertains locals and visitors. You can order his famous conch soup, or conch in a number of other ways, including steamed or curried. He's also known for his savory kettle of curried goat, or you may prefer freshly caught seafood or fish, depending on the catch. Unless you order shellfish, most dishes are rather inexpensive.

Norman Manley Blvd. ✆ **876/957-4330** or 957-9072. Main courses $14–$46. AE, MC, V. Daily 9am–10pm.

Rockhouse Restaurant ★ INTERNATIONAL This is a gorgeous setting for enjoying some of the best food in Negril. Set on the premises of the previously recommended Rockhouse (p. 359), it was developed by a team of Australian and Italian entrepreneurs who designed a bridgelike span, equivalent to a railway trestle, high above the surging tides of a rocky inlet on Negril's West End. You may get a touch of vertigo if you lean over the railing. This place attracts a hip international crowd. Enjoy a drink or two at the bar, which is built with glossy tropical hardwoods and coral stone, before your meal. Menu items, which are always supplemented with daily specials, might include a seasonal platter of smoked marlin or an upscale version of Jamaican peppered pork with yams.

In the Rockhouse, West End Rd. ✆ **876/957-4373.** Reservations required for dinner in high season. Main courses $10–$45. AE, MC, V. Daily 7am–10pm.

INEXPENSIVE

Chicken Lavish ★ JAMAICAN Chicken Lavish, whose name we love, is the best of the low-budget eateries. Just show up on the doorstep of this place along the West End beach strip, and see what's cooking. Curried goat is a specialty, as is fresh fried fish. The red snapper is caught in local waters. But the big draw is the restaurant's namesake, the chef's special Jamaican chicken. It's amazingly consistent, fried or served with curry or sweet-and-sour sauce. The chef will tell you, and you may agree, that it's the best on the island. Ironically, this utterly unpretentious restaurant has achieved something like cult status among counterculture travelers who have eaten here since the 1970s. You can dine on the roofed veranda or ask for takeout.

West End Rd. ✆ **876/957-4410.** Main courses $5–$30. AE, MC, V. Daily 10am–11pm.

Fun on & off the Beach

BEACHES Beloved by the hippies of the 1960s, **Seven Mile Beach** ★★ is still going strong, but it's no longer the idyllic retreat it once was. Resorts attracting an international crowd now line this beach. Nudity, however, is just as prevalent as it's always been, especially along the stretch near Cosmo's. On the western tip of the island, the white powdery sand stretches from Bloody Bay in Hanover to Negril Lighthouse in Westmoreland. Clean, tranquil aquamarine waters; coral reefs; and a backdrop of palm trees add to the appeal. When you tire of the beach, you'll find all sorts of resorts, clubs, beach bars, and open-air restaurants. Vendors will try to sell you everything from Red Stripe beer to ganja. Many of the big resorts have nude beaches as well.

GOLF **Negril Hills Golf Club,** Sheffield Road (✆ **876/957-4638;** www.negrilhillsgolfclub.com), is Negril's only golf course. It may not have the cachet of such Montego Bay courses as Tryall, but it's the only golf course in western Jamaica. Greens fees for this 18-hole, par-72 course are $58, and club rental is $18. Carts and caddies, which are not obligatory, cost $35 and $14, respectively. Anyone can play, but advance reservations are recommended before 7am.

HORSEBACK RIDING Horseback riding, heretofore confined to the north shore, has come to Negril. For a close encounter with the natural beauty of this part of Jamaica, head for **Rhodes Hall Plantation,** signposted at the eastern edge of the resort (✆ **876/957-6422;** www.rhodesresort.com). The guided 2-hour excursions here ramble across the most scenic spots on the outskirts of Negril. Along the way, you'll pass some of the richest vegetation in the Caribbean, including breadfruit, guava, and even wild tobacco plants. Costs average $60 for a beach ride or $50 for a mountain ride. There is a free pick-up service.

WATERSPORTS **Watersports equipment** is easily available at any of at least seven associated kiosks that operate at strategic intervals along the sands of Seven Mile Beach. The best area for **snorkeling** is off the cliffs in the West End. The coral reef here is extremely lively, with marine life visible at a depth of about 3 to 5m (9¾–16 ft.). The waters are so clear and sparkling that just by wading in and looking down, you can see lots of marine life. The fish are small but extremely colorful.

Negril has the best and most challenging **scuba diving** in Jamaica. Unusual dive sites within an easy boat ride of Negril include **Shallow Plane,** the site of a Cessna aircraft that crashed in 15m (49 ft.) of water, and which is a diving attraction today; an underwater cave, **Throne Room,** which allows divers to enter at one end and ascend into the open air at the other; and two separate sites, each about 20m (66 ft.) underwater, known as **Shark's Reef** and **Snapper Drop.** Each of these is loaded with flora and fauna whose species change as the elevations change.

Negril Scuba Centre, in the Negril Escape Resort, One Love Drive (✆ **876/957-0392;** www.negrilscubacenter.com), is the most modern, best-equipped scuba facility in Negril. A professional staff of internationally certified scuba instructors and dive masters guides divers through Negril's colorful coral reefs. Beginners' dive lessons are offered daily, as well as multiple-dive packages for certified divers. (Dives range from $40 to $250.) Full scuba certifications and specialty courses are also available.

Negril After Dark ★

Negril is not without nightspots, though you're likely to spend most evenings enjoying the entertainment in your own resort. Fun places are easy to find, as nearly *everything* is on Norman Manley Boulevard, the only major road in Negril.

See "Where to Dine," above, for details on **Rick's Café** and **Margaritaville. The Jungle,** in Mariner's Negril Beach Club (✆ **876/957-4005;** www.junglenegril.com), is the most crowded, horny, exuberant, and famous dance club in Negril, with a penchant for attracting sports and music-industry celebrities. Its slogan? "Unleash the Animal." The scene gets so mobbed during spring break that movie crews have flown in from the U.S. to film it. Most of the perspiration here is spilled on the ground level, where four bars and dance floors rock 'n' roll with music that varies according to the night's theme. Head for the upper level for the much-needed "cool-downs" that, at least here, have developed into a laid-back art form all their own. Red Stripe and rum punches are the drinks of choice for a crowd that really seems to enjoy their estrogen and testosterone highs. Fortunately, security at least appears tight, with a prominent sign in front that declares, NO PROSTITUTES OR GIGOLOS, NO DRUGS, NO SOLICITING, NO MISCONDUCT and a forbidding-looking bar that locks the place up tighter than a jail during off-hours. The cover charge is $10 for men (referred to on signs at the entrance as TARZANS) and $8 for women (referred to as JANES). The Jungle Arcade is a gaming room with around 100 slot machines. The club is open Wednesday to Saturday 8:30pm until the last patron staggers back to his or her hotel.

Alfred's Ocean Palace, Norman Manley Boulevard (✆ **876/957-4735;** www.alfreds.com), draws mainly locals, but visitors are welcome. Set directly on the beach, it attracts primarily a young party crowd, but if you're 80, you'll still be warmly embraced, your cold Red Stripe waiting. The $7 cover is for shows, and in addition to grabbing a drink, you can order a bite to eat until midnight. Particularly interesting is the beach-party area, with a stage for live reggae and jazz acts. You can also boogie on the dance floor inside, shaking to hits you'll hear at clubs stateside.

Risky Business, Norman Manley Boulevard (✆ **876/957-3008;** www.riskybusinesses.com), sits a few feet from the waves. It can be sleepy or manic, depending on the music. In season you can order burgers and sandwiches, and the Red Stripe is cheap year-round. It's mostly a young hangout with parties Monday, Thursday, and Saturday beginning at 9pm. There's no cover.

Mary's Bay Boat Bar & Grill, West End Road (✆ **876/454-2284**), the brainchild of a U.S. ex-pat, William H. Miller, is about a 10-minute walk west from the center of Negril. This popular bar opens onto a panoramic sweep of Negril's Seven Mile Beach. It has a wide selection of drinks and serves an array of hot, tasty Jamaican dishes. Live reggae music is presented on Tuesday night after 9pm. The bar is also a magnet during the day, with showers and lockers, chaise longues, and an Internet cafe. Boat charter services—featuring fishing, snorkeling, and sunset cruises—also operate out of here.

Another watering hole gaining renown is **Ivan's Bar,** at the Catcha Falling Star Resort in the West End (✆ **876/957-0045**), named after the infamous Hurricane Ivan that struck Jamaica in 2004. Because of limited seating, the bar is open only to guests of the inn—and their friends—or else those who called and made dinner reservations. The bartenders make the best soursop martini on island. The kitchen turns out such delights as coconut pimento chicken or seafood linguini. Sometimes the heavy drinking lasts until the sun comes up over the drunken revelers.

OCHO RIOS ★

This north-coast resort is a 2-hour drive east of Montego Bay or west of Port Antonio. Ocho Rios was once a small banana and fishing port, but tourism became the leading industry long ago. Short on charm, it's now Jamaica's cruise-ship capital. The bay is dominated on one side by a bauxite-loading terminal and on the other by a range of hotels with sandy beaches fringed by palm trees.

Ocho Rios and neighboring Port Antonio have long been associated with Sir Noël Coward (who invited the world to his doorstep) and Ian Fleming, creator of James Bond. (See p. 365 for details about their homes here.)

Frankly, unless you're a cruise passenger, you may want to stay away from the major attractions when a ship is in port. The duty-free markets are overrun then, and the hustlers become more strident in pushing their crafts and junk souvenirs. Dunn's River Falls becomes almost impossible to visit at those times.

However, Ocho Rios has its own flavor and offers a range of sports, including a major fishing tournament every fall, in addition to a wide variety of accommodations.

In our view, you go to Ocho Rios only if you want to stay put at one of the resorts: It is home to some of the leading inns of the Caribbean, as well as two stellar Sandals properties. When in the area, we prefer to stay away from the center of Ocho Rios, at a resort in Runaway Bay or something really special like Ian Fleming's Goldeneye.

Essentials

GETTING THERE If you're going to Ocho Rios, you fly into the **Sangster Airport** in Montego Bay. Some hotels, particularly the larger resorts, will arrange for airport transfers from that point. Be sure to ask when you book.

By taxi, a typical one-way fare from Montego Bay to Ocho Rios is around $140. Always negotiate and agree on a fare *before* getting into the cab.

If your hotel does not provide transfers, you can go by bus for a $25 one-way fare. We recommend **Tour Wise** (✆ **876/974-2323** in Ocho Rios). The bus will drop you off at your hotel; the trip takes 1 hour and 45 minutes.

You can rent a car for the 108km (67-mile) drive east along Route A1 (see "Getting Around" under "Essentials," at the beginning of this chapter).

VISITOR INFORMATION The local office of the **Jamaica Tourist Board** is at Office no. 3 in the Ocean Villa Plaza on Main Street (✆ **876/974-2582**). It is open Monday to Friday 8:30am to 5pm.

MEDICAL SERVICES The nearest hospital is **St. Ann's Bay Hospital** (✆ **876/972-0150**), 11km (6¾ miles) west of the city. The most central pharmacy is **Ocho Rios Pharmacy,** Shop 67 in Ocean Village Plaza (✆ **876/974-2398**), open Monday to Saturday 9am to 7:30pm and Sunday 9am to 6pm.

Where to Stay

More and more discerning travelers to Jamaica are renting private villas such as the **Cottage at Te Moana** (✆ **876/974-2870;** www.harmonyhall.com), lying a half-hour drive east of Ocho Rios and inland from the little town of Oracabessa. The seaside bungalow is owned by Peter and Annabella Proudlock, who also run the Harmony Hall Art Gallery. Their rental contains an outdoor shower, a hammock-lined veranda, a loft-style bedroom, and a full kitchen, costing $120 in off season or $150 in winter. There is a 3-night minimum stay required.

VERY EXPENSIVE

Couples Sans Souci Resort & Spa ★★★ If a cookie-cutter Sandals is the last thing you want, head for this classier beachfront joint. Winner of four diamonds from AAA, this pink, cliff-side luxurious resort is 5km (3 miles) east of town on a forested plot of land abutting a good white-sand beach. There's a separate clothing-optional beach, a mineral bath big enough for an elephant, and a labyrinth of catwalks and bridges stretching over rocky chasms filled with surging water.

Each unit has a veranda or patio, copies of Chippendale furniture, plush upholstery, and subdued colonial elegance. Some contain Jacuzzis. Accommodations range from standard bedrooms to vast suites with large living and dining areas, plus kitchens. Deluxe touches include glazed-tile floors, luxurious beds, and marble bathrooms with whirlpool tubs. You'll enjoy the food at the elegant Casanova restaurant.

Rte. A3 (P.O. Box 103), St. Mary, Jamaica, W.I. www.couples.com. ✆ **800/268-7537** in the U.S., or 876/994-1206. Fax 876/994-1544. 150 units. Winter $735–$1,560 double; off season $645–$1,000 double. Rates are all-inclusive. AE, DISC, MC, V. Children 15 and under not allowed. **Amenities:** 4 restaurants; 6 bars; golf; health club; 2 Jacuzzis; 4 outdoor pools; room service; sauna; spa; 2 tennis courts (lit); watersports equipment/rentals. *In room:* A/C, TV, hair dryer, minibar, MP3 docking station, Wi-Fi (free).

Goldeneye ★★ Few hotels in the world manage to be so luxurious and yet so appealingly informal as this intimate retreat. It surrounds the villa where the most famous secret agent in the world, James Bond (007), was created in 1952 by then-owner Ian Fleming. Fleming built the imposing but simple main house in 1946 and wrote each of the 13 original James Bond books there. In the early 1990s, music-publisher-turned-hotelier Chris Blackwell bought and restored the by-then dilapidated property to its original modernist dignity. Fleming's original desk remains. The oversize Indonesian furniture is placed among memorabilia from the most famous spy movies in the world. The main house is usually rented only as a three-bedroom whole for extended house parties, often to rock stars and other celebs.

You're more likely to rent one of the four additional villas that were built on the surrounding property. Each evokes a tropical version of a billionaire's summer camp in Maine, thanks to a juxtaposition of indoor and outdoor spaces, sofas, and well-chosen decorative pieces. Each unit has a fully equipped kitchen. All drinks, food, and most activities are included in the price. Masonry paths lead to a nearby beach.

Oracabessa, St. Mary, Jamaica, W.I. www.goldeneye.com. ✆ **800/688-7678** in the U.S. and Canada, or 876/975-3354. Fax 876/975-3620. 5 villas. Winter $960 1-bedroom villa, $1,200 2-bedroom villa, $6,000 Ian Fleming main house; off season $640 1-bedroom villa, $780 2-bedroom villa, $4,400 Ian Fleming main house. Rates are all-inclusive. AE, MC, V. **Amenities:** Babysitting; outdoor pool (for Ian Fleming house guests); room service; tennis court (lit); watersports equipment/rentals; Wi-Fi (free). *In room:* A/C, TV, kitchenette, minibar.

Jamaica Inn ★★★ Built in 1950, the gracious beachfront Jamaica Inn is a series of long, low buildings set in a U shape near the sea, 2km (1¼ miles) east of town. Sir Noël Coward, arriving with Katharine Hepburn or Claudette Colbert, was a regular, and Errol Flynn and Ian Fleming used to drop in. It's an elegant anachronism, a true retro hotel, and has remained little changed in 4 decades, avoiding the glitter of all-inclusive resorts like Sandals. Lovely patios open onto the lawns, and the bedrooms are reached along garden paths. Guest rooms are spacious, with colonial two-poster beds, quality carved-wood period pieces, and balconies with balustrades that offer nice views. The beach is a wide, champagne-colored strip; close to the shore, the sea is almost too clear to make snorkeling an adventure, but farther out it's rewarding. The European-trained chef prepares both refined international and Jamaican dishes.

Main St. (P.O. Box 1), Ocho Rios, Jamaica, W.I. www.jamaicainn.com. ✆ **800/837-4608** in the U.S., or 876/974-2514. Fax 876/974-2449. 47 units. Winter $480–$780 double, from $1,165 cottage; off season $250–$380 double, from $560 cottage. AE, MC, V. Children 12 and under not allowed. **Amenities:** Restaurant; 2 bars; babysitting; exercise room; outdoor pool; room service; spa; watersports equipment/rentals. *In room:* A/C, ceiling fan, Wi-Fi (free).

Royal Plantation Spa & Golf Resort ★★ This stately inn, a rival of the Jamaica Inn, has fallen under the Sandals umbrella and become the chain's most upmarket property in Jamaica. The hotel entrance evokes the antebellum South. You drive up a sweeping driveway and enter through a colonnaded portico. A complete renovation has brought major improvements to the rooms and public areas, and added a full-service European spa. Accommodations are all suites, each opening onto the ocean views. Bedrooms are handsomely equipped with such extras as plush cotton robes, daily *New York Times,* fax service, Internet connections, CD players, and the like. Guests have full exchange privileges with the two other Sandals resorts in the area. The cuisine is far superior to that at the other Sandals properties, and the atmosphere less rowdy.

Main St. (P.O. Box 2), Ocho Rios, Jamaica, W.I. www.sandals.com. ✆ **888/SANDALS** (726-3257) in the U.S., or 876/974-5601. Fax 876/974-5912. 74 units. Year-round $480–$1,500 double, from $950 suite. Rates include meals, complimentary greens fees, airport transfers, and unlimited access to scuba diving and other watersports. AE, DISC, MC, V. Children 17 and under not allowed. **Amenities:** 3 restaurants; bar; exercise room; golf at nearby Upton Golf & Country Club; room service; spa; 2 tennis courts (lit); watersports equipment/rentals. *In room:* A/C, TV, CD player, hair dryer, Internet ($15 per day), minibar, MP3 docking station.

EXPENSIVE

Couples Tower Isle ★★ In 1949 Tower Isle hotel opened as Jamaica's first year-round resort and first beach resort. Throughout the 1950s and 1960s, it was a haven for movie stars and various celebrities. In 2008, after a $25-million renovation, it has made a comeback as a couples-only resort. It is set on 7.6 hectares (19 acres) of beautiful beachfront property, with five gourmet restaurants as well as spacious and romantically decorated bedrooms and suites. Accommodations come in a wide range of choices, with the oceanfront accommodations at the higher price level. In general, this is a classier operation than the more mass-market Sandals (at least, the Dunn's River and Ocho Rios versions). Some guests slip away from the resort, which lies an 18-minute drive (8km/5 miles) east of Ocho Rios, to Couples' private island to bask in the buff. A shuttle boat transports visitors to this beautiful little island with a fine sandy beach, a bar, and a pool. Security guards keep the gawkers from bothering guests.

Tower Isle, Rte. A3 (P.O. Box 330), St. Mary, Jamaica, W.I. www.couples.com. ✆ **800/268-7537** in the U.S., or 876/975-4271. Fax 876/975-4439. 226 units. Winter $680–$760 double, $775–$950 suite; off season $600–$685 double, $695–$855 suite. Rates are per couple, per night, and include all meals, drinks, and activities. 3-night minimum (though most guests book by the week). AE, DISC, MC, V. Children 17 and under not allowed. **Amenities:** 5 restaurants; 4 bars; bikes; golf; health club; 4 Jacuzzis; outdoor pool; room service; sauna; spa; 4 lit tennis courts; watersports equipment/rentals. *In room:* A/C, TV, hair dryer, MP3 docking station, Wi-Fi (free).

Jewel Dunn's River ★★ Located on a wide, sugary beach, this newly opened Jamaican beach resort lies between the center of Ocho Rios and St. Ann's Bay. The property sprawls across 10 well-landscaped hectares (25 acres), offering an array of facilities and restaurants. A couples-only resort, it has become a magnet for honeymooners. The elegant and well-furnished guest rooms are scattered among the six-story main buildings, two lanai buildings, and a five-story west wing. Extras include spacious balconies, walk-in closets, and king-size beds. Dining options range from the formal Platinum Setting to the casual Aquamarina Beach Bar & Grill. At night the attraction is the magical Emerald Tree Lounge, which lights up each night.

Route A3 (P.O. Box 858), Ocho Rios, Jamaica, W.I. www.jeweldunnsriverresort.com. ✆ **800/587-1854** or 876/972-7400. Fax 876/972-7402. 250 units. Winter $515–$615 double, $965–$1,165 suite; off season $370–$550 double, $900–$1,100 suite. Rates are all-inclusive. AE, DISC, MC, V. **Amenities:** 6 restaurants; 5 bars; concierge; exercise room; 3 Jacuzzis; 2 outdoor pools; spa; 4 tennis courts (lit); watersports equipment/rentals. *In room:* A/C, TV, CD player, hair dryer, Internet ($11 per day).

Sandals Grande Ocho Rios Beach & Villa Resort ★ This all-inclusive resort is located 2km (1¼ miles) southeast of town, set on 18 hectares (44 acres) of tropical gardens on a private estate dotted with red-tile villas. A great house in the hills overlooks the Caribbean. Across from the imposing gate near the resort's entrance are the white sands of a private beach. All but a handful of the accommodations are in one-, two-, or three-bedroom villas, each with a small pool, a fully equipped kitchen, and a shaded terrace. Honeymoon villas have their own whirlpools. Thirty-six units are traditional single or double rooms on the third floor of the great house. Accommodations are roomy, decorated in Caribbean colors, and have high ceilings. They're well furnished, with particularly fine beds.

Main St. (P.O. Box 728), Ocho Rios, St. Ann, Jamaica, W.I. www.sandals.com. © **888/SANDALS** (726-3257) in the U.S. and Canada, or 876/974-5691. Fax 876/974-5700. 530 units. Year-round $320–$455 double; $455–$2,755 suite. Rates are per couple and all-inclusive. AE, MC, V. Children 15 and under not allowed. **Amenities:** 11 restaurants; 12 bars; 5 Jacuzzis; 7 outdoor pools; 2 saunas; scuba diving, 6 tennis courts (lit). *In room:* A/C, TV, hair dryer, kitchenette, minibar, Wi-Fi ($16 per day).

MODERATE

Hibiscus Lodge Hotel This intimate little inn offers more value for your money than any other resort at Ocho Rios. Perched precariously on a cliff along the shore 3 blocks from the Ocho Rios Mall, the inn has character and charm. Mallards Bay Beach, shared by residents of some of the biggest hotels in Ocho Rios, lies within a 3- to 4-minute walk. All medium-size bedrooms, either doubles or triples, have small, shower-only bathrooms; ceiling fans; and verandas opening to the sea. After a day spent in a pool suspended over the cliffs or lounging on the large sun deck, guests can enjoy a drink in the unique bar with swinging chairs. The owners provide dining at the Almond Tree Restaurant (see below).

83 Main St. (P.O. Box 52), Ocho Rios, St. Ann, Jamaica, W.I. www.hibiscusjamaica.com. © **876/974-2676.** Fax 876/974-1874. 26 units. Winter $150–$160 double, $190 triple; off season $140–$150 double, $170 triple. Rates include breakfast. AE, MC, V. **Amenities:** Restaurant; bar; Jacuzzi; outdoor pool; room service; tennis court (lit). *In room:* A/C, ceiling fan, TV, hair dryer, no phone, Wi-Fi (in some; $10 per day).

High Hope Estate ★ Because this hotel is so intimate, whether you like it will depend on whether you click with the owner and the other guests. Basically, it's an upscale private home in the style of the British colonial world at its most rarefied that accepts paying guests. The estate's 15 hectares (37 acres), set 165m (541 ft.) above the coast and 11km (6¾ miles) west of Ocho Rios, thrive with flowering plants, as well as memories of such luminaries as Sir Noël Coward, who used to play the grand piano that graces one of the public areas. There are absolutely no planned activities. Bedrooms are a delight—spacious, well thought out, and exceedingly comfortable. The staff is on hand to help supervise children, maintain the property, and prepare meals for anyone who gives advance notice. The nearest beach is a 10-minute ride away.

16 Top Rd. (P.O. Box 11), St. Ann's Bay, Jamaica, W.I. www.highhopeestate.com. © **876/972-2277.** Fax 876/972-1607. 5 units. Year-round $125–$185 double. Rates include breakfast. MC, V. **Amenities:** Restaurant; babysitting; outdoor pool; room service. *In room:* Ceiling fan, TV, CD player, hair dryer, minibar, Wi-Fi (free).

Where to Dine

Walkerswood Caribbean Foods (© **876/917-2318;** www.walkerswood.com), tucked away in the hills of St. Ann, gives a 45-minute tour that includes a meal at its on-site cafe. Part of the tour involves a stop at a wattle-and-daub hut where "Mother Thyme" shares herbal secrets of healing. Another part lets you look in on some of the company's nearly two dozen sauces being made. Call the number above to make arrangements for this unique tour.

EXPENSIVE

The Dinner Terrace at The Jamaica Inn ★★ CONTINENTAL/CARIBBEAN The timeless and discreetly upscale dining presentations at the Jamaica Inn seem to have endured better than many of this hotel's counterparts. There is, quite simply, nothing more upscale and dignified in town. A dinner here may recall aspects of earlier, more graceful eras: It can start in the elegant, wood-paneled bar area, or on the moonlit terrace, for predinner drinks. Then migrate into the open-sided (or, weather permitting, open-air) dining room that's steeped in formal and undeniably upscale service rituals—the kind of venue where Sir Winston Churchill could (and frequently did) get in touch with colonial Jamaican posh. The menu changes nightly, and nonresidents who opt to dine here are expected to reserve a table in advance. In 2004 age-old rules were modernized, allowing men to abandon their jackets and neckties in favor of well-groomed shirts with collars and long pants during the dinner hour.

Main St. ✆ **876/974-2514.** Reservations required. Set-price 5-course menu $75 without drinks. AE, MC, V. Daily 7:30–9pm.

Le Papillon Restaurant and the Caviar Bar at the Royal Plantation ★★★ CONTINENTAL This is the most aggressively upscale restaurant, with the most "fussed-over" cuisine, in Ocho Rios. It's marketed as the most prestigious dining option within any Sandals resort in Jamaica, and unlike most other members of the Sandals chain, this one is open to visitors who make a reservation. The venue works hard to impress, and in most cases succeeds, albeit with an occasionally somewhat heavy-handed emphasis on its own glamour. It's located on the upper floor of what looks like a great house on steroids, whose neoclassical symmetry opens into a breathtaking decor that rivals some of the museums of Europe. At the top, past a bevy of formally dressed guardians, you'll find the only caviar-and-champagne bar in the Caribbean. (That's right: Don't ask for a Red Stripe, not here.) Small jars of caviar are opened like holy relics—dispensed with pomp, fanfare, and ceremony. In the artfully decorated Le Papillon, amid cut-velvet wallpaper imported from France, within a room that evokes oceans of good taste, you'll enjoy formal meals with superb cuisine. Begin, perhaps, with roasted quail with an apple compote and black-pepper glaze, or tiger shrimp prepared three different ways (tempura, Cajun sauté, and jerk style); move on to Caribbean-style lobster soup with black-pepper rum and crème fraîche. Main courses include a rock lobster spring roll; sea scallops on a skewer served with angel-hair pasta; a confit of duck with tamarind glaze and apple chutney; and one of the most upscale versions of surf and turf anywhere.

In the Royal Plantation, Main St. ✆ **876/974-5601.** Reservations required. Main courses $42–$62; in Caviar Bar, caviar costs depend on market conditions; champagne $150–$300 per bottle, $180 for a half bottle. AE, DC, MC, V. Tues–Sun 7–10pm.

MODERATE

Almond Tree Restaurant JAMAICAN/CONTINENTAL The Almond Tree is a two-tiered patio restaurant with a tree growing through the roof. Lobster thermidor is the tastiest item on the menu, but we also like the bouillabaisse (made with conch and lobster). Other excellent choices are the roast suckling pig, medallions of beef, and a fondue bourguignon. Jamaican plantation rice is a local specialty. The wine list offers a variety of vintages, including Spanish and Jamaican. Have a cocktail in the unique "swinging bar"—with swinging chairs, that is.

In the Hibiscus Lodge Hotel, 83 Main St., St. Ann's Bay. ✆ **876/974-2813.** Reservations recommended. Main courses $12–$30. AE, MC, V. Daily 7–11pm.

Evita's Italian Restaurant ★ ITALIAN A 5-minute drive south of the commercial heart of Ocho Rios, in a hillside residential neighborhood that enjoys a panoramic view over the harbor and beachfronts, this is one of the most fun restaurants along the north coast of Jamaica. Its soul and artistic flair come from Eva Myers, the convivial former owner of some of the most legendary bars of Montego Bay, who established her culinary headquarters in this green-and-white gingerbread Jamaican house in 1990. An outdoor terrace adds additional seating and enhanced views. More than half the menu is devoted to pastas, including almost every variety known to northern and southern Italy. The fish dishes are excellent—especially the snapper stuffed with crabmeat and the lobster and scampi in a buttery white-cream sauce. Italian (or other) wines by the bottle might accompany your main course.

Eden Bower Rd. ✆ **876/974-2333.** www.evitasjamaica.com. Reservations recommended. Main courses $12–$35. AE, MC, V. Daily 11am–11pm.

Toscanini's ITALIAN Coming from a long line of restaurateurs, co-owners chef P.G. Ricci and headwaiter (his sister) Lella Ricci bring style and a Continental sophistication to their food service and preparation. The restaurant occupies the airy and gracious street level of a 19th-century stone pavilion, whose upper floors function as an upscale art gallery. The menu offers many classic Italian dishes, supplemented by ever-changing specials, depending on what's fresh at the market. The best of the many specialties include spaghetti with lobster *penne all' ortolana* (vegetarian pasta with goat cheese and herbs); crespelle (oven-baked crepes with chopped callaloo and cheese); and local catch of the day with Acqua Pazza sauce (roasted tomatoes, fish reduction, white wine, and herbs). There's an ongoing emphasis on fresh fish and shellfish, especially lobster. The chef also caters to vegetarians. All this good food is backed up by a fine wine list.

Harmony Hall, Tower Isles on the North Coast Hwy. (Rte. A3), 6km (3¼ miles) east of Ocho Rios. ✆ **876/975-4785.** Reservations recommended. Main courses $15–$28; pasta dishes $13–$32. AE, MC, V. Tues–Sun noon–2pm and 7–10:30pm. Closed 1 week in June and 1 week in Sept.

INEXPENSIVE

Margaritaville Ocho Rios ☺ JAMAICAN Lying in the Island Village, a shopping and entertainment complex, this is one of the largest restaurants ever constructed on the north coast, seating 450 diners and drinkers. A high-energy bar and grill, Margaritaville provides all-day family fun with the entertainment continuing late at night. Attractions include a rooftop whirlpool tub, a 30m-long (98-ft.) water slide, and a freshwater pool, along with three bars and a trading post. The decor is rustic West Indian, with an Afro-Cuban aura. Of course, being a Jimmy Buffett dive, expect the world-famous tropical margaritas and those delectable Cheeseburgers in Paradise. There's dancing here—reggae-disco style—at night.

Turtle Beach Rd. (at the cruise-ship docks). ✆ **876/675-8800.** www.margaritavillecaribbean.com. Main courses $14–$19; burgers and salads $11–$16. AE, MC, V. Restaurant daily 9am–9pm. Bar daily 8am–4:30am.

Miss T's Kitchen ★ 🎁 JAMAICAN For real down-home Jamaican cooking, no one in Ocho Rios does it quite as authentic as this little dive right off Main Street, attracting both culinary-curious locals and visitors. The chef gives a special name to each dish. The best appetizer is called "Stamina," made of fish simmered with spicy roasted pumpkin and herbs, enriched with coconut milk. "Swaggerific" is ackee and lobster simmered in a blend of herbs and Jamaican curry. "Mema Mi Tell Yu" is actually braised oxtail seasoned with island spices and herbs in a creamy coconut sorrel sauce with vegetables. Fresh seafood temptations include curried shrimp or grilled lobster. Instead of Miss T, you get the cooking of Staford Anderson, veteran chef here for 25 years.

65 Main St. ✆ **876/795-0099.** Main courses $7-$30. No credit cards. Mon–Sat 9am–9pm.

Ocho Rios Village Jerk Centre ★ JAMAICAN At this open-air restaurant, you can get the best jerk dishes along this part of the coast. When only a frosty Red Stripe beer can quench your thirst and your stomach is growling for the fiery taste of Jamaican jerk seasonings, head here—and don't dress up. The place isn't fancy; it's the food that counts. Fresh daily specials are posted on a chalkboard menu on the wall. The dishes are hot and spicy, but not *too* hot; hot spices are presented on the side for those who want to go truly Jamaican. The barbecue ribs are especially good, and fresh fish is a delight, perfectly grilled—try the red snapper. Vegetarian dishes are also available on request, and if you don't drink beer, you can wash it all down with natural fruit juices.

Da Costa Dr. ✆ **876/974-2549.** Jerk pork $4 ¼ lb., $16 1 lb.; whole jerk chicken $16. MC, V. Daily 10am–11pm.

Hitting the Beach

The most idyllic sands are at the often-overcrowded **Mallards Beach,** in the center of Ocho Rios and shared by hotel guests and cruise-ship passengers. Locals may steer you to the white sands of **Turtle Beach,** which is smaller, more desirable, and not as overcrowded as Mallards.

The most popular spot (stay away when cruise ships are in port!) is **Dunn's River Beach,** located below the famous falls. Another great spot is **Jamaica Grande's Beach,** which is open to the public. Parasailing is a favorite sport here.

Our favorite beach is at Goldeneye, writer Ian Fleming's former home, now a hotel. Follow the trail of 007 and head for **James Bond Beach** (✆ **876/975-0119**), east of Ocho Rios at Oracabessa Beach. For $5 adults, $3 children, nonguests can enjoy its sand strip any day except Monday. There's a watersports rental center here as well.

You might also escape the crowds at Ocho Rios and head to the lovely beach at nearby Runaway Bay. (See, "Runaway Bay," p. 374.)

Exploring the Area

A scenic drive south of Ocho Rios along Route A3 takes you inland through **Fern Gully** ★, a lush gorge. Originally a riverbed, the main road now winds up some 210m (689 ft.) among a profusion of wild ferns, a tall rainforest, hardwood trees, and lianas. There are hundreds of varieties of ferns, and roadside stands offer fruits and vegetables, carved-wood souvenirs, and basketwork. The road runs for about 6km (3¾ miles). At Moneague, a small town, the A1 continues south into the interior of Jamaica, but it also heads back north along a route to the west of the southbound A3. If you take the A1 north, you'll come to the coast on the north shore at St. Ann's Bay.

Heading up A1 north, you'll pass the ruins of **Edinburgh Castle,** lying 13km (8 miles) southwest of Claremont, the major town on the route back. These ruins—not worth a detour, but of passing interest if you're driving by—are a local curiosity.

This 1763 lair was the former abode of one of Jamaica's most famous murderers, a Scot named Lewis Hutchinson, who used to shoot passersby and toss their bodies into a deep pit. At his so-called "castle," really a two-story house, Hutchinson invited his victims inside. There he would wine and dine them before murdering and then robbing them. The authorities got wind of his activities. Although he tried to escape by canoe, Hutchinson was captured and hanged at Spanish Town on March 16, 1773. Evidently proud of his achievements (evidence of at least 43 bodies was found), he left 100 British pounds and instructions for a memorial to be built in his honor. It never was.

These castle ruins can be viewed on the northern outskirts of the village of Bensonton, near the Bensonton Health Club.

In **St. Ann's Bay,** the site of the first Spanish settlement on the island, you can see the **statue of Christopher Columbus,** cast in his hometown of Genoa and erected near St. Ann's Hospital on the west side of town, close to the coast road. There are a number of Georgian buildings in the town. We think that the **Courthouse** near the parish church, built in 1866, is the most interesting.

Brimmer Hall Estate Some 34km (21 miles) east of Ocho Rios, in the hills 3km (2 miles) from Port Maria, this 1817 estate is an ideal place to spend a day. You can swim in the pool and sample a wide variety of brews and concoctions. The Plantation Tour Eating House offers typical Jamaican dishes for lunch, and there's a souvenir shop with a good selection of ceramics, art, straw goods, woodcarvings, rums, liqueurs, and cigars. You can also take a tour around the working plantation in a tractor-drawn jitney to see the tropical fruit trees and coffee plants; the knowledgeable guides will explain the various processes necessary to produce the fine fruits of the island. This is far more interesting than the trip to Croydon Plantation in Montego Bay, so if you're visiting both places and have time for only one plantation, make it Brimmer Hall.

Port Maria, St. Mary's. ✆ **876/974-2244.** Tours $25. Reservations required 3 days in advance. Tours Mon–Fri 9am–3pm.

Coyaba Gardens & Museum & Mahoe Falls Two kilometers (1¼ miles) south of the center of Ocho Rios, at an elevation of 126m (413 ft.), this park and museum were built on the grounds of the former Shaw Park plantation. The word *coyaba* comes from the Arawak name for paradise. Coyaba is a Spanish-style museum with a river and gardens filled with native flora, a cut-stone courtyard, fountains, and a crafts shop and bar. The museum displays a collection of artifacts from the Arawak, Spanish, and English settlements in the area.

Shaw Park Rd. ✆ **876/974-6235.** www.coyabagardens.com. Admission to the garden $10 adults, $5 ages 12 and under. Daily 9am–5pm. Take the Fern Gully–Kingston Rd., turn left at St. John's Anglican Church, and follow the signs to Coyaba, just .4km (¼ mile) farther.

Dunn's River Falls For a fee, you can relax on the beach or climb with a guide to the top of the falls. You can splash in the waters at the bottom of them or drop into the cool pools higher up between the cascades of water. A beach restaurant serves lackluster snacks and drinks, and dressing rooms are available. If you're planning to climb the falls, wear sneakers or sport sandals to protect your feet from the sharp rocks and to prevent slipping. Climbing the falls with the crowds is a chance to experience some 180m (591 ft.) of cold but clear mountain water. In contrast to the heat swirling around you, the splashing water hitting your face and bare legs is cooling on a hot day. The problem here is slipping and falling, especially if you're joined to a chain of hands linking body to body. In spite of the slight danger, there seem to be few accidents. The falls aren't exactly a wilderness experience, with all the tour buses carrying cruise-ship passengers here. The place is always overrun.

Rte. A3. ✆ **876/974-5944.** www.dunnsriverja.com. Admission $15 adults, $12 ages 2–11. Daily 8:30am–4pm. From the center of Ocho Rios, head west along Rte. A3.

Firefly ★ This vacation retreat was the home of Sir Noël Coward and his longtime companion, Graham Payn, who, as executor of Coward's estate, donated it to the Jamaica National Heritage Trust. The recently restored house is more or less as it was on the day Sir Noël died in 1973. His Hawaiian-print shirts still hang in the closet of his austere bedroom, with its mahogany four-poster. The library contains a collection of his books, and the living room is warm and comfortable, with big armchairs and two grand pianos (where he composed several famous tunes). Guests stayed at Blue Harbour, a villa closer to Port Maria; they included Evelyn Waugh, Sir Winston Churchill, Errol Flynn, Sir Laurence Olivier, Vivien Leigh, Claudette Colbert, Katharine Hepburn, Mary Martin, and the Queen Mother. Paintings by the noted playwright/actor/author/composer adorn the walls. An open patio looks out over the pool and the sea. Across the lawn, Sir Noël is buried under a simple marble gravestone.

Grants Town, in St. Mary, 32km (20 miles) east of Ocho Rios above Port Maria. ✆ **876/725-0920.** Admission $10 adults, free for children 11 and under. Daily 9am–5pm.

Harmony Hall This was the centerpiece of a sugar plantation in the late 19th century. Today it has been restored and is the focal point of an art gallery and restaurant that showcases the painting and sculpture of Jamaican artists, as well as a tasteful array of arts and crafts. Among the featured gift items are Sharon McConnell's Starfish Oils, which contain natural additives harvested in Jamaica. The gallery shop also carries the Reggae to Wear line of sportswear, designed and made on Jamaica, and Anabella boxes (for jewelry).

Tower Isles on Rte. A3, 6km (3¾ miles) east of Ocho Rios. ✆ **876/974-2870.** www.harmonyhall.com. Free admission. Gallery Tues–Sun 10am–6pm.

Island Village and Island Village Shopping Center ★ Scattered over 2 hectares (5 acres) on a beachfront within a few steps of the city's cruise-ship terminal is a replica of an idealized Jamaican village, complete with elaborate gingerbread, hundreds of feet of boardwalk, and a medley of psychedelic colors that glow, rainbow style, in the streaming sunlight. It's not without its own Disney-ish theme-park overtones—**sound stages** are strategically scattered within the sightlines of **bars** that serve the kind of high-octane cocktails that could fuel a heavily loaded jetliner from here to Kingston. Music and hotel impresario Christopher Blackwell, who takes credit for the "discovery" and marketing of Bob Marley, is half-owner of this venture—thus, you won't find any shame here about emphasizing reggae as both a lifestyle and an artistic venue.

Within the compound are about 35 **shops** selling clothing, books, souvenirs, "reggae wear," and Bob Marley memorabilia, as well as four or five restaurants and bars. Small-scale reggae presentations occur spontaneously, often when a cruise ship is in port, and large-scale **blockbuster concerts** are scheduled about once a month and are usually attended by hundreds, or even thousands. Except when there's a world-class concert—usually when there's no cruise ship in port—there's no admission charged for entrance to the compound, but an alert security staff ensures that "panhandlers, pickpockets, and lowlifes" (at least, those residing in Jamaica) are kept off the premises. Access to the beachfront—with its own floating trampoline—costs $5 per person.

Island Village, Turtle River Rd. ✆ **876/675-8995.** Free admission. Daily 9am–midnight.

Prospect Plantation This working plantation adjoins the 18-hole Prospect Mini Golf Course. A visit to this property is an educational, relaxing, and enjoyable experience. On a leisurely tour by covered jitney through the scenic beauty of Prospect, you'll readily see why this section of Jamaica is called "the garden parish of the island." You can view the many trees planted by such visitors as Sir Winston Churchill, Henry Kissinger, Charlie Chaplin, Pierre Trudeau, and Sir Noël Coward. You'll learn about and see pimento (allspice), bananas, cassava, sugar cane, coffee, cocoa, coconut, pineapple, and the famous leucaena ("Tree of Life"). You can even sample some of the exotic fruit and drinks.

Horseback riding ($64 per person for 1½ hr.) is available for adults on three scenic trails at Prospect. Dolphin Cove Tours runs a jitney bus tour to the plantation from the center of Ocho Rios Monday to Saturday at 10:30am, 2pm, and 3:30pm.

Rte. A3, 5km (3 miles) east of Ocho Rios, in St. Ann. ✆ **876/994-1058.** www.prospectplantationtours.com. Tours $25 adults, free for children 7 and under. Tours Mon–Sat 10:30am, 2pm, and 3:30pm.

Rainforest Bobsled Jamaica at Mystic Mountain ★★ Jamaica's most scenic attractions lie just a 5-minute drive west of Ocho Rios, including an Olympian joy ride—no snow required. The ride stretches for 100 acres, from the coast road near the entrance to Dunn's River Falls to more than 700 feet above sea level at the peak of Mystic Mountain. You can explore four attractions here: the **Sky Explorer,** the **Bobsled Jamaica,** the **Zipline,** and the **Waterslide.** The Sky Explorer is a chairlift that takes you to the top of Mystic Mountain, at 700 feet. Here you'll find a rural train depot and a swimming pool with a lookout tower. A Caribbean restaurant features plenty of spicy jerk specialties. The summit is also the launch pad for the zipline tree Tranopy tour, featuring rides of almost 400 feet. You soar above dense forest of almond, pimento, and Poinciana trees. Accessible via the Sky Explorer is the Bobsled ride, which will take you on a wild journey as you plummet down the mountainside before coming to a halt in a cool, shaded glade. You're taken on a 1,000m-long (3,280-ft.) gravity drive through the rainforest on custom-designed, high-tech sleds. Jamaicans made this bobsled ride famous at the 1988 Winter Olympics, inspiring the movie *Cool Runnings*.

Mystic Mountain. ✆ **866/759-8726** or 876/974-3990. www.rainforestadventure.com. Bobsled $62 per person; zipline $104 per person; Sky Explorer $42 per person; all-in-one tranopy $125 per person (covers all three main attractions). ***Note:*** The Waterslide is free, but you have to take the Sky Explorer into the park to go down the Waterslide. Daily 9am–5pm.

Shopping

For many, Ocho Rios provides an introduction to Jamaica-style shopping. After surviving the ordeal, some visitors may vow never to go shopping again. Literally hundreds of Jamaicans pour into Ocho Rios to peddle items to cruise-ship passengers and other visitors. Be prepared for aggressive vendors. Pandemonium greets many an unwary shopper, who must also be prepared for some fierce haggling. Every vendor asks too much at first, which gives them the leeway to "negotiate" until the price reaches a more realistic level. Is shopping fun in Ocho Rios? A resounding no. Do cruise-ship passengers and land visitors indulge in it anyway? A decided yes.

In general, the shopping is better in Montego Bay. If you're not going there, wander the Ocho Rios crafts markets, although much of the merchandise is repetitive.

SHOPPING CENTERS & MALLS There are a number of shopping plazas in Ocho Rios. We've listed them because they're here, not because we recommend them. They include the **New Ocho Rios Plaza,** in the center of town, with some 60 shops; opposite is the **Taj Mahal Mall,** with 26 duty-free stores. **Island Plaza** is another major shopping complex, as is the **Mutual Security Plaza,** with some 30 shops.

Ocean Village Shopping Centre (✆ **876/974-2683**) is one of the originals, with numerous boutiques, food stores, a bank, sundries purveyors, travel agencies, and service facilities. The **Ocho Rios Pharmacy** (✆ **876/974-2398**) sells mostly proprietary brands, perfumes, and suntan lotions, among its many wares. Nearby is the major competitor of Ocean Village, the **Coconut Grove Shopping Plaza,** which is linked by walkways and shrubs. The merchandise here consists mainly of local craft items, and this center is often overrun with cruise-ship passengers. Ocean Village is slightly bigger and more upscale—we prefer it.

Just east of Ocho Rios, the **Pineapple Place Shopping Centre** is a collection of shops in cedar-shingle-roofed cottages set amid tropical flowers.

The **Ocho Rios Craft Park** has 135 stalls. A vendor will weave a hat or a basket while you wait, or you can buy a ready-made hat, hamper, handbag, place mats, or lampshade. Other stands stock hand-embroidered goods and will make small items while you wait. Woodcarvers work on bowls, ashtrays, statues, and cups.

Island Plaza, right in the heart of Ocho Rios, has some of the best Jamaican art—all paintings are by local artists. You can also purchase local handmade crafts (be prepared to haggle), carvings, ceramics, kitchenware, and the inevitable souvenir T-shirts.

SPECIALTY SHOPS One of the best bets for shopping is **Soni's Plaza,** 50 Main St., which is the address of all the following recommended shops. **Casa de Oro** (✆ **876/974-5392;** www.casadeoro.com) specializes in duty-free watches, fine jewelry, and classic perfumes. **Gem Palace** (✆ **876/974-2850**) is the place to go for diamond solitaires, tennis bracelets, and 14-karat gold chains. **Mohan's** (✆ **876/974-9270**) offers one of the best selections of 14-karat and 18-karat gold chains, rings, bracelets, and earrings. **Soni's** (✆ **876/974-2303**) focuses strictly on souvenirs, from coffee mugs to T-shirts. **Trinkets and Treasures** (✆ **876/974-9268**) has a little bit of everything: Blue Mountain coffee, film, cigars, and hand-embroidered linen tablecloths. **Jewels and Time Duty Free Fine Jewelry** (✆ **876/675-8762;** www.jewelsandtime.com) beats most competition with its name-brand watches and jewelry.

RUNAWAY BAY

Once a mere satellite of Ocho Rios, Runaway Bay, about 15km (9¼ miles) to the west, has become a destination in its own right, with white-sand beaches that are much less crowded than those in Ocho Rios. Since you're so far removed from the action, such as it is, in Ocho Rios, you stay at Runaway Bay mainly if you're interested in hanging out at a particular resort. It is especially recommended if you want to escape from the hordes descending on Ocho Rios, where cruise-ship crowds and aggressive vendors can intrude on your solitude.

Most people who stay at Runaway Bay stay at one of the all-inclusives, where meals are included. If you're not staying at such a resort, you can dine at **Runaway Heart Country Club,** which is open to nonguests; otherwise, you can dine in Ocho Rios.

This part of Jamaica's north coast has several distinctions: It was the first part of the island seen by Columbus, the site of the first Spanish settlement on the island, and the point of departure of the last Spaniards leaving Jamaica following their defeat by the British.

Where to Stay & Dine

Breezes Resort & Spa—Rio Bueno ★ This is one of the most historically evocative all-inclusive resorts in Jamaica, lying on a prime stretch of sandy, 320m (1,050-ft.) beachfront. Set on 34 hectares (84 acres) of land near Buena Vista, a 15-minute drive west of Runaway Bay, it's a re-creation of a 19th-century Jamaican Victorian village, with gingerbread architecture. A courthouse replica has entertainment, and benches line the town square, where artisans display their handiwork. The old Jamaica that's portrayed is a rather sanitized, Disney version. Yet this is not a place for children; it is a primarily adult retreat. Accommodations are in 12 blocks of three-story buildings, each filled with wicker furniture. All the spacious units have private patios or verandas and face the ocean; blocks one through six are closer to the beachfront, and blocks five and six face a strip of sand designated as a "clothing-optional" area. Beds are very comfortable, with fine linen; all rooms are equipped with CD players and radios.

Rio Bueno, Trelawny, Jamaica, W.I. www.breezes.com. ✆ **877/273-3937** in the U.S., or 876/954-0000. Fax 876/518-6748. 226 units. Winter $305–$635 double; off season $295–$630 double. Rates are all-inclusive. AE, DC, DISC, MC, V. Children 15 and under not allowed. **Amenities:** 5 restaurants; 7 bars; dance club; bikes; 9-hole golf course; health club; squash; 4 Jacuzzis; 2 outdoor pools; room service; sauna; spa; 3 tennis courts; watersports equipment/rentals; Wi-Fi ($20 per day). *In room:* A/C, TV, hair dryer, minibar.

Breezes Runaway Bay Resort & Golf Club ★ This stylish resort is all-inclusive. Passing through a park filled with tropical trees and shrubbery leads to the clubhouse. The lobby is the best re-creation of the South Seas on Jamaica, with hanging wicker chairs and totemic columns. There's a minijungle with hammocks and a nearby nude beach, in addition to the lovely stretch of sandy beach right out front. The resort lies 3km (2 miles) east of Paradise Beach and just next door to the town's second-best beach, Cardiffall. Guest rooms are spacious, with a light, tropical motif. They're fitted with local woods, cool tile floors, and private balconies or patios. The most elegant are the suites, with Jamaican-made four-poster beds. Live music emanates from the stylish Terrace every evening at 7pm, and a nightclub offers live shows 6 nights a week at 10pm. The club offers exchange and day-pass privileges with Hedonism III, immediately next door.

P.O. Box 58 (10km/6¼ miles west of Ocho Rios), Runaway Bay, Jamaica, W.I. www.breezes.com. ✆ **877/273-3937** in the U.S., or 876/973-4825. Fax 876/516-4155. 266 units. Winter $360–$640 double; off season $320–$430 double. Rates include all meals, drinks, and activities. AE, DC, DISC, MC, V. Children 13 and under not allowed. **Amenities:** 5 restaurants; 4 bars; bikes; exercise room; golf; 3 Jacuzzis; outdoor pool; room service; 4 tennis courts; watersports equipment/rentals. *In room:* A/C, TV, hair dryer, minibar (in some), Wi-Fi ($15 per hr.).

FDR (Franklyn D. Resort) ★ ☺ Located on Route A1, 27km (17 miles) west of Ocho Rios, FDR is an all-inclusive that's the number-one choice if you're traveling with children. FDR lies 3km (2 miles) east of Paradise Beach and about .4km (¼ mile) east of Cardiffall. Its own no-name beach stretches for about 180m (591 ft.), a mixture of stone and sand. The resort, named after its Jamaican-born owner and developer, Franklyn David Rance, is on 2 hectares (5 acres) of flat, sandy land dotted with flowering shrubs and trees, on the main seaside highway. Each of the Mediterranean-inspired buildings has a terra-cotta roof, a loggia or an outdoor terrace, Spanish marble in the bathrooms, a kitchenette, and a personal attendant (called a vacation nanny), who cooks, cleans, and cares for children. Although neither the narrow beach nor the modest pools are the most desirable on the island, and most rooms lack a sea view, many visitors appreciate the spacious units and the resort's wholehearted concern for kids.

Main St. (P.O. Box 201), Runaway Bay, St. Ann, Jamaica, W.I. www.fdrholidays.com. ✆ **888/337-5437.** Fax 876/973-6987. 76 units. Winter $300–$490 per person double; off season $280–$350 per person double. Rates are all-inclusive. Children 5 and under stay free in parent's suite; children 6–15 $50 extra each. AE, MC, V. **Amenities:** 4 restaurants; 3 bars; dance club; babysitting; bikes; children's center; health club; Jacuzzi; 2 outdoor pools; tennis court (lit); watersports equipment/rentals. *In room:* A/C, ceiling fan, TV, kitchen, Wi-Fi (free).

Runaway Bay H.E.A.R.T. Hotel ★ This place wins, hands down, as the bargain of the north coast. One of Jamaica's few training and service institutions, the club and its adjacent academy are operated by the government to provide a high level of training for young Jamaicans interested in the hotel trade. The helpful staff of both professionals and trainees offers the finest service of any hotel in the area. Runaway lies a 30-minute drive east of Paradise Beach and a 5-minute drive to Cardiffall. Free shuttles are offered only to Cardiffall. The good-size rooms are bright and airy. The accommodations open onto private balconies with views of well-manicured tropical gardens or vistas of the bay and golf course. Guests enjoy having a drink in the piano bar (ever had a cucumber daiquiri?) before heading for the dining room, the Cardiff Hall Restaurant, which serves superb Jamaican and Continental dishes.

Ricketts Ave. (P.O. Box 98), Runaway Bay, St. Ann, Jamaica, W.I. www.runawayheart.com.jm. ✆ **876/973-6674,** 973-6867, or 973-6868. Fax 876/973-4704. 56 units. Winter $95–$110 double, $100–$110 junior suite, $195–$215 2-bedroom suite; off season $90–$100 double, $93 junior suite, $181 2-bedroom suite. Breakfast and dinner $37 per person. AE, DISC, MC, V. **Amenities:** Restaurant; 3 bars; exercise room; outdoor pool; Wi-Fi (free). *In room:* A/C, TV.

Super Fun Beach Resort & Spa ★ Following a chain format established in Negril, this latest beachfront Hedonism bills itself as a "truly active (and slightly wicked!) vacation." Though this branch of Hedonism isn't as rowdy and raunchy as the Negril branch—it's a little more serene and isolated from the action in town—it's still for the serious party person who likes to drink all night, hang out at the beach all day, and go wild at those toga parties. Set on 6 hectares (15 acres) of landscaped gardens on the eastern end of Runaway Bay, it features ocean views from all rooms and an all-inclusive package deal. The resort has its own private, slightly rocky beach stretching for some 180m (591 ft.); a part of the beach is often nude. It's a 15-minute drive east of Paradise Beach and a 10-minute walk west of Cardiffall. Bedrooms are roomy and freshly decorated, with Jamaica's first-ever block of "swim-up" rooms. Single guests are paired up with a roommate of the same sex or have to pay a single supplement. Unique in Jamaica, the resort offers a circus workshop that features a flying trapeze, juggling, a trampoline "clinic," and various unicycle and bike-balancing acts.

Runaway Bay, Jamaica, W.I. www.superfunresort.com. ✆ **877/467-8737** in the U.S., or 876/973-4100. Fax 876/973-5402. 225 units. Winter $1,630–$2,512 double, $2,775–$3,500 suite; off season $1,554–$2,250 double, $2,575–$2,965 suite. Rates are all-inclusive for 2 guests for 7 nights. AE, DC, DISC, MC, V. Children 17 and under not allowed. **Amenities:** 4 restaurants; 6 bars; exercise room; 3 Jacuzzis; 3 large outdoor pools; room service; sauna; 3 tennis courts (lit); watersports equipment/rentals. *In room:* A/C, TV, CD player, hair dryer.

Beaches & Outdoor Activities

The two best beaches at Runaway Bay are **Paradise Beach** and **Cardiffhall Lot Public Beach.** Both wide, white-sand strips are clean and well maintained—ideal spots for a picnic. If you're staying in Ocho Rios and want to escape the crowds, come here. There is a great natural beauty to this part of Jamaica, and many foreigners, especially Canadians, seek it out. You don't get a lot of facilities, however, so you'd better bring along whatever you need. Since there are no lifeguards, be careful, especially if you're with children.

Runaway Bay offers some of the best **snorkeling** in Jamaica. The reefs are close to shore and swarming with marine life, including enormous schools of tropical fish such as blue chromis, triggerfish, small skate rays, and snapper. All the major resorts offer equipment.

Jamaica's most complete **equestrian center** is the **Chukka Caribbean Adventures,** at Richmond Llandovery, St. Ann (✆ **876/953-6699;** www.chukkacaribbean.com), less than 6km (3¾ miles) east of Runaway Bay. A 1-hour trail ride costs $74. A vast array of other options—the most on the north coast—are also offered, including river kayaking safaris at $65.

Seeing the Sights

Columbus Park Museum, on Queens Highway, Discovery Bay (no phone), is a large, open area between the main coast road and the sea at Discovery Bay. Just pull off the road and walk among the fantastic collection of exhibits; admission is free. There's everything from a canoe made from a solid piece of cottonwood—the way Arawaks did it more than 5 centuries ago—to a stone cross that was originally placed on the Barrett Estate (14km/8¾ miles east of Montego Bay) by Edward Barrett, brother of poet Elizabeth Barrett Browning. You can see a tally, used to count bananas carried on men's heads from plantation to ship, as well as a planter's strongbox with a weighted lead base to prevent its theft. Other items are 18th-century cannons, a Spanish water cooler and calcifier, a fish pot made from bamboo, a corn husker, and a water wheel. Pimento trees, which produce allspice, dominate the park, which is open Monday to Friday 8am to 4pm, Saturday 8am to noon.

You can also visit the **Seville Great House,** Heritage Park (✆ **876/972-2191**). Built in 1745 by the English, it contains a collection of artifacts once used by everybody from the Amerindians to African slaves. In all, you're treated to an exhibit of 5 centuries' worth of Jamaican history. Modest for a great house, it has a wattle-and-daub construction. A small theater presents a 15-minute historical film about the house on request. It's open daily from 9am to 5pm; admission is $5 for adults, $2 for children 12 and under.

PORT ANTONIO ★

Port Antonio, sometimes called the Jamaica of 100 years ago, is a verdant, somewhat bustling seaport on the northeast coast, 101km (63 miles) northeast of Kingston. It's a mecca of the titled and the wealthy, including stars like Kate Moss, Robin Williams, and Glenn Close.

This small town is like many on the island: clean but cluttered, with sidewalks around a market filled with vendors, and tin-roofed shacks competing with old Georgian and modern brick and concrete buildings. At the market, you can browse for local craftwork, spices, and fruits.

Travelers used to arrive by banana boat and stay at the Titchfield Hotel (which burned down). Captain Bligh landed here in 1793 with the first breadfruit plants, and Port Antonio claims that the ones grown in this area are the best on the island. Visitors still arrive by water, but now it's in cruise ships that moor close to Navy Island, and the passengers come ashore just for the day.

Navy Island and the long-gone Titchfield Hotel were owned for a short time by Errol Flynn. The story is that after suffering damage to his yacht, he put into Kingston for repairs, visited Port Antonio by motorbike, fell in love with the area, and in due course acquired Navy Island (some say he won it in a bet). Later he either lost or sold it and bought a nearby plantation, Comfort Castle. He was much loved and admired by the Jamaicans and was totally integrated into the community. They still talk of him in Port Antonio—his reputation for womanizing and drinking lives on.

We find Port Antonio one of the more relaxed retreats in Jamaica, certainly not as undiscovered as it was when William Randolph Hearst or J. P. Morgan visited, but a virtual Shangri-La compared to Ocho Rios or Montego Bay. It also has some of the finest beaches in Jamaica and has long been a center for some of the Caribbean's best deep-sea fishing. It's a good place to go to get away from it all.

Essentials

GETTING THERE If you're going to Port Antonio, you can fly into the **Donald Sangster Airport** in Montego Bay or the **Norman Manley International Airport** in Kingston. Some hotels, particularly the larger resorts, will arrange for airport transfers from that point. Be sure to ask when you book. Port Antonio has its own small airfield. There are no regularly scheduled flights into the resort—only private charters.

You can rent a car for the 214km (133-mile) drive east along Route A1 (see "Getting Around" under "Essentials," at the beginning of this chapter), but we don't advise this 4-hour drive for safety's sake, regardless of which airport you fly into.

If you take a taxi, the typical one-way fare from Montego Bay is $120, but always negotiate and agree upon a fare before you get into the cab.

MEDICAL FACILITIES The **Port Antonio General Hospital** is at Naylor's Hill (✆ **876/993-2646**).

Where to Stay

Despite its charms, Port Antonio is suffering increasingly from a lack of business as travelers are drawn to the more famous Negril, Ocho Rios, and Montego Bay. Many of the hotels are forced to fill up empty rooms with low-cost tour groups hailing from everywhere from Italy to Canada. Because of this, we've found that some of the hotels in the area are showing signs of wear and deterioration.

Goblin Hill Villas at San San ★ This green and sunny hillside—once said to shelter goblins—is now filled with Georgian-style vacation homes on San San Estate. The pool is surrounded by a vine-laced arbor, which lies just a stone's throw from an almost impenetrable forest. A long flight of steps leads down to the crescent-shaped sands of San San beach. This beach is now private, but guests of the hotel receive a pass. Everything has the aura of having last been fixed up in the 1970s, but the resort is still comfortable. The accommodations are town-house style; some have ceiling fans and king-size beds, some have twin beds, and none have phones. The generally roomy units are filled with handmade pine pieces, along with a split-level living and dining area with a fully equipped kitchen. Housekeepers prepare and serve meals and attend to chores in the villas.

San San (P.O. Box 26), Port Antonio, Jamaica, W.I. www.goblinhillvillas.com. ✆ **800/472-1148** in the U.S., or 876/925-8108. Fax 876/925-6248. 28 units. Winter $155–$255 1-bedroom villa, $235–$325 2-bedroom villa; off season $135–$195 1-bedroom villa, $200–$250 2-bedroom villa. AE, MC, V. **Amenities:** Bar; babysitting; outdoor pool; room service; smoke-free rooms; 2 tennis courts (lit). *In room:* A/C, ceiling fan, TV, fridge, kitchen, no phone, Wi-Fi (free).

Hotel Mocking Bird Hill ★ A 10km (6¼-mile) drive east of Port Antonio, this charming, homey, and well-maintained inn competes effectively with hotels and resorts that are larger, grander, and sometimes much more pretentious. The place is an enclave of good taste, reasonable prices, and ecological consciousness. Set about 180m (591 ft.) above the coastline on a hillside laden with tropical plants, within a 5-minute drive from Frenchman's Cove Beach, the hotel attracts a clientele of mostly European visitors who revel in the artsy and ecologically alert setting. The accommodations are tasteful and at their best, understatedly elegant, with neatly kept shower-only bathrooms, balconies or verandas, spinning ceiling fans, mosquito netting, and views that sweep over the rainforest down to the sea. Much of the interior, including its separately recommended restaurant (Mille Fleurs; see below), is decorated with artworks, many executed by Barbara Walker, one of the owners. There are massage options available on-site, as well as day hikes and classes in painting and drawing.

Mocking Bird Hill (P.O. Box 254), North Coast Hwy. (east of Port Antonio), Port Antonio, Jamaica, W.I. www.hotelmockingbirdhill.com. ✆ **876/993-7134.** Fax 876/993-7133. 10 units. Winter $190–$425 double; off season $138–$320 double. AE, MC, V. **Amenities:** Restaurant; bar; outdoor pool; room service. *In room:* Ceiling fan, hair dryer, no phone, Wi-Fi (free).

Jamaica Heights Resort ★ The funkiest, most amusing, and hippest guesthouse in town might be full of rock stars from Düsseldorf or up-and-coming filmmakers cranking out tomorrow's indie fave. The very worldly owner, Helmut Steiner, former professor of literature and philosophy in Berlin, and his wife, Charmaine, maintain this affordable but sophisticated retreat. It's set at the top of a rutted and very steep series of roads. The resort is not on a beach but provides transportation to two of the finest beach strips of sand at Port Antonio, Frenchman's Cove and San San. Scattered amid the wedge-shaped 3-hectare (7½-acre) property are a half-dozen buildings, each white-walled with shutters, gazebos, climbing vines, and a pavilion for meditating over views of the forested terrain that cascades down to Port Antonio's harbor. The garden sports exotic palms, a stream with its own waterfalls, and the most elegant Ping-Pong pavilion in the world. The minimalist accommodations are spotless; each has a four-poster bed and funky lighting fixtures.

Spring Bank Rd., Port Antonio, Jamaica, W.I. www.jahsresort.com. ✆ **876/993-3305.** 8 units. Year-round $75–$175 double. No credit cards. **Amenities:** Restaurant; outdoor pool; watersports equipment/rentals. *In room:* Ceiling fan, no phone, Wi-Fi (free).

Rio Vista Resort Villas ★★ Featured in *Condé Nast Traveler,* this place is ideal for a luxurious vacation, a honeymoon, or even an off-the-record weekend. Six kilometers (3¾ miles) west of Port Antonio (most of the luxe properties lie to the east), Rio Vista is only 3km (2 miles) from the little local airstrip, nestled between the Rio Grande River and the Caribbean Sea. On a 4-hectare (10-acre) estate planted with tropical fruits, it offers handsomely furnished one- and two-bedroom cottages with vaulted ceilings, plus a honeymoon villa with a river view. The setting is a garden of flowers, spices, and sweet-smelling herbs. A housekeeper services each cottage and can assist with meals, and candlelit dinners can be arranged.

St. Margarets Bay (P.O. Box 4), Port Antonio, Jamaica, W.I. www.riovistajamaica.com. ✆ **876/993-5444.** Fax 876/993-5445. 5 villas. Year-round $65–$85 double; $115–$155 suite. Children 12 and under stay free in parent's room. MC, V. **Amenities:** Restaurant; bar; outdoor pool; rafting; room service. *In room:* A/C, TV, kitchen, Wi-Fi (free).

Where to Dine

All hotel restaurants welcome nonguests for dinner, but reservations are required.

Mille Fleurs ★★ CARIBBEAN This restaurant is terraced into a verdant hillside about 180m (591 ft.) above sea level, with sweeping views over the Jamaican coastline and the faraway harbor of Port Antonio. Sheltered from the frequent rains but open on the side for maximum access to cooling breezes, it features candlelit dinners, well-prepared food, and lots of New Age charm. Lunches include sandwiches, salads, grilled fish platters, and soups. At night you might feast on fresh lobster or tender lamb and beef dishes, even savory rabbit or smoked marlin. The restaurant has been praised by *Gourmet* magazine for its dishes. You may want to try the coconut-and-garlic soup, and the fish with spicy mango-shrimp sauce is a specialty. Breads and most jams are made on the premises. Two dishes are vegetarian.

In the Hotel Mocking Bird Hill, North Coast Hwy. ✆ **876/993-7267.** Reservations recommended. Main courses $25–$47; lunch platters $10–$40. AE, MC, V. Daily 8:30–10:30am, noon–2:30pm, and 7–9:30pm.

Norma's at the Marina ★★ JAMAICAN/CONTINENTAL Established in 2005, this is a branch of an upscale, Jamaica-wide restaurant chain made famous by a Jamaica-born, Florida-trained matriarch (Norma Shirley), who has been the subject of more publicity in the culinary press than any equivalent entrepreneur in Jamaica. The restaurant sprawls between two oversized gazebos that mark both ends of a brick-floored beachside terrace inside the fenced-in compound of the Port Antonio marina. Your meal might be served outdoors, on the above-mentioned terrace, or one floor above ground level, within a high-ceilinged, mahogany-trimmed dining room that's open to the breezes on two sides. Menu items are elegant and flavorful, representing the best of modern and creative Jamaican cuisine, and include crab back salad, elegant slices of smoked marlin, a "reggae salad" studded with sautéed shrimp, several different versions of grilled fish, teriyaki-flavored rib-eye steak, wood-smoked pork riblets with a tamarind-flavored honey sauce, pan-seared butterfish filets, and grilled lobster with lime-flavored herb butter.

At the Port Antonio Marina. ✆ **876/993-9510.** www.normasatthemarina.com. Reservations recommended. Main courses $10–$19. MC, V. Tues–Sat 10am–10pm; Sun 11am–8pm.

A Dip in the Blue Lagoon

The young Brooke Shields made the film *The Blue Lagoon* in a calm, protected cove 15km (9¼ miles) east of Port Antonio. The water is so deep, nearly 6m (20 ft.) or so, that it turns a cobalt blue; there's almost no more scenic spot in all of Jamaica. The Blue Lagoon, with its small, intimate beach, is a great place for a picnic. (You can pick up jerk pork at various shacks along the Boston Beach area.)

Hitting the Beach

Port Antonio has several white-sand beaches, including the famous **San San Beach,** which has gone private. Guests of certain hotels are admitted with a pass; otherwise, the fee is $8.

Boston Beach is a free public beach, and it often has light surfing; there are picnic tables, as well as a restaurant and snack bar. On your way here, stop and get the makings for a picnic lunch at the most famous area for peppery jerk pork and chicken on Jamaica. These rustic shacks also sell the much rarer jerk sausage. The beach is 18km (11 miles) east of Port Antonio and just east of the Blue Lagoon.

Also free is **Fairy Hill Beach** (Winnifred), but there are no changing rooms or showers here. **Frenchman's Cove Beach** attracts a chic crowd to its white-sand beach, combined with a freshwater stream. Nonguests are charged $3.

Port Antonio After Dark

The **Tree Bar** draws a fashionable crowd to the grounds of Goblin Hill Villas at San San (✆ **876/925-8108**), high on a hill commanding a panoramic view of 5 hectares (12 acres). The aptly named bar is wrapped around huge ficus trees, whose mammoth aerial roots dangle over the drinking area. Giant-leafed pothos climb down the trunks. It's a sort of "Me Tarzan, you Jane" kind of place.

Go at your own risk to the infamous **Roof Club,** 11 West St. (✆ **876/715-5281**). The most crowded and animated nightclub in Port Antonio, it's one floor above street level in a boxy-looking industrial building in the heart of town. Inside, the venue is earthy, raunchy, crowded, and boozy, with enough secondhand ganja smoke to get virtually anyone high. Recorded (and, more rarely, live) reggae and soca music blares at high volumes. Expect a neopsychedelic decor of mirrors, UV lighting, and free-form Day-Glo artwork. A visit here is not for the squeamish or the faint-hearted, and it's a good idea to come with a friend and/or ally. Try to stay relatively sober, keep your wits about you, and enjoy the slow-moving gyrations of ordinary folks who—sometimes with the help of a spliff or two—get involved in the beat of the music and groove accordingly. Beers cost from $2.50 each. It's open nightly from around 6pm, but most of the genuine hanging out happens after 11pm, especially from Thursday through Sunday.

KINGSTON

Kingston, the largest English-speaking city in the Caribbean, is the capital and cultural, industrial, and financial center of Jamaica. It's home to some 660,000 people, including those living on the plains between Blue Mountain and the sea.

The buildings here are a mixture of the modern, graceful, old, and just plain ramshackle. It's a busy city, as you might expect, with a natural harbor that's the seventh largest in the world. The University of the West Indies has its campus on the edge of the city.

Few other cities in the Caribbean carry as many negative connotations for North American travelers as Kingston, thanks to widely publicized, and sometimes exaggerated, reports of violent crime. Marry that with urban congestion, potholed roads, and difficult-to-decipher road signs that make it hard to navigate, and you've got a bad reputation.

But if you're an urban dweller who copes with everyday life in, say, New York, Atlanta, or Los Angeles, you know how to deal with city life, and Kingston doesn't have to be that scary. It offers resources and charms that can't be found anywhere else. It is here that Jamaica is at its most urban and confident, its most witty, its most exciting, and its most challenging. No other place in Jamaica offers as many singles bars, dance clubs, and cultural outlets—it's the nation's creative cauldron. If you're truly interested in Jamaican culture, Kingston can be very stimulating, as it's very far removed from the tourist-oriented economies of Negril, Ocho Rios, and Montego Bay.

We've carefully screened the recommendations contained within this guidebook, eliminating any that lie within the most dangerous neighborhoods. So keep an open mind about Kingston—it can be a lot of fun and very exciting.

Essentials

GETTING THERE See "Getting There," under "Essentials," at the beginning of this chapter, for details on the airlines that serve Kingston's international airport.

GETTING AROUND Because Kingston is a rather confusing place to negotiate, many visitors rely on taxis.

MEDICAL FACILITIES The **University Hospital** of the West Indies is at Mona (✆ **876/927-1620**). **Moodie's Pharmacy** is in the New Kingston Shopping Centre (✆ **876/926-4174**).

Where to Stay

Jamaica Pegasus ★ A favorite with business travelers, the Jamaica Pegasus is located in the banking area of Kingston, which is also a fine residential area. After a major renovation, the hotel is now better than ever and is the site of many conventions and social events. The hotel combines British style with Jamaican warmth, arranging watersports and sightseeing. Each of the well-furnished bedrooms is of moderate size and decorated in dark tones, often brown, making you yearn for the lighter pastel look of most Caribbean hotel bedrooms. Several floors of luxuriously appointed suites form the Knutsford Club, which offers special executive services. The 4pm tea service is a bit of a social event among some residents. The premier restaurant is the Columbus. The Brasserie is the hotel's informal restaurant that opens onto the swimming pool, where a splashing fountain cools the air. It adjoins a circular bar near the pool, at which occasional barbecues are prepared.

81 Knutsford Blvd., Kingston 5, Jamaica, W.I. www.jamaicapegasus.com. ✆ **876/926-3691.** Fax 876/929-0593. 310 units. Year-round $300–$370 double; $370 junior suite; $400 royal suite. AE, DC, DISC, MC, V. **Amenities:** 3 restaurants; 2 bars; exercise room; Internet (free); outdoor pool; room service; 2 tennis courts (lit). *In room:* A/C, TV, hair dryer, minibar, Wi-Fi (free).

Spanish Court Hotel ★ When this place opened its doors in 2009, it became the first new hotel in Kingston in more than 40 years. The hotel stands on the site of the former Spanish Court Shopping Center and is a completely modern structure, very urban in style. Its accommodations are spacious and accessorized with Jamaican-made fabrics and furnishings. Suites have such extras as safes, coffee machines, blackout blinds, even an oval-shaped tub and shower. On the ground-floor lobby, the Gallery Café serves Continental and Jamaican specialties. The architectural highlight is a Sky Terrace, with an infinity lap pool and a sweeping veranda with chaise longues and shade umbrellas. The terrace opens onto a panoramic view of Kingston.

1 St. Lucia Ave., Kingston 5, Jamaica, W.I. www.spanishcourthotel.com. ✆ **876/926-0000.** Fax 876/926-1613. 107 units. Year-round $170 double; $219 junior suite; $319 suite. Rates include continental breakfast. AE, MC, V. **Amenities:** Cafe; bar. *In room:* A/C, TV, hair dryer, minibar (in some), MP3 docking station (in some), Wi-Fi (free).

Terra Nova All Suite Hotel ★ This house is on the western edge of New Kingston, near West Kings House Road. Built in 1924 for a young bride, it was converted into a hotel in 1959. It was the birthplace of well-known hotelier and Island Records mogul Chris Blackwell. Set in 1 hectare (2½ acres) of gardens with a backdrop of greenery and mountains, it's now one of the best small Jamaican hotels, although the rooms are rather basic and not at all suited for those who want a resort ambience. Most of the bedrooms are in a newer wing. The Regency, with a marble floor and wide windows, serves local and international food.

17 Waterloo Rd., Kingston 10, Jamaica, W.I. www.terranovajamaica.com. ✆ **876/926-2211.** Fax 876/929-4933. 35 units. Year-round $145–$580 suite. AE, MC, V. **Amenities:** 2 restaurants; coffee shop; 2 bars; exercise room; outdoor pool; room service. *In room:* A/C, TV, hair dryer, minibar (in some), Wi-Fi (free).

IN NEARBY PORT ROYAL

Morgans Harbour Hotel On the premises of this yachtie favorite is a 200-year-old redbrick building once used to melt pitch for His Majesty's navy, a swimming area defined by docks and buoys, and a series of wings whose eaves are accented with hints of gingerbread. Set on 9 hectares (22 acres) of flat and rocky seashore, the resort contains the largest marina in Kingston, plus a breezy waterfront restaurant and a popular bar (where ghost stories about the old Port Royal seem especially lurid as the liquor flows on Friday night). Longtime residents claim that the ghosts of soldiers killed by a long-ago earthquake are especially visible on hot and very calm days, when British formations seem to march out of the sea. The simple bedrooms are suitable for an overnight stay.

Port Royal, Kingston 1, Jamaica, W.I. ✆ **800/448-8355** in the U.S., or 876/967-8040. Fax 876/967-8061. 61 units. Year-round $140 double; $425 suite. AE, MC, V. Take the public ferryboat that departs every 2 hr. from near Victoria Pier on Ocean Blvd.; many visitors arrive by car or taxi. **Amenities:** Restaurant; bar; 2 outdoor pools; room service. *In room:* A/C, TV, hair dryer, Internet (free), minibar.

Where to Dine

Norma's on the Terrace ★★ JAMAICAN This is the creation of Jamaica's most famous businesswoman, Norma Shirley, purveyor of food to stylish audiences as far away as Miami. It's housed beneath the wide porticos of the gallery surrounding Kingston's most famous monument, Devon House. Ms. Shirley has taken the old, woefully dusty gardens and transformed them into something you'd find on a manicured English estate. Menus change with the season but usually reflect Ms. Shirley's penchant for creative adaptations of her native Jamaican cuisine. Stellar examples include Jamaican chowder with crabmeat, shrimp, conch, and lobster; grilled whole red snapper encrusted with herbs and served with a thyme-and-caper sauce; and grilled smoked pork loin in a teriyaki/ginger sauce, served with caramelized apples. The hearty breakfast here—of American and international dishes—is the best in town.

In Devon House, 26 Hope Rd. ✆ **876/968-5488.** Reservations recommended. Main courses $9–$42. AE, DISC, MC, V. Mon–Sat 10am–10pm.

Redbones the Blues Café ★★ 🎁 JAMAICAN The name alone lured us to this elegant place, which is the only restaurant in Kingston with cuisine as good as Norma's on the Terrace. All aglow in yellow and peach hues, Redbones is in a former Spanish colonial house. You're greeted with pictures of jazz greats on the wall, everybody from Billie Holiday to Louis Armstrong. A cozy bar, its ceiling studded with records, is installed in someone's former bedroom. Owners Evan and Betsy Williams give standard Jamaican dishes a new twist. Ask for *bammy,* a cassava dish crowned with sautéed shrimp, or a platter of stuffed crab backs, a delectable selection on a tri-color salad. A spinach callaloo with cream cheese is encased in a divine strudel. Seafood pasta is laden with shrimp, lobster, and salmon in a creamy coconut sauce. The best item on the menu is spicy lamb chops in a guava glaze. Live jazz—or something—is always going on.

21 Braemar Ave. ✆ **876/978-8262.** www.redbonesbluescafe.com. Reservations required. Main courses $19–$38. AE, MC, V. Mon–Fri noon–11pm; Sat 6–11pm.

Hitting the Beach

You don't really come to Kingston for beaches, but there are some here. To the southwest of the sprawling city are black-sandy **Hellshire Beach** and **Fort Clarence.** Both of these beaches are very popular with the locals on weekends. Both have changing rooms, heavy security, and numerous food stands. The reggae concerts at Fort Clarence are legendary on the island.

Just past Fort Clarence, the fisherman's beach at **Naggo Head** is an even hipper destination, or so Kingston beach buffs claim. After a swim in the refreshing waters, try out one of the food stands selling "fry fish" and *bammy* (cassava bread). The closest beach to the city (although it's not very good) is **Lime Cay,** a little island on the outskirts of Kingston Harbour, reached after a short boat ride from Morgan's Harbour at Port Royal.

Exploring the Town

Even if you're staying at Ocho Rios or Port Antonio, you may want to visit Kingston for the sights or to make a trip to nearby Port Royal and Spanish Town.

From Kingston, you can make excursions into the Blue Mountains (see below).

IN TOWN

One of the major attractions, **Devon House,** 26 Hope Rd. (✆ **876/929-6602**), was built in 1881 by George Stiebel, a Jamaican who made his fortune mining in Latin America, becoming one of the first black millionaires in the Caribbean. A striking classical building, the house has been restored to its original beauty by the Jamaican National Trust. The grounds contain crafts shops, boutiques, two restaurants, shops that sell the best ice cream in Jamaica (in exotic fruit flavors), and a bakery-and-pastry shop with Jamaican puddings and desserts. The main house also displays furniture of various periods and styles. Admission to the main house is $8; hours are Monday to Saturday 9am to5pm. Admission to the grounds (the shops and restaurants) is free.

Almost next door to Devon House are the sentried gates of **Jamaica House,** residence of the prime minister, a fine, white-columned building set well back from the road.

Continuing along Hope Road, at the crossroads of Lady Musgrave and King's House roads, turn left and you'll see a gate on the left with its own personal traffic light. This leads to **King's House,** the official residence of the governor-general of

Jamaica, the queen's representative on the island. The outside and front lawn of the gracious residence, set in 80 hectares (198 acres) of well-tended parkland, is sometimes open for viewing Monday to Friday from 10am to 5pm. The secretarial offices are housed next door in an old wooden building set on brick arches. In front of the house is a gigantic banyan tree in whose roots, legend says, *duppies* (ghosts) take refuge when they're not living in the cotton trees.

National Library of Jamaica (formerly the West India Reference Library), Institute of Jamaica, 12 East St. (✆ **876/967-1526**), a storehouse of the history, culture, and traditions of Jamaica and the Caribbean, is the finest working library devoted to West Indian studies in the world. It has the most comprehensive, up-to-date, and balanced collection of materials on the region, including books, newspapers, photographs, maps, and prints. It's open Monday to Thursday from 9am to 5pm, Friday from 9am to 4pm.

Bob Marley Museum, 56 Hope Rd. (✆ **876/927-9152;** www.bobmarley-foundation.com), is the most-visited sight in Kingston, but if you're not a Marley fan, it may not mean much to you. The clapboard house with its garden and high surrounding wall was the famous reggae singer's home and recording studio until his death on May 11, 1981. You can tour the house and view assorted Marley memorabilia, and you may even catch a glimpse of his children, who often frequent the grounds. Hours are Monday to Saturday from 9:30am to 4pm. Admission is $20, and $10 ages 4 to 12. It's reached by bus no. 70 or 75 from Halfway Tree, but take a cab to save yourself the hassle of dealing with Kingston public transport.

IN PORT ROYAL

From West Beach Dock in Kingston, a ferry ride of 20 to 30 minutes will take you to Port Royal, whose name in pirate lore conjures up visions of swashbuckling pirates led by Henry Morgan, swilling grog in harbor taverns. This was once one of the largest trading centers of the New World, with a reputation for being the wickedest city on earth. Blackbeard stopped here regularly on his Caribbean trips. But it all came to an end on June 7, 1692, when a third of the town disappeared underwater after a devastating earthquake. Nowadays, Port Royal, with its memories of the past, has been designated by the government for redevelopment as a tourist destination.

Today Port Royal is a small fishing village at the end of the Palisades strip. Some 2,000 residents live here with what many locals claim are a "lot of ghosts." Port Royal's seafaring traditions continue, and it's known for its seafood and ramshackle and much-battered architecture of yesterday. Once there were six forts here with a total of 145 guns, some of which can be seen today. Only Fort Charles still stands, however.

Fort Charles (✆ **876/967-8438**) has withstood attack, earthquake, fire, and hurricane. Built in 1656 and later strengthened by Morgan for his own purposes, the fort was expanded and further armed in the 1700s, until its firepower had more than 100 cannons, covering both the land and the sea approaches. In 1779, Britain's naval hero, Horatio Lord Nelson, was commander of the fort and trod the wooden walkway inside the western parapet as he kept watch for the French invasion fleet. Scale models of the fort and ships of past eras are on display. The fort is open daily from 9am to 5pm; admission is $5.

Part of the complex, **Giddy House,** once the Royal Artillery storehouse, is another example of what the earth's movements can do. Walking across the tilted floor is an eerie and strangely disorienting experience.

IN SPANISH TOWN

From 1662 to 1872, Spanish Town (19km/12 miles west of Kingston on A1) was the capital of the island. Originally founded by the Spaniards as Villa de la Vega, it was sacked by Cromwell's men in 1655, and all traces of Roman Catholicism were obliterated. The English cathedral, surprisingly retaining a Spanish name, **St. Jago de la Vega** (✆ **876/986-4405**), was built in 1666 and rebuilt after being destroyed by a hurricane in 1712. As you drive into the town from Kingston, the ancient cathedral catches your eye with its brick tower and two-tiered wooden steeple, which was not added until 1831. Since the cathedral was built on the foundation and remains of the old Spanish church, it is half English and half Spanish, and displays two distinct styles: Romanesque and Gothic. Of cruciform design and built mostly of brick, it's one of the most interesting buildings on the island. The black-and-white marble stones of the aisles are interspersed with ancient tombstones, and the walls are heavy with marble memorials that almost chronicle Jamaica's history, dating back as far as 1662.

After visiting the cathedral, walk 3 blocks north along White Church Street to Constitution Street and the **Town Square.** This little square is surrounded by towering royal palms. On the west side is old **King's House,** gutted by fire in 1925, although the facade has been restored. This was the residence of Jamaica's British governors until 1872, when the capital was transferred to Kingston.

Beyond the house is the **Jamaica People's Museum of Craft & Technology,** Old King's House, Constitution Square (✆ **876/907-0322**), open Monday to Thursday from 9:30am to 4:30pm and Friday 8:30am to 3:30pm. Admission is $1.50. The garden contains examples of old farm machinery, an old water-mill wheel, a hand-turned sugar mill, a fire engine, and more. An outbuilding houses a museum of crafts and technology, together with a number of smaller agricultural implements. In the small archaeological museum are old prints, models, and maps of the town's grid layout from the 1700s.

The streets around the old Town Square contain many fine Georgian town houses intermixed with tin-roofed shacks. Nearby is the **market,** so busy in the morning that you may find it difficult, almost dangerous, to pass through. It provides, however, a bustling view of Jamaican life.

Shopping

Downtown Kingston, the old part of the town, is centered around **Sir William Grant Park,** formerly Victoria Park, a showpiece of lawns, lights, and fountains. Covered arcades lead off from King Street, and everywhere are teeming masses of people going about their business. There are some beggars and the inevitable hucksters who sidle up and offer "hot stuff, mon," frequently highly polished brass lightly dipped in gold and offered at prices as high as real gold.

For many years, the richly evocative paintings of Haiti were viewed as the most valuable contribution to Caribbean arts. There is on Jamaica, however, a rapidly growing perception of itself as one of the artistic leaders of the Third World. An articulate core of Caribbean critics is focusing the attention of the art world on the unusual, eclectic, and sometimes politically motivated paintings produced here.

Frame Centre Gallery, 10 Tangerine Place (✆ **876/926-4644;** www.framecentregallery.com), is one of the most important art galleries on Jamaica. Its founder and guiding force, Guy McIntosh, is widely respected today as a patron of the

Jamaican arts. There are three viewing areas and a varied collection of more than 300 works.

Kingston Crafts Market, at the west end of Harbour Street (reached via Straw Ave., Drummer's Lane, or Cheapside), is a large, covered area of small stalls, selling all kinds of island crafts: wooden plates and bowls; pepper pots made from *mahoe* (the national wood of the island); straw hats, mats, and baskets; batik shirts; banners for wall decoration, inscribed with the Jamaican coat-of-arms; and wood masks with elaborately carved faces. You should bargain a bit, and vendors will take something off the price (but not very much).

The **Shops at Devon House,** 26 Hope Rd., ring the borders of a 200-year-old courtyard once used by slaves and servants. It's associated with one of the most beautiful and historic mansions on Jamaica, a building owned by the Jamaican National Trust. The best shop is **Things Jamaican** (**✆ 876/926-1961**), showcasing the crafts of the country and carrying a food section that features island-made sauces and spices. **Wassi Art** (**✆ 876/906-5016**) exhibits locally made ceramics.

THE BLUE MOUNTAINS ★★★

Just a short drive north of Kingston is some of the most varied and unusual topography in the Caribbean, a beautiful mountain range laced with rough rivers, streams, and waterfalls. The 78,000-hectare (192,742-acre) **Blue Mountain–John Crow Mountain National Park** is maintained by the Jamaican government. The mountainsides are covered with coffee fields, producing a blended version that's among the leading exports of Jamaica. For the nature enthusiast, the mountains reveal a complex series of ecosystems that change radically as you climb from sea level into the fog-shrouded peaks.

The most popular, the most scenic, and our favorite climb begins at **Whitfield Hall** (**✆ 876/878-0514;** www.whitfieldhall.com), a high-altitude hostel and coffee estate about 10km (6¼ miles) north of the hamlet of Mavis Bank. Reaching the **summit of Blue Mountain Peak** (900m/2,952 ft. above sea level) requires about 3½ hours each way. Of course, there are much shorter variations if you don't want to see "everything." En route, hikers pass through acres of coffee plantations and forest, where temperatures are cooler than you might expect, and where high humidity encourages thick vegetation. Along the way, watch for an amazing array of bird life, including hummingbirds, many species of warblers, rufous-throated solitaires, yellow-bellied sapsuckers, and Greater Antillean pewees.

Dress in layers and bring bottled water. If you opt for a 2am departure in anticipation of watching the sunrise from atop the peak, carry a flashlight as well. Sneakers are usually adequate, although many climbers bring their hiking boots. Be aware that even during the "dry" season (Dec–Mar), rainfall is common. During the "rainy" season (the rest of the year), fogs and mists are frequent.

At no point do we recommend that you hike alone in the Blue Mountains, even if you're an experienced hiker. Weather conditions can change rapidly, and hiking maps are, in general, very poor. Since there are so few discernible landmarks, it is easy to lose your way.

Security is a major concern for an unaccompanied hiker, especially for those hiking on the Kingston side of the mountain. A guide will not only clear an overgrown path for you, but also may keep you out of harm's way. Bandits might rob you and then disappear into the vast wilderness of the Blue Mountains, where they are hard, if not impossible, to track down. If you appeal to local authorities, you will probably face indifference and a belated suggestion that "you should have used a guide." A better bet involves engaging one of Kingston's best-known specialists in eco-sensitive tours, **Sunventure Tours,** 30 Balmoral Ave., Kingston 10 (✆ **876/960-6685;** fax 876/929-5694; sunventuretours.com). The staff here can always arrange an individualized tour for you or your party, but offers a mainstream roster of choices as well. The **Blue Mountain Sunrise Tour** involves a camp-style overnight in one of the most remote and inaccessible areas of Jamaica. For $150 to $250 per person, participants are picked up at their Kingston hotels and driven to an isolated ranger station, Wildflower Lodge, that's accessible only via four-wheel-drive vehicle, in anticipation of a two-stage hike that begins at 2pm. Cost of the tour depends on the number of participants. A simple mountaineer's supper is served at 6pm around a campfire at a ranger station near Portland Gap. At 2am climbers hike by moonlight and flashlight to a mountaintop aerie that was selected for its view of the 5am sunrise over the Blue Mountains. Climbers stay aloft until around noon that day, then head back down the mountain and return to their hotels by 4pm. A 4-hour trek, costing from $90 to $145 per person, can also be arranged.

Blue Mountain Bike Tours (✆ **876/974-7075;** www.bmtoursja.com) offers all-downhill bike tours through the Blue Mountains—you pedal only about a half-dozen times on this several-mile trip. Visitors are driven to the highest navigable point in the Blue Mountains, where they are provided bikes and protective gear. Breakfast, lunch, snacks, and lots of information about coffee, local foliage, and history are provided. The cost is about $98 per person. The tours run Monday to Saturday, departing at 9am and returning around 5pm.

Where to Stay

Strawberry Hill ★★ 🎁 Music-industry-mogul-turned-hotelier-extraordinaire Chris Blackwell has re-created an idealized version of Jamaica that he remembered from his childhood. The setting is a former coffee plantation in the Blue Mountains, on precariously sloping rainforest terrain 930m (3,051 ft.) above the sea. Views from its terraces overlook the capital's twinkling lights. Eco-sensitive and fully contained, the resort has its own power and water-purification system, a small-scale spa, and elaborate botanical gardens. This exclusive resort considers itself kind of a "home away from home for five-star Robinson Crusoes." Maps and/or guides are provided for tours of nearby coffee plantations, hiking and mountain biking through the Blue Mountains, and tours by night or by day of the urban attractions of nearby Kingston. Accommodations are lavishly nostalgic, draped in bougainvillea and Victorian-inspired gingerbread, and outfitted with gracious mahogany furniture like that of a 19th-century Jamaican great house. Local craftspeople fashioned the cottages and furnished them with canopied four-poster beds and louvered mahogany windows.

New Castle Rd., Irish Town, Blue Mountains, Jamaica, W.I. www.islandoutpost.com. ✆ **800/688-7678** in the U.S., or 876/944-8400. Fax 876/944-8408. 12 units. Winter $295–$595 double; off season $195–$395 double. Rates include all meals. AE, DISC, MC, V. Guests are personally escorted to the hotel in a customized van or via a 7-min. helicopter ride. It's a 50-min. drive from the Kingston airport or 30 min. via mountain roads from the center of the city. **Amenities:** Restaurant; bar; babysitting; bikes; outdoor pool; room service; sauna; spa. *In room:* TV, hair dryer, kitchenette (in some), Wi-Fi (free).

Whispering Bamboo Cove The prices at Strawberry Hill are not for everyone. Frugal travelers who want to stay in the Blue Mountains head for this inn, a 40km (25-mile) drive from the center of Kingston, on the scenic south coast of Morant Bay. The rooms are midsize and comfortably furnished with traditional Jamaican furnishings. The cheapest units are cooled by ceiling fans and have no balconies; others are air-conditioned and have balconies opening onto the seafront. A homemade Jamaican breakfast is served in the elegant dining room, and if you give notice, a lunch or dinner of island fare, specializing in seafood, is offered. The hotel opens onto a private beach with good swimming in a reef-protected area.

105 Crystal Dr. (P.O. Box 2), Retreat, Jamaica, W.I. www.discoverjamaica.com/whisper.html. ✆ **876/982-1788.** Fax 876/734-1049. 15 units. Year-round $50–$90 double. MC, V. **Amenities:** Dining room; private beach. *In room:* A/C (in some), ceiling fan, Wi-Fi (free).

MARTINIQUE

Of all the French West Indies, Martinique is truly France in the Tropics, and we're talking Gauloise cigarettes and gendarmes directing traffic. Martinique is one of the Caribbean's most beautiful islands, with its white-sand beaches and lush rainforests. It is part of the Lesser Antilles and lies in the semitropical zone; the western shore faces the Caribbean, and its eastern shore fronts the more turbulent Atlantic.

15

Beaches Martinique has five bays, dozens of coves, and miles of sandy beaches riddled with sandy beaches. Scuba divers flock to the waters at **Pointe Figuier** to the east of Ste-Luce, while swimmers head to the inviting beaches of **Trinité.**

Things to Do Wander the streets of Fort-de-France, with its iron-grille-work balconies overflowing with flowers, like New Orleans meets the French Riviera. Discover Martinique's pre-Columbian past at the **Musée Departemental d'Archeologie et de Prehistoire de la Martinique.** Catch a beguine dance performance by **Les Grands Ballets Martiniquais.**

Eating & Drinking A mouthwatering Francofied Creole cuisine infuses the restaurants in Martinique. Throughout the island you can indulge in inventive takes on dozens of fish, freshwater crayfish, and jumbo prawns. Local produce is equally inviting, with breadfruit, sweet potatoes, and yucca enhancing many dishes.

Nature Martinique is known for is rugged, mountainous terrain. Mountains are covered with tropical forests, impenetrable in many places. The volcano **Montagne Pelée** rises through tropical flowers, baby ferns, plumed bamboo, and valleys so deeply green you'll think you're wearing cheap sunglasses. The island's lush rainforest is a haven for hummingbirds, blackbirds, and mongooses.

ESSENTIALS

For information about Martinique in advance of your departure, contact the **Martinique Department of the French Government Tourist Office,** at 825 Third Ave., 29th Floor, New York, NY 10022 (✆ **212/838-6887** or 838-7800). Other points of contact within the U.S. and the rest of the world include **French Government Tourist Offices** at 9454 Wilshire Blvd., Ste. 210, Beverly Hills, CA 90212 (✆ **310/271-6665**); or 205 N. Michigan Ave., Ste. 3770, Chicago, IL 60601 (✆ **312/327-0290**). In Britain, contact the **French Government tourist office** at

Martinique

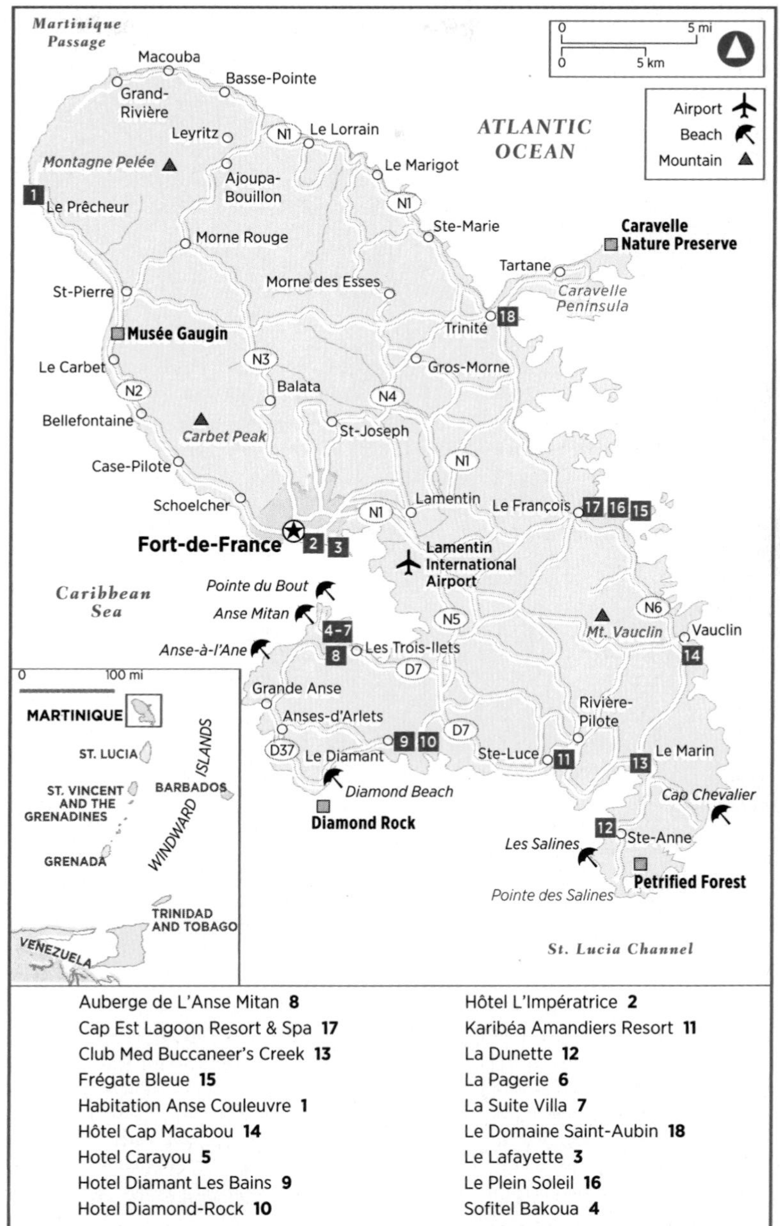

Martinique Passage
Macouba
Grand-Rivière
Basse-Pointe
Leyritz
N1
Le Lorrain
Montagne Pelée
Ajoupa-Bouillon
Le Marigot
1
Le Prêcheur
Morne Rouge
Ste-Marie
ATLANTIC OCEAN
0 5 mi
0 5 km
Airport
Beach
Mountain
Caravelle Nature Preserve
Tartane
Caravelle Peninsula
St-Pierre
Morne des Esses
18
Trinité
Musée Gaugin
N3
Gros-Morne
Le Carbet
N2
Balata
N4
Bellefontaine
St-Joseph
Carbet Peak
Case-Pilote
Schoelcher
Lamentin
Le François
17 16 15
Fort-de-France
2 3
Lamentin International Airport
Caribbean Sea
Pointe du Bout
Anse Mitan
4-7
Anse-à-l'Ane
8
Les Trois-Ilets
N5
D7
N6
Mt. Vauclin
Vauclin
14
0 100 mi
MARTINIQUE
ST. LUCIA
ST. VINCENT AND THE GRENADINES
BARBADOS
WINDWARD ISLANDS
GRENADA
TRINIDAD AND TOBAGO
VENEZUELA
Grande Anse
Anses-d'Arlets
D37
Le Diamant
9 10
Rivière-Pilote
Ste-Luce
11
13
Le Marin
Diamond Beach
Diamond Rock
Cap Chevalier
12
Ste-Anne
Les Salines
Petrified Forest
Pointe des Salines
St. Lucia Channel
Auberge de L'Anse Mitan 8
Cap Est Lagoon Resort & Spa 17
Club Med Buccaneer's Creek 13
Frégate Bleue 15
Habitation Anse Couleuvre 1
Hôtel Cap Macabou 14
Hotel Carayou 5
Hotel Diamant Les Bains 9
Hotel Diamond-Rock 10
Hôtel L'Impératrice 2
Karibéa Amandiers Resort 11
La Dunette 12
La Pagerie 6
La Suite Villa 7
Le Domaine Saint-Aubin 18
Le Lafayette 3
Le Plein Soleil 16
Sofitel Bakoua 4

Lincoln House, 300 High Holborn, London WC1V 7JH (✆ **020/7061-6631**). In Canada, the organization's name and address is **Maison de la France Canada,** 1800 McGill College Ave., Ste. 1010, Montréal, Quebec H3A 3J6 (✆ **514/876-9881**). For information about Martinique on the Web, go to **www.martinique.org**. For Web-derived information about *la France métropolitaine* (mainland France), click on **www.franceguide.com**.

Getting There

BY PLANE **Airport Martinique Aimé Césaire** (✆ **596/42-18-05**) is outside the village of Lamentin, a 15-minute taxi ride east of Fort-de-France and a 40-minute taxi ride northeast of Les Trois-Ilets peninsula (the island's densest concentration of resort hotels). Most flights to Martinique require a transfer on a neighboring island—usually Puerto Rico, Antigua, or Barbados; from there another stopover or transfer in Guadeloupe is often required. Nonstop flights to any of the French islands from the U.S. mainland are rare.

Passengers living in the southeast United States can take a weekly direct flight on **Delta** (✆ **800/241-1212** in the U.S. and Canada; www.delta.com) from Atlanta. Many passengers from other parts of America fly into Atlanta to make this connection. Otherwise, **Air France** (✆ **800/237-2747** in the U.S. and Canada; www.airfrance.com) flies to Martinique several times a week from Miami, with stopovers in either Haiti or Guadeloupe. Many passengers also fly to San Juan on various airlines, connecting to Martinique on **American Eagle** (✆ **800/433-7300** in the U.S. and Canada; www.aa.com).

Other smaller airlines flying to Martinique include **Air Antilles Express** (✆ **0890/64-86-48;** www.airantilles.com), flying in from Guadeloupe or St. Maarten; and **Air Caraïbes** (✆ **590/82-47-56**), also flying in from Guadeloupe and St. Maarten.

British Airways (✆ **800/247-9297** in the U.S. and Canada, or 0870/850-9850 within the British isles; www.britishairways.com) flies separately and daily to both Antigua and Barbados from Gatwick in London. From either of those Caribbean islands, **LIAT** (✆ **888/844-LIAT** [5428]; www.liatairline.com) connects to Martinique. LIAT also flies into Martinique from other islands.

BY FERRY One particularly evocative means of travel between Martinique and Guadeloupe involves taking one of the motorized catamarans that are maintained by a local operator, **Express des Iles.** Carrying between 395 and 495 passengers, depending on the boat, they require 3¾ hours of waterborne transit, which includes an intermediate stopover on either Dominica or Terre-de-Haut, in the Iles des Saintes. The company usually operates three passages a week and sometimes more, between the two largest islands of the French West Indies.

Morning departures from Pointe-à-Pitre for Fort-de-France are usually at 8am (Sat at 11:30am, Sun at 10am), and departures from Fort-de-France for Pointe-à-Pitre are usually at 1pm, although the schedule can vary unexpectedly according to the season and the day of the week. Fares are 100€ round-trip or 67€ one-way (52€ one-way for children 11 and under). For details and reservations, contact **Express des Iles,** Gare Maritime, de Bergevin, 97110 Pointe-à-Pitre, Guadeloupe (✆ **590/91-52-15**), or **Terminal Inter-Iles,** Bassin de Radoub, 97200 Fort-de-France, Martinique (✆ **596/42-04-05**).

Getting Around

BY RENTAL CAR Unless you never plan to leave the beach, you probably want to rent a car to explore the island. Martinique has several local car-rental agencies, but clients have complained of mechanical difficulties and billing irregularities. We recommend renting from one of the U.S.-based firms. Driving in Martinique is on the right side of the road. ***Note:*** An international driver's license is required.

Budget has an office at 30 rue Ernest-Desproges, La Baie, Cruise Terminal, Fort-de-France, in addition to one at Lamentin (✆ **800/472-3325** in the U.S. and Canada, or 596/42-04-04; www.budget-martinique.com). **Avis** is located at Airport Martinique Aimé Césaire (✆ **800/331-1084** in the U.S. and Canada, or 596/42-11-00; www.avis-antilles.fr), as is **Hertz** (✆ **800/654-3001** in the U.S. and Canada, or 596/51-01-01; www.hertzantilles.com).

Regardless of which company you choose, you'll be hit with a value-added tax (VAT) of 8.5% on top of the final bill, plus either a charge of around 25€ if you ask the car to be delivered to your hotel, or an airport pickup charge of about 20€ if you retrieve your car at the airport. Collision damage waivers (CDWs), which eliminate some or all of your financial responsibility in the event of an accident, cost between 12€ and 25€ per day at Budget and Hertz, and usually a bit more at Avis. Of these three car-rental companies, the rates at Budget tend to be the least expensive, although that depends on a wide array of seasonal variations.

BY TAXI Local laws demand that any bona-fide Martiniquais cab must contain a working meter. For specific itineraries—wherein a passenger tells the driver where he or she wants to go—the meter must be "on" and functioning. The island's largest dispatcher advises us that if a taxi driver quotes a flat rate to a passenger instead of activating the meter, you're being robbed, and you should immediately get out and find another cab. For an idea of prices, taxi rates between Fort-de-France and any hotel of La Pointe du Bout are 65€, but only 50€ from Airport Martinique Aimé Césaire to any hotel of La Pointe du Bout. For a general tour of the island, prices are negotiable with the driver. Between 7pm and 6am, a 40% surcharge is assessed.

The rule about using a taxi's meter does not apply to passengers who want to hire a taxi for a **general tour** of the island. If that is your goal, expect to pay from 50€ per hour for up to four passengers, depending on the itinerary and routing you negotiate with the driver. Frankly, we find touring the island by taxi so expensive, and so easily corrupted by the whims of the individual driver, that we advise visitors to rent their own car for the day, driving themselves—armed with a good map—around the island's many rutted but often panoramic roads.

Taxi companies include **Airport Taxi Stand** (✆ **596/42-16-66**) or **Madinina Taxis** (✆ **596/70-40-10**), the latter offering more luxurious cars, such as a Mercedes-Benz.

BY BUS & TAXI COLLECTIF There are two types of buses operating on Martinique. Regular buses, called ***grands busses,*** hold about 40 passengers and cost 2€ to 2.50€ anywhere within the city limits of Fort-de-France. To travel beyond the city limits, nine-passenger ***taxis collectifs*** are used. These are privately owned minivans that traverse the island and bear the sign TC. Their routes are flexible and depend on passenger need. A one-way fare from Fort-de-France to Ste-Anne is about 8€ to 10€. *Taxis collectifs* depart from the heart of Fort-de-France from the parking lot of Pointe Simon. There's no phone number to call for information about this unpredictable means of transport, and there are no set schedules. Traveling in a *taxi collectif* is for the adventurous—these vehicles are crowded and not very comfortable.

Carnival

If you like masquerades and dancing in the streets, you should be here to attend **Carnival,** or Vaval, as it's known here. Most of the celebrations associated with Carnival occur, depending on when Lent falls, for 5 days in either late February or early March, but there is also usually some form of celebration or contest conducted for the six Sundays prior. Most visible of these is the election of the **Carnival Queen,** a contest that's usually held the first Sunday before the actual week of Carnival. Each village prepares costumes and floats. Weekend after weekend, frenzied celebrations take place, reaching fever pitch just before Lent. Fort-de-France is the focal point for Carnival, but the spirit permeates the whole island. On Ash Wednesday, the streets of Fort-de-France are filled with ***diablesses,*** or she-devils (portrayed by members of both sexes). Costumed in black and white, they crowd the streets to form King Carnival's funeral procession. As devils cavort and the rum flows, a funeral pyre is built at La Savane. When it's set on fire, the dancing of the she-devils becomes frantic (many are now thoroughly drunk). Long past dusk, the cortege takes the coffin to its burial, ending Carnival until next year.

BY FERRY The least expensive—and most colorful—way to transfer between Fort-de-France and the hotel and tourist district of Pointe du Bout is via one of the *vedettes* (ferryboats) that depart from rue de la Liberté in Fort-de-France. Transit costs 4.30€ one-way or 6.50€ round-trip. Schedules for the ferryboats, at least 20 of which run at regular (usually 60-min.) intervals every day between 6:30am and 9pm, are printed in the free visitor's guide *Chouboulоute,* in French and English, which is distributed by the tourist office. However, because the ferries are so frequent, most visitors dispense with attempting to understand the schedule altogether, and meander down to the waterfront to wait for the next boat.

There's a smaller ferryboat that runs between Fort-de-France and the unpretentious resorts of Anse Mitan and Anse-à-l'Ane, both across the bay and home to many two- and three-star hotels and modest Creole restaurants. The boat departs from rue de la Liberté in Fort-de-France at intervals of between 20 and 30 minutes every day from 7:30am to 6pm. The trip takes about 20 minutes. One-way and round-trip passage cost 3.80€ and 6€, respectively. If seas are extremely rough, or if there's a hurricane warning, all ferryboat services may be suspended. For more information, call **Vedettes Madinina** (© **596/63-06-46**).

[FastFACTS] MARTINIQUE

Banks Most of the banks of Martinique maintain the following hours: Monday to Friday 7:30am to noon and 2:30 to 4pm. A few of them have opted to close on Wednesday afternoon. Others maintain a policy of remaining closed all day Monday, but opening their doors every Saturday morning between 7:30am and noon. There are about a dozen ATMs in Fort-de-France, at least three at Lamentin Airport, and a scattering of others throughout the island, usually in such touristed areas as Pointe du Bout, Le Diamant, and Ste-Anne.

Currency Because Martinique falls under the same monetary system as mainland France, the island uses the **euro (€)** as its mode of exchange. The rate of exchange at press time was 1€ to US$1.42. **Change Caraïbes** maintains full-service foreign currency divisions, as well as ATMs, at both Lamentin Airport (✆ **596/42-17-11**) and 4 rue Ernest Deproge, in the center of Fort-de-France (✆ **596/60-28-40**). Banks give better exchange rates than hotels. *Prices in this chapter are quoted in euros.*

Customs Items for personal use, such as tobacco, cameras, and film, are admitted without formalities or tax if not in excessive quantity.

Documents U.S. and Canadian citizens need a valid passport. A return or ongoing ticket is also necessary. British citizens need only an identity card.

Electricity Electricity is 220-volt AC (50 cycles), the same as that used on the French mainland. However, check with your hotel to see if it has converted the electrical voltage and outlets in the bathrooms (some have). If it hasn't, bring your own transformer and adapter for U.S. appliances.

Emergencies Call the **police** at ✆ **17,** report a **fire** by dialing ✆ **18,** and summon an **ambulance** at ✆ **17** or **18.**

Hospitals There are about 18 hospitals and clinics on the island, and there's a 24-hour emergency room at the island's largest, **Hôpital Pierre Zobda-Quitman,** Châteauboeuf, 5km (3 miles) south from Fort-de-France (✆ **596/55-20-00**), on the road to Lamentin Airport.

Information The **Tourist Office of Fort-de-France** is at 76 rue Lazare Carnot in Fort-de-France (✆ **596/60-27-73;** www.tourismefdf.com).

Language French, the official language, is spoken by almost everyone. The local Creole patois uses words borrowed from France, England, Spain, and Africa. In the wake of increased tourism, English is occasionally spoken in the major hotels, restaurants, and tourist organizations—but don't count on driving around the countryside and asking for directions in English.

Liquor Laws Liquor is sold in grocery and liquor stores on any day of the week. It's legal to have an open container in public, though the authorities will be very strict with any littering, disorderly behavior, or drunk driving.

Pharmacies Try the **Pharmacie de la Paix,** at the corner of rue Perrinon and rue Victor-Schoelcher in Fort-de-France (✆ **596/71-94-83**), open Monday to Friday from 7:15am to 6:15pm and on Saturday from 7:45am to 1pm.

Safety Crime is hardly rampant on Martinique, yet there are still those who prey on unsuspecting tourists. Follow the usual precautions, especially in Fort-de-France and in the tourist-hotel belt of Pointe du Bout. It's wise to protect your valuables and never leave them unguarded on the beach.

Taxes & Service Charges Most hotels include a 10% service charge in the bill; all restaurants include a 15% service charge. Also added onto your hotel bill is a resort tax known locally as *une taxe hotelière,* which ranges from 1.50€ to 2€ per person per night, depending on the hotel's rating and category.

Telephone To call Martinique from the United States, dial **011** (the international access code), then **596** (the country code for Martinique), and then, if it's a conventional (that is, noncellular) phone, dial 596 again, followed by the six-digit local number. If the number you're calling is a cellphone, dial 011, followed by 596, followed by 696, followed by the six-digit local number. To call the United States from Martinique, dial **19-1,** then the area code, then the seven-digit local number. To make a call within Martinique, dial 0596 followed by the six-digit local number.

Time Martinique is on Atlantic Standard Time year-round, 1 hour earlier than Eastern Standard Time except when daylight saving time is in effect in the U.S.—then Martinique time is the same as on the East Coast of the United States.

Tipping Restaurants generally add a 15% service charge to all bills, which you can supplement if you think the service is outstanding. Some hotels also add a 10% service charge to your bill. Tip taxi drivers at least 15% of the fare.

Water The water is safe to drink throughout the island, but most residents stick to bottled water anyway.

Weather The climate is relatively mild—the average temperature is in the range of 75°F to 85°F (24°C–29°C).

FORT-DE-FRANCE

With its iron-grille-work balconies overflowing with flowers, Fort-de-France, the largest town on Martinique, seems like a cross between New Orleans and a town on the French Riviera. It lies at the end of a large bay surrounded by green hills.

The proud people of Martinique are even more fascinating than the town of Fort-de-France, although today the Creole women are likely to be seen in jeans instead of their traditional turbans, Empress Joséphine–style gowns, and massive, jouncing earrings.

Narrow streets climb up the steep hills, where houses have been built to catch the overflow of the capital's more than 100,000 inhabitants.

Where to Stay

Don't stay in town if you want a hotel near a beach. If you do opt to stay in Fort-de-France, you'll have to take a ferryboat to reach the beaches at **Pointe du Bout** (see "Pointe du Bout & Les Trois-Ilets," later in this chapter). The one exception is the Hôtel La Bâtelière, in the suburb of Schoelcher, which opens onto a small beach.

Hôtel L'Impératrice Favored by businesspeople without unlimited expense accounts, this stucco-sided, five-story hotel faces a landscaped mall in the heart of town, near the water's edge. The much-renovated L'Impératrice was originally built in the 1950s and named in honor of one of Martinique's most famous exports, Joséphine. Its balconies overlook the traffic at the western edge of the sprawling promenade known as La Savane. The small- to medium-size guest rooms are modern and functional. The front rooms tend to be noisy, but they offer a look into life along La Savane. Don't expect outstanding service—almost no one speaks English, and much of the staff seems a bit jaded. But despite the confusion in the very noisy lobby, you might end up enjoying this hotel's unpretentiousness.

Place de la Savane, 15 rue de la Liberté, 97200 Fort-de-France, Martinique, F.W.I. www.limperatricehotel.fr. ✆ **596/63-06-82.** Fax 596/72-66-30. 22 units. Winter 120€–160€ double; off season 110€–145€ double. Rates include breakfast. AE, MC, V. **Amenities:** Restaurant; bar. *In room:* A/C, TV, hair dryer, Wi-Fi (free).

Le Lafayette After 10pm, you'll enter this modest downtown hotel through its entrance on rue Victor-Hugo; during daylight hours, you'll use a larger entrance that opens onto rue de la Liberté, and climb a short flight of terra-cotta steps to reach the simple lobby. Don't expect grandeur; this hotel's snob appeal is practically nonexistent. The hotel was renovated, and its bedrooms are tidy and clean. Most units contain comfortable twin beds, with small pure-white, shower-only bathrooms. The overall impression is neat but simple and unpretentious. The inn is the oldest continuously operating hotel on Martinique, originally built in the 1940s with quasi–Art Deco hints that are now slightly dowdy.

5 rue de la Liberté, 97200 Fort-de-France, Martinique, F.W.I. www.lelafayettehotel.com. ✆ **596/73-80-50.** Fax 596/60-97-75. 24 units. Year-round 65€ double; 75€ triple. AE, MC, V. **Amenities:** Restaurant; bar. *In room:* A/C, TV, Wi-Fi (in some; free).

Where to Dine

Le Dôme ★★ 🎁 FRENCH/ANTILLEAN Set on the top (eighth) floor of a hotel in the Valmenière district, midway between Fort-de-France's commercial center and the airport—and far from the neighborhoods and haunts visited by tourists—this place caters almost exclusively to business travelers, many from the French mainland. Outfitted with a contemporary decor and hues of red, it boasts large bay windows, through which diners enjoy a view that sweeps along the island's coastline. Menu items blend traditional French cuisine with Antillean ingredients, sometimes in very creative ways. You might begin with such temptations as foie gras or cannelloni filled with salmon. Salads, big and generous with fresh greens, are also a feature. An excellent pasta dish is studded with salmon or scallops, and you can also order roast lamb, or else beef with a Creole sauce.

In the Hôtel Valmenière, ave. des Arawaks. ✆ **596/75-75-75.** Reservations recommended. Main courses 18€–33€; business lunch 32€. AE, DC, MC, V. Sun–Fri 12:30–2pm and 7:30–10pm; Sat 7:30–10pm. Bus: 7.

Soup Bar du Centre Ville FRENCH/GERMAN If Martinique has a counterculture cafe, this is it, evoking a tavern in New York's Greenwich Village in the 1950s. The island's most avant-garde artwork decorates the walls. In the heart of Fort-de-France just behind Le Marche aux Epices (the spice market), the tavern is operated by its German-born owner, Mr. Loutchous. He sees that goulash and German beer are on the menu. True to its namesake, the bar is known for its big, hearty bowls of soup, each a meal unto itself. One island soup specialty is called *soupe z'habitant,* which is a purée of green vegetables with pig tails added for that extra punch. Other regional soups—called *des soups du pays*—are a regular feature, including both tripe soup and *pied de veau* (cow-foot soup). You can also order regular main dish platters of food, including lasagna with seafood, plus an array of freshly made salads.

120 rue Martine, Fort-de-France. ✆ **596/60-48-96.** Reservations not needed. Main courses 7€–12€; meal-size salads 11€–20€. AE, DC, MC, V. Daily 6pm–1am.

ON THE OUTSKIRTS

Le Brédas ★★ FRENCH/MARTINIQUAIS/INTERNATIONAL A gastronomic landmark attracting a clientele from miles around, this restaurant occupies a modern, white-walled Creole house, positioned in a verdant and isolated location to the northeast of Fort-de-France. Cuisine changes every 3 months, as envisioned by the creative talent of Martinique-born Chef Brédas and the restaurant's charming manager, Marie-Julie. You might find the régime here a refreshing and rather stylish break from too constant a diet of mainstream Creole cuisine. The best examples might include a mille-feuille (Napoleon) of foie gras with yellow bananas, filets of a local whitefish (cobia) with a risotto of green rice, and yam cakes served with morels and Madeira sauce. Most of the pottery, plates, and tilework within the restaurant were manufactured locally, by local artisans.

Entrée Presqu'ile, Rivière Blanche, St. Joseph. ✆ **596/57-65-52.** Reservations required. Main courses 30€–35€. AE, DC, MC, V. Tues–Sat 7:30–11pm.

Sports & Outdoor Pursuits

If it's a beach you're looking for, take the ferry to **Pointe du Bout** (see "Pointe du Bout & Les Trois-Ilets," below). The island's only **golf course** is in Les Trois-Ilets, also discussed in the next section.

HIKING Inexpensive guided hikes are offered by the **Parc Naturel Régional de la Martinique,** 9 bd. Général-de-Gaulle, Fort-de-France (✆ **596/64-42-59**). This organization also gives out maps of recommended hikes within Martinique and offers advice about routings and access to departure points for walks and hill treks.

Exploring the Town

At the heart of town is **La Savane,** a broad garden with many palms and mangos; playing fields, walks, and benches; plus shops and cafes lining its sides. In the middle of this grand square stands a statue of Joséphine, "Napoleon's little Creole," made of white marble by Vital Debray. Joséphine poses in a Regency gown and looks toward Les Trois-Ilets, where she was born. The statue was decapitated in 1991, probably because islanders felt she championed slavery. Near the harbor, at the edge of the park, you'll find vendors' stalls with handmade crafts, including baskets, beads, bangles, woodcarvings, and straw hats.

Your next stop could be the 1875 **Cathédrale St-Louis,** on rue Victor-Schoelcher. The religious centerpiece of the island, it's an extraordinary iron building, which has been likened to "a sort of Catholic railway station." A number of the island's former governors are buried beneath the choir loft.

A statue in front of the Palais de Justice is of the island's second main historical figure, **Victor Schoelcher,** who worked to free the slaves in the late 19th century. **Bibliothèque Schoelcher,** 1 rue de la Liberté (✆ **596/70-26-67**), also honors this popular hero. Functioning today as the island's central government-funded library, the elaborate structure was first displayed at the Paris Exposition of 1889. The Romanesque portal, the Egyptian lotus-petal columns, even the turquoise tiles were imported piece by piece from Paris and reassembled here. It's open Monday 1 to 5:30pm, Tuesday to Friday 8:30am to 5:30pm, and Saturday 8:30am to noon.

Fort St-Louis, built in the Vauban style on a rocky promontory, guards the port. **Fort Tartenson** and **Fort Desaix** also stand on hills overlooking the port.

Musée Departemental d'Archeologie et de Prehistoire de la Martinique, 9 rue de la Liberté (✆ **596/71-57-05**), has preserved Martinique's pre-Columbian past and has relics from the early settlers, the Arawaks and the Caribs. The museum has exhibits from the years from 3000 B.C. to A.D. 1635, but stops shortly after the arrival of the first French colonials in the early 1600s. In other words, it's mostly an ethnological museum. The museum faces La Savane and is open Monday 1 to 5pm, Tuesday to Friday 8am to 5pm, and on Saturday 9am to noon. Admission is 3.05€ for adults, 1.52€ for children 3 to 11 and 2.29€ students.

Le Musée Régional d'Histoire et d'Ethnographie, 10 bd. de Général-de-Gaulle, in Fort-de-France (✆ **596/72-81-87**), is devoted to an illumination of the island's agrarian past (and the slave culture that made it possible). Expositions showcase the early-20th-century volcanic eruption that leveled St-Pierre, slavery and its effects on the island's society, and explorations of the sugar-cane industry. It's open Tuesday from 2 to 5pm; Saturday from 8:30am to noon; and Monday and Wednesday to Friday from 8:30am to 5pm. Entrance costs 3€ for adults and .75€ for children 11 and under. Entrance is free for anyone with a valid student ID.

MARTINIQUE'S TRADITIONAL dances

The sexy and rhythmic **beguine** was *not* an invention of Cole Porter. It's a dance of the islands—though exactly which island depends on whom you ask. Popular wisdom and the encyclopedia give the nod to Martinique, though Guadeloupeans claim it as their own, too.

Everybody who goes to Martinique wants to see the show performed by **Les Grands Ballets Martiniquais,** a troupe of about two dozen dancers, along with musicians, singers, and choreographers, who tour the island regularly. Their performances of the traditional dances of Martinique have been acclaimed in both Europe and the United States. With a swoosh of gaily striped skirts and clever acting, the dancers capture all the exuberance of the island's soul. The group has toured abroad with great success, but they perform best on their home ground, presenting tableaux that tell of jealous brides and faithless husbands, demanding overseers and toiling cane cutters. Dressed in traditional costumes, the islanders dance the spirited **mazurka,** which was brought from the 18th- and 19th-century ballrooms of Europe, and, of course, the exotic beguine.

Les Grands Ballets Martiniquais usually perform at area hotels, but schedules vary, so check locally. The cost of dinner and the show is from 50€. Most performances are at 8:30pm, with dinners at the hotels beginning at 7:30pm. The show is free for guests of the hotel where the troupe is performing. In addition, the troupe gives miniperformances aboard visiting cruise ships.

Sacré-Coeur de Balata Cathedral, at Balata, overlooking Fort-de-France, is a copy of the one looking down from Montmartre upon Paris—and this one is just as incongruous, maybe more so. It's reached by going along route de la Trace (Rte. N3). Balata is 10km (6¼ miles) northwest of Fort-de-France.

A few minutes away on Route N3, **Jardin de Balata** (© **596/64-48-73**) is a tropical botanical park created by Jean-Philippe Thoze on land that the jungle was rapidly reclaiming around a Creole house that belonged to his grandmother. He restored the house, furnishing it with antiques and engravings. The garden contains a profusion of flowers, shrubs, and trees. It's open daily from 9am to 6pm. Admission is 12.50€ for adults, 7€ for children 3 to 12, and free for children 6 and under.

Shopping

Your best buys on Martinique are French luxury imports, such as perfumes, fashions, Vuitton luggage, Lalique crystal, and Limoges dinnerware. Sometimes (but don't count on it) prices are as much as 30% to 40% below those in the United States.

You're usually better off shopping in the smaller stores, where prices are 8% to 12% lower on comparable items, and paying in euros.

Fort-De-France After Dark

The most exciting after-dark activity is seeing a performance of the folkloric troupe **Les Grands Ballets Martiniquais** (see "Martinique's Traditional Dances," above).

The popularity of individual bars and dance clubs in Martinique rises and falls almost monthly. Many of them charge a cover between 10€ and 15€, although that's often ignored if business is slow—and if you're an appealing physical specimen. A nightclub and restaurant where anyone can be a star, at least for a few minutes, is **Maximus,** Immeuble Les Corneaux, Le Lamentin (© **596/50-16-37**).

If you're on the party circuit around Martinique, you are likely to find the most action at **Crazy Nights,** Ste-Luce (✆ **596/68-56-68**), a wild dance parlor that on weekends can attract hundreds of patrons, each bent on having one "crazy night." Jazz is showcased at the **Calebasse Café,** 19 bd. Allègre, Le Marin (✆ **596/74-69-27**), which sometimes features its own Billie Holiday clone. Meals are served, and the place is packed on Saturday nights. Live performances on Thursday around 10:30pm are a regular feature at **Les Soirees de l'Amphore,** Anse-Mitan (✆ **596/66-03-09**), a small restaurant and minibar. Funk, disco, and soul are all featured.

If you want to gamble, head for Martinique's major casino, **Casino Bâtelière Plaza,** at Schoelcher (✆ **596/61-73-23**), a 10-minute drive from the center of Fort-de-France. You'll need a passport; men do not need a jacket or tie. A special area reserved just for slot machines is open daily, without charge, from 10am to 3 or 4am. A more formal gambling area, with poker, roulette, and blackjack, is open from 8pm to 3am. There's a restaurant on-site. This is the larger, newer, and more crowded of the two casinos in Martinique, with 140 slot machines, compared to the 40 slots at the Casino des Trois-Ilets (see "Pointe du Bout After Dark," later in this chapter). But that might change if and when the new casino at Trois-Ilets opens.

On a cultural note, **L'Atrium,** boulevard Général-de-Gaulle, Fort-de-France (✆ **596/60-78-78**), is the venue for major island cultural events, including dance and music. The theatrical presentations, of course, are in French. You can ask on island what might be happening at the time of your visit. For a not-always-up-to-date rundown on what's cooking entertainment-wise, click on **www.martinique.no-scoop.com**.

POINTE DU BOUT ★ & LES TROIS-ILETS

Pointe du Bout is a narrow peninsula across the bay from the busy capital of Fort-de-France. It's the most developed resort area of Martinique, with at least four of the island's largest hotels, an impressive marina, about a dozen tennis courts, countless pools, facilities for horseback riding, and all kinds of watersports. There's also a handful of independent restaurants, a casino, boutiques, and, in nearby Les Trois-Ilets, a Robert Trent Jones, Sr.–designed golf course. Except for the hillside that contains the Sofitel Bakoua, most of the district is flat and verdant, with gardens and rigidly monitored parking zones. All the hotels listed below are near the clean white-sand beaches of Pointe du Bout. Some of the smaller properties are close to the white-sand beaches of Anse Mitan. Les Trois-Ilets, the birthplace of Joséphine, the empress of France and wife of Napoleon Bonaparte, lies at the base of the peninsula on the bay.

Getting There

If you're driving from Fort-de-France, take Route 1, which crosses the plain of Lamentin—the industrial area of Fort-de-France and the site of the international airport. Often the air is filled with the fragrance of caramel, from the large sugar-cane factories in the surrounding area. After about 30km (19 miles), you reach Les Trois-Ilets. Five kilometers (3 miles) farther on your right, take Route D38 to Pointe du Bout.

For the **ferry service,** see "Getting Around," earlier in this chapter, for details.

Where to Stay

EXPENSIVE

Hotel Bakoua ★ Airline crews fill up many of the rooms at the Sofitel Bakoua, a hotel known for the beauty of its landscaping and its somewhat isolated hillside location. It consists of four low-rise buildings in the center of a garden. Built in 1967 and renovated several times since, accommodations come in a wide range of sizes, from small to spacious, and are comfortable. Rooms have balconies or patios.

Pointe du Bout, 97229 Trois-Ilets, Martinique, F.W.I. www.accorhotels.com. ✆ **800/221-4542** in the U.S., or 596/66-02-02. Fax 596/66-00-41. 138 units. Year-round 380€–480€ double, from 750€ suite. AE, DC, MC, V. **Amenities:** 2 restaurants; 2 bars; babysitting; outdoor pool; room service; 2 tennis courts (lit); watersports equipment/rentals. *In room:* A/C, TV, hair dryer, minibar, Wi-Fi (free).

Hotel Carayou ★ ☺ This hotel is popular with families because of its children's programs, and it prides itself on its lush gardens and glamorous garden setting opening onto a small beach. The accommodations aren't the most attractive in the area, but they are housed in a series of three-story outbuildings, each encircled by large lawns dotted with coconut or palm trees and flowering shrubs. The seaside rooms are the best, and some of the units are air-conditioned. Against a setting of wood trim and whitewashed walls, the rooms are generally small but well maintained.

Pointe du Bout, 97229 Trois-Ilets, Martinique, F.W.I. www.hotel-carayou.com. ✆ **596/66-04-04.** Fax 596/66-00-57. 207 units. Winter 145€–260€ double; off season 90€–150€ double. AE, DC, MC, V. **Amenities:** 2 restaurants; bar; children's program; outdoor pool; tennis court (lit); watersports equipment/rentals. *In room:* A/C (in some), TV, hair dryer, Wi-Fi (free).

La Suite Villa Although not on the beach, this compound of two-level suites and three private villas opens onto a panoramic sweep over the bay to Fort-de-France. Run by artistic owners, the boutique hotel crowns a hilltop opening onto Les Trois-Ilets. Suites in the hotel are spacious, with sleek modern appointments. Each of the villas include two or three bedrooms, and are dressed in colorful hues in traditional Creole style, with private garden terraces and an outdoor shower. The on-site restaurant presents a carefully prepared series of French and Creole specialties. The bar is often filled with local painters and sculptors who showcase their work here. A fixed-price menu of 38€ is featured nightly.

Route du Fort d'Alet, Ansé Mitan, Trois-Ilets 97229, Martinique, F.W.I. www.la-suite-villa.com. ✆ **596/59-88-00.** Fax 596/59-88-10. 6 suites, 9 villas. Winter 280€-320€ suite; 340€-420€ villa; off season 240€-280€ suite; 300€-370€ villa. AE, MC, V. **Amenities:** Restaurant; bar; outdoor pool; room service. *In room:* DVD player, kitchen (in some), Wi-Fi (free).

MODERATE

Hotel La Pagerie The facilities here are relatively modest compared to those in some of the larger and more expensive hotels of Pointe du Bout, but guests can compensate by visiting the many restaurants, bars, and sports facilities in the area. Set close to the gardens of the Hotel Bakoua (see above) and a 26km (16-mile) drive from the airport, this hotel offers comfortably modern bedrooms. Although the walls are thin, the units are neat and uncomplicated, with tile floors, small fridges, and balconies with views opening onto the bay. About two-thirds of the units contain tiny kitchenettes, at no extra charge. The accommodations are outfitted with floral prints, low-slung furnishings, and louvered closets. Guests usually walk 5 minutes to Hotel Carayou (see above) for watersports and access to the beach.

Pointe du Bout, 97229 Trois-Ilets, Martinique, F.W.I. www.hotel-lapagerie.com. ✆ **596/66-05-30.** Fax 596/66-00-99. 94 units. Winter 160€ double; off season 85€ double. Rates include buffet breakfast. AE, MC, V. **Amenities:** Restaurant; bar; outdoor pool; Wi-Fi (4€ for 2 hr.). *In room:* A/C, TV, fridge, kitchenette (in some).

INEXPENSIVE

Auberge de L'Anse Mitan You don't get anything special here, but the price is right, and many guests like this hotel's location at the isolated end of a road whose more commercial section is laden with restaurants and bustles at night. The hotel was built in 1930 but has been renovated several times by the hospitable Athanase family. What you get today is a three-story concrete structure. Six of the units are studios with kitchens and TVs; all have showers. Rooms are boxy, but the beds are comfortable.

35 rue des Anthuriums, L'Anse Mitan, 97229 Trois-Ilets, Martinique, F.W.I. www.auberge-ansemitan.com. ✆ **596/66-01-12.** Fax 596/66-01-05. 18 units. Winter 70€–90€ double, 65€ studio, 90€–110€ triple; off season 55€ double, 50€ studio, 70€ triple. Rates include breakfast. AE, DC, MC, V. **Amenities:** Wi-Fi (free). *In room:* A/C, TV (in studios), kitchenette (in studios), Wi-Fi (in studios; free).

Where to Dine

There isn't a great choice of restaurants, but here's the pick of the litter.

Au Poisson d'Or CREOLE Its position near the entrance of the resort community of Pointe du Bout makes it easy to find. There's no view of the sea, and the traffic runs close to the edge of the veranda and terrace, but the reasonable prices and the complete change of pace make up for that. The rustic dining room offers such classics as grilled fish cooked in Creole sauce, poached local fish with coconut milk, and flan. These ordinary dishes are prepared with flair and served with style.

12 rue des Bougainvilliers, L'Anse Mitan. ✆ **596/66-01-80.** Reservations recommended. Main courses 11€–16€; prix-fixe lunch 14€. AE, MC, V. Tues–Sat noon–2pm and 7–9:30pm; Sun noon–2pm. Closed July.

Fleur de Sel FRENCH/CREOLE/INTERNATIONAL In a restored colonial home from the 19th century, this sophisticated eatery combines French cooking techniques with Caribbean fresh produce. Papaya gives a zest to traditional foie gras ravioli, while the fish tartare is enlivened with fresh mango and chopped, locally grown cucumbers. Foi gras as an appetizer is served on gingerbread with caramelized apples. Winning high praise is the salmon lacquered with ginger. Some dishes take inspiration from Alsace in France, as evoked by the *choucroute Marinere* (shellfish on a cabbage confit with a Riesling sauce).

27 av. De l'Impératrice Joséphine, Bourg, Les Trois-Ilets. ✆ **596/68-42-11.** Fax 596/68-42-13. www.antillesresto.com/restaurant/fleur-de-sel. Reservations recommended. Menu Fleu de Sel 38€; menu degustation 52€. MC, V. Mon–Sat 7:30–11pm.

Havana Café FRENCH Set in Pointe du Bout, amid the densest concentration of tourist hotels and leisure facilities of Martinique, this cafe evokes an idealized version of Cuba in its most decadent period, just before the rise to power of Fidel. Amid a color scheme of bright yellow and blue, and prefaced with a big American sedan, painted yellow, from the early 1960s, a mostly French-born staff serves stiff drinks as well as meal-size salads, burgers, grilled cutlets, and heaping platters of mussels. There's a selection of raw tartars of fish, and a house cheeseburger called the Havana Burger. And for anyone nostalgic for metropolitan France, there's a short list of *des galettes,* the buckwheat crepes endemic to Brittany that are stuffed, Breton style, with savory or sweet fillings that include ham and cheese or ice cream with chocolate sauce. Some kind of music, either live or recorded, rocks-'n'-rolls the place every evening between 9:30pm and midnight, during which time it takes on the aura of a holidaymaker's singles bar. There's another beachside branch of this place, **Havana Plage,** at Grand Anse, Anse d'Arlets (✆ **596/69-07-38**), with the same menu items, prices, and hours, but Le Cabestar Café is the more animated of the two.

In the Village Creole, Pointe du Bout. ✆ **596/66-15-93.** Main courses 12€–18€. MC, V. Daily 9am–11:30pm.

La Villa Creole ★ CREOLE/FRENCH This restaurant, which lies a 3- or 4-minute drive from the hotels of Pointe du Bout, has thrived since the late 1970s, offering a colorful, small-scale respite from the island's high-rise resorts. Set within a simple but well-maintained Creole house, with no particular views other than the small garden that surrounds it, the restaurant serves fairly priced set-price menus of such staples as *accras de morue* (beignets of codfish), *boudin Creole* (blood sausage), and *feroce* (a local form of pâté concocted from fresh avocados, pulverized codfish, and manioc flour). A special delight is the red snapper either prepared with tomato sauce or grilled. If Creole food doesn't appeal to you, there's also a short list of dishes inspired by the traditional cuisine of mainland France, focusing on such Gallic staples as scallops tatin, red tuna with shallots, chicken Colombo, and magret of duck with foie gras sauce. Owner Guy Bruère-Dawson, a singer and guitarist, entertains as you dine.

18 rue des Anthuriums, L'Anse Mitan. ✆ **596/66-05-53.** Reservations recommended. Main courses 14€–25€; vegetarian menu 19€; gourmet menu 39€. AE, MC, V. Tues–Sat noon–2pm and 7–10:30pm.

Le Pacha ★ FRENCH/CARIBBEAN Le Pacha is in a seafronting building that's virtually hidden from the landward side by a thick screen of palm trees and vegetation. Inside, in an environment painted in tones of pink, orange, and variations of green, you'll find a dedication to creative cuisine that's directly affected by the French Alps origins of the creative team who run the place. The same menu is offered at lunch and dinner. Alongside pizzas and salads, the menu includes such elaborate creations as a duet of fish (Atlantic mackerel and Caribbean *balahou*) served with orange sauce, a trio of foie gras, ostrich with fresh chanterelles, and roast half lobster with aioli sauce. A deeply upholstered leather sofa near the entrance functions as a kind of throne at this place, supposedly allowing any Jean, Philippe, or Pierre to feel like a *pacha,* or sultan, in his own right. Le Pacha is a short walk from the departure point for the ferryboats heading to and from Fort-de-France.

19 rue des Anthuriums, Anse Mitan. ✆ **596/66-02-99.** Reservations recommended. Main courses 16€–25€. DC, MC, V. Mon–Sat 6–10:30pm.

Hitting the Beach

The clean white-sand beaches of **Pointe du Bout,** site of the major hotels of Martinique, were created by developers and tend to be rather small. Most of the tourists head here, so the narrow beaches are among the island's most crowded. It doesn't help that Pointe du Bout also has several marinas lining the shore and serves as the docking point for the ferry from Fort-de-France. Even if you don't find a lot of space on the beach, with its semiclear waters, you will find toilets, phones, restaurants, and cafes galore. The waters suffer from industrial usage, although apparently the pollution is not severe enough to prevent people from going in. You'll often see the French standing deep in the water, smoking cigarettes—not our idea of an idyllic beach vacation.

To the south, the golden-sand beaches at **Anse Mitan** are far less crowded and more inviting, with cleaner waters. But the steepness of Martinique's shoreline leaves much to be desired by its swimmers and snorkelers. The water declines steeply into depths, no reefs ring the shores, and fish are rarely visible. Nonetheless, beaches here are good for sunbathing. The neighboring beach is **Anse-à-l'Ane,** an ideal place for a picnic.

Sports & Outdoor Pursuits

GOLF Robert Trent Jones, Sr., designed the 18-hole **Golf de l'Impératrice-Joséphine,** at Trois-Ilets (✆ **596/68-32-81**), a 5-minute drive from Pointe du Bout and about 30km (19 miles) from Fort-de-France. The only golf course on Martinique has greens that slope from the birthplace of Joséphine across rolling hills down to the sea. Amenities include a pro shop, a bar, and a restaurant. Greens fees are 55€ for 18 holes. There are also three tennis courts, which cost 15€ per hour.

HORSEBACK RIDING The premier riding facility on Martinique is **Ranch Jack,** Esperanze, Trois-Ilets (✆ **596/68-37-69**). It offers morning horseback rides for both experienced and novice riders, at a cost of 54€ for a 4-hour ride (either daily 8:30am–12:30pm or 2:30–6pm). Jacques and Marlene Guinchard make daily treks across the beaches and fields of Martinique, with a running (English-language) explanation of the history, fauna, and botany of the island. Cold drinks are included in the price, and transportation is usually free to and from the hotels of nearby Pointe du Bout. Four to 15 participants are needed to book a tour. This is an ideal way to discover both the botany and geography of Martinique.

JET SKIING Also on the grounds of the Hotel Carayou is an outfit specializing in jet-skiing, **Jet Caraibes** (✆ **596/66-09-31**). A 30-minute rental of a jet ski costs 60€ for 1 or 2 persons for 30 minutes.

SCUBA DIVING & SNORKELING The beachfront of the **Hotel Carayou** (p. 401) is the headquarters for the island's best dive outfit, **Espace Plongée Martinique** (✆ **596/66-01-79;** www.espace-plongee-martinique.com), which welcomes anyone who shows up, regardless of where they're staying. Daily dive trips, depending on demand, leave from Le Kalenda's pier every day at 8am, returning at noon, and departing again at 2pm, returning at 5pm. Popular dive sites within a reasonable boat ride, with enough diversity and variation in depth to appeal to divers of all levels of proficiency, include La Baleine (the Whale) and Cap Salomon. A dive shop stocks everything you'll need to take the plunge, from weight belts and tanks to wet suits and underwater cameras. Uncertified divers pay 55€ for a *baptême* ("baptism"), which consists of instruction and practice time in the hotel's swimming pool, followed by a brief experience with a scuba tank in open water.

Certified divers pay 50€ for a one-tank dive, or around 90€ for a full-day excursion to Baie de St-Pierre (St. Peter's Bay) on Martinique's northern coast. Here the excursion includes two dives (morning and afternoon, in different spots), excursions in a minibus to sites of natural beauty along the north coast, and continental breakfast and a picnic lunch. It departs whenever at least five participants show sufficient interest, at 8am. Participants return to the Kalenda the same day at 5:30pm.

Coral, fish, and ferns abound in the semiclear waters around the Pointe du Bout hotels, and snorkeling equipment is usually available free to hotel guests.

WINDSURFING An enduringly popular sport in the French West Indies, *la planche à voile* (windsurfing) is available at most of the large-scale hotels. One of the best equipped (and longest lived) of Martinique's windsurfing centers is **Windsurf Club Martinique,** which occupies a site directly on the beachfront of the Hotel Carayou (✆ **596/66-19-06**). Lessons cost 100€ for 3 hours, and boards, depending on their make and model, rent for 60€ for 3 hours. A 10-hour rental costs 185€.

A Visit to Les Trois-Ilets

Marie-Josephe-Rose Tascher de la Pagerie was born here in 1763. As Joséphine, she was to become the wife of Napoleon I and empress of France from 1804 to 1809. Six years older than Napoleon, she pretended that she'd lost her birth certificate so he wouldn't find out her true age. Although many historians call her ruthless and selfish, she is still revered by some on Martinique as an uncommonly gracious lady. Others have less kind words for her—Napoleon is said by some historians to have "reinvented" slavery, and they cite Joséphine's influence.

Thirty kilometers (19 miles) south of Fort-de-France, you reach Les Trois-Ilets, a charming little village. Two kilometers (1¼ miles) outside the village, turn left to La Pagerie, where the small **Musée de La Pagerie** (✆ **596/68-33-06**) has been installed in the former estate kitchen, where Joséphine gossiped with her slaves and played the guitar. Regrettably, most of the other buildings associated with this once-thriving plantation were destroyed in a hurricane. Visitors today can see mementos of Joséphine's childhood, including the bed she slept in as a teenager and a passionate letter from Napoleon. The collection was compiled by Dr. Robert Rose-Rosette. Still remaining are the partially restored ruins of the Pagerie sugar mill and the church (in the village itself) where she was christened in 1763. The museum is open Tuesday to Friday 9am to 5:30pm, and Saturday and Sunday 9:30am to 12:30pm and 3 to 5pm; it's closed in September. Admission is 5€ for adults, 1.50€ for children 12 and under.

Modern artists and local potters banded together in 2005 to form a cooperative of shops, galleries, and studios at **Trois-Ilets Pottery** (✆ **596/63-03-44**), at La Pagerie, next to the Musée de La Pagerie. You can shop for one-of-a-kind items such as a clay lamp hand painted in Creole colors.

Maison de la Canne, Pointe Vatable (✆ **596/68-32-04**), is on the road to Trois-Ilets. Located on the premises of an 18th-century distillery, its permanent exhibitions demonstrate the sweeping role sugar cane played in the economic and cultural development of Martinique. It's open Tuesday to Thursday 8:30am to 5:30pm; Friday to Saturday 8:30am to 5pm; Sunday 9am to 5pm. Admission is 3€ for adults, .75€ for children 5 to 12, and free for children 4 and under.

The marina complex has a number of fashionable boutiques; several sell handicrafts and curios from Martinique. They're sometimes of good quality but are quite expensive, particularly the enameled jewel boxes and some of the batiks of natural silk.

Pointe du Bout After Dark

For such a popular resort area, nightlife is mostly confined to bars. Other entertainment options are sporadic, including offerings at the **Havana Café,** Village Creole, Pointe du Bout (✆ **596/66-15-93**). If you like a party atmosphere, head for the **Coconuts Club,** Quartier Laugier, Rivière Salée (✆ **596/68-20-49**). This is a three-in-one threat—bar/lounge, restaurant, and dance club. **L'Amphore,** a piano and karaoke bar, is found at the rear of Hotel Bakoua, Pointe du Bout (✆ **596/66-03-09**).

Martinique's **Casino des Trois-Ilets** is at 24 rue des Bougainvilliers (✆ **596/66-00-30**), where you can try your luck on the slot machines daily from 11am to 3am. Roulette and *les grands jeux* (blackjack) are open nightly from 8pm to 3am; visitors must present ID or a passport.

THE SOUTH LOOP

South of Pointe du Bout, you can find sun and beaches. Resort centers here include Le Diamant and Ste-Anne. From Trois-Ilets you can follow a small curved road that brings you to **Anse-à-l'Ane, Grande Anse,** and **Anses-d'Arlets.** At any of these places, you'll find small beaches, which are quite safe and usually not crowded.

Anses-d'Arlets

The scenery is beautiful here. Brightly painted fishing boats known as *gommiers* draw up on the white-sand beach, and the nets are spread out to dry in the sun. Children swim and adults fish from the good-size pier. The waters off Anses-d'Arlets are a playground for divers, with a wide variety of small tropical fish and colorful corals.

The area has been a choice spot for weekend second homes for many years and is now becoming a destination for tourists. The little village features a pretty steepled church, a bandstand for holiday concerts, and a smattering of modest little dining spots. Aficionados of Martinique come here to see the "way it used to be" on the island. Unspoiled and folkloric, the hamlet still retains its *charm typique Martiniquaise.*

From Anses-d'Arlets, panoramic Route D37 takes you to Le Diamant.

Le Diamant

Set on the island's southwestern coast, about 40 minutes by taxi from the airport, this village offers a good beach, open to the prevailing southern winds. The village is named after one of Martinique's best-known geological oddities, **Le Rocher du Diamant (Diamond Rock),** a barren offshore island that juts upward from the sea to a height of 172m (564 ft.). Sometimes referred to as the Gibraltar of the Caribbean, it figured prominently in a daring British invasion in 1804, when British mariners carried a formidable amount of ammunition and 110 sailors to the top. Despite frequent artillery bombardments from the French-held coastline, the garrison held out for 18 months, completely dominating the passageway between the rock and the coast of Martinique. Intrepid foreigners sometimes visit Diamond Rock, but the access across the strong currents of the channel is risky.

Diamond Beach ★★★, on the Martinique mainland, offers a sandy bottom, verdant groves of swaying palms, and many different surf and sunbathing possibilities. The district has developed into a resort, scattered with generally small hotels.

WHERE TO STAY

Hotel Diamant Les Bains This is an unpretentious, family-style hotel with direct access to a sandy beach. From the edge of the resort's pool, you can enjoy a view of the offshore island of Diamond Rock. Twenty units are in outlying motel-style bungalows set either in a garden or beside the beach; the others are in the resort's main building, which also houses the restaurant and bar. Accommodations have furnished terraces or patios, white-tile floors, small fridges, and built-in furniture made from polished fruitwood. Most rooms are medium in size except for the small units on the second floor of the main building, which are often rented to business travelers from the French mainland. The best are the 10 rustic bungalows directly above the beach.

Rond-point du Neg Marron, 97223 Le Diamant, Martinique, F.W.I. ✆ **596/76-40-14.** Fax 596/76-27-00. 27 units. Winter 100€ double, 123€ bungalow; off season 80€ double, 90€ bungalow. Rates include continental breakfast. MC, V. Closed Sept. **Amenities:** Restaurant; bar; outdoor pool; Wi-Fi (free). *In room:* A/C, TV, fridge.

Hotel Diamond-Rock On 2 hectares (5 acres) of forested land, 3km (2 miles) outside the village and 29km (18 miles) south of Fort-de-France, this low-rise building is in one of the most beautiful districts on Martinique. It's the ultimate in laissez-faire management—guests, often tour groups from France, are basically left to themselves. Guest rooms, housed in four three-story wings, face either the pool or the coast, with its view of Diamond Rock. The inviting units have tropical decor, white-tile floors, whitewashed walls, roomy closets, and rattan furnishings, plus adequate desk space. Outside the hotel, the narrow neighboring white-sand beaches aren't too crowded.

Pointe de la Cherry, 97223 Le Diamant, Martinique, F.W.I. www.diamondrockhotel.com. ✆ **596/76-42-42.** Fax 596/76-22-87. 181 units. Year-round 250€ double. Rates include full board. AE, MC, V. **Amenities:** 2 restaurants; bar; large outdoor pool; 2 tennis courts (lit); watersports equipment/rentals. *In room:* A/C, TV, hair dryer, Wi-Fi (7€ per hr.).

Ste-Luce

Between Le Diamant and Ste-Anne lies this sleepy fishing village, which is known for its fine beaches of white sand. Scuba divers flock to the waters at Pointe Figuier to the east of Ste-Luce. Most visitors come here to lodge at the hotel below or just to enjoy the beaches. You can also visit **Ecomusée de Martinique,** Anse Figuier (✆ **596/62-79-14**), which exhibits artifacts unearthed from the days of the earliest settlers, the Carib and Arawak Indians. Entrance is 3€ for adults, .75€ children 5 to 12 and students; hours are Tuesday to Thursday 8:30am to 5:30pm, Friday and Saturday 8:30am to 5pm, and Sunday 9am to 5pm.

WHERE TO STAY

Karibéa Amandiers Resort This is our favorite of three interrelated, side-by-side resorts, each of which is managed by the France-based Karibea Hotel Group. Opening directly onto the sea and a beach, it's a winning choice and imbued with a tropical ambience and a welcoming staff. In the south, this property enjoys a scenic location on a natural cove with a beach. Accommodations are found in buildings rising three floors, the upper levels reached by stairs in lieu of an elevator. The main feature of the hotel is its lovely pool, and the entire complex is set in well-landscaped tropical gardens. Many units open onto balconies and are equipped with full kitchenettes. Cane furniture and West Indian decorative motifs are used throughout. Each room comes with two bathrooms with shower. This hotel's two sister resorts are the **Karibéa Amyris** and the **Karibéa Caribéa,** each within walking distance, and clients tend to mingle around the amenities of all three. When their room count is combined, the three hotels have a total of 298 units.

Quartier Désert, 97228 Ste-Luce, Martinique, F.W.I. www.hotel-caribbean-karibea.com. ✆ **596/62-32-32.** Fax 596/62-11-92. 273 units. Winter 190€ double; off season 160€ double. AE, MC, V. **Amenities:** 2 restaurants; 2 bars; 3 outdoor pools; snorkeling; 2 tennis courts (lit). *In room:* A/C, TV, hair dryer, Wi-Fi (3€ per hr.).

Le Marin

This is the yachting capital of Martinique, lying between Ste-Luce and Ste-Anne, about an hour south from the capital of Fort-de-France. Here pleasure boats fill the protected harbor. There is also a Jesuit church from 1766 crowning the hill overlooking town, with a stone ruin next to it. From Le Marin, a signposted narrow road leads to **Cap Chevalier (Cape Knight),** one of the most panoramic lookout points on Martinique, lying about 1.5km (1 mile) from town. Waterfront restaurants specializing in seafood and clubs fill the town of Le Marin itself.

WHERE TO STAY

Club Med Buccaneer's Creek ★ Set on a tranquil cove at the southernmost tip of Martinique, Club Med is designed as a series of outbuildings evocative of a Creole village. It is set on a 22-hectare (54-acre) former pirate's hideaway at Buccaneer's Creek, amid a forest of coconut palms. The property fronts a beach of white sand with views of Diamond Rock off shore. Features include a modern spa, an "infinity edge" pool, and a beach *palapa* for yoga and fitness classes. Bedrooms are midsize and furnished tastefully and comfortably, but far from lavishly. The hotel staff provides an activity-filled agenda for its guests and a respectable cuisine of Antillean and French dishes. All winter rates include chartered round-trip flights from Atlanta, with supplements charged for flights winging in from other parts of the country to hook up with the Atlanta-based flights. In the off season, rates do not include airfare.

Pointe Marin, 97227 Ste-Anne, Martinique, F.W.I. www.clubmed.com. ✆ **888/932-3582** in the U.S., or 596/76-72-72. Fax 596/76-57-00. 293 units. Year-round 3,270€–4,500€ all-inclusive double 1 week (including round-trip passage from Atlanta). AE, DC, MC, V. **Amenities:** 2 restaurants; 3 bars; dance club; 2 outdoor pools; tennis court (lit); watersports equipment/rentals. *In room:* A/C, TV, Wi-Fi (5€ for 1 hr. or 25€ per day).

WHERE TO DINE

Le Zanzibar ★ 🎁 FRENCH/SEAFOOD/NORTH AFRICAN There's nothing finer in the south of Martinique than sitting on the second-floor veranda of this restaurant, drinking tropical punch and overseeing the yacht-clogged harbor. The restaurant is built in the courtyard style of a Moroccan *riad*. Also in the North African style, both the bar and restaurant are a series of alcoves for intimate dining and drinking. In the background, a DJ spins lounge music as you study the menu. The chef works his magic with sea bass, sea urchins, and a porc filet pignon with honey and ginger sauce. We especially like the roast duck with mango. If you didn't go for the chicken tagine, you can also order grilled shrimp, saffron-flavored cod filets on a bed of leeks, or other main-dish specialties.

Comptoir des Boucaniers, 11 bd. Allègre, Le Marin. ✆ **596/74-08-46.** Reservations required. Main courses 12€–21€. DISC, MC, V. Thurs–Sat and Mon noon–2:30pm; Thurs–Tues 7–10:30pm.

Ste-Anne

From Le Marin, an 8km (5-mile) drive brings you to Ste-Anne, at the extreme southern tip of Martinique. This sleepy little area is known for the white-sand beaches of Les Salines. (Those to the north are more grayish in color.) In many ways, these are Martinique's finest. The climate is arid, and the beaches are almost always sunny, perhaps too much so at midday. The name comes from Etang des Salines, a large salt pond forming a backdrop to the strip of sand. Manchineel trees are found at the southeastern end of the beach. ***Warning:*** Under no circumstances should you go under these trees for protection in a rainfall. When it's sunny you can seek shade here, but when it rains, drops falling from the poisonous tree will be like acid on your skin.

Holidays and weekends tend to be crowded, as many islanders and their families flock to this beach, which is just not big enough to handle the hordes.

Les Salines is also the site of Martinique's only real gay beach. Drive to the far end of the parking lot, near the sign labeled PETITE ANSE DES SALINES. Here you'll find a trail leading through woods to a sun-flooded beach often populated by naked gay men, with an occasional lesbian couple. Technically, there are no legal nudist beaches on Martinique, so it's possible you could be arrested for going nude, although authorities don't seem to enforce this. (Throughout the island, however, the European custom of topless bathing is not uncommon on any of the beaches or even around hotel pools.)

Ste-Anne opens onto views of the Sainte Lucia Canal, and nearby is the Petrified Savanna Forest, which the French call **Savane des Petrifications.** It's a field of petrified volcanic boulders in the shape of logs. The eerie, desertlike site is studded with cacti.

WHERE TO STAY

La Dunette A three-story motel-like stucco structure directly beside the sea, this hotel draws guests who appreciate its simplicity and its isolation from the more built-up resort areas of other parts of Martinique. An unpretentious seaside inn with summery decor and basic bedrooms painted in bright tropical colors, the hotel is accented with a garden filled with flowers and tropical plants. The furnishings are casual and modern, although some rooms are quite small.

97227 Ste-Anne, Martinique, F.W.I. www.ladunette.com. ✆ **596/76-73-90.** Fax 596/76-76-05. 18 units. Winter 110€ double; off season 80€ double. Rates include continental breakfast. AE, MC, V. **Amenities:** Restaurant; bar; watersports equipment/rentals; Wi-Fi (free). *In room:* A/C, TV, hair dryer.

Le François

Along the east coast of Martinique, you can stop over in Le François to visit the **Musée Rhum Clement** at the Domaine de l'Acajou (✆ **596/54-62-07**), about 2km (1¼ miles) south of the village center. The setting for this museum is an outmoded distillery in the cellar of an 18th-century mansion with period furnishings that the Clement Rum Company closed in the early 1990s, when it shifted its production to a newer plant 6km (3¾ miles) away (which cannot be visited). A Columbus exhibit is set up in caves, and other exhibits trace the institution of slavery in the islands. Products of the Clement rum distillery are prominently displayed for purchase, and tastings of some of the rums are available. The museum is in a botanic park; you could easily spend 2 or 3 hours exploring the exhibits and grounds. It's open daily from 9am to 5:30pm. Admission is 7€ for adults, 4€ for ages 7 to 18, and free for ages 6 and under.

Directly south of Le François, with Mt. Vauclin looming in the background, is the little fishing village of Vauclin, where you can find a good luncheon stopover, or else a place for a vacation retreat.

WHERE TO STAY

Rooms can also be rented at La Maison de L'Ilet Oscar (see "Dining," below).

Cap Est Lagoon Resort & Spa ★★★ Set on the island's east coast between the fishing hamlets of Vauclin and Le François—5km (3 miles) from either of them—this is the poshest and most cutting-edge hotel on Martinique. Scattered across nearly 3.5 hectares (8¾ acres) of gently sloping palm-studded beachfront, it's composed of 18 veranda-fronted one- and two-story villas housing 50 well-designed suites. This is as top of the line as you'll find in the French West Indies outside of St. Barts. It's the only government-rated five-star hotel on Martinique, and the only Relais & Châteaux in either Martinique or Guadeloupe. The venue is very French, artfully permissive, and luxurious. Topless sunbathing for women is permitted on the beach or beside any of the pools. Views throughout the resort extend outward over a coral reef to the wide blue seas. Construction and design emulates Creole models elsewhere, with ample use of louvered doors and tropical hardwoods. Each unit has a landscaped terrace or balcony. Besides the showpiece public pool, there are 36 plunge pools.

Quartier La Prairie Cap Est, 97240 Le François, Martinique, F.W.I. www.capest.com. ✆ **800/735-2478** in the U.S. and Canada, or 596/54-80-80. Fax 596/54-96-00. 50 suites. Year-round 400€–1,250€ suite. Rates include buffet or American breakfast. AE, DC, MC, V. Closed Sept to mid-Nov. **Amenities:** 2 restaurants; bar; dock for mooring of private yachts and sailboats; fishing; outdoor pool; 36 plunge pools; room service; spa; tennis court (lit). *In room:* A/C, TV, hair dryer, minibar, Wi-Fi (suites only; free).

Frégate Bleue ★ 🎁 This is the closest thing to a European B&B on the island. It's a calm and quiet choice, with touches of personal, old-fashioned charm. It's not the place for vacationers looking for nightlife and lots of activities—it's for escapists who don't mind the 10-minute drive to the beaches of St-François or the prevailing sense of isolation. Much of this ambience is the work of owner Yveline de Lucy de Fossarieu, an experienced veteran of the hotel industry. Her house is a 5-minute drive inland from the sea, and it overlooks several chains of deserted offshore islands (including Les Ilets de St-François and Les Ilets de l'Impératrice). Bedrooms are small but cozy. The site is perched in a quiet residential neighborhood high on a hill. Each room has either a terrace or a balcony, with sweeping views over the coast.

Frégate Est 4, 97240 Le François, Martinique, F.W.I. www.fregatebleue.com. ✆ **596/54-54-66.** Fax 596/54-78-48. 11 units. Winter 170€–240€ double, 240€ suite; off season 125€–160€ double, 160€ suite. Rates include breakfast. AE, MC, V. **Amenities:** Restaurant; outdoor pool. *In room:* A/C, ceiling fan, TV, kitchenette, Wi-Fi (free).

Hôtel Cap Macabou Set about 50 paces from a good beach, Martinique's newest hotel opened in November 2008 in a three-story format that features a large veranda for each of the units. Painted a shade of pale yellow, with lots of exposed brick, it's the only hotel within 24km (15 miles), but within a quiet fishing village (Le Vauclin) that has traditionally been home to scores of expatriate French "mainlanders." Life here is calm, quiet, and unpretentious, with lots of emphasis on families preparing their own meals within their own kitchens, which are positioned on each unit's veranda, along with a dining table and chairs. Management is particularly proud of the oversize swimming pool and its romantic, even theatrical lighting, as well as the beauty of the nearby beach. Decor within the accommodations includes simple, contemporary furniture; tones of white and off-white; and an occasional painting or memento by a local artist. Don't overlook this place as a nightlife option: Every Friday and Saturday night, the hotel's "second" restaurant opens in a spot adjacent to the pool for disco evenings, attended by locals from the neighborhood. The "main" restaurant is open to both residents and outsiders every day from noon to 3pm and 7:30

to 10pm. Main courses cost 15€ to 20€ and focus on international, French, and Creole cuisine.

Petit Macabou, 97280 Le Vauclin, Martinique, F.W.I. www.capmacabou.com. ✆ **596/74-24-24.** Fax 596/78-67-01. 44 units. Year-round 135€-155€ double; 290€-320€ suite. AE, DC, MC, V. **Amenities:** 2 restaurants; 2 bars; outdoor pool. *In room:* A/C, ceiling fan, kitchen, Wi-Fi (free).

Le Plein Soleil ★★ If a celebrity visits Martinique, chances are, he or she will check into this luxurious retreat, which has been featured in several magazines, mostly the French press. The serene location is on the more tranquil eastern coast, close to the village of Le François and near several good beaches. (There's a beach within a walk of about 275m/902 ft. and a formal-looking swimming pool, but in most cases, whatever distractions and diversions appeal to you, you'll have to organize on your own.) The retreat enjoys a hilltop perch, with views of the ocean (though in rainy weather, the road to Le Plein Soleil is often rough riding). The hotel also attracts a sophisticated clientele to its deluxe restaurant (see below).

Some units for rent are in Creole cottages painted in flamboyant colors. Some rooms are small but others are generous, and each comes with a terrace from where panoramic vistas unfold. Other accommodations are in two-level bungalows, each with a private plunge pool. The decoration and furnishings come, in large part, from Thailand.

Pointe Thalémont, 97240 Le François, Martinique, F.W.I. www.hotelpleinsoleil.fr. ✆ **596/38-07-77.** Fax 596/65-58-13. 16 units. Winter 170€-315€ double; off season 130€-250€ double. Breakfast 18€ per person. MC, V. 5km (3 miles) north of Le François, follow signs first to Le Robert, then veer eastward when you see the signs to Thalémont, Mansarde, and Plein Soleil. **Amenities:** Restaurant; bar; outdoor pool; room service. *In room:* A/C, TV, fridge, Wi-Fi (free).

WHERE TO DINE

La Maison de L'Ilet Oscar ★ INTERNATIONAL/FRENCH Inside an antique Creole house, this establishment lies on a nearly adjacent island off the southeast coast of Martinique; you access it by motorboat from the marina at Le François. If you make advance reservations, you'll be taken on a 12-minute boat ride to the island, stopping at an emerald-colored tidal pool where legend says that Joséphine, wife of Napoleon I, once went swimming. You'll then head to the island's only dwelling, a one-story wood-sided house that was originally built in 1898 on nearby Ilet Thierry, then disassembled and floated, beam by beam, across to Ilet Oscar and reassembled there in 1935. Menu items focus on Creole specialties like an all-fish menu, an all-shrimp menu, or an all-lobster menu, but if you desire food inspired by the traditions of mainland France, Brittany-born Jean-Louis de Lussy and his staff will whip you up avocados stuffed with crayfish, magret of duckling, or whatever else happens to be in the larder. If you want to overnight, the four bedrooms (all with shower, toilet, and double sinks) rent for 150€ to 244€ double, with breakfast included. None has TV, phone, or air-conditioning.

L'Ilet Oscar (B.P. 12), 97240 Baie du François, Martinique. ✆ **696/45-33-30.** Reservations essential 1 day in advance. Fixed-price menu 45€-55€. Round-trip transport from Le Marina du François 50€ for up to 6 passengers. AE, MC, V. Daily 11am-3pm and 6-9:30pm (dinner only for hotel guests). Closed Sept.

Le Bélem/Le Campêche ★★ FRENCH/ANTILLEAN Two of the best-recommended dining spots in Martinique lie on the Atlantic coastline. If you arrive for lunch, you'll be steered toward the less expensive and less formal of the two, Le

Campêche, an oceanfronting outdoor bistro where good-looking people in teeny bathing suits are not at all out of the ordinary. Menu items focus on tried-and-true Creole specialties, as well as salads, pastas, and well-prepared grilled fish and meats.

At Le Bélem, a romantic eatery noted for its wine list and its "gastronomic" interpretation of all things French and Antillean, dinners are more elaborate and more formal. Begin, perhaps, with a spicy shrimp gazpacho, or else foie gras on freshly baked gingerbread. You might for a main opt for a succulent version of magret of duckling with foie gras, or else linguine with scallops and truffles. Another artful dish is spiny lobster prepared three different ways: roasted with vanilla-flavored butter; as lobster ravioli; and served cold, in gelatin, with caviar.

In the Cap Est Lagoon Resort & Spa, Quartier La Prairie Cap Est. ✆ **596/54-88-11** for Campêche, **596/54-88-00** for Bélem. Reservations strongly recommended for nonresidents. Main courses 25€–40€ in Le Bélem, 15€–30€ in Le Campêche. AE, DC, MC, V. Le Bélem daily 7:30–10pm. Le Campêche daily noon–2:30pm. Closed Sept.

Le Plein Soleil ★★ 🎁 INTERNATIONAL With the noteworthy exception of the Cap Est Lagoon Resort & Spa (see above), this is the most upscale and elegant hotel in this part of Martinique. The owners have spent lots of money reworking the layouts, upgrading the accommodations, and revamping the restaurant. Meals here are taken on the wide veranda of a 1880s French colonial–style house that sits on a hillside about 90m (295 ft.) from the sea. Your host is Jean-Christophe Yo-Yo, who will organize your meal (if you phone in your intentions a day in advance) and cook the sublime food. Menu items combine the aesthetics of France and the Antilles. Among the best examples are a terrine of foie gras; an herb-enriched combination of scallops and dorado (mahimahi) in puff pastry; and a well-prepared filet of beef served with red-butter sauce.

Pointe Thalémont. ✆ **596/38-07-77.** Reservations required 1 day in advance. Fixed-price lunches 35€, dinners 45€. MC, V. Mon–Thurs 7:30–9:30pm; Fri–Sat 12:30–2:30pm and 7:30–9:30pm; Sun 12:30–2:30pm.

THE NORTH LOOP

As we swing north from Fort-de-France, our main targets are **Le Carbet, St-Pierre, Montagne Pelée,** and **Leyritz.** However, we'll sandwich in many stops along the way.

From Fort-de-France, there are three ways to head north to Montagne Pelée. The first is to follow Route N4 up to St-Joseph. From there take the left fork for 5km (3 miles), and then turn onto Route D15 toward Le Marigot.

Another option is to take Route N3 through the vegetation-rich *mornes* (hills) to Le Morne Rouge. This road is known as "Route de la Trace" and is now the center of the Parc Naturel Régional de la Martinique.

Yet a third route to Montagne Pelée is via Route N2 along the coast, and the order in which we'll list the towns along the way is as follows. Near Fort-de-France, the first town you reach is **Schoelcher.** Farther along Route N2 is **Case-Pilote,** and then Bellefontaine. This portion, along the most popular drive in Martinique—from Fort-de-France to St-Pierre—is very reminiscent of the way the French Riviera used to look. **Bellefontaine** is a small fishing village, with boats stretched along the beach. Note the many houses also built in the shape of boats.

Le Carbet

Leaving Bellefontaine, an 8km (5-mile) drive north will deliver you to Le Carbet. Columbus landed here in 1502, and the first French settlers arrived in 1635. In 1887, Gauguin lived here for 4 months before going to Tahiti. You can stop for a swim at an Olympic-size pool set into the hills, or watch the locals scrubbing clothes in a stream. The town lies on the bus route from Fort-de-France to St-Pierre.

Set in 4 hectares (10 acres) of tropical gardens, **Aqualand Martinique,** Route des Pitons, Le Carbet (✆ **596/78-40-00;** www.aqualand-mq.fr), lies on the road to St-Pierre, about an hour's drive from Fort-de-France. It features eight nautical attractions, with three especially designed for children. The big hit is a wave pool that can go from almost unnoticed sways to real breakers. Other attractions range from super slaloms to water slides, water beds, and even a minipark for kids to experience the adult attractions but on a smaller scale. Fast-food options here, including crepes and freshly made salads, are the best on the island. The park is open daily June, July, and August 10am to 5pm; admission is 20€ for adults, 16€ for children 3 to 12.

WHERE TO DINE

Chez les Pecheurs SEAFOOD/CREOLE This is arguably the most fun beach restaurant on island. The highlight occurs on Friday and Sunday nights when local bands play music on the beach as diners dance in the sand. On Saturday night a DJ rules the nighttime music. The owners used to be fishermen before they opened this seafood joint. The chef's specialty is a fisherman's platter, offering the best catch of the day. Tuna and lobster are often featured, and fresh crayfish can be seen grilling. A regional plate of rice and beans accompanies most dishes.

Plage de Grande Anse, Le Carbet. ✆ **596/76-98-39.** www.antillesresto.com/restaurant/les-pecheurs. Reservations not needed. Main courses 12€–18€. MC, V. Daily noon–4pm and 7–10pm.

Le Petibonum ★ 🎁 FRENCH/CARIBBEAN This funky beach joint comes as a delightful surprise. Guy Ferdinand, a tall islander who once worked in Florida, claims he drew inspiration from South Beach before opening this laid-back joint that serves well-prepared food in addition to drinks, including the island's most perfect mojito (even Ernest Hemingway would surely approve if he could come back). Everything is informal here, and many guests combine a dip in the sea with food and drink. For appetizers try the garlic-laced snails, or else foie gras with a fruity chutney made of fresh bananas and pears. For the main course, try the filet mignon, a tender duck breast, or tuna with a sesame sauce, or scallops and crayfish in a vanilla sauce. A live band plays on Saturday night.

Quartier Le Coin, Le Carbet. ✆ **596/78-04-34.** Main courses 15€–21€. MC, V. Daily 10am–10:30pm (until 11:30pm Sat–Sun).

St-Pierre ★

At the beginning of this century, St-Pierre was known as the "Little Paris of the West Indies." Home to 30,000 inhabitants, it was the cultural and economic capital of Martinique. On May 7, 1902, the citizens read in their daily newspaper that "Montagne Pelée does not present any more risk to the population than Vesuvius does to the Neapolitans."

However, on May 8, at 8am, the southwest side of Montagne Pelée exploded into fire and lava. At 8:02am, all 30,000 inhabitants were dead—that is, all except one. A

Photo Ops

Martinique is a photographer's dream—certainly the French fashion magazines know it, because crews are always around on shoots. The most picturesque sites are La Savane, in Fort-de-France; St-Pierre, the best place to photograph towering Montagne Pelée; La Pagerie, with its decaying ruins of a sugar factory; and the panoramic overlooks along La Trace, a serpentine road winding through the entire rainforest.

convict in his underground cell was saved by the thickness of the walls. When islanders reached the site, the convict was paroled and left Martinique to tour in Barnum and Bailey's circus.

St-Pierre never recovered its former splendor. It could now be called the Pompeii of the West Indies. Ruins of the church, the theater, and some other buildings can be seen along the coast.

Musée Volcanologique, rue Victor-Hugo, St-Pierre (✆ **596/78-15-16**), was created by the American volcanologist Franck Alvard Perret, who turned the museum over to the city in 1933. Here, in pictures and relics dug from the debris, you can trace the story of what happened to St-Pierre. Dug from the lava is a clock that stopped at the moment the volcano erupted. The museum is open daily from 9am to 5pm; admission is 2€, free for children 7 and under. About a kilometer (½ mile) away, higher up the mountain and clearly signposted, is a modern-looking museum, **Le Centre de Decouverte des Sciences de la Terre** (✆ **596/52-82-42**), containing exhibits about the region's seismology and geology, replete with public-service warnings about what to do in the event of another explosion. It's open Tuesday to Sunday 9am to 5pm September to June, and 10am to 6pm in July and August. Admission is 5€ for adults, 3€ students and children 6 to 16, and free for children 5 and under.

WHERE TO DINE

Le Fromager ★ 🎁 CREOLE/FRENCH Set less than 1km (½ mile) east of the center of St-Pierre, this indoor-outdoor villa, owned by the René Dement family, welcomes luncheon guests with a humor and charm that's part French, part Martiniquais. The restaurant, which resembles a covered open-air pavilion, has a sweeping view of the town. Recommended dishes include marinated octopus, crayfish, and whatever grilled fish is available that day. This is a good lunch stopover during your tour of the island.

Route de Fonds-St-Denis, Quartier St. James, St-Pierre. ✆ **596/78-19-07.** Reservations recommended on Sun. Main courses 8€–15€. MC, V. Tues–Sun 8am–5pm.

Le Precheur

From St-Pierre, you can continue along the coast north to Le Prêcheur. Once the home of Madame de Maintenon, the mistress of Louis XIV, it's the last village along the northern coast of Martinique. Here you can see hot springs of volcanic origin and the **Tombeau des Caraïbes (Tomb of the Caribs),** where, according to legend, the collective suicide of many West Indian natives took place after they returned from a fishing expedition and found their homes pillaged by the French.

WHERE TO STAY & DINE

Habitation Anse Couleuvre Few other hotels in Martinique boast as colorful an agrarian and colonial past as the farm on which this much-restored, much-rebuilt, small-scale manor house stands. Much of what you'll see today dates from 50 years ago, but between the 17th and early 20th centuries, the site functioned as a working plantation with scores of workers, thousands of cocoa plants, and a reputation for rum, cocoa, and citrus byproducts that extended as far away as France and, later, the U.S. Today the retreat sits in an isolated beach-fronting location about 35 bumpy, potholed kilometers (22 miles) from the hamlet of Prêcheur, near the extreme northern tip of Martinique. Ringed with airy verandas, it's a shadow of its former grandeur, but a relaxing and isolated bastion of Creole nostalgia. On the premises is a restaurant that's open to the public every day for fixed-price lunches at 22€ to 32€, from 11am to 4pm. Dinners, priced at 48€ to 58€, are available only to residents of the hotel, from 7:30 to 9:30pm. Don't come here looking for luxury, since it's cozy, down-home, and laissez-faire.

Anse Couleuvre, 97250 Prêcheur, Martinique, F.W.I. www.anse-couleuvre.com/nos_prestations.php. ✆ **596/52-97-74.** 4 units. Year-round 110€–140€ double. Rates include breakfast. No credit cards. Closed Sept–Nov. **Amenities:** Restaurant; bar; offshore excursions w/local fishermen. *In room:* Ceiling fan.

Montagne Pelee ★

A panoramic and winding road (Rte. N2) takes you through a tropical rainforest. The curves are of the hairpin variety, and the road is not always kept in good shape. However, you're rewarded with tropical flowers, baby ferns, plumed bamboo, and valleys so deeply green you'll think you're wearing cheap sunglasses.

The village of **Morne Rouge,** right at the foot of Montagne Pelée, is a popular vacation spot for Martiniquais. From here on, a narrow and unreliable road brings you to a level of 750m (2,461 ft.) above sea level, 480m (1,575 ft.) under the round summit of the volcano that destroyed St-Pierre. Montagne Pelée itself rises 1,373m (4,505 ft.) above sea level.

If you're a serious mountain climber and you don't mind 4 or 5 hours of hiking, you can scale the peak, though you should hire an experienced guide to accompany you. Remember, this is a real mountain, rain is frequent, and temperatures drop very low. Tropical growth often hides deep crevices in the earth, and there are other dangers. The park service maintains more than 150km (93 miles) of trails. Although the hikes up from Grand-Rivière or Le Prêcheur are generally the less arduous of the three options leading to the top, most visitors opt for departures from Morne Rouge because it doesn't take as long to finish the trip. It's steeper, rockier, and more exhausting, but you can make it in just 2½ hours versus the 5 hours it takes from the other two towns. There are no facilities other than these villages, so it's vital to bring water and food with you. Your arduous journey will be rewarded at the summit with sweeping views over the sea and panoramas that sometimes stretch as far as mountainous Dominica to the south. As for the volcano, its deathly eruption in 1902 apparently satisfied it—for the time being.

Upon your descent from Montagne Pelée, drive down to **Ajoupa-Bouillon,** one of the most beautiful towns on Martinique. Abounding in flowers and shrubbery with bright yellow-and-red leaves, this little village is the site of the remarkable **Gorges de la Falaise.** These are minicanyons on the Falaise River, up which you can travel to reach a waterfall. Ajoupa-Bouillon also makes a good lunch stop.

Grand-Riviere

After Basse-Pointe, the town you reach on your northward trek is Grand-Rivière. From here you must turn back, but before doing so, you may want to stop for a bite to eat.

WHERE TO DINE

Yva Chez Vava ★ 🎁 FRENCH/CREOLE Directly west of Basse-Pointe, in a low-slung building painted the peachy-orange of a paw-paw fruit, Yva Chez Vava is a combination private home and restaurant. It represents the hard labor of three generations of Creole women. Infused with a simple country-inn style, it was established in 1979 by a well-remembered, long-departed matron, Vava, whose daughter, Yva, is now assisted by her own daughter, Rosy. Family recipes are the mainstay of this modest and very ethnic bistro. A la carte items include Creole soup, crayfish, shark steak, and various *colombos* (curries). Local delicacies include *z'habitants* (crayfish), *vivaneau* (red snapper), *accras de morue* (codfish beignets), roasted or curried goat, and court bouillon of fish. Occasionally available during certain periods are the very ethnic, and not-to-everyone's taste, *aceras de titiris,* hundreds of tiny *des titiris* (barely visible fish) which are caught with nets as they swarm in the nearby river. These—heads, skeletons, and all—are mixed with flour, herbs, and spices, and deep-fried in oil into *aceras* (fritters).

Before or after their meal, clients can bathe in the nearby river or walk to an unnamed strip of sand, the nearest beach, which lies about .4km (¼ mile) from the restaurant.

Bd. Général-de-Gaulle. ✆ **596/55-72-55.** Reservations recommended. Main courses 10€–30€. AE, MC, V. Thurs–Tues noon–3:30pm.

Ste-Marie

Heading south along the coastal road, you'll pass Le Marigot en route to the little town of Ste-Marie. **Musée du Rhum Saint-James,** route de l'Union at the Saint James Distillery (✆ **596/69-50-37**), displays engravings, antique tools and machines, and other exhibits tracing the history of sugar cane and rum from 1765 to the present. Guided tours of the distillery are offered daily from February to June at 10am, 11:30am, and 1:30pm. Tours cost 5€ per person. Admission to the museum (daily 9am to 5pm, regardless of whether the distillery is functioning) is free. Rum is available for purchase on-site.

From here you can head out the north end of town and loop inland a bit for a stop at Morne des Esses, or continue heading south straight to Trinité.

Trinite

Passing through Morne des Esses, continue south, then turn east; or from Ste-Marie, head south along the coastal route (N1), to reach Trinité. The town is the gateway to the Caravelle peninsula, where the **Caravelle Nature Preserve,** a well-protected peninsula jutting into the Atlantic Ocean from the town of Trinité, has safe beaches and well-marked trails through tropical wetlands and to the ruins of historic Château Debuc. It offers excellent hiking and one of the only safe beaches for swimming on the Atlantic coast. It would hardly merit an actual stop, however, were it not for the Domaine Saint Aubin.

WHERE TO STAY & DINE

Le Domaine Saint Aubin ★ This restored three-story Victorian house is architecturally one of the loveliest inns in the Caribbean. With fancy gingerbread, the hotel was originally built in 1920 of brick and poured concrete as a replacement for a much older wood-sided house, which served as the seat of a large plantation. It sits on a hillside above sugar-cane fields and the bay, 3km (2 miles) from the village of Trinité itself. The nearest beach is Plage Cosmy, lying 1.5km (1 mile) from the hotel. The bedrooms are spacious and modern, with 19th-century furnishings, and there are some family rooms as well.

97220 Trinité, Martinique, F.W.I. www.ledomainesaintaubin.com. ✆ **596/69-34-77.** Fax 596/69-41-14. 28 units. Winter 160€–220€ double; off season 100€–145€ double. MC, V. **Amenities:** Exercise room; outdoor pool. *In room:* A/C, Wi-Fi (free).

La Table de Mamy Nounou FRENCH/ANTILLEAN Set less than 1km (½ mile) east of the fishing village of Tartane, this is the most easterly restaurant in the most easterly hotel on La Caravelle peninsula. The setting, as created and maintained by a team of English-speaking expatriates from the French mainland, is idyllic, a renovated complex perched within a hill-hugging compound of veranda-fronted buildings overlooking the sea. The restaurant is the main allure of the well-managed and carefully maintained Hotel Caravelle.

Lunches are faster, and less elaborately orchestrated, than the candlelit dinners, where guests linger longer within an ambience that falls midway between what you'd expect on the French mainland and what you find in Fort-de-France. Menu items change frequently but might include a *colombo* (spicy Creole stew) concocted from fish, or chicken; braised filets of red mullet with tropical fruits; or, depending on the mood of the chef, classic dishes such as foie gras. Desserts might feature a semi-moist version of chocolate cake, or perhaps a rum-and-orange-flavored soufflé. There's dining on the veranda, easy access to a garden, and, from virtually all points, a sweeping view of the sea.

On-site are 15 studio apartments, each with telephone, air-conditioning, ceiling fans, a kitchenette, and TV. Accommodations rent for 61€ to 84€ double.

In the Hotel Caravelle, Rte. du Château Dubuc, L'Anse l'Etang, Trinité. ✆ **596/58-07-32.** www.hotel-la-caravelle-martinique.com. Reservations recommended for nonresidents of the hotel. Lunch platters and salads 16€–22€; fixed-price dinner 25€. MC, V. Wed–Mon noon–2pm and 7–9:30pm. Closed June and Sept.

16 PUERTO RICO

No one gets bored on Puerto Rico, which pulsates with more life than any other island in the Caribbean. There's something going on here 24/7 for visitors of all tastes. Puerto Rico has a wide array of watersports, golf courses, resorts, and casinos; there's more dance and music clubs than anywhere in the Caribbean; and the shopping is among the most developed and varied, with bargains that rival those of St. Thomas. Puerto Rico also has cultural and historic treasures, picturesque and refreshing mountain towns, virgin rainforest, and all the attractions of a big city metropolis in San Juan.

ESSENTIALS

Visitor Information

For information before you leave home, visit **www.gotopuertorico.com** or contact the **Puerto Rico Tourism Company** offices at La Princesa Building, Paseo La Princesa 2, Old San Juan, PR 00902 (✆ **800/866-7827** or 787/721-2400; www.seepuertorico.com).

Other Tourism Company offices are located at **Luís Muñoz Marín Airport** (✆ **787/791-1014**), open December to April daily from 9am to 10pm, May to November daily 9am to 8pm; and **La Casita,** at Plaza de la Darsena, Old San Juan, near Pier 1, where the cruise ships come in (✆ **787/722-1709**). This office is open Saturday through Wednesday from 8:30am to 8pm, Thursday and Friday 8:30am to 5pm.

There are several tourism-related websites on Puerto Rico, including the official Puerto Rico Tourism Company site at www.seepuertorico.com. Some of the best are dedicated to specific areas: the **Tourism Association of Rincón** (www.rincon.org), **The Vieques Travel Information Portal** (www.enchanted-isle.com), and **Discover Culebra** (www.culebra-island.com). **Puerto Rico Travel Maps** (www.travelmaps.com) offers useful interactive and downloadable travel maps, while **EyeTour Puerto Rico** (http://places.eyetour.com) offers travel videos of sites, attractions, hotels, and restaurants. Ask for a copy of ***Qué Pasa,*** the official visitors' guide, which is distributed free at many hotels and restaurants. ***Bienvenidos,*** a publication of the Puerto Rico Hotel & Tourism Association, is also chock-full of up-to-date visitor information and is also distributed free at island hotels.

Puerto Rico

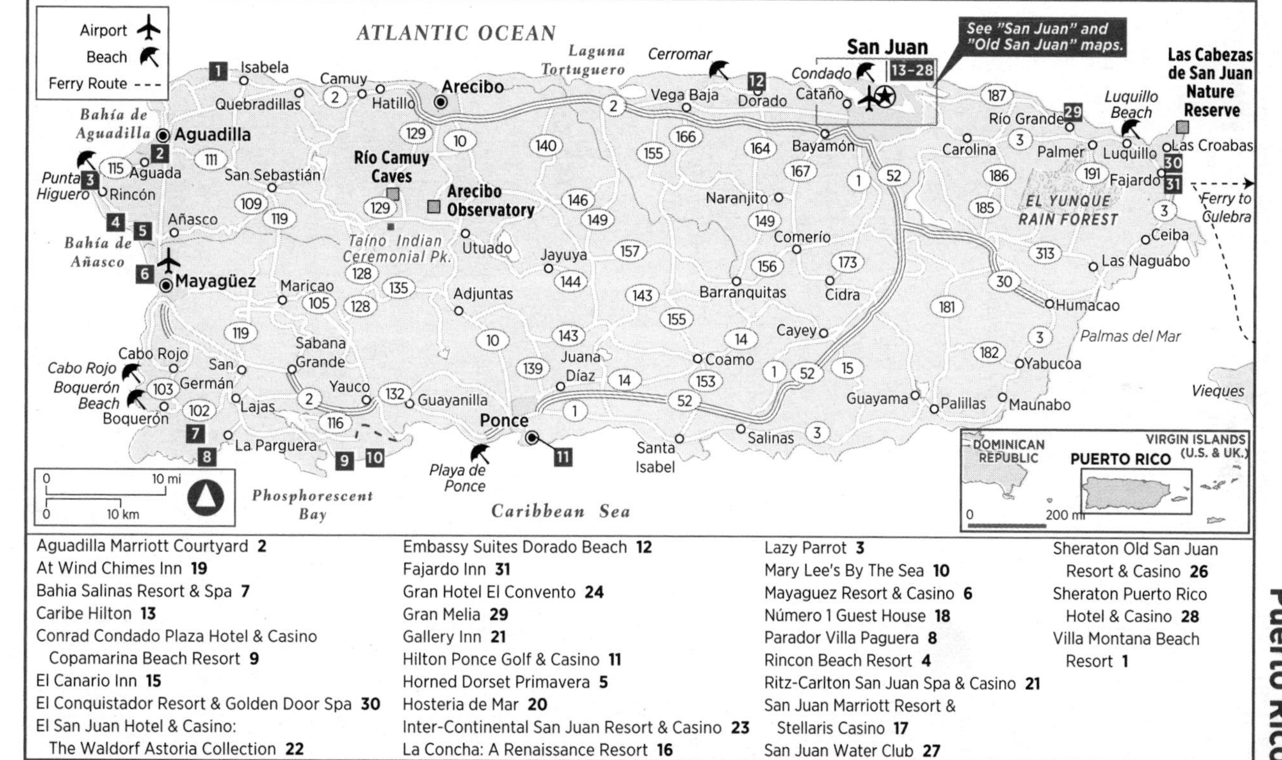
Airport
Beach
Ferry Route
ATLANTIC OCEAN
Caribbean Sea
See "San Juan" and "Old San Juan" maps.
San Juan
13-28
Las Cabezas de San Juan Nature Reserve
Bahía de Aguadilla
Bahía de Añasco
Laguna Tortuguero
Phosphorescent Bay
Cerromar
Condado
Luquillo Beach
Punta Higuero
Cabo Rojo
Boquerón Beach
Playa de Ponce
Isabela
Camuy
Quebradillas
Hatillo
Arecibo
Aguadilla
Aguada
Rincón
San Sebastián
Añasco
Mayagüez
Río Camuy Caves
Arecibo Observatory
Taíno Indian Ceremonial Pk.
Utuado
Jayuya
Adjuntas
Maricao
Sabana Grande
Yauco
Guayanilla
Ponce
Juana Díaz
San Germán
Lajas
Boquerón
La Parguera
Vega Baja
Dorado
Cataño
Bayamón
Naranjito
Comerío
Barranquitas
Cidra
Cayey
Coamo
Santa Isabel
Salinas
Guayama
Palillas
Maunabo
Yabucoa
Humacao
Palmas del Mar
Las Naguabo
Ceiba
Fajardo
Luquillo
Palmer
Río Grande
Carolina
Las Croabas
EL YUNQUE RAIN FOREST
Ferry to Culebra
Vieques
DOMINICAN REPUBLIC
PUERTO RICO
VIRGIN ISLANDS (U.S. & UK.)
0 200 mi
0 10 mi
0 10 km
Aguadilla Marriott Courtyard 2
At Wind Chimes Inn 19
Bahia Salinas Resort & Spa 7
Caribe Hilton 13
Conrad Condado Plaza Hotel & Casino
Copamarina Beach Resort 9
El Canario Inn 15
El Conquistador Resort & Golden Door Spa 30
El San Juan Hotel & Casino:
The Waldorf Astoria Collection 22
Embassy Suites Dorado Beach 12
Fajardo Inn 31
Gran Hotel El Convento 24
Gran Melia 29
Gallery Inn 21
Hilton Ponce Golf & Casino 11
Horned Dorset Primavera 5
Hosteria de Mar 20
Inter-Continental San Juan Resort & Casino 23
La Concha: A Renaissance Resort 16
Lazy Parrot 3
Mary Lee's By The Sea 10
Mayaguez Resort & Casino 6
Número 1 Guest House 18
Parador Villa Paguera 8
Rincon Beach Resort 4
Ritz-Carlton San Juan Spa & Casino 21
San Juan Marriott Resort &
Stellaris Casino 17
San Juan Water Club 27
Sheraton Old San Juan
Resort & Casino 26
Sheraton Puerto Rico
Hotel & Casino 28
Villa Montana Beach
Resort 1

Getting There

The **Luis Muñoz Marín International Airport** in Isla Verde has 63 daily flights to 20 U.S. cities and nonstop service to Caracas, Madrid, Toronto, London, and Panama. In 2009, 8.3 million passengers moved through it, and the airport services more than 20 airlines.

American Airlines (✆ **800/433-7300** in the U.S. and Canada; www.aa.com) offers daily nonstop flights to San Juan from Chicago, Dallas–Fort Worth, Hartford, Los Angeles, Miami, Newark, New York (JFK), Orlando, and Fort Lauderdale, plus flights to San Juan from both Montréal and Toronto, with changes in Chicago or Miami. In 2011 it discontinued nonstop service between San Juan and Boston, Philadelphia, Baltimore, Tampa, and Santo Domingo, Dominican Republic, bringing its daily flight average from 25 to 18, but increased service on popular routes like Miami and New York.

AirTran Airways (✆ **800/247-8726;** www.airtran.com) flies nonstop twice a day to San Juan from Tampa.

Delta (✆ **800/221-1212** in the U.S. and Canada; www.delta.com) has several daily nonstop flights from Atlanta: four on Monday, Tuesday, and Wednesday; five on Thursday and Friday; and six on Saturday and Sunday. Flights into Atlanta from around the world are frequent, with excellent connections from points throughout Delta's network in the South and Southwest. It also has nonstop flights daily from Detroit, Memphis, Minneapolis/St. Paul, and New York.

United Airlines (✆ **800/538-2929** in the U.S. and Canada; www.united.com) offers one daily nonstop flight from Chicago and Philadelphia to San Juan. United also offers flights to San Juan from both Memphis and Minneapolis, with a schedule that varies according to the season and the day of the week.

US Airways (✆ **800/622-1015** in the U.S. and Canada; www.usairways.com) has two daily direct flights between Charlotte, North Carolina, and San Juan. The airline also offers three daily nonstop flights to San Juan from Philadelphia, and one daily nonstop Saturday and Sunday flight to San Juan from Pittsburgh.

Continental Airlines (✆ **800/231-0856** in the U.S. and Canada; www.continental.com) flies nonstop daily from Newark and Houston. The airline also flies from Newark direct to the northwestern airport outside Aguadilla, should you wish to begin your tour of Puerto Rico in the west. In winter service is increased to daily flights. Continental offers one weekly flight from Detroit to San Juan.

JetBlue (✆ **800/538-2583** in the U.S. and Canada; www.jetblue.com) flies nonstop to San Juan from New York's JFK Airport; Fort Lauderdale; Orlando; Jacksonville; Tampa; Washington, D.C.; and Boston. There is also direct service to Aguadilla from New York and connecting service to several other East Coast stops. The airline also serves dozens of other U.S. cities, including Boston, Las Vegas, San Diego, and Seattle.

Spirit Air (✆ **800/772-7117** in the U.S. and Canada; www.spiritair.com) offers two daily nonstop flights from Orlando and one from Fort Lauderdale to San Juan, plus connecting flights to several other cities. It also has a nonstop flight to Aguadilla.

Canadians can fly **Air Canada** (✆ **888/247-2262** in the U.S. and Canada; www.aircanada.com) from either Montréal or Toronto to San Juan.

Puerto Rico is still a major transportation hub of the Caribbean, with the best connections for getting anywhere in the islands, but service in this area has also seen cuts. In addition to **American Eagle** (✆ **800/433-7300** in the U.S. and Canada;

www.aa.com), **Cape Air** (✆ **800/352-0714** in the U.S. and Canada; www.flycapeair.com) links two of the major islands of the U.S. Virgin Islands, St. Thomas and St. Croix, as well as Tortola in the B.V.I., with San Juan. American Eagle cut service in 2011 from San Juan to Haiti, Trinidad, and the Dominican Republic resorts of La Romana and Puerta Plata, among other routes, cutting its average daily flights from 33 to 23.

British travelers can take several **British Airways** (✆ **800/247-9297** in the U.S. and Canada; www.britishairways.com) connecting flights to San Juan from London. There are also several connections to San Juan from Europe via Continental, American, and United. **Iberia** (✆ **800/772-4642** in the U.S. and Canada, or 902/400-500 in Spain; www.iberia.com) has three weekly nonstop flights from Madrid to San Juan, leaving on Sunday, Tuesday, and Saturday. American has nonstop flights on Sunday and Tuesday.

Getting Around

BY PLANE **Cape Air** (✆ **800/352-0714** in the U.S. and Canada; www.flycapeair.com) flies from Luis Muñoz Marín International Airport to Mayagüez, Ponce, and Vieques several times a day. It also offers many flights daily to St. Thomas, St. Croix, and Tortola.

Seaborne Airlines (✆ **888/359-8687** in the U.S. and Canada; www.seaborneonline.com) offers daily links between St. Croix and St. Thomas with San Juan, as well as service to Vieques. The one-way cost from the U.S. Virgin Islands to Puerto Rico ranges from $90 to $150 per person; planes are small, carrying 15 to 19 passengers, but flights are frequent, often with more than 50 flights a day. Seaborne serves both the LMM and Isla Grande airports in San Juan.

LIAT (✆ **800/844-LIAT** [5428] in the U.S. and Canada; www.liatairline.com) provides an air link to the Lesser Antilles islands.

BY RENTAL CAR Puerto Rico offers some of the most scenic drives in all the Caribbean. Driving is the best way to discover its little hidden beaches, coastal towns, mountain villages, vast forests, and national parks. In fact, if you want to explore the island in any depth, driving a private car is about the only way, as public transportation is woefully inadequate.

Of course, if you want to stay only in San Juan, having a car is not necessary. You can get around San Juan on foot or by bus, taxi, and, in some cases, hotel minivan. There's also now the Tren Urbano, an elevated rail from the outskirts of Santurce through metro San Juan and its western suburbs.

Driving in Puerto Rico, depending on the routes you take, can lead to a number of frustrating experiences. Local drivers are often dangerous; older coastal highways provide the most scenic routes but are often congested; and in the mountainous interior, some roads are just too narrow to drive, especially circuitous routes that swing along cliff sides. However, modern highways now circumvent nearly the entire island, extending even to the center of the island. And authorities have been cracking down on speeding and reckless driving, which has improved conditions somewhat. ***Warning:*** Distances are often posted in kilometers rather than miles (1 mile = 1.61km), but speed limits are displayed in miles per hour.

Reliable local agencies include **Target Car Rental** (✆ **800/934-6457;** www.targetrentacar.com) and **Charlie Car Rental** (✆ **800/289-1227;** www.charliecars.com). Larger players are also here: **Avis** (✆ **800/331-1212** in the U.S. and Canada, and 800/230-4898 or 787/253-5926 in Puerto Rico; www.avis.com), **Budget**

(✆ **800/527-0700** in the U.S., or 800/472-3325 outside the U.S.; www.budget.com), or **Hertz** (✆ **800/654-3001** in the U.S. and Canada, or 787/791-0840; www.hertz.com). Each of these companies offers minivan transport to its office and car depot. Be alert to the minimum-age requirements for car rentals in Puerto Rico. Avis, Hertz, and Budget require renters to be 21 or older.

BY PUBLIC TRANSPORTATION ***Públicos*** are cars or vans that provide low-cost transportation. They usually operate only during daylight hours, carry up to six passengers at a time, and charge rates that are loosely regulated. Although prices are low, this option is slow and inconvenient, with frequent and erratic stops, and is used primarily by locals who cannot afford any other means.

Most *públicos* operate from a town's main square. In San Juan, main staging areas include Old San Juan's Plaza Colón, Santurce, and Río Piedras. Information about *público* routes between San Juan and Mayagüez is available from **Lineas Sultana,** Calle Esteban González 898, Urbanización Santa Rita, Río Piedras (✆ **787/765-9377**). Information about *público* routes between San Juan and Ponce is available from **Choferes Unidos de Ponce,** Terminal de Carros Públicos, Calle Vive, Ponce (✆ **787/764-0540**). Major public car centers, from which several routes can be taken, are outside the airport in Isla Verde and outside Old San Juan. Fares from San Juan to Ponce cost about $20; from San Juan to Mayagüez, it's $35.

SIGHTSEEING TOURS **Puerto Rico Tours,** Condo Inter-Suite, Ste. 5M, Isla Verde, San Juan (✆ **787/306-1540** or 791-5479), offers specially conducted private sightseeing tours of Puerto Rico, including trips to the rainforest, Luquillo Beach, the caves of Camuy, and other attractions, such as a restored Taíno Indian village.

Backstage Partners (✆ **787/791-0099;** fax 787/748-0583; www.backstagepartners.com) offers customized tours that take in a wide range of island attractions, including eco-tours, deep-sea fishing, scuba diving and snorkeling, safaris, and golf packages.

Other leading escorted tour operators include **Atlantic San Juan Tours** (✆ **787/644-9841;** www.puertoricoexcursions.com), which covers all the major sights of the island, from Ponce to El Yunque; and **Sunshine Tours** (✆ **787/698-9667;** www.puerto-rico-sunshinetours.com), which covers much of the same ground as the others. **Legends of Puerto Rico** (✆ **787/605-9060;** www.legendsofpr.com) hosts personalized tours, specializing in entertaining cultural and nature adventure tours.

If you'd like to experience Puerto Rico on horseback, **Hacienda Caribalí** (✆ **787/889-5820** or 889-4954; www.haciendacarabalipuertorico.com), offers 2-hour tours on majestic Paso Fino horses that take riders along the Mamayes River in the shadow of El Yunque rainforest for $60. The 600-acre ranch also offers four-track and mountain-bike tours, and has a go-kart track. **Tropical Trail Rides** (✆) **787/872-9256;** www.tropicaltrailrides.com) gives beach tours on Paso Fino horses at a beautiful locale in Isabela, which has cavernous cliffs and tropical forests, as well as at the 2,200-acre Hacienda Campo Rico in Carolina, in the San Juan metropolitan area. There are a number of tours, including a sunset ride, but most last 2 hours. Prices start at $40.

Several other tour operators cater to special tastes, including **Castillo Tours & Travel Service,** 101 Calle Doncella, Punta Las Marias, San Juan (✆ **787/791-6195;** www.castillotours.com), which is known for some of the best deep-sea fishing, and rainforest and catamaran tours.

Special Events

The **Casals Festival,** staged annually in late February and early March, is the Caribbean's most celebrated cultural event. The bill at San Juan's Performing Arts Center includes an array of international guest conductors, orchestras, and soloists who come to honor the memory of Pablo Casals, the renowned cellist who was born in Spain to a Puerto Rican mother and who died in Puerto Rico in 1973. Tickets range from $20 to $80; a 50% discount is offered to students, seniors, and persons with disabilities. Tickets are available through the **Puerto Rico Symphonic Orchestra** in San Juan (✆ **787/721-7727**), the **Luis A. Ferré Performing Arts Center** (✆ **787/620-4444**), or **Ticket Center** (✆ **787/792-5000**). Information is also available from the **Casals Festival** (✆ **787/721-8370;** www.festcasalspr.gobierno.pr). The festivities take place from late February to early March.

Old San Juan's **San Sebastián Street Festival** takes place along the street that bears its name over a long weekend in mid-January (coinciding with Martin Luther King, Jr.'s birthday). It's one of the biggest parties in the Caribbean—with art, live music, food, and dancing from day to night to day again. Call ✆ **787/721-2400.**

The Puerto Rico Heineken Jazz Festival (787/277-9200; www.prheinekenjazz.com) turned 20 in 2010; for 2 decades, it has hosted the biggest names in Latin jazz and related music to an intimate San Juan venue during a long weekend in late spring.

The island's **Carnival** celebrations feature float parades, dancing, and street parties in the week leading up to Ash Wednesday. The festivities in **Ponce** are marked by masqueraders wearing brightly painted horned masks, the crowning of a Carnival queen, and the closing "burial of the sardine." Hotel rates go up at this time of year, sometimes considerably. For more information, call the Ponce Cultural Development Office at ✆ **787/284-4141.**

San Juan also hosts several culinary festivals that are worth attending. **The SoFo Culinary Fest** takes place in June and December in Old San Juan. Four blocks near Calle Colón are closed down for a culinary street party with about 40 restaurants serving delicacies of all stripes alfresco.

Eco Xcursion Aquatica, Route 191, Km 1.7, Río Grande, Fajardo (✆ **787/888-2887**), offers some of the best rainforest hikes and mountain-bike tours for both individuals and groups. It also offers kayak tours to one of several **bioluminescent bays ★★** in Fajardo, where you enter the water at dusk and paddle through calm water teeming with small marine organisms that respond to the slightest touch by glowing an eerie greenish yellow. **Las Tortugas Adventures,** P.O. Box 1637, Canóvanas (✆ **787/809-0253** or 787/637-8356; www.kayak-pr.com), also runs tours to Fajardo's biobay, as well as river tours of the rainforest and Piñones wetlands, and kayaking/snorkeling trips to deserted beaches, rimmed with reefs and teeming schools of tropical fish. **Aventuras Tierra Adentro** (✆ **787/766-0470;** www.aventuraspr.com) offers the best island adventure tours, focusing on hiking through virgin forests, rock climbing, or cliff jumping. Four different adventures are offered, costing $150 per person, which includes transportation from San Juan. Most of the jaunts take place on weekends.

Banks Most major U.S. banks have branches with **ATMs** in the cities and are open Monday to Friday from 8:30am to 4pm. Bank branches in malls are also open on Saturday from 8:30am to 6pm and Sunday from 9am to 3pm.

Currency The **U.S. dollar** is the coin of the realm. Canadian currency is accepted by some big hotels in San Juan, although reluctantly. *Prices in this chapter are quoted in U.S. dollars.*

Documents Since Puerto Rico is part of the United States, American citizens do not need a passport or visa. Canadians and citizens of the United Kingdom must have a passport.

Electricity The electricity is 110-volt AC (60 cycles), the same as in the United States and Canada.

Emergencies Call ✆ **911.**

Language English is understood at the big resorts and in most of San Juan, though it's polite to at least greet people in Spanish and ask if they speak English before you make assumptions. Out in the island, Spanish is still *número uno,* but there's someone everywhere who speaks English.

Safety Use common sense and take precautions. Muggings are rare in tourist areas, so you should confine your moonlit-beach nights to the fenced-in and guarded areas around some of the major hotels. The countryside of Puerto Rico is safer than San Juan, but caution is always the rule. Avoid narrow little country roads and isolated beaches day or night.

Taxes There's a government tax of 9% in regular hotels or 12% in hotels with casinos. The airport departure tax is included in the price of your ticket. There is a 7% sales tax on most items.

Telephone Puerto Rico is on the North American telephone system; the most common area code is **787,** but a newer **939** also exists. Place a call to or from Puerto Rico just as you would from within the United States or Canada.

Time Puerto Rico is on Atlantic Standard Time year-round, putting it 1 hour ahead of U.S. Eastern Standard Time. In winter, when it's noon in Miami, it's 1pm in San Juan. But during daylight saving time on the U.S. East Coast, Puerto Rico and the East Coast keep the same time.

Tipping Some hotels add a 10% service charge to your bill. If they don't, you're expected to tip for services rendered. Tip as you would in the United States (15%–20%).

Water The water in Puerto Rico is generally safe to drink, although you may prefer bottled water. Many locals do.

Weather Puerto Rico is cooler than most of the other Caribbean islands because of its northeast trade winds. Sea, land, and mountain breezes also help keep the temperatures at a comfortable level. The climate is fairly stable all year, with an average temperature of 76°F (24°C). The only variants are found in the mountain regions, where the temperature fluctuates between 66°F and 76°F (19°C–24°C), and on the north coast, where the temperature ranges from 70°F to 80°F (21°C–27°C). There is no real rainy season, but August is the wettest month.

SAN JUAN ★★★

San Juan, Puerto Rico's buzzing capital, preserves the island's Spanish heritage in its colonial neighborhoods. The cobblestone streets of Old San Juan teem with restaurants and shops and a large concentration of art galleries and museums. New San Juan has its charms as well, particularly in its more storied residential architecture in Santurce and Miramar. Golden sand fronts the coastal areas of Ocean Park and Isla

Verde, where peaceful sunsets rub shoulders with a nightlife that rocks until the early morning.

Things to Do Escape the high-rises and highways of central San Juan for the cobbled streets in the walled city of **Old San Juan**, lined with Spanish townhouses decorated with wrought-iron balconies. **Castillo de San Felipe del Morro**, perched on a rocky promontory, provides a view of the entire city. San Juaneros head to the golden sands of **Isla Verde Beach** to swim and snorkel in the calm, clear waters. Hop on a ferry and tour the nearby Bacardi Distillery. At nearby **Luquillo Beach**, families swim in the calm waters.

Shopping Expect to find bargains galore in Puerto Rico, from luxury goods to local crafts. Browse the couture emporiums on **Avenida Ashford** in **Condado**, or look for trendy clothes and electronics at **Plaza Las Americas**, the biggest mall in the Caribbean. A stroll down the narrow side streets of **Old San Juan** reveals shops filled with ***vejigantes*** (painted Carnival masks), unique souvenirs, books and jewelry.

Nightlife & Entertainment Nightlife starts late, with high-rollers rolling the dice in San Juan's **casinos** and Latin beats pouring out from funky beach bars on **Isla Verde**. In **Old San Juan**, head uphill to **Calle San Sebastián** and **Calle Cristo** for a lively mix of bars and restaurants. To get into the clubs and discos, be sure to dress to impress. On Sunday nights, sip rum cocktails and watch the sun set over Old San Juan in the evocative **Paseo de la Princesa**.

Restaurants & Dining San Juan holds many global culinary surprises including splash-worthy steakhouses and sushi emporiums in **Isla Verde**, or casual Italian and Mexican eateries in **Condado**. Sample the island's rustic ***criolla*** cuisine, a blend of Spanish and African influences, in rustic spots in **Old San Juan**. Fresh catches of red snapper (*chillo*) and dolphinfish (*dorado*) are two widely available local favorites. Street-food aficionados will delight in **codfish fritters** or deep-fried cheese. Wash it down with black coffee, ***Cuba Libre*** rum cocktails, or cold beer.

San Juan Essentials

ARRIVING Dozens of taxis line up outside the airport to meet arriving flights, so you rarely have to wait. The island's **Puerto Rico Tourism Company** (**© 787/999-2100** for the transportation division) sets flat rates between the Luís Muñoz Marín Airport and major tourist zones as follows: from the airport to any hotel in Isla Verde, $10; to any hotel in the Condado district, $15; and to any hotel in Old San Juan, $19. At the airport, a dispatcher will give you a ticket with the fare. A 50¢ fuel charge began to be levied on all fares in February 2011. There are also baggage fees (50¢ for the first three bags, $1 for every bag after). Tips of between 10% and 15% of that fare are expected.

There are a number of companies offering limousine service, from Lincoln Town Car limousines to deluxe stretch Hummers. Service must be prearranged. A simple airport pickup to a San Juan hotel can cost from $100 to $125. Other trips are generally $70 to $125 an hour, with most vehicles sitting six. Many companies offer tours, with drivers doubling as guides, to places such as Old San Juan or El Yunque. They are listed in the telephone guide under *limosinas.*

VISITOR INFORMATION Tourist information is available at the **Luís Muñoz Marín Airport** (**© 787/791-1014**) daily from 9am to 10pm (Dec–Apr) and 9am to 8pm (May–Nov). Another office is at **La Casita,** Pier 1, Old San Juan

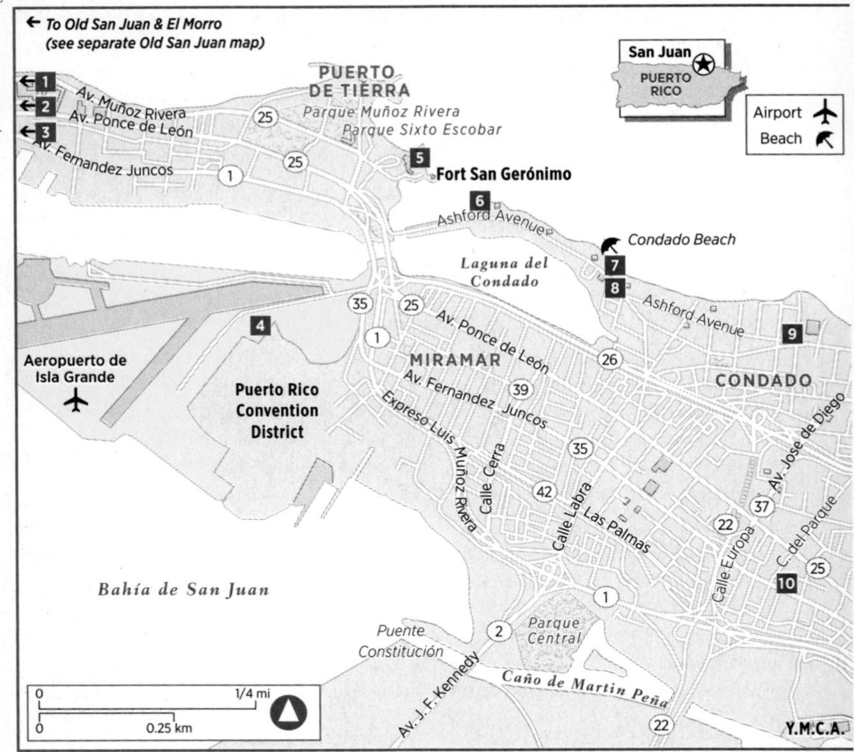

(✆ **787/722-1709**), open Saturday to Wednesday 9am to 8pm, and Thursday and Friday 8:30am to 6:30pm.

ORIENTATION **Old San Juan** sits on an elevated headland at the end of a peninsula leading into the sprawling city of San Juan. Leaving the historic zone (a 2.5-sq.-km/1-sq.-mile area bordered by San Juan Bay and the Atlantic Ocean) over land to the east, the next neighborhood is **Puerta de Tierra,** which contains important government buildings like the Capitol and the Supreme Court; a huge park and a public beach; plus two of the island's most famous hotels, the Caribe Hilton and the Normandie. It's also a literal translation of its name, a bridge of land connecting the historic district with the rest of San Juan. Once you pass through this area, you'll either go to **Miramar,** a beautiful residential neighborhood that also encompasses the city's waterfront redevelopment project (which already contains a convention center, with new hotels, luxury residences, and other amenities under construction), or you'll travel over a bridge to **Condado,** another narrow strip of land bordered by a saltwater lagoon and the Atlantic beachfront. It is lined with luxury hotels, gourmet restaurants, snazzy nightclubs, and great shops. Farther east is **Ocean Park,** a lovely residential area with a great beach that is perhaps the city's best-kept secret. There

At Wind Chimes Inn **11**
Caribe Hilton **5**
Conrad Condado Plaza Hotel & Casino **6**
El Canario Inn **8**
El San Juan Hotel & Casino **14**
Gran Hotel El Convento **1**
Gallery Inn at Galería San Juan **2**
Hosteria del Mar **12**
Inter-Continental San Juan Resort & Casino **15**
La Concha **7**
Numéro 1 Guest House **10**
Ritz-Carlton San Juan Spa & Casino **13**
San Juan Marriott Resort & Stellaris Casino **9**
Sheraton Old San Juan Hotel & Casino **3**
Sheraton Puerto Rico Hotel & Casino **4**
The Water Club **16**

are now more reasons than ever to visit **Santurce,** for decades San Juan's traditional downtown and which is now being revitalized after decades of neglect, with new movie houses, concert halls, museums, restaurants, and nightclubs. **Isla Verde** is home to some of the Caribbean's most upscale resort hotels and San Juan's widest, most populous beach. The international airport lies to the east. **Hato Rey,** the city's financial district, has great restaurants, concert venues, movie houses, and nightclubs. **Río Piedras** is host to the University of Puerto Rico, a botanical gardens, and a thriving shopping district and marketplace.

GETTING AROUND Walking is the best way to get around Old San Juan. The historic core of the old city is very compact. If your feet tire of the old cobblestone streets, board one of the free open-air trolleys that slowly make their way through the old city. You can board a trolley at any point along its route (either side of Calle Fortaleza or Calle San José are good bets), or you can go to La Puntilla for departures.

It's great walking through most neighborhoods as well. But if you are traveling from one area to another, you'll want to take a bus, taxi, or rental car. The **Metropolitan Bus Authority** (**© 787/767-7979**) operates buses in the greater San Juan area. Bus stops are marked by upright metal signs or yellow posts that say PARADA. Bus terminals in San Juan are in the dock area and at Plaza de Colón. The fare is 75¢. Three routes are particularly useful for tourists, plying a route from Old San Juan to other San Juan tourism districts: The A5 goes to downtown Santurce, Ocean Park, and Isla Verde; the B21 down Condado's Ashford Avenue, and then on to downtown San Juan, the city's financial district Hato Rey, and the Plaza Las Americas mall; and the C53, which heads to the Convention Center District, then down Condado's oceanfront drive and on into Isla Verde. Call for more information about routes and schedules. The private **MetroBus** operates a few key express routes from Old San Juan to Río Piedras for 50¢.

Taxi prices are zoned for many tourist areas in San Juan, but they also operate by meter for trips not covered by the set fees. The fixed rates are spread across five zones and three other destinations and range in price from $9 to $22. Taxis should have a posted schedule of these rates. For metered rides, the initial charge for destinations in the city is $1.75, plus 10¢ for each 1⁄10 mile and $1 for every suitcase. Taxis are invariably lined up outside the entrance to most of the island's hotels, and if not, a staff member can almost always call one for you. If you want to arrange a taxi on your own, call the **Cooperative Major Taxi** (✆ **787/723-2460**), **AAA Asociacion Servicios Taxi Capetillo** (✆ **787/758-7000**), or **Rochdale Taxi Cabs** (✆ **787/721-1900**). There are also established fees for taxi rides from San Juan to island destinations: From San Juan to Fajardo, it's $80; to Ponce, $125; and to Mayagüez, $160. The complete list is available on the Puerto Rico Tourism Company website (www.gotopuertorico.com/puerto-rico-taxis.php). For complaints or questions, contact the **Puerto Rico Tourism Company** (✆ **787/999-2100** for the transportation division).

Tren Urbano (✆ **787/690-6688;** www.eltrenurbano.com) the first mass-transit project in the history of Puerto Rico, opened in 2005, linking San Juan (though not Old San Juan) to its suburbs such as Bayamón and Guaynabo. The system provides an easy mode of transportation to the most congested areas of metropolitan San Juan. During rush hour (5–9am and 3–6pm), the train operates every 5 minutes; otherwise, it runs every 10 minutes. There is no service daily from 11pm to 5am. The fare was lowered to 75¢ from $1.50 one-way, so that it is on par with bus fares. From the airport, it's possible to take the AMA-B40 bus to the Tren Urbano, a 15-minute ride. For one fare, you can transfer from the train to bus to go beyond its reach.

Where to Stay

All hotel rooms on Puerto Rico are subject to a 9% to 11% tax, which is not included in the rates listed in this chapter. Most hotels impose a 10% service charge; many also impose a "resort fee" of between 12% and 22% of the cost of your room. Packages can save you a lot of money, especially if you want to stay at one of the big resorts.

IN OLD SAN JUAN

Expensive

Gran Hotel El Convento Puerto Rico's most famous hotel came back to life after a 1997 restoration, and it remains one of the most charming historic hotels in the Caribbean and a quintessential Old San Juan experience. The core of the building was constructed in 1651 as the New World's first Carmelite convent, but over the years it played many roles, from a dance hall to a flophouse to a parking lot for garbage trucks. It first opened as a hotel in 1962. The restoration has returned the property to its past glory while injecting it with an urban, up-to-date feel, very much like Old

San Juan itself. Its fourth-floor rooftop has a small pool, adjacent Jacuzzi, and a big sun terrace with blessed views of the nearby Catedral de San Juan (p. 448), as well as views of the bay and the Atlantic. The lower two floors feature a collection of shops, bars, and restaurants, all worth staying for a while. A late-afternoon wine-and-cheese offering is served on a beautiful midfloor dining area, spilling onto an outdoor terrace overlooking Calle Cristo. The midsize accommodations include Spanish-style furnishings, throw rugs, beamed ceilings, paneling, and Andalusian terra-cotta floor tiles. Each unit contains king-size, queen-size, or two double or twin beds, fitted with fine linens. The small bathrooms, with tub/showers, contain scales and second phones. For the ultimate in luxury, there is Gloria Vanderbilt's restored suite, which goes for $1,490 in the high season and $1,190 in the summer season, or the Pablo Casals suite, which runs around $680 year-round. Room no. 508 is a corner room with panoramic views.

Calle del Cristo 100, San Juan, PR 00901. www.elconvento.com. ✆ **800/468-2779** or 787/723-9020. Fax 787/723-9944. 68 units. Winter $260–$380 double, from $645 suite; off season $190–$250 double, from $525 suite. AE, DC, DISC, MC, V. Parking $20. Bus: Old City Trolley. **Amenities:** 4 restaurants; 3 bars; fitness center; Jacuzzi; small rooftop plunge pool. *In room:* A/C, TV, hair dryer, Wi-Fi (free).

Sheraton Old San Juan Hotel & Casino ★ This may be convenient for cruise-ship passengers wanting to spend a few nights in San Juan before or after a cruise, but don't expect Old City charm. Opened in 1997, this dignified nine-story waterfront hotel was part of a $100-million renovation of San Juan's cruise-port facilities. Backed by buildings erected by the Spanish monarchs in the 19th century, the hotel sits on the bay coast, where it hosts the city's busiest and most modern cruise-ship terminals. It remains a good option for cruise travelers wanting to extend their trip with a stay in San Juan. Most of the major cruise ships dock nearby. On days when cruise ships pull into port, the hotel's lobby and bars are likely to be jammed with passengers stretching their legs after a few days at sea. Most of the lobby level here is devoted to a mammoth casino. Take a pass on the hotel restaurants; you are steps from SoFo (South Fortaleza St. near Plaza Colón), which has some of the finest eateries in the city.

Calle Brumbaugh 100, San Juan, PR 00901. www.sheratonoldsanjuan.com. ✆ **800/325-3535** or 787/721-5100. Fax 787/721-1111. 240 units. Winter $170–$220 double, $230–$250 suite; off season $160–$190 double, $210 suite. AE, DC, DISC, MC, V. Valet parking $21. Bus: Old City Trolley. **Amenities:** 2 restaurants; 3 bars; fitness center; Jacuzzi; outdoor pool; casino; room service; smoke-free rooms. *In room:* A/C, TV, hair dryer, minibar.

Moderate

Casablanca Hotel This funky, beautiful inn, with a North African air, is a great addition to the Old Town's bustling retail area. The lobby and public areas have beautiful mosaic tile, a mix of restored antiques, contemporary furnishings, bold artwork, and wrought-iron lanterns. Guests are as eclectic as the interiors, and both make for a great experience. You are in the middle of SoFo, with great places to eat from dawn to past midnight just steps from your front door, and right near all the area nightclubs, bars, museums, and other attractions. On weekend nights, it can get noisy, so don't stay here if you want to go to bed early. There's a lot of space in which to hang out and meet other guests, and the new Rick's Café is a great addition. The rooftop is a pleasant enough place to work on a tan. If you don't need a beach and you can't afford El Convento, this is another option.

Calle Fortaleza 316, San Juan, PR 00901. www.hotelcasablancapr.com. ✆ **787/725-3436.** Fax 787/725-3435. 35 units. Year-round $95–$240 double. $5 continental breakfast. AE, MC, V. Bus: Old City Trolley. **Amenities:** Restaurant; bar; business center; reading lounge. *In room:* A/C, cable TV, MP3 docking station, Wi-Fi (free).

Gallery Inn at Galería San Juan ★ This unique hotel's location and ambience are unbeatable. The inn rambles through a 300-year-old building overlooking Old San Juan's northern sea wall. There are sweeping sea views, as well as the vista across the colonial city rooftops, extending all the way down to San Juan Bay. Verdant courtyards, interior gardens, and patios and terraces appear around every bend one takes in the inn. The chatter of tropical birds and the murmur of fountains complete the atmosphere in the Caribbean's most whimsically bohemian hotel. In the 1700s, it was the home of an aristocratic Spanish family, but today Jan D'Esopo and Manuco Gandia created this inn out of their home and Jan's art studio. The entire inn is covered with clay and bronze figures, as well as other original art by Jan, and each guest room also functions as gallery space, with Jan's original silk screens, paintings, and prints on display. We suggest booking one of the least expensive doubles; even the cheapest units are fairly roomy and attractively furnished, with good beds. The rooftop Wine Deck has the best view in Old San Juan. Classical music concerts are often held in the Music Room and are free for guests. A small pool has also been added to the property.

Calle Norzagaray 204–206, San Juan, PR 00901. www.thegalleryinn.com. ✆ **866/572-ARTE** (2783) or 787/722-1808. Fax 787/977-3929. 22 units, some with shower only. Year-round $140–$265 double; $280–$350 suite. Off-season specials available. Rates include continental breakfast and 6pm wine-and-cheese reception. AE, DC, MC, V. 6 free parking spaces, plus parking on the street. Bus: Old City Trolley. **Amenities:** Breakfast room. *In room:* A/C, hair dryer.

Hotel Milano There's not much remarkable about this hotel built from a 1920s warehouse, except clean, modern facilities at a good price in a great location, right near all the restaurants and bars along South Fortaleza Street. You enter a wood-sheathed lobby at the end of Calle Fortaleza before ascending to one of the clean, well-lit bedrooms. The simple, modern rooms have cruise-ship-style decor and unremarkable views, and there's excellent Wi-Fi access. The rooftop terrace has outstanding views and is a great spot to relax or enjoy breakfast. The best rooms are on the upper floors overlooking the street. Plus, you're in SoFo, home to some of Puerto Rico's best restaurants.

Calle Fortaleza 307, San Juan, PR 00901. www.hotelmilanopr.com. ✆ **877/729-9050** or 787/729-9050. Fax 787/722-3379. 30 units. Winter $105–$195 double; off season $85–$145 double. Sat night surcharge: $25 high season, $15 low season. $5 continental breakfast. AE, MC, V. Bus: Old City Trolley. **Amenities:** Rooftop terrace cafe; smoke-free rooms; Wi-Fi (free). *In room:* A/C, TV, fridge, hair dryer.

IN PUERTA DE TIERRA

Caribe Hilton ★ The hotel that first put Puerto Rico on the world tourism map when it opened in 1949 is still one of the most up-to-date spa and convention hotels in San Juan. This deluxe beauty, which has kept fresh with several dazzling renovations over the years, has a private beach and huge tropical garden and sits on a choice piece of Atlantic coastline outside Old San Juan.

Rooms have been substantially upgraded, with larger-than-expected bathrooms with a tub/shower, as well as comfortable, tropical-inspired furniture. In the Caribe Terrace Bar, you can order the bartender's celebrated piña colada, which was once enjoyed by movie legends Joan Crawford and Errol Flynn. An oceanfront spa and fitness center, **Las Olas,** features such tantalizing delights as couples massages, body wraps, hydrotherapy tub treatments, and soothing cucumber sun therapies.

1 Calle San Geronimo, San Juan, PR 00901. www.caribe.hilton.com. ✆ **800/445-8667** or 787/721-0303. Fax 787/724-6992. 812 units. Winter $245–$330 double; off season $230–$310 double; year-round $430–$2,030 suite. Children 16 and under stay free in parent's room (maximum 4 people per room). AE, DC, DISC, MC, V. Valet parking $20; self-parking $15. Bus: B21. **Amenities:** 5 restaurants; 2 bars; babysitting; children's activities and playground; health club; room service; smoke-free rooms. *In room:* A/C, TV, hair dryer, minibar, Wi-Fi (free).

IN MIRAMAR

Sheraton Puerto Rico Hotel & Casino ★ This property is an integral part of the Puerto Rico Convention District, and it seems as if you can see the imposing yet graceful convention center arch out any window you look. The two properties both embrace big glass spaces, open to the amazing sky and the futuristic yet tropical landscape surrounding it, and even a bit of the Atlantic Ocean crashing in the distance. The hotel facilities—which include the island's largest casino and a fabulous health club and spa—are first-rate, but this is still primarily a convention hotel, appropriate for those who plan on spending a lot of time at the adjacent convention center. The good news is the property will probably surpass most guests' expectations. The public interiors are subdued and stylish, and the good taste extends to the guest rooms, which are more comfortable and spacious than the average hotel room, especially the hotel beds. It's within a mile of most good city beaches, as well as Old San Juan and Plaza Las Americas, but that mile feels a lot longer when you are on vacation. You are better off at one of the resorts right on the Condado or Isla Verde beaches than staying here, unless you are spending your mornings at the convention center.

200 Convention Blvd., San Juan, PR 00907. www.sheratonpuertoricohotelcasino.com. ✆ **866/325-3535** or 787/993-3500. Fax 787/993-3505. 503 units. Winter $200–$325 double, $330–$500 suite; off season $140–$225 double, $290–$480 suite. Children 16 and under stay free in parent's room (maximum 4 people per room). AE, DC, DISC, MC, V. Valet parking $20; self-parking $15. Bus: C53. **Amenities:** 3 restaurants; 2 bars; babysitting; health club; casino; room service; smoke-free rooms; complete spa. *In room:* A/C, TV, hair dryer, minibar, Wi-Fi (free).

IN CONDADO

Expensive

Conrad Condado Plaza Hotel & Casino ★ This is one of the busiest hotels on Puerto Rico, with enough facilities and restaurants to keep visitors occupied. It's a favorite of business travelers, tour groups, and conventions, but it also attracts independent travelers. Spacious guest rooms and multiple lobbies recently benefited from a $65-million makeover; the rooms have private terraces and are bright and airy with deluxe beds and large, modern bathrooms. The property sprawls across Ashford Avenue, so it overlooks both the Condado Lagoon and the sector's Atlantic coastline. The hotel also has one of the city's most popular casinos and some of its finest dining spots. Right outside the casino is the Eight Noodle Bar, a favorite late-night snacking spot for San Juan's party set, with its kitchen open from noon to 4am daily. One of the island's most renowned chefs, Wilo Benet, has brought two of his signature restaurants here: Pikayo (p. 442) and Varita.

Av. Ashford 999, San Juan, PR 00907. www.condadoplaza.com. ✆ **888/722-1274** or 787/721-1000. 570 units. Winter $229–$329 double, $359–$729 suite; off season $159–$249 double, $209–$620 suite. AE, DC, DISC, MC, V. Valet parking $15; self-parking $10. Bus: C53 or B21. **Amenities:** 5 restaurants; 3 bars; children's activities; health club; 3 Jacuzzis; 3 outdoor pools; casino; room service; smoke-free rooms; spa; 2 tennis courts; watersports equipment/rentals. *In room:* A/C, TV, hair dryer, minibar.

La Concha: A Renaissance Resort ★★ The reopening of this hotel—50 years to the day from when it first opened to rave reviews in December 1958—took 7 years and carried a $220-million price tag, but it was well worth it. Thank former San Juan mayor and governor Sila Calderón and the Puerto Rico Architects Association for stopping the wrecking ball on this one. This renovation completes the comeback of Condado, with oceanfront rooms that feel as if they are part of the horizon, and a multilevel infinity-pool area and adjoining beaches that form a dreamscape in which guests willfully lose themselves. The water motif extends to the cascading fountain at its entrance, the fountains surrounding an open-air deck, and views of the sea from every vantage point. The lobby's Italian marble, white furniture, and huge window to the sea also pull the resort's exteriors and interiors together. The signature shell structure, which sits on the beach surrounded by water, is home to Perla restaurant, a seafood restaurant run by prominent local chef Dayn Smith. The hotel's lobby bar is a great spot for tapas and wine, and the casino sits just off it. Surrounded by designer boutiques and trendy restaurants, La Concha has been a local hot spot since it reopened, and its lobby area always has the sound of Latin rhythms.

Guest rooms have the latest high-tech gadgets; understated natural wood and beige interiors form a canvas for the beautiful views and tropical prints on the walls.

Av. Ashford 1077, San Juan, PR 00907. www.laconcharesort.com. ✆ **877/524-7778** or 787/721-7500. Fax 787/977-4019. 248 units. Winter $290–$360 double, $410–$520 suite; off season $180–$250 double, $230–$445 suite. AE, DC, DISC, MC, V. Valet parking $15; self-parking $10. Bus: C53 or B21. **Amenities:** 5 restaurants; 3 bars; children's activities; health club; 3 Jacuzzis; 3 outdoor pools; casino; 24-hr. room service; smoke-free rooms; spa; 2 tennis courts; watersports equipment/rentals; rooms for those w/limited mobility. *In room:* A/C, flatscreen TV, hair dryer, MP3 docking station, Wi-Fi (free).

San Juan Marriott Resort & Stellaris Casino ★ This centrally located hotel is on one of the Condado's nicest beaches and within walking distance of two parks and the best restaurants in the sector. The tallest building on the Condado, this 21-story landmark packs lots of postmodern style and has an open, comfortable lobby area. A hit with families and kids, it has extensive children's activities and a pool with two water slides. It also has a jumping casino and lobby area, the scene of big-band and Latin jazz performances. Even the sports bar by the pool is active, with sports fans from up and down the East Coast. The guest rooms are generally spacious, with good views of the water, and each comes with a tiled bathroom with a tub/shower. The pastel tones of the comfortable bedrooms are a bit too washed out for our taste, but that's the only legitimate gripe about this property. Junior suites have a living area with a sofa bed. We can't say enough about its great location in the best part of Condado, which is not immediately apparent to visitors. It's an easy walk to anywhere you want to go. And the staff is among the friendliest in town.

Av. Ashford 1309, San Juan, PR 00907. www.marriott.com. ✆ **888/817-2033** or 787/722-7000. Fax 787/722-6800. 525 units. Winter $255–$315 double, $420–$745 suite; summer $190–$285 double, $315–$640 suite. Suite rate includes breakfast. AE, DC, DISC, MC, V. Valet parking $20; self-parking $16. Bus: B21 or A5. **Amenities:** 3 restaurants; 3 bars; babysitting; health club; Jacuzzi; 2 pools; casino; room service; sauna; 2 tennis courts. *In room:* A/C, TV, hair dryer, minibar, Wi-Fi (free).

Moderate

At Wind Chimes Inn ★ ☺ This restored and renovated Spanish manor, 1 short block from the beach and 3½ miles from the airport, is one of the best guesthouses on the Condado. Upon entering a tropical patio, you'll find tile tables surrounded by palm trees and bougainvillea. There's plenty of space on the deck and a covered lounge for relaxing, socializing, and eating breakfast. Dozens of decorative wind chimes add melody to the daily breezes. The good-size rooms offer a choice of size, beds, and kitchens; all contain ceiling fans and air-conditioning. Beds are comfortable and come in four sizes, ranging from twin to king-size. The shower-only bathrooms, though small, are efficiently laid out. Families like this place not only because of the accommodations and the affordable prices, but because in three of the suites, they can also prepare light meals, cutting down on food costs. A sister property, **Acacia Seaside Inn,** right around the block, is also recommended. One of Condado's finest, and most low-key, beaches is a block away.

Av. McLeary 1750, Condado, San Juan, PR 00911. www.atwindchimesinn.com. ✆ **800/946-3244** or 787/727-4153. Fax 787/728-0671. 22 units. Winter $110–$155 double, $155 suite; off season $75–$130 double, $130 suite; holiday weekends $125–$185 double, $185 suite. AE, DISC, MC, V. Parking $10. Bus: B21 or A5. **Amenities:** Bar; outdoor pool; room service. *In room:* A/C, ceiling fan, TV, kitchen (in some).

Atlantic Beach Hotel With the pink piano in the lobby long gone, Puerto Rico's most famous gay hotel has recently undergone a quiet transformation, with a sweeping renovation of guest rooms and a change in attitude that aims to take advantage of its distinction as the only small hotel on the beach in Condado. The five-story hotel still welcomes its core gay clientele, but it's also reaching out to "open-minded" straight couples and business travelers looking for clean, comfortable, attractive rooms right on the beach at a good price. Renovations have extended to a bar and restaurant, and the whole property is in a handsome, subdued style, much like the new direction the property has taken. Some of the rooms are smaller than others, so paying a little more will get you more space plus a beach view. The bar and restaurant on the back deck, which sits about 20 feet above the beach, are still a great place to have a drink, but the flamboyant shows and weekend afternoon happy hours of debauchery are now a thing of the past. The spacious apartments are a good alternative for business travelers or small groups, and one of the best bargains in the Condado.

Calle Vendig 1, Condado, San Juan, PR 00907. www.atlanticbeachhotel.net. ✆ **787/721-6900.** Fax 787/721-6917. 36 units, all with shower only; 6 apartments. Winter $80–$110 double, off season $70–$100 double; year-round $750-$1,250 per week apt. AE, DISC, MC, V. Parking $10 per day. Bus: B21. **Amenities:** Restaurant; bar; beach chairs and umbrellas; Wi-Fi (free); rooms for those w/limited mobility. *In room:* A/C, TV.

El Canario Inn This little bed-and-breakfast, originally built as a private home, is one of the best values along the high-priced Condado strip. The location is just 1 block from the beach (you can walk there in your bathing suit). This well-established hotel lies directly on the landmark Ashford Avenue, center of Condado action, and is close to casinos, nightclubs, and many restaurants in all price ranges. Although surrounded by megaresorts, it is a simple inn, with rather small but comfortable rooms and good maintenance by a helpful staff. All units are nonsmoking and have small, tiled, shower-only bathrooms. You can relax on the hotel's patios or in the whirlpool area, which is surrounded by tropical foliage. There is no elevator. Affiliated with the nearby El Canario by the Lagoon and El Canario by the Beach, which are also recommended, this is the most charming of the three El Canario properties. El Canario by the Sea is right around the block.

Av. Ashford 1317, Condado, San Juan, PR 00907. www.canariohotels.com. ✆ **800/533-2649** or 787/722-3861. Fax 787/722-0391. 25 units. Winter $105–$150 double; off season $80–$110 double. $3 energy fee. $10 weekend surcharge Fri–Sat. Rates include continental breakfast, newspaper. AE, DC, MC, V. Bus: B21 or A5. *In room:* A/C, TV.

IN OCEAN PARK

Hosteria del Mar ★ The hotel boasts medium-size oceanview rooms. Those on the second floor have balconies; those on the first floor open onto patios. The decor is invitingly tropical, with wicker furniture, good beds, pastel prints, and ceiling fans. The bathrooms are small but efficient, some with shower, some with tub only. There are standard and oceanview rooms, suites with kitchenettes, and apartments with full kitchens and living rooms. Our favorite unit is no. 201, with a king-size bed, private balcony, kitchenette, and view of the beach; it's idyllic for a honeymoon. There's no pool, but you are right on the beach. Uvva is one of the hardest-working restaurants in the city, open from 8am to 10pm; it has a large menu of upscale breakfast and lunch choices, and also throws in some cutting-edge, creative world cuisine. On a beachfront street completely enveloped by a canopy of trees, this is one of San Juan's most charming spots. Given the setting, the place is simple, but it puts out its own elegance and warm hospitality.

Calle Tapía 1, Ocean Park, San Juan, PR 00911. www.hosteriadelmarpr.com. ✆ **877/727-3302** or 787/727-3302. Fax 787/268-3302. hosteria@caribe.net. 27 units. Winter $140–$180 double, $230–$240 suites; off season $80–$140 double, $180–$210 suite. Children 11 and under stay free in parent's room. AE, DC, DISC, MC, V. Bus: C53 or A5. **Amenities:** Restaurant; room service. *In room:* A/C, TV, kitchenette (in 3 units), Wi-Fi.

Número 1 Guest House ★★ As a translation of its name implies, this is the best of the small-scale, low-rise guesthouses in Ocean Park. It was originally built in the 1950s as a private beach house in a prestigious residential neighborhood adjacent to the wide sands of Ocean Park Beach. A massive renovation transformed the place into the closest thing in Ocean Park to the kind of stylish boutique hotel you might find in an upscale California neighborhood. Much of this is thanks to the hardworking owner, Esther Feliciano, who cultivates within her walled compound a verdant garden replete with splashing fountains, a small swimming pool, and manicured shrubbery and palms. Stylish-looking bedrooms (all of which are nonsmoking) contain tile floors, wicker or rattan furniture, comfortable beds, and tiled, shower-only bathrooms. Some repeat clients, many of whom are gay, refer to it as their fantasy version of a private villa beside a superb and usually convivial beach. The staff can direct you to watersports emporiums nearby for virtually any tropical watersport. Although it lacks the staggering diversity of the big hotels of the nearby Condado or Isla Verde, some guests value its sense of intimacy and small-scale charm.

Calle Santa Ana 1, Ocean Park, San Juan, PR 00911. www.numero1guesthouse.com. ✆ **866/726-5010** or 787/726-5010. Fax 787/727-5482. 13 units. Mid-Dec to Apr $150–$300; Aug–Oct $90–$200; May–July and Nov to mid-Dec $100–$260 double. $20 weekend surcharge Fri–Sun. $20 each additional occupant of a double room. Rates include continental breakfast. AE, MC, V. Bus: C53 or A5. **Amenities:** Restaurant; bar; outdoor pool; room service. *In room:* A/C, ceiling fan, TV, hair dryer, minibar, Wi-Fi (free).

IN ISLA VERDE

El San Juan Hotel & Casino: The Waldorf Astoria Collection ★ ☺ Despite formidable competition by the Ritz-Carlton for elite and sophisticated travelers, this posh resort still has the power to dazzle. The beachfront hotel is surrounded by 350 palms, century-old banyans, and gardens. It lies on a 2-mile-long golden sandy beach with aquamarine water that is the finest in San Juan. Lined with luxury hotels and condominiums, the beach is always full of activity and has great watersports activities.

The lobby is the most opulent and memorable in the Caribbean. Entirely sheathed in red marble and hand-carved mahogany paneling, the public rooms stretch on almost endlessly. No other hotel in the Caribbean offers such a rich diversity of dining options and such high-quality food, especially at La Piccola Fontana (p. 444). And with live music and DJs playing at nightclubs nearly every night and a beautiful casino, El San Juan is still the place to be seen in the city.

The large, well-decorated rooms are outfitted with the latest in high-tech. The Vista guest rooms are bright and tropical, while the Lanai rooms are imbued with honey-hued woods and rattans, with darker wooden doors, windows, and other furnishing. Bathrooms have all the amenities and tub/showers; a few feature Jacuzzis. The oceanfront Lanai rooms overlook the fern-lined paths of the resort's tropical garden.

Av. Isla Verde 6063, San Juan, PR 00979. www.waldorfastoriacollection.com. ✆ **800/925-3673** or 787/791-1000. Fax 787/791-0390. 382 units. Winter $319–$669 double, $900–$2,300 suite; off season $170–$550 double, from $770–$2,070 suite. AE, DC, DISC, MC, V. Valet parking $15; self-parking $10. Bus: A5, C53. **Amenities:** 7 restaurants; 4 bars; babysitting; children's programs; health club; 2 outdoor pools; casino; 24-hr. room service; sauna and steam room; spa; tennis courts; watersports equipment/rentals; rooms for those w/limited mobility. *In room:* A/C, TV w/in-house movies, hair dryer, minibar, MP3 docking station, Wi-Fi (free).

Inter-Continental San Juan Resort & Casino We love the pool area and the cafe overlooking the beach. Along with a recent face-lift, which included the rooms and public areas, the hotel's staff also has dramatically improved service. The comfortable, medium-size rooms have balconies and terraces, and tastefully conservative furnishings. Executive Club–level rooms carry additional features, such as complimentary meals and drinks. The pool area is one of the finest in San Juan, and it fronts one of the city's prettiest and most active beaches. The oceanside Ciao Mediterranean Café is one of the best spots in the city for an afternoon drink, lunch, or snack. Sit on a table along the boardwalk overlooking the beach in the shade of towering palm trees. Guests will want to venture elsewhere for nightlife, however, which is all nearby.

Av. Isla Verde 5961, Isla Verde, PR 00979. www.ichotelsgroup.com. ✆ **888/424-6835** or 787/791-6100. Fax 787/253-2510. 402 units. Winter $280–$430 double, $700–$1,045 suite; off season $170–$350 double, $425–$745 suite. Children 15 and under stay free in parent's room. AE, DC, DISC, MC, V. Valet parking $22; self-parking $16. Bus: A5 or C53. **Amenities:** 3 restaurants; lounge; babysitting; health club; the Caribbean's largest free-form pool; whirlpool; room service; sauna; scuba diving; Wi-Fi (free). *In room:* A/C, TV, hair dryer, minibar.

Ritz-Carlton San Juan Spa & Casino ★★★ ☺ The Ritz-Carlton is one of the most spectacular deluxe hotels in the Caribbean. Set on 8 acres of prime beachfront within a 5-minute drive from the airport, it appeals to both business travelers and vacationers. The hotel decor reflects Caribbean flavor and the Hispanic culture of the island, with artwork by prominent local artists. More visible, however, is an emphasis on Continental elegance. Some of the most opulent public areas feature wrought-iron balustrades and crystal chandeliers.

Beautifully furnished guest rooms open onto ocean views or the gardens of nearby condos. Rooms are very large, with excellent furnishings, fine linens, and dataports. The marble bathrooms are exceptionally plush, with tub/showers, scales, bathrobes, and deluxe toiletries. Preferred accommodations are in the ninth-floor Ritz-Carlton Club, which has a private lounge and personal concierge staff.

The scope and diversity of dining here is second only to that at the El San Juan Hotel & Casino (see above), and as for top-shelf dining venues, the Ritz-Carlton has no equal. Renowned gourmet chains BLT Steak and Il Mulino of New York are both located here. The hotel also houses one of Puerto Rico's largest casinos, and it's most stylishly elegant. This is a great spot for families, with a full range of children's activities and a great beach for kids, as well as lots of watersports options for active families.

Av. de los Gobernadores (State Rd.) 6961, Isla Verde, PR 00979. www.ritzcarlton.com. ✆ **800/542-8680** or 787/253-1700. Fax 787/253-1777. 416 units. Winter $440–$660 double; off season $230–$510 double; year-round $1,109–$1,530 suite. AE, DC, DISC, MC, V. Valet parking $22; self-parking $17. Bus: A5. **Amenities:** 5 restaurants; 3 bars; nightclub; babysitting; children's program; health club; large pool; Caribbean's largest casino; room service; spa; 2 tennis courts. *In room:* A/C, TV, hair dryer, minibar.

The San Juan Water & Beach Club Hotel ★★ A refreshing change from the megachain resorts of San Juan, this ultrachic hotel is hip and contemporary. Although avant garde, the design is never off-putting. The illuminated lobby might recall *2001: A Space Odyssey,* but it's still warm and friendly. Behind glass are "waterfalls," even on the elevators, and inventive theatrical-style lighting is used to bring the outdoors inside. The one-of-a-kind glass art doors are from Murano, the famed center of glassmaking, outside Venice. A drawback is that rooms are smaller than most, and so is the closet and dresser space. The hotel overlooks Isla Verde's best beach area. Unique features are the open-air 11th-floor exotic bar with the Caribbean's only rooftop fireplace. There's a rooftop pool and sundeck; it's like swimming in an ocean in the sky. This hotel is super pet-friendly: It offers four-legged friends complimentary doggie bags and their owners welcome drinks. Grooming, walking, and massage services are available.

Calle José M. Tartak 2, Isla Verde, San Juan, PR 00979. www.waterbeachclubhotel.com. ✆ **888/265-6699** or 787/253-3666. Fax 787/728-3610. 84 units. Year-round $165–$205 double, $305 suite. AE, DC, DISC, MC, V. Bus: A5 or B21. **Amenities:** Restaurant; 2 bars; fitness center; Jacuzzi; outdoor rooftop pool; room service; smoke-free rooms. *In room:* A/C, TV, hair dryer, Wi-Fi (free), minibar.

Where to Dine

IN OLD SAN JUAN

Expensive

Aquaviva ★★ LATINO/SEAFOOD Located on Calle Fortaleza near Plaza Colón, at the entrance of Old San Juan, this cool, turquoise-colored restaurant features action sometimes as frenetic as the three large replicas of three *aquaviva* (jellyfish), quivering with illumination, each painstakingly manufactured from stained glass specifically for this site. Bioluminescent drinks are served at the bar, and the hip raw bar here features sushi and a host of ceviches, including one made with dorado, mango and lemon juices, and another with marlin and garlic. The hot and cold appetizer towers are great for small groups (fried oysters, coconut-flavored shrimp, fried octopus, and calamari). The best main courses include grilled wild salmon on corn arepas with tomato marmalade and the fried snapper with lobster *mofongo*.

Calle Fortaleza 364. ✆ **787/722-0665.** Reservations not accepted. Main courses $17–$32. AE, MC, V. Mon–Wed 11am–4pm and 6–11pm; Thurs–Sat 11am–4pm and 6pm–midnight; Sun 11am–4pm and 4–11pm. Bus: Old City Trolley.

Carli Café Concierto ★ INTERNATIONAL This stylish restaurant is owned by Carli Muñoz; the gold disc hanging on the wall attests to Carli's success in his previous role as a pianist for the Beach Boys. Nowadays, he entertains his dinner guests nightly with a combination of standards, romantic jazz, and original material on his grand piano, or along with a small jazz combo. Diners can sit outside on the Plazoleta, where they can enjoy a panoramic view of the bay, or they can eat inside against a backdrop of a tasteful decor of terra-cotta walls and black marble tables. There is a wide selection of tapas and appetizers, including a plantain-crusted calamari in a dark sesame sauce. Entrees include a salmon-and-shrimp linguini in a creamy brandy sauce, rosemary jus lamb chops, and blackened ahi tuna with Cajun spices. The bar, with its mahogany and brass fittings, is an ideal spot to chill out. The concert starts every night at 8pm.

Edificio Banco Popular, Calle Tetuán 206 (off Plazoleta Rafael Carrión). ✆ **787/725-4927.** www.carlisworld.com. Reservations recommended. Main courses $14-$36. AE, V. Mon-Fri 3:30-11pm; Sat 4-11:30pm. Bus: M2 or M3.

Il Perugino ★★ ITALIAN Located across from Hotel El Convento, this is Puerto Rico's finest Italian restaurant, serving the cuisine inspired by chef and owner Franco Seccarelli's homeland of Umbria. The homemade pastas deliver the Italian classics to perfection: thin pasta with pancetta, tomatoes, and onions; and the spinach and ricotta gnocci with fresh tomatoes. For a starter, opt for the warm goat cheese with pesto or the calamari stuffed with shrimp and fresh white fish. Seccarelli shines with his pheasant breast alla Cacciatora, baby veal chops in white wine and rosemary, and the rack of lamb with fresh herbs and a rich red-wine sauce. Homemade desserts are also delicious, and wine comes from a cellar in a converted dry well in the center of the restaurant. Service is impeccable and friendly.

Calle Cristo 105. ✆ **787/722-5481.** Reservations recommended. Main courses $25-$38. AE, DISC, MC, V. Thurs-Sat 11:30am-2:30pm; Tues-Sun 6:30-11pm. Bus: Old City Trolley.

Parrot Club ★★ NUEVO LATINO/CARIBBEAN This bistro and bar, owned by husband-and-wife team Emilio Figueroa and Gigi Zafero, is bright and colorful, as inventive as its Nuevo Latino cuisine, which, like the setting, delivers a new take on Puerto Rican and Cuban traditions. Latin cookery—a delicious blend of Spanish, Taíno, and African influence—is brought to lofty heights here, but the genuinely friendly and (usually) efficient service really sets it apart from the competition. Start out with coriander crab fritters with Caribbean tartar sauce, or the stewed beef and root vegetable nachos; ceviche lovers might opt for the excellent tuna, salmon, and mahimahi ceviche, with lime and charred tomato. Main-course standouts include grilled churrasco with yellow tomato chimichurri and sautéed potatoes, and the plantain-crusted mahimahi with sweet-yellow-pepper beurre blanc sauce and Peruvian potatoes. You have to try the Parrot Passion, made from lemon-flavored rum, triple sec, oranges, and passion fruit.

Calle Fortaleza 363. ✆ **787/725-7370.** Reservations not accepted. Main courses $10-$23 lunch, $18-$36 dinner. AE, DC, MC, V. Mon-Fri 11am-4pm and 6-11pm; Sat-Sun 9-11am and 6-11pm. Closed 2 weeks in Sept. Bus: Old City Trolley.

Toro Salao ★ SPANISH TAPAS With dark-wood interior and a Spanish colonial facade, bullfighting posters, and splashes of red, this is the kind of place Ernest Hemingway would have written home about. Toro Salao, "the salty bull" in Spanish, is another restaurant by Emilio Figueroa and Gigi Zaferos (owners/creators of the Parrot Club, Dragonfly, and Aquaviva, among others) that seamlessly matches the cuisine with the restaurant ambience. There's something for everyone, so I always take family here; we gorge on flatbread pizza with artichokes and Mediterranean olives; a *papas bravas* (spicy potatoes) redux that wasn't overly spicy; and seared octopus with sundried tomato vinaigrette. There's nothing better than the crisp and clean mussels in a chunky green salsa and the sweet veal meatballs with romesco sauce and plantains. Full meals include paella seafood with chicken and sausage, seared pork with coriander, and classic churrasco. Order a pitcher of sangria, among San Juan's finest, which comes in several inventive varieties, including a tropical-fruit version, which adds flavor without ever losing the essence of this Spanish tavern standard.

Calle Tetuan 367. ✆ **787/722-3330.** Reservations not accepted. Main courses $22–$35; tapas $12–$25. AE, MC, V. Mon–Fri 11:30am–midnight; Sat–Sun 9am–midnight. Bus: Old City Trolley.

Moderate

Dragonfly ★★ LATIN/ASIAN FUSION One of San Juan's hottest restaurants, the place has been compared to both an Old San Francisco bordello and a Shanghai opium den, descriptions that evoke as much the lusty appeal and addictive power of its cuisine as the red-walled interior, a world of fringed lamps and gilded mirrors behind beaded curtains. It's good for a late meal, as the portion sizes, called *platos,* or plates, are somewhere between appetizers and entrees. The Asian marinated churrasco with wasabi fries and the Amarillo dumplings in citrus dipping sauce are must-haves. Other standouts: seared tuna in green-peppercorn sauce; tempura rock shrimp tacos; and Chino Latino lo mein, with Puerto Rican fried chicken chunks. This is the island's first Latin-Asian menu, and it remains one of the best anywhere—still one of the city's trendiest nights out.

Calle Fortaleza 364. ✆ **787/977-3886.** Reservations not accepted. Main courses $12–$25. AE, MC, V. Mon–Wed 6–11pm; Thurs–Sat 6pm–midnight. Bus: Old City Trolley.

El Picoteo ★★ 📷 SPANISH Spilling across a front and interior terrace overlooking the courtyard of the historic El Convento Hotel, this is the best place in the Old Town to savor some drinks and tapas while watching the action near Calle San Sebastián. On most nights, there's a parade of people walking up and down Calle Cristo in front of the restaurant as they go back and forth to the bars and restaurants just up the hill. We love the spicy potatoes *(papas bravas),* the shrimp in garlic sauce, and the brick-oven pizza, but there are also full meals, like seafood paella. With 80 tapas to choose from, there's also real Spanish flavor here, in such dishes as garbanzo salad, sausages, various ceviches, fresh octopus, and the best selection of cheese in the city. The setting amid Spanish colonial facades and wildly blooming bougainvillea is one of the Old Town's most charmed. It's equally inviting for a weekend lunch. Try the champagne-laced sangria. Dinner is festive, especially Thursday evenings, when there is a live flamenco show.

In El Convento Hotel, Calle del Cristo 100. ✆ **787/723-9202.** Reservations recommended. Main courses $6–$32; paella $20–$35. AE, MC, V. Tues–Sun noon–midnight. Bus: Old City Trolley.

Old Harbor Brewery Steak and Lobster House ★ AMERICAN San Juan's only microbrewery also has top-drawer tavern fare in an upscale mariner setting. Brewmaster Brad Mortensen handcrafts five distinct house beers, as well as seven seasonal beers, on the premises in state-of-the-art brewing facilities. The restaurant specializes in top-quality steaks and fresh Puerto Rican spiny lobster. The cuts are served steakhouse style with a choice of sauces (the mushroom and chimichurri is recommended) and a la carte sides (favorites are the Lyonnise potatoes and asparagus with béarnaise). The hanging tender steak was as promised, and the New York strip was flavorful and cooked to perfection. Caribbean lobster is lighter than Maine lobster, and the version served here is among the best on the island; go with the citrus beurre blanc sauce rather than the coconut, almond-spiced rum. The rich French onion and lobster bisque soup are rich and hearty, and rather a rarity in the Caribbean. I'll vouch for the high quality of the Santo Viejo pilsner and Old Harbor pale ale. The restaurant dates to the 1920s, when it housed the New York Federal Bank, and it was beautifully restored before reopening in 2005. A classic tavern setup surrounds the elegant brew vats, but the place is formal, with fully dressed tables, classic black and white tiles, and metal and wooden finishings.

Calle Tizol 202 (near Recinto Sur). ✆ **787/721-2100.** www.oldharborbrewery.com. Reservations recommended. Platters and main courses $14–$38. AE, MC, V. Daily 11:30am–1am. Bus: Old City Trolley.

Raíces ★ PUERTO RICAN Don't let the apparent touristy trappings fool you: It's not the cheapest meal in town, but it's among the tastiest and most authentic, and we recommend it for a big taste of Puerto Rican cuisine. These are Caguas boys in the kitchen, so enjoy the rustic Puerto Rican setting—beautifully outfitted with local arts and crafts—and the waitresses and waiters decked out in beautiful folkloric dress. It's a perfect fit for its location near the cruise-ship docks, but the first location was in Caguas, which is decidedly untouristy. The "typical festival" combines a number of classic island treats, like meat turnovers, stuffed fried plantain fritters, codfish fritters, and mashed cassava, but you'll also want to try the delicious plantain soup. The stuffed *mofongo* entrees are the real specialty here; along with the typical stuffed chicken or shrimp, the options range to breaded pork, skirt steak, and Creole-style mahimahi. If you want hearty fare, the chicken or shrimp *asopao* is another option. The coconut flan and guava cheesecake do not disappoint. Traditional Puerto Rican music, with occasional live salsa on Thursday nights, further compliments the experience.

Calle Recinto Sur 315. ✆ **787/289-2121.** www.restaurantraices.com. Reservations not necessary. Main courses $10–$26. AE, MC, V. Mon–Fri 11am–4pm and 6–11pm; Sat 11am–11pm; Sun noon–10pm. Bus: Old City Trolley.

Tantra ★ INDO-LATINO So sway to the world-beat music, enjoy the culinary cultural clash, and forget what country you are in. Set in the heart of "restaurant row" on Calle Fortaleza, this restaurant, on the first floor and courtyard of a Spanish colonial mansion, is decorated in Asian colors and handicrafts with Hindu and Buddhist imagery. The ethnic setting fits the sophisticated fusion of Latino with South Indian cuisine, a blend of slow-cooked tandoori with Puerto Rico–derived flavors, from India-born chef and owner Ramesh Pillai. The sesame-masala-crusted sushi tuna with peanut sauce is as good as it sounds; other raves include fried coconut sesame jumbo shrimp with Indian noodles, chicken tikka masala with naan (flatbread), and rice and chicken rolls with passion fruit sauce. The house tandoori chicken sticks to tradition but then throws in manchego and mozzarella cheese, guayaba fruit, guava-flavored dip, and naan. There's also belly-dancing shows on many nights. It's also a place for drinks and late-night snacks for local hipsters and tourists on the prowl; the kitchen stays open with a limited late-night menu, and the bar is often packed until the wee hours. An appropriate way to begin a meal here is to order one of the best martinis we've ever had—a concoction flavored with cinnamon and cloves.

Calle Fortaleza 356. ✆ **787/977-8141.** Reservations only for groups. Main courses $13–$25. AE, MC, V. Mon 3pm–3am; Tues–Sat noon–3am; Sun noon–midnight. Bus: Old City Trolley.

Inexpensive

Caficultura ★ CAFE/BISTRO Any time's a good time to indulge yourself at this beautiful "espresso bar and marketplace kitchen" on Plaza Colón, a fitting temple to the richness of Puerto Rican coffee. It opens early, offers a great respite from the heat of the day for lunch or a snack, and can be counted on most evenings for a delicious tapas menu and nightly special. A "less is more" approach is evident in everything from its stonewashed walls, tiled floors, and wooden doors and furnishings, to its limited yet satisfying menu of Puerto Rican coffee, beer, wine, and alcoholic beverages. You can always get a *cortadito* (espresso topped with steamed milk) or some guayaba cake, but there is also smoked ham and eggs, coconut French toast, and fruit salads for breakfast, as well as gourmet sandwiches like roasted beef loin with baked tomato and caramelized onion or turkey breast with manchego cheese and bacon, with a spring salad, for lunch. Recent nightly specials have included churrasco with sautéed vegetables and baked potato; stir-fried rice with chicken and vegetables; and penne pasta with chicken and broccoli, manchego cheese, and root vegetable cream sauce. Tapas standouts include the assorted fried vegetable appetizer, the shrimp ceviche with cassava fritters, and the Spanish sausage in wine sauce. The baristas and waitstaff are as charming as the ornate chandeliers hanging from the high ceilings and the expertly hewn prints on the walls. Like the best of Old San Juan, Caficultura pays homage to Puerto Rican tradition while remaining very current.

Calle San Francisco 401 (on Plaza Colón). ✆ **787/723-7731.** Reservations not necessary. Main courses $3–$9 breakfast, $6–$12 lunch; evening tapas $4–$18. AE, MC, V. Sun–Wed 7am–4pm; Thurs–Sat 7am–4pm and 6–11pm. Bus: Old City Trolley.

La Bombonera ★ PUERTO RICAN This place offers exceptional value in its homemade pastries, well-stuffed sandwiches, and endless cups of coffee—and it has done so since 1902. Its atmosphere evokes turn-of-the-20th-century Castille transplanted to the New World. The food is authentically Puerto Rican, homemade, and inexpensive, with regional dishes such as rice with squid, roast leg of pork, and seafood *asopao* (a thick rice soup). For dessert you might select an apple, pineapple, or prune pie, or one of many types of flan. Service is polite, if a bit rushed, and the place fills up quickly at lunchtime.

Calle San Francisco 259. ✆ **787/722-0658.** Reservations recommended. Main courses $6–$18; American breakfast $4.50–$6.45. AE, MC, V. Daily 7:30am–8pm. Bus: Old City Trolley.

IN PUERTA DE TIERRA

El Hamburger ★ AMERICAN This no-frills burger stand offers tasty grilled burgers and hot dogs, cold beer, and perfectly golden french fries and onion rings. From its perch overlooking the Atlantic on the oceanfront drive into San Juan, the grill has become a late-night local favorite for those leaving the bars of Old San Juan and is also popular for a bite during work or after the beach. A really good, cheap opportunity to soak up some real local atmosphere, the ramshackle wooden establishment is the kind of burger joint that has disappeared throughout much of the United States with the advent of the modern fast-food restaurant. One of its joys lives on here with a selection of condiments—onions, relish, thick tomatoes, pickles—brought to your table with your burger. There's a patch of palm trees on the undeveloped coastal bluff across the street, and the ocean breeze flows all through the white wooden building. It's always packed, but service is still superfast and the conversation animated.

Av. Muñoz Rivera 402. ✆ **787/721-4269.** Reservations not accepted. Burgers from $3.50. No credit cards. Sun–Thurs 11am–11pm; Fri–Sat 11am–1am. Bus: A-5 or M-1.

Morton's The Steakhouse ★★ STEAKHOUSE The same great Morton's steaks in a dazzling room overlooking the oceans, and service that matches the settings. The chain of gourmet steakhouses was founded in 1978 by Arnie Morton, former executive vice president of the *Playboy* empire. Beef lovers, from Al Gore to Liza Minnelli, know they'll get quality meats perfectly cooked at Morton's. Carts laden with everything from prime Midwestern beefsteaks to succulent lamb or veal chops are wheeled around for your selection, but prime-rib lovers will want to try it here; a 24-ounce porterhouse is another specialty worthy of the hype. Nothing beats the house shrimp cocktail or smoked Pacific salmon for starters. Fresh and delicious seafood and vegetable dishes, shellfish, and chicken round out the menu. For dessert gravitate to one of the soufflés, such as raspberry or Grand Marnier. There are frequent specials and a beautiful bar known for its stiff drinks and smart conversation.

In the Caribe Hilton, Calle San Geronimo 1. ✆ **787/977-6262.** www.mortons.com/sanjuan. Reservations required. Main courses $20–$40. AE, DC, DISC, MC, V. Daily 5–11pm. Bus: B21.

IN CONDADO

Expensive

Budatai ★★★ LATIN/ASIAN The home of Puerto Rico's "Iron Chef" mixes local flavors with Asian ingredients to deliver one of San Juan's finest dining experiences. Scrumptiously situated in an Art Deco town house overlooking an oceanfront park at the heart of Condado's redevelopment revival, Budatai's muted brown interior is as stylish as the designer boutiques surrounding it. With wall-size windows inside and a rooftop terrace, diners have great views and are pampered with oversize tables and leather chairs. Chef Roberto Trevino, who fell just short against Mario Batali on the Food Network's *Iron Chef America* (the secret ingredient was catfish), reworks the Nuevo Latino and Asian fusion concepts he developed at Old San Juan's Parrot Club, Dragonfly, and Aquaviva restaurants and kicks up the portion sizes. Get started with the sesame-crusted pork-wrapped asparagus with a soy mayonnaise, an explosion of flavor and texture; or if sushi's your thing, the geisha roll—lobster, cream cheese, jicama, and meringue kisses. The soy-glazed salmon with coconut hash artfully balances the salty and sweet, while the veal sirloin with lobster and mashed Asian potatoes is as rich as it sounds. Skip the lo mein with *chicharon de pollo* and the karate pork chop, which are not bad, just ordinary. The waitstaff is friendly, efficient, and knowledgeable about the menu and extensive wine list. The second-floor bar and lounge is a hot spot for the city's young and beautiful, especially on weekends.

Av. Ashford 1056, Condado. ✆ **787/725-6919.** www.budatai.com. Main courses $24–$35. AE MC, V. Mon–Wed 11:30am–11pm; Thurs–Sat 11:30am–midnight; Sun 11:30am–10pm. Bus: A5, C53.

Great Taste ★★ CHINESE This is the place where the island's Chinese community goes to eat dim sum, and with good reason, as this restaurant has been serving up among the best Chinese food on the island for decades. (It also has a sushi bar.) Set in a 1970s glass-and-aluminum condominium, the dining room is spacious, comfortable, and bright, with Japanese prints, huge lobster tanks, and an enviable view over the Condado lagoon. Come here for the Chinese; everything you try, from the cashew chicken to the Peking duck to the shrimp in lobster sauce, will be excellent. If dim sum's your thing, this is the best on the island: Try the sticky rice in lotus leaf, skewered beef, and steamed vegetable dumplings. Sunday specials attract droves of diners from the local Chinese community and elsewhere with a refined sense of what good dim sum is all about.

Av. Ashford 1018. ✆ **787/721-8111.** Reservations recommended. Main courses $8–$30. AE, MC, V. Daily 11am–midnight. Bus: B21 or C53.

Pikayo ★★★ PUERTO RICAN FUSION This is an ideal place to go for the next generation of Puerto Rican fusion cuisine. Pikayo not only keeps up with the latest culinary trends, but it also often sets them, thanks to the inspired guidance of owner and celebrity chef Wilo Benet. Formal but not stuffy, and winner of more culinary awards than virtually any other restaurant in Puerto Rico, Pikayo is a specialist in the *criolla* cuisine of the colonial age, emphasizing the Spanish, Indian, and African elements in its unusual recipes. Appetizers include escargot in a wild mushroom fricassee, tuna "pegao" in a chipotle chile sauce, and cheese empanadillas with truffle mojito. The adventurism continues through the main courses, with blackened salmon with tomato-onion compote and mustard beurre blanc, and the veal scaloppine with sweet-pea risotto and julienne prosciutto. The Caribbean lobster tail is served with chorizo sausage and a gaunabana beurre blanc sauce—pricey, but delicious.

At the Conrad Condado Plaza, Av. Ashford 999. ✆ **787/721-6194.** www.wilobenet.com. Reservations recommended. Main courses $29–$65. AE, DC, MC, V. Daily 6–11pm. Bus: B21 or C53.

Ummo Restaurant ★ ARGENTINE The dark-wood and stone interior perfectly suits this sizzling Argentine restaurant specializing in *parrilladas*—grill platters of steak, chicken, blood sausage, and pork cutlets. There's also tasty Italian food, grilled fish and vegetable platters, and a good wine collection. For starters, the house specialty is antipasto platters for couples or groups, with assorted meat, cheese, and seafood combinations. There's often a singer/piano player performing inside, as well as the soccer game of the moment on the slick flatscreen TVs by the bar. The front terrace is a pleasant place for a meal, and you can watch the crowd saunter down Ashford Avenue. If it's really what you are after, a grilled steak or chicken platter might be more satisfying than a mixed grill platter, which tends to be heavy on the grilled sausage and pork cuts. The restaurant strikes a really great balance between the formal and relaxed in its ambience.

Av. Ashford 1351. ✆ **787/722-1700.** Reservations recommended. Main courses $17–$32. Mixed grill platters *(parrilladas)* $36–$44 for 2, $72–$88 for 4. AE, MC, V. Daily 11am–1am. Bus: B21.

Moderate

Via Appia ★ PIZZA/ITALIAN A favorite of *sanjuaneros* with a craving for Italian, Via Appia offers praiseworthy food at affordable prices. Its pizzas are among the best on the island, and basic pasta dishes like baked ziti, lasagna, and spaghetti taste like somebody's Italian grandmother prepared them. However, the restaurant really shows its stuff with dishes like clams *posillipo* (clams in a light tomato sauce), veal and peppers, broiled sirloin with red-wine mushroom sauce, and the delectable chicken français. The house sangria is tasty and packs a punch, and the house wine is good and helps keep a meal here in the budget category. A wine bar and more formal dining room have been added to the original deli-like main building, but the place to sit is on one of the two terraces fronting the establishment.

Av. Ashford 1350. ✆ **787/725-8711.** Main courses and pizzas $9–$30. AE, MC, V. Mon–Fri 11am–11pm; Sat–Sun 11am–midnight. Bus: A5, C53, or B21.

IN SANTURCE

Bistro de Paris ★★ FRENCH This upscale version of a classic Paris bistro sits across from Puerto Rico's beautiful art museum, and the growing legend of its classic French cuisine attracts a huge local following. The restrained beige-and-green bistro has a front terrace under shaded awnings and a dining room with huge glass windows and doors all around. Roomy and comfortable chairs and tables are the only things not authentic about the place. Basic genre dishes like French onion soup, Niçoise salad, and mussels Provençal are executed with perfection. The boneless whole trout in meunière sauce was the best fish one member of our party ever tried, and the shrimp blazed with pastis liquor, ratatouille, and sun-dried tomatoes also knocked some socks off. A big question every night is whether to go for the strip loin with tomatoes Provençal or the steak au poivre. The crème brûlée is fantastic, but the warm apple tart also reigns supreme.

Plaza de Diego, Av. José de Diego 310. ✆ **787/721-8925.** Reservations recommended. Main courses $25-$37; weekend brunch $17. AE, MC, V. Sun and Tues-Thurs noon-10pm; Fri-Sat noon-midnight. Bus: A5.

IN OCEAN PARK

Pamela's ★ 🎁 CARIBBEAN FUSION The food here matches its impressive setting on a white-sand beach free of the high rises that dominate much of the city's coast. It's simply the best place to eat on the beach in San Juan, with a menu that takes flavors from distinct Caribbean cuisines and wraps them around classic Continental fare. The result is appetizers like guava toasted sesame chicken satay, smoked-chicken sour-apple spring rolls, and spicy Jamaican jerked calamari. Main courses include sun-dried tomato *escabeche* codfish and the massive New York strip steak, crusted with a plantain-and-manchego coating. Diners can eat in a courtyard, marked by hand-painted tiles and stone fountains, or take a table under a palm tree outside and listen to the rumble of the ocean. Tasty snacks, sandwiches, and salads, and a full-service bar make this a great spot for a beach break, too.

In the Número 1 Guest House, Calle Santa Ana 1. ✆ **787/726-5010.** Reservations recommended. Main courses $8-$24 lunch, $25-$29 dinner. AE, MC, V. Daily noon-3pm and 7-10:30pm. Tapas daily 3-7pm. Bus: A5, C53.

Repostería Kasalta SPANISH/PUERTO RICAN This is the most widely known of San Juan's cafeterias/bakeries/delicatessens. You'll enter a cavernous room flanked with sun-flooded windows and a long row of display cases filled with meats, sausages, and pastries appropriate to the season. Patrons line up to place their orders at a cash register, then carry their selections to one of the many tables. Knowledge of Spanish is helpful but not essential. Among the selections are steaming bowls of Puerto Rico's best *caldo gallego,* a hearty soup laden with collard greens, potatoes, and sausage slices, served in thick earthenware bowls with hunks of bread. Also popular are Cuban sandwiches (sliced pork, cheese, and fried bread), steak sandwiches, a savory octopus salad, and an assortment of perfectly cooked omelets. Paella Valenciano is a Sunday favorite.

Calle McLeary 1966. ✆ **787/727-7340.** Reservations not accepted. Main courses $5-$22; full American breakfast $4-$9; soups $3-$6; sandwiches $5-$10. AE, DC, MC, V. Daily 6am-10pm. Bus: A5 or C53.

IN ISLA VERDE

Expensive

BLT Steak ★★ STEAKHOUSE French chef Laurent Tourondel takes the American steakhouse to new highs with an awesome selection of Black Angus, Prime and Kobe beef, as well as chicken, lamb, veal, and fresh fish. There's nothing fancy here—just the best steakhouse fare you can imagine, prepared by a chef with the talent to match the quality of the ingredients. Start with some littleneck clams from the raw bar and the crab cakes, then order the signature bone-in sirloin steak, which is among the finest cuts on the island. The sautéed Dover sole is an old-school classic that hits its mark. The potato gratin and parmesan gnocchi is especially tasty, as well as the roasted tomatoes and poached green beans. Steaks are served with a selection of sauces, including chimichurri, béarnaise, peppercorn, and horseradish. The blueberry lemon pie makes for a refreshing finale. There's also peanut-butter chocolate mousse with banana ice cream and warm coconut bread pudding with rum ice cream if you dare.

In the Ritz-Carlton San Juan Hotel, Spa & Casino, Av. de los Gobernadores (State Rd.) 6961. ✆ **787/253-1700.** Reservations required. Main courses $22–$88; fixed-price menus $45–$75. AE, DC, DISC, MC, V. Sun–Thurs 6–10:30pm; Fri–Sat 6–11pm. Bus: A5.

La Piccola Fontana ★ NORTHERN ITALIAN Just off a luxurious wing of El San Juan Hotel (p. 434), this restaurant delivers plate after plate of delectable food nightly. From its white linens to its classically formal service, it enjoys a fine reputation. The food is straightforward, generous, and extremely well prepared. You'll dine in one of two neo-Palladian rooms whose wall frescoes depict Italy's ruins and landscapes. Menu items range from the appealingly simple (grilled filets of fish or grilled veal chops) to more elaborate dishes such as gnocchi with braised *osso buco* ragout, or *linguine scogliere,* with shrimp, clams, and seafood. Grilled medallions of filet mignon are served with braised arugula, Parmesan cheese, and balsamic vinegar.

In El San Juan Hotel & Casino, Av. Isla Verde 6063. ✆ **787/791-0966.** Reservations required. Main courses $29–$75. AE, MC, V. Daily 6–11pm. Bus: A5 or C53.

Moderate

Metropol CUBAN/PUERTO RICAN/INTERNATIONAL This is part of a restaurant chain known for serving the island's best Cuban food, although the chefs prepare a much wider range of dishes. Metropol is the happiest blend of Cuban and Puerto Rican cuisine we've ever had. The black-bean soup is among the island's finest, served in the classic Havana style with a side dish of rice and chopped onions. Endless garlic bread accompanies most dinners, including Cornish game hen stuffed with Cuban rice and beans, or perhaps marinated steak topped with a fried egg (reportedly Castro's favorite). Smoked chicken and chicken-fried steak are also heartily recommended; portions are huge. Plantains, yucca, and all that good stuff accompany most dishes. Finish with a choice of thin or firm custard. Most dishes are at the low end of the price scale.

Club Gallistico, Av. Isla Verde. ✆ **787/791-4046.** www.metropolpr.com. Main courses $10–$30. AE, MC, V. Daily 11:30am–11:30pm. Bus: C53 or A5.

Soleil Beach Club Piñones ★★ 🎁 CARIBBEAN When it opened in 1997, Soleil was a pioneer in operating a fine-dining establishment among the barbecues, wooden shacks, and open-air bars of the Piñones dining scene. More than a decade later, Soleil still rules from its roost amid the sand dunes and palm trees of the undeveloped beach it fronts. Soak in that breeze and listen to those waves from a table or the bar on the oceanfront terrace, and have a drink as the sun goes down before dinner. The food here's as good as its rustic beachfront surroundings. For starters we like the fish skewers with mango sauce and the coconut-breaded shrimp in aioli sauce. The surf-and-turf pairs Argentinean-style skirt steak with shrimp, baby octopus, mahimahi, and scallops. The halibut is served in an Oriental beurre blanc sauce and cassava *mofongo;* the tuna is grilled, topped with a tropical fruit salsa, and served with cilantro-jasmine rice. This is the best oceanfront dining in San Juan and one of the best in Puerto Rico. Today the restaurant hosts corporate dinners and special events, with facilities for concerts and live shows, a dance floor, and a DJ area. There's also Wi-Fi Internet service.

Rd. 187 Km 4.6, Piñones. ✆ **787/253-1033.** www.soleilbeachclub.com. Reservations recommended. Lunch and dinner main courses $13–$39; lunch specials $7–$10. AE, DISC, MC, V. Sun–Thurs 11am–11pm; Fri–Sat 11am–2am. Call ahead to arrange free transportation to and from your hotel in the Soleil Beach Club van.

Hitting the Beach

Puerto Rico has silky white-sand beaches fronted by the warmest blue sea, windswept rocky coastlines splitting surging tides, and classic palm-fringed shores pummeled by Atlantic waves that are the stuff of surfer dreams. Many of the beaches are alternately fierce or calm, depending on the weather or the time of year, and many are fronted by aquamarine waters brimming with reefs and tropical fish.

Some San Juan beaches can get crowded, especially during summer and holiday weekends, but for most of the week, they are deliciously roomy. It's rare to find yourself alone on a beach in San Juan, but if you do, be careful: Petty crime is a reality you need to keep in mind. The city beaches are actually very safe, friendly, and well-protected places. They are also surprisingly pretty; Ocean Park and Pine Grove are among the most charming beaches in all of Puerto Rico, for example.

All beaches on Puerto Rico, even those fronting the top hotels, are open to the public. Public bathing beaches are called ***balnearios*** and charge for parking and for use of facilities, such as lockers and showers. Beach hours in general are 8:30am to 5pm Wednesday to Saturday with a $3 to $4 parking fee per car. For more information, contact the **Compañía de Parques Nacionales de Puerto Rico,** Av. Fernández Juncos 1611, Santurce (✆ **787/622-5200;** www.parquesnacionalespr.com). Hours and pricing vary. Most have bathrooms, showers, snack bars, and other public facilities (including parking areas).

There are two public beaches in the San Juan area with lifeguards, bath and changing rooms, and showers. **El Escambrón public beach** (Av. Muñoz Rivera, Pda. [*parada,* or stop] 8, Puerta de Tierra; ✆ **787/721-6133;** Wed–Sun and holidays 8:30am–5pm; parking $3.20) is right next to the Caribe Hilton and surrounded by two sprawling parks. There's a great swimming beach protected by reefs and rock formations jutting out of the water. There's good snorkeling around the rocks, with lots of fish. The famed El 8 surf spot is just to the west. There's a snack bar and a full-scale restaurant located here. The other public beach is **Isla Verde public beach** (Av. de los Gobernadores; ✆ **787/791-8084;** Tues–Sun 8:30am–5pm; parking $4), a huge expanse of white sand and tranquil waters between Isla Verde and Piñones. There are lifeguards; changing rooms, bathrooms, and showers; and picnic areas and barbecue grills, as well as an on-site restaurant.

Swimmers, Beware

You have to pick your spots carefully if you want to swim along many San Juan beaches, especially Condado Beach. The waters at the beach beside the Condado Plaza Hotel are calmer than in other areas because of a coral breakwater. The beach near the Marriott is not good for swimming because of rocks, a strong undertow, and occasional rip tides. There are no lifeguards except at public beaches. Ocean Park is better to swim, but can still be hazardous when the tides kick up. Isla Verde Beach is generally much calmer, especially at its eastern end. The surf off Piñones, further east, may be the most treacherous of all.

Famous with beach buffs since the 1920s, **Condado Beach ★★** put San Juan on the map as a tourist resort. Backed up against high-rise hotels, it seems more like Miami Beach than any other beach in the Caribbean. All sorts of watersports can be booked at the activities desk of the hotels. A small beach near the Condado Plaza hotel is the only one with lifeguards, which are on duty from 8:30am to 5pm. There are also outdoor showers. The beaches in the rest of the Condado are much nicer, but as there are no lifeguards and the surf can get rough, particularly by the San Juan Marriott; swimmers should exercise caution. There are powerful rip tides here that have been responsible for past drownings. There are no public toilets here. People-watching is a favorite sport along these golden strands, which stretch from the Ventana del Mar park to beyond the Marriott. The best stretch of beach in Condado runs from the Ashford Presbyterian hospital to Ocean Park. The area behind the Atlantic Beach Hotel (p. 433) is popular with the gay crowd; the beach farther along, with Marriott (p. 432) guests and surfers, is also pretty, but with extremely rough waters at times.

One of the most attractive beaches in the Greater San Juan area is **Ocean Park Beach ★★**, a mile of fine gold sand in a neighborhood east of Condado. This beach attracts young people, travelers looking for a guesthouse rather than the large hotel experience, and those looking for a big gay crowd. The beach runs from Parque del Indio in Condado all the way to the Barbosa Park in the area known as El Ultimo Trolley and offers paddle tennis, kite-boarding, and beach volleyball. You can grab lunch and refreshments from several area guesthouses, and vendors walk up and down the beach selling cold beer, water, and soft drinks, and even snacks like fried seafood turnovers. Farther east, there's no real beach at **Punta Las Marías,** but it's one of the favorite launch points for windsurfers.

Isla Verde Beach ★★ is the longest and widest in San Juan. It is ideal for swimming, and it, too, is lined with high-rise resorts a la Miami Beach. Many luxury condos are on this beachfront. Isla Verde is good for watersports, including parasailing and snorkeling, because of its calm, clear waters, and many kiosks will rent you equipment, especially by the El San Juan (p. 434). There are also cafes and restaurants at hotels and more reasonably priced individual restaurants nearby.

Isla Verde Beach extends from the end of Ocean Park to the beginning of a section called Boca Cangrejos. The most popular stretch is probably behind the El San Juan and Inter-Continental San Juan (p. 435) hotels. But Pine Grove Beach, behind the Ritz-Carlton (p. 435), is a great swimming beach and very popular as well, particularly with surfers and sailors.

Sports & Outdoor Pursuits

SCUBA DIVING The continental shelf, which surrounds Puerto Rico on three sides, is responsible for an abundance of coral reefs, caves, sea walls, and trenches for scuba diving and snorkeling. Introductory courses for beginners start at $125; two-tank dives for experienced divers begin at around $85, but most cost at least $125.

In San Juan, try **Caribe Aquatic Adventures,** Normandie Hotel San Juan, Calle 19 1062, Villa Nevarez (✆ **787/281-8858**), or **Ocean Sports,** Av. Isla Verde 77 (✆ **787/268-2329**).

SNORKELING Snorkeling is better in the outlying portions of the island than in overcrowded San Juan. But if you don't have time to explore greater Puerto Rico, you'll find that most of the popular beaches have pretty good visibility and kiosks that rent equipment. Snorkeling equipment generally rents for $15. If you're on your own in the San Juan area, one of the best places is the San Juan Bay Marina, near the Caribe Hilton.

Watersports desks at the big San Juan hotels at Isla Verde and Condado can generally make arrangements for instruction and equipment rental, and can also lead you to the best places for snorkeling, depending on where you are in the sprawling metropolis. If your hotel doesn't offer such services, you can contact **Caribe Aquatic Adventures** (see "Scuba Diving," above), which caters to both snorkelers and scuba divers. Still, even if you are staying in San Juan and want to go snorkeling, you are better off taking a day trip to Fajardo, where you'll get a real Caribbean snorkeling experience, with tranquil, clear water and stunning reefs teeming with tropical fish. (See "Fajardo & the East," later in this chapter.)

Several operators offer day trips (10am–3:30pm) leaving from Fajardo marinas, but transportation to and from your San Juan hotel can also be arranged. Prices start at around $69 per person, or $99 including transportation to and from San Juan.

WINDSURFING & KITEBOARDING Great windsurfing and kiteboarding advice and lessons are available at **Velauno,** Calle Loíza 2430, Punta Las Marías, San Juan (✆ **787/728-8716;** www.velauno.com). The instructors will also rent equipment, with prices starting at about $75 daily. A 1-hour beginner lesson costs $70, and other courses on offer range from 1 to 10 hours. The staff here will guide you to the best windsurfing, which is likely to be the Punta Las Marías in the Greater San Juan metropolitan area. Office hours are Monday to Friday 10am to 7pm, Saturday 11am to 7pm. Other spots on the island for windsurfing include Santa Isabel, Guánica, and La Parguera in the south; Jobos and Shacks in the northwest; and the island of Culebra off the eastern coast.

Exploring the Historic Sites of San Juan

The Spanish moved to Old San Juan in 1521, and the city played an important role as Spain's bastion of defense in the Caribbean. Today the streets are narrow and teeming with traffic, but a walk through El Viejo San Juan makes for a good stroll. It's also the biggest and best collection of historic buildings, stretching back 5 centuries, in all the Caribbean. You can do it in less than a day, but only if you are willing to skim the surface. To truly do this gem justice, plan to spend several days exploring this culturally rich area. In a 7-square-block landmark area in the westernmost part of the city, you can see many of Puerto Rico's chief historical attractions and do some shopping along the way.

CHURCHES

Capilla de Cristo The chapel was built to commemorate what legend calls a miracle. In 1753 a young rider lost control of his horse in a race down this very street during the fiesta of St. John's Day, plunging over the precipice. Moved by the accident, the secretary of the city, Don Mateo Pratts, invoked Christ to save the youth—and had the chapel built when his prayers were answered. Today it's a landmark in the Old Town and one of its best-known monuments. The chapel's gold-and-silver altar can be seen through its glass doors. Since the chapel is open only on Tuesdays, most visitors have to settle for a view of its exterior.

Calle del Cristo (directly west of Paseo de la Princesa). ✆ **787/722-0861.** Free admission. Tues 8am–5pm. Bus: Old City Trolley.

Catedral de San Juan San Juan Cathedral was begun in 1540 and has had a rough life. Looting, lacking funds, and hurricanes have continually hampered its construction and reconstruction. Over the years, a circular staircase and two adjoining vaulted Gothic chambers have been added. Many beautiful stained-glass windows escaped pillagers and natural disasters. In 1908 the body of Ponce de León was disinterred from the nearby Iglesia de San José and placed here in a marble tomb near the transept, where it remains. Since 1862 the cathedral has contained the wax-covered mummy of St. Pio, a Roman martyr persecuted and killed for his Christian faith. To the right of the mummy is a bizarre wooden statue of Mary with four swords stuck in her bosom. The cathedral faces Plaza de las Monjas (the Nuns' Square), a shady spot where you can rest and cool off.

Calle del Cristo 153 (at Caleta San Juan). ✆ **787/722-0861.** Free admission. Daily 8am–5pm; Mass at 9 and 11am. Bus: Old City Trolley.

FORTS

Castillo de San Felipe del Morro ★ ☺ Called "El Morro," this fort stands on a rocky promontory dominating the entrance to San Juan Bay. In 1992 the parklike grounds around El Morro were restored to their 18th-century appearance and are ideal for walks. Constructed in 1540, the original fort was a round tower, which can still be seen deep inside the lower levels of the castle. More walls and cannon-firing positions were added, and by 1787 the fortification attained the complex design you see today. This fortress was attacked repeatedly by both the English and the Dutch.

The U.S. National Park Service protects the fortifications of Old San Juan, which have been declared a World Heritage Site by the United Nations. With some of the most dramatic views in the Caribbean, you'll find El Morro an intriguing labyrinth of

Jogger's Trail or Romantic Walk

El Morro Trail, a jogger's paradise, provides Old Town's most scenic views across the harbor. The first part of the trail extends to the San Juan Gate. The walk then goes by El Morro, a 16th-century fort, and eventually reaches a scenic area known as Bastion de Santa Barbara. The walk passes El Morro's well-preserved walls, and the trail ends at the entrance to the fortress. The walkway is designed to follow the undulating movement of the ocean, and sea grapes and tropical vegetation surround benches. The trail is romantic at night, when the walls of the fortress are illuminated. Stop in at the tourist office for a map, and set off.

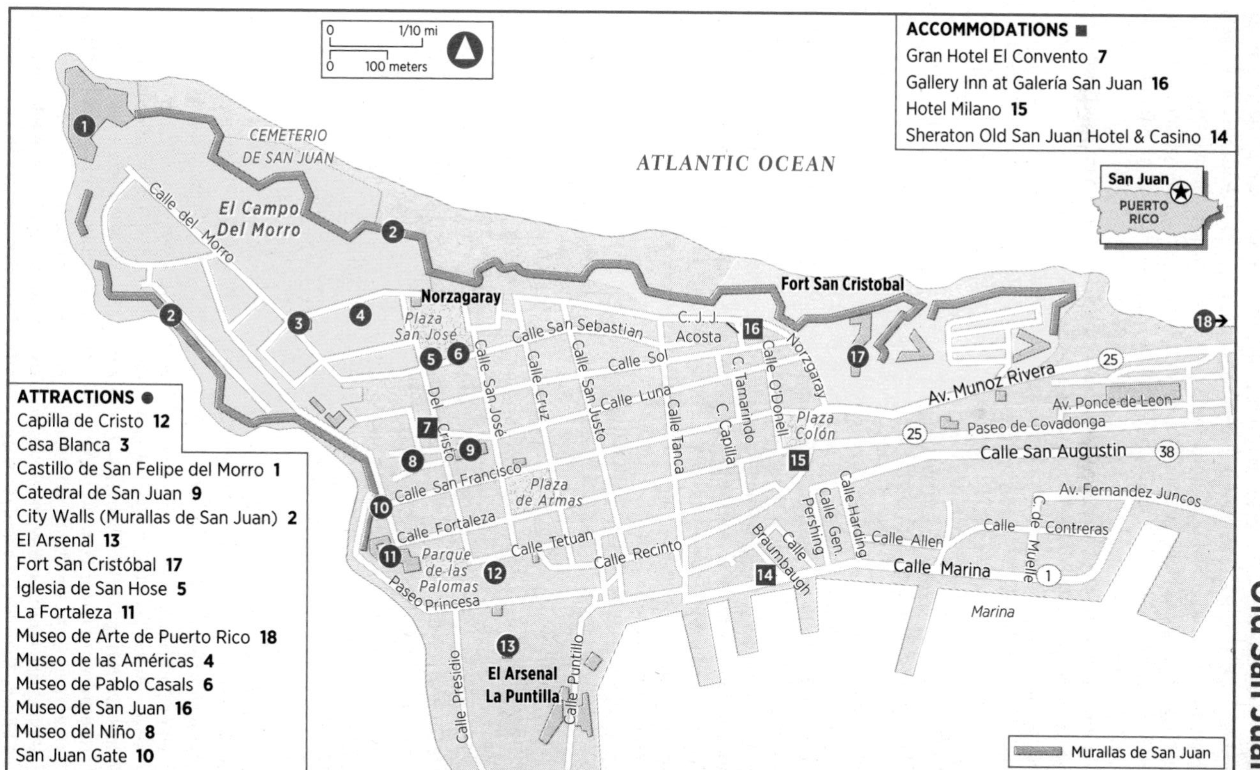
0 1/10 mi
0 100 meters
ACCOMMODATIONS ■
Gran Hotel El Convento 7
Gallery Inn at Galería San Juan 16
Hotel Milano 15
Sheraton Old San Juan Hotel & Casino 14
ATLANTIC OCEAN
San Juan
PUERTO RICO
CEMETERIO DE SAN JUAN
El Campo Del Morro
Calle del Morro
Norzagaray
Plaza San José
Fort San Cristobal
C. J. J. Acosta
Calle San Sebastian
Calle Sol
Calle Luna
Calle San José
Calle Cruz
Calle San Justo
Calle Tanca
C. Tamarindo
C. Capilla
Calle O'Donell
Norzgaray
Plaza Colón
Av. Munoz Rivera
Av. Ponce de Leon
Paseo de Covadonga
Calle San Augustin
Av. Fernandez Juncos
Del Cristo
Calle San Francisco
Plaza de Armas
Calle Fortaleza
Calle Tetuan
Calle Recinto
Calle Braumbaugh
Calle Gen. Pershing
Calle Harding
Calle Allen
Calle Contreras
C. de Muelle
Calle Marina
Marina
Parque de las Palomas
Paseo Princesa
Calle Presidio
El Arsenal La Puntilla
Calle Puntillo
ATTRACTIONS ●
Capilla de Cristo 12
Casa Blanca 3
Castillo de San Felipe del Morro 1
Catedral de San Juan 9
City Walls (Murallas de San Juan) 2
El Arsenal 13
Fort San Cristóbal 17
Iglesia de San Hose 5
La Fortaleza 11
Museo de Arte de Puerto Rico 18
Museo de las Américas 4
Museo de Pablo Casals 6
Museo de San Juan 16
Museo del Niño 8
San Juan Gate 10
Murallas de San Juan

dungeons, barracks, vaults, lookouts, and ramps. Historical and background information is provided in a video in English and Spanish. The nearest parking is the underground facility beneath the Quincentennial Plaza at the Cuartel de Ballajá (Ballajá barracks), on Calle Norzagaray. Sometimes park rangers lead hour-long tours for free, although you can also visit on your own. With the purchase of a ticket here, you don't have to pay the admission for Fort San Cristóbal (see below) if you visit during the same day.

Before going into the citadel, you can visit the new $2-million **San Juan National Historic Site** (✆ **787/729-6960**), which is open daily from 9am to 5pm, charging $3 for adults (free for ages 15 and under). The center is connected via two tunnels to Fort San Cristóbal and was created from a strategic military base used in World War II. Visitors view a 12-minute film about the fortifications. A photo exhibit, a gift shop, and other exhibits are of interest.

At the end of Calle Norzagaray. ✆ **787/729-6777.** www.nps.gov/saju. Admission $3 adults, free for children 15 and under. Daily 9am–6pm. Bus: A5, B21, or B40.

Fort San Cristóbal ★ This huge fortress, begun in 1634 and reengineered in the 1770s, is one of the largest the Spanish ever built in the Americas. Its walls rise more than 150 feet above the sea. Together San Cristóbal and El Morro, which are linked by nearly half a mile of monumental walls and bastions filled with cannon-firing positions, protected San Juan against attackers coming by land. A complex system of tunnels and dry moats connects the center of San Cristóbal to its "outworks," defensive elements arranged layer after layer over a 27-acre site. You'll get the idea if you look at the scale model on display. The fort is administered and maintained by the National Park Service.

Be sure to see the **Garita del Diablo,** or the Devil's Sentry Box, one of the oldest parts of San Cristóbal's defenses, and famous in Puerto Rican legend. The devil himself, it is said, would snatch away sentinels at this lonely post at the edge of the sea. In 1898 the first shots of the Spanish-American War in Puerto Rico were fired by cannons on top of San Cristóbal during an artillery duel with a U.S. Navy fleet. Sometimes park rangers lead hour-long tours for free, although you can visit on your own.

In the northeast corner of Old San Juan (uphill from Plaza de Colón on Calle Norzagaray). ✆ **787/729-6777.** www.nps.gov/saju. Admission $3 adults, free for children 15 and under for 1 fort; $5 pass (valid for 7 days) available for both forts. Daily 9am–6pm. Bus: A5, B21, or B40; then the free Old City Trolley from Covadonga station to the top of the hill.

OTHER HISTORIC SITES

The **city walls** around San Juan *(murallas de San Juan)* were built in 1630 to protect the town against both European invaders and Caribbean pirates, and indeed were part of one of the most impregnable fortresses in the New World. Even today they're an engineering marvel. At their top, notice the balconied buildings that served for centuries as hospitals and also residences of the island's various governors. The thickness of the walls averages 20 feet at the base and 11 feet at the top, with an average height of 39 feet. Between Fort San Cristóbal and El Morro, bastions were erected at frequent intervals. The walls come into view as you approach from San Cristóbal on your way to El Morro. To get here, take the C45 or A5 bus.

San Juan Gate, at Calle San Francisco and Calle Recinto Oeste, was built around 1635, just north of La Fortaleza, several blocks downhill from the cathedral, and was the main gate and entry point into San Juan—that is, if you arrived by ship in the 18th century. The gate is the only one remaining of the several that once pierced the fortifications of the old walled city. To get here, take the Old City Trolley.

Casa Blanca Ponce de León never lived here, although construction of the house (built in 1521) is sometimes attributed to him. The house was erected 2 years after the explorer's death, by the order of his son-in-law, Juan García Troche. The parcel of land was given to Ponce de León as a reward for services rendered to the Crown. His descendants lived in the house for about 2½ centuries, until the Spanish government took it over in 1779 for use as a residence for military commanders. The U.S. government also used it as a home for army commanders. On the first floor, the Juan Ponce de León Museum is furnished with antiques, paintings, and artifacts from the 16th through the 18th centuries. In back is a garden with spraying fountains, offering an intimate and verdant respite from the monumental buildings of Old San Juan.

Calle San Sebastián 1. ✆ **787/725-1454.** Admission $2. Tues–Sat 9am–noon and 1–4:30pm. Bus: Old City Trolley.

El Arsenal The Spaniards used shallow craft to patrol the lagoons and mangroves in and around San Juan. Needing a base for these vessels, they constructed El Arsenal in the 19th century. It was at this base that they staged their last stand, flying the Spanish colors until the final Spaniard was removed in 1898, at the end of the Spanish-American War. Changing art exhibitions are held in the building's three galleries.

La Puntilla. ✆ **787/724-0700.** Free admission. Wed–Sun 8:30am–4:30pm. Bus: Old City Trolley.

La Fortaleza The office and residence of the governor of Puerto Rico is the oldest executive mansion in continuous use in the Western Hemisphere; it has served as the island's seat of government for more than 3 centuries. Yet its history goes back even further, to 1533, when construction began on a fortress to protect San Juan's Spanish settlers during raids by Carib tribesmen and pirates. The original medieval towers remain, but as the edifice was subsequently enlarged into a palace, other modes of architecture and ornamentation were also incorporated, including baroque, Gothic, neoclassical, and Arabian. La Fortaleza has been designated a national historic site by the U.S. government. Thirty-minute tours of the gardens and building are conducted in English and Spanish. Informal but proper attire is required.

Calle Fortaleza 52 (overlooking San Juan Harbor). ✆ **787/721-7000,** ext. 2358. Free admission; tours of the gardens and building $3 (given every 30 min. and conducted in English and Spanish) Mon–Fri 9:30am–4:30pm. Bus: Old City Trolley.

MUSEUMS

Museo de Arte de Puerto Rico ★★ One of Puerto Rico's most important galleries is a state-of-the-art showcase for the island nation's rich cultural heritage as reflected mainly by its painters. Located in Santurce, the museum features a permanent collection and temporary exhibitions. All the important modern island artists are represented, including the best known, Angel Botello (1913–86), but also such contemporaries as Rafael Tufiño (1922–2008) and Arnaldo Roche Rabell (b. 1955). Prominent local artists from the past also star—for example, Francisco Oller (1833–1917), who brought a touch of Cézanne and Camille Pissarro to Puerto Rico. (Oller actually studied in France with both of these Impressionists.) Another leading star of the permanent collection is José Campéche, a late-18th-century classical painter. The museum is like a living textbook of Puerto Rican art, beginning with its early development and going on to showcase camp aspects such as the poster art created here in the mid–20th century.

Av. Jose de Diego 299, Santurce. ✆ **787/977-6277.** www.mapr.org. Admission $6 adults; $3 students, seniors, and children; free for seniors 75 and older and children 4 and under. Tues and Thurs–Sat 10am–5pm; Wed 10am–8pm; Sun 11am–6pm. Bus: A5 or B21.

Museo de las Américas ★ This museum showcases the artisans of North, South, and Central America, featuring everything from carved figureheads of New England whaling ships to dugout canoes carved by Carib Indians in Dominica. It is unique in Puerto Rico and well worth a visit. Also on display is a changing collection of paintings by artists throughout the Spanish-speaking world, some of which are for sale, and a permanent collection called "Puerto Rican *Santos,*" donated by Dr. Ricardo Alegría.

Sala Cuartel de Ballajá (at Calle Norzagaray and Calle del Morro). ✆ **787/724-5052.** Admission $3 adults; $2 students with ID, children 11 and under and seniors 65 and over. Tues–Wed and Sun 10am–4pm; Thurs–Fri 9am–4pm. Bus: Old City Trolley.

Museo de Arte e Historia de San Juan Located in a Spanish colonial building at the corner of Calle MacArthur, this cultural center was the city's main marketplace in the mid–19th century. Local art is displayed in the east and west galleries, and audiovisual materials reveal the history of the city. Sometimes major cultural events are staged in the museum's large courtyard. English- and Spanish-language audiovisual shows are presented Tuesday to Friday every hour on the hour from 9am to 4pm. Some of the city's finest young artists show here.

Calle Norzagaray 150. ✆ **787/724-1875.** Free admission, but donations accepted. Tues–Fri 9am–4pm; Sat–Sun 10am–4pm. Bus: To Old San Juan terminal, then the Old City Trolley.

Museo de Pablo Casals This museum is devoted to the memorabilia left to the people of Puerto Rico by the musician Pablo Casals. The maestro's cello is here, along with a library of videotapes (which can be played upon request) of some of his festival concerts. This small 18th-century house also contains manuscripts and photographs of Casals. The annual Casals Festival draws worldwide interest and internationally known performing artists; it's held in late February or early March.

Plaza San José, Calle San Sebastián 101. ✆ **787/723-9185.** Admission $1. Tues–Sat 9:30am–5:30pm. Bus: Old City Trolley.

Shopping ★★

U.S. citizens don't pay duty on items they purchase in Puerto Rico and bring back to the United States. However, a 7% sales tax is placed on pretty much everything. But you can find great bargains on Puerto Rico, where the competition among shopkeepers is fierce.

The streets of the Old Town, such as Calle Fortaleza, Calle San Francisco, and Calle del Cristo, are the major venues for shopping. After years of trying, local restrictions on operating hours of stores, aimed at protecting small businesses and the religious nature of Sundays in Roman Catholic Puerto Rico, were finally overturned in 2010. Shops and stores are now free to open anytime except between 6 and 11am Sunday mornings. In general, malls in San Juan are open Monday to Saturday 9am to 9pm and Sunday from 10am to 7pm. In tourism districts like Old San Juan and Condado, most stores still close by 7 pm, but Old Town shops remain open late whenever cruise ships are at harbor. There are now more 24-hour grocery stores and pharmacies, and Wal-Mart has instituted the concept at a few stores in suburban San Juan.

Local handicrafts still abound in Puerto Rico, and your best bets are prints, paintings, and sculptures by Puerto Rican artists, including the revered *santos,* carved wooden renderings of the saints and other religious figures, which are coveted by art collectors and said by the devout to have healing powers and the ability to perform *milagros,* or miracles. There is also Mundillo lace, coffee, and rum.

Large, modern, and always up to date, **Plaza Las Americas,** the largest mall in the Caribbean, is located in the financial district of Hato Rey, right off the Las Americas Expressway. The complex has more than 300 shops. There are also several top-notch restaurants, a full cineplex, plus art galleries and food stores. If you want a break from the sun (or if it's raining), there are entertainment options here for all.

ART

If you're interested in acquiring Puerto Rican art, there are many possibilities. **Galería Botello ★**, Calle del Cristo 208 (✆ **787/723-9987;** www.botello.com), is a contemporary Latin American gallery, a living tribute to the late Angel Botello, one of Puerto Rico's most outstanding artists. His paintings and bronze sculptures, evocative of his colorful background, are done in a style uniquely his own. On display are his and other local artists' paintings and sculptures, as well as a large collection of antique Puerto Rican *santos.*

Galería Exodo, Calle del Cristo 200B (✆ **787/725-4252;** www.galeriaexodo.com), is an exciting gallery showing work from young contemporary island and regional artists, many of whom are not afraid to engage in bold experimentation. The work ranges from Radamés Rivera's limestone and coral art pieces that could have existed at the time of the dinosaurs, to Yolanda Velasquez's vibrant abstract paintings. Over 40 artists, from Cuba to Mexico, showcase work here.

Gallery Inn, Calle Norzagaray 204–206 (✆ **787/722-1808**), specializes in the sculpture and paintings of Jan D'Esopo, a Connecticut-born artist who has spent most of her life in Puerto Rico. Many of her fine pieces are in bronze.

COFFEE & SPICES

Spicy Caribbee, Calle del Cristo 154 (✆ **787/725-4690**), offers the best selection of Puerto Rican coffee, which has a good reputation among aficionados. It also has the Old Town's best array of hot, spicy sauces of the Caribbean.

FASHION

Nono Maldonado, Av. Ashford 1112, midway between the Condado Plaza and the Ramada Hotel (✆ **787/721-0456**), is named after its owner, a Puerto Rican designer. Selling both men's and women's clothing, it has everything from socks to dinner jackets, as well as ready-to-wear versions of Maldonado's twice-a-year collections. **Polo Ralph Lauren Factory Store,** Calle del Cristo 201 (✆ **787/722-2136**), has prices that are often 35% to 40% less than what you'd find on the U.S. mainland. You can get even greater discounts on irregular or slightly damaged garments. **Dooney & Bourke Factory Store,** Calle del Cristo 200 (✆ **787/289-0075**), has bargains on its complete line of high-quality leather wear, from handbags to briefcases, wallets, and belts.

Hecho a Mano, Av. Ashford 1126 (✆ **787/722-5322;** www.hechoamanopro.com), stocks beautiful ethnic clothing for women, using island fabric but also that from Guatemala, Indonesia, India, and Africa. Styles range from willowy dresses and wraps in tribal patterns, to more modern, tropical-fashion party dresses. It has gorgeous clothes, plus handmade jewelry and other interesting finds. The ambience in the store is wonderful, complete with incense, world music, and the beautiful sales staff outfitted in the store's fashion. Founded in 1993, the company prides itself on its dealings with its artisans and its efforts to undertake practices and designs in harmony with nature. The brand now has 12 locations, including in Condado and Plaza Las Américas.

The friendliest, trendiest surf shop in town, **Lost Surf Shop,** Av. Ashford 1129. Condado (✆ **787/723-4750**) has what you need—from boards to surf wax—to hit the waves. If you are just interested in looking good on the beach, this is your place, too. The store features top-of-the-line surf wear and beach fashion, but there are frequent specials on quality goods, and some real bargains can be had. Come here for great sunglasses and other accessories.

GIFTS, ARTS & CRAFTS

Butterfly People ★, Calle de la Cruz 152, 2nd Floor (✆ **787/723-2432;** www.butterflypeople.com), is a gallery in a handsomely restored building in Old San Juan. Butterflies, sold here in artfully arranged boxes, range from $35 for a single mounting to thousands of dollars for whole-wall murals. The butterflies are preserved and will last forever. The dimensional artwork is sold in limited editions and can be shipped worldwide. Most of these butterflies come from farms around the world, some of the most beautiful hailing from Indonesia, Malaysia, and New Guinea.

Bóveda, Calle del Cristo 209 (✆ **787/725-0263**), is a long, narrow space crammed with exotic jewelry, clothing, greeting cards of images of life in Puerto Rico, antiques, Mexican punched tin and glass, and Art Nouveau reproductions, among other items.

Get a taste of the beauty of Puerto Rican culture at **Mundo Taíno,** Calle San José 151 (✆ **787/274-3601**), an appropriately bright and friendly shop with local jewelry, statues, prints, fabrics, and other handicrafts, plus music and literature. You can also get a CD with rainforest sounds, gourmet coffee, local sweets, rum, and other delicacies. It's run by a young, helpful, and friendly staff who know their stuff.

Olé, Calle Fortaleza 105 (✆ **787/724-2445**), deserves an *olé.* Browsing this store is a learning experience. Practically everything comes from Puerto Rico or Latin America. If you want a straw hat from Ecuador, hand-beaten Chilean silver, Christmas ornaments, or Puerto Rican *santos,* this is the place.

Puerto Rican Arts & Crafts ★, Calle Fortaleza 204 (✆ **787/725-5596**), set in a 200-year-old colonial building, is one of the premier outlets on the island for authentic artifacts. Of particular interest are papier-mâché carnival masks from Ponce. Taíno designs inspired by ancient petroglyphs are incorporated into most of the sterling-silver jewelry sold here. There's an art gallery in back, with silk-screened serigraphs by local artists, and a gourmet Puerto Rican food section with such items as coffee, rum, and hot sauces. The store also exhibits and sells small carved *santos,* laboriously carved by artisans in private studios around the island.

JEWELRY

Bared & Sons ★, Calle Fortaleza 206 at the corner of Calle San Justo (✆ **787/724-4811**), now in its 4th decade, is the main outlet of a chain of at least 20 upscale jewelry stores on Puerto Rico. On the ground floor are gemstones, gold, diamonds, and watches. One floor up, there's a monumental collection of porcelain and crystal. It's a great source for hard-to-get and discontinued patterns from Christofle, Royal Doulton, Wedgwood, Limoges, Royal Copenhagen, Lalique, Lladró, Herend, Baccarat, and Daum.

Ron Bacardi

No trip to Puerto Rico is complete without a tour of the Bacardi Rum Factory, where they show you how they make the liquid gold and ply you with free drinks. There's an interesting historic tour and a shop where you will be tempted to buy way more bottles than you can possibly carry home or drink.

Casa Bacardi Visitor Center, across the bay from San Juan on Route 165 in Cantaño (© 787/788-8400; www.casabacardi.org), offers free tours Monday through Saturday from 9am to 4:30pm (last tour at 4:15pm), and Sunday from 10am to 5pm (last tour at 3:45pm).

San Juan After Dark

THE PERFORMING ARTS

Qué Pasa, the official visitor's guide to Puerto Rico, lists cultural events, including music, dance, theater, film, and art exhibits. It's distributed free by the tourist office. Local English-language media also announce events on the local **WOSO** 1030 AM radio station.

Puerto Rico Coliseum, Calle Arterial 500, Hato Rey (**© 866/994-0001;** www.coliseodepuertorico.com), also known as the **Jose Agrelot Coliseum,** is a modern state-of-the-art venue that hosts artists such as Sting, the Rolling Stones, Elton John, and Iron Maiden. It even has big family-friendly productions such as Disney's *Princesses on Ice,* and hosts fashion shows and bridal expos. During Christmas season, there's ice-skating. To find out who's playing and how to get your tickets, log on to its website or visit **TicketPop** (**© 787/294-0001;** www.ticketpop.com).

The Centro de Bellas Artes venues in Santurce (**© 787/620-4444**)—the **Luis A. Ferre Center for the Performing Arts** and **Festival Hall**—has classical music, opera, and dance performances. The facility is large, but the venues always feel cozy since there are multiple theaters within the center. Tickets for live performances can be purchased at **Ticket Center** in Plaza Las Americas (**© 787/792-5000;** www.tcpr.com) or at **TicketPop** (**© 787/294-0001;** www.ticketpop.com).

Another cultural venue in San Juan is **Teatro Tapía,** Avenida Ponce de León (**© 787/721-0180**), across from Plaza de Colón, one of the oldest theaters in the Western Hemisphere (built around 1832). Much of Puerto Rican theater history is connected with the Tapía, named after the island's first prominent playwright, Alejandro Tapía y Rivera. Various productions, some musical, are staged here throughout the year and include drama, dance, and cultural events. You'll have to call the box office (Mon–Fri 9am–6pm) for specific information. Tickets generally start at $20 to $30.

THE CLUB & MUSIC SCENE

Like any major metropolitan city, today's hip joint is tomorrow's empty venue. One of the fun parts of a visit to a vibrant destination like San Juan is that there are nearly endless possibilities for evening entertainment. Follow the crowd to the newest hottest salsa club, hippest jazz bar, or wildest party, or swim against the tide and scout out a cozy nook or quiet bar to make your own personal hot spot. Condado's **La Concha** hotel (p. 432), a renovated wonder of tropical modernism, is a great place to have drinks and munch on tapas throughout the lobby and adjacent multilevel pool area, replete with water fountains, tropical vegetation, and designer seating. The

TO THE mountains

The best way to catch a glimpse of the central mountains from San Juan is to head south along the Luis A. Ferré Expressway (Hwy. 52). You can take an afternoon drive and have dinner as the sun sets in the mountains; from some vantage points, the view goes all the way to the coast. A favorite stop is **Guavate.** Take the exit for Route 184, which winds through rolling farmland and farther up along a mountain stream flowing through the lush **Carite State Forest.** In addition to the eateries, the sector is famous for local arts and crafts, and plants and flowers that are sold from stands along the roadway. While the area began gaining fame years ago for a cluster of restaurants outside the natural reserve's main entrance, the string of *lechoneras* (pig-roasting restaurants) has now extended along the entire route from the expressway. The best restaurants, however, have a certain rustic charm in addition to their utilitarian nature. Some look like wooden tropical chalets with blooming flowers, while others are set in front of a stream gushing through a lush mountainside. **Los Amigos,** at the expressway exit, is for those who want to dive in to the genuine experience, and make a quick escape. (On Sunday afternoons, especially around Christmas season, traffic is often clogged along the country road.) It has among the best food we've had here, and though utterly unscenic (like a restaurant converted from a gas station), it draws a lively crowd from early on. Our favorites include **La Casa del Guanime** (Rte. 184 Km 27.5; ✆ **787/744-3921**), **El Rancho Original** (Rte. 184 Km 27.5; ✆ **787/747-7296**), **Los Pinos** (Rte. 184 Km 27.7; ✆ **787/286-1917**), and **El Mojito** (Rte. 184 Km 32.9; ✆ **787/738-8888**). The truth is, however, that we have been rarely disappointed in any of the restaurants we visited.

Most have live music on weekend afternoons, so whether your taste runs from salsa to merengue to local *jíbaro* country music, or to something more contemporary, may play a big role in your choice. Also, the road carves through a lush forest, and a string of restaurants along its right-hand side is set in front of the mountain stream; several have dining rooms overlooking the stream, and in the quieter ones, its gurgling is the only music you'll hear.

The atmosphere is important, but the main thing about Guavate is the food: roast pork and chicken, fried rice and pigeon peas, boiled root vegetables soaked in oil and spices, and blood sausage. This is traditional Puerto Rican mountain food, but the level of the cooking keeps getting better every time we return. The roast turkey (yes, they keep it juicy) is a healthy alternative to the pig; it has recently been showing up *escabeche* style, drenched in olive oil, garlic and onions, roasted peppers, and herbs—absolutely delicious. If you have more time, you can head farther into the mountains, to Cayey and Aibonito, charming towns with fine restaurants.

lobby of **El San Juan Hotel & Casino** (p. 434) in Isla Verde remains one of the city's best centers of nightlife. On Thursday and Friday nights, young professionals gather in the streets surrounding the **Plaza del Mercado** in Santurce, which are lined with open-air bars, many playing loud Latin music.

Bar Gitano, Av. Ashford 1302, Condado (✆ **787/294-5513**) is the kind of spot you might find off the Plaza Mayor in Madrid, with authentic Spanish tapas and fine Spanish wines and sangrias, and every bit as stylish as an Almodóvar film. A new spot for San Juan's ever fashionable party crowd, the bar also serves top notch food and hosts live flamenco music.

Brava and Ultra Lounge, in El San Juan Hotel & Casino, Av. Isla Verde 6063, Isla Verde (✆ **787/791-2781**), attracts the young and privileged, local celebs, and urbane visitors who mix it up on the club's dance floor to house, reggaeton, and Latin music styles. The nightclub is designed in the form of a circle, with a central dance floor and a wraparound balcony, where onlookers and voyeurs—a 25-to-45-year-old age group—can observe the activities on the floor below. There's also a laid-back lounge area for conversation and table service. It has one of the best sound systems in the Caribbean, and its stage is often the scene of memorable performances. You can find it right off the hotel's lively lobby and casino, and it's open Thursday through Saturday from 10pm until 5am.. Guests of the hotel enter free; otherwise, there's a $15 cover (bus no. A5).

Club Laser, Calle del Cruz 251 (✆ **787/722-7581**), has been hopping for nearly 2 decades through various transformations. A huge cavernous place in the middle of town, there's salsa, boca, reggaeton, and other Caribbean styles depending on the night. The club attracts a large local crowd, as well as regular customers who work on the cruise-ship lines, and young people from throughout the world. The cover ranges from $10 to $15, but ladies often enter free.

The **Nuyorican Café,** Calle San Francisco 312 (✆ **787/977-1276;** www.nuyoricancafepr.com), has live music nearly every night of the week. This place specializes in Puerto Rican and Cuban salsa and Latin jazz, but there's also rock *en español,* reggae, theatrical performances, art exhibits, and a damn good kitchen (the pizza is one of the island's best).

Rumba, Calle San Sebastián 152 (✆ **787/725-4407**), has a full bar up front, a huge back room with a stage for a live band, and a dance floor. It's so photogenically hip that it was selected as the site for the filming of many of the crowd scenes within *Dirty Dancing: Havana Nights.* It's a great venue for live music, with excellent salsa, Latin jazz, and other tropical music. The crowd ranges from college kids to well-dressed graybeards who remember the music back in its 1970s heyday; the common denominator is the love of the music and dance. It's open Thursday to Saturday 8pm to 4am (bus: Old City Trolley).

Several restaurants in San Juan have live music on certain days of the week. The **Parrot Club** (p. 437) has live Latin jazz and salsa a few nights weekly. **Carli Café Concierto** (p. 436) has live jazz nightly at 9pm; **Barrachina,** Calle Fortaleza 104 (✆ **787/725-7912**) has a live flamenco music and dance show nightly. **La Playita,** Calle Amapola 6, (✆ **787/791-9115**), in Isla Verde, hosts weekend troubadours, while **Yerba Buena,** Av. Ashford 1350, Condado (✆ **787/721-5700**), has Latin Jazz on Monday nights and Cuban salsa Fridays.

THE BAR SCENE

Graffiti and business cards cover the walls of **El Batey,** Calle del Cristo 101 (✆ **787/725-1787**), the Old Town's favorite dive bar for decades. There's a great jukebox and a view of the procession up and down Calle del Cristo during weekend nights. Drawings of the legends of this storied watering hole are hung in its main room. There's always somebody to talk to at the bar, which draws an eccentric local crowd and independent-minded visitors. Patrons play chess and backgammon as well. The jukebox has great classic and psychedelic rock, some great Sinatra, and some priceless jazz standards by the likes of Duke Ellington and Charlie Parker.

La Sombrilla Rosa, Calle San Sebastián 154 (✆ **787/725-5656**), is a nice neighborhood bar with daily happy hours, a relaxed atmosphere with friendly staff and patrons, and good music. Weekdays until 3pm, it serves great *comida criolla* at prices ranging from $5.50 to $8—basic stuff like steak and onions, and grilled chicken, everything with rice and pink beans and *tostones* (fried plantains). It's open from 9:30am to 3pm for lunch, then from 7pm to at least 3am nightly (bus: Old City Trolley).

Watch the sun set over San Juan from the **Wet Bar,** San Juan Water & Beach Club, Calle José M. Tartak 2 (✆ **787/725-3666**), on the roof of the Water Club boutique hotel. It features jazz music and the Caribbean's only rooftop fireplace for those nippy nights in winter when you want to drink outside. The sensuous decor here includes striped zebra-wood stools, futons, pillowy sofas, and hand-carved side tables. The walls feature Indonesian carved teak panels. It overlooks the brilliant Isla Verde coastline and its palm-fringed beachfront below. Latin rhythms mix with R&B standards and world rhythms. You can order sushi under the stars or some other delicacies from a limited menu. The Wet Bar is open Thursday to Saturday 7pm to 1am (bus no. A5).

CASINOS ★★

Gambling is big in Puerto Rico. Many people come here to do little more than that. As a result, there are plenty of options. Unlike European casinos, visitors don't need to flash passports or pay admission to enter. Nearly all the large hotels in San Juan, Condado, and Isla Verde offer casinos, and there are other large casinos at some of the bigger resorts outside the metropolitan areas. The atmosphere in the casinos is casual, but you shouldn't show up in bathing suits or shorts. Most of the casinos open around noon and close at 4am. Guest patrons must be at least 18 years old to enter.

The casino generating all the excitement today is the 18,503-square-foot **Ritz-Carlton Casino,** Avenida de los Gobernadores, Isla Verde (✆ **787/253-1700**), the largest casino in Puerto Rico. It combines the elegant decor of the 1940s with tropical fabrics and patterns. This is one of the plushest and most exclusive entertainment complexes in the Caribbean. It features traditional games such as blackjack, roulette, baccarat, craps, and slot machines.

In Old San Juan, you can try your luck at the **Old San Juan Hotel & Casino,** Calle Brumbaugh 100 (✆ **787/721-5100**), where five-card stud competes with some 240 slot machines and roulette tables. There's a stately gaming parlor just off the lobby at the **El San Juan Hotel & Casino** (one of the most grand), Av. Isla Verde 6063 (✆ **787/791-1000**), and the **Condado Plaza Hotel & Casino,** Av. Ashford 999 (✆ **787/721-1000**), remains one of the city's busiest and most exciting casinos.

THE NORTH COAST ★

Dorado—the name itself evokes a kind of magic—is a small town with some big resorts, a world of storied luxury hotels and villas unfolding along Puerto Rico's north shore west of San Juan. For decades the Hyatt Cerromar and Dorado Beach formed the epicenter of this world, storied resorts housed in classic quarters with world-class facilities along a stunning coastal stretch of rolling palm groves and white-sand beaches. Currently, vacation and golf clubs are operated on the former site, and there are plans to renovate the old resort buildings and reopen as a luxury resort. The **Arecibo Observatory** offers a *Star Wars*–type experience, set amid lush jungle. The **Río**

Camuy Cave Park offers visitors a look at a splendid network of caves and underground rivers that twist through limestone and lush forest.

Getting There

The destinations listed can be gotten to by taking Expwy. 22 west from San Juan toward Arecibo. Take exit 22A to get to **Dorado,** by taking Route 165 N. The **Arecibo Observatory** lies farther west. Take Route 22 until you reach Arecibo, then head south on Route 10. Take exit 75B and follow the signposts along a roller-coaster journey on narrow two-lane roads. First you will go right on Route 652 and take a left on Route 651. Proceed straight through the intersection of routes 651 and 635, and then turn left at the cemetery onto Route 625, which will lead you to the entrance of the observatory. The **Río Camuy Cave Park** also lies south of Arecibo. Take Route 129 southwest from Arecibo to the entrance of the caves, which are at Km 18.9 along the route, north of the town of Lares. Like the observatory, the caves lie approximately 1½ hours west of San Juan.

Where to Stay

Embassy Suites Dorado del Mar Beach & Golf Resort ★ This beachfront property in Dorado lies less than 2 miles from the center of Dorado, with easy access to the San Juan airport. It is the only all-suite resort in Puerto Rico, and it has been a success since its opening in 2001. The property offers two-room suites with balconies and 38 two-bedroom condos. The suites are spread over seven floors, each spacious and furnished in a Caribbean tropical motif, with artwork and one king-size bed or two double beds. Most of them have ocean views of the water. Each condo has a living room, kitchen, whirlpool, and balcony. The hotel attracts many families because of its very spacious accommodations. It also attracts golfers because of its Chi Chi Rodriguez signature par-72, 18-hole golf course set against a panoramic backdrop of mountains and ocean.

Dorado del Mar Blvd. 210, Dorado, PR 00646. www.embassysuitesdorado.com. ✆ **800/EMBASSY** (362-2779) or 787/796-6125. Fax 787/796-6145. 212 units. Year-round $200–$240 suite; $260–$485 1-bedroom villa; $360–$560 2-bedroom villa. AE, DC, DISC, MC, V. **Amenities:** 2 restaurants; bar and grill; golf course; outdoor pool; room service; tennis court. *In room:* A/C, TV, hair dryer, kitchenette.

Where to Dine

Salitre Mesón Costero ★★ SEAFOOD Hands down, this is the best restaurant in the Arecibo area. Taste the salt of the sea in the breeze blowing through this charming oceanfront restaurant's terrace dining area, and in the smacking-fresh seafood served here. The dining room has big windows overlooking the coast, and there's also a comfortable bar. This is a great place to watch the sunset. The house specialty, *mamposteado de mariscos,* features mussels, shrimp, and freshly caught fish, octopus, or calamari in rice. Its seafood-stuffed *mofongo* platters and the whole red snapper with *tostones* are hard to beat.

Rte. 681 Km 3.8, ✆ **787/816-2020.** www.salitre.com. Reservations not necessary. Main courses $9–$25. MC, V. Daily 11am–11pm.

Hitting the Beach & the Links

The courses at the **Dorado Beach Resort & Club** (✆ **787/278-1993**), designed by Robert Trent Jones, Sr., match the finest anywhere. The two original courses, known as East and West, were carved out of a jungle and offer tight fairways bordered by trees and forests, with lots of ocean holes. His son, Robert Trent Jones, Jr., oversaw a renovation of the East course in 2010, followed by the West course. The somewhat newer and less noted Sugarcane and Pineapple courses, now called the Plantation Club, feature wide fairways with well-bunkered greens and an assortment of water traps and tricky wind factors. Each is a par-72 course; the longest is 7,047 yards. On the Pineapple and Sugarcane courses, regular green fees are $135; on the East and West courses, they rise to $195. All are open daily from 7am until dusk. Golf carts are included for all courses, and the two pro shops have both a bar and snack-style restaurant.

Just outside Dorado is one of Puerto Rico's best public beaches, **Cerro Gordo,** Route 690, Vega Alta (✆ **787/883-2730**). There's a $3-per-car parking fee here; hours are Wednesday through Sunday and holidays 8:30am to 5pm. There are also several beaches known for their surf breaks, the most famous being **Los Tubos** in Manatí.

FAJARDO & THE EAST

From San Juan, the new Roberto Sánchez Vilella (Rte. 66) Expressway takes you to Canvóvanas. You'll pass lush **El Yunque Rainforest;** the nearby town of **Río Grande,** home to luxury resorts and world-class golf courses; and **Luquillo Beach,** one of the island's best and most popular public stretches of sand. At the island's northeast corner is Fajardo, a mariner's paradise, with seven marinas, and the gateway to the Caribbean boater's paradise that stretches east through the U.S. and British Virgin Islands. It's also home to one of the region's most spectacular resorts, El Conquistador (see below), and beautiful beaches and other natural wonders.

Getting There

El Conquistador staff members greet all guests at the San Juan airport and transport them to the resort. Guests can take a taxi or a hotel courtesy car, or they can drive a rental car to Luquillo Beach. The Río Mar and Sol Melía resorts also provide transportation. The cost of a taxi from the San Juan airport averages around $75.

Driving from San Juan, take Route 26 or the Baldorioty de Castro Expressway East to Carolina, where you will pick up Route 66, or the Roberto Sánchez Vilella Expressway. The $1.50 toll road will take you farther along Route 3, putting you in Canóvanas. Go right (east) on Route 3. For El Yunque, exit at Route 191, a two-lane highway that heads south into the forest, and take it for 3 miles, going through the village of Palmer. As the road rises, you enter the El Yunque Caribbean National Forest. You can stop in at the El Portal Tropical Forest Center to pick up information (see "El Yunque Tropical Rainforest," below).

Right beyond the El Yunque turnoff, on the left is the exit for Río Grande's resort area, with the **Sol Melía** and **Trump International Golf** properties. Farther down Route 3 lie Luquillo Beach and Fajardo.

Where to Stay

El Conquistador Resort & Golden Door Spa ★★ ☺ El Conquistador is a destination unto itself. Its array of facilities sits on 499 acres of forested hills sloping down to the sea. Accommodations are divided into five separate sections united by their Mediterranean architecture and lush landscaping. Most lie several hundred feet above the sea. At the same altitude, a bit off to the side, is a replica of an Andalusian hamlet, Las Casitas Village, which seems straight out of the south of Spain. These pricey units, each with a full kitchen, form a self-contained enclave.

A short walk downhill takes you to a circular cluster of tastefully modern accommodations, Las Olas Village. And at sea level, adjacent to an armada of pleasure craft bobbing at anchor, is La Marina Village, whose balconies seem to hang directly over the water. The accommodations are outfitted with comfortable furniture, tropical colors, and robes. All the far-flung elements of the resort are connected by serpentine, landscaped walkways, and by a railroad-style funicular that makes frequent trips up and down the hillside.

One of the most comprehensive spas in the Caribbean, the Golden Door, maintains a branch in this resort. The hotel is sole owner of a "fantasy island" (Palomino Island), with caverns, nature trails, horseback riding, and watersports such as scuba diving, windsurfing, and snorkeling. Free private ferries at frequent intervals connect the island, which is about half a mile offshore, to the main hotel. There's also a 25-slip marina. The hotel operates an excellently run children's club, with activities planned daily. The resort has opened up a water park that's a hit with the kids (and the young at heart), with water slides, a lazy river, and a large pool. It's on the harbor level, right by the water, below the pool's main deck.

Av. Conquistador 1000, Fajardo, PR 00738. www.elconresort.com. ✆ **888/543-1282** or 787/863-1000. Fax 787/863-6500. 918 units. Winter $200–$370 double, $740–$1,200 suite, $490–$1,200 Las Casitas villa; off season $150–$270 double, $540–$810 suite, $390–$790 Las Casitas villa. MAP (breakfast and dinner) packages are available. Children 16 and under stay free in parent's room. AE, DC, DISC, MC, V. Self-parking $16 per day; valet parking $21. **Amenities:** 12 restaurants; 8 bars; nightclub; children's programs; dive shop; fishing; golf course; health club; 35-slip marina; 7 pools; casino; room service; sailing; smoke-free rooms; spa; 7 Har-Tru tennis courts. *In room:* A/C, TV, fridge, hair dryer, minibar.

The Fajardo Inn ★ A good base for visiting El Yunque, this inn is ideal for those who are seeking a location in the east and don't want to pay the prices charged at the El Conquistador (see above). Lying on a hilltop overlooking the port of Fajardo, this *parador* evokes a Mediterranean villa with its balustrades and grand staircases. The midsize bedrooms, most of which open onto good views, are spotless, and each has a small shower-only bathroom. The inn and its pool are handsomely landscaped. The on-site Star Fish restaurant specializes in Creole and Continental cuisine, especially fresh fish, with indoor and outdoor dining. The Blue Iguana Mexican Grill & Bar is a casual pub with good food. Coco's Park is a new pool area, with activities like a beach pool, a slide, a Jacuzzi, tennis, basketball, and miniature golf. It's separated from the rest of the hotel, so as not to disturb the relative tranquillity of the rest of the grounds.

Parcela Beltrán 52, Puerto Real, PR 00740. www.fajardoinn.com. ✆ **888/860-6006** or 787/860-6000. Fax 787/860-5063. 105 units. Year-round $110–$175 double; $175–$300 suite. AE, DISC, MC, V. 15-min. walk east of the center of Fajardo. **Amenities:** 2 restaurants; 2 bars; pool; room service; snorkeling and diving arranged. *In room:* A/C, TV, hair dryer.

Gran Melía Puerto Rico ★★★ ☺ Checking into this pocket of posh on the Miquillo de Río Grande peninsula is the best reason for heading east of San Juan. An all-suite luxury resort, it has set new standards for comfort, convenience, and amenities along the Atlantic northeastern shoreline. Set amid gardens of 40 acres, it opens onto the white sands of the mile-long shoreline of Coco Beach. From watersports to two 18-hole golf courses, the resort has everything on-site, including whirlpool baths and massage tables. Spa treatments revitalize and rejuvenate.

You can also wander the globe in the widely varied restaurants, ranging from Italian to Southeast Asian. Naturally, the chefs also prepare locally caught seafood imbued with Creole flavor. One restaurant serves only Caribbean and Puerto Rican cuisine, whereas another offers its take on contemporary California. Yet another serves Teppanyaki dinners with an adjoining sushi bar. Bedrooms and suites are spacious and furnished luxuriously. There's a lot to do here: world-class golf, a full-service spa, a slew of watersports possibilities. The staff is great at organizing water polo and beach volleyball games, and you can take salsa and merengue dancing lessons by the pool. It's a big reason why this resort is a cut above some competitors, and why you will have so much fun here. We're still talking about our stunning come-from-behind beach volleyball victory nearly a year later.

Coco Beach Blvd. 200, Río Grande, PR 00745. www.gran-melia-puerto-rico.com. © **877/476-3542** or 787/809-1770. Fax 787/809-1785. 582 units. Winter $180–$350 suite for 2; off season $145–$265 suite for 2. AE, DISC, MC, V. **Amenities:** 6 restaurants; 3 bars; babysitting; 2 golf courses; fitness center; kids' clubs; 2 outdoor pools; casino; room service; sauna; smoke-free rooms; spa; 3 tennis courts (lit). *In room:* A/C, TV, hair dryer, kitchenette, minibar.

Where to Dine

Brass Cactus AMERICAN/REGIONAL On a service road adjacent to Route 3 at the western edge of Luquillo, within a boxy-looking concrete building that's in need of repair, is one of the town's most popular bar/restaurants. Permeated with a raunchy, no-holds-barred spirit, this amiable spot has thrived since the early 1990s, when it was established by an Illinois-born bartender who outfitted the interior with gringo memorabilia. It's a great American-style pub, where you can hear rock 'n' roll or catch a game on television. Menu items include king crab salad; tricolor tortellini laced with chicken and shrimp; several kinds of sandwiches, burgers, and wraps; and platters of churrasco, T-bone steaks, chicken with tequila sauce, barbecue pork, and fried mahimahi. A second location has opened in Canóvanas along Highway 3 that has a children's area where they can play video games or do other activities, leaving you to eat in peace. We love the barbecue here, especially the ribs in the Jack Daniels sauce. Portions are large.

In the Condominio Complejo Turistico, Rte. 3, Luquillo. © **787/889-5735.** www.thebrasscactus.com. Reservations not necessary. Main courses $14–$20; sandwiches $7–$9. MC, V. Sun–Thurs 11am–11pm; Fri–Sat 11am–midnight.

Sandy's Seafood Restaurant & Steak House ★ SEAFOOD/STEAKS/PUERTO RICAN The concrete-and-plate-glass facade is less obtrusive than that of other restaurants in town, and the cramped, Formica-clad interior is far from stylish. Nonetheless, Sandy's is one of the most famous restaurants in northeastern Puerto Rico, thanks to the wide array of luminaries—U.S. and Puerto Rican political figures, mainstream journalists, beauty-pageant winners, and assorted slumming rich—who travel from as far away as San Juan to dine here. Set about a block from the main square of the seaside resort of Luquillo, it was founded in 1984 by Miguel Angel, also known as Sandy.

Platters, especially the daily specials, are huge—so copious, in fact, that they're discussed with fervor by competitors and clients alike. The best examples include fresh shellfish, served on the half-shell; *asopaos;* four kinds of steak; five different preparations of chicken, including a tasty version with garlic sauce; four kinds of gumbos; paellas; a dozen preparations of lobster; and even jalapeño peppers stuffed with shrimp or lobster.

Calle Fernandez García 276. ✆ **787/889-5765.** Reservations recommended. Main courses $8–$25; lunch special (Mon–Fri 11am–2:30pm) $5. AE, MC, V. Wed–Mon 11am–9:30pm (or until 11pm, depending on business).

Exploring the Area: Golf, Sailing, Isles & Beaches

Some of the best snorkeling in Puerto Rico is in and around Fajardo. Its public beach, **Playa Seven Seas,** is an attractive and sheltered strip of sand. Nearby, reachable through a path at the western end the public beach, lie **Playa Escondido (Hidden Beach),** a small white-sand cover with coral reefs in aquamarine waters, and gorgeous **El Convento Beach,** stretching out along the miles-long undeveloped coastline between Fajardo and Luquillo. The water plunges steeply just offshore, and it is pocked with large reefs, which draw even large fish to the brink of the beach.

Luquillo Beach ★★★, Puerto Rico's finest beach, is palm-dotted and crescent-shaped, opening onto a lagoon with calm waters and a wide, sandy bank. It's very crowded on weekends but much better during the week. There are lockers, tent sites, showers, picnic tables, and food stands that sell a sampling of the island's *frituras* (fried fare), especially cod fritters and tacos. The beach is open from 8:30am to 5pm Wednesday through Sunday, plus holidays.

You can also snorkel and skin-dive (see below) among the living reefs with lots of tropical fish. Offshore are coral formations and spectacular sea life—eels, octopuses, stingrays, tarpon, big puffer fish, turtles, nurse sharks, and squid, among other sea creatures.

Fajardo is also known for sailing, and the best way to experience this is by taking one of the sailing/snorkeling excursions in luxury catamarans leaving from its marinas. Most have a cash bar serving drinks and refreshments, a sound system, and other creature comforts. Typically, after a nice sail, the cat will weigh anchor at different snorkeling spots and then in sheltered waters near one of the scores of small islands lying off Fajardo's coast, the perfect spot for a swim or sunbathing. Most trips include lunch, which usually is served on a beach. The boats know the best reefs and hot spots for bigger fish and will plan the trip according to weather conditions and other variables. A huge reef extending east to Culebra protects the ocean off Fajardo's coast, which makes for calm seas with great visibility.

Inquire at your hotel desk about operators providing service there. There are many reputable companies. We and friends have all been satisfied with **Traveler Sailing Catamaran** (✆ **787/853-2821**), **East Island Excursions** (✆ **787/860-3434**), and **Catamaran Spread Eagle** (✆ **787/887-8821**). **Erin Go Bragh Charters** (✆ **787/860-4401;** www.egbc.net) offers similar day trips aboard a 50-foot sailing ketch, which is an equally pleasurable experience.

The Río Grande–Fajardo area is quickly becoming the golf hot spot in Puerto Rico, which itself is known as the Ireland of the Caribbean because of the number and quality of its greens. Tom Kite and Bruce Besse designed two 18-hole courses for the **Trump International Golf Club Puerto Rico,** 100 Clubhouse Dr. (✆ **787/657-2000;** www.trumpgolfclubpuertorico.com). You face a spectacular vista of fairways, lakes, and the Atlantic beyond, with four 9-hole loops, each with its own character, which fan out from the Caribbean's largest clubhouse. Another nice option in town is the **Bahia Beach Resort and Golf Club,** Route 187 Km 4.2 (✆ **787/809-8920;** www.bahiabeachpuertorico.com), with greens fees weekdays at $225 and weekends at $275. Robert Trent Jones, Jr., renovated the course with a breathtaking

el yunque TROPICAL RAINFOREST

Some 25 miles east of San Juan lies the **Caribbean National Forest ★★★**, known as El Yunque, the only tropical forest in the U.S. National Forest Service system. It was given its status by President Theodore Roosevelt. Within its 27,664 acres are some 240 tree species (only half a dozen of which are found on the mainland U.S.). In this world of cedars and satinwood, draped in tangles of vines, you'll hear chirping birds, see wild orchids, and perhaps hear the song of the tree frog, the *coquí.* The entire forest is a bird sanctuary and may be the last retreat of the rare Puerto Rican parrot.

El Yunque offers a number of **walking and hiking trails,** high above sea level. The most scenic is the rugged El Toro Trail, which passes through four different forest systems en route to the 3,536-ft. Pico El Toro, the highest peak in the forest. The signposted El Yunque Trail leads to three of the recreation area's most spectacular lookouts. The Big Tree Trail is an easy walk to panoramic La Mina Falls. Just off the main road is La Coca Falls, a sheet of water cascading down mossy cliffs. You can be fairly sure you'll encounter rain—more than 100 billion gallons of rain falls here annually—but showers are usually brief, and there are plenty of shelters in the park.

Nearby, the Sierra Palm Interpretive Service Center has maps and information, and arranges for guided tours. A 45-minute drive southeast from San Juan (near the intersection of rtes. 3 and 191), El Yunque is a popular half-day or full-day outing. Major hotels provide guided tours.

El Portal Tropical Forest Center, Route 191, Río Grande (✆ **787/888-1880**), an $18-million exhibition and information center, has 10,010 square feet of exhibition space. Three pavilions offer exhibits and bilingual displays. The actor Jimmy Smits narrates a documentary called *Understanding the Forest.* The center is open daily from 9am to 5pm, and it charges an admission of $3 for adults and $1.50 for children 11 and under.

new design that was inaugurated in April 2008. It runs along lush beachfront, from the tip of Loíza River to the mouth of the Espíritu Santo River. The **Wyndham Río Mar Beach Resort** (see below) has two world-class courses that stretch out in the shadow of El Yunque rainforest along a dazzling stretch of coast. **El Conquistador**'s (p. 460) golf offerings are also well regarded.

To the Lighthouse: Exploring Las Cabezas de San Juan Nature Reserve ★

Better known as El Faro or "the Lighthouse," this preserve in the northeastern corner of the island, north of Fajardo off Route 987, is one of the most beautiful and important areas on Puerto Rico. A number of different ecosystems flourish in the vicinity. Surrounded on three sides by the Atlantic Ocean, the 311-acre site encompasses forestland, mangroves, lagoons, beaches, cliffs, offshore cays, and coral reefs. El Faro serves as a research center for the scientific community. It's home to a vast array of flora and fauna, including sea turtles and other endangered species.

Laguna Grande, within the reserve, is one of the world's best bioluminescent bays, along with one on the neighboring island of Vieques. The presence of multitudes of tiny organisms, called dinoflagellates, in the protected bay is responsible for the nocturnal glow of its waters. They feed off the red mangroves surrounding the water. Kayaking through the bay at night should be on your bucket list. We highly recommend **Las Tortugas Adventures,** P.O. Box 1637, Canóvanas (✆ **787/809-0253;** http://kayak-pr.com).

The nature reserve is open Wednesday to Sunday; reservations are required, so call before going. For **reservations** throughout the week, call ✆ **787/722-5882;** for reservations on Saturday and Sunday, call ✆ **787/860-2560** (reservations on weekends can be made only on the day of your intended visit). Admission is $7 for adults, $4 for seniors and children 5 to 12; children 4 and under are free. Guided tours are conducted in Spanish at 9:30, 10, and 10:30am, and in English at 2pm.

Vieques & Culebra

Long the best-kept secret of local travelers and a few in-the-know visitors from the East Coast, Puerto Rico's island municipalities Vieques and Culebra are finally getting their due. Now known as the Spanish Virgin Islands, the towns remain blissfully undeveloped. You will find sandy beaches and breathtaking coastal waters, as well as low prices. Vieques has a bit more action than Culebra, but both are places to kick back and relax.

The U.S. military controlled vast swaths of both islands for extended periods. Nature reserves have been built on former military training areas.

The **Puerto Rico Ports Authority** operates ferries to Vieques and Culebra from Fajardo; the trip takes about an hour. The round-trip fare is $4.50 for adults, $2 for children. Call ✆ **800/981-2005** or 787/863-0705.

Both islands have a number of guesthouses and fine restaurants, aimed at the most basic to the most refined tastes and budgets.

PONCE & THE SOUTHWEST

Puerto Rico's second-largest city, Ponce ("the Pearl of the South"), was named after Loíza Ponce de León, grandson of Ponce de León. Today it's Puerto Rico's principal shipping port on the Caribbean Sea, located 74 miles southwest of San Juan. The city is well kept and attractive, with many plazas, parks, and public buildings. It has the air of a provincial Mediterranean town. Look for the *rejas* (framed balconies) of the handsome colonial mansions.

Ponce is a city, not a beach resort, and should be visited mainly for its sights, but a mere 20 minutes west are some of Puerto Rico's finest beaches in the towns of Guánica, La Parguera, and Boquerón.

Essentials

GETTING THERE Flying from San Juan to Ponce five times a day, **Cape Air** (✆ **800/352-0714** in the U.S. and Canada; www.flycapeair.com), a small regional carrier, offers flights for $154 round-trip. Flight time is 25 minutes.

If you're driving, take Las Américas Expressway south to the Luis A. Ferré Expressway (Hwy. 52), then continue south. Once you pass over the central mountain range and reach the south coast, you will continue west until Ponce. The trip takes about 1½ hours.

VISITOR INFORMATION Maps and information can be found at the **tourist office,** Edificio Jose Dapena (© **787/841-8160**). It's open daily from 9am to 5pm. There is also a tourist information office in **Parque de Bombas**, the city's famous Victorian firehouse on Plaza de las Delicias, the main plaza in its historic district.

Where to Stay

Bahia Salinas Beach Resort & Spa ★ This intimate inn in Cabo Rojo, in the far southwestern corner of Puerto Rico, is bordered by a mangrove reserve, bird sanctuaries, and salt flats in the undeveloped coastal region near the Cabo Rojo Lighthouse. Salt mineral waters, similar to those of the Dead Sea, supply water for the on-site Jacuzzi and for treatments at its Cuni Spa, which gives a full range of beauty and relaxation treatments. There is ample opportunity for jogging and hiking in the natural surroundings, as well as all sorts of watersports. It is near many white-sand beaches, including the town's large public beach. The **Agua al Cuello** restaurant excellent, and the **Bohemio Bar** has an enviable view of the sea and unstoppable blenders. The bedrooms are midsize to large and are furnished in the so-called "hacienda" Puerto Rican style, which means wooden colonial-style furniture and four-poster beds. The place is well run and maintained.

Rd. 301 Km 11.5, Sector El Faro, Cabo Rojo, PR 00622. www.bahiasalinas.com. © **787/254-1212.** Fax 787/254-1215. 22 units. Year-round $195–$205 double. Children 11 and under stay free in parent's room. AE, MC, V. **Amenities:** Restaurant; bar; high-speed Internet access (free); 2 outdoor pools; room service (noon–9pm); rooms for those w/limited mobility. *In room:* A/C, TV.

Copamarina Beach Resort & Spa ★★ Charming, low-key, and discreetly elegant, the Copamarina spreads out easily along a landscaped palm grove, with gentle waters and offshore cays, a large pool, and shady grounds. The attractively decorated units have tile floors, lots of exposed wood, and louvered doors with screens that open onto large verandas or terraces. Everything is airy and comfortable. Bathrooms are large and up-to-date. The fine-dining restaurant, Alexandra, serves great food, and it's less formal than most San Juan restaurants of similar quality and staffed by a hardworking crowd of young people. Full-service diving, watersports, and nature and sports tours are available. The hotel also offers guests all-inclusive options. We recommend renting a car and trying some of the local restaurants in Guánica and other coastal villages you will visit while staying here.

Rte. 333 Km 6.5, Caña Gorda (P.O. Box 805), Guánica, PR 00653. www.copamarina.com. © **800/468-4553** or 787/821-0505. Fax 787/821-0070. 106 units. Winter $190–$240 double; off season $145–$185 double; year-round $295–$395 suite, $722–$1,000 villa. AE, DC, MC, V. From Ponce, drive west along Rte. 2 to Rte. 116 and go south to Rte. 333, then head east. **Amenities:** 2 restaurants; bar; babysitting; health club; 2 outdoor pools; room service; tennis courts. *In room:* A/C, TV, fridge, hair dryer.

Hilton Ponce Golf & Casino Resort ★★ On a 74-acre tract of land right on the beach, this is the best full-service hotel in southern Puerto Rico—but has begun showing its wear and tear recently. A 10-minute drive from downtown, near the La Guancha waterfront district, the hotel has a 27-hole golf course, a sprawling pool area, lush grounds, and spacious rooms, done up in attractive tropical style with great amenities and furnishings. Even basic rooms have private balconies and roomy, gleaming bathrooms. There's a playground and pool for the kids, a fitness and health club, a busy casino, and a lively lobby area. The resort has a business center and other services for business travelers.

Av. Caribe 1150 (P.O. Box 7419), Ponce, PR 00716. www.hilton.com. ✆ **800/445-8667** or 787/259-7676. Fax 787/812-2182. 153 units. Year-round $160–$190 double; $375–$660 suite. AE, DC, DISC, MC, V. Valet parking $10; self-parking $4.50. **Amenities:** 2 restaurants; 2 bars; nightclub; bikes; children's program; fitness center; 27-hole golf course; playground; lagoon-shaped pool ringed w/gardens; casino; room service; 2 tennis courts. *In room:* A/C, TV, hair dryer, minibar.

Mary Lee's by the Sea ★ An informal collection of cottages, houses, and apartments are scattered across a beautiful seaside bluff. Several sizes fit groups of all numbers. Whimisically decorated and artfully erratic, the ambience is low-key. A dock and kayaks are located along the mangrove-choked coastline. There are several offshore cays and beautiful snorkeling and diving spots offshore. The Guánica Dry Forest is also nearby. The place is quiet, secluded, and appropriate for low-key vacationers looking for privacy. There isn't a bar or restaurant here, but each unit has a modern kitchen and an outdoor barbecue pit. The rooms are serviced weekly, although guests can arrange daily maid service for an extra fee.

Rte. 333 Km 6.7 (P.O. Box 394), Guánica, PR 00653. www.maryleesbythesea.com. ✆ **787/821-3600.** Fax 787/821-0744. 11 units. Year-round $80–$120 double; $100–$140 studio and 1-bedroom apt; $160–$200 2-bedroom apt; $250 3-bedroom house. MC, V. From Ponce, take Rte. 2. When you reach Rte. 116, head south toward Guánica. The hotel is signposted from the road. *In room:* A/C, kitchen, no phone.

Parador Villa Parguera ☺ Guests enjoy a view of the harbor and can take a dip in the swimming pool. The restaurant is known for its seafood dinners. Every unit has either a balcony or a terrace. Bathrooms are rather cramped but well maintained, and each has either a shower or a tub. This place is gregarious and convivial. There's a dock right outside the restaurant where boats tie up, which is convenient because the thing to do here is to hire a boat and explore the beautiful shallow coast, replete with reefs and tropical sea life.

Rd. 304 Km 303, La Parguera (P.O. Box 273), Lajas, PR 00667. www.villaparguera.net. ✆ **787/899-7777.** Fax 787/899-6040. 74 units, all with either shower or tub. Year round $107–$165 double. 2 children 9 or under stay free in parent's room. AE, DC, DISC, MC, V. Drive west along Rte. 2 until you reach the junction with Rte. 116; then head south along Rte. 116 and Rte. 304. **Amenities:** Restaurant; bar; babysitting; pool; rooms for those w/limited mobility. *In room:* A/C, TV.

Where to Dine

Alexandra ★ INTERNATIONAL This is a genuinely excellent restaurant with a kitchen team turning out delectable dishes that include sautéed shrimps in roasted garlic cream sauce, lobster tail in mustard and mango sauce with provencial plantain fries, and Cornish hen in warm bacon relish over fried risotto. The interior is air-conditioned but tropical in its feel, providing a welcome dose of relaxed glamour.

In the Copamarina Beach Resort, Rte. 333 Km 6.5, Caña Gorda. ✆ **787/821-0505.** Reservations recommended. Main courses $17–$36. AE, DC, DISC, MC, V. Sun–Thurs 6–10:30pm; Fri–Sat 6–11pm.

Archipiélago ★★ PUERTO RICAN/SEAFOOD The new place to be in Ponce is this sixth-floor restaurant, which serves innovative *criolla* and Continental fusion cuisine. The interior dining area is as smart and modern as the menu, with subdued tones and an expansive glass window that brings the Plaza las Delicias below right into the room. There are two outdoor terraces that will make you feel lost in Europe as you look out at the cathedral and the Victorian firehouse. If you are with a group, start out with the Archipiélago platter, which has fried manchego cheese and tomato jam, fried local cheese with guava and prosciutto ham, fried plantains topped with stewed shredded meat, mushroom caps stuffed with pesto, and fried calamari. The lobster in Creole sauce and the chicken stuffed with sun-dried tomatoes, mushrooms, and Italian cheese were both excellent. There are also simple vegetarian dishes, burgers, and straight-up Puerto Rican classics. The desserts are the chef's specialty, and it showed in the coffee crème brulée and the Puerto Rican strudel with dark rum caramel sauce. There is also a lounge area and bar, so this is a one of the city's top nightspots as well.

Calle Cristina 76, Ponce. ✆ **787/812-8822**. Reservations recommended. Main courses $14–$37. AE, DC, MC, V. Wed–Sun 5pm–1am.

Galloway's ★ CREOLE/CONTINENTAL This is our favorite restaurant in Boquerón, right near the center of town but set back along the water. Sit in the back dining room that is on a dock over Boquerón Bay. It's a great spot for a fresh seafood meal as you watch one of those perfect western sunsets. This is a casual spot, but the food is first-rate. Try the fresh whole fried red snapper and boiled Caribbean lobster. While much of the menu is typical of the area, specializing in local cuisine and seafood, you'll also find great ribs, steaks, and pub fare. The bar near the entrance is a good spot to mix with locals and expats, and to pick up tips on area activities. On weekends there's often live music.

Calle José de Diego 12, Poblado de Boquerón, Cabo Rojo. ✆ **787/254-3302.** Reservations not necessary. Main courses $10–$29. AE, MC, V. Thurs–Tues noon–midnight.

La Casita SEAFOOD The town's most consistently reliable and popular restaurant has flourished since the 1960s in a simple wooden building. Inside lots of varnished pine acts as a decorative foil for platters of local and imported fish and shellfish. Filets of fish can be served in any of seven different styles; lobster comes in five. Even the Puerto Rican starchy staple of *mofongo* comes in versions stuffed with crab, octopus, shrimp, lobster, and assorted shellfish. Begin with fish chowder, a dozen cheese balls, or fish croquettes. End with coconut-flavored flan. Don't expect grand service or decor, but rather a setting where food is the focus.

Calle Principal 304, La Parguera. ✆ **787/899-1681.** Reservations not necessary. All main courses $8. AE, MC, V. Tues–Sun 11am–10:30pm. Closed 2 weeks in Sept.

Seeing the Sights

More than 1,000 buildings in town have been restored to their historical stature, with Ponce's downtown area among the largest historic zones in the hemisphere. Architectural styles combine neoclassical with "Ponce Creole" and Art Deco, giving the town a distinctive ambience.

Museo de Arte de Ponce ★, Av. de las Americas 23–25 (✆ **787/848-0505;** www.museoarteponce.org), reopened in November 2011 after a stunning $30-million renovation that brings a substantially richer experience to visitors. The renovation added an extension and retrofit of the original building, designed by Edward Durell Stone (who also designed the John F. Kennedy Center for the Performing Arts in Washington, D.C.) and has been called the "Parthenon of the Caribbean." The permanent collection, which has grown to more than 4,500 works, is arranged thematically. The vast collection represents the principal schools of American and European art of the past 5 centuries, including a growing number of contemporary works, with an emphasis on local and regional artists.

The most dramatic new addition is surely *Brushstrokes in Flight*, a 28-foot tall painted aluminum sculpture created by Pop Art exponent Roy Lichtenstein in 1984 that has been erected in front of the museum. The work was donated by the artist's foundation with the support of his family and is the artist's most important public work in the Caribbean and Latin American region. The late Luís A. Ferré, the former governor who founded the pro-statehood New Progressive Party, donated the museum to the people of Puerto Rico. Its most famous piece is probably Lord Frederic Leighton's *Flaming June*.

The museum charges $6 for adults and $3 for seniors, students, and children 12 and under. The museum is open Wednesday to Monday, from 10am to 6pm. There are guided tours in English and Spanish from 11am to 2pm, and audio guides are available.

Most visitors head for the **Parque de Bombas,** Plaza de las Delicias (✆ **787/284-4141** or 284-3338). This fantastic old black-and-red firehouse was built for a fair in 1883. It's open daily 9am to 5pm; admission is free. The Victorian structure sits on **Plaza de las Delicias,** the city's main square, which also contains the gorgeous marble and bronze **Lion Fountain.** Modeled after a famous fountain in Barcelona, Spain, it was made for the 1939 New York World's Fair and later purchased by the mayor of Ponce.

Around the corner from the firehouse, a trail will lead you to the **Cathedral of Our Lady of Guadalupe,** Calle Concordia/Calle Union, Plaza de las Delicias (✆ **787/842-0134**). Designed by architects Francisco Porrata Doría and Francisco Trublard in 1931, and featuring a pipe organ installed in 1934, it remains an important place for prayer. It's open Monday to Friday from 6am to 12:30pm, Saturday and Sunday from 6am to noon and 3 to 8pm.

El Museo Castillo Serrallés ★ About 2 miles north of the center of town is the largest and most imposing building in Ponce, constructed high on El Vigía Hill during the 1930s by the Serrallés family, owners of a local rum distillery. One of the architectural gems of Puerto Rico, it is the best evidence of the wealth produced by the turn-of-the-20th-century sugar boom. Guides will escort you through the Spanish Revival house with Moorish and Andalusian details. Highlights include panoramic courtyards, a baronial dining room, a small cafe, and a souvenir shop. There's the soaring Cruz del Vigía (Virgin's Cross) observation tower: Built in 1984 of reinforced concrete to replace a 19th-century wooden cross in poor repair, this modern 100-ft structure bears lateral arms measuring 69ft long and an observation tower (accessible by elevator), from which you can see all of the natural beauty surrounding Ponce. Make sure to take a break in the beautifully tranquil Japanese garden, with bonsai plantings and elevated bridges running between ponds and streams. The staff also created a butterfly garden.

El Vigía 17. ✆ **787/259-1774.** Admission $9 adults, $4.50 seniors, $4 children and students (includes all attractions on El Vigía Hill). Tues–Sun 9:30am–5pm.

Hacienda Buena Vista Built in 1833, this hacienda preserves an old way of life, with its whirring water wheels and artifacts of 19th-century farm production. Once it was one of the most successful plantations on Puerto Rico, producing coffee, corn, and citrus. It was a working coffee plantation until the 1950s, and 86 of the original 499 acres are still part of the estate. The rooms of the hacienda have been furnished with authentic pieces from the 1850s.

Rte. 123 Km 16.8. ✆ **787/722-5882** (weekdays) or 787/284-7020 (weekends). Tours $7 adults, $4 children and seniors. Reservations required. 2-hr. tours Wed–Sun 8:30am, 10:30am, 1:30pm (in English), and 3:30pm. A 30-min. drive north of Ponce, in the small town of Barrio Magüeyes, between Ponce and Adjuntas.

San Germán, Puerto Rico's second-oldest town, has been compared to a small-scale outdoor museum. Dating from 1512, San Germán has a small but beautiful historic area, which climbs over hilly streets carved from ancient ship's ballast. There are Spanish colonial (1850s), Creole (1880s), neoclassical (1910s), Art Deco (1930s), and international (1960s) buildings lining the streets. The highlight is the **Iglesia Porta Coeli (Gate of Heaven) ★** (✆ **787/892-0160**), the church that sits atop a hill at the eastern end of a cobble-covered square, the Parque de Santo Domingo. Dating from 1606 and built in a style inspired by the Romanesque architecture of northern Spain, this is one of the oldest churches in the New World. Sheathed in a layer of salmon-colored stucco, it contains a museum of religious art with extraordinary works. The original ceiling is hewn from palm-wood and tough ausobo-wood beams. Admission is $1. The church is open Wednesday through Sunday from 8:30am to noon and 1 to 4:30pm.

Tibes Indian Ceremonial Center Bordered by the Río Portuguéz and excavated in 1975, this is the oldest cemetery in the Antilles. It contains some 186 skeletons, dating from A.D. 300, as well as pre-Taíno plazas from A.D. 700. The site also includes a re-created Taíno village, seven rectangular ball courts, and two dance grounds. The arrangement of stone points on the dance grounds, in line with the solstices and equinoxes, suggests a pre-Columbian Stonehenge. Here you'll also find a museum, an exhibition hall that presents a documentary about Tibes, a cafeteria, and a souvenir shop. Guided tours in English and Spanish conducted through the grounds.

Rte. 503 Km 2.2, Tibes. ✆ **787/840-2255.** Admission $3 adults, $2 children. Tues–Sun 9am–4pm. 2 miles north of Ponce.

Beaches & Outdoor Pursuits

La Guancha is a sprawling boardwalk around Ponce's bayside harbor area near the Ponce Hilton (p. 466). Several eateries are located here, and it is the scene of free concerts and other events at night. During the afternoon, families come here to fly kites or ride bicycles, and hundreds of yachts and pleasure craft tie up here, which is also home to the Ponce Yacht Club. A ferry runs from La Guancha to **Caja de Muertos,** or **Coffin Island,** an uninhabited cay that's covered with mangrove swamps and ringed with worthwhile beaches. It has great snorkeling.

Costa Caribe Golf & Country Club ★★ (✆ **787/812-2650**), on the site of the Hilton Ponce Golf & Casino Resort (p. 466), is one of Puerto Rico's finest golf courses. The 27 holes laid out in former sugar-cane fields overlook the ocean; charges are $89 ($79 for guests) to play 18 holes.

Some of Puerto Rico's best beaches are in the area. In **Guánica,** try either **Caña Gorda** or **Playa Santa.** Another must is the public beach at **Boquerón.** At **La Paguera,** the thing to do is rent a boat and visit an offshore cay or go snorkeling near huge coral reefs just offshore. Southern Puerto Rico has a great reputation among **scuba divers** because of a 20-mile continental shelf that drops off a few miles off the southern coast.

Guánica Forest Reserve ★★ (✆ **787/821-5706**) is the best-preserved subtropical ecosystem on the planet. UNESCO has named Guánica a World Biosphere

Reserve. Some 750 plants and tree species grow in the area. The Cordillera Central cuts off the rain coming in from the heavily showered northeast, making this a dry region of cacti and bedrock, a perfect film location for old-fashioned western movies. It's also ideal country for birders. Some 50% of all of the island's terrestrial bird species can be seen in this dry and dusty forest.

RINCON & THE NORTHWEST ★

At the westernmost point of the island—about 6¼ miles north of Mayagüez and a little over 93 miles west of San Juan—Rincón has one of the most exotic beaches on the island, drawing surfers from around the world. In and around this small fishing village are some unique accommodations. Nearby towns Aguadilla and Isabela also boast beautiful beaches, untrammeled natural areas, and great accommodations. The whole northwest corner of the island forms the Caribbean's best surfing destination.

Getting There

If you rent a car at the San Juan airport, it will take approximately 2½ hours to drive here via the busy northern Route 2, or 3 hours via the scenic mountain route (no. 52) through Ponce to the south. We recommend the southern route.

In addition, there are two flights daily from San Juan to Mayagüez on **Cape Air** (✆ **800/352-0714** in the U.S. and Canada; www.flycapeair.com) and **American Eagle** (✆ **800/433-7300** in the U.S. and Canada; www.aa.com). These flights take 40 minutes, and round-trip fare is $180. From the Mayagüez airport, Rincón is a 30-minute drive to the north on Route 2 (go left or west at the intersection with Rte. 115).

Where to Stay

Horned Dorset Primavera ★★★ This is the most sophisticated hotel on Puerto Rico and one of the most exclusive and elegant small properties anywhere in the Caribbean. The Relais & Châteaux property is set on 8 acres and opens onto a secluded semiprivate beach. Built on the massive breakwaters and seawalls erected as part of a century-old railroad, the hacienda evokes an aristocratic Spanish villa, with wicker armchairs, hand-painted tiles, ceiling fans, seaside terraces, and cascades of flowers. The Primavera Suites (getaways that lack electronics) and the Horned Dorset Residences (which are more fully equipped and furnished) ramble amid lush gardens. The decor is tasteful, with four-poster beds and brass-footed tubs (with showers) in marble-sheathed bathrooms. Rooms are spacious and luxurious, with Persian rugs over tile floors, queen-size sofa beds in the sitting areas, and fine linens and tasteful fabrics on the elegant beds. The Casa Escondida villa, set at the edge of the property, adjacent to the sea, is decorated with an accent on teakwood and marble. Some of the units have private plunge pools; others offer private verandas or sun decks. Each contains high-quality reproductions of colonial furniture by Baker. The hotel's two restaurants are excellent but quite pricey.

Apartado 1132, Rincón, PR 00677. www.horneddorset.com. ✆ **800/633-1857** or 787/823-4030. Fax 787/823-5580. 55 units. Winter $600–$1,070 suites, $770–$1,385 residences; holidays $700–$1,270 suites, $970–$1,585 residences; summer $360–$770 suites, $470–$880 residences. AE, MC, V. Children 11 and under not accepted. **Amenities:** 2 restaurants; bar; fitness center; library; kayaking (free); massage; 3 outdoor pools (1 infinity); limited room service. *In room:* A/C, hair dryer.

The Lazy Parrot Set within an unlikely inland neighborhood, this place is nonetheless one of the best spots in Rincón to stay. It looks like a nondescript storefront from outside, but climb its stairs and you enter an oasis of tropical tranquillity. "Value" rooms are located on the first floor. They are clean, well-organized, and comfortable, if not overly large. They have no view, but each has either a deck, patio, or balcony, and an attractive decor of light, natural colors. The upstairs "panoramic" rooms have a view to the pretty Cadena Hills and the coast, and overlook the pool area. Definitely pay the extra cost for an upstairs room if privacy is important to you. The other rooms are close to the interior lobby and restaurant. The Rum Shack, which serves light fare and drinks poolside, can be a lot of fun at night. This is one of the better-managed properties in town. Though its inland location is not a drawback, you should rent a car anyway to explore other nearby beaches. The pool area is among the best in town.

Rd. 413 Km 4.1, Barrio Puntas, Rincón, PR 00677. www.lazyparrot.com. ✆ **800/294-1752** or 787/823-5654. Fax 787/823-0224. 21 units. Year-round $125 double value rooms; $165 double panoramic rooms. The smallest room goes for $99 single or double. Rates include continental breakfast. AE, DISC, MC, V. **Amenities:** 2 restaurants; bar; babysitting; gift shop w/local crafts; pool; limited room service; Wi-Fi (free). *In room:* A/C, TV, fridge.

Marriott Courtyard Aguadilla ☺ The whole family will love this hotel, with a pool, an aquatics playground, and spacious guest rooms, near some of the prettiest beaches on the island, and right around attractions like the Camuy Caves, Arecibo Observatory, a local water park, and an ice-skating rink. Beautiful beaches ring the coast here from Isabela to the east and Rincón to the west. It's built on the old Ramey Air Force Base, near a coastal suburb. Great location and facilities make a good base to explore the northwest.

West Parade/Belt Rd., Antigua Base Ramey, Aguadilla, PR 00603. www.marriott.com. ✆ **888/236-2427** or 787/658-8000. Fax 787/658-8020. 152 units. Year-round $150–$180 double. AE, MC, V. **Amenities:** 2 restaurants; 2 bars; babysitting; fitness center; 2 pools; room service. *In room:* A/C, TV, Wi-Fi (free).

Rincón Beach Resort ★ Romantic lovebirds and families check into this secluded hideaway. At this beachfront resort, an open-air boardwalk stretches along the coastline at the end of an "infinity pool." It's perhaps the most welcoming place along the western coastline, with a sheltered beachfront. The staff can help you arrange everything from watersports to golf. Guests meet fellow guests in the lobby bar, and later enjoy a savory Caribbean cuisine in Brasas Restaurant, with its open-air terrace. You're given a choice of oceanview or poolview units, and can also rent well-furnished one- and two-bedroom apartments. The decor is tropical throughout, with vibrant colors. It is in a remote location, far from the most traveled Rincón beaches and the center of town, but with a great restaurant, a poolside bar and grill, watersports, and other activities, it does not matter.

Rte. 115 Km 5.8, Añasco, PR 00610. www.rinconbeach.com. ✆ **866/598-0009** or 787/589-9000. Fax 787/589-9040. 118 units. Winter $260–$300 double, $355 junior suite, $459 1-bedroom suite, $650 2-bedroom suite; Summer $210–$250 double, $315 junior suite, $405 1-bedroom suite, $575 2-bedroom suite. Rates include continental breakfast. AE, DISC, MC, V. **Amenities:** Restaurant; grill; 3 bars; babysitting; gym; outdoor pool; smoke-free rooms; rooms for those w/limited mobility. *In room:* A/C, TV, Internet access (free), fridge, hair dryer, kitchenette (in suites).

Villa Montana Beach Resort ★ 🎁 This breathtaking property is set on a 35-acre beachfront plot. The rooms and villas are spread across Caribbean-style plantation buildings with large verandas and balconies. The buildings have cathedral ceilings, peaked tin roofs, and interior courtyards. The facades use muted pastel colors, and rooms are beautifully decorated with a subdued tropical aesthetic and have large terra-cotta tile. There are two beautiful pools and a 3-mile beach, where it's possible to practice every watersport you can imagine. You can also hike through tropical forests, ride horses, go biking, or use the climbing wall on the property. There's a health club, a spa, and sports facilities like basketball courts. Both restaurants, Eclipse and O, have quality food but are on the expensive side. The grounds are lush and beautiful, and there are numerous tropical birds. This is a place to kick way back.

Rd. 4466 Km 1.9, Barrio Bajuras, Isabela, PR 00662. www.villamontana.com. ✆ **787/872-9554.** Fax 787/872-9553. 60 units. Year-round $200–$400 double, $400–$600 villas. AE, MC, V. **Amenities:** 2 restaurants; bar; babysitting; basketball court; volleyball court; climbing wall; laundry service; 2 pools; spa; store; tennis court; watersports equipment/rentals.

Where to Dine

The Lazy Parrot Restaurant ★★ INTERNATIONAL With an inventive menu and a beautiful laid-back setting high up in this beautiful coastal village, this is one of Rincón's finest restaurants. The menu mixes Caribbean and European flavors for optimal impact, and diners sit in an open-air terrace with panoramic views of the pool area, the tropical garden, and green mountains. Try the coconut red-curry crab cakes with papaya slaw, or the fried calamari and roasted garlic in marinara sauce to start. If you want meat, the grilled rib-eye in bordelaise sauce won't disappoint, and seafood lovers will lap up the Caribbean bouillabaisse (a mix of shellfish and mahimahi with avocado and local vegetables).

Rd. 413 Km 4.1, Barrio Puntas, Rincón. ✆ **787/823-0101.** AE, DISC, MC, V. Main courses $20–$36. Daily 5:30–10pm.

Tamboo Tavern and Seaside Grill Restaurant AMERICAN/CARIBBEAN This tavern and restaurant at Beside the Pointe Guesthouse on Sandy Beach is the favored hangout for the young and beautiful beach crowd and surfing enthusiasts from the island and across the planet. It's a great place to eat, offering good food and a beautiful setting no matter who you are. Beachfront dining does not get realer than this. Tables are stretched along a deck running along the beach, with tables spread out among the palm trees. It's basic steaks, ribs, and lots of seafood, but it's well prepared and tastes extra great while you're breathing in the sea and the salt. The mahimahi in caper sauce and grilled Caribbean lobster are both recommended, and you might want to start out with a platter of the mixed Puerto Rican appetizers. Burgers, wraps, and salads are also available for lunch and dinner.

Rd. 413 Km 4, Sandy Beach, Rincón. ✆ **787/823-8550.** Reservations not accepted. Main courses $16–$26; lunch items $7–$12. MC, V. Restaurant Thurs–Tues noon–9:30pm. Bar daily noon–2am.

Hitting the Beach

Rincón is no longer a sleepy coastal village attracting surfers and bohemian travelers. They, of course, are still coming, but a building boom has brought a wave of new condo, hotel, and luxury vacation residence projects, which has attracted more and more visitors here over the past decade. In fact, the town is beginning to worry about the pace of development and its effect on the beautiful natural resources here.

There's still a lot of space to get lost in, though, with the surrounding hills on one side and water on the town's other three borders. With over a dozen beaches in town; great surfing, sailing, and snorkeling; and an ever-better nightlife and cultural scene, it's not hard to see why this place is so popular. It continues evolving as a destination, reinforcing the fact it's one of the best stops to make in Puerto Rico.

There are 8 miles of beachfront in Rincón, and each little spot seems to have its own name: **Maria's, Indicator, Domes,** the **Point, Steps-Tres Palmas, Dog Man's**—the reasons behind the names are varied. One stems from the hulk of an abandoned nuclear power plant just off the beach, another for an old man who lived nearby.

Part of the town's appeal is that it has both rough surfing beaches and tranquil Caribbean coastal areas. Along the north side of Rincón, the Atlantic coast gets large, powerful waves, while other beaches are tranquil, perfect for snorkeling. Yet many beaches provide both, depending on the time of year.

Windsurfing (and, increasingly, kiteboarding) is also extremely popular here. Excellent scuba, snorkeling, parasailing, and sailing are also available in Rincón, making it one of the most active of Caribbean destinations.

Endangered humpback whales winter here, attracting a growing number of whale-watchers from December to March. The lighthouse at El Faro Park is a great place to spot these mammoth mammals.

To the north, **Aguadilla** has great beaches and other natural blessings, for an active vacation experience. And it makes a good base from which to explore the area, with lots of hotels, restaurants, a good infrastructure, a fairly large mall, and lots of attractions, like a water park and golf course.

Isabela's coastline is also beautiful, with dirt roads weaving between cliffs and white beaches, set off by dramatic rock formations and submerged coral reefs that send surf crashing skyward. This is an area of saltwater wells and blowholes, through which dramatic eruptions of saltwater spew from submerged sea caves. **Jobos** is a large beach with a famed surf break at its western end, but kids can frolic along more protected areas along this mammoth shore. There are also guesthouses and restaurants here, and on summer and holiday weekends, it has a party atmosphere.

While Rincón has wider name recognition, Aguadilla and Isabela have equally good surf spots. In fact, the Puerto Rican Pipeline is actually composed of beaches in the three towns. **Gas Chambers, Crash Boat, Surfer's** and **Wilderness** rule in Aguadilla, while the preferred spots in **Isabela** include **Jobos, Middles** and **Shacks.** The best time to surf is from November through March, but summer storms can also kick up the surf. In the summer season, however, when the waves diminish, these northwest beaches double as perfect spots for windsurfing and snorkeling, with calm waters filled with coral reefs and marine life. The towns are quite close together, and the string of beaches through both really forms a single destination.

The northwest is a mecca for surfing aficionados, but it's also a great place to learn the sport. **The Rincón Surf School,** P.O. Box 1333, Rincón (✆ **787/823-0610;** www.rinconsurfschool.com), offers beginners lessons or can teach surfers how to improve their performance. One lesson costs $95, and there are also 2-day ($180), 3-day ($260), and 5-day ($390) packages. A private 2-hour lesson is $150, and $75 each for two people. The school also arranges surf vacation packages in conjunction with the Casa Verde Guesthouse. **Puntas Surf School,** P.O. Box 4319, HC-01 Calle Vista del Mar (✆ **939/697-8040** or 787/366-1689; www.puntassurfschool.com), is another great option. It's run by Melissa Taylor and Bill Woodward, whose love of the sport is infectious, and they say they can teach would-be surfers of any age, from 5 to 105. Private lessons cost $45 per hour, $75 for 2 hours. Group rates and package deals are also available. Board rentals are $25 per day, $60 for three days, $100 for a week. A professional photographer takes photos of lessons for sale.

There are many surfing outfitters in town, and one of the most established is the **West Coast Surf Shop,** Calle Muñoz Rivera 2E, Rincón (© **787/823-3935;** www.westcoastsurf.com), open daily 9am to 6pm. The **Hot Wavz Surf Shop,** Maria's Beach (© **787/823-3942**), rents long boards as well as boogie boards. Prices for board rentals start at around $25 daily. Snorkeling gear can also be rented at these shops.

In Aguadilla, check out **Aquatica Underwater Adventures,** Route 110 Km 10 (outside gate 5 of Rafael Hernández Airport), Aguadilla (© **787/890-6071**). It is a full-service dive and surf shop, but it also rents equipment and gives lessons in scuba and surfing. The outfit also runs mountain-bike excursions to the Guajataca Forest. Prices depend on season and group size, but surf lessons cost from $45 to $65 for 1½ hours, and a two-tank scuba dive is from $75 to $125. Bicycle tours cost around $65 per person and last up to 3 hours. Surf and scuba equipment rentals run from $20 to $45 per day, while bicycles are $25 per day.

The **Hang Loose Surf Shop,** Route 4466 Km 1.2, Playa Jobos, Isabela (© **787/872-2490;** Tues–Sun 10am–5pm), is well stocked with equipment. It gives surf lessons ($60 per hour private lesson) and rents boards for $25 daily. The shop is owned by Werner Vega, a great big-wave rider, who is one of Puerto Rico's premier board shapers.

SABA

17

Saba is different from all the other islands in the Caribbean, in that it is the top of a mountain (the rest of the landmass is undersea), with winding mountain roads and little villages clinging to its sides. More and more divers are flocking here to the last of the "virgin" dive locales, with some of the best sites in the Lesser Antilles.

Diving & Snorkeling Saba is one of the world's finest diving and snorkeling destinations. Dive sites teem with colorful coral and other sea creatures. Dive up to 110 feet at **Saba Marine National Park,** which circles the island. The park also has several marked spots for snorkelers; the adventurous should try the **snorkel trail.**

Things to Do Climb the 1,064 hand-hewn steps up to **Mount Scenery,** traversing a rainforest where wild orchids bloom along with giant elephant ears, palms, ferns, and mangoes. Explore **the Bottom,** the island capital, a charming Dutch village of chimneys, gabled roofs, and gardens.

Eating & Drinking Despite it size, this little island serves up plenty of savory Caribbean dishes and fresh seafood. Indulge in almond-crusted snapper in an eco-lodge or sea-bass filet on a rooftop terrace with panoramic valley views.

Nature Saba is as beautiful above the water as it is below. Hike to the top of **Mount Scenery,** where you'll pass through a lush rainforest of palms, bromeliads, lianas, and tree ferns. For Saba's most panoramic views head to **Crispeen Track.**

ESSENTIALS

Visitor Information

Saba Tourist Board, located in the heart of Windwardside (✆ **599/416-2231;** fax 599/416-2350; www.sabatourism.com), is open Monday to Friday 8am to 5pm.

Getting There

BY PLANE You'll have to get to St. Maarten before you can get to Saba. **American Airlines** (✆ **800/433-7300** in the U.S. and Canada; www.aa.com) flies nonstop from New York's JFK; **Continental Airlines** (✆ **800/231-0856** in the U.S. and Canada; www.continental.com) flies out of Newark. From Queen Juliana Airport on St. Maarten, you can take the 12-minute hop to Saba on **Winair** (✆ **866/466-0410** in the U.S.

and Canada, or 599/545-4237; www.fly-winair.com). There are at least five flights per day, depending on volume; fares are from $115 round-trip.

Saba's **Juancho Yrausquin Airport** (✆ **599/416-2255;** www.b-v-i.com/saba airport/default.htm) is one of the shortest landing strips in the world, stretching only 394m (1,293 ft.) along the aptly named Flat Point, one of the few level areas on the island.

Many guests at hotels on St. Maarten fly over to Saba on the morning flight, spend the day sightseeing, and then return to St. Maarten on the afternoon flight. Winair connections can also be made on Saba to both St. Kitts and St. Eustatius.

BY BOAT You can also take a high-speed ferry from St. Maarten's Pelican Marina at Simpson Bay to Fort Bay on Saba; you'll arrive in about an hour. ***The Edge*** (✆ **599/544-2640;** www.sabatourism.com) departs Wednesday to Sunday at 9am, returning at 5pm, making a day trip to Saba possible. Sometimes the waters are turbulent, making passengers seasick. The round-trip fare is $75 per person or $50 one-way if returning on a different day from your departure. There is also a port fee of $12 per passenger.

Getting Around

BY TAXI Taxis meet every flight. Up to four people are allowed to share a cab. The fare from the airport to Windwardside is $8, or $15 to the Bottom. A taxi from Windwardside to the Bottom costs $6.50. There is no central number to call for service. Taking a taxi ride on Saba is likely to involve you in local life—it's decidedly informal here. Don't be surprised if your driver interrupts the trip to rush a sick child to a plane to be flown to a hospital or pick up an old man to take him up the hill because he's fallen and hurt himself.

BY RENTAL CAR None of the major U.S. firms operates on Saba, partly because most visitors opt to get around by taxi. In the unlikely event that you should dare to drive a car on Saba, locally operated companies include **Caja's Car Rental,** the Bottom (✆ **599/416-2388**), starting at $55 per day and including a full tank of gas and unlimited mileage. Some insurance is included in the rates, but you might be held partly responsible in the event of an accident. Because of the very narrow roads and dozens of cliffs, it's crucial to exercise caution when driving on Saba. Note that traffic moves on the right.

BY HITCHHIKING Hitchhiking has long been an acceptable means of transport on Saba, where everybody seemingly knows everybody else. And if you hitchhike, you'll probably get to know everybody else, too.

ON FOOT The traditional means of getting around on Saba—walking—is still much in evidence. Just don't do the walk from the Bottom up to Windwardside unless you're fairly fit and have shoes with good traction, particularly after a recent rain.

[FastFACTS] SABA

Banks The main bank on the island is **First Caribbean International,** Windwardside (✆ **599/416-2216**), open Monday to Friday from 8:30am to 3:30pm. The **Royal Bank of Trinidad and Tobago** is another option. It's located at Windwardside (✆ **599/416-2454**) and is open Monday to Friday 8:30am to 3pm.

Currency Saba, like the other islands of the Netherlands Antilles, uses the **Netherlands Antilles guilder (NAf),** valued at 1.78 NAf to US$1 (1 NAf = 55¢). However, U.S. money is accepted by almost everybody here. *As such, prices in this chapter are quoted in U.S. dollars.*

Customs You don't have to go through Customs in Saba; it's a free port.

Documents The government requires that all visitors have a passport, plus a return or ongoing ticket.

Electricity Saba uses 110-volt AC (60 cycles), so U.S.-made appliances don't need transformers or adapters.

Emergencies Call ✆ **599/416-3289** for an ambulance, and ✆ **599/416-3237** for the police.

Hospital Saba's hospital complex is the **A. M. Edwards Medical Centre,** the Bottom (✆ **599/416-3239** or 416-3289).

Language The official language is Dutch, but English is widely spoken.

Pharmacies Try the **Pharmacy,** A. M. Edwards Medical Centre, the Bottom (✆ **599/416-3239**), open Monday to Friday 8am to 1pm and 2 to 5:30pm, and Saturday 10am to noon.

Safety Crime on this island, where everyone knows everyone else, is practically nonexistent. But who knows? A tourist might rob you. It is always wise to safeguard your valuables.

Taxes The government imposes a 5% tourist tax on hotel rooms, plus a 3% "turnover tax" on all rooms. If you're returning to St. Maarten or flying over to Statia, you must pay a $6 departure tax. If you're going anywhere else, a $20 tax is imposed. A service charge of 10% to 15% will be added to your restaurant bill.

Telephone To call Saba from the United States, dial **011** (the international access code), then **599** (the country code for the Netherlands Antilles), and finally **416** (the area code for all of Saba) and the four-digit local number. To make a call within Saba, only the four-digit local number is necessary.

Time Saba is on Atlantic Standard Time year-round, 1 hour earlier than Eastern Standard Time. When the United States is on daylight saving time, clocks on Saba and the U.S. East Coast read the same.

Water The water on Saba is generally safe to drink.

Weather Temperatures from January to April average 69°F to 83°F (21°C–28°C). The rest of the year, temperatures range from 70°F to 88°F (21°C–31°C).

WHERE TO STAY

If you're looking for a hotel on the beach, you've come to the wrong island. Saba's only beach, Well's Bay Beach, is tiny and can be reached from most hotels only via a $10 taxi ride.

Cottage Club ★ Small, intimate, and immersed in Saba's architectural and aesthetic traditions, this hotel complex sits on a steeply sloping and carefully landscaped terrain, a 2-minute walk from the center of the island's capital. Designed of local stone and set at an altitude above the other buildings of the complex, the lobby is filled with a collection of island antiques and lace curtains.

Each medium-size studio apartment has a semiprivate patio, a living-room area, and a queen-size bed. These units are housed in clapboard replicas of antique cottages—two studios per cottage—with red roofs, green shutters, white walls, and yellow trim. The interiors are breezy, airy, and comfortable. If you'd like a room with an ocean view, request nos. 1 or 2. There's no bar or restaurant on the premises, but a nearby supermarket will deliver supplies on request.

Windwardside, Saba, N.A. www.cottage-club.com. ✆/fax **599/416-2386.** 10 cottages. Winter $120 studio apt for 2; off season $110 studio apt for 2. 3rd and 4th person free. Children 12 and under stay free in parent's room. Dive packages available. DISC, MC, V. **Amenities:** Outdoor pool. *In room:* Ceiling fan, TV, kitchenette (in some).

Ecolodge Rendez-Vous This nature lover's retreat is buried deep in the rainforest off the Crispeen Trail. A small, family-operated eco-resort, it is enveloped by lush vegetation and is the perfect hideaway, especially since its accommodations can be kept mosquito-free. The owners prefer to say that they are not a hotel, but a lifestyle based on a close encounter with nature, with an aim of "rediscovery of a sense of self." Accommodations are spread across nearly a dozen small Saban-style cottages, each with a private deck and hammock. You live as Sabans used to—that is, by candlelight after dark. The lodge is solar-powered, coming with "sun showers." Most of the vegetables served in the restaurant, and certainly the herbs, are homegrown, as are the fruits, such as Surinam cherries and bitter skin oranges.

Crispeen Track, Windwardside, Saba, N.A. www.ecolodge-saba.com. ✆ **599/416-3888** or 416-3348. Fax 599/416-3299. 11 units. Winter $85–$105 double; off season $75–$95 double. Extra person $10. Add $10 for kitchenette. Dive packages available. MC, V. **Amenities:** Restaurant; bar; hot tub; outdoor pool. *In room:* Kitchenette (in some), no phone.

El Momo ★ The most eco-friendly place to stay on island is this cluster of small wooden cottages enveloped by tropical gardens 475m (1,558 ft.) up Booby Hill. The Robinson Crusoe–like nature retreat is about a 10-minute walk from Windwardside. Decorated with original artwork, cottages are filled with handmade wooden furniture and colorful fabrics. In 2008 the resort became the first 100% smoke-free hotel on Saba. The owners make their own banana rum and vanilla rum liqueurs, which you can purchase on-site.

Booby Hill, Windwardside, Saba, N.A. www.elmomocottages.com. ✆ **599/416-2265.** 7 cottages, 5 with bathroom. Year-round $65–$105 double. **Amenities:** Vegetarian snack bar; outdoor pool. *In room:* Ceiling fan, kitchen (in some), no phone, Wi-Fi (free).

Juliana's This hostelry is set on a hillside, and each guest room is modern, immaculate, and simply but comfortably furnished. All have access to a sun deck and balconies opening onto beautiful views of the Caribbean, except nos. 1, 2, and 3, which are in the rear. Opt for one of the upper-level rooms (nos. 7, 8, or 9), as they offer the best views. Also available are a two-and-a-half-room apartment, complete with kitchenette; and a renovated original Saban cottage, with two bedrooms, a spacious living room, a dining room, a TV, and a fully equipped kitchen.

Windwardside, Saba, N.A. www.julianas-hotel.com. ✆ **866/783-3319** or 599/416-2269. Fax 599/416-2389. 12 units. Winter $110–$170 double, $220 apt, $220 cottage; off season $120–$155 double, $200 apt, $200 cottage. Extra person $30. Dive packages available. DISC, MC, V. **Amenities:** Restaurant; bar; babysitting; outdoor pool. *In room:* Ceiling fan, TV, fridge, hair dryer, kitchen/kitchenette (in some), minibar, no phone, Wi-Fi (free).

Queen's Gardens Resort ★ This is still a classy joint, sitting on a lofty perch. One of the most massive engineering projects in Saba's recent memory included the placement of a rock-sided terrace on this plot of forested, steeply sloping land 360m (1,181 ft.) above the sea. The result is a well-conceived cluster of white-walled, red-roofed bungalows angled for sweeping views and surrounding the semicircular edges of the largest pool on Saba, with north-facing views over the island's capital and the sea. From a distance, the compound evokes a fortified village in Iberia. All accommodations are suites, with a combination of Dutch colonial and Indonesian furnishings. The most elegant place to stay is a villa for up to six guests. Most units are split-level, with large living rooms; all have kitchenettes and fine king-size or queen-size beds. A few suites have a Jacuzzi overlooking the coast and sea.

1 Troy Hill Dr. (P.O. Box 4), the Bottom, Saba, N.A. www.queensaba.com. ✆ **599/416-3494.** Fax 599/416-3495. 12 units. Year-round $200–$300 double; $895 villa. AE, MC, V. **Amenities:** Restaurant; bar; babysitting; dive shop; outdoor pool. *In room:* Ceiling fan, TV, kitchen, minibar, Wi-Fi (free).

Scout's Place Right in the center of Windwardside, this funky dive resort is hidden from the street and set on the ledge of a hill. With only 13 rooms, it's still the second-largest inn on the island. The old house has a large, covered, open-air dining room, where every table has a view of the sea. It's informal, with a decor ranging from Surinam hand-carvings to red-and-black wicker peacock chairs to silver samovars. Guest rooms open onto an interior courtyard filled with flowers, and each has a view of the sea. The rooms are small and rather plain, except for the four-poster beds; many have linoleum floors and tiny TVs. The best units are on the lower floor, as they have French doors opening onto balconies fronting the ocean. You can also opt for a two-bedroom cottage with living room and full kitchen.

Windwardside (P.O. Box 543), Saba, N.A. www.sabadivers.com. ✆ **866/656-7222** in the U.S., or 599/416-2740. Fax 599/416-2741. 13 units. Winter $110–$125 double, $145–$205 cottage; off season $95–$120 double, $145–$185 cottage. Rates include continental breakfast. MC, V. **Amenities:** Restaurant; bar; dive shop; outdoor pool. *In room:* Ceiling fan, TV, fridge, Wi-Fi (free).

Shearwater Resort ★★ This is Saba's only luxurious hotel. The hotel opened in 1994 as Willard's of Saba and immediately began to attract large numbers of visitors, among them celebrities who might not have set foot on the island before. Guest rooms have *Casablanca*-like ceiling fans. Furnishings are of a high standard, and every item was revamped in 2011. Because the hotel is in a garden high on a hill overlooking the island's southwestern coastline, each room has sweeping views and almost constant ocean breezes. Much care went into the design, making use of everything from cedar from the U.S. Northwest to original island paintings. The least expensive units are the two rooms in the main building, which are quite spacious. The other five units are in a concrete building designed in the island's distinctive style, with red roofs, white walls, and green shutters. For the most luxurious living, ask for the VIP Room overlooking the pool, with its own large balcony. Lower cliff-side units are the smallest but have good views from their private balconies. Honeymooners prefer the Room in the Sky.

The hotel restaurant is recommended (below).

Booby Hill, Saba, N.A. www.shearwater-resort.com. ✆ **599/416-2498.** Fax 599/416-2482. 8 units. Winter $195 double, $235–$275 suite; off season $175 double, $215–$250 suite. AE, DISC, MC, V. Children 12 and under not allowed. **Amenities:** Restaurant; bar; exercise room; Jacuzzi; outdoor pool; room service; tennis court (lit). *In room:* TV/DVD, CD player, MP3 docking station, no phone, Wi-Fi ($15 per day).

WHERE TO DINE

Bistro del Mare ★★ NORTHERN ITALIAN In the Shearwater Resort (see above), this bistro is one of the island's best dining spots. It takes a menu of time-tested Italian recipes and somehow manages to infuse dishes with the freshness of the Caribbean. In an intimate setting, you can sample the island's best antipasti, especially the lightly floured and flash-fried calamari served with a garlic aioli. Steamed mussels come in a spicy garlic and tomato broth. From the tasting menus, you can take a culinary tour of Italy with creative dishes paired with specially selected "tasting pours" designed to complement each dish. Favorites among the specialties include fennel-crusted veal scaloppini with a truffled potato gratin, or else seared red snapper in an orange tarragon sauce laced with coconut milk and served with a ginger and chive-studded risotto.

In the Shearwater Resort, Booby Hill. ✆ **599/416-2498.** Reservations required. Main courses $20–$43; 3-course tasting menu $75; 4-course tasting menu $90. AE, DISC, MC, V. Tues–Sat 5:30–9:30pm.

Brigadoon Pub & Eatery ★ CARIBBEAN/AMERICAN The island's best restaurant is in this century-old colonial building with an open front. Your hosts, Trish Chammaa and her husband, Michael (he labors over the hot stove), are virtual legends on the island. Whenever possible, local ingredients are used, including herbs, spices, fruits, and farm-fresh vegetables. Fresh local fish and lobster (prices vary) are generally the best things to order. Steaks are flown in weekly. Other recommended dishes include mahimahi (dolphin) with citrus-butter sauce and Thai shrimp in a coconut-curry sauce. The closing time listed below is not hard and fast. The owner closes the joint "whenever all the customers leave," even if it's really late.

Windwardside. ✆ **599/416-2380.** Reservations not accepted. Main courses $15–$44. AE, DC, MC, V. Wed–Mon 6:30–9:30pm.

Queen's Gardens Restaurant ★ INTERNATIONAL The on-site restaurant at Queen's Gardens Resort (p. 480), this place is not only the most romantic on island, but also surfaces near the top in quality of produce and skill in preparation. After the dinner plates are hustled away, diners dance under the moonlit night—when not enjoying musical evenings or parties around the pool. Some of the chef's inventive dishes are the best on island, notably lobster or duck breast sautéed in guavaberry liqueur. The sautéed Queen's Garden chicken is another specialty. The grilled lamb chops are given extra zest with a cranberry-thyme sauce.

In the Queen's Garden Resort, 1 Troy Hill Dr., the Bottom. ✆ **599/416-3494.** www.queensaba.com. Reservations required. Main courses $22–$35. AE, MC, V. Mon 7–10am and 11am–2pm; Tues–Sun 7–10am, 11am–2pm, and 6–9pm.

Rainforest Restaurant ★ 🎁 CARIBBEAN Getting here is half the fun. The restaurant lies at the end of a mountain road, where you then take a 10-minute hike down the Crispeen Track via the Mt. Scenery Trail to come to this oasis in a rainforest. At the heart of the previously recommended Ecolodge (see above), the restaurant serves the freshest produce on island. Most of the vegetables, certainly the herbs, are homegrown, including fruits such as Surinam cherries and bitter-skin oranges. Outdoor seating is provided on a terrace overlooking a fish pond. Start, perhaps, with a jerk chicken and papaya salad. For a main course, you might order such tasty dishes as red-curry coconut shrimp or almond-crusted snapper, perhaps a steak kebab. Every Tuesday evening, an Indonesian *rijstafel* night is held, with a combination of about a dozen different dishes. The homemade ice creams are prepared from fresh fruits on the island, including soup sop and mango.

In the Ecolodge Rendez-vous, Crispeen Track, Windwardside. ✆ **599/416-3348.** Reservations recommended. Main courses $19–$27. AE, DC, MC, V. Tues–Sun noon–2:30pm and 6:30–9pm.

Restaurant Eden ★ 🎁 FUSION/SEAFOOD In the center of Windwardside, this rooftop restaurant is one of the more inviting on island, with tropical plants and a rustic deck overlooking the valley, the vegetable garden, a gazebo, and the mountains in the distance. A bakery is attached, and many islanders visit during the day for coffee and some of the more delectable baked goods in Saba. For dinner try the homemade rolls with a sun-dried tomato, which can be followed by the soup of the day, perhaps that Parisian bistro favorite of frog legs or escargots. Main courses come with scalloped potatoes or fries and might feature a sea bass filet in a white wine and dill sauce, or pan-fried rack of lamb in a garlic-laced rosemary sauce. Finish off with a Caribbean delight—a chocolate brownie with pecans, vanilla ice cream, and whipped cream.

Lambee's Place, Windwardside. ✆ **599/416-2539.** www.edensaba.com. Reservations recommended. Main courses $18–$37. MC, V. Wed–Mon 5:30–9:30pm (or later).

Scout's Place INTERNATIONAL/CARIBBEAN This is a popular dining spot among day-trippers to the island, so you should have your driver stop by early to make a reservation for you. Lunch is simple, good, and filling, and the prices are low. The sandwiches are the island's best, made with fresh-baked bread. Locals come from all over the island to sample them. Dinner is more elaborate, with tables placed on an open-sided terrace, the ideal spot for a drink at sundown. Fresh seafood is a specialty, as is curried goat. Every day a selection of homemade soups is also offered, perhaps pumpkin or pigeon pea. Scout's chef is proud of his ribs as well. Fresh local fruits and vegetables are used whenever possible. Even if you don't like the food, it's the best place on the island to catch up on the latest gossip.

In the Scout's Place hotel, Windwardside. © **599/416-2740.** Reservations recommended. Lunch $10–$18; fixed-price dinner $10–$27. MC, V. Mon–Sat 7:30am–11pm; Sun 7:30am–3pm.

SPORTS & OUTDOOR PURSUITS

If it's beaches you're seeking, forget it. It's better to remain on St. Maarten. Sports here are limited primarily to diving and hiking.

Diving & Snorkeling ★★

Circling the entire island and including four offshore underwater mountains (seamounts), the **Saba Marine Park,** Fort Bay (© **599/416-3295**), preserves the island's coral reefs and marine life. The park is zoned for various pursuits. The all-purpose recreational zone includes **Well's Bay Beach,** Saba's only beach, but it's seasonal, disappearing with the winter seas only to reappear in late spring. There are two anchorage zones for visiting yachts and Saba's only harbor. The five dive zones include a coastal area and four seamounts, 2km (1¼ miles) offshore. In these zones are more than two dozen marked and buoyed dive sites and a snorkeling trail. You'll plunge into a world of coral and sponges, swimming with parrotfish, doctorfish, and damselfish.

The **snorkel trail** is not for the neophyte. It can be approached from Well's Bay Beach, but only from May to October. Depths of more than 450m (1,476 ft.) are found between the island and the seamounts, which reach a minimum depth of 27m (89 ft.). There's a $3-per-dive visitor fee. Funds are also raised through souvenir sales and donations. The park office at Fort Bay is open Monday to Friday 8am to 5pm, Saturday and Sunday 10am to 2pm. There's a fully operational decompression chamber/hyperbaric facility in the Fort Bay harbor.

Sea Saba Dive Center, Windwardside (© **599/416-2246;** www.seasaba.com), has nine experienced instructors eager to share their knowledge of Saba Marine Park and its famous deep and medium-depth pinnacles, walls, spur-and-groove formations, and giant boulder gardens. Their two 12m (39-ft.), uncrowded boats are best suited for a comfortable day on Saba's waters. Daily boat dives are made between 9:30am and 1:30pm, allowing a relaxing interval for snorkeling. Courses range from resort through dive master. Extra day and night dives can be arranged. A one-tank dive costs $55; a two-tank dive costs $100.

Saba Deep Dive Center, P.O. Box 22, Fort Bay, Saba, N.A. (© **599/416-3347;** www.sabadeep.com), is a full-service dive center that offers scuba diving, snorkeling, equipment rental/repair, and tank fills. Mike Myers and his staff of NAUI and PADI instructors and dive masters make an effort to provide personalized service and great diving, whether you're an old pro or a first-timer. A certification course goes from $350 to $395. A single-tank dive costs $50; a two-tank dive, $100. Night dives are $65. The center is open daily from 7am to 4pm. On the same property, the **In Two Deep Restaurant** and the **Deep Boutique** offer air-conditioned comfort, a view of the harbor area and the Caribbean Sea, good food and drink, and a wide selection of clothes, swimwear, lotions, and sunglasses. The restaurant is open for breakfast and lunch.

Hiking ★

Saba is as beautiful above the water as it is below. It offers many trails, for both beginners and more experienced hikers, all reached by paths leading off from "the Road." There's nothing more dramatic than the hike to the top of **Mount Scenery,** a volcano

A Roller-Coaster Road

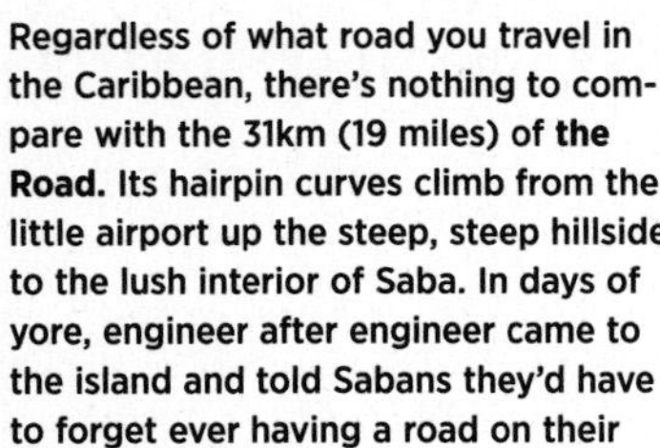

Regardless of what road you travel in the Caribbean, there's nothing to compare with the 31km (19 miles) of the Road. Its hairpin curves climb from the little airport up the steep, steep hillside to the lush interior of Saba. In days of yore, engineer after engineer came to the island and told Sabans they'd have to forget ever having a road on their volcanic mountain. However, Josephus Lambert Hassell, a local, had high hopes. In the 1930s, he began to take a correspondence course in engineering while he plotted and planned the Road. Under his guidance, his fellow islanders built the Road over the next 2 decades or so. In recent years, it's been necessary to reconstruct the Road, but it's there, waiting to thrill you. At the top of the Road stands Windwardside, at 541m (1,775 ft.), Saba's second-largest settlement and the island's midpoint.

that erupted 5,000 years ago. Allow at least 3 hours and take your time climbing the 1,064 sometimes-slippery chiseled-rock and concrete steps up to the cloud-reefed mountain. You'll pass through a lush rainforest of palms, bromeliads, elephant ears, heliconia, mountain raspberries, lianas, and tree ferns. Queen Beatrix of the Netherlands climbed these steps in her pumps and, upon reaching the summit, declared: "This is the smallest and highest place in my kingdom." On a clear day, you can see the neighboring islands of St. Kitts, St. Eustatius, St. Maarten, and even St. Barts. Ask your inn to pack you a picnic lunch, and bring water. The higher you climb, the cooler it grows, a drop of about 1°F (.5°C) every 100m (328 ft.); on a hot day, this can be quite an incentive. It's recommended that you seek guidance from the **Saba Conservation Foundation,** Fort Bay (✆ **599/416-3295**), which provides data on 18 botanical trails. A full-day hike through Mount Scenery costs from $40 per person.

One of our favorite hikes—with some of Saba's most panoramic views—is the **Crispeen Track,** reached from Windwardside as the main road descends to the hamlet of St. John's. Once at St. John's, the track heads northeast going through a narrow but dramatic gorge covered in thick tropical foliage. The vegetation grows lusher and lusher, taking in banana and citrus fields. As you reach the higher points of a section of the island called **Rendezvous,** the fields are no longer cultivated and begin to resemble a rainforest, covered with such flora as philodendron, anthurium, and the wild mammee. Hiking time to Rendezvous is about an hour.

If you don't want to explore the natural attractions of the island on your own, the **Saba Tourist Office,** P.O. Box 527, Windwardside (✆ **599/416-2231**), can arrange tours of the tropical rainforests. Jim Johnson (✆ **599/416-2630**), a fit, 40-ish Saban guide, conducts most of these tours and knows the terrain better than anyone else on the island. (He's sometimes difficult to reach, however.) Johnson will point out orchids, golden heliconia, and other flora and fauna, as well as the rock formations and bromeliads you're likely to see. Tours can accommodate one to eight hikers and usually last about half a day; depending on your particular route and number of participants, the cost can be anywhere from $50 to $100 per person. Actual prices, of course, are negotiated.

EXPLORING THE ISLAND

The first jeep arrived on Saba in 1947. Before that, Sabans went about on foot, climbing from village to village. Hundreds of steps had been chiseled out of the rock by the early Dutch settlers in the 1640s.

The villages here are storybook affairs: Tidy white houses cling to the mountainside, and small family cemeteries adjoin each dwelling. Lace-curtained, gingerbread-trimmed cottages give a Disneyland aura.

Past villages, the Road goes over the crest to **the Bottom.** Derived from the Dutch word *botte,* which means "bowl-shaped," this town is nestled on a plateau 250m (820 ft.) above the sea, which is surrounded by rocky volcanic domes. It's also the official capital of Saba, a charming Dutch village of chimneys, gabled roofs, and gardens.

From the Bottom, you can take a taxi up the hill to the mountain village of **Windwardside,** perched on the crest of two ravines about 541m (1,775 ft.) above sea level. This village of red-roofed houses, the second-most important on Saba, is the site of the two biggest inns and most of the shops. A little beyond Windwardside, a set of 1,064 hand-hewn steps scales the side of **Mount Scenery ★★**, going through a rainforest where wild orchids bloom along with giant elephant ears, palms, ferns, and mangoes.

From Windwardside, you can climb steep steps cut in the rock to yet another village, **Hell's Gate,** teetering on the edge of a mountain. There's also a serpentine road from the airport to Hell's Gate, where you'll find the island's largest church. Only the most athletic climb from here to the lip of the volcanic crater.

SABA AFTER DARK

If you want to do a lot of partying on your vacation, you might want to consider another island. Saba is known for its tucked-away, relaxed, and calm atmosphere. However, don't be too dismayed; there's still something to do at night.

Scout's Place, Windwardside (✆ **599/416-2740;** www.sabadivers.com), is the place to hang out if you want to relax, enjoy a drink, and have a laugh, especially on weeknights. A hotel and restaurant, Scout's Place moonlights as a local watering hole, entertaining tourists and locals with a distinct Saban/Caribbean atmosphere. You won't do much dancing (well, that actually depends on how much you've had to drink), but it's much better than the weeknight alternative: nothing. It's open daily from 7am to around 11pm (but actual closing hours depend on business or the lack thereof). There's no cover.

A British-style pub with a nautical motif, **Saba's Treasure,** Windwardside (✆ **599/416-2819;** www.sabastreasure.com), is the new social center of the island. Robbie Lynn, a local artist, designed and built the structure himself. He decorated the walls with old magazine articles about Saba's maritime past. Expats and visitors alike flock here at night, mainly for the beer but also for the well-stuffed sandwiches and stone-oven pizzas.

If you'd like to combine the ambience of a British pub with a saloon that might have been found in the Arizona Badlands, head for **Swinging Doors,** Windwardside (✆ **599/416-2506**), Saba's good ol' boy watering hole, where locals start consuming the brew at 9am and keep drinking until late at night (no set closing hour). If you get hungry along the way, go for the jalapeño poppers.

18

ST. BARTHÉLEMY

St. Barts: Two words synonymous with glitz, glamour, and gorgeous beaches. A taste of the French Riviera in the Caribbean, St. Barts is eternally chic. Visitors come for pampering without pomp, inimitable French flair, world-class beaches, and the promise of eternal sun and blue skies (it rarely rains). In spite of its tony reputation, the island diligently maintains its quaintness, warmth, and an almost old-fashioned storybook quality.

Beaches St. Barts has some 21 white-sand beaches, and while all are public and free, few are crowded, even in high season. The best known is **St-Jean Beach,** a sun-splashed crescent split by the Eden Rock promontory. The uncrowded strand at **Gouverneur Beach,** on the southern coast, is gorgeous and ringed by steep cliffs. Equally fine is Grande Saline Beach, to the east; lack of shade doesn't deter the nude sunbathers.

Things to Do You can snorkel in the calm waters of secluded **Colombier** or in the protected bay at **Petite Anse,** which teems with colorful aquatic life. Kite-surfing is one of the most popular sports here—study with former champions to get the hang of it on **Grand Cul-de-Sac.** Old-fashioned **Corossol Beach** offers a calm, protected beach and a charming little seashell museum. South of Gustavia, **Shell Beach** is awash with small, exquisite seashells; rocky outcroppings protect the beach from strong waves.

Eating & Drinking Hot young chefs keep ratcheting up the excellence quotient on the St. Barts' dining scene. Yes, it can be expensive to dine out, but the budget-bound can eat well on the filling and affordable lunchtime ***plats du jour*** (special of the day) at casual restaurants. Alternatively, do takeout, St. Barts style, from one of the excellent epicurean takeout delis, or ***traiteurs.***

Shopping Duty-free St. Barts offers French perfumes, haute couture, crystal, porcelain, watches, and other luxuries from designer brands like Bulgari, Cartier, Dior, and Hermès, especially at Gustavia's **Quai de la République**—nicknamed "rue du Couturier." For island crafts, look for intricately woven straw goods (baskets, bags, bonnets) and striking art naïf, including models of Creole *cazes* and fishing boats.

ESSENTIALS

Visitor Information

Comité du Tourisme de Saint-Barthélemy, St. Barts' official tourism agency, was founded in 2008, when the island became a French overseas collectivity and no longer a French *commune* under the administration of

Guadeloupe. Its website is **www.saintbarth-tourisme.com** (or www.cttsb.org). In St. Barts, the tourist office is located adjacent to La Capitanerie (the Port Authority Headquarters) on the pier, quai du Général-de-Gaulle, Gustavia (© **590/27-87-27**).

On island, pick up a copy of ***Ti Gourmet;*** this solid little guide is packed with invaluable information on absolutely everything. Online, the **Insiders' Guide to St. Barthélemy** (www.sbhonline.com) offers very instructive readers' forums and trip reports. The web-only ***St. Barths Online*** (www.st-barths.com) offers details on arts, dining, shopping, and nightlife listings.

Getting There

BY PLANE The flight from St. Maarten is just 10 minutes long, but for many people, landing on a tiny airstrip between two volcanic hills and braking mere feet from sunbathers on the beach is 10 minutes of terror. The makeshift landing strip at St-Jean airport on St. Barts is just 661.5m (2,170 ft.) long and accommodates only STOL (short takeoff and landing) aircrafts no bigger than 19-seaters. Even on these small planes, landing on St. Barts has often been compared (and not favorably) to touching down on an aircraft carrier. The pilot must divebomb between two mountains (one with a giant white Swedish cross), then pull up abruptly: no extra charge for the thrill ride. (In fact, any pilot who plans to land in St. Barts is required to qualify for a special permit first.) No landings or departures are permitted after dark.

There are no nonstop flights to St. Barts from North America. From the United States, the principal gateways are St. Maarten, St. Thomas, and Guadeloupe. Most people from the U.S. or Canada first fly to St. Maarten; for details on getting to St. Maarten, see chapter 22. From St. Maarten, **Windward Islands Airways International** (known by everybody as **Winair;** © **866/466-0410** in the U.S. and Canada, or 590/27-61-01; www.fly-winair.com) offers 10 to 20 daily flights to St. Barts. One-way passage costs around 64€—but that figure excludes taxes and surcharges, which can double the cost (including inflated fees for credit card charges). Flight duration is a mere 10 minutes.

A recommended carrier is **St. Barth Commuter** (© **590/27-54-54;** www.stbarthcommuter.com), which flies four flights Monday through Saturday (two on Sun) from little L'Espérance Airport in Grand Case, St. Martin (one-way fares 60€ adults, 45€ children 2–11). It flies once daily from St. Maarten's Princess Juliana Airport (one-way fares 65€ adults, 50€ children 2–11). (The founder and CEO of St. Barth Commuter is Bruno Magras, a member of one of St. Barts' founding families and current president of the nation's 16-member Territorial Council.)

Airline Advice

Always reconfirm your return flight from St. Barts with your interisland airline. If you don't, your reservation will be canceled. *Note:* On rare occasions, a flight will be rescheduled if the booking doesn't meet its fuel quota. Also, don't check your luggage all the way through to St. Barts, or you may not see it for a few days. Instead, check your bags to your gateway connecting destination (usually St. Maarten), then take your luggage to your interisland carrier and recheck it to St. Barts. Just in case, pack a change of clothes, any required medicine, and a bathing suit in your carry-on.

Tradewind Aviation (✆ **800/376-7922;** www.tradewindaviation.com) offers two daily first-class charter flights to St. Barts from San Juan, Puerto Rico; the flight is an hour long and roundtrip cost (including taxes and surcharges) is $395 per person Monday through Thursday and $495 per person Friday through Sunday.

Air Caraïbes (✆ 590/82-47-47 or 590/27-71-90; www.aircaraibes.com) flights depart four or five times a day from Pointe-à-Pitre's Pôle Caraïbes Aéroport in Guadeloupe. Round-trip passage to St. Barts starts at 236€; trip time is 45 minutes.

BY BOAT The **Voyager** vessels (✆ **590/87-10-68;** www.voy12.com or www.voyager-st-barths.com) make frequent (usually twice daily, sometimes more) runs between St. Barts and either side of St. Maarten/St. Martin. The schedule varies according to the season (and the seas), but the ***MV Voyager II*** usually departs Marigot Harbor for St. Barts every morning and evening. ***MV Voyager I*** travels from Oyster Pond to Gustavia two to four times daily. Advance reservations are a good idea; fares run around 50€ to 58€ adults, 30€ children 2 to 12 one-way (plus taxes). The trip can take around 45 minutes and can be rough; it's recommended that those with weak tummies take seasickness medication before the trip.

The technologically advanced, speedy, and more luxurious and stable 65-foot aluminum mono-hull ***Great Bay Express*** (✆ **590/27-60-33;** www.sbhferry.com) offers daily 20- to 40-minute crossings between St. Maarten's Bobby's Marina, in Philipsburg, and Gustavia. The boat can carry 130 passengers. Reservations are essential; the round-trip fare is 56€ to 95€ adults, 40€ to 50€ children 2 to 11 (plus taxes).

Getting Around

BY TAXI Taxis meet all flights and can be expensive, even though destinations aren't far from one another. Dial ✆ **590/27-75-81** or 590/27-66-31 for taxi service. A typical rate, from the airport to Cul-de-Sac, is 20€. Fares between 8pm and 6am and on Sundays and holidays are 50% higher. Taxi service must be arranged between midnight and 6am—call ahead. There are taxi stands at the airport and in Gustavia.

The government imposes official fares on tours by taxi. Many travelers simply approach a likely looking taxi driver and ask him to show them around. The official rates for one to three passengers are 45€ for 45 minutes, 54€ for 60 minutes, and 60€ for 90 minutes. For four or more passengers, add 8€ to each of the above-mentioned prices.

BY RENTAL CAR A rental car is an essential in St. Barts; it's really the best way to come and go as you please. You can reserve one yourself or have your hotel rent one for you. A number of rental agencies are located at the airport, although most rental agencies are happy to deliver cars straight to your hotel or villa. Many resorts keep an assortment of rental cars on-site, ready to go. Others, like Le Sereno, even include a rental car in your resort rates. All valid foreign driver's licenses are honored.

Star Location Car Rentals (✆ **690/42-28-42**) offers rates with a 1€=US$1 equivalency—still a good deal for Americans at press time. It's located right at St-Jean Airport, with a wide range of rental cars, from automatic-drive Suzuki SUVs and four-wheel-drives to stick-shift vans. Rates run from 38€ to 130€ a day, depending on the season. Also at the airport is **Gumbs Car Rental** (✆ **590/27-75-32**), a longtime island car rental company with a fleet of 65 cars; the reasonable rates start at around 20€ a day. Those with an itch to drive a Mini Cooper convertible around the island can rent one for around 120€ a day from **Pure Rental,** on rue du Roi Oscar II, in Gustavia (✆ **590/27-64-76**).

St. Barthélemy

Budget (✆ **800/472-3325** in the U.S., or 590/29-62-40; www.st-barts.com/budget) rents various 4WD Suzukis and automatic Daihatsus for 60€ a day, with unlimited mileage. Be sure to reserve at least 3 business days before your arrival.

Hertz (✆ **800/654-3001** in the U.S. and Canada; www.hertzstbarth.com) operates on St. Barts through a local dealership, **Henry's Car Rental,** with branches at the airport and in St-Jean (✆ **590/27-71-14**). It offers open-sided Suzuki Samurais for 65€ a day, and more substantial Suzuki Sidekicks for 70€ to 90€ per day.

At **Avis** (✆ **800/331-1212** in the U.S. and Canada, or 590/27-71-43; www.avisstbarth.com), you'll need a reservation a full month in advance during high season. In the winter, cars range from 68€ to 98€ a day. In the off season, rentals are 44€ to 90€ a day.

Note: For Budget, Hertz, and Avis, if you reserve your car in the U.S., you will be charged in dollars, not euros.

DRIVING ST. BARTS Driving is on the right and maximum speed is 50kmph (31 mph); seatbelts are required. Never drive with less than half a tank of gas on St. Barts. There are only two gas stations on the island, and both are closed on Sunday: one near the airport (7:30am–noon and 2–7pm—with an all-night automatic pump that usually accepts MasterCard and Visa), and another in Lorient (7:30am–noon and 2–5pm).

Driving on St. Barts is an interesting experience, with corkscrewing roller-coaster roads (all two-lane) and blind corners sometimes announced by signs without words, just an exclamation point! Unless you're comfortable driving up and down steep hills with ease in a standard four-on-the-floor, I say opt for an automatic car. Slow down as you maneuver 90-degree curves, and don't let tailgating motorbikes and scooters push you into speeding up. (And be on the lookout for motorbikes and scooters pulling out into traffic.) Also: If you plan to park on the road, say, in St-Jean, amid tight traffic, be sure to pull in your driver's side rear-view mirror, or you might find it sheared off when you return. Happy driving!

BY MOTORBIKE & SCOOTER **Denis Dufau** operates two affiliates (✆ **590/27-70-59** and 590/27-54-83). A helmet is provided (and required—it's the law), and renters must either leave an imprint of a valid credit card or pay a deposit. Rental fees vary from 24€ to 35€ per day, depending on the size of the bike. (Four-wheeling quads are becoming a popular choice.) For all but the smallest models, presentation of a valid driver's license is required, and you must be 21 or older.

JOGGING/BY BICYCLE St. Barts is not the ideal place to ride a bike or go for a roadside run. The two-lane roads have narrow-to-nonexistent shoulders and few sidewalks, traffic can be heavy, and you'll be huffing and puffing up and down steep hills and around corkscrew bends. Serious joggers can resort to their hotel fitness rooms or head to the newly resurfaced track around the soccer field in St-Jean Carenage (behind the St-Jean firehouse). Gustavia is also a good place to jog when traffic is light.

[FastFACTS] ST. BARTHÉLEMY

Banks The two main banks, both of which have **ATMs,** are **Banque Française Commerciale,** rue du Général-de-Gaulle, Gustavia (✆ **590/27-62-62,** or ✆ **590/27-87-75** in St-Jean); and the **Banque Nationale de Paris,** rue du Bord de Mer (✆ **590/27-63-70**). Open hours for both are Monday to Friday from 8am to noon and 2 to 3:30pm.

Currency The euro is the official currency, although U.S. dollars are accepted just about everywhere. At press time 1€ equaled US$1.42. *Prices in this chapter are quoted in euros.*

Documents U.S., British, and Canadian citizens need a passport to enter St. Barts. If you're flying in, you'll need to present your return or ongoing ticket. Citizens of the European Union need only an official photo ID, but passports are always recommended.

Electricity The electricity is 220-volt AC (50 cycles); U.S.-made appliances will require adapter plugs and transformers.

Emergencies Dial ✆ **17** for **police** or **medical** emergencies, ✆ **18** for **fire** emergencies.

Hospital St. Barts is not the greatest place to find yourself in a medical emergency. Except for vacationing doctors escaping their own practices in other parts of the world, it has only seven resident doctors and about a dozen on-call specialists. The island's only hospital, with the only emergency facilities, is the **Hôpital de Bruyn,** rue Jean-Bart (✆ **590/27-60-35**), about .4km (¼ mile) north of Gustavia. Serious medical cases are often flown to St. Maarten, Martinique, Miami, or wherever the person or his/her family specifies.

Language The official language is French, but English is widely spoken.

Pharmacies The **Pharmacie de Saint-Barth** is on quai de la Republique, Gustavia (✆ **590/27-61-82**). Its only competitor is the **Pharmacie de l'Aeroport,** adjacent to the airport (✆ **590/27-66-61**). Both are open Monday through Saturday from 8am to 7:30pm; on Sunday, one or the other remains open for at least part of the day.

Safety Crime is extremely rare on St. Barts; it's one of the safest islands in the Caribbean. But it's always wise to protect your valuables. Don't leave them unguarded on the beach or in parked cars, even if locked in the trunk.

Taxes You're assessed a 4€ departure tax if you're heading for another French island. Otherwise, you'll pay 8€. (These taxes are included in your airline ticket.) There is no sales tax and no tax on restaurant meals. Hotels now tack on a 5% tourist tax.

Telephone St. Barts is linked to the Guadeloupe telephone system. To call St. Barts from the United States, dial **011** (the international access code), then **590** (the country code for Guadeloupe), then **590** again, and finally the six-digit local number. To make a call within St. Barts, dial only the six-digit local number, and ignore the prefix 590. To reach an AT&T operator from anywhere on the island, dial ✆ **0800-99-00-11.** To reach **MCI,** dial ✆ **0800-99-00-19,** and to reach **Sprint,** dial ✆ **0800-99-00-87.**

Time When standard time is in effect in the United States and Canada, St. Barts is 1 hour ahead of the U.S. East Coast. When daylight saving time is in effect in the U.S., clocks in New York and St. Barts show the same time.

Tipping Hotels usually add a service charge of 10% to 15%; always ask if this is included in the price you're quoted. Restaurants add a 15% service charge. Taxi drivers expect a tip of 10% of the fare.

Water The water on St. Barts is generally safe to drink.

Weather The climate of St. Barts is ideal: dry, with an average temperature of 72°F to 86°F (22°C–30°C).

WHERE TO STAY

St. Barts has some 30 hotels, most of which trend toward boutique—the largest property on island has only 65 rooms. Hotels and resorts throughout the island, with some exceptions, are pricey, and a service charge of between 10% and 15% is usually added to your bill. Tack on a weak dollar, and St. Barts can be an expensive place to vacation for North Americans. If you're looking for ways to cut costs, consider visiting in the shoulder or low seasons. Off-season rates plummet and often include a rental car for stays of a week or more. In March it's difficult to find a spot to stay on St. Barts unless you've made reservations far in advance, but check in during May, and you'll have the run of the place. Many resorts offer terrific money-saving packages (especially during the off season), advertised via e-mail, Facebook, or Twitter. Note that a number of properties close between August and October.

Very Expensive

Carl Gustaf ★★★ The "Goose," as it's affectionately known, has always been *the* spot for sunset cocktails. Gustavia's most glamorous hotel has ratcheted up the glam factor, with its gleaming restaurant and bar, state-of-the-art spa, and a four-bedroom suite, the 2,600-square-foot Royale Suite. The hotel oversees the town's harbor from a steep hillside. Each of the hotel's 14 suites is in one of a dozen pink or green, red-roofed villas. Access to each building is via a central staircase, which can test the stamina of even the most active guests. The wood-frame units are angled for maximum views of boats bobbing far below in the bay and panoramic sunsets, best

Renting a Villa in St. Barts

If you choose to rent a villa in St. Barts instead of going the hotel route, you won't be alone. St. Barts has some 450 **villas, beach houses, and apartments** for rent by the week or month. Villas are dotted in and around the island's hills—very few are on the beach. Instead of an oceanfront bedroom, you get a panoramic view. Rentals, priced in U.S. dollars, can range from a one-room "studio" villa away from the beach for $980 per week in off season, up to $40,000 per week for a minipalace at Christmas. Most rentals average between $2,500 and $4,000 a week in the high season, between mid-December and mid-April, with discounts of 30% to 50% the rest of the year. One of the best agencies to contact for villa, apartment, or condo rentals is **St. Barth Properties,** 12 Washington St., Ste. 201, Franklin, MA 02038 (✆ **800/421-3396** or 508/528-7727 in the U.S. and Canada; www.stbarth.com). Peg Walsh, a longtime aficionado of St. Barts, and her capable son, Tom Smyth, will let you know what's available. She can also make arrangements for car rentals and air travel to St. Barts and can book babysitters and restaurant reservations. Another excellent option with similar rates and services is **Wimco,** P.O. Box 1481, Newport, RI 02840 (✆ **800/449-1553** or 401/849-8012; www.wimco.com), which has some 250 villa properties to rent.

enjoyed from the plunge pool on the private patio bisecting each suite. Bedrooms are luxuriously furnished: You'll feel like a pasha as you swan about on Italian marble floors under a pitched ceiling. Beaches are a 10-minute walk away. In **Victoria's,** Chef Emmanuel Motte has revitalized the classic French kitchen.

Rue des Normands, 97099 Gustavia, St. Barthélemy, F.W.I. www.hotelcarlgustaf.com. ✆ **866/297-2153** in the U.S., or 590/29-79-00. Fax 590/27-82-37. 14 units. Winter 1,150€–3,550€ suite; off season 750€–2,600€ suite. Rates include continental breakfast. AE, MC, V. **Amenities:** Restaurant; bar; outdoor pool; room service; sauna; spa; watersports equipment/rentals (extensive). *In room:* A/C, TV/DVD, CD player, fax, fridge, hair dryer, kitchen (in Royale Suite only), kitchenette (in 1- and 2-bedroom suites only), minibar (in spa suite only), MP3 docking station, private plunge pools, Wi-Fi (free).

Eden Rock ★★★ Greta Garbo checked in as Suzy Schmidt for a 3-day holiday and ended up staying 3 weeks. That was eons ago, but this legendary hotel still exerts a magnetic pull on the rich and fabulous. Eden Rock occupies one of St. Barts's most spectacular sites, a quartzite promontory cleaving St-Jean Bay into two white-sand crescents. When the island's former mayor, Remy de Haenen, paid $200 for the land some 60 years ago from an old woman, she ridiculed him for paying too much. Today Eden Rock is one of the Caribbean's most glamorous addresses. The individually decorated accommodations either climb the rock or are perched steps from the water on either side. The original "Rock" rooms are stuffed with antiques, family heirlooms, silver fixtures, steamer trunks, and four-poster beds. The newer units include eight suites with decks opening onto the beach, as well as five one- to three-bedroom beach houses with outdoor Jacuzzis and plunge pools (two have full swimming pools). The 450-sq.-m (4,844-sq.-ft.) Howard Hughes Suite, atop the Main House on "the rock," has hardwood floors, three verandas offering 360-degree panoramas, and two bathrooms clad in welded copper. Opened in 2010, the Rockstar Suite is a 1,486-sq.-m (16,000-sq.-ft.) stunner with four master suites, a screening room, a fully equipped recording studio, a pool table, a private pool, and a dedicated butler. Cost: $130,000 per week.

For lunch, head to the casual beachfront Sand Bar. Dinner is served up at the swanky On the Rocks Restaurant. The Eden Rock Gallery showcases local and international artists.

Baiede, 97133 St-Jean, St. Barthélemy, F.W.I. www.edenrockhotel.com. ✆ **855/333-6762** in the U.S. and Canada, or 590/29-79-99. Fax 590/27-88-37. 33 units. Winter 685€–1,025€ double, from 1,295€ suite; off season 490€–645€ double, from 785€ suite. Extra person 6 and over 125€. Rates include VIP airport transfers and buffet breakfast. AE, MC, V. Closed Aug 30–Oct 8. **Amenities:** 2 restaurants; bar; babysitting; fitness center; room service; watersports activities. *In room:* A/C, TV/ DVD, hair dryer, kitchen (in some), minibar (in some), MP3 docking station, private plunge pools (in some), Wi-Fi (free).

Hôtel Guanahani & Spa ★★★ ☺ St. Barts's largest hotel would be a jewel of a small boutique hotel anywhere else. Don't let its casual good nature fool you: Guanahani defines excellence. Service is as good here as you'll get anywhere, with a warm, friendly staff that knows what you need before you know it yourself.

This hotel enjoys a spectacular situation on its own peninsula bracketed by two scenic beaches, one facing the Atlantic Ocean, the other, the Grand Cul-de-Sac Bay, overlooking Marigot Bay. The intimately scaled resort spills down a lush hillside to the spacious beach. The rich, saturated colors make the cool monochrome of other luxe resorts look prosaic by comparison. The lobby alone beckons with teal walls, pink/orange furniture, blue-sky trim—all grounded by an earthy wooden floor. It's a warm, boldly conceived tropical palette that manages to avoid tropical-resort clichés.

Of the resort's 69 rooms, 36 are suites—and 14 of these have private pools. Guanahani has several free-standing modern Creole cottages that offer space and privacy. The two restaurants—airy, alfresco Indigo and Le Bartolemo—offer creative Continental cuisine. Kids are welcomed, with children's programs and a big box of beach toys. On-site, the **Clarins Spa ★** is first-rate, with its own good-size swimming pool. Up above the spa is the Caribbean equivalent of a Parisian garret: The Wellness Suite is a private, self-contained haven, with a terrace and views of Grand Cul-de-Sac from every window; it has a fabulous stone sink that's practically primal, and an outdoor shower with a pebbled floor.

In 2010, Guanahani underwent major renovations on 20 rooms near the beach. ***Note:*** The resort is not for those with mobility problems; the sometimes steep and rambling layout is not particularly pedestrian-friendly.

Grand Cul-de-Sac, 97133 St. Barthélemy, F.W.I. www.leguanahani.com. ✆ **800/216-3774** in the U.S., or 590/27-66-60. Fax 590/27-70-70. 69 units. Winter 595€–965€ double, from 1,090€ suite; off season 360€–600€ double, from 700€ suite. Rates include full American breakfast and round-trip airport transfers. AE, MC, V. **Amenities:** 2 restaurants; 3 bars; babysitting; horseback riding; butler services (villas only); children's programs (ages 2–6); concierge; fitness center; Jacuzzi; 2 outdoor pools; room service; spa; 2 tennis courts; watersports equipment/rentals; Wi-Fi (free). *In room:* A/C, ceiling fan, TV/ DVD, hair dryer, minibar, MP3 docking station.

Hôtel St. Barth Isle de France ★★ Effortless elegance distinguishes this family-run hotel, which continues to rack up awards for its luxurious lodging and excellent service. It opens right onto glorious Flamands Beach. The architecture blends the richly saturated colors of Corsica with Caribbean and New England influences. Guest rooms are unusually spacious for St. Barts. Each top-notch unit contains a private patio or terrace overlooking the pool, beach, or lavishly landscaped grounds. Beds are outfitted with fine linens. Commodious marble-clad bathrooms are equipped with dual basins, large tubs (some with whirlpool jets), and showers. For a sense of privacy, you might opt for the Hillside Bungalow, which overlooks the gardens and has a terrace; or the Fisherman's Cottage, with two en-suite bedrooms, a kitchenette, and its own interior courtyard. Four new 139-sq.-m (1,500-sq.-ft.) one-bedroom suites open onto the beach and come with private infinity plunge pools, fully equipped kitchens, and stone bathtubs.

The on-site Spa at Isle de France, created by Molton Brown, and quintessential beachfront *boîte,* La Case de l'Isle (island-tinged French fare), complete the memorable experience.

B.P. 612, 97098 Baie des Flamands, St. Barthélemy, F.W.I. www.isle-de-france.com. ✆ **800/810-4691** in the U.S., or 590/27-61-81. Fax 590/27-86-83. 40 units. Winter 845€–1,280€ double, from 1,545€ suite; off season 525€–795€ double, from 1,055€ suite. Rates include continental breakfast. AE, MC, V. Closed Sept to Oct 15. **Amenities:** Restaurant; bar; babysitting; exercise room; 2 outdoor pools; room service; spa; tennis court. *In room:* A/C, ceiling fan, TV, fridge, hair dryer, minibar, MP3 docking station, Wi-Fi (free).

Le Sereno ★★ Opening onto Grand Cul-de-Sac Beach, this intimate all-suites hotel is a chic and stylish retreat. The suites are both relaxingly understated and exquisitely a la mode, with all the extra touches and modcons that make for luxe living (signature robes and linens from Porthault, plasma TVs, personal iPods)—but some suites are better than others. Definitely ask for the Grand Suite Plage room nos. 20 to 35: They are the same category as the other Grand Suite Plage rooms (and a step up from the simple Garden Rooms), but much, much roomier. The pool and the **Restaurant des Pecheurs ★** are the resort's social hubs. The trio of three-bedroom villas above the hotel are so spectacular, they almost make humpback whales passing by seem ho-hum (almost). Each villa comes with a pool, a personal butler, and unparalleled views of Grand Cul-de-Sac. Inside are sleek designer kitchens stocked with Le Creuset pots and pans; music plays underwater in the pools. A complimentary rental car is included in the rates in low season.

Grand Cul-de-Sac, 97099 St. Barthélemy, F.W.I. www.lesereno.com. ✆ **888/LESERENO** (537-3736) in the U.S., or 590/29-83-00. Fax 590/27-75-47. 37 units. Winter 680€–1,190€ suite, 1,330€–2,330€ villa; off season 480€–780€ suite, 990€–1,930€ villa. Rates include breakfast and airport transfers. AE, MC, V. **Amenities:** Restaurant; 2 bars; gym & spa; outdoor pool; room service; watersports equipment/rentals. *In room:* A/C, TV, bar, fridge, hair dryer, MP3 docking station, Wi-Fi (free).

Le Toiny ★★★ At Le Toiny, you don't have to see or be seen by anyone—even breakfast arrives in a hush, set out on a patio table sheathed in crisp linens and silver cutlery. From every vantage point—even reflected in your bathroom mirror—the sea/sky/mountain vista is soul-stirring. One of the Caribbean's most glamorous resorts, this Relais & Châteaux enclave has but 15 villas, scattered among a half-dozen buildings clinging to a gently sloping hillside overlooking the windswept Toiny coast. Abundant flowering shrubs protect privacy-seekers from prying eyes. Each sumptuous suite features its own private plunge pool, tropical-wood floors, teak and mahogany furnishings, espresso machines, Villeroy & Boch tubs, and beds swaddled in Frette linens. Outside, the patios's plunge pool overlooks hills and sea, with bougainvillea spilling out of big blue pots. Giant bathrooms have impeccable hand-painted moldings and colorful tiles. Le Toiny now has direct beach access—a pleasant 5-minute path through a coconut grove—but the waters at Toiny Beach can be rough. In the new Serenity Spa Cottage, you can get a spa treatment featuring spa products from Le Ligne of St. Barts. The outstanding restaurant, Le Gaïac (see "Dining," below), remains the island's gold standard.

Anse de Toiny, 97133 St. Barthélemy, F.W.I. www.hotelletoiny.com. ✆ **800/278-6469** in the U.S., or 590/27-88-88. Fax 590/27-89-30. 15 units. Winter 1,250€–1,680€ suite, 2,780€ villa; off season 520€–930€ 1-bedroom suite for 2 guests, 1,210€–1,800€ villa. Rates include breakfast and hotel transfers. AE, DC, MC, V. Closed Sept 1 to Oct 25. **Amenities:** Restaurant; bar; babysitting; bikes; concierge; fitness center; outdoor pool; room service; spa; watersports equipment/rentals. *In room:* A/C, TV/DVD, hair dryer, kitchenette, minibar, MP3 docking station, private plunge pool, Wi-Fi (free).

Expensive

Baie des Anges ★ For beach lovers, it's hard to imagine a more appealing spot. Opening right onto the gorgeous white sands of Flamands Beach, this retreat is cooled by trade winds and has a laid-back, carefree atmosphere, as opposed to some of the snootier spots on the island. Surrounded by gardens, the two-story, ocean-fronting property is relatively simple but has its own charms. If your sinks must be clad in cool marble and your beds in Porthault, this is not the place for you. The simple, spacious, and newly refreshed accommodations are attractive and comfortable, decorated in sea colors of blue and green and with handsome king-size beds (some four-poster), kitchenettes, and private terraces. You can opt for a room opening onto the sea or the courtyard with its pool, where guests can be found when the Atlantic waves get too rough for swimming. For such a small place, the inn has a first-rate restaurant, La Langouste, where nonguests can dine for lunch and dinner on Creole or French specialties. The hotel posts its rates in U.S. dollars.

Baie des Anges, Flamands, 97133 St. Barthélemy, F.W.I. www.hotelbaiedesanges.fr. ✆ **590/27-63-61.** Fax 590/27-83-44. 10 units. Winter $415–$565 double, $460–$625 triple; off season $230–$370 double, $265–$420 triple. MC, V. **Amenities:** Restaurant; bar; babysitting; pool; room service. *In room:* A/C, ceiling fan, TV, hair dryer, kitchenette, Wi-Fi (in some).

Hotel Christopher ★★ Set on a dramatic, sun-splashed promontory above the sea, this Pointe Milou hotel has undergone a smart new renovation and kept its prices down in the process. With views over the blue Atlantic and two excellent restaurants, the Christopher represents real value on pricey St. Barts. A lifestyle hotel that's "contemporary but not intimidating," the Christopher serves up a supremely relaxed atmosphere against a background of precise service. The hotel is not adjacent to the beach (guests must drive 10 min. to reach Plage de Lorient) but it has the biggest pool on the island, a sprawling, low-slung pair of interconnected ovals facing the sea. The Christopher is an exciting work in progress, and by the time you read this, most of the 42 rooms will have been stylishly renovated, including 19 chic new suites with rainforest showers built into ceilings, bleached louvered ceilings, and square tubs built for two. Much here is impeccably and sustainably sourced: Floors are a cool concrete composite; tables and benches were made from recycled timber from Indonesia; and beds are swathed in organic Belgian coverlets. Open for breakfast and dinner, Taino sits right on the lip of the sea and serves a French-Caribbean "ingredients cuisine," with homemade croissants and fish smoked in-house. Lunch is served barefoot-style at Mango, a 60-seat spot where tables are literally set down in the sand. The resort is largely a couples' retreat in high season, but families are welcomed the rest of the year.

Pointe Milou (B.P. 571), 97133 St. Barthélemy, F.W.I. www.hotelchristopher.com. ✆ **590/27-63-63.** Fax 590/27-92-92. 42 units. Winter 350€–850€ double, 550€–1,200€ suite; off season 300€–370€ double, 400€–580€ suite. Rates include full American breakfast. Extra person/bed 100€. 1 child 3 and under stays free in parent's room. AE, MC, V. Closed Sept to Nov 14. **Amenities:** 2 restaurants; 2 bars; babysitting; gym; outdoor pool; room service; watersports equipment/rentals. *In room:* A/C, ceiling fan, TV, hair dryer, minibar, Wi-Fi (free)

Hotel Emeraude Plage ★ Location, location, location: It doesn't get more central than this, right on St-Jean's golden sands. The hotel has one villa, two cottages, four suites, and 21 bungalows, all connected by a maze of outdoor walkways. Rooms are drenched in white, with accents in brown (curtains) and beige (the tile floors). All come with fully equipped kitchens for maximum self-catering options. The only real public space is a book-filled reception and a small outdoor bar/restaurant on a deck facing that beach, with Eden Rock perched on a rock to the right and planes zooming in on the left. The Club Eau de Mer is open for breakfast, light lunch, and sunset cocktails.

Baie de St-Jean, 97133 St. Barthélemy, F.W.I. www.emeraudeplage.com. ✆ **590/27-64-78.** Fax 590/27-83-08. 11 units. Winter 370€–910€ bungalow, 580€ cottage, 1,290€ villa; off season 275€–760€ bungalow, 470€ cottage, 1,080€ villa. Extra person 100€. AE, MC, V. **Amenities:** Babysitting; concierge; watersports equipment/rentals; Wi-Fi (in lobby; free). *In room:* A/C, ceiling fan, TV, CD player, hair dryer.

La Banane ★ This former disco is still a social nexus. La Banane is not on the beach; in fact, it's located just off a shopping-center parking lot on the outskirts of Lorient. But this intimate little gem manages to feel like a secluded hideaway. That's in large part because of the layout and dense jungle landscaping; road traffic feels far, far away. It's all pillowed in a garden of banana trees, palms, frangipani, jasmine, and bougainvillea. Nine bungalows are scattered around the pool and lobby, the resort nerve center, where guests gravitate and become fast friends as they lounge amid smartly curated modernist furniture (including Le Corbusier–inspired pieces that look both snappy and irresistibly comfy). Rooms have pop-art floors, four-poster beds, and colorful mosaic tiles in the bathrooms. Bathrooms open onto patios or private gardens so that taking a shower becomes a perfumed ritual in tropical flora.

Baie de L'Orient, 97133 St. Barthélemy, F.W.I. www.labanane.com. ✆ **590/52-03-00.** Fax 590/59-02-76. 7 units. Winter 485€–585€ double; off season 385€–485€ double. Extra person/bed 70€. Rates include breakfast and airport shuttle. AE, MC, V. Closed Sept–Oct. Children 12 and under not allowed. **Amenities:** Bar; 2 outdoor pools; room service; watersports equipment/rentals. *In room:* A/C, ceiling fan, TV/DVD, CD player, hair dryer, minibar, Wi-Fi (free).

Les Ilets de la Plage ★ ☺ Homey and warm, set on a serene stretch of St-Jean Beach (even with the planes arriving and departing next door), Les Ilets is a charming departure from resort sleek and chic. In the lexicon of typical beach resort landscaping, Les Ilets is a sweet anomaly. The property faces out toward curving beach and deep blue sea, but the surrounding terrain is more like the sun-dappled and slightly overgrown summer backyards of bygone days. Les Ilets has 11 cottage-style villas, with one-, two-, and three-bedroom units (only four one-bedroom villas are directly on the beach), all with fully equipped kitchens. Interiors have a spartan grace, with tile floors, whitewashed wooden walls, and crisp linens. The villas are very private—and in that location, you're just a short stroll away from great St-Jean restaurants and shopping. Off-season rates offer great value for the two- and three-bedroom villas.

Baie de St-Jean, 97133 St. Barthélemy, F.W.I. www.lesilets.com. ✆ **590/27-88-57.** Fax 590/27-88-58. 11 units. Winter 450€–610€ 1-bedroom villa, 690€–800€ 2-bedroom villa, 710€–900€ 3-bedroom villa; off season 200€–350€ 1-bedroom villa, 300€–335€ 2-bedroom villa, 325€–370€ 3-bedroom villa. AE, MC, V. **Amenities:** Babysitting; concierge; outdoor pool; watersports equipment/rentals. *In room:* A/C, ceiling fan, TV/DVD/VCR (available on request), CD player, hair dryer, kitchen, Wi-Fi (free)..

Tom Beach Hotel This small, bustling hotel opens onto a popular section of St-Jean Beach; next door are windsurfing and watersports rentals. A festive atmosphere prevails, so if you're an early-to-bed type, this may not be for you. The flamboyantly painted villas are enveloped by a Caribbean garden and painted in bright pastels. Bedrooms are spacious and stylish, each adorned with draped four-poster beds and opening onto terraces complete with wet bars. Hit the **Pink Parrot** beach bar or the hotel's popular **La Plage** restaurant.

Baie de St-Jean, 97133 St-Barthélemy, F.W.I. www.tombeach.com. ✆ **590/27-53-13.** 12 units. Winter 450€–690€ double; off season 290€–480€ double. AE, MC, V. **Amenities:** Restaurant; bar; Internet (free); outdoor pool. *In room:* A/C, TV/DVD, hair dryer, minibar.

Moderate

Hostellerie des Trois Forces ★ Breton astrologer Hubert Delamotte (a Gemini) and his wife, Ginette, created this hilltop sanctuary dedicated to enriching the flow between life's primary three forces: mind, body, and spirit. The inn occupies panoramic grounds in Vitet, about a 10-minute drive from Cul-de-Sac and Lorient beaches. The gingerbread bungalows are staggered to maximize privacy and sweeping ocean vistas. Each is named for a sign of the zodiac and decorated with the appropriate color scheme. Holistic services include massage therapy, yoga, past-life regression therapy, and psychic readings. Hubert believes "the stomach is a spiritual gate," and his on-site restaurant's French fare earned him membership in France's prestigious gastronomic order Confrérie de la Marmite d'Or.

Morne Viet, 97133 St. Barthélemy, F.W.I. www.3forces.net. ✆ **590/27-61-25.** Fax 590/27-81-38. 7 cottages. Winter 270€ double; off season 170€ double. AE, MC, V. **Amenities:** Restaurant; bar; outdoor pool. *In room:* A/C, kitchenette (in 2 units), minibar.

Le P'tit Morne ★ This is hardly the most luxurious or stylish lodging on an island that's legendary for its glamorous five-star hotels. But the hotel's government-rated three-star format, its moderate rates, and the warm welcome extended by its island-born owners, Mr. and Mrs. Felix and daughter Marie-Joëlle, make it a worthy vacation site. It's a 10-minute drive from the beach. The colonial-style guest rooms are filled with completely unpretentious furniture and comfortable king-size beds. It offers plenty of elbow room, and units were built to catch the trade winds.

Colombier (P.O. Box 14), 97095 St. Barthélemy, F.W.I. www.timorne.com. ✆ **590/52-95-50.** Fax 590/27-84-63. 14 units. Winter 185€–230€ double; off season 95€–150€ double. AE, MC, V. Closed Sept. **Amenities:** Babysitting; room service. *In room:* A/C, TV, fridge, kitchen.

Le Village St-Jean ★ This family-owned cottage colony hideaway, 2km (1¼ miles) from the airport toward St-Jean, offers charm, warmth, and comfort. Just a 5-minute drive uphill from St-Jean Beach, this is one of the best values on this high-priced island. A collection of stone-and-redwood buildings scattered about a flower-filled garden and hillside holds five handsomely furnished hotel rooms (fridge only) and 20 cottages and three villas with well-equipped kitchens, tiled bathrooms, sun decks or gardens, tiered living rooms, and balconies with retractable awnings and hammocks strategically placed to enjoy the breezes. An infinity pool comes with killer views of the sea. The Well-Being Cottage holds a gym and a relaxation room for massages and other body treatments.

Colline de Saint-Jean (B.P. 623), 97133 St. Barthélemy, F.W.I. www.villagestjeanhotel.com. ✆ **590/27-61-39.** Fax 590/27-77-96. 30 units. Winter 220€ double, 260€–650€ 1-bedroom cottage, from 620€ 2-bedroom cottage; off season 135€ double, 170€–350€ 1-bedroom cottage, 400€ 2-bedroom cottage. Extra person 50€–70€. Rates include continental breakfast. AE, MC, V. **Amenities:** Restaurant; bar; babysitting; gym; Jacuzzi; outdoor pool; room service; Wi-Fi (free). *In room:* A/C, ceiling fan, fridge, hair dryer, kitchen (except hotel rooms).

Les Ondines sur la Plage ★ ☺ This postmodern all-suites hotel, sequestered by a private garden lagoon opening onto Grand Cul-de-Sac Beach, has a kid-pleasing fish-shaped freshwater pool. The five one-bedroom and two two-bedroom suites are enormous by St. Barts standards. Most suites have terrific ocean views, and all feature such necessities as fully equipped kitchens (two-bedroom units even have washer/dryer and dishwasher). Creative touches extend to modish kitchens and track-lit bathrooms (stunning bas-relief moldings and mosaics).

Grand Cul-de-Sac, 97133 St. Barthélemy, F.W.I. www.stbarth-lesondineshotel.com. ✆ **590/27-69-64.** Fax 590/52-24-41. 7 units. Winter 350€–690€ double; off season 215€–450€ double. Rates include continental breakfast and airport transfers. AE, MC, V. Closed Sept–Oct. **Amenities:** Outdoor pool; room service; watersports equipment/rentals. *In room:* A/C, ceiling fan, TV/DVD, hair dryer, kitchen, Wi-Fi (free).

Salines Garden Cottages ★ 🎁 This is excellent value on pricey St. Barts. Guests stay in stylish gingerbread *cazes* (traditional Creole houses), three with kitchenettes, nestled amid flowering trees and bushes just steps from one of the island's finest beaches. Each has a private tiled terrace shaded by bougainvillea. Interiors have brilliant batik fabrics, island crafts in various media, and four-poster or cast-iron beds. Asian and African antiques, collected by the peripatetic owners, enliven public spaces and grounds. Romantics and independent types can cherish utter seclusion while finding sustenance at two good restaurants within walking distance—and Salines beach is just minutes away.

Salines, 97133 St. Barthélemy, F.W.I. www.salinesgarden.com. ✆ **590/51-04-44.** Fax 590/27-64-65. 5 units. Winter 140€–190€ double; offseason 90€–120€ double. Extra person 30€–50€. Rates include continental breakfast, airport transfers, taxes, and service charges. AE, MC, V. **Amenities:** Babysitting; outdoor pool. *In room:* A/C, ceiling fan, kitchen (in some), hair dryer.

Inexpensive

La Normandie 🏷 This modest, unassuming, family-owned Antillean inn has undergone a transformation: No longer a plain Jane, the Normandie has become a stylish boutique inn with modern rooms. The owners, however, are committed to keeping the rates down, and lucky for you—this is very good value. A Brazilian-wood deck connects the two buildings that hold the guest rooms. The Normandie is located near the intersection of two major roads, about 200m (656 ft.) from Lorient Beach.

Rte. de Saline, L'Orient, 97133 St. Barthélemy, F.W.I. www.normandiehotelstbarts.com. ✆ **590/27-61-66.** Fax 590/27-98-83. 8 units. Winter 175€ double; off season 125€ double. Rates include continental breakfast and afternoon wine. AE, DC, MC, V. **Amenities:** Outdoor pool. *In room:* A/C, TV (in some), fridge, Wi-Fi (free).

WHERE TO DINE

Fueled by young French chefs and hotel dining rooms that keep ratcheting up the excellence quotient, the St. Barts dining scene is superb. It's also really, really expensive, and prized tables are often booked along with hotel reservations in high season. But the island is not just about five-star hotel dining. You can eat very well at the many casual beachfront, hilltop, and harborside restaurants. Many of the island's most popular spots offer an affordable and filling lunchtime *plat du jour* (daily special) for 10€ to 12€. Restaurants offering *plats du jours* include **La Marine** and the **Wall House** in Gustavia, and **The Hideaway** in St-Jean.

Virtually all the restaurants on St. Barts include a 15% service charge (*service compris*). **Note:** *Entrée* is the French term for appetizer; *plat* means main course.

In Gustavia

Bonito Saint Barth ★ FRENCH/ASIAN FUSION Formerly La Mandala, Bonito Saint Barth has been transformed into a striking ceviche bar/fusion restaurant. White is the new black here, with crisp white tablecloths and painted white wicker offset by blue-and-white pillows. A candlelit, white-on-white lounge with nightly DJs has ramped up the hipness quotient. The location alone—a house on Gustavia's steepest street with a dining deck overlooking a swimming pool—guarantees memorable sunset cocktails.

Rue Lubin Brin. ✆ **590/27-96-96.** www.ilovebonito.com. Reservations recommended. Main courses 22€–34€. MC, V. Thurs–Tues 7–11pm; sushi and cocktails 5–7pm.

Eddy's ★  CREOLE For some 15 years, charismatic Eddy Stackelborough has satisfied in-the-know locals and regulars with simple, honest island fare (green papaya salad, shrimp curry barbecued ribs, chicken in coconut sauce, passion fruit mousse). The setting resembles a Caribbean translation of *The Secret Garden:* It's a virtual jungle punctuated by ethno-tropic trappings. It's a miracle how Eddy keeps prices affordable by most standards (perhaps the roving location keeps rents down).

Rue du Centenaire (near rue Général-de-Gaulle). ✆ **590/27-54-17.** No reservations accepted. Main courses 15€–22€. No credit cards. Mon–Sat noon–10:30pm.

La Route des Boucaniers ★ FRENCH/CREOLE Having written a five-volume primer, owner/chef Francis Delage is considered an authority on Creole cuisine. The decor evokes a rum shack—there's even a boat wreck—and the fare is simple but hearty. The restaurant has a prime perch overlooking Gustavia harbor. The menu

TRAITEURS: GOURMET FOOD to go

Dining on St. Barts is expensive, so one way to stretch your food budget (other than cooking) is getting takeout from the island's gourmet *traiteurs*. This being St. Barts, however, these takeout spots go way beyond the classic Continental picnic of bread, cheese, and a bottle of wine: This is highfalutin' grub, equally at home on a beach picnic or a candlelit dinner as on your villa terrace. **La Rôtisserie**—which has two stores: **Gustavia** (rue du Roi Oscar II; ✆ **590/27-63-13**) and **St-Jean** (✆ **590/29-75-69**)—is a boulangerie, patisserie, bakery, and more, selling wine, mustard, pâté, herbs, caviar, chocolate, and exotic oils and vinegars, as well as takeout *plats du jours* from pâtés to *pissaladière* (onion tart); the Gustavia store is open daily 7am to 7pm; the St-Jean location is open 6am to 8pm. **Maya's To Go** (✆ **590/29-83-70**), across from the airport, offers creative and homey takeout specialties like meatloaf sandwiches, sesame chicken noodles, wahoo ceviche, and tuna tataki. It's open Tuesday to Sunday 7am to 7pm. Also in St-Jean, **Kiki-é Mo** (✆ **590/27-90-65**; www.kikiemo.com) sells pizzas, pastas, and panini—and great espresso; it's open 9am to 10pm. **La Route des Boucaniers,** the harborside restaurant in Gustavia, does delicious French/Creole takeout meals (✆ **590/27-73-00**). If you want to stock up on basic supplies and groceries, St. Barts has a number of grocery stores with excellent selections of imported French delicacies, good wines, and snacks. The **Marche-U supermarket** (which recently replaced the old **Match**) is located directly across from the airport; it's open on Sundays.

offers spiny lobster; coq au vin de Bourgogne; sea scallops and shrimp with crispy risotto and passion fruit sauce; and a traditional West Indian chicken Colombo curry with Creole sauce. The *assiete Creole* (spicy Caribbean platter) is a tasty seafood platter of codfish fritters, conch gratin, marinated Bonito puff pastry of crab, and a *feroce d'avocat* (local avocado recipe and green salad).

Rue de Bord de Mer, Gustavia. ✆ **590/27-73-00.** Reservations required in winter. Main courses 20€–28€. AE, MC, V. Daily 10am–10pm.

Pipiri Palace ★ FRENCH/CREOLE The twinkling lights and dense gardens fronting a classic Creole cottage make this a romantic spot in the heart of Gustavia. It's a lush, lively spot, with the gregarious owner, Pierrot, presiding over the nightly action. The barbecued ribs and grilled rock lobster are specialties, but the local fish, served in a lemony butter sauce or Colombo style, is equally good. Start with the lobster bisque or homemade foie gras.

Rue Général-de-Gaulle. ✆ **590/27-53-20.** Reservations recommended. Main courses 19€–33€. MC, V. Mon–Sat 6:30–10pm. Closed June–Oct.

Wall House ★★ FRENCH/CREOLE New ownership has not diminished the Wall House traditions of warm service, lively ambience, and bistro fare with flair at reasonable prices. The harbor setting certainly doesn't hurt. In taking over the reins of this local favorite, owners Bernard and Julien Tatin have proven to be warm, gracious hosts. The menu retains a lively mix of ingredients and influences: Look for bacon-wrapped roasted monkfish filet in a black pepper sauce; sautéed foie gras with rhubarb compote in a gingerbread sauce; and the divinely creative lobster and mozzarella on crispy polenta bruschetta with pesto. The three-course prix-fixe menus (29€) and daily *plats du jours* (10€–12€) are remarkable values.

La Pointe. ✆ **590/27-71-83.** www.wallhouserestaurant.com. Reservations recommended. Main courses 18€–28€. AE, MC, V. Mon–Sat noon–2pm and 7–9:30pm; Sun 7–9:30pm. Closed June–Oct.

In the St-Jean Beach Area

The Eden Rock hotel (p. 492) has two excellent dining choices: The chillingly expensive **On the Rocks** ★ serves dinner high above Baie St-Jean, and **The Sandbar** ★ offers lunch down on the beach. Call ✆ **590/29-79-99** for reservations.

The Hideaway ★ INTERNATIONAL How can you not love a place that advertises "corked wine, warm beer, lousy food, view of the car park," with a staff "hand-picked from the sleaziest dives, mental institutions, and top-security prisons?" Savvy locals and celebrity regulars know that the sound system, food, and prices rock at this beloved haunt, nicknamed Chez Andy after Brit owner Andrew Hall. Worthy specialties include a duck gizzard salad dressed in a house dressing; shrimp Creole; pastas; and thin-crust pizzas from the wood-burning oven. Andy will finish off your evening (and you) with a bottomless carafe of free vanilla or orange rum.

Vaval Center, St-Jean. ✆ **590/27-63-62.** Reservations recommended. Main courses 16€–24€. AE, MC, V. Tues–Sat noon–2:30pm and 7–10:30pm; Sun 7–10:30pm.

In the Toiny Coast Area

Le Gaïac ★★★ FRENCH This swooningly romantic restaurant is for folks who want to dine among the rich and famous at Le Toiny (p. 494), one of St. Barts's most expensive hotels. Here's the shocker: You don't have to be rich *or* famous to enjoy the restaurant's seamless, pampered service. The elegant open-air pavilion has sweeping views of the blue-black sea. Lunchtime menu items—black truffle and Parmesan spaghetti, perhaps, or a yellowtail snapper in a lemongrass emulsion—are simple yet exquisitely prepared, and the sumptuous all-you-can-eat "Brunch du Toiny" (43€) is a must. Dinner courses might include a lighter-than-air tuna and salmon tartar with wheatberries. For the main course, try the fricassee of Maine lobster and cepe mushroom, or lamb served in three different Creole styles. A Tuesday-night Fishmarket Menu lets you pick your fresh filet—which is then lightly grilled—and your choice of sauce, whether a creamy tomato or an old-fashioned *moutarde*. It's all first-rate, from the food to the setting to the impeccable service.

In Hôtel Le Toiny, Anse de Toiny. ✆ **590/27-88-88.** Reservations recommended in winter. Main courses 20€–29€ lunch, 30€–40€ dinner. AE, DC, MC, V. Mon–Sat 7:30–10:30am, noon–2:30pm, and 7–10pm; Sun 11am–2:30pm. Closed Sept 1 to Oct 23.

At Morne Lurin

Santa Fe ★ FRENCH This informal restaurant is set atop one of the highest points on the island, overlooking Gouverneur Beach, making it a prime spot for sunset cocktails on the wraparound decks. For decades this place was known as a good burger joint. It still serves a great burger, but the rest of the menu has headed upmarket, specializing in French dishes along with barbecued meats and fresh fish. In addition to the catch of the day, opt for the côte de veau or the flavorful tomato tart.

Morne Lurin. ✆ **590/27-61-04.** Reservations not accepted. Main courses 19€–60€. MC, V. Thurs–Tues noon–2:30pm and 6–11pm.

In the Grande Saline Beach Area

Le Grain de Sel ★ CREOLE Set on a wooden deck overlooking the old salt ponds of Salines, Grain de Sel has a sun-dappled, treehouse appeal. It's a casual place that's popular with the locals, but the crowd ranges from families to hipsters, all tucking into delicious, well-priced Creole classics. The seafood is well-prepared, and you can't go wrong with the shrimp, here grilled on kebabs with a buttery herb sauce or swimming in a heady beer sauce. Local fish is grilled or cooked in a tomatoey Creole sauce. Entrees come with traditional rice and peas.

Plage de Saline. ✆ **590/52-46-05.** Reservations recommended. Main courses 16€–27€. MC, V. Daily 11:30am–4pm and 7–10:30pm.

Le Tamarin ★ FRENCH/CREOLE The perfect place for a lazy afternoon on the beach, this open-air bistro sits amid rocky hills and forests on the road to Plage de Saline, in a thatched gingerbread cottage with a teak-and-bamboo interior. Lunch is the more animated meal, with customers dining in T-shirts and bathing suits. If you have to wait, savor an aperitif in one of the hammocks stretched under a tamarind tree—or even take a dip in the swimming pool. A new menu focuses on light, summery fare.

Plage de Saline. ✆ **590/27-72-12.** Reservations required for dinner. Main courses 25€–34€. AE, MC, V. Wed–Mon noon–4pm and 7–10:30pm.

In the Grand Cul-de-Sac Beach Area

A casual beachside favorite, **O'Corail Restaurant ★** (✆ **590/29-33-27**) opened in April 2008 on the sands between Le Sereno and the former La Gloriette in front of the Ouanalao Dive shop. It has views out over Grand Cul-de-Sac and good, fresh-tasting food, from burgers to lobster salad to paninis. It's open for breakfast and lunch Tuesday to Sunday, and dinner Friday and Saturday nights.

Bartoloméo ★★ FRENCH/MEDITERRANEAN It's located inside one of the island's most exclusive hotels, Guanahani (p. 493). But Bartoloméo manages to be unthreatening, informally sophisticated, and gracefully upscale. It's a lovely setting, half inside a Creole cottage under a lime wainscoted ceiling and half outside on a wooden deck beneath the blue-black sky. Cream-colored walls are romantically lit. The food is impeccable. If you want *poisson,* try the basted swordfish tataki in lemon and salt, with baby bok choy. For meat-lovers, there's the 10-hour confit of suckling lamb knuckle-joint. Starters include St. Barts lobster ravioli in a foamy caper juice; the curry shrimp cannellone wrapped in braised cabbage and pasta is simply fantastic. Spaghetti with clams comes to the table tangled in sprigs of dill and sprays of foam, as if it had just washed up out of the sea.

In the Hôtel Guanahani, Grand Cul-de-Sac. ✆ **590/27-66-60.** Reservations recommended, especially for nonguests. Main courses 32€–44€. AE, DC, MC, V. Daily 7:30–10pm.

Le Restaurant des Pêcheurs ★ FRENCH/SEAFOOD The house restaurant at Le Sereno (p. 494) resort is a lively spot during the day, but at night it takes on a more somber tenor. The joint is not jumping—at least not when I was there. Maybe it's the liberally spaced seating, good for privacy-loving diners but not so good for communal feng shui. The food doesn't disappoint, however; there's a deft hand in the kitchen, for sure. But it's pricey for what is essentially a fish house. The menu features a catch of the day, both local (29€) and imported Atlantic/Mediterranean (45€). Starters include a deeply flavored gazpacho and a lobster trio of carpaccio, mini spring roll, and charlotte with mango dressing. For mains, try the giant prawns in garlic and herb sauce; risotto with grilled scallops, leeks, and green asparagus; or lamb shank with Caribbean vegetables.

In Le Sereno hotel, Grand Cul-de-Sac. ✆ **590/29-83-00.** Reservations recommended, especially for nonguests. Main courses 22€–48€. AE, MC, V. Daily 7am–10:30pm.

ST. BARTS'S BEACHES

St. Barts has some 21 white-sand beaches. Few are crowded, even in winter; all are public and free. Topless sunbathing is common (nudity is officially permitted on two). The liveliest and best known is **St-Jean Beach ★★**, which is actually two beaches divided by the Eden Rock promontory. It offers watersports, restaurants, a few hotels, and snorkeling west of the rock. Just to the east is **Lorient Beach ★**, on the north shore, quiet and calm, with shaded areas. An offshore reef tames breakers, save on the wilder western end, where locals and surfer dudes hang out.

The largest beach on the island is lovely **Flamands Beach ★**, to the west, dotted with a few small hotels and in some areas shaded by lantana palms.

For a beach with hotels, restaurants, and watersports, **Grand Cul-de-Sac Beach ★**, on the northeast shore, fits the bill. It's narrow and protected by a reef. The shallow lagoon waters aren't great for swimming, but the breezy conditions make it ideal for wind- and kitesurfing.

North of Gustavia, the rather unromantic-sounding **Public Beach** is a combination of sand and pebbles more popular with boaters than swimmers. There is no more beautiful place on the island, however, to watch the boats at sunset. Also in Gustavia, **Shell Beach** is awash with lovely little seashells—or it is when the conditions are right. Rocky outcroppings protect the beach from strong waves. It's also the site of popular **Do Brazil,** a favored lunch spot.

In the picturesque fishing village of Corossol, **Corossol Beach** offers a typical glimpse of French life, St. Barts style, facing a bay dotted with bobbing boats. This is a calm, protected beach, with brown sand and a charming little **seashell museum.**

Southeast of Gustavia, **Gouverneur Beach ★★**, on the southern coast, can be reached by driving south from Gustavia to Lurin. Turn at the popular **Santa Fe** restaurant (p. 501; stop for drinks on the way back to savor sensational sunset views) and head down a narrow road. The uncrowded strand is gorgeous, ringed by steep cliffs overlooking St. Kitts, Saba, and Statia (St. Eustacius), but there's no shade. You'll find excellent snorkeling off the point.

Grande Saline Beach ★★, to the east of Gouverneur Beach, is reached by driving up the road from the commercial center in St-Jean; a 10-minute walk from the parking lot over a rocky pathway, and you're here. Lack of shade doesn't deter the nude sunbathers.

Colombier Beach ★★ is difficult to get to but well worth the effort. It can be reached only by boat or by taking a rugged goat path from Petite Anse past Flamands Beach, a 30-minute walk. The lookouts here are breathtaking; several adjacent coves are patrolled only by peacocks and mules. Shade, seclusion, and snorkeling are found here, and you can pack a lunch and spend the day. Locals call it Rockefeller's Beach because for many years, David Rockefeller owned the surrounding property.

More than one local has driven us past the fiercely beautiful **Grand Fond,** on the Toiny Coast, overlooking a rock-strewn beach and crashing surf. On the other side of the two-lane road is a mossy green hill that rises sharply; here, goats serenely graze pastoral cliffsides.

SPORTS & OUTDOOR PURSUITS

FISHING Anglers are fond of the waters around St. Barts. From March to July, they catch mahimahi; in September, wahoo. Atlantic bonito, barracuda, and marlin also turn up. **Yannis Marine,** Gustavia (✆ **590/29-89-12;** www.yannismarine.com), charters a 50-foot Sunseeker Carmarque outfitted for deep-sea sport fishing. A half-day trip for nine guests costs 1,300€, which includes a captain, fuel, snacks, open bar, and fishing equipment. Yannis also offers boat rentals, snorkeling trips, and island excursions; sunset cruises (7–11 guests) cost 850€ to 900€.

KITESURFING Kitesurfing is fast becoming one of the most popular sports here. Former champion Enguerrand Espinassou gives expert lessons at **7e Ciel of St. Barth Kitesurf School,** at the Ouanalao Dive center (see below) on Grand Cul-de-Sac (✆ **690/69-26-90**), open daily from 8am to 5pm. Kitesurfing costs 300€ for a 3-hour lesson, 450€ for a 5-hour lesson, and 800€ for 10 hours. Reservations are recommended, especially in high season.

SAILING Charter the beautiful ***Lone Fox,*** a wooden sailing yacht built in 1957, for a day of sailing, swimming, snorkeling, and exploring the St. Barts coastline. You'll have a captain and crew on board to do all the heavy lifting. The maximum number of guests is eight; a full-day charter is 1,400€ (✆ **690/33-27-91;** www.lonefoxcharters.com).

SCUBA DIVING **Marine Service,** quai du Yacht-Club, in Gustavia (✆ **590/27-70-34**), is the island's most complete watersports facility. It operates from a one-story building at the edge of a marina on the opposite, quieter side of Gustavia's harbor. Catering to both beginners and advanced divers, the outfit is familiar with at least 20 unusual sites scattered throughout the protected offshore Réserve Marine de St-Barth. The most interesting include Pain de Sucre off Gustavia harbor and the remote **Grouper,** west of St. Barts, close to the uninhabited cay known as Île Forchue. The only relatively safe wreck dive, the rusting hulk of ***Kayali,*** a trawler that sank in deep waters in 1994, is recommended for experienced divers. A resort course, including five open-water dives, costs 280€. A "scuba review," for certified divers who are out of practice, also goes for 75€, while a one-tank dive for certified divers begins at 60€. Multidive packages are available.

SNORKELING Hundreds of shallow areas right off beaches such as Anse des Cayes teem with colorful aquatic life. You can also test your luck at hundreds of points offshore. **Marine Service,** quai du Yacht-Club, Gustavia (see above), runs daily snorkeling expeditions. Half- and full-day group excursions aboard a 13 or 14m (42- or 46-ft.) catamaran, including snacks, open bar, all equipment, and exploration of two separate snorkeling sites, costs from 72€ per person. They also rent snorkeling gear and can direct you to good snorkeling sites.

SHOPPING

Duty-free St. Barts offers liquor and French perfumes at some of the lowest prices in the Caribbean—often cheaper than in France itself. You'll find good buys, albeit a limited selection, in haute couture, crystal, porcelain, watches, and other luxuries. Gustavia's **rue de la République** is lined with designer boutiques, including Bulgari, Cartier, Giorgio Armani, Louis Vuitton, and Hermès.

Aside from Gustavia, St-Jean is the island's center of shopping action, with several small shopping plazas along the main road leading toward L'Orient: **Les Galeries du Commerce, La Villa Creole, La Sodexa,** and **L'Espace Neptune,** each filled with small boutiques. We actually find St-Jean a more satisfying shopping experience than Gustavia—less of the chillingly pricey international brands, and more of the real-life St. Barts clothing we covet: flirty kurtas and gypsy dresses; sexy, slouchy jersey separates in dusky tones; gold and silver sandals or bejeweled flip-flops. **La Savane Commercial Center,** across from the airport, has grocery stores, an electronics store, and a handful of boutiques.

As for island crafts, the little old ladies from the fishing village of Corossol have long made intricately braided straw goods (baskets, bags, bonnets) from the dried fronds of the latanier palm. You can find these delicately woven crafts for sale along the harborside quai in Gustavia.

Keep in mind that most shopkeepers open around 9 or 10am but close midday for an extended *dejeuner* (lunch) that may last until 2 or 3pm. Closing time is around 7pm.

There are **officially designated sales seasons,** generally the month of May and from mid-October to mid-November. Much of everything is deeply discounted, including couture—so expect to find great deals during these times.

ST. BARTS AFTER DARK

Most visitors consider a sunset aperitif followed by dinner under the stars enough of a nocturnal adventure. But the island has a lively lounge and live-music scene that can go into the wee hours. Here are a few of the best-known hot spots.

In Gustavia, one of the most popular gathering places is **Le Select,** rue de la France (✆ **590/27-86-87**), a 50-year-old institution named after its more famous granddaddy in the Montparnasse section of Paris. Locals love this classic dive with the friendly vibe. It's a glorified shanty, though most patrons congregate at tables in the open-air garden (called "Cheeseburgers in Paradise" in homage to honorary St. Barthian Jimmy Buffett), where a game of dominoes might be under way as you walk in. You never know who might show up here—Mick Jagger, perhaps? It's closed Sundays.

Former French tennis star and singer/performer Yannick Noah is one of the owners of **Do Brazil** ★ (✆ **590/29-06-66;** www.dobrazil.com), right on the Plage de Shell Beach. This bar and cafe is a great place to hang out after a swim on Shell Beach. It serves a French-Thai cuisine and a sampling of French-Brazilian dishes.

Le Bête à Z'Ailes ★ (also known as the Baz Bar), on the harbor in Gustavia (✆ **590/92-74-09**), is a sushi bar and live-music club, where an eclectic assortment of bands play soul, jazz, blues, urban folk, and indie tunes, accompanied by excellent fusion food.

Draped in red, **Le Ti St. Barth,** Pointe Milou (✆ **590/27-97-71;** www.ksplaces.com) calls itself a Caribbean tavern, and the setting, in a pitched-roof Creole-style cottage, manages to be both charming and sexy at once. The club has a fashion show nightly at 11pm in high season.

Le Ti St. Barth's Carole Gruson transformed the **Le Yacht Club,** rue Jeanne d'Arc (✆ **590/27-68-91;** www.ksplaces.com), into a favored haunt of the dawn patrol, with breathtaking harbor views through billowing white drapes.

ST. EUSTATIUS

In days gone by, the little Dutch island of St. Eustatius was the busiest port in the Caribbean, a kind of Pirates of the Caribbean scene with some 200 to 300 sailing vessels anchored in the harbor on any given day. Called "Statia," this Dutch-held island, a mere 21-sq.-km (8¼-sq.-mile) pinpoint in the Netherlands Antilles, still basks in its 18th-century heritage as the "Golden Rock." One of the true backwaters of the West Indies, it's slowly awakening to tourism.

Beaches Statia's beaches are small, narrow strips of volcanic sand. The best beaches are on the tranquil Caribbean side. Swimmers will find the beige and black sands of **Orange Beach** suitable for a leisurely swim, while **Crook Castle Beach** draws beachcombers for the blue beads underneath the sands.

Things to Do Encounter a tropical forest filled with wild orchids and fruit trees on a hike around the Quill, an extinct volcano. Visit the lush showcase of Statia's fauna and flora at **Miriam C. Schmidt Botanical Garden,** or wander around the cliffs of **Fort Oranje,** built in 1636.

Eating & Drinking Though a small island, Statia serves up an eclectic array of flavors, from Caribbean and French to Italian and Chinese. Casual restaurants abound, as is the laidback nature of the island.

Diving & Snorkeling Statia's reefs teem with corals and all sorts of marine life. Head to **Crack in the Wall** to see pinnacle coral shoot up from the ocean floor of the ocean. Darting among the reefs are barracudas, eagle rays, black-tip sharks, and other large fish.

ESSENTIALS

Visitor Information

On the island, the **tourist bureau** is located at Fort Oranje (✆/fax **599/318-2433**), open Monday to Friday 8am to noon and 1 to 5pm (Fri until 4:30pm). Statia's official website is **www.statiatourism.com**.

Getting There

St. Eustatius can be reached from Dutch St. Maarten's Queen Juliana Airport via the 20-seat planes of **Winair** (✆ **866/466-0410** in the U.S. and Canada, or 599/545-4237; www.fly-winair.com). The little airline has an excellent safety record. Always reconfirm your return passage once

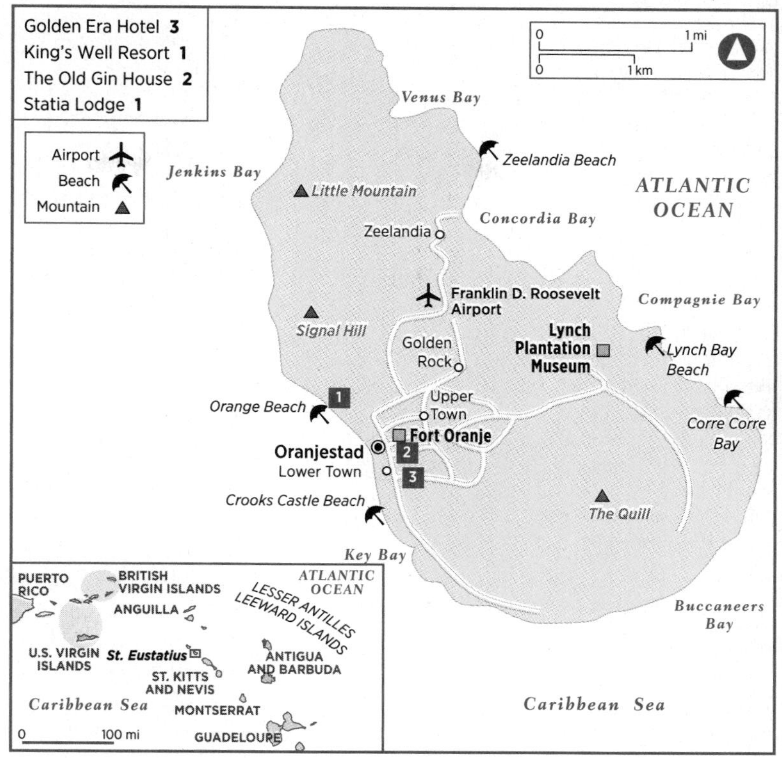

you're on Statia. Several flights a day take only 16 minutes to hop the waters to Statia's **Franklin Delano Roosevelt Airport** (✆ **599/318-2887**). There are usually three flights a day between Statia and Saba, and two per week between Statia and St. Kitts, but schedules are irregular. To be sure of getting to another island from Statia, you'll want to go to St. Maarten first.

Getting Around

BY TAXI Taxis meet all incoming flights. Taxi rates are low, no more than $10 from the airport to your hotel. On the way to the hotel, your driver may offer himself as a guide. If you book a 2- to 3-hour tour (long enough to cover all the sights on Statia), the cost is about $80 per vehicle. To summon a taxi, call **Taxi Servia** (✆ **599/318-2620**) or **Ausvan Taxi** (✆ **599/318-1300**).

BY RENTAL CAR **Rainbow Car Rental** (✆ **599/318-2811**) or **Walter's** (✆ **599/318-2719**) are your best bets if you want to reserve a car in advance. Drivers must be 21 years old and present a valid license and credit card. Walter's rents only cars.

[Fast FACTS] ST. EUSTATIUS

Banks **First Caribbean International Bank,** Upper Town (✆ **599/318-2392**), is open Monday to Friday 8:30am to 3:30pm. The **Windward Islands Bank,** Upper Town (✆ **599/318-2846**), is open Monday to Friday 8:30am to noon and 1:30 to 3:30pm. The banks have **ATMs.**

Currency The official unit of currency is the **Netherlands Antilles guilder (NAf),** at NAf 1.78 to each US$1 (1 NAf = 55¢), but nearly all places will quote you prices in U.S. dollars. *As such, prices in this chapter are quoted in U.S. dollars.*

Customs There are no Customs duties because the island is a free port.

Documents To be on the safe side, all citizens of any country should travel the Caribbean with a valid passport.

Electricity It's 110-volt AC (60 cycles), the same as in the United States.

Emergencies For the police, call ✆ **911;** for an ambulance, call ✆ **912;** in case of fire, call ✆ **912.**

Hospital A licensed physician is on duty at the **Queen Beatrix Medical Center,** 25 Princessweg, Oranjestad (✆ **599/318-2211**).

Language Dutch is the official language, but English is commonly spoken.

Safety Although crime is rare, it's wise to secure your valuables and take the kind of discreet precautions you would anywhere. Don't leave valuables unguarded on the beach.

Taxes & Service Charges There's a $5.65 tax if you're returning to the Dutch-held islands of St. Maarten or Saba; if you're going elsewhere, the tax is $12. Hotels on Statia collect a 7% government tax, plus a 3% turnover tax. Most hotels, guesthouses, and restaurants add a 10% to 15% service charge.

Telephone To access **AT&T Direct** for calls to the United States from Statia, call ✆ **001-800/225-5288.** To call Statia from the U.S., dial **011** (the international access code), then **599** (the country code for the Netherlands Antilles), and finally **318** (the area code for Statia) and the four-digit local number. To make a call within Statia, only the four-digit local number is necessary.

Time St. Eustatius operates on Atlantic Standard Time year-round. When all time zones are on standard time, 6pm in Oranjestad is 5pm in New York. During daylight saving time, the island keeps the same time as the U.S. East Coast.

Water The water here is generally safe to drink.

Weather The average daytime temperature ranges from 78°F to 82°F (26°C–28°C). The annual rainfall is 1.1m (43 in.).

WHERE TO STAY

Don't expect deluxe hotels or high rises—Statia is strictly for escapists. Guests are sometimes placed in private homes.

Golden Era Hotel Set directly on the water, this 1960s hotel is clean, serviceable, and comfortable. Twelve units offer full or partial sea views. (The most stunning panorama is from no. 205.) All accommodations are spacious, with king-size or queen-size beds, although the look is that of a rather dated motel room. Regrettably, the shower-only bathrooms are so tiny that it's hard to maneuver. You can, if you wish, sit on the toilet and wash your face at the same time. Lunch and dinner are served daily in the simply decorated bar and dining room.

Bay Rd., Lower Town, Oranjestad, St. Eustatius, N.A. www.statiatourism.com/goldenera. ✆/fax **599/318-2455.** 20 units. Year-round $135–$150. AE, DISC, MC, V. **Amenities:** Restaurant; bar; outdoor pool. *In room:* A/C, ceiling fan, TV, fridge.

King's Well Resort ★ This small resort is the best address on Statia, surpassing the Old Gin House (see below). Set on the Caribbean side of the island, less than 1km (½ mile) north of Oranjestad, this secluded choice occupies about .3 hectare (¾ acre) on an oceanfront cliff, 20m (66 ft.) above the surf. If you're looking for a laid-back, escapist vacation, this is your place. (Your nearest neighbors are in the local cemetery.) Most views look to the southwest, ensuring colorful sunsets that tend to be enhanced by drinks served from the bar at the King's Well Restaurant (see below). Just below the hotel is a breeding bay for fish and octopus. The owner has several friendly pet dogs on the property. There are no room keys, so don't expect much security. The accommodations are small and rather sparsely furnished, and each is unique. The units in the rear are larger and face the sea, and those in front open onto a shared seaview balcony. This resort might not be suitable for very young children, as there is no guard around the pool.

Oranjebaai, St. Eustatius, N.A. www.kingswellstatia.com. ✆/fax **599/318-2538.** 12 units. Year-round $120–$150 double. Rates include breakfast. DISC, MC, V. **Amenities:** Restaurant; boating; fishing; Jacuzzi; outdoor pool. *In room:* A/C (in some), ceiling fan, TV, fridge, Wi-Fi (free).

The Old Gin House ★ For years the premier resort of Statia, the Old Gin House is a historic landmark. The inn is a faithful reconstruction of an 18th-century building that once housed a cotton gin. The bricks that went into the construction were once used by sailing ships as ballast. Surrounded by tropical gardens, including palms and bougainvillea, the hotel enjoys a central but tranquil location. All the good-size bedrooms are comfortably furnished, with queen-size beds and direct-dial phones.

Oranjebaai 1, St. Eustatius, N.A. www.oldginhouse.com. ✆ **599/318-2319.** Fax 599/318-2135. 18 units. Year-round $155–$205 double; $330 suite. Rates include breakfast. AE, DISC, MC, V. **Amenities:** 2 restaurants; 2 bars; babysitting; dive shop; outdoor pool. *In room:* A/C, TV, fridge (in some), Wi-Fi (free).

Statia Lodge ★ This is real Caribbean living in one of 10 exotic wooden bungalows with an outdoor freshwater pool overlooking the sea not far from the center of Oranjestad. The views from this colony of buildings are the most panoramic on Statia. On a clear day, you can see the island of Nevis in the distance, and the Quill volcano looms in the distance. Cottages are cozy and attractively furnished, with French doors opening onto a patio. Teakwood furnishings and tiles on the floors add a bit of style, as ceiling fans overhead keep you cool. A scooter is included in double rentals, and a car for three or four guests sharing a bungalow.

White Wall, Oranjestad, St. Eustatius, N.A. www.statialodge.com. ✆ **599/318-1900.** Fax 599/318-2873. 10 units. Year-round $150 double (includes a scooter rental); $230 quad (includes a car rental). MC, V. **Amenities:** Bar; outdoor pool. *In room:* Ceiling fan, kitchen, no phone.

WHERE TO DINE

Blue Bead Restaurant & Bar ★ FRENCH/WEST INDIAN Across from the waterfront, in relatively simple surroundings, this little eatery serves some of the best homemade food on the island. Set amid 18th-century ruins at Gallows Bay, it's decorated in bright Caribbean colors. Try to get a table on the veranda, with its potted palms. Dig into such local delights as mussels with french fries. Salt-cod fritters—and tasty ones, at that—are a specialty. If you drop in for lunch, you can choose from a selection of well-made sandwiches, among other offerings, and the pizza oven is kept piping hot at night. Locals end their meal with a taste of the house special, homemade vanilla rum. On Friday nights, fresh seafood is a feature. Island families frequent the place on Saturday night.

Bay Rd., Lower Town, Oranjestad. ✆ **599/318-2873.** Reservations recommended. Main courses $12–$29. AE, MC, V. Daily 7am–9:30pm.

Chinese Bar & Restaurant ASIAN/CARIBBEAN This place caters to locals and serves standard Chinese-restaurant fare with a bit of local flavor—the curried shrimp, for example. The atmosphere is very laid-back. For instance, even though the terrace isn't set up for dining, you can request to have your table moved there for an alfresco meal. The portions are hearty and range from the typical sweet-and-sour pork and a variety of shrimp dishes to chop suey and chow mein. This is the best place on the island for vegetarian food.

Princessweg, Oranjestad. ✆ **599/318-2389.** Main courses $5–$17. No credit cards. Daily 11am–midnight.

King's Well Restaurant INTERNATIONAL The restaurant here is more successful than the simple hotel in which it's housed (see above). Set less than 1km (½ mile) north of Oranjestad, and perched on a cliff about 20m (66 ft.) above the surf, it features an open kitchen and great sunset panoramas. Enjoy a fruity drink from the rustic bar before your meal. Lunches feature deli-style sandwiches and a selection of platters form the dinner menu, which is more elaborate. Dishes might include veal *cordon bleu* (thin slices of ham and Swiss cheese sandwiched between scallops of veal, then breaded and sautéed), fresh lobster, pan-fried grouper or snapper with parsley-butter sauce, plus a few German dishes like Jaeger schnitzel (veal sautéed in burgundy with mushrooms). Be sure to finish with the homemade apple strudel.

In the King's Well Resort, Oranjebaai. ✆ **599/318-2538.** Reservations required. Main courses $14–$32. DISC, MC, V. Daily 6–7:30pm.

Ocean View Terrace ★ CARIBBEAN/SEAFOOD This pleasant restaurant is set within a billowing, open-sided tent, inside the courtyard of the government's guesthouse, part of historic Fort Oranje. Diners sit amid dozens of hanging plants and historical artifacts and get a sweeping view of the sea. Menu items are firmly grounded in local culinary traditions but usually include well-prepared versions of local seafood, especially dishes made from shrimp and lobster. Specific examples, based on the whim of the chef, might include shrimp in either a garlic- or a curry-flavored sauce; teriyaki fish; a medley of chicken dishes; and, if you want to go native, several versions of goat and oxtail, including curried and stewed. Lunches, which include a range of salads and sandwiches, tend to be simpler than the more elaborate food featured at dinner.

In Fort Oranje. ✆ **599/318-2934.** Reservations recommended. Main courses $10–$30. DISC, MC, V. Mon–Sat 8am–2pm and 6:30–9pm.

The Old Gin House Restaurant ★ INTERNATIONAL/FRENCH/ASIAN Escape here for some of the more imaginative, exotic dishes on an island that tends to be devoted to a basic Antillean cuisine. It's a popular spot for divers, who can usually be found at the bar (Mooshay Pub) watching Winston prepare their favorite drinks. This beautiful old bar is in the main building, a former warehouse that once housed sugar, cotton, and indigo. The dining room and kitchen are also here. You can enjoy a candlelit dinner by the pool if the weather cooperates. Fresh lobster appears almost daily on the menu in winter, and the catch of the day, which can be grilled, typically includes red snapper, mahimahi, and kingfish. Fishermen bring their catch right to the door of the kitchen to sell.

In the Old Gin House, Oranjebaai 1. ✆ **599/318-2319.** Reservations required. Main courses $10–$28. AE, MC, V. Daily 7–10:30am, 11:30am–2pm, and 6:30–9pm.

STATIA'S BEACHES

Most of Statia's beaches are small, narrow strips of sand, either volcanic black or a dull, mudlike gray. Regrettably, the best beaches are not on the tranquil Caribbean side, but on the turbulent Atlantic side, where the waters are often too rough for swimming.

Beachcombers delight, however, in their search for the fabled **blue-glass beads,** which were manufactured in the 1600s by a Dutch West Indies Company. They were used as money for the trading of such products as tobacco, cotton, rum—and even slaves. These beads, which are real collector's items, are often unearthed after a heavy rainfall or tropical storm.

Orange Beach, also called Smoke Alley Beach, lies on the Caribbean side of the island directly off Lower Town. This is one of the small volcanic beaches on the southwest shore, with beige or black sands and waters suitable for a leisurely swim. You virtually have the beach to yourself until late afternoon, when locals start to arrive for a dip.

Also on the leeward, or Caribbean, side is **Crooks Castle Beach,** south of Oranjestad. The waters, filled with giant yellow sea fans, sea whips, and pillar coral, attract snorkelers, while beachcombers are drawn to the many blue beads that have been unearthed here.

On the southeast Atlantic side of the island, **Corre Corre Bay** has a strip of dark golden sand. It's about half an hour down Mountain Road and is worth the trip to get here, although the waters are often too churned up for comfortable swimming. Two bends north of this beach, the light-brown-sand **Lynch Bay Beach** is more sheltered from the wild swells of the Atlantic. Nonetheless, the surf here is almost always rough, plus there's a dangerous undertow; this beach is better for sunbathing than swimming.

Also on the Atlantic side, **Zeelandia Beach** is 3km (2 miles) long and filled with very dark-beige and volcanic-black sand. One tourist promotion speaks of its "exciting Atlantic surf and invigorating trade winds" but fails to warn of the dangerous undertow. Only one small designated section is safe for swimming. The beach is suitable, however, for wading, hiking, and sunbathing. It's almost always deserted.

SPORTS & OUTDOOR PURSUITS

HIKING Hiking is the most popular outdoor activity on the island. Those with enough stamina can climb the slopes of the **Quill,** the highest point on Statia. Its extinct volcanic cone harbors a crater filled with a dense tropical rainforest, containing towering kapok trees and a dozen or more species of wild orchids, some quite rare. It's also home to at least 50 species of bird life, including the rare blue pigeon, known to frequent the breadfruit and cottonwood trees here. Islanders once grew cocoa, coffee, and cinnamon in the crater's soil, but today bananas are the only crop. The **tourist office** (✆ **599/318-2433**) will supply you with a list of a dozen trails of varying degrees of difficulty and can also arrange for a guide. You'll have to negotiate the fee; it's usually $10 and up.

Catching Crabs Means Something Different Here

We're perfectly serious: If you're interested, you can join Statians in a crab hunt. The Quill's crater is the breeding ground for these large crustaceans. At night they emerge from their holes to forage, and that's when they're caught. Either with flashlights or relying on moonlight, crab hunters climb the Quill, catch crabs, and take them home to prepare the local delicacy, stuffed crab. Your hotel can usually hook you up with this activity.

WATERSPORTS **Scubaqua Dive Center** is a full PADI diving center on Fishermen's Beach in Lower Town (✆ **599/318-2435;** www.scubaqua.com), offering everything from beginning instruction to dive master certification, costing $450. Its professional staff guides divers of all experience levels to spectacular walls, untouched coral reefs, and historic shipwrecks. Scubaqua offers one- and two-tank boat dives, costing $40 to $80. Equipment is $20 a day. Night dives and snorkel trips are also available.

Statia is mostly a divers' island, but there is some decent **snorkeling** on the Caribbean side. You can explore the remnants of an 18th-century man-of-war and the walls of warehouses, taverns, and ships that sank below the surface of Oranje Bay more than 200 years ago. The best place to go is **Crooks Castle Beach,** southwest of Lower Town. Any dive shop can rent you snorkeling gear.

EXPLORING THE ISLAND

Oranjestad stands on a cliff looking out on a beach and the island's calm anchorage, where in the 18th century, you might have seen 200 vessels offshore. **Fort Oranje** was built in 1636 and restored in honor of the U.S. bicentennial celebration of 1976. Perched atop the cliffs, its terraced rampart is lined with the old cannons.

Miriam C. Schmidt Botanical Garden ★, Upper Company (www.statiapark.org), is the best place in Statia for a picnic lunch, lying on the Atlantic side of the Quill. The garden sprawls across 21 lush hectares (52 acres) and is a haven for the island's fauna and flora. A ranger is on hand Monday to Friday in the morning (hours vary) to give visitors a tour of the gardens, requesting a $5 donation. Tours last 90 minutes and take in the Sensory Garden, Palm Garden, Lookout Garden, and a bird trail. More information about the gardens can be obtained from the **St. Eustatius National Parks Foundation** at Gallows Bay (✆ **599/318-2884**).

A final site for the adventurers is the **Quill ★★**, the volcanic cone of an extinct volcano, rising 5km (3 miles) south of Oranjestad on the main highway. In the crater of this 610m (2,001-ft.) volcano is a primeval rainforest. You can hike down into its depths, which now are part of the first official national park created in the Netherlands Antilles. The park consists of the Quill itself, plus the White Wall, a limestone formation on the south side of the volcano.

The park also covers the Boven area, covering five hills in the northern tier of the island. Rangers offer guided tours of the park and maintain a network of 10 trails in the Quill sector. The cost is $10 for a 3- to 4-hour guided hike, including the national-park visitor fee. Arrangements can be made at the **visitor center** near the harbor at

Gallows Bay (✆ **599/318-2884**). The center is open Monday to Thursday 7am to 5pm, Friday 7am to 4pm.

St. Eustatius Historical Foundation Museum, Upper Town (✆ **599/318-2288**), is also called the Donker House in honor of its former tenant, Simon Donker. After British Admiral Rodney sacked Statia for cooperating with the United States, he installed his own headquarters here. Today the 18th-century house and museum stands in a garden, with a 20th-century wing crafted from 17th-century bricks. There are exhibits on the process of sugar refining and shipping and commerce, a section devoted to the pre-Columbian period, archaeological artifacts from the colonial period, and a pair of beautiful rooms furnished with 18th-century antiques. In the annex is a massive piece of needlework by American Catherine Mary Williams, showing the flowers of Statia. The museum is open Monday to Thursday from 9am to 5pm, Friday 9am to 3pm, and Sunday 9am to noon (closed Sat). Admission is $3 for adults, $1 for children.

A few steps away, a cluster of 18th-century buildings surrounding a quiet courtyard is called **Three Widows' Corner.**

Nearby are the partially restored ruins of the first **Dutch Reformed church,** on Kerkweg (Church Way). To reach it, turn west from Three Widows' Corner onto Kerkweg. Tilting headstones record the names of the characters in the island's past. You can climb to the top level of the tower and see the bay as lookouts did many years before.

Statia once had a large colony of Jewish traders, and you can explore the ruins of **Honen Dalim,** the second-oldest Jewish synagogue in the Western Hemisphere (see p. 221 for information on the oldest). Built around 1740 and damaged by a hurricane in 1772, the synagogue stands beside Synagogpad, a narrow lane whose entrance faces Madam Theatre on the square.

The walls of a *mikvah* (ritual bath) rise beside the **Jewish burial ground** on the edge of town. Most poignant is the memorial of David Haim Hezeciah de Lion, who died in 1760 at the age of 2 years, 8 months, 26 days; carved into the baroque surface is an angel releasing a tiny songbird from its cage.

You can also visit **Lynch Plantation Museum** at Lynch Bay (✆ **599/318-2338**), but you'll have to call to arrange a tour. Donations are accepted; otherwise, admission is free. Locals still call this place the Berkel Family Plantation, although today it's a museum depicting life on Statia a century ago, through antiques, fishing and farming equipment, pictures, and old Bibles. Usually, Ismael Berkel is on hand to show you around Monday to Friday 9am to 5pm. This is still very much a residence rather than some dead, dull museum.

SHOPPING

At **Mazinga Gift Shop,** Fort Oranjestraat, Upper Town (✆ **599/318-2245**), you'll find an array of souvenirs—T-shirts, liquor, costume jewelry, 14-karat-gold jewelry, cards, drugstore items, beachwear, office supplies, children's books, handbags, and paperback romances. You may have seen more exciting stores in your life, but this is without parallel for Statia. You can buy books, office supplies, and stationery at the **Paper Corner,** Van Tonningenweg, Upper Town (✆ **599/318-2208**).

ST. EUSTATIUS AFTER DARK

As for after-dark fun, Statia ain't Las Vegas. Nightlife pickings here are among the slimmest in the Caribbean. Weekends are the best—maybe the only—time to go out. **Smoke Alley Bar & Grill,** Lower Town, Gallows Bay (© **599/318-2002**), is an open-air beach bar with live music on Friday night; it's open Monday to Saturday 6 to 11pm. For local flavor, try **Cool Corner,** Wilhelminaweg, Uppertown, Oranjestad (© **599/318-2523**), across from the St. Eustatius Historical Foundation Museum, in the center of town.

ST. KITTS & NEVIS

The two islands that make up the tiny nation of St. Kitts and Nevis are often referred to as sisters. Both have lush landscapes, including rainforests, and a cultural heritage from 18th-century sugar plantation economies. Long-dormant volcanoes dominate, and most beaches lack the crowds of more popular Caribbean islands. Big sister St. Kitts is by far the most visited; however, it's still possible to find untamed scenery in its trio of mountain ranges. Little sister Nevis is a sleepy getaway perfect for leaving your worries behind.

Beaches St. Kitts's beaches vary from black sand in the island's north, to gray or white sand in the south. **Friar's Bay Beach,** a favorite of many locals, is also good for families, thanks to its calm waters and food stands. With its reef-protected waters, ideal for both swimming and snorkeling, **Pinney's Beach** on Nevis is one of the grandest in the Caribbean. A lagoon that evokes the South Pacific awaits near the beach's windward edge.

Things to Do To get a breathtaking view of the best panorama in the Caribbean, visit the **Brimstone Hill Fortress** on St. Kitts, which commands a view of six islands: Nevis, Montserrat, Saba, St. Eustatius, St. Martin, and St. Barts. The **St. Kitts Scenic Railway** follows old sugarcane tracks on a tour of the island's most spectacular scenery. Journey through a rainforest and local villages on a hike or mountain-bike ride on Nevis' 14.5km (9-mile) **Upper Round Road.**

Eating & Drinking In St. Kitts and Nevis, it's best to eat island style, whether it's **seafood** with West Indian curry or **goat water**—goat stew with vegetables and dumplings. Head to Rawlins Plantation Inn on St. Kitts for West Indian fare with a stunning view, or The Golden Lemon for house specialties such as **lobster** from Dieppe Bay or **rum-beef stew**. Try a **rum punch** and enjoy the sunshine at the Double Deuce, a casual beach bar and restaurant on Nevis.

Nature Beyond the sandy beaches, natural attractions are abundant on both islands. On St. Kitts, adventurous types hike up **Mount Liamuiga** through the rainforest to the crater rim of a dormant volcano. Among the trees of the cloud forest are a variety of rare birds, as well as green vervet monkeys. **Dive sites** off the western coast of Nevis vary from thermal vents to the high shoals near **Booby Island,** where Southern stingrays and hawksbill turtles are found.

ESSENTIALS

Visitor Information

Information is available from the **Explore St. Kitts** stateside offices at 414 E. 75th St., New York, NY 10021 (✆ **800/582-6208** or 212/535-1234).

In **Canada,** an office is located at 133 Richmond St., Ste. 311, Toronto, ON M5H 2L3 (✆ **416/368-6707**), and in the **United Kingdom** at 10 Kensington Court, London W8 5DL (✆ **020/7376-0881**).

The website for St. Kitts is **www.stkittstourism.kn**. The equivalent website for Nevis is **www.nevisisland.com**.

[Fast FACTS] ST. KITTS & NEVIS

Banks The most convenient bank, with **ATM** services, is the **St. Kitts-Nevis-Anguilla National Bank** on Central Street in Basseterre (✆ **869/465-2204**). Other ATMs are at Port Zante, the shopping mall adjacent to the cruise-ship piers in downtown Basseterre, and at the Marriott Resort in Frigate Bay. Funds are dispensed, depending on the machine, in either U.S. dollars or Eastern Caribbean dollars.

Currency The local currency is the **Eastern Caribbean dollar (EC$),** pegged at EC$2.67 to the U.S. dollar (EC$1 = US37¢). Many prices, however, including those of hotels, are quoted in U.S. dollars. Always determine which "dollar" locals are talking about. *Prices in this chapter are quoted in U.S. dollars.*

Customs You are allowed in duty-free with your personal belongings. Sometimes luggage is subjected to a drug check. If you clear Customs in one of the islands, you don't have to do it again if you visit the other.

Documents U.S., British, and Canadian citizens need a passport. A return or ongoing ticket is mandatory.

Electricity Electricity on St. Kitts is 230-volt AC (60 cycles), so you'll need an adapter and a transformer for U.S.-made appliances. However, most hotels on the islands have outlets that will accept North American appliances. Check with your hotel to see if it has converted its voltage and outlets.

Emergencies Dial ✆ **911** for emergencies, ✆ **333** for fire department.

Language English is the language of both islands, and it is spoken with a decided West Indian lilt; patois is commonly spoken as well.

Safety This is still a fairly safe place to travel. Most crimes against tourists—and there aren't a lot—are robberies on Conaree Beach on St. Kitts, so exercise the usual precautions. It's wise to safeguard your valuables, and women should not go jogging alone along deserted roads. Crime is rare on Nevis.

Taxes The government imposes a 9% tax on rooms and meals, plus another $22 airport departure tax. (You don't pay the departure tax when you travel between St. Kitts and Nevis.)

Telephone The area code for St. Kitts and Nevis is **869.** You can make calls to or from the United States as you would for any other area code in North America. To access **AT&T Direct,** call ✆ **800/225-5288;** to reach **MCI,** dial ✆ **800/888-8000.**

Time St. Kitts and Nevis are on Atlantic Standard Time year-round. This means that in winter, when it's 6am in Basseterre, it's 5am in New York. When the United States goes on daylight saving time, St. Kitts and Nevis are on the same time as the East Coast of the United States.

Tipping Most hotels and restaurants add a service

charge of 10% to cover tipping. If not, tip 10% to 15%.

Water The water on St. Kitts and Nevis is so good that in the 1970s, Baron de Rothschild's chemists selected St. Kitts as their only site in the Caribbean to distill and produce CSR (Cane Sugar Rothschild), a pure sugar-cane liqueur. In the 1700s, Lord Nelson regularly brought his fleet to Nevis just to collect water, and Nevis still boasts of having Nelson spring water.

Weather St. Kitts and Nevis are tropical, and the warm climate is tempered by the trade winds. The average air temperature is 79°F (26°C); the average water temperature, 80°F (27°C). Dry, mild weather is usually experienced from November to April; May to October is hotter and rainier.

ST. KITTS

St. Kitts's major crop is sugar, a tradition dating from the 17th century. But tourism may overwhelm it in the years to come, as its southeastern peninsula, site of the best white-sand beaches, has been set aside for massive resort development. Most of the island's other beaches are of gray or black volcanic sand.

The Caribs, the early settlers, called the island Liamuiga, or "fertile isle." Its mountain ranges reach up to nearly 1,200m (3,937 ft.), and its interior contains virgin rainforests, alive with hummingbirds and wild green vervet monkeys. The monkeys were brought in as pets by the early French settlers but were set free when the British took control of the island in 1783. These native African animals have proliferated and can be seen at the Estridge Estate Behavioral Research Institute. The British brought in mongooses to control rats in the sugar-cane fields, only to discover that the predators slept during the rats' most active forays. Wild deer are found in the mountains.

The capital of St. Kitts, **Basseterre,** lies on the Caribbean shore near the southern end of the island, about 2km (1¼ miles) from the airport. Its white colonial houses with toothpick balconies look like a Hollywood version of a West Indian port.

Essentials

GETTING THERE In 2007 several airlines stepped up their nonstop service from the North American mainland into St. Kitts. American was one of these, reinstating nonstop service from New York's JFK airport twice per week, and inaugurating once-per-week nonstop service into St. Kitts from Miami. This supplements service that had existed previously, including **US Airways** (✆ **800/622-1015** in the U.S. and Canada; www.usairways.com) Saturday service from both Philadelphia and Charlotte to St. Kitts. Otherwise, you have to connect through Antigua, St. Maarten, or Puerto

Sweet Treat

At some point during your visit, you should eat sugar directly from the cane—and an occasional vendor, some of them positioned in downtown Basseterre at the corner of Fort and Cayon Streets, will sell you a stalk for around $2. Strip off the hard exterior of the stalk, bite into it, chew on the tasty reeds, and swallow the juice. It's best with a glass of rum. Tourist officials are quick to point out that the local economy is no longer based exclusively on sugar cane in particular, or on agriculture in general, but you'll nonetheless spot lots of flourishing sugar-cane fields, especially in isolated regions of (northwestern) St. Kitts.

Party Times in St. Kitts

Carnival in St. Kitts is celebrated not in the days leading up to Ash Wednesday, but from Christmas Eve to January 2. The festivities include parties, dancing, talent shows, and the crowning of the Carnival Queen. The final day of the celebration is known as "Last Lap" and features a repeat of many of the activities, including a multitude of bands jamming in the streets of Basseterre.

Another popular party time is the **St. Kitts Music Festival,** held the last weekend in June (Thurs–Sun). The soca/calypso night is usually the festival's opening event, and its most popular. You can also hear reggae, jazz, rhythm and blues, and gospel performances over the 4 days. For more information, call the Department of Tourism at ✆ **869/465-4040.**

Rico. **American Airlines** (✆ **800/433-7300** in the U.S. and Canada; www.aa.com) has dozens of daily flights to its hub in San Juan. From there, American's commuter partner, **American Eagle,** makes four daily nonstop flights into St. Kitts.

Winair (✆ **866/466-0410** in the U.S. and Canada, or 599/54-54237; www.fly-winair.com) flies to St. Kitts from St. Maarten. The Antigua-based carrier **LIAT** (✆ **888/844-LIAT** [5428]; www.liatairline.com) flies to St. Kitts from Antigua, Puerto Rico, and St. Maarten. Winair has two daily flights between Nevis and St. Kitts.

Air Canada (✆ **888/247-2262** in the U.S. and Canada, or 514/422-5000; www.aircanada.ca) flies from Toronto to Antigua. **Excel Airlines** (✆ **0892/231-300;** www.xl.com) flies about once a week from London's Gatwick to Antigua. From Antigua, you can make connections on LIAT or Winair (see above).

You can also use the **interisland ferry service** between St. Kitts and Nevis. Ferry schedules follow no obvious patterns and are subject to change without notice. The fare is $8 round-trip for any of the ferryboats that participate in the frequent runs. In addition, in 2007 car-ferry service was inaugurated between St. Kitts and Nevis, with a departure between the two islands once per day throughout the year. For specific schedules, call ✆ **869/466-4618** or click on **www.boatschedule.leytonms.com**.

GETTING AROUND Since most **taxi** drivers are also guides, this is the best means of getting around. You don't even have to find a driver at the airport—one will find you. Drivers also wait outside the major hotels. First, however, you must agree on the price, since taxis aren't metered. Also, ask if the rates are in U.S. or Eastern Caribbean dollars. The fare from the airport to Basseterre is about $7; to Sandy Point, $12; to Frigate Bay (site of the Marriott Hotel), around $12. Tours of the island, each lasting around 2½ hours and appropriate for one to four passengers, cost around $80 each. For more information, call the **St. Kitts Taxi Association** (✆ **869/465-8487**).

Avis, Irishtown Bay Road (✆ **800/331-1084** in the U.S. and Canada, or 869/465-6507; www.avisstkitts.com), charges from $40 to $80 per day or $260 to $480 per week, plus $15 per day for collision damage, with a $950 deductible and a surcharge of $1.50 per day. The company offers free delivery service to either the airport or any of the island's hotels; drivers must be between 25 and 75. Avis will arrange for a rental exchange if you also go to Nevis.

Avis's most impressive competitor is **Thrifty Rent-a-Car,** located at the corner of Central Street and West Independence Square Street, in the center of Basseterre

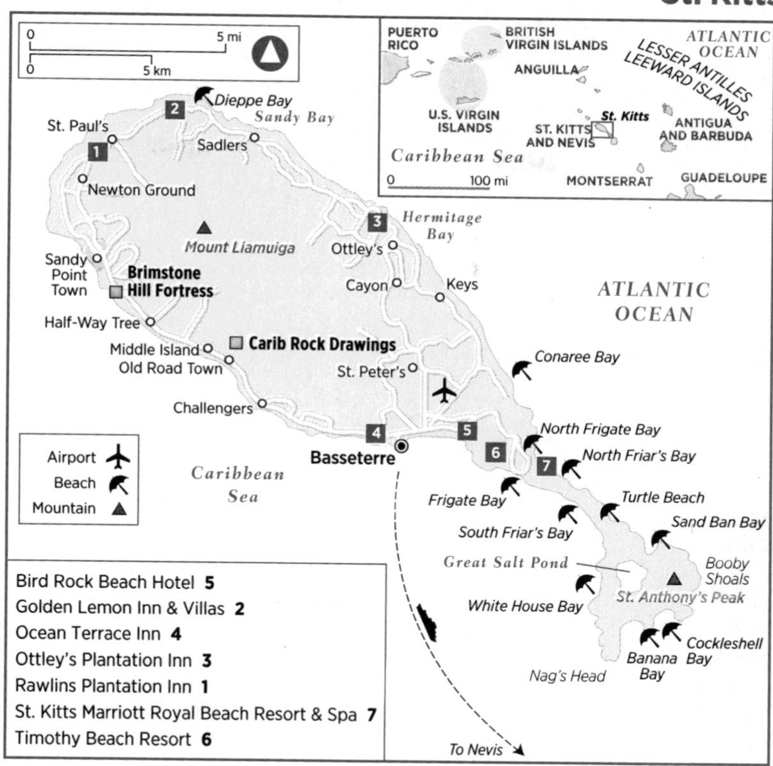

(✆ **869/465-2991,** or 465-3160 for their airport branch). Prices rival those at Avis, and quality of cars is generally very good.

C & C Economy Car Rentals, Liverpool Row, Basseterre (✆ **869/465-8449**), is a local company offering cars and jeeps starting at $40 to $60 per day. Tax and insurance are extra ($10 per day for collision damage, $750 deductible). This might be your best deal on the island.

Remember: Driving is on the left! You'll need a local driver's license, which can be obtained at the **Traffic Department,** on Cayon Street in Basseterre, for $24. Usually a member of the staff at your car rental agency will drive you to the Traffic Department to get one.

FAST FACTS **Banks** on St. Kitts are open Monday to Thursday from 8am to 2pm, Friday from 8am to 4pm, and Saturday from 8:30 to 11am. You can place **international telephone calls,** including collect calls, at **LIME,** Cayon Street, Basseterre (✆ **869/465-1000**), Monday to Wednesday from 8am to 5pm, Thursday and Friday 8am to 4pm, and Saturday from 9am to noon.

The most centrally located pharmacy is **City Drug,** Central Street in Basseterre (✆ **869/465-2156**), open Monday to Wednesday and Friday to Saturday from 8am to 7pm, Thursday from 8am to 5pm, and Sunday from 8 to 11am.

There's a 24-hour **emergency room** in Basseterre at **Joseph N. France General Hospital,** Buckley's Site (✆ **869/465-2551**).

Explore St. Kitts, the island's tourist board, operates at Pelican Mall, Bay Road in Basseterre (✆ **869/465-4040**). It's open Monday to Friday 7:30am to 5pm.

Where to Stay

VERY EXPENSIVE

Golden Lemon Inn & Villas ★★ Sophisticated and elegant describe both the Golden Lemon and its clientele. The resort's centerpiece is a much-restored, much-altered French colonial manor house with an 18th-century Georgian upper story, set within a coconut grove near a black volcanic-sand beach, on the otherwise isolated northwest coast of St. Kitts. Flanking the great house are the Lemon Court and Lemon Grove Condominiums, each painted a neon shade of lemon-gold, where you can rent luxuriously furnished suites surrounded by manicured gardens; most have private pools. The venue is a wee bit faded from its glory days when this kind of upscale-bohemian venue was a novelty in these parts. The spacious rooms are furnished with antiques and always contain fresh flowers, but are not air-conditioned. Bedrooms have been redecorated with new fabrics, rugs, and accessories. Many beds are raised four-posters draped in mosquito netting in the old plantation style; each is equipped with fine linen. The larger villas have sunken tubs, kitchens, and dishwashers.

Dieppe Bay, St. Kitts, W.I. www.goldenlemon.com. ✆ **800/633-7411** in the U.S., or 869/465-7260. Fax 869/465-4019. 26 units. Winter $320 double, $350 1-bedroom villa, $385–$540 2-bedroom villa; off season $215 double, $235 1-bedroom villa, $270–$365 2-bedroom villa. Rates include American breakfast. Extra person $150. Honeymoon packages available. AE, MC, V. Closed Sept to mid-Oct. Children 18 and under not usually accepted. **Amenities:** Restaurant; horseback riding; outdoor pool (lit); room service; tennis court; watersports equipment/rentals. *In room:* A/C (in 2), ceiling fan, fridge, hair dryer, Internet (free), kitchenette (in villas).

Ottley's Plantation Inn ★★★ This is the island's finest, most appealing, and most stylish place to stay. It's historically evocative and infinitely intimate, and invariably leaves a visitor with the impression that enormous amounts of love, tenderness, loyalty, and devotion have been showered upon the place by the resident innkeepers, long-ago refugees from the bookselling business in Princeton, New Jersey, the Keusch family. Ten kilometers (6¼ miles) north of the airport, and near a rainforest, it occupies a 14-hectare (35-acre) site that functioned during the 17th century as a plantation. Those seeking historically evocative charm will appreciate the rooms within the gracefully restored 1832 great house. Other units include free-standing cottages and a series of hideaway and very romantic suites, each with a view of the sea, a private plunge pool, and furniture that's artfully appropriate to the setting and the 19th-century flair in which this place excels. Regardless of their location and category, rooms are elegantly appointed and very spacious, with queen- or king-size beds. Guests enjoy body polishing or body wraps at the trendy Mango Orchard Spa set in a replica of a traditional wood-framed Antillean cottage called a chattel house.

Ottley's Village (P.O. Box 345), St. Kitts, W.I. www.ottleys.com. ✆ **800/772-3039** in the U.S., or 869/465-7234. Fax 869/465-4760. 24 units. Winter $345–$555 double, $830 suite, $1,090–$1,620 villa; off season $230–$385 double, $550 suite, $770–$1,090 villa. $100 per person daily for half-board (breakfast and dinner). Wedding, honeymoon, and other packages available. AE, DISC, MC, V. Children 9 and under discouraged. **Amenities:** Restaurant; 2 bars; shuttle to beach; babysitting; bikes; croquet; Jacuzzi; outdoor pool; room service; spa; tennis court (lit). *In room:* A/C, ceiling fan, TV (DVD by request), hair dryer, minibar (in some), Wi-Fi (free).

Rawlins Plantation Inn ★★ This hotel in the verdant uplands above Dieppe Bay is situated among the ruins of a muscovado sugar factory on the northeast coast, with a good sandy beach just a short drive away. Isolated and rural in flavor, and dominated by the artfully gaunt masonry smokestack of the long-ago sugar cane distillery, this former plantation enjoys cool breezes from both ocean and mountains. Behind the 5 hectares (12 acres) of manicured lawns and gardens, the land segues into a rainforest and Mount Liamuiga. Accommodations lie within the original core of either the main house or what used to be the distillery, or within pleasantly decorated outbuildings. There's no air-conditioning, but ceiling fans and cross-ventilation keep the place comfortable. Each unit, generous in size, is decorated in a Caribbean country-house style with antiques, stone or white walls, floral prints, local art, and rattan furnishings. Many bedrooms have mahogany four-posters.

Mount Pleasant (P.O. Box 340), St. Kitts, W.I. www.rawlinsplantation.com. ✆ **869/465-6221.** Fax 869/465-4954. 12 units. Winter $280–$295 double, $390 Sugar Mill honeymoon suite, $665 2-bedroom cottage; off season $185–$200 double, $280 Sugar Mill honeymoon suite, $445 2-bedroom cottage. Wedding packages available. Rates include breakfast, dinner, afternoon tea, and laundry service. MC, V. Closed Aug–Oct. Children 11 and under not allowed. **Amenities:** Restaurant; bar; outdoor pool (lit); tennis court. *In room:* Ceiling fan, hair dryer, no phone, Wi-Fi (free).

EXPENSIVE

St. Kitts Marriott Resort & The Royal Beach Casino ★★ ☺ This is the largest and most unselfconsciously "mass market" resort on St. Kitts, a sprawling but well-managed behemoth that entered the scene in 2003. Its design evokes the Mediterranean with its tile roofs and lush landscaping. Its modernity is a long way from such historical resorts as Ottley's and Rawlins (see both above). In the center, a few steps down from the lobby, is a replica of Columbus's *Santa Maria,* surrounded by a reflecting pool and some waterfalls. The location, with its adjacent Royal Beach Casino, is near the narrowest part of St. Kitts, close to Atlantic-fronting beaches. Its 9 hectares (22 acres) include an 18-hole golf course designed by Canadian-born Tom McBroom and one of the largest casinos in the Caribbean. The decor of this sprawling resort is self-tabbed as "Euro-Caribbean," with vague references to the Italian Renaissance within its pastel-colored sprawl and richly patterned marble floors. Most of the tasteful, comfortable, and elegant accommodations are within a five-story central core, but there are also various low-rise "outbuildings" between the main building and the sea.

858 Frigate Bay Rd., Frigate Bay, St. Kitts, W.I. www.marriott.com. ✆ **800/228-9290** in the U.S., or 869/466-1200. Fax 869/466-1201. 443 units. Winter $255–$380 double, $410–$640 suite; off season $165–$240 double, $265–$410 suite. AE, DC, DISC, MC, V. **Amenities:** 8 restaurants; 6 bars; nightclub; babysitting; children's programs; 18-hole golf course; health club; 3 outdoor pools; whirlpool; casino; room service; sauna; full-service spa; 4 tennis courts (lit). *In room:* A/C, TV, fridge, hair dryer, Wi-Fi ($15 per day).

MODERATE

Bird Rock Beach Hotel Built in the mid-1980s as a small inn, but expanded and enlarged many times since then, this resort is set on steeply sloping terrain beside a secluded, half-moon-shaped beach 3km (2 miles) southeast of Basseterre. The small hotel is uncomplicated and easygoing. Seven coral-colored and angular buildings each have six to eight accommodations. It's a good example of a carefully maintained West Indian–owned resort where guests, despite the handful of organized activities, are very much on their own. Views from most bedroom balconies are either of the Bay of Basseterre and the capital, or of the water stretching toward Nevis. All units have private patios or balconies and rather bland furniture inspired by the Tropics. Bedrooms carry out the Caribbean motif with flowery fabrics and paintings of birds. Each superior room has one king-size or two double beds, and each studio suite offers a queen-size bed plus a sofa bed and a kitchenette. Apartments have full kitchens.

Basseterre (P.O. Box 227), St. Kitts, W.I. www.birdrockbeach.com. ✆ **877/244-6285** in the U.S., or 869/465-8914. Fax 869/465-1675. 46 units. Winter $105–$135 double, $225 2-bedroom suite, $300 3-bedroom suite; off season $90–$105 double, $165 2-bedroom suite, $215 3-bedroom suite. AE, MC, V. **Amenities:** 3 restaurants; 2 bars; dive shop; outdoor pool; room service. *In room:* A/C, TV, fridge (in some), hair dryer, kitchenette (in some), Wi-Fi (free).

Ocean Terrace Inn ★ This inn is affectionately known as the "OTI" by its mainly business clients. If you want to be near Basseterre, it's the best hotel within a reasonable walking distance of downtown and the port, with oceanfront verandas and a view of the harbor and the capital. It's so compact that a stay here is like a house party on a cruise ship. Terraced into a landscaped hillside above the edge of Basseterre, the hotel also has a garden and well-kept grounds. Each of the handsomely decorated rooms has a light, tropical feel and overlooks a well-planted terrace. Bedrooms are a wide variety of sizes and are tidily maintained. The hotel also offers apartments at the Fisherman's Wharf and Village, a few steps from the nearby harbor. These units are filled with most of the comforts of home.

Wigley Ave. (P.O. Box 65), Fortlands, St. Kitts, W.I. www.oceanterraceinn.com. ✆ **800/524-0512** or 869/465-2754. Fax 869/465-1057. 69 units. Winter $135–$165 double, $150–$320 suite; off season $120–$145 double, $135–$290 suite. Dive, honeymoon, and eco-safari packages available. AE, DC, MC, V. Go west along Basseterre Bay Rd. past the Cenotaph. **Amenities:** 3 restaurants; 3 bars; exercise room; Jacuzzi; 3 outdoor pools; room service; sauna; watersports equipment/rentals. *In room:* A/C, ceiling fan (in some), TV, fridge, hair dryer, kitchenette (in some), Wi-Fi (free).

Rock Haven Bed & Breakfast ★★ 🎁 Only a 2-minute drive from the beaches of Frigate Bay, this cozy little Caribbean-style home offers warm hospitality, with views of ocean and beaches. There are only a couple of suites, each spacious and well maintained, with a full bathroom and plenty of beach towels. Double louvered doors open onto your own private patio adorned with flowers. You sleep in a colonial bed draped in mosquito netting. The breakfast, hosted by the owners, is one of the best on the island, with such treats as fluffy French toast, banana pancakes, home-baked ham, cheese or mushrooms omelets, and a host of other goodies. If you want breakfast like an islander, opt for the salted codfish with fried ripe plantains.

Frigate Bay (P.O. Box 821), St. Kitts, W.I. www.rock-haven.com. ✆ **869/465-5503.** Fax 869/466-6130. 2 units. Winter $175 double; off season $155 double. Rates include breakfast. MC, V. **Amenities:** Airport transfers (free). *In room:* A/C (in one), hair dryer, kitchen (in one), Wi-Fi (free).

Timothy Beach Resort ☺ Located at the foot of a green mountain 5km (3 miles) east of Basseterre, this condo resort is a family favorite, with lots of children, most of them 12 and under, running around underfoot. Though short on atmosphere, it's on one of St. Kitts's finest beaches. Naturally, the most sought-after units are those opening directly onto the beach, which offers swimming, sailing, and watersports. There's also a pool, and an 18-hole golf course is just a short drive away. The rooms are furnished in a Caribbean motif, and the larger accommodations have kitchens. Units here are timeshares, so there are no routine extras.

Frigate Bay (P.O. Box 1198), Basseterre, St. Kitts, W.I. www.timothybeach.com. ✆ **877/94-BEACH** (942-3224) or 869/465-8597. Fax 869/466-7085. 60 units. Winter $140–$165 double, $230 1-bedroom suite, $345 2-bedroom suite; off season $110–$125 double, $165 1-bedroom suite, $240 2-bedroom suite. AE,

MC, V. **Amenities:** Restaurant; bar; babysitting; golf (nearby); outdoor pool. *In room:* A/C, TV, fridge, hair dryer, kitchenette (in some), Wi-Fi (free).

Where to Dine

VERY EXPENSIVE

The Beach House ★★★ FUSION This deluxe restaurant, arguably the best on the island, is the advance salvo of the spectacular development of Christophe Harbour on the southwest peninsula, which is expected to sprawl across 1,100 hectares (2,718 acres), and will include a Tom Fazio golf course atop Priddies Plateau, a megayacht harbor, and a marina village, as well as several five-star hotels. In the meantime, you can get an advance preview of the place by dining here.

A variety of international cuisine is deftly offered, including French, Mediterranean, American, and even the South Pacific. Patrons can treat themselves to such starters as duck foie gras pâté with Caribbean fruit salsa, or shrimp tempura with a spinach aïoli. A look at the mains is a culinary voyage of discovery—a Turtle Beach bouillabaisse, peppercorn-crusted sea bass, or lemon-grass ginger-pork stew in a coconut silk base.

Turtle Beach. ✆ **869/469-5299.** www.stkittsbeachhouse.com. Reservations required. Main courses $30–$45. AE, MC, V. Lunch Tues–Sat 11:30am–3pm; dinner Mon–Sat 5:30–10pm. Closed Sun.

The Royal Palm ★★ CARIBBEAN FUSION On the grounds of Ottley's Plantation Inn (p. 520), the Royal Palm is a favorite, serving St. Kitts's most creative and most innovative cuisine. It also has a colorful setting: Gaze through the early-19th-century stone arches to the ocean on one side, and Mount Liamuiga and the inn's veranda-ringed great house on the other. The menu changes daily. If they're available, you may start with roasted vegetable torte or chili-flavored shrimp corn cakes. The lobster quesadillas, made with local lobster, are worth crossing the island to sample. Main courses are impeccably prepared, especially the French roast of lamb and the breast of chicken Molyneux with almonds, country ham, mozzarella, and mushroom stuffing.

In Ottley's Plantation Inn, north of Basseterre, on the east coast. ✆ **869/465-7234.** Reservations required. Main courses $12–$34 lunch, $36–$50 dinner; Sun champagne brunch $36; prix-fixe dinner $66. AE, MC, V. Mon–Sat 8–10am, noon–3pm, and 6–8:30pm; Sun 11am–2pm and 6–8:30pm.

EXPENSIVE

The Golden Lemon ★ CONTINENTAL/CREOLE The food is very good and the service polite in this fine hotel (p. 520) on the northern coast. It's especially appropriate as a lunch stop on a tour of the island. Dinner is served in an elegant, candlelit dining room, in the garden, or on the gallery. The hotel's sophisticated owner created many of the recipes. The menu changes daily but is likely to include baked Cornish hen with ginger, fresh fish of the day, and Creole sirloin steak with a spicy rum sauce. Vegetarian dishes are also available. Dress is casually chic.

In the Golden Lemon Inn, Dieppe Bay. ✆ **869/465-7260.** Reservations usually required; walk-ins accepted if space available. Main courses $38–$49 lunch; fixed-price dinner $55; Sun brunch $30. AE, MC, V. Mon–Sat 7:30–10am, 11am–3pm, and 6–11pm; Sun noon–3pm and 7–10pm.

Marshall's ★ 🎁 JAMAICAN/INTERNATIONAL Jamaica-born chef Verral Marshall infuses the island's local cuisine with his own spice and flair. Installed around the pool area of Horizons Villa Resort, steeply uphill from the Marriott, and built on the foundations of the ruined, long-gone British-built Fort Tyson, his restaurant overlooks Frigate Bay and the relatively nearby island of Nevis. It's quite romantic at night, with beautifully laid tables, flickering candles, and a definite sense of very hip and very romantic charm. You'll get a warm welcome, excellent service, and good food. The fish depends on the catch of the day, but menu items that are usually readily available include crab cakes in rémoulade sauce, seafood "coquille St. Kitts" in a white-wine-and-cream sauce, seared scallops in olive oil with butter-lemon sauce, and roast of duck with raspberry sauce. Prices are a bit steep but, overall, worth it for an evening out on the island.

Frigate Bay. ✆ **869/466-8245.** www.marshalls-stkitts.com. Reservations recommended. Main courses $19–$38. AE, DISC, MC, V. Jan–Apr Mon–Fri 11:30am–3pm and 6–10pm, Sat 6–10pm; May–Dec Mon–Sat 6–10pm.

Serendipity ★★ INTERNATIONAL One of the newest and most-talked-about restaurants on St. Kitts occupies the tidy and well-ordered premises of a modern house in the uplands above the Ocean Terrace Inn (p. 522), on the outskirts of Basseterre. Here English expatriates Pauline Horton and Alexander Jones, from within a yellow-and-blue dining room and an open-air veranda, serve well-prepared food that many locals have highly praised. Menu items include coconut-flavored shrimp, snapper or grouper prepared any way you specify, and duck in red-wine sauce. Lunches are a bit less formal, focusing on dishes that include Caesar salads garnished with your choice of grilled shrimp, or chicken, sandwiches, and burgers.

3 Wigley Ave., Fortlands, Basseterre. ✆ **869/465-9999.** www.serendipitystkitts.com. Reservations recommended. Main courses $21–$45; lunch salads and platters $7–$13. AE, DC, MC, V. Tues–Fri 11:30am–3pm and 6–9:30pm; Sat–Sun 6–9:30pm.

The Waterfalls Restaurant ★ CARIBBEAN/INTERNATIONAL Some of the finest cuisine in Basseterre is found here. The views from the open-air veranda—especially at night when the harbor is lit up—are also some of the best around. We prefer the real downhome island dishes; international specialties tend to be more bland. Dinner might include tasty fish cakes, accompanied by breaded carrot slices, creamed spinach, a stuffed potato, a cornmeal dumpling known as a johnnycake, and a green banana in a lime-butter sauce, topped off by a tropical fruit pie and coffee. The less daring can stick with chateaubriand.

Ocean Terrace Inn, Wigley Ave. (P.O. Box 65), Fortlands. ✆ **869/465-2754.** Reservations recommended. Main courses $17–$35. AE, MC, V. Daily 6:30–10pm. Drive west on Basseterre Bay Rd. to Fortlands.

MODERATE

Ballahoo Restaurant ★ CARIBBEAN Overlooking the town center's Circus Clock and the most charming traffic roundabout in the Caribbean, the Ballahoo lies in the heart of St. Kitt's capital, on the second story of an antique stone building. Open on one side to breezes and a view over the main square, and aggressively unpretentious (it evokes, in some ways, a Caribbean luncheonette), it is one of the coolest places in town on a hot afternoon, thanks to sea breezes. One of the most reliable dishes is blue parrotfish filet, but the house special is sexy, succulent conch in garlic butter. The chef also makes chili, baby back ribs, sandwiches, burgers, steaks, and breakfast omelets. Seafood platters, such as chili shrimp or fresh lobster, are served with coconut salad and rice. For more elegant fare, there's Italian-style chicken breast topped with pesto, tomatoes, and cheese and served with pasta and salad, or the salade niçoise (anchovies, eggs, and potatoes topped with fresh fish). The service is casual. Because of its central location and general appeal, this restaurant also draws the cruise-ship crowd.

The Circus, Fort St., Basseterre. ✆ **869/465-4197.** Reservations recommended. Salads, sandwiches, and *rotis* (Caribbean burritos) $13–$20; platters and main courses $11–$34. MC, V. Mon–Sat 8am–10pm.

Glimbara Diner CARIBBEAN Don't expect grand cuisine from this everyday eatery. Established in 1998 in a simple family-run guesthouse in the heart of Basseterre, it has become a local favorite, thanks to the hardworking staff and down-to-earth food. Small and cozy, and painted in shades of blue, white, and gray, it serves Creole cuisine that varies with the mood and inspiration of the cook. Examples might include large or small portions of the stewlike goat water, pumpkin or bean soup, and several kinds of fried or grilled fish, which might be accompanied by coleslaw or green salad. American-style platters, including hamburgers and hot dogs, are usually served with fries and soda. Ask for a local fruit punch known as *fairling* or the bottled sugary grapefruit drink called Ting.

In the Glimbara Guesthouse, Cayon St., Basseterre. ✆ **869/465-1786.** Main courses $12–$30. AE, MC, V. Daily 8am–10pm.

Reggae Beach Bar & Grill ★ CARIBBEAN This is a great place to hang out during the day, feeding the 600-pound pig, Wilbur, the bar's mascot. Near Turtle Beach, this laid-back bar and dining joint is operated by a fifth-generation Kittitian, Gary Pereira, who is one of the most welcoming hosts on island. He will feed you well without turning you into a beach bum like Wilbur. Kick back on the wooden deck, while dining on locally caught and freshly grilled lobster or else the catch of the day, often red snapper, with a side of rice and peas. Conch fritters and coconut shrimp are also island delights. The bartender shakes up St. Kitts's best mango margarita, and there is live music on Sunday afternoon. If you don't want to hang at the bar, you can rent snorkeling gear, Hobie Cats, and even kayaks.

Cockleshell Beach, S.E. Peninsula Rd. ✆ **869/762-5050.** www.reggaebeachbar.com. Main courses $10–$32. AE, DC, MC, V. Daily 10am–6pm.

Hitting the Beaches

Most visitors to St. Kitts are primarily concerned with its beaches. The narrow peninsula in the southeast that contains the island's salt ponds also boasts the best white-sand beaches. All beaches, even those that border hotels, are open to the public. However, to use the beach facilities of a hotel, you must first obtain permission and will probably have to pay a small fee.

Until the Dr. Kennedy Simmonds Highway (named for the nation's first prime minister)—a 10km (6¼-mile) road beginning in the Frigate Bay area—opened to the public in 1989, it was necessary to take a boat to enjoy the beautiful, unspoiled beaches of the southeast peninsula. To travel this road is one of the pleasures of a visit to St. Kitts. Not only will you see some of the island's most beautiful scenery, but you'll also pass lagoonlike coves and fields of tall guinea grass. If the day is clear (and it usually is), you'll have a panoramic vista of Nevis. The best beaches along the peninsula are **Frigate Bay, Friar's Bay, Sand Bank Bay ★, White House Bay, Cockleshell Bay,** and **Banana Bay.** Of all these, Sand Bank Bay gets our nod as the finest strip of sand.

Both Cockleshell Bay and Banana Bay also have their devotees. Together these two beaches run a distance of 3km (2 miles), all with powder-white sands. So far, in spite of several attempts, this area hasn't filled with high-rise resorts.

A live steel band plays on Sundays from 12:30 to 3pm at the **Turtle Beach Bar and Grill,** Turtle Bay, making this the place for afternoon cocktails on the beach.

For excellent **snorkeling,** head to somewhat rocky White House Bay, which opens onto reefs. Schools of rainbow-hued fish swim around a tugboat sunk long ago—a stunning sight.

South Friar's Bay is lovely, and many locals consider it their favorite. Frigate Bay, with its powder-white sand, is ideal for swimming, windsurfing, and water-skiing.

You may also want to visit **Great Salt Pond** at the southeastern end of St. Kitts. This is an inland beach of soft white sand, opening onto the Atlantic Ocean in the north and the more tranquil Caribbean Sea in the south.

The beaches in the north of St. Kitts are numerous but are of gray volcanic sand and are much less frequented than those of the southeast peninsula. Beachcombers like to visit them, and they can be ideal for sunbathing, but swimming is much better in the southeast, as waters in the north, sweeping in from the Atlantic, can often be turbulent.

The best beach on the Atlantic side is **Conaree Bay,** with a narrow strip of gray-black sand. Bodysurfing is popular here. **Dieppe Bay,** another black-sand beach on the north coast, is good for snorkeling and windsurfing, but not for swimming. This is the site of the island's most famous inn, the Golden Lemon (p. 520), which you might want to visit for lunch. ***Warning:*** If you should be on this beach during a tropical shower, do not seek shelter under the dreaded manchineel trees, which are poisonous. Rain falling off the leaves will feel like acid on your skin.

Sports & Outdoor Pursuits

GOLF The **Royal St. Kitts Golf Course,** Frigate Bay (✆ **869/466-2700;** www.royalstkittsgolfclub.com), is an 18-hole championship course that covers 64 hectares (158 acres). It features 10 water hazards, not including the Caribbean Sea and the Atlantic Ocean, which border it. It's open daily from 7am to 6pm. Greens fees are $150 to $180 for 18 holes. A bar and an on-site restaurant open daily at 7am. The course is part of the St. Kitts Marriott Resort (p. 521).

HORSEBACK RIDING **Trinity Stables** (✆ **869/465-3226**) charges $60 for a half-day tour through a rainforest. You might also get to see the wild lushness of the North Frigate Bay area and the rather desolate Conaree Beach. You must call for a reservation; you'll be told where to meet and offered advice, including what to wear.

SCUBA DIVING, SNORKELING & OTHER WATERSPORTS Some of the best dive spots include **Nag's Head,** at the south tip of St. Kitts, an excellent shallow-water dive starting at 3m (9¾ ft.) and extending to 21m (69 ft.). A variety of tropical fish, eagle rays, and lobster is found here. The site is ideal for certified divers. Another good spot for diving is **Booby Shoals,** off the southeast Atlantic coast near Cockleshell Bay. Booby Shoals has abundant sea life, including nurse sharks, lobster, and stingrays. Dives are up to 9m (30 ft.) in depth, ideal for both certified and resort divers.

A variety of activities is offered by **Pro Divers,** at Turtle Beach (✆ **869/660-3483;** www.prodiversstkitts.com). You can swim, float, paddle, or go on scuba-diving and snorkeling expeditions from here. A two-tank dive costs $105; night dives go for $80. A PADI certification course is $420, with a resort course going for $125. Snorkelers can also sign up for a 3-hour trip costing $50.

Exploring the Island

The British colonial town of **Basseterre** is built around a so-called **Circus,** the town's round square. A tall green Victorian clock stands in the center of the Circus.

After Brimstone Hill Fortress, **Berkeley Memorial Clock** is the most photographed landmark of St. Kitts. In the old days, wealthy plantation owners and their families used to promenade here.

Try to visit the **marketplace,** especially on a Saturday morning. Here country people bring baskets brimming with mangos, guavas, soursop, mammee apples, and wild strawberries and cherries just picked in the fields. Tropical flowers abound.

Another major landmark is **Independence Square.** Once an active slave market, it's surrounded by private homes of Georgian architecture.

You can negotiate with a taxi driver to take you on a tour of the island, costing from $80 for a 3-hour trip; most drivers are well versed in the lore of the island. You might want to make lunch reservations at either the Rawlins Plantation Inn or the Golden Lemon (p. 523). For more information, call the **St. Kitts Taxi Association,** the Circus, Basseterre (✆ **869/465-8487,** until 10pm).

The island's most popular attraction is the **St. Kitts Scenic Railway ★** (✆ **869/465-7263;** www.stkittsscenicrailway.com). In double-decker and air-conditioned railcars, you're taken on a panoramic tour of the most spectacular scenery the island has to offer. The upper level features a spacious, open-air observation deck. The narrow-gauge railway follows the old sugar-cane train tracks, taking in the best vistas of mountains and the Caribbean Sea. You can enjoy a service bar and live musical entertainment. The train is boarded at Needsmust Station. This is certainly the quickest and easiest way to see "St. Kitts in a nutshell," especially if you're a cruise-ship passenger with limited time. The 50km (31-mile) ride costs $89 for adults, half-price for children. Trips last 3½ hours, with departure daily at 8:10am. Sometimes a second daily tour will be announced if business merits it.

If you want to go on a "safari" in the sky, **Sky Safari Tours** at Wingfield Estate (✆ **869/466-4259;** www.skysafaristkitts.com), on the site of an old sugar plantation, leads cable-line treks that zip through St. Kitts Rainforest at speeds of up to 80kmph (50 mph), from as high up as 76m (250 ft.) above the ground. Most tours vary from 1½ to 2 hours, costing $89 per person and $65 for children 14 and under. Tours begin at 8am daily, shutting down around 4 or 5pm when the last cable line comes in.

Brimstone Hill Fortress ★ (✆ **869/465-2609**), 14km (8¾ miles) west of Basseterre, is a major stop. This historic monument, among the largest and best preserved in the Caribbean, is a complex of bastions and barracks ingeniously adapted to the top and upper slopes of a steep-sided 240m (787-ft.) hill. The fortress dates from 1690, when the British attempted to recapture Fort Charles from the French. Admission is $8 for adults, $4 for children.

Today the fortress is the centerpiece of a national park, with nature trails and a diverse range of plant and animal life, including the **green vervet monkey.** It's also a photographer's paradise, with views of mountains, fields, and the Caribbean Sea. On a clear day, you can see six neighboring islands. Visitors can enjoy self-guided tours among many ruins and restored structures, including the barrack rooms at Fort George, which contain an interesting museum. The gift shop stocks prints of rare maps and paintings of the Caribbean. Admission is $8, half price for children. The Brimstone Hill Fortress National Park is open daily from 9:30am to 5:30pm.

You can visit the site where a large tamarind tree in the hamlet of **Half-Way Tree** once marked the boundary between the British- and French-held sectors. It was near the hamlet of **Old Road Town** that Sir Thomas Warner landed with the first band of settlers and established the first permanent colony to the northwest at Sandy Point. Sir Thomas's grave is in the cemetery of St. Thomas Church.

A sign in the middle of Old Road Town points the way to **Carib Rock Drawings,** all the evidence that remains of the former inhabitants. The markings are on black boulders, and the pictographs date from prehistoric days.

Into the Volcano

Mount Liamuiga was dubbed "Mount Misery" long ago, but it sputtered its last gasp around 1692. This dormant volcano on the northeast coast is one of the major highlights for hikers on St. Kitts. The mountain's peak often lies under cloud cover.

The ascent to the volcano is usually made from the north end of St. Kitts at Belmont Estate. The trail winds through a rainforest and travels along deep ravines up 788m (2,585 ft.) to the rim of the crater. The actual peak is at 1,138m (3,734 ft.). Figure on 5 hours of rigorous hiking to complete the round-trip walk.

The caldera itself is some 120m (394 ft.) from its rim to the crater floor. Many hikers climb down into the dormant volcano, but the trail is steep and slippery, so be careful. At the crater floor is a tiny lake, along with volcanic rocks and various vegetation.

Greg's Safaris (**© 869/465-4121;** www.gregsafaris.com) is the most competent and best-accessorized trekking outfitter in St. Kitts, maintaining seven different four-wheel-drive Land Rovers for access to some of the island's toughest terrain. Owner and founder Greg Pereira charges $95 per person for 9-hour hiking tours of remote regions of his island, recommending that participants be reasonably fit and that they carry a dry shirt (the one you'll wear will get drenched with perspiration) and a waterproof bag or knapsack for transport of bottled water and your camera. Hikes go up the sides of Mount Liamuiga ("fertile isle" in Carib) and include a picnic lunch and a rum-based drink or two at the conclusion of the day's hiking. Treks include a guide and running commentary on the island's topography, sociology, ecology, and history. The same outfit also offers half-day rainforest explorations for $65 per person.

Shopping

The good buys here are local handicrafts, including leather (goatskin) items, baskets, and coconut shells. Some good values can also be found in clothing and fabrics, especially Sea Island cottons. Store hours vary but are likely to be Monday to Saturday from 8am to noon and 1 to 4pm.

If your time is limited, head first for the **Pelican Shopping Mall,** Bay Road, which contains some two dozen shops. Opened in 1991, it also offers banking services, a restaurant, a philatelic bureau, and the administrative offices of the St. Kitts Tourist Office. Some major retail outlets in the Caribbean, including Little Switzerland, have branches here. Also check out the offerings along the quaintly named **Liverpool Row,** which has some unusual merchandise, and **Fort Street.**

Associated with the island's burgeoning cruise-ship industry, **Port Zante** is a shopping mall built just after the turn-of-the-millennium directly on landfill that was dumped into what old-timers designated as Horseshoe Harbor. Cruise ships can berth at quays immediately adjacent to Port Zante, in a way that's replicated in Barbados, and whose role model the St. Kittitians copied. The *Queen Mary* stops frequently, disgorging passengers who shop, shop, shop. Port Zante, whose name derives from an ancient Greek myth, is the home of about 60 shops, with emphasis on things that glitter, especially jewelry. Although there are dozens of shops purveying upscale goods, one of the noteworthy, best-established shops is **Linen and Gold** (**© 869/465-9766**), which offers a limited selection of gold and silver jewelry, usually in bold modern designs. But the real appeal of this shop is its tablecloths, doilies, and napkins, laboriously handcrafted in China from cotton, linen, and polyester. The workmanship is as intricate as anything you'll find in the Caribbean.

Ashburry's, the Circus/Liverpool Row, Basseterre (© **869/465-8175**), is a local branch of a chain of luxury-goods stores based on St. Maarten. This well-respected emporium sells fragrances, fine porcelain, Baccarat crystal, designer handbags, watches, and jewelry at prices 25% to 30% below what you might pay in retail stores in North America; the selection is similar to dozens of equivalent stores throughout the Caribbean.

Spencer Cameron Gallery, 10 N. Independence Sq., Basseterre (© **869/465-1617**), is set on a dusty plaza ringed with businesses and residential clapboard-sided houses, near the center of Basseterre, and with an exterior brightly painted in tropical colors, this is a leading art gallery. On display are scenes of St. Kitts and Nevis by Brit Rosie Cameron-Smith, along with works by a handful of other mostly West Indian artists. Rosey ("a good-natured English lass in the Tropics") is well known on the island for her paintings of Kittitian Carnival clowns, monkeys, and figurative work, and she also produces greeting cards, postcards, calendars, and lithographs.

The finest gallery on St. Kitts is **Kate Design,** Mount Pleasant (© **869/465-7740;** www.katedesign.com), set in a carefully restored West Indian house, on a hillside below the Rawlins Plantation (p. 521). Virtually all the works on display are by English-born Kate Spencer, who is well known throughout North America and Europe. Her paintings of island scenes range in price from $200 and have received critical acclaim. Also for sale is a series of Ms. Spencer's silk-screened scarves, each crafted from extra-heavy stonewashed silk.

Island Hopper (known as "The Big Shop of the Little Island"), the Circus, below the popular Ballahoo Restaurant (p. 524), Basseterre (© **869/465-1640**), is one of St. Kitts's most patronized shops, with the biggest inventory of any store on the island. Notice the all-silk, shift-style dresses from China and the array of batiks made on St. Kitts. About half of the merchandise is from the islands.

Caribelle Batik, at Romney Manor, Old Road, about 15km (9¼ miles) west of Basseterre (© **869/465-6253;** www.caribellebatikstkitts.com), is the most unusual factory in St. Kitts. It was built around 1625 as a manor house for sugar baron Lord Romney. For years, it has been used as the headquarters and manufacturing center for a local clothier, Caribelle Batik, whose tropical cottons sell widely to cruise-ship passengers and tourists from at least three outlets in the eastern Caribbean. The merchandise ranges from scarves to dresses, along with an extensive collection of wall hangings and cushions. In 1995 a tragic fire and hurricane completely gutted the historic building. The manor has now been rebuilt and extended. Consider a stopover here if only to admire the 2 hectares (5 acres) of lavish gardens, where 30 varieties of hibiscus, rare orchids, huge ferns, and a 250-year-old saman tree still draw horticultural enthusiasts. Entrance to the gardens is free.

St. Kitts After Dark

The **Ocean Terrace Inn's Fisherman's Wharf,** Fortlands (© **869/465-2754**), has a live band every Friday from 8 to 10pm. It's not "after dark," but the **Turtle Beach Bar and Grill,** Turtle Bay (© **869/469-7611**), on the southeast peninsula, offers a live steel band daily from 12:30 to 3pm; on Saturday, it's beach disco time. There's no cover at either place.

A few other nightspots come and go (mostly go). Currently, islanders hang out at **Bobsy's** (✆ **869/466-6133**), clearly signposted from the roads leading into Frigate Bay. Another local dive, **Henry's Night Spot,** Dunn's Cottage, Main Street, Cayon (✆ **869/465-3508**), has a loyal following, as does the **Oasis Sports Bar,** at Frigate Bay (✆ **869/466-1814**), where a medley of large-screen TVs broadcast current or repeat views of major sports events from the worlds of American or European football, baseball, or basketball. At the Marriott Resort at Frigate Bay (p. 521), the **Royal Beach Casino** (✆ **869/466-5555**) lures gamblers to its large casino with slot machines and games of chance with croupiers. For the high roller, there are private salons. And if you opt for an exploration of the casino within Marriott, you might as well explore a bit, since that resort contains at least six bars.

NEVIS

It's a tough job, but somebody's got to do it. That is, make a choice between St. Kitts and Nevis, the "Sisters of the Caribbean." Although both islands have their charms, we cast our vote for Nevis. Separated by a 3.2km (2-mile) channel from St. Kitts, Nevis, like its twin, is volcanic (dormant, that is) and has golden-sand beaches. But for rustic charm and a certain old plantation bucolia, it is becoming a secret address for celebrities and the discerning travelers who shun overpopulated islands such as Barbados or Puerto Rico.

Nevis is the sleeper of the Caribbean. With its old-fashioned West Indian charm and its intimate island inns, it is a rustic alternative to St. Barts—but doesn't charge those celestial prices. Nevisians will tell you that Kittitians are more interested in the dollar and more anxious for hotel development. To cinch their argument, Nevisians like to point out that overstressed Kittitians take the ferryboat over to Nevis for their R&R weekends and for public holidays.

A local once said that the best reason to go to Nevis was to practice the fine art of *limin'*. To him, that meant doing nothing in particular. Limin' might still be the best reason to venture over to Nevis. If you want to lie out in the sun, head for reef-protected Pinney's Beach, a 5km (3-mile) strip of dark-gold sand set against a backdrop of palm trees with panoramic views of St. Kitts.

Columbus sighted Nevis in 1493. The explorer called it Nuestra Señora de Las Nieves—"Our Lady of the Snows"—because its peak is often shrouded in clouds, making it look snow-capped. From St. Kitts the island appears to be a perfect cone, rising gradually to a height of 970m (3,182 ft.). A saddle joins the tallest mountain to two smaller peaks, Saddle Hill (375m/1,230 ft.) in the south and Hurricane Hill (only 75m/246 ft.) in the north.

Centuries before the British settled the island in 1628, Nevis was a habitat for the friendly Arawaks and later the fierce Caribs. These native populations were replaced with the arrival of the British, who established sugar and tobacco plantations beginning in the mid-1600s. In the ensuing decades, both the Spanish and the French battled the British for control of the island, the British finally winning out in this tug-of-war in 1783 when both Nevis and St. Kitts came under British control. The two-island nation would remain under British control until independence was achieved in 1983.

Nevis's beauty has remained relatively unspoiled. Coral reefs rim the shoreline, and there's mile after mile of palm-shaded white-sand beaches. Natives of Nevis, for the most part, are descendants of African slaves.

The volcanic island is the birthplace of Alexander Hamilton, the American statesman who wrote many of the articles contained in *The Federalist Papers* and who was

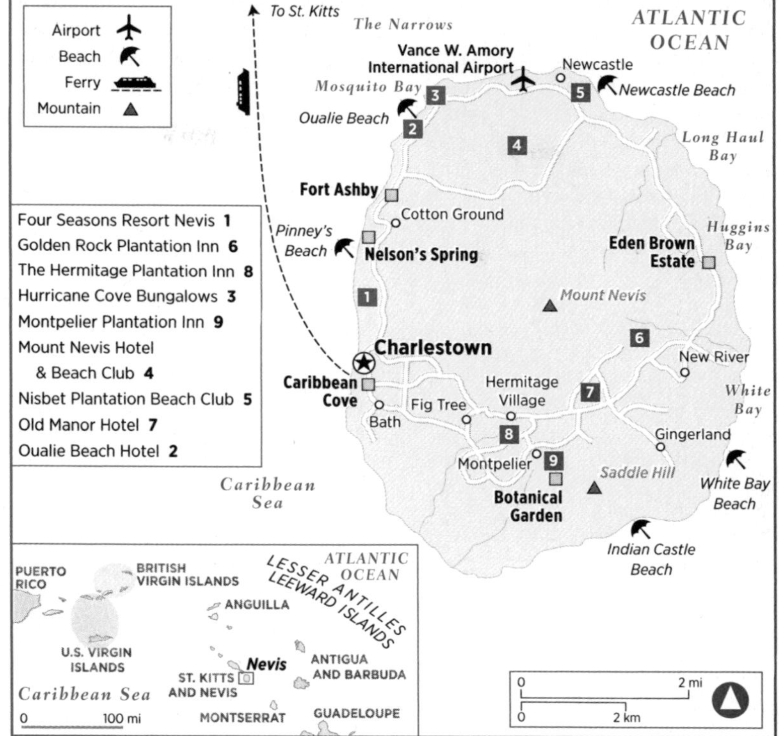

George Washington's treasury secretary. Nevis is also the island on which Admiral Horatio Lord Nelson married Frances Nisbet, a local widow, in 1787, an episode described in James Michener's *Caribbean* (the facts are romanticized, of course).

In the 18th century, Nevis's hot mineral springs made it the leading spa of the West Indies. The island was also once peppered with prosperous sugar-cane estates, but they're gone now—many have been converted into some of the most intriguing hotels in the Caribbean. Sea Island cotton is the chief crop today.

On the Caribbean side, **Charlestown,** the capital of Nevis, was fashionable in the 18th century, when sugar planters were carried around in carriages and sedan chairs. A town of wide, quiet streets, this port gets busy only when its major link to the world, the ferry from St. Kitts, docks at the harbor.

Essentials

GETTING THERE There are no nonstop flights to Nevis from North America. To get here, you'll have to stop or change planes in Antigua, St. Maarten, or Puerto Rico. **American Airlines** (✆ **800/433-7300** in the U.S. and Canada; www.aa.com) has dozens of daily flights to San Juan. From here you can catch a propeller plane to Nevis, arriving on Nevis at the **Vance W. Amory International Airport,** which has a single runway. You can also fly into Nevis from San Juan, Puerto Rico, on two daily flights operated by **American Airlines** (see above). The airport is located on the north side of the island—just 15 minutes outside the capital of Charlestown and less than 30 minutes from all the major resorts, hotels, and plantation inns on the island.

For information on traveling to Nevis by ferry, see "Getting There," under "St. Kitts," earlier in this chapter.

GETTING AROUND **Taxi** drivers double as guides, and you'll find them waiting at the airport or the ferry dock. The fare between Newcastle Airport and Charlestown is $25; between Charlestown and Old Manor Estate, $15; and from Charlestown to Pinney's Beach, $6. Between 10pm and 6am, 50% is added to the prices. Call ✆ **869/469-1042** for more information.

You can arrange for a **rental car** from a local firm through your hotel. Or you can check with **TDC Car Rental,** on the Bay Front in Charlestown (✆ **869/469-1005**), a local outfit that's loosely allied with Thrifty (✆ **800/367-2277**) in the U.S.; or **Nevis Car Rental,** Newcastle, near the airport (✆ **869/469-9837**). Another reliable firm is **Noel's Courtesy Garage,** Farms Estate (✆ **869/469-5199**), which is convenient to guests in hotels east of Charlestown, including Hermitage, Montpelier, Old Manor, and Golden Rock. To drive on Nevis, you must obtain a permit from the traffic department, which costs $25 and is valid for 3 months. Car rental companies will handle this for you. ***Remember:*** Drive on the left side of the road. The road that encircles Nevis has been improved and resurfaced.

FAST FACTS **Banks** are usually open Monday to Thursday 8am to 2pm, and Friday 8am to 3pm. Normal **store hours** are Monday to Saturday 8am to 4pm. Most are closed Sunday.

The **post office** is on Main Street in Charlestown. It's open Monday to Friday 8am to 3pm. Virtually every phone on the island allows you to make international phone calls—in fact, the ease of international access from within your accommodation is so widespread that few opt to travel to the LIME office anymore.

If you need a pharmacy, try **Evelyn's Drugstore,** Charlestown (✆ **869/469-5278**), open Monday to Saturday 8am to 6:30pm, Saturday from 8am to 7pm, and Sunday for only 1 hour, from 7 to 8pm, to serve emergency needs.

There's a 24-hour **emergency room** at **Alexandra Hospital,** Government Road, in Charlestown (✆ **869/469-5473**). For police, fire, or medical emergencies, dial either ✆ **911** or **5391** from any island phone.

The **Nevis Tourism Authority** is on Main Street in Charlestown (✆ **869/469-7550**).

For more information, search **www.nevisisland.com**.

Where to Stay

VERY EXPENSIVE

Four Seasons Resort Nevis ★★ ☺ This hotel is, hands down, the most luxurious, most upscale, most prestigious choice on the island. Even so, discerning travelers have detected a problem or two, especially when conventions dominate or raucous families check in. Located on Nevis's west coast, it's set in a palm grove beside Pinney's Beach, the finest sandy beach on Nevis. On an island known for its small and intimate inns, this low-rise resort, built in 1991, stands out as the largest and best-managed hotel, with the most complete sports facilities (including a fabulous golf course) and even the best children's program. Designed in harmony with the surrounding landscape and an intense devotion to the integrity and well-being of the local ecology, the accommodations offer conservative mahogany furniture, touches of marble, carpeting, and wide patios or verandas overlooking the beach, the golf course, or Mount Nevis. Public rooms are rather formal and more than a bit British in their look and appointments, a kind of Belgravia (London) meets the Tropics, with plenty of deep, comfortable sofas and wide-open views of the gardens. Guest rooms are spacious, with generous closet space, full-length mirrors, luxurious upholstery and fabrics, and king-size or double beds. The Alexander Hamilton and the Horatio Nelson suites are filled with antiques and memorabilia of these two figures.

Pinney's Beach (P.O. Box 565), Charlestown, Nevis, W.I. www.fourseasons.com/nevis. ✆ **800/332-3442** in the U.S. and Canada, or 869/469-1111. Fax 869/469-1112. 196 units. Winter $455–$750 double, from $1,300 suite; off season $345–$575 double, from $845 suite. Up to 2 children 17 and under stay free in parent's room. AE, DC, MC, V. **Amenities:** 4 restaurants; 2 bars; babysitting; horseback riding; children's programs; 18-hole golf course; health club; Jacuzzi; 3 outdoor pools; room service; sauna; spa; 10 tennis courts (lit); watersports equipment/rentals. *In room:* A/C, TV, hair dryer, minibar, Wi-Fi ($10 per day).

The Hermitage Plantation Inn ★★ This much-photographed, frequently copied historians' delight is said to be the oldest all-wood house in the Antilles and was built amid the high-altitude plantations of Gingerland in 1740. Some say it once hosted Alexander Hamilton and Horatio Nelson. Today former Philadelphian Richard Lupinacci and his wife, Maureen, have assembled here one of the best collections of antiques on Nevis. Wide-plank floors, intricate latticework, and high ceilings add to the hotel's beauty. The accommodations are in 12 cozily rustic wood-sided cottages, each evoking an old-fashioned summer cottage in Maine. Many contain huge four-poster beds, colonial-style louvered windows, and the distinct sense that the clients who adore this place have raised more than one generation of children among the trees and verdant landscaping of an inn that's on everybody's list of the most appealing small hotels in the Caribbean. The most luxurious and expensive unit is a yellow manor house on .2 hectares (5 acres) of private gardens with its own ceramic-tile pool, three large bedrooms furnished with antique canopy beds, oversize bathrooms with dressing rooms, a comfortable living room, a dining room, and a full kitchen. Complimentary beach transportation is provided because the best nearby beach is a 15-minute drive away.

St. John's Parish, Nevis, W.I. www.hermitagenevis.com. ✆ **800/682-4025** in the U.S., or 869/469-3477. Fax 869/469-2481. 15 units. Winter $325–$390 double, $450 cottage, $790 manor-house villa; off season $150–$180 double, $245 cottage, $650 manor-house villa. Rates include breakfast. AE, MC, V. Take the main island road 6km (3¾ miles) from Charlestown. **Amenities:** Restaurant; bar; horseback riding; outdoor pool; room service; tennis court (lit). *In room:* Ceiling fan, TV (in some), fridge, hair dryer, kitchen/kitchenette (in some), Wi-Fi (free).

Montpelier Plantation Inn ★★ One of the Plantation Inns of Nevis, the Montpelier stands in the hills, 210m (689 ft.) high, with grandstand views of the ocean. The 18th-century plantation is in the center of its own 12-hectare (30-acre) estate, which contains 4 hectares (10 acres) of ornamental gardens surrounding the cottage units. Admiral Horatio Nelson married Frances Nisbet at this historic sugar plantation back in 1787. Accommodations are generally spacious and brightened with fresh flowers and luxuries like comfortable chairs and dressing tables. Tasteful fabrics in contemporary colors are used. The guest rooms contain bamboo tables and chairs, as well as mahogany writing desks and cedar wall closets. Today the look is one of minimalist chic, as befits the 21st century. Most of the elegant bedrooms have four-poster beds. Service is among the best on island. The staff will even unpack your clothing, press your garments, and put them away for you. Montpelier by the Sea is the hotel's private .8-hectare (2-acre) beach, featuring waterfront dining and beverages in an old Nevisian house.

St. John Figtree (P.O. Box 474), Montpelier, Nevis, W.I. www.montpeliernevis.com. ✆ **888/334-7609** or 869/469-3462. Fax 869/469-2932. 17 units. Winter $520–$580 double, $780 suite, $1,220 2-bedroom suite; off season $320–$380 double, $580 suite, $920 2-bedroom suite. Rates include breakfast and afternoon tea. AE, MC, V. Closed Aug–Sept. Children 7 and under not allowed. **Amenities:** 3 restaurants; 2 bars; babysitting; outdoor pool; room service; spa; tennis court (lit); watersports equipment/rentals. *In room:* A/C, fridge, hair dryer, MP3 docking station, Wi-Fi (free).

Mount Nevis Hotel & Beach Club ★ ☺ Originally established in 1989, this family-owned and -run resort—built on the site of a lime plantation—is on the slopes of Mount Nevis, a 5-minute drive southwest of the Vance Amory International Airport. Small-scale, with touches of genuine charm, it's an inn rather than a full-blown resort, but with absolutely none of the 18th-century references that so richly permeate such competitors as the Hermitage Plantation (p. 533) or the Nisbet Plantation (below). It's known for the quality of its accommodations, for its panoramic views, and for serving some of the best food on Nevis. Near the historic fishing village of Newcastle, it offers standard rooms, junior suites, and, most plush of all, a series of "supervisor suites," the latter with fully equipped kitchens and enough space for at least four guests, making it an ideal family choice. The rooms have ceiling fans and are furnished in a tropical motif, with wicker and colorful island prints. The Mount Nevis Beach Club offers a site directly astride the waters of Newcastle Bay and features a beach pavilion, bar, and restaurant. A shuttle bus interconnects the hotel with its beach facilities.

Shaws Rd., Newcastle (P.O. Box 494), Charlestown, Nevis, W.I. www.mountnevishotel.com. ✆ **869/469-9373.** Fax 869/469-9375. 54 units, 16 with kitchens. Winter $350–$450 double or junior suite, $450 1-bedroom suite, $740 2-bedroom suite; off season $250 double or junior suite, $300 1-bedroom suite, $560 2-bedroom suite. Rates include breakfast. Children stay free in parent's room. AE, MC, V. **Amenities:** 2 restaurants; bar; babysitting; exercise room; outdoor pool; room service. *In room:* A/C, TV/DVD (in some), fridge, hair dryer, kitchen (in some), Wi-Fi (free; in some).

Nisbet Plantation Beach Club ★★ A respect for fine living prevails in this gracious estate house on a coconut plantation, which is the only plantation-style house that lives up to the grace notes of Montpelier Plantation Inn (p. 537). This is the former home of Frances Nisbet, who, at the age of 22, married Lord Nelson. This is the only plantation hotel in Nevis that opens directly onto the beach—a kilometer or so (½ mile) of pulverized coral sand against a backdrop of palm trees. The present main building (that is, the great house) was rebuilt on the foundations of the original 18th-century manor house. The ruins of a circular sugar mill stand at the entrance, covered with bougainvillea, hibiscus, and poinciana. Gingerbread and fretwork-trimmed guest cottages, each with between two and four units, are set in a palm grove. All rooms are brightly decorated and beautifully appointed.

Newcastle, St. James's Parish, Nevis, W.I. www.nisbetplantation.com. ✆ **800/742-6008** in the U.S. and Canada, or 869/469-9325. Fax 869/469-9864. 36 units. Winter $655–$880 double; off season $365–$625 double. Rates include MAP (breakfast and dinner) and afternoon tea. AE, MC, V. Turn left out of the airport and go 2km (1¼ miles). **Amenities:** 3 restaurants; 2 bars; babysitting; exercise room; golf at Four Seasons; outdoor pool; snorkeling; spa; tennis court (lit). *In room:* A/C, ceiling fan, hair dryer, minibar, Wi-Fi (free).

EXPENSIVE

Golden Rock Inn ★ This place doesn't have the polish and glaze of other choices here, but it offers downhome qualities and quiet charm. This former sugar estate, built in 1815, lies in the lush hills only a 15-minute drive east of Charlestown. Set on 40 tropical hectares (99 acres), it fronts a 10-hectare (25-acre) garden. Guests live in fairly spacious surroundings, in a setting of pineapple friezes, island crafts, family heirlooms, and tile flowers. Fabrics are island made, with tropical flower designs. Cottages are scattered about the garden, and each has a four-poster king-size bed made of bamboo or mahogany. Rooms have large porches with views of the sea as well. The original stone tower windmill has been turned into a duplex honeymoon suite (or accommodations for a family of four). The hotel lies at the beginning of a rainforest walk; it takes about 3 to 4 hours to follow the trail round-trip (the hotel provides a map). For the equestrian, horseback riding can be arranged. If you want to go to the beach, the complimentary hotel shuttle will take you to either Pinney's Beach (on the leeward side) or White Bay Beach (also known as Windward Beach), which has good surfing.

Charlestown (P.O. Box 493), Nevis, W.I. www.golden-rock.com. ✆ **869/469-3346.** Fax 869/469-2113. 12 units. Winter $260–$325 double; off season $200–$235 double. AE, MC, V. Closed Sept. **Amenities:** 2 restaurants; bar; beach shuttle; babysitting; outdoor pool; watersports equipment/rentals. *In room:* Ceiling fan, hair dryer, no phone, Wi-Fi (free).

Hurricane Cove Bungalows This cluster of self-contained bungalows is set on a hillside with a world-class ocean view, a far better sight than the complex's rather ramshackle facade. It's located on the northernmost point of Nevis, a 5-minute drive west of the airport. Each bungalow is wood-sided and vaguely Scandinavian in design, with a tile roof and a massive foundation that anchors it into the rocky hillside. No meals are served, but each unit has a full kitchen, and there's a poolside barbecue grill. Each bungalow has a queen-size bed, a covered porch, and a ceiling fan. A freshwater pool is built into the foundation of a 250-year-old fortification, and the beach lies at the bottom of a steep hillside. The three-bedroom villa has its own small, but private, pool.

Oualie Beach, Nevis, W.I. www.hurricanecove.com. ✆/fax **869/469-9462.** 12 units. Winter $245–$410 1-bedroom bungalow, $375–$435 2-bedroom bungalow, $685 3-bedroom villa; off season $165–$325 1-bedroom bungalow, $255–$330 2-bedroom bungalow, $495 3-bedroom villa. MC, V. **Amenities:** Babysitting; outdoor pool; snorkeling. *In room:* Ceiling fan, fridge, kitchen, no phone (in most).

Old Manor Hotel ★ Thanks to its construction around an abandoned sugar mill, this plantation-style inn evokes the aura of a long-gone way of life better than any of its competitors. East of Charlestown and north of Gingerland, at a cool and comfortable elevation of 240m (787 ft.), the Old Manor Hotel has an old-world grace, but because the Florida-based owners aren't always on the premises, it lacks the hands-on attention to detail that you'll get elsewhere on the island. The forested plot of land on which the hotel sits was granted to the Croney family in 1690 by the king of England. The estate thrived as a working sugar plantation until 1936. Beneficiary of many renovations (in the 1980s, much of this place was partially ruined), the hotel is cheerful and historical. Accommodations contain wide-plank floors of tropical hardwoods, reproduction furniture, and high ceilings. Only three of the units contain TVs—but in light of the historic authenticity of the place, many of the guests actually prefer the silence.

Gingerland (P.O. Box 70), Nevis, W.I. www.oldmanornevis.com. ✆ **869/469-3445.** Fax 869/469-3388. 13 units. Winter $290 double, $380 suite; off season $220 double, $280 suite. Rates include full breakfast. Extra person $50–$70. AE, MC, V. **Amenities:** Restaurant; bar; Jacuzzi; outdoor pool; sauna. *In room:* Ceiling fan, hair dryer, kitchenette (in some), minibar, Wi-Fi (free).

Oualie Beach Hotel This complex of Creole-style, congenially weather-beaten cottages is set on flatlands adjacent to the white sands of its namesake, the island's second-most famous beach. It's often fully booked several months in advance by European sun-worshippers who come here for the beach and only because of the beach, expecting very little else. Each medium-size unit is well maintained and simple, with tiled floors and small fridges; a few have kitchenettes. Extras include full-length mirrors, mahogany furnishings, and double or four-poster queen-size beds. The resort's centerpiece is its well-recommended restaurant and bar (p. 539), where doors open directly onto a view of the beach.

Oualie Beach, Nevis, W.I. www.oualiebeach.com. ✆ **869/469-9735.** Fax 869/469-9176. 32 units. Winter $280–$360 double; off season $215–$270 double. Children 15 and under stay free in parent's room. AE, DC, DISC, MC, V. **Amenities:** Restaurant; bar; babysitting; bikes; watersports equipment/rentals. *In room:* A/C, TV, fridge, kitchen (in studios), minibar, Wi-Fi (free).

Where to Dine

VERY EXPENSIVE

Coral Grill ★★ CARIBBEAN/STEAK In the Four Seasons Resort (p. 532), this upscale restaurant with its fusion cuisine is the most elegant, elaborate, largest, and finest dining room in Nevis. Definitely save it for your grandest night out. Decorated in a Caribbean interpretation of French Empire design, the dining room opens onto rows of beveled glass windows on three sides. There's a fireplace, and the walls are appointed with local art. The island's top-rated chefs are in command in the kitchen, turning out marvelous dishes of fresh seafood and exquisite cuts of meat. The island's best selection of hot and cold appetizers is presented nightly, ranging from a Caribbean spiny lobster cocktail with creole mayonnaise to black mussels steamed with chardonnay and fresh herbs. From the char-grill emerges the best beef on island, especially Black Angus with exceptional marbling, a firm texture, and a ruby-red color. The chefs also serve that gourmet favorite, Wagyu beef, named for a breed of cattle originally from Japan. Berkridge pork on the menu is most flavorful, succulent, and consistently delicious. This "Black Hog" type of pork is hailed as the world's finest. From the sea swims line-caught wahoo steak or a swordfish mignon.

In the Four Seasons Resort Nevis, Pinney's Beach. ✆ **869/469-1111.** Reservations required. Main courses $32–$58. AE, DC, MC, V. Daily 6–10pm.

The Hermitage Plantation Inn ★★ INTERNATIONAL At this restaurant, you can combine an excellent dinner with a visit to the oldest house on Nevis, and one of the island's most unusual hotels (p. 533). No other restaurant on Nevis gives as strong an impression of being the extension of a stylish, elegant, somewhat "clubby" private home, and the presence, on-site, of the owners adds enormously to its sense of welcome, stylishness, and cheer. Meals are served on the latticed porch of the main house, amid candles and good cheer. Maureen Lupinacci, who runs the place with her husband, Richard, combines Continental recipes with local ingredients. Enjoy a before-dinner drink in the British colonial–style living room, then move on to the likes of lemon-grass-and-lime-flavored fish cakes with papaya-scented mayonnaise; ragout of snapper flavored with lemon grass and lime; marinated shrimp on black-bean cakes; and a delectable version of cold rum soufflé. One of the social and culinary highlights occurs every Wednesday, in season, when slow-roasted pig elicits many curious comments.

In the Hermitage Plantation Inn, St. John's Parish. ✆ **869/469-3477.** Reservations required. Lunch platters $12–$20; fixed-price dinners $35–$50. AE, MC, V. Daily 8–10:30am, noon–2:30pm, and 7–9:30pm. Go south on the main island road from Charlestown.

Miss June's ★★ CARIBBEAN/INTERNATIONAL This charming venue, midway between the Four Seasons Resort and the airport, is the private home of June Mestier, a Trinidad-born grande dame, and probably wouldn't exist if it had not been for Oprah Winfrey's enthusiasm. While visiting Nevis, Oprah heard that Mestier was the finest cook on the island and arranged a private dinner; after being served an excellent meal, Oprah urged her to open a restaurant.

A dinner in Mestier's West Indian house, which is adorned with latticework, requires advance reservations; some visitors call before they even arrive on Nevis. Guests at these dinner parties assemble for canapés and drinks in an airy living room, then sit down for soup and sherry. The tables hold from four to eight diners, and the silver and porcelain are quaintly elegant and charmingly mismatched. Fish and wine follow. All this is followed with samples of about 20 to 40 buffet dishes that hail from Trinidad, New Orleans, India, and the French isles. Mestier's comments on the food are one of the evening's most delightful aspects. After dinner, guests retire to a lounge for coffee, chocolates, and port. Many visitors find a meal here to be one of the highlights of their visit to Nevis.

Jones Estate, Jones Bay. ✆ **869/469-5330.** Reservations required. Fixed-price 5-course meal $95. MC, V. Wed and Fri beginning around 7pm; dinner served at 8pm.

Montpelier Plantation Inn ★ INTERNATIONAL This hotel restaurant provides what's generally considered the finest and perhaps most interesting dining on the island. You sit by candlelight on the verandas of a grand old West Indian mansion, overlooking floodlit gardens, the lights of Charlestown, and the ocean. We consider it more than just a dining experience, as it incorporates aesthetics and a vivid sense of Nevis's late-18th- and early-19th-century cultural and mercantile importance as well. Lobster and fish are served the day the catch comes in, and the foreign and Nevisian chefs conspire to produce delectable tropical dishes. On a recent visit, the best menu items started with a crispy seafood cake, followed by five-spice duck with a honey flavor and a vegetable-filled mandarin pancake. Other members of our party enjoyed the seared filet of mahimahi with sauce vert and garlic-cream potatoes. Cape Brandy pudding with Chantilly cream was everybody's favorite dessert. There's limited seating for dinner, so try to show up on time. An excellent and well-balanced wine list is available. An additional dining choice with approximately the same menu is the Sugar Mill, which is open only on a somewhat haphazard schedule and only during certain nights a week. Torches line your pathway as you head up to the elegantly decorated mill, with its mahogany antiques and crystal sconces.

Montpelier. ✆ **869/469-3462.** Reservations required. Main courses lunch $12–$35; fixed-price dinner $70. AE, MC, V. Daily 8:30–10:30am, 11:30am–2:30pm, and 7–9:30pm. Closed Aug–Sept.

EXPENSIVE

Bananas Bistro ★ CARIBBEAN Charming and whimsical, this isolated and romantic dining hideaway is reached after a bouncing, axle-breaking detour to the wooded highlands above Hamilton Plantation, about 4km (2½ miles) east of Charlestown. Here, within a tropical garden that's ringed with a fence and a gate, lies a traditional, veranda-ringed Nevisian cottage. Views of the surrounding terrain and the sea from here are fabulous, even though at night, you're likely to see an occasional light within an otherwise isolated, underpopulated landscape. Begin a meal here with a Bertini, the house cocktail (something akin to a passion fruit martini), then move to such entrees as bourbon-soaked baby back spare ribs, Moroccan-style lamb shanks with garlic-flavored mashed potatoes, or any of several varieties of Thai-style curries.

Decor within this Nevisian cottage includes Turkish carpets, exposed stone, and a winning combination of English and Caribbean antiques.

Upper Hamilton Estate. ✆ **869/469-1891.** Reservations recommended. Main courses $25–$40. MC, V. Mon, Wed, and Fri 5:30–9:30pm.

Coconut Grove ★★ FRENCH/PACIFIC RIM This is a hot choice, and its tables are eagerly sought out by discerning palates. Located in a coconut grove on Nevis's beast beach, the building itself looks like a hut from Tahiti. It was the creation of restaurateur Gary Colt and his wife, Karin, whose wine collection is one of the finest in the southern Caribbean, with some 4,000 bottles. You dine under a roof of thatched palm fronds in a rough timbered structure. A crying Buddha emerges from the root of a teak tree. All this is but a backdrop for one of the best cuisines on island. Quality ingredients and first-rate dishes emerge from the kitchen, demonstrated by such dishes as a seafood napoleon with shrimp and lobster in a Madras-curry sauce, or sliced flank steak in a cabernet sauvignon butter sauce with a side of truffle-laced mashed potatoes. You might also sample the chicken breast with a pistachio dressing, a divine marriage. Finish off with crème brûlée, a dessert specialty, although the chocolate almond tart is also sublime. The poolside bar and grill downstairs features live music most nights.

Main Island Rd., Nelson's Spring (off Pinney's Beach). ✆ **869/469-1020.** Reservations required. Main courses $8–$18 lunch, $22–$42 dinner. MC, V. Daily 11am–3pm and 6:30–10pm.

Mango ★ WEST INDIAN At the previously recommended Four Seasons Resort (p. 532), this beach bar and restaurant has the most panoramic outdoor deck for dining in Nevis. The music's hot, and the drinks, especially those rum punches, are among the island's most alluring. Both hotel guests and visitors drop in here for a "sundowner," enjoying the gorgeous sunsets. Since it lies only a short stroll from the golf course, sportsmen also frequent the place. Their favorite libation is a Tipsy Palmer.

The dishes are creative, and spices from the island's fertile soil play a large part in the flavoring. Coconut, mango, and passion fruit also appear in some dishes. Start with such inventive appetizers as pumpkin soup with honey-butter croutons, or else spiny lobster fritters in a Calypso hot-pepper sauce. Some of the seafood is taken straight from the boat into the kitchen. A specialty is a Gallows Bay fish pot, Nevisian style, baked in foil and served with organic vegetables. Baby back ribs appear with a Jamaican rum barbecue sauce. And don't forget a side of green papaya slaw.

Pinney's Beach. ✆ **869/469-1111.** Reservations recommended. Main courses $22–$40. AE, DC, MC. Daily noon–3pm and 6–10pm.

MODERATE

Double Deuce ★ SEAFOOD/WEST INDIAN With its decor of boats and fishing scenes, Papa Hemingway would surely have made this beach bar his local during his stay in Nevis. Mark Roberts trained at the deluxe Montpelier (p. 537) but decided to go it on his own at this jumping eatery on the water. Mark even catches some of the fish he serves himself. Karaoke rules on Thursday night, so Double Deuce can also become your fun spot for the whole evening. The location is half a mile down Pinney's Beach from the Four Seasons. The day's specials are posted on a blackboard menu and are likely to feature line-caught wahoo and snapper. Locals claim the cook's cheeseburger is the best in the southern Caribbean: It's a half-pound of organic beef buried under a landslide of cheddar and served with a secret pineapple-and-wild-honey sauce.

Pinney's Beach. ✆ **869/469-2222.** www.doubledeuce.com. Reservations required. Main courses $12–$40. No credit cards. Daily 9am–midnight.

The Gallipot ★ CARIBBEAN British expats Julian and Tracy Rigby, who sailed around the Caribbean for a while before establishing this place near Oualie Beach, are now among the island's best chefs. Their well-chosen and carefully prepared menu is backed up by a sophisticated wine list. Open only 4 days a week, they have often entertained celebrities, including Meryl Streep. Menu items feature a wide variety of fish that's smoked in house according to whatever comes in fresh that week. Angus steaks, the best on Nevis, arrive regularly from the U.S. and are prepared any way you want them. There's also a selection of spicy curries, vegetarian dishes, and beef and chicken main courses. Desserts are made fresh daily, featuring cheesecakes and such delights as a mocha and chocolate torte.

Jones Estate. ✆ **869/469-8230.** Reservations recommended. Main courses $10–$15 lunch, $15–$32 dinner. AE, MC, V. Thurs–Sun noon–2:30pm and 6–10pm; Sun noon–2:30pm. Closed July–Oct.

Oualie Beach Hotel INTERNATIONAL/CARIBBEAN This restaurant is the centerpiece of the Oualie Beach Hotel (p. 536), the only lodging adjacent to Oualie Beach. The airy building has a bar area and a screened-in veranda just a few steps from the ocean. Every day the chef prepares a creative menu with real Caribbean flair, so you may want to study it closely before ordering. The pleasant staff also makes recommendations. The chef prepares several lobster dishes, and the Creole conch stew is the island's best. Pastas appear frequently, along with some fairly bland international dishes such as chicken breast with rice, fries, or salad. Special nights are Tuesdays, which feature a barbecue surf-and-turf buffet along with a live band; Friday and Saturday nights with another band; and Super Sunday (the last Sun of the month) with steel-band music and beach activities such as the greasy pole. An array of brightly colored rum drinks is available, and you can get a reasonably priced breakfast or lunch here, too.

In the Oualie Beach Hotel. ✆ **869/469-9735.** Reservations required for dinner. Main courses $7–$12 breakfast, $12–$20 lunch, $20–$35 dinner; Tues night buffet $35. AE, MC, V. Daily 7–10am, noon–3pm, and 6:30–9pm.

INEXPENSIVE

Rodney's Cuisine ★ 🎁 CARIBBEAN "I cook from the earth," says Rodney Elliott, an island woman who uses recipes handed down from generation to generation. She keeps her dining room spotless and has flamboyantly decorated it in bright red, yellow, and green. A religious woman, she uses placemats with the Lord's Prayer (in both Spanish and English) printed on them. Actually a stew, her "goat water" is the best on island, with tender hunks of meat and breadfruit simmered in a rich smoky broth. The catch of the day is steamed and served with johnnycakes or *mussa* (a polenta-like side dish made with cassava meal). A plate of her "cook up" will get you chicken, saltfish, and peas and rice along with cold glasses of mauby, a ginger drink made from bark. Another specialty is "breadfruit cheesy," a cross between a cheese soufflé and mashed breadfruit.

Charlestown. ✆ **869/663-1644.** Main courses EC$28–EC$45. No credit cards. Mon–Sat 6:30am–8:30pm.

Hitting the Beaches

There are several fabulous public beaches on the island as well. The best one—in fact, one of the best in the Caribbean—is the reef-protected **Pinney's Beach ★★**, which has crystal-clear water, golden sands, and a gradual slope. It's no accident that the Four Seasons (p. 532) chose this location for its chic and superexpensive Nevis resort. Beaches are public on Nevis, and hotels are forbidden to restrict access. However, hotels can protect their private grounds from trespassers.

Pinney's is just a short walk north of Charlestown on the west coast. You'll have 5km (3 miles) of sand (often virtually to yourself) that culminates in a sleepy lagoon, set against a backdrop of coconut palms. It's almost never crowded, and its calm, shallow waters are perfect for swimming and wading, which makes it a family favorite. It's best to bring your own sports equipment; the hotels along this beach have only limited gear that may be in use by its guests. You can go snorkeling or scuba diving here among damselfish, tangs, grunts, blue-headed wrasses, parrotfish, and other species. The beach is especially beautiful in the late afternoon, when flocks of cattle egrets fly into its north end to roost at the freshwater pond at **Nelson's Spring.**

If you're going to be around for a few days, you might want to search out the other beaches as well, notably beige-sand **Oualie Beach,** known especially for its diving and snorkeling. The location is north of Pinney's and just south of Mosquito Bay. The beach is well maintained and rarely crowded; you can purchase food and drink, as well as rent watersports equipment, at the Oualie Beach Hotel (p. 536).

Indian Castle Beach, at the southern end of Nevis, has active surf and a swath of fine-gray sand. Indian Castle is definitely for escapists—chances are, you'll have the beach all to yourself except for an indigenous goat or two, who may be very social and interested in sharing your picnic lunch.

Newcastle Beach is by the Nisbet Plantation (p. 534), at the northernmost tip of the island on the channel that separates St. Kitts and Nevis. Snorkelers flock to this strip of soft beige sand set against a backdrop of coconut palms.

The beaches along the east coast aren't desirable. They front Long Haul Bay in the north and White Bay in the south. These bays spill into the Atlantic Ocean and are rocky and too rough for swimming, although they're rather dramatic to visit if you're sightseeing. Of them all, **White Bay Beach** (sometimes called Windward Beach), in the southeastern section, east of Gingerland, is the best (especially for surfers). But be careful, as the waters can become turbulent suddenly.

Sports & Outdoor Pursuits

BOATING **Scuba Safaris,** an outfit that operates independently on the premises of the Oualie Beach Hotel (p. 536), offers boat charters to Turtle Beach, which can make for a great day's outing; it costs $65 round-trip (minimum of four people). Although it gives preference to guests of the Four Seasons (p. 532), another good boat outfitter is **Leeward Islands Charters** (© **869/465-7474;** www.stkittsleewardislandscharters.com). The captain, Lennox, also built the boat, a 15m (49-ft.) catamaran called *Caona*. A typical cruise is across the 3.2km (2-mile) passage to St. Kitts, where the snorkeling is better than it is on the western side of Nevis.

In 2007, recognizing that the smooth, unjagged coastline of Nevis does not offer an abundance of anchorage spots for oceangoing yachts, the Port Authority of Nevis sank at least 100 permanent moorings deep into the sea bed off the island's relatively sheltered western shore. A key component of each of those moorings is a 5m (16-ft.) aluminum "corkscrew," which is screwed into the seabed with barged-in equipment in ways that cause a minimum amount of damage to the marine ecology. All that's recognizable from the surface is a bright yellow buoy, a talisman which yacht owners prize, and pay steep rentals for, as a means of providing at least some kind of shelter from tides and howling storms. Most of these buoys lie in 18m (59 ft.) of water, enough for the draft of even very large yachts, which from now on can be moored safely offshore Nevis's northwest coast, in a series of staggered moorings positioned offshore in an unbroken string between Charlestown and Oualie.

FISHING **Nevis Water Sports** (✆ **869/662-9166;** www.fishnevis.com) offers the best deep-sea fishing aboard its custom 9m (30-ft.) fishing boat. The boat holds up to six; a 4-hour trip costs $500, while an 8-hour trip is $1,000. Snorkeling trips are available for $50 per person, including equipment.

GOLF The **Four Seasons ★★★** (p. 532), Pinney's Beach (✆ **869/469-1111;** www.fourseasons.com/nevis/golf), has one of the most challenging and visually dramatic golf courses in the world. Designed by Robert Trent Jones, Jr. (who called it "the most scenic golf course I've ever designed"), this 18-hole championship course wraps around the resort and offers panoramic ocean and mountain views at every turn. From the first tee (which begins just steps from the sports pavilion), through the 660-yard, par-5 18th green at the ocean's edge, the course is, in the words of one avid golfer, "reason enough to go to Nevis." Nonguests of the hotel pay $205 for 18 holes. Rental clubs are available at $40 for 9 holes, or $70 for 18 holes.

HIKING & MOUNTAIN CLIMBING Hikers can climb **Mount Nevis,** 970m (3,182 ft.) up to the extinct volcanic crater, and enjoy a trek to the rainforest to watch for wild monkeys. This hike is strenuous and is recommended only for those in good shape. Ask your hotel to pack a picnic lunch and arrange a guide (who will charge about $35 per person). The hike takes about 5 hours; at the summit, you'll be rewarded with views of Antigua, Saba, St. Eustatius, St. Kitts, Guadeloupe, and Montserrat. Reaching the summit means scrambling up near-vertical sections of the trail, requiring handholds on not-always-reliable vines and roots. It's definitely not for anyone afraid of high places. Information on guides can also be obtained at the **Nevis Historical and Conservation Society,** based at the Museum of Nevis History, Main Street, Charlestown (✆ **869/469-5786;** www.nevis-nhcs.org). **Sunrise Tours,** Gingerland (✆ **869/469-2758;** www.nevisnaturetours.com), is run by a husband-and-wife team, Lynell and Earla Liburd, who offer an unusual assortment of hikes, not just the usual climbs around the slopes of Mount Nevis. They'll take you to little-known areas such as Devil's Copper, New River Spring, and three magnificent waterfalls. Rainforest and hidden ruins are also part of their hikes, which also include trips to rarely visited local villages.

If you're looking for a local to guide you through the logistics of virtually any aspect of Nevis, consider **Top to Bottom** (✆ **869/469-9080;** www.walknevis.com). For a fee that's fair and equitable, they'll accompany you on any of at least a half-dozen walking tours either through downtown Charlestown or through some of the most vertiginous and isolated terrain on the island. Dialogues focus on the island's history, flora, fauna, natural topography, and ecology.

SCUBA DIVING & SNORKELING Some of the best dive sites on Nevis include **Monkey Shoals,** 3km (2 miles) west of the Four Seasons (p. 532). This is a beautiful reef, starting at 12m (39 ft.), with dives up to 30m (98 ft.) in depth. Angelfish, turtles, nurse sharks, and extensive soft coral can be found here. The **Caves** are on the south tip of Nevis, a 20-minute boat ride from the Four Seasons. A series of coral grottoes with numerous squirrelfish, turtles, and needlefish make this ideal for both certified and resort divers. **Champagne Garden,** a 5-minute boat ride from the Four Seasons, gets its name from bubbles created from an underwater sulfur vent. Because of the warm water temperature, large numbers of tropical fish are found here. Finally, **Coral Garden,** 3km (2 miles) west of the Four Seasons, is another beautiful coral reef with schools of Atlantic spadefish and large sea fans. The reef is at a maximum depth of 21m (69 ft.) and is suitable for both certified and resort divers.

Snorkelers should head for Pinney's Beach. You might also try the waters of Fort Ashby, where the settlement of Jamestown is said to have slid into the sea; legend has it that you can still hear the church bells and see the underwater town when conditions are just right. So far, no diver, to our knowledge, has ever found the conditions just right.

Scuba Safaris, Oualie Beach (✆ **869/469-9518;** fax 869/469-9519; www.scubanevis.com), on the island's north end, offers PADI scuba diving and snorkeling in an area rich in dive sites. It also offers resort and certification courses, dive packages, and equipment rental. A one-tank scuba dive costs $69; a two-tank dive, $99. Full certification courses cost $400 to $550 per person. Snorkeling trips cost $50 per person (minimum of four people).

TENNIS There are no public courts on Nevis. Guests at the big hotels play on their courts for free. Nonguests can play on the courts at the **Hermitage Plantation** (p. 533; ✆ **869/469-3477**). Tennis is free for those who visit the restaurant. There's also a somewhat battered public tennis court in Charlestown, immediately adjacent to the Secondary School, which can be used—if the net is up at all—without charge during daylight hours only.

WINDSURFING The waters here are often ideal for this sport, especially for beginners and intermediates. **Windsurfing Nevis,** at the Oualie Beach Hotel (p. 536; ✆ **869/469-9682**), offers the best equipment, costing $25 for 1 hour.

Exploring the Island

It's a good idea to negotiate with a taxi driver to take you around Nevis. The distance is only 58km (36 miles), but you may find yourself taking a long time if you stop to see specific sights and talk to all the people who will want to chat with you. A 3-hour sightseeing tour around the island will cost $65; the average taxi holds up to four people. No sightseeing bus companies operate on Nevis, but a number of individuals own buses that they use for taxi service. Their names are known to the reception staff at every hotel on Nevis, so if you're interested, make the proper enquiries. You can also call **Nevis Taxi Service** (✆ **869/469-5621**) for information.

The major attraction is the **Museum of Nevis History,** in the simple but gracefully proportioned stone house where Alexander Hamilton was born, on Main Street in Charlestown (✆ **869/469-5786;** www.nevis-nhcs.org), overlooking the bay. The lava-stone house by the shore has been restored. The museum, dedicated to the history and culture of Nevis, houses the island's archives. Hours are year-round Monday to Friday from 9am to 4pm, and also on Saturday mid-December to mid-April from 9am to noon. Admission is $5 for adults, $2 for children 5 to 12.

Eden Brown Estate, East Coast Road, about 2km (1¼ miles) from New River, is said to be haunted. It was once the home of a wealthy planter whose daughter was to be married, but her husband-to-be was killed in a duel at the prenuptial feast. The mansion was then closed forever and left to the ravages of nature. Today it's a rather spooky-looking ruin. Only the most adventurous ever come here on a moonlit night.

At one time, Sephardic Jews from Brazil made up a quarter of the island's population, and it's believed that Jews introduced sugar production to the Leeward Islands. Outside the center of Charlestown, at the lower end of Government Road, the **Jewish Cemetery** has been partially restored and is the resting place of many of the early shopkeepers of Nevis. Most of the tombstones date from 1690 to 1710. There's no attendant on duty, and few local residents seem to know a lot about this place. Unless you look very carefully, its location isn't immediately obvious.

One of the island's best attractions is the 4-hectare (10-acre) **Botanical Garden of Nevis** (✆ **869/469-3509;** www.botanicalgardennevis.com), 5km (3 miles) south of Charlestown on the Montpelier Estate. Rainforest plants grow in re-created Mayan ruins on a hillside site overlooking the Caribbean. A retired Philadelphia businessman, Joseph Murphy, has spent some $8 million on these gardens, containing, among other treasures of nature, 100 species of palms from Madagascar, Asia, and Hawaii, along with 70 varieties of orchids. In the Kew Gardens–like greenhouse, you can see rainforest flora and waterfalls. The on-site restaurant, **Martha's Tea House,** operated and maintained by the Montpelier Plantation Inn (p. 533), serves an English tea with scones and double Devon cream. You can also order a ploughman's lunch (French bread, pickled onions, and cheese), barbecue chicken breast, mahimahi, or tuna salad. If you patronize the restaurant or gift shop, you don't have to pay the admission of $10 adults, or $7 children 6 to 12 (free for children 5 and under), to the gardens. The garden is open Monday to Saturday from 9am to 5pm.

Nevis Jockey Club organizes and sponsors thoroughbred races every month. Local horses, as well as some brought over from other islands, fill out a typical five-race card. If you want to have a glimpse at what horse racing must have been like a century or more ago, you'll find the Nevis races a memorable experience. For information, contact Richard Lupinacci, a Jockey Club officer and owner and operator of the Hermitage Plantation (p. 533).

Fothergill's Nevisian Heritage Village (✆ **869/469-5521**), is a collection of historic structures moved to this site, with an old sugar mill as its centerpiece. Among the attractions are a blacksmith's workshop, a rum store, and a cobbler's outpost, along with replicas of buildings ranging from African-style slave huts to thatched shelters once inhabited by the Caribs. The village is open daily 8am to 4pm, charging an admission of $2.

Shopping

For original art, visit **Eva Wilkin Gallery,** Clay Ghaut, Gingerland (✆ **869/469-2673**). Wilkin was the island's most famous artist; even Prince Charles showed up to look at her work. Until her death in 1989, she painted island people, local flowers, and scenes of Nevis life. Prints are available in some of the local shops, but originals sell for $150 and up. You can visit her former atelier, on the grounds of an old sugar-mill plantation near Montpelier.

In a stone building about 60m (197 ft.) from the wharf, near the marketplace, **Nevis Handicraft Cooperative Society,** Cotton House, Charlestown (✆ **869/469-1746**), contains locally made gift items, including unusual objects of goatskin, local wines made from a variety of fruits grown on the island, hot-pepper sauce, guava cheese, jams, and jellies.

Island Fever, Main Street in Charlestown (✆ **869/469-9613**), has a tasteful and varied selection of items that might range from puppets and batiks from Indonesia to caftans, informal ware, steel drums, painted fish, or handmade jewelry. It's closed in September.

Some newcomers develop a fascination for the local postage stamps during their time on island, interpreting them as a combination of nostalgia for the British Commonwealth, pride of independent nationhood, and a celebration of the natural beauty of Nevis. Postage stamps issued under the auspices of the **Nevis Philatelic Bureau** are available for sale at the philatelic office, on Market Street (✆ **869/469-5535**), about a 2-minute walk from the main Post Office (also on Market St.) Especially prized are stamps commemorating the late Princess Diana, Alexander Hamilton, or anything to do with Nevis's flora, underwater fauna, and architecture. Because of their relative rarity (if not in Nevis, then within the world at large), Nevisian collectors' stamps sell for a slight premium over their face value.

A craftsperson worthy of mention is **Kennedy Tyrell** (✆ **869/469-3442**), who sells hand-carved wooden figures of monkeys, birds, pineapples, and other objects from his workshop along the road in Zion's Village, in Zion, on the eastern side of Nevis.

Nevis After Dark

Nightlife is not the reason to visit Nevis. Summer nights are quiet, but there's organized entertainment in winter, often steel bands performing at the major hotels.

Most action takes place at the **Four Seasons Resort,** Pinney's Beach (p. 532; ✆ **869/469-1111**), on Friday and Saturday nights.

Oualie Beach Hotel, Oualie Beach (p. 536; ✆ **869/469-9735**), offers a live string band entertaining guests.

Another Friday night "jump-up" is at the **Water Department Barbecue,** Pump Road, Charlestown (no phone), to help raise money for the department. Tents go up in the late afternoon and meat goes on the grill. Some of the best barbecue chicken and ribs on island is served here.

Wednesday night is all the rage at **Eddy's Bar & Restaurant,** Main Street in Charlestown (✆ **869/469-5958**), which serves the best conch fritters in town. Karaoke and dancing to music spun by an island DJ last way past midnight.

Finally, **Sunshine's Beach Bar,** Pinney's Beach (✆ **869/469-5817**), is an ultra-informal shack perched provocatively a few paces away from the property line that divides terrain belonging to the Four Seasons Resort from the rest of the world at large. As such, the place attracts clients of that überupscale resort. It's appealingly raffish (that is, battered and makeshift)—the kind of place with recorded reggae music, a leashed vervet monkey who may or may not be interested in the cache of bananas the staff provides, and rum-based drinks so strong they're virtually psychedelic. (One of these is the Killer Bee. Try two of them, and you'll know why.) Why does this place have such a distinctive name? It's thanks to the charm and verve of its resident owner, Rastaman Llewellyn ("Sunshine") Caines.

ST. LUCIA

21

St. Lucia (Loo-sha) remains relatively unspoiled, a checkerboard of green-mantled mountains, valleys, wild orchids, and fishing villages. The island has a mixed French and British heritage, but there's a hint of the South Pacific about it as well. Music reverberates throughout St. Lucia, and the savory smells of a rich cuisine waft through Marigot Bay and Soufrière. A favorite stop-off for island-hoppers, yachties and jet-setters, St. Lucia offers volcanic rock beaches, lush fruity landscapes, and a lively nightlife of limbo, jazz, and rum punch.

Things to Do Roll out your towel on the beige sand of popular **Reduit Beach** or the seclusion of **Marigot Bay,** ringed by emerald hills. Try to spot whales off **Vigie Cove,** or dive below the surface at **Anse Chastanet.** The Atlantic trade winds make for challenging windsurfing in **Anse de Sables Bay,** while beginners can try **Cas en Bas** beach at **Gros Islet.** Away from the beach, take a therapeutic mud bath at the sulfur springs of **Soufrière,** discover St. Lucia's agricultural past at **La Sikwe Historical Sugar Mill and Plantation,** or watch butterflies flit about at the **Maria Islands Nature Reserve.**

Shopping In the capital city, Castries, you can stock up on hot sauce, spices, and luscious fruits and vegetables at the bustling **public market,** or bring back pottery, wood carvings, and silk-screened textiles from the shops along **William Peter Boulevard** and **Bridge Street.** Head to **Rodney Bay** for original artworks and antique prints, and **Soufrière** for batik clothing.

Nightlife & Entertainment Hotels and resorts provide the mainstay of local nightlife, with DJs spinning everything from calypso, soca, and reggae to hip-hop, Latin, and rock at clubs and discos. Drink with the yachting crowd and expats in **Marigot Bay,** or dance the night away with the jet-setters at clubs in **Castries.** Friday-night jump-ups are weekly street parties, where rum, reggae, and grilled fish flow. Gatherings in **Gros Islet** and **Anse la Raye** keep it hopping until the wee hours.

Eating & Drinking Creole flavors inspire much of the local cuisine. Taste traditional dishes such as **green figs, saltfish,** and **callaloo** soup along with **curries** and **pepperpot stews.** Fresh foods abound, from fruits like **mangoes, papayas,** and **coconuts,** and fish, including lobster and marlin. Dine on haute cuisine at the higher-end resorts and restaurants in **Castries,** or join the locals in **Dennery** for their Saturday night fish fiesta.

ESSENTIALS

Visitor Information

In the **United States,** the St. Lucia Tourist Board office is located at 800 Second Ave., Ste. 910, New York, NY 10017 (© **800/456-3984** or 212/867-2950). In **Canada,** information is provided at the tourist board at 8 King St. East, Ste. 709, Toronto, ON M5C 1B5 (© **416/362-4242**).

On the island, the main tourist office is at Sureline Building, Vive Boutielle, Castries (© **758/452-4094**). In **Soufrière,** there's a branch on Bay Street (© **758/459-7419**). St. Lucia information is on the Web at **www.stlucianow.com**.

Getting There

The island maintains two separate airports, whose different locations cause endless confusion to many newcomers. Most international long-distance flights land at **Hewanorra International Airport** (**UVF;** © **758/454-6355**) in the south, 72km (45 miles) from Castries. If you arrive here and you're booked into a hotel in the north, you'll spend about an hour and a half traveling along the potholed East Coast Highway. Many hotels arrange transfers to and from the airport, but if not, taxis are available; the average fare is $20 to $85 for up to four passengers. Many visitors now prefer to take helicopter flights from Hewanorra International Airport to their resorts rather than endure the long, stomach-churning car ride. **St. Lucia Helicopters** (© **758/453-6950;** www.stluciahelicopters.com) offers flights between Castries and Hewanorra Airport or Soufrière, costing $145 per person one-way. Flights can also be arranged to the Jalousie Plantation (p. 552), which has its own helicopter pad.

Flights from other parts of the Caribbean usually land at the smaller, somewhat antiquated **George F. L. Charles Airport** (formerly known as Vigie; © **758/452-1156**), in the northeast. Its location just outside Castries affords much more convenient access to the capital and many of the island's hotels. It is a long (about an hour and a half), twisting drive to lodging in and around Soufrière, but you'll pass through beautiful terrain and quaint fishing villages along the way.

American (© **800/433-7300** in the U.S. and Canada; www.aa.com) flies nonstop Monday, Thursday, and Sunday from New York's Kennedy Airport to Hewanorra. American also flies daily from Miami to St. Lucia.

Delta (© **800/241-4141** in the U.S. and Canada; www.delta.com) flies once daily from Friday to Tuesday from Atlanta.

American Eagle (© **800/433-7300** in the U.S. and Canada, or 758/452-1820; www.aa.com) serves George F. L. Charles Airport with nonstop flights from San Juan, Puerto Rico. Connections from all parts of the North American mainland to the airline's enormous hub in San Juan are frequent and convenient. American also offers some good package deals.

US Airways (© **800/622-1015** in the U.S. and Canada; www.usairways.com) flies two times a week from Philadelphia to St. Lucia's Hewanorra Airport.

Air Canada (© **888/247-2262** in the U.S. and Canada; www.aircanada.ca) has nonstop weekly flights to St. Lucia's Hewanorra Airport that depart from Toronto or Montréal.

British Airways (© **800/247-9297** in the U.S.; www.britishairways.com) offers two flights a week from London's Gatwick Airport to St. Lucia's Hewanorra Airport.

Almond Morgan Bay **8**
Almond Smugglers Cove **2**
Anse Chastanet **15**
Auberge Seraphine **11**
Bay Gardens Beach Resort **4**
Bay Gardens Hotel **9**
Bay Gardens Inn **5**
Body Holiday at Le SPORT **4**
Coco Palm Hotel **5**
Coco Kreole **5**
Coconut Bay Resort & Spa **22**
Cotton Bay Village **3**
East Winds Inn **6**
Harmony Suites **10**
Hummingbird Beach Resort **19**
The Inn on the Bay **14**
Jade Mountain Club **14**
Jolousie Plantation **21**
Ladera Resort **20**
Le Haut Plantation **16**
Mago Estate Hotel **17**
Margot Bay Hotel **12**
Royal St. Lucian **7**
Sandals Grande St. Lucian Spa & Beach Resort **1**
Sandals Regency St. Lucia **12**
Stonefield Estate Villa Resort & Spa **18**
Ti Kaye Village Resort **13**
Villa Beach Cottages **7**
Windjammer Landing Villa Beach Resorts **6**

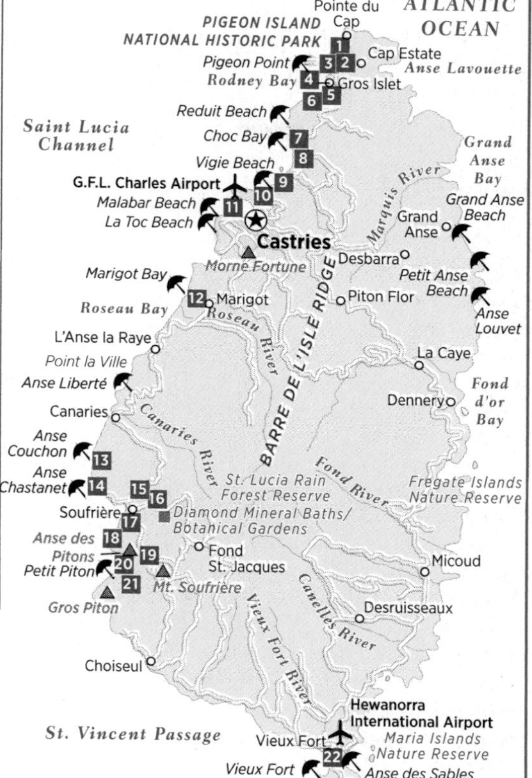

LIAT (© **888/844-LIAT** [5428]; www.liatairline.com) has small planes flying from many points throughout the Caribbean into George F. L. Charles Airport. Points of origin include such islands as Barbados, Antigua, St. Thomas, St. Maarten, and Martinique. On some LIAT flights, you may visit all these islands before arriving in St. Lucia.

Air Jamaica (© **800/523-5585** in the U.S. and Canada; www.airjamaica.com) serves the Hewanorra Airport with nonstop service from New York's JFK 4 days a week.

WestJet (✆ **888/WESTJET** [937-8538]; www.westjet.com) offers nonstop service from Toronto to St. Lucia. Flights head out from mid-December to April, arriving in a Boeing 737 at St. Lucia's Hewanorra International Airport.

Getting Around

BY TAXI Since driving St. Lucia's unmarked, bad roads is rather difficult, a taxi is recommended for all but the most adventurous. Taxis are ubiquitous and most drivers are eager to please. The drivers have special training that allows them to serve as guides. Their cabs are unmetered, but the government fixes tariffs for all standard trips. Typical fares—say, from Castries to Hewanorra Airport—are $90, or else from Castries to Rodney Bay, $20 to $25. Always ask if the driver is quoting a rate in U.S. dollars or Eastern Caribbean dollars (EC$). For more information, call the **Taxi Association** at ✆ **758/454-6136.**

BY RENTAL CAR **Avis** (✆ **800/331-1084** in the U.S. and Canada, or 758/452-2700 or 452-2202; www.avisstlucia.com), **Traders Auto Rentals** (✆ **758/452-0233**), and **Hertz** (✆ **800/654-3001** in the U.S. and Canada, or 758/452-0679; www.hertz.com) have offices at (or will deliver cars to) both of the island's airports. Each also has an office in Castries and, in some cases, at some of the island's major hotels.

Avis's rates begin at $85 per day, and Hertz's begin at $92 per day. You can sometimes save money by booking through one of the local car rental agencies, where rates begin at $60 per day, depending on size. Try **C.T.L. Rent-a-Car,** Gros Islet Highway, Rodney Bay Marina (✆ **758/452-0732**). **Cool Breeze Car Rental,** New Development, Soufrière (✆ **758/459-7729**), is also a good bet if you're staying in the south. Prices are $45 and up.

Remember: Drive on the left, and try to avoid some of the island's more obvious potholes. Drive carefully, and honk your horn while going around the blind hairpin turns. You'll need a St. Lucia driver's license ($20), which you can purchase at either airport when you pick up your rental car.

BY BUS **Minibuses** (with names like Lucian Love) and **jitneys** connect Castries with such main towns as Soufrière, for $2.60, and Vieux Fort ($1.90). They're cheap, but they're generally overcrowded and often filled with produce on its way to market. Buses for Cap Estate, in the northern part of the island, leave from Jeremy Street in Castries, near the market. Buses going to Vieux Fort and Soufrière depart from Bridge Street in front of the department store.

BY HELICOPTER In addition to providing the fastest mode of transport on this island (preferred by such visitors as Harrison Ford), **St. Lucia Helicopters** (✆ **758/453-6950;** www.stluciahelicopters.com) offers the island's most dramatic sightseeing. The 10-minute North Island Tour, costing $85 per person, flies you over Castries, the major resort hotels, the elegant Cap Estate homes, Pigeon Point, Rodney Bay, Rat Island, and the more turbulent Atlantic coast. The longer 20-minute South Island Tour, costing $140 per passenger, flies over Castries, the banana plantations, beautiful Marigot Bay, fishing villages, the lush rainforest, the Pitons, the Soufrière volcano, and even remote waterfalls, rivers, and lush valleys. Another tour, combining both the north and south, costs $175 per person.

[Fast FACTS] ST. LUCIA

Banks Banks are open Monday to Thursday from 8am to 3pm, Friday from 8am to 5pm, and Saturday 8am to noon. **ATMs** can be found at all bank branches, transportation centers, and shopping malls.

Currency The official monetary unit is the **Eastern Caribbean dollar (EC$),** which is pegged at EC$2.67 per U.S. dollar (EC$1 = 37¢). Nearly all hotels, restaurants, and shops accept U.S dollars. Always ascertain which dollar prices are listed. *Prices in this chapter are quoted in U.S. dollars.*

Customs At either airport, Customs may be a hassle if there's the slightest suspicion, regardless of how ill-founded, that you're carrying illegal drugs.

Documents U.S., British, and Canadian citizens need valid passports, plus an ongoing or return ticket.

Electricity St. Lucia runs on 220–230 volts AC (50 cycles), so bring an adapter if you plan to use U.S. appliances. Some hotels are wired for U.S. appliances. Ask when you book.

Emergencies Call the police at ✆ **999.** For an ambulance or in case of fire, call ✆ **911.**

Internet Convenient Internet outlets at Rodney Bay Marina, Gros Islet, include **Snooty Agouti** (✆ **758/452-0321**), **Cyber Connections** (✆ **758/450-9309**), and **Destination St. Lucia** (✆ **758/452-8531**).

Hospitals There are 24-hour emergency rooms at **St. Jude's Hospital,** Vieux Fort (✆ **758/454-6041**), and **Victoria Hospital,** Hospital Road, Castries (✆ **758/452-2421**).

Language English is the official tongue, but islanders often speak a French-Creole patois similar to that heard on Martinique.

Pharmacies The best is **M&C Drugstore,** Bridge Street, in Castries (✆ **758/458-8147**), open Monday to Friday 8am to 5pm, and Saturday 8am to 1pm.

Safety St. Lucia has its share of crime, like every other place these days. Use common sense and protect yourself and your valuables. If you've got it, don't flaunt it! Don't pick up hitchhikers if you're driving around the island. The use of narcotic drugs is illegal, and possession or sale of drugs could lead to stiff fines or jail.

Taxes The government imposes an 8% occupancy tax on hotel rooms, and there's a $26 departure tax for both airports. Children 11 and under don't pay departure tax.

Telephone The area code for St. Lucia is **758.** Make calls to or from St. Lucia just as you would with any other area code in North America. On the island, dial all seven digits of the local number. To access **AT&T Direct,** call ✆ **800/225-5288;** to reach **MCI,** dial ✆ **800/888-8000.**

Time St. Lucia is on Atlantic Standard Time year-round, placing it 1 hour ahead of New York. However, when the United States is on daylight saving time, St. Lucia matches the clocks of the U.S. East Coast.

Tipping Most hotels and restaurants add a 10% service charge. (Ask if it's been included in the initial hotel rate you're quoted.) If you're pleased with the service in a restaurant, by all means, supplement with an extra 5%. Taxi drivers expect 10% of the fare.

Water Water here is generally considered safe to drink; if you're unsure or have a delicate constitution, stick to bottled water.

Weather This little island, lying in the path of the trade winds, has year-round temperatures of 70°F to 90°F (21°C–32°C).

WHERE TO STAY

Most of the leading hotels on this island are pretty pricey; you have to really search for the bargains. However, many of the big resorts here are frequently featured in packages. Once you reach your hotel, chances are good you'll feel pretty isolated, which is exactly what most guests want. Many St. Lucian hostelries have kitchenettes where you can prepare simple meals. Prices are usually quoted in U.S. dollars. Most hotels also add a 10% service charge. (Ask if it's been included in the initial hotel rate you're quoted.)

The All-Inclusives

Almond Morgan Bay ★ ☺ This all-inclusive resort sits beside Choc Bay on an 89-hectare (220-acre) site 4.8km (3 miles) north of Castries. Very sports- and entertainment-oriented, with a well-organized children's club, the hotel is suitable for singles, couples of any persuasion, and families. Sit-down meals in any of the on-site restaurants focus on artfully small portions and an innovative cuisine. The club's core is a wooden building with decks overlooking a free-form pool. The accommodations are in three- and four-story wings, each pleasantly and comfortably outfitted in English colonial furniture. The grounds are artfully landscaped and seem to descend in a funnel-shaped cone toward a complex of swimming pools and a sandy beach. Each features one king-size bed or twin beds, plus patios or terraces.

Choc Bay, Gros Islet (P.O. Box 2167), Castries, St. Lucia, W.I. www.almondresorts.com. ✆ **800/4-ALMOND** (425-6663) or 758/450-2511. Fax 758/450-1050. 345 units. Year-round $2,695–$4,720. Rates are double all-inclusive for 7 nights. AE, DC, MC, V. **Amenities:** 4 restaurants; 4 bars; dance club; airport transfers $14–$75; babysitting; children's club; fitness center; Internet cafe; 4 outdoor pools; watersports equipment/rentals. *In room:* A/C, TV, hair dryer, Wi-Fi (free).

Anse Chastanet Resort ★★★ This is not only St. Lucia's premier dive resort, but it's also an exceptional Caribbean inn. It lies 29km (18 miles) north of Hewanorra International Airport (a 50-min. taxi ride), 3km (2 miles) north of Soufrière on a forested hill, and a 103-step climb above palm-fringed Anse Chastanet Beach. The main building—surrounded by coffee trees and coconut palms—is decorated in a rambling island style. Guests can also stay on the beach in spacious accommodations styled like West Indian plantation villas. Other units, constructed like octagonal gazebos, have views of the Pitons. The large rooms are comfortably appointed with locally made furniture. The resort offers two dozen exclusive "infinity suites," a "resort within a resort," with their own reception area. Rooms have only three walls, to allow for an unobstructed view of the Pitons and the Caribbean.

Anse Chastanet Beach (P.O. Box 7000), Soufrière, St. Lucia, W.I. www.ansechastanet.com. ✆ **800/223-1108** in the U.S., or 758/459-7000. Fax 758/459-7700. 49 units. Winter $495–$905 double, from $955 suite; off season $330–$665 double, from $695 suite. Winter rates include breakfast and dinner. AE, MC, V. Children 9 and under not accepted in winter. **Amenities:** 2 restaurants; 2 bars; airport transfers $20–$80; bikes; gym; spa; tennis court; watersports equipment/rentals. *In room:* Ceiling fan, fridge, hair dryer, minibar, no phone, Wi-Fi (free).

Body Holiday at LeSPORT ★★ This is the most idyllic place in the southern Caribbean for a spa holiday. Even if you don't want a spa holiday, LeSPORT would qualify as a first-rate beach resort. This is an adults-only retreat in a tropical environment. All sorts of treatments are offered, including many different forms of massage and aromatherapy, even yoga and ayurvedic treatments. The rates include daily treatments. Your selection of a bedroom determines the price, ranging from rather standard rooms to deluxe oceanview junior suites. The accommodations themselves come in various shapes and sizes: The best units open onto well-furnished balconies overlooking the sea; others have garden views. What you won't get in your room is a TV set. The cuisine is first rate, especially that served at Tao (p. 563). Greens fees are free at the adjacent St. Lucia Golf Resort & Country Club (p. 564), and all sorts of watersports and outdoor recreation are featured, even such unusual pursuits as archery.

Cap Estate, Gros Islet, Castries, St. Lucia, W.I. www.thebodyholiday.com. ✆ **800/544-2883** in the U.S. or Canada, or 758/457-7800. Fax 758/450-0171. 153 units. Year-round $675–$860 double (per day). Rates all-inclusive. AE, MC, V. **Amenities:** 3 restaurants; 2 bars; airport transfers $90; gym; 2 outdoor pools; room service; spa; 2 tennis courts; watersports equipment/rentals. *In room:* A/C, fridge, hair dryer, MP3 docking station, Wi-Fi (free).

Coconut Bay Beach Resort & Spa ★★★ ☺ On the island's southern shore, and very close to Hewanorra Airport, this sprawling oceanfront resort has emerged as one of the most frequently recommended mass-market, all-inclusive hotels on the island. It features a water park with two four-story-high water slides and a handful of swimming pools which, while not the most dramatic on St. Lucia, are among the largest. There's also a lazy 230m (755-ft.) stream that runs sleepily through the property. Unlike some resorts, Coconut Bay welcomes singles, couples (of all persuasions), and families. There is an array of constant activities, including nightly entertainment from local bands. Spanning 34 lushly planted hectares (84 acres), Coconut Bay is fringed with coconut palms and opens onto Savannes Bay. Rooms are long and narrow, each with at least a partial ocean view (those on the fourth floor have unobstructed vistas). Units also come with separate sitting areas and a private balcony.

Vieux Fort, St. Lucia, W.I. www.coconutbayresortandspa.com. ✆ **877/352-8898** or 758/459-6000. Fax 758/456-9900. 260 units. Winter $280–$325 double; off-season $255–$320 double. Extra adult $45; extra child 17 and under $45–$75. Rates are all-inclusive. AE, DC, MC, V. **Amenities:** 3 restaurants; 4 bars; dance club; free airport transfers from Hewanorra; children's activity center; fitness center; 3 outdoor pools; spa; 4 tennis courts; water park. *In room:* A/C, TV, fridge (in some), hair dryer, Internet ($10 per day).

Cotton Bay Village ★★ ☺ On the northeast of St. Lucia, 18km (11 miles) north of Castries, this property has a series of luxury suites, town houses, and villas. Some of its larger units are available with a pool cottage. Furnished in an eclectic style, the plantation features units with designer kitchens and living rooms, even state-of-the-art entertainment systems. Town houses or villas come with their own private pool and spa. The resort would be ideal for honeymooners, but it also caters to children 3 to 14 with its Humming Bird Kids Club. Its Casuarina Spa and Fitness Center features an outdoor treatment gazebo and even a rooftop restaurant, Heaven.

Cap Estate, Cotton Bay, St. Lucia, W.I. www.cottonbayvillage.com. ✆ **888/237-7915** in the U.S., or 758/456-5700. Fax 758/450-9518. 74 units. Winter $370–$925 double suite, $1,290–$2,715 town house or villa; off season $275–$620 double suite, $415–$1,310 town house or villa. Rates all-inclusive. AE, MC, V. **Amenities:** 2 restaurants; 2 bars; airport transfers $30–$95; children's club; fitness center; golf club privileges; outdoor pool; room service; watersports equipment/rentals. *In room:* A/C, TV/DVD player, kitchen (in suites), private pool (in villas), Wi-Fi (free).

East Winds Inn ★ 🎁 Low-key and classy, and lying a short drive south of Rodney Bay, this is a cottage colony on 2.8 hectares (7 acres) of landscaped terrain. It employs a staff of 10 gardeners, who keep the grounds kempt, and a management team that runs the place like a private club. A series of cinder-block and wood-built cottages are private and well maintained, each containing two separate units. Each is comfortable but deliberately simple, and not as plush as you might expect from a place with such an upscale clientele. The resort's social center is the rock-trimmed restaurant and bar, each of them fronting La Brelotte Bay (also known as East Winds Beach). Both areas are permeated with just a whiff of what you might have expected in Tahiti.

La Brelotte Bay, Gros Islet (P.O. Box 1477), Castries, St. Lucia, W.I. www.eastwinds.com. © **758/452-8212.** Fax 758/452-9941. 30 units. Winter $850–$910 double, $1,050 suite; off season $470–$670 double, $670–$800 suite. Rates are all-inclusive. AE, MC, V. **Amenities:** Restaurant; bar; outdoor pool; free (nonmotorized) watersports; Wi-Fi (free). *In room:* A/C, ceiling fan, fridge.

Jade Mountain ★★ Iconoclastic and intensely theatrical, Jade Mountain is one of the most dramatic and thought-provoking pieces of postmodern design on St. Lucia. Imagine a curvaceous organic form sinuously poised between the base of a rocky cliff and a hilltop stretching down a forested hillside to the sea. Also imagine about a dozen 30m-long (98-ft.) steel and masonry catwalks, each poised in midair between the cliff face and the mahogany louvers of a building. Every accommodation is a suite, each surface of which is sheathed with granite, tropical hardwood, stainless steel, copper, and tilework. Each accommodation also comes with a private infinity pool. The only thing missing within these plush and artfully minimalist suites is a wall separating the suite's interior from the wide-open view of the Pitons, the forested shoreline, and the sea.

Anse Chastanet Beach (P.O. Box 4000), Soufrière, St. Lucia, W.I. www.jademountainstlucia.com. © **800/223-1108** in the U.S., or 758/459-7000. Fax 758/459-7700. 24 suites. Winter $1,000–$2,500 double; off season $900–$1,950 double. Breakfast and dinner $75 per person extra. DC, DISC, MC, V. Children 15 and under not allowed. **Amenities:** Restaurant; bar; airport transfer $20–$80; exercise room; private infinity pool for each suite; spa; shared amenities with Anse Chastenet (see above). *In room:* Ceiling fan, fridge, hair dryer, minibar, no phone, Wi-Fi (free).

The Jalousie Plantation ★★ Perched within a seemingly endless grove of coconut palms in the Val des Pitons, this is an elegant resort for visitors looking for privacy. It originated in the late 1990s, sprawling across one of the most desirable building sites in St. Lucia. The property is so large (130 hectares/321 acres) that vans circulate to shuttle guests around. An ongoing renovation of the headquarters and the tile-roofed villas has added 52 units. Many of the resort's accommodations are in individual villas or villa suites (slightly larger, with separate sitting rooms) that dot the hillside. Villas and suites have private plunge pools. In addition to the villas, 12 Sugar Mill double rooms are in two buildings; they're slightly smaller but still have private terraces, ***Note:*** There is talk of a change of management, which might bring about different policies or even a name change to "Sugar Beach."

Forbidden Beach, La Baie de Silence (P.O. Box 251), Soufrière, St. Lucia, W.I. www.jalousieplantation.com. © **800/235-4300** in the U.S. (for reservations only), or 758/456-8000. Fax 758/459-7667. 112 units. Winter $590–$990 double, from $610–$2,200 villa; off season $240–$590 double, $550–$1,500 villa. Breakfast and dinner $100 per person extra. Honeymoon, dive, and spa packages available. AE, MC, V. **Amenities:** 4 restaurants; 4 bars; on-site disco (Fri–Sat only); airport transfers $20–$80; babysitting; children's programs; 3-hole golf course; health club; outdoor pool; room service; spa; 4 Laykold tennis courts (lit); watersports equipment/rentals. *In room:* A/C, TV, hair dryer, minibar, Wi-Fi (free).

Ladera ★★ The Ladera is an exercise in luxurious simplicity on St. Lucia's southwest end, frequently a retreat for the rich and famous. There are no phones or TVs in the rooms. Outside the town of Soufrière, this hideaway is perched on a rocky, vertiginous clifftop 330m (1,083 ft.) above sea level. Sandwiched between the Pitons, the resort has views that sweep over Jalousie Bay—the most stunning vista you'll find on St. Lucia. Thanks to the prevailing winds, architects designed the place without any wall separating the bedrooms from the views: Clients sleep without air-conditioning, beneath mosquito netting on four-poster beds. Don't come here for the beach—it's a 15- to 20-minute complimentary shuttle ride away. Accommodations are constructed of tropical hardwoods, stone, and tile, and are furnished with 19th-century French furniture, wicker, and accessories built by local craftspeople. All units afford total privacy and have indoor gardens and plunge pools, plus showers. To get a room here in the winter, reserve 4 months in advance. Children 14 and under are not encouraged here, except during Christmas week.

Soufrière (P.O. Box 225), St. Lucia, W.I. www.ladera.com. ✆ **866/290-0978** in the U.S. and Canada, or 758/459-7323. Fax 758/459-5156. 27 units. Winter $615–$1,025 suite, from $1,075 2-bedroom villa suite; off season $380–$810 suite, from $840 2-bedroom villa suite. 5-night minimum Dec 23–29; 3-night minimum Jan to mid-Apr. Rates all-inclusive. AE, MC, V. Closed mid-Sept to mid-Oct. **Amenities:** Restaurant; bar; airport transfers $20–$80; horseback riding; outdoor pool; private plunge pools; room service; spa; watersports equipment/rentals. *In room:* Fridge, hair dryer, no phone, Wi-Fi (free).

Royal St. Lucian ★★ ☺ A fine resort with a deluxe spa, the Royal St. Lucian lies north of Castries. Standing in its own gardens of royal palms and tropical foliage, it opens onto a dramatic lobby. All the accommodations are luxury suites, the best of which have sea views and balconies. There are eight even more spacious suites right at beachfront, each with a private terrace. Some of the units are split-level, with cream-colored tile floors, rattan furniture, and woven rugs. Everywhere you look, the setting is lush. The food is among the best hotel cuisine on the island, and candlelit beach dinners are featured. Jazz can be heard in the chic cocktail lounge, and the spa offers everything from hydrotherapy to herbal body wraps.

Rodney Bay (P.O. Box 977), Castries, St. Lucia, W.I. www.rexresorts.com. ✆ **800/255-5859** in the U.S., or 758/452-9999. Fax 758/452-9639. 96 units. Winter $450–$1,030 double; off season $255–$895 double. Rates all-inclusive. AE, DC, DISC, MC, V. **Amenities:** 3 restaurants; 2 bars; babysitting; children's programs; fitness center & health club; outdoor pool; room service; sauna; spa; 2 tennis courts; watersports equipment/rentals. *In room:* A/C, TV, hair dryer, minibar, Wi-Fi (free).

Sandals Grande St. Lucian Spa & Beach Resort ★★ This is the best accessorized of the three Sandals resorts on island. The luxury resort lies adjacent to the causeway on the northern tip of St. Lucia, linking the "mainland" with Pigeon Island, with the Caribbean Sea on one side and the Atlantic Ocean on the other. Set on a landscaped 1-hectare (2½-acre) lagoon, the megaresort occupies a site 10km (6¼ miles) northwest of Castries at Rodney Bay. With a private golden sandy beach, the most lavish lagoon-style swimming pool on the island, a state-of-the-art spa, and a choice of six restaurants, many find it hard to tear themselves away from the grounds. Even the least expensive bedrooms are spacious, with antique reproductions in an English colonial plantation style. The fourth-floor rooms have better views, service, and space, and are more comfortable overall. For the ultimate in luxury, ask for one of the two dozen "swim-up" units with their own free-form pools and terraces.

Pigeon Island Causeway, Gros Islet, St. Lucia. W.I. www.sandals.com. ✆ **888/726-3257** in the U.S., or 758/455-2000. Fax 758/455-2001. 301 units. Winter $3,865–$5,755 double, from $7,350 suite; off season $3,300–$5,445 double, from $7,350 suite. Rates are double all-inclusive for 7 days. AE, DISC, MC, V. Children not accepted. **Amenities:** 5 restaurants; 12 bars; night club; free airport transfers; exercise room; golf privileges; 5 outdoor pools; room service; spa; 4 tennis courts (lit); watersports equipment/rentals. *In room:* A/C, TV, hair dryer, Internet ($15 per day).

Sandals Regency St. Lucia Golf Resort & Spa ★★ The Sandals chain opened this clone of its all-inclusive formula in 1993 on a forested 85-hectare (210-acre) peninsula whose highest altitudes slope steeply down to the sea. Although not as spiffy as the more cutting-edge (and custom-built) Sandals Grande St. Lucian in the tourist zone at Rodney Bay, the Regency nonetheless claims elegant antecedents, having originally been built as St. Lucia's first large-scale resort, the Cunard La Toc. Catering to couples regardless of sexual preference and with lots of on-site entertainment, the hotel is near Castries, a few steps from St. Lucia's major golf course. The resort's centerpiece is a gazebo-fringed pool that incorporates two waterfalls, a swim-up bar, and a dining pavilion. Larger-than-expected guest rooms contain king-size four-poster beds with mahogany headboards, and balconies or patios.

La Toc Rd. (P.O. Box 399), Castries, St. Lucia, W.I. www.sandals.com. ✆ **888/726-3257** in the U.S., or 758/452-3081. Fax 758/453-7089. 331 units. Winter $2,610–$3,760 double, $5,355 suite; off season $2,730–$3,950 double; $4,900 suite. Rates are double all-inclusive for 7 days. AE, DISC, MC, V. Children 17 and under not allowed. **Amenities:** 7 restaurants; 10 bars (2 swim-up); nightclub; free airport transfers; 9-hole golf course; health club; 4 outdoor pools; room service; spa; 5 tennis courts (lit); watersports equipment/rentals. *In room:* A/C, TV, hair dryer, Internet ($15 per day).

Smugglers Cove ★ ☺ This village-style, all-inclusive resort lies on a 24-hectare (59-acre) estate with a sandy beach on the northwest coast of St. Lucia, fronting a lovely bay. Millions of dollars have been poured into its renovations, whose major features are the best tennis courts on island at the St. Lucia Racquet Club and the best children's program. Whether you rave or rant about your bedroom will depend on your room assignment, as accommodations come in five different categories, ranging from fairly simple yet comfortable units to better equipped, more spacious, and better furnished rooms. The location is adjacent to the St. Lucia Golf Resort and Country Club (p. 564), where guests of Smugglers get three free 18-hole rounds of golf. The place is a bustling beehive of activity and may not be suitable for those seeking a tranquil retreat. There is a vast array of land activities and watersports, and the restaurants offer a varied cuisine. There is also live entertainment nightly.

Smugglers Cove, Cap Estate, Gros Islet, St. Lucia, W.I. www.smugglerscove.com. ✆ **758/450-0551.** Fax 758/450-8625. 360 units. Year-round $2,575–$3,185 per person. Rates all-inclusive for 7 nights. AE, DC, MC, V. **Amenities:** 4 restaurants; 4 bars; airport transfer $100; children's program; gym; Internet; 6 outdoor pools; room service; spa; watersports equipment/rentals. *In room:* A/C, TV, hair dryer, Wi-Fi (free).

Expensive

Calabash Cove Resort & Spa ★★ Romance is in the air at this luxurious beachfront boutique resort and spa, set on a hillside along the private Bonaire Bay Accommodations offer private balconies with views; from some units, you can even see Martinique in the distance to the north. Bedrooms are elegantly furnished and quite stylish, and are rented in three different categories—water's-edge cottages, swim-up junior suites, and oceanview junior suites. The Ti Spa, Fitness Center, and Beauty Parlor adjoin "Sweetwaters," the resort's 100-foot infinity-edge designer pool. On-site is the Windsong, a restaurant opening onto panoramic water views and featuring seasonally inspired dishes made from local ingredients whenever possible. Live island music is often heard in the convivial C-Bar. All accommodations offer a private Jacuzzi, including secluded plunge pools, outdoor rain showers, and a hammock for those lazy island days.

Bonaire Estate, Marisule, Gros Islet, St. Lucia, W.I. www.calabashcove.com. ✆ **758/456-3500.** Fax 758/450-4603. 26 units. Winter $425–$1,055 double; off season $370–$775 double. AE, MC, V. **Amenities:** Restaurant; bar; concierge; kayaks; outdoor pool; room service. *In room:* A/C, TV, hair dryer, Wi-Fi (free).

Marigot Bay Hotel ★★ Splashy and hedonistic, this sprawling resort 8km (5 miles) south of Castries opens onto what author James Michener called "the most beautiful bay in the Caribbean." It occupies a landscaped 3-hectare (7½-acre) site that stands upward from a marina and across the water, a 5-minute ferryboat ride to the nearest good beach. The bulky timbering, dark-stained wooden sheathing and the stalwart masonry foundations evoke alpine Europe more than the Caribbean. Indonesian four-poster beds and dark-wood furnishings fill the rooms, each with big bathrooms with walk-in "drench shower." Suites come with full kitchens and living rooms, and half of them also have plunge pools. The 57 suites can be subdivided into 124 conventional double rooms.

Marigot Bay (P.O. Box MG7227), Castries, St. Lucia, W.I. www.discoverystlucia.com. ✆ **877/384-8037** in the U.S. or Canada, or 758/458-5300. Fax 758/458-5299. 122 units. Winter $340–$815 double, $490–$2,150 suite; off season $275–$915 double, from $525 suite. AE, MC, V. **Amenities:** 3 restaurants and snack bars; 3 bars; babysitting; 2 outdoor pools; room service; spa; watersports equipment/rentals. *In room:* A/C, TV, DVD player (in some), hair dryer, kitchen, minibar, Wi-Fi (free).

Stonefield Estate Villa Resort & Spa ★ 🎁 Nestled at the base of Petit Piton, this former cocoa plantation is for escapists. In the southwestern part of the island, it stands on its own 10 hectares (25 acres), complete with a nature trail and some of the island's most striking panoramas, lying near the little fishing village of Soufrière, and close enough to the Jalousie Plantation that Stonefield guests can use the beach there, a free 5-minute shuttle ride away. Each of the on-site cottages has its own tropic-toned color scheme, character, privacy, and rambling verandas; each is surrounded with forested greenery. The estate here has one of the island's oldest archeological artifacts, a petroglyph from 350 B.C. Each accommodation comes with antiques, high ceilings, and fully furnished kitchens. Villas range in size from one to three bedrooms.

Stonefield Villas (P.O. Box 228), Soufrière, St. Lucia, W.I. www.stonefieldvillas.com. ✆ **758/459-7037.** Fax 758/459-5550. 17 units. Winter from $495 1-bedroom villa, from $550 2-bedroom villa, from $860 3-bedroom villa; off season from $340 1-bedroom villa, from $665 2-bedroom villa, from $770 3-bedroom villa. MC, V. Children 4 and under not allowed. **Amenities:** Restaurant; bar; airport transfers $70–$90; babysitting; outdoor pool; room service; snorkeling. *In room:* A/C (in 8 units), kitchen, no phone, Wi-Fi (free).

Ti Kaye Village Resort ★★ 🎁 It's special, it's fun, and there's nothing like it on St. Lucia. An elite, intimate retreat, it sprawls across a clifftop overlooking the Caribbean and evokes a laid-back Creole village between Castries and Soufrière. A hideaway, it stands on a bit more than 6 hectares (15 acres) of lushly planted grounds. The resort offers beautifully furnished and comfortable bedrooms in individual cottages trimmed in fretwork, or else a dozen units in somewhat less ornate and less private duplex cottages. Each accommodation comes with a spacious porch with a hammock. Bedrooms are furnished with four-posters along with a private open-air garden shower, and 11 of the accommodations (a third of the total) have their own plunge pool. A wooden staircase, 167 steps down, leads to a secluded cove of white sands.

Anse Cochon (P.O. Box GM669), St. Lucia, W.I. www.tikaye.com. ✆ **758/456-8101.** Fax 758/456-8105. 33 units. Winter $280–$490 double; off season $190–$350 double. Rates include full breakfast. AE, DC, MC, V. Children 11 and under not allowed. **Amenities:** 2 restaurants; bar; free airport transfers; exercise room; outdoor pool; watersports equipment/rentals. *In room:* A/C, CD player, fridge, hair dryer, MP3 docking station, Wi-Fi (free).

Windjammer Landing Villa Beach Resort ★ ☺ A sprawling cluster of villas, this bustling resort opening onto a beautiful bay is spread across 22 tropical hectares (54 acres) north of Reduit Beach, about a 15-minute drive north of Castries. Although it's one of the largest resorts on island, it nonetheless is a tranquil and luxurious retreat. Windjammer draws both honeymooners, who occupy the more secluded villas, and families with children. The resort was designed with a vaguely Andalusian/Moorish motif, heavily influenced by Caribbean themes; tropical colors predominate, with wicker and rattan furniture. White villas climb a forested hillside above a 305m (1,000-ft.) stretch of white-sandy beach. This is an all-suite/villa resort (the villas have private plunge pools). The roomy villas offer separate living and dining rooms, plus full kitchens. All bedrooms open onto sun terraces. The resort also contains more restaurants per capita than most of its competitors.

Labrelotte Bay (P.O. Box 1504), Castries, St. Lucia, W.I. www.windjammer-landing.com. ✆ **877/522-0722** in the U.S., or 758/456-9000. Fax 758/452-9454. Winter $250–$400 double, $460 1-bedroom villa, $675–$820 2-bedroom villa; off season $180–$200 double, $250 1-bedroom villa, $480–$700 2-bedroom villa. AE, DISC, MC, V. **Amenities:** 5 restaurants; 4 bars; airport transfers $25–$180; babysitting; children's programs; exercise room; Jacuzzi; 4 outdoor pools; room service; 2 tennis courts (lit); watersports equipment/rentals. *In room:* A/C, ceiling fan, TV, fridge, hair dryer, Internet (free), kitchen (only in the villas), minibar.

Moderate

Bay Gardens Beach Resort ★ This hotel is grander, plusher, and closer to the beach than its older sister, the also-recommended Bay Gardens Hotel (p. 558), with which it shares the same owners. Rated as a four-star deluxe property, it opened in 2007 with a configuration of rooms that could, depending on how the interior partitions were arranged, contain either 72 conventional bedrooms or 36 one-bedroom suites. Both hotels are owned by Berthia Parle, an imposing matriarch who's often prominently featured in the press as a kind of "voice" during St. Lucian elections. The compound's central core is painted in tones of lime and tangerine, and arranged around a convivial set of swimming pools, both of them adjacent to the "wider" end of Reduit Beach. Inside, rooms contain a mixture of Caribbean, postmodern, and tropical colors and furnishings.

Reduit Beach, Rodney Bay Village, Gros Islet, St. Lucia, W.I. www.baygardensbeachresort.com. ✆ **877/620-3200** or 758/457-8500. Fax 758/457-8400. 72 units. Mid-Dec to May $185–$470 double, from $255 1-bedroom suite; off season $155–$415 double, from $225 1-bedroom suite. AE, MC, V. **Amenities:** 2 restaurants; 3 bars; deli; Jacuzzi; outdoor pool; scuba diving. *In room:* A/C, TV/DVD, CD player, fridge, hair dryer, kitchen (in suites), Wi-Fi (free).

Coco Kreole At Rodney Bay, one of the most scenic parts of St. Lucia, this greatly expanded hotel is an affiliate of Coco Palm (see above). Reduit Beach, one of the best on island, lies only a 5-minute walk from the property. The government-rated four-star boutique hotel blends classic French Caribbean Creole decor with modern amenities. Bedrooms are handsomely appointed in a breezy Caribbean style. A regional island cuisine is a feature of the on-site Ti Bananne Caribbean Bistro.

Rodney Bay, St. Lucia, W.I. www.cocokreole.com. ✆ **877/655-2626** or 758/456-2800. Fax 758/452-0773. 20 units. Winter $145–$290 double; off season $125–$280 double. Rates include continental breakfast. AE, DC, MC, V. **Amenities:** Bar; outdoor pool; room service. *In room:* A/C, TV, CD player, fridge, hair dryer, MP3 docking station, Wi-Fi (free).

Coco Palm Hotel ★ Perched on a grassy terrace above Reduit Beach, Coco Palm offers low-key and affordable chic within a Dutch colonial decor. It's the latest creation of Caribbean guru Allen Chastanet, who co-founded the Island Outpost group that also operates Coco Kreole (see below). Rooms are spread across a three-story building in candy colors of lemon and lime. Of special note here are seven "swim-up rooms," with a private terrace linked to the hotel's serpentine pool. The bedrooms and suites are decorated with plantation-style furniture, local paintings, and glass-walled showers. The top-floor suites open onto roof decks with views of the village restaurants.

Rodney Bay Blvd., Rodney Bay Village (P.O. Box GM605). St. Lucia, W.I. www.coco-resorts.com. ✆ **877/655-2626** in the U.S., or 758/456-2800. Fax 758/452-0733. 80 units. Winter $155–$370 double, $325–$370 suite; off season $125–$280 double, $280–$330 suite. AE, MC, V. **Amenities:** Indoor/outdoor restaurant/bar; outdoor pool. *In room:* A/C, TV, fridge, hair dryer, MP3 docking station, Wi-Fi (free).

Harmony Suites This complex of two-story buildings offers well-maintained accommodations at reasonable rates, a short walk from one of the island's finest beaches at Reduit. The suites—decorated in rattan, wicker, and florals—sit adjacent to a saltwater lagoon. Each unit offers a patio or balcony with views of moored yachts, the lagoon, and surrounding hills. Those on the top floor have more privacy. All suites, except the VIP/honeymoon units, have sofa beds. Each VIP suite features a double Jacuzzi, a four-poster queen-size bed on a pedestal, a sun deck, white rattan furnishings, and a bidet. Eight of the suites contain kitchenettes, complete with beverage makers, fridges, and wet bars—ideal for families on a budget.

Rodney Bay Lagoon (P.O. Box 155), Castries, St. Lucia, W.I. www.harmonysuites.com. ✆ **888/790-5264** in the U.S., or 758/452-8756. Fax 758/452-8677. 30 units. Winter $180–$335 suite; off season $135–$265 suite. Extra person $35. AE, MC, V. Children 11 and under not allowed. **Amenities:** Restaurant; bar; outdoor pool; room service. *In room:* A/C, TV, hair dryer, kitchenette (in some), minibar, Wi-Fi (free).

The Inn on the Bay This small-scale inn perched 90m (295 ft.) above the waters of Marigot Bay makes for a romantic escape. It's the creative statement of Montréal-born Normand Viau and his wife, Louise Boucher. Abandoning careers as a lawyer and social worker, respectively, they designed the hotel themselves, modeling its blue roof and veranda-ringed style on the island's plantation-house tradition. Today the centerpiece of their establishment is an open-air terrace, site of a small pool and semiprivate dinners available only to hotel guests. Bedrooms, with 3m (9¾-ft.) ceilings, are spacious, comfortably furnished, and airy. Each has a ceiling fan and ample windows for cross-ventilation.

Seaview Ave., Marigot Bay (P.O. Box RB2377), Castries, St. Lucia, W.I. www.saint-lucia.com. ✆ **758/451-4260.** Fax 928/438-3828. 5 units. Winter $215 double; off season $175 double. Rates include breakfast. MC, V. Children 17 and under not allowed. **Amenities:** Breakfast room; outdoor pool; room service. *In room:* Ceiling fan, fridge, hair dryer, kitchenette, no phone.

La Haut Resort ★★ If you're adventurous, you can skip all the fancy resorts recommended and stay on a 21-hectare (52-acre) working plantation 2.4km (1½ miles) from the town of Soufrière, nestled on a lush mountain on the west coast. In a former life, the estate was a cocoa and coconut plantation, but today it is a farm growing fruits and vegetables, many of the ingredients plucked from the fields to appear on the hotel's menus. Everything from oranges to breadfruit, from soursops to cashew nuts, flourish here. Guests stay either in the century-old main house or in a guest cottage converted from a copra house. From the estate, panoramic views of the Pitons unfold. Four of the units offer standard comfort, the rest being more luxurious, but all are inviting. The open-air restaurant, with its vista, serves both Creole and international dishes, everything from fresh lobster to the catch of the day (often flying fish).

Soufrière (P.O. Box 304), St. Lucia. W.I. www.lahaut.com. © **888/790-5264** in the U.S., or 758/459-7008. Fax 758/459-5975. 16 units. Winter $125–$275 double, $375 cottage for 4; off season $90–$150 double, $180 cottage for 4. AE, DC, DISC, MC, V. **Amenities:** Restaurant; bar; 2 outdoor pools. *In room:* Ceiling fan, fridge, no phone, Wi-Fi (free).

Mago Estate Hotel ★ This is a true Caribbean Shangri-La, ideal for a honeymoon. Just above the fishing village of Soufrière and overlooking the Pitons, this glamorous little inn is run by German-born Peter Gloger. A 5-minute walk from the beach, the property is surrounded by tropical trees, including *mago* (patois for mango), mahogany, papaya, *maracuya* (passion fruit), and banana. Each of the accommodations has only three walls; the other side of the room is open to a view of the mountains and sea. Guests sleep in four-poster beds underneath ceilings of painted clouds, with mosquito netting for protection from insects. Each unit comes with a spacious private terrace. The most desirable units are four large bedrooms with teakwood furnishings or handcrafted antiques, along with plunge pools, hammocks, and large sliding doors opening to the terrace and pool.

Soufrière (P.O. Box 247), St. Lucia, W.I. www.magohotel.com. © **758/459-5880.** Fax 758/459-7352. 18 units. Winter $250–$350 double, $390–$775 suite; off season $200–$280 double, $312–$620 suite. Rates include breakfast and beach shuttle service. AE, MC, V. **Amenities:** Dining room; bar; outdoor pool; room service. *In room:* A/C (in some), fridge, minibar, no phone, Wi-Fi (in suites, free).

Villa Beach Cottages ★ The charm of this place derives from its small scale and its personalized sense of intimacy. The location is at the northern end of St. Lucia, 6.4km (4 miles) from Castries. Between the beach and the coastal road is a postmodern row of gingerbread-adorned town houses, each state of the art, with a balcony overlooking the water. Cottages are rentable for self-catering clients who prefer to spend quiet days reading and swimming, and who usually cook their own meals on-site. Kitchens within each unit are better and more contemporary than those within many modern U.S. condos in, say, Florida, and decor is well maintained and comfortable. There's no restaurant on-site, but a "resident chef" will, with 24 hours advance warning, arrive to prepare meals.

John Compton Hwy., Choc Bay (P.O. Box 129), Castries, St. Lucia, W.I. www.villabeachcottages.com. © **758/450-2884.** Fax 758/450-4529. 20 units. Winter $200–$350 double; off season $190–$285 double. AE, DISC, MC, V. **Amenities:** Outdoor pool. *In room:* A/C, hair dryer, kitchen.

Inexpensive

Auberge Seraphine This two-story, 1990s-era, concrete-sided building painted cerulean blue and white is a 15-minute walk from Vigie Beach, overlooking the marina and the harbor of Castries. Owned and operated by the St. Lucia–born Joseph family, whose hotel skills were honed during a long sojourn in England, the hotel offers well-maintained but simple accommodations. They're generally spacious and often decorated with bright colors and tropical prints. Most activities surround an open terrace whose surface is sheathed with terra-cotta tiles ringing a small round-sided pool. Don't expect too many extras, as the place's charm derives from its simplicity.

Vieille Bay (P.O. Box 390), Castries, St. Lucia, W.I. www.aubergeseraphine.com. © **758/453-2073.** Fax 758/451-7001. 28 units. Year-round $120–$140 double. AE, MC, V. **Amenities:** Restaurant; bar; outdoor pool; room service. *In room:* A/C, TV, hair dryer, Wi-Fi (free).

Bay Gardens Hotel ★ This hotel, which is not to be confused with its better-equipped and spiffier twin, the Bay Gardens Beach Resort (p. 556), offers one of the best values, as well as some of the best service, on the island. It's not right on the sands, but Reduit Beach, one of St. Lucia's finest, is a 5-minute walk or a complimentary 2-minute shuttle ride away. Bay Gardens opens onto a large atrium lobby with a designer fountain pool and bamboo furnishings. The medium-size bedrooms in vivid florals contain a terrace or balcony, and tropical art and accessories. Families might rent one of the eight apartments, each a self-contained unit with a kitchenette. Look for weekly rum punches, barbecues, Caribbean buffets, and live music on occasion.

Rodney Bay (P.O. Box 1892), Castries, St. Lucia. W.I. www.baygardenshotel.com. ✆ **877/620-3200** in the U.S., or 758/457-8007. Fax 758/452-9747. 89 units. Winter $110–$135 double, $140–$280 suite; off season $100–$120 double, $135–$230 suite. MAP (breakfast and dinner) $45 per person extra. 1 child stays free in parent's room. AE, MC, V. **Amenities:** Restaurant; 2 bars; airport transfers $20–$80; babysitting; library; Jacuzzi; 2 outdoor pools; room service. *In room:* A/C, TV, fridge, hair dryer, kitchenette, minibar, Wi-Fi (free; in some).

Bay Gardens Inn In the heart of Rodney Bay, near Reduit Beach, this inn enjoys a prime location and prices which, when compared to its neighbors, are relatively inexpensive. Its proximity to Rodney Bay Marina puts it at the heart of the action. The inn is small and modern, with a 1.2m-deep (4-ft.) freshwater pool. The most desirable rooms are called Bay View Superior, each with a spacious queen-size bed. Units also open onto a private balcony or terrace.

Rodney Bay, St. Lucia, W.I. www.baygardensinn.com. ✆ **877/620-3200** in the U.S. and Canada, or 758/457-8006. Fax 758/452-9747. 33 units. Winter $95–$144 double; off season $90–$110 double. AE, DC, DISC, MC, V. **Amenities:** Restaurant; bar; babysitting; shuttle to beach; outdoor pool; day spa w/ limited facilities. *In room:* A/C, TV, fridge, hair dryer, Wi-Fi (free).

Hummingbird Beach Resort ★ Set on .3 hectare (¾ acre) of landscaped grounds, this is a small and carefully maintained inn that has direct access to a sandy strip of beachfront, on the northern edge of Soufrière. Bedrooms are sheathed in white stucco and accented with varnished hardwoods like mahogany. Views are of the water or the soaring nearby heights of Petit Piton and the rugged landscape of southern St. Lucia. Each unit has a ceiling fan and mosquito netting that's artfully draped over the elaborately carved bedsteads. There's a restaurant, Lifeline, on the premises (p. 561).

Soufrière (P.O. Box 280), St. Lucia, W.I. www.istlucia.co.uk. ✆ **888/790-5264** in the U.S. and Canada, or 758/459-7985. Fax 758/459-7033. 10 units, 7 with bathroom. Winter $90–$100 double without bathroom, $240–$300 double with bathroom, $300 suite; off season $50–$70 double without bathroom, $140–$250 double with bathroom, $165 suite. Rates include continental breakfast. AE, DISC, MC, V. **Amenities:** Restaurant; bar; airport transfers $60–$75; babysitting; access to nearby health club; outdoor pool; room service. *In room:* A/C (in some), ceiling fan, TV, Wi-Fi (free).

WHERE TO DINE

Instead of fancy wine, many locals drink the local beer, Piton, which has won many coveted international prizes, including both a silver medal and a gold medal in 2006 in international beer competitions held in the city of Prague. The other regional alcohol is Bounty Rum, a quality, light-golden rum with a smooth, full-bodied taste. It's known as "the Spirit of St. Lucia."

In Castries

The Coal Pot ★★ SEAFOOD/CARIBBEAN It's our favorite restaurant within Castries or on its outskirts, a place that's simultaneously elegant and earthy, within a rustic, even raffish setting that's firmly infused with a conscious European flair.

Established in 1968 and managed today by Michelle—daughter of the original founder—and her French-born husband, Xavier, who's the chef, it occupies a woodsy-looking low-slung bungalow whose veranda parallels the waterfront of Vigie Bay, a relatively shallow harbor that's suitable for small-scale, old-fashioned fishing boats and is not far from Vigie Airport. Fresh local fish will be accompanied with your choice of sauces, including garlic butter, Creole, ginger, or coconut-flavored curry sauce. Grilled meats include succulent versions of duck breast, or filet steak with black peppercorn or mushroom sauce. Start a meal here with fish chowder, pumpkin-callaloo soup, or St. Lucian–style crab backs. Also consider, perhaps at lunch, a niçoise salad with fresh tuna, a Caesar salad garnished with grilled chicken or shrimp, or boiled local saltfish served with ripe green figs.

Vigie Marina, Castries. © **758/452-5566.** www.coalpotrestaurant.com. Reservations recommended. Main courses EC$40–EC$82 lunch, EC$65–EC$115 dinner. AE, MC, V. Mon–Fri noon–2:45pm and 6:30–9:45pm; Sat 6:30–9:45pm.

Jacques Waterfront Dining ★★ SEAFOOD/CARIBBEAN In this part of St. Lucia, we prefer the Coal Pot (see above), which lies immediately across the tiny harbor. But for an almost-as-good pick, consider this foremost competitor. Its owner, chef Jacky Rioux, has traveled the world, picking up ideas for a fusion cuisine that combines market-fresh ingredients with French cooking methods. Local fishermen are always bringing him unusual catches from the sea, which he shapes into such dishes as conch in a curried coconut sauce. Among our favorite of his main courses are boneless chicken breast stuffed with smoked salmon in a citrus-butter sauce, or oven-baked kingfish with a white-wine-and-sweet-pepper sauce. The chef mixes his own spices and seasonings and is a talented sauce maker. He even smokes his own fish and meat. His open-air garden restaurant overlooks Vigie Cove.

Vigie Marina. © **758/458-1900.** www.jacquesrestaurant.com. Reservations required. Main courses EC$32–EC$55 lunch, EC$60–EC$95 dinner. AE, MC, V. Mon–Sat 11:30am–2:30pm and 7–11pm.

At Marigot

Chateau Mygo House of Seafood ★ CREOLE/EAST INDAIN A dockside table at this spot overlooking Marigot Bay is perhaps the most romantic choice for dining on the island. Chef-owner Shaid Rambally successfully manages to blend East Indian and Caribbean cookery into a series of tasty dishes. At lunch you can order the grilled catch of the day, or feast on freshly made salads, sandwiches, or burgers. At night the chef-owner's wife, Doreen, struts her stuff, drawing on three generations of Creole and East Indian recipes. Fresh ingredients such as mangos, papayas, okra, taro root, and plantains flavor such dishes as red snapper, mahimahi, or Caribbean lobster. The château also boasts the best sushi bar on the West Coast—try a spicy tuna roll or the crunchy calamari roll. Sashimi can also be ordered, along with 20 different thin-crust pizzas; the lobster pizza alone is worth the journey across island. Live music and dancing add to the fun.

Marigot Bay. © **758/451-4772.** www.chateaumygo.com/house-of-seafood.html. Reservations recommended for dinner. Main courses $14–$28. MC, V. Daily 8am–11pm.

Rainforest Hideaway ★★ INTERNATIONAL By virtually everyone's reckoning, this is the best restaurant at Marigot Bay, where the competition from a half-dozen other restaurants is stiff. Its owner and executive chef is England-derived Jim Verity, whose parents are intimately associated with the blockbuster resort Discovery Bay, just across the harbor. To reach the restaurant from Marigot Bay's only access road, hop aboard any of the water taxis that ply the waters of the bay at regular intervals. The cost of the ferryboat is included in the price of your dinner. About 90% of the restaurant is on a deck stretching out into the harbor. Menu items are as good as they'll get on St. Lucia and are likely to include, among others, Thai-style coconut and pumpkin soup, a carpaccio of fresh tuna with a wasabi-and-soy glaze, chili-infused shrimp and scallops with a Parmesan-flavored risotto, and cinnamon-crusted duck breast with a reduction of orange juice and coconut milk.

Marigot Bay. ✆ **758/286-0511.** www.rainforesthideawaystlucia.com. Reservations required. 2-course fixed-price menu EC$130; 3-course fixed-price menu EC$160. MC, V. Mon–Sun 6–10pm. Closed Sept.

At Anse Cochon

Ti Kaye Restaurant ★★ INTERNATIONAL There's a lot to like about this mostly Creole-style restaurant, where a high ratio of staff to diners make meals here effortless and charming, and where much of the ambience might remind you of a meal within the private homes of one of the attentive waitstaff. You'll dine on smallish tables decked with plaid napery, within dim illuminations. The staff recites daily specials that augment the regular offerings listed on the menu. These include mushroom-and-chive-flavored risotto; spicy Caribbean pepper pot; grilled breast of chicken with cassava and coconut flavoring; and Cowboy Coffee Steak, wherein upscale cuts of beef are dry-rubbed with ground coffee and garlic.

Anse Cochon. ✆ **758/456-8101.** Reservations required. Main courses $24–$35. MC, V. Daily noon–3pm and 7–9pm.

In the Soufriere Area

Dasheene Restaurant & Bar ★ CARIBBEAN/INTERNATIONAL This is one of the most widely heralded restaurants on St. Lucia, and it has the most dramatic setting. Inspired by the best of the Caribbean/Creole kitchen and the innovations of California, this mountaintop hideaway offers some of the island's most refined and creative cuisine. Be warned that, after dark, a dress code for men (who should at least wear long pants with a collared shirt) is strictly enforced. From any of a series of timbered terraces that seem cantilevered up the sloping hill that's the site of this place, you can start with such tantalizing appetizers as St. Lucia fish pot consommé, or the green-papaya-and-pumpkin fritters with a lettuce rémoulade dressing. We prefer the fisherman's catch of the day, often red snapper or kingfish. It's served with your choice of a mild jerk butter or lemon-caviar butter. A local way of preparing steak, called Mojo Steak, is marinated in a lime-and-pepper seasoning before it's pan-seared. The chocolate rum mousse for dessert makes for a festive evening.

In the Ladera resort, between Gros Ilet and Petit Piton, Soufrière. ✆ **758/459-7323.** Reservations required. Main courses $30–$35; fixed-price lunch $20. AE, DISC, MC, V. Daily noon–2:30pm and 6:30–9:30pm.

Lifeline Restaurant at the Hummingbird CARIBBEAN/INTERNATIONAL This restaurant is the best part of the Hummingbird Beach Resort complex (p. 559). Tables are set on a stylish veranda adjacent to the sands of Hummingbird Beach. The cuisine focuses on such West Indian dishes as Creole-style conch, lobster, burgers, steaks, and filets of both snapper and grouper, punctuated with such American staples as burgers and BLTs. A tiny gift shop on the premises sells batik items crafted by staff members. Joyce Alexander Stowe is the undisputed matriarch who's in charge here.

At the Hummingbird Beach Resort, on the waterfront just north of the main wharf at Soufrière. ✆ **758/459-7232.** Main courses $22–$54. AE, DISC, MC, V. Daily 7am–11pm.

The Mango Tree INTERNATIONAL Because of its isolation north of Soufrière, in the island's southern tier, this place is sometimes sought out as a luncheon or "sundowner" stop for motorists touring the island's southern fringe. It's set within an octagonal building overlooking the sea and the Pitons. Menu items taste better (what doesn't?) when accompanied with any of the party-colored drinks emanating from the bar, but even if you're tee-totaling, they'll still hit the spot. Tasty menu items include jumbo shrimp in a crispy chili-pepper-and-sesame-seed crust, a julienne of lamb with Asian spices, St. Lucian–style fish broth, curried chicken, pork chops with a sauce flavored with local beer, and blackened fish filets.

At the Stonefield Estate Villas, Soufrière. ✆ **758/459-5648.** Reservations recommended. Main courses $21–$42. MC, V. Daily 11am–4pm and 6:30–9:30pm.

In Rodney Bay

The Charthouse AMERICAN/CREOLE In a large building with a sky-lit ceiling and a mahogany bar, the Charthouse is one of the oldest restaurants in the area and one of the island's most popular. It was built several feet above the bobbing yachts of the lagoon, without walls, to allow an optimal view of the water. The helpful staff serves simple, honest, good food in large portions. The specialties might include pumpkin soup, St. Lucian crab backs, baby back ribs, and fresh local lobster. (Sept–Apr, you can often witness the live lobster being delivered from the boat at around 5pm.) If you fancy a well-cooked charcoal-broiled steak, you'll see why this dish made the restaurant famous. Of course, traditionalists visit the Charthouse for one reason—its roast prime rib of beef, which is good, but never better here than in the U.S.

Reduit Beach, Rodney Bay. ✆ **758/452-8115.** Reservations required. Main courses $20–$41. AE, MC, V. Daily 5–10:30pm.

The Edge ★★★ CARIBBEAN FUSION Many of the toughest critics in St. Lucia cite this as the island's best and most creative pocket of upscale gastronomy, and we agree. Swedish-born chef Bobo Bergström is the island's culinary star. There are many oddities about this place: It's unexpectedly perched in an unlikely looking, low-slung building on the grounds of an undistinguished middle-bracket hotel (Harmony Suites, p. 557) in the touristic thick of Rodney Bay Village. It contains the first and only sushi bar on St. Lucia. If sushi is not your thing, you'll want to proceed deeper into the artfully simple, bistrolike interior of this place. Bobo is one of the world's premier advocates of European-fused Caribbean cuisine. Your delightful meal might include a trio of ceviches; duck breast with star anis on sesame croutons with guava dressing; a mousseline of scallops and shrimp served with fried scallops and shrimp and a tomato-colada sauce; or jerk-marinated and grilled tenderloin of beef with a carrot-and-yam tarte. An intriguing dessert is a house-style piña-colada-flavored "Tira Mi Su."

In the Harmony Suites Hotel, Rodney Bay Village. ✆ **758/450-3343.** www.edge-restaurant.com. Reservations recommended. Main courses $26–$40; 5-course "Eurobbean" fusion tasting menu $72; sushi $5–$12 per portion. MC, V. Daily noon–3pm and 6:30–10pm. Closed Sept.

The Lime on the Bay CARIBBEAN/AMERICAN This popular bar and restaurant is for "limin'," local jargon for hanging out. While you enjoy savory meals and lime-infused cocktails, you'll be entertained by a DJ or live entertainment. Try the spicy jerk chicken, inspired by Jamaica and served with a breadfruit salad, or the char-grilled freshly caught fish of the day, which might be red snapper. You can drop in during the day and pick up provisions for a picnic, as well. Next door is aptly named The Late Lime, which lives up to its name (patrons often pile out at daybreak).

Rodney Bay. ✆ **758/452-0761.** Main courses $20–$30. DC, MC, V. Mon and Wed–Thurs 3pm–midnight; Fri–Sun 11am–2am.

Tao ★★ ASIAN/CARIBBEAN On a second-floor veranda on the edge of Cariblue Beach, this gem of a restaurant lies on the grounds of the Body Holiday at LeSPORT (p. 550). Although this is an all-inclusive resort undergoing transformation, the restaurant is open to the public, with diners sitting out on a moonlit night enjoying the trade winds. Its fusion cuisine blends imaginative specialties of the West Indies with the best of such countries as Bali, Thailand, or Indonesia. Start with a lobster spring roll with mango coulis, or a deluxe sushi and sashimi platter. For mains the Pacific Rim seafood bouillabaisse is the island's best, with lemon grass and chili flavors cooked with fresh fish; there's also conch, jumbo shrimps, and scallops. The tamarind-flavored lamb is an invariable success, as is the hibachi-grilled pork tenderloin marinated with miso paste and served with a gratin of eggplant.

Cap Estate. ✆ **758/450-8551.** Reservations required. Main courses $32–$48. AE, DC, MC, V. Daily 1st seating 7pm, 2nd seating 9:30pm.

ST. LUCIA'S BEACHES

Since most of the island hotels are built right on the beach, you won't have to go far to swim. All beaches are open to the public, even those along hotel properties. However, if you use any of the hotel's beach equipment, you must pay for it. We prefer the beaches along the western coast, as the rough surf on the windward (east) side makes swimming potentially dangerous. The best hotels are all on the western coast for good reason.

One of the best beaches is **Pigeon Point Beach** ★, off the north shore, part of the **Pigeon Island National Historic Park** (see "Exploring the Island," below). The small beach here has white sand and is an ideal place for a picnic. Pigeon Island is joined to the mainland of St. Lucia by a causeway, so it's easy to reach.

The most frequented beach is **Reduit Beach** ★★, at Rodney Bay, 2km (1¼ miles) of soft beige sand fronting very clear waters. Many watersports kiosks can be found along the strip bordering Royal St. Lucian Hotel. With all its restaurants and bars, you'll find plenty of refueling stops.

Choc Bay is a long stretch of sand and palm trees on the northwestern coast, convenient to Castries and the big resorts. Its tranquil waters lure swimmers and especially families (including locals) with small children.

The 3km (2-mile) white-sand **Malabar Beach** runs parallel to the George F. L. Charles Airport runway, in Castries, to the Rendezvous resort. **Vigie Beach,** north of Castries Harbour, is also popular. It has fine beige sands, sloping gently into crystalline water. **La Toc Beach,** just south of Castries, opens onto a crescent-shaped bay containing golden sand.

Marigot Bay is the quintessential Caribbean cove, framed on three sides by steep emerald hills and skirted by palm trees. There are some small but secluded beaches here. Some of the Caribbean's most expensive yachts anchor in this bay.

One of the most charming and hidden beaches of St. Lucia is the idyllic cove of **Anse Chastanet,** north of Soufrière. This is a beach connoisseur's delight. Towering palms provide shade from the fierce noonday sun, and lush hills are a refreshing contrast to the dark sandy strip.

The dramatic crescent-shaped bay of **Anse des Pitons** is at the foot of and between the twin peaks of the Pitons, south of Soufrière. The Jalousie Plantation (p. 552) transformed the natural black-sand beach by covering it with white sand; you walk through the resort to get to it. It's popular with divers and snorkelers. While here, ask about a very special beach reached only by boat: the black volcanic sands and tranquil waters of **Anse Couchon.** With its shallow reefs, excellent snorkeling, and picture-postcard charm, this beach has become a hideaway for lovers. It's south of Anse-le-Raye.

You'll find miles of white sand at the beach at **Vieux Fort,** at the southern end of the island. Reefs protect the crystal-clear waters here, rendering them tranquil and ideal for swimming. At the southern end of the windward side of the island is **Anse des Sables,** which opens onto a shallow bay swept by trade winds that are great for windsurfing.

SPORTS & OUTDOOR PURSUITS

CAMPING Camping is now possible on St. Lucia courtesy of the **Environmental Educational Centre,** a division of the St. Lucia National Trust (© **758/452-5005**). This reserve features 12 campsites along a beautiful stretch of beach on historic Anse Liberté, in the fishing town of Canaries, 40km (25 miles) southwest of Castries and 13km (8 miles) north of Soufrière. At present you must bring your own tent, paying $25 to $75 per night to rent the site. There are nearby community bathrooms and community cooking areas. The reserve has 8km (5 miles) of hiking trails; staff members give tours of the area and explain the rich history of the Anse Liberté, which literally translated means "freedom harbor."

DEEP-SEA FISHING The waters around St. Lucia are known for their game fish, including blue marlin, sailfish, mako sharks, and barracuda, with tuna and kingfish among the edible catches. Most hotels can arrange fishing expeditions. Call **Mako Watersports** (© **758/452-0412**), which offers half-day fishing trips for $99 per person or full-day trips from $400. **Captain Mike's** (© **758/452-7044;** www.captmikes.com) also conducts fishing trips, renting boats by the half-day for $450 to $550, or a whole day in the $800-to-$1,000 price range.

GOLF St. Lucia has an 18-hole golf course (6,815 yd., par-71) at the **St. Lucia Golf Resort and Country Club,** Cap Estate, at the northern end of the island (© **758/450-8523;** www.stluciagolf.com). In winter greens fees are $145 for 18 holes or $105 for 9 holes; these charges are lowered in summer to $120 for 18 holes or $95 for 9 holes. Carts are included, and clubs can be rented for $50. Hours are from 6:30am to 6pm daily, and reservations are needed.

HIKING A tropical rainforest covers a large area in the southern half of St. Lucia, and the St. Lucia Forest and Lands Department manages it wisely. This forest reserve divides the western and eastern halves of the island. There are several trails, the most popular of which is the **Barre de l'Isle Trail,** located almost in the center of St. Lucia, southeast of Marigot Bay; it's a fairly easy trail that even children can handle. There are four panoramic lookout points with dramatic views of the sea where the

Atlantic and the Caribbean meet. It takes about an hour to walk this 2km-long (1.25-mile) trail, which lies about a 30-minute ride from Castries. Guided hikes can usually be arranged through the major hotels or through the **Forest and Lands Department** (© **758/450-2078**).

HORSEBACK RIDING North of Castries is the island's oldest riding establishment—**Trim's National Riding Stable,** Cas-en-Bas, Gros Islet (© **758/450-8273;** www.trimsnationalridingacademy.com). Its activities range from trail rides to beach tours, and the stable even offers horse-drawn carriage tours of Pigeon Island. Rides are $45 for an hour, $60 for 2 hours, or $80 for a 3-hour beach ride with a barbecue.

SCUBA DIVING In Soufrière, **Scuba St. Lucia,** in the Anse Chastanet Resort (© **758/459-7755;** www.scubastlucia.com), offers one of the world's top dive locations at a five-star PADI dive center. At the southern end of Anse Chastanet's .4km-long (¼-mile) secluded beach, it features premier diving and comprehensive facilities for divers of all levels. Some of the most spectacular coral reefs of St. Lucia, many only 3 to 6m (9¾–20 ft.) below the surface, lie a short distance from the beach.

Many PADI instructors offer five dive programs a day. Photographic equipment is available for rent (film can be processed on the premises), and instruction is offered in picture taking. Experienced divers can rent any equipment they need. PADI certification courses are available for $650. A 2- to 3-hour introductory lesson costs $95 and includes a short theory session, equipment familiarization, development of skills in shallow water, a tour of the reef, and all equipment. Single dives cost $40. Hours are from 8am to 6pm daily.

Another full-service scuba center is available on St. Lucia's southwest coast at the **Jalousie Plantation,** at Soufrière (© **758/456-8000**). The PADI center offers dives in St. Lucia's National Marine Park; there are numerous shallow reefs near the shore. The diver certification program is available to hotel guests and other visitors ages 12 and up. Prices range from a single dive for $40 to $85, to a certification course for $550 to $800. There's a daily resort course for noncertified divers that includes a supervised dive from the beach; it costs $95. A 10-dive package is $400; a six-dive package is $300. All prices include equipment, tax, and service charges.

TENNIS The best place for tennis on the island is the **St. Lucia Racquet Club,** adjacent to Club St. Lucia (© **758/450-0551**). It's one of the finest tennis facilities in the Lesser Antilles. Its seven illuminated courts are maintained in state-of-the-art condition, and there's also a good pro shop on-site. You must reserve 24 hours in advance. Guests of the hotel play for free; nonguests are charged $12 per hour. Tennis racquets rent for $8 per hour.

The **Jalousie Plantation,** at Soufrière (© **758/456-8000**), has a good program. Vernon Lewis, the top-ranked player in St. Lucia, is the pro. You'll find four brand-new Laykold tennis courts (three lit for night play). Hotel guests play for free (though they pay for lessons). Nonguests can play for $25 per hour.

OTHER WATERSPORTS The best all-around watersports center is **St. Lucian Watersports,** at the Rex St. Lucian Hotel (© **758/452-8351**). Water-skiing costs $20 for a 10- to 15-minute ride (three rounds). Windsurfers can be rented for $25 per half-hour. Snorkeling is free for guests of the hotel; nonguests pay $10 per hour for equipment.

EXPLORING THE ISLAND

With lovely little towns, beautiful beaches and bays, mineral baths, and banana plantations, you won't tire of exploring St. Lucia. You can even visit a volcano.

Most hotel front desks will make arrangements for tours that take in all the major sights of St. Lucia. For example, **Sunlink Tours,** Reduit Beach Avenue (**© 758/456-9100;** www.sunlinktours.com), offers many island tours, including full-day boat trips along the west coast of Soufrière, the Pitons, and the volcano; the cost is $100 per person. One of the most popular jaunts is a rainforest ramble for $90 by jeep. There's also a daily shopping tour for $30. The company has tour desks and/or representatives at most of the major hotels.

Castries

The capital city has grown up around its **harbor,** which occupies the crater of an extinct volcano. Charter captains and the yachting set drift in here, and large cruise-ship wharves welcome vessels from around the world. Because several devastating fires (most recently in 1948) destroyed almost all the old buildings, the town today looks new, with glass-and-concrete (or steel) buildings rather than the French colonial or Victorian look typical of many West Indian capitals.

Castries may be architecturally dull, but its **public market** is one of the most fascinating in the West Indies, and our favorite people-watching site on the island. It goes full blast every day of the week except Sunday and is most active on Friday and Saturday mornings. The market stalls are a block from Columbus Square along Peynier Street, running down toward the water. The local women dress traditionally, with cotton headdresses; the number of knotted points on top reveals their marital status. (Ask one of the locals to explain it to you.) The luscious fruits and vegetables of St. Lucia may be new to you; the array of colors alone is astonishing. Sample one of the numerous varieties of bananas: On St. Lucia, they're allowed to ripen on the tree, and taste completely different from those picked green and sold at supermarkets in the United States. You can also pick up St. Lucian handicrafts such as baskets and unglazed pottery here.

One of the highlights of Castries is **Derek Walcott Square,** a dignified and verdant rectangle that's bordered with, among others, the public library and the island's most visible Catholic church, the Cathedral (see below). Derek Walcott, born in St. Lucia in 1930, won a Nobel Prize for literature. Plaques within the park honor Walcott with a verse from his epic poem, *Ste. Lucie*: *"Moi c'est gens Ste. Lucie: C'est la*

Rainforest Sky Rides

A Rainforest Aerial Tram Adventure ★★ is the greatest scenic adventure on the island. Gondolas safely glide you through and over the treetops of this oceanic rainforest. Dense thickets of vegetation merge with cascades of flowers such as lavender stars, orange bursts, and white magnolias. Sixteen open-air gondolas seat up to eight passengers, with one guide each. The cost is $72 for adults or $62 for children 2 to 12. The ride is just one of several rainforest excursions offered by **Rainforest Sky Rides,** Reduit Gros Islet, Rodney Bay (© 758/458-5151; www.rainforest adventure.com).

moi sortie, is there that I born." A few steps away is a plaque commemorating another island-born luminary, Sir William Arthur Lewis (1915–79), winner of a Nobel Prize for economics, whose face appears on some of the nation's EC$100 bills. Both of the commemorative plaques are virtually within the shadow of a 500-year-old "Simon-tree" (a local name for a local species), which anyone in the park will happily point out as proof of the fertility of the island's soil and climate.

One of the most important French-built religious buildings in the West Indies is the **Cathedral,** immediately to the edge of the park. Built during the 19th century of wrought iron, cast iron, and stone under the supervision of several generations of hard-working, long-suffering priests, it's covered with an almost surreal mélange of French Catholic and West Indian iconography. Notice on one wall the frescoes commemorating the "Martyrs of Uganda" who were slaughtered by the forces of dictator Idi Amin.

To the south of Castries looms **Morne Fortune,** the inappropriately named "Hill of Good Luck." In the 18th century, some of the most savage Caribbean battles between the French and the British took place here. You can visit the military cemetery, a small museum, the old powder magazine, and the Four Apostles Battery (a quartet of grim muzzle-loading cannons). Government House, now the official residence of the governor-general of St. Lucia, is one of the few examples of Victorian architecture that escaped destruction by fire. The private gardens are beautifully planted, aflame with scarlet and purple bougainvillea. Morne Fortune also offers what many consider the most **scenic lookout** perch in the Caribbean. The view of the harbor of Castries is panoramic: You can see north to Pigeon Island or south to the Pitons; on a clear day, you may even spot Martinique. To reach Morne Fortune, head east on Bridge Street.

Pigeon Island National Historic Park ★

St. Lucia's first **national park** is joined to the mainland by a causeway. On its west coast are two white-sand beaches (see "Beaches," above). There's also a restaurant, Jambe de Bois, named after a wooden-legged pirate who once used the island as a hideout.

Pigeon Island offers an **Interpretation Centre,** equipped with artifacts and a multimedia display on local history, ranging from the Amerindian occupation of A.D. 1000 to the Battle of the Saints, when Admiral Rodney's fleet set out from Pigeon Island and defeated Admiral De Grasse in 1782. The Captain's Cellar Olde English Pub lies under the center and is evocative of an 18th-century English bar.

Pigeon Island, only 18 hectares (44 acres), got its name from the red-neck pigeon, or ramier, that once colonized this island in huge numbers. Now the site of a Sandals Hotel (p. 553) and interconnected to the St. Lucian "mainland" with a causeway, the island offers pleasant panoramas but no longer the sense of isolated privacy that reigned here prior to its development. Parts of it, those far from the hotel on the premises, seem appropriate for nature walks. For more information, call ✆ **758/452-5005,** or visit www.slunatrust.org/pigeon_island.php.

Rodney Bay ★

This scenic bay is a 15-minute drive north of Castries. Set on a man-made lagoon, it has become a chic center for nightlife, hotels, and restaurants—in fact, it's the most active place on the island at night. Its marina is one of the top watersports centers in the Caribbean, and a destination every December for the Atlantic Rally for Cruisers, when yachties cross the Atlantic to meet and compare stories.

Marigot Bay ★

Movie crews, including those for Sophia Loren's *Fire Power,* have used this bay, one of the most beautiful in the Caribbean, for background shots. Thirteen kilometers (8 miles) south of Castries, it's narrow yet navigable by yachts of any size. Here Admiral Rodney camouflaged his ships with palm leaves while lying in wait for French frigates. The shore, lined with palm trees, remains relatively unspoiled, although some building sites have been sold. It's a delightful spot for a picnic. A 24-hour ferry connects the bay's two sides.

Soufriere

This little fishing port, St. Lucia's second-largest settlement, is dominated by two pointed hills called **Petit Piton** and **Gros Piton ★★★**. The Pitons, two volcanic cones rising to 738m and 696m (2,421 ft. and 2,283 ft.), have become the very symbol of St. Lucia. Formed of lava and rock, and once actively volcanic, they are now covered in green vegetation. Their sheer rise from the sea makes them a landmark visible for miles around, and waves crash at their bases. It's recommended that you attempt to climb only Gros Piton, but doing so requires the permission of the **Forest and Lands Department** (**© 758/450-2078**) and the company of a knowledgeable guide.

Near Soufrière lies the famous "drive-in" volcano, **Mount Soufrière ★★**, a rocky lunar landscape of bubbling mud and craters seething with sulfur. You literally drive your car along a winding, forested road into a millions-of-years-old crater. From the parking lot, you'll walk uphill, along a closely monitored trail peppered with park rangers and, from observation platforms, get a view in the near distance of bubbling sulfur springs and pools of hissing steam. The most visible of these is **Gabriel's Pool,** which was named in honor of a 1960s-era St. Lucian tour guide, Gabriel, whose weight collapsed the chalky surface of the congealed mud close to the hot springs. Ever since then, one of the pools has borne his name, and ever since, visitors are strictly prohibited from getting too close to the steamy depths. Entrance to the crater and the vicinity of the pools costs $5 per person and includes the services of your guide, who will point out the blackened waters, among the few of their kind in the Caribbean. Hours are Monday to Friday 8:30am to 4:30pm; for more information, call **© 758/459-7200.**

Nearby are the **Diamond Mineral Baths** (**© 758/459-7155;** www.diamondstlucia.com) in the **Diamond Botanical Gardens ★**. Deep in the lush tropical gardens is the Diamond Waterfall, one of the geological attractions of the island. Created from water bubbling up from sulfur springs, the waterfall changes colors (from yellow to black to green to gray) several times a day. The baths were constructed in 1784 on the orders of Louis XVI, whose doctors told him these waters were similar in mineral content to the waters at Aix-les-Bains; they were intended to provide recuperative effects for French soldiers fighting in the West Indies. The baths have an average temperature of 106°F (41°C). For $10 you can bathe and try out the recuperative effects for yourself. There is a $5 entrance fee. Hours are Monday to Saturday 10am to 5pm, Sunday 10am to 3pm.

Discovering "Forgotten" Grande Anse

The northeast coast is the least visited and least accessible part of St. Lucia, but it contains dramatic rockbound shores interspersed with secret sandy coves. The government has set Grand Anse aside as a nature reserve so that it will never be developed. The terrain is arid and can be unwelcoming, but it is fascinating nonetheless. Grande Anse is home to some rare bird species, notably the white-breasted thrasher, as well as the fer-de-lance, the only poisonous snake on the island (but visitors report rarely seeing them). Its beaches—Grande Anse, Petite Anse, and Anse Louvet—are nesting grounds for endangered sea turtles, including the hawksbill, the green turtle, the leatherback, and the loggerhead. Nesting season lasts from February to October. Many locals tackle the poor road in a four-wheel-drive vehicle, especially the bumpiest part from Desbarra to Grande Anse.

From Soufrière in the southwest, the road winds toward Fond St-Jacques, where you'll have a good view of mountains and villages as you cut through St. Lucia's Cape Moule-Chique tropical rainforest. You'll also see the Barre de l'Isle divide.

Nature Reserves

The fertile volcanic soil of St. Lucia sustains a rich diversity of bird and animal life. Some of the richest troves for ornithologists are in protected precincts off the St. Lucian coast, in either of two national parks: Fregate Islands Nature Reserve and the Maria Islands Nature Reserve.

The **Fregate Islands** are a cluster of rocks a short distance offshore from Praslin Bay, midway up St. Lucia's eastern coastline. Barren except for tall grasses that seem to thrive in the salt spray, the islands were named after the scissor-tailed frigate birds *(Fregata magnificens)* that breed here. Between May and July, large colonies of the graceful birds fly in well-choreographed formations over islands that you can visit only under the closely supervised permission of government authorities. Many visitors believe that the best way to admire the Fregate Islands (and to respect their fragile ecosystems) is to walk along the nature trail that the St. Lucian government has hacked along the clifftop of the St. Lucian mainland, about 45m (148 ft.) inland from the shoreline. Even without binoculars, you'll be able to see the frigates wheeling overhead. You'll also enjoy eagle's-eye views of the unusual geology of the St. Lucian coast, which includes sea caves, dry ravines, a waterfall (during the rainy season), and a strip of mangrove swamp.

The **Maria Islands** are larger and more arid, and are almost constantly exposed to salt-laden winds blowing up from the equator. Set to the east of St. Lucia's southernmost tip, off the town of Vieux Fort, their biodiversity is strictly protected. The approximately 12 hectares (30 acres) of cactus-dotted land that make up the two largest islands (Maria Major and Maria Minor) are home to more than 120 species of plants, lizards, butterflies, and snakes that are believed to be extinct in other parts of the world. These include the large ground lizard *(Zandolite)* and the nocturnal, nonvenomous kouwes snake *(Dromicus ornatus)*.

The Marias are also a bird refuge, populated by such species as the sooty tern, the bridled tern, the Caribbean martin, the red-billed tropicbird, and the brown noddy, which usually nests under the protective thorns of prickly pear cactus.

For more information, contact the **St. Lucia National Trust** (**© 758/452-5005;** www.slunatrust.org).

SHOPPING

Most of the shopping is in **Castries,** where the principal streets are William Peter Boulevard and Bridge Street. Many stores will sell you goods at duty-free prices (providing you don't take the merchandise with you, but have it delivered to the airport or cruise dock). There are some good (but not remarkable) buys in bone china, jewelry, perfume, watches, liquor, and crystal.

Built for the cruise-ship passenger, **Pointe Seraphine,** in Castries, has the most comprehensive collection of shops on the island, along with offices for car rentals, organized taxi service (for sightseeing), a *bureau de change,* a philatelic bureau, an information center, and international phones. Cruise ships berth beside cement piers immediately adjacent to the shopping center. The complex was designed as a labyrinth of arcades and cottages (each capped with terra-cotta roof tiles) that meander amid landscaping in a kind of extended garden. Access to the compound requires that you present a cruise pass or an airline ticket to the shopkeeper when purchasing duty-free goods. Visitors can take away their purchases, except liquor and tobacco, which will be delivered either to the airport or to your cruise ship, depending on your means of transport. The compound is open in winter Monday to Friday 8am to 5pm and Saturday 8am to 2pm; off season, hours are Monday to Saturday 9am to 4pm. It has extended hours when cruise ships are in port.

On Gros Islet Highway, 3km (2 miles) north of Castries, **Gablewoods Mall** contains three restaurants and one of the island's densest concentrations of shops.

Local products of note include an inventory of at least seven kinds of locally distilled rums from **La Belle Creole** (also known as Wilco, Ltd.) Most visible is a delicious version flavored with coconut, and **Seventh Heaven,** a variety that's (informally and unofficially) advertised for its powers as an aphrodisiac, thanks to the combination of ginger, local herbs, and aromatic bark (suggestively known as *bois bandé*) that go into it.

ST. LUCIA AFTER DARK

Friday-night "jump-ups" are weekly street parties where islanders let it rip. These jump-ups, especially for guests of all-inclusives, offer a real opportunity to get out and mix with the locals. For reggae and hot times, head for the gatherings at **Gros Islet,** attracting both St. Lucians and the visiting yachties from Rodney Bay. You won't go hungry: Stall after stall hawks barbecued meats along with such sides as rice 'n' beans and a tuber called dasheen, as seafood sizzles over hot coals and the smell of barbecued chicken whets appetites. More jump-ups take place at **Anse la Raye** on St. Lucia's western shore. Rum and reggae flow from about 6pm to midnight or beyond. Stalls along the Anse la Raye waterfront often sell fresher and better seafood than you get in the upmarket dining rooms of the all-inclusives—conch, lobster, mahimahi, and even "potfish." Islanders claim that if you drink a "sea-moss shake" (seaweed, milk, sugar, and fruit), you'll keep jumping up throughout the night. In the winter, at

St. Lucia Jazz

Amazingly, the St. Lucia Jazz Festival ★★★ is now ranked number two in the Caribbean, eclipsed only by Trinidad's Carnival. It takes place every May. Leading jazz artists from all over the world descend on St. Lucia at this time, offering varied shows that range from New Age jazz to rhythm and blues. Shows range from formal performances to late-night open-air venues. The tourist office has complete details of the festival, and information is also available online at www.stluciajazz.org. There's a downside to all this: Many hotels take advantage of all these arrivals to jack up room prices.

least one hotel has a steel band or calypso music every night of the week. Otherwise, check to see what's happening at the **Green Parrot** (✆ **758/452-3399**), in Castries.

If you'd like to go barhopping, begin at **Shamrocks Pub,** Rodney Bay (✆ **758/452-8725**). This Irish-style pub is especially popular among boaters and gets really lively on weekends.

At Marigot Bay, where the 1967 version of *Doctor Doolittle,* starring Rex Harrison, was filmed, the memory is perpetuated at **Doolittle's,** part of the Marigot Beach Club Hotel (✆ **758/451-4974**), lying 14km (8¾ miles) south of Castries. The Marigot Bay ferry takes you to the palm-studded peninsula of the resort; tickets cost $1.90. On Saturday nights—when Doolittle's offers a lavish seafood and barbecue buffet along with a steel band—this is the best place to be on the island. You can come here for drinks (try the Singapore Slings), or for dishes like chunky pumpkin soup, jerk chicken, or lobster and coconut shrimp Creole.

22 ST. MAARTEN/ ST. MARTIN

Two nations, one island: St. Martin/St. Maarten is an exotic cocktail of French, Dutch, and Caribbean influences set in a sparkling necklace of aquamarine seas. You can stay in charming Creole cottages or sprawling beachside resorts—and you will dine very well, whether at casual beach barbecues or grand temples of French gastronomy. You can snorkel in gin-clear waters, sip rum punches, and soak up the sun on your choice of 39 beaches.

Things to Do Wander the cobblestone streets of **Philipsburg,** the capital of Dutch St. Maarten. On the French side, take in the views over the charming village of **Marigot** and its jewel-like harbor from the hillside ruins of **Fort Louis.** Discover your inner Tarzan on a zip line flight through the jungle canopy at **Loterie Farm.**

Eating & Drinking A concentration of top-notch restaurants has given tiny **Grand Case** the title of "Gourmet Capital of the Caribbean." Mix with the locals at open-air barbecue joints known as ***lolos***—a St. Martin institution—for hearty and delicious helpings of barbecued ribs, lobster, chicken, or fish grilled on split metal drums, all for under $20, a real bargain on pricey St. Martin.

Shopping Browse **duty-free shops** in Philipsburg for cameras, watches and local Guavaberry rum. **Front Street** has a mind-boggling display of high-end shops, from Tiffany to Tommy Hilfiger. On the French side, browse boutiques and designer shops on the narrow streets around the **Marina Port la Royale. Harborside,** a lively morning market buzzes with vendors selling spices, fruit, and handicrafts. Wander the curved staircases in **Le West Indies Mall** to browse big-name boutiques, from Escada to Lacoste.

Relaxing The island's pristine beaches invite barefoot strolls, snorkeling offshore reefs, or sunning to a reggae beach-bar beat. Watch the sun rise on **Dawn Beach,** or head to **Pinel Island** for a dip in a serene lagoon. Relax over cocktails in the island's bars and lounges, from rickety rum shops to neon-lit nightclubs. In downtown Philipsburg, **soca** and ***zouk*** (French Creole music) spill out of clubs and bars. Saucy beach bars on **Orient Bay** host barbecues with steel bands and sunset cocktails.

ESSENTIALS

Visitor Information

For information on **Dutch St. Maarten,** go to **www.vacationstmaarten.com**. For information on **French St Martin,** go to **www.stmartinisland.org** or **www.st-martin.org**. You can also contact the **St. Maarten Tourist Bureau,** 675 Third Ave., Ste. 1807, New York, NY 10017 (✆ **800/786-2278** or 212/953-2084). For information on French St. Martin, contact the **St. Martin Promotional Bureau,** 825 Third Ave., New York, NY 10022. In Canada, the office for information about the Dutch side of the island is located at 703 Evans Ave., Ste. 106, Toronto, ON M9C 5E9 (✆ **416/622-4300**). For information about the French side of the island, contact 1981 Ave. McGill College, Ste. 490, Montréal, Québec H3A 2W9 (✆ **514/288-4264**).

Once on St. Maarten, go to the **Tourist Information Bureau,** Vineyard Office Park, 33 W. G. Buncamper Rd., Philipsburg, St. Maarten, N.A. (✆ **599/54-22337**), open Monday to Friday from 9am to 5pm.

The tourist board on French St. Martin, called the **Office du Tourisme,** is at Route de Sandy Ground, Marigot, 97150 St. Martin (✆ **590/87-57-21**), open Monday to Friday from 8am to 1pm and 2:30 to 5:30pm.

Getting There

American Airlines (✆ **800/433-7300** in the U.S. and Canada; www.aa.com) offers more options and more frequent service into St. Maarten than any other airline—currently one daily nonstop flight from New York's JFK and one from Miami. Additional nonstop daily flights into St. Maarten are offered by American and its local affiliate, **American Eagle,** from San Juan.

Continental Airlines (✆ **800/231-0856** in the U.S. and Canada; www.continental.com) has daily nonstop flights out of its hub in Newark, New Jersey, during the winter months (flight times vary in low season).

Delta Airlines (✆ **800/241-4141** in the U.S. and Canada; www.delta.com) flies in from Atlanta and New York City (through Atlanta).

United (✆ **800/538-2929** in the U.S. and Canada; www.united.com) also offers flights from New York.

US Airways (✆ **800/428-4322** in the U.S. and Canada; www.usairways.com) offers nonstop daily service from Philadelphia and Charlotte to St. Maarten.

JetBlue Airways (✆ **800-JETBLUE** [538-2583] in the U.S.; www.jetblue.com) has one daily nonstop flight from New York's JFK into St. Maarten.

Spirit Airlines (✆ **800/772-7117** in the U.S. and Canada; www.spiritair.com) has nonstop service from Fort Lauderdale to St. Maarten.

Air Caraïbes (✆ **590/52-05-10;** www.aircaraibes.com) offers flights from Paris's Orly airport into St. Maarten.

Caribbean Airlines (✆ **800/920-4225** in the U.S. and Canada, or 599/54-67660 on St. Maarten; www.caribbean-airlines.com), the national airline of Trinidad and Tobago (replacing the now-defunct BWIA), has flights from New York, Miami, Toronto, and London with connections to St. Maarten.

St. Maarten/St. Martin

ST. MAARTEN

ACCOMMODATIONS ■
Divi Little Bay Beach Resort **10**
Holland House Beach Hotel **4**
The Horny Toad Guesthouse **12**
La Vista Beach Resort **11**
Mary's Boon Beach Resort **12**
Pasanggrahan Royal Guest House **3**
Princess Heights **1**
Sonesta Great Bay Beach Hotel & Casino **8**
Sonesta Maho Beach Hotel & Casino **13**
Westin St. Maarten Dawn Beach Resort & Spa **2**

DINING ◆
Antoine **7**
Beau Beau's **34**
Chesterfields **9**
La Gondola **14**
L'Escargot **6**
Mr. Busby's Beach Bar **35**
Oualichi **5**
Rare **14**
Saratoga **12**
Skipjack's Seafood Grill, Bar & Fish Market **12**
Temptation **14**
Topper's **12**

ST. MARTIN

ACCOMMODATIONS ■
Alamanda Resort **35**
Club Orient Naturist Resort **33**
Esmeralda Resort **32**
Grand-Case Beach Club **26**
Green Cay Villas **35**
Hotel Beach Plaza **20**
Hotel La Plantation **34**
Hotel L'Esplanade **24**
La Samanna **15**
Le Domaine de Lonvilliers **29**
Le Petit Hotel **25**
Radisson Blue Resort Marina & Spa, St. Martin **30**

DINING ◆
Chez Yvette **36**
Claude Mini-Club **21**
La Belle Epoque **19**
La Cigale **16**
La Vie en Rose **19**
Le Bistro Caraïbes **23**
Le Cottage **27**
Le Pressoir **27**
Le Santal **17**
L'Oizeau Rare **19**
Mario's Bistro **18**
Sol é Luna **31**
Spiga **28**
Sunset Café **26**
Tastevin **22**

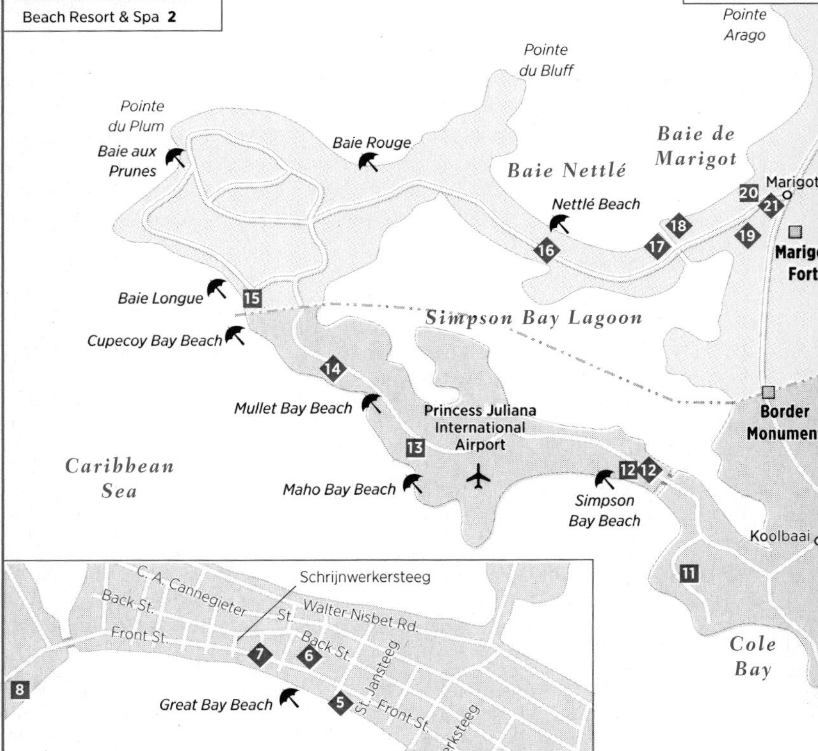

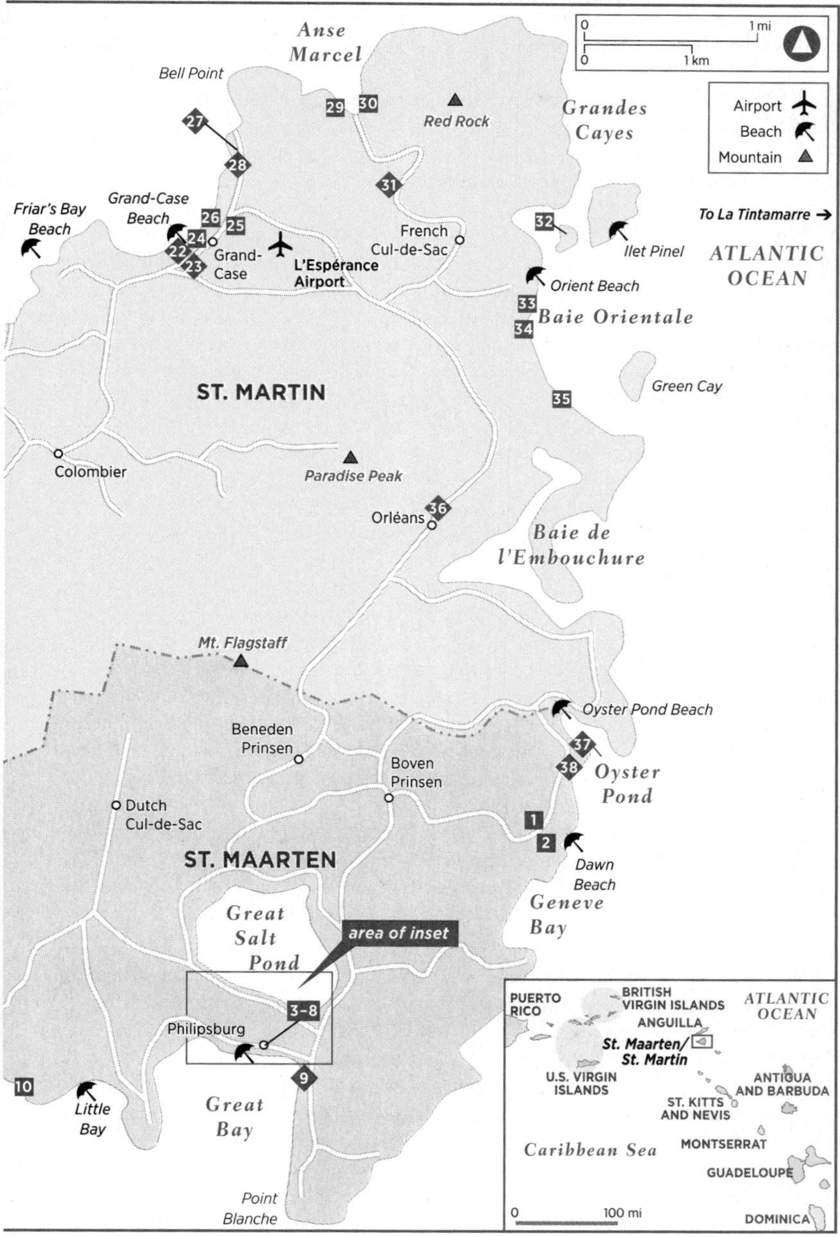
Anse Marcel
Bell Point
Red Rock
Grandes Cayes
Airport
Beach
Mountain
0
1 mi
0
1 km
Friar's Bay Beach
Grand-Case Beach
Grand-Case
L'Espérance Airport
French Cul-de-Sac
To La Tintamarre →
Ilet Pinel
ATLANTIC OCEAN
Orient Beach
Baie Orientale
Green Cay
ST. MARTIN
Colombier
Paradise Peak
Orléans
Baie de l'Embouchure
Mt. Flagstaff
Oyster Pond Beach
Beneden Prinsen
Boven Prinsen
Oyster Pond
Dutch Cul-de-Sac
ST. MAARTEN
Dawn Beach
Geneve Bay
Great Salt Pond
area of inset
Philipsburg
Little Bay
Great Bay
Point Blanche
PUERTO RICO
BRITISH VIRGIN ISLANDS
ATLANTIC OCEAN
ANGUILLA
St. Maarten/ St. Martin
U.S. VIRGIN ISLANDS
ANTIGUA AND BARBUDA
ST. KITTS AND NEVIS
Caribbean Sea
MONTSERRAT
GUADELOUPE
0
100 mi
DOMINICA

The regional airline **LIAT** (✆ **888/844-5428** in the U.S. and Canada; www.liatairline.com) has direct daily 40-minute flights and connecting flights into St. Maarten from its hub in Antigua. From St. Martin, LIAT offers ongoing service to a number of other islands, including Antigua, St. Croix, Puerto Rico, St. Kitts, and Dominica.

One airline specializes in flying the short routes of the northeastern Caribbean islands, from Tortola to Montserrat. **Winair** (✆ **866/466-0410** in the U.S. and Canada, or 599/54-54237; www.fly-winair.com) offers island trips from its main gateway at the Princess Juliana International Airport.

Getting Around

BY TAXI Most visitors use taxis at some point to get around the island. Taxis are plentiful at Princess Juliana International Airport; taxi stands are conveniently located just outside the airport Arrivals section. Taxis are unmetered on both sides of the island (although drivers are required to carry government-issued rate sheets based on two-person occupancy), so always determine the rate before getting into a cab.

Rates are slightly different depending on which side of the island the taxi is based, though both Dutch and French cabs service the entire island. **St. Maarten taxis** have minimum fares for two passengers, and each additional passenger pays $4 extra. One piece of luggage per person is allowed free; each additional piece is $1 extra. Typical fares around the island are as follows: Princess Juliana Airport to Grand Case, $25 for up to two passengers and all their luggage; Marigot to Grand Case, $15; Princess Juliana airport to anywhere in Marigot, $15 to $20; Princess Juliana Airport to the Maho Beach Hotel, $6; and Princess Juliana Airport to Philipsburg, about $15. ***Note:*** Fares are 25% higher between 10pm and midnight, and 50% higher between midnight and 6am.

St. Martin taxi fares are also for two passengers, but plan to add about $1 for each suitcase or valise, and $2 for each additional person. These fares are in effect from 6am to 10pm; after that they go up by 25% until midnight, rising by 50% after midnight. On the French side, the fare from Marigot to Grand Case is $15; from Princess Juliana Airport to Marigot and from Princess Juliana Airport to La Samanna, $15.

For late-night cab service on St. Maarten, call ✆ **147.** To reach the **Taxi Dispatch offices** in St. Maarten, call ✆ **599/54-67759** (airport) or ✆ **599/54-22359** (Philipsburg). On the French side of the island, **Taxi Service & Information Center** operates at the port of Marigot (✆ **590/87-56-54**).

BY RENTAL CAR A car is the best way to experience and explore St. Maarten/St. Martin. Renting a car here couldn't be easier; car rental agencies are a dime a dozen, with locations at the airports and throughout the island. Renting a car is also a cost-efficient way to see the island, with rates starting around $30 or 21€ a day, with unlimited mileage, and short distances between towns.

Many visitors rent cars when they arrive at Princess Juliana International Airport. A good number of car rental agency kiosks are located on the Arrivals floor of the airport and along Airport Road. To get around the law (strictly enforced by St. Maarten taxi drivers' union) that forbids anyone from picking up a car at the airport, every rental agency parks its cars at a location nearby. When you rent a car at one of the agency kiosks on the Arrivals floor of the Princess Juliana Airport, you will be taken by company shuttle 5 to 10 minutes away to pick up your car.

Tip: Always ask how far away from the airport rental cars are located; some of the smaller agencies are a couple of miles away—which can turn into a long trip when traffic is heavy around the airport.

Car rental agencies at the airport include **Budget** (**© 800/472-3325** in the U.S. and Canada, or 599/54-54030 on the Dutch side; www.budget.com), **Avis** (**© 800/331-1212** in the U.S. and Canada, 599/54-22847 on the Dutch side, or 590/87-50-60 on the French side; www.avis-sxm.com), **Hertz** (**© 800/654-3001** in the U.S. and Canada, or 590/54-54541 on the Dutch side; www.hertz.com), and **Alamo/National** (**© 877/222-9058** in the U.S. and Canada, or 599/54-55546 on the Dutch side; www.nationalcar.com). Also at the Princess Juliana airport are **Best Deal Car Rental** (**© 866/826-2205** or 599/54-53061; www.bestdealscarrental.com) and **Safari Car Rentals** (**© 800/736-6917** or 599/54-53185; www.safaricarrentals.com).

Budget (**© 599/54-54030**) also has an office at the cruise-ship terminal.

All these companies charge roughly equivalent rates. The major car rental agencies require that renters be at least 25 years old.

Many rental agencies will also deliver cars directly to your hotel, where an employee will complete the paperwork. Some hotels, like La Samanna (p. 584), actually have a fleet of cars to rent on the premises—but try to reserve well in advance because supply is limited.

Driving is on the right side of the road. Seat belts and child car seats are mandatory. International road signs are observed, and there are no Customs formalities at the border between the French and Dutch sides—in fact, you might not even realize you crossed the border.

Expect traffic jams in and around Philipsburg during rush hours—particularly in the Simpson Bay area when the Simpson Bay drawbridge is raised to let boat traffic through (six times daily in high season). Tune your car radio to **Island 92** (91.9 FM) for traffic updates.

BY BUS Traveling by public bus (more like a minivan) is a reasonable means of transport on St. Maarten/St. Martin if you don't mind a bit of inconvenience and overcrowding. Buses run daily from 5am to midnight and serve most major locations on both sides of the island. The most popular run is from Philipsburg on the Dutch side to Marigot on the French side. Privately owned and operated, minibuses tend to follow specific routes; the fare is $2 ($2.50 8pm–midnight). Buses accept both dollars and euros.

[FastFACTS] ST. MAARTEN/ST. MARTIN

Banks Banks affiliated with the **Cirrus** (**© 800/424-7787;** www.mastercard.com) and **PLUS** (**© 800/843-7587;** www.visa.com) ATM networks are located on St. Maarten/St. Martin. Check the following banks' websites for locations of ATMs (also called ABMs for "automated banking machines"): **Windward Island Bank** (www.wib-bank.net), **Scotiabank** (www.scotiabank.com), **First Caribbean Bank** (www.firstcaribbeanbank.com), and **RBTT N.V.** (www.rbtt.com). The international airport in St. Maarten has two ATMs (WIB and RBTT) on the Arrivals floor. A Scotiabank branch is located at the cruise terminal building at Pointe Blanche, St. Maarten. ***Note:*** Keep in mind that ATMs in St. Maarten give you a choice of dollars or euros, while ATMs on St. Martin dispense only euros.

Business Hours On the Dutch side, most banks are open Monday to Friday 8:30am to 3:30pm, Saturday 9am to noon. On the French side, they are usually open Monday to Friday 8:30am to 1:30pm. It's easy to find ATMs. On the Dutch side, several banks are clustered along Front Street in Philipsburg. On the French side, most banks are along rue de la République in Marigot. Although French St. Martin stores open around 9am and close around 7pm, most shopkeepers close for an extended lunch break from around 12:30 to 2pm or even later. Dutch side stores stay open continuously from 9am to 6pm (and later).

Currency U.S. dollars are widely accepted, and prices in hotels and most restaurants and shops are most often designated in dollars as well. On the French side, the official monetary unit is the **euro (€)**, with most establishments widely quoting and accepting either dollars or **Netherlands Antilles florin (NAf) guilders** as well. At press time, the U.S. dollar was trading at $1.42 to 1€. *Prices throughout this chapter are given in U.S. dollars for establishments on the Dutch side, and in euros or dollars for establishments on the French side.*

Documents U.S., British, and Canadian citizens should have a passport, plus an ongoing or return ticket and a confirmed hotel reservation.

Electricity Dutch St. Maarten uses the same voltage (110-volt AC, 60 cycles) with the same electrical configurations as the United States, so adapters and transformers are not necessary. On French St. Martin, 220-volt AC (50 cycles) prevails, so you'll usually need transformers and adapters. To simplify things, many hotels on both sides of the island have installed sockets suitable for both European and North American appliances.

Emergencies For emergencies, call ✆ **911.** On the **Dutch** side, call the **police** at ✆ **599/54-22222** or an **ambulance** at ✆ **599/54-22111;** to report a **fire,** call ✆ **911** or ✆ **120.** On the **French** side, you can reach the **police** by dialing ✆ **17** or **590/87-50-10.** In case of **fire,** dial ✆ **18.** For an **ambulance,** dial ✆ **15.**

Hospitals On the Dutch side, go to the **St. Maarten Medical Center,** Welegen Rd., Cay Hill (✆ **599/54-31111;** www.sintmaarten-medicalcenter.com). On the French side, the local hospital is **Hospital Louis-Constant Fleming,** near Marigot in Concordia (✆ **590/52-25-25**).

Language The language on the St. Maarten side is officially Dutch, and it's officially French on St. Martin. But most people speak English, especially on the Dutch side. A French-based patois is spoken by a small segment of the local populace, as are French Creole, Spanish, and Papiamento.

Liquor Laws On both sides of the island, liquor is sold in grocery and liquor stores on any day of the week. It's legal to have an open container in public, though the authorities are very strict about littering, disorderly behavior, and drunk driving.

Safety Petty crime has become a concern on St. Maarten, with thefts and break-ins on the rise. Travelers are urged to lock their cars and lodging doors and windows at all times. Visitors should exercise common sense and take basic precautions, including being aware of one's surroundings, avoiding walking alone after dark or in remote areas, and locking all valuables in a rental or hotel safe. Also, let that deserted, isolated beach or road remain so.

Taxes & Service Charges For departures to international destinations from Princess Juliana Airport on the Dutch side, there's a departure tax of $30 ($10 if you're leaving the island for St. Eustatius or Saba; if you're leaving by ferry from Marigot Pier to

Anguilla, the departure tax is $4). There is a 3€ departure tax for departures from L'Espérance Airport on the French side. ***Note:*** The departure tax is often included in the airfare. On St. Maarten, a government tax of 5% is added to your hotel bill. On top of that, many hotels tack on a service charge of between 10% and 15%. Hotels on French St. Martin add a 10% service charge and a *taxe de séjour,* a local room tax of 4% to 5%.

Telephone **To call Dutch St. Maarten:** Dial the international access code (011 from the U.S.; 00 from the U.K., Ireland, or New Zealand; or 0011 from Australia), then **599** (the country code for the Netherlands Antilles), followed by **54** and the five-digit local number. To make a local call on Dutch St. Maarten, dial **54,** then the five-digit local number. But if you're calling "long distance" from the Dutch side of the island to the French side of the island, dial **00,** followed by **590590** (the most prevalent international access code for French St. Martin) or, for cellular phones, **590690,** followed by the six-digit local number.

Note: If you're on the French side of the island and want to call anyone on the Dutch side, dial **00,** followed by **599,** then **54** and the five-digit local number. Know in advance that calls between the French and Dutch sides are considered long-distance calls and are much, much more expensive than you might have imagined, considering the relatively short distance.

To call French St. Martin (which is linked to the Guadeloupe telephone system): Dial the international access code (011 from the U.S.; 00 from the U.K., Ireland, or New Zealand; or 0011 from Australia), then **590** (the country code for Guadeloupe), then **590** again, and then the six-digit local number. To make a call from French St. Martin to any point within French St. Martin, no codes are necessary; just dial the local six-digit French number.

To make international calls: From St. Maarten/St. Martin and St. Barts, first dial 00 and then the country code (U.S. or Canada 1, U.K. 44, Ireland 353, Australia 61, New Zealand 64). Next, dial the area code and local number. For example, if you wanted to call the British Embassy in Washington, D.C., you would dial 00-1-202-588-7800. From Anguilla to the U.S., dial 1, then the number.

On the Dutch side, there are facilities for overseas calls, but from the French side you cannot make collect calls to the States, and there are no coin-operated phones. At the Marigot post office, you can purchase a *telecarte,* giving you 40 units. A typical 5-minute call to the States takes up to 120 units. There are two public phones at the Marigot tourist office from which it's possible to make credit card calls. There are six public phones at the post office.

For directory assistance: Dial 150 if you're looking for a number inside St. Maarten/St. Martin, and dial 0 for numbers to all other countries.

For operator assistance: If you need operator assistance in making a call, dial 0 if you're trying to make an international call or call a number within St. Maarten/St. Martin.

Toll-free numbers: There are no toll-free numbers on St. Maarten/St. Martin, Anguilla, or St. Barts, and calling a 1-800 number in the States from them is not toll-free. In fact, it costs the same as an overseas call.

Time Zone St. Maarten and St. Martin operate on Atlantic Standard Time year-round. In winter, if it's 6pm in Philipsburg, it's 5pm in New York. During daylight saving time in the United States, the island and the U.S. East Coast are on the same time.

Tipping Most hotels on both sides on the island add a 10% or 15% service charge to your bill; make sure you're clear on whether it's already included in the original price quoted to you. Most restaurants automatically add a service charge to your bill. If service has not been added (unlikely), it's customary to tip around 15% to 20%. Porters and bellmen expect $1 or 1€ per bag. Taxi drivers should receive 10% of the fare, more if they offer touring or other suggestions.

Water The water on the island is safe to drink. In fact, most hotels serve desalinated water.

Weather The island has a year-round temperature of about 80°F (27°C).

WHERE TO STAY

In Dutch St. Maarten

Timeshares comprise some 60% of the St. Maarten accommodations market. What this means is that you may be competing for rooms with timeshare owners, who generally get first dibs.

Keep in mind that a government tax of 5% is added to your hotel bill. On top of that, many hotels tack on a service charge of between 10% and 15%. Ask whether taxes are included in the rates you're quoted.

VERY EXPENSIVE

Westin St. Maarten Dawn Beach Resort & Spa ★ When this sprawling resort opened in early 2007, one local said it looked like a prison had been plopped down on Dawn Beach. To be fair, the hotel's colonnaded beachfront facade is much more elegant than its character-free backside. And the huge freshwater infinity pool fronting Dawn Beach is truly lovely. This is St. Maarten's top lodging option, and the 306 mostly oceanview guest rooms (and six suites) have all the pampering pluses you'd expect from a Westin, including trademark Heavenly Bed mattresses—and the rates cover a range of budgets. The lobby has a spiffy Frank Lloyd Wright feel, although it's joined at the hip by a clanging casino. Facilities include a full-service, European-style spa, fitness center, retail shops with duty-free shopping, two oceanfront restaurants, watersports, and meeting facilities. The Westin has a popular **Sunday champagne brunch** in the **Ocean** restaurant (noon–3pm; $48 per person).

144 Oyster Pond Rd., St. Maarten, N.A. www.starwoodhotels.com. ✆ **800/WESTIN-1** (937-8461) or 599/54-36700. Fax 599/54-36004. 314 units. Winter $410–$580 double, $1,050–$3,150 suite; off season $325–$545 double, $735–$1,200 suite. AE, MC, V. **Amenities:** 2 restaurants; 2 lounges; babysitting; concierge; fitness center; outdoor pool; casino; room service; spa. *In room:* A/C, TV, hair dryer, minibar, Wi-Fi ($15/day; $50/week).

EXPENSIVE

Divi Little Bay Beach Resort ★ Built on a slender peninsula about a 10-minute drive east of the airport, this timeshare resort/hotel originated as a simple guesthouse in 1955 and soon became famous as the vacation home of the Netherlands's Queen Juliana, Prince Bernhard, and Queen Beatrix. It's been beaten and battered by hurricanes over the years—the beach bar, Gizmo's, was wiped out in 2008 by Hurricane Omar—but it remains the stalwart flagship of the Divi chain. The rooms and public spaces have been nicely renovated and freshened up. The architecture evokes a European seaside village, with stucco walls and terra-cotta roofs, and touches of Dutch colonial here and there. In the upper reaches of the property are the ruins of Fort Amsterdam, once Dutch St. Maarten's most prized military stronghold and today a historical site. The resort is carefully landscaped, and Divi improved the nearby beach after it suffered massive erosion. Divi has a shopping promenade and an art gallery.

Accommodations are airy, accented with ceramic tiles and pastel colors, and each has its own private balcony or patio; suites (and studios) have fully equipped kitchens—the only units that don't have kitchens are the beachfront doubles. The luxury Casita one-bedroom suites even have iPod docking stations. The resort offers a variety of meal plans, including an all-inclusive option.

Little Bay Rd. (P.O. Box 961), Philipsburg, St. Maarten, N.A. www.divilittlebay.com. ✆ **800/367-3484** in the U.S., or 599/54-22333. Fax 599/54-24336. 225 units. Winter $230–$290 double, $270–$330 1-bedroom suite, $475 2-bedroom suite; off season $180–$220 double, $180–$250 1-bedroom suite, $370 2-bedroom suite. Children 14 and under stay free in parent's room. AE, DC, MC, V. **Amenities:** 3 restaurants; bar; activities coordinator; dive shop; gym; Internet (in Bayview Café); 3 outdoor pools; spa; 2 tennis courts (lit); watersports center and equipment/rentals (extensive). *In room:* A/C, TV (DVD in some), CD player (in some), hair dryer, Jacuzzi (in suites), kitchen (in suites), MP3 docking station (in some).

Holland House Beach Hotel ★ The lobby of this polished, well-run "city" hotel runs uninterrupted from bustling Front Street to Great Bay Beach. The public areas are quite stylish, with creamy adobe walls hung with rotating local and Dutch artworks. The lively global clientele enjoys the little touches (free international newspapers, beach chairs, and freshwater beach shower). Most rooms have gorgeous polished hardwood floors and large, arched balconies. The one-bedroom penthouse includes a kitchenette, large-screen TV, DVD, and fax machine. The $36 surcharge is well worth it for the popular oceanview rooms, but weekly stays in any unit lasso huge savings.

The **Ocean Lounge,** the alluring beachfront restaurant and bar (crowned by a billowing tent), is a great spot to sip a cocktail night or day. Fresh fish is the chef's specialty.

43 Front St. (P.O. Box 393), Philipsburg, St. Maarten, N.A. www.hhbh.com. ✆ **800/223-9815** in the U.S., or 599/54-22572. Fax 599/54-24673. 54 units. Winter $230–$310 double, $425 1-bedroom suite, $650 penthouse; off season $175–$310 double, $295 1-bedroom suite, $560 penthouse. Weekly rates available. AE, MC, V. **Amenities:** Restaurant; bar; watersports equipment/rentals. *In room:* A/C, ceiling fan, TV, fridge, hair dryer, Wi-Fi (free).

Princess Heights ★ In the hills above Dawn Beach, which lies just across the road, this all-suites condo hotel has heart-stopping panoramic views. Princess Heights is reached after a 10-minute drive from Philipsburg. Opening onto St. Barts in the distance, the suites are big and tastefully furnished, each with one or two bedrooms and separate living rooms opening onto balconies and sumptuous views. Living rooms have not only foldout sofas but foldout chairs as well. Granite-topped counters, clay-tiled terraces, marble floors throughout, and fully equipped kitchens make for a comfortable, convenient stay, and the hillside location spells privacy. The only hitch: You have to walk 5 minutes down a steep path or drive to get to Dawn Beach. In 2008 the hotel added 36 oceanview deluxe suites on the hillside slightly above the original building. Ask for one—the rooms are the hotel's spiffiest.

156 Oyster Pond Rd., Oyster Pond, St. Maarten, N.A. www.princessheights.com. ✆ **800/881-1744** in the U.S., or 599/54-36858. Fax 599/54-36007. 51 units. Winter $285 studio, $350–$450 suite; off season $160–$210 studio, $225–$375 suite. Children (2 maximum) 11 and under stay free in parent's room. Extra person $35–$45. AE, DISC, MC, V. **Amenities:** Babysitting; fitness center; Internet; outdoor pool. *In room:* A/C, flatscreen TV, hair dryer, Jacuzzi, kitchen (in suites), kitchenette (in studios), minibar.

Sonesta Great Bay Beach Resort & Casino ★ ☺ Built in 1968, the second-oldest hotel in St. Maarten (after Divi) is ideally located a few minutes' walk from downtown Philipsburg. Some say that it's looking a tad dowdy and overdue for refreshment. No matter: The public spaces, pools, beaches, and bars are always buzzing with activity—and the setting inside a sexy curve of Great Bay beach is hard to beat. This resort was smartly designed around that priceless crescent of beach. You get harbor views virtually anywhere and everywhere you plop yourself; whether you're eating breakfast in the alfresco **Bay View** restaurant, sunning beside the infinity pool, or having dinner at the **Molasses** restaurant, the lights on the bay shimmer like diamonds. All rooms have the standard decorative tropical trappings, but budget travelers can save big by choosing a room with a "mountain" view (a parking lot, some shrubbery, and, in the distance, the hills of St. Maarten) over one with ocean views. The suites include kitchens and sofa beds. Friendly management, extensive watersports options, and an enviable location make this a good choice for families.

19 Little Bay Rd. (P.O. Box 910), Philipsburg, St. Maarten, N.A. www.sonesta.com/greatbay. ✆ **800/766-3782** in the U.S., or 599/54-22446. Fax 599/54-23859. 257 units. Year-round $135–$440 double; $245–$775 suite. AE, DC, DISC, MC, V. **Amenities:** 3 restaurants; 4 bars; babysitting; children's program; dive shop; fitness center; Internet cafe; 2 Jacuzzi; 3 outdoor pools; casino; spa; tennis court (lit); watersports equipment/rentals (extensive). *In room:* A/C, ceiling fan, satellite TV, fridge (in some), hair dryer, kitchenette (in some), Wi-Fi (free).

Sonesta Maho Beach Hotel & Casino ★ Separated into three distinct sections, this megaresort is the island's largest hotel and practically a self-contained village. It's the closest thing on either the Dutch or French side to a Vegas-style blockbuster, and it's right in the thick of the Maho Bay action. The hotel is always packed with conventioneers and tour groups, but constant refreshments keep things polished. Set on a 4-hectare (10-acre) tract that straddles the often congested coastal road adjacent to the crescent-shaped Maho Beach, the hotel's scattered structures are painted a trademark cream and white. Rooms in the Ocean Terrace building are large and comfortably furnished. Inside the main building, the premier rooms on floors 6 through 9 were refreshed in 2010 in pleasing hues of dusty lavender/rose and orange-browns. Suites have Jacuzzi tubs that open onto the bedroom and sea-and-sky views. Each has Italian tiles, plush upholstery, a walk-in closet, and soundproofing that buffers the thundering boom of planes taking off at nearby Princess Juliana airport several times a day.

The hotel contains three restaurants. The **Point** is good for steak and seafood; the open-air **Palms** is a casual beachfront cafe; the **Ocean Terrace** has all-day buffets. The glitzy **Casino Royale,** across the street, includes a cabaret theater for glitzy shows and **Tantra** (formerly the Q Club), one of the island's hottest late-night dance spots. On the resort's street front, the Maho Promenade is filled with shops open late, restaurants (including Cheri's Café), a scuba-diving center, even a classy gentleman's club.

1 Rhine Rd., Maho Beach, St. Maarten, N.A. www.sonesta.com/mahobeach. ✆ **800/766-3782** in the U.S., or 599/54-52115. Fax 599/54-53180. 537 units. Year-round $135–$470 double, $280–$620 suite. AE, DC, DISC, MC, V. **Amenities:** 3 restaurants; 1 nightclub; babysitting; children's program; fitness center; 2 outdoor pools; casino; room service; spa; 4 tennis courts. *In room:* A/C, TV, fridge (in some), hair dryer, Wi-Fi (free).

MODERATE/INEXPENSIVE

The Horny Toad Guesthouse This homey, welcoming place is run by Maine expat Betty Vaughan. Although the hotel is near the airport, the roar of jumbo jets is heard only a few times a day. Children 7 and under are not allowed, but families with older children are welcome, and repeat visitors quickly become part of the Horned Toad family. Seven well-maintained units lie in an amply proportioned beachside house originally built in the 1950s as a private home by the island's former governor. The eighth room is in half of an octagonal "round house," with large windows and views of the sea. Guest rooms range from medium-size to spacious, and each has a fully equipped kitchen and a king-size bed. The guesthouse has no pool, no restaurant, and no organized activities of any kind, but the beach is just steps away, and the island of Saba lies off in the distance. Join the other guests in impromptu get-togethers around the barbecue pavilion.

2 Vlaun Dr., Simpson Bay, St. Maarten, N.A. www.thehornytoadguesthouse.com. © **800/417-9361** in the U.S., or 599/54-54323. Fax 599/54-53316. 8 units. Winter $200 double; off season $110 double. Extra person $40 in winter, $25 off season. MC, V. No children 6 and under allowed. **Amenities:** Smoke-free rooms. *In room:* A/C, ceiling fan, kitchen, Wi-Fi (free).

La Vista Resort This small timeshare resort lies at the foot of Pelican Cay. For a fee, guests can use the more elaborate facilities of the nearby Pelican Resort, with its casino, shops, and spa. The West Antillean–style resort consists of two parts—La Vista, a 2-minute walk from a good sandy beach, and La Vista Beach, which is on the beach. Rooms at La Vista come in seven different categories, including a junior suite, deluxe suite, and penthouse. Each suite has a fully equipped kitchenette or kitchen, and all have panoramic ocean views. The rooms at La Vista Beach come in studios and two-bedroom apartments, and all open directly onto the beach. Our preference is the one-bedroom Antillean cottage with a front porch (suitable for four). The **Hideaway Bar & Restaurant** serves well-prepared French cuisine adjacent to the pool, with live entertainment several nights a week.

53 Billy Folly Rd., Pelican Cay (P.O. Box 2086), Simpson Bay, St. Maarten, N.A. www.lavistaresort.com. © **599/54-43005.** Fax 599/54-43010. 50 suites. Winter $180–$210 junior and deluxe suites, $235–$330 suite for 4, $270–$300 penthouse, $210 cottage; off season $140–$160 junior and deluxe suites, $175–$225 suite for 4; $200–$215 penthouse, $160 cottage. Extra person $20. Children 12 and under stay free in parent's room. AE, DISC, MC, V. **Amenities:** Restaurant; bar; outdoor pool. *In room:* A/C, TV, hair dryer, kitchen or kitchenette, Wi-Fi (free).

Mary's Boon Beach Resort ★ Nestled in tropical greenery, Mary's Boon is one of those endearing places that draw loyal guests year after year. The small, convivial bar, an informal watering hole for local movers and shakers from nearby Simpson Bay, has a fizzy happy hour. In business for 40-plus years, Mary's Boon enjoys direct access to 3 miles of lovely, uncrowded beach with powdery white sand. Even better, its owner has beautified the rooms and added spa services, and is going as green as possible on an island that doesn't even recycle (yet). He has succeeded without undermining the inn's charming, offbeat ambience.

Mary's Boon is right near the airport, so guests have to deal with the plate-rattling sounds of jets taking off at various times during the day. But it's also just minutes from casinos, shops, and restaurants. Every room varies architecturally, but all have verandas or terraces; a number have big cherrywood beds and Balinese woodcarvings. Those directly facing the sea enjoy high ceilings and gentle breezes. Renovated rooms are equipped with full fridges, granite countertops, stainless steel appliances, and flatscreen TVs. Upstairs, room nos. 201 through 205 are particularly spacious, opening up to the sea on one side and the garden on the other. **Tides,** the modest beach restaurant and bar, offers satisfying, good-value food that reveals a sure hand in the kitchen—it should, as the head chef, Leona, has been cooking here for 36 years!—and its perch over the beach, with the sea breeze wafting in, is tonic for what ails you.

117 Simpson Bay Rd., St. Maarten, N.A. www.marysboon.com. © **877/260-7483** in the U.S., or 599/54-57000. Fax 599/54-53403. 37 units. Winter $135–$300 double (studio and 1-bedroom suite), $250–$425 2-bedroom suite; off season $75–$275 double, $135–$415 2-bedroom suite. Extra person $35. MC, V. Take the first right turn as you head from the airport toward Philipsburg, then follow the signs to Mary's Boon. **Amenities:** Restaurant; bar; babysitting; outdoor pool; room service; spa; Wi-Fi (free). *In room:* A/C, ceiling fan, TV, hair dryer, kitchen or kitchenette.

Pasanggrahan Royal Guest House ★ Construction is ongoing at this wooden West Indian–style guesthouse, built in 1904 as the summer home of the Dutch Queen Wilhelmina. A new five-story addition, with underground parking, a spa, and 19 new rooms, was scheduled for completion in 2012. Pasanggrahan enjoys a prime spot on the beach in Philipsburg, sandwiched between busy, narrow Front Street and the harborside boardwalk, and set back and shaded under tall trees. The interior has a gracious, Victorian decor, filled with peacock bamboo chairs, Indian spool tables, and a gilt-framed oil portrait of the queen. The small- to medium-size accommodations have queen-size, double, or king-size beds with four-poster designs; some are in the main building, and others are in an adjoining annex. The finest have genuine colonial flair, with antique secretaries and four-posters swaddled in mosquito netting; madras valances; hand-stitched quilts; beamed ceilings; and still-life paintings.

Set among lush palms is the harborfront **Pasanggrahan Restaurant** ★, which specializes in family-style dinners and fresh fish caught by the hotel's own deep-sea charter fishing boat. Even if you aren't staying here, this is a peaceful, shady oasis for lunch or a cocktail after a day wrestling the cruise-ship hordes in downtown Philipsburg. The food is good and fresh, and the view of the harbor from the old wooden veranda, with Fort Amsterdam in the distance, never quits.

19 Front St. (P.O. Box 151), Philipsburg, St. Maarten, N.A. www.pasanroyalinn.com. ✆ **599/54-23588.** Fax 599/54-22885. 38 units. Winter $160–$250 double; off season $100–$250 double. Extra person $75 winter, $55 off season. DISC, MC, V. Closed Sept. **Amenities:** Restaurant; 2 bars; Internet (free). *In room:* A/C, ceiling fan, TV, fridge, kitchenette (in some).

In French St. Martin

Hotels on French St. Martin add a 10% service charge and a *taxe de séjour*; this local room tax is 4% to 5%. Expect higher rates during Christmas week. ***Note:*** Rates are quoted in either euros or dollars, depending on how establishments quoted them at press time.

VERY EXPENSIVE

Green Cay Villas ★ This gated hillside community overlooking the sweep of Orient Bay features 16 fully equipped three-bedroom villas, each with a private pool, at (comparatively) bargain rates, especially off season. Each can be configured into individual units; even the one-bedroom contains a modern kitchen. The design emphasizes cool blues, pristine off-whites, and rich tropical accents mirroring sea, sand, and sunset. White and natural wicker and hardwood furnishings are juxtaposed with boldly hued art naïf, throw pillows, fabrics, ceramics, and whimsical touches like painted parrots dangling from high coffered ceilings.

Parc de la Baie Orientale (B.P. 3006), 97150 St. Martin, F.W.I. www.greencayvillas.com. ✆ **866/592-4213** in the U.S., or 590/87-38-63. Fax 590/87-39-27. 16 units. Winter $630 1-bedroom suite, $825 2-bedroom suite, $950 3-bedroom villa; off season $420 1-bedroom suite, $550 2-bedroom suite, $660 3-bedroom villa. Rates include continental breakfast. 4-night minimum. MC, V. **Amenities:** Gym; private pool in each suite. *In room:* A/C, TV, VCR, hair dryer, Internet, kitchen, Wi-Fi (free).

La Samanna ★★★ La Samanna has earned a reputation as a world-class complex where the cognoscenti come to relax and unwind. With low-lying Mediterranean-style villas spread out over a long stretch of Baie Longue, one of St. Martin's finest beaches, this Orient-Express resort is lovely indeed. The sweeping views from the hotel's signature restaurant are stunning, and the colonial-style lobby and bar are handsomely atmospheric. Regardless of their size, most rooms feature private terraces. Suites and villas have spacious bedrooms with luxurious beds, fully equipped kitchens, living and dining rooms, and large patios. The bathrooms are spacious and well designed, with bidets and hand-painted Mexican tiles. Five state-of-the-art specialty suites have private terraces with Baie Longue views. For the ultimate in luxury, eight villas have private wraparound infinity pools and rooftop terraces with magnificent views. The three- or four-bedroom villas come with private concierge service, private beach cabanas, and VIP airport transfers.

Despite the price tag, La Samanna isn't stuffy; everyone is treated royally here. Guests enjoy dinner on a candlelit terrace spectacularly perched above Baie Longue—the ambience is pure French Riviera. (***Note:*** Children 6 and under are not permitted in the main restaurant for dinner.) The wine cellar, Le Cave, holds some 14,000 bottles. The poolside grill serves lunch daily and dinner 2 nights a week. If you can't make dinner in the main restaurant, you can enjoy the same great views during the sumptuous **buffet breakfasts ★**, as delicious as the setting—and included in room rates. With the curve of Baie Longue stretched out below, there are few better ways to start the day.

Baie Longue (B.P. 4077), 97064 St. Martin CEDEX, F.W.I. www.lasamanna.com. ✆ **800/957-6128** in the U.S., or 590/87-64-00. Fax 590/87-87-86. 81 units. Winter $995 double, $1,925–$5,275 suite; off season $450–$680 double, from $850 suite; year-round from $3,000 villa. Extra person $75. Children 11 and under stay free in parent's room. Rates include full buffet breakfast. AE, MC, V. Closed late Aug to late Oct. **Amenities:** 2 restaurants; 2 bars; babysitting; fitness center; 2 freshwater outdoor pools; room service; spa; 3 tennis courts (lit); watersports equipment/rentals (extensive). *In room:* A/C, ceiling fan, TV/DVD, CD player (in some), hair dryer, minibar, plunge pool (in some), Wi-Fi (free).

EXPENSIVE

Alamanda Resort ★ Small and intimate, like a European beachfront inn, the Alamanda opens onto Orient Bay's beautiful beach. The resort is a cluster of Creole *cazes,* or little houses, surrounding a lushly landscaped outdoor pool quite near the beach. If the Alamanda has a drawback, it's that not all rooms have ocean views. Bedrooms are spacious and done up in soothing earth tones, with decorative accents in bold colors from sunflower yellow to tomato red, or pineapple patterns. The king-size beds have elegant bones, often a four-poster. The best accommodations are the two-bedroom duplexes with a second bathroom. Our favorite place to dine here is at **Kakao Beach** beachfront restaurant, featuring both Creole and European specialties in a laid-back Caribbean atmosphere. A less expensive choice is **Cafe Alamanda,** with an inventive tropical cuisine served at poolside.

Baie Orientale (B.P. 5166), 97071 St. Martin, F.W.I. www.alamanda-resort.com. ✆ **800/622-7836** in the U.S. or 590/52-87-40. Fax 590/52-87-41. 42 units. Winter $375–$490 double, $600 2-bedroom duplex, $710–$790 suite; off season $270–$340 double, $440 2-bedroom duplex, $450–$500 suite. Extra person $50. Up to two children 11 and under stay free in two parents' room. AE, MC, V. Closed Sept. **Amenities:** 2 restaurants; 2 bars; babysitting; concierge; gym; outdoor pool; room service; 2 tennis courts; watersports equipment. *In room:* A/C, ceiling fan, TV, hair dryer, kitchenette, Wi-Fi (free).

Esmeralda Resort ★ This hillside compound of well-maintained Creole-inspired villas clings to sloping terrain that's interspersed with lush gardens. It's just a 25-minute taxi ride northeast of Princess Juliana airport. Opening onto Orient Beach, the Esmeralda blossomed into a full-scale resort in the early 1990s, offering views over Orient Bay and French flair. Each of the 18 Spanish Mission–style, tile-roofed villas can be configured into four separate units through lockouts between rooms. Villas are outfitted with a king-size or two double beds, a kitchenette, a terrace, and a private entrance. Each villa has its own communal pool, which creates the feeling of a private club. The suites (one to five bedrooms) are luxuriously spacious.

The Astrolabe, with its award-winning chef, Stephane Decluseau, serves fine French-Caribbean specialties at breakfast and dinner daily. For lunch, the hotel provides an ID card that you can use for discounts at any of a half-dozen restaurants along Orient Bay.

Baie Orientale (B.P. 5141), 97071 St. Martin, F.W.I. www.esmeralda-resort.com. ✆ **590/87-36-36.** Fax 590/87-35-18. 65 units. Winter $375–$550 double, $690–$1,020 suite; off season $270–$370 double, $440–$600 suite. Extra person 12 and over $80. Children 11 and under free in parent's room. AE, MC, V. Closed Sept. **Amenities:** 2 restaurants; bar; babysitting; horseback riding (nearby); 18 outdoor pools; room service; 2 tennis courts; watersports equipment/rentals (extensive). *In room:* A/C, ceiling fan, TV, Internet (free), fridge, hair dryer, kitchenette.

Grand Case Beach Club ★ This bundling of red-roofed buildings sits between two beaches just a short stroll from the action in "downtown" Grand Case. Draped in bougainvillea, the resort is immaculately maintained, and you can't beat the views. Families will particularly appreciate the gated entrance (making the lovely Petite Plage practically private) and 24-hour security guard/video surveillance. All rooms and suites have been newly refreshed and feature well-stocked kitchens with granite counters and private balconies or patios (the best offering smashing views of Anguilla). Little extras include a sampling of island-music CDs and a bottle of wine at check-in. The general manager is conscientious, cordial, and helpful, qualities he inculcates in the staff.

The **Sunset Café,** set spectacularly on the rocks overlooking the water, serves hearty food at reasonable prices for breakfast, lunch, and dinner daily.

Grand Case, 97150, St. Martin, F.W.I. www.grandcasebeachclub.com. ✆ **800/344-3016** in the U.S., or 590/87-51-87. Fax 590/87-59-93. 73 units. Winter $320–$395 studio double, $375–$530 1-bedroom suite, $530–$565 2-bedroom suite; off season $150–$220 studio double, $170–$283 1-bedroom suite, $280–$295 2-bedroom suite. Rates include continental breakfast. Children 11 and under stay free in parent's room. Extra person $35. AE, MC, V. **Amenities:** Restaurant; bar; fitness center; outdoor pool; tennis court; watersports equipment/rentals (extensive). *In room:* A/C, ceiling fan, TV, CD player, hair dryer, kitchen.

Hotel Beach Plaza This is the best hotel within a reasonable distance of Marigot's commercial heart. The three-story building centers on a soaring atrium festooned with live banana trees and climbing vines. It's within a cluster of buildings composed mostly of condominiums. Built in 1996, and painted in shades of blue and white, the hotel is set midway between the open sea and the lagoon, giving all rooms water views. The white interiors are accented with varnished, dark-tinted woods and a tropical motif. Each room contains a balcony, tile floors, native art, and simple hardwood furniture, including a writing desk and comfortable beds. The hotel's restaurant, **Le Corsaire,** serves French food except for the all-you-can-eat buffets two nights a week, which feature Creole classics and seafood, respectively.

Baie de Marigot, 97150 St. Martin, F.W.I. www.hotelbeachplazasxm.com. ✆ **800/221-5333** in the U.S., or 590/87-87-00. Fax 590/87-18-87. 144 units. Winter 220€–379€ double, 448€–506€ suite; off season 150€–295€ double, 342€ suite. One child 11 and under stays free in parent's room. Rates include buffet breakfast. AE, MC, V. **Amenities:** Restaurant; 2 bars; babysitting; bikes; outdoor pool; room service; watersports equipment/rentals (extensive). *In room:* A/C, TV, fridge, hair dryer, Wi-Fi (free).

Hotel La Plantation ★ Although it's a few minutes' walk from the gorgeous white-sand beach, this is one of the most attractive and appealing hotels at Orient Bay. It's set on a steep, meticulously landscaped slope. Seventeen colonial-style villas are scattered around the tropically landscaped grounds and pool; each villa contains a suite and two studios, which can be rented separately or combined. The spacious units are furnished in a colorful Creole theme, complete with hand-painted or hand-stenciled murals, and each sports its own oceanview terrace. Studios have kitchenettes and queen-size or twin beds; the suites have separate bedrooms with king-size beds, big living rooms, full kitchens, and beautifully tiled full bathrooms. **Café Plantation** serves French and Creole dinners. At lunch, clients use an in-house "privilege card" to buy French/Creole/international meals at any of five beach-front restaurants loosely associated with the resort.

C 5 Parc de La Baie Orientale, Marigot, 97150 St. Martin, F.W.I. www.la-plantation.com. ✆ **590/29-58-00.** Fax 590/29-58-08. 52 units. Winter $340–$360 studio for 2, from $510 suite; off season $200–$210 studio, from $275 suite. Children 11 and under stay free in parent's room. Rates include buffet breakfast. DISC, MC, V. Closed Sept 1 to mid-Oct. **Amenities:** Restaurant; beach bar and grill; babysitting; bikes; horseback riding; concierge; health club; outdoor pool; 2 tennis courts; watersports equipment/rentals; Wi-Fi (free; in public spaces). *In room:* A/C, ceiling fan, TV, CD player (in some), fridge, hair dryer, kitchen or kitchenette.

Hôtel L'Esplanade ★★ This lovely, beautifully managed small hotel just gets better and better. Along with its sister hotel, Le Petit (p. 588), it's easily one of the nicest places to stay on the entire island. A collection of suites set on a steep slope above the village of Grand Case, L'Esplanade has the feel of a boutique inn on a French hillside. Flowered vines frame terraces with views of the village and sea below. The resort is connected by a network of steps and terraced gardens; cascades of bougainvillea drape walls accented with hand-painted tiles and blue slate roofs. The lovely pool is just steps down the hill, and access to a beach is via a 6-minute walk down a winding pathway. There's no restaurant, but the village of Grand Case is famous for its many fine dining options. All guest rooms have private terraces that angle out toward the sea and the sun setting behind Anguilla. Each individually decorated unit contains a kitchen with up-to-date cookware, Italian porcelain tile floors, beamed ceilings, plasma-screen TVs, DVDs, mahogany and wicker furniture, and very comfortable queen- or king-size beds (many four-poster). Slate and tumbled-marble bathrooms are beautifully equipped. The loft suites on the upper floors are worth the extra charge—they include a sofa bed downstairs, an upstairs master bedroom with a king-size bed, and a partial bathroom downstairs. The cordial owners, Marc and Kristin Petrelluzzi, have completely redone every suite; additional, even posher villas are in the works.

Grand Case (B.P. 5007), 97150 St. Martin, F.W.I. www.lesplanade.com. ✆ **866/596-8365** in the U.S., or 590/87-06-55. Fax 590/87-29-15. 24 units. Winter $395 studio, $445–$495 loft, $495 suite; off season $245 studio, $295–$345 loft, $345 suite. Extra person $70 winter, $50 off season. AE, MC, V. **Amenities:** Bar (winter); babysitting; outdoor pool. *In room:* A/C, ceiling fan, TV, CD player, hair dryer, Internet (free), kitchen, minibar.

Le Domaine de Lonvilliers ★ This attractive resort sprawls over 60 hectares (148 acres) of palm-fringed gardens and follows the lovely curve of the beach at Anse Marcel. It and the neighboring Radisson (originally one hotel) are the only inhabitants of this beguiling, secluded cove. The comfortable rooms are done in cool creams and browns or bold reds set against ivory walls and white tile floors. All have spacious bathrooms and either a private balcony or terrace. In its beachside restaurant, **La Table du Marché,** the hotel has the Caribbean twin to the St-Tropez original.

Anse Marcel, 97150 St. Martin, F.W.I. www.hotel-le-domaine.com. ✆ **590/52-35-35.** Fax 590/29-10-81. 141 units. Winter 280€–500€ double, 560€–1,450€ suite; off season 235€–420€ double, 470€–1,090€ suite. Extra person 60€. 1 child 11 and under stays free in parent's room. Rates include buffet breakfast. DISC, MC, V. Closed Sept 1 to mid-Oct. **Amenities:** Restaurant; beach bar; lounge; fitness center; outdoor pool; room service; spa; 2 tennis courts; watersports equipment/rentals (extensive). *In room:* A/C, TV, kitchen (in some), Wi-Fi (free).

Le Petit Hotel ★ 🎁 This thoughtfully designed hotel opens directly onto the sands of Grand Case Beach. It practically defines casual chic. It shares the same strong management, meticulous attention to detail, and sense of stylish comfort that distinguishes its sister property, L'Esplanade (see below). Furnishings and accents are sourced from around the globe, including hand-painted tiles throughout the public spaces and hallways, and Balinese teak and Brazilian mahogany. Natural wicker beds are topped with white down duvets and Frette linens. The smallish bathrooms are mostly shower only, and the kitchenettes have a microwave, a fridge, and a two-burner stovetop, but no oven. Each has a huge, beautifully appointed terrace or balcony overlooking the beach. The overall effect is one of serene sanctuary. Though there's no restaurant, the town's superb dining options are steps away.

248 bd. de Grand Case, Grand Case, 97150 St. Martin, F.W.I. www.lepetithotel.com. ✆ **590/29-09-65.** Fax 590/87-09-19. 10 units. Winter $415–$455 double, $525 suite; off season $265–$305 double, $375 suite. Extra person (including children) $50–$70. Rates include continental breakfast. AE, MC, V. **Amenities:** Babysitting; activities desk. *In room:* A/C, ceiling fan, TV, CD player, fridge, hair dryer, kitchenette, Wi-Fi (free).

Radisson Blu Resort Marina & Spa, St. Martin ★★ ☺ This 250-room property is now a full-fledged Radisson Blu—which means it trends a little more upscale and boutiquey than standard Radisson-branded properties. It's the only resort on island with direct access to a full-service marina, and the setting is a beaut: tucked inside the half-moon of the cove at Anse Marcel, with the lights of Anguilla twinkling across the sea. The location inside this secluded cove and the property's sheer sense of space (7.3 hectares/18 acres) give it a real getaway feel. The infinity, zero-entry pool is spectacular: at 93m (305 ft.) it's the largest freshwater pool on island. The hotel is suite-heavy (63 suites), and most of the units face the flower-filled courtyard; if you want a full ocean view from your patio, ask for a room at the end of the East and West buildings. Every room has a patio/balcony and the trademark Radisson "Sleep Number" Bed; bathrooms have been handsomely updated. Le Spa has five treatment rooms and two full cabanas for outside treatment; you can choose the color of your lighting and even bring your iPod. The main restaurant, C Le Restaurant (see "Dining," below), is set alongside the Baie des Froussards, where sailboats are silhouetted against the starry sky. Radisson will arrange watersports excursions that leave straight from the resort marina—you don't have to go through St. Maarten. You can get to the Radisson the prosaic way (by taxi) or the cool way: by water taxi ($45 one-way adult; $30 children 3–12) straight from the airport to the resort in the *ScoobiTWO* catamaran.

Anse Marcel (B.P. 581), 97056 St. Martin CEDEX, F.W.I. www.radissonblu.com/resort-stmartin. ✆ **800/333-3333** in the U.S. or Canada, or 590/87-67-00. Fax 590/87-30-38. 252 units. Winter 340€–420€ double, 590€–630€ suite; off season 210€–300€ double, 390€–550€ suite. Children 11 and under stay free in parent's room. Rates include full breakfast. AE, DC, DISC, MC, V. **Amenities:** 2 restaurants; 2 bars; ATM; babysitting; bocce court; children's program w/clubhouse & playground; concierge; fitness center; volleyball; full-service marina; 2 pools; spa; watersports center/dive center. *In room:* A/C, flatscreen TV/DVD, hair dryer, minibar, MP3 docking station, Wi-Fi (free).

MODERATE

Club Orient Naturist Resort ★ Occupying an isolated spot, this is the only true nudist resort in the French West Indies, but it's not a particularly wild, swinging place. Celebrating more than 30 years of business, it's clean, decent, middle-class, family friendly even. Very few singles check in, in fact. Many of the guests are older and very conservative—just looking for a quiet, reclusive getaway to walk around naked. There's no pool on the premises, but the chalets are right on an excellent beach, with plentiful activities to facilitate hanging out (in every sense). Accommodations, set in red-pine chalets imported from Finland, sport a basic IKEA-meets-campground-cabin look, though the decor has been spruced up. All have outside showers, and most have both front and back porches. At Papagayo Restaurant, you can dine alfresco; the popular 5-to-7pm happy hour allows guests to compare, er, notes. However, each unit has a kitchenette, and there's a general store, **La Boutique,** on-site if you want to cook your own meal.

1 Baie Orientale, 97150 St. Martin, F.W.I. www.cluborient.com. ✆ **877/456-6833** in the U.S., or 590/87-33-85. Fax 590/87-33-76. 136 units. Winter 215€–230€ studio and suite, 330€–360€ chalet, 750€ villa; off season 135€–190€ studio and suite, 185€–280€ chalet, 450€–560€ villa. Extra person 12 and over 25€. Children 11 and under stay free in parent's room. AE, DC, DISC, MC, V. **Amenities:** 2 restaurants; 2 bars; babysitting; fitness center; library; 2 tennis courts (lit); wellness center (w/spa treatments); watersports equipment/rentals (extensive). *In room:* A/C, ceiling fan, kitchen, Wi-Fi (free).

WHERE TO DINE

In Dutch St. Maarten

Rates are quoted in dollars on Dutch St. Maarten. Unlike in French St. Martin, restaurants do not include a service charge, and gratuities are appreciated.

VERY EXPENSIVE

Rare ★★ STEAKHOUSE Dino Jagtiani, the whiz behind the adjacent Temptation (see below), opened this take on the classic chophouse in 2005. The futuristic-yet-retro space is wittily designed. The only steakhouse in St. Maarten to carry USDA Prime dry-aged certified Angus beef, Rare offers choices from a 12-ounce filet mignon to a 28-ounce porterhouse. Those seeking lighter fare can savor sashimi-grade tuna with wasabi mash, or Parmigiano-crusted salmon. Anyone could make a meal of the home-baked bread and dips (hummus, pesto, tapenade). Dino's creativity truly shines in sauces (nine, including chipotle-ketchup and spicy peanut). Desserts include an inspired s'mores cobbler, with chocolate, graham crackers, marshmallow crust, caramel, and vanilla ice cream.

Atlantis Casino, Cupecoy. ✆ **599/54-55714.** www.chefdino.com. Reservations required. Main courses $25–$45. AE, DISC, MC, V. Mon–Sat 6:30–10:30pm.

Temptation ★★★ NOUVEAU CARIBBEAN The name may sound like a strip club, but this innovative gem is one of the finest restaurants on island. Owner/chef Dino Jagtiani, who hails from a multigenerational East Indian family, is a native and graduate of the prestigious Culinary Institute of America. His mother, Asha, graciously greets diners "as if it were our house, only for 100 guests." Dino's Asian-inspired cuisine is exciting, often utilizing unorthodox pairings. Main courses include "Quack Quack l'Orange," orange-ginger-glazed crispy duck breast with Asian veggie stir-fried rice; chicken-'n'-shrimp pad Thai; and veal *osso bucco* braised in red wine. You'll find the perfect wine complement on one of the island's top wine lists.

Atlantis Casino, Cupecoy. ✆ **599/54-55714.** www.chefdino.com. Main courses $34–$38. AE, MC, V. Tues–Sun 6:30–10:30pm.

EXPENSIVE

Antoine ★ FRENCH In a lovely seaside setting, Antoine serves comforting bistro food with sophistication and style. The handsome room is decked with jungle-themed Haitian masterworks, Delft tile, hurricane lanterns, old phonographs, and towering floral arrangements. Start with the chef's savory kettle of fish soup, escargots de Bourgogne, or the almost translucent sea scallops Nantaise. You can't go wrong with the baked red snapper filet delicately flavored with shallots and a white-wine butter sauce; shrimp scampi flambéed with Pastis; or grilled local lobster. And desserts are satisfyingly sinful. Antoine is also open for lunch, serving pastas, burgers, sandwiches, and salads, and has a basic kids' menu.

119 Front St., Philipsburg. ✆ **599/54-22964.** www.antoinerestaurant.com. Reservations recommended. Main courses $9–$24 lunch, $19–$40 dinner; lobster thermidor $46. AE, DISC, MC, V. Daily 11am–10pm.

La Gondola ★★ ITALIAN In a large, warmly lit room, guests dine on fresh pasta dishes and impeccably prepared Italian classics. The decor gives the place a swooning "mamma mia" ambience: The overriding palette is bordello red, unabashedly accented by neoclassical cherubs and gilt. The food, too, hews to the tried-and-true. But the minestrone is pitch-perfect, and the tomato sauce sparkles. For something richly decadent, try the lobster ravioli in a lobster sauce—it's not overkill, trust me—or the baked veal manicotti. The congenial staff makes the dining experience a real pleasure.

Atlantis Casino, Cupecoy. ✆ **599/54-53938.** www.lagondola-sxm.com. Reservations recommended. Main courses $18–$32. AE, MC, V. Daily 6–10pm.

L'Escargot ★★ FRENCH/CREOLE You can't miss the wildly painted shutters and tropical Toulouse-Lautrec murals of revelers on the yellow exterior of this 160-year-old Creole cottage. The high spirits continue within, thanks to the colorful, candlelit decor and mellow staff, which does double duty performing the Friday night cabaret drag show, *La Cage aux Folles*. The chef is deft with fish, particularly classic preparations like meunière, and hearty bistro classics. The *coeur de filet a la confiture d'oignons* (filet of beef served in a sweet-onion dressing perfumed with grenadine) will melt in your mouth. And, oh yes, snails, with at least six preparations on the menu (try the sampler plate), including *sur champignons* (in fresh mushroom caps), *en croustade au safran* (in a crust with chardonnay and saffron sauce), and in cherry tomatoes with garlic butter. It's a temple to garlic and color and bonhomie—and a memorable evening out in Philipsburg.

96 Front St., Philipsburg. ✆ **599/54-22483.** www.lescargotrestaurant.com. Reservations recommended. Main courses $19–$30. AE, DISC, MC, V. Mon–Fri 11am–3pm; daily 6–10pm.

Saratoga ★ INTERNATIONAL/SEAFOOD This restaurant, owned and run by Culinary Institute of America grad John Jackson, occupies a beautiful setting, with a Spanish colonial–style exterior and gleaming mahogany inside. Seating is either indoors or on a marina-side veranda. The food is beautifully presented. Although the menu changes frequently, it leans toward light and healthy, with some six different salads, a gazpacho with lobster, and lots of grilled local fish. Not that fat is banned: If you're looking for decadent, opt for the linguine primavera, here prepared with *both* smoked ham and bacon. Yum. Jackson dips into Thai and classic Chinese preparations, including salt-and-pepper-fried whole black seabass.

Simpson Bay Yacht Club, Airport Rd. ✆ **599/54-42421.** www.sxmsaratoga.com. Reservations recommended. Main courses $24–$37. AE, MC, V. Mon–Sat 6:30–10pm. Closed Aug to mid-Oct.

MODERATE

The harborfront **Pasanggrahan Restaurant,** 19 Front St., Philipsburg (✆ **599/54-23588;** www.pasanroyalinn.com), in the Pasanggrahan Inn (p. 584), is a peaceful, shady oasis for lunch or a drink. The food is good and fresh, and the views of Great Bay are wonderful.

Chesterfields ★ CARIBBEAN/INTERNATIONAL The "house" restaurant at the Great Bay Marina is the ideal spot for après snorkeling or sailing. Set right on the dock of the marina, with boats cruising in and salt air wafting, Chesterfields has an appealingly roughhewn, nautical feel, with wooden tables and walls tacked with mounted fish. A friendly staff oversees the comings and goings of sunburned sailors, grizzled captains, and day-trippers revitalized after a morning of exploring offshore islets. Look for standard pub fare such as burgers, steaks, salads, and sandwiches, as well as island specialties like garlic shrimp, stuffed mahimahi, and conch chowder. The food is good and hearty—testament to Chesterfields' nearly 30 years of solid customer service.

Dock Maarten, Great Bay Marina, Philipsburg. ✆ **599/54-23484.** www.chesterfields-restaurant.com. Main courses $8-$16 lunch, $16-$23 dinner. DISC, MC, V. Mon–Wed 7:30am–10pm; Thurs–Sun 9am–10pm.

Mr. Busby's Beach Bar/Daniel's by the Sea ★ ISLAND Little more than a few wooden *palapas* set in the sand on Dawn Beach, Mr. Busby's is *the* place to relax and let your hair down with a cross section of St. Maarteners. Cooled by shady palms and sea breezes, this is just what it purports to be: a *beach bar,* but it's also a fine breakfast and lunch destination. It's a lively spot, but nowhere near as rowdy as the beach bars around, say, Maho. Sit back and sip a Carib beer against a backdrop of lilting reggae or calypso music. Mr. Busby's is serious about its food, however, and it shows. Homemade johnnycakes, eggs to order, and a pitch-perfect bloody Mary make this one of the top breakfast spots on island. Lunch is jumping, too, with a menu that includes grilled Saba lobster, shrimp kebab over rice, conch or lobster salad, and Busby's own barbecued ribs. Be sure to sample the potato salad; it's addictive. After the 4-to-6pm happy hour (try the guavaberry colada), the space becomes **Daniel's by the Sea,** which offers solid Italian fare. The restaurant is located next door to the Oyster Bay Beach Resort.

Dawn Beach. ✆ **599/54-36828.** Main courses $8–$20 Mr. Busby's, $16–$32 Daniel's. DISC, MC, V. Mr. Busby's daily 7:30am–5pm. Daniel's 6–10pm.

Oualichi ★ CARIBBEAN/PIZZA/BURGERS With a prime spot on the Philipsburg waterfront, this brasserie is a local favorite. The best seating is on the patio, where you can watch cruise-ship passengers nervously roll by on Segways. Giant cruise shops docked across the waters of Great Bay compete with sailboats, catamarans, and clanking rust buckets for your attention, but it's the sparkling waters set against mossy-green cliffs that truly mesmerizes. The menu is a fusion of pub food (excellent pizzas), island classics (mahimahi and rice), and French specialties. The ambience is fairly pedestrian, but that view! And the food is very good, making this a solid choice for a filling lunch—you can even take a dip in the bay between courses. *Oualichi* was the island's original Arawak name, meaning "land of women" after its sinuous hills.

St. Rose Arcade, Front St., Philipsburg. ✆ **599/54-24316.** Main courses $13–$30. AE, MC, V. Mon–Wed 9am–6pm; Thurs–Sun 9am–10pm.

SkipJack's Seafood Grill, Bar & Fish Market ★ SEAFOOD Of the many shipshape seafood spots on Simpson Bay, this pleasant, breezy spot is one of the best. You can pick your fish on ice and both Maine and Caribbean lobster from a tank and pool, then enjoy the breezes on the handsome and expansive wooden deck, from which you can watch the big yachts muscle their way in and out of Simpson Bay. The entrees taste like they jumped from the sea to your plate, from blackened grouper to shrimp pot pie. The steamed shrimp, hot and piled on the plate, was some of the best I've ever had. Other excellent starters include tuna carpaccio, a hearty New England clam chowder, a lobster and crab salad, and crab cakes with caper mayo. SkipJack's does justice to its namesake, the old-time single-mast fishing boats that plied the Chesapeake.

Airport Rd., Simpson Bay. ✆ **599/54-42313.** www.skipjacks-sxm.com. Main courses $18–$25. MC, V. Daily noon–10:30pm. Closed Sun lunch.

Topper's ★ AMERICAN Other travelers first clued us in to this spot, raving about the big, delicious steaks and well-poured drinks served up by a gentleman of a certain age in what was essentially a roadside Creole shack. Topper's is indeed a hoot, but someone in the kitchen has a real touch with beef—where else on St. Maarten will you find delicious and tender brisket, served with homemade mashed potatoes and whisky carrots? Other classics include Caesar salad, shrimp cocktail, and meatloaf. The steaks are indeed big and good, and the atmosphere is fun. Best of all, the prices are reasonable for pricey St. Maarten.

113 Welfare Rd., Simpson Bay. ✆ **599/54-43500.** www.sxmtoppers.com. Reservations recommended. Main courses $13–$24. AE, MC, V. Mon–Sat 11am–10pm.

INEXPENSIVE

Travelers in the know (and those who watch the Travel Channel's Anthony Bourdain as he chases his appetite around the globe) are already clued in to **Hilma's Windsor Castle,** located on the main road in Simpson Bay. Even by shack standards, Hilma's is rudimentary, basically a minitrailer with an awning and four stools. Hilma's specialty? Johnnycakes filled with all sorts of delicious things, like ham, eggs, and cheese. The star is the saltfish johnnycake, spiced with peppers and onions ($2). Hilma's is open Monday through Saturday 7:30am to 3pm.

In French St. Martin

Note: Rates are quoted in either euros or dollars, depending on how establishments quoted them at press time. Prices include taxes and a 15% service charge, but you may want to add an extra gratuity if the service warrants it.

VERY EXPENSIVE

La Cigale ★★ FRENCH Celebrating 10 years in the business, this family-run establishment provides a winning combination of innovative French fare and tropical flair, a beachfront setting, and warmth and intimacy. Tucked away behind the Laguna Beach hotel at the end of an alley, congenial Olivier Genet's bistro is worth a potential wrong turn or three to find. He recruited his parents from the Loire Valley to help him run the tiny operation: Mama is the hostess, papa the pastry chef (bravo to both for the molten chocolate cake soufflé). The setting and ambience are casual, but chef Stéphane Istel's subtly seasoned food is anything but. Try the *crottin de Chavignol en nougatine* (goat cheese in phyllo pastry) with nuts and honey; seabass filet Provençal style; or rack of lamb baked in thyme, cabbage, and garlic. Olivier will ply you with several home-brewed rum *digestifs* and anecdotes of his Sancerre upbringing.

Route des Terres Basses, Baie Nettlé. ✆ **590/87-90-23.** www.restaurant-lacigale.com. Reservations required. Main courses 26€–33€. MC, V. Mon–Sat 6–10:30pm.

Le Cottage ★ FRENCH/CREOLE This perennial favorite in a town loaded with worthy contenders is set in what looks like a private house on the inland side of the main road running through Grand Case. Its atmosphere is at least partly influenced by Burgundy-born sommelier Stéphane Emorine, who shows a canny ability to recommend the perfect wine to complement the French-Caribbean cuisine. Meals begin dramatically with mini tasting menus (the "taste of tuna," say, includes sashimi- and sushi-grade tuna). Mains include both rustic *cuisine du terroir* (such as roasted rack of lamb with breaded lamb sweetbreads dusted in panko) and Creole-influenced dishes, including monkfish and sautéed squid with chorizo, olives, and preserved tomatoes. A four-course lobster tasting menu includes lobster mousse, lobster fritters, lobster salad, and lobster risotto.

97 bd. de Grand Case, Grand Case. ✆ **590/29-03-30.** www.restaurantlecottage.com. Reservations recommended. Main courses 25€–32€; lobster tasting menu 57€. AE, DC, MC, V. Daily 6–11pm.

Le Santal ★ FRENCH The approach to this dazzler is through a ramshackle, working-class Marigot suburb, a sharp contrast to the glam interior filled with mirrors, fresh flowers, ornately carved chairs, Villeroy & Boch china, and Christofle silver. Try to nab one of the coveted oceanfront tables, occupied at one time or another by the likes of Robert de Niro, Brooke Shields, Arab sheiks, and minor royalty. Sadly, you will no longer be greeted by owner Jean Dupont; he passed away in 2005, but his wife and children continue to run the restaurant. The fare focuses on the classics. The crepe stuffed with lobster meat, mushrooms, and scallions in a white-wine crawfish butter sauce is a formidable starter; the grilled whole red snapper flambéed in Pastis with fennel beurre blanc is deboned at your table. Superb chateaubriand au poivre is flambéed in aged Armagnac and coated with béarnaise. End your evening with crêpes Suzette prepared the old-fashioned way, tableside—a charming touch.

40 rue Lady Fish, Sandy Ground. ✆ **590/87-53-48.** www.restaurantlesantal.com. Reservations recommended. Main courses $38–$49. AE, MC, V. Daily 6–10:30pm (lunch by advance reservation for groups of 6 or more).

Mario's Bistro ★★ FRENCH The setting defines romance, with tables staggered along a balcony overlooking Sandy Ground Bridge. The greeting from Martyne Tardif couldn't be warmer, and her husband, Mario, inspires passion with his architectural presentations and inventive cooking spiced with Asian, Moroccan, and Southwestern accents. Start with hoisin-braised duck roll and cacao foie gras, or the sautéed lobster tails in puff pastry. For mains, try the crab-crusted baked mahimahi, or bouillabaisse with green Thai curry and lemon grass. ***Note:*** Mario's does not have high chairs or booster seats for kids, although you're welcome to bring your own.

Sandy Ground Bridge, Marigot. ✆ **590/87-06-36.** www.mariosbistro.com. Reservations recommended. Main courses 24€–35€. DISC, MC, V. Mon–Sat 6:30–10:30pm. Closed Aug–Sept.

Sol é Luna ★★★ FRENCH This lovely, family-run Creole *caze* is virtually pillowed in luxuriant greenery, with smashing Anse Marcel views. Set back from the road, it can be tricky to find, but the incomparable ambience, service, and food make "Sun and Moon" the perfect place for a romantic dinner. The light yet intensely flavored dishes combine Asian influences and classic French preparations. You might start your meal with a roll of monkfish with pecans and red curry, or homemade crab cakes. Lamb braised for 7 hours melts off the bone, and lobster ravioli is served with saffron, basil, and spinach, and drizzled with a cream sauce. Delicious desserts like banana crunchy cake with chocolate mousse are followed by a mini tasting of artisan rums (plum and passion fruit, vanilla and ginger). The hideaway also offers handsomely appointed **studios and suites** ($726–$860/week).

61 Mont Vernon, Cul-de-Sac (above Anse Marcel). ✆ **590/29-08-56.** www.solelunarestaurant.com. Main courses 28€–35€. MC, V. Daily 6–10pm. Closed mid-June to mid-July and mid-Sept to Oct.

EXPENSIVE

Claude Mini-Club ★ CREOLE/FRENCH For more than 3 decades, this has been an enduring favorite with locals and discerning visitors. Built around the trunks of old coconut palms, the building has the feel of a treehouse. The Haitian decor—including colorful murals of local scenes—captures much of the vibrancy of that island. A big terrace opens onto the sea. Authentic Creole offerings include *lambi* (conch) in zesty tomato stew and *accras* (cod fritters) in shallot sauce, but you can also find entrecôte in green-peppercorn sauce, veal escalope with fresh morels, and such classic desserts as banana flambé and crème brûlée. The restaurant stages the island's best buffets, featuring such crowd pleasers as roast suckling pig, roast beef, quail, chicken, red snapper, and Caribbean lobster, accompanied by carafes of wine.

Bd. de la Mer, Marigot. ✆ **590/87-50-69.** Reservations required. Main courses 18€–30€; buffet 42€. AE, MC, V. Mon–Sat 11am–3pm and 6–10pm. Closed Sept.

La Vie en Rose ★★ FRENCH The dining room in this balconied second-floor restaurant evokes a tropical version of Paris in the 1920s, thanks to flower boxes, gilt mirrors, arches, ceiling fans, candlelight, and time-honored culinary showmanship to match the show-stopping harbor views. The menu is classic French, although Caribbean undertones creep in. Lunches are relatively simple affairs, with an emphasis on fresh meal-size salads, simple grills like beefsteak with shallot sauce, brochettes of fresh fish, and pastas. Dinners are more elaborate (attracting a dressier crowd) and might begin with a lobster salad with passion fruit dressing. Main courses include grilled filet of red snapper simmered in a champagne sauce with pumpkin risotto; breast of duck in a foie gras sauce; lobster paired with boneless rabbit in honey-vanilla sauce; and an unusual version of roasted rack of lamb in a mushroom and truffle sauce. The lobster bisque in puff pastry is a must.

Bd. de France at rue de la République, Marigot. ✆ **590/87-54-42.** Reservations recommended. Main courses 10€–18€ lunch, 19€–33€ dinner. AE, DISC, MC, V. Mon–Sat noon–3pm and 6:30–10pm; Sun 6:30–10pm.

Le Bistro Caraïbes ★ FRENCH/CARIBBEAN Brothers Thibault and Amaury Mezière, former chefs at Paul Bocuse's restaurant in Lyon, have been cooking at this charming spot for more than 15 years. Fresh lobster and the catch of the day are their specialties. Start with the homemade smoked salmon on toast points, or the hot goat cheese in a pastry crust. You can do lobster any number of ways (in butter, simply grilled, or as thermidor), or go for the fisherman's platter in a rich bouillabaisse-style lobster sauce. A classic crème brûlée or the warm chocolate cake topped with hazelnut ice cream and coffee sauce provides an elegant finish.

81 bd. de Grand Case, Grand Case. ✆ **590/29-08-29.** www.bistrotcaraibes.com. Reservations recommended. Main courses 21€–27€. MC, V. Daily 6–10:30pm; closed Sat May–Dec.

Le Pressoir ★★ FRENCH This restaurant occupies a charming 19th-century Creole house painted yellow and blue. It's a gingerbread confection, with periwinkle shutters, mango walls hung with homey island paintings (many for sale), carved hardwood chairs, and lace doilies as lampshades. The kitchen presents an artful combination of old and new French cuisine. Standout standards include lobster ravioli in a

Grand Case: Foodie Haven

No other town in the Caribbean features as many restaurants per capita as the village of Grand Case, set near St. Martin's northernmost tip. Don't be put off by the town's ramshackle, feet-in-the-sand appearance: Behind the peeling clapboards are French-, Italian-, and American-style restaurants managed by some very sophisticated cooks.

passion fruit cream sauce, seafood tagliatelle, grilled sea scallops with foie gras and truffles, and grilled beef tenderloin in a Camembert sauce.

30 bd. de Grand Case, Grand Case. ✆ **590/87-76-62.** Reservations recommended. Main courses 18€–35€. AE, MC, V. Daily 6–10:30pm. Closed Sun in low season.

MODERATE

Chez Yvette ★ WEST INDIAN/CREOLE In a Creole cottage trimmed in gingerbread, Yvette's is the one place almost universally recommended by the locals we asked for dining advice. It's home cooking, St. Martin style, with superbly prepared mains like fish, conch, goat stew, ribs, and stewed chicken served with heaping platters of rice and peas, and sides of freshly made johnnycakes. Yvette passed away several years ago, but her husband, Felix, is the master chef in charge. For those looking for an authentic island meal, this is it.

Orleans, French Quarter. ✆ **590/87-55-57.** Main courses $20. No credit cards. Call for hours.

La Belle Epoque FRENCH/PIZZA You won't find a better perch to watch the boats in the Marigot marina than this blue-awning boardwalk cafe. After window-shopping in Marigot, stop by for Belgian beers or a glass of proper rosé; grilled Creole specials; pastas; fish; steak; or utterly scrumptious special minipizzas (8€–18.50€), with a multitude of toppings. It's open for breakfast, serving omelets, pastry, and juices.

Marina Port la Royale, Marigot. ✆ **590/87-87-70.** www. sxm-marinaroyale.com/belle_epoque. Main courses, salads, and sandwiches 14€–24€. MC, V. Daily 7:30am–11pm (from 5pm on Sun).

L'Oizeau Rare ★ FRENCH The "Rare Bird" serves up creative French cuisine in a blue-and-ivory antique house on a Marigot hillside with garden views. At lunch, served on the covered terrace, you can choose from a number of salads and crispy pizzas and fish and meat courses (say, shrimp fricassee flamed with Pastis)—not to mention what is described as a "formidable" hamburger with homemade french fries. Dinner choices include fresh fish, such as snapper or grouper; roasted rack lamb with garlic breadcrumbs and fresh herbs; or penne with a shrimp and sea-scallop fricassee. There are numerous daily specials and prix-fixe options, and the wine list features French options at moderate prices. Many guests come here at sundown to enjoy the harbor view over a Kir Royale and a cigar from the extensive selection.

Bd. de France, Marigot Harbor. ✆ **590/87-56-38.** www.marigotwaterfront.com/oizeaurare. Reservations recommended. Main courses 15€–24€ lunch, 18€–25€ dinner. AE, MC, V. Mon–Sat 11:30am–3pm and 6:30–10:30pm. Closed June.

Spiga ★★ ITALIAN The gracious husband-and-wife team of Ciro Russo (a native of Lecco, Italy) and Lara Bergamasco (second-generation St. Maarten restaurant royalty) have crafted the finest Italian restaurant on the island. Simple elegance reigns, starting with the charming 1914 Creole home. You can dine inside, where

Lolos: Local Barbecue Joints

Open-air barbecue stands are a St. Martin institution, dishing out big, delicious helpings of barbecued ribs, lobster, chicken, or fish grilled on split metal drums; garlic shrimp; goat stew; rice and peas; cod fritters; and johnnycakes—all from $10 to $20, a real bargain on pricey St. Martin. In Grand Case, the two best, Talk of the Town (✆ 590/29-63-89) and Sky's the Limit (✆ 690/35-67-84), have covered seating, a waitstaff, and sea views. Several excellent *lolo*-style Creole restaurants are found in Marigot facing the marketplace and ferry port, including Le Goût and Chez Coco—but my favorite is Enoch's Place (✆ 590/29-29-88), which serves terrific garlic shrimp (10€), stew chicken (10€), and stew conch (8€); each platter comes with savory rice and peas, cooked plantain, and salad. Derrick Hodge's Exclusive Bite (no phone) is right by the city's scenic cemetery. The Dutch side has its own versions. For lunch try Mark's Place (no phone) in Philipsburg's Food Center Plaza parking lot; after 6pm head for Johnny B's Under the Tree (no phone) on Cay Hill Road in Cole Bay.

dark-stained wooden doors and windows frame salmon-pink walls, or on the candlelit patio. Try the deeply flavorful tomato and basil lobster bisque and the handmade pappardelle with braised beef-and-mushroom sauce. A hearty cioppino is filled with shrimp, scallops, and fish in a tomatoey shellfish broth. The roast pork tenderloin comes wrapped in smoked pancetta. End the evening with a vanilla-bean crème brûlée and raspberry panna-cotta, washed down with fiery grappa.

4 rte. de l'Espérance, Grand Case. ✆ **590/52-47-83.** www.spiga-sxm.com. Reservations recommended. Main courses $17–$32. DISC, MC, V. Daily 6–10:30pm. Closed Tues May–Nov.

Sunset Café FRENCH/INTERNATIONAL This open-air restaurant straddles the rocky peninsula dividing Grand Case Beach from Petite Plage. Tables are set along a narrow terrace that affords sweeping views of the setting sun, when spotlights play on the water. It's a nice, breezy spot to dine and watch the waves roll in. The chef/operator, Brittany-born Alexandre Pele, has a résumé that includes cooking stints at the Savoy in London and La Samanna (p. 584) here on French St. Martin. His emphasis is on seafood and French classics at reasonable prices. At lunch you can choose from more basic fare—sandwiches, burgers, pastas, salads—as you watch herons dive-bombing for their own meal.

In the Grand Case Beach Club, Grand Case. ✆ **590/29-43-90.** Reservations recommended for weekend dinners in winter. Main courses 11€–38€ lunch, 17€–26€ dinner. AE, MC, V. Daily 7am–midnight.

Tastevin ★ FRENCH/CARIBBEAN With a warm, beautifully candlelit ambience, Tastevin is a favorite of locals and visitors alike. You dine on a garden terrace overlooking Grand Case Bay. Daily specials are listed on the blackboard out front, but often include fresh fish like mahimahi, red snapper, or grouper in a classic French or Asian-infused sauce. The two vegetarian dishes are among the best items on the menu; try the white-bean-and-vegetable pan with wild rice and mango, local squash in curry, potato, black olive, and sun-dried tomatoes napoleon; and sweet potato pancakes. Tastevin is known for its extensive and detailed wine list.

86 bd. de Grand Case, Grand Case. ✆ **590/87-55-45.** www.letastevin-restaurant.com. Reservations recommended. Main courses 17€–30€. AE, MC, V. Daily noon–2pm and 6–10pm. Closed Tues May–Nov.

ST. MAARTEN/ST. MARTIN BEACHES ★★

Coves scissor the island's rugged coastline; with 39 beautiful beaches of varying length and hue, it's fairly easy to find a place to park your towel. All beaches are public, though access is often via a rutted dirt road and/or through a fancy resort. Beaches on the western leeward half are generally hotter and calmer; those on the eastern windward side, predictably, breezier with rougher swells (when not reef-protected). All beaches on the French side of the island allow topless sunbathing, although the Dutch side is becoming more liberal. ***Warning:*** If a beach is too secluded, be careful. It's unwise to carry valuables; robberies have been reported on some remote strips.

On Dutch St. Maarten

Popular **Cupecoy Beach ★** is close to the Dutch-French border at the island's southwest tip. It's a string of three sand beaches set against a backdrop of caves, rock formations, and dramatically eroded limestone cliffs. Locals come around with coolers of cold beer and soda for sale. The beach has two parking lots, one near Cupecoy and Sapphire beach clubs, the other a short distance to the west; parking costs $2. You must descend stone-carved steps to reach the sands. Cupecoy is also the island's major gay beach. Clothing is optional toward the northwest side of the beach. ***Warning:*** The steep drop-off and high swells make the beach hazardous for young children and weak swimmers; prevailing weather affects not only the surf, but the sand's width. The Cupecoy area is seeing considerable new development and, with it, disturbing reports of wastewater runoff onto the beaches.

The next strand down (west of the airport) is palm-shaded, white-sand **Mullet Bay Beach ★**, framed in sea grapes. Once it was the busiest beach on the island, but St. Maarten's largest resort, Mullet Bay, has been shuttered (save for a timeshare section) since Hurricane Luis in 1995, so it's never crowded, though locals flock here on weekends. Watersports equipment can be rented at a local kiosk, and two beach bars sell refreshments. The snorkeling is not bad along the rocks.

Near the airport, **Maho Beach,** at the Sonesta Maho Beach Hotel and Casino (p. 582), is a classic Caribbean crescent, with vendors hawking colorful wares and locals inviting you to impromptu beach barbecues. This is one of the island's busiest beaches, buzzing with windsurfers—and buzzed by jumbo jets that nearly decapitate the palm trees. When you spot a 747 coming into view, hang on to your hats, towels, and partner.

West of Philipsburg before you reach the airport, the 2km-long (1¼-mile) white sands of crescent-shaped **Simpson Bay Beach** ring the lagoon and are set against a backdrop of brightly hued fishing boats, yachts, and condominiums. This beach is ideal for a stroll or a swim (beware the steep drop-off), with calm waters and surprisingly few crowds.

Great Bay Beach ★ is best if you're staying along Front Street in Philipsburg. This 2km-long (1¼-mile) beach is sandy and calm; despite bordering the busy capital, it's surprisingly clean and a nice place to kick back after shopping, admiring the cruise ships from one of many strategic bars along the new boardwalk. On a clear day, you'll have a view of Saba. Immediately to the west, at the foot of Fort Amsterdam, is picturesque **Little Bay Beach,** but it can be overrun with tourists disgorged by the cruise ships. You can actually climb up to the site of Fort Amsterdam itself. Built in

A Grand Day on the Isle of Pinel ★★

Imagine a secluded tropical island where bathers swim in a smooth, gin-clear lagoon fringed by palm trees and a curtain of jade mountains. Gentle surf laps a beach dotted with *palapas* and parasols. The scent of barbecued meat and coconut oil commingle with the salt air. Welcome to **Ilet Pinel,** a tiny islet a short boat ride from Orient Beach. A day trip to this uninhabited island is highly recommended. You'll find two delightful beach bistros, each with its own section of beach chairs and umbrellas (20€ for the day). Among them, **Karibuni ★ (✆ 690/39-67-00)** is the country's longest-running beach bar. Small ferryboats ($6 per passenger) run from the French Cul-de-Sac on St. Martin's northeast coast to Pinel daily on the hour from 9am to 4pm (to 5pm on Sun). Watch for the last return trip at 4:30pm. For more information, go to **www.visitpinel.com.** Or hop aboard a **Wind Adventures** catamaran from Orient Beach for a "One Day in Pinel" snorkeling safari **(✆ 590/29-41-57; www.wind-adventures.com;** from 50€ per person for the day for 1–3 people).

1631, it was the first Dutch military outpost in the Caribbean. The Spanish captured it 2 years later, making it their most important bastion east of Puerto Rico. Only a few of the fort's walls remain, but the view is panoramic.

On the east side of the island, **Dawn Beach ★** is noted for its underwater life and incredible sunrises, with some of the island's most beautiful reefs immediately offshore. Dawn has plenty of wave action, but it's suitable for swimming and snorkeling. Dawn Beach is now the site of the **Westin Resort.** This, in addition to the expansion of **Oyster Bay Resort,** has somewhat diminished its peaceful allure, but its remarkable reef, soft pearly sand, and views of St. Barts remain unchanged.

On French St. Martin

Baie Longue (Long Bay) ★, on the west coast, is supremely conducive to R&R. Chic, expensive La Samanna hotel (p. 584) opens onto this beachfront, but it's otherwise blissfully undeveloped and uncrowded. The reef-protected waters are ideal for snorkeling, but beware the strong undertow and steep drop-off. Baie Longue is to the north of Cupecoy Bay Beach, reached via the Lowlands Road. Don't leave valuables in your car, as break-ins have been reported along this stretch of highway.

Isolated **Anse des Pères (Friar's Bay Beach) ★** lies at the end of a winding, bumpy country road; its clearly signposted entrance intersects with the main highway between Grand Case and Marigot. This is a pretty, less-visited beach with ample parking. Shelling, snorkeling, and sunset-watching are all favored. Two beloved beach bars organize raucous themed bashes. Stop in at **Kali's Beach Bar** (**✆ 590/49-06-81**), a thatched bamboo hut splashed in Rasta colors, where Kali himself serves some of the island's best barbecue. Kali hosts "full-moon parties," featuring reggae bands on the beach along with a bonfire and plenty of drink. ***Tip:*** Have one of the staff here point you in the direction of relatively undiscovered **Anse Heureuse (Happy Bay) ★**, a 10-minute walk north through underbrush over a hill from Friar's Bay (pause to drink in the views of Anguilla). It richly deserves the name, thanks to the tranquillity, fine snorkeling, and white-sand beach.

Grand Case Beach, a long, narrow ribbon in the middle of Grand Case, is a small, pleasant beach that can get crowded on weekends but has none of Orient Beach's carnival-like atmosphere. The waters are very calm, so swimming is good—although it's become a popular parking spot for visiting boats. A large section of the water has been roped off for kids to swim safely. Dining choices along the Caribbean's "Restaurant Row" run from *lolos* (essentially, barbecue shacks) to gourmet bistros. For something in between, try **Calmos Café,** where you can watch the sun set over the beach with your feet in the sand and a drink in your hands.

To the east of Grand Case, follow the winding road up and over Pigeon Pea Hill. The spectacular setting of **Anse Marcel** comes into view. This lovely cove is home to two resorts, the **Radisson Blu St. Martin** (p. 588) and **Le Domaine de Lonvilliers** (p. 587). The beach itself is protected, with shallow waters ideal for families. You can swim here or take a hike for 1½ hours north over a hill and down to one of the island's most pristine beaches, **Baie de Petites Cayes.** This is the most idyllic spot on St. Martin for a picnic. A ribbon of brilliant white sand beckons, and the waters ripple from sapphire to turquoise. Part of the fun is the hike itself, with panoramic views stretching all the way to Anguilla.

On the east coast, **Baie Orientale (Orient Beach)** ★ is where the action is. It's also a beauty of a beach. Eating, drinking, and people-watching qualify as sports, and many beach bistro/bars offer not only grilled crayfish Creole, but also live music, boutiques (with fashion shows), massages, parasailing, jet-ski rentals, kiteboard instruction, and more. Of those beach bars marketing themselves as "The Five Stars of Orient Bay," **Waïkiki Beach** (✆ **590/87-43-19**) is a favorite of the well-heeled St. Barts set, who down caviar with Belvedere shots. **Kontiki** (✆ **590/87-43-27**) has two sections: the main eatery and the Tiki Hut, serving a mix of dishes from jerk chicken to paninis, quesadillas, and sushi. **Bikini Beach** (✆ **590/87-43-25**), which also stays open for dinner, has a menu that runs from hamburgers to Spanish-style paella studded with lobster. Its southern end contains the naturist resort, **Club Orient.**

Baie de l'Embouchure ★, embracing **Le Galion** and **Coconut Grove beaches,** just south of Orient, is part of the St. Martin Réserve Sous-Marine Régionale, established to protect migrant waterfowl habitats and rebuild mangrove swamps. A coral reef encloses the bay: The calm, shallow water (you can wade up to 100m/328 ft. out) makes it ideal for small children—and it's the only beach on the French side where topless sunbathing is discouraged. Tiki carvings and blue umbrellas mark the appealing **Le Galion Restaurant** (also known as Chez Pat after owner Pat Turner; ✆ **590/87-37-25**). Up in the hills facing the bay is a handsome white house that was long the home of Romare Bearden, the celebrated American artist and collagist.

SPORTS & OUTDOOR PURSUITS

DEEP-SEA FISHING The waters here teem with tuna, wahoo, snapper, grouper, jack, pompano, yellowtail, marlin, and other big game fish. The island hosts several highly regarded competitions, including March's Marlin Cup and June's Billfish Tournament, which lure an international roster of entrants. The crew from **Lee's Roadside Grill,** on Welfare Road 84, Simpson Bay (✆ **599/544-4233;** www.leesfish.com), knows where to catch the big boys, since they supply their own wildly popular seafood grill. Charter one of its 9.3m (31-ft.) Bertrams for a half-, three-quarter-, or full-day excursion with a minimum of four people (maximum six). Drinks are included in the half-day trip ($150 per person), and lunch and drinks are included in the three-quarter- and full-day excursions ($200 and $250 per person respectively). And yes, they'll cook your trophy up at the restaurant for no extra cost.

GOLF The **Mullet Bay Golf Course** (✆ **599/54-52850**) is the island's only golf course. It's a battered 18-hole Joseph Lee–designed course whose fate has hung in the balance, based on ongoing court battles, for years. The ruins of the Mullet Bay resort surround the course. The island's flagship resort was severely damaged by Hurricane Luis in 1995, and no one has ever gotten around to cleaning up the mess (more to the point: no one will take financial responsibility for the cleanup). But golfers find their way here anyway and putter along on the lumpy, unkempt course. Greens fees are $50 for 9 holes or $80 for 18 holes; rental carts are $50.

SCUBA DIVING Although the nearby island of **Saba** is considered to be the area's top dive sight, the scuba diving is good around **St. Martin,** with reef, wreck, night, cave, and drift diving; the depth of dives is 6 to 21m (20–66 ft.). Off the northeastern coast on the French side, dive sites include Ilet Pinel, for shallow diving; Green Key, a barrier reef; and Tintamarre, for sheltered coves and geologic faults. To the north, Anse Marcel and neighboring Anguilla are good choices. The waters around **St. Maarten** waters offer dive wrecks, including the 1770 British man-of-war, **HMS *Proselyte,*** which came to a watery grave on a reef 2km (1¼ miles) off Philipsburg in 1801. Most of the big resorts have facilities for scuba diving and can provide information about underwater tours, photography, and night diving.

LeRoy French, the larger-than-life owner of the island's oldest dive shop, **Ocean Explorers,** at Kim Sha Beach (✆ **599/54-45252;** www.stmaartendiving.com), is still diving more than a half-century after he caught the bug (using some of Cousteau's first Aqua Lungs). The personalized touch—he takes a maximum of six divers—costs a bit more ($53–$59 single-tank dive, $98–$104 double-tank) and means reservations are essential. Ocean Explorers also offers day trips to the island of Saba ($90–$115).

One of the island's premier dive operations is **Scuba Fun,** whose dive center is at the Great Bay Marina, Dock Maarten, Philipsburg (✆ **599/54-23966;** www.scubafundivecenter.com). It offers morning and afternoon dives in deep and shallow water, wreck dives, and reef dives. A resort course for first-time divers with reasonable swimming skills costs 75€ and includes instruction in shallow water and a one-tank dive above a coral reef. A morning two-tank dive (certified divers only) costs 85€.

In Grand Case, the multinational staff at **Octopus Diving** (✆ **590/29-11-27;** www.octopusdiving.com) provides PADI courses, night dives, and underwater photography to some 30 dive sites around the island. One-site dives go for $99 per dive, and two-site dives for $85 to $99 per dive, all equipment included.

Dive Safaris, at Simpson Bay (✆ **599/54-52401;** www.divestmaarten.com), offers competitive rates and a full range of PADI certification courses, including specialty instruction in marine habitats, photography, and wreck diving. Those wanting to get up close and personal with sharks can don chain-mail-like armor to feed the sharks in their "Shark Awareness Dives" ($80 per person). Rates are $50 to $55 for single-tank dives; $95 to $100 for double-tank dives; and $75 for night dives.

SNORKELING ★★ The calm waters ringing the island's shallow reefs and tiny coves make it a snorkeler's heaven. The waters off the northeastern shores of French St. Martin have been classified as a regional underwater nature reserve, **Réserve Sous-Marine Régionale,** which protects the area around Flat Island (also known as Tintamarre), Ilet Pinel, Green Key, Proselyte, and Petite Clef. Equipment can be rented at almost any hotel, and most beaches have watersports kiosks.

Eagle Tours, at Bobby's Marina in Philipsburg (✆ **599/54-36237** or 54-23323; www.sailingsxm.com) offers snorkeling, kayaking, lagoon sailing, and sightseeing tours aboard its fleet of seaworthy vessels. The 23m (76-ft.), custom-designed *Golden Eagle* catamaran (originally built for the prestigious Whitbread Around the World Race) cruises to various deserted strands and cays for snorkeling and soaking up both tropical ambience and drinks (the pampering service includes a floating bar—you *will* be dancing or leading a conga line by the end of the trip). The flatboat *Explorer* stops in Marigot for shopping before heading home; mimosas and rum punches flow copiously. The Friday jaunt ($99 per person) sails to Tintamarre and Creole Rock, puts in at Grand Case for lunch, then stops by Baie Longue for a final cooling dip. Transportation to and from your hotel is included.

Both **Scuba Fun** and **Octopus Diving** (see "Scuba Diving," above) provide guided snorkeling trips to the island's teeming offshore reefs. Snorkeling trips with Scuba Fun cost 30€ for a half-day, plus 7.50€ for equipment rental. Snorkeling trips to two sites with Octopus Diving cost $40 (including all equipment).

WINDSURFING Most windsurfers gravitate to the eastern part of the island, most notably Coconut Grove/Le Galion Beach, Orient Beach, and, to a lesser extent, Dawn Beach, all in French St. Martin. The top outfitter here, **Tropical Wave,** Le Galion Beach, Baie de l'Embouchure (✆ **590/87-37-25;** www.sxm-orientbeach.com/chezpat), capitalizes on the near-ideal combination of wind and calm waters. Pat rents Mistrals for 20€ an hour, with instruction offered at 30€ an hour, and 45€ for a 2-hour beginner course. They also rent snorkeling gear, pedal boats, and kayaks (tours can be arranged).

Wind Adventures (formerly Club Nathalie Simon), on Orient Beach (✆ **590/29-41-57;** www.wind-adventures.com), is one of the Caribbean's premier windsurfing schools. Lessons cost 120€ for 1- to 3-hour lessons. Kite trips for the experienced to Green Cay start at 95€. Wind Adventures also rents windsurfers and Hobie Cats and offers both safaris and instruction (with excellent multilesson discounts).

SHOPPING ★★

In Dutch St. Maarten

Not only is St. Maarten a free port, but it also has no local sales taxes. Prices are sometimes lower here than anywhere else in the Caribbean, except possibly St. Thomas. The best buys are in electronics, jewelry, watches, and cameras. In general, Dutch side shops stay open from 9am to 6pm

Except for the boutiques at resort hotels, the main shopping area is in the center of **Philipsburg.** Most of the shops are on **Voorstraat (Front Street),** which stretches for about 2km (1¼ miles) and is lined with stores. More shops are along the little lanes, known as *steegijes,* that connect Front Street with **Achterstraat (Back Street),** another shoppers' haven.

Del Sol St-Maarten, 23 Front St. (✆ **599/54-28784**), sells men's and women's sportswear. Embedded into the mostly black-and-white designs are organic crystals that react to ultraviolet light, which transforms the fabric into a rainbow of colors. Step back into the shadows, and your T-shirt will revert to its original black-and-white design. The same technology is applied to yo-yos, which shimmer psychedelically when you bob them up and down.

The Belgian Chocolate Box, 109 Old St. (© **599/54-28863**), is the best of its kind on island. It's always busy here, especially when cruise ships are berthed at nearby piers.

Guavaberry Emporium, 8–10 Front St. (© **599/54-22965;** www.guavaberry.com), sells the rare "island folk liqueur" of St. Maarten, which for centuries was made only in private homes. Sold in square bottles, this rum-based liqueur is made with guavaberries grown on the hills in the center of the island. The liqueur has a fruity, woody, smoky tang. Some people prefer it blended with coconut as a guavaberry colada, or splashed in a glass of icy champagne. The charming Creole cottage also contains exotic natural perfumes and hot sauces.

Sint Maarten National Heritage Foundation Shop, 7 Front St. (© **599/54-24917;** www.museumsintmaarten.org) is a modest museum gift shop with some of the most original gift items around. It has interesting crafts by local artists, including Christmas ornaments, as well as books, maps, and helpful guides to historic sights.

In French St. Martin

Many day-trippers come over to Marigot from the Dutch side of the island just to visit the French-inspired boutiques and shopping arcades. Because St. Martin is also a duty-free port, you'll find some of the best shopping in the Caribbean here as well. Whether you're seeking jewelry, perfume, or St-Tropez bikinis, you'll find it in one of the boutiques along **rue de la République** and **rue de la Liberté** in Marigot.

Prices are often quoted in U.S. dollars, and salespeople frequently speak English. Credit cards and traveler's checks are generally accepted. French St. Martin stores open around 9am and close around 7pm, but most shopkeepers take an extended lunch break from around 12:30 to 2pm or later.

At Marigot's harborside, a lively **morning market** on Wednesday and Saturday hosts vendors selling clothing, spices, and handicrafts. There's a cookie-cutter quality to the crafts, with many of the vendors offering the same (imported) goods, but it's a good spot to pick up spices, colorful and inexpensive children's clothes, and the occasional good-quality craft.

At **Marina Port la Royale,** mornings are bustling: Boats board guests for picnics on deserted beaches, and a dozen little restaurants ready for the lunch crowd. Marina Royale is peppered with narrow warrens and alleyways where boutiques sell everything from designer clothes to jewelry.

The waterfront **Le West Indies Mall** (© **590/51-04-19**) is a marbled stone-wood-and-concrete structure with arches, skylights, curved staircases, and gazebos galore—a hushed, icily ornate contrast to the steamy, ramshackle market across the street. But it does concentrate 22 big-name boutiques, from Escada to Lacoste. You'll also find a branch of the venerable gourmet shop **Hédiard** (established in Paris in 1854), where you can purchase champagne, caviar, and foie gras; its aromatic tea room is a delightful stop for fresh pastries. Smaller complexes include **Galerie Périgourdine** and **Plaza Caraïbes,** which houses Cartier, Longchamp, and Hermès outposts.

L'Atelier, 28 Marina Port la Royale (© **590/87-13-71**), showcases clothing and accessories (shoes, belts, and bags) from well-known European designers and is stocked with the latest Paris fashions. **Havane Boutique,** 50 Marina Port la Royale (© **590/87-70-39**), is a hyperstylish menswear store, more couture than ready-to-wear. **Serge Blanco "15" Boutique,** Marina Port la Royale (© **590/29-65-49**), is a relatively unknown name in North America, but in France, Blanco is revered as one of the most successful rugby players of all time. His menswear is sporty, fun, and elegant. Clothes include polo shirts, shorts, shoes, and latex jackets.

Ma Doudou (✆ **590/87-30-43**) occupies a tiny shack virtually obscured by overgrown foliage in the town of Cul-de-Sac. Call ahead unless you're in the neighborhood, as it keeps irregular hours. *Ma Doudou* means "my darling" in Creole patois, which certainly describes the collectible hand-painted bottles containing rum-filled candies, spices, jams, and 20 flavored rums.

Roland Richardson Paintings and Prints, 6 rue de la République (✆ **590/87-84-08**), has a beautiful gallery. Known for luminous landscapes, portraits, and still lifes, Roland Richardson's clearest influence is the 19th-century Barbizon School of Impressionists. A native of St. Martin and one of the Caribbean's premier artists, he works in numerous media—oil, watercolors, pastels, charcoal, even batik and stained glass. His work has been exhibited in nearly 100 one-man and group shows in museums and galleries around the world. Richardson is also the resident artist at **La Samanna resort** (p. 584), where he has a changing collection of works.

ST. MAARTEN/ST. MARTIN AFTER DARK ★★

This is a sunny, good-time place, where after-dark activities begin early—usually starting with a sundowner on one of the Caribbean's most beautiful beaches.

To find out what's on during your stay, get the **Thursday edition** of *The Daily Herald,* which runs an "Out and About" section and lists of upcoming events.

Look for appearances around the island by the "king of soca," **T-Mo** (full name: Timothy iKing T-Moi van Heyningen)—literally, a six-time winner of the title of Soca Monarch. Another popular local musician, calypso king **Beau Beau**—known as St. Maarten's Frank Sinatra—can be seen most nights singing and dancing with the Beaubettes at his eponymous seafood restaurant at the **Oyster Bay Beach Resort** (✆ **599/54-36049;** www.beaubeaus.com).

BEACH BARS & NIGHTCLUBS The island has a number of beachside bars—from bare-bones shacks to more elaborate affairs—that are great spots for soaking up the island scenery, sipping sundowners, and listening to reggae, calypso, and soca music. The legendary **Sunset Beach Bar,** Airport Beach (✆ **599/54-53998;** www.sunsetbeachbar.com), lies directly on the beach and is mobbed most afternoons and evenings. No one seems to mind the roar of airplane engines from aircraft that seem to fly just a few dozen feet overhead. A live band plays reggae or calypso music every Sunday—expect a good-time party atmosphere.

Another Maho hot spot is **Bliss,** 2 Beacon Hill Rd. (✆ **588/54-53996;** www.bliss-sxm.com), an open-air nightclub where Miami Beach–style disco chic rules. A giant Jumbotron trained on the dance floor lets you admire your own fancy footwork.

A contender for most popular bar on island, **Cheri's Café,** Rhine Rd. 45, Maho Beach (✆ **599/54-53361**), is that rare tourist trap that also appeals to locals. The open-air pavilion in the heart of Maho offers music and live entertainment 6 nights a week.

In Grand Case, **Calmos Café ★**, bd. de Grand Case 40 (✆ **590/29-01-85;** www.calmoscafe.com), is a funky and low-key beach shack that draws a laid-back crowd for sunset cocktails in the sand. Management posts a sign that says NO SNOBS near the entrance. It also has good, affordable food. It's open daily from 10am to midnight.

CASINOS St. Maarten has 14 casinos, but don't expect aircraft-hangar-size rooms or Vegas overkill. Most of the island casinos are relatively low-key affairs, as befits the casual island vibe.

Princess Casino ★, Port de Plaisance Resort, Cole Bay (© **599/54-44311;** www.princesscasinosxm.com), wins the prize for overall elegance, as evidenced by the dressier crowd and handsome neoclassical design. Princess has more than 650 slots and 20 table games, from craps to blackjack. Dining options include Peg Leg Pub, a fine buffet, and a sushi bar.

Atlantis World Casino ★, Rhine Rd. 106, Cupecoy (© **599/54-54601;** www.atlantisworld.com), is St. Maarten's homage to Las Vegas, with some of the best of the island restaurants (Rare [p. 589] and Temptation [p. 589]), but also a posh interior with all the big table games, along with 500 slot and video-poker machines.

Casino Royale ★, at the Sonesta Maho Beach Resort (p. 582) on Maho Bay (© **599/54-52590;** www.playmaho.com), is the island's largest, glitziest gaming emporium. The casino offers baccarat, minibaccarat, and more than 200 slot machines. It's open daily from 1pm to 6am. In the same building is the island's loudest dance club, **Tantra** (formerly the Q-Club), with wraparound catwalks, multiple bars, and colored lights. It's open nightly from around 10pm.

ST. VINCENT & THE GRENADINES

23

St. Vincent is undeveloped when compared to neighboring St. Lucia, and it's not as lush as Grenada and Dominica, but it has its own beauty. It has only enough attractions to absorb a day or two of your time, but the offshore islands of the Grenadines are the best sailing waters in the Caribbean, even topping the British Virgin Islands—the yachting crowd seems to view St. Vincent merely as a launching pad for the 65km (40-mile) string of the Grenadines.

Beaches Swimmers and snorkelers will find plenty action on **Indian Bay Beach,** a rocky, golden expanse of sand and reef-protected tranquil waters. Hang with the beautiful people on **Macaroni Beach,** Mustique's favorite haven of turquoise water and pure white sand.

Things to Do Immerse yourself in such tropical exotics as teak, almond, cinnamon, nutmeg, cannonball, and mahogany trees at the **Botanic Gardens.** Panoramic views unfold in all directions along **Leeward Highway.**

Eating & Drinking You'll find West Indian cuisine and fresh seafood throughout St. Vincent & the Grenadines. Dine on lobster salad at the famous Basil's Bar & Restaurant or lobster crepes on a waterfront terrace.

Nature Journey through **Marriqua Valley**, one of the lushest valleys of the Caribbean, where you'll pass by winding rivers, deep forests, terraced farms, freshwater streams, and boys on donkeys.

ST. VINCENT

Essentials

VISITOR INFORMATION

In the United States, you can get information at the **St. Vincent and Grenadines Tourist Office,** 801 Second Ave., 21st Floor, New York, NY 10017 (© **800/729-1726** or 212/687-4981; www.stvincent.com). The website for St. Vincent and the Grenadines is **www.discoversvg.com**.

Special Events

Late June brings St. Vincent's weeklong Carnival, one of the largest such celebrations in the eastern Caribbean. The festivities include steel-band and calypso competitions, parades, costumes, and the crowning of the king and queen of the carnival. The fun extends through the first 2 weeks in July, culminating in a huge street party.

On St. Vincent, the local **Department of Tourism** is on Upper Bay Street, Government Administrative Centre, Kingstown (✆ **784/457-1502**). Hours are Monday to Friday from 8am to 4pm.

GETTING THERE

In the eastern Caribbean, St. Vincent—the "gateway to the Grenadines" (the individual islands are discussed later in this chapter)—lies about 160km (99 miles) west of Barbados. There are no direct flights. The best connections are through Barbados and Antigua. From Barbados you can take **LIAT** (✆ **888/844-LIAT** [5428] in most of the Caribbean, or 784/458-4841; www.liatairline.com), which connects the islands of Grenada and St. Lucia with St. Vincent, Bequia, Union Island, and Antigua.

American Eagle (✆ **800/433-7300** in the U.S. and Canada, or 784/456-5555; www.aa.com) flies nonstop from San Juan, Puerto Rico, to Canouan, one of the most visited of the Grenadines.

Dependable **SVG Airways** (✆ **800/624-1843** or 784/457-5124; www.svgair.com) makes daily shuttle runs from St. Vincent to the satellite islands of Mustique, Union, and Canouan, with per-person fares ranging from $46 to $85 round-trip, plus a fuel surcharge. To connect with those Grenadine islands with airports, separate charter arrangements can be made from Union Island. The price of these chartered flights is less than you might expect and often matches the fares on conventional Caribbean airlines.

GETTING AROUND

BY TAXI Because of the bad roads, most visitors use taxis to get around. The government sets the rates, but taxis are unmetered, so be sure to agree on the fare before getting in. Figure on spending $5.60 to $20 or more to go from the airport to your hotel. You should tip about 12% of the fare.

You can also hire taxis to take you to the island's major attractions. Most drivers seem to be well-informed guides. (It won't take you long to learn everything you need to know about St. Vincent.) You'll spend from $20 per hour for a car holding two to four passengers.

BY RENTAL CAR Driving on St. Vincent is a bit of an adventure because of the narrow, twisting roads (sound your horn as you make the sharp hairpin turns). ***Most important:*** Drive on the left. If you present your valid driver's license from home at the police department, on Bay Street in Kingstown, and pay a $19 fee, you'll get a temporary permit to drive.

Avis (✆ **800/331-1084** in the U.S. and Canada; www.avis.com) has a branch at the airport. One local rental firm is **Star Garage,** on Grenville Street in Kingstown (✆ **784/456-1743**). Make sure your car has a spare tire, because the roads are full of potholes.

BY BUS Flamboyantly painted "alfresco" buses travel the principal roads of St. Vincent, linking the major towns and villages. The price is low, depending on where you're going, and the experience will connect you with the locals. The central departure point is the bus terminal at the New Kingstown Fish Market. Fares range from 35¢ to $2.20.

[FastFACTS] ST. VINCENT & THE GRENADINES

Banks Most banks are open Monday to Thursday from 8am to either 1 or 3pm; and Friday from either 8am to 5pm, or 8am to 1pm and then 3 to 5pm. There are a few banks with ATMs on Halifax Street in Kingstown on St. Vincent (plus one at the airport), and there are also a few on Bequia and Union Island.

Currency The official currency of St. Vincent is the **Eastern Caribbean dollar (EC$),** pegged at EC$2.67 per U.S. dollar (EC$1 = 37¢). Most restaurants, shops, and hotels will accept payment in U.S. dollars or traveler's checks. *Prices in this chapter are quoted in U.S. dollars.*

Documents British, Canadian, and U.S. citizens should have a passport and a return or ongoing airplane ticket.

Electricity Electricity is 220-volt AC (50 cycles), so if you're traveling with U.S. appliances, you'll need an adapter and a transformer. Some hotels have transformers, but it's best to bring your own.

Emergencies In an emergency, dial ✆ **999** or **911.**

Hospitals There is one hospital on St. Vincent in Kingstown: **Milton Cato Memorial General Hospital** (✆ **784/456-1185**), Hospital Road.

Language English is the official language.

Liquor Laws Liquor can be sold on any day of the week. It's legal to have an open container on the beach as long as you don't get rowdy or litter.

Pharmacies On St. Vincent, try the **People's Pharmacy,** Greenville Street, Kingstown (✆ **784/456-1170**), open Monday to Saturday from 8am to 8pm. There are a few other drugstores in Kingstown as well.

Post Office The **General Post Office,** on Halifax Street in Kingstown (✆ **784/457-1744**), is open Monday to Friday from 8am to 3pm and Saturday from 8 to 11:30am. There are smaller post offices in 56 districts throughout the country, including offices on the Grenadine islands of Bequia, Mustique, Canouan, Mayreau, and Union Island.

Safety St. Vincent and its neighboring islands of the Grenadines are quite safe. Even in Kingstown, the capital of St. Vincent, chances are slim you'll encounter serious crime. However, take the usual precautions and never leave valuables unguarded.

Taxes & Service Charges The government imposes an airport departure tax of $16 per person. A 10% government occupancy tax is charged for all hotel accommodations. Hotels and restaurants almost always add a 10% to 15% service charge; ask whether it's included in the initial hotel rates you're quoted. If it's not already added at a restaurant, tip at that rate.

Telephone To call St. Vincent or the Grenadines from the United States, dial **1,** then **784** (the area code for St. Vincent), and then the local seven-digit number. Once on St. Vincent, you can access **AT&T Direct** at ✆ **800/225-5288.** To reach **MCI,** dial ✆ **800/888-8000.**

Time Both St. Vincent and the Grenadines operate on Atlantic Standard Time year-round: When it's 6am on St. Vincent, it's 5am in

New York. During daylight saving time in the United States, St. Vincent keeps the same time as the U.S. East Coast.

Water In St. Vincent and the Grenadines, stick to bottled water.

Weather The climate of St. Vincent and the Grenadines is pleasantly cooled by the trade winds year-round. The tropical temperature is in the 78°F-to-82°F (26°C–28°C) range. The rainy season is July to October.

Where to Stay

Don't expect high-rise resorts here. The places are small and comfortable, not fancy, and you usually get a lot of personal attention from the staff.

If you want a luxurious resort, head for the Grenadines. Except for Young Island, most resorts here are fairly simple affairs, and since most people are in St. Vincent for only a night or two, you may prefer to be located directly in the center in the capital of Kingstown.

VERY EXPENSIVE

Young Island Resort ★★ On its own private island off Villa Beach, this resort is as good as it gets in St. Vincent. It's far more stylish and comfortable than its nearest competitor, Grand View Beach Hotel (p. 609). This 14-hectare (35-acre) resort, its grounds full of lush fruit trees, white ginger, hibiscus, and ferns, is supposedly where a Carib tribal chieftain kept his harem. It lies just 180m (591 ft.) off the south shore of St. Vincent; a ferry makes the 5-minute run from the pier right on Villa Beach. The beach has brilliant white sand. Set in a tropical garden are romantic wood-and-stone Tahitian cottages (all for couples), with bamboo decor and outdoor showers in little rock grottoes (open but hidden from public view). Floors are of tile and terrazzo, covered with rush rugs. The spacious accommodations come with queen- or king-size beds (rarely a twin) and generous storage. Some units open onto the beach; others are on a hillside.

Young Island (P.O. Box 211), St. Vincent, W.I. www.youngisland.com. ✆ **800/223-1108** in the U.S. and Canada, or 784/458-4826. Fax 784/457-4567. 29 units. Winter $530–$1,150 double, $1,075–$1,225 suite; off season $470–$860 double, $890–$935 suite. Rates include breakfast and dinner. Ask about packages. AE, MC, V. Closed Sept. **Amenities:** Restaurant; 2 bars; babysitting; access to nearby health club; Internet (free); outdoor pool; spa; tennis court; watersports equipment/rentals. *In room:* Ceiling fan, fridge, hair dryer, no phone.

EXPENSIVE

Bequia Beach Hotel ★★ The newest hotel on island, a boutique one at that, was inspired by Oliver Messel's stylish villas on the exclusive island of Mustique. Enveloped by tropical gardens, the compound, with its own secluded beach area, offers a choice of a dozen spacious suites or villas. You can also rent a double room, each well furnished in a tropical style. Each room features a private terrace, most of which overlook the pool. The villas come with a combined living room and kitchenette, perfect for families. On Saturday nights, a lobster fest is staged on the beach, and live music is presented 2 nights a week in winter. The hotel boasts two restaurants: the Blue Tropic, on a hillside, and the Bagatelle, right on the beach.

Friendship Bay, St. Vincent, W.I. www.bequiabeach.com. ✆ **784/458-1600.** Fax 784/458-1700. 30 units. Year-round $180–$225 double, $350 suite, $300–$395 villas. Rates include continental breakfast. AE, DC, MC, V. **Amenities:** 2 restaurants; 2 bars; exercise room; outdoor pool; spa; tennis court (lit); watersports equipment/rentals. *In room:* A/C, kitchenette (in some), Wi-Fi (free).

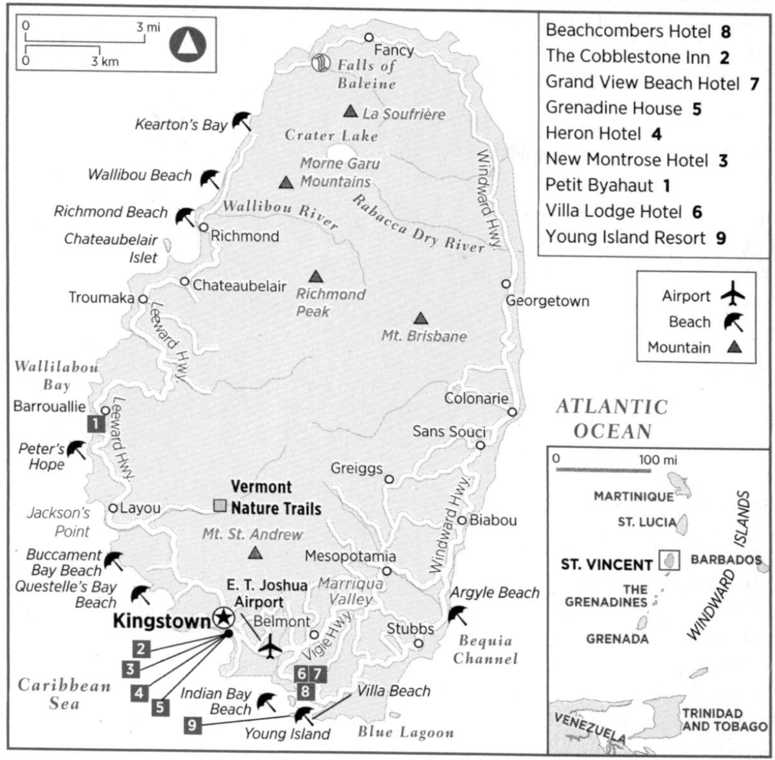

Grand View Beach Hotel ★ Owner/manager F. A. (Tony) Sardine named this place well: The "grand view" promised is of islets, bays, yachts, Young Island, headlands, lagoons, and sailing craft. This resort is set on 3 hectares (7½ acres) of gardens, just steps from the beach. The 19th-century plantation house is a large, white two-story mansion. Most bedrooms are of medium size and comfortable, opening onto views. The most luxurious and spacious rooms, some of which have wide terraces and faraway views of the Grenadines, are in the Mediterranean-style modern wing. The other units are on the upper level of a former great house and have a B&B feel.

Villa Point (P.O. Box 173), St. Vincent, W.I. www.grandviewhotel.com. ✆ **784/458-4811.** Fax 784/457-4174. 19 units. Winter $175–$215 double; off season $130–$170 double. Breakfast and dinner $55 per person extra. AE, MC, V. **Amenities:** 2 restaurants; 2 bars; exercise room; outdoor pool; room service; sauna; squash court; tennis court. *In room:* A/C, TV, hair dryer, Wi-Fi (free).

Grenadine House ★★ Set in a residential hillside suburb of Kingstown Park, this elegant little inn overlooks the town and botanical gardens. It's built on the site of St. Vincent's oldest guest house, from 1781 (and once the home of the island's governor). Today it's a modern guest house with well-furnished bedrooms that are spacious and furnished in part with wicker pieces and tropical designs. From the wide porches, panoramic views of Kingstown and the boat-filled harbor can be seen. You're a $4 taxi ride from the center of town or the nearest good beach.

Kingstown Park (P.O. Box 2523), Kingstown, St. Vincent, W.I. www.grenadinehouse.com. ✆ **866/659-8351** or 784/458-1800. Fax 784/458-1333. 20 units. Winter $200–$290 double; summer $180–$270 double. MC, V. **Amenities:** Restaurant; bar; gym; Internet (free); outdoor pool. *In room:* Ceiling fan.

MODERATE

Villa Lodge Hotel Set on a residential hillside a few minutes southeast of the center of Kingstown and the airport, this place is a favorite of visiting businesspeople. Because of its access to a beach and its well-mannered staff, it evokes the feeling of a modern villa. It's ringed with tropical, flowering trees and shrubs growing in the gardens. The air-conditioned rooms have ceiling fans, king-size beds, and comfortable rattan and local mahogany furniture. The hotel also rents eight apartments in its Breezeville Apartments complex next door, charging $150 for a double in winter and $135 for a double in summer.

Indian Bay (P.O. Box 1191), St. Vincent, W.I. www.villalodge.com. ✆ **800/448-8355** in the U.S., or 784/458-4641. Fax 784/457-4468. 19 units. Winter $130–$150 double, $150 apt; off season $115–$135 double, $135 apt. Breakfast and dinner $45 per person extra. AE, DISC, MC, V. **Amenities:** Restaurant; bar; babysitting; outdoor pool; room service. *In room:* A/C, ceiling fan, TV, fridge, hair dryer, kitchenette (in some), Wi-Fi (free).

INEXPENSIVE

Beachcombers Hotel ★ Richard and Flora Gunn operate this B&B in a tropical garden right on the beach. Three chaletlike buildings house the small to medium-size accommodations, all with private bathrooms and tasteful decor. The rooms are spotless and well maintained. Try for nos. 1, 2, or 3, as they open onto the water. Two units have small kitchenettes, and there is also a penthouse suite. The hotel has a health spa (Mrs. Gunn is a massage and beauty therapist) with a steam room, sauna, facials, and aromatherapy. The Beachbar & Restaurant, a favorite gathering place for locals, fronts an open terrace and has excellent food.

Villa Beach (P.O. Box 126), St. Vincent, W.I. www.beachcombershotel.com. ✆ **784/458-4283.** Fax 784/458-4385. 32 units. Year-round $90–$130 double; $150–$275 penthouse suite. Rates include breakfast. AE, MC, V. **Amenities:** Restaurant; bar; babysitting; outdoor pool; sauna; spa. *In room:* A/C, ceiling fan, TV, fridge (in some), Internet (free), kitchenette (in some).

The Cobblestone Inn Originally built as a warehouse for sugar and arrowroot in 1814, the core of this historic hotel is made of stone and brick. Today it's one of the most famous hotels on St. Vincent, known for its labyrinth of passages, arches, and upper hallways. To reach the high-ceilinged reception area, you pass from the waterfront through a stone tunnel into a chiseled courtyard. At the top of a massive sloping stone staircase, you're shown to one of the simple, old-fashioned bedrooms. The most spacious is no. 5, but it opens onto a noisy street. Meals are served on a third-floor aerie, high above the hotel's central courtyard. The hotel is convenient to town, but it's a 5km (3-mile) drive to the nearest beach.

Bax St. (P.O. Box 867), Kingstown, St. Vincent, W.I. www.thecobblestoneinn.com. ✆ **784/456-1937.** Fax 784/456-1938. 19 units. Year-round $75 double; $95 triple; $95 suite. AE, MC, V. **Amenities:** 2 restaurants; 2 bars; room service. *In room:* A/C, TV (in some), Wi-Fi (free).

Heron Hotel This hotel—renovated in 2006—is in one of St. Vincent's historic buildings. In spite of modern improvements, it still exudes a sense of old-fashioned timelessness you simply won't find in modern resorts. Built of local stone and tropical hardwoods, it served as a warehouse in the late 18th century and then later provided lodgings for colonial planters doing business along the wharves of Kingstown. Some of the simple and rather small rooms overlook an inner courtyard; others face the street. Room no. 15 is the largest. Although you don't get grand comfort here, the price is hard to beat, and the staff is hospitable.

Upper Middle St. (P.O. Box 226), Kingstown, St. Vincent, W.I. ✆/fax **784/457-1631.** 8 units. Year-round $75 double. AE, MC, V. **Amenities:** Restaurant; bar. *In room:* A/C, TV, fridge, Wi-Fi (free).

New Montrose Hotel ★ A real discovery, this bright, sunflower-yellow hotel lies on the northern fringe of town. The beach is a short ride away and there is no on-site pool, but what you will find is a handsomely furnished and comfortable room at an affordable price in a tranquil location. Accommodations have such extras as a full-length mirror closet, smoke detector, and good lighting. Some of the units have refrigerators or even a fully equipped kitchenette. The Caribbean/international dishes at the Mont Rose restaurant are good, so you can eat in if you don't want to wander the streets of Kingstown at night.

New Montrose (P.O. Box 215), Kingstown, St. Vincent, W.I. www.newmontrosehotel.com. ✆ **784/457-0172.** Fax 784/457-0213. 25 units. Year-round $70 double; $120 2-bedroom family suite. AE, MC, V. **Amenities:** Restaurant; bar; room service; spa. *In room:* A/C, fridge, kitchenette, Wi-Fi (free).

Where to Dine

Most guests eat at their hotels on the Modified American Plan (breakfast and dinner), and many Vincentian hostelries serve authentic West Indian cuisine. There are also a few independent restaurants, but not many.

Basil's Bar & Restaurant ★ SEAFOOD/INTERNATIONAL This enclave is set beneath the previously recommended Cobblestone Inn, a former sugar warehouse. The air-conditioned interior is accented with exposed stone and brick, soaring arches, and a rambling mahogany bar, which remains open throughout the day. The food is quite acceptable, but nowhere near as good as that enjoyed by Princess Margaret or Mick Jagger at Basil's more famous bar on Mustique (p. 622). The menu might include lobster salad, shrimp in garlic butter, sandwiches, hamburgers, and barbecued chicken. Dinners feature grilled lobster, shrimp cocktail, grilled red snapper, and grilled filet mignon, all fairly standard dishes of the international repertoire. You can order meals here throughout the day and late into the evening.

Bay St., Kingstown. ✆ **784/457-2713.** www.basilsbar.com. Reservations recommended. Main courses $20–$40. AE, MC, V. Daily 7am–10pm.

Bounty AMERICAN/WEST INDIAN In the redbrick Troutman Building in the center of Kingstown, you'll find the extremely affordable Bounty serving the local workers. (The true power-lunch venue is Basil's, recommended above.) Fill up on pastries, *rotis* (Caribbean burrito), sandwiches, homemade soups, pastas, quiche, and pizza. The cooking is as simple as the surroundings. A tasty collection of juices includes passion fruit. An on-site gallery and gift shop sells works by local artists.

Egmont St., Kingstown. ✆ **784/456-1776.** Pastries and sandwiches 40¢–$5; breakfast (all day) $7; lunch $7. No credit cards. Mon–Fri 7:30am–4:30pm; Sat 7:30am–1:30pm.

Cobblestone Rooftop Bar & Restaurant CARIBBEAN If you're shopping or sightseeing in Kingstown, this waterfront restaurant with a view serves some of the best meals in town. You climb three flights of stairs to reach the dining room, which was installed in an original Georgian building once used as a sugar warehouse. The food is good and fresh, using island produce when available. Starters include homemade soups of the day and a selection of salads, including chicken, tuna, or fresh fruit. Sandwiches and burgers are on the menu, but you can also order complete meals. The grilled catch of the day is a specialty, and you can also order stewed chicken or roast beef.

Upper Bay St., Kingstown. ✆ **784/456-1937.** All main courses $8. AE, DC, MC, V. Daily 7am–3pm.

The French Verandah ★ FRENCH/INTERNATIONAL The island's finest dining is at one of the candlelit tables on the waterfront terrace of Mariners Hotel, overlooking Villa Beach. There is an elegance to the service and setting, the cuisine is well crafted, and the ingredients first-rate. There is a harmonious blending of regional dishes and French favorites, such as a choice between Vincentian callaloo and conch soup or else snails in garlic butter. Many international dishes also appear in the chef's repertoire, including lobster crepes or fish salad Tahitian style. Our favorite main courses are the grilled yellowfin tuna or the shrimp in a mango-and-coconut salsa, the latter with real island flavor. Classic French main courses also appear on the menu, including grilled beef tenderloin with a black-pepper sauce.

Villa Bay. ✆ **784/457-4000.** Reservations recommended. Main courses $23–$43. AE, MC, V. Daily 6:30am–11pm.

L'Auberge des Grenadines ★ FRENCH/CARIBBEAN On the waterfront opening onto Admiralty Bay, this operation is popular with yachties, locals, and visitors alike. With its wood tables and high ceilings, it offers as a special feature a lobster tank. With your guaranteed fresh catch, the lobster can be grilled to your specifications. The couple who runs the place consistently turns out excellent fare, including appetizers such as salads made with fresh conch or goat cheese. The mussels come all the way from New Zealand, and they are awash in garlic and butter. For a main course, we go for the lobster flamed with old dark rum, or the seafood platter with the likes of shrimp, mussels, fresh white fish, and lobster. The seafood curry has mussels, shrimp, and lobster cooked delectably in coconut milk.

Belmont Walkway, Belmont. ✆ **784/457-3555.** www.caribrestaurant.com. Reservations recommended in winter. Main courses $10–$35; fixed-price menu $30–$42. MC, V. Daily 11:30am–9:30pm.

Sapodilla Room ★ CARIBBEAN On a hillside overlooking Kingstown, this is intimate dining on island at its best. Much of the produce served here comes from the lush tropical island itself. The air-conditioned restaurant lies on the ground floor. The evening begins in the West Indies Bar, which evokes an old British pub; it's decorated with movie-star photographs. Later you are shown to your table to peruse the daily menu, including the catch of the day. The chef makes succulent pastas and has a winning way with an array of meat and poultry dishes. He successfully imbues each dish with island flavor.

Kingstown Park, Kingstown. ✆ **784/458-1800.** Reservations required. Main courses $18–$30. MC, V. Daily 7-10am, noon–3pm and 7–8:30pm.

Vee Jay's Rooftop Diner & Pub WEST INDIAN/INTERNATIONAL This restaurant does a thriving business, thanks to its well-prepared food. Even though the restaurant has moved to a ground-floor location opposite the Bayview parking lot, it retains its original name from when it was a rooftop eatery. Lunches stress traditional Creole recipes using fresh fish, chicken, mutton, beef, and goat. Dinners are more international and may include lobster, excellent snapper with lemon-butter and garlic sauce, steaks with onions and mushrooms, and several savory preparations of pork. Every Friday there's a barbecue and a steel band after 6pm. In addition, 60 different drinks are featured at the bar.

Lower Bay St., Kingstown. ✆ **784/457-2845.** Reservations recommended for dinner. Main courses $12–$25; lunch platters $5–$15. AE, MC, V. Mon–Sat 9am–10pm.

Young Island Resort Restaurant ★★ CARIBBEAN/CONTINENTAL St. Vincent's best dining is on this 14-hectare (35-acre) private island lying off Villa Beach that's reached by a 5-minute scenic ride on the hotel's launch (p. 608). An evening at this restaurant, under thatched kiosks near the beach and surrounded by tropical gardens, will be your most romantic night on St. Vincent. Patrons are treated to lavish and elegant buffets twice a week. Fresh local fish, fruit, and vegetables are served. We always enjoy their freshly baked bread—banana, raisin, cinnamon, wheat, coconut, or just plain white, with lots of butter. The lunch menu changes frequently but is likely to feature the catch of the day. Go in the evening for the most glamorous experience and order the five-course dinner, which changes nightly.

Young Island. ✆ **784/458-4826.** Reservations required. Main courses $16–$19 lunch, $20–$50 dinner; Sun lunch buffet $31; Sat barbecue buffet $68. AE, MC, V. Daily 7am–11pm.

Exploring the Island

BEACHES

All beaches on mainland St. Vincent are public, and many of the best border hotels, where you can order drinks or lunch. Most of the resorts are in the south, where the beaches have golden-yellow sand. The only real white-sand beach is on Young Island, which is private (see p. 608 for a review of Young Island Resort). Many of the beaches in the north have sands of a lava-ash color. The safest swimming is on the leeward beaches; the surf on the windward or eastern beaches is often rough and can be quite dangerous.

The island's most popular strip is narrow **Villa Beach,** only a 10-minute drive from Kingstown. Its tranquil waters make swimming safe, and there are numerous simple cafes and watersports stands. Unfortunately, this beach can barely accommodate the crowds who flock here; weekends can be particularly bad.

Nearby **Indian Bay Beach** is similar to Villa Beach and also attracts lots of Vincentians on weekends. Monday to Thursday, however, you'll probably have plenty of room on this narrow strip. The sand is slightly golden but tends to be rocky. The reef-protected tranquil waters are ideal for both swimming and snorkeling. You'll find both bars and restaurants here.

Heading north from Kingstown, you'll reach **Buccament Bay Beach,** where the waters are clean, clear, and tranquil enough for swimming. This beach is very tiny, however, and it has black volcanic sand. In the same area, **Questelle's Bay Beach** (pronounced Keet-*ells*) is also on the leeward, tranquil Caribbean side of the island. This black-sand beach, next to Camden Park, is very similar to Buccament Bay.

Only die-hards head for the beaches on the east coast, or windward side, where the big breakers roll in from the Atlantic. Don't plan to go swimming in these rough waters; you might just enjoy a beach picnic instead. The best beaches, all with black

All This & Johnny Depp, Too

While scouting a location for its *Pirates of the Caribbean* movie series, Disney officials settled on St. Vincent for its virtually untouched coastline that seemingly belongs back in the 1800s.

volcanic sand, are found at **Kearton's Bay, Richmond Beach,** and **Peter's Hope,** all reached along the leeward highway running up the west coast of St. Vincent.

SPORTS & OUTDOOR PURSUITS

FISHING It's best to go to a local fisherman for advice, but your hotel can also arrange a trip for you. It's sometimes possible to accompany a fisherman on a trip, perhaps 6 or 8km (3¾ or 5 miles) from shore. A modest fee should suffice. The fishing fleet leaves from the leeward coast at Barrouallie. People have been known to return to shore with everything from a 15cm (6-in.) redfish to a 6m (20-ft.) pilot whale. Visitors don't need a fishing license.

HIKING Exploring St. Vincent's hot volcano, **La Soufrière,** is an intriguing adventure. As you travel the island, you can't miss its cloud-capped splendor. The most recent eruption was back in 1979, when it spewed ashes, lava, and hot mud that covered the vegetation on its slopes. Belching rocks and black curling smoke filled the blue Caribbean sky. About 17,000 people were evacuated from a 15km (9¼-mile) ring around the volcano.

At the rim of the crater, you'll be rewarded with one of the most panoramic views in the Caribbean—that is, if the wind doesn't blow too hard and make you topple over into the crater itself! ***Warning:*** Use extreme caution. Looking inside, you can see the steam rising from the crater.

Even if you're an experienced hiker, don't attempt to explore the volcano without a guide. Wear suitable hiking clothes, and be sure that you're in the best of health before making the arduous journey. The easiest route is the 5km-long (3-mile) eastern approach from Rabacca. The more arduous trail, longer by 2km (1¼ miles), is the western trail from Chateaubelair. The round-trip to the crater takes about 5 hours.

St. Vincent Forestry Headquarters, in the village of Campden Park, about 5km (3 miles) from Kingstown along the west coast (© **784/457-8594**), provides information about hiking to La Soufrière. It's open Monday to Friday from 8am to noon and 1 to 4pm. **HazEco Tours** (© **784/457-8634;** www.hazecotours.com) offers guided hikes up to La Soufrière, costing $85 per person, including drinks and lunch.

If you don't want to face Soufrière, the best hikes are the **Vermont Nature Trails.** These marked trails (get a map at the tourist office) take you through a rainforest and pass long-ago plantations reclaimed by nature. If it's your lucky day, you might even see the rare St. Vincent parrot with its flamboyant plumage. Wear good hiking shoes and lots of mosquito repellent.

SAILING & YACHTING ★★ St. Vincent and the Grenadines are one of the great sailing centers of the Caribbean. If you want to go bareboating, you can obtain a fully provisioned yacht. If you're a well-heeled novice, you can hire a captain and a crew. Rentals are available for a half-day, a full day, overnight, or even longer.

The longest-established yacht-chartering company in St. Vincent, **Barefoot Yacht Charters,** Blue Lagoon (© **784/456-9526;** www.barefootyachts.com), is better than ever and is now granting substantial discounts for last-minute or walk-in bookings. The outfitter has a fleet of 25 yachts run by the American Sailing Association and offers charters with or without a crew. Its operation is at its own custom-built marina with docks and moorings, along with a restaurant opening onto a panoramic vista of Bequia. There's even an Internet cafe. In winter, and depending on the vessel rented, rates range from $425 to $900 per day, with off-season prices going from $255 to $540. We also recommend **Nicholson Yacht Charters ★★** (© **305/433-5533,** or 268/460-1530 from Antigua; www.nicholson-charters.com). Prices at Nicholson are roughly comparable to those at Barefoot Yacht Charters.

SNORKELING & SCUBA DIVING ★★ St. Vincent's 30 or so dive sites are sprinkled along its leeward shore, where you might spot seahorses and frogfish. The best area for snorkeling and scuba diving is the Villa/Young Island section on the southern end of the island.

Dive St. Vincent, on the Young Island Cut (✆ **784/457-4928;** www.divestvincent.com), has been owned and operated by a transplanted Texan, Bill Tewes, since 1984. St. Vincent's oldest and best dive company, it now has an additional shop, **Grenadines Dive,** at the Sunny Grenadines Hotel on Union Island (✆ **784/458-8138;** www.grenadinesdive.com). Also try **Dive Canouan,** at the Tamarind Beach Hotel on Canouan Island (✆ **784/528-8030;** www.canouandivecenter.com). It offers dive/snorkel trips as well as sightseeing day-trips and dive instruction. Single-tank dives go for $110, or else $95 per tank if you're taking more than five dives, including all equipment and instructors and/or dive-master guides. Dive packages are also available.

KINGSTOWN

Though lush and tropical, the capital isn't as architecturally significant as Grenada's St. George's. There are some English-style houses, many of which look as though they belonged in Penzance or Cornwall rather than the Caribbean. This is a chief port and gateway to the Grenadines, and you can see the small boats and yachts that have dropped anchor here. On Saturday morning, the **market** at the south end of town is at its most active.

At the top of a winding road on the north side of Kingstown, **Fort Charlotte** was built on Johnson Point around the time of the American Revolution. The ruins aren't much—the reason to come here is the view. The fort sits atop a steep promontory some 190m (623 ft.) above the sea. From its citadel, you'll have a sweeping view of the leeward shores to the north, Kingstown to the south, and the Grenadines beyond. On a clear day, you can even see Grenada. Three cannons used to fight off French troops are still in place and there's a series of oil murals depicting the history of black Caribs. Admission is free, and the fort is open daily 6am to 6pm.

The second major sight is the **Botanic Gardens ★**, on the north side of Kingstown at Montrose (✆ **784/457-1003**). Founded in 1765 by Gov. George Melville, these are the oldest botanic gardens in the West Indies. You'll see 8 hectares (20 acres) of such tropical exotics as teak, almond, cinnamon, nutmeg, cannonball, and mahogany; some of the trees are more than 200 years old. One of the breadfruit trees was reputedly among those original seedlings brought to this island by Captain Bligh in 1793. There's also a large *Spachea perforata* (the Soufrière tree), a species believed to be unique to St. Vincent and not found in the wild since 1812. The gardens are open daily from 6am to 6pm; admission is free, but a tour guide costs $3.70.

THE LEEWARD HIGHWAY ★★

The leeward, or sheltered, west side of the island has the most dramatic scenery. North of Kingstown, you rise into lofty terrain before descending to the water again. There are views in all directions. Here you can see one of the finest petroglyphs in the Caribbean: the massive **Carib Rock,** with a human face carving dating from A.D. 600.

Continuing north, you reach **Barrouallie,** where there's a Carib stone altar. Even if you're not into fishing, you might want to spend some time in this village, where whalers still occasionally set out in brightly painted boats armed with harpoons. While Barrouallie may be one of the few outposts in the world where whaling is legal,

Vincentians claim that it doesn't endanger an already endangered species, as so few are caught each year. If one is caught, it's an occasion for festivities.

The highway continues to **Chateaubelair,** the end of the line. Here you can swim at attractive **Richmond Beach** before heading back to Kingstown. In the distance, the volcano, La Soufrière, looms menacingly.

The adventurous set out from here to see the **Falls of Baleine,** 12km (7½ miles) north of Richmond Beach on the northern tip of the island, accessible only by boat. Baleine is a freshwater falls that comes from a stream in the volcanic hills. If you're interested in making the trip, check with the tourist office in Kingstown for tour information.

MARRIQUA VALLEY ★

Sometimes known as the Mesopotamia Valley, the Marriqua Valley is one of the lushest cultivated valleys in the eastern Caribbean. Surrounded by mountain ridges, the drive takes you through a landscape planted with nutmeg, cocoa, coconut, breadfruit, and bananas. The road begins at the Vigie Highway, east of the airport. Surrounded by mountain ridges, it opens onto a panoramic view of Grand Bonhomme Mountain, rising 954m (3,130 ft.). At Montréal you'll come upon natural mineral springs, where you can have lunch and take a dip. Only rugged vehicles should make this trip.

Around Kingstown you can also enjoy the **Queen's Drive,** a scenic loop into the high hills to the east of the capital. From here the view is panoramic over Kingstown and its yacht-clogged harbor to the Grenadines in the distance.

SHOPPING

St. Vincent isn't a shopping destination, but while you're here, you might pick up some of the Sea Island cotton fabrics and clothing that are local specialties. Vincentian artisans also make pottery, jewelry, and baskets.

Since Kingstown consists of about 12 small blocks, you can walk, browse, and see about everything in a single morning. Try to be in town for the colorful, noisy **Friday morning market.** You might not purchase anything, but you'll enjoy the riot of color.

If you're searching for regional souvenirs, head for **St. Vincent Craftsmen's Centre,** on Frenches Street in Kingstown (✆ **784/457-2516**), a 4-minute walk from the wharf. Here islanders sell handmade items such as place or floor mats, along with straw products, local paintings, and St. Vincent dolls.

At **Sprott Brothers,** Homeworks, Bay Street (✆ **784/457-1121**), you can buy clothing designed by Vincentians, along with an array of silk-screened T-shirts and even Caribbean-made furniture.

St. Vincent Philatelic Services, Dee's Service Building, Bay Street (✆ **784/457-1911**), is the largest operating bureau in the Caribbean, and its issues are highly acclaimed by stamp collectors around the world.

ST. VINCENT AFTER DARK

Most nightlife centers on the hotels, where activities usually include barbecues and dancing to steel bands. In season, at least one hotel seems to have something planned every night. Beer is extremely cheap at all the places noted.

Aquatic Club, adjacent to the departure point of the ferryboat from St. Vincent to Young Island (✆ **784/458-4205**), is the loudest and most raucous nightspot on St. Vincent; it often features live reggae, soca, or calypso. It's a source of giddy fun to its fans. On Saturday nights, things heat up by 11pm and continue to the wee hours.

Predictably, the hotel with the best entertainment is **Young Island Resort,** Young Island (p. 608; ✆ **784/458-4826**), which in winter hosts live musical entertainment on Wednesday nights. A string band is brought in on Friday night for the manager's sunset cocktail party. Local musicians play on instruments made of bottles, gourds, and bamboo. The week's events are climaxed on Saturday with steel-band music and a barbecue dinner.

If you're in St. Vincent on a Friday night around 8pm, join the locals for a "jump-up" called **Caliaqua Culture Pot,** on the Main Road in Caliaqua. This is really a street party with lots of beer drinking and barbecue, followed by dancing to local bands.

THE GRENADINES

Essentials

GETTING THERE

BY PLANE Four of the Grenadines—Bequia, Mustique, Union Island, and Canouan—have small airports. Service from St. Vincent is by small interisland carriers. **SVG Air** (**© 800/624-1843** or 784/457-5124; www.svgair.com), one of the longest-established airlines in the region, will fly you in modern five- to nine-seaters to any island within the eastern Caribbean. From St. Vincent the one-way fare to Canouan or Union Island is $45.

BY BOAT The ideal way to go, of course, is to hire your own yacht, as many wealthy visitors do. A far less expensive option is to take a mail, cargo, or passenger boat, as the locals do, but you'll need time and patience. The ferry dock at Kingstown is at the cruise-ship terminal. The most visited island by ferry is Bequia, costing $10 for the 1-hour trip. Two companies compete on this route: **Admiralty Transport** (**© 784/458-3348;** www.admiralty-transport.com) and the **MV *Bequia Express*** (**© 784/458-3472**). Several daily trips are made Monday to Saturday beginning at 8am in St. Vincent; the last trip back from Bequia is at 5pm. On Sunday the schedules are curtailed, but there are usually two trips—one for morning departures, another for an evening sail.

Some adventurers prefer to take the mail boat, **MV *Barracuda*** (**© 784/455-9835**), sailing Monday and Thursday mornings from St. Vincent, stopping at Canouan, Mayreau, and Union islands. On Saturday a round-trip takes in every island. The one-way fare to Canouan is $12, to Mayreau $12, and to Union Island $14.

Bequia ★★

Only 18 sq. km (7 sq. miles) of land, Bequia (*Beck*-wee) is the largest of the Grenadines. It's the northernmost island in the chain (only 14km/8¾ miles south of St. Vincent), offering quiet lagoons, reefs, and long stretches of nearly deserted beaches. Its friendly population of some 5,000 is descended from seafarers and other early adventurers. Some 10% are of Scottish ancestry, living mostly in the Mount Pleasant region. A feeling of relaxation and informality prevails.

ESSENTIALS

GETTING AROUND Most visitors find it unnecessary to rent a car, as roads are atrocious. Those wanting to see more of the island might consider a taxi guide. Before going to your hotel, drop in at the **Tourist Information Centre** and ask for a driver who's familiar with the attractions of the island (all of them are). You should negotiate the fare in advance. **Rental cars,** owned by locals, are available at the port, or you can hire a **taxi** at the dock to take you around the island or to your hotel. Taxis are

Special Events

The Easter Regatta is held over Easter weekend, with boat races, food, and music. Bequia's Carnival celebrations are a 4-day affair, held just before St. Vincent's party in late June.

reasonably priced, but an even better bet are the so-called **dollar cabs,** which take you anywhere on the island for a small fee. They don't seem to have a regular schedule—you just flag one down.

VISITOR INFORMATION The **Tourist Information Centre** is at Port Elizabeth (✆ **784/458-3286;** www.bequiatourism.com). Hours in winter are Monday to Friday 8:30am to 6pm, Saturday 9am to 2pm, and Sunday 9am to noon; off season hours are Monday to Friday 9am to 5:30pm, Saturday 8:30am to 2pm, and Sunday 9am to noon.

BANKS There are a few bank branches on Bequia, mostly in Port Elizabeth. All have ATMs.

WHERE TO STAY

Firefly Plantation Bequia ★★★ Set on an 11-hectare (27-acre) sugar plantation dating from the 1700s, this is a gem of a little Caribbean inn. Composed of three buildings, it overlooks Bequia's only banana plantation, which is also riddled with orange trees, mangoes, and guavas. You can stroll through a coconut palm grove to the white sandy beach at Spring Bay. The location is 3km (2 miles) north of Port Elizabeth. The buildings housing the rooms were constructed on a hillside—expect some steep climbs—to capture the trade winds. Bedrooms are beautifully furnished in exquisite taste, with mosquito netting draped over four-poster beds in the colonial plantation style.

Spring Bay, Bequia, the Grenadines, St. Vincent, W.I. www.fireflybequia.com. ✆ **784/458-3414.** Fax 784/457-3305. 10 units. Winter $495 double; off season $395 double. AE, DC, MC, V. **Amenities:** Restaurant; bar; outdoor pool; tennis court; watersports equipment/rentals. *In room:* A/C, hair dryer, minibar, MP3 docking station, Wi-Fi (free).

The Frangipani ★★ This local favorite of yachties is a great hangout, its ambience created by James Mitchell, longtime prime minister of the island chain. The core of this pleasant guesthouse originated as the home of a 19th-century sea captain. Since it was transformed into a hotel, it has added accommodations that border a sloping tropical garden in back. The complex overlooks the island's historic harbor, Admiralty Bay. The five rooms in the original house are smaller and much less glamorous (and less expensive) than the better-outfitted accommodations in the garden. The garden units are handcrafted from local stone and hardwoods, and have tile floors, carpets of woven hemp, wooden furniture (some made on St. Vincent), and balconies.

Guests can play tennis or arrange scuba dives, sailboat rides, or other watersports nearby. The nearest scuba outfitter, **Dive Adventures,** is fully accredited by PADI (✆ **784/458-3826;** www.bequiadiveadventures.com). A single dive costs $60, a two-tank dive $102.

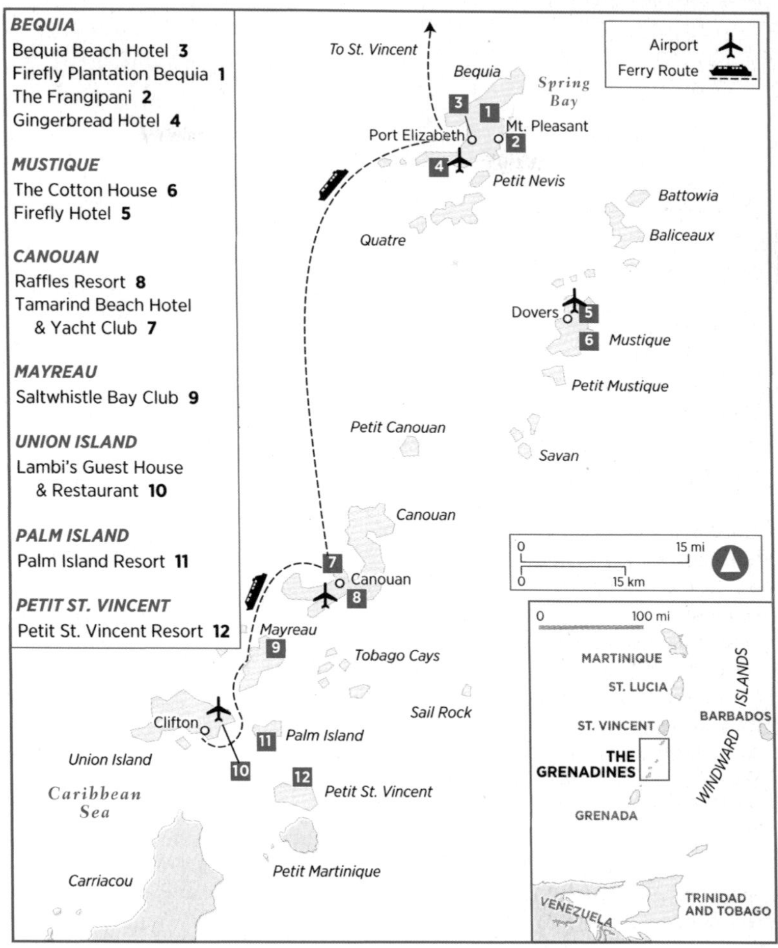

Admiralty Bay (P.O. Box 1), Bequia, the Grenadines, St. Vincent, W.I. www.frangipanibequia.com. ✆ **784/458-3255.** Fax 784/458-3824. 15 units, 10 with bathroom. Winter $75 double without bathroom, $165–$250 double with bathroom; off season $60 double without bathroom, $120–$180 double with bathroom. AE, MC, V. **Amenities:** Restaurant; bar; babysitting; boating; nearby dive shop; limited room service; tennis court; private yacht charter. *In room:* TV, ceiling fan, fridge (in some), no phone, Wi-Fi (free).

WHERE TO DINE

The food here is good and healthy—lobster, chicken, and steaks from such fish as mahimahi, kingfish, and grouper, plus tropical fruits, fried plantains, and coconut and guava puddings made fresh daily. Even the beach bars are kept spotless.

Frangipani ★ CARIBBEAN/INTERNATIONAL This waterside dining room, always full of yachties, is one of the best restaurants on the island. With the exception of the juicy steaks imported for barbecues, only local food is used in the specialties. Lunches, served throughout the day, include sandwiches, salads, and seafood platters. Dinner specialties include homemade soup, conch chowder, baked chicken with rice-and-coconut stuffing, lobster, and an array of fresh fish. A Thursday-night barbecue with live entertainment is an island event.

In the Frangipani Hotel, Port Elizabeth. ✆ **784/458-3255.** Reservations required for dinner. Main courses $4–$10 breakfast, $4–$24 lunch, $10–$33 dinner; fixed-price dinner $20–$50. AE, MC, V. Daily 7:30–10:30am, 11am–3pm lunch, and 6:30–9:30pm. Closed Sept.

L'Auberge des Grenadines ★ FRENCH/CARIBBEAN On the north side of Admiralty Bay, this little shack with a panoramic harbor view serves French cuisine with Creole accents. Yachties are especially fond of the place, often dropping in to make a selection from the lunchtime blackboard. The live lobster pool lets you know immediately that lobster is the house specialty, and it can be cooked to your preference. French-born Jacques Thevenot and his Vincentian wife, Eileen, will guide you through the menu of locally caught seafood, island-grown vegetables, and other dishes. During lunch you can order salads, burgers, and sandwiches. The auberge also rents three well-furnished bedrooms, costing $40 to $60 a night in winter or $30 to $50 a night in the off season. These are among the most affordable bedrooms on island.

Hamilton, Admirality Bay, Port Elizabeth. ✆ **784/458-3201.** Reservations required for dinner. Main courses $8–$19; fixed-price lunch $30–$37. AE, MC, V. Daily 11am–3pm and 6:30–9:30pm.

Mac's Pizzeria PIZZA Locals swear by this joint, claiming it serves the best pizza in the Grenadines, and we believe them. Piping hot from the oven, pizzas have been perfuming the night air here since 1980. You're given nearly 20 delectable toppings, even lobster if you're feeling flush. And if you don't like pizza (highly unlikely), you'll find an array of other items here, including homemade soups, succulent pastas, and conch fritters flavored with curry. Since Mac's is also a bakery, you can enjoy such treats as lime pie with a shortbread crust, hearty banana bread, or else homemade ice creams in tropical flavors.

Belmont Walkway, Admiralty Bay, Port Elizabeth. ✆ **784/458-3474.** Reservations required for dinner. Main courses $16–$24. AE, DC, MC, V. Daily 11am–3pm and 6:30–9:30pm. Closed Mon May–Nov.

EXPLORING BEQUIA

Obviously, the secluded beaches are at the top of everyone's list of Bequia's attractions. As you walk along the beaches, especially near Port Elizabeth, you'll see craftspeople building boats by hand, a method passed on by their ancestors. Whalers sometimes still set out from here in wooden boats with harpoons. Some beaches require a taxi ride. You might check out the uncrowded, pristine white sands at **Friendship Bay,** where you can rent watersports equipment or order a drink from the bar at the hotel. **Industry Bay** and **Lower Bay** are both gorgeous beaches shaded by palm trees, offering good swimming and snorkeling.

Dive Bequia, Gingerbread House, Admiralty Bay (P.O. Box 326), Bequia (✆ **784/458-3504;** www.divebequia.com), specializes in diving and snorkeling on the lush reefs of Bequia, where you might spot manta rays. Scuba dives cost $70 for one dive or $106 for two dives in the same day; a 10-dive package goes for $525. A four-dive open-water certification course is $525. Snorkeling trips are $30 per person, and these prices include all the necessary equipment.

The main harbor village, **Port Elizabeth,** is known for its safe anchorage, Admiralty Bay. The bay was a haven in the 17th century for the British, French, and Spanish navies, as well as for pirates. Descendants of Captain Kydd (or Kidd) still live on the island. Today the yachting set anchors here.

SHOPPING

Anyone on the island can show you the way to the workshops of **Sargeant's Model Boatshop Bequia,** Front Street, Port Elizabeth (✆ **784/458-3344**), west of the pier past the oil-storage facility. Sought out by yacht owners looking for a scale-model reproduction of their favorite vessel, Lawson Sargeant is the self-taught woodcarver who established this business. The models are carved from white pine and mahogany, and then painted brilliant colors. When a scale model of the royal family's yacht, *Britannia,* was commissioned in 1985, it required 5 weeks of work. You can pick up a model of a Bequia whaling boat for much less.

Mustique ★★★

This island of luxury villas, which someone once called "Georgian West Indian," is so remote and small that it would be unknown—if it didn't attract the likes of Paul Newman, Mick Jagger, Raquel Welch, Richard Avedon, Tommy Hilfiger, and Prince Andrew, many of whom have cottages here. Its most famous resident was the late Princess Margaret.

The island, privately owned by a consortium of businesspeople, is only 5km (3 miles) long and 2km (1¼-miles) wide, and it has only one major hotel (the Cotton House). It's located 24km (15 miles) south of St. Vincent. After settling in, you'll find many good white-sand beaches against a backdrop of luxuriant foliage. Our favorite is **Macaroni Beach,** where the water is turquoise, the sands are pure white, and a few trees shade the picnic tables. If you've come over on a day trip, you might go to **Britannia Bay,** which is next to the jetty and close to Basil's Bar (p. 622).

On the northern reef of Mustique lies the wreck of the French liner *Antilles,* which ran aground on the Pillories in 1971. Its massive hulk, now gutted, can be seen cracked and rusting a few yards offshore—an eerie sight.

If you want to tour the small island, you can rent a **Mini-Moke** (a small golf-cart-like car) to see some of the most elegant homes in the Caribbean, including the late Princess Margaret's place, **Les Jolies Eaux (Pretty Waters).**

GETTING THERE & GETTING AROUND

This posh island is serviced by **Mustique Airways,** which runs only private charter flights. For information and reservations, call **SVG Airways** at ✆ **784/456-6793**.

Once here, you can call a taxi (✆ **784/488-8000,** ext. 448), but chances are someone at the Cotton House (below) will already have seen you land.

WHERE TO STAY

The Cotton House ★★★ The Caribbean's most exclusive hotel is as casually elegant and sophisticated as its clientele. The 18th-century main house is built of coral and stone, and it was painstakingly restored, reconstructed, and redecorated by Oliver Messel, uncle by marriage to Princess Margaret. The antique loggia, arched louvered doors, and cedar shutters set the style. The decor includes everything from Lady Bateman's steamer trunks to a scallop-shell fountain on a quartz base. Guests go between two beaches, each only a couple of minutes away on foot—Endeavour Bay, on the leeward side, with calmer waters, and L'Ansecoy, on the other side. Guest rooms are in five fully restored Georgian houses, a trio of cottages, a newer block of four rooms, and a five-room beach house, all of which open onto windswept balconies or patios. The Tower Suite is one of the most luxurious of the accommodations, filling the entire second floor. The most expensive residence is Cotton Hill, a two-bedroom villa with a private pool.

Endeavour Bay, Mustique (P.O. Box 349), the Grenadines, St. Vincent, W.I. www.cottonhouse.net. ✆ **888/452-8380** in the U.S., or 784/456-4777. Fax 784/456-5887. 17 units. Winter $815–$1,675 double, from $1,565 suite; off season $520–$995 double, from $1,115 suite. Rates include MAP (breakfast and dinner). AE, MC, V. **Amenities:** 2 restaurants; 3 bars; babysitting; horseback riding; exercise room; outdoor pool; room service; spa; 2 tennis courts; watersports equipment/rentals. *In room:* A/C, hair dryer, minibar, Wi-Fi (free).

Firefly Hotel ★ This stone house, constructed in 1972, is one of the first homes ever built by an expatriate English or North American on Mustique. It functioned as a simple, not particularly glamorous B&B until the late 1990s, when Sussex-born Elizabeth Clayton spent huge sums of money to upgrade and enlarge the hotel and its restaurant. Although it contains only five bedrooms, it thrives as one of the most consistently popular and animated bars and restaurants (see below) on an island where lots of the expatriate residents enjoy partying into the wee hours. Each of the rooms has Caribbean decor, ceiling fans, mahogany furniture, an antique four-poster bed, and a bathroom with a plunge pool.

Britannia Bay (P.O. Box 349), Mustique, the Grenadines, W.I. www.fireflymustique.com. ✆ **784/488-8414.** Fax 784/488-8514. 5 units. Year-round $900–$1,200 double. Rates are all-inclusive. AE, MC, V. Children 11 and under not allowed. **Amenities:** Restaurant; bar; free airport transfers; 2 outdoor pools; room service; tennis (nearby); snorkeling. *In room:* A/C, hair dryer, minibar, MP3 docking station, Wi-Fi (free).

WHERE TO DINE

Basil's Beach Bar ★ SEAFOOD/CARIBBEAN Nobody ever visits this island of indigenous farmers and fishermen without spending a night at Basil's, which looks straight out of the South Seas with its wooden deck, open-air dance floor, and thatched roof. Built on piers above the sea, the beach bar is a popular gathering place for yachties sailing the Grenadines. Some people come for drinks and the panoramic view, but Basil's also has a reputation as one of the finest seafood restaurants in the Caribbean. Everything is simple but well prepared. You can dine under the open-air sunscreens or in the sun. On Wednesday night in winter, you can jump-up at a barbecue, and there's live music on Mondays. A boutique is also on the premises.

13 Britannia Bay. ✆ **784/488-8350.** www.basilsmustique.com. Reservations recommended. Main courses $20–$47. AE, MC, V. Daily 8am–10pm. Bar daily 8am until "very late."

The Restaurant at Firefly ★ FRENCH/INTERNATIONAL This is one of the island's most consistently popular restaurants, characterized by its bright tropical colors and open-air terraces, a busy bar area where you're likely to see Mustique's glitterati at play, and a menu that's the byproduct of a European-trained chef whose earlier venues were very grand and very prestigious. Some of the establishment's tried-and-true dishes include spicy Caribbean crab cakes and pineapple-shrimp curry with rice. Other entrees change with the season and the inspiration of the chef. The drink associated with this place is the Firefly Special, made with coconut cream, two kinds of rum, fresh papaya, and nutmeg. Don't miss the banana flambé.

In the Firefly Hotel, Britannia Bay. ✆ **784/488-8414.** Reservations recommended for dinner. Main courses $48. AE, MC, V. Daily 8am–10pm. Bar daily 8am–midnight.

Canouan ★★

In the shape of a half-circle, Canouan rises from its sandy beaches to the 240m-high (787-ft.) peak of Mount Royal in the north, where you'll find unspoiled forests of white cedar. Twenty-three kilometers (14 miles) south of St. Vincent and 32km (20 miles) north of Grenada, Canouan has a population of fewer than 2,000 people, many of whom fish for a living and live in **Retreat Village,** the island's only village.

Only 6×2km (3¾×1¼ miles), Canouan is surrounded by long ribbons of absolutely gorgeous powdery white-sand beaches and blue lagoons. The surrounding coral reefs teem with life, making for great diving. As for snorkeling, it's the best this side of the Maldives.

GETTING THERE

Reaching Canouan by air is slightly different from traveling to the other islands of the Grenadines. **American Eagle** (✆ **800/433-7300** in the U.S. and Canada, or 784/456-5555) flies nonstop from San Juan to Canouan. **SVG Air,** in St. Vincent (✆ **800/624-1843** or 784/457-5124), makes two daily flights to Canouan at a cost of $396 round-trip.

WHERE TO STAY

Canouan Resort ★★ Named after the famous hotel of Singapore, this villa-studded resort opens onto a beautiful white-sand beach set on 120 hectares (297 acres). Opening onto Carenage Bay, each of the accommodations is a villa suite. The golf course has been extended to a full 18 holes, and a deluxe European-style casino has been added. Each suite comes with its own private terrace. Decorated in pastels, the bedrooms have a light, airy, tropical feel. Rooms come in a variety of categories, from deluxe through luxurious suites. The Caribbean's largest hotel pool is one of the allures.

Carenage Bay, Canouan, St. Vincent, W.I. www.canouan.com/resort.asp. ✆ **784/458-8000.** Fax 784/458-8885. 156 units. Winter $1,800–$4,600 double suite; off season $550–$2,600 double suite. AE, MC, V. **Amenities:** 4 restaurants; 4 bars; boat excursions; children's club; exercise room; 18-hole golf course; 2 pools (outdoor and children's); casino; room service; spa; 4 tennis courts. *In room:* A/C, TV, hair dryer, kitchenette (in some), minibar, Wi-Fi (free).

Tamarind Beach Hotel & Yacht Club ★ Italian-owned and -managed, this idyllic inn opens onto the long white sands of Grand Bay Beach. Thatched-roof bungalow-style hideaways, each enveloped by tropical gardens, are called seaside hideaways here—and so they are. Rooms have private balconies or patios, wicker furnishings, louvered wooden doors, and wood walls. Whirling ceiling fans go night and day. The staff provides several thoughtful touches, such as leaving a tropical fruit basket in your bedroom. The staff will help you arrange "island safaris" to such neighboring sandy strips as the Tobago Cays. Although everything is imported, the food is good and is served at water's edge on an open terrace with a view of the boats.

Charlestown, Canouan, St. Vincent, W.I. www.canouan.com/tamarind.asp. ✆ **784/458-8044.** Fax 784/458-8851. 39 units. Winter $550–$650 double, $630–$750 suite; off season $260 double, $495 suite. MAP (breakfast and dinner) $140 per person extra. Children 11 and under stay free in parent's room. AE, MC, V. **Amenities:** 2 restaurants; 2 bars; babysitting; dive shop; sailing; scuba diving; spa; windsurfing. *In room:* A/C, ceiling fan, TV (in some), fridge, hair dryer, minibar, Wi-Fi (free).

WHERE TO DINE

Jambu's ★ CHINESE/ASIAN The best Chinese and Asian food in this tiny archipelago nation is served here at the chic Canouan Resort (above). Many of the dishes have flavors familiar to Singaporeans. With these Far East flavors, regional ingredients are often used as well, making for some intriguing combinations. It's a true East-meets-West kitchen. The Chinese "tapas" alone would make a meal unto themselves—coconut seafood *tom yam* soup, pan-seared marinated duck with hoisin sauce in rice-paper rolls, or delectable soft-shell crab and lobster wontons. The barracuda served comes from the Caribbean, but the red-chili curry paste is from the Pacific. Lemon-grass-crusted lamb chops are another celestial delight. Opt for a beach-bordering table, where candles flicker in the trade winds at the island's most romantic spot.

In the Canouan Resort, Carenage Bay. ✆ **784/458-8000.** Reservations required. Main courses $13–$56 lunch, $47–$52 dinner. AE, MC, V. Daily 7-10:30am, noon–3pm, and 7–10pm.

DIVING & GOLF

Spread over more than 24 hectares (59 acres) with panoramic sea views, **Trump International Golf Club ★★★**, at the Canouan Resort on Carenage Bay (p. 623; ✆ **784/458-8000**), is an 18-hole, par-72 championship course designed by Jim Fazio. The course soars 252m (827 ft.) above sea level to the 13th tee, and holes 11 to 15 teeter on a knife's-edge ride. Several golf magazines have named this course one of the best in the world. Greens fees for 18 holes are $220 for hotel guests or $300 for visitors. Available at the pro shop are carts, rental clubs, and even golf instruction.

The best dive center is **Canouan Dive Center,** next to the previously recommended Tamarind Beach Hotel, at Charlestown (✆ **784/528-8030;** www.canouandivecenter.com), offering scuba diving for all levels of experience. The island itself has some of the finest diving in the southern Caribbean, and you can also go on dives to the Tobago Cays, Mayreau, and Union Island. This is a full PADI resort, offering training by master scuba divers. With equipment, prices range $95 to $110 per one-tank dive, or $95 per dive if more than five dives are booked; PADI courses cost from $175 to $875, depending on your requirements.

Mayreau ★

A tiny cay, 4 sq. km (1½ sq. miles) of land, Mayreau is a privately owned island shared by a hotel and a little hilltop village of about 250 inhabitants. It's on the route of the mail boat that plies the seas to and from St. Vincent (see "Getting There," under "The Grenadines," earlier in this chapter). It's completely sleepy unless a cruise ship anchors offshore and hustles its passengers over for a lobster barbecue on the beach.

WHERE TO STAY & DINE

Saltwhistle Bay Club ★ 🎁 Slightly less formal and expensive than the Petit St. Vincent Resort on Petit St. Vincent (see below), to which it's frequently compared, Saltwhistle Bay Club caters to escapists with money. You can spend your days lolling in one of the hammocks strung among the trees in the 8-hectare (20-acre) tropical garden, perhaps taking a swim off the expanse of white-sand beaches that curve along both the leeward and windward sides of the island, or the staff will take you to a little uninhabited island nearby for a Robinson Crusoe–style picnic. Set back from the beach, the accommodations were built by local craftspeople, using local stone and tropical woods like purpleheart and greenheart. Inside, the spacious cottages have an almost medieval feel, with thick stone walls and dark-wood furnishings.

Mayreau Island, the Grenadines, St. Vincent, W.I. www.saltwhistlebay.com. ✆ **784/458-8444.** Fax 784/458-8944. 10 units. Winter $480 double; off season $360 double. Rates include breakfast and dinner. AE, MC, V. Closed Sept–Oct. Take the private hotel launch from the airport on Union Island ($60 per person round-trip). **Amenities:** Restaurant; bar; babysitting; room service; watersports equipment/rentals. *In room:* Ceiling fan, hair dryer, no phone.

Union Island

Midway between Grenada and St. Vincent, Union Island is one of the southernmost of the Grenadines. It's known for its dramatic 270m (886-ft.) peak, Mount Parnassus, which yachters can see from miles away. For those cruising in the area, Union is the port of entry for St. Vincent. Yachters are required to check in with Customs upon entry.

ESSENTIALS

GETTING THERE The island is reached by chartered or scheduled aircraft, cargo boat, private yacht, or mail boat. (See "Getting There," under "The Grenadines," earlier in this chapter).

WHERE TO STAY & DINE

Lambi's Guest House & Restaurant CREOLE/SEAFOOD *Lambi* means "conch" in Creole patois, and if you've never tried this shellfish, this is a good place to do so. Built partially on stilts on the waterfront in Clifton, this is also one of the best places to sample the local cuisine. You can order various fresh fish platters, depending on the catch of the day, and lobster is frequently available. You can also order chicken, steak, lamb, or pork chops, but all this is shipped in frozen. Fresh vegetables are used whenever possible. In winter a steel band entertains nightly in the bar. Other entertainment includes limbo dancers or fire dancing.

Upstairs are 41 dormitory-style rooms for rent, each with two double beds, ceiling fans, and a tiny, tiny bathroom. They go for $26 single, $35 double, and $60 triple.

Clifton Harbour, Union Island, the Grenadines, St. Vincent, W.I. © **784/458-8549.** Main courses $15–$35. MC, V. Daily 7am–11pm.

Palm Island ★

Is this island a resort, or is the resort the island? Casual elegance prevails on these 52 hectares (129 acres) in the southern Grenadines. Surrounded by five white-sand beaches, this private island is sometimes called Prune, so we can easily understand the more appealing name change. This little islet offers complete peace and quiet, with plenty of sea, sand, sun, and sailing.

To get to Palm Island, you must first fly to Union Island. From Union Island, a hotel launch will take you to Palm Island.

WHERE TO STAY

Palm Island Resort ★★★ Tranquillity reigns at this all-inclusive resort with its five white-sand beaches. This exclusive and remote retreat has come a long way since its founder, John Caldwell ("Coconut Johnny"), began planting palms here to give the island a lush, tropical look. The posh retreat consists of a cluster of units contained in 22 Caribbean cottages. Bedrooms capture the spirit of the Grenadines, occupying both standard guest rooms and "treehouses," each with custom-designed bamboo and rattan furnishings, and balconies or patios opening onto the view. The romantic treehouses have high-peaked ceilings, breezy balconies, and four-poster bamboo beds. In addition to the regular accommodations, the Plantation House boasts four bedrooms, each with queen-size beds. Children are allowed April to December.

Palm Island, the Grenadines, St. Vincent, W.I. www.palmislandresortgrenadines.com. © **866/237-2157** in the U.S. and Canada, or 784/458-8824. Fax 784/458-8804. 45 units. Winter $855–$935 double, $1,010–$1,365 cottages and suites; off season $725 double, $850–$1,155 cottages and suites. Rates are all-inclusive. AE, MC, V. **Amenities:** 2 restaurants; 2 bars; bikes; exercise room; outdoor pool; tennis court; watersports equipment/rentals. *In room:* A/C, hair dryer, minibar, no phone, Wi-Fi (free).

Petit St. Vincent ★

A private island 6km (3¾ miles) from Union Island in the southern Grenadines, this speck of land is rimmed with white-sand beaches. On 45 hectares (111 acres), it's an out-of-this-world corner of the Caribbean that's only for self-sufficient types who want to escape just about everything.

The easiest way to get to Petit St. Vincent is to fly to Union Island via St. Vincent. Make arrangements with the hotel to have its "PSV boat" pick you up on Union Island. This is the southernmost of St. Vincent's Grenadines.

WHERE TO STAY

Petit St. Vincent Resort ★★★ This nautical-chic resort lies on a lush 45-hectare (111-acre) property. It's the only place to stay on the island. Open to the trade winds, this self-contained cottage colony was designed by a Swedish architect, Arne Hasselquist, who used purpleheart wood and the local stone, blue bitch (yes, that's right), for the walls. Some cottages are built on a hillside, with great views, and some are set close to the beach. Cottages open onto big outdoor patios and are cooled by trade winds and ceiling fans. Each of the spacious accommodations has an ample living area, two daybeds, a good-size bedroom with two queen-size beds, Caribbean-style wicker and rattan furnishings, and a large patio with a hammock. For payment, personal checks are accepted and preferred. When you need something (perhaps a picnic lunch made up for your day on the beach), you simply write out your request, place it in a slot in a bamboo flagpole, and run up the yellow flag.

Petit St. Vincent, the Grenadines, St. Vincent, W.I. www.psvresort.com. ✆ **800/654-9326** or 954/963-7401. Fax 954/963-7402. 22 units. Winter $903–$1,070 cottage for 2; off season $709–$903 cottage for 2. Rates are all-inclusive. AE, MC, V. Closed Sept–Oct. **Amenities:** Dining room; bar; babysitting; fitness trail; room service; tennis court; watersports equipment/rentals. *In room:* Ceiling fan, hair dryer, minibar, no phone, Wi-Fi (free).

TRINIDAD & TOBAGO

24

One of the most industrialized nations in the Caribbean, Trinidad draws more business travelers than tourists and entertaining a booming cruise-ship industry. Trinidad's population is a mosaic—you'll find descendants of Hindustanis, Javanese, Lebanese, Africans, and Creole mixes. But all come together at Carnival, when Trinidad erupts in a riot of color and sound, lilting steel pans moving the party along. Tobago, it's tiny cousin, is an unspoiled paradise of lush, natural beauty, where amber sunsets sink into gin-clear waters.

Beaches While the island has an extensive coastline, most beaches are undeveloped and remote, far removed from the capital. The closest of the better beaches, **Maracas Bay,** is delightful. Encircled by mountains, it has white sand, swaying coconut palms, and crystal-clear waters. On Tobago, sunbathers share space with giant leatherback turtles on the sandy shores of **Turtle Beach.**

Things to Do Port-of-Spain can be explored on foot and includes a varied sampling of colonial architectural styles, including the **"Magnificent Seven"** row of mansions. **Carnival** is an amazing spectacle of dazzling costumes and gaiety. Hundreds of sequined and feathered masqueraders parade through the cities to the sounds of calypso and furious steel-band competitions. **Pitch Lake,** a wonder of the natural world, is an expansive deposit of asphalt with a surface like elephant skin.

Eating & Drinking Leave your hotel restaurant behind and head to local hot spots where you can dine on island specials like **stuffed crabs** and ***chip-chip***, tiny clamlike shellfish (you may want to skip the armadillo and opossum stews). Spicy ***rotis*** (Caribbean burritos) filled with vegetables or ground meat make a hearty, filling lunch, and the drink of choice is a fresh **rum punch** flavored with locally produced Angostura Bitters. Except for a handful of fancy places, dress tends to be very casual.

Nature The island landscape is a fertile wonder of flora and fauna—with 700 varieties of orchids and 400 species of birds. The sanctuary **Pointe-à-Pierre Wild Fowl Trust** is tucked away in an unlikely setting: near an oil refinery. Despite the seemingly inhospitable clime, wildfowl flourish amid luxuriant vegetation such as myrtle and mango trees; look closely and you may spot a toucan. **Caroni Bird Sanctuary** is a mangrove swamp and home to clouds of scarlet ibis, the national bird of Trinidad and Tobago.

ESSENTIALS

Visitor Information

The tourism website for both Trinidad and Tobago is **www.tdc.co.tt**. Once in Trinidad, you can visit **Maritime Centre,** 29 10th Ave., Barataria (✆ **868/675-7034;** www.tdc.co.tt), or the kiosk at **Piarco International Airport,** Piarco (✆ **868/669-5196**).

On Tobago, go to the **Tobago Division of Tourism,** N.I.B. Mall, Level 3, Scarborough (✆ **868/639-2125**), or the information desk at **Crown Point Airport** (✆ **868/639-0509**). You can also check **www.visittobago.gov.tt**.

[FastFACTS] TRINIDAD & TOBAGO

Currency The official currency is the **Trinidad and Tobago dollar (TT$).** As regards the U.S. dollar, TT$1 = 15¢. Stated inversely, that means that $1 is worth TT$6.26 in Trinidadian currency. As regards the British pound, at press time, TT$1 equaled 10p and £1 = TT$10.10. When you get to Trinidad or Tobago, be sure to predetermine what currency is being referred to whenever rates are quoted—most places in T&T will accept the Trinidad and Tobago dollar or the U.S. dollar. Smaller local establishments may prefer Trinidad and Tobago dollars. *Prices in this chapter are quoted in U.S. dollars.*

Customs To avoid the long delays inherent in clearing Trinidad's Customs (reportedly the worst delays in the southern Caribbean), it helps to arrive during the day. Visitors may bring in 200 cigarettes or 50 cigars plus 1 quart of spirits.

Documents Citizens of the United States, Britain, and Canada need passports and an ongoing or return ticket to enter Trinidad and Tobago. A visa is not required for tourist or business stays of 90 days or less. Save the carbon copy of the immigration card you'll fill out when you arrive; you'll have to return it to immigration officials when you depart.

Electricity The electricity is either 110- or 230-volt AC, so ask when making your hotel reservations if you'll need transformers and/or adapters.

Embassies & High Commissions In Port-of-Spain on Trinidad, the **U.S. Embassy** is at Public Affairs Section, 7–9 Marli St. (✆ **868/822-5585**), and 15 Queen's Park West (✆ **868/622-6371;** Tues–Thurs 1–4pm); the **Canadian High Commission** is situated at Maple House, 3–3A Sweet Briar Rd., St. Clair (✆ **868/622-6232**); and the **British High Commission** is found at 19 St. Clair Ave., St. Clair (✆ **868/350-0444**).

Emergencies On both Trinidad and Tobago, call the **police** at ✆ **999;** to report a **fire** or summon an **ambulance,** dial ✆ **990.**

Language English is the official language, although you'll hear it spoken with many different accents, especially British. Chinese, French, Spanish, Hindi, and Trinibagianese—a local dialect—are also spoken.

Safety Like neighboring countries such as Colombia and Venezuela, Trinidad is importing a dangerous kidnapping culture. High unemployment and easy money lure newcomers to the kidnapping industry. No one, including tourists, is immune. There is no sure way to prevent kidnappings, but do take the usual precautions—avoid lonely beaches and walking alone at night.

As a general rule, Tobago is safer than Trinidad. Crime does exist on Tobago, but it's not of raging dimensions. If you can, avoid the downtown streets of Port-of-Spain at night, especially those around Independence Square, where muggings have been reported. Evening jaunts down Wilson Street and the Market of Scarborough are also discouraged. Visitors are open prey for pickpockets during Carnival, so be alert during large street parties. It is wise to safeguard your valuables; never leave them unattended at the beach or even in a locked car.

Taxes & Service Charges The government imposes a 15% value-added tax (VAT) on room rates. It also imposes a departure tax of TT$100, or $15, on every passenger age 6 and over, and it must be paid in local currency. The big hotels and restaurants add a 10% to 15% service charge to your final tab.

Telephone The area code for Trinidad and Tobago is **868.** Make calls to or from the islands as you would to any other area code in North America. On either island, just dial the local seven-digit number. For **MCI** call ✆ **800/888-8000,** for **Sprint** ✆ **800/877-8000,** and for **AT&T** ✆ **800/872-2881.**

Time Trinidad and Tobago are in the Eastern Standard Time zone but don't follow daylight saving time; when all time zones are on standard time, time here is the same as the U.S. East Coast. During daylight saving time in the United States, T&T is 1 hour behind (when it's 6am on the East Coast, it's 5am in T&T).

Tipping Tip taxi drivers 10% to 15% of the fare, and tip waiters 10% to 15% of the cost of a meal. Tip skycaps and bellboys $1 per bag.

Water On Trinidad and Tobago, stick to bottled water.

Weather Trinidad has a tropical climate all year, with constant trade winds maintaining mean temperatures of 84°F (29°C) during the day and 74°F (23°C) at night. It rarely gets above 90°F (32°C) or below 70°F (21°C). The rainy season runs from May to November, but it shouldn't deter you from visiting; the rain usually lasts no more than 2 hours before the sun comes out again. However, carry along plenty of insect repellent if you visit then.

TRINIDAD

Trinidad is completely different from the other Caribbean islands, which is part of its charm and appeal. It's not for everyone, though. Because **Port-of-Spain,** the capital, is one of the most bustling commercial centers in the Caribbean, more business travelers than tourists are drawn here. The island—approximately 80km (50 miles) long and 65km (40 miles) wide—does have beaches, but the best of them are far away from the capital. The city itself, with a population of about 120,000, is hot, humid, and somewhat dirty. With the opening of its $2-million cruise-ship complex, Port-of-Spain has become a major port of call for Caribbean cruise lines.

Although Port-of-Spain, with its shopping centers, fast-food joints, modern hotels, and active nightlife, draws mixed reviews, the countryside is calmer. Far removed from the traffic jams of the capital, you can explore the fauna and flora of the island. It's estimated that there are some 700 varieties of orchids alone, plus 400 species of birds.

The people are part of the attraction on Trinidad, the most cosmopolitan island in the Caribbean. The island's polyglot population includes Syrians, Chinese, Americans, Europeans, East Indians, Parsees, Madrasis, Venezuelans, and the last of the original Amerindian settlers of the island. You'll also find Hindustanis, Javanese, Lebanese, African descendants, and Creole mixes. In all there are about 1.2 million inhabitants, whose language is English, although you may also hear the local dialect, Trinibagianese.

Essentials

GETTING THERE From the United States, there are nonstop flights to Trinidad from both New York and Miami aboard **American Airlines** (✆ **800/433-7300** in the U.S. and Canada; www.aa.com). Check with **Continental Airlines** (✆ **800/231-0856** in the U.S. and Canada; www.continental.com) for routings from other cities such as Washington, D.C., and Houston.

In addition, **Air Canada** (✆ **888/247-2262** in the U.S. and Canada, or 868/669-4065; www.aircanada.ca) flies Tuesday, Thursday, Saturday, and Sunday nonstop from Toronto to Trinidad, and **British Airways** (✆ **800/247-9297** in the U.S. and Canada; www.britishairways.com) has three flights a week (Wed, Thurs, and Sat), leaving year-round from London's Gatwick Airport.

Caribbean Airlines (✆ **800/920-4225** in the U.S. and Canada; www.caribbean-airlines.com), the national carrier, offers service from New York, Miami, and Philadelphia to Port-of-Spain. The airline also flies from Toronto in Canada and from London in the U.K.

Trinidad is the transfer point for many passengers to Tobago. For information about getting to Tobago, see "Tobago," later in this chapter.

Arrivals are at Trinidad's Piarco International Airport, which is about a 30-minute drive east of Port-of-Spain.

GETTING AROUND Trinidad **taxis** are unmetered, and they're identified by their license plates, which begin with the letter H. There are also "pirate taxis" as well: private cars that cruise around like regular taxis and pick up passengers. Whether you take an official taxi or a pirate taxi, make sure you agree on the fare beforehand; otherwise, you're likely to get ripped off. **Maxi Taxis,** or **vans,** can also be hailed on the street. A fare from Piarco Airport into Port-of-Spain generally costs $20 during the day, $35 at night. Call **Phone-A-Taxi** (✆ **868/628-TAXI** [8294]) for taxi information or to order a cab.

To avoid the anxiety of driving, you can **hire a local driver** for your sightseeing jaunts. Although it costs more than doing it yourself, it alleviates the hassles of badly marked (or unmarked) roads and the sometimes-bizarre local driving patterns. Most drivers will serve as guides. Their rates, however, are based on route distances, so get an overall quotation and agree on the actual fare before setting off.

If you're brave enough to set out via **rental car,** arm yourself with a good map and **never forget to drive on the left.** Visitors with a valid international driver's license or a license from the United States, Canada, France, or the United Kingdom may drive without extra documentation for up to 3 months.

Since the island is one of the world's largest exporters of asphalt, Trinidad's 7,245km (4,502 miles) of roads are well paved. However, outback roads should be avoided during the rainy season, as they're often narrow, twisting, and prone to washouts. Inquire about conditions, particularly if you're headed for the north coast. The fierce traffic jams of Port-of-Spain are legendary, and night driving anywhere on the island is rather hazardous.

The major U.S.-based car rental firms currently have no franchises on the island, so you'll have to make arrangements with a local firm (go over the terms and insurance agreements carefully). Count on spending about $50 to $100 per day or more, with unlimited mileage included. Your best bet is one of the firms maintaining offices at Piarco Airport. These include **Southern Sales Car Rentals** (✆ **868/675-2424**), **Thrifty** (✆ **800/847-4389** in the U.S. and Canada, or 868/669-0602;

Trinidad

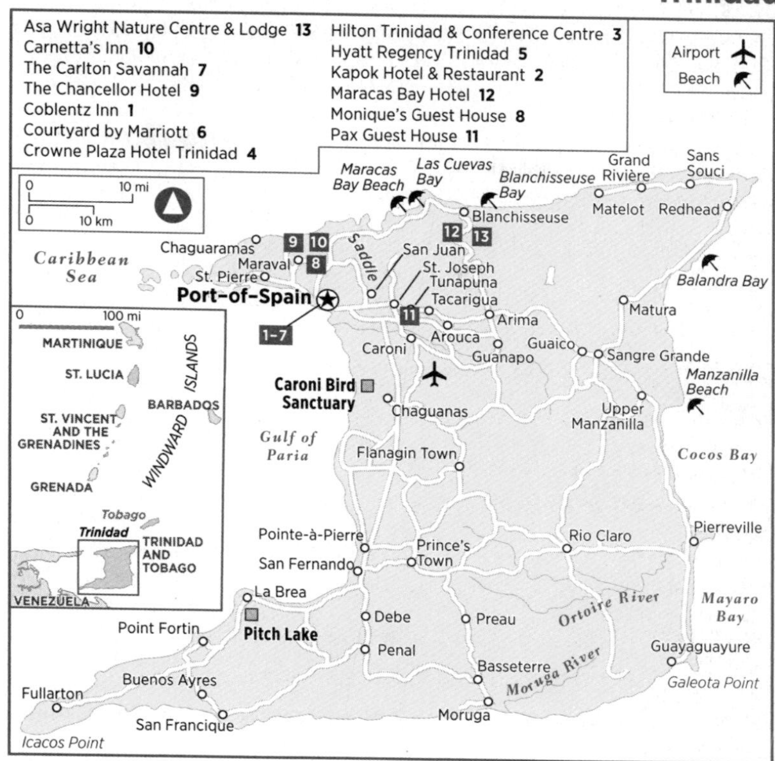

www.thrifty.com), and the simply named **Auto Rentals** (© **868/669-2277**). ***Warning:*** Although these local car rental firms technically accept reservations, a car may not be waiting for you even if you reserve ahead of time.

All the towns of Trinidad are linked by regular **bus service** from Port-of-Spain. Fares are low (about 30¢–$1.90 for runs within the capital). However, the old buses are likely to be very overcrowded. Try to avoid them at rush hours and beware of pickpockets.

FAST FACTS Most **banks** are open Monday to Thursday from 8am to 2pm and Friday from 9am to noon and 3 to 5pm. **Citibank** has offices at 12 Queen's Park East, Port-of-Spain (© **868/625-1046** or 625-1049), and 18–30 High St., San Fernando (© **868/652-3691**). **Republic Bank Ltd.,** 9–17 Park St. (© **868/625-4411**), and **Royal Bank of Trinidad & Tobago Ltd.,** Royal Court, 19–21 Park St. (© **868/625-7288**), are two of the many banks in Port-of-Spain with **ATMs.** You'll also find ATMs at some big supermarkets.

There is no 24-hour **pharmacy.** In Port-of-Spain, **Starlite Drugs** at Four Roads, Diego Martin (© **868/632-0516**), is open Monday to Saturday from 8am to 9:30pm.

THE CARNIVAL OF TRINIDAD

Called the "world's most colorful festival," the **Carnival of Trinidad** (www.ncctt.org) is a spectacle of dazzling costumes and gaiety. Hundreds of bands of masqueraders parade through the cities on the Monday and Tuesday preceding Ash Wednesday, bringing traffic to a standstill. The island seems to explode with music, fun, and dancing.

Some of the Carnival **costumes** cost hundreds of dollars. "Bands" might depict the birds of Trinidad, such as the scarlet ibis and the keskidee, or a bevy of women might come out in the streets dressed as cats. Costumes are often satirical and comical.

Trinidad, of course, is the land of **calypso,** which grew out of the folk songs of the African-West Indian immigrants. The lyrics command great attention, as they're rich in satire and innuendo. The calypsonian is a poet-musician, and lyrics have often toppled politicians from office. In banter and bravado, the calypsonian gives voice to the sufferings and aspirations of his people. At Carnival time, the artist sings his compositions to spectators in tents. There's one show a night at each of the calypso tents around town, from 8pm to midnight. Tickets for these are sold in the afternoon at most record shops.

You can attend rehearsals of **steel bands** at their headquarters, called panyards, beginning about 7pm. Preliminary band competitions are held at the grandstand of Queen's Park Savannah in Port-of-Spain and at Skinner Park in San Fernando, beginning 2 weeks before Carnival.

Carnival parties, or **fetes,** with three or four orchestras at each one, are public and are advertised in the newspaper. For a really wild time, attend a party on Sunday night before Carnival Monday. To reserve tickets, contact the **National Carnival Committee,** Queen's Park Savannah, Port-of-Spain, Trinidad (✆ **868/627-1357;** www.ncctt.org). Hotels are booked months in advance, and most inns raise their prices—often considerably—over Carnival.

The **Port-of-Spain General Hospital** is located at 169 Charlotte St. (✆ **868/623-2951**). Medical care is sometimes limited, and physicians and health-care facilities expect immediate cash payment for services.

The main **post office** (✆ **868/669-4360**) is on Wrightson Road, Port-of-Spain, and is open Monday to Friday from 8am to 4:30pm.

Where to Stay

The number of hotels on Trinidad is limited, and you shouldn't expect your Port-of-Spain room to open directly onto a white-sand beach. The nearest beach is a long, costly taxi ride away. Hotels are booked months in advance of Carnival (the week before Ash Wednesday), and they raise their rates, often considerably, at this time.

VERY EXPENSIVE

Asa Wright Nature Centre & Lodge ★ 🎁 There really isn't anything else like this in the Caribbean. Known to bird-watchers throughout the world, this center sits on 74 remote hectares (183 acres) of protected land at an elevation of 360m (1,181 ft.) in the rainforested northern mountain range of Trinidad, 15km (9¼ miles) north of Arima, beside Blanchisseuse Road. Hummingbirds, toucans, bellbirds, manakins, several varieties of tanagers, and the rare oilbird are all on the property. Back-to-basics accommodations are available in the lodge, in the 1908 Edwardian main house, and in the cottages on elevated ground above the main house. Even though they offer less privacy, we prefer the two rooms in the main house, which are more atmospheric and are outfitted with dark-wood antiques and two king-size beds each. Furnishings in the cottages are rather plain but comfortable. Guided tours are available on the nature center's grounds, which contain several well-maintained trails and a natural waterfall with a pool.

Spring Hill Estate, Arima, Trinidad, W.I. (for reservations, Caligo Ventures, P.O. Box 6356, Key West, FL 33041). www.asawright.org. ✆ **800/426-7781** in the U.S., or 868/667-4655. Fax 868/667-4540. 24 units. Winter $430 double; off-season $250–$340 double. Rates include all meals. MC, V. Children 11 and under not accepted. **Amenities:** Restaurant; airport transfers $60 per person; Internet (free). *In room:* Ceiling fan, no phone.

The Carlton Savannah ★★★ Nestled on a mountain, Cascade, this boutique hotel challenges both the Hyatt and the Hilton for supremacy. The luxe property overlooks the green space of Queen's Park Savannah in the central business district of Port-of-Spain. Balconies open onto lush bamboo and flora. Thick walls and black-out draperies shut out noise and light, if that is your desire. Bedrooms are spacious and elegantly furnished, with either king- or queen-size beds with silky duvets. Suites are the most elegant in Trinidad, with a kitchen and dining area. The hotel service is the island's best. Its restaurant, Ca-Sa, is a gourmet retreat; its rooftop and bar rises 13 floors high; its Indaba Bar features jazz and the blues; and its Santosha Spa focuses on both physical and mental therapy, soothing your senses with the feel of being in a rainforest.

2-4 Coblentz Ave, Port-of-Spain, Trinidad, W.I. www.thecarltonsavannah.com. ✆ **868/621-5000.** Fax 868/621-5001. 157 units. Winter $230–$300 double, from $390 suite; off season $150–$180 double, from $300 suite. AE, DC, MC, V. **Amenities:** 2 restaurants; 2 bars; airport transfers $35; exercise room; outdoor pool; room service. *In room:* A/C, TV/CD player, hair dryer, Internet (free), minibar, MP3 docking station.

Courtyard by Marriott ★ This chain hotel has almost no Trinidadian atmosphere but is a top choice for convenience, service, and comfort, attracting a lot of business travelers, although it's suitable for vacationers as well. The location next to the Movie Towne Shopping Center and the Hasley Crawford National Stadium is convenient to shopping stores and restaurants, and central to the city center. Bedrooms, spread across four floors, are stylish, comfortable, and spacious, with the best in-house entertainment in town. The hotel specializes in plush bedding—crisp linens, thick mattresses, custom comforters, and fluffy down/feather pillows.

Invaders Bay, Audrey Jeffers Hwy., Port-of-Spain, Trinidad, W.I. www.marriott.com. ✆ **800/321-2211** in the U.S. and Canada, or 868/627-5555. Fax 868/627-6317. 119 units. Year-round $210–$280 double; from $320 suite. AE, DC, MC, V. **Amenities:** Restaurant; bar; exercise room; indoor pool; room service. *In room:* A/C, TV, fridge, hair dryer, Wi-Fi ($12 per day).

Crowne Plaza Hotel Trinidad ★ This bland but modern 14-story hotel is a favorite with business travelers, who tolerate the noise and congestion for the convenient location, a 5-minute walk from the city center. The renovated bedrooms, tastefully decorated in pastels, contain private balconies and two double beds. The hotel has two executive floors and such luxuries as trouser presses, magnifying mirrors, mahogany furniture, and brass lamps. An on-site restaurant, 360°, is the only revolving restaurant on island, providing a striking view of the city.

Wrightson Rd. at London St. (P.O. Box 1017), Port-of-Spain, Trinidad, W.I. www.ichotelsgroup.com. ✆ **877/227-6963** in the U.S. and Canada, or 868/625-3361. Fax 868/625-4166. 245 units. Year-round $155–$225 double; $395 suite. Rates include breakfast. AE, MC, V. **Amenities:** 2 restaurants; bar; babysitting; exercise room; outdoor pool; room service. *In room:* A/C, TV, hair dryer, Wi-Fi ($10 per day).

Hilton Trinidad & Conference Centre ★★ ☺ The lobby is on the uppermost floor, while the guest rooms are staggered in rocky but verdant terraces that sweep down the steep hillside. The location just above Queen's Park Savannah affords most of its rooms a view of the sea and mountains. The higher rooms are cheaper than lower ones. This is not the greatest Hilton in the world, or even in the Caribbean, but all rooms still meet international first-class standards, with queen-size or twin beds, balconies, and generous closet space. Accommodations in the main wing are the most sought-after, as they have good views over Queen's Park Savannah. Executive-floor rooms have upgraded services and amenities.

Lady Young Rd. (P.O. Box 442), Port-of-Spain, Trinidad, W.I. www.hiltoncaribbean.com. ✆ **800/445-8667** in the U.S. and Canada, or 868/624-3211. Fax 868/624-4485. 412 units. Year-round $189–$239 double; $350–$1,020 suite. AE, MC, V. **Amenities:** 2 restaurants; 4 bars; babysitting; children's activities; fitness center; 2 outdoor pools; room service; sauna; 2 tennis courts. *In room:* A/C, TV, hair dryer, kitchen (in some), minibar, MP3 docking station, Wi-Fi ($15 per day).

Hyatt Regency Trinidad ★★★ This gigantic hotel is designed as both a convention and business hotel, and a ritzy property for the leisure traveler. With an infinity pool and terrace overlooking the Gulf of Paria, it boasts more facilities than any other hotel on island, with the best spa and fitness center. In the heart of Port-of-Spain, the hotel's midsize to spacious bedrooms evoke streamlined elegance, comfort, and style, with ample working desks. Some rooms have scenic balconies, and all come with bamboo floors, frosted-glass showers, and 32-inch TVs, with both wireless and wired Internet connections.

1 Wrightson Rd., Port-of-Spain, Trinidad, W.I. www.trinidad.hyatt.com. ✆ **800/492-8804** or 868/623-2222. Fax 868/821-6401. 428 units. Year-round $170–$340 double; from $350 suite. AE, MC, V. **Amenities:** Restaurant; 2 bars (1 poolside); deli/patisserie; fitness center & spa; outdoor pool; room service. *In room:* A/C, TV, hair dryer, minibar, MP3 docking station, Wi-Fi ($14 per day).

MODERATE

The Chancellor Hotel Designed for the business traveler, this lovely little inn is also ideal for vacationers. In the valley of St. Ann's, the hotel sits in lush landscaped gardens studded with palms. An Iberian-style courtyard filled with sculptures and a cascading waterfall emptying into a swimming pool is one of the hotel's more attractive features. Each of the accommodations is tastefully and comfortably furnished with batik quilts, wall hangings, and teak-wood desks. The beds are Victorian style.

5 St. Ann's Ave., St. Ann's, Trinidad, W.I. www.thechancellorhotel.com. ✆ **868/623-0883.** Fax 868/623-0883. 22 units. Year-round $180–$260 double; $270–$350 suite. AE, MC, V. **Amenities:** Restaurant; 2 bars; outdoor pool; room service. *In room:* A/C, TV, hair dryer, Internet ($15 per day).

Coblentz Inn ★ In the residential suburb of Cascade, right outside Port-of-Spain, stands this little boutique hotel of charm and a certain grace. Each accommodation is decorated in an individual and whimsical theme—the Central Room evokes the opulence of Indian palaces and the colorful marketplaces of Asia; the Government House Room pays tributes to past governor generals and visiting royalty; and the Cocoa House Room is inspired by the amber and gold leaves of the cocoa tree. A complimentary, fully stocked minibar is part of the deal, and the on-site restaurant, Battimamzelle, is one of Port-of-Spain's best (p. 637).

44 Coblentz Ave., Cascade, Trinidad, W.I. www.coblentzinn.com. ✆ **868/621-0541.** Fax 868/624-7566. 16 units. Year-round $205–$225 double. Rates include continental breakfast. AE, MC, V. **Amenities:** Restaurant; room service. *In room:* A/C, TV, CD player, hair dryer, kitchenette, minibar, Wi-Fi (free).

Kapok Hotel & Restaurant ★ This modern but unpretentious nine-floor hotel, in the residential suburb of St. Clair, is an efficient, well-maintained operation run by the Chan family. It's located away from the worst traffic of the city, near the zoo and the Presidential Palace, and just north of Queen's Park Savannah. From its lounge, you'll have panoramic views of the Savannah and the Gulf of Paria. The comfortably appointed, spacious rooms have wicker furnishings. For a hotel of this price range, it comes as a surprise to find phones with voice mail, and even room service until 10pm. In the back is an expanded pool area with a bistro/bar, waterfall, garden, menagerie, and sun deck.

16–18 Cotton Hill, St. Clair, Trinidad, W.I. www.kapokhotel.com. ✆ **868/622-5765.** Fax 868/622-9677. 94 units. Year-round $175–$200 double; $220–$240 suite. Additional person $16 per night. Rates include continental breakfast. AE, MC, V. **Amenities:** 2 restaurants; exercise room; outdoor pool; room service. *In room:* A/C, TV, hair dryer, Internet (free), kitchenette (in some).

INEXPENSIVE

Carnetta's Inn ★ This home is in the suburb of Andalusia in the cool and scenic Maraval neighborhood, about a 15-minute ride from the central business district and a 45-minute ride to Maracas Beach, the most popular sand strip on island. It's owned by Winston and Carnetta Borrell—both have a wealth of information about touring the island (he was a former director of tourism), and both are keen naturalists. Winston is a gardener, filling his property with orchids, ginger lilies, and anthuriums, among other plant life. Carnetta grows her own herbs to produce some of the finest meals around. The rooms have floral themes and are furnished in a tropical style. For the most privacy, request a guest room on the upper floor. Our preferred nest is Le Flamboyant, opening onto the little inn's patio. Most of the rooms are medium in size.

99 Saddle Rd., Maraval, Trinidad, W.I. www.carnettasinn.com. ✆ **868/628-2732.** Fax 868/628-7717. 14 units. Year-round $90 double; $110 with kitchen. Rates include breakfast. MC, V. **Amenities:** Restaurant; bar; room service. *In room:* A/C, TV, kitchenette (in some), Wi-Fi (free).

Maracas Bay Hotel If you'd like to sightsee in Trinidad and also be on the beach, Maracas Bay Hotel is a decent choice. It's the only beachfront hotel in all of Trinidad, and even here, you'll have to walk across the coastal road to reach the sands. Owned and operated by a local family, it's nestled in a valley on sloping terrain across the road from Maracas Bay. It's only 11km (6¾ miles) north of Port-of-Spain, but dense traffic and a winding road mean at least a 45-minute drive from the commercial center of the capital. There's a bar/lounge accented with Hindu art and an unpretentious dining room. Bedrooms contain simple furnishings, white-and-blue walls, and terra-cotta tile floors, and each unit has two queen-size beds. The beach, a wide strip of white sand bordered by palm trees, is a lovely oasis from the bustle of Port-of-Spain.

Maracas Bay Rd., Maracas, Trinidad, W.I. www.maracasbay.com. ✆ **868/669-1914.** Fax 868/669-1643. 32 units. Year-round $85–$110 double. AE, MC, V. **Amenities:** Restaurant; bar; room service. *In room:* A/C, no phone.

Monique's Guest House ☺ In the lush Maraval Valley just an 8-minute (5km/3-mile) drive north of the center of Port-of-Spain, Monique's offers 20 bungalow-style rooms. Some are large enough to accommodate up to four people, and 10 rooms offer kitchenettes with their own porches. The biggest are nos. 25 and 26, which can sleep up to six, though everyone would feel a bit crowded. Families are fond of booking rooms here because of the kitchenettes. Accommodations have open balconies so you can enjoy the tropical breezes and scenic hills. The air-conditioned dining room and bar offers a medley of local and international dishes, and Maracas Beach is only a 25-minute drive away.

114–116 Saddle Rd., Maraval, Trinidad, W.I. www.moniquestrinidad.com. ✆ **868/628-3334.** Fax 868/622-3232. 20 units. Year-round $90 double; $110 double with kitchenette; $100–$120 triple. MC, V. **Amenities:** Restaurant; bar; airport transfers $40; babysitting. *In room:* A/C, TV, kitchenette (in some), Wi-Fi (free).

Pax Guest House There are a few drawbacks here, but this hilltop building is one of the more attractive and affordable options in the Greater Port-of-Spain district. You'll need transportation to get to most of the clubs, restaurants, and nightlife options. Otherwise, this elevated, antiques-filled guesthouse is idyllic for panoramic views. Hiking trails begin right on the property. Bedrooms are a bit no-frills but are reasonably comfortable and well maintained. In the old-fashioned tradition, afternoon tea is still served in the courtyard.

Mt. St. Benedict, Tunapuna, Trinidad, W.I. www.paxguesthouse.com. ✆ **868/662-4084.** 18 units. Year-round $75–$85 double. Rates include breakfast. MC, V. **Amenities:** Dinner offered; tennis court. *In room:* TV (in some), no phone, Wi-Fi (free).

Where to Dine

The food in Trinidad should be better, considering all the different culinary backgrounds that shaped the island. But being as it is, we recommend sticking to local specials like stuffed crabs and *chip-chip* (tiny clamlike shellfish). Skip the armadillo and opossum stews. Spicy *rotis* (Caribbean burritos) filled with vegetables or ground meat seem to be everyone's favorite lunch, and the drink of choice is a fresh rum punch flavored with Angostura Bitters. Except for a few fancy places, dress tends to be very casual.

VERY EXPENSIVE

Chaud ★★★ FUSION Chef Khalid Mohammed is hailed as the finest chef in Trinidad. Everyone from Bill Clinton to Donald Trump has hailed his culinary skill. For recipes, his "beat" is the world, but mostly he uses his imagination in creating dishes served at this elegant restaurant in a restored house across from Queen's Park Savannah. Never in Trinidad have we tasted such dishes as guava barbecue shrimp and creamy cheddar grits with applewood-smoked bacon or a tasting of three tartares—yellowfin tuna, Atlantic salmon, and Chilean sea bass. And these are just starters. How many diners have ever had seared foie gras with coconut butter and pineapple marmalade? For a main course, you can opt for such delights as tamarind-glazed double-cut pork chop with harmonious flavoring, or a maple-glazed double duck breast with apple butter. Desserts just might be some of the best you've had, especially coconut lime marble cheesecake, or the banana crème brûlée with burnt honey-almond praline ice cream.

2 Queen's Park W., Port-of-Spain. ✆ **868/623-0375.** www.chaudkm.com. Reservations required. Main courses $32–$72. AE, DC, MC, V. Mon–Sat 11:30am–3pm and 6–10:30pm.

EXPENSIVE

Angelo's ★ ITALIAN This 1920s gingerbread colonial building makes an elegant setting for the excellent cuisine here. The chefs search for quality ingredients and allow their natural flavors to shine. The chefs will prepare Caribbean dishes, but only by request. Otherwise, it features an ever-changing menu filled with succulent pastas, fresh seafood, and meat dishes such as tender veal, along with sumptuous Italian desserts.

38 Ariapita Ave., Woodbrook. ✆ **868/628-5551.** Reservations recommended. Main courses $19–$47. MC, V. Mon–Fri 11:30am–2:30pm and 6:30–10:30pm; Sat 6:30–10:30pm.

Apsara ★ NORTHERN INDIAN Marie Kavanagh welcomes you graciously to her restaurant, the name of which translates as "heavenly dancer." An island painter, Sarah Beckett, has decorated the place with her contemporary take on Moghul art. The skilled chefs are from India, bringing with them their exotic palette of spices. The menu is widely varied—almost too large—but the dishes are a delight, especially tandoori specialties like jumbo shrimp marinated in yogurt, fresh lime juice, and Indian spices. We're also fond of the tender lamb cooked in a rich curry sauce. Many dishes will please vegetarians. Some of the main courses emerge from the oven on a sizzling platter—try *machi masala,* a hot and spicy fish cooked in a rich and aromatic sauce. Most meals end with the masala tea flavored with clove, cardamom, and cinnamon.

13 Queen's Park E., Port-of-Spain. ✆ **868/623-7659.** Reservations required. Main courses $22–$65. AE, MC, V. Daily 11am–11pm.

Battimamzelle ★ 🎁 ☺ CARIBBEAN/INTERNATIONAL The name of this restaurant, which means "dragonfly" in the local dialect, sets the whimsical tone for this joint. Its decor—red and yellow walls adorned with flower paintings and red lampshades with imprints of *battimamzelles* on them—is often called "Mexicanish." For his inspiration, the chef roams the world, offering Greek-style lamb (but stuffed with Moroccan sausage) served with fruits, nuts, and couscous. The barbecued kingfish is brushed with fresh guava and served with pumpkin. The delightful Cornish hens come with a fricassee of wild mushrooms, and the 22-ounce "cowboy" rib-eye steak is tantalizingly provided with hash browns and sizzling onions. A kiddie menu is also offered on request. Most dishes are priced at the lower end of the scale.

In the Coblentz Inn, 44 Coblentz Ave., Cascade. ✆ **868/621-0541.** Reservations required. Main courses $18–$55. AE, MC, V. Daily 11am–3pm and 6–10:30pm. Closed Dec 22–29.

Mélange ★★ SPANISH/AMERINDIAN Drawing upon the heritage of the early settlers, including the Amerindians and the Spanish, chef Moses Reuben creates the most imaginative and some of the most tantalizing specialties on island. He has a surprising list of delicacies under his chef's toque, including a main course of succulent filet of chicken breasts to which smoked herring and a fruity tomato sauce laced with star fruit is added. The dish is accompanied by dasheen, a locally popular root vegetable. It is not just his main dishes but also his appetizers that show care for quality produce and taste. Try his curried fresh crab on a shell filled with tasty miniature dumplings: The dish is scrumptious, as are his freshly made desserts that always delight you, even as you take in the calories.

40 Ariapita Ave., Woodbrook, Port-of-Spain. ✆ **868/628-8687.** Reservations required. Main courses $32–$48; fixed-price lunch menu $28. AE, MC, V. Mon 11:30am–2:30pm; Tues–Fri 11:30am–2:30pm and 7–10:30pm; Sat 7–10:30pm.

Restaurant Singho CHINESE This restaurant, with an almost mystically illuminated bar and aquarium, is on the second floor of one of the capital's largest shopping malls, midway between the commercial center of Port-of-Spain and the Queen's Park Savannah. For Trinidad, the food isn't bad. In fact, it's better than your typical chop-suey-and-chow-mein joint; many of the dishes are quite tasty and spicy. A la carte choices include shrimp with oyster sauce, stewed or curried beef, almond pork, and spareribs with black-bean sauce. The to-go service is one of the best in town. The Wednesday-night buffet offers an enormous selection of main dishes, along with heaps of rice and fresh vegetables, and dessert.

Long Circular Mall, Level 5, Port-of-Spain. ✆ **868/628-2077.** Main courses $10–$35; Wed night buffet $20. MC, V. Daily 10am–2am.

Tamnak Thai ★★ THAI/ASIAN In the landmark center at Queen's Park Savannah, this upmarket restaurant in a restored colonial home is the island nation's finest Asian restaurant, specializing in the regional fare of Thailand. Refined dishes are beautifully served in an elegant, luxuriant, and tasteful setting, especially if you select a table on the patio. The kitchen makes the most of excellent ingredients, fashioning them into subtle dishes like red-curry chicken in coconut milk or stir-fried lobster with spring onions. Our favorite dish is the steamed mussels in a clay pot with fresh herbs such as lemon grass. If you're with a large party, you can order a selection of hors d'oeuvres that are full of zest and flavor. Many dishes are very spicy, filled with fiery chilies, but there are also milder choices.

13 Queen's Park E., Port-of-Spain. ✆ **868/625-9715.** Reservations required. Main courses $8–$32; set lunch $16;. AE, MC, V. Mon–Fri 11am–3pm and 6–11pm; Sat–Sun 6–11pm.

MODERATE

Veni Mangé ★★ 🎁 CREOLE/INTERNATIONAL Originally built in the 1930s and set about 2km (1¼ miles) west of Port-of-Spain's center, Veni Mangé (which means "come and eat") is painted in coral tones and has louvered windows on hinges that ventilate the masses of potted plants. It was established by two of the best-known women in Trinidad, Allyson Hennessy and her sister, Rosemary Hezekiah. Allyson, the Julia Child of Trinidad, hosts a daily TV talk show that's broadcast throughout the island. Start with the bartender's special, a coral-colored fruit punch that's a rich, luscious mixture of papaya, guava, orange, and passion fruit juices. The authentic callaloo soup, according to Trinidadian legend, can make a man propose marriage. With a menu that changes daily, the main courses might be curried crab, a West Indian hot pot (a variety of meats cooked Creole style), or perhaps a vegetable lentil loaf. The helpings are large, but if you still have room, order the pineapple upside-down cake.

67A Ariapita Ave., Port-of-Spain. ✆ **868/624-4597.** www.venimange.com. Reservations recommended. Main courses $19–$22. AE, MC, V. Mon–Tues and Thurs 11:30am–3pm; Wed and Fri 11:30am–3pm and 7–10pm.

Hitting the Beach

Trinidad isn't thought of as beach country, yet it has more beach frontage than any other island in the West Indies. The only problem is that most of its beaches are undeveloped and in distant, remote places, far removed from Port-of-Spain. The closest of the better beaches, **Maracas Bay,** is a full 29km (18 miles) from Port-of-Spain on the North Coast Road. It's a delight to visitors, with its protected cove and quaint fishing village. The crowds and the strong current are the only drawbacks. Facilities include restrooms and snack bars.

Farther up the North Coast Road is **Las Cuevas Bay,** which is far less crowded. The narrow beach is set against a backdrop of palm trees. There are changing rooms and vendors selling luscious tropical-fruit juices.

To reach the other beaches, you'll have to go a bit farther, perhaps to **Blanchisseuse Bay** on the North Coast Road. This narrow strip of sand set against palms is an excellent spot for a picnic, although there are no facilities.

Bodysurfers frequent **Balandra Bay** on the northeast coast, but the waters generally aren't good for more pedestrian swimming.

Manzanilla Beach, along the east coast of Trinidad, north of Cocos Bay and south of Matura Bay, is not ideal for swimming, either. Nonetheless, it has some picnic facilities, and the view of the water is dramatic.

Sports & Outdoor Pursuits

For serious golf and tennis, we recommend that you try another island.

DEEP-SEA FISHING Some of the best fishing in the Caribbean is possible in the waters off the northwest coast of Trinidad—or, at least, Franklin D. Roosevelt used to think so. Try **Hard Play Fishing Charters,** 13 the Evergreen, Auchenskeoch, Buccoo (✆ **868/639-7108** or 868/682-3474; www.hardplay.net). Your skipper is "Frothy" De Silva, who charges $440 for 4-hour trips, or $110 per hour for a maximum of 9 hours, on his 12m (39-ft.) vessel, *Hard Play.* Another good possibility is **Dillon's Fishing Charter,** Crown Point (✆ **868/637-8635** or 868/678-3195), offers half-day charters for $495 and full-day charters for $850, which include drinks and lunch. Along with record catches in blue marlin, fishermen pursue wahoo, mahimahi, kingfish, and barracuda.

GOLF The oldest golf club on the island, **St. Andrew's Golf Course,** Moka Estate (✆ **868/629-0066;** www.golftrinidad.com), is in Maraval, about 3km (2 miles) from Port-of-Spain. This 18-hole course has been internationally acclaimed ever since it hosted the 1976 Hoerman Cup Golf Tournament. There's a full-service clubhouse on the premises. Greens fees are $75 for 18 holes. Club rental costs $25. Hours are daily 6am to 6pm.

Exploring the Island

ORGANIZED TOURS

Sightseeing tours are offered by **Trinidad & Tobago Sightseeing Tours,** 165A Western Main Rd., St. James (✆ **868/628-1051;** www.trintours.com), in late-model sedans with a trained driver/guide. Several different tours are offered, including a daily city tour that takes you past (but not inside) the main points of interest of Port-of-Spain. The 2½-hour tour costs $40 per person for two.

You'll see tropical splendor at its best on a Port-of-Spain/Maracas Bay/Saddle Road jaunt, tours lasting 3½ hours. The tour begins with a drive around Port-of-Spain, passing the main points of interest in town and then going on through mountain scenery. The cost is $52 per person.

PORT-OF-SPAIN ★

One of the busiest harbors in the Caribbean, Trinidad's capital, Port-of-Spain, can be explored on foot. Start out at **Queen's Park Savannah ★**, on the northern edge of the city. "The Savannah" consists of 80 hectares (198 acres), complete with soccer, cricket, and rugby fields, and vendors hawking coconut water and *rotis.* This area was once a sugar plantation, but a fire in 1808 swept it and destroyed hundreds of homes.

Among the Savannah's outstanding buildings is pink-and-blue **Queen's Royal College ★**, containing a clock tower with Westminster chimes. Today a school for boys, it stands on Maraval Road at the corner of St. Clair Avenue. The Roodal clan's family home—affectionately called the "**gingerbread house**" by Trinidadians—is on the same road. It was built in the baroque style of the French Second Empire.

Nearby stands **Whitehall,** a former private mansion turned into the office of the prime minister of Trinidad and Tobago. In the Moorish style, it was erected in 1905 and served as the U.S. Army headquarters here during World War II. These houses, including Hayes Court, the residence of the Anglican bishop of Trinidad, and others, form what is known as the **"Magnificent Seven" ★** big mansions standing in a row.

On the south side of Memorial Park, a short distance from the Savannah and within walking distance of the major hotels, stands the **National Museum and Art Gallery,** 117 Frederick St. (**© 868/623-5941**), open Tuesday to Saturday from 10am to 6pm, Sunday from 2 to 6pm. The free museum contains a representative exhibition of Trinidad artists, including an entire gallery devoted to Jean Michel Cazabon (1813–88); permanent collections of artifacts giving a general overview of the island's history and culture; examples of Amerindian archaeology; British historical documents; and a small natural-history exhibition including geology, corals, and insect collections. There's also a large display filled with costumes dedicated to the colorful culture of Carnival.

At the southern end of Frederick Street, the main artery of Port-of-Spain's shopping district, stands **Woodford Square.** The gaudy **Red House,** a large neo-Renaissance structure built in 1906, is the seat of the government of Trinidad and Tobago. Nearby stands **Holy Trinity Cathedral,** with a Gothic look reminiscent of the churches of England.

Another of the town's important landmarks is **Independence Square,** dating from Spanish days. Now mainly a parking lot, it stretches across the southern part of the capital from Wrightson Road to the **Cathedral of the Immaculate Conception.** This Roman Catholic church was built in 1815 in the neo-Gothic style and consecrated in 1832.

The cathedral has an outlet that leads to the **Central Market,** on Beetham Highway on the outskirts of Port-of-Spain. Here you can see all the spices and fruits for which Trinidad is known. It's one of the island's most colorful sights, made all the more so by the wide diversity of people who sell wares here.

North of the Savannah, the **Royal Botanical Gardens** (**© 868/622-4221;** www.bgci.org) covers 28 hectares (69 acres) and is open daily from 8am to 4pm; admission is free. The park is filled with flowering plants, shrubs, and rare and beautiful trees, including an orchid house. Seek out the raw beef tree: An incision made in its bark is said to resemble rare, bleeding roast beef. Guides will take you through and explain the luxuriant foliage. In the gardens is the **President's House,** official residence of the president of Trinidad and Tobago. Victorian in style, it was built in 1875.

Part of the gardens is the **Emperor Valley Zoo** (**© 868/622-3530**), in St. Clair, which shows a good selection of the fauna of Trinidad, as well as some exotic animals from around the world. The star attractions are a family of mandrills, a reptile house, and open bird parks. You can take shady jungle walks through tropical vegetation. Admission is $1.60 for adults, 80¢ for children 3 to 12, and free for children 2 and under. It's open daily from 9am to 6pm.

AROUND THE ISLAND

One of the most popular attractions in the area is the **Asa Wright Nature Centre ★** (p. 632; **© 800/426-7781** in the U.S., or 868/667-4655; www.asawright.org). If you're not a guest of the hotel, you can call and reserve a space for its noonday lunch for $22 Monday to Saturday or $32 on Sunday. It's also possible to reserve one of the daily guided tours of its sanctuary at 10:30am or 1:30pm, which cost $10.

On a peak 330m (1,083 ft.) above Port-of-Spain, **Fort George** was built by Gov. Sir Thomas Hislop in 1804 as a signal station in the days of the sailing ships. Once reached only by hikers, today it's accessible by an asphalt road. From its citadel, you can see the mountains of Venezuela. Locals refer to the climb up the winding road as "traveling up to heaven." The drive is only 15km (9¾ miles), but to play it safe, allow about 2 hours.

Pointe-à-Pierre Wild Fowl Trust, Le Riene Town House, Flagstaff Hill, Long Circular Road (✆ **868/658-4200,** ext. 2512), is a 10-hectare (25-acre) bird sanctuary, 2 hours by car south of Port-of-Spain. The setting is unlikely, near an industrial area of the state-owned Petrotrin oil refinery, with flames spouting from flare stacks in the sky. However, in this seemingly inhospitable clime, wildfowl flourish amid such luxuriant vegetation as crape myrtle, flamboyant soursop, mango trees, and even black sage bushes said to be good for high blood pressure. You can spot the yellow-billed jacana, plenty of Muscovies, and, if you're lucky, such endangered species as the toucan or the purple gallinule. Admission is $2 adults, $1 children 3 to 12, and 50¢ kids 2 and under. Hours are Monday to Friday 8am to 5pm, Saturday and Sunday by appointment only from 10:30am to 1:30pm.

Enhanced by the blue and purple hues of the sky at sunset, clouds of scarlet ibis, the national bird of Trinidad and Tobago, fly in from their feeding grounds to roost at the 104-sq.-km (40-sq.-mile) **Caroni Bird Sanctuary ★** (✆ **868/645-1305**), a big mangrove swamp interlaced with waterways. The setting couldn't be more idyllic, with blue, mauve, and white lilies; oysters growing on mangrove roots; and caimans resting on mud banks. Visitors are taken on a tour through these swamps to see the birds (bring along insect repellent). The most reliable tour operator is **James Meddoo,** Bamboo Grove Settlement, 1 Butler Hwy. (✆ **868/662-7356**), who has explored the swamps for some 25 years. His 2½-hour excursion leaves daily at 4pm and costs $10 per person, or $5 for kids 5 to 11. The sanctuary is about a half-hour drive (11km/6¾ miles) south of Port-of-Spain.

Pitch Lake ★ is on the west coast of Trinidad, with the village of Le Brea on its north shore. To reach it from Port-of-Spain, take the Solomon Hocoy Highway. It's

EVOCATIVE OF INDIA

Visiting the little town of Chaguanas—located south of Port-of-Spain and the Parco International Airport—is like taking a shopping trip to India. To get there, drive out Uriah Butler Highway and look for the turn-off sign to **Chaguanas.** This was the birthplace of the Nobel Prize–winning novelist V. S. Naipaul.

As you come in on Main Road, you'll think you've miraculously arrived in Calcutta. A hodgepodge of shops sell Indian clothing, jars of spicy chutney, and Bollywood music. The gem of shops is **Radika's Pottery,** 183 Edinburgh Village (✆ **868/665-4267**), run for three generations by the Pickal family, which is acclaimed around the world for its exquisite pottery—jugs, pots, candle holders, and more. Even Naipaul is a fan of this pottery, which is exhibited at international art fairs.

If you're in town for lunch, head for the very simple but good **Indo-Chinese Vegetarian Restaurant** on Main Road (✆ **868/665-6928**).

about a 2-hour drive, depending on traffic. One of the wonders of the world, with a surface like elephant skin, the lake is 90m (295 ft.) deep at its center. It's possible to walk on its rough side, but we don't recommend that you proceed far. Legend has it that the lake devoured a tribe of Chayma Amerindians, punishing them for eating hummingbirds in which the souls of their ancestors reposed. The lake was formed millions of years ago, and it's believed that at one time, it was a huge mud volcano into which muddy asphaltic oil seeped. Churned up and down by underground gases, the oil and mud eventually formed asphalt. According to legend, Sir Walter Raleigh discovered the lake in 1595 and used the asphalt to caulk his ships. Today the bitumen mined here is used to pave highways throughout the world. You can tour Pitch Lake on your own, paying an admission of $5 per person. **Trinidad & Tobago Tours** (✆ **868/628-1051**) runs guided tours of the lake for $70 per person. You'll find some bars and restaurants at Le Brea.

The **Saddle ★** is a humped pass on a ridge dividing the Maraval and the Santa Cruz valleys. Along this circular run, you'll see luxuriant grapefruit, papaya, cassava, and cocoa trees. Leaving Port-of-Spain by Saddle Road, going past the Trinidad Country Club, you pass through Maraval Village and St. Andrew's Golf Course (p. 639). The road rises to cross the ridge at the spot from which the Saddle gets its name. After going over the hump, you descend through Santa Cruz Valley (rich with giant bamboo), into San Juan, and back to the capital along Eastern Main Road or Beetham Highway. You'll see panoramic views in every direction; the 29km (18-mile) tour takes about 2 hours.

Nearly all cruise-ship passengers are hauled along Trinidad's "Skyline Highway," the **North Coast Road.** Starting at the Saddle, it winds for 11km (6¾ miles) across the Northern Range and down to Maracas Bay. At one point, 30m (98 ft.) above the Caribbean, you'll see on a clear day as far as Venezuela to the west or Tobago in the east—a sweep of some 160km (99 miles).

Most visitors take this route to the beach at **Maracas Bay,** the most splendid beach on Trinidad. Enclosed by mountains, it has the charm of a Caribbean fantasy: white sands, swaying coconut palms, and crystal-clear water (see "Hitting the Beach," above).

Shopping

One of the largest **bazaars** of the Caribbean, Port-of-Spain has luxury items from all over the globe, including Irish linens, English china, Scandinavian crystal, French perfumes, Swiss watches, and Japanese cameras. Even more interesting are the Asian bazaars, where you can pick up items in brass. Reflecting the island's culture are calypso shirts, sisal goods, woodwork, cascadura bracelets (made from the scales of the cascadura fish), silver jewelry in local motifs, and saris. For souvenirs, visitors often like to bring back figurines of limbo dancers, Carnival masqueraders, or calypso singers.

Stechers, Gulf City Complex (✆ **868/657-6993**), is the best bet for luxury items—crystal, watches, jewelry, perfumes, Georg Jensen silver, Lladró, Wedgwood, Royal Doulton, Limoges, and Royal Albert. You can find other branches at Long Circular Mall and West Mall. You can also pay a last-minute call at their tax-free airport branches or at the cruise-ship complex at the Port-of-Spain docks.

Y. De Lima, 83 Queen St. (✆ **868/623-1364**), is a good store for watches, but the main focus is local jewelry. Its third-floor workroom will make whatever you want in jewelry or bronze. You might emerge with anything from steel drum earrings to a hibiscus blossom brooch.

Art Society of Trinidad & Tobago, 26 Taylor St., Woodbrook (© **868/622-9827;** www.artsocietytt.org), showcases island artists who work in various media, including painting and sculpture. The best of the islanders' artistic statements are showcased here, and something new and fresh is always on exhibit, from "Shango-Baptist imagery" to paintings reflecting the East Indian backgrounds of its creators.

Lovers of Caribbean art also flock to the **101 Art Gallery,** 101 Tragarete Rd. (© **868/628-4081;** www.101artgallery.com), in Port-of-Spain. This is the best showcase for the hottest local talent. Local artist Sarah Beckett's work is so influential that her abstract oils appear on regional stamps. Often you can meet some of the artists here, especially on Tuesday evenings during openings.

The Market, 10 Nook Ave., St. Ann's (© **868/624-1181**), is one of the most fashionable shopping complexes on Trinidad. Some 20 boutiques represent the best jewelers, designers, and art dealers on the island. You'll find a wide assortment of clothing, cosmetics, bags, shoes, china, tableware, handicrafts, and accessories. The complex forms an interconnected bridge among the Normandie Hotel and Restaurant, and the restaurant Vidalia.

Trinidad After Dark

The most popular spot on the weekends, although busy any night, is **Trotters,** at Maraval and Sweet Briar roads, St. Clair (© **868/627-8768;** www.trotters.net). This is a rustic, earthy, and multilevel English-style sports bar and pub with an eatery on the upper level. The bartenders stock more than 25 beers from around the world, and the pub has 30 TV monitors blaring at all times. There's pub grub, of course, such as barbecue ribs and chicken. Friday night a DJ is brought in for your listening pleasure. There is no cover.

Known for its pop-rock nights, **HiRPM,** Gulf City Mall, South Trunk Road, La Romain (© **868/652-3760**), is located slightly out of town, reached by heading south of Port-of-Spain, following the South Trunk Road to the mall. Attracting mostly a 21-to-35 age group, it features different entertainment on different nights—for example, techno night on Tuesday, and rock bands on Wednesday. Club nights are on weekends, when there is a great mix of music and a gyrating dance party. On Saturday the action begins at noon and doesn't stop until Sunday morning.

You can catch us having a beer at **Mas Camp Pub,** corner of French Street and Ariapita Avenue, Woodbrook (© **868/623-3745**). This place has a big stage where some of the best live bands in Trinidad frequently appear (or a DJ rules the night). There's also a reliable kitchen dishing up local specialties. **More Vino ★**, 23 O'Connor St., Woodbrook (© **868/622-8466**), is known for its array of different wines and as a rendezvous point for the smart set of young professionals. Gossip fills the air, and patrons sip cocktails on the terrace, or else retreat to the air-conditioned interior.

Local joints come and go with alarming frequency, but locals continue to flock to the live music at the **Base,** Main Street (no phone), at Chaguaramas, a 20-minute drive or taxi ride west of Port-of-Spain. This nightclub takes its name from its former role as a World War II air base and is open Friday and Saturday night (no set hours). Also on this former airfield is the Base's competitor, **Anchorage,** Point Gourde Road (© **868/634-4334**), a popular gathering spot for "sundowners." Later on, groups head across the base to **Pier 1,** Williams Bay (© **868/634-4426**), for dancing.

TOBAGO

Tobago is 30km (19 miles) northeast of Trinidad, and the two islands are connected by frequent flights. Long known as a honeymooner's paradise, Tobago's idyllic natural beauty makes it one of the greatest escapes in the Caribbean. It has forests of breadfruit, mango, cocoa, and citrus through which a chartreuse-colored iguana will suddenly dart. It's for those who like a generous dose of sand, sun, and solitude in a mellow atmosphere. Snorkelers especially will find plenty to entertain them.

Unlike bustling Trinidad, Tobago is sleepy, and Trinidadians come here, especially on weekends, to enjoy the wide, sandy beaches. The legendary home of Daniel Defoe's Robinson Crusoe, Tobago is only 43km (27 miles) long and 12km (7½ miles) wide. The people are hospitable, and their tiny villages seem to blend in with the landscape.

The island's villagelike capital and main port, **Scarborough,** lies on the southern coast. Surrounded by mountains, its bay provides a scenic setting, but the town itself is rather plain. Most of the shops are clustered in streets around the local market.

Essentials

GETTING THERE Combining services with BWIA, **LIAT** (✆ **888/844-LIAT** [5428]; www.liatairline.com) offers direct service to Tobago from either Barbados or Grenada. There are also regular flights from Trinidad to Tobago on **Tobago Express** (✆ **868/631-8015**). **British Airways** (✆ **800/247-9297** in the U.S. and Canada; www.britishairways.com) flies weekly from London to Tobago.

Tobago's small **airport** at Crown Point (✆ **868/639-0509**) is near the island's southwestern tip.

It's possible to travel between Trinidad and Tobago by **ferry service,** although the trip takes 5½ to 6 hours. Call the **Port Authority of Trinidad and Tobago** (✆ **868/639-2417** in Scarborough, or 868/625-3055 in Port-of-Spain; www.patnt.com) for departure times. The round-trip fare is $18, or else $26 round-trip for a double-occupancy cabin.

GETTING AROUND From the airport to your accommodations, you can take a **taxi,** which will cost $25 to $80, depending on the location of your hotel (taxis are unmetered). You can also arrange (or have your hotel do it for you) a **sightseeing tour** by taxi. Rates must be negotiated on an individual basis.

If you want to do extensive touring, we recommend a car, as attractions are very spread out. Options include **Rattan's Car Rentals,** at Crown Point Airport (✆ **868/639-8271**), and **Singh's Auto Rentals,** Grafton Beach Resort (✆ **868/639-0030**). One final possibility is **Thrifty,** at the airport or at the Rex Turtle Beach Hotel, Courtland Bay, Black Rock (✆ **868/639-8507**). Daily charges range from $50 to $85 a day.

Inexpensive **public buses** travel from one end of the island to the other several times a day. Expect an unscheduled stop at any passenger's doorstep, and never be in a hurry. Fares are $1.

FAST FACTS Most **banks** are open Monday to Thursday from 8am to 2pm, and Friday from 8am to 1pm and 3 to 5pm. **RBTT Bank Limited,** on Burnett Street (✆ **868/639-2404**), and **Republic Bank Ltd.,** on Carrington Street, Scarborough (✆ **868/639-2811**), both have **ATMs.**

You can send mail from the island post offices: **Tobago Post Office,** Teal Building, Milford Road, Scarborough (✆ **868/660-7377**).

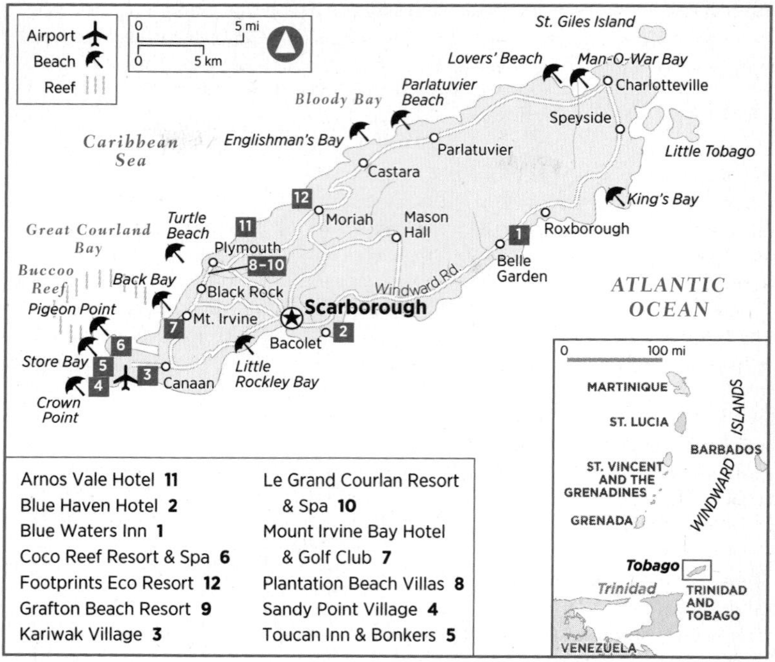

Tobago

Arnos Vale Hotel **11**
Blue Haven Hotel **2**
Blue Waters Inn **1**
Coco Reef Resort & Spa **6**
Footprints Eco Resort **12**
Grafton Beach Resort **9**
Kariwak Village **3**
Le Grand Courlan Resort & Spa **10**
Mount Irvine Bay Hotel & Golf Club **7**
Plantation Beach Villas **8**
Sandy Point Village **4**
Toucan Inn & Bonkers **5**

For **tourist information,** contact the Tourism Division of the Tobago House of Assembly at the airport office (✆ **868/639-0509**), or at the main office at NIB Mall in Scarborough (✆ **868/639-2125;** www.visittobago.gov.tt or www.mytobago.info).

Scarborough Regional Hospital is on Fort George Street, Scarborough (✆ **868/639-2551**). Medical care is sometimes limited, and physicians and health-care facilities expect immediate cash payment for services.

Where to Stay

To save money, it may be best to take the breakfast and dinner (MAP) plan when reserving a room. There's a 10% value-added tax (VAT) on all hotel bills, and often a service charge of about 10%. In addition, there is a 15% service charge on other hotel charges (other than the room rate) and on restaurant bills. Don't forget to ask if the VAT and service charge are included in the prices quoted to you.

VERY EXPENSIVE

Blue Haven Hotel ★ It's made a comeback. In the 1950s, it was the hottest ticket in town. Rita Hayworth and Robert Mitchum even stayed here when they made *Fire Down Below* in 1957. In romantic legend, the inn stands at the place where Robinson Crusoe was stranded in 1659 in the Defoe novel. Elegantly furnished bedrooms open onto panoramic views of the water—the inn is, in fact, surrounded on three sides by the sea and opens onto a secluded beach of fine white sands. Guests walk on wooden floors, and there's a glass wall separating the bedrooms

from the sleekly modern bathrooms. Guests have several options for lodging, ranging from standard doubles to deluxe suites, plus two-bedroom villas with a private pool. All accommodations come with private balconies with ocean views.

Bacolet Bay, Scarborough, Tobago, W.I. www.bluehavenhotel.com. ✆ **868/660-7400.** Fax 868/660-7900. 55 units. Winter $240–$275 double, $355 suite, $585 2-bedroom villa; off season $185–$220 double, $275 suite, $425 2-bedroom villa. Children 2 and under stay free in parent's room. AE, DISC, MC, V. **Amenities:** Restaurant; 2 bars; babysitting; children's playground; exercise room; outdoor pool; room service; spa; tennis court; watersports by special arrangement; Wi-Fi (free). *In room:* A/C, TV, hair dryer, minibar.

Coco Reef Resort & Spa ★★ This is one of the largest beachfront hotels on the island, and it has a certain South Florida pizzazz. It's on Tobago's northern shore, near the airport. Most accommodations are in the two- and three-story main building, although about a half-dozen villas are scattered over the surrounding acreage. The designer incorporated a number of environmentally friendly features and used some recycled materials. The bedrooms are spacious, airy, and filled with wicker furniture. Most rooms have an intricately trimmed balcony. The hotel offers 15 suites with large balconies and patios overlooking the Caribbean and lush tropical gardens. The complex is near a trio of the island's best beaches—Store Bay, Pigeon Point, and Coconut Beach itself, just steps from your room.

Coconut Bay (P.O. Box 434), Scarborough, Tobago, W.I. www.cocoreef.com. ✆ **868/639-8571.** Fax 868/639-8574. 137 units. Winter $425–$510 double, from $750–$4,000 suite or villa; off season $325–$415 double, from $615–$2,500 suite or villa. MAP (breakfast and dinner) $66 per person extra, $45 for children 5–12. Extra person $82 per day. AE, MC, V. **Amenities:** 2 restaurants; 2 bars; babysitting; health club; outdoor pool; room service; spa; tennis court (lit); watersports equipment/rentals. *In room:* A/C, TV, hair dryer, minibar, Wi-Fi ($15 per hour).

Le Grand Courlan Spa Resort ★★★ Operated by the same owners as the Grafton Beach Resort (see below), this pricey hotel is definitely five-star and definitely deluxe. For those who want to live in style but don't want a megaresort, the Courlan is a good choice. It's named for the bay on the western edge of the island on which it sits. A soft, sandy beach is at its door, and everything is set against a backdrop of bougainvillea, white frangipani, and hibiscus. Constructed to fit in with its natural surroundings, the hotel was built of stone and teak harvested from farms on Trinidad, then furnished with handcrafted mahogany pieces and decorated with original artwork. The floors are covered in Italian porcelain tile, and the ceilings are made from Guyanan hardwood. The bedrooms are handsomely tropical in decor, with two phones, king-size beds, and large balconies.

Stonehaven Bay, Black Rock (P.O. Box 25), Scarborough, Tobago, W.I. www.legrandtobago.com. ✆ **868/639-9667.** Fax 868/639-0030. 86 units. Year-round $260–$575 double. Includes all meals and beverages, and 1 spa treatment or scuba dive daily. AE, MC, V. **Amenities:** 2 restaurants; bar; dive shop; fishing; golf privileges; Internet (free); outdoor pool; sauna; spa; 2 tennis courts (lit); watersports equipment/rentals. *In room:* A/C, TV, fridge, hair dryer, minibar.

Plantation Beach Villas ★ At the edge of a tropical rainforest, between a bird sanctuary and the Caribbean, this pink-and-white cottage complex stands above a palm-fringed beach. The resort is reminiscent of the plantation era, with its British colonial architecture, rocking chairs on the front porch, four-poster beds, and louvered doors. Two sailing buddies and native Tobagonians, Jennifer Avey and Brenda Farfan, created this little gem, furnishing it with handmade pieces and original artwork. Each spacious villa has three bedrooms, a trio of baths with showers, and a

teak-covered front porch with a sea view. It's like living in your own private vacation retreat. The site is a 15-minute drive from the airport.

Stonehaven Bay Rd., Black Rock (P.O. Box 435), Scarborough, Tobago, W.I. www.plantationbeachvillas.com. ✆ **800/633-7411** in the U.S., or 868/639-9377. Fax 868/639-0455. 6 units. Winter $580–$710 for up to 4 persons, $670–$765 for up to 5 or 6 persons; off season $400 for up to 4 persons, $500 for up to 5 or 6 persons. AE, MC, V. **Amenities:** Restaurant; bar; babysitting; outdoor pool. *In room:* A/C, TV, CD player, kitchenette, Wi-Fi (free).

EXPENSIVE

Arnos Vale Hotel ★ This inn—one of the first hotels of Tobago's modern tourist age—sprawls over 180 hectares (445 acres) of very private land. It's named after a township in England, although tour groups from Italy often fill up its chambers. This place was once a closely guarded secret, but it was a long time ago that the late Princess Margaret honeymooned here. The other celebs who used to flock here are off in Anguilla these days. Rooms, each with a private patio or veranda, are furnished with a wide spectrum of furniture, including some pieces dating back to the early 1960s, retained because many clients appreciate their slightly battered charm. Only a few of the units are actually on the beach. Suites are in a handful of individual bungalows. Most of the socializing occurs at the likable bar.

Arnos Vale Rd. (P.O. Box 208), Scarborough, Tobago, W.I. www.arnosvalehotel.com. ✆ **868/639-2881.** Fax 868/639-4629. 29 units. Winter $150 double, $190–$235 suite; off season $105 double, $170–$200 suite. MAP (breakfast and dinner) $78 per person extra. No credit cards. **Amenities:** 2 restaurants; 2 bars (1 swim-up); babysitting; outdoor pool; tennis court (lit). *In room:* A/C, Internet ($7 per hr.), minibar (in some).

Blue Waters Inn ★ ☺ Attracting nature lovers, this family-run property on the northeastern coast of Tobago is nestled along the shore of Batteaux Bay, where a private 300m-long (984-ft.) beach beckons guests. This rustic retreat extends onto acres of tropical rainforest with myriad exotic birds, butterflies, and other wildlife. The building's entrance almost appears to drop over a cliff, and birds may actually fly through the open windows of the driftwood-adorned dining room. It's a very informal place, so leave your fancy resort wear at home. The inn now offers several units with kitchenettes, suitable for families. The second-floor rooms offer lovely views of the water. The inn is about 40km (25 miles) from the airport, a 75-minute drive along narrow, winding country roads.

Batteaux Bay, Speyside, Tobago, W.I. www.bluewatersinn.com. ✆ **800/448-8355** in the U.S., or 868/660-4341. Fax 868/660-5195. 38 units. Winter $250–$280 double, $380 efficiency, $590 2-bedroom efficiency; off season $160–$280 double, $290 efficiency, $460 2-bedroom efficiency. MAP (breakfast and dinner) $35 per person extra. AE, MC, V. **Amenities:** Restaurant; bar; babysitting; watersports equipment/rentals. *In room:* A/C, hair dryer, Internet (free).

Footprints Eco Resort ★ The island's first eco-resort sprawls across some 24 hectares (59 acres) on Culloden Bay. A local doctor and his daughter carved this "environmentally responsible" resort out of a dense forest of cocoa and fruit trees in 1997. The result is a rustic and charming compound of wood-sided, thatch-roofed cottages. Each unit is artfully built of recycled lumber, with an emphasis on native termite-resistant hardwoods such as wallaba and teak. Accommodations are rough-hewn but comfortable, with a hammock for classic island lounging, wooden floors, and a lot of idiosyncratic charm. Rooms range from standard doubles to king superior units with fridges. Nature trails fan out across the nearby hills, and good beaches include Courland Bay and Castara Bay, a 15-minute drive away.

Golden Lane, Culloden Bay Rd., Tobago, W.I. www.footprints-resort.com. ✆ **868/660-0416.** Fax 868/660-0027. 15 units. Winter $115–$140 double, $225–$300 villa; off season $95–$115 double, $185–$225 villa. AE, MC, V. **Amenities:** Restaurant; bar; babysitting; exercise room; Jacuzzi; 2 outdoor pools; room service; spa. *In room:* A/C, ceiling fan, TV (in some), kitchenette (in some), minibar (in some).

Grafton Beach Resort ★ Still going strong—although it's now outclassed by many others—this complex sprawls across a beach shoreline set against a backdrop of palms. It draws the most European clientele on the island and is under the same ownership as the neighboring and superior Le Grand Courlan Spa Resort (p. 646; Grafton guests can use Courlan's spa). Rooms are in three- and four-story buildings scattered over 2 hectares (5 acres) descending to a white-sand beach. The well-furnished units contain ceiling fans, sliding-glass doors opening onto balconies, and handcrafted teak furniture. The resort's pool is ringed with cafe/restaurant tables, and there is a swim-up bar. Limbo dancing and calypso, or some other form of entertainment, is featured nightly.

Black Rock (P.O. Box 25), Scarborough, Tobago, W.I. www.graftontobago.com. ✆ **868/639-0191.** Fax 868/639-0030. 106 units. Year-round $120–$180 double; $224–$280 per person suite. Rates are all-inclusive. AE, MC, V. **Amenities:** 3 restaurants; 3 bars (1 swim-up); golf privileges; outdoor pool; watersports equipment/rentals. *In room:* A/C, ceiling fan, TV, fridge, hair dryer, Wi-Fi (free).

Mount Irvine Bay Hotel & Golf Club ★★ This 6-hectare (15-acre) resort stands on the site of an 18th-century sugar plantation. The surrounding Mount Irvine Golf Course is one of the finest courses in the Caribbean. Although Mount Irvine retains a loyal clientele, Le Grand Courlan Spa Resort (p. 646) and the Hilton surpassed it long ago. The center of the resort is a luxurious oval pool and the ruins of a stone sugar mill. The grounds slope down to a good sandy beach. On the hill leading to the beach are the newer and better-maintained cottage suites, covered with heliconia. Most accommodations are in the main building, a two-story, hacienda-inspired wing of rather large but standard guest rooms, each with a view of green lawns and flowering shrubbery. Some of the better units have Queen Anne–style furniture with two- and four-poster beds.

Mount Irvine (P.O. Box 222), Scarborough, Tobago, W.I. www.mtirvine.com. ✆ **868/639-8871.** Fax 868/639-8800. 105 units. Winter $195 double, $300 cottage, $460 1-bedroom suite; off season $150 double, $250 cottage, $380 1-bedroom suite. MAP (breakfast and dinner) $47 per person extra. AE, MC, V. 8km (5 miles) northwest of the airport. **Amenities:** 3 restaurants; 6 bars; exercise room, 18-hole golf course; Internet cafe; outdoor pool; room service; sauna; 2 tennis courts (lit); watersports equipment/rentals. *In room:* A/C, TV, fridge (in some), hair dryer, Wi-Fi (free).

MODERATE

Kariwak Village ★ 🎁 This cluster of cottages evoking the South Pacific is about a 6-minute walk from the beach on the island's west end and a 2-minute drive from the airport. The name is a combination of the two native tribes that originally inhabited Tobago, the Caribs and the Arawaks. In this "village," Cynthia and Allan Clovis run a holistic haven as well as an inn. Come here, among other reasons, for Hatha Yoga, Qi Gong, and various stretching and relaxing exercises. Two on-site massage therapists give you all your favorite massages. If you're a vegetarian headed for Tobago, this is the place for you. You can even walk through Cynthia's garden, where she grows fresh herbs and vegetables for the meals served here. Nine of the accommodations are hexagonal cabanas with two rooms each, opening onto the pool. The units are quite spacious, with king-size beds. Live entertainment is provided on Friday and Saturday.

Store Bay Local Rd. (P.O. Box 27), Crown Point, Tobago, W.I. www.kariwak.com. ✆ **868/639-8442.** Fax 868/639-8441. 24 units. Winter $165 double; off season $120 double. Children 12 and under stay free in parent's room. MAP (breakfast and dinner) $40 per person extra. AE, MC, V. **Amenities:** Restaurant; bar; yoga; Jacuzzi; outdoor pool. *In room:* A/C, hair dryer.

INEXPENSIVE

Sandy Point Village This miniature vacation village resembles a Riviera condominium complex. It's just a 5-minute ride from the airport, but its shoreside position on the island's southwestern coast makes it seem remote. Airport noise, however, can be a problem. The little village of peaked and gabled roofs is landscaped all the way down to the sandy beach, where the rustic Steak and Lobster Grill serves meals throughout the day and evening. The fully equipped accommodations have patios that open toward the sea, living and dining areas with Jamaican wicker furniture, and satellite TV. All but six of the units (those at poolside) contain kitchenettes, and each has a shower-only bathroom. Some of the studios have a rustic open stairway leading to a loft with bunk beds, with a twin-bedded room on the lower level as well.

Crown Point, Tobago, W.I. www.sandypt.net. ✆ **868/639-8533.** Fax 868/639-8496. 45 units. Winter $75 double, $90 2-bedroom apt; off season $65 double, $80 2-bedroom apt. Children 11 and under $15 extra. AE, MC, V. **Amenities:** Restaurant; bar; bikes; dive shop; exercise room; Jacuzzi; outdoor pool; sauna; watersports equipment/rentals. *In room:* A/C, TV, kitchenette (in most).

Toucan Inn & Bonkers ★ This combination restaurant and hotel is one of Tobago's best values. An inn of charm and grace, it is close to the airport and surrounded by attractively landscaped gardens. If you stay here, you'll be just a short drive from some of the island's best sandy beaches. The staff is helpful in directing you. Bedrooms are done in a modern style with comfortable though streamlined furniture; rooms come in various shapes and sizes, each with a queen-size bed or two twins. The hotel offers an option of well-furnished bedrooms with tiled shower bathrooms. The cluster of rooms facing the garden is more secluded, but even so, many guests prefer the cabanas around the pool. Teak furnishings predominate in the bedrooms. On-site Bonkers is one of the most frequented restaurants and bars in Tobago.

Store Bay Local Rd. (P.O. Box 452), Crown Point, Tobago, W.I. www.toucan-inn.com. ✆ **868/639-7173.** Fax 868/639-8933. 20 units. Winter $110–$130 double; off season $90–$110 double. AE, MC, V. **Amenities:** Restaurant; bar; babysitting; outdoor pool. *In room:* A/C, hair dryer.

Where to Dine

EXPENSIVE

Arnos Vale Water Wheel Restaurant INTERNATIONAL This restaurant occupies the weathered premises of a former 19th-century water mill used to crush sugar cane. You'll dine in the wheelhouse, with an antique oven and the wheel's original machinery still in place, while overlooking the verdant banks of the Franklin River. Menu items include Cornish hen, shaved-pear-and-Parmesan salad, deviled chicken, honey-roasted duck breast, caramelized breast of chicken with polenta and callaloo sauce, grilled fish served with a medley of sauces, and at least three different shrimp and lobster dishes. Three times a week, there's a performance of live Trinidadian/Tobagan music and dance; the animated sounds perk up the otherwise calm and quiet landscape of chirping tree frogs and splashing water.

Franklyn Rd., Arnos Vale Estate. ✆ **868/660-0815.** www.arnosvalehotel.com/waterwheel.htm. Reservations recommended. Main courses $24–$37. AE, MC, V. Daily 8:30am–10:30pm. 5-min. drive from the Arnos Vale Hotel.

The Blue Crab ★ 🎁 CARIBBEAN/INTERNATIONAL One of our favorite restaurants in the capital, this family-run spot occupies an Edwardian-era house with an oversize veranda. The menu makes the most of local ingredients and regional spices, and is dictated by whatever is available that day in the marketplace. The good, homemade food includes fresh conch, stuffed crab backs, an array of Creole meat dishes grilled over coconut husks, flying fish in a mild curry-flavored batter, shrimp with garlic butter or cream, and a vegetable rice dish of the day. Lobster sometimes appears on the menu.

5 Robinson St., Scarborough. ✆ **868/639-2737.** www.tobagobluecrab.com. Dinner reservations required 24 hr. in advance. Main courses $7–$10 lunch, $24–$31 dinner. AE, MC, V. Mon–Fri noon–3pm; Mon, Wed, and Fri dinner by reservation only.

Cafe Havana CUBAN/ASIAN For a change of pace, this restaurant features specialties from Havana, with some delicacies from Asia as well. It lies on three levels, each offering a panoramic view of the ocean. Its mojitos, a favorite drink of Cuban aficionado Ernest Hemingway, are among the best in the island. In a tropical setting, you can order the daily catch caught in Bacolet Bay. Seafood platters are a feature, backed up by homemade bread and fresh pasta. A specialty is callaloo soup with fresh crabmeat in a broth of coconut milk. A main dish delight is the piña colada dolphin steaks with pineapple purée and fresh herbs.

In the Half-Moon Blue Hotel, 73 Bacolet St., Scarborough. ✆ **868/639-3551.** www.halfmoonblue.com. Reservations required. Main courses $18–$35. MC, V. Daily 7:30am–11pm.

Dillon's ★ INTERNATIONAL Set in a simple house near the Coco Reef Resort (p. 646) and the airport, this restaurant is run by one of Tobago's leading operators of a deep-sea-fishing boat. Consequently, the fish is sure to be fresh. There's both an indoor, air-conditioned room with framed memorabilia of the island's tradition of steel-pan music, and an outdoor terrace with views over the garden. Menu items include fresh snapper with lemon-butter sauce; tenderloin steak with a spinach-bacon ragout; pan-fried or grilled shrimp served with grilled Parmesan polenta, basmati rice, and a tomato/basil sauce; curried shrimp in coconut sauce and mango chutney; and a lobster crepe with white-wine sauce and fresh herbs.

Milford Rd., near Crown Point. ✆ **868/639-8765.** Reservations recommended. Main courses $19–$48. AE, DISC, MC, V. Mon–Fri 6–10pm. Closed 6 weeks May–June.

Tamara's ★ CREOLE/INTERNATIONAL One of the most appealing restaurants on Tobago occupies a two-tiered, stone-and-timber gazebo whose curved edges are open on all sides for maximum exposure to cool breezes and views of the nearby sea. It serves some of Trinidad and Tobago's most sophisticated food, based on West Indian traditions with lots of international touches. Start, perhaps, with homemade veal-and-bacon terrine, or pan-fried shrimp with wilted greens and wasabi sauce. Try the lamb loin on couscous, the charcoal-grilled ocean snapper with a creamy mushroom-and-lemon-grass sauce, or most definitely the pork tenderloin garnished with a lima-bean ragout. The menu changes every 2 days.

In the Coco Reef Resort, Coconut Beach. ✆ **868/639-8571.** Reservations recommended. Breakfast $19; lunch buffet $26; fixed-price dinner $50. AE, MC, V. Daily 7am–10pm.

MODERATE

The Cocoa House ★ WEST INDIAN/TOBAGONIAN Proud of its eco-sensitivity (waste water and paper trash are recycled here), this restaurant is a worthy choice for its allegiance to tried-and-true Tobagonian food that's prepared in a style endorsed by many of the island's matriarchs and grandmothers. Its name comes from its unusual roof, made from the fronds of the timit palm. On balmy evenings, the roof retracts (just as it might at an old-fashioned cocoa-pod-drying room), allowing views of the setting sun and, a bit later, of the moon and stars. Well-flavored dishes include jerk versions of shrimp, chicken, and pork; duck with either orange or pineapple sauce; and *pelau,* a French-inspired dish that combines chicken and beef bound together with rice. For a dish that many Tobagonians remember from their childhood, try pork and dumplings.

In Footprints Eco Resort, Golden Lane, Culloden Bay Rd. ✆ **868/660-0416.** www.footprints-resort.com. Dinner reservations required. Main courses $7–$14 lunch, $12–$24 dinner; breakfast $5–$9. AE, MC, V. Daily 8am–9pm.

Kariwak Village Restaurant ★ CARIBBEAN Even if you're not a guest here, consider visiting at dinnertime. The chefs prepare one of the choicest menus on the island, a four-course repast that changes nightly, based on what's best and freshest at the market. On our latest rounds, we began with creamy breadfruit soup, followed by freshly grilled fish, rice, stuffed butternut pumpkin, and *christophene* (Caribbean squash). The price even includes dessert and coffee. In an open-air setting, you can enjoy recorded music from Trinidadian steel bands. The owner, Cynthia Clovis, grows herbs and vegetables in an on-site organic garden. The Friday or Saturday evening buffet is one of the best spreads on the island, with live music to boot. Shrimp and steak are favorites, but don't overlook the green-banana salad seasoned with fresh herbs.

In the Kariwak Village hotel, Store Bay Local Rd., Crown Point. ✆ **868/639-8442.** www.kariwak.com. Reservations recommended. Breakfast $11; lunch $14; 4-course dinner $31. AE, MC, V. Daily 7am–11pm.

La Tartaruga ★ ITALIAN/SEAFOOD/VEGETARIAN Born in Milan, Lombardian Gabriele de Gaetano has brought the flavors of his homeland to remote Tobago and has infused the island with marvelous change-of-pace dining. The eatery is casual yet elegant, with lots of color used along with local artwork. The island's most gracious host, Gaetano "table hops," always concerned about your welfare and whether you like his food. (Diners almost invariably tell him how tasty and flavorful his Italian-inspired cuisine is.) Perhaps he can't find all the authentic ingredients needed for his food, but he succeeds admirably nonetheless. His ravioli won our hearts until we tasted his tagliatelle with lobster, made all the tastier with the use of Trinidadian capers in wine and fresh cream. For a main course, we heartily endorse the mixed seafood grill of lobster, shrimp, and calamari, among other delights. Many of the dishes will appeal to the vegetarian in all of us. Desserts are homemade fresh daily and are luscious. Everything is backed up by the best wine menu on the island.

Buccoo Rd., Buccoo. ✆ **868/639-0940.** www.latartarugatobago.com. Reservations recommended. Main courses $7–$38. AE, MC, V. Mon–Sat 6:30–10pm.

Hitting the Beach ★★

On Tobago you can still feel like Robinson Crusoe in a solitary sandy cove—at least until Saturday, when the Trinidadians fly over for a weekend on the beach.

Pigeon Point, on the northwestern shore, is the best-known bathing area, with a long coral beach. It's public, but to reach it, you must enter a former coconut estate, which charges a fee of $1.60. Set against a backdrop of royal palms, this beach is becoming increasingly commercial. Facilities include food kiosks, crafts shops, a diving concession, paddleboat rentals, changing rooms in thatched shelters, and picnic tables. Pigeon Point is also the jumping-off point for snorkeling cruises to **Buccoo Reef.**

Another good beach, **Back Bay,** is an 8-minute walk from the Mount Irvine Bay Hotel (p. 648) on Mount Irvine Bay. Along the way, you'll pass a coconut plantation and an old cannon emplacement. Snorkeling is generally excellent, even in winter. There are sometimes dangerous currents, but you can always explore Rocky Point Beach and its brilliantly colored parrotfish. In July and August, the surfing is the finest in Tobago; it's also likely to be good in January and April. Stop in Scarborough for picnic fixings, which you can enjoy at the picnic tables here; a snack bar sells cold beer and drinks.

Great Courland Bay is known for its calm, gin-clear waters, and is flanked by **Turtle Beach,** named for the turtles that nest here. Near Fort Bennett and south of Plymouth, Great Courland Bay is one of the longest sandy beaches on the island and the site of several hotels and a marina.

The locals and the fishing boats make the setting at half-moon-shaped **Parlatuvier Beach** (on the north side of the island) more bucolic than the swimming. If you can't stand crowds, head for **Englishman's Bay,** on the north coast just west of Parlatuvier. We don't know why this beach is virtually deserted: It's charming, secluded, and good for swimming, and there have been no reports of muggings despite the seclusion.

Near the little fishing village of Charlotteville, **Man-O-War Bay** is one of the finest natural harbors in the West Indies. It has a long, sandy beach and a government-run rest house. Sometimes local fishermen will hawk the day's catch (and clean it for you as well). Nearby **Lovers' Beach** is accessible only by boat and is famous for its pink sand, formed long ago from crushed sea shells. Negotiate a fee with one of the local boatmen; expect to pay around $25.

The true beach buff will head for **King's Bay** in the northeast, south of the town of Speyside near Delaford. Against a backdrop of towering green hills, the crescent-shaped grayish-sand beach is one of the best places for swimming.

Sports & Outdoor Pursuits

GOLF Tobago is the proud possessor of an 18-hole, 6,800-yard course at Mount Irvine. Called the **Tobago Golf Club** at the Mount Irvine Estates (✆ **868/639-8871**), it covers 60 breeze-swept hectares (148 acres) and was featured in the *Wonderful World of Golf* TV series. Even beginners agree the course is friendly to duffers. Guests of the Mount Irvine Bay Hotel (p. 648) are granted temporary membership, use of the clubhouse and facilities, and a 15% discount on greens fees. The course is also open to nonguests, who pay $55 for 18 holes or $35 for 9 holes. Cart rentals are $42 for 18 holes or $23 for 9 holes. **Tobago Plantations Golf & Country Club,** Hampden Road, Lowlands (✆ **868/631-0875**), lies on a 303-hectare (749-acre) estate that was previously a sugar-cane plantation. Some holes on this par-72, 7,000-yard course follow the coastline. Greens fees, including golf cart, are $100 for 18 holes, $50 for 9 holes.

SCUBA DIVING, SNORKELING & OTHER WATERSPORTS ★★ The unspoiled reefs off Tobago teem with a great variety of marine life. Divers can swim through rocky canyons 20 to 40m (66–131 ft.) deep, underwater photographers can shoot pictures they won't find anywhere else, and snorkelers can explore the celebrated **Buccoo Reef** (off Pigeon Point), which teems with gardens of coral and hundreds of fish in the waist-deep water. Even nonswimmers can wade knee-deep in the waters. Remember to protect your head and body from the sun, and to guard your feet against the sharp coral. Nearly all the major hotels arrange boat trips here. After about half an hour at the reef, passengers reboard their boats and go over to **Nylon Pool,** with its crystal-clear waters. Here in this white-sand-bottom spot, about 2km (1¼ miles) offshore, you can enjoy a dip in water only 1m (3¼-ft.) deep.

Wreck divers have a new adventure to enjoy with the sinking of the former ferryboat *Maverick,* in 30m (98 ft.) of water near Mount Irvine Bay Hotel on Tobago's southwest coast.

Dive Tobago, Pigeon Point (© **868/660-7767;** www.divetobago.com), is the oldest and most established operation on Tobago, run by Jay Young, a certified PADI instructor. It offers easy resort courses, single dives, and dive packages, along with equipment rentals. A basic resort course costs $75, although for certification you must pay $450. A one-tank dive goes for $45.

Tobago Dive Experience, at the Manta Lodge, Speyside (© **868/660-4888;** www.tobagodiveexperience.com), offers scuba dives, snorkeling, and boat trips. All dives are guided, with a boat following. Exciting drift dives are available for experienced divers. A one-tank dive costs $50 without equipment, a two-tank dive starts at $90, and a resort course costs $75.

TENNIS The best courts on the island are at the **Mount Irvine Bay Hotel** (p. 648; © **868/639-8871**). Nonguests may use one of the two courts here for $6 per hour. There is an additional $4 light fee on request.

Exploring the Island

If you'd like a close-up view of Tobago's many rare and exotic tropical birds, as well as a range of other island wildlife and lush tropical flora, naturalist-led field trips are the answer. Each 5-hour trip leads you to forest trails and coconut plantations, along rivers and past waterfalls; one excursion even goes to two nearby islands. Trips cost $8 to $13. For details, contact **Newton George,** Speyside (© **868/660-5463** or 868/754-7881; www.newtongeorge.com).

Tobago's capital, **Scarborough,** need claim your attention only briefly before you climb up the hill to **Fort King George,** about 130m (427 ft.) above the town. Built by the English in 1779, it was later captured by the French, then tossed back and forth among various conquerors until a hurricane devastated the city in 1847. You can view the ruins of a military hospital and also see artifacts displayed at the **Tobago Museum** (© **868/639-3970**), in the fort's old barracks. Admission is $1, and hours are Monday to Friday 8:30am to 4:30pm.

From Scarborough you can drive northwest to **Plymouth,** Tobago's other town. Perched on a point at Plymouth is **Fort James,** which dates from 1768. Now it's mainly in ruins.

From Speyside in the north, you can make arrangements with a local fisherman to go to **Little Tobago ★**, a 180-hectare (445-acre) offshore island whose bird sanctuary attracts ornithologists. The 20-minute crossing is likely to be rough, but the effort is worth it. Threatened with extinction in New Guinea, many birds—perhaps 50 species—were brought over to this little island in the early part of last century. The islet is arid and hilly, with a network of marked trails.

Off Pigeon Point in the south is **Buccoo Reef ★★**, where sea gardens of coral and hundreds of fish can be seen in waist-deep water (see "Sports & Outdoor Pursuits," above). This is the natural aquarium of Tobago, offering the island's best **snorkeling** and **scuba diving.** Nearly all the major hotels arrange boat trips here.

Shopping

In Tobago's capital, Scarborough, you can visit the local **market** Monday to Saturday mornings. Scarborough's stores have a limited range of merchandise, more to tempt the browser than the serious shopper.

Farro's, Wilson Road (no phone), across from the marketplace, offers the tastiest condiments on the island, packed into little straw baskets for you to carry back home. Sample the delectable lime marmalade, any of the hot sauces, the guava jelly, and most definitely the homemade tamarind chutney.

If you're seeking handicrafts, especially straw baskets, head for the **Shaadijas Souvenir & Gift Shop,** Port Mall (✆ **868/660-1000**), also in Scarborough.

Cotton House Fashion Studio, Old Windward Road, Bacolet (✆ **868/639-2727**), is the island's best choice for "hands-on" appreciation of the fine art of batik. In the Indonesian tradition, melted wax is brushed onto fabric, resisting dyes and creating unusual colors and designs. This outlet contains the largest collection of batik clothing and wall hangings on Tobago. Dying techniques are demonstrated to visitors, who can then try their skills.

The Tobago Art Gallery, Hibiscus Drive, Lowlands (✆ **868/631-1424;** www.tobagoartgallery.com), across from the Tobago Hilton, features the works of at least 10 artists. On permanent exhibit upstairs is a collection of island watercolors by Rachel Superville and her husband, Martin. Sculptures and a number of handicrafts are also sold here.

Tobago After Dark

Your best bet for entertainment is at the **Mount Irvine Bay Hotel** at Mount Irvine Bay (p. 648; ✆ **868/639-8871**), where you might find some dance action or a steel band performing by the beach or pool.

Grafton Beach Resort at Black Rock owns one of the island's most charming bars, **Buccaneer's Beach Bar** (✆ **868/639-0191;** www.buccaneersbeachbar.com), across from the resort. Here you'll find a wide wood terrace sheltered by a grove of almond trees. Daily specials written up on a surfboard include burgers, fried fish, and the like (don't expect the elegant beachside Creole cooking of Martinique). The resort itself offers cabaretlike entertainment nightly. Try to catch the local troupe, Les Couteaux Cultural Group, which performs a version of Tobagonian history set to dance.

Want some local action? Try **Bonkers** ★, Store Bay Road at Crown Point (✆ **868/639-7173**), a lively bar where you'll hear the best soca, reggae, or jazz on the island. If you've been "bad," the DJ might order you to walk the gangplank into the pool.

TURKS & CAICOS

The Turks and Caicos Islands (TCI) are a coral-reef paradise. Even with the advent of real tourist development and the bustle of construction—particularly on the main island of Providenciales (nicknamed "Provo")—the beauty and tranquillity of this island chain remain intact. What has put Turks and Caicos on the map are the beautiful beaches—224 miles of them, to be precise—and the magnificent underwater life.

Beaches The beaches of Turks and Caicos owe much of their natural good looks to the surrounding unspoiled coral reef ecosystem. Twelve-mile **Grace Bay Beach** is Provo's most beautiful stretch of sand. From Provo you can take a beach excursion to the island's offshore cays, the **Caicos Cays,** to find pristine sand dollars. On **Grand Turk, Governor's Beach** is a wide swathe of soft, pearly sand under the shade of casuarina pines.

Things to Do Dive experts have cited these islands as among the world's best scuba-diving sites. The big action is on **Grand Turk** along the **Wall,** where the western edges of the island plunge 2,133.5m (7,000 ft.) into deep water. Snorkeling is world-class as well; head to coral gardens by boat, or snorkel right off Grace Bay at **Bight Reef.** Conditions are also ideal for parasailing, windsurfing, and stand-up paddleboarding. Visit **Little Water Cay,** a nature preserve for indigenous rock iguanas.

Eating & Drinking You will eat very well in Provo on cuisines from around the world, but if it's local flavor you're craving, head to Provo's **Blue Hills,** where casual beach shacks serve such regional favorites as peas 'n' rice, curry fish, johnnycakes, and conch. Head to **Da Conch Shack** for fresh conch fritters, conch stew, and conch chowder, or try the Wednesday night fish fry at **Smokey's on Da Bay.**

Nightlife & Entertainment The party vibe on Provo is easygoing and laid-back. For prime sunset viewing, the Grace Bay Club's beachfront **Lounge** has a glowing fire pit, and the **Infinity Bar** is a sleek ribbon of black marble inset with sexy blue lights. Enjoy ripsaw music at the **Wednesday and Sunday barbecues** at the **Osprey Beach Hotel** in Grand Turk.

ESSENTIALS

Visitor Information

The **Turks and Caicos Tourist Board** (www.turksandcaicostourism.com) has offices in Stubbs Diamond Plaza, Providenciales (✆ **649/946-4970**), and Front Street, Cockburn Town, Grand Turk (✆ **649/946-2321**). The New York City office is now overseen by Pamela Ewing (✆ **800/241-0824**). In Canada the tourist board has an office at 81 Rumsey Rd., Toronto, ON (✆ **866/413-8875** or 416/642-9771).

[Fast FACTS] TURKS & CAICOS ISLANDS

Banks Branches and ATMs of **First Caribbean International Bank** (✆ **649/946-4245;** www.firstcaribbeanbank.com) and **Scotiabank** (✆ **649/946-4750;** www.scotiabank.com) are at convenient and central locations on both Provo and Grand Turk.

Currency The **U.S. dollar** is the official currency. *Prices in this chapter are quoted in U.S. dollars.*

Customs On arriving, you may bring in 1 liter of liquor or wine, 200 cigarettes, 50 cigars, or 8 ounces of tobacco duty-free. There are no restrictions on cameras, film, sports equipment, or personal items, provided they aren't for resale. Absolutely no spear guns or Hawaiian slings are allowed, and the importation of firearms without a permit is also prohibited. Illegal imported drugs bring heavy fines and lengthy terms of imprisonment.

Documents U.S. and Canadian citizens must have a passport or a combination of a birth certificate and photo ID, plus a return or ongoing ticket, to enter the country. Citizens of the United Kingdom, Commonwealth countries of the Caribbean, the Republic of Ireland, and E.U. countries must also have a current passport.

Electricity The electric current on the islands is 110 volts (60 cycles) AC. European appliances will need adapters.

Emergencies Call ✆ **911** or **999** for an **ambulance,** to report a **fire,** or to contact the **police.**

Language The official language is English.

Safety Although crime is minimal in the islands, petty theft does take place, so protect your valuables, money, and cameras. Don't leave luggage or parcels in an unattended car. Beaches are also vulnerable to thievery.

Taxes A departure tax of $35 is levied on all persons 3 and over leaving the islands (the tax is generally rolled into the price of your airline ticket). Also, the government collects an 11% occupancy tax, applicable to all hotels, guesthouses, and restaurants in the 40-island chain. Hotels generally add a 10% to 15% service charge on top of the government tax.

Telephone To call Turks and Caicos, dial **1** and then the number. To call a phone carrier in the U.S., dial **0,** then **1,** and then the number. The country code for the TCI is **649.** The international-operator telephone service is ✆ **115.** Local directory assistance is ✆ **118.**

Time The islands are in the Eastern Standard Time zone, and daylight saving time is observed.

Tipping Many hotels automatically add 10% to 15% to your bill to cover service. If individual staff members perform various services for you, it is customary to tip them something extra. If you take an island tour, watersports

The Turks & Caicos Islands

charter, or beach excursion, tip your guide 10% to 20%, depending on the level of service you receive. In restaurants, 15% is appropriate unless a service charge has already been added; if in doubt, ask. Tip taxi drivers 10% to 15%.

Water Government officials insist that the water in Turks and Caicos is safe to drink. Nonetheless, stick to bottled water, especially if you have a delicate stomach.

Weather The average temperature here is 82°F (28°C), dropping to 77°F (25°C) at night. The cooling breezes of the prevailing trade winds prevent the climate from being oppressive. The islands receive approximately 53cm (21 in.) of rainfall annually.

PROVIDENCIALES (PROVO) ★★★

Affectionately known as **Provo,** Providenciales is bounded by stunning turquoise seas and white-sand beaches that stretch for miles along the northeast coast. It is protected by a barrier reef that attracts swimmers, divers, and boaters.

The island's commercial center, Provo is at the heart of the nation's fast-paced development. But the island's premier beach, the 19km (12-mile) strand known as **Grace Bay** (named the "World's Leading Beach" 4 years running in the World Travel Awards), has long, languid stretches dotted with seabirds and puffs of clouds. On the powdery sands of Grace Bay, it's easy to feel you've really gotten away from it all.

Essentials

GETTING THERE Provo is the most easily reached island in the nation because of the frequency of flights. The main point of entry for international flights into Turks and Caicos is **Providenciales International Airport** (www.visitprovidenciales.com); Grand Turk also has an international airport. The Provo airport was undergoing a major upgrade at press time and welcoming new airlines to the burgeoning TCI market. Both **Continental Airlines** (✆ **800/523-3273;** www.continental.com) and **JetBlue** (✆ **800/538-2583;** www.jetblue.com) launched nonstop air service to Provo in winter 2011. Continental offers daily flights between Newark and Provo, while JetBlue has daily nonstop service from New York's JFK airport and Saturday flights from Boston's Logan airport.

American Airlines (✆ **800/433-7300** in the U.S. and Canada; www.aa.com) flies regular nonstop flights from New York, Boston, and Miami. Other airlines serving the islands include **Air Canada** (✆ **888/247-2262** in the U.S. and Canada; www.aircanada.ca), which has direct flights from Toronto, Montréal, and Ottawa; **Bahamas Air** (✆ **800/222-4262;** www.bahamasair.com); **British Airways** (✆ **800/247-9297** in the U.S., or 0870/850-9850 in the U.K.; www.britishairways.com), which flies nonstop from London on Sundays; **Delta** (✆ **800/241-4141** in the U.S. and Canada; www.delta.com), which flies nonstop daily from Atlanta; and **US Airways** (✆ **800/622-1015** in the U.S. and Canada; www.usairways.com), which flies nonstop from Charlotte (daily), Boston, and Philadelphia.

WestJet (✆ **888/937-8538;** www.westjet.com) recently added twice-weekly service from Montréal and Toronto. **Air Turks & Caicos** (✆ **649/946-4181;** www.airturksandcaicos.com) flies regularly between Provo and Jamaica, Haiti, the Dominican Republic, and the Bahamas.

GETTING AROUND Most of Provo's lodgings are an easy 15- to 20-minute taxi ride from the airport. The days of the free hotel **transfers** to and from the airport are over, however—your hotel can arrange a taxi transfer, but for a charge (or the fee discreetly folded into your hotel rate); otherwise, plenty of **taxis** are on hand to meet arriving flights. If for some reason none are around, call your hotel or the **Provo Taxi Association** (✆ **649/946-5481**). Cabs are metered and rates set by the government, but not all taxi drivers turn on their meters, so it's a good idea to negotiate the fare before you leave the airport—or anytime, for that matter. Expect to pay around $22 to $25 (plus tip) per couple (additional person $7.50) for a taxi ride from the airport to the Grace Bay area. Most taxis are vans equipped to carry more than one group of passengers, so it stands to reason that the more people are onboard, the lower the rate per couple.

Taxis are expensive—just jumping from one section of Grace Bay to another can run into double figures—and they're plentiful on Provo, but there are no designated taxi stands. We've hailed down taxis in the road on a number of occasions, however. If you find a taxi driver you like, ask for his or her card or jot down the number on the side of the van, and avail yourself of his or her services throughout your trip (taxi drivers are also happy to show you around the island—be sure to negotiate the fee upfront). Some Provo hotels include complimentary shuttle service around the Grace Bay area.

Because the island is so large and its hotels and restaurants are so far-flung, you might find a **rental car** useful on Providenciales, but be warned: Renting a car on the TCI is not particularly cheap, either.

Three major U.S.–based car rental agencies with a franchise in the Turks and Caicos Islands are **Budget,** with two Provo locations: the airport, and downtown Provo, in the Town Centre Mall (✆ **800/472-3325** in the U.S., or 649/946-4079 or 946-5400; www.budgetrentacar.com); **Avis,** with a branch at the airport (✆ **800/331-1212** in the U.S. and Canada, or 649/946-4705; www.avis.tc); and **Hertz** affiliate **Mystique Car Rental,** located at the Ports of Call shopping complex on Grace Bay Road, and on Old Airport Road, 2 minutes from the airport (✆ **649/941-3910;** www.hertztci.com). Cars rent for $40 to $225 a day (depending on the vehicle); collision-damage insurance costs $10 to $12 a day. The government will collect a $16 tax for each rental contract, regardless of the number of days you keep the car.

In the British tradition, **cars on all the islands drive on the left.** You need only a valid driver's license from your home country to rent a vehicle.

Bicycling is an ideal way to get around the flat Grace Bay area. Most people ride bikes on the sidewalks running along both sides of the paved roads. Many resorts, including Royal West Indies (p. 669), the Grace Bay Club, and the Sands at Grace Bay (p. 670), offer complimentary bikes for their guests. **Caicos Wheels,** Queens Landing Plaza, Grace Bay (✆ **649/242-6592;** www.caicoswheels.com), rents bikes (as well as scooters) in Providenciales. It will drop off and pick up bicycles at your resort; bikes cost $15/per day (deposit required).

FAST FACTS Branches and ATMs/ABMs of **First Caribbean International Bank** (✆ **649/946-4245;** www.firstcaribbeanbank.com) and **Scotiabank** (✆ **649/946-4750;** www.scotiabank.com) are at central locations on Provo. **First Caribbean** has 24-hour ABM service at the main branches of its bank on Provo and a branch in the Saltmills shopping complex on Provo's Grace Bay Road. **Scotiabank** has 24-hour ATMs at four locations on Provo: at the Provo airport check-in hall; at the Graceway Gourmet on Grace Bay Road; next to the Graceway IGA on Leeward Highway; and at Petro Plus on Millennium Highway. **Turks & Caicos Banking Company (TCBC)** has opened a branch (with ATM) in Provo's Regent Village on Grace Bay Road (✆ **649/941-4994;** http://turksandcaicos-banking.com).

Providenciales (Provo)

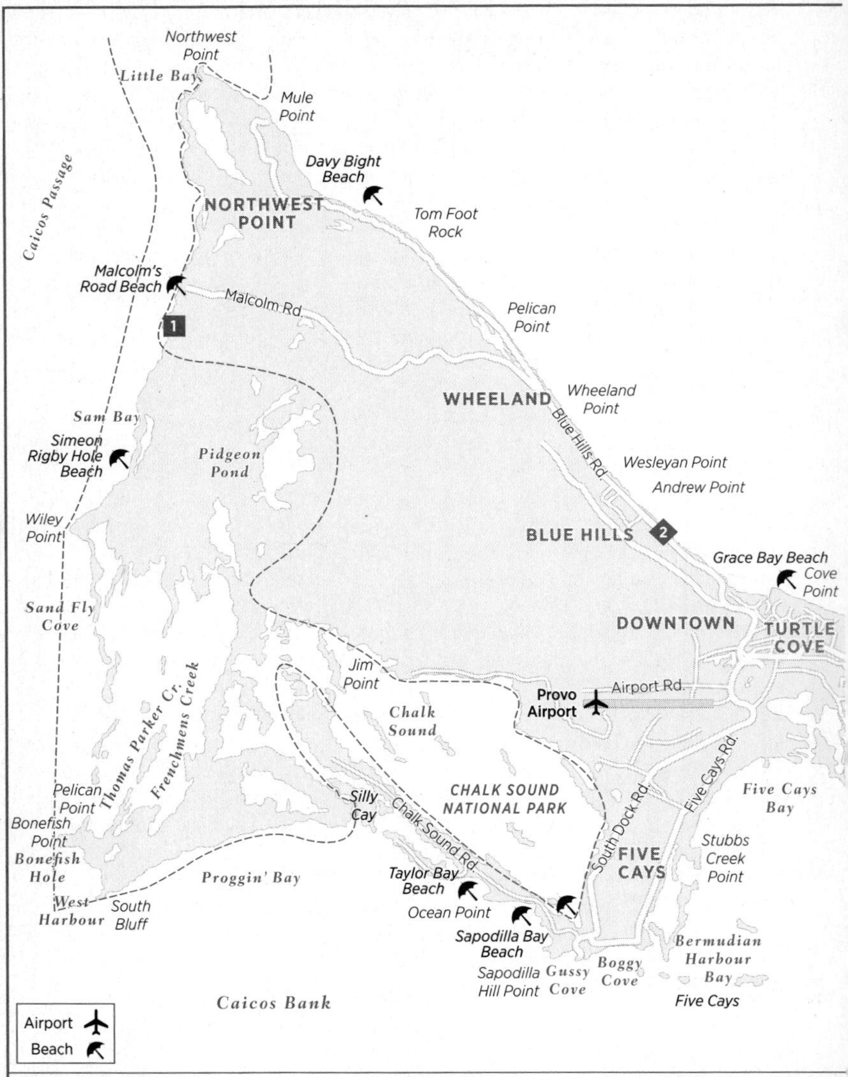

Northwest Point
Little Bay
Mule Point
Davy Bight Beach
Caicos Passage
NORTHWEST POINT
Tom Foot Rock
Malcolm's Road Beach
Malcolm Rd.
1
Pelican Point
WHEELAND
Wheeland Point
Blue Hills Rd.
Sam Bay
Simeon Rigby Hole Beach
Pidgeon Pond
Wesleyan Point
Andrew Point
Wiley Point
BLUE HILLS
2
Grace Bay Beach
Cove Point
Sand Fly Cove
DOWNTOWN
TURTLE COVE
Jim Point
Airport Rd.
Provo Airport
Chalk Sound
Thomas Parker Cr.
Frenchmens Creek
Pelican Point
CHALK SOUND NATIONAL PARK
Silly Cay
Chalk Sound Rd.
South Dock Rd.
Five Cays Rd.
Five Cays Bay
Bonefish Point
Bonefish Hole
FIVE CAYS
Stubbs Creek Point
Proggin' Bay
Taylor Bay Beach
West Harbour
South Bluff
Ocean Point
Sapodilla Bay Beach
Bermudian Harbour Bay
Sapodilla Hill Point
Gussy Cove
Boggy Cove
Five Cays
Caicos Bank

Airport
Beach

ACCOMMODATIONS ■

Amanyara **1**
Beaches Turks & Caicos Resort & Spa **5**
Caribbean Paradise Inn **14**
Club Med Turkoise **17**
The Gansevoort Turks + Caicos **3**
Grace Bay Club **15**
Parrot Cay **18**
Point Grace **11**
The Regent Grand **12**
The Regent Palms **7**
Royal West Indies Resort **16**
The Sands at Grace Bay **10**
Sibonné Beach Hotel **9**
The Somerset **8**
The Veranda **6**
The West Bay Club **4**

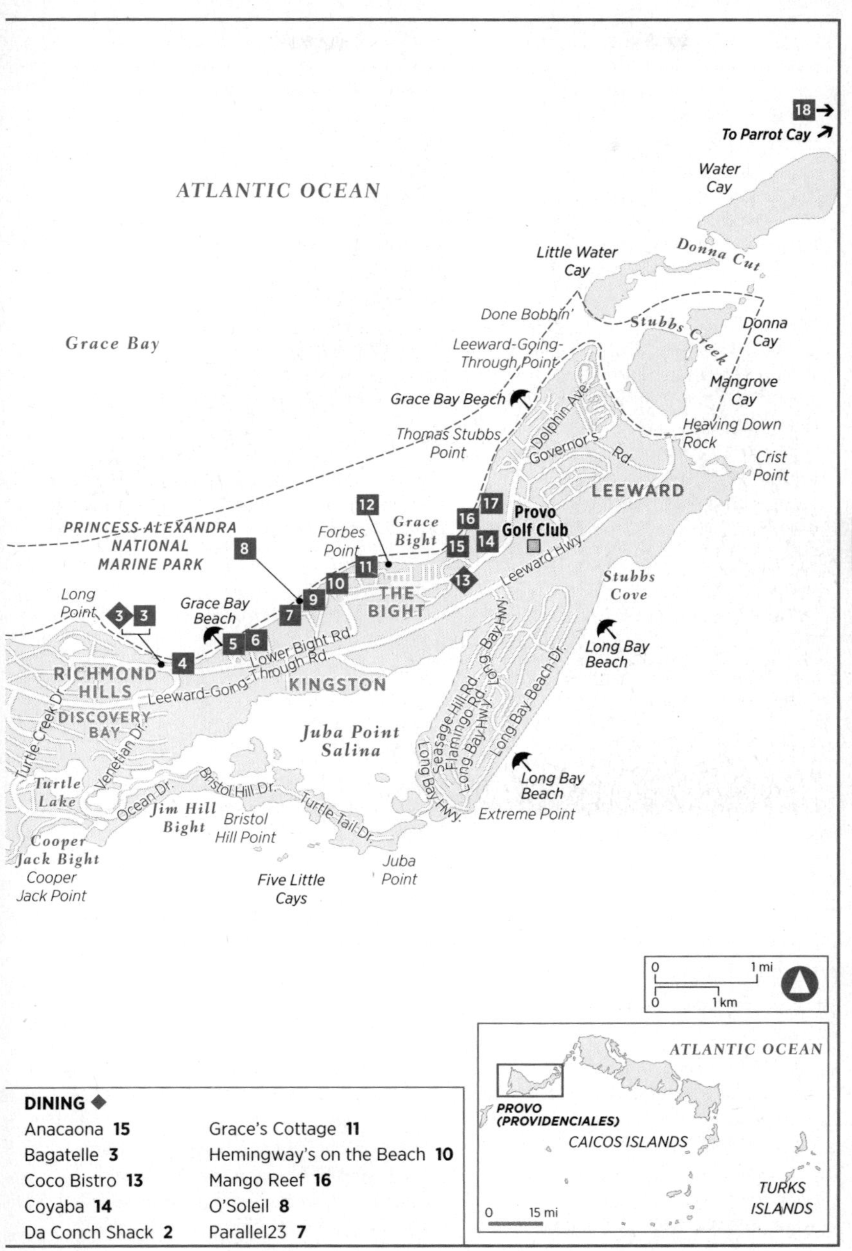
ATLANTIC OCEAN
18 →
To Parrot Cay
Water Cay
Donna Cut
Little Water Cay
Done Bobbin'
Stubbs Creek
Donna Cay
Grace Bay
Leeward-Going-Through Point
Mangrove Cay
Grace Bay Beach
Heaving Down Rock
Thomas Stubbs Point
Dolphin Ave.
Governor's Rd.
Crist Point
LEEWARD
12
17
16
Provo Golf Club
PRINCESS ALEXANDRA NATIONAL MARINE PARK
Forbes Point
Grace Bight
15
14
8
11
Leeward Hwy.
13
Stubbs Cove
10
Long Point
THE BIGHT
9
Grace Bay Beach
3
3
7
Long Bay Beach
5
6
Lower Bight Rd.
4
Leeward-Going-Through Rd.
RICHMOND HILLS
KINGSTON
Turtle Creek Dr.
DISCOVERY BAY
Venetian Dr.
Juba Point Salina
Long Bay Hwy.
Seasage Hill Rd.
Flamingo Rd.
Long Bay Beach Dr.
Turtle Lake
Bristol Hill Dr.
Long Bay Beach
Ocean Dr.
Jim Hill Bight
Bristol Hill Point
Turtle Tail Dr.
Extreme Point
Cooper Jack Bight
Cooper Jack Point
Five Little Cays
Juba Point
0 1 mi
0 1 km
ATLANTIC OCEAN
PROVO (PROVIDENCIALES)
CAICOS ISLANDS
TURKS ISLANDS
0 15 mi
DINING ◆
Anacaona 15
Bagatelle 3
Coco Bistro 13
Coyaba 14
Da Conch Shack 2
Grace's Cottage 11
Hemingway's on the Beach 10
Mango Reef 16
O'Soleil 8
Parallel23 7

Finding Sundries on Grace Bay

Forgotten an essential toiletry, crave a snack or a soft drink, or need sunscreen or bug repellent? The Grace Bay area can be a tough place to locate such little conveniences—vending machines are virtually nonexistent, and convenience stores and groceries are few and far between. (And resorts often charge inflated prices for snacks and little extras.) Cause for celebration is the opening of a full-service grocery store right on Grace Bay Road. The **Graceway Gourmet** (✆ 649/333-5000), across the street from the Seven Stars Resort in central Grace Bay (at Dolphin Ave.), is impressively stocked and more conveniently located than its (larger) sister grocery store, the **Graceway IGA,** on Leeward Highway (reachable by car or taxi). The Graceway Gourmet has basic supplies, fresh produce, meats and seafood, a salad bar, a deli, a coffee bar, even Wi-Fi; it's open 7 days a week from 7am to 9pm. It also has a Saturday farmer's market selling fresh produce from North Caicos! A few other well-placed convenience stores within walking distance of most resorts in and around Grace Bay supply the essentials and more—including brand-name snacks and candy bars; beer, wine, and liquor; magazines; and even local crafts. The following are open daily from around 9am to 6pm:

- **The Sand Dollar** at the Sands on Grace Bay
- **Sand Castle Convenience Store** at Ocean Club East
- **Neptune's Nectar** in back of Ports of Call shopping village

In April 2010, **Turks & Caicos Island Hospital,** the nation's first modern hospital, opened its two centers: the **Cheshire Hall Medical Centre** (on Providenciales) and the **Cockburn Town Medical Center** (on Grand Turk). **Grace Bay Medical Centre** is an urgent-care medical facility in Providenciales at Neptune Plaza, Allegro Road (✆ **649/941-5252,** or 649/231-0525 for emergencies).Call ✆ **911** or **999** for an emergency, or ✆ **649/946-4259** if you need the **police.**

The **Provo Post Office and Philatelic Bureau** is located at the corner of Airport Road in downtown Providenciales. It's open Monday to Thursday from 8am to 4pm and Friday from 8am to 3:30pm.

Where to Stay

Provo's 19km (12-mile) Grace Bay is where the majority of the islands' resorts and hotels are situated. Keep in mind that many resorts have minimum-stay requirements in the high season and during the Christmas holidays.

VERY EXPENSIVE

Amanyara ★★★ The first Amanresorts property in the West Indies was such a big deal when it opened in early 2006 that *Travel + Leisure* magazine devoted an entire cover article to it. This is unfussy luxury, with Amanresorts' trademark purity of form, integrity of materials, and obeisance to eco-principles. The prices are heart-stopping, but no detail has been left to chance. Classically aligned wooden buildings appear to float on the surrounding reflecting pools. The bar has a teepee-style ceiling that soars toward the sunlight. The infinity pool, of speckled black Indonesian lava, is rimmed by linen-wrapped sofa beds.

The 40 individual pavilions are stand-alone houses, utterly private; a few have ocean views. Wraparound patios are enveloped in native scrub brush, sea grape, and sea ox-eye daisies. It's very earthbound, if not for the exceptional gadgets: Flip open your laptop and go online, groove to the surround-sound Bose system, or switch on the flatscreen TV as you soak in the freestanding bathtub.

The restaurant serves a menu with Asian-Mediterranean influences either inside or on a candlelit patio; the Beach Club serves lunch and afternoon meals. The smiling resort staff love children; management is happy to provide not only cribs and nannies, but Diaper Champs, toddler stools, and training potties—the kitchen even makes homemade baby food! But in my experience, most of the time, crying babies and unruly toddlers do not a happy Amanyara clientele make—and who can blame them? Guests come here for stress-free R&R and deeply pampered serenity.

All that peace and quiet is tied to location as well: The resort lies on the island's northwest shore, a fairly isolated spot reached by traveling a winding two-lane road some 25 minutes from the airport. If you're keen on exploring the island, know that you're a good 30- to 40-minute drive from the action in Provo.

Note that the resort has three privately owned three-, four-, and five-bedroom villas. Each villa is centered around its own infinity pool and has a personal cook and housekeeper (winter $5,600–$13,950; off season $4,300–$11,700).

Northwest Point, Providenciales, Turks and Caicos, B.W.I. www.amanyara.com. ✆ **866/941-8133** or 649/941-8133. Fax 649/941-8132. 40 private pavilions. Winter $1,550–$2,150; off season $1,200–$1,800. Ask about Christmas holiday rates. Children 12 and under stay free in parent's pavilion. AE, MC, V. **Amenities:** 2 restaurants; bar/lounge; afternoon tea; babysitting; fitness center; outdoor pool; Serenity Villa (spa, beauty services, and yoga classes); screening room; 2 clay tennis courts; watersports equipment. *In room:* A/C, TV, DVD/CD player, hair dryer, minibar/fridge, Wi-Fi (free).

Grace Bay Club ★★★ ☺ This luxury boutique resort sets the bar for exemplary service in the TCI. Opened in 1993, it's one of the island's oldest hotels, but constant refreshment by one of the finest management teams in the Caribbean underscores its commitment to excellence. You'll get plenty of pampering for your money—and a whopping repeat business proves they're doing things right. It doesn't hurt that the resort sits on the largest oceanfront acreage on Grace Bay (4.5 hectares/11 acres).

The hotel has accomplished the neat trick of creating three hotels in one (all with fabulous Grace Bay views): 1) the romantic 21-suite hotel with its own pool and bar and restaurant (Anacaona); 2) four low-density villas containing 38 upscale, family-friendly condos, positioned directly on the beach with their own pool and restaurant (Grill Rouge); and 3) the newest addition, the Estate at Grace Bay Club, 22 custom-designed ultraluxe oceanfront residences fronting a lap pool and a poolside bar/restaurant. The Estate's 7,000-square-foot penthouse is utterly stunning, with four oceanfront bedrooms, a media room, and terraces for sublime views all around.

The Grace Bay Club personifies easy elegance, with a sun-burnished Mediterranean look and feel. Each of the villa accommodations has travertine-tile floors, custom-made imported furnishings, deep private patios, and oceanfront views. Each suite (except junior suites) and penthouse has its own state-of-the-art kitchen (granite countertops, stainless steel appliances), washing machine, and dryer. The four 446-sq.-m (4,779-sq.-ft.) penthouses have outdoor Jacuzzis, among other luxuries. Spa specialists offer Euro-Asian treatments at the 465-sq.-m (5,005-sq.-ft.) **Spa Anani** (open 9am–6pm).

The hotel's main restaurant, **Anacaona**, is one of Provo's top restaurants—but no kids 12 and under, please. Families can dine in the adjacent **Grill Rouge,** which offers casual alfresco dining with grilled seafood, panini, salads, and a kids' menu. The beachfront **Lounge,** with its Hamptons-style white-cushion seating and glowing fire pit, is one of the best spots on the island to have a cocktail and watch the sunset on Grace Bay; it now serves a tapas menu. But for sheer heat, check out the sexy **Infinity Bar,** which boasts the longest bar in the Caribbean, a sleek ribbon of black stone set with twinkling blue lights.

The children's program, **Kid's Town** (for kids 5–12), offers a full menu of half- or full-day excursions, including snorkeling, sailing, eco-activities, and kayaking; a dinnertime "campout" on the beach may include hot dogs and s'mores by a campfire.

1 Grace Bay Circle Rd. (P.O. Box 128), Providenciales, Turks and Caicos, B.W.I. www.gracebayclub.com. ✆ **800/946-5757** in the U.S., or 649/946-5050. Fax 649/946-5758. 59 units. Hotel: Winter $1,150 junior suite, $1,250–$1,750 1-bedroom suite, $2,100–$2,600 2-bedroom suite; off season $650–$850 junior suite, $750–$1,300 1-bedroom suite, $1,250–$1,950 2-bedroom suite. Villas: Winter $950 junior suite, $1,750 1-bedroom suite, $2,100–$2,600 2-bedroom suite, $3,330 3-bedroom suite, $6,050–$8,500 penthouse; off season $550–$700 junior suite, $1,050–$1,300 1-bedroom suite, $1,250–$1,950 2-bedroom suite, $1,950–$2,450 3-bedroom suite, $3,600–$6,550 penthouse. Estate: Winter $1,300–$10,000; off season $800–$7,500. Ask about Christmas holiday rates. Extra person $150–$180. Rates include full breakfast. AE, DC, DISC, MC, V. Closed Sept. **Amenities:** 2 restaurants; 3 bars; bikes; fitness center; Jacuzzi; 2 outdoor pools; room service; spa; 2 tennis courts (lit); watersports equipment (extensive). *In room:* A/C, ceiling fan, TV/DVD/CD player, hair dryer, kitchen (excluding junior suites), washer/dryer (excluding junior suites), Wi-Fi (free).

Parrot Cay ★★★ This luxury resort is a favored retreat of celebrities, but you don't have to be a movie star to enjoy Parrot Cay's warm embrace and high service standards—standards that are impeccably maintained. Parrot Cay defines excellence. The resort lies on an isolated and private 400-hectare (988-acre) island—reputedly a former pirate's lair—with a powdery white-sand beach. The compound features 10 white colonial-style buildings, each with a terra-cotta tile roof. Rooms have louvered doors that open onto terraces or verandas, oyster-white walls with tongue-and-groove paneling, and mosquito netting over four-poster beds. The spacious tiled bathrooms are beautifully appointed with a big tub and a shower, and the spa's Invigorate toiletries. The best units are the roomy, handsome beach houses and villas, which offer utter privacy and direct access to the beach, not to mention plunge pools and hardwood verandas. Beach villas (one to three bedrooms) are even roomier, with swimming pools and kitchenettes.

Many come to Parrot Cay for the sublime treatments in the COMO Shambhala holistic spa, the finest spa in the Caribbean, a wood pavilion wrapped in a sea of glass that looks out over the marsh wetlands. In addition, the resort has an infinity pool and access to scuba diving, Hobie Cats, snorkeling, kayaks, and water-skiing. Kids' activities are available as well.

The Terrace restaurant, in the resort's main building, serves breakfast and dinner, specializing in Mediterranean cuisine. Lunch and dinner are served in Lotus, a romantic torch-lit poolside restaurant with Southeast Asian–inspired cuisine (along with regular-Joe lunch favorites like hamburgers); both restaurants offer a healthful Shambhala spa menu. The bountiful breakfasts at the Terrace were among the best we had in Provo.

Parrot Cay (P.O. Box 164), Providenciales, Turks and Caicos, B.W.I. www.parrotcay.com or http://parrotcay.como.bz. ✆ **866/388-0036** in the U.S., or 904/288-0036. Fax 904/288-6125. 60 units. Winter $940–$1,180 double, $1,995 1-bedroom suite, $3,510 1-bedroom beach house, $4,235–$7,565 beach villa; off season $695–$1,030 double, $1,210–$1,635 1-bedroom suite, $2,480–$2,785 1-bedroom beach house, $3,145–$5,810 beach villa. Ask about Christmas holiday rates. Extra person 13 and over $210. Rates include full American breakfast and return airport transfers by car and hotel boat (commercially scheduled flights only). AE, MC, V. Reached by a 30-min. private boat ride north from Provo, leaving from Leeward Marina. **Amenities:** 2 restaurants; 2 bars; babysitting; fitness center; Jacuzzi;

nature trail; outdoor pool; room service; sauna; spa; 2 tennis courts; watersports equipment (extensive). *In room:* A/C, ceiling fan, TV/DVD, radio/CD player, hair dryer, kitchenette (in some), minibar, Wi-Fi (free).

The Regent Palms ★★★ Opened in early 2005, the Palms is one of Grace Bay's classiest lodgings, with some of the most handsomely appointed rooms on the island. But don't let its cool good looks intimidate you. Yes, the neo-Palladian centerpiece of the resort is referred to as "the Mansion"—but beneath that elegant facade is a congenial Turks and Caicos ambience and a level of service that few resorts on the island can match. It also has one of the Caribbean's top spas in the gorgeous 2,323-sq.-m (25,005-sq.-ft.) Regent Spa; many of its 17 treatment rooms are in white-tented cabanas classically arranged around an outdoor reflecting pool.

The resort has two main gathering spots: the infinity pool and Plunge, the pool bar and lunch restaurant. Plunge has a sunken dining terrace and a swim-up bar—as you lie around the serpentine pool, you can check your e-mail and drink a toast to another tough day at the beach. The Mansion (fashioned after the theatrical Caribbean estates designed by Oliver Messel, the late British stage designer who also created Princess Margaret's "cottage" in Mustique) has a different feel entirely—more like a Tuscan villa overlooking a moonlit summer garden. The Mansion houses a clubby wood-paneled bar and the resort's main restaurant, **Parallel23,** which serves tropical-fusion cuisine from an open kitchen; the restaurant's half-moon terrace fronts **Palm Place,** with shops on either side of a palm-lined courtyard.

Grace Bay Rd. (P.O. Box 681), Providenciales, Turks and Caicos, B.W.I. www.regentturksandcaicos.com or www.regenthotels.com/hotels/tcturks. ✆ **866/877-7256,** 649/946-8666 or 305/532-7900 (Christmas holiday reservations only). Fax 649/946-5502. 72 units. Winter $650–$675 double, $850–$1,400 1-bedroom suite, $1,675–$2,075 2-bedroom suite, $2,750 3-bedroom suite, $1,725–$3,075 penthouse; off season $400–$475 double, $700–$825 1-bedroom suite, $1,150–$1,275 2-bedroom suite, $1,600–$1,725 3-bedroom suite, $1,425–$2,325 penthouse. Inquire about Christmas holiday rates. Children 11 and under stay free in parent's room. Rates include continental buffet breakfast. AE, MC, V. **Amenities:** 2 restaurants; 2 bars; babysitting/nanny service; Conch Kritters Club; croquet pitch; fitness center (personal trainers available on request); yoga, Pilates, and meditation studio; Jacuzzi; infinity pool; room service; sauna; spa; Plexipave tennis courts; watersports equipment (extensive). *In room:* A/C, ceiling fan, TV (flat-panel LCD TVs in penthouses), hair dryer, full kitchens w/Viking appliances (in suites and penthouses), MP3 docking station, minibar, Wi-Fi (free).

The Somerset ★★★ ☺ Is it just us, or is minimalist chic a bit of a tired beach-resort cliché these days? Maybe that's why the Somerset stands out, its colorful Italianate style in striking contrast to all that cool monochrome. This 5-year-old resort looks and feels like an old-timer, in the best sense. The monumental neo-Tuscan architecture gives the place a solid feel, anchored by sweeping stone staircases and spraying fountains. Suites have solid-wood French doors and are furnished in a rich palette. If all this sounds prohibitively snooty, trust us: This is one of the friendliest, most relaxing spots on the island—it hums along with maximum efficiency and minimum drama. The Somerset is smaller and quieter than its neighbor, the Regent Palms (see above), and when the sun goes down, the pool is magically lit and palms sway in the night breeze. It's the very essence of serene tropical comfort.

The spacious rooms and suites are available in three accommodations categories: Estate, Stirling House, and Garden Cottage. The four blocks of oceanview Estate suites comprise four full-floor suites per block (except the penthouse, which has two floors); each suite has a Viking grill and hot tub on its balcony. The Stirling House is composed of 24 units, including both standard doubles (garden views) and suites (ocean views), and the 13 Garden Cottage units are duplexes with basement garages and garden views. Every suite has Viking equipment and appliances in the fully equipped kitchens, DVD/CD surround-sound music system (even on the balconies), travertine marble floors, and personal wine coolers. Each of the three penthouses has roof terraces with hot tubs and 360-degree views. The resident restaurant, **O'Soleil,** has terrific food and service (see "Dining," below), but the elegant white-on-white interior feels a little too frosty; we prefer to dine alfresco on one of the restaurant's two handsome terraces. The lap pool stretches to the sea, with reverse currents (and underwater audio). An infinity pool near the edge of the dunes is a magnet for kids—and the poolside grill is a great meeting-spot for families.

Grace Bay, Providenciales, Turks and Caicos, B.W.I. www.thesomerset.com. ✆ **877/887-5722** or 649/946-5900. 54 units. Winter $1,700–$4,000 Estate Villas, $500–$2,100 Stirling House suites and rooms, $350–$1,650 Garden Cottage suites; summer $830–$3,000 Estate Villas, $275–$2,400 Stirling House suites and rooms, $500–$1,100 Garden Cottage suites. Rates include continental breakfast. Children 11 and under (maximum of 2) stay free in parent's room. Extra person $100. AE, DISC, MC, V. **Amenities:** 2 restaurants; pool bar; babysitting/nanny service; concierge; croquet pitch; infinity pool; room service; watersports equipment. *In room:* Zoned A/C, TV, semiprivate elevators, hair dryer, private outdoor Jacuzzi (Estate suites), full kitchen w/Viking appliances (in suites), MP3 docking station, Wi-Fi (free).

The Veranda ★★ ☺ This sprawling all-inclusive opened in February 2010 and already feels like a classic. It's divided into two main zones, the family-friendly West Village and the adult-oriented East Village. The center of the resort is occupied by the Veranda House, an uninspired multilevel structure encircling a courtyard. Opt instead for a stay in one of the two- or three-story cottages. The pastel-hued clapboard houses trimmed in gingerbread make the Veranda look more like a neighborhood in Key West or Nantucket than a posh resort. Rockers on wooden porches and picket fences entwined with bougainvillea complete the picture. All of which is to say: There's nothing like it on Grace Bay. But step inside your room, and it's resort elegance all the way, in a plumped-up, English-cottage vein. Look for beamed and wainscoted ceilings, plump bedding, and tastefully upholstered reproduction furnishings. (Note that most bathrooms have showers, not tubs.) The eight stand-alone beachfront houses are da bomb: Wrapped in flower-bedecked white picket fencing, each cottage has some 371.5 sq. m (4,000 sq. ft.) of handsomely appointed living space and its own "front yard" with a plunge pool. The Veranda covers quite a bit of territory, but intimate zones set around landscaped green lawns make it feel more like a small town. The main restaurant, the Marin, faces the beach—this is the beating heart of the Veranda, with firepits aglow at night, a bar illuminated in sultry blue lights, and a second-story Sky Lounge where you can star-gaze while you sip.

Grace Bay, Providenciales, Turks and Caicos, B.W.I. **www.theverandatci.com.** ✆ **800/946-5757** in the U.S., or 649/339-5050. Fax 649/946-5758. 169 units. Call about winter rates; off season $460 double, $635 1-bedroom suite, $885 2-bedroom suite, $1,060 3-bedroom suite. Rates are all-inclusive. AE, DISC, MC, V. **Amenities:** 2 restaurants; 2 bars; coffee/pastry shop; babysitting; bikes; kids' program, playroom, and sandbox; concierge; fitness center; 3 pools; spa; watersports equipment (extensive); Wii game room. *In room:* A/C, TV, hair dryer, full kitchen (except studios), Playstation, washer/dryer (except studios), Wi-Fi (free).

EXPENSIVE

Beaches Turks & Caicos Resort & Spa ★ ☺ This Grace Bay megaresort remains a perennial favorite among families. And with a whopping 620 units, it's remarkable that it all chugs along as smoothly as it does. The grounds are beautifully maintained, kids look deliriously happy, and weddings are held on-site on an almost daily basis. It's a winning formula: Rooms are nearly impossible to come by in high season without reservations made long in advance.

This resort is part of the Sandals chain of all-inclusive hotels, though unlike at most Sandals, families with kids are welcome here—and welcome with a bang. Actors dressed as characters from *Sesame Street*—Elmo and his friends—are on hand to thrill the little ones as part of "The Caribbean Adventure with Sesame Street" activities for kids 5 and under. The Kids Camp has daylong activities for children 6 to 12. Older kids can lose themselves in free, unlimited play at the Xbox 360 Game Garage interactive gaming center. Tweens and teens can groove to DJ-spun sounds (and vie for one of the four VIP cabanas) at Club Liquid.

The all-inclusive designation means you get a lot for your money: all meals and drinks; excellent watersports; winning service from a staff of nearly 800 employees; a full-service nursery with cribs, swings, rockers, and a coterie of nannies; and even a spa, the Red Lane (daily 8am–8pm). Gratuities are included for everything, so you don't have to worry about doling out tips all day. Note, however, that you'll pay extra for many spa treatments, certain scuba-diving courses and excursions, and international telephone calls.

Accommodations come in 12 different categories and a variety of configurations. All rooms and suites have king-size beds. The higher-category suites have four-poster beds, a "Premium Bar" and a fully stocked refrigerator based on your personal requests, and 8am-to-8pm concierge service. The luxury suites offer 24-hour butler service, with professionally trained butlers catering to your every whim. The largest unit, the French Village three-bedroom suite, can accommodate up to 11 people. The resort's newest section is the all-suites Italian Village, featuring a 1,115-sq.-m (12,002-sq.-ft.) pool with a giant water park (with wave pool) and 168 spanking-new family suites.

Food is available somewhere on the premises 24 hours a day, but room service is offered only in the butler-service suites. In general, the food is plentiful, if not particularly inspired. Among the 16 restaurants, you can get Italian (Giuseppe), Tex-Mex (Arizona's), seafood (Schooners), or Asian (Kimonos). For the kids, the very cool Bobby D's is a 1950s-style diner with burgers, hot dogs, and spaghetti.

Lower Bight Rd. (P.O. Box 186), Providenciales, Turks and Caicos, B.W.I. www.beaches.com. ✆ **888/232-2437** in the U.S., or 649/946-8000. Fax 649/946-8001. 620 units. Winter $420–$510 double, $640 1-bedroom suite, $1,200 2-bedroom suite for 4, $1,680 3-bedroom family suite; off season $385–$440 double, $575–$675 1-bedroom suite, $1,090 2-bedroom suite for 4, $1,525 3-bedroom family suite. Prices based on 2 nights (minimum stay). Rates are all-inclusive. AE, DISC, MC, V. **Amenities:** 10 restaurants; 7 bars; babysitting; children's center w/pool; fitness center; basketball; volleyball; Internet cafe; nurses' station; 8 outdoor pools; 2 saunas; spa; 4 tennis courts (lit); watersports equipment (extensive). *In room:* A/C, ceiling fan, TV, CD players, fridge, hair dryer, in-room bars (in concierge rooms), Wi-Fi (free).

Club Med Turkoise ★ Set on 28 hectares (69 acres) of sun-blasted scrubland on a white strip of beachfront overlooking Grace Bay, this adults-only all-inclusive resort was one of the pioneers of Grace Bay when it opened in 1984. To be honest, the oldest resort on the island is showing its age. The landscaping is negligible, the food serviceable at best, and from the outside, the accommodations look more like a church camp than a beach resort. Miked music kicks in around sunset, and it's certainly noisier and more hyperactive than anything else on Grace Bay. But who cares? Even in the low season, the resort is packed with happy campers, filled to capacity when other resorts are half-full. Its appeal lies in its mix of nonstop activity and communal fun. Singles and couples come here to play in the sun—and this sprawling beachside campus has plenty of toys, including a flying trapeze.

The village-style cluster of basic two- and three-story accommodations contains comfortable, colorful rooms with twin or king-size beds, all designed with beachfront living in mind. The "all-inclusive" designation means that meals are included, as well as most drinks—except the really good stuff, like champagne, certain premium liquors and wines, and canned and bottled drinks (be sure to check the fine print before you book). Among the three restaurants, Grace Bay serves breakfast, lunch, and dinner buffet style, and Lucayan offers a la carte meals and is open in the evening only (7:15–8:45pm; reservations required). Most meals are served at long, communal tables.

Grace Bay, Providenciales, Turks and Caicos, B.W.I. www.clubmed.us. ✆ **800/258-2633** in the U.S., or 649/946-5500. Fax 649/946-5497. 290 units. Winter $1,545–$1,722 per person weekly; off season $1,300–$1,600 per person weekly. Rates are all-inclusive. AE, MC, V. Children 17 and under not allowed. **Amenities:** 3 restaurants; 2 bars; open-air nightclub; gym; basketball; flying trapeze; softball; trampoline; volleyball; outdoor pool; 8 tennis courts (4 lit); watersports equipment (extensive); wellness center w/spa treatment rooms; Wi-Fi (free). *In room:* A/C, flatscreen TV, clock radio/CD player, hair dryer, minifridge.

The Gansevoort Turks + Caicos ★★★ The Gansevoort brand projects effortless chic. The resorts have an ingrained urbanity—no wonder, since the line's flagship hotel is the Gansevoort in Manhattan's Meatpacking District. Trendiness aside, these are superbly run hotels that dispense a healthy sense of hospitality. The Gansevoort Turks + Caicos has the hipness quotient down, but it also has a killer Grace Bay setting, to which every one of the 91 rooms daily genuflects. The sun-blasted pool is a marvel in beachside feng shui; it's the nerve center of the resort, dotted with personal "floating islands." Rooms are smartly outfitted, with electric blackout blinds, LCD TVs, and cutting-edge kitchens loaded with Liebherr, Gaggenau, and Bosch appliances; play "find the fridge" (it's camouflaged in the cabinetry). Bathrooms have glass-encased rain showers. And can we say that the big, deep tubs filled from a spigot high in the ceiling make us very happy? The "wow" factor hits the roof (literally) with four 344-sq.-m (3,700-sq.-ft.) three-bedroom penthouses—wraparound terraces, designer kitchens, personal concierge, a veritable VIP buffet. The Bagatelle Bistrot brings a sure, sophisticated touch to the island dining scene. But the breezy vibe is all Provo—especially at night, when the palms rustle in the trade winds and warm candlelight softens any urban edges.

Grace Bay, Providenciales, Turks and Caicos, B.W.I. www.gansevoortturksandcaicos.com. ✆ **888/844-5986** in the U.S., or 649/941-7555. Fax 309/210-9091. 91 units. Winter $575–$750 double, $950–$5,000 suite; off season $350–$600 double, $600–$5,000 suite. Rates include continental breakfast. Children 11 and under stay free in parent's room. Extra person $100. AE, MC, V. **Amenities:** Restaurants; 2 bars; babysitting; children's program; concierge; fitness center; outdoor pool; room service; spa; watersports equipment (extensive). *In room:* A/C, ceiling fan, TV/DVD, CD player, hair dryer, kitchen (suites), kitchenettes (studios), MP3 docking station, washer/dryer (suites), Wi-Fi (free).

Point Grace ★★★ This boutique hotel opened in 2000 on a lyrical crescent of Grace Bay beachfront. In a little over 10 years, Point Grace has perfected an almost effortless graciousness and racked up one award after another. The motif is British colonial, and resort services and amenities are first-rate, ranging from twice-daily maid service to midday sorbets on the beach. Don't expect the joint to be jumping: Even at its liveliest, generally during cocktail hour around the pool bar, this is a haven of quiet serenity. (Some say *too* quiet.) The Thalasso Spa at Point Grace (daily 9am–6pm) is a full-service on-site spa that offers spa treatments using sea mud and seaweed, among other delicacies, in whitewashed cottages open to the sea breezes—easily some of the best massages on the island.

The complex features spacious one-, two-, three-, and four-bedroom suites and penthouses, furnished with Indonesian teak, and brightened by crisp white Frette linens; many are decorated with 200-year-old wall hangings from India. Hand-painted tile and mahogany grace the rooms, and each suite has a beautifully appointed kitchen and a washer/dryer.

Tucked away in a candlelit garden is **Grace's Cottage** (p. 672), perhaps the most romantic spot to dine on an island filled with romantic restaurants.

Grace Bay (P.O. Box 700), Providenciales, Turks and Caicos, B.W.I. www.pointgrace.com. ✆ **866/924-7223** in the U.S., or 649/946-5096. Fax 649/946-5097. 28 units. Winter $625–$675 cottage suite, $1,197 oceanfront suite, $1,520–$1,790 Atlantic suite, $2,050 Cotton Cay suite, $2,870 Big Cameron Cay suite; off season $475–$525 cottage suite, $695–$915 oceanfront suite, $835–$1,365 Atlantic suite, $1,260–$1,560 Cotton Cay suite, $1,765–$2,185 Big Cameron Cay suite. Ask about Christmas holiday rates. Rates include continental buffet breakfast; complimentary house cocktails and hors d'oeuvres at the pool bar 5–6pm; and airport transfers. AE, DISC, MC, V. **Amenities:** 2 restaurants; 2 bars; babysitting; bikes; concierge; Internet (free); outdoor pool; room service; oceanfront spa; watersports equipment. *In room:* A/C, TV, CD/DVD player, hair dryer, Internet (free), kitchen, minibar, washer/dryer.

The Regent Grand ★ Occupying a central spot along oceanfront Grace Bay, this all-suites resort is an impressive property of classical design, with a breathtaking centerpiece of a pool (the biggest in the TCI), a tennis court, and a shopping-and-restaurant complex next door in Regent Village. The suites are large and comfortably furnished and have everything you need—including fully equipped kitchens—even if layouts are a little uninspired. That's okay; you'll have every amenity under the sun and a swell piece of beachfront to play on.

Grace Bay Rd. (P.O. Box 124), Providenciales, Turks and Caicos, B.W.I. www.theregentgrandresort.com. ✆ **877/537-3314** or 649/941-7770. Fax 649/941-7771. 54 units. Winter $489 double, $795–$1,360 1-bedroom suite, $1,060–$1,885 2-bedroom suite, $2,185–$2,875 3-bedroom suite; off season $3,455 double, $655–$1,050 1-bedroom suite, $760–$1,540 2-bedroom suite, $1,840–$2,300 3-bedroom suite, $1,425–$2,325 penthouse. Inquire about Christmas holiday rates. Extra person $50 ($80 holidays). Children 11 and under stay free in parent's room. Rates include continental breakfast delivered to the suite and airport transfers. AE, MC, V. **Amenities:** 2 restaurants; 2 bars; babysitting; bikes; fitness center; pool; room service; spa; two tennis courts (lit); watersports equipment (extensive). *In room:* A/C, ceiling fan, TV/DVD, hair dryer, full kitchens, Wi-Fi (free).

MODERATE

Royal West Indies Resort ★ ☺ This is one of the most reliable condo-hotel resorts on Grace Bay, offering family-friendly lodging and a enviable location on prime beachfront, right next door to Club Med. The property is pillowed in manicured gardens, the centerpiece of which is a large pool enveloped in tropical foliage. It's a pretty big place, with 99 units, but the spacious suites are situated in intimate groupings of low-rise buildings spread out over the property. Guests have a choice of oceanfront, oceanview, studio, or gardenview one- and two-bedroom suites. Suites have balconies or patios and good-size kitchenettes. The interiors have been nicely refurbished with comfortable, well-maintained furnishings and good linens. Even if you're not a guest, we strongly recommend a meal at Mango Reef (see "Dining," below), the casual poolside restaurant with consistently fresh, delicious food.

Grace Bay (P.O. Box 482), Providenciales, Turks and Caicos, B.W.I. www.royalwestindies.com. ✆ **800/332-4203** in the U.S., or 649/946-5004. Fax 649/946-5008. 99 units. Winter $285–$425 studio, $385–$625 1-bedroom suite, $525–$795 2-bedroom suite; off season $225–$345 studio, $275–$445 1-bedroom suite, $485–$545 2-bedroom suite. Extra person 13 or over $35 per night. Children 12 and under stay free in parent's room. AE, DISC, MC, V. **Amenities:** Restaurant; bar; babysitting; bikes; Jacuzzi; 2 outdoor pools; watersports equipment (extensive); Wi-Fi (free; in lobby and hot spot). *In room:* A/C, ceiling fan, TV, hair dryer, kitchen, washer/dryer.

The Sands at Grace Bay ★★ ☺ The Sands has always been a popular choice on Grace Bay, but a topnotch refurbishment—including the construction of an elegant freestanding lobby—has put it in another league altogether. This sprawling all-suites condo resort is set on a sweet stretch of Grace Bay Beach. Suites have been tastefully and luxuriously updated, with granite countertops, marble sinks, and fine linens. The landscaped gardens and pools are impeccably maintained—this is one well-managed property. Choose from studio, one-bedroom, two-bedroom, or three-bedroom suites—each of which is fully appointed, with screened terraces. The suites also have full kitchens (studios have kitchenettes) and washer/dryers—great for family stays. The Sands is the site of one of the island's most popular beachfront restaurants, Hemingway's (p. 673), and the Spa Tropique at the Sands.

Grace Bay (P.O. Box 681), Providenciales, Turks and Caicos, B.W.I. www.thesandstc.com. ✆ **877/777-2637** in the U.S., or 649/946-5199. Fax 649/941-3133. 116 units. Winter $285–$460 studio, $460–$710 1-bedroom suite, $560–$710 2-bedroom suite, $800–$1,200 3-bedroom suite; off season $185–$330 studio, $330–$530 1-bedroom suite, $430–$580 2-bedroom suite, $530–$830 3-bedroom suite. Children 11 and under stay free in parent's room (maximum of 2). AE, DISC, MC, V. **Amenities:** Restaurant; bar; supermarket shuttle ($8 per person round-trip); babysitting; bikes; dive shop; fitness center; Jacuzzi; 3 outdoor pools; spa services; tennis court; watersports equipment (extensive). *In room:* A/C, ceiling fan, TV, hair dryer, kitchen (in some), kitchenette (in studios), washer/dryer, Wi-Fi (free).

The West Bay Club ★★ For those who want top-notch accommodations in a prime location more than having a splashy destination restaurant, state-of-the-art spa, or sizzling lounge scene, the West Bay Club represents fantastic value on beachfront Grace Bay. Opened in 2009, this Lower Bight property has a decidedly more laidback feel than the Gansevoort, its neighbor to the west, but its rooms are plenty swell. The West Bay Club has some of the biggest suites on Grace Bay, sheathed in marble floors and outfitted with 46-inch flat-panel TVs, DVD/CD surround-sound theater systems, MP3 docks, full kitchens with stainless steel appliances and granite countertops, oceanfront terraces, and a surplus of closet space. Particularly good value are the multibedroom suites and the glamorous penthouses, the largest of which are 353 sq. m (3,800 sq. ft.), with Grace Bay views that go on forever. By design, the hotel amenities are quite modest—the pool is smallish, the simple restaurant has only nine tables (but the food is fresh and delicious), and the bar is just a smattering of stools. Here the emphasis is firmly on luxe rooms and a prime location along Grace Bay. It all purrs along with the expert guidance of the warm and unpretentious management, a husband-and-wife team offering Mom-and-Pop luxe.

Lower Bight Rd., Grace Bay, Providenciales, Turks and Caicos, B.W.I. www.thewestbayclub.com. ✆ **866/607-4156** in the U.S., or 649/946-8550. Fax 649/941-8695. 46 units. Winter $300 studio, $495–$520 1-bedroom suite, $595–$695 2-bedroom suite, $975 3-bedroom suite, $1,100–$1,265 penthouse; off season $235 studio, $400–$450 1-bedroom suite, $500–$595 2-bedroom suite, $690 3-bedroom suite, $795–$900 penthouse. Extra person $75 per night. Rates include European breakfast. AE, DISC, MC, V. **Amenities:** Restaurant; bar; babysitting; bikes; concierge; fitness center; pool; room service; spa; watersports equipment. *In room:* A/C, ceiling fan, TV, DVD/CD player, hair dryer, kitchen (except studios), MP3 docking station, washer/dryer (except studios), Wi-Fi (free).

INEXPENSIVE

Caribbean Paradise Inn This intimate, cozy inn is a real find, considering it's only a 2-minute walk from lovely Grace Bay Beach *and* the low rates include a breakfast buffet. It has also been a hub of activity since chef Paul Newman moved the popular restaurant **Coyaba** (see "Dining," below) to the adjoining bar/patio area; even though the restaurant is run independently from the inn, the lively dining scene gives the place a jolt of electricity. Two stories of rooms overlook the pool and a nice tropical courtyard. Rooms come with tile floors and a king or two full beds, with either a patio or balcony; the small bathrooms have showers only. Jean Luc Bohic is the personable owner.

Grace Bay (P.O. Box 673), Providenciales, Turks and Caicos, B.W.I. www.caribbean-paradise-inn.com. ✆ **877/946-5020** in the U.S., or 649/946-5020. Fax 649/946-5022. 17 units. Winter $147–$168 double; off season $118–$135 double. Extra person $35. Children 4 and under stay free in parent's room. Rates include buffet breakfast. MC, V. **Amenities:** Bar; babysitting; outdoor freshwater pool; watersports equipment. *In room:* A/C, ceiling fan, TV, fridge, hair dryer, minibar, Wi-Fi ($10/day).

Sibonné Beach Hotel ★ One of the first lodgings constructed on the fabulous sands of Grace Bay Beach, this hotel is a fantastic value, as long as you don't expect a big laundry list of amenities or the taciturn staff to shower you with love. What it does have is a comfortable, informal vibe; alluring courtyard gardens; and knockout Grace Bay views. It's considerably more charming and personable than any chain-style hotel, with rooms done up in a light, breezy decor. For a stupendous deal on Grace Bay, book the one-bedroom upstairs apartment, detached from the actual hotel. It has a full kitchen, with pots, pans, plates, the works; a separate living room; a big, comfortable bed; and two oceanfront patios, one screened, one open—you'll feel as if you have your own sunny beachfront cottage within spitting distance of the million-dollar sands of the Regent Palms (p. 665). On-site is the Bay Bistro, a casual beachside restaurant offering exceptional breakfast, lunch, and dinner fare; and Junior's Bar, where bartender extraordinaire Junior Brown presides. ***Note:*** Sibonné does not accept children 12 and under in the winter or holiday season.

Grace Bay (P.O. Box 144), Providenciales, Turks and Caicos, B.W.I. www.sibonne.com. ✆ **800/528-1905** in the U.S., or 649/946-5547. Fax 649/946-5770. 29 units. Winter $125–$235 double, $375 apt; off season $110–$205 double, $285 apt. Rates include continental breakfast. Extra person $45, children 11 and under $35. AE, MC, V. No children 12 and under in winter or holiday season. **Amenities:** Restaurant; bar; outdoor pool. *In room:* A/C, ceiling fan, TV, fridge, hair dryer, Wi-Fi (free).

Where to Dine

VERY EXPENSIVE

Anacaona ★★★ CARIBBEAN Set beneath thatched-roof *palapas* and the starry evening sky, this is one of the top dining options in Provo. Among its winning attributes is an unbeatable location directly facing the Grace Bay Beach. Next door are Grace Bay Club's (p. 663) two buzzing bars, the Lounge and the Infinity Bar, where you can enjoy a drink before dinner and watch the sun set. Tabletop candles and flickering lights from free-standing torches deepen the romance of the setting. The menu changes regularly, but you might start with the trio of conch (conch tacos, conch tempura, conch Creole) or the tuna tartare; main courses rely heavily on seafood, particularly fish—try the mahimahi in papillotte or seared filet of red snapper. No children 11 and under.

In the Grace Bay Club, 1 Grace Bay Circle Rd. ✆ **649/946-5050.** Reservations recommended. Main courses $28–$33. AE, MC, V. Daily 6:30–9pm.

Bagatelle ★★★ FRENCH/MEDITERRANEAN With nods to South Beach and downtown Manhattan, this urbane spot takes TCI dining to a whole new level, with serious food and a serious wine list served up in a monochromatic indoor/

outdoor space dotted with towering palm trees. The ambience is crisp and relaxed all at once, with a sizzling up-tempo soundtrack that heats up as the day progresses. But in the evening, when the sky is a canopy of stars and shadows dance in the breeze, you are very much aware that you are in Provo—and Provo at its most seductive. Start with the *crevettes à la Thai* (grilled black tiger prawns); a cracked conch seared with a Vietnamese red-pepper glaze; or the hearty West Indian vegetable curry. Meats are impeccably prepared, like the roasted pork porterhouse or the two-person *côte de boeuf* (beef rib steak). The chef is a wizard with fish; he'll even cook up your own catch with a little advance notice. Only a year old, this may be Provo's top destination restaurant.

In the Gansevoort Turks + Caicos, Lower Bight Rd. ✆ **649/946-5746.** www.gansevoorttc.com. Reservations recommended. Main courses $31–$43. AE, MC, V. Sun–Thurs 7am–10pm; Fri and Sat 7am–11pm.

Coco Bistro ★★★ MEDITERRANEAN/CARIBBEAN This perennial favorite is so hot in the high season, it famously turned away Bruce Willis and company (no reservation, alas). Coco Bistro is set in a former plant nursery that has since grown into the largest palm grove on the island. It's a magical spot: You dine outside under the palms, candles twinkling. The food is as memorable as the ambience. Among the tasty starters, try conch, garlic, and potato soup scented with saffron; grilled shrimp satay on sugar-cane skewers; or Peking duck egg rolls. For mains try the roast rack of Colorado lamb with a pomegranate molasses and macadamia-nut crust; soft-shell-crab tempura; or a zesty West Indian curry, brimming with chicken and shrimp.

Grace Bay Rd. ✆ **649/946-5369.** www.cocobistro.tc. Reservations recommended. Main courses $28–$39. DISC, MC, V. Tues–Sun 6–10:30pm.

Coyaba Restaurant ★★ CONTINENTAL/CARIBBEAN When this popular gourmet restaurant moved from its longtime spot in Coral Gardens in October 2007, it barely missed a beat—it remains one of the island's most popular dining destinations. Its location on the patio fronting the Caribbean Paradise Inn may not be as roomy as its previous locale, but that hasn't kept chef Paul Newman from flexing his inventive culinary chops. Newman prepares some of the island's freshest and best seafood; his West Indian dishes show a strong European influence. Start with coconut tempura shrimp in Barcelo-honey-rum sauce, or the conch and seafood chowder. For a main course, the fish dishes are exuberantly flavored and exquisitely cooked; the Coyaba-style lobster thermidor is formidable.

Next to the Caribbean Paradise Inn, Grace Bay. ✆ **649/946-5186.** www.coyabarestaurant.com. Reservations required. Main courses $32–$39. AE, MC, V. Wed–Mon 6–10pm.

Grace's Cottage ★★ CARIBBEAN/CONTINENTAL This buttery-yellow Victorian cottage with gingerbread trim and lacy latticework is pure enchantment. The restaurant seats only 62 people, but most every night it's filled with hand-holding couples soaking up the palpable romantic ambience. Inside you can enjoy an aperitif at the mahogany bar before dinner. Dine on the cottage terrace, or on one of the patios nestled in tropical vegetation amid softly illuminated lighting. After a sojourn serving a somewhat misguided menu of high-wire (and often goofy) culinary creations, Grace's Cottage has bounced back, with executive chef Vincent Poitevin preparing food that is both flavorful and satisfying. You might start with the Thai shellfish bisque, or a nori tempura wrap of tuna and foie gras; mains include a slow-roasted South Caicos red snapper on a bed of jambalaya rice, and the duxelle-encrusted rack of lamb on a wild-mushroom risotto.

In the Point Grace Hotel, Grace Bay. ✆ **649/946-5096.** Reservations required. Main courses $22–$45. AE, MC, V. Daily 6:30–10:30pm.

O'Soleil ★★★ INTERNATIONAL/ISLAND You know a place is good when the other local chefs start talking it up. This showcase space is draped in white and accented with marble floors, crystal chandeliers, and vaulted ceilings, a departure from the island-style interiors of other local spots. The decor veers ever so slightly into Carmela Soprano territory—and all that white and crystal makes it feel a little chilly. We prefer to dine on the alfresco terraces. The patio out front faces the croquet lawn, and the terrace in the back is enveloped in greenery and a soothing waterfall wall. But no matter where you eat, the food is splendid, prepared with flair and confidence by one of the island's few female chefs, Lauren Callighen. Start with the tequila-cured salmon or the pistachio-crusted, pan-fried scallops. Entrees include a curried grouper in a lime curry sauce; a Caribbean shrimp tagliatelle; and terrific New York strip steak, here in a wild-mushroom demi-glace. Service is superb.

In the Somerset on Grace Bay resort, Grace Bay. ✆ **649/946-5900.** Reservations recommended. Main courses $28–$40. AE, DC, MC, V. Daily 7:30–10:30am and 6–10pm.

EXPENSIVE

Hemingway's on the Beach ★ CARIBBEAN/INTERNATIONAL This casual open-air place is reliably good, and the ocean-side location is a big enticement. Yes, for a certain discriminating diner used to getting a decent glass of house wine, Hemingway's comes up short. But the coconut shrimp is light and tasty, and if local lobster is in season, order it here, grilled to perfection. Hemingway's is also a fine lunch choice, serving a terrific mango shrimp salad over Provo lettuce with mango chutney; a very respectable hamburger; and satisfying chicken and chips—marinated and fried Caribbean jerk chicken breast with the restaurant's signature seasoned fries. At night torches and candlelight heighten the ambience. A bell mounted on a pole on the upper deck of the restaurant is there to ring if anyone spots JoJo the resident dolphin cruising Grace Bay.

At the Sands at Grace Bay. ✆ **649/941-8408.** Reservations required. Main courses $17–$34. AE, MC, V. Daily 8am–10pm.

Mango Reef ★ ☺ CARIBBEAN/INTERNATIONAL This cheerful, laid-back spot is not luxe by any means and has no ocean views (you dine on a covered terrace overlooking the pool and landscaped gardens at the Royal West Indies Resort, p. 669). But if you come for lunch or dinner, you may find yourself surrounded by TCI movers and shakers chowing down heartily. That's because the food is delicious and won't drain your bank account dry. It's a big menu, with plenty of seafood, including conch (fritters, chowder, salad, and cracked) and a Red Queen snapper curry. Caribbean pork comes with fresh pineapple salsa. At lunch you can also choose among panini, wraps, fajitas, burgers, and sandwiches. It's a kid-friendly spot, too.

In the Royal West Indies Resort, Grace Bay Rd. ✆ **649/946-8200.** www.mangoreef.com. Reservations recommended. Main courses $21–$32. AE, MC, V. Daily 8am–10pm.

Parallel23 ★★★ TROPICAL FUSION/INTERNATIONAL Try to snag a table on the restaurant terrace, entwined in flower vines and lit by gas lamps specially ordered from a shop in New Orleans. It's a bewitching setting, overlooking the glittering Palm Place courtyard. The menu neatly balances top-end foods (impeccably sourced aged steaks and Wisconsin veal) with creative, reasonably priced nightly specials. It's a thoughtful menu, with lots of nifty touches (the butter is whipped with Parmesan and truffle oil). Starters include yellowfin tuna sashimi or pan-seared foie gras. On the grill menu, you choose your grilled meat and then sides and toppings. The attached Green Flamingo Bar (open noon–midnight) has the kind of overstuffed sofas and dark-grain wood you'd find in a gentleman's club in some exotic colonial outpost.

In the Regent Palms resort, Grace Bay. ✆ **649/946-8666.** Reservations required. Main courses $18–$38. AE, MC, V. Daily 7–10:30am and 6–10:30pm.

INEXPENSIVE

Da Conch Shack ★ CONCH/CARIBBEAN This sunny spot is set in and around a whitewashed beach shack on a sandy bluff above Blue Hills Beach. Next door is the open-air RumBar, separated by more sand and white picnic tables. Down below, in the shallow aquamarine waters, small conch pens hold live conch. The pens are refreshed daily by fishermen. Conch this fresh and well-prepared is a revelation, and here's it's served any number of ways, whether as superb conch fritters, conch curry, or conch chowder. Equally good is the curry chicken, the lobster (in season), shrimp, or local grouper. Some people come straight here from the airport, kick off their shoes, and order up a platter of conch and an icy Turk's Head lager.

Blue Hills. ✆ **649/946-8877.** www.conchshack.tc. No reservations. Main courses $12–$14; lobster $28. MC, V. Daily 11am–9pm.

Hitting the Beach

It's no hype: The beaches of Turks & Caicos are some of the most beautiful on the planet, thanks in large part to one of the few remaining unspoiled coral reef ecosystems in the Caribbean—or the world, for that matter. This, the third-largest coral reef system on the planet, helps act as a breakwater against ocean surges for these islands, keeping the coastal waters calm and clear. It makes its presence known on land as well: Coral is literally the soft white sand beneath your feet.

Starting at Leeward and running all the way to Thompson Cove, **Grace Bay Beach ★★★** is Provo's finest beach and, some say, one of the most beautiful beaches on the planet. Alongside 19km (12 miles) of spectacular, powdery-soft white sand are gin-clear, blue-green seas that are extremely tranquil and free of rocks, making the beach ideal for young kids. Many resorts have developed along its edge, so you won't have these sands all to yourself, but all beaches in the TCI are free to the public. Although there are no public facilities on the beach, the hotels themselves come in handy—most have oceanside bars and restaurants with restrooms.

Another way to see some of the area's finest beaches is to take a beach excursion that delivers you to one of the luscious **Caicos Cays** just off Provo for a few hours of leisurely beachcombing (see below).

Watersports & Outdoor Pursuits

BEACH EXCURSIONS One of the most popular watersports activities in the Provo area is a **beach excursion ★★**, offered by a number of charter-boat operators. Charter boats leave out of Heaving Down Rock marina, on Provo's northeast shore. Recommended operators include **Silver Deep** (✆ **649/946-5612;** www.silverdeep.com), **Big Blue Unlimited** (✆ **649/946-5034;** www.bigblueunlimited.com), and **Sail Provo** (✆ **649/946-4783;** www.sailprovo.com). A favorite beach excursion may involve a half-day or full day out on the Caicos Cays and might include **snorkeling,** a **shelling stopover** on one of the uninhabited cays, and a **visit to Little Water Cay.** Also known as Iguana Island, Little Water Cay is an uninhabited nature reserve set up to protect the island's 2,000 rock iguanas, an endangered species of lizards indigenous to the TCI. Eco-tours and kayaking trips in and around North and Middle Caicos are also popular excursions.

FISHING **Silver Deep** (✆ **649/946-5612;** www.silverdeep.com) offers top fishing excursions, with both half- and full-day expeditions, usually for bonefishing or bottom fishing. Tackle and bait are thrown in.

GOLF **Provo Golf & Country Club ★**, on Grace Bay Road (✆ **649/946-5833;** www.provogolfclub.com), is one of only two golf courses in the country (the other is on Grand Turk). The 6,560-yard, par-72, 18-hole course was designed by Karl Litten of Boca Raton, Florida. A driving range and putting greens are also available. Inside the clubhouse is a full-service restaurant and bar called **Fairways Bar & Grill.** Greens fees are $165 per person for 18 holes; the price includes the use of a shared golf cart, which is mandatory (ask about discounted afternoon and twilight rates Nov–March). Golf clubs can be rented for $30 to $60 per set (18 holes).

KITEBOARDING & WINDSURFING Kiteboarding (aka kitesurfing) has taken off on Turks and Caicos, where conditions are excellent: The calms waters are protected by a coral reef, the seas are uncrowded, and winds can be very cooperative. You can get kite-boarding or windsurfing lessons and/or equipment rentals directly on Grace Bay beach from **Windsurfing Provo** (Ocean Club East resort; ✆ **649/241-1687;** www.windsurfingprovo.tc; $40/hr. and $150/day) or **KiteProvo** (✆ **649/242-2927;** www.kiteprovo.com), with IKO- and PASA-certified instructors Mike Haas and Terri Tapper. Both Windsurfing Provo and KiteProvo offer 3-hour Kiteboarding Fundamentals lessons for $225/per person an hour. **Big Blue Unlimited** (✆ **649/946-5034;** www.bigblueunlimited.com) also offers kiteboarding expeditions, lessons, and rentals.

SAILING Sailing excursions are offered by many charter groups, most notably **Sail Provo** (✆ **649/946-4783;** www.sailprovo.com). It sails 14m or 16m (46- or 52-ft.) catamarans on half- or full-day excursions. One of the most frequented is a sailing and snorkeling trip for $68 (children 3–11 $40) that's offered on Monday, Wednesday, and Saturday, and includes a tour of Little Water Cay, or "Iguana Island." A full-day cruise Tuesday to Friday costs $150 (children 3–11 $80), including a lunch buffet served onboard. Sail Provo also offers sunset cruises and glowworm cruises.

SCUBA DIVING Dive experts, including the late Jacques Cousteau, have cited these islands as among the 10 best dive sites in the world. Why is the diving so good in the Turks and Caicos? A number of reasons: great visibility (often more than 30m/98 ft.), gentle seas, a barrier reef that runs the full length of the island's 27km (17-mile) north coast, dramatic vertical underwater "walls" where the coral is big and healthy and marine life congregates, and a local government committed to protecting its natural assets—much of the coastal waters around Provo are protected national parkland. The water is warm and calm much of the year.

Around Provo and the Caicos Islands, the popular diving spots include **Grace Bay, Northwest Point** (a 4.8km/3-mile strip of excellent dive sites with a vertical drop-off to 2,100m/6,890 ft.); **Pine Cay; West Caicos** (with miles of 1,800m/5,906-ft. vertical walls); and **French Cay** (more 1,800m/5,906-ft. vertical drop-offs). For extensive information about each of these sites, check out **Art Pickering's Provo Turtle Divers,** Turtle Cove (✆ **800/833-1341** for reservations, or 649/946-4232; www.provoturtledivers.com), the oldest dive operation in the islands. Both **Big Blue Unlimited** (✆ **649/946-5034;** www.bigblueunlimited.com) and **Dive Provo**

(✆ **800/234-7768** in the U.S., or 649/946-5040; www.diveprovo.com) offer technical and recreational scuba diving, instruction, and equipment rental.

Most dive operators rent scuba tanks, plus backpacks and weight belts (included in the dive cost). In general, a single-tank dive costs $75, a night dive goes for $75, and a morning two-tank dive is $109. Many offer technical diving and PADI training, with full instruction and resort courses. An open-water PADI referral course goes for $400.

SNORKELING The snorkeling is as good as it is on Provo and the Caicos Islands for the same reasons the diving is exalted. This is a great place to learn to snorkel—the waters are clean, clear, temperate, and gentle, and the marine life is rich and thriving. A number of watersports operators offer snorkeling trips (or combination snorkeling/beach excursions) off Grace Bay or in and around the Caicos Cays, a short (30-min.) trip from Provo. **Caicos Adventures** takes you farther still, on 4.6m-wide (15-ft.) powered catamarans, to superb snorkeling spots in West Caicos and French Cay, both about an hour's boat ride from Leeward (✆ **649/941-3346;** www.caicosadventures.com).

You can even find great snorkeling opportunities right on Grace Bay. Grab your snorkel and fins (most hotels offer complimentary equipment) and head down the beach to one of Grace Bay's two snorkeling spots, **Smith's Reef** and **Bight Reef,** both in the Princess Alexandra National Park, off the northwest corner of Provo.

The **Bight Reef Snorkel Trail** has underwater trail signs that describe corals and how they grow. Water depth ranges from 1m to 5m (3¼–16 ft.), and visitors can view mobile species like yellowtail snappers, big jolthead porgies, and sand-sifting mojarras.

STAND-UP PADDLEBOARDING Turks and Caicos have ideal conditions for stand-up paddleboarding, one of the fastest-growing board sports in the world. It's pretty much what the name implies: You stand up on a thick surfboard and propel yourself through the water with a long paddle. Cruise along in calm, flat waters along the shoreline or through peaceful mangrove channels. **Big Blue Unlimited,** ever at the forefront of eco-sensitive activities, offers stand-up paddleboarding expeditions and rentals (✆ **649/946-5034;** www.bigblueunlimited.com).

Exploring the Island

Provo has little in the way of historic or cultural attractions; for a real feel for the rich heritage of the TCI, you'll need to head to **Grand Turk** (see below).

Chalk Sound, a landlocked lagoon west of Five Cays Settlement, is now a public park. **Sapodilla Bay** and **Taylor Bay** are part of Chalk Sound National Park. These beautiful, shallow bays along Provo's southwest coastline have soft, silty bottoms and warm water.

Shopping

Art Provo, Regent Village, Grace Bay Road (✆ **649/941-4545**), has a large selection of paintings by local artists, pottery, baskets, jewelry, and glass. **Bamboo Gallery,** Caicos Café Plaza, Grace Bay Road (✆ **649/946-4748**), is one of the island's leading art galleries, with a large inventory of Haitian art.

Crafts and products made in the TCI are sold at the modest **Turks & Caicos National Trust Shop,** Grace Bay Plaza, Grace Bay Road (✆ **649/941-3536;** www.

tcinationaltrust.org), including native pottery, fanner-grass baskets, silvertop-palm bags, model Caicos sloops, and more. Get your rock iguana T-shirts here!

Provo After Dark

The nightlife on Provo can't compete with the late-night revelry of, say, Aruba or St. Maarten. The TCI is a fairly conservative place, overall, where the party vibe is easy-going and laid-back. But it does offer a number of quality nighttime diversions. The **Casablanca Casino,** Grace Bay Road, Providenciales (✆ **649/941-3737;** www.thecasablancacasino.com), offers roulette, blackjack, poker, craps, and baccarat.

Smokey's on Da Bay in Provo's Blue Hills has a Wednesday-night fish fry (✆ **649/241-4343**). Join the locals for happy hour at the **Sharkbite,** Turtle Bay Marina (✆ **649/941-5090;** www.thesharkbite.com), which also serves pub grub and West Indian favorites. The island's only Irish pub, **Danny Buoy's,** Grace Bay Road (✆ **649/946-5921;** www.dannybuoys.com), has imported beers on tap, darts, and pool tables.

For prime sunset viewing, the Grace Bay Club's beachfront **Lounge** (p. 663) has white-cushion seating and a glowing fire pit, and sister lounge the **Infinity Bar,** the longest bar in the Caribbean, is a sleek ribbon of black marble inset with sexy blue lights (✆ **649/946-5050**). Check out the Gansevoort's **Beach Lounge** (p. 668) and the resort's **Bagatelle Bistrot** (✆ **649/941-7555**) for late-night action.

Catch live music on the terrace at **O'Soleil** (✆ **649/946-5900**) at the Somerset Resort (p. 665) Saturdays; reggae during sunset cookouts at the **Alexandra resort** (✆ **649/946-5807**); and **Hemingway's** (✆ **649/941-8408)** for live music three nights a week.

GRAND TURK ★★

If you think Providenciales is laid-back, prepare yourself for the *really* relaxed world of Grand Turk. Grand Turk is a low-key charmer with architectural remnants of the islands' colonial past. If you love to scuba dive or snorkel, have a thing for sun-drenched beaches and ridiculously beautiful seas, and crave a relaxed, back-to-basics departure from the pricey boutique-resort scene, a visit is highly recommended.

Grand Turk continues to recover from a devastating direct hit by Hurricane Ike in September 2008. The island's lodgings are open for business, however, and the surrounding coral reef and undersea "Wall" are reportedly recovering as well, good news for divers and snorkelers who make pilgrimages here from around the globe to explore Grand Turk's spectacular marine waters.

Grand Turk is the capital of the Turks and Caicos Islands, although it is no longer the financial and business hub of the island nation, having lost that position to Provo. It is no longer the transportation hub, either; Provo receives 95% of international airplane landings. Grand Turk may not be the center of action anymore, but it has a genial charm: It's a laid-back, budget-friendly destination with world-class diving, white-sand beaches, and a small-town vibe.

Where Provo is the glittering, bustling center of 21st-century TCI, Grand Turk is its historic heart. In fact, many scholars believe that Grand Turk was the site of Columbus's first landfall in October 1492. Its heritage as a bustling salt-raking center in the 19th century is most evident in charming **Cockburn** (*Coe*-burn) **Town,** the business center of this tiny (11×3.2km/6¾×2-mile) island. Take time to tour Cockburn Town's **historic section,** particularly Duke and Front streets, where 200-year-old structures crafted of wood and limestone line the waterfront. Stroll the area and soak in the vintage architecture behind picket fences, the crimson bougainvillea, the funky beachfront bars, the wet suits hanging out to dry.

Governor's Beach is a fine place for swimming and watching massive cruise ships steam in over the horizon and dock at the **Grand Turk Cruise Center** (see "Exploring the Island," below), which welcomed some 500,000 cruise-ship passengers to this sleepy little island in 2009. In spite of all this revved-up activity, Grand Turk remains its dreamy, laid-back self. Stay for a couple of days, and you'll be waving to familiar faces on the street, calling the local dogs by name, and settling into your new favorite spot on Duke Street to watch the sunset over a Turks Head beer.

Essentials

VISITOR INFORMATION The **Turks and Caicos Tourist Board** (www.turksandcaicostourism.com) has an office in Grand Turk (Front St., Cockburn Town; ✆ **649/946-2321**). Office hours are Monday to Friday from 8:30am to 4:30pm.

GETTING TO GRAND TURK Your likely point of entry into the Turks and Caicos Islands will be the **Providenciales International Airport** (www.provoairport.com). To get to Grand Turk or Salt Cay, you will take a **domestic flight** on one of the interisland airlines or a charter plane from the Provo airport into Grand Turk International Airport (also known as J.A.G.S. McCartney International Airport). Several daily flights between Provo and Grand Turk are offered by the domestic airline **Air Turks & Caicos** (✆ **649/941-5481,** or 946-1667 on Grand Turk; www.airturksandcaicos.com). The flight from Provo to Grand Turk takes 25 minutes and costs from $135 to $160 round-trip.

GETTING AROUND GRAND TURK **Taxis** are always available at the Grand Turk airport. The fare is $10 to $12 from the airport to most inns and resorts. Staff at your hotel can summon a taxi for you if you need one. Most drivers are happy to give visitors an island tour; expect to pay around $50 to $60 for a 45-minute tour.

On Grand Turk, you can rent cars (as well as scooters, bicycles, and snorkeling gear) at **Tony's Car Rental,** located at the Grand Turk International Airport (✆ **649/964-1879;** www.tonyscarrental.com). Cars and jeeps rent for $70 to $95 a day, scooter rentals cost $40 a day, and bike rentals are $20 a day. Tony's also offers scooter tours of the island.

FAST FACTS Both **First Caribbean International Bank** (✆ **649/946-2831**) and **Scotiabank** (✆ **649/946-4750**) have 24-hour ATM service at their main branches in Cockburn Town.

In April 2010, **Turks & Caicos Island Hospital,** the nation's first modern hospital, opened two centers, one of which is the **Cockburn Town Medical Center** on Grand Turk. **Grand Turk Hospital** is on Hospital Road in Grand Turk (✆ **649/946-2040**).

The **Grand Turk Post Office** (✆ **649/946-1334**) is located in Cockburn Town. It's open Monday to Friday from 8am to 4pm.

Where to Stay

Don't expect a lineup of luxury resorts, a la Provo; the accommodations on Grand Turk are, for the most part, comfortable but modest, with prices to match.

Bohio Dive Resort ★ This resort has a terrific location directly overlooking Pillory Beach, the very spot where some historians believe Christopher Columbus first made landfall during his 1492 voyage to the New World. The main focus here is the hotel's in-house dive operation, with on-site PADI instructors and dive masters. Each of the serviceable 12 rooms and four suites, located in a separate building from the main section of the resort, has its own balcony with sea views; the suites have kitchenettes. The resort restaurant, Guanahani, serves breakfast, lunch, and dinner daily; the menu includes local favorites like conch chowder as well as standard Continental fare—they'll even cook your day's catch for you. Or you can sample the bar menu, with burgers, fish, and conch (offered daily all day long) over a specialty Bohio cocktail at the convivial Ike and Donkey Beach Bar, built on the site of the original dive shack, which was blown away by Hurricane Ike in 2008. The hotel offers 3- to 7-night dive/stay packages; check the website for the latest rates.

Front St. (P.O. Box 179), Grand Turk, Turks and Caicos, B.W.I. www.bohioresort.com. ✆ **649/946-2135.** Fax 649/946-1536. 16 units. Winter $190 double, $225 suite; low season $165 double, $195 suite. Children 2 and under stay free in parent's room. Children 3–12 $35 extra a night. AE, MC, V. **Amenities:** Restaurant; bar; bikes; dive instructors and dive shack; outdoor pool; watersports equipment; Wi-Fi (free; in restaurant and bar). *In room:* A/C, ceiling fan, TV, fridge (in doubles), hair dryer, kitchenette (in suites).

Grand Turk Inn ★★ These are the top accommodations in Grand Turk. Sisters Katrina Birt and Sandy Erb, veterans of the Key West inn scene, discovered the charms of Grand Turk and the excellent bones of this handsome Bermudian-style 150-year-old former Methodist manse, which they lovingly renovated. The five suites are spacious and ultracomfortable, with king- or queen-size beds dressed in soft linens; all have full kitchens and private bathrooms. The second-floor Pelican Suite can sleep up to four people. A big upper-floor sun deck overlooking the sea provides the perfect venue from which to watch humpback whales pass by in the winter.

Front St. (P.O. Box 9), Grand Turk, Turks and Caicos, B.W.I. www.grandturkinn.com. ✆ **649/946-2827.** Fax 649/946-1066. 5 units. Winter $300 double; summer $250 double. Rates include continental breakfast. AE, DISC, MC, V. No children 15 or under. **Amenities:** Bikes. *In room:* A/C, ceiling fan, TV/DVD, hair dryer, kitchen, Wi-Fi (free).

Osprey Beach Hotel ★ This landmark hotel is set along a white-sand beach for easy swimming and snorkeling. Twenty-seven refurbished rooms occupy modern two-story town houses, each with oceanfront verandas; 10 spacious units are located across the street in the Atrium. All of the Queen suites have full kitchens; the rest have kitchenettes or minifridges. Rooms on the upper floors are larger and have higher ceilings, and many have unobstructed views of the turquoise sea. The lower rooms have easy access to the beach. Lunch and dinner are served poolside (the menu features seafood, steaks, and local favorites like conch chowder); also poolside is the popular Birdcage Bar. Joan's Deli and Boutique offers specialty sandwiches, wraps, salads, and coffees served by the capable Joan from Captain Zheng's (see below); it's located in the Atrium. On Sunday and Wednesday nights, the whole of Duke Street and beyond congregates for the poolside barbecue buffet ($14–$30) and the rollicking ripsaw music of "dive-master troubadour" Mitch Rolling and the High Tide.

1 Duke St. (P.O. Box 216), Grand Turk, Turks and Caicos, B.W.I. www.ospreybeachhotel.com. ✆ **649/946-2666.** Fax 649/946-2817. 37 units. High season $195–$235 double, $115–$150 courtyard rooms (in Atrium); low season $165–$190 double, $100–$135 courtyard rooms (in Atrium). Extra person $30 per

day. Children 11 and under stay free in parent's room. Dive/hotel packages available. AE, MC, V. **Amenities:** 2 restaurants; bar; outdoor pool; watersports equipment; Wi-Fi (free; around pool and restaurant). *In room:* A/C, ceiling fan, TV, fridge, kitchenette (in some).

Where to Dine

Don't miss the **Wednesday-** and **Sunday-night poolside barbecues** at the **Birdcage,** in the Osprey Beach Hotel (p. 679) on Duke Street. The restaurant is also open for dinner (✆ **649/946-2666**).

Captain Zheng's CHINESE Dine on freshly made Chinese classics amid softly draped linens and Oriental lanterns. The menu changes regularly, but you may find Sichuan chili mountain chicken, garlic shrimp and squid, and Peking duck. As the menu says, no MSG!

At the Salina Houses, Close Haul Rd. (south of Duke St.). ✆ **649/242-2436.** Main courses $11–$23; Peking duck $30. No credit cards. Tues–Sat 6–10 pm.

Jack's Shack Beach Bar & Grill Just north of the cruise port, Jack's is a fun spot to spend a beach day, with lounge chairs, floats, a volleyball net, tantalizing barbecue scents, spine-stiffening rum drinks, and a companionable island vibe. The chef serves up tasty jerk chicken, fish stew, steamed conch, and other local specialties. Jack's is open only those days when cruise ships are in port.

South Base (500m/1,640 ft. north of the cruise center). ✆ **649/232-0099.** www.jacksshack.tc. Main courses $5–$12. MC, V. 7am–7pm only when cruise ships are in.

The Sandbar CARIBBEAN/BURGERS This casual, friendly watering hole set above the beach is a social hub for locals and visitors—and a dog or two lying in the cool sand. It's owned by two vivacious Canadian sisters, Tonya and Katya, who also run the **Manta House B&B** (✆ **649/946-1111;** www.grandturk-mantahouse.com), across the street. The menu is much more interesting than a beach bar's need be, with lobster quesadilla, cracked conch, shrimp and chips, and very respectable burgers.

Duke St. ✆ **649/946-1111.** Main courses $10–$18. MC, V. Sun–Fri noon–late (food served noon–3pm and 6–9pm).

Secret Garden SEAFOOD/CARIBBEAN Tucked in the covered backyard garden of the Salt Raker Inn, this casual eatery is a local favorite. Flattened by Hurricane Ike, it's been rebuilt (this time with concrete underpinnings) but has retained its dreamy tropical-garden atmosphere and reliable kitchen. Lunch specials are tasty and include grouper sandwich, barbecued chicken, and even a hearty spaghetti Bolognese. Evening entrees include grouper, seafood pasta, garlic shrimp, cracked conch, or curry goat, with a side of peas 'n' rice, of course.

1 Duke St. ✆ **649/946-2260.** Reservations recommended in winter. Main courses $12–$21; lunch specials $9–$18. MC, V. Tues–Sun 7–10am, noon–2:30pm, and 7–9:30pm.

Scuba Diving & Snorkeling ★★

Some of the finest **scuba diving** in the archipelago is around Grand Turk—in fact, a breathtakingly short .8km to 1.6km (½–1 mile) offshore (a 5-to-10-min. boat ride away). The action is at the **Wall,** where the western edges of the island (and its necklace of coral reef) plunge dramatically 2,134m (7,001 ft.) into deep water, actually the leeward side of the Turks Island Passage (also known as the Columbus Passage), which lies between the Turks Islands and the Caicos Islands. Scuba divers flock here to enjoy panoramic wall dives on the vertical sides of the reefs. The diving sites of the Wall have colorful names like Coral Garden, the Aquarium, the Library, and even McDonald's (for its coral arch). You'll even see humpback whales as they migrate south through the Turks Island Passage in the winter.

Snorkeling can be good right off many Grand Turk beaches, including **Governor's Beach, White Sands Beach,** and **Pillory Beach** (in front of the Bohio Dive Resort). One popular activity is a **snorkeling trip to Gibbs Cay,** an uninhabited cay where snorkelers can swim with native stingrays in shallow water; most local dive operators (see section below for contact information) offer snorkeling trips to Gibbs Cay for around $60 per person. The dive shops discussed below all rent snorkel gear.

DIVE OPERATORS

The owners and operators of the following dive companies are experienced divers on the island, and they know where to find marine life in a kaleidoscope of colors. They work with novices—offering good beginning courses and training—as well as experienced divers of all skill levels. Rates below are per person.

Blue Water Divers, on Front Street (✆/fax **649/946-2432;** www.grandturkscuba.com), offers single dives, PADI registration, and dive packages, and even runs trips to Salt Cay. These people are top-rate and will tell you many facts and legends about diving in their country (like the fact that the highest mountain in the Turks & Caicos is 2,400m/7,874 ft. tall, but only the top 42m/138 ft. are above sea level!). A single-tank dive costs $45, with a two-tank dive going for $85; a night dive costs $55. Trips to Salt Cay and Gibbs Cay cost $60. Full PADI certification is $400. (Mitch Rolling, the Blue Water Divers dive master, is also the guitarist who plays at the Osprey Beach Hotel (p. 679) with the ripsaw band High Tide.)

Cecil Ingham's Sea Eye Diving, on Duke Street (✆ **649/946-1407**), is convenient to most hotels in town. It offers two-tank morning dives at $75 to $80. An afternoon single-tank dive costs $45, and a single-tank night dive goes for $55. Rental equipment is also available. NAUI and PADI courses at all levels are offered. A full-certification course goes for $400, including training equipment and boat checkout dives. Dive packages that include accommodations can be arranged at your hotel. Snorkeling and cay trips are available for nondivers.

Oasis Divers, on Duke Street (✆ **649/946-1128;** www.oasisdivers.com), offers complete dive-master services, with dive adventures along the Wall, night dives, trips to Gibbs Cay, snorkeling trips, trips to Salt Cay, and dive/accommodations packages. A morning two-tank dive costs $86; a night dive is $55. An instruction course and dive from your resort is $110; a trip to Salt Cay is $50, and a trip to Gibbs Cay is $55.

Grand Turk native Smitty Smith is the expert instructor and guide with **Grand Turk Diving** (✆ **649/946-1559;** www.gtdiving.com), which offers dive/lodging packages, a resort course ($150; equipment included), and full scuba certification ($450; equipment included). Two single-tank morning dives cost $75.

Exploring the Island

People mainly travel to Grand Turk to swim, snorkel, dive, and do little but soak up the sun. But now that the cruise ships have arrived, local tour operators are offering a mind-numbing assortment of new activities and tours, including horseback-riding trips, jeep safaris, kayaking trips, and dune-buggy tours.

It's a pleasant bike ride to the Northwest Point to see the cast-iron **Grand Turk Lighthouse,** which was brought in pieces from the United Kingdom, where it had been constructed in 1852. Its old lens is on display in the Turks & Caicos National Museum (see below).

Conch World Opened in 2009, this combination theme park, commercial conch farm, and educational complex is located in what was described by one local as a "way-off-the-beaten-path" spot along bumpy dirt roads; the only signpost is an arrow pointing the way. Conch World is generally only open when cruise ships are in port. It features a video on the history of the conch in the TCI; some 200 onshore holding tanks containing juvenile conch of different ages; and the full-grown conches Sally and Jerry, transferred here after a hurricane leveled its sister conch farm in Provo. The complex also includes the Pink Pearl Gift Shop.

South Creek Sound. ✆ **649/946-1228.** Tour $17.

Grand Turk Cruise Center The 5.7-hectare (14-acre) cruise-ship terminal is a fair distance away from the heart of Cockburn Town. The terminal was designed by the folks at Carnival Cruise Lines to resemble a colorful Bermudian-style village out of the early 19th century, much like Cockburn Town might have looked in the early 1800s. The center is planted smack-dab on Governor's Beach, with a 172m-long (564-ft.) main pier; hundreds of deck chairs along the beach; a huge Jimmy Buffet's Margaritaville (with lagoonlike pool and private poolside cabanas); and the Grand Turk FlowRider—a fast-moving artificial-wave pool. The terminal's main building is distinguished by four prominent vintage-style chimneys and shops designed to resemble the wooden "salt houses" of the salt era. Many of the shops are locally owned and sell island crafts and gifts. It all lies mute and still until the arrival of a 2,000-passenger ship, which shows up on the empty horizon just as the sun comes up—a watery behemoth that gets eye-poppingly bigger as it approaches the island. A miniature train takes arriving cruise passengers to Governor's Beach. Cruise guests can tour Cockburn Town by beach buggy, horse-drawn carriage, moped, or shuttle taxi. They can participate in one of many shore excursions (scuba diving, snorkeling, horseback riding) available through local tour operators. Independent-minded travelers who prefer to explore the island on their own can rent a car at the Cruise Center's car-rental office, or hire one of the local taxi drivers to give them a tour. ***Note:*** The cruise center is open only on days when ships come in (now averaging 4–5 days a week).

Waterloo Rd. ✆ **649/946-1040.** www.grandturkcc.com.

Turks & Caicos National Museum ★ This is the country's first (and only) museum. It occupies a 150-year-old residence, Guinep House, originally built by Bermudian wreckers from timbers salvaged from ships wrecked on nearby reefs. Today about half of its display areas are devoted to the remains of the most complete archaeological excavation ever performed in the West Indies, the wreck of a Spanish caravel (sailing ship) that sank in shallow waters sometime before 1513. Used to transport enslaved local Lucayans, the boat is similar to vessels built in Spain and Portugal during the 1400s (like Columbus' expeditionary *Pinta,* which some people believe it may be). Today the remains are referred to simply as the Wreck of Molasses Reef. Although only 2% of the hull remains intact, the exhibits contain a rich legacy of the everyday (nonbiodegradable) objects used by the crews and officers.

The remainder of the museum is devoted to exhibits on the island's salt industries, its plantation economy, and pre-Columbian inhabitants. The natural-history exhibit features a 2×6m (6½×20-ft.), three-dimensional reproduction of a section of the Grand Turk Wall, the famous reef with the dramatic vertical drop-off.

Guinep House, Front St., Cockburn Town, Grand Turk. ✆ **649/946-2160.** www.tcmuseum.org. Admission $5 nonresidents, free for full-time island residents. Mon–Sat 9am–1pm.

Grand Turk After Dark

Wednesday and Sunday barbecues at the Osprey Beach Hotel on Duke Street (p. 679) feature music by Mitch Rolling and the High Tide.

26 THE U.S. VIRGIN ISLANDS

The U.S. Virgin Islands lie in two bodies of water: St. John is entirely in the Atlantic Ocean, St. Croix is entirely in the Caribbean Sea, and St. Thomas spans the Atlantic and the Caribbean. Directly in the belt of the subtropical, easterly trade winds, these islands enjoy one of the most perfect year-round climates in the world.

ESSENTIALS

Visitor Information

For general information, visit **www.usvitourism.vi** or call © **800/372-USVI** (8784).

Before you go, contact the **U.S. Virgin Islands Division of Tourism,** at One Penn Plaza, Ste. 3525, New York, NY 10001 (© **212/502-5300**). Branch offices are located at 245 Peachtree Center Ave., Marriott 1 Tower, Ste. MB-05, Atlanta, GA 30303 (© **404/688-0906**); 500 N. Michigan Ave., Ste. 2030, Chicago, IL 60611 (© **312/670-8784**); 2655 Le Jeune Rd., Ste. 907, Coral Gables, FL 33134 (© **305/442-7200**); 3460 Wilshire Blvd., Ste. 412, Los Angeles, CA 90010 (© **213/739-0138**); and 444 N. Capital St., Ste. 305, Washington, DC 20009 (© **202/624-3560**).

Getting There

It's possible to fly from the mainland of the U.S. directly to St. Thomas and St. Croix, but the only way to get to St. John is by a ferry from St. Thomas, or from Jost Van Dyke or Tortola in the British Virgin Islands.

TO ST. THOMAS OR ST. CROIX **American Airlines** (© **800/433-7300** in the U.S. and Canada; www.aa.com) offers frequent service to St. Thomas and St. Croix from the U.S. mainland, with three daily flights from New York to St. Thomas in high season. Passengers originating in other parts of the world are usually routed to St. Thomas through American's hubs in Miami or San Juan, Puerto Rico, both of which offer nonstop service (often several times a day) to St. Thomas. (American Eagle has 12 nonstop flights daily from San Juan to St. Thomas.)

Delta (© **800/221-1212** in the U.S. and Canada; www.delta.com) offers two daily nonstop flights between Atlanta and St. Thomas in winter, as well as three nonstop flights weekly between Atlanta and St. Croix.

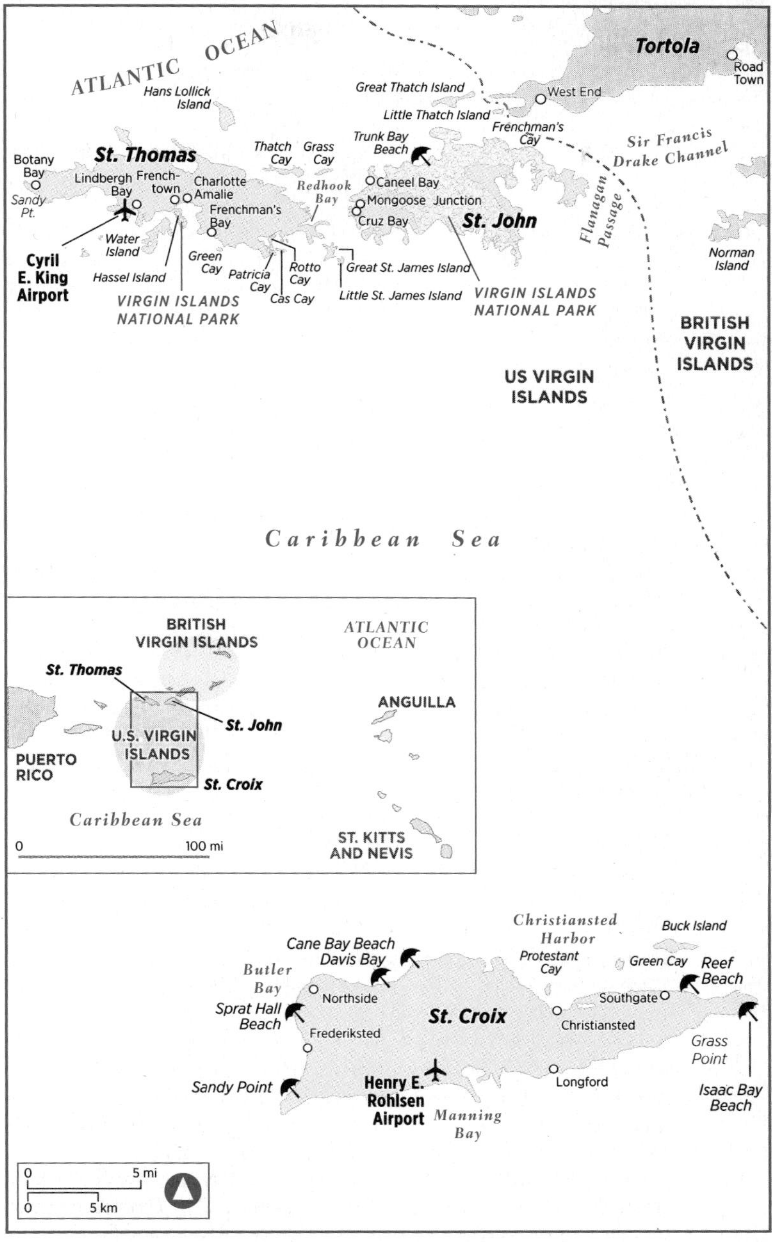
ATLANTIC OCEAN
Tortola
Road Town
West End
Great Thatch Island
Little Thatch Island
Frenchman's Cay
Sir Francis Drake Channel
Hans Lollick Island
St. Thomas
Botany Bay
Sandy Pt.
Lindbergh Bay
French-town
Charlotte Amalie
Frenchman's Bay
Water Island
Cyril E. King Airport
Hassel Island
Green Cay
Patricia Cay
Cas Cay
Rotto Cay
Thatch Cay
Grass Cay
Redhook Bay
Trunk Bay Beach
Caneel Bay
Mongoose Junction
Cruz Bay
St. John
Great St. James Island
Little St. James Island
VIRGIN ISLANDS NATIONAL PARK
VIRGIN ISLANDS NATIONAL PARK
Flanagan Passage
Norman Island
BRITISH VIRGIN ISLANDS
US VIRGIN ISLANDS
Caribbean Sea
BRITISH VIRGIN ISLANDS
ATLANTIC OCEAN
St. Thomas
St. John
ANGUILLA
U.S. VIRGIN ISLANDS
PUERTO RICO
St. Croix
Caribbean Sea
0
100 mi
ST. KITTS AND NEVIS
Christiansted Harbor
Buck Island
Cane Bay Beach
Davis Bay
Protestant Cay
Green Cay
Reef Beach
Butler Bay
Northside
Southgate
Sprat Hall Beach
St. Croix
Christiansted
Frederiksted
Grass Point
Sandy Point
Henry E. Rohlsen Airport
Longford
Isaac Bay Beach
Manning Bay
0
5 mi
0
5 km

US Airways (© **800/622-1015** in the U.S. and Canada; www.usairways.com) has one nonstop daily flight from Philadelphia to St. Thomas, and an additional flight on Saturday.

Cape Air (© **800/352-0714** in the U.S. and Canada; www.flycapeair.com) has service between St. Thomas and Puerto Rico. This Massachusetts-based airline offers 5 to 12 flights daily. Cape Air has expanded its service to include flights from San Juan to St. Croix and flights between St. Croix and St. Thomas.

United Airlines (© **800/538-2929** in the U.S. and Canada; www.united.com) has nonstop service on various days to St. Thomas from Chicago and Washington, D.C.

Continental Airlines (© **800/231-0856** in the U.S. and Canada; www.continental.com) has daily flights from Newark to St. Thomas.

A **ferry** service between Charlotte Amalie in St. Thomas and Puerto Rico, with a stop in St. John, is available about once every 2 weeks. The trip takes about 2 hours, costing $125 round-trip. For more information, call © **340/776-6282** or 787/863-0582, or visit www.vinow.com.

TO ST. CROIX FROM ST. THOMAS **American Airlines** (© **800/433-7300** in the U.S. and Canada; www.aa.com) has eight flights a day, costing $246 one-way between St. Thomas and St. Croix, with a stopover in San Juan. In addition, **Seaborne Airlines** (© **888/359-8687** in the U.S. and Canada, or 340/773-6442; www.seaborneairlines.com) offers 21 round-trip flights daily, going for $100 one-way and $125 round-trip. Flight time is 25 minutes.

TO ST. JOHN The easiest and most common way to get to St. John is by **ferry** (© **340/776-6282;** www.vinow.com), which leaves from the Red Hook landing pier on St. Thomas's eastern tip; the trip takes about 20 minutes each way. Beginning at 6:30am, boats depart more or less every hour. The last ferry back to Red Hook departs from St. John's Cruz Bay at noon. The service is frequent and efficient enough that even cruise-ship passengers temporarily anchored in Charlotte Amalie can visit St. John for a quick island tour. The one-way fare is $27 for adults, $22 for children 5 to 11. Schedules change without notice, so call in advance.

To reach the ferry, take the **Vitran** bus from a point near Market Square (in Charlotte Amalie) directly to Red Hook. The cost is $1 per person each way. In addition, privately owned taxis will negotiate a price to carry you from virtually anywhere to the docks at Red Hook.

If you've just landed on St. Thomas and want to go straight to the ferry dock, your best bet is to take a cab from the airport (Vitran buses run from Charlotte Amalie but don't serve the airport area). After disembarking from the ferry on St. John, you'll have to get another cab to your hotel. Depending on the traffic, the cab ride on St. Thomas could take 30 to 45 minutes, at a fare between $20 and $24.

It's also possible to board a **boat** for St. John directly at the Charlotte Amalie waterfront for a cost of $10 to $15 each way. The ride takes 45 minutes. The boats depart from Charlotte Amalie at 7:15am and continue every 2 hours, until the last boat departs around 5:30pm. (The last boat to leave St. John's Cruz Bay for Charlotte Amalie departs at 3:45pm.) Call © **340/776-6282** for more information.

[Fast FACTS] THE U.S. VIRGIN ISLANDS

Banks Banks are generally open Monday to Thursday 9am to 3pm and Friday 9am to 6pm. It's not hard to find a bank with an **ATM** on St. Thomas or St. Croix.

Currency The **U.S. dollar** is the unit of currency in the Virgin Islands. *Prices in this chapter are quoted in U.S. dollars.*

Customs Every U.S. resident can bring home $1,600 worth of duty-free purchases, including two cases of liquor per adult. If you go over the $1,600 limit, you pay a flat 5% duty, up to $1,000. You can also mail home gifts valued at up to $100 per day, which you don't have to declare. (At other spots in the Caribbean, U.S. citizens are limited to $400 or $600 worth of merchandise and a single bottle of liquor.)

Documents U.S. and Canadian citizens are required to present some proof of citizenship to enter the Virgin Islands, such as a birth certificate with a raised seal along with a government-issued photo ID. A passport is not strictly required, but carrying one is a good idea. The requirements for other citizens are the same as for foreigners entering the U.S. mainland; travelers from the United Kingdom, Australia, and New Zealand need valid passports but not visas.

Electricity It's the same as on the U.S. mainland: 120-volt AC (60 cycles). No transformer, adapter, or converter is needed for U.S. appliances.

Emergencies In an emergency, dial ✆ **911.**

Liquor Laws Liquor is sold 7 days a week, but it is not permitted on beaches.

Safety The U.S. Virgin Islands have more than their share of crime. Travelers should exercise extreme caution both day and night, especially in the back streets of Charlotte Amalie on St. Thomas, and in Christiansted and Frederiksted on St. Croix. Muggings are commonplace. Avoid strolling at night, especially on the beaches.

Taxes There is no departure tax for the U.S. Virgin Islands. Hotels add on a 10% tax. (Always ask if it's included in the original price you're quoted.)

Telephone The phone system for the U.S. Virgin Islands is the same as on the U.S. mainland. The area code is **340.** To reach **Sprint,** dial ✆ **800/877-8000,** and to reach **MCI,** dial ✆ **800/888-8000.**

Time The U.S. Virgins are on Atlantic Standard Time, which is 1 hour ahead of Eastern Standard Time. However, the islands do not observe daylight saving time, so in the summer during daylight saving time, the Virgin Islands and the U.S. East Coast are on the same time. In winter, when it's 6am in Charlotte Amalie, it's 5am in Miami.

Tipping Tip as you would on the U.S. mainland (15% in restaurants, 10%–15% to taxi drivers, $2 per round to bartenders, at least $1 or $2 per day for chambermaids). Some hotels add a 10% to 15% surcharge to cover service, so check before you wind up paying twice.

Water Most visitors drink the local tap water with no harmful aftereffects. Those with more delicate stomachs might want to stick to bottled water.

Weather From November to February, temperatures average about 77°F (25°C). Sometimes in August, the temperature peaks in the high 90s (mid-30s Celsius), but the subtropical breezes keep it comfortably cool in the shade. The temperature in winter may drop into the low 60s (mid-teens Celsius), but this rarely happens.

ST. THOMAS ★

St. Thomas is the busiest cruise-ship harbor in the West Indies. Bustling Charlotte Amalie, with its white houses and bright red roofs glistening in the sun, is one of the most beautiful towns in the Caribbean. It's most famous for shopping, but the town is also filled with historic sights, like Fort Christian, an intriguing 17th-century building constructed by the Danes. Outside of town, the beaches are renowned for their white sand and calm, turquoise waters, including the very best of them all, Magens Bay.

Things to Do Pretty 18th-century buildings surround the harbor of the active port of **Charlotte Amalie,** where warehouses once filled with pirate booty still stand. Watch butterflies flutter at the **Butterfly Farm,** or see the colorful Caribbean water world from an ***Atlantis*** submarine dive. Explore island history in the redbrick **Fort Christian.** Laze in the white sands at **Magens Bay,** or seek shade under the coconut palms of **Secret Harbour** on the East End. For a little seclusion, try **Limetree Beach** or **Vessup Bay.**

Shopping Spend freely at the designer boutiques and jewelry stores of **Charlotte Amalie.** Sift through pottery, silk-screened fabrics, candles, and watercolors at **Tillett Gardens,** or duck into the warehouses on **Main Street** for island trinkets and clothing. When you tire of French perfumes and Swiss watches, head for **Market Square** for ackee, cassava, and breadfruit, or buy local crafts and souvenirs from nearby **Havensight Mall. Duty-free shopping** bargains include china, crystal, perfumes, jewelry (especially emeralds), Haitian art, clothing, watches, and items made of wood.

Nightlife & Entertainment St. Thomas sizzles with the most extensive nightlife in the U.S. or British Virgin Islands. **Charlotte Amalie** still swings with waterfront pubs and bars, but much of the action has shifted to the bars and restaurants of **Frenchtown.** The big hotels have the most lively options, and after a day in the hot sun, you can wind down with a cocktail and local fungi band playing traditional music on homemade instruments.

Eating & Drinking St. Thomas adds an eclectic mix of cuisines—including American, Italian, Mexican, and Asian—to its spicy Caribbean palate. **Charlotte Amalie** is dense with restaurants, but the **East End** has a variety of spots as well. Seafood specialties abound, such as "ole wife" and yellowtail at waterfront dining rooms, or splurge on Coral Bay crab cakes served with island rémoulade on an elegant terrace. Most local restaurants serve **johnnycake,** a popular fried, unleavened bread.

Carnival

The annual **Carnival** celebration, held after Easter, is a spectacular event, with echoes of the islanders' African heritage. "Mocko Jumbies," people dressed as spirits, parade through the streets on stilts nearly 20 feet high. Steel, calypso, and fungi (folk) bands; "jump-ups" (Caribbean hoedowns); and parades bring the event to life. Events take place islandwide, but most of the action is on the streets of Charlotte Amalie. Contact the visitor center in St. Thomas (p. 690) for a schedule of events.

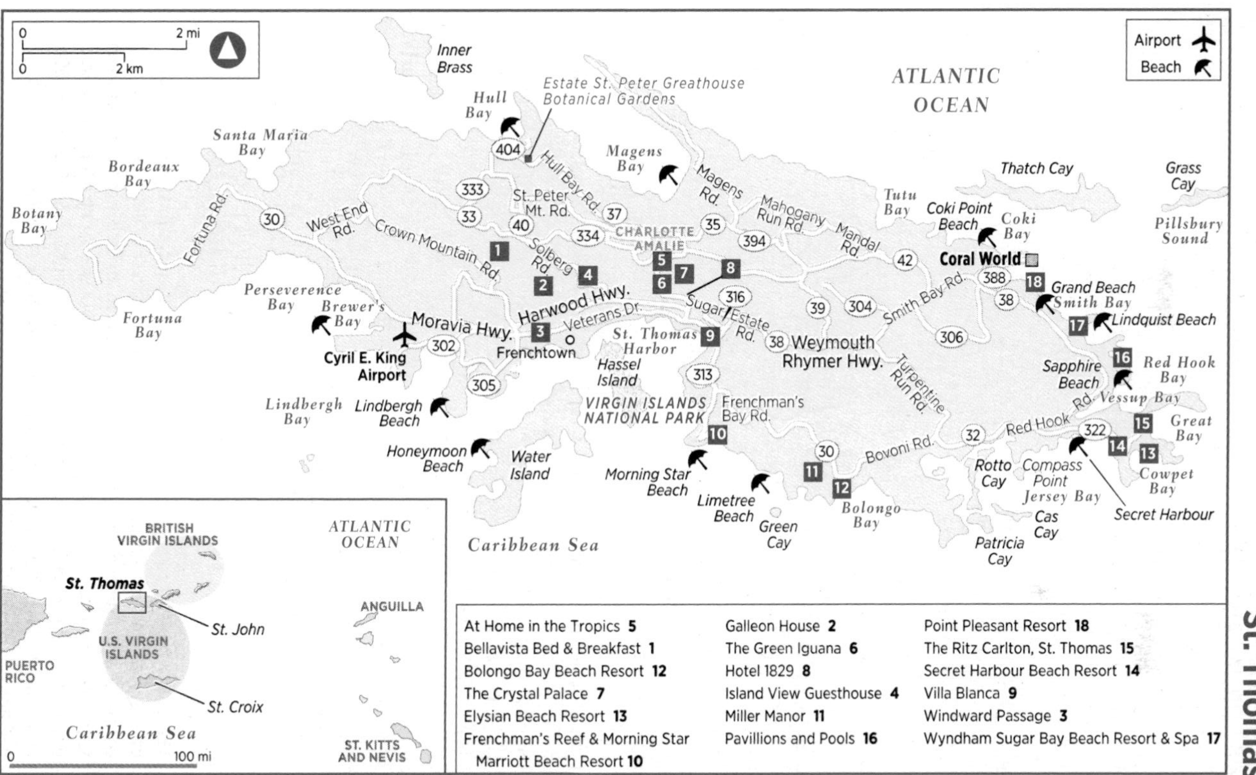
0 2 mi
0 2 km
Airport
Beach
ATLANTIC OCEAN
Inner Brass
Hull Bay
Estate St. Peter Greathouse Botanical Gardens
Santa Maria Bay
Bordeaux Bay
Botany Bay
Fortuna Rd.
Fortuna Bay
30
West End Rd.
Crown Mountain Rd.
333
33
404
St. Peter Mt. Rd.
40
Hull Bay Rd.
37
334
Solberg Rd.
Magens Bay
Magens Rd.
CHARLOTTE AMALIE
35
394
Mahogany Run Rd.
Mandal Rd.
Tutu Bay
42
Thatch Cay
Coki Point Beach
Coki Bay
Coral World
Grass Cay
Pillsbury Sound
Perseverence Bay
Brewer's Bay
Cyril E. King Airport
302
Moravia Hwy.
Harwood Hwy.
Veterans Dr.
Frenchtown
305
St. Thomas Harbor
Hassel Island
Sugar Estate Rd.
316
39
304
Smith Bay Rd.
388
38
Grand Beach
Smith Bay
Lindquist Beach
38
Weymouth Rhymer Hwy.
306
313
Turpentine Run Rd.
Sapphire Beach
Red Hook Bay
Red Hook Rd.
Vessup Bay
Great Bay
Lindbergh Bay
Lindbergh Beach
VIRGIN ISLANDS NATIONAL PARK
Frenchman's Bay Rd.
Honeymoon Beach
Water Island
Morning Star Beach
Limetree Beach
Green Cay
30
Bovoni Rd.
Bolongo Bay
32
322
Rotto Cay
Compass Point
Jersey Bay
Cas Cay
Patricia Cay
Cowpet Bay
Secret Harbour
Caribbean Sea
BRITISH VIRGIN ISLANDS
ATLANTIC OCEAN
St. Thomas
St. John
U.S. VIRGIN ISLANDS
PUERTO RICO
St. Croix
ANGUILLA
Caribbean Sea
ST. KITTS AND NEVIS
0 100 mi
At Home in the Tropics 5
Bellavista Bed & Breakfast 1
Bolongo Bay Beach Resort 12
The Crystal Palace 7
Elysian Beach Resort 13
Frenchman's Reef & Morning Star Marriott Beach Resort 10
Galleon House 2
The Green Iguana 6
Hotel 1829 8
Island View Guesthouse 4
Miller Manor 11
Pavillions and Pools 16
Point Pleasant Resort 18
The Ritz Carlton, St. Thomas 15
Secret Harbour Beach Resort 14
Villa Blanca 9
Windward Passage 3
Wyndham Sugar Bay Beach Resort & Spa 17

Essentials

VISITOR INFORMATION At 78 Estate Contant 1-2-3, across from the Nisky Shopping Center, on the waterfront in downtown Charlotte Amalie, the **Department of Tourism** (✆ **340/774-8784**) is open Monday to Friday 8am to 5pm. There are also **welcome centers** at both of the island's cruise-ship terminals.

GETTING AROUND **Taxis** are unmetered, but fares are controlled and widely posted, and each taxi is, at least officially, supposed to carry a copy of those fares inside. However, we still recommend that you determine a fare with the driver before you get into the car. A typical fare—say, from Havensight Mall to Magens Bay for a day at the beach—runs to $8.50 per person, or $6 per person in a shared cab. Surcharges, one-third of the price of the excursion, are added after midnight. You'll pay $1 to $2 per bag for luggage. For 24-hour radio-dispatch taxi service, call ✆ **340/774-4077** (www.islandertaxiservice.com). If you want to hire a taxi and a driver (who may just be a great tour guide) for a day, expect to pay about $50 per person for 2 hours of sightseeing in a shared car, or from $50 per hour for two to four people.

Taxi vans transport 8 to 12 passengers to multiple destinations on the island. It's cheaper to take a van instead of a taxi if you're going between your hotel and the airport. The cost for luggage ranges from $1 to $2 per bag.

Buses, called **Vitrans,** leave from street-side stops in the center of Charlotte Amalie, fanning out east and west along all the most important highways. They run between 5:30am and 8pm daily, but waits can be very long, and this is a difficult way to get about. A ride within Charlotte Amalie is 75¢, and anywhere else $1. For schedule and bus-stop information, call ✆ **340/774-5678.**

St. Thomas has many leading North American **car rental firms** at the airport, and competition is stiff among the following: **Avis** (✆ **800/331-1084** in the U.S. and Canada, or 340/778-9355; www.avis.com), **Budget** (✆ **800/472-3325** in the U.S. and Canada, or 340/778-4663; www.budget.com), **Hertz** (✆ **800/654-3001** in the U.S. and Canada, or 340/778-1402; www.hertz.com), and **Thrifty** (✆ **800/367-2277** in the U.S. and Canada, or 340/776-1500; www.thrifty.com).

You can often save money by renting from a local agency, although vehicles aren't always as well maintained. Try **Dependable Car Rental,** No. 12 Lindberg Bay, behind the Bank of Nova Scotia and the Medical Arts Complex (✆ **800/522-3076** or 340/774-2253; www.dependablecar.com), which will pick up renters at the airport or their hotel; or the aptly named **Discount Car Rental,** 14 Harwood Hwy., outside the airport on the main highway (✆ **877/478-2833** or 340/776-4858; www.discountcar.vi), which grants drivers a 12% discount on rivals' rates. There is no tax on car rentals in the Virgin Islands, but if you opt to retrieve your rental car at the airport, as opposed to any of the other island locations, you'll pay a 12% airport pickup fee.

FAST FACTS **Roy Lester Schneider Regional Hospital,** 9048 Sugar Estate, Charlotte Amalie (✆ **340/776-8311;** www.rlshospital.org), a 5-minute drive east of the town's commercial center, is the largest hospital, with the best-equipped emergency room.

Where to Stay

Remember that hotels in the Virgin Islands slash their prices in summer by 20% to 60%. Unless otherwise noted, the rates listed below do *not* include the 10% government tax.

VERY EXPENSIVE

Frenchman's Reef & Morning Star Marriott Beach Resort ★★ Lying 3 miles east of Charlotte Amalie on the south shore, this is the largest hotel on island—and one of the best, although not as plush as the Ritz-Carlton (see below). The megaresort is divided into two sections, both lying on a bluff overlooking the Caribbean: the less expensive Frenchman's Reef, and the more upscale Morning Star. Oddly, the suites are in the high-rise Frenchman's Reef, not in the low-rise Morning Star annex. All units have private balconies and are midsize to spacious, with tasteful, comfortable furnishings. Facilities devoted to the good life are everywhere; you take a glass-enclosed elevator to reach a secluded beach.

5 Estate Bakkeroe, Flamboyant Point, St. Thomas, U.S.V.I. 00801. www.marriott.com. ✆ **800/524-2000** or 340/776-8500. Fax 340/715-6191. 450 units. Winter $360–$745 double, from $760 suite; off season $300–$629 double, from $600 suite. AE, DC, MC, V. **Amenities:** 7 restaurants; 6 bars; babysitting; health club; 3 outdoor pools; room service; spa; 2 tennis courts (lit); watersports equipment/rentals. *In room:* A/C, TV, fridge, hair dryer, Wi-Fi ($7 per day).

Ritz-Carlton St. Thomas ★★★ ☺ Fronted by white-sand beaches, on 30 acres of steeply sloping terrain near the extreme southeastern tip of St. Thomas, its architecture evokes a *palazzo* in Venice. Originally built by another hotel chain, and skillfully adapted and expanded to the Ritz-Carlton's specifications, it's the most prestigious and desirable hotel on the island, with landscaped gardens, bubbling fountains, and occasionally hidden courtyards evoking the feel of a sprawling Mediterranean villa.

Regardless of room (some are better accessorized and more plush than others), each accommodation has been fully renovated and painted in tones of butter and mahogany. Most of the accommodations are in six three-story villa annexes, each designed with vaguely Mediterranean motifs. Both the landscaping and the public rooms have been considerably upgraded, including the Ritz-Carlton spa. A wide variety of cardiovascular and weight-training equipment was also added. A $58 resort fee is assessed to include watersports, even Wi-Fi, and other activities.

6900 Great Bay, St. Thomas, U.S.V.I. 00802. www.ritzcarlton.com. ✆ **800/542-8680** or 340/775-3333. Fax 340/775-4444. 180 units. Winter $660–$880 double, from $1,290 suite; off season $380–$570 double, from $700 suite. AE, DC, DISC, MC, V. **Amenities:** 4 restaurants; 3 bars; babysitting; children's programs; health club; Jacuzzi; 2 outdoor pools; room service; spa; 2 tennis courts (lit); watersports equipment/rentals. *In room:* A/C, TV, minibar, Wi-Fi (free).

Wyndham Sugar Bay Resort & Spa ★★ ☺ At the eastern end of the island, on a desirable 32-acre plot of steeply sloping terrain, within a 5-minute ride of Red Hook, this well-maintained, much-improved hotel caters very clearly to a conservative, mainstream clientele who often opt to bring their families and young children along with them on holiday. Since about 60% of the guests who stay here opt for a full-board plan, it is, in effect, the largest all-inclusive hotel on St. Thomas. It has panoramic views that sweep out over the sea from its position atop a rocky headland, although its secluded beach is really too small for a resort of this size. Many of the attractive rooms are decorated with rattan pieces and pastels. This is not the most cutting-edge or stylish hotel on the island, but after a renovation in 2006, guest rooms have modern carpeting, Balinesian furnishings, electronics, wall treatments, and state-of-the-art plumbing. The hotel has one of only two casinos (slot machines only) on the island, and the hotel's spa, Journeys, is the largest full-service spa in the U.S. Virgins.

6500 Estate Smith Bay, St. Thomas, U.S.V.I. 00802. www.wyndham.com. ✆ **877/999-3223** or 340/777-7100. Fax 340/777-7200. 294 units. Winter $590–$685 double, from $1,250 suite; off season $500–$615 double, from $1,050 suite. Rates are all-inclusive. Ask about packages and various meal plans. AE, DC, DISC, MC, V. **Amenities:** 3 restaurants; 3 bars; coffee shop; babysitting; children's club; exercise room; Internet (70¢ per min.); 3 outdoor pools; casino (slot machines only); sauna; spa; 4 Laykold tennis courts (lit); watersports equipment/rentals. *In room:* A/C, ceiling fan, TV, fridge, hair dryer.

EXPENSIVE

Bolongo Bay Beach Resort ★ This is an unpretentious, middle-bracket, barefoot kind of place, a well-established St. Thomas all-inclusive (one of only two on the island) whose name translates as "beautiful" from a dialect spoken in the Congo. Deeply entrenched since it was established in 1974, it boasts a half-moon-shaped, 1,000-foot-long white-sand beach—a bit rocky—and a cluster of pink two- and three-story buildings, plus some motel-like units set directly on the sands. The resort has a tightly knit management group consisting of second-generation family members and their spouses and children. There's a social center consisting of a smallish pool and a beachfront bar, replete with palm fronds and timber-built structures that evoke a mixture of a Polynesian treehouse and a Palladian pavilion, within easy reach of a bar and a definite sense of family-maintained laissez-faire. It's a relatively small property, but it offers most of the facilities of a big resort. Many guests check in on the continental plan, which includes breakfast; others opt for plans that include all meals, drinks, a sailboat excursion to St. John, and use of scuba equipment. Rooms are simple, summery, and filled with a kind of conservative but comfortable furniture.

7150 Bolongo, St. Thomas, U.S.V.I. 00802. www.bolongobay.com. ✆ **800/524-4746** or 340/775-1800. Fax 340/775-3208. 65 units. Winter $210–$355 double; off season $185–$310 double. Ask about other packages and various meal plans. AE, MC, V. **Amenities:** 2 restaurants; 2 bars; babysitting; children's programs (ages 4–12); exercise room; basketball courts; 2 outdoor pools; sauna; 2 tennis courts (lit); watersports equipment/rentals. *In room:* A/C, ceiling fan, TV, fridge, hair dryer, kitchenette (in some), Wi-Fi (free).

Elysian Beach Resort ★ This 1980s-era timeshare resort on Cowpet Bay in the East End, a 30-minute drive from Charlotte Amalie, is imbued with a certain European resort chic. The beautiful white-sand beach is the most compelling reason to stay, but you might also come if you're looking for tranquillity and seclusion without the razzle-dazzle of other east end resorts. The thoughtfully planned bedrooms contain balconies, and four offer sleeping lofts reached by a spiral staircase. The decor is tropical, with rattan and bamboo furnishings, ceiling fans, and natural-wood ceilings. The rooms are in a bevy of four-story buildings connected to landscaped gardens. All units are one- or two-bedroom suites. Designer fabrics and white ceramic-tile floors make the tropical living quite grand. Try to avoid rooms in buildings V through Z, as they are some distance from the beach and close to the noisy traffic of the coastal road. Robert's American Grill serves American food, while the less formal Ainsley's Café features cocktails, West Indian and international food, burgers, and salads.

6800 Estate Nazareth (Cowpet Bay), St. Thomas, U.S.V.I. 00802. www.elysianbeachresort.net. ✆ **866/620-7994** or 340/775-1000. Fax 340/776-0910. 180 units. Winter $220–$265 double, $460 suite; off season $215–$260 double, $400 suite. AE, DC, DISC, MC, V. **Amenities:** 2 restaurants; 2 bars; exercise room; volleyball; outdoor pool; sauna; spa; tennis court (lit); watersports equipment/rentals. *In room:* A/C, TV, hair dryer, kitchenette, Wi-Fi ($10 per day).

Pavilions and Pools ★ This unpretentious resort is ideal for those who want to run around as nude as Adam and Eve, Eve and Eve, or Adam and Adam. It dates from the mid-1970s, when the concept of a condo unit with its private plunge pool was new and novel. You stay within your own walled garden, within an apartment whose floor-to-ceiling glass doors open onto a small but strictly private pool. After checking in and following a wooden and concrete pathway to an individual unit, you don't have to see another soul until you leave, if you so desire—the fence and gate around your space are that high. Your swimming pool is flanked on two sides with a deck and plenty of tropical greenery, but very few, if any, have views of the sea. The resort lies 6¾ miles east of Charlotte Amalie. The place is cozy and appealing, albeit in some cases a bit battered, but definitely not posh or particularly cutting-edge. The resort lies steeply uphill from Sapphire Bay, one of the island's best beaches, although you'll have to walk across the grounds of a neighboring resort to reach it.

6400 Estate Smith Bay, St. Thomas, U.S.V.I. 00802. www.pavilionsandpools.com. ✆ **800/524-2001** or 340/775-6110. Fax 340/776-5694. 25 units. Winter $325–$350 double; off season $250–$275 double. Rates include continental breakfast. AE, MC, V. **Amenities:** Restaurant; 25 outdoor pools; watersports equipment/rentals; Wi-Fi (free). *In room:* A/C, ceiling fan, TV/DVD/CD player, fridge, hair dryer, kitchen.

Point Pleasant Resort ★ This is a very private resort on Water Bay, on the northeastern tip of St. Thomas, just a 5-minute walk from lovely Stouffer's Beach. These condo units, which are rented when their owners are not in residence, are set atop a 15-acre bluff with flowering shrubbery, century plants, frangipani trees, secluded nature trails, old rock formations, and lookout points. The villa-style accommodations have light and airy furnishings, mostly rattan and floral fabrics. From your living room, you'll have a gorgeous view over Tortola, St. John, and Jost Van Dyke. The restaurant, Agavé Terrace (p. 699), is one of the most consistently reliable on the island.

6600 Estate Smith Bay, St. Thomas, U.S.V.I. 00802. www.pointpleasantresort.com. ✆ **800/524-2300** or 340/775-7200. Fax 340/776-5694. 128 units. Winter $300–$320 junior suite, $320–$395 deluxe suite, $550–$570 2-bedroom suite; off season $180 junior suite, $195–$255 deluxe suite, $355 2-bedroom suite. Ask about package deals. Children 11 and under stay free in parent's room. AE, DC, DISC, MC, V. **Amenities:** 2 restaurants; 2 bars; exercise room; Internet (free); 3 outdoor pools; snorkeling. *In room:* A/C, ceiling fan, TV, kitchen.

Secret Harbour Beach Resort ★ This all-suites resort from the early 1970s is on the stunning white-sand beach at Nazareth Bay, just outside Red Hook Marina. Each of its pink-fronted contemporary annexes (four on the beachfront and an additional three on a hillside near the beach) has southwestern exposure (great for sunsets), and each unit has a private deck or patio. You'll be just steps from the sand, and great snorkeling is right offshore. There are three types of accommodations, each outfitted according to the tastes and budgets of its individual owner: studio apartments, one-bedroom suites, and two-bedroom suites. Each studio apartment has a bedroom/sitting-room area, patio, and dressing-room area; each one-bedroom suite has a living/dining area, a separate bedroom, and a sun deck; and each luxurious two-bedroom suite has two bathrooms with tub/showers and a private living room. Honeymooners are likely to show up in the winter months.

The Blue Moon Café (p. 696) serves simple American dishes at lunch. At dinner look for some of the best steaks on the island and the fresh catch of the day.

6280 Estate Nazareth, Charlotte Amalie, St. Thomas, U.S.V.I. 00802. www.secretharbourvi.com. ✆ **340/775-6550.** Fax 340/775-1501. 60 units. Winter $365–$395 double, $375–$465 suite; off season $195–$265 double, $245–$335 suite. Children 12 and under stay free in parent's room. AE, MC, V. **Amenities:** Restaurant; bar; exercise room; Internet (free); Jacuzzi; outdoor pool; 3 tennis courts (lit); watersports equipment/rentals. *In room:* A/C, TV, hair dryer, kitchen.

Windward Passage This well-managed, upgraded hotel is at the edge of Charlotte Amalie. It's favored by business travelers, sports fans, musicians, and politicians from neighboring islands. If you don't mind the sense of standardized rooms, chain-hotel style, you can get some comfortable accommodations here. Rooms are priced with premiums charged for water-fronting views, so ask for an "island view" if you want to economize.

Veterans Dr. (P.O. Box 640), St. Thomas, U.S.V.I. 00804. www.windwardpassage.com. ✆ **800/524-7389** or 340/774-5200. Fax 340/774-1231. 151 units. Winter $275–$325 double, $300–$375 suite; off season $172–$223 double, $225–$265 suite. AE, DC, MC, V. **Amenities:** Restaurant; bar; exercise room; outdoor pool; room service; spa; watersports equipment/rentals. *In room:* A/C, TV, fridge, hair dryer, Wi-Fi (free).

MODERATE

At Home in the Tropics ★ This is one of the best-run and most comfortable B&Bs in Charlotte Amalie. Since it is a traditional West Indian house, only one room deep, each accommodation opens onto a panoramic view of Charlotte Amalie harbor. The structure dates from 1803, when it was the barracks for the personal guard of the Danish governor. Handsomely restored, the bedrooms are attractively furnished in an airy Caribbean motif. The setting is in the midst of many of the island's elegant mansions and gardens. Guests are given their own key to the locked gate for the courtyard property. The property is small, and the swimming pool is deep, so kids 12 and under are discouraged.

1680 Dronningens Gade, Charlotte Amalie (P.O. Box 6877), St. Thomas, U.S.V.I. 00804. www.athome inthetropics.com. ✆ **340/777-9857.** Fax 340/774-3890. Winter $225–$245 double; off season $205–$225 double. Rates include breakfast. AE, MC, V. **Amenities:** Outdoor swimming pool. *In room:* A/C, ceiling fan, hair dryer, Wi-Fi (free).

Villa Blanca ★ Small, intimate, charming, and just a wee bit battered, this hotel lies east of Charlotte Amalie on 3 secluded acres of residential hilltop land, among the most panoramic areas on the island, with views over the harbor and the green rolling hills. The hotel's main building served as the private home of its present owner, Blanca Terrasa Smith, between 1973 and 1985. After the death of her husband, Mrs. Smith added a 12-room annex in the garden and opened her grounds to paying guests. Today a homey, caring ambience prevails. Each room contains tile floors, a ceiling fan and/or air-conditioning, a well-equipped kitchenette, and a private balcony or terrace with sweeping views either eastward to St. John or westward to Puerto Rico and the harbor of Charlotte Amalie. On the premises are a freshwater pool and a large covered patio where you can enjoy the sunset. The closest beach is Morning Star Bay, about a 4-mile drive away.

4 Raphune Hill (Rte. 38), Charlotte Amalie (P.O. Box 7505), St. Thomas, U.S.V.I. 00801. www.villablanca hotel.com. ✆ **800/231-0034** or 340/776-0749. Fax 340/779-2661. 14 units. Winter $135–$145 double, $145 cottage; off season $95–$105 double, $105 cottage. Rates include continental breakfast. AE, DISC, MC, V. **Amenities:** Outdoor pool; sportfishing. *In room:* A/C and/or ceiling fan, TV, hair dryer, kitchenette, Wi-Fi (free).

INEXPENSIVE

Bellavista Bed & Breakfast ★★ It's a bit pricey, but if you want to live with a certain luxury, B&B style, this is about as good as it gets on the island. Nestled on Denmark Hill, this restored island estate overlooks Charlotte Amalie and its historic harbor. You are only a 5-minute walk into town, or else a 7-minute drive to the premier beach of Magens Bay. Bedrooms have an architectural charm embellished with an eclectic tropical decor. The romantic bedrooms have names such as Bambooshay or J'ouvert Gardens. The former master bedroom, for example, is decorated with jewel-toned fabrics and bamboo accents, the bed adorned with a demi-canopy trimmed in mosquito netting. The best rooms open onto a private balcony with a view.

2713 Murphy Gade 12–14, St. Thomas, U.S.V.I. 00802. www.bellavista-bnb.com. ✆ **888/333-3063** or 340/714-5706. 4 units. Winter $195–$245 double; off season $175–$235 double. MC, V. Rates include breakfast. **Amenities:** Concierge; outdoor pool. *In room:* A/C, ceiling fan, TV, fridge, hair dryer, Wi-Fi (free).

The Crystal Palace This is one of the few B&Bs on St. Thomas. It occupies what was rebuilt in 1932 on early 19th-century foundations after a series of fires and hurricanes that left other parts of the island homeless. Today its owner is the kindly but crusty Ronnie Lockhart, president of the St. Thomas & St. John Friends of Denmark Society, Inc., who showcases the home he was raised in as a genuinely historical but somewhat battered mansion. There's a stateliness to this elegant antique monument, whose foot-thick masonry walls defy most attempts to drill through them. Views from the covered balconies of this place sweep out over the city and the harbor. Furnishings include a mixture of the modern, the prosaic, the serviceable, and the genuinely antique, scattered rather formally amid souvenirs from the Lockhart family of long ago. Only two of the building's five accommodations contain a private bathroom—the others are shared facilities in the corridors.

12 Crystal Gade, Synagogue Hill (P.O. Box 12200), St. Thomas, U.S.V.I. 00802. www.crystalpalaceusvi.com. ✆ **866/502-2277** or 340/777-2277. 4 units, 2 with bathroom. Winter $120 double without bathroom, $150 double with bathroom; off season $100 double without bathroom, $120 double with bathroom. Rates include breakfast. AE, DISC, MC, V. *In room:* A/C, TV, no phone, Wi-Fi (free).

Galleon House The rates at Galleon House are among the most competitive on St. Thomas, and the resident managers (Canadian Sandy Rankin and his Tennessee-born wife, Martha) are especially helpful. It consists of a wood-sided "main house" (from around 1850) and a concrete-sided annex (built in the early 1980s), site of most of the accommodations. You'll walk up a long flight of stairs to reach a concrete terrace that doubles as the reception area. The small rooms are within scattered hillside buildings. The best accommodations have panoramic views from private verandas. Breakfast is served on a veranda overlooking the harbor, and Magens Beach is a 15-minute drive from the hotel.

31 Kongens Gade (P.O. Box 6577), Charlotte Amalie, St. Thomas, U.S.V.I. 00804. www.galleonhouse.com. ✆ **800/524-2052** or 340/774-6952. Fax 340/774-6952. 13 units, 11 with bathroom. Winter $85 double without bathroom, $110–$160 double with bathroom; off season $75 double without bathroom, $90–$125 double with bathroom. Rates include full breakfast. AE, MC, V. **Amenities:** Outdoor pool; snorkeling. *In room:* A/C, ceiling fan, TV, Wi-Fi ($5 per hr.).

The Green Iguana ★ Sitting on Blackbeard's Hill, in the center of Charlotte Amalie, this is one of the best-run and most economical inns on the island. There's a remnant within the construction from a much older building, but much of what you'll see today is an unpretentious concrete structure from the 1970s and 1980s. Bedrooms have panoramic views of the harbor, the constantly arriving cruise ships, and the other Virgin Islands. The little inn lies only a 5-minute walk from the town's shops, restaurants, and bars, and Magens Beach is a 10-minute drive over the hill. Bedrooms are midsize and done in a tropical motif with wicker. You have a choice of a king-, queen-, or twin-size bed.

1002 Blackbeard's Hill, Charlotte Amalie, St. Thomas, U.S.V.I. 00802. www.thegreeniguana.com. ✆ **855/448-2621** or 340/776-7654. Fax 340/777-4312. 9 units. Winter $140–$170 double; off season $125 double. AE, MC, V. *In room:* A/C, ceiling fan, fridge, hair dryer, kitchenette, Wi-Fi (free).

Hotel 1829 ★ This national historic site is one of the leading small hotels in the Caribbean. It was designed in a Spanish motif, with French grillwork, Danish bricks, and sturdy Dutch doors. Danish and African labor completed the structure in 1829 (hence the name), and since then it has entertained the likes of Edna St. Vincent Millay and Mikhail Baryshnikov. The place stands right in the heart of town, on a hillside 3 minutes from Government House. Magens Bay Beach is about a 10-minute drive. It's a bit of a climb to the top of this multitiered structure—there are many steps, but no elevator. Amid a cascade of flowering bougainvillea are the upper rooms, which overlook a central courtyard with a miniature pool. The rooms in the main house are well designed and attractive, and most face the water. All have wood beams and stone walls. The smallest units, in the former slave quarters, are the least comfortable. Children 11 and under aren't really encouraged here.

Kongens Gade (P.O. Box 1567), Charlotte Amalie, St. Thomas, U.S.V.I. 00804. www.hotel1829.com. ✆ **800/524-2002** or 340/776-1829. Fax 340/776-4313. 15 units. Winter $105–$155 double, from $145 suite; off season $80–$125 double, from $190 suite. Rates include continental breakfast. DISC, MC, V. **Amenities:** Bar; small outdoor pool. *In room:* A/C, TV, fridge, hair dryer, no phone, Wi-Fi (free).

Where to Dine

The St. Thomas dining scene is among the best in the West Indies; however, meals tend to be expensive, and the best spots (with a few exceptions) are outside Charlotte Amalie and can be reached only by taxi or car.

IN CHARLOTTE AMALIE

Banana Tree Grille ★★ INTERNATIONAL Hip, urbanized, and deeply entrenched among the island's mover-and-shaker stratum, this is our favorite restaurant in St. Thomas. It's perched on a covered veranda whose sides, unless they're louvered shut during inclement weather, are open to the night air and the shimmering lights of Charlotte Amalie's harbor. Set at the base of Bluebeard's Castle (you'll have to walk through some of the 18th-c. stone corridors to reach it), the place serves up candlelit dinners, sweeping views over the busy harbor, and a decor that includes genuine banana plants artfully scattered through the two dining rooms. The cuisine is creative, the patrons usually sophisticated and laid-back. Start with one of the aptly named "fabulous firsts," such as bacon-wrapped horseradish shrimp, grilled and dancing over mango glaze. The house specialties, lobster-tail tempura with orange-sambal sauce and mango-mustard-glazed salmon, are particularly good. If it's offered, try the aioli lamb shank, another specialty; the meat is slowly braised in Chianti and served with aioli sauce over vegetables and garlic mashed potatoes. The desserts are truly decadent. The bar opens at 5pm. The effervescent Liz Buckelew, a hardworking entrepreneur, is the gracious, affable, and gregarious owner.

In Bluebeard's Castle, Bluebeard's Hill. ✆ **340/776-4050.** www.bananatreegrille.com. Reservations required. Main courses $20–$56. AE, MC, V. Tues–Sun 5:30–9:30pm.

Blue Moon Café CREATIVE AMERICAN For idyllic dining in an open-air setting, this beachfront restaurant claims, with some degree of accuracy, one of the most memorable settings for panoramic sunset views; *Wine Spectator* twice recognized the Blue Moon Café as having the most romantic setting in St. Thomas. The menu, based on market-fresh ingredients, is changed twice seasonally. The list of food is geared to appeal to a wide range of palates, beginning with such tropical starters as coconut-honey shrimp with a guava dipping sauce, or a portobello-mushroom-and-goat-cheese tart with field onions. Tiptop foodstuffs are handled with imagination and appear in zestful combinations like mahimahi with pecans, bananas, and a coconut-rum sauce; and grilled scallops with a tomato-basil risotto and fresh asparagus. For lunch you can enjoy burgers, wraps, salads, and sandwiches.

In the Secret Harbour Beach Resort, 6280 Estate Nazareth. ✆ **340/779-2262.** www.bluemooncafevi.com. Reservations required. Main courses $17–$36. AE, DC, DISC, MC, V. Daily 8am–10pm.

Grande Cru/Wikked/Fat Turtle ★ INTERNATIONAL This trio of the genuinely intriguing restaurants of Charlotte Amalie lie side by side beside the WICO docks, immediately adjacent to where some of the world's biggest cruise ships moor. Each of the three is part of a fast-evolving marina/hotel/condo development, Yacht Haven Grande. The most expensive, formal, and elegant of the three restaurants is Grande Cru, whose meticulously crafted dining room manages to be both romantic and jazzy at the same time. Tables spill outdoors onto a covered veranda that's open to a view of privately owned yachts. Look for stylish menu items that include braised short ribs on horseradish and lemon risotto; pistachio and basil-crusted goat cheese on greens with a truffle-flavored vinaigrette; and a succulent version of roasted chicken with preserved lemon and sun-dried tomatoes.

The charming middle-bracket contender within the group is Wikked, a breezy, amiable, and likable restaurant that some of the local boat and condo owners have transformed into their favorite. And the most raucous and animated is Fat Turtle, a booze-and-burger joint that's a favorite with the college crowd looking for flavorful grub, very stiff drinks, and large-screen TVs broadcasting sporting events.

In the Yacht Haven Marina. ✆ **340/775-7263** for Grande Cru, **340/775-8953** for Wikked, or **340/714-3566** for Fat Turtle. www.grandecruvi.com, www.wikkedrestaurant.com, or www.fat-turtle.com. Reservations recommended at Grande Cru, not necessary at Wikked or Fat Turtle. Main courses $24–$35 at Grande Cru, $11–$42 at Wikked and Fat Turtle. AE, MC, V. Grande Cru Mon–Fri noon–3pm and 5:30–10pm; Sat–Sun 5:30–10pm. Wikked Mon–Sat 11am–10pm; Sun 9am–10pm. Fat Turtle daily 11am–10pm (bar open till 2am).

Hervé Restaurant & Wine Bar ★ AMERICAN/CARIBBEAN/FRENCH A panoramic view of Charlotte Amalie and a historic setting are side benefits—it's the cuisine that matters. Hervé Paul Chassin is a restaurateur with a vast classical background. In an unpretentious setting, he offers high-quality food at reasonable prices. There are two dining areas: a large open-air terrace, and a more intimate wine room. Start with the pistachio-encrusted brie, shrimp in a stuffed crab shell, or conch fritters with mango chutney. For a main course, try the house special bouillabaisse, or a delectable black-sesame-crusted tuna with a ginger/raspberry sauce. There are also nightly specials of game, fish, and pasta. Desserts are divine—you'll rarely taste a creamier crème caramel or a lighter, fluffier mango or raspberry cheesecake.

Next to Hotel 1829, Government Hill. ✆ **340/777-9703.** www.herverestaurant.com. Reservations required. Main courses $9–$48 lunch, $21–$49 dinner. AE, MC, V. Mon–Fri 11am–3pm; daily 6–10pm.

Petite Pump Room ★ WEST INDIAN/INTERNATIONAL This restaurant is housed on the second floor of the industrial-looking ferryboat terminal at the edge of the harborfront in Charlotte Amalie, departure point for boats headed off to the British Virgin Islands and St. Croix. Established in 1963 by the then-owner of the famous Pump Room restaurant in Chicago, it does a thriving breakfast and lunch business among local boat owners and downtown office workers. The draw is some of the best West Indian cooking on island, a cuisine that takes the preparation of callaloo greens very seriously (they're fabulous), and the nuances of pounded conch steak and grouper with fries with devotion. If you want something international (that is, American), the menu lists club sandwiches, steaks, chicken dishes, and burgers, but virtually everyone who comes here orders the West Indian food. Examples? Stewed oxtail or chicken, or fried potfish with Creole sauce, always served with your choice of pigeon peas and rice, mashed potatoes, dumplings, macaroni and cheese, mushrooms with vegetables, fried plantains, or two different kinds of potatoes.

In the Edward Wilmoth Blyden Building, Veterans Dr. © **340/776-2976.** www.petitepumproom.com. Breakfasts $7-$13; sandwiches and salads $8-$18; platters $12-$21. Daily 7am-4:30pm.

Virgilio's ★ NORTHERN ITALIAN Virgilio's is the best northern Italian restaurant in the Virgin Islands. Its neobaroque interior is sheltered under heavy ceiling beams and brick vaulting. A well-trained staff serves meals against a backdrop of stained-glass windows, crystal chandeliers, and soft Italian music. The *cinco peche* (clams, mussels, scallops, oysters, and crayfish simmered in a saffron broth) is delicious, and the fettuccine Alfredo is one of the best we've tasted. Classic dishes are served with a distinctive flair—the lamb shank, for example, is filled with a porcini-mushroom stuffing and glazed with a roasted garlic aioli. The marinated grilled duck is served chilled. You can also order individual pizzas. The place also does a thriving take-away business as well.

18 Dronningens Gade (entrance on a narrow alley running between Main and Back sts.). © **340/776-4920.** Reservations recommended. Main courses $13-$29 lunch, $23-$50 dinner. AE, MC, V. Mon-Sat 11:30am-10:30pm.

IN FRENCHTOWN

Bella Blu ★ MEDITERRANEAN/SEAFOOD To the immediate west of Charlotte Amalie, this restaurant's 14 tables overlook the harbor. For years Bella Blu enjoyed fame throughout the Caribbean under the name Alexander's, serving a rather heavy (for the Tropics) Austrian cuisine. Under new owners, the fare is lighter and focuses on the sunny flavors of the Mediterranean. To begin with, you might try the tuna tartare or one of the Moroccan dishes. The cooks are whizzes at concocting superb creations from lamb, veal, and seafood. The menu changes based on seasonal shopping and what's good and fresh at the marketplace.

Frenchtown Mall. © **340/774-4349.** Reservations recommended. Main courses $9-$24 lunch, $9-$34 dinner. AE, MC, V. Mon-Sat 11:30am-4pm and 5:30-10pm.

Craig & Sally's ★ INTERNATIONAL This Caribbean cafe is set in an airy, open-sided pavilion, with views of the sea and sky. Dishes range from pasta to seafood, with influences from Europe and Asia. You can try such light dishes as filet of salmon with a lemon-grass-flavored mayonnaise, or perhaps the pan-seared trout with fresh mushrooms. The lobster-stuffed twice-baked potatoes are inspired, and the wine list is the most extensive and sophisticated on St. Thomas. The menu changes daily.

3525 Honduras. © **340/777-9949.** www.craigandsallys.com Reservations recommended. Main courses $15-$34. MC, V. Wed-Fri 11:30am-3pm and 5:30-10pm; Sat-Sun 5:30-10pm.

Oceana ★ INTERNATIONAL/SEAFOOD This upscale (but not stuffy) restaurant is a hip and stylish enclave popular with locals. It occupies what was, during the Danish occupation, the Russian consulate. Outfitted with slabs of carefully oiled paneling and painted in bright blues and greens inspired by the ocean, it offers two distinctly different venues. The street level has a wine-cum-singles bar, where small platters of food (blini, crostini, and cheese platters) and tapas specifically designed to go with the changing array of wines help foster convivial after-work chitchat. Upstairs, within a relaxed but relatively formal dining room, candles and oil lamps flicker amid bouquets of flowers. Menu items focus mainly on fish, but a fair number of beef and lamb dishes appear as well. Our favorites include spicy shrimp served with a cup of Andalusian-style gazpacho; house-marinated salmon (gravlax); mussels in white-wine sauce; pan-fried freshwater trout from Idaho; oven-roasted sea bass with a white wine, thyme, and olive-oil sauce; grilled sirloin of lamb; several different preparations of Caribbean lobster; and New York strip, porterhouse, and filet mignon steaks. For sheer delight, visit the "tasting table," a long bar that offers an array of such concoctions as portobellos topped with bacon bits and goat cheese, or smoked oyster, crab, and avocado salad—even a wild rice and lamb manchego. You can dine on either floor.

In the Villa Olga, 8 Honduras. ✆ **340/774-4262.** www.oceana.vi. Reservations recommended. Main courses $25–$48; tapas $12–$20. AE, DC, MC, V. Thurs–Tues 5:30–10pm.

ON THE NORTH COAST

The Old Stone Farmhouse AMERICAN/INTERNATIONAL Set in a wooded valley close to the 11th hole of the Mahogany Run Golf Course, the old-fashioned building that contains this restaurant dates from the 1750s. Once it was a stable for a nearby Danish sugar plantation. Ceiling fans and breezes blowing through the valley keep the place cool, while golfers and those who love them indulge from an eclectic menu that takes advantage of the best seasonal produce. The fresh fish dishes are always the best option. Begin, perhaps, with grilled portobello mushrooms with Asian duck. Many regulars come here for the well-prepared steak.

Mahogany Run. ✆ **340/777-6277.** www.oldstone.rummi.com. Reservations recommended. Main courses $19–$32. AE, MC, V. Tues–Sun 5:30–9:30pm.

Romano's Restaurant ITALIAN Located near Coral World, this hideaway is owned by New Jersey chef Tony Romano, who specializes in a flavorful and herb-laden cuisine that makes a nice change from Caribbean food. House favorites include *linguine con pesto,* four-cheese lasagna, a tender and well-flavored *osso buco* (veal shanks), scaloppine Marsala, and broiled salmon. All desserts are made on the premises. With exposed brick and well-stocked wine racks, this restaurant always seems full of happy, lively diners.

6501 Red Hook Plaza. ✆ **340/775-0045.** www.romanosrestaurant.com. Reservations recommended. Main courses $24–$42; pastas $24–$27. MC, V. Mon–Sat. 6–10:30pm. Closed Sept, 4 days in Apr for Carnival, 4 days in Dec, and New Year's Day.

IN & AROUND RED HOOK BAY (THE EAST END)

Agavé Terrace ★ CARIBBEAN Perched high above a steep and heavily forested hillside on the eastern tip of St. Thomas, one of the island's best restaurants offers a sweeping panorama and unparalleled romance. The house drink is Desmond Delight, a combination of Midori, rum, pineapple juice, and a secret ingredient. After a few Delights, try the house appetizer, an Agavé sampler for two, which includes portions of crabmeat, conch fritters, and shrimp cocktail. The catch of the day features three different fish, which can be prepared in any of seven different ways with a choice of nine sauces. Some of our favorite meals here include Chef Nakata's jerk chicken and Coral Bay crab cakes served with rémoulade. There are also vegetarian selections. The wine list is extensive. A live steel-drum band draws listeners Tuesday and Thursday nights.

In the Point Pleasant Resort, 6600 Estate Smith Bay. ✆ **340/775-4142.** www.agaveterrace.com. Reservations recommended. Main courses $20–$38. AE, DC, MC, V. Daily 6–10pm.

Caribbean Saloon AMERICAN Yachties from the American Yacht Harbor dine and drink here, enjoying the good times, which might be watching sports on the widescreen TVs or listening to live music on the weekends. It's arguably the most active joint in Red Hook. The nearby fishing fleet always brings in the catch of the day, which is often grilled to your specifications. The luncheon fare is mostly appetizers, sandwiches, and burgers. Dinner gets more elaborate, including such tasty appetizers as crab cakes with a shrimp sauce, or conch fritters. Soups and fresh salads are followed by an array of ribs, chicken, pasta dishes, steaks, chops, and seafood. The baby back ribs are the perennial favorite, as is the filet mignon in a burgundy wine sauce. Mahimahi, swordfish, and lobster tail invariably appear on the menu in a variety of cooking methods, often served blackened. There's a late-night menu, which is available only from 10pm to 4am.

American Yacht Harbor, Building B, Red Hook. ✆ **340/775-7060.** www.caribbeansaloon.com. Main courses $17–$37. MC, V. Daily 11am–10:30pm.

Coco Blue ★★ CARIBBEAN This Red Hook eatery, a sister restaurant of Havana Blue (p. 701), comes up with a new take on Caribbean cuisine. Creative chef James "Black Magic" Crowther features an inventive menu of such delights as calamari with a coconut and lime aioli; spring rolls with jalapeño and grilled pineapple, graced with tamarind chutney; or blackened fish tacos with a sweet-chili-glazed bacon and a citrus crème fraîche. And that's just the appetizers. A soup of the day highlights local produce and flavors. The island's best sushi rolls include everything from local Caribbean wahoo to spicy tuna. The highlights of the main courses include white-wine-marinated sea bass with a shiitake sauté, or lemon-grass-glazed salmon with a cilantro essence. Mahimahi is wrapped in banana leaves and served with a coconut black rice and a banana pepper buerre blanc. Ever had piña colada chicken? You can here.

American Yacht Harbor, Red Hook. ✆ **340/774-7253.** Reservations recommended. Main courses $16–$28; 6-course menu $85. AE, MC, V. Mon–Sat 11:30am–2:30pm and 5:30–10:30pm; Sun 5:30–10:30pm.

Duffy's Love Shack ★ 🎁 AMERICAN/CARIBBEAN You can mingle with locals at this loud, animated, raucous, and aggressively pickup-oriented singles bar. Things get particularly busy here on weekends, when, as the evening wears on, the customers virtually become the entertainment, sometimes dancing on the tabletops and consuming inordinate amounts of liquor. Yes, Duffy's also serves food, standard American dishes with Caribbean flavors. The restaurant is open-air, with lots of bamboo and a thatched roof over the bar. Even the menu appears on a bamboo stick, like an old-fashioned fan. Start with honey-barbecued ribs, then move on to pork Cuban. After midnight, a late-night menu (mainly sandwiches) appears. The bar business is huge, and the bartender is known for his lethal rum drinks. You can ask about the Lobster Lunacy parties, but since things get fairly loony around here anyway, it probably won't make much of a difference.

6500 Red Hook Plaza. ✆ **340/779-2080.** www.duffysloveshack.com. Main courses $9–$20. No credit cards. Daily 11:30am–2am.

Fungi's on the Beach CARIBBEAN This funky native bar opens onto Pineapple Beach. It's a lot of fun, and the burgers are some of the juiciest on the island. You can also order Caribbean specialties like conch in butter sauce, yellowtail snapper Creole, johnnycakes, plantains, rice and beans, and callaloo soup. Stewed chicken is a local favorite. The place has an outdoorsy atmosphere with a reggae theme. Nightly entertainment—reggae and more reggae—is also a feature.

Point Pleasant Rd., East End. ✆ **340/775-4142.** Main courses $7–$24. AE, MC, V. Daily 11:30am–10pm.

Havana Blue ★★ CUBAN/PACIFIC RIM/FUSION This, one of our favorite restaurants on St. Thomas, is a chic and stylish venue on the second floor of an airy, open-sided pavilion directly beside the beach on the grounds of the Morning Star annex of the Marriott resort (p. 691). Accented with highly theatrical uplighting and yards of sheer white muslin, it presents a well-trained staff and a sophisticated urban-hipster menu that is the island's most inspired. An inventive crew labors away in the kitchen, running wild in its culinary imagination. Cool cigars, hip drinks (mango mojitos), and a chic decor draw serious foodies to this cutting-edge restaurant, where chef Omar Sanchez intoxicates with his aromas and flavors. After launching yourself with the black-bean hummus, duck-meat crepe with jalapeño-and-espresso sauce, or the tuna tartare with a soy-lime vinaigrette, it's on to such delights as breaded chicken breast stuffed with manchego cheese and diced jalapeños; a mojito-glazed skirt steak; or a miso-crusted sea bass. Or how about ancho-chili-rubbed beef filet with espresso sauce? Desserts are worth crossing the island for, if it means Cuban chocolate cake with coconut ice cream, or warm banana and macadamia spring rolls with a strawberry balsamic purée.

In the Frenchman's Reef & Morning Star Marriott Beach Resort, 5 Estate Bakkeroe. ✆ **340/715-2583.** www.havanabluerestaurant.com. Reservations required. Main courses $28–$42. AE, DC, MC, V. Daily 5:30–10:30pm.

Molly Malone's IRISH/CARIBBEAN Within a replica of an old-fashioned clapboard-sided house, and tucked away within a back alley of Red Hook's American Yacht Harbor, you can join the good ol' boys and dig into the best baby back ribs on the island. No one can drink more brew than the boisterous crowd that assembles here every night to let the good times roll. But despite this place's reputation as the most popular Irish pub and bistro on the island, the food is surprisingly good. Chili with cheese, bangers and mash, Philadelphia-style hoagies, oversized Caesar salads, and "Whale of a Tale" seafood platters are deservedly popular. If you're nostalgic for the Emerald Isle, go for the shepherd's pie. The conch fritters are the best in the East End, and an Irish/Caribbean stew is a nightly feature.

6100 Red Hook Quarters. ✆ **340/775-1270.** Main courses $10–$28. AE, MC, V. Daily 7am–11pm (until midnight on weekends).

Hitting the Beach

Chances are, your hotel will be right on the beach or very close to one. All the beaches in St. Thomas are public, and most lie anywhere from 1¾ to 5 miles from Charlotte Amalie.

THE NORTH SIDE The gorgeous white sands of **Magens Bay ★★** lie between two mountains 3 miles north of the capital. The turquoise waters here are calm and ideal for swimming, and the snorkeling is also good. The beach is no secret, and it's usually terribly overcrowded, though it gets better in the midafternoon. Changing facilities, snorkeling gear, lounge chairs, paddleboats, and kayaks are available. There is no public transportation to get here from Charlotte Amalie (though some hotels provide shuttle buses); take Route 35 north all the way. The gates to the beach are open daily from 5am to 6pm. (After 4pm, you'll need insect repellent.) Admission is

Two Great Escapes

Water Island, ½ mile off the coast from the harbor of Charlotte Amalie, is the fourth-largest island of the U.S. Virgins, with 494 acres of land. At palm-shaded **Honeymoon Beach,** you can swim, snorkel, sail, water-ski, or sunbathe, then order lunch or a drink from the beach bar (Sat–Sun only). A ferry (✆ **340/690-4159**) runs between Crown Bay Marina and Water Island several times a day; it's $5 for a one-way ticket, $10 per person round-trip. **Crown Bay Marina** (✆ **340/774-2255**) is part of the St. Thomas submarine base.

In the same bay, and even closer to shore, is **Hassel Island.** It's almost completely deserted, and it is protected as part of a U.S. National Park. There are no hotels or services of any kind here, and swimming is limited to narrow, rocky beaches. Even so, many visitors hire a boat to drop them off for an hour or two. A hike along part of the shoreline is a welcome relief from the cruise-ship congestion of Charlotte Amalie. Bring water and food if you plan to spend more than 3 hours here.

$3 per person, plus $1 per car. Don't bring valuables, and certainly don't leave anything essential in your parked car.

A marked trail leads to **Little Magens Bay,** a separate, clothing-optional beach that is especially popular with gay and lesbian visitors. This is also former President Clinton's preferred beach on St. Thomas. (No, he doesn't go nude.)

Coki Point Beach, in the northeast, near Coral World, is good, but whenever more than one cruise ship is in port, it can get very, very crowded. In our opinion, the best time to visit this beach, as a means of avoiding the congestion of the "high noon" hours (and whether cruise ships are in port or not), is mornings from 8 to 10am and afternoons from 3 to 6pm. It's noted for its warm, crystal-clear water, ideal for swimming and snorkeling. (You'll see thousands of rainbow-hued fish swimming among the beautiful corals.) Locals even sell small bags of fish food, so you can feed the sea creatures while you're snorkeling. Informal shacks serve fresh food, including just-caught fish, at ramshackle picnic tables. Kiosks rent beach chairs and snorkel gear, and there are outdoor showers as well as toilets. Of course, there are the inevitable hair braiders. From the beach, there's a panoramic view of offshore Thatch Cay. Concessions can arrange everything from water-skiing to parasailing. An East End bus runs to Smith Bay and lets you off at the gate to Coral World and Coki. Watch out for pickpockets.

Also on the north side is luscious **Grand Beach,** one of the island's most beautiful. It opens onto Smith Bay and is near Coral World. Many watersports are available here. The beach is right off Route 38.

THE EAST END Small and special, **Secret Harbour** is near a collection of condos. With its white sand and coconut palms, it's the epitome of Caribbean charm. The snorkeling near the rocks is some of the best on the island, and it is likely you'll spot a hawksbill turtle foraging for some sea anemones for lunch. Kiosks rent gear for watersports, and a beachside restaurant offers snacks and drinks. No public transportation stops here, but it's an easy taxi ride east of Charlotte Amalie heading toward Red Hook.

Sapphire Beach is set against the backdrop of the Sapphire Beach Resort and Marina, where you can have lunch or order drinks. There are good views of offshore cays, and St. John, a large reef, is close to the shore. Windsurfers enjoy this beach. The all-day beach party that goes on here is the best on island. Snorkel gear, beach chairs, Sunfish, and kayaks can be rented from various kiosks, and there is also a bar, plus a restaurant, toilets, and an outdoor shower. Just off the beach, there is good snorkeling over a shallow reef populated by conch, eagle rays, and starfish, among other species. The best place for snorkeling here is at Prettyklip Point. Take the East End bus from Charlotte Amalie, going via Red Hook. Ask to be let off at the entrance to Sapphire Bay; it's not too far to walk from here to the water.

White-sand **Lindquist Beach** isn't a long strip, but it's one of the island's prettiest. It's between Wyndham Sugar Bay Resort and the Sapphire Beach Resort. Many films and TV commercials have used this photogenic beach as a backdrop. It's not likely to be crowded, as it's not very well known.

THE SOUTH SIDE **Morning Star Beach** (also known as Frenchman's Bay Beach) is near the Frenchman's Reef & Morning Star Marriott Beach Resort (p. 691), about 1¾ miles east of Charlotte Amalie. Here, among the often-young crowds of visitors (many of whom are gay), you can don your skimpiest bikini. Sailboats, snorkeling equipment, and lounge chairs are available for rent. The beach is easily reached by a cliff-front elevator at Frenchman's Reef.

Limetree Beach, set against a backdrop of sea-grape trees and shady palms, lures those who want a serene spread of sand where they can bask in the sun and even feed hibiscus blossoms to iguanas. Snorkeling gear, lounge and beach chairs, towels, and drinks are available. There's no public transportation, but the beach can easily be reached by taxi from Charlotte Amalie.

WEST OF CHARLOTTE AMALIE Near the University of the Virgin Islands in the southwest, **Brewer's Bay** is one of the island's most popular beaches and the site of an occasional political rally or protest, as well as Carnival parties. The strip of white-coral sand is almost as long as the beach at Magens Bay. Unfortunately, this isn't the place for snorkeling. Vendors sell light meals and drinks. From Charlotte Amalie, take the Fortuna bus heading west; get off at the edge of Brewer's Bay, across from the Reichhold Center.

Lindbergh Beach, which has a lifeguard, restrooms, and a bathhouse, lies immediately adjacent to the Island Beachcomber Hotel and is used almost exclusively by

Hidden Beach Discoveries

At this point, you'd think all the beaches in overrun St. Thomas had been discovered. But there are two less-trampled strands of sand we recently came upon. A sparkling beach of white sand, Vessup Bay, is at the end of Bluebeard's Road (Rte. 322) as it branches off Route 30 near the hamlet of Red Hook. Against a rocky backdrop, the beach curves around a pristine bay studded with vegetation, including cacti, agave plants, and sea grape. One end of the beach is less populated than the other. A watersports concessionaire operates here. Another find is Hull Bay, on the north shore, just west of overcrowded Magens Bay. Surfers are attracted to the waves along the western tip of Hull Bay, and local St. Thomas fishermen anchor in the more tranquil strands. Part of the beach is in shade. Don't expect much in the way of watersports, but there is a combined restaurant and open-air bar.

locals. Its location is close to the airport. Westward-facing, the beach is perfect for catching a sunrise, but except near the rocky promontories on either side of its boundaries, it's not generally considered good for snorkeling. Drinks are served on the beach. Take the Fortuna bus route west from Charlotte Amalie.

Sports & Outdoor Pursuits

DEEP-SEA FISHING The U.S. Virgins have excellent deep-sea fishing—some 19 world records (8 for blue marlin) have been set in these waters. Outfitters abound at the major marinas, like Red Hook. We recommend angling off the ***Fish Hawk*** (**✆ 340/775-9058**), which Captain Al Petrosky sails out of Fish Hawk Marina Lagoon on the East End. His 48-foot diesel-powered craft is fully equipped with rods and reels. For all equipment (as well as sodas and beers, but not meals), you'll pay $650 per half-day for up to six passengers. Full-day excursions start at $1,200.

SAILING **American Yacht Harbor,** Red Hook (**✆ 340/775-6454;** www.igy-americanyachtharbor.com), can refer both bareboat and fully crewed charters. It leaves from the east end of St. Thomas in Vessup Bay. The harbor is home to numerous boat companies, including day-trippers, fishing boats, and sailing charters. Another reliable outfitter is **Charter Yacht League,** at Gregory East (**✆ 800/524-2061** in the U.S., or 340/774-3944; www.vicl.org).

SCUBA DIVING The best scuba-diving site off St. Thomas, especially for novices, has to be **Cow and Calf Rocks,** off the southeast end (45 min. from Charlotte Amalie by boat); here you'll discover a network of coral tunnels riddled with caves, reefs, and ancient boulders encrusted with coral. The ***Cartanser Sr.,*** a sunken World War II cargo ship that lies in about 36 feet of water, is beautifully encrusted with coral and now home to myriad colorful fish. Another popular wreck dive is the ***Maj. General Rogers,*** the stripped-down hull of a former Coast Guard cutter.

Experienced divers may want to dive at exposed sheer rock pinnacles like **Sail Rock** and **French Cap Pinnacle,** which are encrusted with hard and soft corals, and frequented by lobsters and green and hawksbill turtles. They are also exposed to open-ocean currents that can make these very challenging dives.

St. Thomas Diving Club, 7147 Bolongo Bay (**✆ 877/538-8734** in the U.S., or 340/776-2381; www.stthomasdivingclub.com), is a full-service, PADI five-star IDC center, the best on the island. An open-water certification course, including four scuba dives, costs $450. An advanced open-water certification course, including five dives that can be accomplished in 2 days, goes for $450. You can also enjoy local snorkeling for $55.

Dive In!, in the Sapphire Beach Resort & Marina, Smith Bay Road/Route 36 (**✆ 866/434-8346,** ext. 2144, in the U.S., or 340/777-5255; www.diveinusvi.com), is a well-recommended complete diving center that offers some of the finest services in the U.S. Virgin Islands, including professional instruction (beginner to advanced), daily beach and boat dives, custom dive packages, snorkeling trips, and a full-service PADI dive center. An introductory resort course costs $105, with a one-tank dive going for $80 and two-tank dives for $110. A six-dive pass costs $300.

SEA KAYAKING **Virgin Island Ecotours/Mangrove Adventures** (**✆ 877/845-2925** or 340/779-2155; www.viecotours.com) offers half-day kayak trips through a mangrove lagoon on the southern coastline. The cost is $69 per person or $39 for children 11 and under. The professional naturalists who lead the tour allow for 30 to 40 minutes of snorkeling.

SNORKELING ★★ With 30 spectacular reefs just off St. Thomas, this is a terrific destination for snorkeling. We like the waters off **Coki Point ★★**, on the northeast shore of St. Thomas; the coral ledges near Coral World's underwater tower are especially enticing. **Magens Bay** also has great snorkeling year-round. If your hotel doesn't provide snorkel gear, it's easy to rent on most of the island's popular beaches.

You may also want to take a snorkeling cruise. Many leave from the Red Hook and Yacht Haven marinas. The 50-foot yacht ***Nightwind,*** Sapphire Marina (© **340/775-7017;** www.usvi.net/treetops/html/nightwind.html), offers full-day sails to St. John and the outer islands. The price of $125 per adult and $90 for kids 12 and under includes free snorkeling equipment and instruction, plus a continental breakfast, a buffet lunch, and an open bar.

New Horizons, 6501 Red Hook Plaza, Ste. 16, Red Hook (© **800/808-7604** or 340/775-1171; www.newhorizons.daysails.com), offers windborne excursions amid the cays and reefs of the Virgin Islands. The two-masted, 65-foot sloop has circumnavigated the globe and has been used as a design prototype for other boats. A full-day excursion, with continental breakfast, an Italian buffet lunch, and an open bar, costs $120 per person; children 2 to 12, when accompanied by an adult, pay $80. Excursions depart daily, weather permitting, from the Sapphire Beach Resort & Marina. Call ahead for reservations and information. Another vessel, ***New Horizons II,*** a 44-foot custom-made speedboat, runs full-day trips to some of the most scenic highlights of the British Virgin Islands, costing $145 for adults or $95 for children 2 to 12. You will need your passport and will have to pay an additional $30-per-person Customs fee.

You can avoid the crowds by sailing aboard the ***Fantasy,*** Red Hook (© **340/775-5652;** fax 340/775-6256; www.daysailfantasy.com), which departs from the American Yacht Harbor at Red Hook at 9:30am daily. It takes a maximum of six passengers to St. John and nearby islands for swimming, snorkeling, beachcombing, and trolling. Snorkel gear with expert instruction is provided, as is a champagne lunch. The full-day trip costs $140 per person in the summer. A full-day sail for six people costs $840.

Exploring the Island

CHARLOTTE AMALIE ★

The capital, Charlotte Amalie, where most visitors begin their sightseeing, has all the color and charm of an authentic Caribbean waterfront town. In days of yore, seafarers from all over the globe flocked here, as did pirates and members of the Confederacy, who used the port during the American Civil War. (Sadly, St. Thomas was the biggest slave market in the world.) The old warehouses once used for storing pirate goods still stand; today many of them are house shops.

Fort Christian This imposing structure, which dates from 1671, dominates the center of town and underwent a complete renovation with many improvements in 2008. It was named after the Danish king Christian V and has been everything from a fort to a governor's residence to a jail. It became a national historic landmark in 1977 but functioned as a police station, court, and jail until 1983. Now a museum, the fort houses displays on the island's history and culture. Cultural workshops and turn-of-the-20th-century furnishings are just some of the exhibits. A museum shop features local crafts, maps, and prints.

In the town center. © **340/776-4566.** http://www.nps.gov/history/nR/travel/prvi/pr29.htm. Admission $3. Mon–Fri 8:30am–4:30pm.

St. Thomas Skyride This cable-car contraption affords visitors a dramatic view of Charlotte Amalie harbor, with a ride to the top of a 700-foot peak whose panoramas sweep out over the complicated topography of the Caribbean's busiest cruise-ship harbor. The aerial tramway, similar to those used at alpine ski resorts, operates six cars, each with an eight-person capacity, for the 15-minute round-trip ride. It transports customers from the Havensight area adjacent to the harborfront to Paradise Point, where they can disembark to visit shops.

Across from Havensight Mall. © **340/774-9809.** http://paradisepointtramway.com. Round-trip $21 adults, $11 children 6–12, free for children 5 and under. Daily 9am–5pm (call in advance for reservations).

Seven Arches Museum Browsers love checking out the private home of longtime residents Philibert Fluck and Barbara Demaras. This is an 18th-century Danish house, restored to its original condition and furnished with West Indian antiques. You can walk through the yellow ballast arches and visit the great room, with its wonderful view of the busiest harbor in the Caribbean. Night-blooming cacti and iguanas are on the roof of some of the quarters.

Government Hill. © **340/774-9295.** www.sevenarchesmuseum.com. Admission $5. Open only by appointment.

ELSEWHERE ON THE ISLAND

Route 30 (the harbor-fronting Veterans Dr.) will take you west of Charlotte Amalie to **Frenchtown.** (Turn left at the sign to the Admiral's Inn.) Early French-speaking settlers arrived on St. Thomas from St. Barts after the Swedes uprooted them. This colorful village of low-rise, mostly modern buildings, many of which service the ships and barges in the nearby harbor, contains a number of restaurants and taverns, and has a reputation as a nightclubbing destination. Because Charlotte Amalie has become somewhat dangerous at night, Frenchtown has picked up its after-dark business and is the best spot for drinking, dancing, dining, and local entertainment.

Coral World Ocean Park ★ Set on a strip of jagged coastline dotted with cement holding tanks for marine life, this aquatic complex was built in 1978 by an Israeli company whose innovative designs became a prototype for later marine parks that followed in other parts of the world. Today one of its immediately visible features is a three-story underwater observation tower positioned 100 feet offshore, directly atop the richly fertile Coki Point Reef. From a vantage point inside, looking out through thick windows, you'll see sponges, fish, coral, and other aquatic creatures in their natural state, carried along in a kind of aquatic ballet by the ocean currents outside.

A circular 80,000-gallon tank, whose perimeter completely surrounds a viewing area that's capped with a dome, creates the feeling of being within a blue-green salon whose decor consists of a direct view of marine life above a coral reef. It is illuminated day and night, with light filtering in through the waters that surround the place.

These are only two of the half-dozen or so distinctly separate distractions you'll encounter within Coral World. Other features include a Nautilus semisubmarine going 6½ feet below the surface of the water. On board, passengers can enjoy close encounters with a sea of coral gardens and rainbow-hued fish outside their portholes, without the feelings of claustrophobia associated with deeper dives. There are also a series of open pools with manta rays or baby sharks; walk-in cages filled with tropical birds; nature trails; and assorted snack bars and a gift shop.

Our favorite attraction at Coral World is a saltwater tank that's home to a colony of sea lions, imported from the coast of Peru and carefully trained for many months

Into the Deep for Nondivers

Nondivers can experience some of the thrills familiar to scuba aficionados by participating in Sea Trek at the Coral World Ocean Park (✆ 340/775-1555; www.coralworldvi.com/activities/sea-trek.html). Admission is $77 for adults, $68 for children, and for that, you get a full undersea immersion. No experience is needed. Participants are given a helmet and a tube to breathe through; the tube is attached to an air source at the observatory tower. You then enjoy a 20-minute stroll in water 18 feet deep. You're on the sea floor taking in the rainbow-hued tropical fish and the coral reefs as you go along. It's a marvelous way to experience the world through the eyes of a fish. Opening times vary throughout the season, so please call ahead.

in Thailand. In one of the most popular and entertaining diversions at Coral World, staff will carefully monitor groups of four swimmers at a time as they "interact" with the tame marine mammals, whose instinct for love, applause, and approval make them stars in their own right.

Coral World's guests can take advantage of adjacent **Coki Beach** for snorkel rentals, scuba lessons, or simply swimming and relaxing. Lockers and showers are available.

6450 Estates Smith Bay. ✆ **888/695-2073** or 340/775-1555. www.coralworldvi.com. Admission $19 adults, $10 children 3–12. Daily 9am–4pm. Coral World is a 20-min. drive from Charlotte Amalie, off Rte. 38.

Estate St. Peter Greathouse Botanical Gardens ★ This estate consists of 11 acres at the foot of volcanic peaks on the northern rim of the island. The grounds are laced with self-guided nature walks that identify some 200 varieties of West Indian plants and trees, including an umbrella plant from Madagascar. From a panoramic deck in the gardens, you can see some 20 of the Virgin Islands, including Hans Lollick, an uninhabited island between Thatched Cay and Madahl Point. The house itself, filled with local art, is worth a visit.

At the corner of Rte. 40 (6A St. Peter Mountain Rd.) and Barrett Hill Rd. ✆ **340/774-2400.** www.greathousevi.com. Admission $5 adults, $2.50 children 11 and under. Daily 8am–4pm.

French Heritage Museum Lying in historic Frenchtown, this museum houses artifacts such as wooden tools, original fishing nets, mahogany antiques, musical instruments, pictures, and memorabilia that document the lives of the people of French descent who lived on St. Thomas.

Frenchtown. ✆ **340/714-2583.** www.frenchheritagemuseum.com. Free admission. Mon–Fri 9am–noon and 1–5pm.

Shopping ★★★

The discounted, duty-free shopping in the Virgin Islands makes St. Thomas a mecca for consumers. It's possible to find well-known brand names here at savings of up to 60% off mainland U.S. prices. But be warned—not all savings are so good. Before you leave home, check prices in your local stores if you think you might want to make a major purchase, so you can be sure that you are, in fact, getting a good deal.

The best deals include china, crystal, perfume, jewelry (especially emeralds), Haitian art, fashion, watches, and items made of wood. St. Thomas is also the best place in the Caribbean for discounts on porcelain, but remember that U.S. brands may often be purchased for 25% off the retail price on the U.S. mainland. Look for the imported patterns for the biggest savings.

Most shops, some of which occupy former pirate warehouses, are open Monday to Saturday from 9am to 5pm. Some stores open Sunday and holidays if a cruise ship is in port. ***Note:*** Friday is the biggest cruise-ship day at Charlotte Amalie (we once counted eight ships in port at once), so try to avoid shopping then. It's a zoo.

Nearly all the major shopping is along the harbor of Charlotte Amalie. Cruise-ship passengers embarking at the WICO docks have immediate access to the **Havensight Mall** at the eastern edge of town; cruise ships embarking at the Crown Bay Marina enjoy convenient access to the relatively new collection of shops at the **Crown Bay Center.** The principal shopping street in the center of Charlotte Amalie is **Main Street,** which is sometimes referred to as Dronningens Gade (its old Danish name). To the north is another merchandise-loaded street called **Back Street,** or Vimmelskaft. Many shops are also spread along the **Waterfront Highway (Kyst Vejen).** Between these major streets is a series of side streets, walkways, and alleys, all filled with shops. You might also browse along Tolbod Gade, Raadets Gade, Royal Dane Mall, Palm Passage, Storetvaer Gade, and Strand Gade.

It's illegal for most street vendors (food vendors are about the only exception) to ply their trades outside the designated area called **Vendors Plaza,** at the corner of Veterans Drive and Tolbod Gade. Monday to Saturday, hundreds of vendors converge here at 8am; they usually pack up around 5pm.

When you completely tire of French perfumes and Swiss watches, head for **Market Square,** also called Rothschild Francis Square. Under a Victorian tin roof, locals with machetes slice open fresh coconuts, while women wearing bandanas sell akee, cassava, and breadfruit.

All the major stores in St. Thomas are located by number on an excellent map in the publication ***St. Thomas This Week,*** distributed free to all arriving plane and boat passengers, and at the visitor center. A lot of the stores on the island either don't have street numbers or don't display them, so look for their signs instead.

Crystal Shoppe ★, in the A. H. Riise Mall, 37 Main St. (**✆ 800/323-7232**; www.crystalshoppe.net), is the largest branch of a four-store family-run chain that has garnered a reputation for fairness and honesty in the decades it's been doing business. It sells huge quantities of crystal and porcelain from around the world; all the big names in glass—Wedgwood, Hummel, Royal Copenhagen, Swarovski, and Rosenthal—are on parade, along with some particularly good pieces from the Swedish firm of Kosta Boda. Its porcelain Lladró figurines from Spain are also a fast-moving item. Of particular interest are the guest lecturers, which the store imports on a rotating basis from factories in Ireland and Sweden. Depending on their expertise, they'll engrave, cut, shape, or autograph their signature stemware or crystal as you watch.

Fabric in Motion, Storetvaer Gade (**✆ 340/774-2006**), culls the globe for fabrics and has a wonderful selection of silky cottons from Liberty's of London, the best Italian linens, and flamboyant batiks from Indonesia. Other tempting items include leather handbags and fun beach bags.

Boolchand's ★★, 31 Main St. (**✆ 340/776-0794;** www.boolchand.com), is the place to go when you're in the market for a camera. Famous throughout the Caribbean, this is the major retailer of not only cameras but also electronics and digital products throughout the West Indies. Now into its eighth decade, it sells all the big names, from Kodak to Leica, from Nikon to Fuji. In the electronics divisions are the latest in DVDs, minidiscs, and other items. There is also a jewelry department and a wide selection of watches.

Bernard K. Passman ★★★, 38A Main St., with branch stores at Havensight Mall and at the Crown Bay Marina (✆ **340/777-4580;** www.passman.com), is the world's leading sculptor of black-coral art and jewelry. After being polished and embellished with gold and diamonds, the coral takes on a rich, warm hue that evokes a semiprecious, lustrous gemstone in its own right. Depending on the piece's size and its workmanship, pieces sell for between $100 and $1 million.

Gallery Camille Pissarro ★, 14 Main St. (✆ **340/774-4621;** www.pissarro.vi), is located in the street-fronting building where Pissarro was born in 1830 and where he lived until he was 26. (Failing to domesticate him into a merchant following in the footsteps of the family business, his family regretfully decided to allow him to pursue his artistic hopes and dreams—and the rest is history.) In three high-ceilinged and airy brick-lined rooms, you can view many prints and originals by local artists. The gallery also sells original batiks, alive in vibrant colors. Paintings and artworks sell for between $50 and $15,000. You'll find this funky, charmingly bohemian place at the top of a flight of uneven steps, a welcome change from the endless rows of jewelry stores on the street outside. Keep climbing—the insights you'll get from owner Janine Wesselmann are worth the uphill trek.

Mango Tango Art Gallery, Al Cohen's Plaza, Raphune Hill, Route 38 (✆ **340/777-3060;** www.mangotango-art.com), is one of the largest galleries on island, closely connected with a half-dozen internationally recognized artists who spend at least part of the year in the Virgin Islands. Original works begin at $500; prints and posters are cheaper.

Gallery St. Thomas, 1 Main St. (✆ **877/797-6363** or 340/777-6363; www.gallerystthomas.com), showcases the works of Virgin Island painters, notably Lucinda Schutt, best known for her Caribbean land and seascapes. At this gallery, Schutt sells artwork beginning at $150 and prints for $18, and teaches painting with watercolors.

Native Arts and Crafts Cooperative ★, Tolbod Gade 1 (✆ **340/777-1153**), is the largest arts-and-crafts emporium in the U.S. Virgin Islands, offering the output of 80 different artisans. It specializes in items small enough to be packed into a suitcase or trunk, such as spice racks, lamps crafted from conch shells, salad bowls, crocheted goods, and straw goods.

Caribbean Marketplace, Havensight Mall, building no. 3 (✆ **340/776-5400**), carries a selection of spices, including the Sunny Caribbee line; a vast array of condiments; and botanical products. Don't expect very attentive service.

A. H. Riise Gift ★, 37 Main St. (✆ **800/315-1600** or 340/776-2303; www.ahriise.com), is St. Thomas's oldest outlet for luxury items and offers the best liquor selection on the island. The store carries fine jewelry and watches from Europe's leading craftspeople, including Bulgari, Omega, Rolex, and Gucci, as well as a wide selection of gold, platinum, and precious-gemstone jewelry. Imported cigars are stored in a climate-controlled walk-in humidor. Waterford, Lalique, Baccarat, and Rosenthal are featured in the china and crystal department. Specialty shops in the complex sell Caribbean gifts, books, T-shirts, food, prints, note cards, and designer sunglasses.

One of the island's most famous outlets, **Al Cohen's Discount Liquors,** Havensight Mall (✆ **340/774-3690**), occupies a big warehouse at Havensight with a huge selection of liquor and wine. The wine department is especially impressive. You can also purchase T-shirts and souvenirs.

Royal Caribbean ★, 33 Main St. (✆ **340/776-4110;** www.royalcaribbean.vi), is one of the largest camera and electronics stores in the Caribbean. It carries Nikon, Minolta, Pentax, Canon, and Panasonic products, plus watches by Seiko, Movado, Corum, Fendi, Philippe Charriol, and Zodiac. There are also leather bags, Mikimoto pearls, and 14- and 18-karat jewelry. Another branch is located at the Havensight Mall (✆ **340/776-8890**).

Often called the Tiffany's of the Caribbean, **Cardow Jewelers ★★**, 39 Main St. (✆ **800/227-3697** or 340/776-1140; www.cardow.com), stocks the largest selection of fine jewelry in the world. This fabulous shop, where more than 20,000 rings are displayed, offers savings because of its worldwide direct buying, large turnover, and duty-free prices. Unusual and traditional designs are offered in diamonds, emeralds, rubies, sapphires, and pearls.

Azura, Havensight Mall (✆ **340/774-2442**), is renowned throughout the Caribbean for its collection of Colombian emeralds, both set and unset. Here you buy direct from the source, which can mean significant savings. The shop also stocks fine watches.

Another good place to browse for gemstones is **Pierre's,** 24 Palm Passage (✆ **340/776-5130;** www.pierresdiamonds.com), one of the most impressive repositories of collector's gemstones in the Caribbean. Look for alexandrites (garnets in three shades of green), spinels (pink and red), sphenes (yellow-green sparklers from Madagascar that are as reflective as high-quality diamonds), and tsavorites (green stones from Tanzania).

Fresh Produce, Riise's Alley (✆ **340/774-0807;** http://freshproduceclothes.com), the California chain famed for its tropical apparel for women, has now invaded St. Thomas. Much of the clothing is dyed like native fruits: banana yellow, pink guava, lime-green mangoes, and zesty orange. A wide array of summer dresses, slacks, shirts, and skirts, along with accessories and handbags, are for sale in this sunny place.

At **Local Color,** Havensight Mall (✆ **340/774-3182;** www.usviweb.com/localcolor), you can outfit yourself in Caribbean attire with a selection of cool, comfortable, and casual styles. Living up to its name, much of the clothing for men, women, and children is in tropical colors inspired by local fruits. Sunglasses and various accessories are also for sale. The store is well stocked with such famous brand names as Jams World, Kipling, and Crocs. There is also a selection of casual jewelry.

Scandinavia Center ★, Havensight Mall (✆ **877/454-8377** or 340/777-8620; www.scandinaviancenter.com), has the best buys in glass, crystal, and ceramics from Denmark and Sweden. All the big names are showcased here, including Royal Copenhagen, Georg Jensen, and Orrefors. You'll also find a good selection of handcrafted glass, sterling silver, stainless steel hollowware, and porcelain figurines. Some of the most modern jewelry in innovative designs is also sold in a section here.

A shop that manages an allegiance to both cutting-edge technology and a strong sense of practical merchandising is **New Age Photo,** in the Crown Bay Center (✆ **340/777-9324**). Don't expect a traditional array of camera and film at this place—it's a lot more evolved than that. For sale is a medley of ornaments, some made from black onyx, some from granite, some from cut crystal, some from clear plastic polymers, which accept lasered-on replicas of any photo you'd present to a staff member. Photos come out looking like fine art and with a sense of depth perception when laser-engraved on their new surface. Electronic images from JPEGs or other electronic media are acceptable for this, and the possibility of creating some high-tech souvenirs of your trip here are endless. Everything in the store costs between $30 and $150, and usually takes 20 minutes of tinkering to bring to fruition.

If you are shopping for a simple souvenir, stop in at **Captain's Corner,** Main Street, across from H. Stern (✆ **340/774-4370;** www.captainscornervi.com), the oldest and biggest souvenir outlet in town. Its most popular item is the Caribbean "map watch," but there is countless other merchandise, including voodoo masks and other island crafts such as handmade items crafted from wood.

Virgin Islands Brewing Company, across from Happy Buzzard at Royal Dane Mall (✆ **340/777-8888;** www.beercollections.com), was founded on St. Croix but has invaded St. Thomas with one local beer, Blackbeard Ale. At the company store, you're given free samples and can purchase six-packs of the home-brewed suds, along with T-shirts, caps, and polo shirts.

Outside of Charlotte Amalie, another noteworthy destination is **Tillett Gardens,** a virtual oasis of arts and crafts—pottery, silk-screened fabrics, candles, watercolors, jewelry, and more. It's on the highway across from Four Winds Shopping Center (take Rte. 38 east from Charlotte Amalie). A major island attraction is the **Jim Tillett Art Gallery and Silk Screen Print Studio ★★** (✆ **340/775-1405;** www.tillettgardens.com), which displays the best work of local artists, including originals in oils, watercolors, and acrylics. The prints are all one-of-a-kind, and prices start as low as $20. The famous Tillett maps on fine canvas are priced from $45.

St. Thomas After Dark

St. Thomas has more nightlife than any other island in the Virgins, U.S. and British—but not as much as you might think. Charlotte Amalie is no longer the swinging town it used to be. Many of the streets are dangerous after dark, so visitors have abandoned all but a few places in town. Most of the action is in **Frenchtown,** which has some great restaurants and bars. However, just as in Charlotte Amalie, some of these little hot spots are along dark, badly lit roads.

Note: Sexual harassment can be a problem in certain bars in Charlotte Amalie, where few single women would want to be alone at night anyway. Any of the major resort hotels are generally safe.

The big hotels, such as Frenchman's Reef & Morning Star Marriott Beach Resort (p. 691) and Bluebeard's, have the liveliest after-dark scenes. After a day of sightseeing and shopping in the hot West Indies sun, sometimes your best bet is just to stay at your hotel in the evening, perhaps listening to a local calypso band. You might also call the **Reichhold Center for the Arts,** University of the Virgin Islands, 2 John Brewer's Bay (✆ **340/693-1559;** www.reichholdcenter.com), or check with the tourist office to see what's on during your visit. Its Japanese-inspired amphitheater is set into a natural valley, with seating for 1,196. Several different repertory companies of music, dance, and drama perform here. Performances usually begin at 8pm. Tickets usually range from $18 to $45, but depending on the attraction, this could vary greatly.

In Charlotte Amalie, head to the **Bar at Paradise Point** (✆ **340/777-4540;** www.paradisepointtramway.com) at sunset. It's 700 feet above sea level, across from the cruise-ship dock, and provides excellent photo ops and panoramic views. A tram takes you up the hill (the St. Thomas Skyride; p. 706). Get the bartender to serve you the specialty, a Bushwacker. Sometimes a one-man steel band is on hand to serenade the sunset watchers. You can also order inexpensive food, such as pizza, hot dogs, and hamburgers.

At the Yacht Haven Grande, **Fat Turtle** ★ (✆ **340/714-3566;** www.fat-turtle.com), is the best waterside hangout in Charlotte Amalie, a rendezvous for yachties, cruise shippers, and young men and women "from everywhere" just hanging out and downing coladas. DJs and dancers rule the night, and sometimes big acts show up, including, on one occasion, the Beach Boys. Friday nights are particularly wild around here. By day it's a more subdued atmosphere, attracting shoppers who come in carrying Gucci or Louis Vuitton totes. Lunch is served here daily from 11am, costing $20 and up, but the place keeps pouring drinks until 2am.

We recommend only a few other places in Charlotte Amalie. They include **Greenhouse,** Veterans Drive (✆ **340/774-7998;** www.thegreenhouserestaurant.com), a bar/restaurant that's raucous enough to appeal to the college crowd and set directly on the waterfront. Happy hour with discounted appetizers and drinks is daily from 4:30 to 7pm. On Tuesday a DJ rules the night.

The scenic **Cabana Bar,** Bluebeard's Hill (✆ **340/774-1600**), overlooking the yacht harbor, hosts piano-bar entertainment on Thursday, Saturday, and Sunday from 7 to 10pm. It's a popular gathering spot for both locals and visitors. Entertainment varies from month to month, but a steel band comes in some nights, while others are devoted to reggae and salsa. It's open Tuesday to Sunday 5:30 to 9:30pm. There's no cover.

During the day, **Iggie's Bolongo,** in the Bolongo Beach Resort, 7150 Bolongo St. (✆ **340/693-2600;** www.iggiesbeachbar.com), is an informal open-air diner, serving hamburgers, sandwiches, and salads. After dark it presents karaoke and offers night volleyball. It's also one of the most active sports bars on island.

West of Charlotte Amalie, in Frenchtown, **Epernay,** 24A Honduras, Frenchtown (✆ **340/774-5348;** www.epernaystthomas.com), next to Bella Blu, is a stylish watering hole with an ocean view. You can order vintage wines and at least six different brands of champagne by the glass. Also available are appetizers, including sushi, main courses ($15–$33), and tempting desserts like chocolate-dipped strawberries.

The popular **Turtle Rock Bar** lies in the Mangrove Restaurant at the Wyndham Sugar Bay Resort & Spa, 6500 Estate Smith Bay (p. 691; ✆ **340/777-7100**). Sunday night is karaoke. Burgers, salads, steaks, and grilled fish are available at the Iguana Grill a few steps away. There's no cover.

Finally, if you're way out on the island's easternmost tip, a legitimate way of exploring the premises of St. Thomas's most upscale hotel involves dropping into the elegant but cozy **Great Bay Lounge,** an airy bar-cum-clubhouse on the grounds of the Ritz-Carlton (p. 691; ✆ **340/775-3333**). One of four restaurants on the grounds of that hotel, it's the most appropriate for late-night downwinding and, as such, welcomes a large percentage of managers from others of the island's resorts. Cocktails and glasses of wine cost from $9 to $25 each, platters of food from $10 to $35 each. It's open daily from 10am to around 11pm or later (depending on business), but we find that it's at its most appealing from 8pm on.

ST. JOHN ★★★

St. John, the smallest and least densely populated of the three U.S. Virgin Islands, is a wonder of untouched rocky coastline, beautiful crescent-shaped bays, and white-sand beaches. Inland, miles of hiking trails lead past the ruins of 18th-century Danish plantations to panoramic views. A smattering of pastel-painted houses, Mongoose

St. John

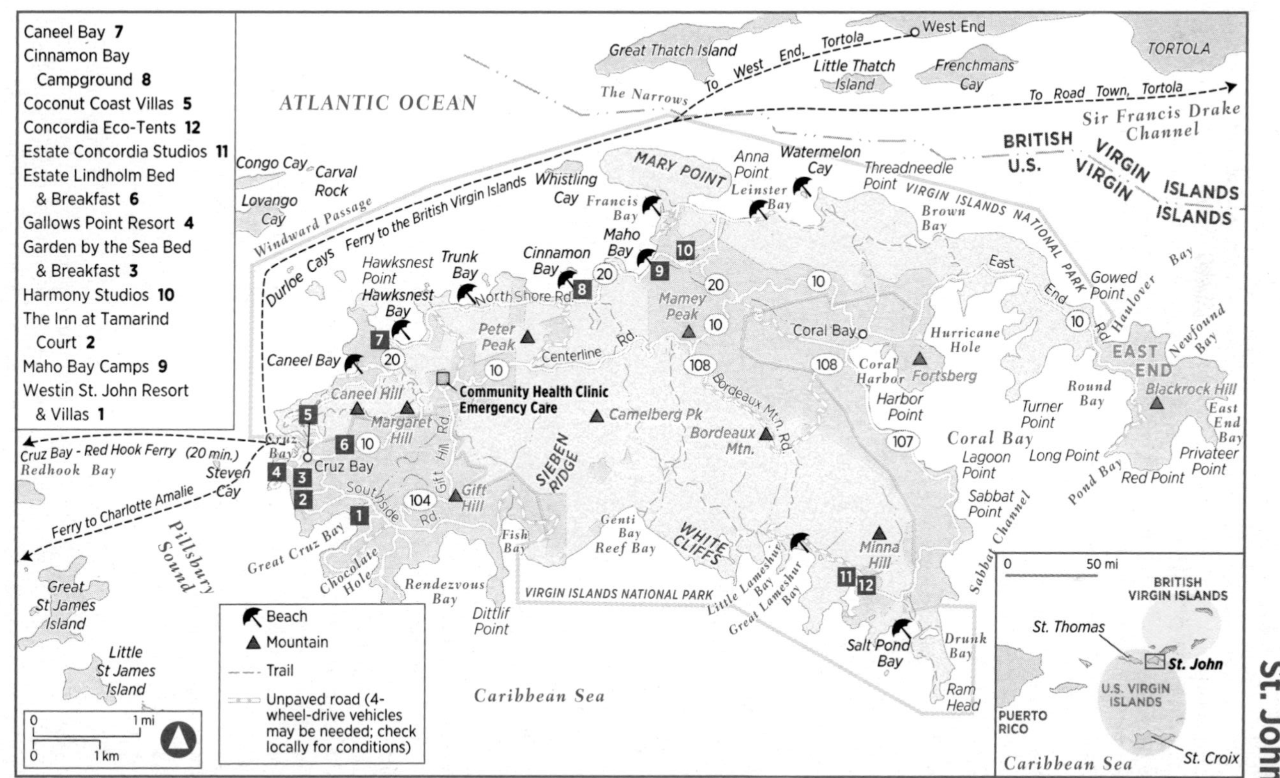
Caneel Bay 7
Cinnamon Bay Campground 8
Coconut Coast Villas 5
Concordia Eco-Tents 12
Estate Concordia Studios 11
Estate Lindholm Bed & Breakfast 6
Gallows Point Resort 4
Garden by the Sea Bed & Breakfast 3
Harmony Studios 10
The Inn at Tamarind Court 2
Maho Bay Camps 9
Westin St. John Resort & Villas 1
Beach
Mountain
Trail
Unpaved road (4-wheel-drive vehicles may be needed; check locally for conditions)
ATLANTIC OCEAN
Caribbean Sea
Great Thatch Island
Little Thatch Island
Frenchmans Cay
TORTOLA
West End
To West End, Tortola
To Road Town, Tortola
The Narrows
Sir Francis Drake Channel
BRITISH VIRGIN ISLANDS
U.S. VIRGIN ISLANDS
Ferry to the British Virgin Islands
Congo Cay
Carval Rock
Lovango Cay
Windward Passage
Durloe Cays
Whistling Cay
MARY POINT
Francis Bay
Maho Bay
Anna Point
Leinster Bay
Watermelon Cay
Threadneedle Point
VIRGIN ISLANDS NATIONAL PARK
Brown Bay
Hawksnest Point
Hawksnest Bay
Trunk Bay
Cinnamon Bay
North Shore Rd.
Caneel Bay
Caneel Hill
Margaret Hill
Peter Peak
Centerline Rd.
Mamey Peak
Community Health Clinic Emergency Care
Camelberg Pk
Bordeaux Mtn.
Bordeaux Mtn. Rd.
Coral Bay
Hurricane Hole
Coral Harbor
Fortsberg
Harbor Point
East End Rd.
Gowed Point
Haulover Bay
Newfound Bay
EAST END
Blackrock Hill
East End Bay
Round Bay
Turner Point
Coral Bay
Long Point
Lagoon Point
Privateer Point
Red Point
Pond Bay
Sabbat Point
Sabbat Channel
Cruz Bay
Cruz Bay - Red Hook Ferry (20 min.)
Redhook Bay
Steven Cay
Ferry to Charlotte Amalie
Pillsbury Sound
Southside Rd.
Gift Hill Rd.
Gift Hill
SIEBEN RIDGE
Great Cruz Bay
Chocolate Hole
Rendezvous Bay
Ditlif Point
Fish Bay
Genti Bay
Reef Bay
WHITE CLIFFS
Little Lameshur Bay
Great Lameshur Bay
Minna Hill
Salt Pond Bay
Drunk Bay
Ram Head
Great St James Island
Little St James Island
0 1 mi
0 1 km
0 50 mi
BRITISH VIRGIN ISLANDS
St. Thomas
St. John
U.S. VIRGIN ISLANDS
PUERTO RICO
St. Croix
Caribbean Sea

Junction shops, and restaurants and bars populate sleepy Cruz Bay. St. John is definitely sleepy, and that's why people love it.

Things to Do Explore island history at the **Annaberg Sugar Plantation Ruins,** a once thriving 18th-century mill and plantation. Hike the 22 trails of the **Virgin Islands National Park** to see archaeological sites dating back to the time of the Taíno people, while enjoying the forest and birdlife. Reefs and wreck dive spots ring the park's deserted beaches. Surrounded by hills, the golden sands of **Hawksnest Bay** seduce visitors as the perfect escape. Follow the underwater **snorkeling** trail at Trunk Bay to see grouper, parrotfish, and snappers.

Shopping Shopping on St. John means a visit to the arts and crafts boutiques and shops of **Cruz Bay,** most of which are clustered at **Mongoose Junction.** Nearby **Wharfside Village** is a complex of courtyards, alleys, and shady patios with a mishmash of boutiques, restaurants, and bars. The most shopping fun takes place on **St. John Saturday,** a spicy, drum-beating feast for the senses, held on the last Saturday of every month. Vendors hawk handmade items, from jewelry and handicrafts to food and clothing.

Nightlife & Entertainment The expatriate hippie crowd has created a mellow scene at **Cruz Bay,** where a few cafes and dive bars invite those who want to drink and gossip with the locals or listen to the occasional live band. Sip trademark **Plantation Punch** (lime and orange juice with three different kinds of rum; bitters; and nutmeg) at a resort bar in **Caneel Bay,** or go celeb-spotting at **Morgan's Mango.** Most people, however, are simply content to have a long, leisurely dinner.

Eating & Drinking St. John's quiet, easygoing pace means that it's not unusual—indeed, it is perfectly acceptable—for dinner to comprise the whole of your evening. As a result, there are some posh options, particularly at the luxury resorts in **Caneel Bay,** where you can eat well on Caribbean, Creole, and Italian. In **Cruz Bay,** seaside bistros serve spicy blackened snapper and flying fish, while **West Indian** huts serve top notch meals with plenty of local color and flavor.

Essentials

GETTING THERE To get to St. John, you take a ferry from St. Thomas. (There are also ferries from the British Virgin Islands.) See "Getting There," at the beginning of this chapter, for information on how to get to St. Thomas, and for details about the ferry to St. John.

VISITOR INFORMATION The **tourist office** (✆ **340/776-6450**) is located near the Battery, a 1735 fort that's a short walk from the St. Thomas ferry dock. It's open Monday to Friday from 8am to 5pm. A **national park visitor center** (✆ **340/776-6201**) is also found at Cruz Bay, offering two floors of information and wall-mounted wildlife displays, plus a video presentation about the culture of the Virgin Islands. It's open daily 8am to 4:30pm.

GETTING AROUND The most popular way to get around is via the local **Vitran** (✆ **340/774-0165**) service, the same company that runs the buses on St. Thomas. Buses run between Cruz Bay and Coral Bay, costing $1 for adults and 75¢ for children.

An open-air **surrey-style taxi** is more fun, however. Typical fares are $9 to Trunk Bay, $11 to Cinnamon Bay, or $14 to Maho Bay. Between midnight and 6am, fares are increased by 50%. Call **Paradise Taxi** at ✆ **340/714-7913** for more information.

The island's undeveloped roads offer some of the best views anywhere. Because of this, many people opt to rent a vehicle (sometimes with four-wheel-drive) to tour the island. Most visitors need a car for only a day or two. ***Remember:*** Drive on the left and follow posted speed limits, which are generally very low.

Unless you need to carry luggage, which should probably be locked away in a trunk, you might consider one of the sturdy, open-sided, jeeplike vehicles that offer the best view of the surroundings and are the most fun way to tour St. John. Note that most of these vehicles have manual transmission, which can be especially tricky in a car built to drive on the left side of the road. They cost $60 to $100 a day.

For a local firm, try **St. John Car Rental,** across from the Catholic church in Cruz Bay (✆ **340/776-6103;** www.stjohncarrental.com).

FAST FACTS If you need a **hospital,** go to **Myrah Keating Smith Community Health Clinic,** 3B Sussanaberg (✆ **340/693-8900**), which can be reached along Route 10, about 1¾ miles east of Cruz Bay.

Where to Stay

There are actually more villa and condo beds available on St. John than there are hotel beds. In addition to the condo and villa complexes reviewed below, **Caribbean Villas & Resorts** (✆ **800/338-0987;** fax 207/510-6308; www.caribbeanvilla.com), the island's biggest real estate agency, is an excellent choice. Villa rentals begin at $1,750 weekly.

VERY EXPENSIVE

Caneel Bay ★★★ Conceived by megamillionaire Laurance S. Rockefeller in 1956, this is the Caribbean's first eco-resort. Though long one of the Caribbean's premier resorts, Caneel Bay is definitely not one of the most luxurious. That means no phones or TVs in the rooms. Nevertheless, the movers and shakers of the world continue to come here, though younger people tend to head elsewhere. To attract more families, young children are now allowed. Go to the Westin St. John Resort & Villas (see below) for glitz and glitter; head here for a touch of class. The resort lies on a 168-acre portion of the national park, offering a choice of seven beaches. Surrounded by lush greenery, the main buildings are strung along the bays, with a Caribbean lounge and dining room at the core. Other buildings housing guest rooms stand along the beaches. Most rooms, however, are set back on low cliffs or headlands. The decor within is understated, with Indonesian wicker furniture.

Virgin Islands National Park (P.O. Box 720), St. John, U.S.V.I. 00831. www.caneelbay.com. ✆ **888/767-3966** in the U.S., or 340/776-6111. Fax 340/693-8280. 166 units. Winter $470–$1,060 double, from $1,410 suite; off season $349–$729 double, $875 suite. 1 child under 13 can stay free in parent's room. AE, MC, V. **Amenities:** 5 restaurants; 2 bars; babysitting; children's center; exercise room; outdoor pool; room service; spa; 11 tennis courts (lit); watersports equipment/rentals. *In room:* A/C, ceiling fan, hair dryer, minibar, no phone, Wi-Fi (free).

Westin St. John Resort & Villas ★★★ ☺ Come here if you like megaresort flash and glitter as opposed to the "old-school ties" of Caneel Bay (see above). This is the most architecturally dramatic and visually appealing hotel on St. John. The complex is set on 35 acres of landscaped grounds on the southwest side of the island. It consists of 21 cedar-roofed postmodern buildings, each with ziggurat-shaped angles and soaring ceilings. Herringbone-patterned brick walkways connect the gardens (with 400 palms imported from Puerto Rico) to the 1,180-foot white-sand beach and one of the largest pools in the Virgin Islands. Some of the stylish accommodations contain fan-shaped windows and curved ceilings. Most units open onto private balconies, and some have their own whirlpools. Villas, of course, offer more space and come with a full kitchenette.

Great Cruz Bay (P.O. Box 8310), St. John, U.S.V.I. 00831. www.westinresortstjohn.com. ✆ **866/716-8108** in the U.S., or 340/693-8000. Fax 340/693-8888. 367 units. Winter $490–$640 double, from $1,000 villa; off season $400–$550 double, from $900 villa. AE, DC, DISC, MC, V. Round-trip shuttle and private ferryboat transfers from St. Thomas airport $100 per adult, $80 ages 4–12. **Amenities:** 3 restaurants; 2 bars; babysitting; children's programs; dive shop; nearby golf; exercise room; outdoor pool; room service; sauna; 6 tennis courts (lit); watersports. *In room:* A/C, TV, hair dryer, Jacuzzi (in some), kitchenette (in some), minibar, Wi-Fi (included in $40 resort fee).

MODERATE/EXPENSIVE

Coconut Coast Villas This is a good choice for families seeking a vacation condo. The spacious accommodations contain two or three bedrooms; some units, however are studios, suitable for couples. The location is a 10-minute walk from Cruz Bay in a quiet suburban neighborhood. There's a small beach, but it's pebbly, and there are some steep steps, so it's not ideal for the mobility-impaired. Extra features include a hot tub, a grill, and laundry facilities. All units are oceanfront with private porches and fully equipped kitchens. Extras include beach chairs, coolers, and beach towels. A minimum stay of 4 nights is required.

Turner Bay, Cruz Bay, St. John, U.S.V.I. 00831. www.coconutcoast.com. ✆ **800/858-7989** or 340/693-9100. 9 units. Winter $300 studio, $390 2-bedroom condo, $560 3-bedroom condo; off season $190–$230 studio, $290–$330 2-bedroom condo, $350–$440 3-bedroom condo. MC, V. **Amenities:** Internet (free); outdoor pool. *In room:* A/C, TV, kitchenette.

Estate Concordia Studios This environmentally sensitive 49-acre development has been widely praised for its integration with the local ecosystem. Its elevated structures were designed to coexist with the stunning southern edge of St. John. The secluded property is nestled on a low cliff above a salt pond, surrounded by hundreds of pristine national-park acres. It's best for those with rental vehicles. Each building was designed to protect mature trees and is connected to its neighbors with boardwalks. The nine studios are contained in five postmodern cottages. Each unit has a kitchen, a shower-only bathroom, a balcony, and a ceiling fan; some have an extra bedroom. On-site management assists with activity suggestions. For information on the on-site **Eco-Tents,** refer to "Campgrounds," below.

20–27 Estate Concordia, Coral Bay, St. John, U.S.V.I. 00830. www.maho.org. ✆ **800/392-9004** in the U.S. and Canada, or 340/715-0501. Fax 340/776-6504. 9 units. Winter $160–$250 double; off season $115–$160 double. MC, V. **Amenities:** Outdoor pool. *In room:* Ceiling fan, kitchen, no phone.

Estate Lindholm Bed & Breakfast ★ 🎁 The island's best B&B grew out of an estate originally settled by Dutch planters in the 1720s. Set among the Danish ruins, Estate Lindholm is a charming guesthouse on a hill overlooking Cruz Bay, each of its nonsmoking bedrooms opening onto a view. The spacious bedrooms are attractively and comfortably furnished, many resting under ceiling beams. Guests can enjoy private balconies as well. On the property is the Asolare restaurant, one of the island's best (p. 719). The staff is helpful in hooking you up with any number of outdoor activities, including everything from sea kayaking to windsurfing.

P.O. Box 1360, Cruz Bay, St. John, U.S.V.I. 00831. www.estatelindholm.com. ✆ **800/322-6335** in the U.S., or 340/776-6121. Fax 340/776-6141. 10 units. Winter $340–$380 double; off season $170–$210 suite. Rates include continental breakfast. AE, DISC, MC, V. **Amenities:** Restaurant; exercise room; outdoor pool. *In room:* A/C, TV, fridge, Wi-Fi (free).

Gallows Point Resort ★ The first complex of buildings you see as you arrive at Cruz Bay is this colony of condos just outside the town. Lying on a 5-acre peninsula, the complex blends into its setting, a tropical landscape with island-style architecture. You're within walking distance of the restaurants and shops of Cruz Bay. In all, there are 15 well-furnished buildings, each structure with four one-bedroom suites, coming with a full kitchen and spacious living area. The best views, of course, are in the apartments on the upper level. Harborside villas tend to get more noise. The beach nearby is small and rocky, so you may want to go farther afield for the sands. The garden suites are one story with sunken living rooms. The property also includes multilevel sunbathing decks. On-site is Zozo's Ristorante (p. 720).

Gallows Point (P.O. Box 58), St. John, U.S.V.I. 00831. www.gallowspointresort.com. ✆ **800/323-7229** or 340/776-6434. Fax 340/776-6520. 60 units. Winter $465–$655 suite; off season $265–$495 suite. AE, MC, V. **Amenities:** Restaurant; bar; outdoor pool. *In room:* A/C, TV/VCR, CD player, hair dryer, kitchen, Wi-Fi (free).

Garden by the Sea Bed & Breakfast ★ Overlooking the ocean, this B&B lies a 10-minute walk south of the little port of Cruz Bay. It has easy access to the north-shore beaches and lies between Frank and Turner bays. From the gardens of the house, a short path along Audubon Pond leads to Frank Bay Beach. Be sure to reserve a room ahead, as it offers only three bedrooms. Artifacts from around the world have been used to furnish the units. Each bedroom features elephant bamboo canopy beds, Japanese fountains, hardwood floors, and well-kept bathrooms. Don't expect phones or TVs, as this is a getaway, not a communications center. The 1970s house is designed in a Caribbean gingerbread style with cathedral beamed ceilings. Breakfast is served on the veranda (try the homemade muffins and quiche).

Cruz Bay (P.O. Box 37), St. John, U.S.V.I. 00831 www.gardenbythesea.com. ✆/fax **340/779-4731.** 3 units. Winter $250–$275 double; off season $160–$200 double. No credit cards. Closed Sept. *In room:* A/C, ceiling fan, hair dryer, no phone, Wi-Fi (free).

Harmony Studios ★ Built on a hillside above the Maho Bay Camps, this is a small-scale cluster of 12 plain, rather basic studios in six two-story houses with views sweeping down to the sea. The complex is designed to combine both ecological technology and comfort; it's one of the few resorts in the Caribbean to operate exclusively on sun and wind power, which means no hot showers in the morning. Most of the building materials are derived from recycled materials, including reconstituted plastic and glass containers, newsprint, old tires, and scrap lumber. The managers and staff are committed to offering educational experiences, as well as the services of a small-scale resort. The studios contain tiled shower-only bathrooms, kitchenettes, dining areas, and outdoor terraces. The studios sit high on a hillside, and the units are built on stilts and linked with wooden walkways and stairs. Expect lots of stairs and lots of climbing—a long, hard slog up from the beach to your studio.

P.O. Box 310, Cruz Bay, St. John, U.S.V.I. 00831. www.maho.org. ✆ **800/392-9004** in the U.S. and Canada, or 340/776-6240. Fax 340/776-6504. 12 units. Winter $225–$250 studio for 2; off season $130–$155 studio for 2. Extra person $25. MC, V. **Amenities:** Watersports equipment/rentals. *In room:* Ceiling fan, kitchenette, no phone.

INEXPENSIVE

The Inn at Tamarind Court Right outside Cruz Bay but still within walking distance of the ferryboat dock, this modest place consists of a small hotel and an even simpler West Indian inn. The inn is pretty basic and won't please you if you're too demanding, but it's one of the few low-cost options on St. John. Bedrooms are small, evoking those in a little country motel. Most have twin beds. Shower-only bathrooms in the inn are shared among the single rooms; units in the hotel have small private bathrooms. The social life here revolves around its courtyard bar and the in-house restaurant under the same name. From the hotel, you can walk to shuttles that take you to the beaches.

South Shore Rd. (P.O. Box 350), Cruz Bay, St. John, U.S.V.I. 00831. www.innattamarindcourt.com. ✆ **800/221-1637** in the U.S., or 340/776-6378. Fax 340/776-6722. 20 units, 14 with private bathroom. Winter $75 single without private bathroom, $150 double with private bathroom, $240 apt for 4 with private bathroom; off season $60–$65 single without private bathroom, $110–$120 double with private bathroom, $170–$190 apt for 4 with private bathroom. Rates include continental breakfast. AE, DISC, MC, V. **Amenities:** Restaurant; bar. *In room:* A/C, ceiling fan, TV, fridge, no phone.

CAMPGROUNDS

Cinnamon Bay Campground ★★ This National Park Service campground is the most complete in the Caribbean. The site is directly on the beach, surrounded by thousands of acres of tropical vegetation. Life is simple here: You have a choice of a tent, a cottage, or a bare site. At the bare campsites, you get just the site, with no fancy extras. Each canvas tent is 10×14 feet and has a floor as well as a number of extras, including all cooking equipment; your linens are even changed weekly. Each cottage is 15×15 feet, consisting of a room with two concrete walls and two screen walls. Each cottage contains cooking facilities and four twin beds with thin mattresses; one cot can be added. Lavatories and cool-water showers are in separate buildings nearby. In winter, guests can camp for a maximum of 2 weeks; the rest of the year, camping is limited to 30 days.

Cruz Bay (P.O. Box 720), St. John, U.S.V.I. 00831. www.cinnamonbay.com. ✆ **800/539-9998** or 340/776-6330. Fax 340/776-6458. 126 units, none with bathroom. Winter $120–$155 cottage for 4, $88 tent site, $30 bare site; off season $77–$100 cottage for 2, $64 tent site, $30 bare site. Extra person $19. AE, MC, V. Closed Sept. **Amenities:** Restaurant; watersports equipment/rentals. *In room:* No phone.

Concordia Eco-Tents On the southern tip of St. John, overlooking Salt Pond Bay and Ram Head Point, these solar- and wind-powered tent-cottages combine sustainable technology with some of the most spectacular views on the island. The light framing, fabric walls, and large screened-in windows lend a treehouse atmosphere to guests' experience. Set on the windward side of the island, the tent-cottages enjoy natural ventilation from the cooling trade winds. Inside, each has two twin beds with rather thin mattresses in each bedroom; one or two twin mattresses on a loft platform; and a queen-size futon in the living-room area. (Each unit can sleep up to six people comfortably.) Each kitchen is equipped with a running-water sink, propane stove, and cooler. In addition, each Eco-Tent has a small solar-powered private shower, rather meager towels, and a composting toilet. The secluded hillside location, surrounded by hundreds of acres of pristine national park land, requires guests to arrange for a rental vehicle.

20–27 Estate Concordia, Coral Bay, St. John, U.S.V.I. 00830. www.maho.org. ✆ **800/392-9004** in the U.S., or 304/715-0501. Fax 340/776-6504. 18 units, 4 wheelchair-accessible. Winter $155–$185 tent; off season $105 tent. Extra person after two $15. MC, V. **Amenities:** Outdoor pool. *In room:* No phone.

Maho Bay Camps ★ Right on Maho Bay, this is an interesting concept in ecology vacationing, where you camp close to nature but with considerable comfort. It's set on a hillside above the beach surrounded by Virgin Islands National Park. To preserve the existing ground cover, all 114 tent-cottages are on platforms, above a thickly wooded slope. Utility lines and pipes are hidden under wooden boardwalks and stairs. Each tent-cottage, covered with canvas and screens, has two twin beds with thin mattresses, a couch, electric lamps and outlets, a dining table, chairs, a propane stove, an ice chest (cooler), linens, thin towels, and cooking and eating utensils. Guests share communal bathhouses. Maho Bay Camps is more intimate and slightly more luxurious than its nearest competitor, Cinnamon Bay (see above).

P.O. Box 310, Cruz Bay, St. John, U.S.V.I. 00830. www.maho.org. ✆ **800/392-9004** in the U.S., or 340/715-0501. Fax 340/776-6504. 114 units, none with bathroom. Winter $135 tent-cottage for 2 (7-night minimum); off season $80 tent-cottage for 2. Extra person $15 winter, $12 off season. MC, V. **Amenities:** Restaurant; watersports equipment/rentals.

Where to Dine

Many of the restaurants here command high prices, but you can lunch almost anywhere more reasonably. Dinner is often an event on St. John, since it's about the only form of nightlife the island has.

EXPENSIVE

Asolare ★★ INTERNATIONAL/ASIAN This is the most beautiful and elegant restaurant on St. John, with the hippest and best-looking staff. It sits on a hill overlooking Cruz Bay and some of the British Virgin Islands. *Asolare* translates as "the leisurely passing of time without purpose," and that's what many diners do here. The chef uses some of the best and freshest ingredients available on island. To begin, try the grilled Asian barbecued shrimp or the squid-and-shrimp medley. For a main course, try the ginger lamb or the peppercorn-dusted filet of beef. Two other truly excellent dishes are the chicken Kiev and sashimi tuna on a sizzling plate with plum-passion-fruit-sake vinaigrette. For dessert, we like the fresh berry dishes and the chocolate pyramid cake.

In the Estate Lindholm Bed & Breakfast, Cruz Bay. ✆ **340/779-4747.** www.asolarestjohn.com. Reservations required. Main courses $29–$38. AE, MC, V. Tues–Sun 6–9pm.

Equator ★ CARIBBEAN/INTERNATIONAL This restaurant lies behind the tower of an 18th-century sugar mill, where ponds with water lilies fill former crystallization pits for hot molasses. A flight of stairs leads to a monumental circular dining room, with a wraparound veranda and sweeping views of a park. In the center rises the stone column that horses and mules once circled to crush sugar-cane stalks. In its center, the restaurant grows a giant poinciana-like Asian tree of the *Albizia lebbeck* species. Islanders call it "woman's tongue tree."

For the most part, the chefs pull off their intriguing flavor combinations. A spicy and tantalizing opener is lemon-grass-and-ginger-cured salmon salad. A classic Caribbean callaloo soup is offered, and the salads use fresh ingredients such as roma tomatoes and endive. Daily Caribbean selections are offered, or you can opt for such fine dishes as seared Caribbean tuna, or penne pasta with shiitake mushrooms and roasted tomatoes in an herb-garlic cream sauce. There's always a dry, aged Angus steak or a grilled veal chop for the more traditional palate.

In the Caneel Bay Hotel, Caneel Bay. ✆ **340/776-6111.** Reservations required. Main courses $24–$44. AE, MC, V. Tues-Sun 6–9pm (check with hotel beforehand, as days and hours vary by season).

La Plancha del Mar ★★ MEDITERRANEAN This discovery is a little bit off the beaten path but worth the journey. It serves hearty food with an exotic twist, and is named *plancha* for its piping-hot iron grill, likely to be sizzling with steak. The house specialty is a churrasco steak with garlic herb fries and a citrus aioli, a tasty treat. Other specialties at night include seared mahimahi with a spicy tomato and basil purée, or a paella à la Plancha studded with tiger prawns, mussels, bits of chicken, and chorizo. Appetizers are some of the best on the island, featuring a toasted pine-nut hummus or a crusted Brie with a strawberry coulis. At lunch you get a selection of pizzas, sandwiches, and wraps, along with an array of appetizers such as flash-fried calamari with a lime and cilantro-laced aioli. Nothing is overpriced or oversauced—the owners believing in preserving the natural flavor of their ingredients.

Rte. 104, Marketplace Shopping Center (outside Cruz Bay). ✆ **340/777-7333.** www.laplanchadelmar.com. Reservations recommended for dinner. Main courses $24–$40. MC, V. Mon–Fri 11:30am–2pm and 5–9pm; Sat 5–9pm.

La Tapa INTERNATIONAL/MEDITERRANEAN There's a tiny bar with no more than five stools, a two-tiered dining room, and lots of original paintings. (The establishment doubles as an art gallery.) Menu items are thoughtful and well conceived, and include fast-seared tuna with a Basque-inspired relish of onions, peppers, garlic, and herbs; filet au poivre, a steak soaked with rum and served with a cracked-pepper sauce and mashed potatoes; and linguine with shrimp, red peppers, and leeks in peanut sauce. Live jazz is offered on Mondays.

Centerline Rd. (across from First Bank), Cruz Bay. ✆ **340/693-7755.** Reservations recommended. Main courses $30–$41. AE, MC, V. Wed–Mon 6–10pm; daily in winter.

Rhumb Lines ★ ☺ CARIBBEAN/PACIFIC RIM In the heart of Cruz Bay, this restaurant, with its West Indian courtyard, has a South Seas ambience. Appetizers are among the island's best, ranging from hot-and-sour grilled duck breast glazed with rum punch to cracked-pepper-crusted tuna over a seaweed salad. The main dishes are full of flavor and are delectable, especially the fresh mahimahi in banana leaf with a gingered banana beurre blanc, or the tenderloin of Cuban pork marinated in garlic and citrus juices. For the adventurous palate, there is a special Pupu menu, with everything from lemon grass and tofu cakes to spicy Szechuan noodles. There is also a kid's menu. The drink menu has some of the most imaginative drinks on island, including Nutty Monkey, made with amaretto and Frangelico whipped together with Irish cream, heavy cream, chocolate, and a whole banana, finished off with a crown of chocolate whipped cream and chopped nuts. You can never go back to a chocolate milkshake at the soda shop after drinking this concoction.

Meada's Plaza, Cruz Bay. ✆ **340/776-0303.** www.rhumblinesstjohn.com. Reservations recommended. Main courses $14–$29. MC, V. Wed–Mon 5:30–10pm; Sunday brunch 10am–2:30pm.

Sweet Plantains Restaurant & Rum Bar ★ CARIBBEAN/CREOLE Cool drinks, a tropical ambience, and authentic flavors lure both locals and visitors to this eatery, where comfort and good food go hand in hand. You can dine alfresco in the sea-bordering courtyard or in a lush tropical garden surrounded by West Indian art. A helpful staff will guide you through the menu, beginning with such appetizers as saltfish cakes with a sweet mango purée, or a spicy crab spread with green plantain chips. A freshly made soup is also featured daily. For a main, you can order tender short ribs of beef, or such specialties as pork tenderloin in a guava barbecue sauce. Choice top-quality beef cuts and game are also featured. Nightly specialties are offered, ranging from curries with a choice of seafood or chicken, or else French Caribbean dishes. The bar has the best selection of Caribbean rums on island.

16118 Little Plantation, Coral Bay. ✆ **340/777-4653.** www.sweetplantains-stjohn.com. Reservations recommended. Main courses $21–$34. MC, V. Wed–Mon 5:30–9pm.

Zozo's Ristorante ITALIAN An in-the-know crowd of locals and visitors flocks to this charming Italian trattoria, with an open-air terrace and a sweeping panoramic view over the sea. It's the kind of place that locals would book to the rafters on holidays such as New Year's Eve or for private celebrations such as birthdays or anniversaries. First-rate ingredients, style, and fresh seasonings contribute to such winning dishes as an eggplant tower (layers of eggplant, fontina, ricotta, and red peppers); little neck clams in white wine, garlic, and plum tomatoes; and lump crab cakes with a roasted-pepper aioli. The pastas are the island's best, especially the lobster ravioli with wild mushrooms and toasted pine nuts, and the basil-infused linguine. Tuck into such fish dishes as a grilled sea bass with an eggplant tapenade in a roasted-garlic-and-shrimp sauce, or pan-seared black grouper with a sauce flavored with orange and fresh basil. Their *osso buco* is slowly simmered in red wine, tomato, and veal stock, and is a tasty main course.

In the Gallows Point Resort. ✆ **340/693-9200.** www.zozos.net. Reservations recommended. Main courses $33–$38. AE, MC, V. Nov–May daily 5:30–9pm; off season Mon–Sat 5:30–9pm.

MODERATE

Morgan's Mango CARIBBEAN The chefs here roam the Caribbean for tantalizing flavors, which they adapt for their ever-changing menu. The restaurant is easy to spot with its big canopy, the only protection from the elements. The bar wraps around the main dining room and offers some 30 frozen drinks. Some think the kitchen tries to do too much with the nightly menu, but it does produce some zesty fare—everything from Anegada lobster cakes to spicy Jamaican pickapeppa steak. Try flying fish served as an appetizer, followed by Haitian voodoo snapper pressed in Cajun spices, then grilled and served with fresh-fruit salsa. Equally delectable is mahimahi in Cruzan-rum-and-mango sauce. The knockout dessert is the mango-banana pie.

Cruz Bay (across from the national-park dock). ✆ **340/693-8141.** Reservations recommended. Main courses $16–$34. AE, MC, V. Daily 5:30–10pm.

Shipwreck Landing SEAFOOD/CONTINENTAL Eight miles east of Cruz Bay on the road to Salt Pond Beach, Shipwreck Landing has palms and tropical plants on a veranda overlooking the sea. The intimate bar specializes in tropical frozen drinks. Lunch features a lot more than just sandwiches, salads, and burgers—try pan-seared blackened snapper in Cajun spices, or the conch fritters. The chef shines at night, offering a pasta of the day along with such specialties as tantalizing Caribbean blackened shrimp. A lot of the fare is routine, including New York strip steak and fish and chips, but the grilled mahimahi in lime butter is worth the trip. Entertainment, mainly jazz, is featured Thursday and Sunday nights, with no cover.

34 Freeman's Ground, Rte. 107, Coral Bay. ✆ **340/693-5640.** Reservations requested. Main courses $16–$26; lunch $9–$17. AE, DISC, MC, V. Daily 11am–9pm (bar until 11pm). Closed Sept–Oct.

INEXPENSIVE

Vie's Snack Shack ★ WEST INDIAN Vie's looks like little more than a plywood-sided hut, but its charming and gregarious owner is known as one of the best local chefs on St. John. Her garlic chicken is famous. She also serves conch fritters, johnnycakes, island-style beans and rice with meat sauce, and coconut and pineapple tarts. Don't leave without a glass of homemade limeade. The place is open most days, but as Vie says, "Some days, we might not be here at all"—so you'd better call before you head out.

East End Rd., Rte. 10 (13 miles east of Cruz Bay). ✆ **340/693-5033.** Main courses $7–$12. No credit cards. Tues–Sat 10am–5pm (but call first!). Closed Oct.

Hitting the Beach

The best beach, hands down, is **Trunk Bay** ★★, the biggest attraction on St. John. To miss its picture-perfect shoreline of white sand would be like touring Paris and skipping the Eiffel Tower. One of the loveliest beaches in the Caribbean, it offers ideal conditions for diving, snorkeling, swimming, and sailing. The only drawback is the crowds (watch for pickpockets). The only way to avoid these hordes is to arrive early in the morning or late in the afternoon. Beginning snorkelers, in particular, are attracted to the underwater trail near the shore (see "Sports & Outdoor Pursuits," below); you can rent snorkeling gear here. Lifeguards are on duty. Admission is $4 per person for those 17 and over. If you're coming from St. Thomas, both taxis and safari buses to Trunk Bay meet the ferry from Red Hook when it docks at Cruz Bay.

Caneel Bay, the stamping ground of the rich and famous, has seven beautiful beaches on its 168 acres, and all are open to the public. **Caneel Bay Beach** is easy to reach from the main entrance of the Caneel Bay resort (p. 715). A staff member at the gatehouse will provide directions. **Hawksnest Beach** is one of the most beautiful beaches near the Caneel Bay properties. It's not wide, but it's choice. Since it's near Cruz Bay, where the ferry docks, it is the most crowded, especially when cruise-ship passengers come over from St. Thomas. Safari buses and taxis from Cruz Bay will take you along Northshore Road.

The campgrounds of **Cinnamon Bay** have their own beach, where forest rangers sometimes have to remind visitors to put their swim trunks back on. This is our particular favorite, a beautiful strip of white sand with hiking trails, great windsurfing, ruins, and wild donkeys. (Don't feed or pet them!) Changing rooms and showers are available, and you can rent watersports equipment. Snorkeling is especially popular; you'll often see big schools of purple triggerfish. This beach is best in the morning and at midday, as afternoons are likely to be windy. A marked **nature trail,** with signs identifying the flora, loops through a tropical forest on even turf before leading up to Centerline Road.

Maho Bay Beach is immediately to the east of Cinnamon Bay, and it also borders campgrounds. As you lie on the sand, you can see a whole hillside of pitched tents. This is also a popular beach, often with the campers themselves.

Francis Bay Beach and **Watermelon Cay Beach** are just a couple more of the beaches you'll encounter traveling eastward along St. John's gently curving coastline. Watermelon is actually an island in Sir Francis Drake Channel, and it's far from a melon, with a reef of rainbow-hued fish surrounding it. It lies right offshore, and you can easily swim across to it along with the starfish gliding through turtle-grass beds. To reach Watermelon, follow the Leinster Bay Trail for .75 miles along the Sir Francis Drake Channel, which is studded with islands. Francis Bay Beach lies near the Annaberg Plantation. Locals come here for Sunday barbecues, and snorkelers explore its shallow reef washing up on the bay's rock-strewn northern shore. Swimming among the algae-covered rocks are the territorial damselfish, French grunts, and even "Christmas tree worms" with their feathery tentacles. The beach at **Leinster Bay** is another haven for those seeking the solace of a private sunny retreat. You can swim in the bay's shallow water or snorkel over the spectacular and colorful coral reef, perhaps in the company of an occasional turtle or stingray.

The remote **Salt Pond Bay** is known to locals but often missed by visitors. It's on the beautiful coast in the southeast, adjacent to **Coral Bay.** The bay is tranquil, but the beach is somewhat rocky. It's a short walk down the hill from a parking lot. (***Warning:*** A few cars have been broken into here.) The snorkeling is good, and the bay has some fascinating tidal pools. The Ram Head Trail begins here and, winding for about 1 mile, leads to a belvedere overlooking the bay. Facilities are meager but include an outhouse and a few tattered picnic tables.

If you want to escape the crowds, head for **Lameshur Bay Beach,** along the rugged south coast, west of Salt Pond Bay and accessible only via a bumpy dirt road. The sands are beautiful, and the snorkeling is excellent. You can also take a 5-minute stroll down the road past the beach to explore the nearby ruins of an old plantation estate that was destroyed in a slave revolt.

Does St. John have a nude beach? Not officially, but lovely **Salomon Bay Beach** is a contender, although park rangers sometimes ask people to put their swimwear back on. Leave Cruz Bay on Route 20 and turn left at the park service sign, about a quarter-mile past the visitor center. Park at the end of a cul-de-sac, then walk along the trail for about 15 minutes. Go early, and you'll practically have the beach to yourself. The beach interests snorkelers of all levels of experience. Also on the north shore and to the immediate south of Salomon is the aptly named **Honeymoon Beach,** where couples often openly display their affection.

Sports & Outdoor Pursuits ★★

St. John is known for the Virgin Islands National Park, as well as for its coral-sand beaches, winding mountain roads, hidden coves, and trails that lead past old, bush-covered sugar-cane plantations. Just don't visit expecting to play golf.

The most complete line of watersports equipment available, including rentals for windsurfing, snorkeling, kayaking, and sailing, is offered at the **Cinnamon Bay Watersports Center,** on Cinnamon Bay Beach (✆ **340/776-6330**). One- and two-person sit-on-top kayaks rent for $15 to $30 per hour. You can also sail away in a 14- or 16-foot Hobie monohull **sailboat** for $30 to $50 per hour.

BOAT EXCURSIONS You can take half- and full-day boat trips, including a full-day excursion to the Baths at Virgin Gorda. **Cruz Bay Watersports** (✆ **340/776-6234;** www.divestjohn.com) offers trips to the British Virgin Islands for $130, including food and beverages. ***Note:*** Be sure to bring your passport for any excursions to the British Virgin Islands.

FISHING Outfitters located on St. Thomas offer sportfishing trips here—they'll come over and pick you up. Call the **Charter Boat Center** (✆ **340/775-7990;** www.charterboat.vi) at Red Hook. Count on spending from $550 to $850 per party for a half-day of fishing.

HIKING St. John has the most rewarding hiking in the Virgin Islands. The terrain ranges from arid and dry (in the east) to moist and semitropical (in the northwest). The island has more than 800 species of plants and 160 species of birds, and more than 20 trails maintained beautifully by the island's crew of park rangers. Much of the land on the island is designated as **Virgin Islands National Park ★★★**. Visitors must stop by the **Cruz Bay Visitor Center,** where you can pick up the park brochure, which includes a map of the park and the *Virgin Islands National Park News,* which has the latest information on park activities. It's important to carry a lot of water and wear sunscreen and insect repellent when you hike.

St. John is laced with a wide choice of clearly marked walking paths. At least 20 of these originate from Northshore Road (Rte. 20) or from the island's main east-west artery, Centerline Road (Rte. 10). Each is marked at its starting point with a pre-planned itinerary; the walks can last anywhere from 10 minutes to 2 hours. Maps are available from the national park headquarters at Cruz Bay.

One of our favorite hikes, the **Annaberg Historic Trail** (identified by the U.S. National Park Service as trail no. 10), requires only about a .5-mile stroll. It departs

Underwater Wonderful

At Trunk Bay, divers and snorkelers can follow the **National Park Underwater Trail** (✆ **340/776-6201**), which stretches for 656 feet and helps you identify what you see—everything from false coral to colonial anemones. You'll pass lavender sea fans and schools of silversides. Rangers are on hand to provide information. There is a $4 admission fee to access the beach.

from a clearly marked point along the island's north coast, near the junction of routes 10 and 20. This self-guided tour passes the partially restored ruins of a manor house built during the 1700s. Signs along the way give historical and botanical data. Visiting the ruins is free. If you want to prolong your hiking experience, take the **Leinster Bay Trail** (trail no. 11), which begins near the point where trail no. 10 ends. It leads past mangrove swamps and coral inlets rich with plant and marine life; markers identify some of the plants and animals.

Near the beach at **Cinnamon Bay,** there's a marked nature trail, with signs identifying the flora. It's a relatively flat walk through a tropical forest, eventually leading straight up to Centerline Road.

The **National Park Service** (✆ **340/776-6201**) provides a number of ranger-led activities. One of the most popular is the guided 2.5-mile **Reef Bay Hike.** Included is a stop at the only known petroglyphs on the island and a tour of the sugar-mill ruins. A park ranger discusses the area's natural and cultural history along the way. The hike starts at 9:30am on Monday, Tuesday, Thursday, and Friday, and costs $21 per person. Reservations are required and can be made by phone (at least 2–3 weeks in advance).

SCUBA DIVING & SNORKELING ★★ **Cruz Bay Watersports,** P.O. Box 252, Cruz Bay, St. John (✆ **340/776-6234;** www.divestjohn.com), is a PADI and NAUI five-star diving center. Certifications can be arranged through a dive master for $750. Beginner scuba lessons start at $100. Two-tank reef dives with all dive gear cost $100, and wreck dives, night dives, and dive packages are available. In addition, snorkel tours are offered daily for $60.

Divers can ask about scuba packages at **Low Key Watersports,** Wharfside Village (✆ **800/835-7718** in the U.S., or 340/693-8999; www.divelowkey.com). All wreck dives offered are two-tank/two-location dives and cost $90, with night dives going for $95. Snorkel tours are also available, at $75 per person.

The best place for snorkeling is **Trunk Bay** (see "Hitting the Beach," above). Snorkeling gear can be rented from the Cinnamon Bay Watersports Center (see above) for $5, plus a $25 deposit. Two other choice **snorkeling spots** around St. John are **Leinster Bay ★★** and **Haulover Bay ★★**. Usually uncrowded Leinster Bay offers some of the best snorkeling in the U.S. Virgins. The water is calm, clear, and filled with brilliantly hued tropical fish. Haulover Bay is a favorite among locals. It's often deserted, and the waters are often clearer than in other spots around St. John. The ledges, walls, and nooks here are set very close together, making the bay a lot of fun for anyone with a little bit of experience.

SEA KAYAKING **Arawak Expeditions,** based in Cruz Bay (✆ **800/238-8687** in the U.S., or 340/693-8312; www.arawakexp.com), provides kayaking gear, healthful meals, and experienced guides for full- and half-day outings. Trips cost $100 and

$65, respectively. Multiday excursions with camping are also available; call the toll-free number if you'd like to arrange an entire vacation with them. These 5-day trips range in price from $1,449 in winter to $1,249 in summer.

WINDSURFING The windsurfing at Cinnamon Bay is some of the best anywhere, for either the beginner or the expert. The **Cinnamon Bay Watersports Center** (see above) rents high-quality equipment for all levels, even for kids. Boards cost $25 to $65 an hour; a 2-hour introductory lesson costs $80.

Exploring the Island

The best way to see St. John quickly, especially if you're on a cruise-ship layover, is to take a 2-hour **taxi tour.** The cost is $50 for one or two passengers, or $25 per person for three or more. Almost any taxi at Cruz Bay will take you on these tours, or you can call the **St. John Taxi Association** (✆ **340/693-7530**).

Many visitors spend time at **Cruz Bay,** where the ferry docks. This village has interesting bars, restaurants, boutiques, and pastel-painted houses. It's a bit sleepy, but relaxing after the fast pace of St. Thomas.

Most cruise-ship passengers dart through Cruz Bay and head for the island's biggest attraction, **Virgin Islands National Park ★★** (✆ **340/776-6201**). The park totals 12,474 acres, including submerged lands and water adjacent to St. John, and has more than 19 miles of hiking trails to explore. See "Sports & Outdoor Pursuits," above, for information on trails and organized park activities.

Other major sights on the island include **Trunk Bay** (see "Hitting the Beach," above), one of the world's most beautiful beaches, and **Fort Berg** (also called Fortsberg), at Coral Bay, which served as the base for the soldiers who brutally crushed the 1733 slave revolt. Finally, try to make time for the **Annaberg Ruins** on Leinster Bay Road, where the Danes maintained a thriving plantation and sugar mill after 1718. It's located off Northshore Road, east of Trunk Bay. Admission is free. On certain days of the week (dates vary), park rangers lead guided walks of the area. For information on the **Annaberg Historic Trail,** see "Sports & Outdoor Pursuits," above.

Shopping ★★

Compared to St. Thomas, St. John's shopping isn't much, but what's here is interesting. The boutiques and shops of Cruz Bay are individualized and quite special. Most of the shops are clustered at **Mongoose Junction,** in a woodsy area beside the roadway, about a 5-minute walk from the ferry dock.

Before you leave the island, you'll want to visit the recently expanded **Wharfside Village** (✆ **340/693-8210;** www.wharfsidevillage.com), just a few steps from the ferry departure point. In this complex of courtyards, alleys, and shady patios is a mishmash of all sorts of boutiques, along with some restaurants, fast-food joints, and bars.

Bamboula, Mongoose Junction (✆ **340/693-8699;** www.bamboulastjohn.com), has an exotic and very appealing collection of gifts from St. John, the Caribbean, India, Indonesia, and Central Africa. The store also has clothing for both men and women under its own label—hand-batiked soft cottons and rayons made for comfort in a hot climate.

Coconut Coast Studios, Frank Bay (✆ **800/887-3798** or 340/776-6944; www.coconutcoaststudios.com), is the studio of Elaine Estern, best known for her Caribbean landscapes. It's 5 minutes from Cruz Bay; walk along the waterfront, bypassing Gallows Point. The outlet also sells calendars, gifts, limited-edition prints, and lithographs. From November to April, the studio hosts a free sunset cocktail party Wednesday 5:30 to 7pm.

At the **Donald Schnell Studio,** Mongoose Junction (✆ **800/253-7107** or 340/776-6920; www.donaldschnell.com), Schnell and his assistants have created one of the finest collections of handmade pottery, sculpture, and blown glass in the Caribbean. The staff can be seen working daily. They're known for their rough-textured coral work. Water fountains are a specialty item, as are house signs and coral-pottery dinnerware.

The **Fabric Mill,** Mongoose Junction (✆ **340/776-6194**), features batik fabrics from around the world. Vibrant rugs; bed, bathroom, and table linens; sarongs; scarves; and handbags are all made here.

R & I Patton Goldsmithing, Mongoose Junction (✆ **800/626-3445** or 340/776-6548; www.pattongold.com), is one of the oldest businesses on the island. Three-quarters of the merchandise here is made on St. John. There's a large selection of jewelry in sterling silver, gold, and precious stones. Also featured are the works of goldsmiths from outstanding American studios, as well as Spanish coins.

St. John After Dark

Bring a good book. When it comes to nightlife, St. John is no St. Thomas. Most people are content to have a leisurely dinner and then head for bed.

Woody's Seafood Saloon, Cruz Bay (✆ **340/779-4625;** www.woodysseafood.com), is the local dive and hangout at Cruz Bay, right by the ferry dock. It draws both expats and a cross-section of island life, from taxi drivers to fishermen. You can come here to eat or drink. The place is particularly popular during happy hour, from 3 to 6pm, featuring dollar beers. It's about the only place on island you can order food as late as 1am. Try the blackened-fish sandwich or the "biggest, baddest cheeseburger on island." The joint's hosts are Chad and Todd Beaty, identical twins. They hire bartenders who are willing to pour alcohol in navels or spray whipped cream "anywhere," and we do mean that literally. The joint jumps Sunday to Thursday 11am to 1am, Friday and Saturday 11am to 2am.

The **Caneel Bay Bar,** at the Caneel Bay resort (p. 715; ✆ **340/776-6111**), has live music Tuesday to Sunday 11am to 11pm. The most popular drinks are the Cool Caneel (local rum with sugar, lime, and anisette) and the trademark Plantation Punch (lime and orange juice with three different kinds of rum; bitters; and nutmeg).

The two places above are very touristy. If you'd like to drink and gossip with the locals, try **JJ's Texas Coast Café,** Cruz Bay (✆ **340/776-6908**), a real dive, across the park from the ferry dock. The margaritas here are lethal. Also at Cruz Bay, check out the action at **Fred's,** on King Street (✆ **340/776-6363**), across from the Lime Inn. Fred's brings in bands and has dancing on Friday nights. It's just a little hole-in-the-wall and can get crowded fast.

The best sports bar on the island is **Skinny Legs,** Emmaus, Route 10, Coral Bay, beyond the fire station (✆ **340/779-4982;** www.skinnylegs.com). This shack made of tin and wood happens to have the best burgers in St. John. (The chili dogs aren't bad, either.) The yachting crowd likes to hang out here, though you wouldn't know it at first glance—it often seems that the richer they are, the scruffier they dress. The bar has a satellite dish, dartboard, and horseshoe pits. Live music is presented on Friday and Saturday nights during high season.

Morgan's Mango (✆ **340/693-8141**) is one of the hottest watering holes on the island (p. 721). It's in Cruz Bay, across from the national-park dock. Count yourself lucky if you get in on a crowded night in winter. The place became famous locally when it turned away Harrison Ford, who was vacationing at Caneel Bay. Thursday is Margarita Night, and Tuesday night is Lobster Night.

Island Blues, Coral Harbour (© **340/776-6800;** www.island-blues.com), lies in the East End. A rough, tough waterhole, it's the best place to meet local characters and expats. In winter there is live music every night—definitely not of the classical concert variety. If you're hungry, you can order daily specials scrawled on chalkboards and served on a terrace overlooking the water. Island specialties include spicy stewed Caribbean chicken served over seasoned rice. The club is open daily from 11:30am, remaining so until the last customer leaves, often in the wee hours of the morning.

ST. CROIX ★★

St. Croix is the largest of the U.S. Virgin Islands, but its easygoing vibe seems unchanged from when the Danish settled here in the late 18th century. Its history is enshrined in colorful buildings of picturesque Christiansted, while smaller and earthier Frederiksted, on the island's rocky east end, comes alive when cruise ships dock and keep the local Cruzan Rum Distillery busy. Inland, the island is a lush feast of mango and mahogany trees, tree ferns, and dangling lianas, ringed by beautiful beaches and rolling hills.

Things to Do Discover St. Croix's Danish colonial history on a walking tour amid brightly painted Georgian buildings in **Christiansted,** then climb to the top of **Fort Christiansvaern** for a view of the harbor. In **Frederiksted,** sample the delights of the **Cruzan Rum Distillery,** or take a boat trip to **Buck Island,** in the middle of a marine sanctuary. Sunbathe on the white sands under swaying palms at **Davis Bay,** follow the footpaths through the private **"Rain Forest,"** or see fine black coral while snorkeling in **Salt River Canyon.**

Shopping **Christiansted** is the shopping hub of St. Croix, where hole-in-the-wall and chic boutiques sell an array of handmade goods, beachwear, and decorative carvings. Along the boardwalk, try the **King's Alley Complex,** a pink-sided compound filled with the densest concentration of shops, for china and leather goods. In **Frederiksted,** look for framed engravings and West Indies antiques in the urban mall at **Frederiksted Pier.**

Nightlife & Entertainment The waterfront bars and clubs at **Christiansted** hum to a lighter groove than they do on St. Thomas, but you can still have a nice night out listening to live reggae and soca, linger over a beer at a hip dive, or listen to DJs spin island sound. Try to catch an exciting performance of the flamboyant **Quadrille Dancers**—watch and learn their steps, then join them on the dance floor.

Eating & Drinking **Christiansted** is filled with a variety of restaurants, so it's not hard to settle into a bistro serving spicy Creole seafood, steaks, or homemade soups. **Frederiksted** features simpler, more laid-back dining rooms where you can sample the local ***funghi*** (fish with cornmeal and gravy), ***daube*** (meat roasted in a pot with spicy seasoning) or ***souse*** (a lime-flavored stock of pig's feet, head, and tail).

Essentials

See "Getting There," at the beginning of the chapter, for details on flights to St. Croix.

VISITOR INFORMATION You can begin your explorations at the **visitor bureau,** 53A Company St., Christiansted (© **340/773-0495;** www.stcroixtourism.com), a yellow building across from the open-air market. It's open Monday to Friday 8am to 5pm.

GETTING AROUND At Henry E. Rohlsen International Airport, official taxi rates are posted. From the airport, expect to pay about $16 to $36 to Christiansted and about $12 to $24 to Frederiksted. Cabs are unmetered, so agree on the rate before you get in. The **St. Croix Taxi Association** (✆ **340/778-1088;** www.stcroixtaxi.com) offers door-to-door service.

Air-conditioned **buses** run between Christiansted and Frederiksted about every 2 hours daily between 5:30am and 8pm. They start at Tide Village, to the east of Christiansted, and go along Route 75 to the Golden Rock Shopping Center. They transfer along Route 70, with stopovers at the Sunny Isle Shopping Center, La Reine Shopping Center, St. George Village Botanical Garden, and Whim Plantation Museum, before reaching Frederiksted. The one-way fare is $1, or 55¢ for seniors. For more information, call ✆ **340/773-1664.**

If your hotel is in Christiansted and you don't plan to do extensive touring around the island, you can manage without a car. But if you plan to get out and explore, a car is the way to go. Many of the roads are quite good. St. Croix offers moderately priced car rentals, even on cars with automatic transmission and air-conditioning. However, because of the island's higher-than-normal accident rate, insurance costs are a bit higher than usual. If you're not covered under your existing insurance policies or by your credit card, you should consider paying for the collision-damage waiver.

Avis (✆ **800/331-1084** in the U.S. and Canada, or 340/778-9355; www.avis.com), **Budget** (✆ **800/472-3325** in U.S. and Canada, or 340/778-9636; www.budgetstrcroix.com), and **Hertz** (✆ **800/654-3001** in the U.S. and Canada, or 340/778-1402; www.rentacarstcroix.com) all maintain headquarters at the airport; look for their kiosks near the baggage-claim areas. In most rural areas, the speed limit is 35 mph; certain parts of the major artery, Route 66, are 55 mph. In towns and urban areas, the speed limit is 20 mph. If you're going into the "bush country," you'll find the roads very difficult. Sometimes the government smoothes the roads out before the rainy season begins (often in Oct or Nov), but they deteriorate rapidly. ***Be warned:*** Driving is on the left.

FAST FACTS If you need medical assistance, go to the **Governor Juan F. Luis Hospital & Medical Center,** 4007 Estate Diamond Ruby, Christiansted (✆ **340/778-6311;** www.jflusvi.org).

Where to Stay

All rooms are subject to an 8% hotel room tax, which is not included in the rates below. If you're interested in a villa or condo rental, contact the places reviewed below or **Vacation St. Croix,** 4000 La Grande Princesse, Ste. 8, Christiansted, St. Croix, U.S.V.I. 00820 (✆ **877/788-0361** or 340/718-0361; fax 340/718-5491; www.vacationstcroix.com), which offers some of the best accommodations on the island. Some are private residences with pools; many are on the beach. They range from one-bedroom units to six-bedroom villas, with prices from $2,000 to $8,800 per week in winter. The minimum stay is 7 nights. These same prices are lowered in off season to $1,800 to $6,900 per week.

VERY EXPENSIVE

The Buccaneer ★★★ ☺ This large, luxurious, family-owned resort has three of the island's best beaches and the best sports program on St. Croix. The property was

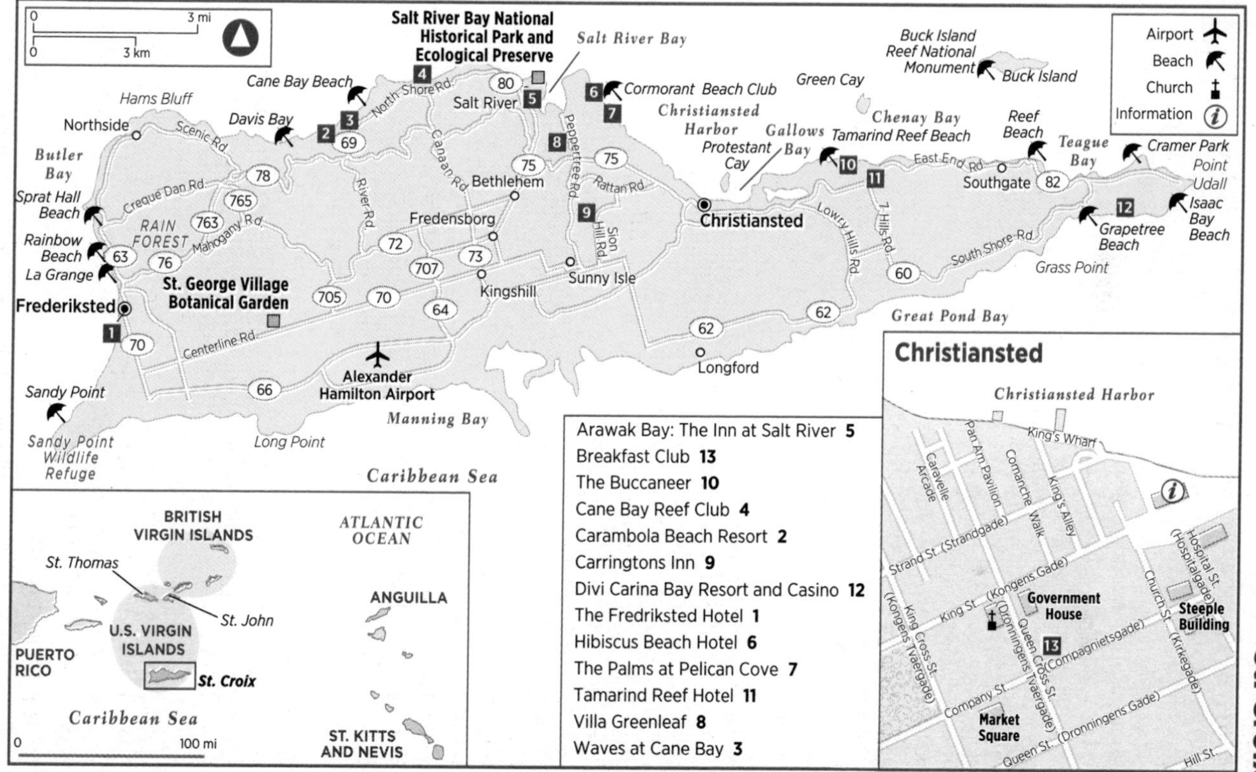
0 3 mi
0 3 km
Salt River Bay National Historical Park and Ecological Preserve
Salt River Bay
Buck Island Reef National Monument
Buck Island
Airport
Beach
Church
Information
Cane Bay Beach
Hams Bluff
Northside
Scenic Rd.
Davis Bay
North Shore Rd.
Salt River
Cormorant Beach Club
Green Cay
Christiansted Harbor
Gallows Bay
Protestant Cay
Chenay Bay
Tamarind Reef Beach
Reef Beach
Teague Bay
Cramer Park
Point Udall
Isaac Bay Beach
Butler Bay
Sprat Hall Beach
Rainbow Beach
La Grange
Creque Dam Rd.
RAIN FOREST
Mahogany Rd.
River Rd.
Canaan Rd.
Bethlehem
Peppertree Rd.
Rattan Rd.
Fredensborg
Sion Hill Rd.
Christiansted
Lowry Hills Rd.
7 Hills Rd.
East End Rd.
Southgate
South Shore Rd.
Grapetree Beach
Grass Point
St. George Village Botanical Garden
Kingshill
Sunny Isle
Frederiksted
Centerline Rd.
Great Pond Bay
Longford
Alexander Hamilton Airport
Sandy Point
Sandy Point Wildlife Refuge
Long Point
Manning Bay
Caribbean Sea
BRITISH VIRGIN ISLANDS
ATLANTIC OCEAN
St. Thomas
St. John
U.S. VIRGIN ISLANDS
ANGUILLA
PUERTO RICO
St. Croix
Caribbean Sea
0 100 mi
ST. KITTS AND NEVIS
Arawak Bay: The Inn at Salt River 5
Breakfast Club 13
The Buccaneer 10
Cane Bay Reef Club 4
Carambola Beach Resort 2
Carringtons Inn 9
Divi Carina Bay Resort and Casino 12
The Fredriksted Hotel 1
Hibiscus Beach Hotel 6
The Palms at Pelican Cove 7
Tamarind Reef Hotel 11
Villa Greenleaf 8
Waves at Cane Bay 3
Christiansted
Christiansted Harbor
King's Wharf
Caravelle Arcade
Pan Am Pavilion
Comanche Walk
King's Alley
Strand St. (Strandgade)
King St. (Kongens Gade)
Government House
Hospital St. (Hospitalgade)
Church St. (Kirkegade)
Steeple Building
King Cross St. (Kongens Tvaergade)
Queen Cross St. (Dronningens Tvaergade)
(Compagnietsgade)
Company St.
Market Square
Queen St. (Dronningens Gade)
Hill St.

once a cattle ranch and a sugar plantation; its first estate house, which dates from the mid–17th century, stands near a freshwater pool. Accommodations are either in the main building or in one of the beachside properties. The baronially arched main building has a lobby opening onto landscaped terraces, with a sea vista on two sides and Christiansted to the west. The rooms are fresh and comfortable, though some of the standard units are a bit small. All have wicker or mahogany furnishings and full bathrooms. The best bathrooms are in the Beachside Doubloons and come complete with whirlpool tubs. A free kid's camp is available year-round.

5007 Estate Shoys (P.O. Box 25200), Gallows Bay (1¾ miles east of Christiansted on Rte. 82), Christiansted, St. Croix, U.S.V.I. 00824. www.thebuccaneer.com. ✆ **800/255-3881** in the U.S., or 340/712-2100. Fax 340/712-2104. 138 units. Winter $288–$560 double, from $430 suite; off season $259–$360 double, from $368 suite. Children 17 and under stay free in parent's room. Rates include American breakfast. AE, DISC, MC, V. **Amenities:** 4 restaurants; bar; babysitting; children's program; 18-hole golf course; exercise room; 2 outdoor pools; room service; spa; 8 tennis courts (2 lit); watersports equipment/rentals. *In room:* A/C, TV, fridge, hair dryer, Wi-Fi (free).

EXPENSIVE

Carambola Beach Resort Extensively renovated, this hotel is set on 27 acres above Davis Bay, about a 30-minute drive from Christiansted. It's one of the largest hotels on St. Croix, and it lies adjacent to an outstanding golf course, in a lovely, lush setting on a white-sand beach whose turquoise waters provide fine snorkeling. Despite its spectacular physical location, this resort doesn't match the Buccaneer's (p. 728) class and style. Guests are housed in red-roofed, two-story buildings, each of which contains six units. The accommodations, each a suite, are furnished in mahogany, with Danish design; each has a balcony partially concealed from outside view, overlooking either the garden or the sea. Rooms have an upscale flair, with louvered doors, tile floors, mahogany trim, and sometimes extras like screened-in porches with rocking chairs. If you want the very finest room, ask for the Davis Bay Suite, which was a former Rockefeller private beach home. Its veranda alone is capable of entertaining 50 people, should that many drop in.

Estate Davis Bay (P.O. Box 3031), Kingshill, St. Croix, U.S.V.I. 00851. www.carambolabeach.com. ✆ **888/503-8760** in the U.S., or 340/778-3800. Fax 340/778-1682. 150 units. Winter $349–$529 suite; off season $249–$379 suite. AE, DISC, MC, V. **Amenities:** 2 restaurants; bar; golf course; exercise room; outdoor pool; whirlpool; spa; 2 tennis courts (lit); watersports equipment/rentals. *In room:* A/C, TV, fridge, hair dryer, kitchenette (in some), Wi-Fi (free).

Divi Carina Bay Resort and Casino ★ Opening onto 1,000 feet of sugar-white beach, this resort brought gambling to the U.S. Virgin Islands. That fact seems to obscure its success as a place of barefoot elegance and a top resort property. Accommodations feature oceanfront guest rooms and villa suites with views of the Caribbean. Rooms are a good size and well equipped, with computer/fax lines, VCRs, a small kitchen, full bathrooms, and balconies. We prefer the accommodations on the ground floor, as they are closer to the water's edge. The 20 villas across the street are about a 3-minute walk from the sands. The most up-to-date building contains 50 oceanfront accommodations with balconies. You can simply go upstairs for a massage at the spa on the top floor.

5025 Estate Turner Hole, Christiansted, St. Croix, U.S.V.I. 00820. www.divicarina.com. ✆ **877/773-9700** in the U.S., or 340/773-9700. Fax 340/773-6802. 180 units. Winter $265–$310 double, from $405 suite; off season $139–$220 double, from $305 suite. Children 15 and under stay free in parent's room. AE, MC, V. **Amenities:** 2 restaurants; 2 bars; babysitting; dive center; health club; 2 outdoor pools; 2 outdoor whirlpools; casino; room service; snorkeling; spa; tennis court (lit). *In room:* A/C, TV, fridge, hair dryer, kitchen (in some); Wi-Fi (free).

Hibiscus Beach Resort ★ This hotel, on one of the island's best beaches, attracts a lively clientele. The accommodations are in six two-story white-and-blue buildings. Each guest room is a retreat unto itself, with a private patio or balcony and a view of the Caribbean, plus tasteful Caribbean furnishings and floral prints. Shower-only bathrooms are small but well maintained. Guests who stay here are a bit isolated and will find a car useful.

4131 La Grande Princesse (about 3 miles northwest of Christiansted, beside Rte. 75, next to the Cormorant), St. Croix, U.S.V.I. 00820. www.hibiscusbeachresort.com. ✆ **800/442-0121** in the U.S., or 340/718-4042. Fax 340/718-7668. 38 units. Winter $200–$295 double; off season $150–$245 double. Honeymoon, dive, and golf packages available. AE, DISC, MC, V. **Amenities:** Restaurant; bar; babysitting; outdoor pool; smoke-free rooms; snorkeling. *In room:* A/C, ceiling fan, TV, hair dryer, minibar, Wi-Fi (free).

Tamarind Reef Hotel A sandy beach at the Tamarind Reef's doorstep and good snorkeling along the reef highlight this property. The resort exudes a fresh, bright new look. Each motel-style room features a garden patio or private balcony, affording guests a view of the blue Caribbean. In addition, 18 of the suites provide fully equipped kitchenettes and accommodate up to four people. Guests can relax by the pool and enjoy cocktails, light lunches, and snacks from the poolside bar and grill. For those who want to explore St. Croix underwater, the hotel offers complimentary watersports equipment. Adjoining the hotel is the Green Cay Marina, where guests can charter boats for deep-sea fishing or sailing expeditions.

5001 Tamarind Reef, Christiansted, St. Croix, U.S.V.I. 00820. www.tamarindreefhotel.com. ✆ **800/619-0014** in the U.S., or 340/7718-4455. Fax 340/718-3989. 39 units. Winter $275–$325 double; off season $200–$300 double. Extra person $35–$50. Children 6 and under stay free in parent's room. Ask about dive, golf, and honeymoon packages. AE, DC, MC, V. **Amenities:** 2 restaurants; bar; outdoor pool; 4 tennis courts (lit); watersports equipment/rentals. *In room:* A/C, ceiling fan, TV, fridge, hair dryer, Internet (free), kitchenette (in some).

Villa Greenleaf ★★ This is one of the best B&Bs on the island, owned and operated by the same staff that made the Greenleaf Inn at Boothbay Harbor one of the leading inns of New England. This snug family retreat still adheres to its New England innkeeping tradition, offering personal service and the elegant ambience of a private home. It's very small, so make reservations well in advance. The building dates from the 1950s, when it was a private home, but it's been completely renovated postmillennium. Four-poster beds are just some of the elegant details associated with the roomy bedrooms of this house. Each of the suites is individually decorated and imbued with muted Caribbean charm and grace. The location is to the west of Christiansted, so you'll need a car for excursions down from the hill.

Island Center Rd. (P.O. Box 675), Montpellier, St. Croix, U.S.V.I. 00821. www.villagreenleaf.com. ✆ **888/282-1001** in the U.S., or 340/719-1958. Fax 340/772-5425. 5 units. Winter $275–$300 double; off season $200–$225 double. Rates include breakfast. AE, DC, MC, V. **Amenities:** Free airport transfers; Jacuzzi; pool. *In room:* A/C, ceiling fan, fridge, hair dryer, no phone, Wi-Fi (free).

MODERATE

Cane Bay Reef Club ★ This is one of the little gems of the island, offering large suites, each with a living room, a full kitchen, and a balcony overlooking the water. It's on the north shore, about a 20-minute taxi ride from Christiansted, fronting the rocky Cane Bay Beach near the Waves at Cane Bay. Sunsets are beautiful, and the snorkeling's great. The decor is breezily tropical, with cathedral ceilings, overhead fans, and Chilean tiles. Bedrooms are spacious, cool, and airy, with comfortable beds; living rooms also contain futons. There's a golf course nearby, and there's a dive shop within walking distance. You can cook in your own kitchen, barbecue, or dine at the in-house restaurant, Bogey's.

P.O. Box 1407, Kingshill, St. Croix, U.S.V.I. 00851. www.canebay.com. ✆ **800/253-8534** in the U.S., or 340/778-2966. Fax 340/778-2966. 9 units. Winter double $150–$250 daily, $970–$1,600 weekly; off season double $110–$160 daily, $700–$990 weekly. Extra person $20. AE, DC, DISC, MC, V. **Amenities:** Restaurant; bar; outdoor pool. *In room:* A/C, ceiling fan, TV, fridge, kitchen, minibar, no phone (in some).

Carringtons Inn ★ 🎁 If you've read stories about celebrities, such as screen legend Maureen O'Hara, who own villas on St. Croix, and you wonder what life is like in them, here's your chance to experience one firsthand. This grandly elegant B&B was once the home of a wealthy family who spent winters here; much evidence of their former lifestyle remains. This is an intimate B&B with personalized attention and five spacious and beautifully furnished guest rooms with first-class private bathrooms. Some rooms have a king-size canopy bed, and wicker furnishings are in tasteful abundance. When guests gather around the pool, a house-party atmosphere prevails. Even your breakfast of such delights as rum-flavored French toast can be served poolside. The staff delivers thoughtful touches such as a full concierge service, bathrobes, and even freshly baked cookies in the evening.

4001 Estate Hermon Hill (1 mile west of Christiansted), St. Croix, U.S.V.I. 00820. www.carringtonsinn.com. ✆ **877/658-0508** in the U.S., or 340/713-0508. Fax 340/719-0841. 5 units. Winter $125–$165 double; off season $100–$125 double. Rates include breakfast. AE, MC, V. **Amenities:** Breakfast room; nearby health club; outdoor pool; nearby tennis courts (lit). *In room:* A/C, ceiling fan, hair dryer, kitchenette (in some), Wi-Fi (free).

The Palms at Pelican Cove ★★ ☺ This family-oriented resort stands on 7 acres of beachfront property at a point 3 miles northwest of Christiansted. Its bedrooms are inviting, in a Caribbean style with an upgraded decor. Designed in a boxy, modern-looking series of rectangles, the resort has outcroppings of exposed natural stone, striking a balance between seclusion and accessibility. Long Reef lies less than 100 feet offshore from the resort's sandy beachfront. The spacious guestrooms have a private balcony or patio with ocean views. Social life revolves around an open-air lounge, bar, and restaurant with sea views.

4126 La Grande Princesse, St. Croix, U.S.V.I. 00820. www.palmspelicancove.com. ✆ **800/548-4460** in the U.S., or 340/718-8920. Fax 340/718-9218. 40 units. Winter $230–$290 double, $290–$320 suite; off season $190–$220 double, $240–280 suite. AE, MC, V. **Amenities:** Restaurant; bar; outdoor pool; room service; scuba-diving lessons. *In room:* A/C, TV, hair dryer, minibar, Wi-Fi (free).

Waves at Cane Bay This intimate and tasteful condo property is about 8 miles from the airport, midway between the island's two biggest towns. It's set on a well-landscaped plot of oceanfront property on Cane Bay, the heart of the best scuba and snorkeling at Cane Bay Beach. The renovated accommodations are within a pair of two-story cement-sided buildings, each directly on the beach. Each of the accommodations is high-ceilinged and relatively large, with a well-equipped kitchenette, a selection of reading material, tiled floors, and a private veranda that's partially or fully concealed from the views of any of the other verandas. Attached to one of the buildings is an open-sided pavilion that functions as a bar and restaurant, open Monday to Saturday for dinner.

Cane Bay (P.O. Box 1749), Kingshill, St. Croix, U.S.V.I. 00851. www.canebaystcroix.com. ✆ **800/545-0603** in the U.S., or 340/718-1815. 12 units. Winter $150–$175 double; off season $110–$130 double. Extra person $20. AE, MC, V. From the airport, go left on Rte. 64; after 1 mile, turn right on Rte. 70; after another mile, go left at the junction with Rte. 75; after 1¾ miles, turn left at the junction with Rte. 80;

follow for 5 miles. **Amenities:** Restaurant; bar; outdoor pool; watersports equipment/rentals. *In room:* A/C, ceiling fan, TV, kitchen, Wi-Fi (free).

INEXPENSIVE

Arawak Bay: The Inn at Salt River ★ This is a purpose-built, modern B&B, lying on the north shore and opening onto panoramic views of Salt River Bay and the Caribbean. Each accommodation comes with a balcony where you can relax and take in the view. There are even telescopes for ship- or star-gazing. Bedrooms are furnished in a simple but comfortable Caribbean motif, with either one king or two full-size beds. A complimentary breakfast includes house specialties and local pastries. The location is convenient to beaches, including Cane Bay, Christiansted, and the airport.

Kingshill (P.O. Box 3475), St. Croix, U.S.V.I. 00851. www.arawakbaysaltriver.co.vi. ✆ **877/261-5385** or 340/772-1684. Fax 340/772-1686. 14 units. Winter $140 double; off season $120 double. AE, DC, MC, V. **Amenities:** Bar; outdoor pool. *In room:* A/C, TV, Wi-Fi (free).

The Breakfast Club ★ Here you'll get the best value of any bed-and-breakfast on St. Croix. This comfortable place combines a 1950s compound of efficiency apartments with a traditional-looking stone house that was rebuilt from a ruin in the 1930s. Each of the units has a cypress-sheathed ceiling, off-white walls, a beige-tile floor, and summery furniture. An on-site chef specializes in banana pancakes and will prepare lunch or dinner on request. When there is a full house count, occasional "party nights" are staged, featuring recorded music.

18 Queen Cross St., Christiansted, St. Croix, U.S.V.I. 00820. ✆ **340/773-7383.** Fax 340/773-8642. 10 units. Year-round $75 double. Rates include breakfast. AE, V. *In room:* A/C (in some), TV, fridge, no phone.

The Frederiksted Hotel This contemporary four-story inn is a good choice for the heart of historic Frederiksted. It's in the center of town, about a 10-minute ride from the airport. Much of the activity takes place in the outdoor tiled courtyard, where guests enjoy drinks. The cheery rooms are like those of a motel on the U.S. mainland, perhaps showing a bit of wear, and with good ventilation but bad lighting. They're done in a tropical motif of pastels and are equipped with small fridges. The best (and most expensive) rooms are those with ocean views; they're subject to street noise but have the best light. The nearest beach is Fort Frederik, a 3-minute walk away.

442 Strand St., Frederiksted, St. Croix, U.S.V.I. 00840. www.frederikstedhotel.dk. ✆ **800/595-9519** in the U.S., or 340/772-0500. Fax 340/719-1272. 36 units. Winter $80–$150 double; off season $80–$140 double. AE, DISC, MC, V. **Amenities:** Restaurant; bar; Internet (free); outdoor pool. *In room:* A/C, TV, fridge.

Where to Dine

IN CHRISTIANSTED

Bacchus ★ STEAKHOUSE/CONTINENTAL In a restaurant dedicated to the god of wine, it's no surprise that the wine menu receives as much attention as the food. Both *Wine Spectator* and *Food & Wine* have praised the cellar here. The decor, the fine service, and the presentation of the dishes make for a fine evening out. The kitchen uses first-class ingredients, many imported, to craft a number of dishes that combine flavor and finesse. To finish, it doesn't get any better than the rum-infused sourdough bread pudding. Most dishes, except lobster, are at the lower end of the price scale.

52 King St. ✆ **340/692-9922.** www.restaurantbacchus.com. Reservations requested. Main courses $24–$70. AE, DC, DISC, MC, V. Tues–Sat 6–10pm.

Elizabeth's at H2O ★★ ☺ AMERICAN At the Hibiscus Beach Resort (p. 731), this restaurant serves a contemporary cuisine and features karaoke and DJs on most nights. A la carte meals are available for three meals a day, with buffet menus varying in price based on the seasons. It's one of the best places in town for breakfast, featuring such delights as buttermilk pancakes, or coconut French toast served with a rum-cream sauce. The talented chef, Jason Gould, is known for such specialties as his five-star rack of lamb, or the island's best crab cakes. He also entices with his saffron coconut mussels and his pistachio-crusted Chilean sea bass; his flourless chocolate torte has even won awards. The restaurant caters more to kids than any other place on island, staging special activities for them, even children's parties.

4131 La Grande Princesse. ✆ **340/718-0735**. www.elizabethsath2o.com. Reservations recommended. Main courses $6–$15 breakfast, $9–$16 lunch, $13–$31 dinner; lunch buffet (Mon–Fri) $9; Sun brunch $16. AE, MC, V. Daily 7:30–11am, 11am–2pm, and 6–9pm.

Harvey's CARIBBEAN Forget the plastic and the flowery tablecloths that give this place a 1950s feel, and enjoy the thoroughly zesty cooking of island matriarch Sarah Harvey, who takes joy in her work and aims to fill your stomach with her basic but hearty fare. Try one of her homemade soups, especially the callaloo or chicken. She'll even serve you conch in butter sauce as an appetizer. For a main dish, you might choose from barbecue chicken, barbecue spareribs, boiled filet of snapper, and sometimes even lobster. For dessert try one of the delectable tarts made from guava, pineapple, or coconut.

11B Company St. ✆ **340/773-3433.** Main courses $6–$22. No credit cards. Mon–Sat 11:30am–3:30pm.

Kendricks ★★ FRENCH/CONTINENTAL Kendricks, the island's toniest restaurant, lies in the historic Quin House complex at King Cross and Company streets. Some of its recipes have been featured in *Bon Appétit,* and deservedly so. You'll immediately warm to specialties like roasted-pecan-crusted pork loin with ginger mayonnaise, or grilled filet mignon with a port-wine demi-glace and red-onion confit. The signature appetizer is king-crab cakes with lemon-pepper aioli.

King Cross St. ✆ **340/773-9199.** www.kendricksdining.com. Reservations recommended. Main courses $26–$39. AE, MC, V. Mon–Sat 6–9:30pm. Closed Mon Sept–Oct.

Luncheria Mexican Food MEXICAN/CUBAN/PUERTO RICAN This restaurant is a bargain. You get the usual tacos, tostadas, burritos, nachos, and enchiladas, as well as chicken fajitas, enchiladas verde, and *arroz con pollo* (spiced chicken with brown rice). Daily specials feature both low-calorie and vegetarian choices (the chef's refried beans are lard-free), and whole-wheat tortillas are offered. The complimentary salsa bar has mild to hot sauces, plus jalapeños. Some Cuban and Puerto Rican dishes appear on the menu, including a zesty chicken curry, black-bean soup, and roast pork. The bartender makes the island's best margaritas.

In the historic Apothecary Hall Courtyard, 2111 Company St. ✆ **340/773-4247.** Main courses $5–$13. MC, V. Mon–Sat 11am–9pm.

Paradise Café DELI/AMERICAN This neighborhood favorite draws locals seeking good food and great value. Its brick walls and beamed ceiling were originally part of an 18th-century great house. New York–style deli fare is served during the day. The homemade soups are savory, and you can add grilled chicken or fish to the freshly made salads. At breakfast you can select from an assortment of omelets, or try the steak and eggs. Dinners are more elaborate. The 12-ounce New York strip steak and the freshly made pasta specialties are good choices. Appetizers include mango chicken quesadillas and crab cakes.

53B Company St. (at Queen Cross St., across from Government House). © **340/773-2985.** Main courses $6–$11 breakfast, $7–$12 lunch, $15–$27 dinner. MC, V. Mon–Sat 7:30am–9pm.

Rum Runners ☺ CARIBBEAN This open-air restaurant sits right on the boardwalk and offers some fabulous views to accompany the excellent dining. The ambience reeks of the Caribbean, and the sound of waves in the background can put even the tensest of people at ease. Excellent choices here include the New York strip steak, the fresh broiled whole lobster, the Caribbean pork tenderloin served with a grilled banana, and one of the house specials: baby back ribs slow-cooked in island spices and Guinness. The younger vacationers can pick from the children's menu.

At the Hotel Caravelle, 44A Queens Cross St. (on the boardwalk). © **340/773-6585.** www.rumrunnersstcroix.com. Reservations recommended. Main courses $15–$34. AE, MC, V. Daily 7–10:30am, 11:30am–3pm, and 5:30–9:30pm; Sun 8am–2pm and 5:30–9:30pm.

Savant ★ CARIBBEAN/THAI/MEXICAN The spicy fusion cuisine here provides a marvelous burst of palate-awakening flavors. The bistro atmosphere is stylish, yet fun and laid-back. Black-and-white photos and other original artwork line the walls of the restaurant. Fresh fish is deftly handled. We gravitate to the tantalizing Thai curries, most of which are mildly spiced. You can ask the chef to "go nuclear" if you prefer hotter food. The red-coconut-curry sauce is one of the best we've ever had on the island. If you're craving an enchilada, try the one stuffed with seafood. The maple-teriyaki pork tenderloin, one of the chef's specialties, is terrific, as are the steak choices. There are only 20 candlelit tables, so call for a reservation as far in advance as you can.

4C Hospital St. © **340/713-8666.** Reservations required. Main courses $14–$39. AE, MC, V. Mon–Sat 6–10pm.

IN FREDERIKSTED

Blue Moon INTERNATIONAL/CAJUN The best little bistro in Frederiksted becomes a hot, hip spot during Sunday brunch and on Friday nights, when it offers entertainment. The 200-year-old stone house on the waterfront is a favorite of visiting jazz musicians, and visitors have discovered (but not ruined) it. It's decorated with funky, homemade art from the U.S., including a trash-can-lid restaurant sign. The atmosphere is casual and cafelike. Begin with the "lunar pie," with feta, cream cheese, onions, mushrooms, and celery in phyllo pastry; or the artichoke-and-spinach dip. Main courses include the catch of the day and, on occasion, Maine lobster. The clams served in garlic sauce are also from Maine. There's also the usual array of steak and chicken dishes. Save room for the brownie ice cream.

7 Strand St. © **340/772-2222.** www.bluemoonstcroix.com. Reservations required. Main courses $23–$29. AE, MC, V. Tues–Fri 11:30am–2pm and 6–9pm; Sat 6–9pm; Sun 11am–2pm.

Uca's Kitchen VEGETARIAN/RASTAFARIAN Don't come here looking for a glamourous setting, as you won't find one. The joint may not look like much, but it's the best vegetarian option on island, and one of the most economical places to dine. Just straight off the cruise dock, Uca's is a local hangout. Try such dishes as the cook's barbecued tofu kebab, or his callaloo with a fungi polenta. The house specialty is a tasty mushroom lasagna. Everything is washed down with fresh tropical fruit juices.

King St., Frederiksted. ✆ **340/772-5063.** Reservations not required. Main courses $10–$15. No credit cards. Daily 12:30pm–midnight.

Villa Morales PUERTO RICAN This inland spot is one of the best Puerto Rican restaurants on St. Croix. You can choose between indoor and outdoor seating areas. No one will mind if you come here just to drink; the cozy bar is lined with memorabilia collected by several generations of the family who maintains the place. Look for a broad cross-section of Hispanic dishes, including many that Puerto Ricans remember from their childhood. These include fried snapper with white rice and beans, stewed conch, roasted or stewed goat, and stewed beef. Meal platters are garnished with beans and rice. Most of the dishes are inexpensive. On special occasions, the owners transform the place into a dance hall, bringing in live salsa and merengue bands.

82C Estate Whim (off Rte. 70, about 1¾ miles from Frederiksted). ✆ **340/772-0556.** Reservations recommended. Main courses $9–$35. MC, V. Thurs–Sat 10am–9pm.

AROUND THE ISLAND

Duggan's Reef CONTINENTAL/CARIBBEAN This is one of the most popular restaurants on St. Croix. It's only a few feet from the still waters of Reef Beach and makes an ideal perch for watching windsurfers and Hobie Cats. At lunch an array of salads, crepes, and sandwiches is offered. The more elaborate night menu features the popular house specialties: Duggan's Caribbean lobster pasta and Irish whiskey lobster. Begin with fried calamari or conch chowder. Main dishes include New York strip steak, fish, and pastas. The local catch of the day can be baked, grilled, blackened Cajun style, or served island style (with tomato, pepper, and onion sauce).

East End Rd., Teague Bay. ✆ **340/773-9800.** www.visitstcroix.com/duggans_reef.html. Reservations required for dinner in winter. Main courses $18–$39; pastas $17–$27. MC, V. Daily 6–9:30pm; Sun brunch 11am–2pm. Bar daily noon–11:30pm.

The Galleon FRENCH/NORTHERN ITALIAN This restaurant, which overlooks the ocean, is a local favorite, and deservedly so. It serves northern Italian and French cuisine, including *osso buco,* just as good as that dished up in Milan. Freshly baked bread, two fresh vegetables, and rice or potatoes accompany main dishes. The menu always includes at least one local fish, such as wahoo, tuna, swordfish, mahimahi, or even fresh Caribbean lobster. You can order a perfectly done rack of lamb, which will be carved right at your table. There's an extensive wine list, including many sold by the glass. Music from a baby grand accompanies your dinner several nights a week, and you can enjoy guitar music on Thursday and Saturday.

East End Rd., Green Cay Marina. ✆ **340/718-9948.** www.galleonrestaurant.com. Reservations recommended. Main courses $22–$40. MC, V. Daily 11am–4pm and 6–10pm; happy hour 4–6pm. Go east on Rte. 82 from Christiansted for 5 min.; after going 1 mile past the Buccaneer, turn left into Green Cay Marina.

The Palms Restaurant ★ CARIBBEAN/INTERNATIONAL Guests appreciate its relaxed atmosphere, well-prepared food, and gracefully arched premises overlooking the sea. The menu changes nightly. The day begins with an American breakfast featuring selections from the griddle and a variety of egg dishes. At lunch, served beachside, you can enjoy freshly made soups, along with sandwiches and salads, as well as fish and chips, burgers, and pastas. Caribbean and American dishes dominate the menu at night, including a specialty, charbroiled rib-eye steak, and daily specials such as locally caught catch of the day, as well as a changing array of beef, pork, chicken, and pasta dishes. At the Mahogany Bar, you can order from a bar menu featuring pizza, burgers, buffalo wings, and fries.

In the Palms at Pelican Cove, 4126 La Grande Princesse. © **340/718-8920.** Reservations recommended. Main courses $6 breakfast, $4–$15 lunch, $9–$24 dinner. AE, DC, MC, V. Daily 7:30–10:30am, 11:30am–2:30pm, and 6:30–9pm.

Sunset Grill ★ CARIBBEAN/AMERICAN This informal spot is on the west coast, near Sprat Hall Plantation. It's the best place on the island to combine lunch and a swim. The restaurant has been in business since 1948, feeding both locals and visitors. Try such local dishes as seafood chowder and the fried fish of the day. These dishes have authentic island flavor, perhaps more so than any other place on St. Croix. You can also get salads and burgers. The bread is baked fresh daily. The owners allow free use of the showers and changing rooms.

Rte. 63 (1 mile north of Frederiksted). © **340/772-5855.** Main courses $17–$32; sandwiches $6–$13. MC, V. Daily 11am–9pm (Sun brunch 10:30am).

Hitting the Beach

The most celebrated beach is offshore **Buck Island** (p. 741), part of the U.S. National Park Service network. Buck Island is actually a volcanic islet surrounded by some of the most stunning underwater coral gardens in the Caribbean. The white-sand beaches on the southwest and west coasts are beautiful, but the snorkeling is even better. Buck Island is home to three kinds of sea turtles and more than 250 species of fish. The islet's interior is filled with such plants as cactus, wild frangipani, and pigeonwood. There are picnic areas for those who want to make a day of it. Boat departures are from Kings Wharf in Christiansted; the ride takes half an hour. John F. Kennedy visited the island as a young man in the 1950s, calling it "one of the finest marine gardens in the Caribbean Sea." When he became president, he proclaimed it a national monument.

Your best choice for a beach in Christiansted is the one at the **Hotel on the Cay.** This white-sand strip is on a palm-shaded island. Lying in only 4 feet of water, the artificial reef here consists of old car parts and conch shells, and has an array of small tropical reef fish, including sergeant majors and French grunts. If you're a more advanced snorkeler, you can head out a bit to where the reef drops off about 15 feet. Here you can encounter squid, octopus, and eagle rays. To get here, take the ferry from the fort at Christiansted; it runs daily from 7am to midnight. The 4-minute trip costs $3 round-trip, free for guests of the Hotel on the Cay. Five miles west of Christiansted is the **Palms at Pelican Cove** (p. 732), where some 1,200 feet of white sand shaded by palm trees attracts a gay and mixed crowd. Since a reef lies just off the shore, snorkeling conditions are ideal.

We highly recommend **Davis Bay** and **Cane Bay,** with swaying palms, white sand, and good swimming. Because they're on the north shore, these beaches are often windy, and their waters are not always tranquil. The snorkeling at Cane Bay is truly spectacular; you'll see elkhorn and brain corals, all some 750 feet off the Cane Bay Wall. Cane Bay adjoins Route 80 on the north shore. Davis Bay doesn't have a reef; it's more popular among bodysurfers than snorkelers. There are no changing facilities.

On Route 63, a short ride north of Frederiksted, lies **Rainbow Beach,** which has white sand and ideal snorkeling conditions. Nearby, also on Route 63, about 5 minutes north of Frederiksted, is another good beach, called **La Grange.** Lounge chairs can be rented here, and there's a bar nearby.

Sandy Point, directly south of Frederiksted, is the largest beach in all the U.S. Virgin Islands. Its waters are shallow and calm, perfect for swimming. Try to concentrate on the sands and not the unattractive zigzagging fences that line the beach. Continue west from the western terminus of the Melvin Evans Highway (Rte. 66).

There's an array of beaches at the east end of the island; they're somewhat difficult to get to, but much less crowded. At **Isaac Bay Beach,** you come upon a tropical paradise, with shallow, calm waters protected by an offshore reef. Snorkelers encounter schools of blue tang, trunkfish, trumpetfish, and other species swimming through forests of sea fans, elkhorn coral, staghorn coral, and other types. If you packed a picnic lunch, this is the spot at which to enjoy it. Windsurfers like **Reef Beach,** which opens onto Teague Bay along Route 82 (East End Rd.), a half-hour ride from Christiansted. You can get food at Duggan's Reef (see above). **Cramer Park** is a special public park operated by the Department of Agriculture. It's lined with seagrape trees and has a picnic area, a restaurant, and a bar. **Grapetree Beach** is off Route 60 (South Shore Rd.). Watersports are popular here.

Sports & Outdoor Pursuits

Some of the best snorkeling, diving, and hiking is found on Buck Island (see "Buck Island," below).

FISHING The fishing grounds at **Lang Bank** are about 10 miles from St. Croix. Here you'll find kingfish, dolphin fish, and wahoo. Using light-tackle boats to glide along the reef, you'll probably turn up jack or bonefish. At **Clover Crest,** in Frederiksted, local anglers fish right from the rocks.

HIKING Scrub-covered hills make up much of St. Croix's landscape. The island's western district, however, includes a dense, 15-acre forest known as the **"Rain Forest"** (though technically it's not a rainforest). The network of footpaths here provides some of the best nature walks in the Caribbean. For more details on hiking in this area, see "The 'Rain Forest,'" below. **Buck Island** (see "Buck Island," below), just off St. Croix, also offers some wonderful nature trails.

The **St. Croix Environmental Association,** Arawak Building, 5032 Anchor Way, Ste. 3, Christiansted (✆ **340/773-1989;** www.stxenvironmental.org), has scheduled hikes costing $10 per person.

HORSEBACK RIDING **Paul and Jill's Equestrian Stables,** 2 Sprat Hall Estate, Route 58 (✆ **340/772-2880;** www.paulandjills.com), the largest equestrian stable in the Virgin Islands, is known throughout the Caribbean for its horses. A 1½-hour trail ride costs $90. Tours usually depart daily in winter at 10:30am and 3pm, and in the off season at 4pm, with slight variations according to demand. Reserve at least a day in advance.

KAYAKING The beauty of St. Croix is best seen on a kayak tour such as those offered by **Caribbean Adventure Tours** (✆ **340/778-1522;** www.stcroixkayak.com). You use stable, sit-on-top ocean kayaks, which are a blast. These enable you to traverse the tranquil waters of Salt River (of Columbus landfall fame) and enjoy the park's ecology and wildlife. The tour, lasting 3 hours, costs $45 per person and includes water and a light snack.

SAFARI TOURS The best are run by **St. Croix Safari Tours** (✆ **800/524-2026** or 340/773-6700) in a 25-passenger open-air bus tour led by a hip tour guide who knows all about the botany, cuisine, and history of the island. Tours crisscross the island with stops at plantation houses, historic Frederiksted, the Salt River landfall of Columbus, and a drive through the "Rain Forest," with a stop for lunch. There are lots of photo ops. The cost of the tour is $55 per person, including admission fees to the botanical garden, rum factory, and museum.

SNORKELING & SCUBA DIVING ★★ Sponge life, black coral (the finest in the West Indies), and steep drop-offs near the shoreline make St. Croix a snorkeling and diving paradise. The island is home to the largest living reef in the Caribbean, including the fabled north-shore wall that begins in 30 feet of water and drops to 13,120 feet, sometimes straight down. See "Hitting the Beach," above, for information on good snorkeling beaches. The **St. Croix Water Sports Center** (see "Windsurfing," below) rents snorkeling equipment for $20 per day if your hotel doesn't supply it.

Buck Island ★★ is a major scuba-diving site, with a visibility of some 100 feet. It also has an underwater snorkeling trail. All the outfitters offer scuba and snorkeling tours to Buck Island. See "Buck Island," below.

Other favorite dive sites include the historic **Salt River Canyon** (northwest of Christiansted at Salt River Bay), which is for advanced divers. Submerged canyon walls are covered with purple tube sponges, deep-water gorgonians, and black coral saplings. You'll see schools of yellowtail snapper, turtles, and spotted eagle rays. We also like the gorgeous coral gardens of **Scotch Banks** (north of Christiansted), and **Eagle Ray** (also north of Christiansted), the latter so named because of the rays that cruise along the wall there. **Cane Bay ★★** is known for its coral canyons.

Davis Bay is the site of the 11,800-foot Puerto Rico Trench. **Northstar Reef,** at the east end of Davis Bay, is a spectacular wall dive, recommended for intermediate or experienced divers only. The wall here is covered with stunning brain corals and staghorn thickets. At some 50 feet down, a sandy shelf leads to a cave where giant green moray eels hang out.

At **Butler Bay,** to the north of the pier on the west shore, three ships were wrecked: the *Suffolk Maid,* the *Northwind,* and the *Rosaomaira,* the last sitting in 100 feet of water. These wrecks form the major part of an artificial reef system that also contains abandoned trucks and cars. This site is recommended for intermediate or experienced divers.

Anchor Dive, Salt River National Park (✆ **800/523-3483** in the U.S., or 340/778-1522; www.anchordivestcroix.com), is located within the most popular dive destination in St. Croix. It operates two boats. The staff offers complete instruction, from resort courses through full certification, as well as night dives. A resort course is $90, with a two-tank dive going for $90. Dive packages begin at $250 for six dives.

Another recommended outfitter is the **Cane Bay Dive Shop** (✆ **340/773-9913**).

WINDSURFING Head for the **St. Croix Water Sports Center** (✆ **800/942-6725** or 340/773-7060), on a small offshore island in Christiansted Harbor and part of the Hotel on the Cay. It's open daily from 10am to 5pm. Here you can rent snorkeling equipment for $20 per day and Yamahas (only with a reservation) that seat two for $60 per half-hour.

Exploring the Island

Taxi tours are the ideal way to explore the island. The cost is around $80 for 2 hours or $100 for 3 hours for up to 4 passengers. All prices should be negotiated in advance.

For more information, call the **St. Croix Taxi Association** (✆ **340/778-1088;** www.stcroixtaxi.com).

CHRISTIANSTED ★★

One of the most picturesque towns in the Caribbean, **Christiansted** is an old, handsomely restored (or, at least, in the process of being restored) Danish port. On the northeastern shore of the island, on a coral-bound bay, the town is filled with Danish buildings erected by prosperous merchants in the booming 18th century. These red-roofed structures are often washed in pink, ocher, or yellow. Arcades over the sidewalks provide shade for shoppers. The whole area around the harborfront has been designated a historic site, including **Government House** (✆ **340/773-1404**), which is looked after by the U.S. National Park Service.

Fort Christiansvaern This fortress overlooking the harbor is the best-preserved colonial fortification in the Virgin Islands. It's maintained as a historic monument by the U.S. National Park Service. Its original four-pronged, star-shaped design was in accordance with the most advanced military planning of its era. The fort is now the site of a military museum, which has exhibits on local Danish military history on the island from the late 1800s to 1917.

THE ST. CROIX HERITAGE TRAIL

A trail that leads into the past, **St. Croix Heritage Trail** (✆ **340/772-0598**), launched at the millennium, helps visitors relive the Danish colonial history of the island. All you need are a brochure and map, available at the **tourist office** at 53A Company St. in Christiansted (✆ **340/773-0495**). This 72-mile itinerary consists mainly of existing roadways and includes a combination of asphalt-covered roads suitable for driving and narrow woodland trails that must be navigated on foot. The brochure will identify everything you're seeing. Many aficionados opt to drive along the route whenever practical, descending onto the footpaths wherever indicated, then returning to their cars for the continuation of the tour. En route you'll be exposed to one of the Caribbean's densest concentrations of historical and cultural sites.

The route connects the two major towns of Christiansted and Frederiksted, going past the sites of former sugar plantations. It traverses the entire 28-mile length of St. Croix, passing cattle farms, suburban communities, even industrial complexes and resorts. It's not all manicured and pretty, but much is scenic and worth the drive. Allow at least a day for this trail, with stops along the way.

Nearly everyone gets out of the car at **Point Udall,** the easternmost point under the U.S. flag in the Caribbean. You'll pass an eclectic mix of churches and even a prison.

The highlight of the trail is the **Estate Mount Washington Plantation** (see "Around the Island," below), a strikingly well-preserved sugar plantation. Another highlight is **Estate Whim Plantation** (see below), one of the best of the restored great houses, with a museum and gift shop. Another stop is along **Salt River Bay,** which cuts into the northern shoreline. This is the site of Columbus's landfall in 1493.

Of course, you'll want to stop and get to know the locals. We recommend a refreshment break at **Smithens Market.** Off Queen Mary Highway, vendors here offer freshly squeezed sugar-cane juice and sell locally grown fruits and homemade chutneys.

On the waterfront. ✆ **340/773-1460.** Admission $3 (also includes admission to the Steeple Building). Mon–Fri 8am–5pm; Sat–Sun 9am–5pm.

Steeple Building This building's full name is the Church of Lord God of Sabaoth. It was built in 1753 as St. Croix's first Lutheran church, and it was deconsecrated in 1831; the building subsequently served as a bakery, a hospital, and a school. Today it houses exhibits relating to island history and culture.

On the waterfront, off Hospital St. ✆ **340/773-1460.** Admission $3 (also includes admission to Fort Christiansvaern). Mon–Fri 8am–5pm; Sat–Sun 9am–5pm.

FREDERIKSTED ★

This former Danish settlement at the western end of the island, about 17 miles from Christiansted, is a sleepy port town that comes to life only when a cruise ship docks at its shoreline. Frederiksted was destroyed by a fire in 1879. Its citizens subsequently rebuilt it with wood frames and clapboards on top of the old Danish stone and yellow-brick foundations.

Most visitors begin their tour at russet-colored **Fort Frederik,** at the northern end of Frederiksted next to the cruise-ship pier (✆ **340/772-2021**). This fort, completed in 1760, is said to have been the first to salute the flag of the new United States. When a U.S. brigantine anchored at port in Frederiksted hoisted a homemade Old Glory, the fort returned the salute with cannon fire, violating the rules of neutrality. It was also here on July 3, 1848, that Gov.-Gen. Peter von Scholten emancipated the slaves in the Danish West Indies in response to a slave uprising led by a young man named Moses "Buddhoe" Gottlieb. A bust of Buddhoe now stands here. The fort has been restored to its 1840 appearance and is today a national historic landmark. You can explore the courtyard and stables. A **local history museum** has been installed in what was once the Garrison Room. Admission is $5, or free for children 15 and under. It's open Monday to Friday from 9am to 3:30pm.

The **Customs House,** just east of the fort, is an 18th-century building with a 19th-century two-story gallery. On the ground floor is the **visitor bureau** (✆ **340/772-0357**), where you can pick up a free map of the town.

BUCK ISLAND ★★★

The crystal-clear water and white-coral sand of **Buck Island,** a satellite of St. Croix, are legendary. Some call this island the single most important attraction of the Caribbean. Only ¼ mile wide and 1 mile long, Buck Island lies 1½ miles off the northeastern coast of St. Croix. A barrier reef here shelters many reef fish, including queen angelfish and smooth trunkfish. In years past, Morgan, Blackbeard, and Captain Kidd frequented the island.

Buck Island's greatest attraction is its **underwater snorkeling trails,** which ring part of the island and provide some of the most beautiful underwater views in the Caribbean. Plan on spending at least two-thirds of a day at this famous ecological site, maintained by the U.S. National Park Service. There are also many **labyrinths and grottoes for scuba divers.** The sandy **beach** has picnic tables and barbecue pits, as well as restrooms and a small changing room.

You can follow **hiking trails** through the tropical vegetation that covers the island. Circumnavigating the island on foot takes about 2 hours. Buck Island's trails meander from several points along its coastline to its sunny summit, affording views over nearby St. Croix. ***A couple of warnings:*** Wear lots of sunscreen. Even more important, don't touch every plant you see. The island's western edge has groves of poisonous manchineel trees, whose leaves, bark, and fruit cause extreme irritation to human skin.

Small boats run between St. Croix and Buck Island. Nearly all charters provide snorkeling equipment and allow for 1½ hours of snorkeling and swimming. **Caribbean Sea Adventures,** in the King Christian Hotel, 59 King's Wharf, Christiansted (✆ **340/773-2628;** www.caribbeanseaadventures.com), conducts two different types of tours. The first option is a half-day tour aboard a glass-bottom boat departing from the King Christian Hotel, daily from 9:30am to 1pm and 1:30 to 5pm; it costs $65 per person. The second is a full-day tour, offered daily from 10:30am to 4pm on a 40-foot trimaran for $95. Included in this excursion is a box lunch.

Captain Heinz (✆ **340/773-3161** or 773-4041) is an Austrian-born skipper with more than 25 years of sailing experience. His trimaran, *Teroro II,* leaves the Green Cay Marina "H" Dock daily at 9am and 2pm, never filled with more than 23 passengers. This snorkeling trip costs $65 for adults, $45 for children 11 and under. The captain is not only a skilled sailor, but also a considerate host. He will even take you around the outer reef for an unforgettable underwater experience.

THE "RAIN FOREST" ★

The island's western district contains a dense, 15-acre forest called the "Rain Forest" (though it's not a real one). The area is thick with mahogany trees, *kapok* (silk-cotton) trees, turpentine (red-birch) trees, *samaan* (rain) trees, and all kinds of ferns and vines. Sweet limes, mangoes, hog plums, and breadfruit trees, all of which have grown in the wild since the days of the plantations, are also interspersed among the larger trees. Crested hummingbirds, pearly eyed thrashers, green-throated caribs, yellow warblers, and perky but drably camouflaged banaquits nest here. The 148-foot Creque Dam is the major man-made sight in the area.

The "Rain Forest" is private property, but the owner lets visitors go inside to explore. To experience its charm, some people opt to drive along Route 76 (Mahogany Rd.), stopping beside the footpaths that meander off on either side of the highway into dry riverbeds and glens. Stick to the most worn footpaths. You can also hike along some of the little-traveled four-wheel-drive roads in the area. Three of the best for hiking are the **Creque Dam Road** (rtes. 58/78), the **Scenic Road** (Rte. 78), and the **Western Scenic Road** (rtes. 63/78).

Our favorite trail in this area takes about 2½ hours one-way. From Frederiksted, drive north on Route 63 until you reach Creque Dam Road, where you turn right, park the car, and start walking. About 1 mile past the Creque Dam, you'll be deep within the forest's magnificent flora and fauna. Continue along the trail until you come to the Western Scenic Road. Eventually, you reach Mahogany Road (Rte. 76), near St. Croix Leap Project. Hikers rate this trail moderate in difficulty.

You could also begin near the junction of Creque Dam Road and Scenic Road. From here, your trek will cover a broad triangular swath, heading north and then west along Scenic Road. First the road will rise, and then descend toward the coastal lighthouse of the island's extreme northwestern tip, **Hams Bluff.** Most trekkers decide to retrace their steps after about 45 minutes of northwesterly hiking. Real die-hards, however, will continue all the way to the coastline, then head south along the coastal road (Butler Bay Rd.), and finally head east along Creque Dam Road to their starting point at the junction of Creque Dam Road and Scenic Road. Embark on this longer expedition only if you're really prepared for a hike lasting about 5 hours.

SANDY POINT WILDLIFE REFUGE ★

St. Croix's rarely visited southwestern tip is composed of salt marshes, tidal pools, and low vegetation inhabited by birds, turtles, and other wildlife. More than 3 miles of ecologically protected coastline lie between Sandy Point (the island's westernmost tip) and the shallow waters of the Westend Saltpond. The area is home to colonies of green, leatherback, and hawksbill turtles. It's one of only two such places in U.S. waters. It's also home to thousands of birds, including herons, brown pelicans, Caribbean martins, black-necked stilts, and white-crowned pigeons. As for flora, Sandy Point gave its name to a rare form of orchids, a brown/purple variety.

This wildlife refuge is open only on Saturday and Sunday from 10am to 4pm. To get here, drive to the end of Route 66 (Melvin Evans Hwy.) and continue down a gravel road. For guided weekend visits, call ✆ **340/773-4554.**

AROUND THE ISLAND

North of Frederiksted, you can drop in at **Sprat Hall,** the island's oldest plantation, or continue along to the "Rain Forest" (see above). Most visitors come to the area to see the jagged estuary of the northern coastline's **Salt River.** The Salt River was where Columbus landed on November 14, 1493. Marking the 500th anniversary of Columbus's arrival, the U.S. Congress created the 902-acre **Salt River Bay National Historical Park and Ecological Preserve.** The park contains the site of the original Carib village explored by Columbus and his men, including the only ceremonial ball court ever discovered in the Lesser Antilles. Also within the park is the largest mangrove forest in the Virgin Islands, sheltering many endangered animals and plants, plus an underwater canyon attracting divers from around the world.

Estate Mount Washington Plantation is the island's best-preserved sugar plantation and a highlight along the St. Croix Heritage Trail. It flourished from 1780 to 1820, when St. Croix was the second-largest producer of sugar in the West Indies. The on-site private residence is closed to the public, but you can arrange to go on a self-guided tour of the 12 acres. There is no admission charge, although donations are appreciated. Know that this is one of St. Croix's more loosely organized cultural attractions, but if you phone in advance (✆ **340/772-1026**), someone might give you permission. The plantation site lies at the very southwestern tip of the island, off Route 63, 1 mile inland from the highway that runs along the Frederiksted coast.

Cruzan Rum Factory This factory distills the famous Virgin Islands rum, which some consider the finest in the world. Guided tours depart from the visitors' pavilion; call for reservations and information. There's also a gift shop.

Estate Diamond, W. Airport Rd. (Rte. 64), Frederiksted. ✆ **340/692-2280.** www.cruzanrum.com. Admission $5 adults, $1 children 11 and under. Tours Mon–Fri 9–11:30am and 1–4pm.

Estate Whim Plantation Museum This restored great house is unique among the many sugar plantations whose ruins dot the island. It's composed of only three rooms. With 4-foot-thick walls made of stone, coral, and molasses, the house resembles a luxurious European château. A division of Baker Furniture Company used the Whim Plantation's collection of models for one of its most successful reproductions, the Whim Museum–West Indies Collection. Upscale reproductions of some of the furniture on display within the Whim Plantation, plus others from the Caribbean, are for sale on-site. Slightly different inventories are available from an associated store in downtown Christiansted: **St. Croix Landmarks Museum Store,** 6 Company St. (✆ **340/713-8102**). For more information, refer to "Shopping," below.

The ruins of the plantation's sugar-processing plant, complete with a restored windmill, also remain.

Centerline Rd. (1¾ miles east of Frederiksted). ✆ **340/772-0598.** Admission $10 adults, $5 children. Wed–Sat 10am–4pm.

St. George Village Botanical Garden This is a 16-acre Eden of tropical trees, shrubs, vines, and flowers. The garden is a feast for the eye and the camera, from the entrance drive bordered by royal palms and bougainvillea to the towering kapok and tamarind trees. It was built around the ruins of a 19th-century sugar-cane-workers' village. Self-guided walking-tour maps are available at the entrance to the garden's great hall. Facilities include restrooms and a gift shop.

127 Estate St. (just north of Centerline Rd., 3¾ miles east of Frederiksted). ✆ **340/692-2874.** www.sgvbg.org. Admission $8 adults, $1 children 12 and under; donations welcome. Daily 9am–5pm.

Shopping ★★★

In **Christiansted,** the emphasis is on hole-in-the-wall boutiques selling one-of-a-kind merchandise. The selection of handmade items is especially strong. Knowing that it can't compete with the volume of Charlotte Amalie on St. Thomas, Christiansted has forged its own identity as the chic spot for merchandise in the Caribbean. All its shops are within about a half-mile of each other. **King's Alley Complex** is a pink-sided compound filled with the densest concentration of shops on St. Croix.

Frederiksted has also become a popular shopping destination. Its urban mall appeals to cruise-ship passengers arriving at Frederiksted Pier. The mall is on a 50-foot strip of land between Strand and King streets, the town's bustling main thoroughfare.

Below are our favorite shops in Christiansted.

At the hip and eclectic **From the Gecko,** 1233 Queen Cross St. (✆ **340/778-9433;** www.fromthegecko.com), you can find anything from hand-painted local cottons and silks to that old West Indian staple, batiks. We found the Indonesian collection here among the most imaginative in the U.S. Virgin Islands—everything from glass jewelry to hemp linens.

Many Hands, 102 Strand St. (✆ **340/773-1990**), sells locally made pottery, art, and handmade jewelry. The collection of local paintings is intriguing, as is the year-round "Christmas tree."

Purple Papaya, 39 Strand St., Pan Am Pavilion (✆ **340/713-9412**), is the best place to go for inexpensive island gifts. It has the biggest array of embroidered T-shirts and sweatshirts on island. Although you're in the Caribbean and not Hawaii, there is a large selection of Hawaiian shirts and dresses, along with beachwear for the whole family, plus island souvenirs.

Royal Poinciana, 1111 Strand St. (✆ **340/773-9892**), looks like an antique apothecary. You'll find hot sauces, seasoning blends for gumbos, island herbal teas, Antillean coffees, and a scented array of soaps, toiletries, lotions, and shampoos. There's also a selection of museum-reproduction greeting cards and calendars, plus educational but fun gifts for children.

About 60% of the merchandise at **Gone Tropical,** 5 Company St. (✆ **340/773-4696;** www.gonetropical.com), is made in Indonesia (usually Bali). Prices of new, semiantique, or antique sofas, beds, chests, tables, mirrors, and decorative carvings are the same as (and sometimes less than) those of new furniture in conventional stores. Gone Tropical also sells art objects, jewelry, batiks, candles, and baskets.

The small West Indian cottage of **Crucian Gold,** 1112 Strand St. (✆ **877/773-5241;** www.cruciangold.com), holds the gold and silver creations of island-born Brian Bishop. His most popular item is the Crucian bracelet, which contains a "True

Lovers' Knot" in its design. The shop also sells hand-tied knots (bound in gold wire), rings, pendants, and earrings.

Sonya Hough of **Sonya Ltd.,** 1 Company St. (✆ **877/766-9284** or 340/773-8924; www.sonyaltd.com), has a group of loyal local fans who wouldn't leave home without wearing one of her bracelets. She's most famous for the sterling silver and gold versions of her C-clasp bracelet. Locals say that if the cup of the C is turned toward your heart, you're taken; if the cup is turned outward, you're available. Prices range from $30 to $3,100.

Coconut Vine, Strand Street (✆ **340/773-1991**), is one of the most colorful and popular little boutiques on the island. Hand-painted batiks for both men and women are the specialty.

For a shopping adventure in Frederiksted, head for the **St. Croix Landmarks Museum Store ★**, 52 Estate Whim (✆ **340/772-0598;** www.stcroixlandmarks.com). The shop focuses on reproductions of some of the antiques on display at the Estate Whim Plantation (p. 743). Also available are framed engravings of the kind of botany you'd expect on St. Croix: paperweights, books, brass candlesticks, and gift items redolent with memories and references to the West Indies.

St. Croix After Dark

St. Croix doesn't have the nightlife of St. Thomas. To find the action, you might have to consult the publication ***St. Croix This Week,*** which is distributed free to cruise-ship and air passengers, and is also available at the tourist office.

Try, if it's taking place, to catch a performance of one of the **Quadrille Dances ★★**, performed by either of two independent, part-time dance troupes based on St. Croix. Hours, performance details, and organization of these dance groups vary widely from season to season, but the basic steps associated with La Quadrille have changed little since the plantation days. The women wear long dresses, white gloves, and turbans, while the men wear flamboyant shirts, sashes, and tight black trousers. At one of these performances, after you've learned the (relatively basic) steps, you might be invited to join the dancers on the floor. Ask at your hotel if and when one of these loosely organized dance troupes might be performing, if at all, during your visit.

If you enjoy gambling, visit the **Divi Carina Bay Casino,** 35 Estate Turner Hole (✆ **340/773-7529;** www.carinabay.com). Set on the grounds of the Divi Carina Bay Resort (p. 730), with which its management is not associated, it's sheltered from the glaring Caribbean sunlight with a glistening white dome inspired by the architecture of the North African desert. Inside, within a decor inspired by the Moroccan casbah, you'll find the only casino in the U.S. Virgin Islands, with 10,000 feet of gaming space, a cafe-style bistro and bar, at least 20 gaming tables, and 300 jangling slot machines. Entrance is free. It's open Monday to Thursday from noon to 4am, and Friday to Sunday 24 hours.

If you're looking to hear some live music, try **Blue Moon,** 7 Strand St. (✆ **340/772-2222;** www.bluemoonstcroix.com), a hip little dive and a good bistro. It's currently the hottest spot in Frederiksted on Fridays, when a five-piece ensemble entertains. On Sunday a live jazz trio performs. There's no cover.

The **Terrace Lounge,** in the Buccaneer (p. 728), Route 82, Estate Shoys (✆ **340/712-2100**), off the main dining room of one of St. Croix's most upscale hotels, welcomes some of the Caribbean's finest entertainers every night, often including a full band.

The Palms Restaurant, 4126 La Grande Princesse (© **340/718-8920**), is set in a resort about 3 miles northwest of Christiansted. You can sit at tables overlooking the ocean or around an open-centered mahogany bar, adjacent to a gazebo. Excellent tropical drinks are mixed here. It is open daily from 7pm until the last customer leaves.

PLANNING YOUR TRIP TO THE CARIBBEAN

27

As with any trip, a little preparation is essential before you start your journey to the Caribbean. This chapter provides a variety of planning tools, including information on how to get there; tips on accommodations; and quick, on the ground resources.

THE ISLANDS IN BRIEF

Anguilla

Although it's developing rapidly as vacationers discover its 19km (12 miles) of arid but spectacular beaches, Anguilla (rhymes with "vanilla") is still quiet, sleepy, and relatively free of racial tensions. A flat coral island, it maintains a maritime tradition of proud fishermen, many of whom still make a living from the sea, catching lobsters and selling them at high prices to expensive resorts and restaurants. Although the island has a handful of moderately priced accommodations, Anguilla is a very expensive destination, with small and rather exclusive resorts. It's as posh as St. Barts, but without all the snobbery. There are no casinos (and that's the way most of the locals want it). In fact, there's not much to do here except lie in the sun, bask in luxury, and enjoy fine dining.

Antigua

Antigua is famous for having a different beach for every day of the year, but it lacks the lushness of such islands as Dominica and Jamaica. Some British traditions (including a passion for cricket) linger, even though the nation became independent in 1981. The island's population of 80,000 is mostly descended from the African slaves of plantation owners. Antigua's resorts are isolated and conservative but very glamorous, its highways are horribly maintained, and its historic naval sites are interesting. Antigua is politically linked to the sparsely inhabited and largely undeveloped island of **Barbuda,** about 50km (31 miles) north. In spite of its small size, Barbuda has two posh, pricey resorts.

Aruba

Until its beaches were "discovered" in the late 1970s, Aruba, with its desertlike terrain and lunarlike interior landscapes, was an almost-forgotten outpost of Holland, valued mostly for its oil refineries and salt factories. Today vacationers come for the dependable sunshine (it rains less here than anywhere else in the Caribbean), the spectacular beaches, and an almost total lack of racial tensions despite a culturally diverse population. The high-rise hotels of Aruba are within walking distance of each other along a strip of fabulous beach. You don't stay in old, converted, family-run sugar mills here, and you don't come for history. You come if you're interested in gambling and splashy high-rise resorts.

Barbados

Originally founded on a plantation economy that made its aristocracy rich on the backs of slave laborers, this Atlantic outpost was a staunchly loyal member of the British Commonwealth for generations. Barbados is the Caribbean's easternmost island, a great coral reef floating in the mid-Atlantic and ringed with glorious beige-sand beaches. Cosmopolitan Barbados has the densest population of any island in the Caribbean, with few racial tensions despite its history of slavery. A loyal group of return visitors appreciates its stylish, medium-size hotels (many of which carry a hefty price tag). Usually, service is extremely good, a byproduct of the British mores that have flourished here for a century. Topography varies from rolling hills and savage waves on the eastern (Atlantic) coast to densely populated flatlands, rows of hotels and apartments, and sheltered beaches in the southwest. If you're looking for a Las Vegas–type atmosphere and fine beaches, go to Aruba. If you want history (there are lots of great houses and old churches to explore); a quiet, conservative atmosphere; and fine beaches, come here.

Bonaire

Its strongest historical and cultural links are to Holland. Although long considered a poor relation of nearby Curaçao, Bonaire has better scuba diving and better bird life than any of its larger and richer neighbors. The terrain is as dry and inhospitable as anything you'll find in the Caribbean, a sparse desert landscape offset by a wealth of marine life that thrives along miles of offshore reefs. The island isn't overly blessed with natural resources, but those coral reefs around most of the island attract divers and snorkelers from all over the world. The casino and party crowds should head for Aruba instead.

The British Virgin Islands (B.V.I.)

Still a British Crown Colony, this lushly forested chain consists of about 50 small, mountainous islands (depending on how many rocks, cays, and uninhabited islets you want to include). Superb for sailors, the B.V.I. are less populated and less developed, and have fewer social problems than the U.S. Virgin Islands. **Tortola** is the main island, followed by **Virgin Gorda,** where you'll find some of the poshest hotels in the West Indies. **Anegada,** a coral atoll geologically different from the other members of the B.V.I., mainly attracts the yachting set. Come here for the laid-back lifestyle, the lovely sandy beaches, the friendly people, and the small, intimate inns.

The Cayman Islands

This trio of islands is set near the southern coast of Cuba. It's a prosperous, tiny nation dependent on Britain for its economic survival and attracting millionaire expatriates from all over the world by means of some very lenient tax and banking laws. Relatively flat and unattractive, these islands are covered with scrubland and swamp, but they have more than their share of expensive private homes and condominiums. Until the millennium, **Grand Cayman** enjoyed one of the most closely knit societies in the Caribbean, although recent prosperity has created some socioeconomic divisions. The warm, crystal-clear waters and the colorful marine life in the offshore reefs surrounding the island attract scuba divers and snorkelers. Many hotels line the luscious sands of Seven Mile Beach.

Curaçao

Because much of the island's surface is an arid desert that grows only cactus, its canny Dutch settlers ruled out farming and made Curaçao (Coo-ra-*sow*) into one of the Dutch empire's busiest trading posts. Until the post–World War II collapse of the oil refineries, Curaçao was a thriving mercantile society with a capital (Willemstad) that somewhat resembled Amsterdam and a population with a curious mixture of bloodlines, including African, Dutch, Venezuelan, and Pakistani. The main language here is Papiamento, a mixture of African and European dialects, though Dutch, Spanish, and English are also spoken. Tourism began to develop during the 1980s, and many hotels have been built since then. The island has a few interesting historic sights, and Willemstad is one of the most charming towns in the Caribbean. If you're choosing among the Dutch ABC islands, go to Aruba for beaches and gambling, Bonaire for scuba diving, and Curaçao for little cove beaches, shopping, history, and its distinctive "Dutch in the Caribbean" culture.

Dominica

An English-speaking island set midway between Guadeloupe and Martinique, Dominica (Doh-mi-*nee*-kah), the largest and most mountainous island of the Windward Islands, is not to be confused with the Dominican Republic (see below). A mysterious, little-visited land of waterfalls, rushing streams, and rainforests, it has only a few beaches, most of which are lined with black volcanic sand. But if you like the offbeat and unusual, you may find this lush island the most fascinating in the Caribbean. Some 85,000 people live here, including 2,000 descendants of the Carib Indians. Roseau, one of the smallest capitals in the Caribbean, is more like an overgrown Creole village than a city. Dominica is one of the poorest islands in the Caribbean, and it has the misfortune of lying directly in the hurricane belt.

The Dominican Republic

Occupying the eastern two-thirds of Hispaniola, the island it shares with Haiti, the mountainous Dominican Republic is the second-largest country of the Caribbean. Long a victim of various military dictatorships, it now has a more favorable political climate and is one of the most affordable destinations in the Caribbean. Its crowded capital is Santo Domingo, with a population of two million. The island offers lots of Latin color, zesty merengue music, and many opportunities to dance, drink, and party. Unfortunately, the contrast between the wealth of foreign tourists and the poverty of locals is particularly conspicuous, and it's not the safest island. For fun in the sun and good beaches, head for La Romana in the southeast, Punta Cana on the easternmost shore, Puerto Plata in the northwest, or any resorts along the Amber Coast in the north.

Grenada

The southernmost nation of the Windward Islands, Grenada (Gre-*nay*-dah) is one of the lushest islands in the Caribbean. With its gentle climate and extravagantly fertile volcanic soil, it's one of the largest producers of spices in the Western Hemisphere. There's a lot of very appealing local color on Grenada, particularly since the political troubles of the 1980s seem, at least for the moment, to have ended. There are beautiful white-sand beaches, and the populace (a mixture of English expatriates and islanders of African descent) is friendly. Once a British Crown Colony but now independent, the island nation also incorporates two smaller islands: Carriacou and Petit Martinique, neither of which has many tourist facilities. Grenada's capital, St. George's, is one of the most charming towns in the Caribbean.

Guadeloupe

Although it isn't as sophisticated or cosmopolitan as the two outlying islands over which it holds administrative authority—St. Barthélemy and the French section of St. Martin—there's a lot of natural beauty in this *département* of mainland France. With a relatively low population density (only 440,000 people live here, mostly along the coast), butterfly-shaped Guadeloupe is actually two distinctly different volcanic islands separated by a narrow saltwater strait, the Rivière Salée. It's ideal for scenic drives and Creole color, offering an unusual insight into the French colonial world. The island has a lot of good beaches, each one different, and a vast national park (a huge tropical forest with everything from wild orchids to coffee and vanilla plants). It's life *à la française* in the tropics, but we'd give the nod to Martinique (see below) if you can visit only one French island.

Jamaica

A favorite of North American honeymooners, Jamaica is a mountainous island that rises abruptly from the sea 145km (90 miles) south of Cuba and about 160km (99 miles) west of Haiti. One of the most densely populated nations in the Caribbean, with a vivid sense of its own identity, Jamaica has a history rooted in the plantation economy and some of the most turbulent and impassioned politics in the Western Hemisphere. In spite of its economic and social problems, Jamaica is one of the most successful black democracies in the world. The island is large enough to allow the more or less peaceful coexistence of all kinds of people within its beach-lined borders—everyone from expatriate English aristocrats to dyed-in-the-wool Rastafarians. Its tourist industry has been plagued by the island's reputation for aggressive vendors and racial tension, but it is taking steps to improve the situation. Overall, and despite its long history of social unrest, increasing crime, and poverty, Jamaica is a fascinating island. It offers excellent beaches, golf, eco-tourism adventures, and fine hotels in all price brackets, making it one of the most popular destinations in the Caribbean, especially since you can find package deals galore.

Martinique

One of the most exotic French-speaking destinations in the Caribbean, Martinique was the site of a settlement demolished by volcanic activity (St. Pierre, now only a pale shadow of a once-thriving city). Like Guadeloupe and St. Barts, Martinique is legally and culturally French (certainly, many islanders drive with a Gallic panache—read: very badly), although many Creole customs and traditions continue to flourish. The beaches are beautiful, the Creole cuisine is full of flavor and flair, and the island has lots of tropical charm. Even more than Guadeloupe, this is the social and cultural center of the French Antilles. If you'd like to visit a charmingly beautiful island with elegant people, the Martiniquaise will wish you *bonjour.*

Puerto Rico

Home to more than four million people whose primary language is Spanish (though English is widely spoken, too), the Commonwealth of Puerto Rico is under the jurisdiction of the United States and has a more or less comfortable mix of Latin culture with imports from the U.S. mainland. It's the most urban island of the Caribbean, with lots of traffic and relatively high crime, though it compensates with great beaches, glittering casinos, hotels in all price brackets, sports and eco-tourism offerings, good hearty food, and sizzling salsa clubs. The island's interior is filled with rainforests and ancient volcanic mountains; the coastline is ringed with gorgeous sandy beaches. The commonwealth also includes a trio of small offshore islands: Culebra, Mona, and Vieques (the last has the most tourist facilities). San Juan, the island's capital, has some of the most extensive and best-preserved Spanish colonial neighborhoods in the New World, with historic sites and much to see and do, and a steady flow of cruise-ship passengers who keep the stores and casinos filled throughout much of the year. You can usually find great package deals through Puerto Rico's hotels and resorts.

Saba

Saba is a cone-shaped extinct volcano that rises abruptly and steeply from the watery depths of the Caribbean. With no beaches or historic sights to speak of, the local Dutch- and English-speaking populace has traditionally made a living from fishing, trade, and needlework, rather than tourism. Hotel choices are limited. Saba's thrifty, seafaring folk can offer insights into the old-fashioned lifestyle of the Netherlands Antilles. There's only one road on the island, and unless you opt to hike away from its edges, you'll have to follow the traffic along its narrow, winding route. Basically, you come here if you want to hang out at your hotel pool, climb up to a rainforest, go diving, and perhaps make a day trip to one of the nearby islands. Saba is a place to visit if you like to collect untouristy islands. You may want to come just for the afternoon—you can do this by plane or trimaran.

St. Barthélemy (St. Barts)

Part of the French *département* of Guadeloupe, lying 24km (15 miles) from St. Martin, St. Barts is a small, hilly island with a population of 7,000 people who live on 34 sq. km (13 sq. miles) of verdant terrain ringed by pleasant white-sand beaches. A small number of African descendants live harmoniously on this chic Caribbean island with descendants of Norman and Breton mariners and a colony of more recent expatriates from Europe. An expensive and exclusive stomping ground of the rich and famous, with a distinctive seafaring tradition and a decidedly French flavor, St. Barts has a lovely "storybook" capital in Gustavia. For sophistication and luxury living, St. Barts is equaled in the Caribbean only by Anguilla, and the price tag isn't cheap. It's a place to visit if you want to wind down from a stressful life.

St. Eustatius (also known as Statia)

Statia is part of the Netherlands Antilles and the Leeward Islands, lying to the south of Dutch St. Maarten. During the 1700s, this Dutch-controlled island ("the Golden

Rock") was one of the most important trading posts in the Caribbean. During the U.S. War of Independence, a brisk arms trade helped to bolster the local economy, but the glamour ended in 1781, when British Admiral Romney sacked the port, hauled off most of the island's wealth, and propelled St. Eustatius onto a path of obscurity—where it remained for almost 200 years, until the advent of tourism. Today the island is among the poorest in the Caribbean, with 21 sq. km (8 sq. miles) of arid landscape, beaches with strong and sometimes dangerous undertows, a population of around 3,000 people, and a sleepy capital, Oranjestad. Out of desperation, the island is very committed to maintaining its political and fiscal links to the Netherlands. This is a destination for people who are interested in American Revolution–era history and who like hanging out around a pool at a friendly, informal local inn. Most people will want to make a day trip to see the historic sites, have lunch, and leave.

St. Kitts & Nevis

The first English settlement in the Leeward Islands, St. Kitts has a rich sense of British maritime history. With 176 sq. km (68 sq. miles) of land, St. Kitts enjoyed one of the richest sugar-cane economies of the plantation age. This island lies somewhat off the beaten tourist track and has a very appealing, intimate charm. A lush, fertile mountain island with a rainforest and waterfalls, it is crowned by the 1,138m (3,734-ft.) Mount Liamuiga, a crater that, thankfully, has remained dormant (unlike the one at Montserrat). St. Kitts is home to some 38,000 people and Brimstone Hill, the Caribbean's most impressive fortress. Come here for the beaches and the history, for lush natural scenery, and to stay at a restored plantation home that's been turned into a charming inn. Lots of sporting activities, ranging from mountain climbing to horseback riding, are also available.

Many Nevisians feel strongly about eventually breaking away from St. Kitts, from which Nevis is separated by 3km (2 miles) of water. Nevis was spotted by Columbus in 1493 on his second voyage to the New World. He called it Nieves—Spanish for "snows"—when he saw the cloud-crowned volcanic isle that evoked for him the snow-capped peaks of the Pyrenees. Known for its long beaches of both black and white sand, Nevis, more than any other island in the Caribbean, has turned its former great houses, built during the plantation era, into some of the most charming and atmospheric inns in the West Indies. It also has the Four Seasons Resort for those who want world-class elegance and service. The capital city of Charlestown looks like a real Caribbean backwater, though it is home to hundreds of worldwide businesses that are drawn to Nevis for its tax laws and bank secrecy.

St. Lucia

St. Lucia (*Loo*-sha), 39km (24 miles) south of Martinique, is the second largest of the Windward Islands. Although in 1803 Britain eventually won control of the island, French influence is still evident in the Creole dialect spoken here. A volcanic island with lots of rainfall and great natural beauty, it has white- and black-sand beaches, bubbling sulfur springs, and beautiful mountain scenery. Most tourism is concentrated on the island's northwestern tip, near the capital (Castries), but the arrival of up to 200,000 visitors a year has altered the old agrarian lifestyle throughout the island. Come here for the posh resorts and the gorgeous beaches, the rainforests, and the lush tropical foliage.

St. Maarten/St. Martin

Lying 232km (144 miles) east of Puerto Rico, this scrub-covered island has been divided between the Dutch (Sint Maarten) and the French (Saint Martin) since 1648. Regardless of how you spell its name, it's the same island on both sides of the unguarded border—though the two halves are quite different. The Dutch side contains the island's major airport, more shops, and more tourist facilities; the French side has some of the poshest hotels and superior food. Both are modern, urbanized, and cosmopolitan, and both suffer from traffic jams, a lack of parking space in the capitals, tourist-industry burnout (especially on the Dutch side), and a disturbing increase in crime. In spite of the drawbacks, there's a lot to attract you here—great beaches, the shopping (some of the Caribbean's best), the gambling, the self-contained resorts, the nonstop flights from the U.S., the nightlife, and some of the best restaurants in the Caribbean. For a day trip from here, you can fly to St. Eustatius or Saba.

St. Vincent & the Grenadines

The natural beauty of this miniarchipelago has long been known to divers and the yachting set, who consider its north-to-south string of cays and coral islets one of the loveliest sailing regions in the world. **St. Vincent** (29km/18 miles long and 18km/11 miles wide) is by far the largest and most fertile island in the country. Its capital is the sleepy, somewhat dilapidated town of Kingstown (not to be confused with Kingston, Jamaica). **The Grenadines,** some 32 neighboring islands, stretch like a pearl necklace to the south of St. Vincent. These include the charming boat-building communities of **Bequia** and **Mustique,** where the late Princess Margaret had a home. Less densely populated islands in the chain include the tiny outposts of **Mayreau, Canouan, Palm Island,** and **Petit St. Vincent,** which was mostly covered with scrub until hotel owners planted much-needed groves of palm and hardwood trees and opened resorts.

Trinidad & Tobago

The southernmost of the West Indies, this two-island nation lies just 11km (6¾ miles) off the coast of Venezuela. Both islands once had sugar-plantation economies and enjoyed fantastic wealth during the 18th century. **Trinidad** is the most industrialized island in the Caribbean, with oil deposits and a polyglot population from India, Pakistan, Venezuela, Africa, and Europe. Known for its calypso music and Carnival celebrations, it is also one of the most culturally distinctive nations in the Caribbean, with a rich artistic tradition. In its 4,662 sq. km (1,800 sq. miles), you'll find a bustling capital (Port-of-Spain), wildlife sanctuaries, and an impressive variety of exotic flora and fauna. What you won't necessarily find are beaches: While Trinidad has some excellent ones, they are far removed from the capital and hard to locate.

For beach life, head for Tobago, which is about 30km (19 miles) northeast of Trinidad. Tiny **Tobago** (14km/8¾ miles wide and 42km/26 miles long) is calmer and less heavily forested, with a rather dull capital (Scarborough) and an impressive array of white-sand beaches. While Trinidad seems to consider tourism only one of many viable industries, Tobago is absolutely dependent on it. Life is sleepy on Tobago, unlike bustling Trinidad. Tobago has coral reefs ideal for scuba diving, rainforests, powdery sands, shoreline drives, lanes of coconut palms, and a soothing get-away-from-it-all atmosphere. We hope it stays that way.

Turks & Caicos

Although these islands are actually part of the Bahamian archipelago—they are to the east of the southernmost islands of the Bahamas, directly north of Haiti and the Dominican Republic—they are governed separately.

Home of Cockburn Town, the capital of Turks and Caicos (*Kayk*-us), **Grand Turk** nevertheless has a small-town atmosphere. The farthest island from Florida, it totals 23 sq. km (8⅘ sq. miles). Grand Turk is ringed by abundant marine life, but most of the island's surface is flat, rocky, and dry. The diving is world class—the main draw for most visitors. Grand Turk has a relatively undeveloped tourist infrastructure, although it offers a scattering of inns and hotels.

One of the larger islands of Turks and Caicos, **Providenciales,** or Provo, is green but arid, with miles of scrubland and stunted trees covering the island's low, undulating hills. Whatever Turks and Caicos has to offer in organized sports is here, including the nation's only golf course, boat tours, and diving excursions. The 19km (12-mile) beach and pristine coastline of Provo were a tourist development waiting to happen. In the late 1970s, hotel megaliths such as Club Med poured money into increasingly popular low-rise eco-conscious resorts. Now Provo's tourist infrastructure far surpasses that of Grand Turk. The island also has the best cuisine and the finest entertainment in Turks and Caicos, but it's still much sleepier than the big developments of Aruba.

The U.S. Virgin Islands

Formerly Danish possessions, these islands became part of the United States in 1917. Originally based on a plantation economy, St. Croix is the largest and flattest of the U.S. Virgins, and St. Thomas and St. John are more mountainous.

All three islands offer stunning beaches, great snorkeling, sailing, and lovely scenery, but they are rather expensive destinations. If you want great shopping and lots of diversions, facilities, bars, restaurants, and modern resort hotels, go to overbuilt **St. Thomas,** sometimes referred to as the shopping mall of the Caribbean. Cruise-ship passengers pass through constantly. **St. Croix** also has good facilities, though not as many as St. Thomas. It's more laid-back, a better place to escape for peace and quiet. **St. John** is most often visited on a day trip from St. Thomas. Much of this island is devoted to a national park, a gift from Laurance Rockefeller to the national park system. Petty crime is on the increase, however—an unfortunate fly in the ointment of this otherwise soothing corner of paradise.

WHEN TO GO

The Weather

The temperature variations in the Caribbean are surprisingly slight, averaging between 75°F and 85°F (24°C–29°C) in both winter and summer. It can get really chilly, however, especially in the early morning and at night. The Caribbean winter is usually like a perpetual May. Overall, temperatures in the mid-80s (high 20s Celsius) prevail throughout most of the region, and trade winds make for comfortable days and nights, even without air-conditioning.

The humidity and bugs can be a problem here year-round. However, more mosquitoes come out during the rainy season, which usually occurs in autumn.

If you come in the summer, be prepared for a really broiling midafternoon sun.

Brochures make people feel that it's always sunny in the Caribbean, and that isn't necessarily the case. Different islands get different amounts of rain. On Aruba it hardly ever rains; on other islands, you can have overcast skies your entire vacation. Winter is generally the driest season, but even then it can be wet in mountainous areas, and you can expect brief afternoon showers, especially in December and January, on Martinique, Guadeloupe, Dominica, St. Lucia, on the north coast of the Dominican Republic, and in northeast Jamaica.

The curse of Caribbean weather, the **hurricane season** lasts—officially, at least—from June 1 to November 30. But there's no cause for panic: Satellite forecasts give enough warning that precautions can be taken.

The High Season & the Off Season

The Caribbean has become a year-round destination. The "season" runs roughly from mid-December to mid-April, which is generally the driest time of year in the Caribbean and the most miserable time of year in the U.S. Northeast and Midwest and in Canada. Hotels charge their highest prices during the peak winter period, and you'll have to make your reservations well in advance—months in advance if you want to travel over Christmas or in the depths of February, especially around U.S. Presidents Day weekend.

The off season in the Caribbean—roughly from mid-April to mid-December (although this varies from hotel to hotel)—is one big summer sale, though it's become more popular in recent years. In most cases, hotels, inns, and condos slash 20% to 50% off their winter rates.

Dollar for dollar, you'll spend less money by renting a summer house or self-sufficient unit in the Caribbean than you would on Cape Cod, Fire Island, or Laguna Beach. You just have to be able to tolerate strong sun if you're considering coming in the summer.

In the off season, the beaches are less crowded, and you can get good deals. But restaurants close, and hotels offer fewer facilities and may even use the off season for construction. Make sure to ask what work is going on, and if you decide to go anyway, ask for a room far away from the noise. If you're single and going during off season, ask for the hotel's occupancy rate. You want crowds!

Because there's such a drastic difference in high-season and off-season rates at most hotels, we've included both on every property we review. You'll see the incredible savings you can enjoy if your schedule allows you to wait a couple of months for your fun in the sun.

GETTING THERE

By Plane

American Airlines (✆ 800/433-7300; www.aa.com) is the major carrier throughout the region. Other airlines serving the islands include **Air Canada** (✆ 888/247-2262 in the U.S. and Canada; www.aircanada.com), **Air Jamaica** (✆ 800/523-5585; www.airjamaica.com), **British Airways** (✆ 800/247-9297 in the U.S., or 0844/493-0787 in the U.K.; www.britishairways.com), **Caribbean Airlines** (✆ 800/920-4225; www.caribbean-airlines.com), **Cayman Airways** (✆ 800/422-9626; www.caymanairways.com), **Continental** (✆ 800/231-0856; www.continental.com), **Delta** (✆ 800/221-1212; www.delta.com), **JetBlue Airways** (✆ 800/538-2583; www.jetblue.com), **LIAT** (✆ 888/844-LIAT [5428] in most of the Caribbean, or 268/480-5601 elsewhere; www.liatairline.com), **United** (© 800/538-2929; www.united.com), and **US Airways/AmericaWest** (© 800/622-1015; www.usairways.com), plus some smaller regional carriers. In each of the island chapters that follow, we list details on which airlines fly the various routes.

By Boat

For detailed information on the cruise lines serving the Caribbean, pick up a copy of *Frommer's Caribbean Ports of Call.*

RESPONSIBLE TRAVEL

Some of the best wildlife cruises are packaged by **Oceanic Society Expeditions** (© **800/326-7491;** www.oceanicsociety.org). Whale-watching jaunts and some research-oriented trips are also featured. You can swim with humpback whales in the Dominican Republic, for example.

Puerto Rico's varied and often hard-to-reach natural treasures have been conveniently packaged into a series of affordable eco-tours. **AdvenTours** (© **787/530-8311;** www.adventourspr.com) features customized private tours with activities like bird-watching, hiking, camping, visits to coffee plantations, and kayaking. **Aventuras Tierra Adentro,** 268 Piñero Ave., San Juan (© **787/766-0470;** www.puertoricoexplore.com), specializes in rock climbing, body rafting, caving, and canyoning, among other activities. **Eco Xcursion Aquatica,** Road 191, Km 1.7, Rio Grande, Fajardo (© **787/888-2887**), offers some of the best rainforest hikes and mountain-bike tours.

Machias Adventures (© **888/427-3497** or 203/454-1243; www.machiasadventures.com) arranges adventure tours to St. Vincent, including hiking up a volcano, sailing with a crew, seeking out the huge variety of bird life, and hiking up a river canyon to a dramatic water pool—perfect for swimming. The cost of these 7-day jaunts is $2,500 per person, based on double occupancy.

Although one could argue that any vacation that includes an airplane flight can't be truly "green," you can go on holiday and still contribute positively to the environment. You can offset carbon emissions from your flight in other ways. Choose forward-looking companies that embrace responsible development practices, helping preserve destinations for the future by working alongside local people. An increasing number of sustainable tourism initiatives can help you plan a family trip and leave as small a "footprint" as possible on the places you visit.

TOURS

Biking

The Dominican Republic is the best mountain-bike destination in the Caribbean. *Bicycling* magazine said the island defies all stereotype with its "towering mountains and miles of single track." The best-organized trips are offered by **Iguana Mama Mountain Bike,** Cabarete (© **809/571-0908;** www.iguanamama.com).

Hiking

Unlike many of its neighboring islands, Jamaica has mountain peaks that climb to 2,220m (7,284 ft.). The flora, fauna, waterfalls, and panoramas of those peaks have attracted increasing numbers of hikers determined to experience the natural beauty

Websites for Divers

For useful information on scuba diving in the Caribbean, check out the website of the **Professional Association of Diving Instructors (PADI)** at **www.padi.com**. This site provides descriptions of dive destinations throughout the Caribbean and a directory of PADI-certified dive operators. *Scuba Diving* magazine also has a helpful website at **www.scubadiving.com**. Both sites list dive package specials and display gorgeous color photos of some of the most beautiful dive spots in the world.

of the island firsthand. Because of the dangers involved, it's often best to go on an organized tour. Good ones are offered by **Sunventure Tours,** 30 Balmoral Ave., Kingston 10, Jamaica, W.I. (✆ **876/960-6685;** www.sunventuretours.com). For more information, refer to "The Blue Mountains," in chapter 14.

Scuba Trips

A number of outfitters offer scuba packages and cruises. **Aqua Hut** (✆ **610/642-3483;** www.aquahut.net) specializes in diving trips throughout the Caribbean for individuals, couples, and families. Its destinations range from the British Virgin Islands to Bonaire. **Island Dreams Tours & Travel** (✆ **800/346-6116;** www.divetrip.com) also offers trips, including itineraries in the Cayman Islands, Bonaire, and Turks and Caicos.

Explorer Ventures (✆ **800/322-3577** or 307/235-0683; www.explorerventures.com) takes divers on its ***Caribbean Explorer II*** to excursions in the waters of The Bahamas, St. Kitts, Turks and Caicos, and Saba. Trips usually last a week.

Another specialist in this field is **Caradonna Worldwide Dive Adventures** (✆ **800/328-2288** or 407/774-9000; www.caradonna.com), which offers adventurous scuba-cruise packages to Bonaire, St. Croix, and St. Kitts, among other islands.

Sea Kayaking

The only outfitter in the Virgin Islands that offers sea-kayaking/island-camping excursions is **Arawak Expeditions,** based in Cruz Bay, St. John (✆ **800/238-8687** in the U.S., or 340/693-8312; www.arawakexp.com). It provides kayaking gear, healthy meals, camping equipment, and two experienced guides. Multiday excursions range from $1,095 to $2,495.

TIPS ON ACCOMMODATIONS

Saving on Your Hotel Room

WATCH OUT FOR THOSE EXTRAS! Nearly all islands charge a government tax on hotel rooms, usually 7½% to 9%, but those rates vary from island to island. When booking a room, make sure you understand whether the price you've been quoted includes the tax. That will avoid an unpleasant surprise when it comes time to pay the bill. Sometimes the room tax depends on the quality of the hotel—it might be relatively low for a guesthouse but steeper for a first-class resort.

Furthermore, most hotels routinely add 10% to 12% for "service," even if you didn't see much evidence of it. That means that with tax and service, some bills are 17% or even 25% higher than the price that was originally quoted to you! Naturally, you need to determine just how much the hotel, guesthouse, or inn plans to add to your bill at the end of your stay, and whether it's included in the initial price.

That's not all. Some hotels slip in little hidden extras that mount quickly. For example, it's common for many places to quote rates that include a continental breakfast. Should you prefer ham and eggs, you will pay extra charges. If you request special privileges, like extra towels for the beach or laundry done in a hurry, surcharges may mount. It pays to watch those extras and to ask questions before you commit.

WHAT THE ABBREVIATIONS MEAN Rate sheets often have these classifications:

- **MAP (Modified American Plan)** usually means room, breakfast, and dinner, unless the room rate has been quoted separately, and then it means only breakfast and dinner.
- **CP (Continental Plan)** includes room and a light breakfast.
- **EP (European Plan)** means room only.
- **AP (American Plan)** includes your room plus three meals a day.

HOTELS & RESORTS Many budget travelers assume they can't afford the big hotels and resorts. But there are so many packages out there and so many frequent sales, even in winter, that you might be pleasantly surprised.

Some hotels are often quite flexible about their rates, and many offer discounts and upgrades whenever they have a big block of rooms to fill and few reservations. The smaller hotels and inns are not as likely to be generous with discounts, much less upgrades.

ALL-INCLUSIVE RESORTS The promises are persuasive: "Forget your cash, put your plastic away." Presumably, everything's all paid for in advance at an "all-inclusive" resort. But is it?

The all-inclusives have a reputation for being expensive, and many of them are, especially the giant **SuperClubs** of Jamaica or even the **Sandals** properties (unless you book in a slow period or the off season).

In the 1990s, so many competitors entered the all-inclusive game that the term now means different things to the various resorts that use this marketing strategy. The ideal all-inclusive is just that—a place where everything, even drinks and watersports, is included. But in the narrowest sense, it means a room and three meals a day, with extra charges for drinks, sports, whatever. When you book, it's important to ask and to understand exactly what's included in your so-called all-inclusive. Watersports programs vary greatly at the various resorts. Extras might include horseback riding or sightseeing.

The all-inclusive market is geared to the active traveler who likes organized entertainment, a lot of sports and workouts at fitness centers, and a lot of food and drink.

If you have children, stay away from Hedonism II in Negril, Jamaica, which lives up to its name. Some Club Meds are targeted more for singles and couples; others aggressively pursue the family market. Some Club Meds have Mini Clubs, Baby Clubs, and Teen Clubs at some of their properties, at least during holiday and summer seasons.

The trick is to look for that special deal and to travel in off-peak periods, which doesn't always mean just from mid-April to mid-December. Discounts are often granted for hotels during certain slow periods, called "windows," most often after the New Year's holiday. If you want a winter vacation at an all-inclusive, choose the month of January—not February or the Christmas holidays, when prices are at their all-year high.

GUESTHOUSES An entirely different type of accommodation is the guesthouse, where most of the Antilleans themselves stay when they travel. In the Caribbean, the term *guesthouse* can mean anything. Sometimes so-called guesthouses are really like simple motels built around swimming pools. Others are small individual cottages, with their own kitchenettes, constructed around a main building in which you'll often find a bar and a restaurant that serves local food. Some are surprisingly comfortable, often with private baths and swimming pools. You may or may not have air-conditioning.

For value, the guesthouse can't be topped. You can always journey over to a big beach resort and use its seaside facilities for only a small charge, perhaps no more than $5. Although they don't have any frills, the guesthouses we've recommended are clean and safe for families or single women. The cheapest ones are not places where you'd want to spend a lot of time, because of their simple, modest furnishings.

RENTING A CONDO, VILLA, OR COTTAGE Particularly if you're a family or a group of friends, a "housekeeping holiday" can be one of the least expensive ways to vacation in the Caribbean, and if you like privacy and independence, it's a good way to go. Accommodations with kitchens are now available on nearly all the islands. Some are individual cottages, others are condo complexes with swimming pools, and some are private homes that owners rent out while they're away. Many (though not all) places include maid service, and you're given fresh linens as well.

In the simpler rentals, doing your own cooking and laundry or even your own maid service may not be your idea of a good time in the sun, but it saves money—a lot of money. The savings, especially for a family of three to six people, or two or three couples, can range from 50% to 60% of what a hotel would cost. Groceries are sometimes priced 35% to 60% higher than on the U.S. mainland, as nearly all foodstuffs have to be imported, but even so, preparing your own food will be a lot cheaper than dining at restaurants.

There are also quite lavish homes for rent, where you can spend a lot and stay in the lap of luxury in a prime beachfront setting.

Many villas have a staff, or at least a maid who comes in a few days a week, and they also provide the essentials for home life, including linens and housewares. Condos usually come with a reception desk and are often comparable to a suite in a big resort hotel. Nearly all condo complexes have pools (some more than one). Like condos, villas range widely in price and may begin at $700 per week for a modest one and go over $50,000 a week for a luxurious one. More likely, the prices will be somewhere in between.

You'll have to approach these rental properties with a certain sense of independence. There may or may not be a front desk to answer your questions, and you'll have to plan your own watersports.

For a list of agencies that arrange rentals, refer to the accommodations sections of the individual island chapters. You can also ask each island's tourist office for good suggestions. Make your reservations well in advance.

Here are a few agencies renting throughout the Caribbean:

- **Villas of Distinction** (✆ **800/289-0900** in the U.S.; www.villasofdistinction.com) offers upscale private villas with one to six bedrooms and a pool. Domestic help is often included. They have offerings on St. Martin, Anguilla, Mustique, Barbados, the U.S. and British Virgins, the Cayman Islands, St. Lucia, Nevis,

Turks and Caicos, St. Barts, and Jamaica. Descriptions, rates, and photos are available online.

- **At Home Abroad** (✆ **212/421-9165;** fax 212/228-4860; www.athomeabroadinc.com) has private upscale homes for rent on Barbados, Dominican Republic, Jamaica, Mustique, St. John, St. Croix, St. Thomas, Tortola, and Virgin Gorda, most with maid service included.
- **Hideaways Aficionado** (✆ **800/843-4433** in the U.S., or 603/430-4433; www.hideaways.com) publishes *Hideaways Guide,* a pictorial directory of home rentals throughout the world, including the Caribbean—especially the British Virgin Islands, the Cayman Islands, Jamaica, and St. Lucia, with full descriptions so you know what you're renting. Rentals range from cottages to staffed villas to whole islands! Other services include yacht charters, cruises, airline ticketing, car rentals, and hotel reservations. Annual membership is $195. Membership information, listings, and photos are available online.
- **Heart of the Caribbean Ltd.** (✆ **800/231-5303** or 262/783-5303; www.hotcarib.com) is a villa wholesale company offering travelers a wide range of private villas and condos on several islands, including St. Maarten/St. Martin, Barbados, U.S.V.I., B.V.I., and St. Lucia. Accommodations range from one to six bedrooms, and from modest villas and condos to palatial estates. Homes have complete kitchens and maid service. Catering and car rentals can also be provided. Rates, listings, and photos are available online.

Landing the Best Room

Somebody has to get the best room in the house. It might as well be you. You can start by joining the hotel's frequent-guest program, which may make you eligible for upgrades. A hotel-branded credit card usually gives its owner "silver" or "gold" status in frequent-guest programs for free. Always ask about a corner room: They're often larger and quieter, with more windows and light, and they often cost the same as standard rooms. When you make your reservation, ask if the hotel is renovating; if it is, request a room away from the construction. Ask about nonsmoking rooms and rooms with views. Be sure to request your choice of twin, queen-, or king-size beds. If you're a light sleeper, ask for a quiet room away from vending or ice machines, elevators, restaurants, bars, and discos. Ask for a room that has been recently renovated or refurbished.

If you aren't happy with your room when you arrive, ask for another one. Most lodgings will be willing to accommodate you.

In resort areas, particularly in warm climates, ask the following questions before you book a room:

- What's the view like? Cost-conscious travelers may be willing to pay less for a back room facing the parking lot, especially if they don't plan to spend much time in their room.
- Does the room have air-conditioning or ceiling fans? Do the windows open? If they do, and the nighttime entertainment takes place alfresco, you may want to find out when showtime is over.
- What's included in the price? Your room may be moderately priced, but if you're charged for beach chairs, towels, sports equipment, and other amenities, you could end up spending more than you bargained for.
- How far is the room from the beach and other amenities? If it's far, is there transportation to and from the beach, and is it free?

[FastFACTS] CARIBBEAN

Customs Each island has specific guidelines on what you can bring in with you; these are detailed in the destination chapters that follow. Generally, you're permitted to bring in items intended for your personal use, including tobacco, cameras, film, and a limited supply of liquor—usually 40 ounces.

Just before you leave home, check with your country's Customs or Foreign Affairs department for the latest guidelines—including information on items that are not allowed to be brought into your home country—since the rules are subject to change and often contain some surprising oddities.

U.S. Customs and Border Protection (www.customs.gov) allows $1,600 worth of duty-free imports every 30 days from the U.S. Virgin Islands; if you go over this amount, you're taxed at 1.5% rather than the usual 3%. The duty-free limit is $800 for other Caribbean Basin destinations. If you visit only Puerto Rico, you don't have to go through Customs at all, since the island is a U.S. commonwealth.

Joint Customs declarations are possible for family members traveling together. For example, for a husband and wife with two children, purchases in the U.S. Virgin Islands become duty-free up to $6,400. Unsolicited gifts can be sent to friends and relatives at the rate of $200 per day from the U.S. Virgin Islands and $100 a day from the other islands. U.S. citizens or returning residents at least 21 years of age traveling directly or indirectly from the U.S. Virgin Islands are allowed to bring in free of duty 1,000 cigarettes, 5 liters of alcohol, and 100 cigars (but not Cuban cigars). Duty-free limitations on articles from other countries are generally 1 liter of alcohol, 200 cigarettes, and 200 cigars.

You should collect receipts for all purchases made abroad. You must also declare on your Customs form the nature and value of all gifts received during your stay abroad. It's prudent to carry proof that you purchased expensive cameras or jewelry on the U.S. mainland. If you purchased such an item during an earlier trip abroad, you should carry proof that you have previously paid Customs duty on the item.

Sometimes merchants suggest a false receipt to undervalue your purchase. ***Beware:*** You could be involved in a sting operation—the merchant might be an informer to U.S. Customs.

If you use any medication that contains controlled substances or requires injection, carry an original prescription or note from your doctor.

For information on what you're allowed to bring home, contact one of the following agencies:

U.S. Citizens: U.S. Customs & Border Protection (CBP), 1300 Pennsylvania Ave. NW, Washington, DC 20229 (✆ **877/287-8667;** www.cbp.gov).

Canadian Citizens: Canada Border Services Agency, Ottawa, Ontario, K1A 0L8 (✆ **800/461-9999** in Canada, or 204/983-3500; www.cbsa-asfc.gc.ca).

U.K. Citizens: HM Customs & Excise, Crownhill Court, Tailyour Road, Plymouth, PL6 5BZ (✆ **0845/010-9000,** or 020/501-261 from outside the U.K.; www.hmrc.gov.uk).

Australian Citizens: Australian Customs Service, Customs House, 5 Constitution Ave., Canberra City, ACT 2601 (✆ **1300/363-263,** or 612/6275-6666 from outside Australia; www.customs.gov.au).

New Zealand Citizens: New Zealand Customs, the Customhouse, 17–21 Whitmore St., Box 2218, Wellington, 6140 (✆ **04/473-6099** or 0800/428-786; www.customs.govt.nz).

Disabled Travelers

Most disabilities shouldn't stop anyone from traveling. There are more options and resources out there than ever before. However, in general, the Caribbean is not easy for persons with disabilities. Attractions and sights, for the most part, don't have elevators, ramps, or wheelchair-accessible toilets. Nor are most hotels constructed for accessibility. If you are contemplating a holiday in the sun, consider the islands of Puerto Rico or one of the U.S. Virgins—St. Thomas, St. Croix, or St. John. As U.S. territories, these islands must abide by the Americans with Disabilities Act. Even so, getting around can be difficult. Transportation is woefully inadequate, and many Caribbean hotels lie in hilly or mountainous regions. However, some resorts have ground-floor bedrooms with wide doors and accessible bathrooms. We've indicated this in the amenities section of the hotel reviews.

Doctors Finding a good doctor in the Caribbean is not a problem, and most speak English. See the "Fast Facts" section in each chapter for specific names and addresses on each individual island.

Family Travel To locate accommodations, restaurants, and attractions that are particularly kid-friendly, look for the "Kids" icon throughout this guide.

Health For preexisting conditions, make sure to pack prescription medications in your carry-on luggage. Carry written prescriptions in generic, not brand-name, form, and dispense all prescription medications from their original labeled vials. Many people try to slip drugs such as cocaine into the Caribbean (or pick them up there). Drugs are often placed into a container for prescription medication after the legal medications have been removed. Customs officials are well aware of this type of smuggling and often check medications if they suspect a passenger is bringing illegal drugs into or out of a country. If you wear contact lenses, pack an extra pair in case you lose one.

Most islands in the Caribbean have hospitals, and most doctors and nurses speak English. However, some smaller islands may send patients to other islands for more specialized care. See the "Fast Facts" section in each chapter for specific hospitals on each individual island.

Tropical Illnesses Infectious hepatitis has been reported on islands such as Dominica and Haiti. Unless you have been immunized for both hepatitis A and B, consult your doctor about the advisability of getting a gamma-globulin shot before you leave. The United States **Centers for Disease Control and Prevention** (✆ **800/232-4636;** www.cdc.gov) provides up-to-date information on necessary vaccines and health hazards by region or country.

Bugs, Bites & Other Wildlife Concerns One of the biggest menaces are "no-see-ums," which emerge mainly in the early evening. You can't see these gnats, but you sure can "feel-um." Window screens can't keep these critters out, so carry bug repellent. Mosquitoes are also a nuisance. Malaria-carrying mosquitoes in the Caribbean are confined largely to Haiti and the Dominican Republic. If you're visiting either, consult your doctor for preventive medicine at least 8 weeks before you leave. Dengue fever is prevalent in the islands, most prominently on Antigua, St. Kitts, Dominica, and the Dominican Republic. To date, no satisfactory treatment has been developed; visitors are advised to avoid mosquito bites—as if that were possible.

Sun/Elements/Extreme Weather Exposure The Caribbean sun can be brutal. Wear sunglasses and a hat, and use sunscreen liberally. Limit your time on the beach the first day. If you do overexpose yourself, stay out of the sun until you recover. If your exposure is followed by fever or chills, a headache, or a feeling of nausea or dizziness, see a doctor. Many of the Caribbean islands are also inside the hurricane belt. Hurricane season officially runs from June 1 to November 30, but always check for weather advisories before you leave. See the "Fast Facts" sections in each chapter for more details.

Insurance For information on traveler's insurance, trip cancelation insurance, and medical insurance while traveling, please visit www.frommers.com/tips.

LGBT Travelers The most gay-friendly Caribbean islands are the U.S. possessions, most notably San Juan, which is hailed as the "gay capital of the Caribbean" and offers gay guesthouses, nightclubs, bars, and dance clubs. To a lesser extent, the U.S. Virgin Islands are welcoming, too.

The French islands—St. Barts, St. Martin, Guadeloupe, and Martinique—are technically an extension of mainland France, and the French have always regarded homosexuality with a certain blasé tolerance. However, don't let your guard down: Severe attacks and hate crimes against gay men have been reported.

The Dutch islands of Aruba and Bonaire are quite conservative, so discretion is suggested. But in a surprise move in 2005, their sister island of Curaçao became the first in the Caribbean to announce that it was embracing the gay and lesbian community, urging such travelers to visit the island as a gay-friendly destination, and some hotels have joined the Gay & Lesbian Travel Association. Even certain nightclubs in Willemstad highlight their gay-friendly atmosphere in an attempt to attract patrons from this community of travelers.

Gay life is fairly secretive in many of the sleepy islands of the Caribbean. Some islands even have repressive antihomosexual laws. Homosexuality is actively discouraged in places like the Cayman Islands, but as a result of pressure from gay advocacy groups, past homophobia is slowly giving way to tolerance. In Barbados homosexuality is illegal, and there is often a lack of tolerance in spite of the large number of gay residents and visitors on the island.

Jamaica is the most homophobic island in the Caribbean, with harsh antigay laws, even though there is a large local gay population. The famous all-inclusive **Sandals** of Jamaica had until 2004 a discriminatory policy of admitting only male-female couples. However, under pressure they were forced to rescind the ban and admit same-sex couples.

Mobile Phones The three letters that define much of the world's wireless capabilities are **GSM (Global System for Mobile Communications),** a big, seamless network that makes for easy cross-border cellphone use. In the U.S., T-Mobile and AT&T Wireless use this quasi-universal system; in Canada, Microcell and some Rogers customers are GSM, and all Europeans and most Australians use GSM. GSM phones function with a removable plastic SIM card, encoded with your phone number and account information. If your cellphone is on a GSM system and you have a world-capable multiband phone such as many Sony Ericsson, Motorola, and Samsung models, you can make and receive calls across civilized areas around much of the globe. Just call your wireless operator and ask for "international roaming" to be activated on your account. Unfortunately, per-minute charges can be high.

For many, **renting** a phone is a good idea. While you can rent a phone from any number of overseas sites, including kiosks at airports and at car-rental agencies, we suggest renting the phone before you leave home. Alternatively, **buying a phone** can be economically attractive, as many nations have cheap prepaid phone systems. Once you arrive at your destination, stop by a local cellphone shop and get the cheapest package; you'll probably pay less than $100 for a phone and a starter calling card. Local calls may be as low as 10¢ per minute, and in many countries incoming calls are free.

For more information on cellphone use in the Caribbean, see the individual "Fast Facts" sections of each chapter, or see www.frommers.com/tips.

Money & Costs Frommer's lists exact prices in the local currency. The currency conversions provided were correct at press time. However, rates fluctuate, so before departing consult a currency exchange website such as **www.oanda.com/currency/converter** to check up-to-the-minute rates.

THE VALUE OF THE EASTERN CARIBBEAN DOLLAR VS. OTHER POPULAR CURRENCIES

EC$	US$	UK£	Euro (€)	NAf	Aus$	NZ$	Can$
1	0.37	0.23	0.27	0.66	0.37	0.50	0.36

On many islands in the Caribbean, the Eastern Caribbean dollar is the legal tender. Other islands count the euro as their official currency; the Antilles use the Netherlands Antillean florin; still others use a host of local moneys (the Barbados dollar, the Jamaican dollar, the Cayman Islands dollar, and so on) as their official currency. But most widely accepted throughout the Caribbean is the U.S. dollar. It is the legal currency of the U.S. Virgin Islands, the British Virgin Islands, and Puerto Rico, and will be recognized just about anywhere you go. As such, throughout this book, prices are listed in U.S. dollars. The only exception occurs in cases where the euro is the official currency of the realm; prices in those chapters will be listed in euros.

You may find certain restaurants and shops present their prices in local currency, but they will still accept U.S. dollars—just make sure that when you inquire about a price, you know the type of dollars quoted. Also be aware that you may receive your change in local currency rather than in U.S. dollars. Finally, keep in mind that you may save some money by converting to the local currency rather than paying in U.S. dollars. For details and specific currency conversions for each island, see the "Fast Facts" sections in the individual island chapters.

In the Caribbean, **ATMs** (automated teller machines), sometimes referred to as "cash machines" or "cashpoints," will most likely offer the best exchange rates. Avoid exchanging money at commercial exchange bureaus and hotels, which often have the highest transaction fees.

Credit cards are widely accepted at hotels and many restaurants throughout the Caribbean. They are another safe way to carry money. They also provide a convenient record of all your expenses, and they generally offer relatively good exchange rates. You can withdraw cash advances from your credit cards at banks or ATMs, but high fees make them a pricey way to get cash. Keep in mind that you'll pay interest from the moment of your withdrawal, even if you pay your monthly bills on time. Also, note that many banks now assess a 1% to 3% "transaction fee" on *all* charges you incur abroad (whether you're using the local currency or your native currency).

It's highly recommended that you travel with at least one major credit card. You must have a credit card to rent a car, and hotels and airlines usually require a credit card imprint as a deposit against expenses.

Beware of hidden credit card fees while traveling. Check with your credit or debit card issuer to see what fees, if any, will be charged for overseas transactions. Recent reform legislation in the U.S., for example, has curbed some exploitative lending practices. But many banks have responded by increasing fees in other areas, including fees for customers who use credit and debit cards while out of the country—even if those charges were made in U.S. dollars. Fees can amount to 3% or more of the purchase price. Check with your bank before departing to avoid any surprise charges on your statement.

For help with currency conversions, tip calculations, and more, download Frommer's convenient Travel Tools app for your mobile device. Go to www.frommers.com/go/mobile and click on the Travel Tools icon.

Passports All travelers arriving from the Caribbean by air, including Americans, are now required to have a passport to enter or re-enter the United States. You'll certainly need identification at some point, and a passport is the best form of ID for speeding through Customs and Immigration. Driver's licenses are not acceptable as a sole form of ID. For up-to-date passport requirements for countries around the world, check out the **Consular Information Sheets** at the U.S. State Department website (http://travel.state.gov).

Allow plenty of time before your trip to apply for a passport; processing normally takes 3 weeks but can take longer during busy periods (especially spring). And keep in mind that if you need a passport in a hurry, you'll pay a higher processing fee.

It is advised to always have at least one or two consecutive blank pages in your passport to allow space for visas and stamps that need to appear together. It is also important to note when your passport expires. Many countries require your passport to have at least 6 months left before its expiration to allow you into the destination.

Safety Each island in the Caribbean has its own safety concerns. In general, if you exercise caution when traveling and safeguard your valuables, you should be okay. For specific safety advisories, see the "Fast Facts" section of each island chapter.

Senior Travel Mention that you're a senior when you make your travel reservations. Many hotels in the Caribbean still offer discounts for seniors, and in most cities, people over the age of 60 qualify for reduced admission to theaters, museums, and other attractions, as well as discounted fares on public transportation.

Telephones Generally, hotel surcharges on long-distance and local calls are astronomical, so you're better off using your **cellphone** whenever you can. See "Fast Facts" under the individual island chapters about calling the destination from your home or calling your home country once you're there.

Visas Visas are usually not required in the Caribbean, but some countries may require you to fill out a tourist card. See the individual island chapters for details.

Index

A

B

C

D

G

H

I

J

M

N

O

P

Q

R

S

T

U

V

W

Y